THE OXFORD HANDBOOK OF

INTERNATIONAL ARBITRATION

THE OXFORD HANDBOOK OF

INTERNATIONAL ARBITRATION

Edited by

THOMAS SCHULTZ

and

FEDERICO ORTINO

Assistant Editor

JASON MITCHENSON

OXFORD
UNIVERSITY PRESS

OXFORD
UNIVERSITY PRESS

Great Clarendon Street, Oxford, OX2 6DP,
United Kingdom

Oxford University Press is a department of the University of Oxford.
It furthers the University's objective of excellence in research, scholarship,
and education by publishing worldwide. Oxford is a registered trade mark of
Oxford University Press in the UK and in certain other countries

First Edition published in 2020

Impression: 1

Published in the United States of America by Oxford University Press
198 Madison Avenue, New York, NY 10016, United States of America

British Library Cataloguing in Publication Data
Data available

Library of Congress Control Number: 2020937004

ISBN 978–0–19–879619–0

Printed and bound by
CPI Group (UK) Ltd, Croydon, CR0 4YY

Contents

Table of Cases

NATIONAL CASES

Australia

Canada

China

France

Germany

Guatemala

Hong Kong

United Kingdom

INTERNATIONAL CASES

Ad-hoc Tribunals

Eritrea–Ethiopia Claims Commission

European Commission

European Court of Human Rights (ECtHR)

European Court of Justice (ECJ)/Court of Justice of the European Union (CJEU)

International Centre for Settlement of Investment Disputes (ICSID)

International Chamber of Commerce (ICC)

International Court of Justice (ICJ)

Permanent Court of International Justice (PCIJ)

Stockholm Chamber of Commerce (SCC)

United Nations Commission on International Trade Law (UNCITRAL)

World Trade Organization

Table of Legislation

TABLE OF STATUTES

TABLE OF EUROPEAN SECONDARY LEGISLATION

Directives

Regulations

TABLE OF INTERNATIONAL INSTRUMENTS

TABLE OF ARBITRATION AND MEDIATION RULES

TABLE OF CODES AND PROCEDURAL RULES OF ARBITRATION

List of Contributors

Frédéric Bachand, Judge, Superior Court of Quebec

Nathalie Bernasconi, Head of Economic Law & Policy programme, International Institute for Sustainable Development

Andrea Bianchi, Professor of International Law, Graduate Institute of International and Development Studies, Geneva

Andrea K. Bjorklund, Associate Dean of Graduate Studies, Full Professor, and L. Yves Fortier Chair, McGill University Faculty of Law

Martin Dietrich Brauch, International Law Adviser, International Institute for Sustainable Development

Stavros Brekoulakis, Professor in International Arbitration, Queen Mary University of London

Tomer Broude, Sylvan M. Cohen Chair in Law, Hebrew University of Jerusalem

†David D. Caron, Professor of International Law, King's College London; Judge, Iran-United States Claims Tribunal

Elena Cima, Scientific Collaborator, Institute for Environmental Governance and Territorial Development, University of Geneva

Tony Cole, Reader in Arbitration and Investment Law, University of Leicester

Jean d'Aspremont, Chair in Public International Law, University of Manchester; Professor of International Law, Science Po Law School Paris

Yves Dezalay, Emeritus Director of Research, Centre National de la Recherche Scientifique

Thomas Dietz, Professor of International Relations and Law, University of Münster

Christopher R. Drahozal, John M. Rounds Professor of Law, University of Kansas

Cédric Dupont, Professor of International Relations, Graduate Institute of International and Development Studies, Geneva

Emmanuel Gaillard, Visiting Professor of Law at Yale Law School and Harvard Law School; Shearman & Sterling

Bryant G. Garth, Distinguished Professor of Law, University of California, Irvine

Fabien Gélinas, Sir William C. Macdonald Chair in Law, McGill University

Myriam Gicquello, PhD student, King's College London

Florian Grisel, Reader in Transnational Law, King's College London; Research Fellow, Centre National de la Recherche Scientifique

Moshe Hirsch, Maria Von Hofmannsthal Chair in International Law, Hebrew University of Jerusalem

Alexis Keller, Professor of Legal and Political History, University of Geneva; Visiting Professor, Sciences Po, Paris

Ursula Kriebaum, Professor of International Law, University of Vienna

Howard Mann, International Institute for Sustainable Development

Makane Moïse Mbengue, Professor of International Law, University of Geneva

Ralf Michaels, Director, Max Planck Institute for Comparative and International Private Law

Alex Mills, Professor of Public and Private International Law, University College London

Loukas Mistelis, Clive M. Schmitthoff Professor of Transnational Commercial Law and Arbitration, Queen Mary University of London

Jason Mitchenson, Level Twenty Seven Chambers

Tibisay Morgandi, Lecturer in International Energy and Natural Resources Law, Queen Mary University of London

Jacqueline Nolan-Haley, Professor of Law, Fordham University

Federico Ortino, Reader in International Economic Law, King's College London

Pietro Ortolani, Assistant Professor in Private Law, Radboud University

François Ost, Emeritus Professor, Saint Louis University Brussels

William W. Park, Professor of Law, Boston University

Jan Paulsson, Michael Klein Distinguished Scholar Chair, University of Miami School of Law; Three Crowns

Lauge N. Skovgaard Poulsen, Associate Professor in International Political Economy, University College London

Deepak Raju, Sidley Austin LLP

Niccolò Ridi, Lecturer in Law, University of Liverpool

Hélène Ruiz Fabri, Director, Max Planck Institute Luxembourg for Procedural Law

David Schneiderman, Professor of Law and Political Science, University of Toronto

Thomas Schultz, Professor of Law, King's College London; Professor of International Arbitration, University of Geneva; Visiting Professor of International Law, Graduate Institute of International and Development Studies, Geneva

Esmé Shirlow, Senior Lecturer in Law, Australian National University

Taylor St John, Lecturer in International Relations, University of St Andrews

Edoardo Stoppioni, Senior Research Fellow, Max Planck Institute Luxembourg for Procedural Law

Anne Van Aaken, Alexander von Humboldt Professor, Chair for Law and Economics, Legal Theory, Public International Law and European Law, University of Hamburg

†V. V. Veeder, Essex Court Chambers; Visiting Professor of International Arbitration, King's College London

Horatia Muir Watt, Professor of Private International Law, Sciences Po Law School, Paris

Sean Wright, Clinical Manager, Lutheran Community Services

Jason Webb Yackee, Professor of Law, University of Wisconsin

Anil Yilmaz Vastardis, Lecturer in Law, University of Essex

CHAPTER 1

ARBITRATION LITERATURE

THOMAS SCHULTZ AND NICCOLÒ RIDI

1.1 Introduction

International arbitration entertains a particular relationship with its own literature—the written knowledge in the field and about the field. This relationship is marked by one big mix, be it in the form of competition[1] or cooperation,[2] of practitioners who use it, legal entrepreneurs who make and change it, and scholars who analyse it, with more or less permanent alternations and confusions of these roles. Of course, Schrödinger's Cat-type problems[3] make some of this intertwinement inevitable: Indeed, can one really analyse it without, by the same token, changing it by giving a certain representation of it? Can one use it without analysing it and, by using it, changing it? Can one make it without, in a sense, using it and at least pretending to analyse it? Not really. But in arbitration, this relationship (call it, quite normatively, expertise-enhancing cross-fertilization or rather mind-narrowing dogmatic collusion, as you will) has a strength that would probably appear curious, and worth investigating, in many other fields in which public interests are at stake.

[1] Yves Dezalay and Bryant G. Garth, *Dealing in Virtue: International Commercial Arbitration and the Construction of a Transnational Legal Order* (University of Chicago Press, 1998).

[2] Florian Grisel, 'Treaty-Making between Public Authority and Private Interests: The Genealogy of the Convention on the Recognition and Enforcement of Foreign Arbitral Awards', (2017) 28 European Journal of International Law 73.

[3] Schrödinger's Cat is a thought experiment suggested by Austrian physicist Erwin Schrödinger, in which a cat is put in a box with a flask of poison. The mechanism releasing the poison is triggered by a system based on quantum mechanics, which, long story short, means that the cat is simultaneously dead and alive, until the researcher opens the box, at which point reality collapses into one of the two possibilities. Observation, the point is for us here, can influence, change the object of the observation by interfering with it. (Of course: 'No animals were harmed during the making of either this experiment or the current chapter.')

This is what this chapter starts doing. It offers to put the starting point of this investigation in knowledge, empirically acquired and then abstractly, intuitively typologized. The chapter moves in two main parts. The first asks questions such as: What sort of literature has the field produced? By whom and citing whom? On what topics? Which journals structure the field, which landmark books have guided it? Who are, citation-wise, the great, impactful authors of international arbitration, and how do they cluster in groups? We seek to answer these questions with a scientometric analysis. The second part of the chapter then offers a typology of the main types of literature that fuel the field, and suggests hopefully credible hypotheses about the factors that determine what gets written, by whom, and where.

1.2 Charting the arbitration literature: a bird's-eye view

1.2.1 The question

Arbitration literature has a long history—one long enough in itself to warrant its study.[4] So far, however, no attempt has been made to examine it and its evolution systematically and with a quantitative approach.

The lack of investigation of this research question is, in and by itself, surprising. Clearly, the literature plays a strong role in shaping the thinking and making of international arbitration law. Beyond extreme views that might see scholarship as directly amounting to a source of law,[5] if a subsidiary and unprivileged one, no arbitration conference, or foyer discussion, would omit mentions of its camps, theories, and schools of thought. The literature is thus, and at the very least, the material evidence of these camps, theories, and schools of thought, and can be taken as the litmus test of how they catch on, evolve, and have a meaningful impact on other thinkers and practitioners.

An alternative way of looking at the same problem suggests that the importance of the research question may go beyond this point. Literature—and scientific literature

[4] See e.g., with reference to investment law and arbitration, Stephan W. Schill, 'W(h)ither Fragmentation? On the Literature and Sociology of International Investment Law', (2011) 22 European Journal of International Law 875.

[5] These questions mainly arise in the field of international investment arbitration in relation to its conceptual vicinity with and necessary application of public international law, the sources of which include (in the most widely accepted formulation, contained in Article 38[1][d] of the ICJ Statute) 'the teachings of the most highly qualified publicist' as subsidiary means for the determinations of rules of law. Ole Kristian Fauchald, 'The Legal Reasoning of ICSID Tribunals: An Empirical Analysis', (2008) 19 European Journal of International Law 301; Sondre T. Helmersen, 'The Use of Scholarship by the WTO Appellate Body', (2016) 7 Goettingen J. Int'l L. 309; Sandesh Sivakumaran, 'The Influence of Teachings of Publicists on the Development of International Law', (2017) 66 International & Comparative Law Quarterly 1.

in particular—is a privileged conduit for the various actors in the social field of international arbitration.[6] It acts, first and foremost, as a channel of learning and communication, through which these actors can portray themselves as 'value providers' for the system, or otherwise shape it by striving to publish activist or justificatory efforts.[7] What is more, and not at all in contradiction with the preceding remarks, it also provides important clues as to the ways in which these actors interact and their overall connectedness.

These assumptions make good sense intuitively, but they must be tested empirically to properly map and measures tendencies and approaches. Facing the open sea of scholarly publishing in international arbitration, we must cast our nets wisely. Enter *scientometrics*.[8] This field was first defined as 'the quantitative methods of the research on the development of science as an informational process'. Methodologically, it is a development of *bibliometrics*, or 'the quantitative methods of the research on the development of science as an informational process'. However, it is specifically concerned with 'the exploration and evaluation of scientific research'.[9]

On the scientometrics market the citation is the main currency.[10] It serves as a flexible unit of measurement, and the measurement has a number of real-world implications—for example, as an index for universities to assess when considering a candidate for a position—and universities, it bears recalling, are one of the traditional 'holding pens' of the members of the arbitral community. The rationale is that citation counts are positively associated with subsequent impact.[11] To take an extreme case, high numbers of citations have even been correlated with the likelihood of being awarded a Nobel prize.[12] Therein, then, lies the connection with influence and social capital.

After parsing citations from scholarly works, a variety of techniques can be used to make the data say something. Most obviously, one can simply count the number of citations that are received by any scholarly work. High citation counts, as we said, are a good predictor of impact, so this already is meaningful, as it suggests how much a given work, and its author, likely have made a dent in the literature, have steered the knowledge in the field in a certain direction. Fine. But this is a bit crude. It is in fact a brutal over-simplification to say that there is one single, common body of knowledge in a field, as if everyone in the field knew roughly the same things, understood them in the same way, believed in the correctness or appropriateness of the same things. In many,

6 E. Gaillard, 'Sociology of International Arbitration', (2015) 31 Arbitration International 1.

7 Ibid. 9.

8 The development of scientometrics as a field is generally credited to Derek de Solla Price. See Derek John de Solla Price, *Little Science, Big Science—and Beyond* (Columbia University Press, 1963).

9 John Mingers and Loet Leydesdorff, 'A Review of Theory and Practice in Scientometrics', (2015) 246 European Journal of Operational Research 1, 1.

10 Ibid.

11 Yves Gingras and Matthew L. Wallace, 'Why It Has Become More Difficult to Predict Nobel Prize Winners: A Bibliometric Analysis of Nominees and Winners of the Chemistry and Physics Prizes (1901–2007)', (2010) 82 Scientometrics 401.

12 Gregory J. Feist, 'Quantity, Quality, and Depth of Research as Influences on Scientific Eminence: Is Quantity Most Important?', (1997) 10 Creativity Research Journal 325, 326.

perhaps most, fields of knowledge, there likely are very few central ideas which really structure the entire field, central ideas which are accepted by everyone in the field. Knowledge in a field is likely better thought of as a set of entangled and partly overlapping clusters of ideas, beliefs, values, and postulates. To make the data show this, and how it plays out in the field of arbitration, we can use essential notions of network analysis to a scientific field: the data now tells us who cites whom or what.[13]

Technically, this can be done through co-authorship analysis, where individual nodes in the network (authors) are given greater connectedness on the basis of the number of works that they have authored together. Or it is possible to consider basic citation analysis, which shifts nodes closer together depending on the number of times two authors tend to cite each other. Still, it is possible to go further, making relatedness a function of how many times two works are cited together (co-citation analysis) or even of the number of times they cite the same works together. The possibilities of course go much further, and the research questions one can address through one such approach are numerous. In the balance of this chapter, we hope to demonstrate the interest of this new methodology, by highlighting latent patterns in the arbitration literature and thus illuminating our overall, bird's-eye picture of it: from an intuitive guess about what happens in arbitration scholarship we can now progressively turn to a more informed, crisper picture.

1.2.2 Measuring arbitration literature

We measure the arbitration literature in two ways. First, we determine which works are the most cited, in absolute terms and over time, for two different time windows (see Tables 1.1 and 1.2). This is, if you will, the equivalent of scouting for the highest summits in a mountain range. In the terms from above, these are, then, the works that likely have had the most impact on the knowledge in and about arbitration, where this knowledge is taken as a single, common whole. Second, we look at what the co-citation network can tell us about the make-up of the world of arbitration literature. This allows us to see 'invisible colleges',[14] and we thus seek to confirm our hypotheses, anticipating encounters with islets, archipelagos, and whole continents. These are the expected clusters of ideas, beliefs, values, and postulates from above, which go beyond the simplistic idea of arbitration knowledge as a single, common whole.

[13] For an overview, see Farideh Osareh, 'Bibliometrics, Citation Analysis and Co-Citation Analysis: A Review of Literature I', (1996) 46 Libri 149; 'Bibliometrics, Citation Anatysis and Co-Citation Analysis: A Review of Literature II', (1996) 46 Libri 217; Howard D. White and Katherine W. McCain, 'Visualizing a Discipline: An Author Co-Citation Analysis of Information Science, 1972–1995', (1998) 49 Journal of the American Society for Information Science 327.

[14] Diana Crane, 'Social Structure in a Group of Scientists: A Test of the "Invisible College" Hypothesis', (1969) 34 American Sociological Review 335; Oscar Schachter, 'Invisible College of International Lawyers', (1977) 72 Nw. UL Rev 217; Markus Gmür, 'Co-Citation Analysis and the Search for Invisible Colleges: A Methodological Evaluation', (2003) 57 Scientometrics 27.

Table 1.1 The most-cited works overall

Cites	Authors	Title	Year	ECC	Cites/ year	Cites/ author	Authorcount	Age
1394	Y. Dezalay, B. G. Garth	Dealing in virtue: international commercial arbitration and the construction of a transnational legal order	1996	1394	60.61	697	2	23
1080	A. Redfern, M. Hunter	Law and practice of international commercial arbitration	2004	1080	72	540	2	15
871	G. Born	International commercial arbitration	2009	871	87.1	871	1	10
867	S. D. Franck	The legitimacy crisis in investment treaty arbitration: privatizing public international law through inconsistent decisions	2004	867	57.8	867	1	15
797	B. O'Neill	A problem of rights arbitration from the Talmud	1982	797	21.54	797	1	37
762	M. S. Miller, E. D. Tribble, N. Hardy, C. T. Hibbert	Diverse goods arbitration system and method for allocating resources in a distributed computer system	1997	762	34.64	191	4	22
759	J. D. M Lew, L. A. Mistelis, S. M. Kröll, S. Kröll	Comparative international commercial arbitration	2003	759	47.44	190	4	16
676	H. Lauterpacht	Private law sources and analogies of international law: with special reference to international arbitration	2002	676	39.76	676	1	17
675	F. Elkouri, E. A. Elkouri, E. P. Goggin, M. M. Volz	How arbitration works	1985	675	19.85	169	4	34
510	J. R. Sternlight	Panacea or corporate tool? Debunking the Supreme Court's preference for binding arbitration	1996	510	22.17	510	1	23
497	A. Cox	Reflections upon labor arbitration	1958	497	8.15	497	1	61
491	P. Fouchard, B. Goldman	Fouchard, Gaillard, Goldman on international commercial arbitration	1999	491	24.55	246	2	20
479	N. Blackaby, C. Partasides	Redfern and Hunter on international arbitration	2009	479	47.9	240	2	10

(continued)

Table 1.1 (Continued)

Cites	Authors	Title	Year	ECC	Cites/ year	Cites/ author	Authorcount	Age
448	S. Mentschikoff	Commercial arbitration	1961	448	7.72	448	1	58
439	D. S. Schwartz	Enforcing small print to protect big business: employee and consumer rights claims in an age of compelled arbitration	1997	439	19.95	439	1	22
380	G. Van Harten	Investment treaty arbitration and public law	2007	380	31.67	380	1	12
372	S. J. Brams	Negotiation games: applying game theory to bargaining and arbitration	2003	372	23.25	372	1	16
370	J. R. Sternlight	Creeping mandatory arbitration: is it just?	2004	370	24.67	370	1	15
357	K. V W. Stone	Mandatory arbitration of individual employment rights: the yellow dog contract of the 1990s	1995	357	14.88	357	1	24
348	I. R. Macneil, R. E. Speidel, T. J. Stipanowich	Federal arbitration law: agreements, awards, and remedies under the Federal Arbitration Act	1994	348	13.92	116	3	25

Table 1.2 The most cited works 2008–2018

Cites	Authors	Title	Year	ECC	Cites/year	Cites/author	Authorcount	Age
871	G. Born	International commercial arbitration	2009	871	87.1	871	1	10
479	N. Blackaby, C. Partasides	Redfern and Hunter on international arbitration	2009	479	47.9	240	2	10
308	C. McLachlan, L. Shore, M. Weiniger	International investment arbitration: substantive principles	2017	308	154	103	3	2
303	M. L. Moses	The principles and practice of international commercial arbitration	2017	303	151.5	303	1	2
219	C. Dugan, D. Wallace, N. Rubins, B. Sabahi	Investor–state arbitration	2011	219	27.38	55	4	8
219	T. J. Stipanowich	Arbitration: the new litigation	2010	219	24.33	219	1	9
217	L. Reed, J. Paulsson, N. Blackaby	Guide to ICSID arbitration	2011	217	27.13	72	3	8
215	C. N. Brower, S. W. Schill	Is arbitration a threat or a boon to the legitimacy of international investment law?	2008	215	19.55	108	2	11
214	M. Goltsman, J. Hörner, G. Pavlov, F. Squintani	Mediation, arbitration and negotiation	2009	214	21.4	54	4	10
212	J. Resnik	Diffusing disputes: the public in the private of arbitration, the private in courts, and the erasure of rights	2014	212	42.4	212	1	5
211	S. D. Franck	Development and outcomes of investment treaty arbitration	2009	211	21.1	211	1	10
188	S. M. J. Mustill, S. C. Boyd	The law and practice of commercial arbitration in England	2009	188	18.8	94	2	10
174	M. Rubino-Sammartano	International arbitration law and practice	2014	174	34.8	174	1	5

(continued)

Table 1.2 (Continued)

Cites	Authors	Title	Year	ECC	Cites/year	Cites/author	Authorcount	Age
165	B. Simma	Foreign investment arbitration: a place for human rights?	2011	165	20.63	165	1	8
164	G. Born	International arbitration: law and practice	2012	164	23.43	82	2	7
149	T. H. Oehmke	Oehmke commercial arbitration	2008	149	13.55	149	1	11
143	A. J. S. Colvin	An empirical study of employment arbitration: case outcomes and processes	2011	143	17.88	143	1	8
142	A. A. P. Bruhl	The unconscionability game: strategic judging and the evolution of federal arbitration law	2008	142	12.91	142	1	11
137	G. Van Harten	Arbitrator behaviour in asymmetrical adjudication: an empirical study of investment treaty arbitration	2012	137	19.57	137	1	7
135	D. S. Schwartz	Mandatory arbitration and fairness	2008	135	12.27	135	1	11

In order to do so, we need, of course, to gather citation data on arbitration literature. (see Figure 1.1) Yet this brings us to a common problem in scientometrics: the quality of the source data. Indeed, citation analyses of this kind are only as good as what is fed into the machine. (Computer scientists, not prone to convoluted literary metaphors, call this the GIGO Principle: Garbage In Garbage Out.) Generally speaking, Clarivate's Web of Science[15] is the preferred source for extracting citation data, which can be downloaded in computer-readable format; but it is by no means perfect. Not only is it not a freely accessible service, but it is also fairly under-inclusive, especially when scholarly works such as books and book chapters are concerned (even Oxford Handbooks). This may be problematic in the context of the arbitration literature, where different sources, some far less formal than others, all have their place.[16] The obvious alternative, Google Scholar, mitigates these problem: it is freely accessible, speedy, and more thorough for the counting of sources such as books and working papers posted on SSRN.[17] It does, however, suffer from the opposite problem: it is prone to over-inclusiveness, duplicate entries, and—most problematically—significant consistency problems with regard to the spelling of names and citation accuracy. In addition to these problems, Google renders automatic mining of its data difficult.

To compensate for these limitations, we combine the two sources. First, we rely on Google Scholar for the first type of analysis, thus benefiting from the broader outlook. For the analysis of the data obtained from this source—in order, then, to count the number of citations—we use software called Publish or Perish, a standard in the field.[18] For the second type of analysis, when we hunt for islands of knowledge, when we conduct co-citation analyses, we rely on Web of Science. Perhaps this does not map the entire field of arbitration, because of the under-inclusiveness of Web of Science. But the parts it does map, it maps very precisely, and we take these parts of the field to be representative of the whole. More precisely with regard to the method, we employ a number of keywords and search expressions designed to capture records relating to both international commercial and investment arbitration, processing them with the VOSViewer software developed by Nees Jan van Eck and Ludo Waltman.[19]

Finally, we should point out that our dataset suffers from an almost inevitable limitation, which has to do with language diversity. Indeed, it is almost impossible to gather data relating to sources published in languages other than English. Although the assumption that the literature not published in English is simply irrelevant seems of

[15] http://webofknowledge.com.

[16] Just as arbitral awards are sometimes sent out to colleagues or mailing lists prior to their formal publishing, the world of academia knows its own informal publication outlets.

[17] Anne-Wil K. Harzing and Ron Van der Wal, 'Google Scholar as a New Source for Citation Analysis', (2008) 8 Ethics in Science and Environmental Politics 61; Nabil Amara and Réjean Landry, 'Counting Citations in the Field of Business and Management: Why Use Google Scholar Rather than the Web of Science', (2012) 93 Scientometrics 553.

[18] Anne-Wil Harzing (2007), 'Publish or Perish', available from: http://www.harzing.com/pop.htm.

[19] Nees Jan van Eck and Ludo Waltman, 'Visualizing Bibliometric Networks', *Measuring Scholarly Impact* (Springer, 2014): https://link.springer.com/chapter/10.1007/978-3-319-10,377-8_13, accessed 27 Apr.2018. The software (free, but not Open Source) can be downloaded from: http://www.vosviewer.com.

course too much of a stretch[20] (it may be telling that names of French cities sometimes function as shorthand for entire schools of thought in arbitration),[21] there seems to be enough anecdotal evidence to suggests that the status of English as the lingua franca of scientific communication may make the limitation a little more tolerable.[22] These inevitable shortcomings notwithstanding, we submit that the data we present maintains its overall illustrative value. Ultimately, Korzybski's general caveat is worth recalling: the map is not the territory—but it resembles it closely, it can still be useful to navigate it.[23]

1.2.3 Reconnaissance

The classic literature on citations and precedents focuses on the reasons for citing and the reasons for citing one specific person or authority. These are interesting questions. But they are not quite ours. Our question, investigated through a scientometric analysis, rather focuses on who is cited together. The reasons for this outlook should be intuitive: as scholars in the field, we know who the players are, but it is only by thinking three-dimensionally, as it were, that we may place them on the checkerboard and better understand their game. (Or as good gossipers would put it, and they have a good grasp of what is intuitively interesting: who does what with whom?)

Consider, for example, the question of who the main authorities are in the field—or rather we should say, already at the level of hypothesis, based on the discussion above, who the main specific authorities are for the specific sub-fields in the literature.

By employing a simple clustering algorithm, we can group together authors who tend to be cited together often. And notice (Figure 1.2) how the groups form, how the clusters are distributed: seasoned practitioners are more likely to be cited alongside seasoned practitioners,[24] and theorists of the legitimacy crisis of investment arbitration alongside, and by, their counterparts north of a border.[25]

No surprise here: these are different communities with different interests and different purposes in their contributions to the social construct that is the arbitration literature (as we will discuss in the second part of this chapter). They seek to construct distinct things and for these distinct constructions enlist distinct co-workers.

[20] With reference to the making of European law scholarship, see Bruno de Witte, 'European Union Law: A Unified Academic Discipline?' in Antoine Vauchez and Bruno de Witte (eds), *Lawyering Europe: European Law as a Transnational Social Field* (Bloomsbury, 2013).

[21] Thomas Schultz, *Transnational Legality: Stateless Law and International Arbitration* (OUP, 2014), 153f.

[22] See in general C. Tardy, 'The Role of English in Scientific Communication: Lingua Franca or Tyrannosaurus Rex?' (2004) 3 Journal of English for Academic Purposes 247.

[23] Alfred Korzybski, *Science and Sanity: An Introduction to Non-Aristotelian Systems and General Semantics* (Institute of General Semantics, 1958), 58.

[24] E.g. Gabrielle Kaufmann-Kohler, David D. Caron, Emmanuel Gaillard, Yas Banifatemi, Michael Reisman, and Gary Born, to name a few, are all likely to be cited together.

[25] Susan D. Franck, 'The Legitimacy Crisis in Investment Treaty Arbitration: Privatizing Public International Law through Inconsistent Decisions', (2005) 73 Fordham Law Review 1521.

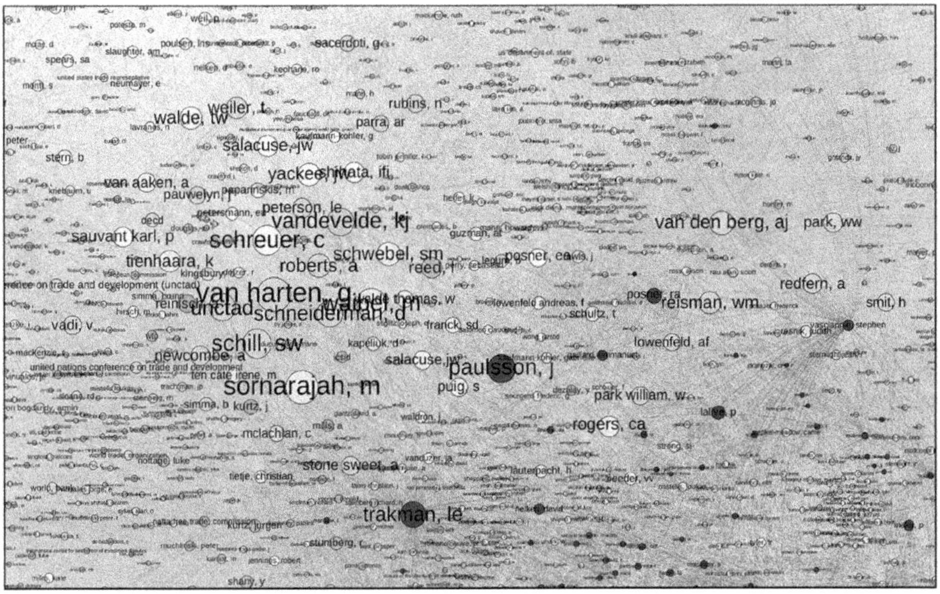

FIGURE 1.1 Citation network. The connections between nodes are, simply put, citations and describe a 'who cites whom' relationship.

But beyond that, we can see that clustering also occurs around books and articles made to serve as 'authorities',[26] as so many referencing totems, connecting together either paradigm adherents or those who attempt to rethink paradigms.[27]

There is more, too: a co-citation network allows us to discern patterns of institutional and mentorship bonds. (From co-workers we have moved here to sidekicks, one might brutally put this.) By unpacking these invisible colleges,[28] one can then identify social factors driving the development and direction of the arbitration literature. This question is best addressed with a sociological approach,[29] but it is worth mentioning in the current discussion too because of the sheer importance of informal networks emerging in the field.[30]

But let us now zoom out. A bird's-eye look at the scientific landscape provides an empirical confirmation of one of our simple assumptions: the arbitration literature is

[26] Christoph H. Schreuer and International Centre for Settlement of Investment Disputes, *The ICSID Convention: A Commentary* (Cambridge University Press, 2001); Zachary Douglas, *The International Law of Investment Claims* (Cambridge University Press, 2009); Rudolf Dolzer and Christoph Schreuer, *Principles of International Investment Law*, 2nd edn (Oxford University Press, 2012).

[27] Stephan W. Schill, *The Multilateralization of International Investment Law* (Cambridge University Press, 2009); Stephan W. Schill (ed.), *International Investment Law and Comparative Public Law* (Oxford University Press, 2010); Anthea Roberts, 'Clash of Paradigms: Actors and Analogies Shaping the Investment Treaty System', (2013) 107 American Journal of International Law 45.

[28] Crane (n. 13); Schachter (n. 13). [29] See Ch. 30 by Moshe Hirsch in this Handbook.

[30] Consider the fact that an authority such as Redfern and Hunter's commentary specifically mentions the practice of circulating awards on mailing lists. See Nigel Blackaby et al., *Redfern and Hunter on International Arbitration* (Oxford University Press, 2015), 568.

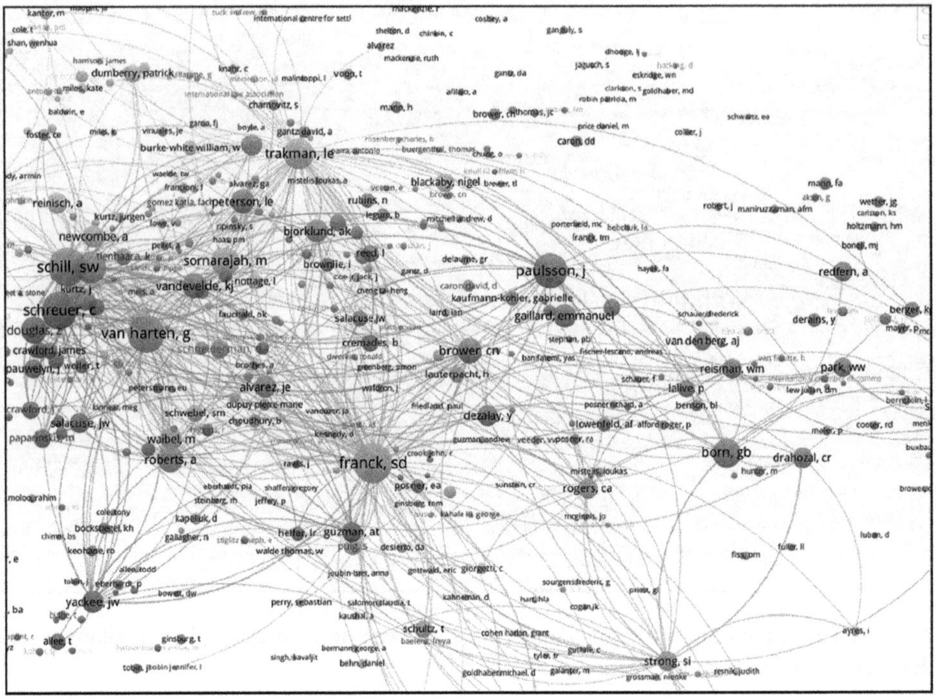

FIGURE 1.2 Co-citation network. Here, authors are connected to each other if they are cited together. In both cases clusters are formed by authors who are more connected to each other—with these two types of relationships—than to the rest of the network.

very much the product of a multiplicity of actors, who thus all appear to contribute to its advancement. To be sure, as Figure 1.3 shows, the affiliations of the producers of the arbitration literature are quite variegated. They do tend, however, to be ultimately limited to a specific set of professional and academic institutions. In this respect, the arbitration literature, a bit like a Möbius band, both reflecting and constituting the field it describes and animates.

Let us explain. Arbitration, as a field, is made in a varied selection of places at the same time. Law schools may still be the chief vehicle of delivery of information about it (yes, 'vehicle of delivery', not necessarily place of production: universities give university authority to the information that transits through them, but they do not necessarily guarantee that the information was produced by university members working with university methods and university objectives). But affiliations with law firms and other institutions of practice are not radically less likely. Now to the important point: the co-citation-based connection with practice seems barely escapable. What Figure 1.3 shows in this regard is the connectedness between academic and professional affiliations (consider the precise composition of the grey-scale clusters to see the point, literally). In other words, it makes it quite clear that scholarly works in the discipline tend to combine influences from both camps—to the point, and hence the metaphor we promised to

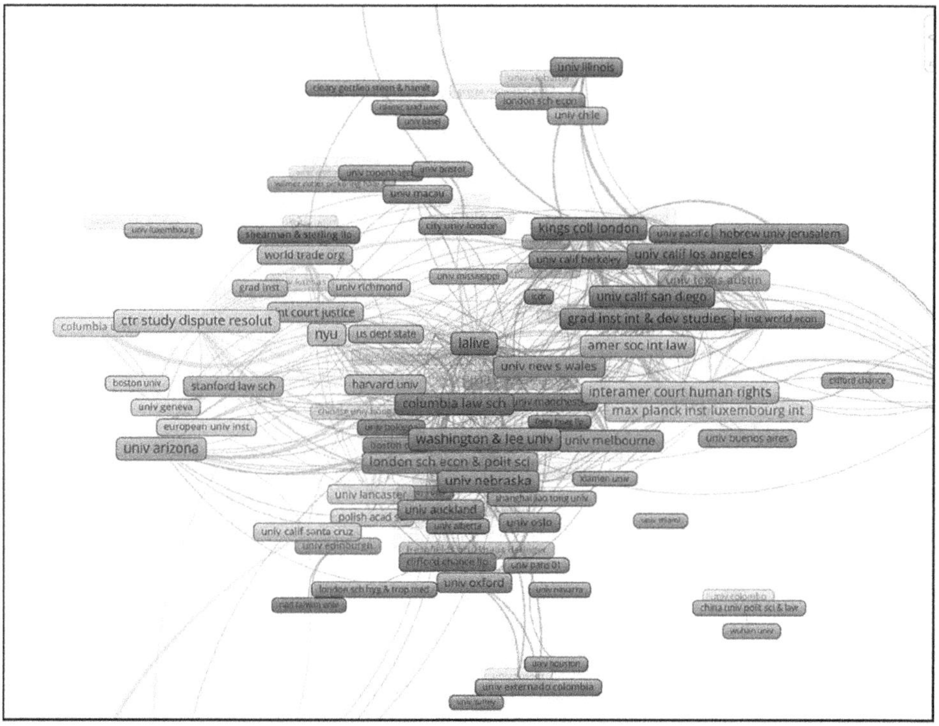

FIGURE 1.3 A co-citation network showing the affiliations of authors commonly cited together.

explain, that it is as difficult to distinguish them as it is to distinguish the two sides of a Möbius band (a band with only one side, with the mathematical property of being unorientable: if you were to walk along the full length of the band, you would come back to your starting point after having walked both sides without ever crossing an edge).

The other meaningful point that emerges from Figure 1.3 is that, to the chagrin of many, no one specific institution is really more central than the others, despite the fact, for instance, that some have a longer tradition in the field.

Co-citation analysis also allows us to make a point about the sources that are more influential in the world of the arbitration literature. As Figure 1.4 shows, the increased focus on questions relating to arbitration under investment treaties makes references to public international law sources far more common. The emerging picture is not, of course, one that suggests isolation of the worlds of investment arbitration on one side and commercial arbitration on the other. Interaction between the two communities is evident. But one may observe differences in citation patterns. For example, the field of investment arbitration shows closer connections with general-purpose law journals and reviews than commercial arbitration does. One thing this means is that investment arbitration is of greater relevance beyond its own specialism than commercial arbitration is; or to take this one step further, its broader societal relevance is more readily recognised.

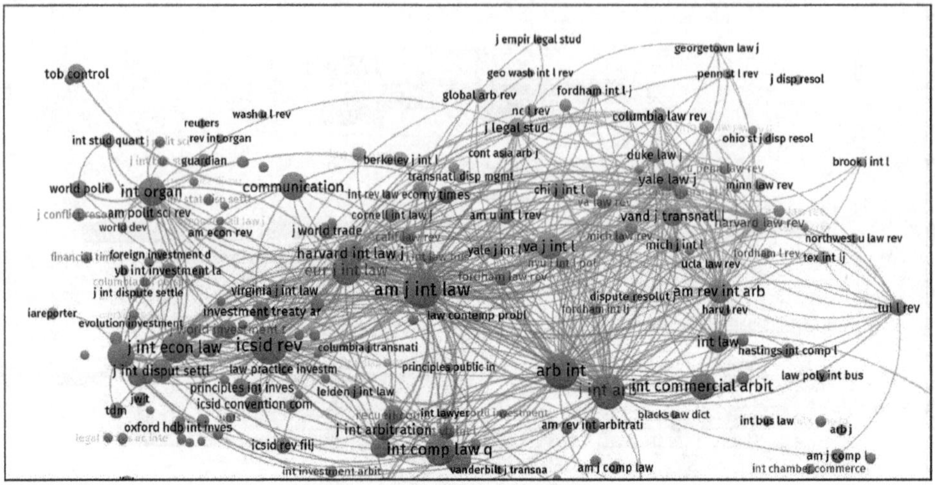

FIGURE 1.4 A co-citation network showing journals that are cited together.

Yes, this is all quite in line with the intuitive understanding of those who know the field, but here the data shows this to be in fact the case and suggests the degree to which this is the case.

The co-citation data also highlights a general divide between law journals on one or the other end of the Atlantic—a tendency that can by the way be observed in a number of other disciplines.[31]

From the perspective of network importance, works on international investment arbitration clearly dominate the landscape. There can be many explanations for this, but the following ones may provide a starting point. First, investment arbitration attracts a wider range of practitioners and academics versed in fields other than commercial arbitration, such as international lawyers. They have found themselves in a position to comment on a larger jurisprudential output, and may have incentives to do so to find a way into the club of those who are regularly appointed. Further, investment awards tend to be public, thus inherently attracting commentary. Finally—for our purposes—investment arbitration is at the centre of broader debates about questions relating to the emergence of transnational legal orders, the nature of international adjudication, the status of the very notion of sovereignty, the rethinking of dispute settlement institutions, and so much more: in short, the societal relevance from above.

As to what gets cited, it is not surprising to find higher citation scores for textbooks, reference works, and commentaries. But even then, distinctions can be made: obviously, citing *Redfern & Hunter*,[32] or even *The International Law of Investment Claims*,[33] may be not quite the same thing, serving not quite the same objective, as citing Sornarajah's

[31] We do not address here the important question of whether citation patterns are related to the need to address a specific community or another. Guglielmo Verdirame, '"The Divided West": International Lawyers in Europe and America', (2007) 18 European Journal of International Law 553.

[32] Blackaby et al. (n. 30). [33] Douglas (n. 26).

The International Law on Foreign Investment.[34] Although singling out the most political of the lot may be a harder question than what would appear at first sight, it is clear that these three works serve very different purposes and audiences.

Consider, for example, the referencing patterns of (and before) investment tribunals. There it is to be expected that an invocation of scholarship will be an invocation of incontrovertible authority—thus, it is not surprising to discover that Schreuer's *Commentary* has been cited so many times.[35]

In a sense then, the important, if obvious, point is this: different actors will rely on different sources, which better match their arguments.[36] And this is true when submitting an argument to a tribunal as it is true when making 'objective' statements about arbitration. So much then for the idea that knowledge, about arbitration here at least, can be truly objective, can be anything else than socially constructed. So much, also, for those who think of themselves as being at the centre of the discipline: if 'the discipline' can be likened to the knowledge, to the literature, then it does not have much of a centre.

Let us briefly return to the Möbius band, to insist on a central argument that runs through this chapter. Although there are obvious differences in these uses of scholarship, they all are deeply intertwined. This is so because the scholarly community and that of arbitration practitioners, which already overlap to a significant degree, interact with each other in a continuous feedback loop guided by incentives of various nature. There is no real distinction between commentators, the readership, and the object of study—all of it is one and the same. Thus, an arbitrator handing down a decision will be mindful of the criticism—sometimes ferocious—that it may encounter, and mindful that future tribunals will have full recollection of it.[37] Often—and the examples are really too many to necessitate examples—arguments made in awards will be rehashed, almost verbatim, in an article or book chapter. On the other side of the barricade—assuming, again, that there is one—linger the same anxieties, as a commentator seeking appointment knows any possibility of appointment to a tribunal may have to survive the intensive vetting of one's scholarly production by a team of law firm associates tasked with

[34] M. Sornarajah, *The International Law on Foreign Investment* (Cambridge University Press, 2004): http://public.eblib.com/choice/publicfullrecord.aspx?p=266,634, accessed 21 July 2016; *The International Law on Foreign Investment*, 3rd edn (Cambridge University Press, 2010).

[35] At the time of writing, Schreuer's commentary had been cited by 161 majority decisions. Schreuer and International Centre for Settlement of Investment Disputes (n. 26); Christoph H. Schreuer, *The ICSID Convention: A Commentary* (Cambridge University Press, 2009).

[36] See e.g. *CC/Devas (Mauritius) Ltd, Devas Employees Mauritius Private Limited and Telecom Devas Mauritius Limited v India*, PCA Case No. 2013-09, Award on Jurisdiction and Merits, para. 436, summarizing India's reliance on Gus Van Harten's work (*Investment Treaty Arbitration and Public Law* (Oxford University Press, 2007)) as critical authority against 'attempts to expand the FET concept beyond the minimum standard of treatment provided by customary international law in the absence of evidence evincing such intention of the Contracting Parties'.

[37] *Waguih Elie George Siag & Clorinda Vecchi v Arab Republic of Egypt*, ICSID Case No. ARB 05 15, Award, 1 June 2009, paras. 498–9 ('The Loewen decision has been the subject of intense scrutiny and criticism by international law scholars and investment arbitration practitioners... Commentators have also stigmatised the Tribunal's application of a rule developed in one particular context... Finally, academics and practitioners have questioned the relevance of the Loewen Tribunal's conclusions').

identifying biases, and may be put into question by a proposal for disqualification at a later stage.[38]

1.3 A FRAMEWORK ON INTERNATIONAL ARBITRATION LITERATURE

Having examined the types of works that tend to be influential, can we infer anything more and further catalogue the types of literature that deal with international arbitration? The sections that follow attempt to provide a general framework to classify these types of scholarly production.

1.3.1 Types of legal literature

It is generally said that the purpose of mostly any academic discipline, be it within hard sciences, social sciences, or humanities, is to articulate propositions.[39] These propositions together form a system of thought,[40] which in turn creates knowledge that is eventually susceptible, if not of verification and falsification,[41] at least of rational assent, of rational approval.[42] In other words, it ultimately seeks to improve our understanding of what has happened and what is likely to happen.[43]

Systems of thought are generally organized around a paradigm,[44] a central idea, a central understanding. The whole purpose of law as a scientific discipline can for

[38] *Urbaser S.A. and Consorcio de Aguas Bilbao Bizkaia, Bilbao Biskaia Ur Partzuergoa v The Argentine Republic*, ICSID Case No. ARB/07/26, Decision on Claimants' Proposal to Disqualify Professor Campbell McLachlan, 12 Aug. 2010. See the interesting reflections on such matters and the potential 'chilling effect' on academic writing made in Stephan Schill, 'Editorial', (2014) 15 Journal of World Investment & Trade 1.

[39] This is of course such a general statement that much of the philosophy of science could be referred to. For useful starting points, see, on law, François Ost, 'Science du droit 540', in André-Jean Arnaud (ed.), *Dictionnaire encyclopédique de théorie et de sociologie du droit* (LGDJ, 1998), and more generally on scientific work, Isabelle Stengers, *Cosmopolitiques, tome 1: La guerre des sciences* (La Découverte and Les Empêcheurs de penser en rond, 1996); Bruno Latour, 'How to Talk About the Body: The Normative Dimension of Science Studies', 10 Body & Society 205 (2004); *Pandora's Hope: Essays on the Reality of Science Studies* (Harvard University Press, 1999).

[40] Imre Lakatos, 'Falsification and the Methodology of Scientific Research Programmes', in Imre Lakatos and Alan Musgrave (eds), *Criticism and the Growth of Knowledge* (Cambridge University Press, 1970).

[41] Karl R. Popper, *Conjectures and Refutations* (Routledge, 1963).

[42] David Hartley, *Observations on Man: His Frame, His Duty and His Expectations* (Richardson, 1749), 324: 'rational assent... to any proposition may be defined as readiness to affirm it to be true, proceeding from a close association of the ideas suggested by the proposition, with the idea or internal feeling belonging to the word truth; or of the terms of the proposition with the word truth.'

[43] See Popper (n. 41).

[44] Thomas Kuhn, *The Structure of Scientific Revolutions*, 2nd edn (University of Chicago Press, 1970).

instance be described as a 'cognitive activity seeking to provide a representation of the legal phenomenon in conformity with the scientific paradigm that was endorsed'.[45] A central paradigm, and often a number of smaller secondary paradigms, structure and validate the thinking in the field. Such paradigms could, for instance, be a central understanding of what arbitration itself is, or a central understanding of core ideas in arbitration, such as consent, or public policy,[46] or competence-competence, or that investment arbitration protects investors, or that investment arbitration multilateralizes bilateral treaties.[47] From this central idea, or ideas, follow rules of truth shared by members of the discipline: inferences from the paradigm about what is legally valid and what is not, what is an accurate explanation of reality and what is not.

It is certain that, after a while, anomalies start to appear that the orthodox paradigms cannot explain. As this happens more and more frequently, the validity of the old paradigm is questioned, and new candidate ideas line up to become the next. Though the old paradigm in place resists for a time, due to various stakes involved and the beliefs and values that undergird this particular paradigm, it eventually resigns, allowing a new one to emerge and determine what is true and what is false in the field, what can be and what cannot, what is legally valid and what is not.[48] In other words, when the system of thought in place no longer provides the best explanation, among competing explanations, of reality, then the system of thought changes, taking us somewhat nearer (when all goes well) to an accurate representation of an observer-independent reality (what philosophers call 'truth').[49] And so our understanding progresses through research. This, in essence, is the scientific theory of law as a scientific discipline.

1.3.1.1 *Persuasion*

Of course, in law generally, much of what is published in law reviews or in law books does not really try to produce knowledge filtered by critical thinking. It rather tries to produce opinion, approximating religion more than social sciences or the humanities (notice the connotation of the word 'doctrine'). In these cases, what counts is our ability to persuade. This type of literature finds inspiration in the art of persuasion.[50] It also may well find *aspiration* in powerful ideological systems, at its most dramatic even espousing logophobia, in the sense of 'a sceptical doctrine about rationality... [where]

[45] Ost (n. 39).

[46] Gus Van Harten, 'Investment Treaty Arbitration, Procedural Fairness, and the Rule of Law', in Stephan W. Schill (ed), *International Investment Law and Comparative Public Law* (Oxford University Press, 2010): http://www.oxfordscholarship.com/view/10.1093/acprof:oso/9780199589104.001.0001/acprof-9,780,199,589,104-chapter-20, accessed 26 July 2016; *Sovereign Choices and Sovereign Constraints: Judicial Restraint in Investment Treaty Arbitration* (Oxford University Press, 2013).

[47] Schill (n. 27).

[48] Kuhn (n. 44).

[49] E.g. Andrea Bianchi, 'Reflexive Butterfly Catching: Insights from a Situated Catcher', in Joost Pauwelyn et al. (eds), *Informal International Lawmaking* (Oxford University Press, 2012), 200–215.

[50] See e.g. James Boyd White, *The Legal Imagination* (University of Chicago Press, 1985), and Austin Sarat, Matthew Anderson, and Cathrine O. Frank, 'Introduction: On the Origins and Prospects of the Humanistic Study of Law', in Austin Sarat, Matthew Anderson, and Cathrine O. Frank (eds), *Law and the Humanities: An Introduction* (Cambridge University Press, 2010), 1–46.

rationality cannot be an objective constraint on us but is just whatever we make it, and what we make it depends on what we value'.[51] Logophobics, to take it to an extreme, 'have developed an arsenal of strategist obfuscate clear thinking, which they deploy whenever pressed by a sceptic'.[52] When only persuasion counts, logical fallacies are not merely condoned. They are practised, refined, admired if they carry the audience. We take into the law review and the law book the craft developed by advocates for courts—developed for their most mesmerizing feats in court, rather than logical conclusiveness. The law reviews and the law books then dispense the labels of 'literature' or 'scholarship'.

Hence a parallel with religions, which prevail not because they provide a better account of reality, but merely because they become stronger, more powerful. The Crusaders certainly seemed to think so. The same happens to legal thinking, which changes not only like paradigms but also like religion. Central ideas in a field can also be imposed by brute force: our central idea is better than yours because I am stronger. I can push it by inundating the field with publications by our gang mates, organizing conferences around our central idea, launching journals that take our approach, by telling our students (in a broad sense) that mine is the only correct way of thinking, exclusively marks the proprieties. Our school eventually prevails over yours.

By way of example, today much bombast and invective and displays of raw lobbying power mark much of the thinking about the question whether, in the context of the Transatlantic Trade and Investment Partnership (TTIP), EU–US investment disputes should be solved by arbitral tribunals or by a permanent international investment court. Much less attention is devoted to, for instance, finding evidence, historical parallels, developing theories that help us understand the difference, and trying to predict what would likely happen.

1.3.1.2 *Scholarly review*

Other forms of legal literature have other sources of inspiration. To see the point, let us first say that we seem to have a general issue with role models when we write on law. That role models often determine, or at least influence, the way we think, the type of thinking we believe is appropriate, is no more than a truism. Then again, the implication of the truism is that, as scholars, it would make sense for us to have as role models exceptional scholars (exceptional as in 'exceptionally good', not as in 'exceptionally famous'), be they in our field or in a neighbouring discipline. Should we not dream of being the person who brought down a central paradigm in our field, or who came up with a new key idea in our discipline? Or at least contribute a small but significant piece to either of these enterprises?

As it happens, much of legal literature seems to identify itself with the work of an appellate court, chastising or complimenting the lower court, engaging in an 'imitation

[51] N. Shackel, 'The Vacuity of Postmodernist Methodology', 36 Metaphilosophy 295 (2005).

[52] M. Pigliucci, 'Logophobia', 33 Skeptical Inquirer 24 (2009).

of judicial idioms, tasks, gestures, professional anxieties, and the like.'[53] Why, really, when we look for a role model for our scholarly activities do we look to individuals who are precisely not scholars, but judges—individuals who are neither more nor less admirable but have a very different social role and whose work is structured by very different constraints and incentives than ours? They—the judges—have the practical task of providing a satisfactory judicial solution to the case at hand and thinking of its broader repercussions.[54] As Pierre Schlag puts it, '[t]heir words... visit legal acts on... parties, and third parties'.[55] We have the intellectual task of providing a satisfactory scholarly treatment of a question that relates to law. They provide decisions; we provide ideas (or just information). The difference matters, be it only because the degree of intellectual sophistication most appropriate to handle these tasks, the suitable ideational toolboxes, are significantly different. Pierre Schlag again, *pace* the judicial profession: 'Judicial discourse is not intellectually edifying. It *is not designed to be*.'[56] A legal decision may be intellectually hogwash, but socially genius, and thus a good decision. Whether the same is true for legal scholarship is entirely more questionable.

1.3.1.3 *Initiative*

Another role model is possibly even more representative of the psychological workings of legal literature. Indeed at other times legal scholars seem to identify themselves with members of parliament, giving the thumbs up to someone's proposal, ridiculing another, taking sides in a project of 'norm-advocacy'.[57] Norm-advocacy is the practice of choosing some norm (a *norm*, not a concept) and doing whatever it takes to have it adopted—adopted by an official body or by a community of other individuals who likewise 'vote' on such norms, which again could be the community of legal scholars. To be clear, we are not arguing that this sort of literature is not useful. It tries to be part of the substance of the law, to shape doctrines, to offer solutions to judges, arbitrators, and legislators, to influence them. That may well be part of our role as *citizens*, here as special citizens because of our specialized knowledge in certain legal areas. But is this our role as scholars? Schlag once more: 'adoption... is oddly treated as a sign of good scholarship as opposed to what it is (or might be)—namely, a sign of good service.'[58]

1.3.1.4 *Reporting on the law and on oneself*

Yet another role model that seems to influence our thinking as legal scholars is that of the journalist. We are in the realm of what we could call reporting or, indeed, 'case-law

[53] P. Schlag, 'Spam Jurisprudence, Air Law, and the Rank Anxiety of Nothing Happening (a Report on the State of the Art)', 97 Georgetown Law Journal 803 (2009), 812.

[54] P. Schlag, 'Anti-Intellectualism', 16 Cardozo Law Review 1111 (1995).

[55] P. Schlag, 'Jurisprudence Noire', 101 Columbia Law Review 1733 (2001), 1739.

[56] Schlag (n. 54), 813 (the emphasis is mine).

[57] P. Schlag, 'A Comment on Thomas Schultz's Editorial', 5 Journal of International Dispute Settlement 235 (2014), 236.

[58] P. Schlag, 'The Faculty Workshop', 60 Buffalo Law Review 807 (2012), 813.

journalism'[59] or legislative journalism: describing cases and legislative amendments, without really using them to form an overarching system of thought, without really trying to rationalize what is being studied. This approach is not necessarily too far away from that of those who focus on the idea that law is not only a theoretical corpus but a social practice too. The way law is actually practised shapes the real-world contents of the law (law on the books is shaped into law in action by practice, as the customary terminology would put it). Thus, the literature sometimes tries to lead the law somewhere by influencing how it is practised. This leads to a type of literature in arbitration that deals with, for instance, how witnesses are and *should* be cross-examined.

Note, however, that writings of this kind may be, in actual fact, reporting on *oneself*. Their purpose is not so much to advance our knowledge of law as a theoretical corpus or as a social practice, and not even to form opinion about a legal matter, as it is to advance our knowledge of the author of the writings: if you need to hire a lawyer who is good at a certain set of legal question, then I am your man. Let us write something that demonstrates how good we master these questions. It is bit like playing the violin in a masterclass. Undoubtedly beautiful to observe. But to be taken for what it is.

1.3.2 Consequences for the arbitration literature

Much of what we have described so far are points that apply to legal literature generally. Let us turn more specifically to arbitration.

First of all, it bears noting that arbitration has grown socially: there are quite more people who write on arbitration today than there were 30 years ago. There are more journals too, and more books. So there is more of it. But is it better?

Certainly, the arbitration literature is more diversified. Although this, too, is an oversimplification, but where there used to be mainly doctrinal work and case-law journalism, there is now, in addition to that, conceptual work, epistemological work, sociological work, socio-legal studies, critical systemic work, and much more. The methods are more diverse (think of the growth of empirical studies, for instance). There are more diverse political discourses about arbitration, discourses about the social values that arbitration sustains, and whether the sustainment of these values is socially, economically, politically a good idea or not. There is more interdisciplinary work, trying to bring into arbitration theoretical developments happening elsewhere, reaching out further into neighbouring fields (political science, economics, philosophy, psychology, literature). This would signal that we have more choices now when we engage in arbitration research. The field has become more ecumenical. Further, there seem to be more people who write on arbitration whose socio-professional recognition does not depend, or depends to a lesser degree, on their *practice* of arbitration. This is of import because our socio-professional interests, inevitably, shape our epistemology, they influence what we consider valid, interesting, admissible research.

[59] Schlag (n. 54), 821ff.

Quite clearly indeed, one's epistemology, what one is ready to recognize as true, valid knowledge, is influenced by one's interests. (In technical philosophical language: theory acceptance is driven by reasons-for-action as much, if not more so, as it is by epistemic reasons.)[60] Again: one's epistemology is influenced by one's interests. Think of a government lawyer, or a former government lawyer, who has interests (psychological or more tangible ones) in promoting or sustaining the power of governments. Such a person, because of his or her interests, is likely to have an epistemology that prevents him from recognizing, possibly even in his or her most candid moments, that non-state actors can create norms of, say, customary international law.[61] If one's interest is that governments stay strong, one's epistemology is likely to be such that only governments can create law, can create norms of international law.

A similar observation can be made about the epistemic community of arbitration—that is, the community of so-called experts that shapes the episteme of arbitration. The community, in other words, that shapes the knowledge we have of the field, the way in which we come to apprehend it theoretically, to use it practically and to explain its operation. That community has become much more diversified, much more fragmented into sub-communities, including for instance the commercial lawyers, the trade lawyers, the public lawyers, and the public international lawyers.[62] These are parallel, juxtaposed communities of individuals who think about international arbitration. These are parallel, juxtaposed drawings of the contours of international arbitration law and practice. They are parallel, juxtaposed epistemic fields. Each sub-community has a somewhat different understanding of arbitration, and they do not necessarily really talk to one another. The stars of one sub-community may have a very different standing in another sub-community—if they are known there at all.

As a result, there are more diverse discourses in arbitration today than there were thirty years ago. This matters because it means more experimentation with new ideas, and thus a greater likelihood that something really new emerges: unconscious thought structures ('epistemological obstacles', in Gaston Bachelard's terminology)[63] become diluted as individuals with more diverse backgrounds join the discussion, and thus stand less in the way of change. There may be less of a 'centre' and a 'periphery' of the

[60] Joseph Raz, *From Normativity to Responsibility* (Oxford University Press 2011), 36–7: 'Reasons for action, I will assume, are facts which constitute a case for (or against) the performance of an action. Epistemic reasons are reasons for believing in a proposition through being facts which are part of a case for (belief in) its truth (call such considerations 'truth-related')... theory acceptance is... acceptance of theories, not belief in them... accepting a proposition is conducting oneself in accord with the belief that there is sufficient reason to act on the assumption that the proposition is true: acceptance of the proposition that P entails belief, but not belief that P. Rather it entails belief that it is justified to act as if P. Thus acceptance combines epistemic and practical reasons, though its target is action rather than belief. Acceptance dominates many areas of practical thought.'

[61] Michael Wood, *Second Report on Identification of Customary International Law*, International Law Commission, A/CN.4/672, 2014.

[62] A. Roberts, 'Clash of Paradigms: Actors and Analogies Shaping the Investment Treaty System', 107 American Journal of International Law 45 (2013).

[63] Gaston Bachelard, *The Formation of the Scientific Mind: A Contribution to a Psychoanalysis of Objective Knowledge* (Clinamen, 2007).

discipline than there used to be—something that is reflected in our empirical study, too. Or rather there are a number of centres which all see some of the rest as periphery—but with more caution, it is contended, than ever before. And, indeed, given the communal and ideational connections between these centres (they are not watertight, they communicate, exchange ideas), meaningful ideas developed in each of these then have the potential to become a candidate for paradigm also in another centre—what in the language of the day we often call cross-fertilization. Epistemological breaks (again Bachelard's terminology[64]) may ensue, as unconscious thought structures become conscious and are abandoned, in the light of the conscious examination now possible, because of their insufficient analytical purchase. A new candidate for paradigm may fare better and take over. These are what we need to make the field progress. These are what is generally considered to make for a healthy scientific discipline.[65]

The bottom line is this: we are probably still far behind other legal fields, such as international law, which clearly is no longer the intellectual wasteland that it was said to be twenty years ago.[66] Arbitration is following a similar route, thanks in part, precisely, to the fact that international lawyers, but also political scientists, economists, and even militant NGOs, have joined the fray.

1.3.2.1 *Determinants of literature*

So what is it that produces the landscape of literature we have described so far? What drives its evolution? Why are some of the aspects of literature we described more present in arbitration, and others less? Why are there things we never do, never say, even though they intuitively seem to be worthwhile pursuits? What are the possible determinants of our scholarly activity in the field of arbitration?

Most things we do in life (or perhaps actually all of them) is governed by incentives and constraints. We want to do certain things and shirk or oppose others. We can do certain things and cannot do certain others. Incentives and constraints determine what we do. It is undisputed that this is a truism, but it is one that has proven remarkably interesting in understanding law itself. The simple idea that there are determinants that make us do what we do is at worst mildly informative and at best illuminating in understanding the behaviour of judges—why do they decide the way they do? Why do they interpret the law the way they do? This is the core of law & economics approaches and of legal realism. It works to understand arbitrator behaviour too.[67] Our claim is that it is at

[64] Ibid. [65] Ost (n. 39).

[66] B. S. Chimni, *International Law and World Order: A Critique of Contemporary Approaches* (Sage, 1993), 15. See also Mariti Koskenniemi, *From Apology to Utopia: The Structure of International Legal Argument* (Lakimiesliiton Kustannus, 1989), xiii; Arthur Nussbaum, *A Concise History of the Law of Nations* (Macmillan, 1947), 293.

[67] T. Schultz, 'Arbitral Decision-Making: Legal Realism and Law & Economics', 6 Journal of International Dispute Settlement 231 (2015); Bruce L. Benson, 'Arbitration', in Boudewijn Bouckaert and Gerrit De Geest (eds), *Encyclopedia of Law and Economics*, vol. 5: V *The Economics of Crime and Litigation* (Edward Elgar, 2000).

least also a quizzical heuristic to understand our own behaviour when we write on arbitration.

To be sure, the ways to account for the different determinants of our behaviour are numerous. We rely on a very general distinction—one uncommon in legal literature, but popular among philosophers: prudential vs moral reasons-for-action.[68] Prudential reasons-for-action relate to the pursuit of an actor's own interests. People act in a certain way for prudential reasons if they believe it is in their interest to do so, that they would be better off if they acted in that way. Put differently, prudential reasons-for-action are reasons potentially or actually influencing someone's behaviour which 'are focused exclusively or primarily on his own interests and only derivatively if at all on the interests of other people'.[69] Behaviour informed by moral reasons-for-action, instead, relies on the belief that it is 'morally' good to act in such a way. Morality is a question of interests, and pursuing it merely means to pursue the advancement of the interests of others. Moral reasons-for-action, then, are reasons potentially or actually influencing someone's behaviour which 'are focused exclusively or primarily on other people's interests and only derivatively if at all on his own interests'.[70]

In other words, we may do something because we believe it is in our own interest to do so (a prudential reason-for-action), or because we believe what we do is good for someone else (a moral reason-for-action). And so we may be torn between two courses of action, one advancing our interests but harming someone else's interests, the other advancing someone else's interests but harming our own. But to be clear, while these two types of reasons-for-action may pull in different directions, as the dilemma we just mentioned illustrates, they need not. They need not conflict, and they are not necessarily mutually exclusive; it is not necessarily one *or* the other. We can also do something because we believe it is good for both us *and* someone else.

Here our endeavour is to develop a heuristic through abstract reasoning, rather than a sociological project. A clarification is thus in order: just as others have used the phrase 'reasons-for-action' elsewhere, here too it refers 'not only to factors that actually do motivate people, but also to factors that *would* motivate them if they were to understand the serviceability of those factors for the furtherance of their general objectives'.[71] In other words, the prevalence of these factors in the actual determinants of actual literature is not a question we investigate, or even could investigate through abstract reasoning: this is an empirical point which would require a lot of social-scientific research, which would lead to a contribution to the sociology of professions. Interesting as this may be, this is not what we do or probably even could do: the research would be shrouded in complications and would require a great number of qualifications, since the actual determinants of concrete pieces of arbitration literature are 'a matter that will hinge on contingent features of human psychology and sociocultural influences'.[72]

[68] See e.g. Immanuel Kant, *Groundwork for the Metaphysics of Morals* (Oxford University Press, 2002, first published 1785), 199.

[69] M. H. Kramer, 'On the Moral Status of the Rule of Law', 63 Cambridge Law Journal 65 (2003), 66.

[70] Ibid. [71] Ibid. [72] Ibid.

In plain English: the interests, incentives and constraints we identify below are interests, incentives, and constraints regardless whether they are actually understood or not, whether they are actually acted upon or not, whether they actually make a difference to the literature or not. Scholars may not be aware of them when they write, or may not be influenced by them in any meaningful fashion for any other reason. Our point is that these reasons are serviceable for certain objectives—not that they are indeed followed.

Let us reiterate our set of questions without the jargon (yet the precisions from above of course still apply): What can the literature on international arbitration be good for? What advances other people's interests when we write on arbitration, and what are these interests? And what advances our own interests when we write on arbitration, and, again, what are these interests? There are things we write that we believe are good for us—us as authors as we write—and there are things we believe are good for other people, for groups that do not include us as a major stakeholder. What are these things? We will review these interests (which are as many determinants of arbitration literature) according to the distinction we just introduced, addressing in turn moral and prudential reasons-for-action.

1.3.2.2 *Pursuing other people's interests*

Probably the most obvious reason-for-action we have when we produce arbitration literature is to advance knowledge and the understanding of arbitration. There is a great array of ways to do this: they range from the simplest reporting of information on minute legal points (the crudest forms of case-law journalism and legislative journalism) to the most daring constructions of systems of thought meant to account for the entire system of arbitration (the most large-scale attempts to bring forward a new candidate for paradigm), and include: offering more or less sophisticated compilations of cases, statutes, and rules; adducing quantitative and qualitative empirical findings; imagining heuristic devices; telling happy anecdotes, and sad ones; whistle-blowing about structural imperfections and professional misconduct; trumpeting major breakthroughs and successes; crafting plain or more rococo and labyrinthine doctrinal accounts; doing actual journalism; and many more. The ways of contributing to our knowledge and understanding of arbitration are variegated in the extreme. Some, of course, are more serviceable than others.

Strictly speaking, this is a moral reason-for-action: we try to advance other people's knowledge and understanding, not our own. We are thus focused primarily on other people's interests, or else we would not publish what we found. (It is true, though, that sometimes the literature in the area reads like a note to self, as if the author wanted primarily to clarify things for himself—or perhaps for one particular client—and then might as well publish it. But let us keep away from this diversion.) So this moral reason-for-action pushes us (if we think in the terms we sketched above) in the direction of articulating propositions, forming systems of thought, and engaging with central ideas, or paradigms, in the field. This may seem all quite plain, and in many ways it is, but it needed reminding, just as the scientific theory of law as a scientific discipline needed reminding above, in order to base the coinage.

Now of course we do not mean that this is the only reason-for-action that makes us publish whatever we believe advances knowledge and understanding, or else we may as well not identify ourselves as the author. As we said above, reasons-for-action are not necessarily mutually exclusive. Several are typically coexistent, and may but need not conflict. This coexistence and conflict is precisely what undergirds our discussion here.

Then there is another quite evident moral reason-for-action we have in our scholarly gymnastics, as we move from the theory/knowledge-oriented to the practice- oriented: we may choose to 'free-lance for the state', to borrow from Pierre Schlag's lexicon.[73] This is an incentive to write, and to write certain things. Our reason here to produce research is to help the state. We try to help the state in its judicial function, by spoon-feeding the courts, clarifying the law for them, presenting it in a way that makes it more expedient to use, pointing out a real or hypothetical decision's consequences and ripple effects we think the court did not or would not see. We try to help the state in its legislative function by canvassing the terrain they may or should move into, by offering solutions, by presenting certain options in a favourable light and others as dramatic mistakes.

All of this of course also applies to arbitration, beyond the state: we may freelance for arbitrators and counsel in arbitration, suggesting (sometimes quite directly by sending through uninvited email attachments or SSRN links) possible arguments to rely on (with or without the hope that they will cite us in return); summarizing entire areas of the law; offering footnote fodder; redesigning processes to makes them faster, easier, more user-friendly—'iPhoning' arbitration, as we suggested elsewhere.[74]

Some of these activities are axiologically neutral. But more often than not they are not: clarifying the law for the courts and arbitral tribunals and parliaments is rarely a neutral operation (not that the articulation of propositions, systems of thought, and paradigms is really neutral either, but there is a difference in degree). When we do this, we really respond to (or our behaviour just happens to be aligned with) the promotion of certain values within the state or within the ecosystem of arbitration. Norm-advocacy projects, as we suggested above, are more or less overt, more or less straightforward political projects.

In international arbitration, and in particular in investment arbitration, many scholarly outputs are quite strongly and directly political: 'the world needs a strong hand to protect investors and investment arbitration is that hand' nicely converts into specific legal norms to be advanced in scholarly fashion; 'investment arbitration overly undermines the policy space of states to advance worthy social projects' translates just as well. You get the point.

And so, much of the backlash-against-arbitration story is an ideational political debate, in the sense that what really fuels the debate is antagonism about the political values that investment arbitration should pursue, our appreciation of its socio-political legitimacy, not a massive exercise of the 'exit strategy' that the various actors could opt for. In other

[73] Schlag (n. 54), 808.

[74] T. Schultz, 'Arbitration as an iPhone, or Why Conduct Academic Research in Arbitration?' 2 Journal of International Dispute Settlement 279 (2011).

words, what is happening is that (political) norm-advocacy projects are being pursued in the literature, projects that growl at the current output of investment arbitration as a political system, much more than treaties are being renegotiated in a way that effectively lashes back at investment arbitration.

These political projects constitute moral reasons-for-action. Whether these are good or bad projects is itself a political (or just possibly economic) question. Whether it is good or bad that the arbitration literature takes such political positions is a more intricate question and probably a barely avoidable fact. What is avoidable is the presentation of such norm- and value-advocacy as being purely technical, neutral, stating the law, clarifying it for the sake of clarity. Granted, the boundaries are not watertight between, on the one hand, neutral technical efficiency and clarification and, on the other hand, other axiological projects; between, on the one hand, descriptive statements and, on the other, normative statements. But too much confusion is just too much.

1.3.2.3 *Pursuing our own interests*

As we already mentioned, it would be an awkward representation of human psychology to state that our actions, even when we write scholarly work, are not influenced by a pursuit of self-interest—prudential reasons-for-action in the language used above. There is nothing wrong in this in the abstract—in the sense of morally wrong. The more intriguing question, of course, is to understand what these interests in the furthering of the self may be and, if taken all together and against the background of any other interests and constraints, assess whether they result in situations that would call for an adjustment, by one means or another, of the overall resultant of all these determinants. In plain English: does the inevitable pursuit of self-interest in the production of literature on international arbitration lead to a situation that we think is better unchanged than changed? The purpose of our reflections, as we also said above (repeatedly, to mark the point) is not an assessment of that resulting situation. They more modestly focus on the identification of the possible interests that we pursue for ourselves when we produce arbitration literature.

I will leave aside the most trivial prudential interests, whose examination yields the least heuristic advancement. These include factors such as the simple pleasure of formulating ideas, of being read by others, of being cited; the prestige that sometimes follows from quantitatively and qualitatively significant scholarly outputs; the deference and authority that may follow from such prestige; the satisfaction derived from advancing our own conception of... almost anything; the interest one may have in advancing the school of thought to which one belongs; the satisfaction derived from exhibiting analytical capacity or other skills valued by those who care about thinking and ideas; the need for faculty members and aspiring faculty members and grant holders to just write something; the need for practising lawyers to market themselves through visible publications, and thus to also just write something; and the pursuit of leisure itself (which is not an incentive to engage in scholarly activity, but to engage in it in a certain way, favouring more efficient, lighter, work). A dissection of the workings of these determinants of the arbitration literature is unlikely to teach us much—except for the fact that there is much that is being written that likely is superfluous, but that already is conventional wisdom. Then again, is it really superfluous? Superfluous means more than enough. But enough for what purposes? Perhaps—undoubtedly in fact—for the purposes of the advancement of knowledge and understanding, but that is a problem regarding moral reasons-for-action. Is what is being produced more than enough for the purposes of our own prudential interests?

Let us introduce here a distinction between two types of prudential reasons-for-action: collective and individual. The former relate to actions that advance directly the interests of a group of which we are, or believe to be, or hope to be, a member, and thus advance indirectly our own interest. The boundaries of the group need not be defined very clearly but it must be smaller than the group of all parties affected in any way by the arbitration literature, or else we are back within the ambit of moral reasons for action. Individual prudential reasons-for-action are those that relate to actions that seek to advance directly our own, individual, interests.

Collective prudential reasons-for-action we may have when we produce literature on arbitration may include, first of all, the protection of the industry of arbitration. If one entertains some form of hope to derive some form of income (or prestige, or visibility, which may be currencies in themselves or may be factors of actual income), at some time, from arbitration practice, as arbitrator, as counsel, as expert, as adviser to any of the preceding, then one has an incentive to write about arbitration, and to write certain things about it.

At its most extreme, this may take the form of attempts to prevent arbitration from disappearing as a business, to prevent it from being replaced by a dispute resolution mechanism designed in such a way as to deny us any possible or meaningful business. To put it simply, it is serviceable for arbitration business to preserve its existence as just that, a business. Now of course, if we are realistic, its disappearance is extraordinarily unlikely to occur anytime soon anyway. It seems a safe bet to say that arbitration as a business will not fold within the lifetime of even the youngest person who reads the current text. But of course the scale of the business is a matter that obtains by degrees.

A much more meaningful threat is that the system of arbitration is altered in such a way as to redistribute the resources, in a way that harms, from a business perspective, those who now benefit the most from it. One may think about it as one would think about electric cars replacing gasoline cars, and what incentives this creates for the leading makers of gasoline motors, or significantly different regulations for the banking industry and what incentives this creates for today's leading financial institutions. This creates an incentive to produce studies that do not protect the auto industry per se, but more precisely the auto industry in its current form, that do not protect the banking industry per se, but more precisely the leading financial institutions, that do not protect the arbitration industry per se, but more precisely the arbitration industry in its current form. This incentive may be more of a problem. Insisting on cars running on nothing other than gasoline for the next decades, on banks remaining regulated the way they are (or were a few years ago) may be a quite damaging stance to take for the industry as a whole in the long term.

So this incentive is a reason to produce literature that is protective not only of arbitration as an institution, but also of the current setup and workings of arbitration. We are unaware of any study that has exhaustively surveyed the sources of critical studies of arbitration, and the respective importance of these sources and the robustness of the criticism; but let us note that much of the most robust criticism of the way arbitration works *today* seems to come steadily from sources outside those who (usually) produce arbitration literature—they come from NGOs, international organizations, governments, journalists. The reaction from those who usually produce arbitration literature to such criticism, in particular to the strongest forms of criticism, seems to lack serious engagement with it, and on a number of occasions withdraws to argumentative fallacies, including ad hominem attacks ('These *people* are not credible'); black or white fallacies ('Either you are in favour of arbitration and you protect it, or you are against it and you want to kill it. If you criticize it, it means you are not in favour of it'); and the use of straw men (misrepresenting the criticism to more easily counter it). Flat-out denials, or at least nearly flat-out ones, abound.

Such argumentative gymnastics might just be an appropriate response to the incentives we have mentioned, but this is more likely so in the short than in the long run. It is not an unlikely proposition that the 'backlash' against arbitration, which at some stage may well have real business consequences, is due as much if not more to the (internal) categorical denials of problems than to an (external) oversensitivity or misunderstanding of them. As John Stuart Mill put it, argument and dissent are of great import, because it is in the collision of half-truths, which is what most of our opinions are, that real truths might emerge[75]—but that requires real collision, in the form of critical thinking.

To be sure, the opposite reason-for-action also exists. If one believes one has no chance of getting any 'job' (in the broadest sense of that word) in the current setup of the system but would ideally wish to obtain one, then one has a reason, an incentive, to change it. A new setup means new opportunities. New cards mean a new game. The more individuals there are who write on arbitration and who do not believe they are able to get a job out of it in the current system, the greater the chance that there will be a higher number of suggestions to change the system.

As we said above, the scale of the business of arbitration is a matter that obtains by degrees. This first means that the more arbitrations there are, the more business there is. If we again focus on our hypothetical individual who entertains the hope of deriving income (or prestige or visibility) from arbitration practice, this individual has an incen-

[75] John Stuart Mill, *On Liberty* (Batoche Books, 2001, first published 1859), 43–4, 50: 'The received opinion may be false . . . or the received opinion being true, a conflict with the opposite error is essential to a clear apprehension and deep feeling of its truth. But there is a commoner case than either of these; when the conflicting doctrines, instead of one being true and the other false, share the truth between them; and the nonconforming opinion [the one not endorsed by the authorities] is needed to supply the remainder of the truth . . . First, if any opinion is compelled to silence, that opinion may, for aught we can certainly know, be true. To deny this is to assume our own infallibility. Secondly, though the silenced opinion be an error, it may, and very commonly does, contain a portion of truth; and since the general or prevailing opinion on any subject is rarely or never the whole truth, it is only by the collision of adverse opinions that the remainder of the truth has any chance of being supplied.'

tive to produce a certain type of literature on arbitration—a type of literature that increases the number of arbitrations. Increasing the size of the pie means increasing the chance of obtaining a bigger slice of it, or of obtaining just some slice. A serviceable response to this incentive may be a scholarly defence of doctrines or opinions resulting in the lowering of jurisdictional standards; or in the firming up of mechanisms that create new avenues to file claims (think of MFN clauses, for instance); or in allowing new types of disputes to be brought to arbitration (think of mass claims, for instance). All of this is good for business—at least in the short run, at least until the last straw breaks the camel's back.

This account is of course a simplification. Indeed the serviceability for business of certain arguments meant to increase the number of arbitrations is more nuanced. Consider the proposals for a Multilateral Investment Court: disparaging reform attempts may well only be useful (from the business perspective we focus on here) if one hopes to obtain appointments as an arbitrator in disputes covered by the new system. If, however, one's hope is to source work more generally in arbitration practice, including as counsel, expert, or consultant in investor–state dispute settlement (ISDS, here in the sense of arbitration and other adjudicative proceedings), this may create a reason to advance the opposite argument. A calculation of interests and likelihood may indeed lead one to the belief that it is a better bet to replace arbitration with a permanent court, because it increases the system's chances of survival in the long term—because, for example, a permanent court may be perceived as more legitimate than arbitration, which may mean less interference from states, and possibly even their assistance, in its expansion. Brutally simplified, a permanent court decreases the opportunities of becoming an arbitrator (there are simply fewer jobs as arbitrators/judges on the investment court), but it may increase the number of cases and thus the opportunities of deriving income from the system as counsel, expert, or consultant.

Increasing the pie of arbitration business is also an incentive to produce another type of literature (beyond, then, arguments that focus on the legal and political hurdles to the existence of arbitrations): literature that relates to what happens during an arbitration. If one hopes to derive income (or prestige, or visibility) from arbitration practice, one has a reason to produce literature that contributes to making arbitrations run more smoothly, more efficiently, to the greater satisfaction of the parties. The point is simple: if the procedures leave the parties more satisfied, they are more inclined and likely to use arbitration again.

But efficiency is a two-edged sword. Efficiency means the quality of being able to deliver a certain result with minimal expenses. Now, the more financial resources are spent by the parties on arbitration, the more there is to be redistributed among the various actors who derive income from it, or hope to. More expenses mean a greater pie. If a person's objective (even if it is one among several objectives) is to increase the likelihood of deriving income from arbitral practice, then that person has a reason (which may be one among several reasons, possibly pulling in different directions) to produce literature which contributes to making arbitration, on the one hand, sufficiently efficient for the parties to want to use it as often as possible and, on the other, as inefficient as possible in order to maximize expenses.

A simple way out of this tension is to move the goalposts. If, again, efficiency means the quality of being able to deliver a certain result with minimal expenses, then moving the goalposts means changing the result we want delivered. It means remodelling the objective, the purpose, the role of arbitration. The purpose of arbitration is not simply to settle a business dispute and allow the parties to get back to business. It is (at least) to settle it in an acceptable way. 'Acceptable' means, in the words of William Park for instance (who includes but goes beyond efficiency)resolving the dispute in an accurate manner (he sometimes calls it 'adjudicatory truth-seeking'),[76] ensuring due process or fairness ('intelligent litigants usually craft their rules with deference to the adage that one person's delay is another's due process'),[77] resulting in a justified, enforceable award.[78] Probably everyone who is involved with arbitration would agree with Park, mostly quite straightforwardly—including the parties. They indeed, and that is the point, most likely adhere to this idea.

The point is that these objectives—at least accuracy and due process—obtain by degrees. When we write on arbitration and hope to derive an income from arbitral practice, one of the incentives we have, one of the prudential reasons-for-action we have to produce a certain type of literature, is to maximize the expected (thus, in several ways, *required*) level of accuracy and due process. We have a reason to progressively alter the social norms in the profession, if not the legal norms, both of which shape the expectations of the parties and thus their willingness to incur costs, so that ever more accuracy and due process is required. (To avoid any misunderstanding: our argument here entails no criticism of Park's position. We explain why just a bit later.)

From a slightly—and really just slightly—different perspective, we have an incentive to produce literature that progressively leads arbitration down the avenue described by Alec Stone Sweet and Florian Grisel: from the initial contractual model of arbitration, in which arbitrators 'resolve discreet dyadic disputes',[79] are the agents of the parties, and are accountable to them only; to the judicial model of arbitration, in which the arbitrators reach beyond the interests of the contracting parties to include 'wider social interests'[80] and become agents of 'the wider stakeholder community',[81] which means the stakeholders of the regime itself including future disputants, arbitration institutions, probably law firms (as distinguished from the parties), etc.; to the constitutional model

[76] W. W. Park, 'Arbitrators and Accuracy', 1 Journal of International Dispute Settlement 25 (2010), 27.

[77] Ibid. 34.

[78] W. W. Park, 'Arbitration in Autumn', 2 Journal of International Dispute Settlement 287 (2010); W. W. Park, 'The Four Musketeers of Arbitral Duty: Neither One-for-All nor All-for-One', 8 Dossiers of the International Chamber of Commerce Institute of World Business Law 25 (2011).

[79] Alec Stone Sweet and Florian Grisel, 'The Evolution of International Arbitration: Delegation, Judicialization, Governance 23', in Walter Mattli and Thomas Dietz (eds), *International Arbitration and Global Governance: Contending Theories and Evidence* (Oxford University Press, 2014).

[80] Ibid. 32. [81] Ibid. 34.

of arbitration, in which arbitrators become agents of a yet 'wider international legal order'[82] and play a role in international governance itself, jumping out of the arbitral regime, as it were, to take into consideration high-level exogenous norms, typically heavily loaded axiologically, from trade, human rights, the protection of the environment, etc. The point for us here is that this evolution from one model to the next entails more 'organizational complexity',[83] more rules and factors and interests to take into consideration, which tends to require more work, and more sophisticated work, thus more nuance, more arguments, more witness evidence, more expert witness evidence—just more. Thus more expenses, and ultimately a greater pie.

Now, to be clear, the fact that we have a prudential reason-for-action to favour certain expectations from arbitral proceedings by no means implies that we may not also have both an epistemic reason for such a position (a reason to genuinely believe it) and a moral reason-for-action for such a position (we defend such a position in scholarly fashion because we mean to advance the interests of the parties or those of a wider community of stakeholders). We do not argue that this sophistication of arbitration is not *also* a moral reason-for-action, that the pursuit of accuracy and due process, or the inclusion of wide social interests and high-level value-charged norms, may not also be good for the parties and beyond. Our arguments in the previous main section of this chapter in fact recognize just as much. Our argument here is simply that this is a reason-for-action we *do* have if one of our purposes is to benefit financially from arbitration practice.

Let us close this section with a light parallel: If the intended result is to drive from London to the Scottish Highlands, a 15-year-old Toyota will do just fine. If the intended result is to drive from London to the Scottish Highlands *comfortably*, then this may lead to the need for a Porsche Cayenne. If we are a car salesman, we have a reason to stress comfort, to enthuse about the evolution towards ever more sophisticated vehicles—in scholarly fashion if we must and can. In a scholarly fashion that may (as we believe is the case in the examples we used) but also may not proceed from a neutral stance on the question whether the Porsche is really needed.

1.4 Conclusion

There are probably few vexations of arbitration that cannot be fixed. And fixing them can certainly be one of the purposes that authors of the literature in the field can set for themselves. From the point of view of most, this would likely constitute a useful, legitimate purpose, which can be served by a great variety of forms of literature alike—from the grandest ideas to the finest fine-tuning. A different question is whether the literature will be able to fix these vexations before they cause serious annoyance—harm

[82] Ibid. 34. [83] Ibid. 23.

to certain parties, to society more generally, to arbitration business itself? Has some such harm not already occurred? It was man's ability to invent which has made human society what it is. And what is indeed already reasonably palpable is the shift in the forms of literature we produce, and in the reasons that make us produce literature in general and certain types of literature in particular. This shift is likely to produce a greater diversity of ideas, knowledge, and opinion. More ways to invent more futures. That, surely, is good news.

PART I

CORNERSTONES

CHAPTER 2

ARBITRATION AND LAW

WILLIAM W. PARK

2.1 Legitimacy in Private Dispute Resolution

2.1.1 Two cautionary tales

The aggregate social and economic consequences of any legal rule or principle reveal themselves with greater crispness when viewed against alternatives adopted in different legal systems. To introduce law's interaction with arbitration, let us consider two lawsuits presenting both parallels and points of divergence. One case unfolds in a tiny country of the Southern hemisphere, while the other arises in a larger and more populous nation on the other side of the globe. The cases reach dramatically different answers on the same basic question: what happens when an arbitration agreement stipulates a form of judicial review not available under applicable national arbitration law?

The first case, *Carr & Brookside*, stemmed from cancellation of an agreement for sale of farming assets in New Zealand.[1] Disappointed business managers blamed their lawyers for mishandling the transaction. Attorney and client agreed to arbitrate the malpractice claim, each participating in arbitration without complaint. The law firm won, the arbitrator having decided that attorney negligence did not cause collapse of the deal. So far, this narrative contains nothing unusual.

The losing client then filed an appeal in court, seeking judicial review of the arbitrator's findings of fact. The arbitration agreement provided for award challenge on 'questions of

[1] *Carr & Brookside Farm Trust Ltd v Gallaway Cook Allan*, [2014] NZSC 75 (2014) (McGrath J). In domestic arbitration, New Zealand allows appeals unless agreed otherwise, while for international arbitration the parties must opt for an appellate regime. In either event, appeals lie only for mistakes of law, not fact. New Zealand Arbitration Act 1996, Sch. 5, Cl. 5 and 10.

law and fact' which went beyond the New Zealand arbitration statute which permits appeals only for errors of law.

The reviewing court saw the valid part of the clause (appeal on law) as inextricably entwined with the invalid portion (appeal on facts), incapable of being severed. Thus the court set aside the award. The client bargained to arbitrate, but on the assumption that another round of argument would be available before a judge if the arbitrator made a mistake. The court found that the scope of appeal went to the heart of their agreement. That expectation could not be met under current law. So all bets were off. The parties' intent had been thwarted and the arbitral award became a nullity.

In the other lawsuit, *Hall Street v Mattel*, the United States Supreme Court considered an arbitration between a landlord and its commercial tenant at odds about responsibility for cleanup costs covering environmental damage. The parties had concluded a stipulation analogous to the one at issue in the New Zealand case, permitting court scrutiny of an arbitrator's mistakes of law and fact.[2]

The U.S. Supreme Court construed the Federal Arbitration Act to preclude such review. Nevertheless, the court left the award itself as an enforceable arbitral decision. The valid portion of the contract (an agreement to arbitrate) was given effect detached from the invalid right of judicial appeal.

Neither the New Zealand nor the American approaches give total satisfaction. Each court ignored at least one element of the litigants' wishes, justifying such disregard in the name of party intent. In the New Zealand story, legislation designed to enhance finality in arbitration, by precluding appeals on questions of fact, resulted in an award becoming irredeemably precarious. Recognizing the parties' wishes for a generous right of appeal meant disregard of their bargain for private dispute resolution.

In contrast, the American approach gave the arbitral decision a binding character never envisioned by the parties, who had agreed explicitly that the arbitrator would *not* have the last word on matters of fact or law. Yet to avoid having the arbitral award serve as mere foreplay to court litigation, the *Hall Street* decision discounted that appellate element of the parties' deal in order to impose an adjudicatory mechanism with limited input from the government judiciary.[3]

[2] *Hall Street Associates v Mattel, Inc.*, 552 U.S. 576 (2008). The contract provided for judicial modification of arbitral findings of fact if unsupported by evidence, or for erroneous conclusions of law. The Federal Arbitration Act was held to provide both a floor and a ceiling for judicial review. The parties could go no lower than judicial monitoring of awards for lack of procedural integrity, on matters like partiality, excess of authority, fraud, or corruption. Nor could they contract for a higher level of review covering simple mistake.

[3] In a colourful concurrence in an earlier case with similar contours, one federal judge accepted application of contractually stipulated review standards (which in the particular related to 'substantial evidence or erroneous legal conclusion'), but suggested that the result should be different if an agreement provided for the judge to review awards 'by flipping a coin or studying the entrails of a dead fowl'. See *LaPine Tech. Corp. v Kyocera Corp.*, 130 F.3d 884, 891 (9th Cir. 1997) (Judge Alex Kozinski). On re-hearing, the same appellate court found that federal judges may review awards only on grounds set forth in the Federal Arbitration Act. See *Kyocera Corp. v Prudential-Bachen T. Servs.*, 341 F.3d 987 (9th Cir. 2003).

Providing lessons in unintended consequences, these cases also operate as prisms to separate key themes in arbitration's legal framework. Modern arbitration law aims to respect freely-accepted bargains to waive recourse to courts. In tandem with that goal, however, judges condition award recognition on scrutiny of the procedural integrity of the arbitral process.

In New Zealand, the search for that procedural integrity led to disregard of the arbitration clause in order to avoid thwarting the parties' expectation of appellate review. In the United States, by contrast, the court considered the totality of party intentions, viewed against the backdrop of federal law, as favouring recognition of the arbitrator's decision, even if flawed in fact or law and not subject to the expected appeal.

Finding the right balance among rival goals does not always yield to facile analysis. In both New Zealand and the United States, courts faced the task of accommodating (or choosing between) two somewhat inconsistent aspects of the agreement: a firm commitment to arbitrate and an expectation that courts would intervene to correct mistakes.

Other competing objectives affect law's interaction with private dispute resolution. Indeed, as discussed below it may be more useful to speak of how 'laws' (plural) intersect with the arbitral process, whether in matters like award recognition, or the conduct of arbitral proceedings and decisions on the substantive merits of the underlying claim.

2.1.2 Three dimensions of law

Without any magic or exclusivity, three sets of questions present themselves with respect to the role of law in arbitration. The first relates to arbitration's legal framework. As suggested in connection with the New Zealand and American cases, modern arbitration law implicates the relationship of judge and arbitrator, primarily with respect to judicial recognition of arbitration agreements and awards, concomitant with the court's monitoring of arbitration's basic fairness.

Dovetailing into arbitration's legal framework, a second role of law relates to the specific procedures by which arbitration proceedings unfold, for example, in presenting evidence or organizing oral hearings. Do arbitrators rely on oral testimony or written witness statements? Or both? What, if any, principles of privilege apply in arbitration? Should arbitrators consider legal theories not advanced by counsel? On occasion, these procedures build on the 'soft law' of professional guidelines and practices.

A third role of law implicates the arbitrator's evaluation of the merits of the disputes itself. New York law governs an insurance policy. English law applies to the construction of a loan agreement. The parties to a joint venture provide that their relationship will be subject to the Swiss Federal Code of Obligations.

Although separate, the three dimensions of law support each other in promoting the efficiency, fairness and legitimacy of cross-border dispute resolution. For example, arbitration's legal framework ('arbitration law' as such) provides signals to arbitrators about the contours of the procedures they can adopt in hearing evidence without jeopardizing the enforceability of their awards due to violations of basic notions of due process. Or, in applying a given national law to decide the merits of a dispute, arbitrators may well consider how a supervising court will react. To take another illustration, in allocating costs at the end of the case, an arbitrator sitting in England could be conflicted between the law of the seat, which imposes 'loser pays' principles, and the law selected by the parties to govern their contract, which gives effect to the pre-dispute agreement that each side bear its own costs in any event.

2.1.3 Circularity in law: reactive and generative elements of legal norms

Laws in living legal systems usually arise in reaction to perceived community needs. Bank regulations, for example, often represent a response to some financial crisis, rather than any 'a priori' or platonic view of how financial institutions should be monitored.

In turn, basic laws often generate their own reality in the form of secondary rules that apply the initial mandates. Fiscal law provides a ready example. The government's need for money begets an income tax, which at first may seem simple enough.[4] However, the tax law itself usually generates supplementary rules related to calculation of revenue, addressing matters like depreciation allowances, foreign tax credits, or limits on business deductions. Other secondary tax rules may seek to encourage certain types of behavior, such as home ownership or educational funding, by allowing deductions for mortgage interest and charitable giving.[5]

Analogously, basic arbitration statutes trigger more complex arbitration law. The initial rules and conventions may respond to grievances when business partners repudiate bargains to arbitrate which courts have not honored. The law mandates that arbitration agreements and awards must be enforced. Those mandates, however, lead to new norms aiming to prevent abuse of arbitration, for example, in the event of arbitrator bias, or rulings that exceed arbitral jurisdiction. If arbitration clauses will be enforced, the process must be fair. But what does 'fairness' mean in its details? May an award vacated in one country still be enforced in another? When must arbitrators disclose prior appointments? When and by whom should determinations be made of arbitrator competence?

What might be called the 'generative' aspect of arbitration law imposes a duty to respect the arbitration commitment. The 'reactive' part of the legal framework consists of principles that make enforcement fair, distinguishing legitimate and illegitimate

[4] In the U.S., federal income tax arrived in 1913 with a simple one-sentence Constitutional Amendment, the 16th, allowing Congress to tax income without regard to census or apportionment among the various states.

[5] Of course, awareness of how one event feeds into another can inform understanding of the human experience beyond law, in areas as diverse as faith and technology. The Protestant Reformation was the child of movable type to the extent that printing made the Bible more available. In turn, printing advanced the Reformation emphasis on understanding Scripture.

arbitral proceedings in a host of matters touching how and when arbitrations may take place.[6]

Performance of the arbitrator's function thus falls within a framework of cases, statutes, and treaties seeking balance between two goals: (i) to prevent disregard of an arbitration commitment; while at the same time (ii) to monitor the arbitral process for conformity to recognized notions of procedural fairness.

As arbitrators decide cases, and judges enforce the ensuing awards, the rules elaborated by each group also create new breeds of cognoscenti, including practitioners and scholars alike. Trained to decorticate a host of legal issues, the arbitration community must confront questions as disarmingly broad as the 'soft law' of arbitral procedure (discussed below), and some as eternal as the impartiality required of arbitrators. Yet others issues remain as frustrating complex (to insiders as well as outsiders) as the jurisdictional notions bearing exotic names like 'separability' and *Kompetenz-Kompetenz*.[7] The following paragraphs aim to provide the reader with a modest appetite for further exploration of at least some of these questions, recognizing the inevitable intertwining of judicial and arbitral proceedings.[8]

2.1.4 Taxonomy: what are we discussing?

Rigorous exploration of how arbitration and law interact begs preliminary inquiry into the nature of both law and arbitration. Determining 'the law' of arbitration requires a nod to the character of law in general,[9] as well as a tentative working definition of the chameleon-like notion of arbitration, a term applied to a multitude of adjudicatory mechanisms unfolding outside government courts. The term 'arbitration' has been

[6] The most obvious questions about legitimacy in arbitration relates to arbitrator bias and the contours of arbitral jurisdiction. However, a range of other questions have arisen over the years, including Sunday hearings. In *Bauer v Bauer*, 507,082/2013 (N.Y. Sup. Ct. 2014), an inheritance dispute was decided by a Beth Din after sitting on Sunday. At the request of the losing side, a Brooklyn judge annulled the award on the basis that arbitrators perform a judicial function and thus must respect §5 of the New York Judiciary Law which says that courts may not be open Sunday. For a similar case coming to a different result, see *Karapschinsky v Rothbaum*, 163 S.W. 290 (Mo. Ct. App. 1914).

[7] See the discussion below of *BG Group v Argentina*, 134 S. Ct. 1198 (2014); William W. Park, *Jurisdiction to Determine Jurisdiction* (13 ICCA Congress Series 55, The Hague 2007) adapted Part II.A in William W. Park, *Arbitration of International Business Disputes*, 2nd edn (Oxford University Press, 2012).

[8] For an example of a single dispute which implicated multiple arbitral and judicial fora, one cannot do much better than the Chevron, Ecuador, and Lago Agrio dispute, which combined treaty-based arbitration, human rights courts, and criminal proceedings, along with national administrative and legislative involvement. A U.S. federal court concluded that corruption had procured a $9 billion Ecuadorian judgment against Chevron for environmental contamination. *Chevron v Donziger*, 974 F.Supp.2d 362 (S.D.N.Y. 2014), affirmed 833 F.3d 74 (2nd Cir. 2016) (Kearse J), cert. denied, U.S. Supreme Court, 19 June 2017.

[9] In a similar vein, see Tai-Heng Chen, 'The Idea of Law: Comments on Douglas M. Johnston, The Historical Foundations of World Order, The Tower and the Arena (2008)', 103 Am. Soc'y Int'l L. Proc. 113 (2009).

pressed into service equally for (a) ordinary commercial quarrels in matters like sales, insurance or construction; (b) nation-to-nation disputes; (c) disagreements between investors and governments; and (d) in certain places (such as the United States) for consumer and employment matters.

The first question ('What is law?') triggers consideration of authoritative dispute resolution processes that include rules and principles informing both substantive conduct and the way judges and arbitrators decide disputes. The inquiry seeks to understand not the laws of science or divinity, but rather how controversies are resolved in a rightful fashion, whether between private parties or individuals and society at large.[10]

Legal systems often implicate elements of compulsion, at least against those who would refuse to do what the law says they must.[11] In arbitration law, compulsion derives from the binding nature of the arbitrator's award, foreclosing otherwise available judicial action. Yet compulsion may be oblique, as with respect to evidentiary norms related to privilege,[12] a matter which can raise significant doctrinal and practical challenges for arbitrations implicating different legal systems.[13]

Moving to the second question, the nature of arbitration, requires recognition that modern arbitration implicates dispute resolution practices with roots in antiquity,[14] taking

[10] Francophones often distinguish between *loi* (an enactment) and *droit* (legitimate norms) which both qualify as 'law' for Anglophones. A tyrant's edict might be law even if contrary to higher authoritative norms. In 1776 the rebellious American colonists rejected the legitimacy of British rule, which was doubtless 'law' from the perspective of Great Britain. Likewise, the British rejected the legitimacy of many American laws until signing the Treaty of Paris in 1783. All of these characterization wrinkles illustrate why the best of minds have sunk beneath the waves of uncertainty trying to explain the notion of law, a quest evoking the warning at the door to Dante's Inferno, *Lasciate ogni speranza, voi ch'entrate* ('Abandon all hope, you who enter here'). See Dante Alighieri, *Divine Comedy*, 'Inferno', III, 9.

[11] See e.g. Frederick Schauer, *The Force of Law* (Harvard University Press, 2015).

[12] Whether characterized as substantive or procedural, attorney–client privilege is normally considered law by most observers. This is so even for international cases where uncertainty exists on proper standards to determine privilege, and with documents created in legal systems that speak not of privilege attached to a document, but of the 'professional secrecy' imposed on an adviser. Even if not subject to direct sanction, arbitrators may violate law by resting decisions on properly privileged documents, or by refusing to consider non-privileged documents. A loser might argue for award annulment either if an arbitrator looked at privileged material or if the arbitrator refused to consider evidence. Although few arbitrators enjoy having awards vacated, annulment punishes the side deprived of a favourable award rather than the errant arbitrator.

[13] One party's home jurisdiction might protect communications with in-house counsel (as in the U.S.), while the other side's might not (as in Switzerland). See generally Annabelle Mŏckesch, *Attorney–Client Privilege in International Arbitration* (Oxford University Press, 2017). Of course, when all counsel come from the same legal culture, they may simply presume a conclusion about the proper law (their own) as e.g. a cross-border dispute arbitrated in Houston with Texas attorneys on both sides. In other cases questions of applicable law may be less obvious, as discussed below.

[14] The Greek dramatist Menander (342–290 BCE) penned a play about an arbitration over custody of a baby found outside Athens, whose necklace was disputed between a shepherd and a charcoal burner. Menander, 'The Arbitration: The Epitrepontes of Menander', trans. Gilbert Murray, 7 Arb. Int'l 72 (1991), 72–5. On arbitration in antiquity, see also Derek Roebuck and Bruno de Loynes de Fumichon, *Roman Arbitration* (HOLO Books, 2004).

special but divergent significance in periods as disparate as the French Revolution,[15] Colonial North America,[16] and today's increasingly globalized economy. At the same time, present-day notions can vary dramatically from country to country.[17]

As a starting point for analysis, one scholar has suggested the idea of arbitration as binding dispute resolution 'accepted with serenity by those who bear its consequences because of their special trust in chosen decision-makers'.[18] In itself, this conception of arbitration says nothing about how legal systems will or should treat arbitration—a matter that doubtless affects usage at different times and places.

The definitional exercise takes on special complexity when moving from the abstract into the realm of the concrete. In agreeing to enforce arbitration awards, most nations endorse a notion of arbitration implicating decisions that may not in fact be 'accepted with serenity' by those who bear their consequences.

More significantly, some countries affix the label 'arbitration' to adjudicatory mechanisms whose participants have little if any 'special trust' in chosen decision-makers. Professional sports presents a striking example of arbitration different in stripe and spirit from that of normal commerce, yet endorsed by law and practice. Although American arbitration law requires a high level of arbitrator impartiality, at least two United States courts have confirmed arbitral awards penalizing football players, even though the 'arbitrator' is none other than the commissioner who himself imposed the administrative sanction for misbehaviour. In a case involving popular New England Patriots quarterback Tom Brady,[19] who was accused of deflating a football to gain an

[15] Bruno de Loynes de Fumichon, 'La passion de la révolution française pour l'arbitrage', Revue de l'arbitrage 3 (2014). England's arbitration history has been chronicled by Derek Roebuck. See Derek Roebuck, *Early English Arbitration* (HOLO Books, 2008); *Mediation and Arbitration in the Middle Ages: England from 1154–1558* (HOLO Books, 2013); *The Golden Age of Arbitration: Dispute Resolution Under Elizabeth I* (HOLO Books, 2015); *Arbitration and Mediation in 17th Century England* (HOLO Books, 2017).

[16] See accounts of the 1640 arbitration between the Plymouth and Massachusetts colonies (William W. Park, Cohasset Marshlands Arbitration (ICCA 2014), at 11) and arbitration by the Governor of New France settling disputes among Iroquois and Algonquian nations (Gilles Havard, *La grande paix de Montréal de 1701* (Recherches amérindiennes au Québec, 1992)). See also Bruce Mann, *Neighbors and Strangers: Law and Community in Early Connecticut* (University of North Carolina Press, 1987); 'The Formalization of Informal Law: Arbitration Before the American Resolution', 59 N.Y.U.L. Rev 443 (1984).

[17] For example, although ad hoc arbitration garners global acceptance, the People's Republic of China appears to require arbitration pursuant to rules of an approved arbitral institution. See Tietie Zhang, 'Enforceability of Ad Hoc Arbitration in China', 46 Cornell Int'l L. J. 361 (2013).

[18] Jan Paulsson, *The Idea of Arbitration* (Oxford University Press, 2013), 1.

[19] *National Football League Management Council v NFL Players Association*, 820 F.3d 527 (2nd Cir. 2016). Court confirmed a four-game suspension for allegedly deflating a ball to facilitate passing. After imposing the suspension as National Football League Commissioner, the same individual (Roger Goodell) donned an arbitrator's cap to hear the complaint brought by the Players Association. Although reference was made to the Federal Arbitration Act for one issue (partiality), the majority opinion focused on 301 of the Labor Management Relations Act, 29 U.S.C. §185(a), permitting federal courts to enforce awards made under collective bargaining agreements. Similarly, *NFL Players Association v NFL Management Council*, 831 F.3d 985 (8th Cir. 2015) upheld an award suspending Minnesota Vikings running back Adrian Peterson for chastising his son with a tree branch. The U.S. Supreme Court has yet to rule directly on the application of the Federal Arbitration Act to collective bargaining arbitration.

advantage in passing, the court applied the 'law of the shop' under collective bargaining agreements, deeming that the player waived any expectation of impartiality.[20]

Such proceedings represent a different type of arbitration (if arbitration even provides the proper label) from the norm in business disputes, where parties and courts alike expect arbitrators to be independent and impartial. The very same jurisdiction that confirmed the award on deflated footballs (notwithstanding obvious partiality in the arbitrator) had earlier imposed a high standard of independence in a commercial case, where an arbitrator failed to investigate business links between a litigant and an affiliate of the arbitrator's company.[21]

In commercial cases, relinquishments of arbitrator independence almost always implicate a specific conflict clearly waived with informed consent,[22] not the type of systemic bias present in American football arbitration.[23]

Faced with such diversity, what should a scholar do to enhance meaningful analysis? Perhaps nothing, except to be clear on the particular context for procedural norms. Sound analysis also recognizes that notions of arbitration diverge precisely because arbitration, like law itself, represents an artifact of the variable human condition, not a fixed element of the mineral world like zircon in the Jack Hills of Western Australia.

With this caveat, let us try to understand the interface of law and arbitration, beginning with revisiting the definition of arbitration as used in international commercial disputes. Whatever usage might be given the word 'arbitration' in other contexts,[24] arbitration of

[20] The court rejected annulment of the award for 'evident partiality' under section 10 of the Federal Arbitration Act, noting that the players knew the Commissioner's role in determining conduct detrimental to professional football. See *National Football League Management Council v NFL Players Association*, 820 F.3d 527, 548 (2nd Cir. 2016).

[21] See the interpretation of section 10 of the Federal Arbitration Act in *Applied Indus. Materials Corp. (AIMCOR) v Ovalar Makine Ticaret Ve Sanayi, A.S.*, 492 F.3d 132 (2d Cir. 2007), discussed further below.

[22] See *Schwartzman v Harlap*, 377 Fed.Appx. 108 (2nd Cir. 2010), affirming in relevant part *Schwartzman v Harlap*, 2009 WL 1009856 (E.D.N.Y. 2009). An American importer of fruit (the *esrog* or *etrog*, used in the Jewish harvest festival Succoth) refused to pay the Israeli grower. The dispute was submitted to arbitration by a rabbi, who decided for the grower. Resisting enforcement, the distributor argued that the rabbi (*qua* arbitrator) was not independent, having provided services (*qua* rabbi) to the grower in certifying the orchard's kosher status, essential to the fruit's marketability. Rejecting the challenge, the court reasoned that the distributor knew the rabbi wore two hats, and thus waived his right to complain. It is not clear that waiver could (or should) extend from lack of independence to prejudgment, e.g. to a rabbi who begins by saying that all Americans lie. Prejudgment strikes at the heart of the arbitral process. See *In re Owners of Steamship Catalina and Owners of Motor Vessel Norma*, [1938] 61 Lloyd's Rep. 360 (London arbitrator referred to Portuguese people as liars in a dispute involving Portuguese witnesses).

[23] Collective bargaining arbitration in the U.S. arose from a perceived judicial animosity towards organized labour in the late 19th c., with the judiciary supporting employers' rights by enjoining strikes and boycotts. The confrontation reached its climax in 1908, when the Supreme Court of the U.S. held that participants in strikes were liable for conspiracy in restraint of trade under the Sherman Act. See *Loewe v Lawlor*, 208 U.S. 274 (1908) and, more generally, Christopher Tomlins, *The State and the Unions* (Cambridge University Press, 1985), 60–65.

[24] Contextual variance in the use of the word 'arbitration' remains vital to understanding the role of law in the arbitral process. Words take meaning in relation to the company they keep, as underscored by the Latin maxim *noscitur a sociis*. Feet run. Noses run. Depositors see a run on the bank. A person

cross-border economic disputes encompasses a brand of forum selection implicating three elements:

(i) dispute resolution by party-selected decision-makers;
(ii) an intention that the process be binding rather than advisory;[25] and
(iii) adjudication of legal claims, rather than answering factual questions.[26]

Although judicial enforcement of the arbitral process remains a matter separate from the 'What is arbitration?' question, modern arbitration almost always implicates a gloss that assumes agreements and awards will be given effect by courts, which in turn expect arbitrators to remain free from prejudgment and to respect the basics of due process and their jurisdictional mandate. Litigants and courts alike normally anticipate that arbitrators will consider witness testimony, documentary exhibits, and publicly available legal authorities, rather than a more random process such as a coin toss or role of dice.[27]

2.2 Arbitration's legal framework

2.2.1 Courts and arbitrators

2.2.1.1 *The golden rule of arbitration law*

Two thousand years ago, a rabbi known as Hillel the Elder was asked to summarize Jewish law while standing on one foot. Daring to meet the test, Hillel articulated his

who says 'I got it' might mean 'I understand' or 'I caught a disease'. Italians sometimes suggest a variant observation: *Dimmi con chi vai e ti dirò chi sei* (Tell me your company, and I'll tell you who you are).

[25] Sometimes painted as a cousin to mediation, arbitration presents a different adjudicatory animal. Mediators facilitate settlement, sometimes with non-binding proposals, leaving the parties free to walk away. Arbitrators impose binding decisions. Each process represents an 'alternative' to lawsuits in government courts (as does duelling, for that matter), but arbitration rests on a commitment to respect the decision-maker's conclusions.

[26] On 'expert determinations', see Association of the Bar in the City of New York, Committee on International Commercial Disputes, *Purchase Price Adjustment Clauses and Expert Determinations: Legal Issues, Practical Problems and Suggested Improvements* (New York City Bar Association, 2013); William W. Park, 'Documentary Credit Dispute Resolution: The Role of Arbitrators and Experts', 12 Int'l Arb. Rep. 15 (1997).

[27] This is not to say that other adjudicatory processes lack legitimacy in different contexts. One recalls Biblical recourse to the *Urim* and *Thummim*, where sacred lots in the breastplate of the High Priest were consulted in moments of national uncertainty. See Exod. 28:30, Num. 27:21, Deut. 33:8, and 1 Sam. 14:41–2, 28:6. On more modern oracles see, Oscar Chase, *Law, Culture, and Ritual: Disputing Systems in Cross-Cultural Context* (New York University Press, 2005), providing a comparative tour beginning with the Azande people of Central Africa, where ritual poison administered to a small chicken will confirm (on death of the chicken) guilt of a couple accused of adultery.

version of the Golden Rule as follows: 'What is hateful to you, do not do to others. That is the whole law. The rest is simply commentary.'[28]

Challenged to provide an analogous synopsis for arbitration law, a modern jurist might suggest the following two-pronged rule for the interaction of courts and arbitrators: 'Judges should recognize bargains to arbitrate, subject to monitoring the fundamental procedural fairness of the arbitral process.' And indeed, most legal systems now follow a version of those twin principles, albeit with variation for disputes (like consumer cases) that require closer attention.

Arbitration analogues of what Rabbi Hillel called 'simply commentary' often end up being less than simple, with broad principles proving difficult to apply in practice. Most generalities risk ignoring key elements in the universe of real life problems,[29] which for arbitration express themselves in a web of treaties, statutes, and cases layered like a Russian nesting doll with one carved figure opening to more diminutive figurines.[30]

Few matters better illustrate the challenges of 'simple commentary' in arbitration than the question of arbitrator independence and impartiality, raised earlier in the American football case. A consensus exists, at least in commercial disputes, that arbitrators must demonstrate independence and impartiality by hearing before deciding, which leads to the suggestion that arbitrators should 'disclose all contacts' with the parties and the case. Such an injunction usually proves unworkable without the context of what contacts will be significant. In an arbitration with Brazil as Respondent, an arbitrator would normally reveal a position in the Brazilian government. Would he also need to tell the Parties that his wife was Brazilian? That he had been sent to Rio while a Midshipman in the United States Navy? On a planet where butterflies flapping wings in Africa trigger weather patterns that later cause Canadian snowstorms, few human experiences will be devoid of impact on an individual's predisposition in deciding cases. The establishment of workable disclosure guidelines implicates a high-wire act between overly lax standards that tolerate appointment of pernicious arbitrators, unable to judge independently, and the alternate route of unrealistic ethical rules that render the arbitrator's position precarious and susceptible to destabilization by litigants engaged in dilatory tactics. Principles of proportionality must operate to permit triage between different types of challenges.

[28] Babylonian Talmud, Shabbat 31a. At approximately the same time, 2,000 years ago, another rabbi voiced similar moral aspirations phrased a bit differently: 'Whatever you want others to do to you, do also to them.' See Matt. 7:12. And well before either Hillel or Jesus, Moses employed yet another formulation: 'Love your neighbor as yourself.' See Lev 19:18.

[29] Richard Feynman, winner of a 1965 Nobel prize for contributions to quantum mechanics, allegedly asserted that the best way to understand a subject was to reduce it to 'freshman level' simplicity. We have no evidence, however, that his students won prizes remaining at that level.

[30] Unlike a *matryoshka*, however, arbitration law often reveals exceptions as capacious as the rules from which they derogate, hedged fore and aft by qualifiers to be pursued by the diligent or the curious.

2.2.1.2 *When should judges not decide cases?*

Most fields of law provide guidance on how to decide disputes. In contrast, the law of arbitration tells courts when *not* to decide cases, in deference to private decision-makers.

Yet decisions to arbitrate often exist in the shadow of one party's second thoughts about the wisdom or the fairness of the agreement. The parties might diverge about what the agreement covers, with one side seeking court assistance in getting the arbitration started or implementing an award. Judges could be asked to determine if the arbitrator can legitimately hear the case, or whether the arbitral proceedings were conducted fairly.

Although contract principles provide a starting point for analysis, any suggestion that arbitration remains only a matter of contract would be misplaced. Arbitration agreements pave the way for something unpredictable: strangers to the dispute (the arbitrators) impose a decision that replaces a court judgment. Thus governments understandably seek to craft special rules about the legitimacy of the process, to ensure that courts do not lend their power to awards resting on a fundamentally unfair proceeding, or awards otherwise violating public policy. In an international context, arbitration law must also address delicate questions of how courts in one jurisdiction should treat the decisions of judges in other countries who vacate or confirm an arbitrator's decision. Moreover, national law may direct courts to take an 'arbitration-friendly' approach, putting a thumb on the scale when the agreement to arbitrate may not be clear,[31] going beyond simply enforcing agreements.

2.2.1.3 *Rival policies*

The juridical wrinkles on arbitration law implicate costs and benefits related to several rival goals, notably: (i) procedural fairness; (ii) litigation finality; (iii) avoiding undue cost in time and money; (iv) accurate awards; and (v) respect for vital public policies. Implementing any one of these goals can curtail the realization of another.[32] As a concomitant to enforcing arbitration agreements, courts monitor procedural fairness in the arbitral process to enhance chances that unbiased arbitrators hear disputes, listening before deciding and staying within the contours of their mission. Inevitably, tensions arise when an arbitrator reaches conclusions at odds with those favoured by

[31] In one case, the U.S. Supreme Court suggested that 'our cases place it beyond dispute that the [Federal Arbitration Act] was designed to promote arbitration'. See the majority opinion by the late Justice Scalia in *AT&T Mobility LLC v Concepcion*, 131 S. Ct. 1740, 1753 (2011). As a matter of intellectual rigour, the notion of 'promoting arbitration' seems a stretch, both in policy and exegesis of the statutory text, by ignoring that arbitration rests on consent, whether express or implied. It might well be, of course, that faced with ambiguity in construing an arbitration clause, a reviewing judge gives the benefit of the doubt to the position that implements an arbitration agreement or award.

[32] Among the inevitable trade-offs in arbitration, few remain more intractable than the need to balance due process and accuracy (allowing each side its say and assisting the arbitrator in reaching a correct result), on the one hand, and the avoidance of undue cost and delay on the other. Almost inevitably, a search for fair and right answers will take time and money. In this connection, one recalls the Latin maxim *Veritas filia temporis* (truth is the daughter of time), attributed by a 2nd-c. Roman grammarian to an unnamed predecessor. 'Alius quidam veterum poetarum, cuius nomen mihi nunc memoriae non est, Veritatem Temporis filiam esse dixit.' See Aulus Gellius, *Noctes Atticae*, XII.11.7.

the reviewing judge, who must decide whether he or she faces a fundamentally unjust result, or just a bad award.

The law also seeks to reduce the prospect that arbitration will run afoul of vital community norms. Treaties and statutes include escape hatches to permit non-recognition of awards that violate public policy.[33] National law often forbids pre-dispute arbitration clauses in sensitive areas, as diverse as consumer contracts[34] and nursing home agreements,[35] from concern that reduced access to courts serves as a tool to oppress weaker parties.

Arbitration law thus raises two competing sets of expectations. On the one hand, courts should give effect to arbitration commitments obtained through informed consent. On the other hand, judges bear a correlative duty to ensure that impartial arbitrators hear before deciding, and respect both contractual limits of their authority and relevant public policy.

2.2.2 Enforcing bargains

Arbitration's statutory framework evolved initially in relation to 'business to business' arbitration,[36] implicating the intervention of national judges in matters such as compelling arbitration and enforcing (or setting aside) arbitral awards. Yet for better or for worse, arbitration law in many countries covers other types of disputes, such as employment and consumer controversies, and investor–state disputes.[37]

[33] See e.g. 1958 New York (United Nations) Convention on Recognition and Enforcement of Foreign Arbitral Awards (New York Convention), Art. V(2)(b).

[34] EU Council Directive 93/13/EEC (1993), Art. 6, requires member states to enact rules precluding unfair contract terms in consumer sales. Art. 3(3) of that Directive refers to an Annex whose examples of unfair terms include requirements that consumers 'take disputes exclusively to arbitration not covered by legal provisions'. In England, the Arbitration Act 1996, sections 89–91, deem arbitration unfair in certain consumer contracts. French law has long distinguished the pre-dispute *clause compromissoire* from the post-dispute *compromis*, the former valid only in contracts between merchants or persons contracting in a professional capacity. See French Code Civil, Art. 2061. The reasoning seems to be that unconscionability lies in allowing merchants, manufacturers, and financial institutions to impose arbitration on weaker parties who presumably cannot make informed choices in this respect.

[35] See U.S. Department of Health and Human Services rules barring long-term care facilities with federal funding from concluding binding pre-dispute arbitration clauses with their residents. See 81 Fed. Reg. 686,866, at 68867 (2016), 42 C.F.R. pt. 483.70(n).

[36] See e.g. Ian MacNeil, *American Arbitration Law* (Oxford University Press, 1992), 139–47.

[37] See the U.S. Supreme Court decision in *BG Group v Argentina*, discussed below. Compare investor-state arbitration proceedings largely independent of domestic courts proceedings under the rules of the World Bank affiliate ICSID, pursuant to the Convention on the Settlement of Investment Disputes between States and Nationals of Other States (1965) (ICSID Convention). See ICSID Convention, Art. 26, discussed in Christoph Schreurer et al., *The ICSID Convention: A Commentary* (Cambridge University Press, 2009), 348ff. The ICSID Convention, Art. 50–52, provides self-contained processes for award interpretation, revision, and annulment. Only in the context of award enforcement do municipal courts play a role. See ICSID Convention, Art. 54–55.

A different legal framework generally covers arbitral resolution of state-to-state disputes,[38] including the Hague Conventions,[39] the OECD initiative on tax treaty arbitration,[40] and ad hoc initiatives such as the treaty to resolve British American disputes following the American Civil War.[41]

2.2.2.1 *The fairness model*

An arbitration agreement permits withdrawal of disputes from national courts in favour of private dispute resolution. When one side ignores its duty to arbitrate, the other side might ask courts to compel arbitration, to stay litigation, or to enforce awards against a loser's assets, raising questions about what the parties agreed and whether proceedings were fair.[42]

At such moments, arbitration law normally includes two limbs: first, to hold parties to their bargains to arbitrate; second, to monitor the basic integrity of the arbitral process, through judicial scrutiny of the award, so that the case will be heard by a fair tribunal

[38] Ulf Franke, Annette Magnusson, and Joel Dahlquist, *Arbitrating for Peace* (Kluwer, 2016), recounting 14 key arbitrations. Early investor–state arbitrations included a mechanism to resolve claims by British creditors against American debtors after establishment of the U.S. in 1776 or 1783, depending on perspective. Art. 6 of the 1794 'Jay Treaty' (negotiated for the U.S. by Chief Justice John Jay) called for commissioners to resolve post-independence differences. See Barton Legum, 'Federalism, NAFTA Chapter Eleven and the Jay Treaty of 1974', 18 ICSID News (2001). The Jay Treaty seems to have produced few awards, however. On another early investor–state arbitration, see Jason Webb Yackee, 'The First Investor–State Arbitration: The Suez Canal Company v Egypt (1864)', 17 J. World Investment and Trade 401 (2016), addressing Egypt's attempt to eliminate the canal's forced labour regime.

[39] The Permanent Court of Arbitration created by the 1899 Hague Convention for the `Pacific Settlement of International Disputes, adopted at the First Hague Peace Conference, convened at the initiative of Czar Nicholas II of Russia, later revised at the second Hague Peace Conference in 1907 called by President Theodore Roosevelt. See generally Arthur Eyffinger, *The 1899 Hague Peace Conference: The Parliament of Man, The Federation of the World* (Martinus Nijhoff, 1999).

[40] OECD, Model Tax Convention on Income and on Capital (2014), Art. 25; OECD, Multilateral Convention to Implement Tax Treaty Related Measures to Prevent Base Erosion and Profit Shifting (2016), Art. 16–26.

[41] The 1871 Washington Convention established a five-member arbitral tribunal in Geneva to address United States claims against Britain for damages arising from attacks on Union ships by Confederate raiders built or serviced in Britain, the most famous being C.S.S. *Alabama*, sunk in 1864 off Normandy. On 14 Sept. 1872, the 'Alabama Claims Tribunal' awarded $15.5 million for damages to shipping, although the case began with a $2 billion claim for indirect damages in prolonging war after the Battle of Gettysburg. Britain accepted arbitration under the shadow of American threats to annex Canada, favored by expansionists like Senator Sumner of Massachusetts. See generally Tom Bingham, 'The Alabama Claims Arbitration', 54 Int'l & Comp. L. Q. 1 (2005); Jan Paulsson, 'The Alabama Claims Arbitration: Statecraft and Stagecraft', in Franke, Magnusson, and Dahlquist (n. 38); †V. V. Veeder, 'The Historical Keystone to International Arbitration', in David D. Caron et al., *Practising Virtue: Inside International Arbitration* (Oxford University Press, 2015), 127, focusing on party-appointed arbitrators Alexander Cockburn and Charles Francis Adams, who sat with colleagues from Brazil, Italy, and Switzerland. See also Bruno de Fumichon and William W. Park, *L'opinion dissidente dans l'affaire Alabama* (forthcoming).

[42] The late Allen Farnsworth aptly subtitled one of his books *The Law of Regretted Decisions*. See E. Allen Farnsworth, *Changing Your Mind: The Law of Regretted Decisions* (Yale University Press, 1998). A similar designation might apply to arbitration law as such, much of which (though not all) implicates determining what the parties intended the arbitrator to decide. See generally Alan Rau, 'Arbitral Jurisdiction and the Dimensions of Consent', 24 Arb. Int'l 199 (2008).

that listens before deciding, stays within its mission, and respects the limits of relevant public policy.

By enforcing arbitration agreements and awards, arbitration statutes fill several functions. First, they send signals to curb judicial hostility toward the ouster of judicial jurisdiction.[43] Second, they enhance predictability in the prerequisites for valid arbitration arrangements and fair proceedings,[44] without which practitioners would face a procedural morass much like the legal hodge-podge governing court selection and foreign judgments.[45] Finally, arbitration acts provide intellectual hooks on which to hang doctrines useful in addressing recurring problems. For example, the principle of 'separability' reduces the prospects of arbitration being sabotaged by fraud allegations unrelated to the arbitration clause itself.[46]

Not all arbitration law makes arbitration agreements easier to enforce than under general contract principles. For example, most statutes and treaties require writing of some sort, often signed.[47] The requirement makes sense, given that it is no small matter to forego one's day in court. A legal system that enforces waivers of recourse to judges will want to ensure that the parties mean what they say. Of course, once a valid commitment to arbitrate exists, arbitration-friendly frameworks reduce wiggle room for escape.

Most major business centres have restricted appeal on the legal and factual merits of a case, or permit waiver of such appeal. On the assumption that an arbitral award should end rather than begin litigation, the emerging trend grants deference to arbitrators' decisions,[48] while retaining mandatory judicial review for defects related to jurisdiction,

[43] In an early case involving an attempt at contractual circumvention of supervisory jurisdiction by English courts, Justice Scrutton declared: 'There must be no Alsatia in England where the King's writ does not run.' See *Czarnikow v Roth, Schmidt & Co*, [1922] 2 KB 478, 488. 'Alsatia' referred to a part of London near Fleet Street that had once been a sanctuary for criminals.

[44] For a thoughtful excursion into how the text of a statute affects decisions on arbitration, see concurrence by Justice Thomas in *AT&T Mobility LLC v Concepcion*. 131 S. Ct. 1740, 1753 (2011), addressing the interaction of sections 2 and 4 in the Federal Arbitration Act.

[45] Although the New York Convention now gives international currency to arbitration awards in over 150 countries, the 2005 Hague Choice of Court Convention has yet to come into effect to give similar effect to decisions of national courts. See also *M/S Bremen v Zapata Off-Shore Co.*, 407 U.S. 1, 9–12 (1972), noting that court selection clauses have historically not been favoured by American courts (and were often declined enforcement) on the ground that they were contrary to public policy.

[46] Separability permits arbitrators to do their job notwithstanding invalidity of the larger contractual framework, with the arbitration clause remaining autonomous from the principal agreement. See Park, *Arbitration of International Business Disputes* (n. 7), 231–95; Alan Rau, 'Everything You Really Need to Know About "Separability" in Seventeen Simple Propositions', 14 Am. Rev Int'l Arb. 1 (2003); *Prima Paint. Corp. v Flood & Conklin Mfg. Co.*, 388 U.S. 395 (1967). Some defects in the contractual framework do affect the arbitration clause, of course, as with forgery or duress. However, if a buyer alleges that a company did not have the assets represented by the seller, that dispute would raise exactly the type of question expected to be resolved under the acquisition agreement's arbitration clause, notwithstanding allegations of misrepresentations that might invalidate the transaction.

[47] New York Convention, Art. II. Compare *Kahn Lucas Lancaster v Lark Int'l Ltd*, 186 F.3d 210 (2nd Cir. 1999) (signature needed for contract with arbitration clause) and *Sphere Drake Ins v Marine Towing*, 16 F.3d 666, 669 (5th Cir. 1994) (no signature needed).

[48] Where appeal on points of law exist, it will usually derive from the parties' opting in (or failure to opt out), or through special regimes to protect consumers and employees against ill-informed choices.

due process and public policy.[49] This 'procedural fairness' model resonates with arbitration's treaty architecture, which gives awards an international currency subject to safeguards for public policy and arbitral authority.[50]

Some countries, notably England, have left a good legislative trail of their path to the procedural fairness paradigm. At one time, English law permitted *de facto* appeal by requiring arbitrators to 'state the case' for court determination. On the assumption that the commercial community had little interest in judges second-guessing arbitrators' decisions, the law in 1979 removed that judicial control on the legal exactness of an award,[51] although flirting with a halfway house of merits appeal in maritime, insurance, and commodities cases, to fertilize development of substantive legal principles in those areas.[52] The current statutory framework, adopted in 1996, eliminated those special categories, leaving appeals on questions of English law only if not 'otherwise agreed', along with mandatory (non-waivable) challenges for defects related to substantive jurisdiction[53] and serious procedural irregularity.[54]

When law diverges from country to country, the disparity often derives not from discord on policy goals, but from the relative weight given to rival risks. French courts, for

[49] Notable jurisdictions include Belgium, England, France, Hong Kong, the Netherlands, Singapore, Sweden, Switzerland, and the U.S., as well as countries that have adopted some form of the UNCITRAL Model Arbitration Law, such as Australia, Bermuda, Canada, and Germany. See Park, *Jurisdiction to Determine Jurisdiction* (n. 7).

[50] New York Convention, Art. V; ICSID Convention, Art. 52–53.

[51] William W. Park, 'Judicial Supervision of Transnational Commercial Arbitration: The English Arbitration Act of 1979', 21 Harv Int'l L.J. 87 (1980); 'The Interaction of Courts and Arbitrators in England', 1 Int'l Arb. Rev 54 (1998); Julian Lew et al. (eds), *Arbitration in England* (Kluwer, 2013).

[52] Those 'special category' disputes were abolished by the 1996 Act.

[53] In any legal system, grounds for challenge of awards can remain difficult to define with intellectual rigour. In particular, the line remains difficult to trace between an arbitrator's simple mistake (a risk assumed by agreeing to arbitrate) and an excess of authority. The English judge Lord Denning once suggested (albeit in an administrative context) that going wrong in law meant exceeding authority, since a tribunal was not authorized to decide in error. See Lord Denning, *The Discipline of Law* (Butterworths 1979). This position was rejected by the House of Lords in 2005 in the *Lesotho Highlands* decision. See *Lesotho Highlands Development Authority v Impreglio SpA*, [2005] UKHL 43. In some instances, challenge may be heard on hybrid grounds such as 'manifest disregard of the law' which falls shy of full appeal, albeit constituting something more than simple excess of authority. See also *Stolt-Nielsen S.A. v AnimalFeeds Int'l Corp.*, 559 U.S. 662, 671 (n. 3) (2010) and 'manifest excess of powers' in ICSID Convention, Art. 52(1)(b).

[54] English Arbitration Act 1996. Section 67 addresses jurisdiction, section 68 serious procedural irregularity, and section 69 error of English law. Notions of 'serious irregularity' causing 'substantial injustice' (section 68) were recently tested in a high-profile case involving a dispute between an American contractor and the British government. See, *Secretary of State for the Home Department v Raytheon Systems Limited* [2015] EWHC 311 (TCC) and [2014] EWHC 4375 (TCC). Raytheon was engaged to design and deliver a new technology system for border control. The Tribunal awarded Raytheon almost £200 million in damages for the government's unlawful termination of the agreement. Rightly or wrongly, the reviewing court annulled the award for procedural irregularity purportedly found in the arbitrators' failure to deal with essential issues. Some institutional rules provide waiver of appeal, which would cover errors of law under section 69. See ICC Arbitration Rules, Art. 34(6). In passing, one might note that the ICC Rules (Art. 33) impose their own internal scrutiny of awards to enhance coherence in reasoning.

example, delay judicial review of an arbitrator's jurisdiction until an award has been made, to reduce prospects for sabotage by dilatory challenges.[55] In comparison, American courts may assess the validity of an arbitration agreement at any moment, to avoid proceedings that ultimately prove futile.[56]

2.2.2.2 *Merits review*

Not all commentators accept the notion that arbitrators should not be second-guessed by judges on the merits of their decisions. In a recent lecture, the Lord Chief Justice of England and Wales suggested that the current arbitration framework in his country reduces the potential for courts to develop law, transforming the common law 'from a living instrument into... an ossuary'.[57] His proposals include liberalizing criteria for granting permission to appeal awards[58] and encouraging greater use of judicial power to decide points of law arising after arbitration begins but before an award.[59]

The view that commercial disputes should fertilize the evolution of law harks back to an earlier framework which allowed appeal on points of law in so-called 'special category' cases arising from admiralty, commodity, and insurance contracts governed by English law.[60] Under this view, litigation constitutes not only a way to settle disputes, but also a means to provide broader behavioral rules to guide business conduct.[61]

The concern for predictability deserves consideration. More appeals permit greater refinement of legal points. However, business managers may feel dismayed by a legal system that sends them to court for another round of hearings after the final award, particularly in international transactions where parties seek to avoid the other side's home courts.[62]

[55] French Code of Civil Procedure, Art. 1448 and 1506.

[56] See *Three Valleys Municipal Water District v E.F. Hutton*, 925 F.2d 1136 (9th. Cir. 1991); *Sandvik A.B. v Advent International Corp.*, 220 F.3d 99 (3rd Cir. 2000).

[57] Lord Thomas of Cwmgiedd, 'Developing Commercial Law Through the Courts: Rebalancing the Relationship Between the Courts and Arbitration', Bailii Lecture (2016), 10, citing a statement by Lord Toulson in a different context in *Kennedy v The Charity Commission*, [2014] 2 W.L.R. 808, 133.

[58] In England, appeals on a question of English law have long been permitted in some form or another, currently provided for under section 69 of the Arbitration Act 1996, albeit with the possibility of the parties opting out. See generally Bernard Rix, 'Judicial Review of the Merits of Arbitration Awards Under English Law', in Julio Betancourt (ed.), *Defining Issues in International Arbitration: Celebrating 100 Years of the Chartered Institute of Arbitrators* (Oxford University Press, 2016), 319.

[59] This power is provided in section 45 of the Arbitration Act 1996.

[60] See section 4 of the Arbitration Act 1979, discussed in the 1993 Departmental Advisory Committee Report on Special Categories reprinted in 9 Arbitration International 405 (1993).

[61] Compare the so-called 'public law model' of litigation discussed in Robert Bone, 'Lon Fuller's Theory of Adjudication and the False Dichotomy Between Dispute Resolution and Public Law Models of Litigation', 75 B.U. Law. Rev 1273 (1995).

[62] In pressing his point, Lord Thomas cited an earlier House of Lords decision that may seem less than convincing. An appeal under the 'case stated' procedure of the time (essentially allowing reversal for mistakes of law) resulted in overturning an award for a German manufacturer that had terminated its British distributors for non-performance. The court criticized the award for taking into account the parties' behaviour, contrary to a rule of English law to the effect that subsequent conduct cannot assist in construing a contract. Although the rule may seem eminently sensible to English barristers, the position remains peculiar to many non-English observers. The effect of the example becomes even more obscure

Concern about development of the law connects with academic criticisms of arbitration in the United States, which rightly or wrongly see the arbitral process as denying vindication of rights to weaker parties.[63] The reasoning of such critics is not always easy to follow. No evidence exists that arbitrators refuse to enforce legal obligations less than judges. Indeed, arbitration in American collective bargaining arose as way to disarm judicial hostility to the rights of labour unions.[64]

2.2.2.3 *Award annulment*

Few areas of arbitration law attract attention as much as the judicial review of arbitral awards in actions to enforce or to vacate the award, as illustrated by the conviction of a managing director of the International Monetary Fund who, when French finance minister, failed to seek annulment of an award in a high-profile business dispute. The decision was viewed as criminal negligence in the exercise of her official functions.[65]

The effect of award annulment outside the arbitral seat remains an enduring source of debate in assessing optimum counterpoise among finality, efficiency, and fairness in arbitration. If a Swiss court sets aside an award made in Geneva, should the award be enforceable in Paris or London? To what extent does annulment at the seat of the proceedings eliminate or restrict the award's effect in other countries? These questions overlap with, but remain distinct from, the debate on the proper grounds for setting awards aside at the arbitral seat.

when reading Lord Reed's observation in the House of Lords that 'the contract is so obscure that I can have no confidence that this is the true meaning'. See *Schuler A.G v Wickman Tool Sales Ltd*, [1974] A.C. 235, 252. One can only imagine how the German manufacturer felt about the award overturned to benefit British interests in relation to a totally obscure contract.

[63] See J. Maria Glover, 'Disappearing Claims and the Erosion of Substantive Law', 124 Yale Law Rev 3052 (2015); Judith Resnik, 'Diffusing Disputes: The Public in the Private of Arbitration, the Private in Courts, and the Erasure of Rights', 124 Yale Law Rev 2804 (2015). In this context, one might note that 30 years earlier the U.S. Supreme Court explicitly declined to indulge the presumption that arbitrators were unable to apply statutory protections of American competition law. See *Mitsubishi Motors Corp. v Soler Chrysler-Plymouth*, 473 U.S. 614 (1985).

[64] See e.g. Tomlins (n. 23), 60–64, noting that the history of American labour relations law derives in large measure from judicial animosity towards the organized labour movement. For a recent application of the principles of labor arbitration, see *National Football League Management Council v National Football League Players Association*, discussed above.

[65] See Landon Thomas, Liz Alderman, and Aurelien Breeden, 'Christine Lagarde Convicted of Negligence', *New York Times* (2016), B1(15). The case implicated allegations of rigged arbitration and a €403 million award in favor of French businessman Bernard Tapie, arising from claims against Crédit Lyonnais in connection with its role in selling his interest in a sporting goods company. See Cour d'appel de Paris, No. 13/13278 (2015). On application for 'recour en révision' the Court found fraudulent collusion between an arbitrator and one of the parties, and quashed the awards ('ordonne la rétractation') pursuant to Art. 1491 of the French Code de Procédure Civile in effect in 2008 when the awards were rendered. The Cour de Cassation ultimately confirmed annulment of the award on 18 May 2017.

French courts take a clear position, giving effect to awards set aside where rendered. On receiving confirmation, an award enters the French legal order with a *res judicata* effect that trumps annulment by the curial courts at the place of proceedings.[66]

Some scholars justify recognition of annulled awards by reference to a free-floating international legal order.[67] Others remain sceptical.[68] In this debate, each side's rhetoric invokes the parties' agreement. If litigants bargain to arbitrate, says one side, why defer to a judicial annulment? In reply, the other side notes that most arbitration clauses specify a geographical venue, implying an expectation of judicial control at the arbitral seat.[69]

A middle position suggests that sound policy treats annulment decisions like other foreign money judgments, respected unless a reason exists to see the vacating judgment as lacking procedural integrity.[70] Initially suggested in an American law review article,[71] this intermediate view has gained traction in recent case law and scholarship.[72]

Dutch and British courts adopt this more nuanced view in recent cases arising from the much-publicized Yukos saga, which in 2014 resulted in $50 billion of awards.[73] In an

[66] *Société Hilmarton Ltd v Société OTV*, Cour de Cassation, Rev Arb. 327 (1994) (note Charles Jarrosson); *PT Putrabali Adyamulia Rena Holding Ltd*, Cour de Cassation, Rev Arb. 507 (2007) (note Emmanuel Gaillard). See Philippe Pinsolle, 'The Status of Vacated Awards in France: the Cour de Cassation Decision in Putrabali', 24 Arb. Int'l 227 (2008); Richard Hulbert, 'When the Theory Doesn't Fit the Facts: A Further Comment on Putrabali', 25 Arb. Int'l 157 (2009).

[67] Emmanuel Gaillard, *Aspects philosophiques du droit de l'arbitrage international* (Académie de Droit International de La Haye, 2008), adapted as *Legal Theory of International Arbitration* (Brill 2010). Compare Jan Paulsson, 'Enforcing Arbitral Awards Notwithstanding Local Standard Annulment', 9(1) ICC Bull. 14 (1998).

[68] Albert Jan van den Berg, 'Enforcement of Arbitral Awards Annulled in Russia', 27(2) J. Int'l Arb. 189 (2010); 'Should Setting Aside of the Arbitral Award be Abolished?', 2014 ICSID Rev 1.

[69] Analogous issues arise for awards confirmed at the arbitral seat but challenged abroad. See *Commissions Imp. Exp. S.A. v Republic of Congo*, 2014 WL 3377337 (D.C. Cir. 2014). A Paris award confirmed in England was presented for enforcement under the District of Columbia Money Judgments Recognition Act. Reversing the lower court, the Court of Appeals held that the Federal Arbitration Act does not preempt a longer limitations period than in the Judgments Act. Compare *Island Territory of Curacao v Solitron Devices, Inc.*, 489 F.2d 1313 (2d Cir. 1973); *Dallah Real Estate & Tourism Holding Co. v Gov't of Pakistan*, [2010] UKSC 46.

[70] For an illustration of a questionable annulment, see *Telecordia Tech. v Telkom SA*, 458 F.3d 172 (3rd Cir. 2006). An ICC award made in South Africa was vacated by a judge who, instead of letting the ICC name a new arbitrator, constituted a replacement tribunal composed of three retired South African judges nominated by the losing South African side.

[71] See Jonathan Mance, 'Arbitration: A Law unto Itself?', 32 Arb. Int'l. 223 (2016); William W. Park, 'Duty and Discretion in International Arbitration', 93 Am. J. Int'l. L. 805 (1999).

[72] See discussion below of the *Yukos* and *Pemex* decisions. See American Law Institute, 'Restatement (Third) U.S. Law of International Commercial Arbitration', Tentative Draft No. 2 (2012), §4–16, comment c: 'Though courts in the United States ordinarily decline to recognize and enforce awards that have been set aside by a court having proper jurisdiction, the Restatement acknowledges that under the [New York and Panama] Conventions a court may in certain exceptional situations confirm, recognize, or enforce an award that has been set aside.'

[73] The Russian energy giant Yukos, once controlled by oligarch Mikhail Khodorkovsky, entered bankruptcy after a tax investigation resulting in its owner being eliminated as a political opponent of Vladimir Putin. In bankruptcy proceedings, Rosneft, an entity controlled by the Russian state, acquired the majority of Yukos's assets, giving rise to multiple arbitrations. The saga drew public attention in July 2014 with awards in three Energy Charter Treaty arbitrations brought against the Russian Federation

earlier stage of the drama, an Amsterdam court confirmed awards made in Moscow that had been vacated by Russian courts, reasoning that foreign annulments should be respected only if they meet minimal criteria for procedural due process.[74] Likewise, the English High Court ruled that annulment at the seat of arbitration does not automatically foreclose enforceability abroad. It would be quite unsatisfactory to give effect to judgments that offended basic 'honesty, natural justice and domestic concepts of public policy'.[75]

American case law has evolved in a similar direction, respecting annulment except upon a showing of irregularity by the vacating court. In 2007 a federal court refused enforcement to an award both made in Colombia and later vacated there because local law did not permit arbitration under the ICC Rules.[76] Six years later, however, a federal court confirmed a Mexican award notwithstanding annulment in Mexico, reasoning that *ex post* application of Mexican procedural law violated basic notions of due process.[77]

2.2.2.4 *Award enforcement and forum law*

The 1958 New York (United Nations) Convention on Recognition and Enforcement of Foreign Arbitral Awards (New York Convention) provides in Art. III that each contracting state shall recognize arbitral awards as binding 'in accordance with the rules of procedure of the territory where the award is relied upon.'[78]

Nevertheless, building on the language referring to 'rules of procedure of the territory where the award is relied upon', some American courts require enforcement of foreign arbitral awards to meet local procedural requirements such as personal jurisdiction[79]

for which the Permanent Court of Arbitration served as Registry. See Stanley Reed, 'Yukos Shareholders Awarded About $50 Billion in Court Ruling', *New York Times* (2014).

[74] *Yukos Capital Sarl v OAO Rosneft*, Court of Appeal of Amsterdam (Enterprise Division) (2009), LJN BI2451 s. 3.10, refusing to recognize the Russian annulment. See Lisa Bench Nieuwveld, 'Yukos v Rosneft: The Dutch Courts find that Exceptional Circumstances Exist' (Kluwer Arbitration Blog 2010).

[75] *Yukos Capital S.A.R.L. v OJSC Rosneft Oil Co.*, [2014] EWHC 2188 (Comm) (Simon J). An earlier English decision, *Yukos Capital S.A.R.L. v OJSC Rosneft Oil Co.*, [2012] EWCA Civ 855 (Rix, Longmore, and Davis JJ) held that Rosneft (the Russian-controlled entity) was not estopped from objecting to award enforcement in England, since public policy issues (the fairness of the Russian annulments) might be decided differently from country to country.

[76] *Termorio S.A. E.S.P. v Electranta S.P.*, 487 F.3d 928 (D.C. Cir. 2007), contradicting an earlier decision (*Chromalloy v Arab Republic*, 939 F. Supp. 907, D.D.C. 1996) that enforced an award made in Cairo but set aside by an Egyptian court.

[77] *Corporación Mexicana de Mantenimiento Integral, S. De R.L. De C.V., v Pemex-Exploración y Producción*, 962 F.Supp.2d 642 (S.D.N.Y. 2013), affirmed *Corporación Mexicana de Mantenimiento Integral, S. De R.L. De C.V., v Pemex-Exploración y Producción*, 832 F.3d 92 (2nd Cir. 2016) (order for rehearing denied), relating to an award made in Mexico in favour of a Mexican subsidiary of a U.S. company against a state-owned Mexican petroleum entity.

[78] New York Convention, Article V, further sets forth grounds for award non-recognition which are traditionally understood as exhaustive. See generally William W. Park and Alexander Yanos, 'Treaty Obligations and National Law: Emerging Conflicts in International Arbitration', 58 Hastings L. Rev 250 (2006), 251–2.

[79] *Base Metal Trading, Ltd v OJSC Novokuznetsky Aluminium Factory*, 283 F.3d 208 (4th Cir. 2002); *Glencore Grain Rotterdam B.V v Shivnath Raj Harnarain Co.*, 284 F.3d 1114 (9th Cir. 2002).

and *forum non-conveniens*,[80] the former deriving from 'due process' requirements of the Fifth and Fourteenth Amendments of the Constitution and the latter constituting a judge-made rule to enhance procedural efficiency. Thus the winning side of an award rendered outside the United States must navigate the intricacies of American constitutional law and civil procedure in a way the drafters of the New York Convention did not likely intend.[81]

In this connection, the drafters of the Restatement (Third) of International Commercial Arbitration appear to accept that enforcement courts must possess personal jurisdiction over the defendant, but part company with cases on *forum non-conveniens*, instead considering the presence of assets in the forum state sufficient to create adjudicative authority for an enforcing court.[82] It is significant that the doctrine of *forum non-conveniens* (unlike jurisdictional limitations) derives simply from a court's inherent power to manage its own docket, dismissing cases when a different forum would be more suitable for the resolution of a particular case. Moreover, in the context of New York Convention, Art. III, *forum non-conveniens* does not easily fit as a 'procedural rule', given that it relates not to how an award will be enforced but to whether it will be enforced at all.

2.2.2.5 *Arbitral jurisdiction: who decides what?*

In allocation of tasks between judges and arbitrators, drafting matters in treaties as in contracts. One investment treaty says that arbitration claims 'may not be filed' until after a local court action has been commenced. Another allows claims to be filed immediately after a dispute arises, but with a proviso that proceedings begin only if local courts have been allowed a year to resolve the matter.

Significant nuances in arbitral jurisdiction were addressed in the well-publicized decision of *BG Group v Argentina*, where the U.S. Supreme Court reviewed an award arising from gas distribution in Buenos Aires.[83] Economic emergency measures in Argentina had 'pesified' gas tariffs by converting dollar-denominated rates into pesos at a third of their value. An UNCITRAL arbitral tribunal sitting in Washington awarded a British investor $185 million for violation of the 'fair and equitable treatment' standard

[80] *Monégasque de Réassurances S.A.M. v NAK Naftogaz of Ukraine*, 311 F.3d 488, 498–501 (2nd Cir. 2002); *Figueiredo Ferraz e Engenharia de Projeto Ltda. v Republic of Peru*, 665 F.3d 384 (2nd Cir. 2011).

[81] See the line of Supreme Court cases elaborating on 'general' and 'specific' notions of 'personal jurisdiction', including *Pennoyer v Neff*, 95 U.S. 714, 720 (1878) ('The authority of every tribunal is necessarily restricted by the territorial limits of the State in which it is established'); *Shaffer v Heitner*, 433 U.S. 186, 197 (1977); *Int'l Shoe Co. v Wash.*, 326 U.S. 310 (1945) ('[D]ue process requires only that in order to subject a defendant to a judgment in personam, if he be not present within the territory of the forum, he have certain minimum contacts with it such that the maintenance of the suit does not offend "traditional notions of fair play and substantial justice"'); *Daimler AG v Bauman*, 134 S. Ct. 746, 754 (2014) (quoting *Int'l Shoe Co. v Wash.*, 326 U.S. 310, 317 (1945)).

[82] Restatement (Third) U.S. Law of International Commercial Arbitration, §4–27(b), Tentative Draft No. 2 (2012) ('Unless forum law provides otherwise, jurisdiction over the defendant in a post-award action may be based on the presence of the defendant's property within the court's jurisdiction, whether or not the property bears any relationship to the underlying dispute').

[83] *BG Group PLC v Argentina.*, 134 S. Ct. 1198 (2014). See also Larry Shore and Amal Bouchenaki, 'Note', Cahiers de l'arbitrage (2012), 675.

in the Argentine investment treaty with the United Kingdom. The treaty allowed arbitration by an investor, but only eighteen months after submitting the dispute to the host country courts. Notwithstanding failure to respect the eighteen-month 'local litigation' rule, the arbitral tribunal rendered an award, reasoning that the emergency decree restricted judicial access so as to preclude a literal application of that provision.

The award was challenged for excess of authority under the Federal Arbitration Act.[84] A majority of the court invoked what it described as ordinary contract principles to require deference to the arbitrators' determination. The 'local litigation' provision was seen as a procedural matter, governing when (not whether) the arbitration begins.

A thoughtful dissent by Chief Justice Roberts reasoned that jurisdictional challenges bear an added layer of complexity for investment treaties and free trade agreements. Each state extends a standing offer to arbitrate, but one which the investor must accept on terms stipulated in the treaty. Until the investor's acceptance of the offer, no agreement to arbitrate can exist, since the investor was not party to the treaty itself. It thus falls to courts to decide whether the offer was accepted, which in the instant case would require judicial consideration of whether a litigation attempt would have been futile.[85]

Sometimes a treaty will contain non-jurisdictional limits on an arbitrators' ability to decide. Such speed bumps, characterized as questions of ripeness, *recevabilité*, or admissibility,[86] may be cured during the arbitration, and do not necessarily bar tribunal authority.[87] An arbitral tribunal might confirm its jurisdiction but delay decision subject to satisfaction of a contractually agreed conciliation mechanism or a deposit for advance on costs.

In a trio of ICSID arbitrations, different tribunals construed the same dispute resolution provision in a treaty between two Turkic nations. The relevant convention language said that disputes not settled amicably within six months after notification 'can be submitted' to arbitration.[88] However, the text continued: 'provided that, *if* the investor

[84] A different scenario would obtain under the ICSID rules, which preclude challenge under the law of the arbitral seat and instead provide for an ad hoc committee convened under the ICSID Convention, Art. 52 and 54.

[85] For some arbitrations, it might be that contracting nations agree that alleged jurisdictional flaws be evaluated by some third body, such as an institution supervising the proceedings, as happens in ad hoc review pursuant to Art. 52 of the ICSID Convention. Whether such designation happens will depend on the facts of each case. In this connection, the concurring opinion of Justice Sotomayor urged that close attention be paid to expressions of intent as articulated by the treaty partners: '[I]f the local litigation requirement at issue here were labelled a condition on the treaty parties' consent to arbitrate, that would… change the analysis as to whether the parties intended the requirement to be interpreted by a court or an arbitrator.' See *BG Group PLC*, 134 S. Ct. 1198, 1214 (2014) (Sotomayor J, concurring).

[86] See e.g. Jan Paulsson, 'Jurisdiction and Admissibility', in Gerald Aksen et al. (eds), *Global Reflections on International Law, Commerce and Dispute Resolution: Liber Amicorum Robert Briner* (ICC, 2005), 601.

[87] Such admissibility restrictions bear a conceptual kinship to defences in the nature of laches, prescription, and statutes of limitations. An arbitrator with jurisdiction to decide a controversy might nevertheless decline to reach the merits, dismissing the claim with prejudice because the claimant has waited too long to file its action.

[88] See *Kiliç İnşaat İthalat İhracat Sanayi Ve Ticaret Anonim Şirketi v Turkmenistan*, Award, ICSID Case No. ARB/10/1 (2013); *Muhammet Çap v Turkmenistan*, Decision on Jurisdiction, ICSID Case No. ARB/12/6 (2015); *İçkale İnşaat Limited Şirketi v Turkmenistan*, Award, ICSID Case No. ARB/10/24 (2016).

has brought the dispute before the courts of justice of the [host state] *and* a final award has not been rendered within one year'.[89] A careful observer will note that an optional 'if' combined with a mandatory 'and' makes the clause anything but clear.[90] From the perspective of logic and grammar, the clause would normally contain either (i) the introductory 'if' to indicate an option ('provided that *if* the investor has brought the dispute to host state courts, a final award has been rendered') or (ii) the conjunctive 'and' to link two necessary events: an action filed in court, plus an award ('provided that the investor brought the dispute to host state courts *and* a final award has been rendered'). However, to combine 'if' with 'and' makes little sense in the context of that provision.

In the first-decided of the cases, a majority dismissed the action after reading the local litigation requirement as a jurisdictional bar.[91] By contrast, the minority arbitrator (whose view was adopted in the two subsequent cases involving the same treaty)[92] stressed the treaty's clear six-month notice period, compelling construction of the litigation requirement as simply an admissibility requirement, which would allow the case to be put into abeyance during the court action.[93]

Of course, some procedural steps, whether provided by contract or by treaty, remain essential to contract formation, and thus preconditions to arbitral authority.[94] Likewise, arbitrators possess discretion on certain procedural matters, but not others.[95] Sound

See generally Mahnoush Arsanjani and W. Michael Reisman, 'Babel and BITs: Divergence Analysis and Authentication in the Unusual Decision of Kiliç v Turkmenistan', in Caron et al. (n. 41), 407; Berk Demirkol, 'Interpretation of the Dispute Settlement Clause in Turkish Investment Treaties with Turkic States', 32 Arb. Int'l 29 (2016).

[89] Emphasis added. Turkey–Turkmeninstan BIT (1997), Art. VII(2) (concluded in two authentic versions, English and Russian).

[90] The English version gives the investor a choice of one of three fora: ICSID, UNCITRAL, or ICC. The Russian version connected the litigation proviso only to ICC arbitration, arguably making it irrelevant to ICSID proceedings. The interpretative task was complicated by the existence of Turkish and Turkmen texts, neither deemed authentic.

[91] In *Kiliç*, an interim ruling had characterized the one-year local court provision as mandatory, reading the word 'if' out of the treaty, in part due to linguistics testimony suggesting pleonastic Russian usage of 'provided that' (при условии) and 'if' (если) translated 'on condition that' an investor file litigation and wait a year.

[92] *Muhammet Çap v Turkmenistan*, Decision on Jurisdiction, ICSID Case No. ARB/12/6 (2015) (unanimous); *İçkale İnşaat Limited Şirketi v Turkmenistan*, Award, ICSID Case No. ARB/10/24 (2016) (with partial dissent).

[93] The minority view in *Kiliç* presents no inconsistency with the dissent of Justice Roberts in *BG Group*. Not only were the treaties different, but so were the questions presented. *BG Group* addressed whether fulfilment of the local litigation requirement was for the courts to decide, an option foreclosed in the *Kiliç* proceedings under the ICSID Rules, which does not permit vacatur by national courts.

[94] If a house painting contract was offered on condition that the contractor post a bond, the painter cannot say that the contract's arbitration clause became effective although the bond was rejected. By contrast, if the contract provided for painting the second floor after payment for the first floor, a dispute about whether the first floor had been painted would fall to the arbitrator. See argument by counsel for Argentina, Oral Argument Transcript (2 Dec. 2013), 51–2 in BG Group Plc v Republic of Argentina, Case No U.S. 12-138 – U.S. Supreme Court.

[95] If an adequate advance on costs must be deposited before proceedings begin, arbitrators would normally be the ones to decide what amount will be sufficient. By contrast, if the contract or treaty requires arbitration in Washington pursuant to the UNCITRAL, it would be a brave judge indeed who

analysis requires attention to the facts of each case, along with the language and structure of the contract or treaty allegedly creating arbitral authority. Few long-term interests will be served by having judges or arbitrators simply incant catchphrases and maxims.

2.2.2.6 *Choice-of-law analysis*

The law applicable to an arbitration flows from accidents of geography, triggered by the country where award recognition is sought against the loser's property, or the venue for arbitration proceedings, with the latter overlapping notions such as arbitral 'seat' or place of award. A search for applicable law can run through a choice-of-law analysis addressing the agreement to arbitrate, as separate from the legal principles controlling the parties' basic commercial relationship. One instance of such *dépeçage* arose in the English decision of *Sulamérica v Enesa Engenheria*, involving claims under insurance policies relating to construction of a hydro-electric plant in Brazil.[96]

Courts in London were asked to restrain litigation in Brazil. From one perspective, applicability of English law seemed a stretch. Contracts among Brazilian companies included an express choice of Brazilian law, with exclusive jurisdiction given to Brazilian courts. Recourse to the law of England became more plausible, however, as the court considered the parties' agreement to arbitrate in London, where the insurers commenced arbitration to contest liability following a policy-holder action in Brazil.

In deciding whether to enjoin the Brazilian litigation, the English court saw the arbitration clause as subject to a law different from that of the substantive contract.[97] Rejecting an implied choice of Brazilian law for the commitment to arbitrate, the court upheld the anti-suit injunction restraining Brazilian litigation, holding that the law of England, as the seat of the arbitration, had the most real connection with the question presented.

Applying Occam's razor, one might suggest simply that a decision to arbitrate in London gives English courts a say in determining whether the arbitration goes forward, with ancillary power to restrain competing litigation. Whether courts elsewhere must respect those determinations remains another question.[98]

would defer to an arbitrator's decision to hear proceedings in Paris under the ICC Rule, absent some special circumstance or further agreement by the parties.

[96] *Sulamérica Cia Nacional de Seguros SA v Enesa Engenheria SA*, [2012] EWCA (Civ), 638.

[97] On the notion of a single law to govern an agreement's material validity, scope, and interpretation, see Rule 57 of *Dicey, Morris & Collins on the Conflicts of Law*, 15th edn (Sweet & Maxwell, 2017. For an exploration of this approach, see William W. Park, 'Rules and Standards in Private International Law, Review Essay of Dicey, Morris and Collins: The Conflict of Laws', 73 Arbitration 441 (2007).

[98] Not all courts take such an approach. See *Cape Flattery Ltd v Titan Maritime*, 647 F.3d 914 (9th Cir. 2011), where a ship owner brought an action against a salvage company seeking indemnity or contribution for damages to a coral reef. The salvage contract provided that '[a]ny dispute arising under this Agreement shall be settled by arbitration in London, England' in accordance with the English Arbitration Act 1996. The court denied the company's motion to compel arbitration, finding that U.S. federal law (not English law) applied to determine whether the parties agreed to arbitrate.

2.3 Arbitral proceedings

2.3.1 Soft law and the conduct of arbitration

Few artifacts of international arbitration prove more elusive than norms governing (or which should govern) the conduct of arbitral proceedings. Matters like rules of evidence and discovery, as between adversaries from different countries, have proved particularly problematic.

In national legal systems, trial by combat gave way to witness testimony and exhibits. Rules were then enacted to create contours for how and when evidence will be considered.

A parallel evolution occurred in arbitration, to foster more efficient private dispute resolution, but with rule creation falling largely to the arbitrators themselves. In addition to determining which side's narrative bears a closer connection to the right answer, arbitrators must configure rules which permit them to get as near as reasonably possible to an understanding of what happened, what a contract says, and what legal duties lie on each side of the controversy.

In pursuing fair and efficient dispute resolution, arbitrators and arbitral institutions have generated a transnational 'soft law' expressed in rules, guidelines, and canons of professional associations, serving to supplement mandatory procedural norms imposed by the harder law (to some minds) of statute and court decision.[99]

As memorials to the experience of those who regularly sit as arbitrators and act as counsel, such international standards both derive from and apply to international arbitration practice. Reflecting and creating normative procedure, soft law enhances legitimacy in arbitration by providing a 'grass roots' quality whereby participants generate their own rules.

Of course, the parties to any arbitration normally remain free to agree on procedural questions, either expressly or by reference to rules applying in default of an agreement otherwise. However, when a particular question eludes consensus, arbitrators must decide the quarrel. Soft law standards provide an analytic tool to balance efficiency and fairness, indicating shared pre-dispute expectations. Written witness statements stand as evidence in chief, with oral hearings devoted to cross-examination. Pre-trial discovery restricts itself to narrow and specific categories of documents. *Ex parte* communication on the case should not take place between arbitrator and counsel. By contrast, a common

[99] Of course, 'soft law' will be influenced by national constraints on what arbitrators can do if they expect awards to be enforced. E.g. the extent of document production required in arbitral proceedings may depend on whether denial of discovery is deemed misconduct. See e.g. *Astra Oil Trading NV v Petrobras America Inc.*, 718 F.Supp.2d 805 (S.D. Texas 2010), holding that under the New York Convention an arbitral tribunal did not unduly refuse extensive discovery. The decision was later reconsidered, but only on whether the Convention applied to a dispute 'entirely between U.S. citizens' (it does not), with Astra deemed to have its principal place of business in California, notwithstanding incorporation under Dutch law. See *Astra v PAI*, 2010 WL 3069793.

culture eludes other questions, such as when and why the loser should pay legal costs of the prevailing party—a matter that has long divided British and American legal traditions.

Some scholars feel uncomfortable with reference to hard and soft law, seeing law as having a binary character, switched on or off, without a dimmer to make norms brighter or softer.[100] Either rules are law, or they are not.

Controversy over whether 'soft law' is law recalls the proverbial debate over whether public international law is really 'law' in the same way as national law. Clearly, differences exist. In genesis and enforcement mechanisms, the 'law of nations' on maritime boundaries, elaborated through state practice, diverges from consumer protection statutes enacted by a state legislatures or city council. Likewise, document production standards in the International Bar Association Rules on Taking Evidence carry a qualitatively different cast from the income tax rates of the Internal Revenue Code. Yet each type of law serves similar purposes, representing part of an authoritative dispute resolution process that includes rules and principles to provide information on decision-making about substantive as well as procedural differences.[101]

The notion of 'soft law' certainly carries risks. International standards can serve as a juridical fig leaf to cover an arbitrator's personal preference, excusing deviation from duty and facilitating an arrogation of power to decide *ex aequo et bono*, or in amiable composition, contrary to the parties' legitimate expectations. In all events, the integrity of the process requires a healthy humility from scholars professing to summarize arbitral standards.

In practice, transnational norms, if properly applied, serve to enhance predictability. They fill procedural gaps, providing norms on questions like document production, witness statements, and conflicts of interest, representing the product of careful and concerted analysis by those who play significant roles in cross-border arbitration.[102]

Soft law can merge into hard law, finding its way into judicial decisions that fill interstices of national statute. One American court case had recourse to the International Bar Association Guidelines on Conflict of Interest in order to give meaning to the term 'evident partiality' in the Federal Arbitration Act.[103] Although not binding as such on federal courts, the Guidelines informed the content of partiality relevant to the proper grounds for award annulment.

[100] W. Michael Reisman, 'Soft Law and Law Jobs', 2 J. Int. Disp. Set. 26 (2011); Thomas Schultz, *Transnational Legality: Stateless Law and International Arbitration* (Oxford University Press, 2014).

[101] On a more playful note, questions about the existence of 'soft law' bring to mind the story of an old New England farmer who met his pastor in the village one Sunday. Disappointed that the parishioner skipped worship, the clergyman asked, 'Enoch, do you believe in baptism?' 'Believe in it?' the farmer repeated. 'Pastor, I've seen it done!'

[102] See e.g. Gabrielle Kaufmann-Kohler, 'Soft Law in International Arbitration: Codification and Normativity', 1 J. Int'l Disp. Set 283 (2010), 297, noting how soft law enjoys a degree of normativity, regarded with deference yet not perceived as mandatory in a classic sense.

[103] See *Applied Indus. Materials Corp. (AIMCOR) v Ovalar Makine Ticaret Ve Sanayi, A.S.*, 2006 WL 1816383 (S.D.N.Y. June 28, 2006) affirmed *Applied Indus. Materials Corp. (AIMCOR) v Ovalar Makine Ticaret Ve Sanayi, A.S.*, 492 F.3d 132 (2nd Cir. 2007).

Each type of law remains uniquely authoritative. Hard law emanates from governments with power to make people pay fines and damages. Soft law commands obedience in large measure because the arbitration community sees merit in principles elaborated by those with experience in the costs and benefits of various procedural practices.[104]

2.3.2 Reinventing civil procedure: three dilemmas

Arbitration is like art, not only because both words begin with the letter 'A' but also because so many people want to be experts, telling others what to do. Often, however, the experienced arbitrator will recollect that the days of his or her greatest certainty (at least about 'best' practices) lay in the simpler world of the first arbitration, before multiple questions posed during intervening decades muddied the waters with the need to reinvent procedure.

New approaches to old problems receive elaboration as different legal cultures and traditions receive consideration in pronouncements of courts, arbitrators, practitioners, and scholars from around the globe.[105]

Language presents special challenges to international arbitrators, particularly in respect of procedural norms. From one language to another, analogous procedural notions may prove false friends. For example, a corporate officer presenting evidence on behalf of the corporation would be a 'witness' for Americans but lack the capacity to testify under French notions of a *témoin*.[106]

Clearly right answers can prove elusive. Yet some solutions will be more or less useful than others in reconciling efficiency and fairness in arbitration procedure. By way of

[104] For example, the International Bar Association Rules in Art. 9(2)(b) provide that an arbitral tribunal shall exclude a document from evidence or production by reason of 'legal impediment or privilege under the legal or ethical rules determined by the Arbitral Tribunal to be applicable'; Art. 9(3)(c) provides that in considering issues of legal privilege the arbitral tribunal may take into account 'the expectations of the Parties and their advisors at the time the... privilege is said to have arisen', but adds for consideration, in Art. 9(3)(e), 'the need to maintain fairness and equality as between the Parties, particularly if they are subject to different legal or ethical rules'.

[105] A recent symposium in New York City employed the term 'twilight issues' in reference to questions to which answers might not be self-evident. See New York International Arbitration Center and Columbia University Center for International Commercial and Investment Arbitration, 'Twilight Issues in International Arbitration: Where Should International Arbitrators Look for Guidance?' (2016). A subline on the conference publicity listed three options for consideration: (i) national law; (ii) no law at all; and (iii) an international standard.

[106] See generally Pierre Mayer, 'Le poids des témoignages dans l'arbitral international', in L.G.D.J., *Mélanges en l'honneur du professeur Bernard Audit* (L.G.D.J., 2014), at 525. The point has been made with force in Yves Derains, 'Langue et langages de l'arbitrage', in Peter Guach, Franz Werro, and Pascal Pichonnaz (eds), *Mélanges en l'honneur de Pierre Tercier* (Schulthess, 2008), 789. Juxtaposing two ways to say 'language' in French (*langue* and *langage*), Derains notes French might be the tongue (*la langue*) for communication in an arbitration built on procedural concepts (*les langages*) drawn from American practice, such as a trial with testimony by 'witnesses' in the American sense. See also Stephan Wilske, 'Linguistic and Language Issues in International Arbitration: Problems, Pitfalls and Paranoia', 9(2) Contemporary Asia Arb. J 159 (2016).

illustration, let us take three instances where responses of courts and arbitrators overlap.

2.3.2.1 *Non-signatories*

One stubborn question implicates when arbitrators should extend their jurisdiction to so-called 'non-signatories', such as company affiliates that did not execute the relevant agreement. Such entities could be joined on a theory such as agency, estoppel, or implied consent. In determining who agreed to arbitrate, judges look for guidance to standards set by their own law, whether in conflict-of-laws principles or in standards for contract validity. Either way, a court starts with the established legal system from which it draws its authority.

By contrast, in cross-border arbitration the genesis of decision-making power derives from no single legal system. Arbitration arises precisely because the parties decided that the dispute should *not* be decided by national courts. The contractually stipulated law, like the law of the arbitral seat, provides assistance for arbitrator analysis of difficult legal questions.

With respect to joinder of a non-signatory, serious conceptual and practical problems arise from looking at the law of the contract or the seat, which can trigger a circular exercise in presuming conclusions. If a corporation never consented to arbitrate under a sales contract signed by its sister company, how can that contract's stipulated law apply? The law of the arbitral seat would be equally foreign to an entity that remained a stranger to the transaction.

If a company or individual contests its agreement to arbitrate, an arbitrator confronts a dilemma not unlike that of the proverbial chicken and egg. Each side will tell a different story about the existence of a bargain to arbitrate. Depending on which story proves correct, the arbitrator either will or will not possess authority.

In evaluating whether the two sides bargained to arbitrate, expressly or impliedly, judges look to norms of their own fora. By contrast, arbitrators in cross-border disputes derive instruction from no single country. The starting point for their authority lies in the parties' agreement, which is the very matter in controversy. Consequently, arbitrators frequently seek guidance in so-called 'transnational norms' or 'international standards' elaborated in practice, as manifested by published awards, or articulated by scholars based on an emerging corpus of principles on joinder of non-signatories.

2.3.2.2 *Cost allocation*

Cost allocation presents a second example of problematic arbitration procedure. In England, a 'loser pays' rule casts a wide net,[107] which can catch reasonable arrangements among sophisticated business managers who wish for something other than the English rule. A contract stipulates arbitration in London as a convenient venue, but with

[107] See English Arbitration Act, sections 59–65, which provides that costs should follow the event, as a general norm, and invalidates pre-dispute agreements to impose on one side the obligation to pay all or part of the costs in any event.

New York law applicable to interpret the agreement, as happens in 'Bermuda Form' insurance policies. In such instances, a conscientious arbitrator falls between Scylla and Charybdis, faced with inconsistent mandates from the *lex loci arbitri* (English Arbitration Act) and the contract (New York law).

2.3.2.3 *Prior decisions*

Clarity can prove elusive with respect to the details of principles such as *res judicata* and issue preclusion. When will (or should) an earlier judgment or award bind an arbitrator deciding a later case? Although many legal systems impose finality for prior decisions, differences remain on questions such as the preclusive effect of reasoning (as opposed to holding) and the right to relief on a theory that could have been, but was not, asserted in an earlier action. Sometimes the parties provide standards to be applied, through choice of an applicable law. Sometimes not, however.

In respect of prior decisions, national law frequently looks to certain 'identities' that preclude re-litigation, such as (i) the same parties; (ii) the same claim (*petita*) (cause of action or prayer for relief); and (iii) the same legal theory (*causa petendi*). Consensus remains elusive on significant key matters, however. Many civil law countries understand the notion of 'claim' (*petita*) narrowly, as a relief sought, permitting a litigant a second bite at the apple. In contrast, common law jurisdictions give the notion of claim a broader scope, opening doors for preclusive effect of the earlier court's determination of issues and reasoning, or the legal and factual premises on which a ruling rests.[108]

2.3.3 A laundry list of dilemmas

By way of further illustration, set forth below are a few of the more common procedural questions which occasionally straddle hard law and soft, in the sense of being posed to international arbitrators and national judges:[109]

[108] William W. Park, 'Soft Law and Transnational Standards in Arbitration: The Challenge of Res Judicata', in Arthur Rovine (ed.), *Contemporary Issues in International Arbitration: The 2015 Fordham Papers* (Brill, 2016). In *Citigroup, Inc. v Abu Dhabi Investment Authority*, 776 F.3d 126 (2nd Cir. 2015), an American court held that *res judicata* must be left for arbitrators to decide, finding that the remedies authorized by the All Writs Act (28 U.S.C. §1651) did not permit a federal court to enjoin an arbitration based on preclusive effect of a prior judgment that confirmed an earlier arbitration award but did not consider its merits. See also Filip de Ly and Audley Sheppard, 'ILA Final Report on Res Judicata in Arbitration', 25 Arb. Int'l 63 (2009); American Law Institute, *Restatement of the Law Third: The U.S. Law of International Commercial Arbitration*, sections 4–9 and 4–10; *Apotex Holdings Inc. & Apotex Inc. v USA*, Award, ICSID Case ARB(AF)/12/1 (2014).

[109] Sometimes a single case raises both issues addressed by courts, as well as arbitral institutions and arbitrators. See *Belize Social Development Bank v Gov of Belize*, 94 F.3d 99 (D.C. Cir. 2015), implicating sovereign immunity in enforcement of an arbitral award, and later (in a decision of the same court issued on 31 Mar. 2017), public policy implicated by an alleged conflict arising from an arbitrator's membership in barristers' chambers whose members once acted adversely to the respondent. Sovereign immunity and the policy challenges were rejected.

- Privilege: Should privilege be considered a question of merits or procedure? Or a mandatory norm of the law of the arbitral seat?[110]
- Ethical dilemmas such as potential conflicts of interest by reason of repeat appointment as arbitrator.[111]
- Disclosure of financial institutions serving as third-party funders.[112]
- Should damages in investor-state arbitration be subject to special legal standards?[113]
- Orders on security for costs.[114]
- The arbitrators' ability to raise new legal issues without consulting the parties.[115]
- Applicable law: methodology in the absence of the parties' choice.
- Mandatory norms (*lois de police*), both substantive and procedural.[116]
- Effects of statutes of limitations and similar time limitations.[117]

[110] See generally Richard Jacobs, Loreli Masters, and Paul Stanley, *Liability Insurance in International Arbitration: The Bermuda Form*, 2nd edn (Hart, 2011), 315–18. Compare David Scorey, Richard Geddes, and Chris Harris, *The Bermuda Form* (Oxford University Press, 2011). See generally Richard Mosk and Tom Ginsburg, 'Evidentiary Privileges in International Arbitration', 50 Int. Com. L. Q. 345 (2001); Norah Gallagher, 'Legal Privileges in International Arbitration', 6 Int'l Arb. L. Rev 45 (2003); Klaus Peter Berger, 'Evidentiary Privileges: Best Practice Standards vs. Arbitral Discretion', 22 Arb. Int'l 501 (2006); Gary Born, *International Commercial Arbitration* (Kluwer, 2009), 1910–14. One decision in the House of Lords (as it then was) referred to privilege as a 'fundamental human right'. See *R (Morgan Grenfell Ltd) v Special Commissioner*, [2003] 1 AC 563; [2002] HL 21, 7.

[111] See the English High Court decision in *H v L & Others*, [2017] EWHC 137 (Comm). The sanitized decision in *H v L* (for which leave to appeal has been granted) implicated appointment of arbitrator 'M' by litigant 'L' in more than one case. Compare the 2014 IBA Guidelines on Conflicts of Interest in International Arbitration.

[112] William W. Park and Catherine Rogers, 'Third-Party Funding in International Arbitration', *Austrian Arbitration Yearbook* (2015), 114. Concern about arbitrator conflicts implicates disclosure of third-party funders. Addressing the request may meet the objection, 'What you don't know can't hurt you'. However, if it transpires that an arbitrator had links with the person paying bills for the prevailing party, the integrity of the process (and validity of the award) would be called into question regardless of what the arbitrator knew at the time.

[113] See *Case Concerning the Factory at Chorzów*, Merits Judgment, PCIJ Rep. Series A No. 7 (1926); *Indemnity Claim*, Merits Judgment, PCIJ Rep. Series A No. 17 (1928), German Interests in Polish Upper Silesia, arising from Polish nationalization of German-owned property in Upper Silesia after the First World War, arbitrated pursuant to a 1922 Geneva Convention. See Ronald Goodman and Yuri Parkhomenko, 'Does the Chorzów Factory Standard Apply in Investment Arbitration? A Contextual Reappraisal', ICSID Review 1 (2017).

[114] See generally Alan Redfern and Sam O'Leary, 'Why It Is Time for International Arbitration to Embrace Security for Costs', 32 Arb. Int'l 397 (2016).

[115] *La Société Commercial Caribbean Niquel v La Société Overseas Mining Investments Ltd*, Paris Cour d'appel, 1st Chamber, 08/23901 (2010), in which an award was vacated because the arbitrators decided damages on the basis of 'lost chance' rather than 'lost profits'.

[116] Putting aside when arbitrators do or should apply norms of a legal system not chosen by the parties, mandatory national norms will have a practical impact in two significant instances: (i) the award needs to be enforced in a country other than the party-selected law (e.g. the American competition law at issue in *Mitsubishi Motors Corp. v Soler Chrysler-Plymouth*, 473 U.S. 614 (1985)); and (ii) the arbitral situs imposes mandatory procedural rules (such as rules for cost allocation in sections 59–65 of the English Arbitration Act 1996).

[117] Compare *Raymond James Financial Services v Phillips*, 126 So.3d 186 (Fl. 2013) (Florida Supreme Court held arbitration proceeding included within statute of limitations) and *Lewiston Firefighters Ass'n v City of Lewiston*, 354 A.2d 154 (Maine 1976) (Maine Supreme Judicial Court held that state statute of

- Impact on arbitral jurisdiction of an alleged bribe in contract procurement.
- Document production requests, which implicate time and money but may also assist decision-making by providing relevant and material information.
- Whether awards must state reasons.[118]
- The propriety of 'summary judgment' by arbitrators.[119]

Answers to fundamental questions can vary not only from one legal system to another, but among judicial circuits within the same country. Such is the case, for example, with respect to principles guiding the type of 'writing' that binds parties to arbitrate.[120]

2.4 The Merits of the Case

2.4.1 Judges and arbitrators

The lion's share of legal analysis in arbitration normally focuses on the substantive merits of the case. Does the applicable law permit contract limitation of damages? Or allow 'double patenting' of intellectual property? Or require liability insurers to approve a reasonable settlement?

Much debate surrounds whether arbitrators apply substantive law differently from judges. The best answer, unlikely to satisfy ideologues, will be 'sometimes'. Much depends on *which* judges are compared with *which* arbitrators. Meaningful analysis begs questions not so much about arbitrators and judges in the abstract, but about how one class of arbitrators rule compared to particular types of judges.[121]

When judges and arbitrators do diverge, variance derives from different starting points for authority, which can yield different calculi of duty. As creatures of the parties' agreement, arbitrators will be less prone than judges to engage in social engineering in a

limitations applied only to 'civil actions' which did not include arbitration, precluding the statute from serving as an automatic bar to recovery).

[118] S. I. Strong, 'Reasoned Awards in International Commercial Arbitration: Embracing and Exceeding the Common Law-Civil Law Dichotomy', 37 Michigan J. Int'l L. 1 (2015).

[119] On summary judgment in international arbitration, see the decision by Mr Justice Blair in *Travis Coal Restructuring Holdings LL.C. v Essar Global Fund Limited*, [2014] EWHC 2510 (Comm.). See also Philip Chong and Blake Primrose, 'Summary Judgment in International Arbitrations Seated in England', 33 Arb Int'l 63 (2017).

[120] See *Kahn Lucas Lancaster v Lark Int'l Ltd*, 186 F.3d 210 (2nd Cir. 1999) (contract signature required to give effect to arbitration clause in contract) and *Sphere Drake Ins. v Marine Towing*, 16 F.3d 666 (5th Cir. 1994) (no signature required). Each case interpreted the significance of a comma in Art. II of the New York Convention. For a recent decision on the effect of a comma in national legislation, see *O'Connor v Oakhurst Dairy*, 2017 WL 957195 (1st Cir. 2017), addressing overtime pay for truckers delivering Maine blueberries.

[121] For common law judicial views, see Tom Bingham, *The Business of Judging* (Oxford University Press, 2000); Antonin Scalia and Bryan Garner, *Reading Law: Interpretation of Legal Texts* (West, 2012).

way that overrides private bargains.[122] It can happen that courts, rather than arbitrators, deviate from contract terms or prior legal precedent by reason of forum concerns on social or economic matters. In a dispute over the price of imported oil, it would not be surprising for a Massachusetts judge to consider the cost of fuel to local residents during a bitter New England winter, whereas the disciplined arbitrator (whether from Boston or from Caracas) would demonstrate fidelity to the parties' shared *ex ante* expectation that contract rights be vindicated.

2.4.2 Two illustrative scenarios

In evaluating baselines for comparison, let us consider two illustrations: one concerning exculpatory clauses inconsistent with applicable law; the other implicating a Texas court and a Texas statute of mandatory application.

2.4.2.1 *Exculpatory clauses*

In a hypothetical joint venture between French and German companies, covering a project in a third country, the contract foresees arbitration in London by a tribunal asked to decide all questions arising under, or related to, the contract. The agreement also provides that (i) neither side shall be liable for negligence, and (ii) no damages will be awarded for lost profits. The parties agree their rights and duties are to be determined according to Swiss law (perceived as neutral), which invalidates contract exclusion of responsibility for gross negligence, although accepting a right to limit damages for lost profits.[123]

As the parties' relationship unfolds, one company complains that the other's gross negligence has caused damages, including lost profits, and requests arbitration. Three world-class arbitrators hear the dispute.

What should be done with the claim for gross negligence? The parties told the arbitrators to exclude liability, but in an agreement whose terms select a governing law invalidating exculpation. Seeking to find the best guide to the parties' intent, an arbitrator would normally decide that specific contract stipulations trump general principles,[124]

[122] Just as not all judges will be cut from the same cloth, not all arbitrators come from the same mould. If the applicable law says that a buyer alleging fraud had only the remedy of rescission, one arbitrator might apply that rule, while another might take the position that he never liked that principle to begin with, and suggest making new law allowing reduction in price. In international arbitration, the temptation to disregard established law often meets the reality that arbitrators, unlike American juries, must explain themselves in a reasoned award that circulates within the business community, thus encouraging fidelity to the parties' shared expectations.

[123] See Swiss *Code des obligations* (Book V, Code Civil), Art. 100(1): 'Est nulle toute stipulation tendant à libérer d'avance le débiteur de la responsabilité qu'il encourrait en cas de dol ou de faute grave' (Any agreement purporting to exclude in advance liability for willful blindness or gross negligence is void).

[124] For a broader musing on specific and general rules, see Antonin Scalia, 'The Rule of Law as the Law of Rules', 56 U. Chicago Law Rev 1175 (1989), contrasting rules of law with personal discretion to do justice, the latter exemplified (according to the late Justice Scalia) in the fair and even-handed decisions

finding an exclusion of damages narrower than a reference to applicable law. Swiss law was chosen to fill gaps, not to contradict explicit contract terms, particularly in a dispute with no connection with Switzerland.[125]

A Boston judge considering a similar dispute may likewise face conflicting directives. Although hesitating to enforce limitations of liability for gross negligence,[126] American law tends to distinguish between situations in which a forum state does, or does not, have an interest in applying its law.[127] A choice of law clause invalidating express provisions of the contract would normally constitute a mistake.[128] Moreover, local policy for invalidating exculpatory clauses serves to protect local residents, not a contract between foreigners with performance abroad.[129]

2.4.2.2 *Punitive damages*

Another juxtaposition of judges and arbitrators arises when courts apply their forum's law even to transactions outside their jurisdiction which would otherwise be subject to a different law. One would expect little variance in the way an English judge and a Bermuda

dispensed by King Louis IX of France sitting under his proverbial oak tree just after having heard Mass. See also Steven Calabresi and Gary Lawson, 'The Rule of Law as a Law of Law', 90 Notre Dame L. Rev 482 (2014).

[125] For many cases, of course, the intent of a choice-of-law clause may be less than evident, having been inserted with little or no research at 02:18 in the morning after a long tussle over the main business points of price and delivery. The construction exercise becomes even more complex if the parties chose to import only part of Swiss law, e.g. the *Code des obligations* (Book V, Code Civil), governing commercial matters. Should arbitrators look to interpretative tools from other parts of Swiss law, such as Art. 2 in Book I of the *Code Civil*, with its well-known prohibition on abuse of rights?

[126] See *Zavras v Capeway Rovers Motorcycle Club*, 687 N.E.2d 1263, 1265 (Mass. App. Ct. 1997), holding gross negligence could not be waived for a racetrack motorcycle crash after the rider agreed not to sue the motorcycle club for injury. American law tends to allow exclusion of consequential damages unless circumstances make such exclusion 'unconscionable' (UCC, section 2–719(3)). See also Mass. Gen. Laws 106 §2–719(3) ('Limitation of consequential damages for injury to the person in the case of consumer goods is prima facie unconscionable but limitation of damages where the loss is commercial is not.'); Restatement (Second) Law of Contracts, §351, which, in comment 'a', provides that when parties expressly exclude or limit consequential damages, freedom of contract means the provision should be enforced.

[127] Restatement (Second) of Conflict of Laws §187, comment (e), distinguishing two situations where parties choose a law making the contract invalid. One is where the forum state serves simply as the place for trial. The other implicates a forum state with an interest apart from its location as the place of trial, where forum state policies operate separate from administration of justice. Comment (b) to Restatement §188 (establishing default rules based on the principle of most significant relationship) states that the parties' expectations that a contract will be valid 'should not be disappointed by application of the local law rule of a state which would strike down [the contract provision] unless the value of protecting the expectations of the parties is substantially outweighed in the particular case by the interest of the state with the invalidating rule in having this rule applied.'

[128] See also Russell Weintraub, 'Choice of Law in Contract', 54 Iowa L. Rev 399 (1968), 410: 'When fully translated, section 187 means that the parties' choice of law will be given effect if it selects the validating law, but not if it selects the invaliding law.'

[129] Thus a thoughtful judge might say that the Massachusetts interest for invalidating exculpatory clauses does not impose itself on foreign parties who have chosen a different result by express contract terms, thus arriving at the same conclusions as an arbitrator. For a French perspective on an analogous problem, see Sylvain Bollée, 'L'impérativité du droit choisi par le parties devant l'arbitre international', Rev Arb. 675 (2016).

arbitrator decide an insurance coverage dispute under a policy governed by English law. What differences did exist derive from individual predispositions, conditioned by factors such as prior work as insurer's counsel, which vary among both arbitrators and judges.

By contrast, a Houston judge might feel compelled to ignore the same New York choice-of-law clause in favour of Texas legal principles declared mandatory by the Texas legislature. In San Antonio, an arbitrator would give a similar response if concerned about his or her award being vacated by courts at the arbitral seat.

Texas imposes punitive damages for bad faith by an insurer in relation to contracts purchased by Texas citizens.[130] Texas judges can hardly ignore such a rule, given the source of their paychecks.

By contrast, outside Texas, judges and arbitrators alike would greet such a rule with scepticism, at least in relation to a contract subject to another legal system where the transaction has no substantial connection with the Lone Star State. The punitive damages might constitute a penalty against public policy by arbitrators or judges in London, particularly if the insurance was purchased from a company they deemed had not done business in Texas.

2.5 An intellectual Hamlet

French poet Paul Valéry described his world as staggering between rival chasms of order and disorder, likened to an intellectual Hamlet,[131] conjuring the indecisiveness of Shakespeare's famous protagonist of that same name.[132] A thoughtful observer notes an analogous tension in international arbitration. In agreeing to arbitrate, parties opt for a private and perhaps idiosyncratic adjudicatory mechanism, which may appear as tending toward disorder.

[130] The Texas Insurance Code authorizes a cause of action for misrepresentation and bad faith in claims handling (Tex. Ins. Code §541.001), and allows treble damages on a finding that the insurer knowingly committed the complained-of act. The statute seems to apply to any policy purchased by a Texas citizen, even if purchased outside the state. Tex. Ins. Code §21.42 provides, 'Any contract of insurance payable to any citizen or inhabitant of this State by any insurance company or corporation doing business within this State shall be held to be a contract made and entered into under and by virtue of the laws of this State relating to insurance, and governed thereby, notwithstanding such policy or contract of insurance may provide that the contract was executed and the premiums and policy (in case it becomes a demand) should be payable without this State, or at the home office of the company or corporation issuing the same.' For application of this provision, see *In re ATP Oil & Gas Corp.*, 2015 A.M.C. 1709 (S.D. Tex. Bankr. 2015), related to the Deepwater Horizon Accident of April 2010, where the Texas Insurance Code applied to a policy with a New York choice-of-law clause.

[131] 'L'Hamlet européen . . . est un Hamlet intellectuel [qui] chancelle entre les deux abîmes, car deux dangers ne cessent de menacer le monde: l'ordre et le désordre.' See Paul Valéry, *La crise de l'esprit* (Athenaeum, 1919), republished in Yves Hersant, *Europe: de l'antiquité au XXe siècle* (Robert Laffont, 2000), 405. Valéry's vision proved tragically accurate as European history unfolded during the next quarter-century.

[132] 'To be, or not to be' forms the opening phrase of a soliloquy by the Prince of Demark in Act III, Scene 1.

At the same time, freedom to opt out of public order requires respect for broader notions of fairness and predictability lurking in expectations of the judicial systems that support the arbitral process. In meeting these expectations, law comes into play in three contexts: (i) a legal framework for enforcing the arbitration; (ii) a set of norms to level the procedural playing field; and (iii) standards for substantive decision-making.

Arbitration's legal framework assists courts in their tightrope walk of recognizing both party autonomy and legitimate public interests, safeguarding basic fairness without second-guessing arbitrators on the merits of a case. Arbitration law seeks counterpoise between two persistent risks: (i) failure to recognize commitments to waive recourse to courts; and (ii) a breakdown in monitoring the basic integrity of the arbitral process. In resolving this tension, arbitration law swings between the risk of weak enforcement mechanisms, permitting disregard of arbitration commitments, and dangers inherent in enforcing arbitration clauses and awards lacking foundations of informed consent or due process.

Sound doctrine lies in finding counterpoise between the precarious and the pernicious, distinguishing between agreements and awards that deserve legal support, and those that do not. Such balance requires appropriate safeguards to monitor fundamental fairness, but without undue interference in the arbitrators' mission to decide the merits of the dispute. Law also inserts itself into arbitration through 'soft law' norms or international standards which provide a more even playing field. Such norms find exploration by professional associations that guide proceedings in default of party agreement. Finally, law supplies substantive standards for making a decision on questions of contract or treaty interpretation that divide the litigants. In this connection, the arbitrator's task will usually resemble that of courts facing similar disputes.

This is not to suggest that arbitration needs law to exist. Nothing stops merchants from making deals to decide cases privately without a legal mechanism to enforce the bargain.[133] Judicial interaction with the arbitral process remains a question separate from the nature of the arbitral process itself, albeit understandably mingled and blended. For homogeneous communities, sanctions for breach of an arbitration agreement lie in social pressures like shunning. In a heterogeneous world, shame may not work as well. Moreover, even close-knit groups seek judicial help resolving property disputes,[134] with courts intervening in Jewish,[135] Muslim,[136] and Christian[137] faith-based arbitration.

[133] See Daniel Markovits, 'Arbitration's Arbitrage: Social Solidarity at the Nexus of Adjudication and Contract', 59 DePaul L. Rev 431 (2010); Lisa Bernstein, 'Opting Out of The Legal System', 21 J. Leg. Stud. 115 (1992); Jerold Auerbach, *Justice Without Law* (Oxford University Press, 1983).

[134] In *Baker v Fales*, 16 Mass. 488 (1820), the court set out a legal framework for resolving property disputes between Unitarian and Trinitarian members in the same Massachusetts congregation.

[135] See *Soleimany v Soleimany*, [1998] EWCA Civ 285 (1998) (father/son carpet-smuggling operations); *Avitzur v Avitzur*, 58 N.Y.2d 108 (1983) (pre-nuptial agreement or *Ketubah* deemed to constitute an arbitration clause, allowing intervention when a husband refused to grant his wife a certificate or *get* allowing remarriage in the Jewish faith).

[136] In *Jivraj v Hashwani*, [2011] UKSC 40 (Ismaili Muslim businessmen agreeing that disputes from a hotel venture would be arbitrated by 'respected members of the Ismaili community').

[137] *Spivey v Teen Challenge of Florida*, 122 So. 3d 986 (Fla. Dist. Ct. App. 2013) (mother's wrongful death action on behalf of son who overdosed after leaving Christian rehabilitation program).

To the business manager, the role of law in arbitration may not be immediately evident. If a dispute involves broken ship engines, delayed completion of a power plant, or disagreement on a bank's net value, the temptation exists to ask arbitrators just to 'get on with it' in determining why engines failed, who goofed in the construction, or what the bank was worth. On reflection, however, injection of law into arbitration should be no mystery even to commercially minded folks. Most merchants seek not only to resolve their fight, but also to resolve it fairly. Corporate executives may not care about nuances between American *res judicata* and French *chose jugée*. Yet they will expect that questions not be endlessly re-litigated, and that arbitrators will exercise independent judgment in applying the contract as written and will address only questions actually presented by the parties. These matters implicate jurisdiction and due process, and a legal framework for judicial review decisions not meeting basic standards of procedural fairness.

Although no playing field will be perfectly level, some will be less so than others. Arbitration law serves to enhance the prospect of a game decided by referees who have no stake in the outcome. In a domestic context, failure to consider arbitration may not matter much. If a Boston seller must sue a Georgia buyer in Atlanta, the dispute will take place within a relatively homogeneous linguistic and procedural context, with proceedings in a variant of the English language according to the Federal Rules of Civil Procedure. However, if the buyer is located not in Atlanta but in Athens, Algiers, or Aix-en-Provence, the court action may proceed not in the language of Shakespeare, but in the tongue of Demosthenes, Mohammed, or Molière. Local counsel must usually be engaged with respect to what, to one side, will be an unfamiliar code of civil procedure, or a judicial system of uncertain integrity.

For international transactions, arbitration justifies itself not so much by speed or economy (although both remain important) but by the enhancement of fairness, in reality and in perception.[138] In its broadest sense, the role of arbitration law thus seeks to balance respect for the parties' agreement to renounce recourse to courts and to arbitrate, and fairness in the process. Thus conceived, arbitration law promotes the type of economic cooperation promoted by reliable follow-through on pre-dispute expectations.

Whether building bridges or providing insurance, mutually productive activity relies on expectations that commitments will be met. Few rational actors invest the same money for the same return without considering whether potential disputes will be decided in a fair forum likely to enforce their bargain. In a world lacking neutral supranational courts of mandatory jurisdiction, the absence of effective arbitration would leave many transactions unconsummated, or concluded at higher cost to reflect a risk premium for the inadequate vindication of rights.

[138] In some instances, perception may be as significant as reality. One study found that in federal civil actions in the United States, foreigners fare better than domestic parties, a counterintuitive finding perhaps explained by a foreign fear of litigation bias that leads overseas litigants to settle rather than continue to judgment unless they have strong cases. See Kevin Clermont and Theodore Eisenberg, 'Xenophilia in American Courts', 109 Harv Law. Rev 1122 (1996).

CHAPTER 3

ARBITRAL JURISDICTION*

ALEX MILLS

3.1 Introduction

3.1.1 The concept and source of arbitral jurisdiction

The term 'jurisdiction' has a wide range of meanings in a variety of legal contexts. In the context of arbitration it typically refers to the 'power' or 'authority' of the arbitral tribunal to decide a dispute. But even this simple definition raises difficult preliminary questions. A decision about whether a tribunal has jurisdiction will frequently be made by the tribunal itself, but that decision is not and cannot be a *source* of its jurisdiction, and cannot be a definitive determination of that jurisdiction, because the authority of that decision depends on the very question under review. A degree of deference may be given to the tribunal's determination of these questions by national courts, as will be explored further below, but self-evidently a tribunal may not confer authority on itself. So where does the jurisdiction of a tribunal come from?

An arbitral tribunal does not (at least typically) have 'power' in a conventional, practical sense—unlike a national court, it cannot directly command the seizure of the person or the property of any party. The 'power' of a tribunal comes more indirectly from two sources. First, the cooperation of national courts, which may readily recognize and enforce arbitral awards and may also act in support of arbitration in various other ways, such as by freezing assets or making other forms of provisional order. Second, the potential reputational consequences of non-compliance with an arbitral award, which may lead a party to comply with it voluntarily. The 'jurisdiction' of an arbitral tribunal is thus ultimately a question for these two communities, which represent the real source of its power. A tribunal will have jurisdiction to the extent that a court or the parties themselves will view its exercise of power as legitimate and requiring compliance. Naturally enough, the view of the parties (and, at least to some extent, the arbitrators) will generally

* Thank you to Dr Ira Lakhman and Camelia Aknouche for helpful research assistance. (I've added the 'Dr' – Ira was a PhD student who has since graduated.)

be based on the position they would expect a national court to take, as it is a national court which would ultimately have the coercive power to enforce the orders of the tribunal, and the question of whether the tribunal exercised its power 'lawfully' in the eyes of national courts will be a significant determinant of whether there would be a reputational cost for non-compliance with its orders. So in most cases a tribunal will be viewed as having jurisdiction where the parties would anticipate a national court taking the position that the tribunal has 'lawful' authority, or a national court has indeed taken that position. Actual cases of judicial intervention may be exceptional, but the *possibility* of a court seizing assets nevertheless provides a foundation for arbitration, both directly and indirectly through its influence on the reputational costs of non-compliance.

The legal framework for arbitration applied by most national courts is of course set out in the New York Convention 1958, and this remains a key basic source of the standards which are applied to determine when an arbitral tribunal is considered to have jurisdiction. For the many questions which remain unanswered or unclear under this Convention, however, different national legal systems may take different views. Where (as in this chapter) we are dealing with an 'international' arbitration, where the parties, the dispute, and/or the dispute settlement process have connections to more than one territory, the issue of 'lawful' authority thus raises two further fundamental questions: *which* national legal system's view of the jurisdiction of the tribunal counts, and *why*? The law governing the arbitration agreement? The law of the seat of arbitration? The law of the place of enforcement of the arbitral award? Or should some non-national standard of law be applied instead? As we will see, this is a highly complex issue which must be confronted not only by national courts (which will not necessarily apply their own law to these issues) but also by the arbitral tribunal itself.

3.1.2 The agreement to arbitrate

It is trite but true to observe that the jurisdiction of an arbitral tribunal depends on the consent of the parties, usually expressed in a contract, in the form of an arbitration agreement.[1] This is an essential feature of the question of arbitral jurisdiction, regardless of the context or the legal order in which the issue is being reviewed.[2] In the words of Lord Hope in the House of Lords:

> As everyone knows, an arbitral award possesses no binding force except that which is derived from the joint mandate of the contracting parties. Everything depends on

[1] See generally e.g. Alex Mills, *Party Autonomy in Private International Law* (Cambridge University Press, 2018), Chapter 6; Andrea Steingruber, *Consent in International Arbitration* (Oxford University Press, 2012); Gary Born, *International Commercial Arbitration*, 2nd edn (Kluwer Law International, 2014), 225 ('The foundation of almost every international arbitration—and of the international arbitral process itself—is an international arbitration agreement'); Nigel Blackaby et al., *Redfern and Hunter on International Arbitration*, 6th edn (Oxford University Press, 2015), para. 2.01 ('The agreement to arbitrate is the foundation stone of international arbitration').

[2] 'Arbitration' mandated by statute, which is perhaps better considered not to be arbitration at all, is not considered in this chapter.

their contract, and if there was no contract to go to arbitration at all an arbitrator's award can have no validity.[3]

The U.S. Supreme Court has similarly observed that 'arbitration is a matter of contract, and a party cannot be required to submit to arbitration any dispute which he has not agreed so to submit'.[4] An arbitration without consent could not, in principle, lead to an award that would be enforced by any court. Most of the issues which arise concerning the jurisdiction of a tribunal are therefore issues of contract law, as explored further below. However, this simple observation masks two complex further dimensions, which are related to the question of the source of arbitral jurisdiction discussed above.

The first is that an arbitration agreement is not an ordinary contract, because it is not concerned with the substantive rights and obligations of the parties. It is a contract through which parties agree on a mechanism to resolve legal disputes which arise between them, as a substitute for national courts, and thereby to determine their substantive rights and obligations. While an arbitration agreement may be viewed as an 'extension' of freedom of contract, it has long been understood that it is therefore importantly distinct from, for example, a contract for mediation or conciliation, which does not establish a binding determination of the rights and obligations of the parties. Consent to arbitration may take a contractual form, but in effect, it involves opting in to an alternative justice system—a system which exists alongside that of national courts.[5] While the foundations of arbitration lie in private law, the function of arbitration is a private replication of the public functions of courts. This has a number of important implications, as explored below.

The second complexity is the question of whether the contract is the *ultimate* basis of arbitration. Should the contract itself be viewed as the foundation of the tribunal's jurisdiction, or should the legal system (or legal systems) which give effect to the contract be considered as a further underlying foundation? As a general matter, where a contract does not have cross-border connections it is relatively intuitive (although not incontrovertible) to say that the agreement between the parties is only binding because it is recognized by the local legal system. If that legal order views the agreement as invalid, the parties do not have obligations arising from it; if it is valid, the precise nature of their obligations is also a matter for that legal order. To put this another way, at least conventionally a 'contract' must have a system of law behind it; without a governing law to give it the status of a contract, it is, to paraphrase the House of Lords, merely a 'piece of paper'.[6] Where a contract has connections with more than one state, however, this

[3] *Fiona Trust v Privalov* (reported as *Premium Nafta Products Ltd v Fili Shipping Company Ltd*), [2007] UKHL 40, [34].

[4] *Steelworkers v Warrior & Gulf Co.*, 363 U.S. 574, 582 (1960).

[5] See classically e.g. Kenneth Carlston, 'Theory of Arbitration Process', 17 Law and Contemporary Problems 631 (1952); Heinrich Kronstein, 'Arbitration is Power', 38 New York University Law Review 661 (1963); Philip McConnaughay, 'The Risks and Virtues of Lawlessness: A "Second Look" at International Commercial Arbitration', 93 Northwestern University Law Review 453 (1999).

[6] *Amin Rasheed Shipping Corporation Appellants v Kuwait Insurance Co*, [1984] AC 50, 65 (Lord Diplock: 'Contracts are incapable of existing in a legal vacuum. They are mere pieces of paper devoid of all legal effect unless they were made by reference to some system of private law').

question becomes more complex. Different legal orders connected with the contract may answer these questions differently; a contract may be valid in one legal order and invalid in another, or it may be interpreted to establish different legal obligations in different contexts. This can make it difficult for parties to know what their obligations are, since they may not know in advance where their disputes are likely to be litigated, or indeed which system of law will be applied. The development of international commercial arbitration might be viewed, at least in part, as a response to these difficulties—ensuring that parties can agree on a single 'neutral' forum to resolve their disputes, so that the inconvenience of having different answers from different national courts can be avoided. But the same issues may arise in relation to arbitration agreements, at least on a traditional analysis—an arbitration agreement may be valid under one legal order and invalid in another. This may make the situation complex for the parties and their arbitrators, as they may not know in advance in which legal order or orders the lawfulness of their actions will be evaluated. To say that an international arbitration derives its authority from a contract therefore raises an additional foundational question—does the characterization of an arbitration agreement as contractually binding depend on a system of national law, and if so, which one?

As will be discussed further, this is far from a simple question, and it goes to the heart of the nature of international commercial arbitration. Gaillard has described three different 'structuring representations' of arbitration, each of which suggests a distinct response to these concerns.[7]

The first is to view arbitration as a replication of the judicial function which is authorized by the legal system of the seat of arbitration, thereby giving priority to the law of the seat. This approach, perhaps most closely associated with F. A. Mann,[8] is referred to as 'monolocal' by Gaillard,[9] and has also been described by Paulsson as the 'territorialist' thesis.[10] Its main criticism is that it does not capture the more complex modern reality of the internationalism of arbitration or of the practice of arbitrators, which readily crosses a variety of national borders and whose validity cannot be derived from or ascribed to a single national legal order. It is indicative of these complexities that the concept of the 'seat' of the tribunal is itself no longer considered a question of fact (the place where the tribunal 'sits' to hold hearings), but rather a 'juridical' question[11] (essentially, identifying the legal order which provides the default and/or non-derogable procedural law for the tribunal, sometimes referred to as the *lex arbitri*)—it is now

[7] Emmanuel Gaillard, *Legal Theory of International Arbitration* (Martinus Nijhoff, 2010). See also Emmanuel Gaillard, 'The Representations of International Arbitration', 1 Journal of International Dispute Settlement 271 (2010).

[8] F. A. Mann is the better way to refer to this author - it is how he is generally known. Mann, 'State Contracts and International Arbitration', 42 British Yearbook of International Law 1 (1967); F. A. Mann, 'Lex Facit Arbitrum', in Pieter Sanders (ed.), *International Arbitration: Liber Amicorum for Martin Domke* (Martinus Nijhoff, 1967).

[9] Gaillard, 'Representations' (n. 7), 279.

[10] Jan Paulsson, 'Arbitration in Three Dimensions', 60 ICLQ 291 (2011); Jan Paulsson, *The Idea of Arbitration* (Oxford University Press, 2013), ch. 2.

[11] Lord Collins and Jonathan Harris, *Dicey, Morris & Collins on The Conflict of Laws*, 15th edn (Sweet and Maxwell, 2012), para. 16–035.

uncontroversial that the venue (or venues) for tribunal hearings may not be the same as the seat.[12]

Given these complexities, a second perspective is to see arbitration as anchored in 'a plurality of national legal orders'. In Gaillard's terminology, this is a 'multilocal' approach;[13] Paulsson has similarly described this as the 'pluralistic' thesis, under which 'arbitration may be given effect by more than one legal order, none of them inevitably essential'.[14] This approach would suggest simply accepting the complexities of different potentially applicable legal orders, acknowledging that 'the powers, duties, and jurisdiction of an arbitral tribunal arise from a complex mixture of the will of the parties, the law governing the arbitration agreement, the law of the place of arbitration, and the law of the place in which recognition or enforcement of the award may be sought'.[15] The unsatisfactory aspect of this approach is that the meaning and validity of an arbitration agreement and arbitral award may vary between legal orders, which may undermine the effectiveness of arbitration in resolving cross-border disputes by leading to conflicting decisions from the tribunal and from different national courts.

The third 'representation' of arbitration suggested by Gaillard (and the approach which he endorses) conceives instead of international arbitration as functioning in an autonomous 'transnational' realm, rather than as part of one or more national legal orders: 'the juridicity of arbitration is rooted in a distinct, transnational legal order, that could be labeled as the arbitral legal order, and not in a national legal system, be it that of the country of the seat or that of the place or places of enforcement.'[16] An arbitration may apply national law, but that does not mean that national law is the source of its authority, and under this view it may therefore equally be open to a tribunal to apply non-national sources of law.[17] Paulsson similarly describes this approach as postulating that 'arbitration is the product of an autonomous legal order accepted as such by arbitrators and judges'.[18] The source of the authority of the tribunal may thus be viewed as the 'contract' itself, existing independently from the endorsement of any system of

[12] For discussion, see e.g. *Shagang South-Asia (Hong Kong) Trading Co Ltd v Daewoo Logistics*, [2015] EWHC 194 (Comm); *Bay Hotel and Resort Ltd v Cavalier Construction Co Ltd*, [2001] UKPC 34.

[13] Gaillard, 'Representations' (n. 7), 279.

[14] Paulsson, 'Three Dimensions' (n. 10), 292.

[15] Blackaby et al. (n. 1), para. 5.02.

[16] Gaillard, *Legal Theory* (n. 7), 35.

[17] See further e.g. Thomas Schultz, *Transnational Legality: Stateless Law and International Arbitration* (Oxford University Press, 2014); Ralf Michaels, 'Roles and Role Perceptions of International Arbitrators', in Walter Mattli and Thomas Dietz (eds), *International Arbitration and Global Governance: Contending Theories and Evidence* (Oxford University Press, 2014), 52 ('If the arbitral award is denationalized, then, functionally, the same is true for the arbitrator: he ceases to be part of a national state and instead becomes integrated in a "global adjudication system." The arbitrator is no longer obliged toward his or any other national state, nor only toward the parties themselves. Instead, he adopts a transnational role within a transnational system into which he is integrated').

[18] Paulsson, 'Three Dimensions' (n. 10), 292. Paulsson also describes a fourth approach under which 'arbitration may be effective under arrangements that do not depend on national law or judges at all'. This is not entirely distinguishable from the third approach, although he argues that in practice it collapses into the second (pluralistic) approach, as non-national law is simply another form of legal ordering.

national law. According to Gaillard, this representation 'corresponds to the international arbitrator's strong perception that they do not administer justice on behalf of any given State, but that they nonetheless play a judicial role for the benefit of the international community'.[19] As will be explored further below, every international arbitration faces this fundamental question of the potentially transnational character of arbitration; and although it is not always expressly dealt with by tribunals or the leading authorities on arbitration, it has a major impact on questions of arbitral jurisdiction.

3.1.3 Outline

An important preliminary point, examined in section 3.2, is the need to distinguish between questions of jurisdiction and admissibility. The former are concerned with the powers of the tribunal, while the latter are concerned with whether the preconditions for commencing arbitral proceedings have been satisfied—and will thus ordinarily be left to a tribunal to determine. There are then two main categories of legal issue which may arise concerning limitations on the jurisdiction of an arbitral tribunal. The first follows from the fact that, as discussed above, the foundations of arbitral jurisdiction lie in the agreement to arbitrate. The most important limitations thus concern the validity and effectiveness of the arbitration agreement, and six distinct issues will be examined in turn in section 3.3. The second, which will be considered in section 3.4, is the existence of subject matter limitations on the possibility of arbitration, often referred to as the question of arbitrability—whether certain types of disputes may not be capable of settlement through arbitration. Although this may also be understood as concerned with the question of the validity of the arbitration agreement, it is distinctive because it is not focused on the parties and whether they have reached agreement but on external legal constraints on the possibility for them to do so. Each of these questions potentially raises two general problems, which are (as already noted above) pervasive concerns relating to arbitral jurisdiction: (i) who should decide, and (ii) what rules they should apply. These general problems are discussed in sections 3.5 and 3.6 respectively, before section 3.7 concludes.

3.2 Jurisdiction and Admissibility

The concept of 'admissibility'—sometimes also referred to as 'conditions precedent to arbitration', or (particularly in the United States, and perhaps slightly unfortunately) as

[19] Gaillard, *Legal Theory* (n. 7), 35.

the question of 'procedural arbitrability'[20]—is related to the concept of jurisdiction, and drawing a distinction between the two sometimes raises difficulties in practice.[21] As discussed above, the question of jurisdiction concerns the power of the tribunal. The question of admissibility is related to the claim, rather than the tribunal, and asks whether this is a claim which can be properly brought. In particular, it considers the question of whether there are any conditions attached to the exercise of the right to arbitrate which have not been fulfilled. Those conditions might be, for example, a limitation period applicable to the right to commence arbitration,[22] or a requirement to mediate and/or negotiate before arbitral proceedings may be commenced[23] (variously referred to as 'cascading', 'waterfall', or 'multi-tier' dispute resolution clauses).[24]

A range of issues may arise relating to such conditions. Requirements which are not sufficiently clearly defined may not be legally effective,[25] and care must also be taken to distinguish those clauses which merely create alternative options, rather than conditions precedent.[26] Issues may also arise as to whether such conditions have been fulfilled, and if not, whether the requirement may have been waived by the conduct of the other party. Limitation periods in the context of arbitration may be contractual as well as statutory, and contractual limitation periods may not always be enforced by the courts.[27] Particularly complex issues may arise where a limitation period operates under a cascading dispute resolution clause—a prior period of mediation may or may

[20] See *Howsam v Dean Witter Reynolds, Inc.*, 573 U.S. 79, 83–86 (2002); for criticism of this terminology, see Jan Paulsson, 'Jurisdiction and Admissibility', in Gerald Aksen et al. (eds), *Global Reflections on International Law, Commerce and Dispute Resolution* (ICC, 2005).

[21] For a general, practically oriented guide to this distinction, see e.g. Chartered Institute of Arbitrators, 'International Arbitration Guidelines 2015/2016: Jurisdictional Challenges' http://www.ciarb.org/guidelines-and-ethics/guidelines/practice-guidelines-protocols-and-rules. See further Gary Born and Marija Šćekić, 'Pre-Arbitration Procedural Requirements: A Dismal Swamp', in David D. Caron et al. (eds), *Practising Virtue: Inside International Arbitration* (Oxford University Press, 2016), 227; Laurent Gouiffès and Melissa Ordonez, 'Jurisdiction and Admissibility: Are We Any Closer to a Line in the Sand?', 31 Arbitration International 109 (2015); Paulsson (n. 20).

[22] See further Andrew Tweeddale and Keren Tweeddale, 'Commencement of Arbitration and Time-Bar Clauses', 75 Arbitration 480 (2009).

[23] See e.g. *HIM Portland LLC v DeVito Builders, Inc.*, 317 F.3d 41 (1st Cir. 2003); *Kemiron Atl., Inc v Aguakem Int'l Inc.*, 290 F.3d 1287, 1291 (11th Cir. 2002); *Channel Tunnel Group v Balfour Beatty Construction Ltd*, [1993] AC 334.

[24] See generally Didem Kayali, 'Enforceability of Multi-Tiered Dispute Resolution Clauses', 27 Journal of International Arbitration 551 (2010); Doug Jones, 'Dealing with Multi-Tiered Dispute Resolution Process', 75 Arbitration 188 (2009); Alexander Jolles, 'Consequences of Multi-Tier Arbitration Clauses: Issues of Enforcement', 72 Arbitration 329 (2006); Dyala Jiménez Figueres, 'Multi-Tiered Dispute Resolution Clauses in ICC Arbitration', 14 ICC Bulletin 71 (2003).

[25] *Sulamerica CIA Nacional de Seguros SA v Enesa Engenharia SA*, [2012] EWCA Civ 638, [22] ('An undertaking to negotiate, or an agreement to strive to settle a dispute amicably, is too uncertain to be enforced, because the court has insufficient objective criteria to decide whether one or both parties have complied with or breached such a provision'); *Wah (aka Alan Tang) v Grant Thornton International Ltd*, [2012] EWHC 3198 (Ch), [57]; but compare *HSBC Institutional Trust Services (Singapore) Ltd v Toshin Development Singapore Pte Ltd*, [2012] SGCA 48; *Holloway v Chancery Mead Ltd*, [2007] EWHC 2495 (TCC), [81]; *Cable & Wireless Plc v IBM United Kingdom Ltd*, [2002] EWHC 2059 (Comm).

[26] See e.g. *NB Three Shipping Ltd v Harebell Shipping Ltd*, [2004] EWHC 2001 (Comm).

[27] This is reflected in e.g. Arbitration Act 1996 (UK), s. 12. This power is in practice exercised sparingly, as it amounts to non-enforcement of the contractual agreement between the parties: *Harbour &*

not count toward the limitation period for arbitration.[28] Difficulties may also arise concerning when an arbitration has actually been commenced for limitation period purposes; the English Courts judge this question flexibly, and do not adopt a strict and technical approach.[29]

The most important consequence of the distinction between issues of jurisdiction and admissibility is that the latter are usually considered not to provide a challenge to the general authority of the parties' agreement to arbitrate. As a result, while a tribunal's decision on jurisdiction cannot be decisive concerning whether such jurisdiction exists (although as discussed below it may be given a degree of deference), the determination of a tribunal on questions of admissibility should generally be considered decisive, where a valid arbitration agreement exists.[30] An arbitral tribunal will therefore normally need to establish its jurisdiction as a precondition for making any decision on admissibility. As a further consequence of this, the general approach is that (on the assumption that the arbitration agreement is exclusive)[31] an arbitral tribunal should be considered to have the exclusive authority to consider questions of admissibility—that these are questions which fall within the purview of the agreement to arbitrate, whose validity is itself not in question, and should not be addressed by a court.[32] The converse principle is also usually followed, which is to say that a national court decision concerning a question of admissibility arising under a valid exclusive arbitration agreement will not necessarily be recognized by an arbitral tribunal, on the basis that such a decision has been made contrary to the arbitration agreement. By contrast, an arbitral tribunal is much more likely to defer to the decision of a court (particularly the courts of the seat of arbitration) concerning questions of arbitral jurisdiction, because (as explored below) that determination, going to the very authority of the tribunal, may legitimately be made by both courts and arbitral tribunals, and the power of the tribunal may ultimately depend on judicial enforcement.

3.3 The Arbitration Agreement: Six Questions

This section focuses on issues relating to the validity or effectiveness of an arbitration agreement. (Strictly speaking we should probably refer to an 'apparent' or 'alleged'

General Works v Environment Agency, [2000] 1 W.L.R. 950; *Thyssen Inc v Calypso Shipping Corp SA*, [2000] 2 All E.R. (Comm) 97.

28 See further e.g. *Wholecrop Marketing Ltd v Wolds Produce Ltd*, [2013] EWHC 2079 (Ch).

29 See further *Seabridge Shipping AB v AC Orsleff's EFTS A/S*, [2000] 1 All E.R. (Comm) 415; Arbitration Act 1996 (UK), s. 14.

30 Paulsson (n. 20).

31 See further section 3.3.5.

32 See e.g. *BG Group plc v Republic of Argentina*, 134 S. Ct. 1198 (2014); *Howsam v Dean Witter Reynolds, Inc.*, 573 U.S. 79, 83–86 (2002); but see *Wah (aka Alan Tang) v Grant Thornton International Ltd*, [2012] EWHC 3198 (Ch).

arbitration agreement, but for the sake of simplicity the term 'arbitration agreement' will be used here even when its existence or validity is contested.) In the United States these issues are sometimes referred to as 'substantive gateway questions',[33] to distinguish them from the procedural gateway questions which are discussed above under the label of 'admissibility' issues. The key point of distinction is that, as a matter of logic, it is unsatisfactory for the issues discussed in this section to be answered exclusively by the arbitral tribunal (which, as discussed below, is not to say that the tribunal cannot answer them at all), because they go to the very authority of that tribunal.

Perhaps the most important general principle here is that of separability (sometimes also referred to as severability), which requires that the validity or effectiveness of the arbitration agreement be determined separately from that of any contract as part of which it may have been agreed. Challenges to the other contractual terms between the parties will thus not necessarily affect the arbitration agreement, and may therefore be matters which should be determined by an arbitral tribunal. The implications of this principle are discussed further in section 3.5.3.

3.3.1 Has an arbitration agreement been reached?

The first and perhaps simplest question which must be asked is whether an arbitration agreement has been reached. This is, at least traditionally, analysed as a question of contractual formation—considering, for example, whether there has been an offer which has been accepted. It may therefore be dependent on the determination of the law applicable to this question, as discussed below. Pursuant to the doctrine of separability, as noted above, we are only concerned here with the question of whether there is an agreement to arbitrate, not whether a substantive contract has been formed. Only challenges which go to the validity of the arbitration agreement may affect the jurisdiction of the tribunal. In many cases such questions may be straightforward, but difficult issues may also be raised, such as where an offer may have been accepted by conduct, or where an offer refers to one party's standard terms and conditions, which include an arbitration agreement. In the first case, the issue may be characterized as whether an agreement has been formed at all, while in the second case the issue may be characterized as whether a validly formed contract incorporates the arbitration agreement. (It is also possible that a failure to incorporate standard terms would invalidate the contract as a whole, because important contractual terms have not been agreed, although a preliminary and incomplete agreement potentially containing an arbitration agreement may

[33] *Howsam v Dean Witter Reynolds, Inc.*, 573 U.S. 79, 83 (2002). The terminology is, however, somewhat contested: for clarification see George Bermann, 'The "Gateway" Problem in International Commercial Arbitration', 37 Yale Journal of International Law 1 (2012).

also be recognized as valid even if other substantive terms remain to be negotiated.)[34] Different legal systems may take different approaches to the question of how much notice is required before terms can be successfully incorporated by reference into a contract, and may even single out arbitration clauses for special treatment in this regard because they involve a waiver of any entitlement to commence judicial proceedings. The recent practice of the English Courts tends to apply the general rules on the incorporation of contractual terms, without any special reference being required to the arbitration agreement,[35] although an exception may apply for charterparty clauses in bills of lading.[36]

Arbitration agreements may be concluded in advance of a dispute arising, typically where they are negotiated as part of the formation of a contractual relationship, or retrospectively, typically where they may form part of ad hoc dispute settlement negotiations.[37] In the latter case, it is possible for an arbitration agreement to be established by conduct as well as through an express agreement (analogous to the concept of submission as applied to the jurisdiction of a court), if an arbitration is commenced by one party and the other party accepts through participating in the proceedings (other than to dispute jurisdiction).[38] Submission by conduct is unusual in the context of arbitration, although an agreement to arbitrate may effectively be formed where two parties have attempted to enter into an express agreement, but have unknowingly failed to do so successfully, and have subsequently arbitrated on the basis of this mutual mistake.[39]

3.3.2 Is the arbitration agreement valid?

The second (and closely related) question which may be raised concerning an arbitration agreement is whether it is 'valid'. Arbitration agreements may raise issues of both formal and substantive validity.[40]

[34] See e.g. *RTS Flexible Systems Ltd v Molkerei Alois Muller GmbH & Co KG*, [2010] UKSC 14; *Pagnan SpA v Feed Products*, [1987] 2 Lloyd's Rep. 601.

[35] *Habas Sinai Ve Tibbi Gazlar Isthisal Endustri AS v Sometal SAL*, [2010] EWHC 29 (Comm).

[36] *Caresse Navigation Ltd v Zurich Assurances Maroc (The Channel Ranger)*, [2014] EWCA Civ 1366; *Sea Trade Maritime Corp v Hellenic Mutual War Risks Association (Bermuda) Ltd (The Athena)*, [2006] EWHC 2530 (Comm), [65]; *AIG Europe (UK) Ltd and others v The Ethniki*, [2000] 2 All ER 566, [37]. See generally Melis Ozdel, 'Enforcement of Arbitration Clauses in Bills of Lading: Where Are We Now?', 33 Journal of International Arbitration 151 (2016).

[37] See further e.g. Born (n. 1), para 2.02; Blackaby et al. (n. 1), para 2.119.

[38] *Gulf Import & Export Co v Bunge*, [2008] 1 Lloyd's Rep. 316; *Baird Textiles Holdings v Marks & Spencer*, [2001] EWCA Civ 274.

[39] *The Amazonia*, [1990] 1 Lloyd's Rep. 236.

[40] See generally e.g. Born (n. 1), ch. 5; Blackaby et al. (n. 1), ch. 2.

Formal validity is concerned with any conditions which relate to how arbitration agreements may be formed, such as requirements that they be in writing or signed. As is well known, the New York Convention 1958 requires that arbitration agreements be in writing.[41] In practice, the trend is to interpret this requirement flexibly, in line with developments in communications technology.[42] The requirement for writing under the New York Convention also does not necessarily mean that unwritten agreements are invalid. Some national laws may require arbitration agreements to be in writing to be valid, but others may recognize the validity of unwritten agreements (by either enforcing such agreements or enforcing arbitral awards made pursuant to such agreements)—the trend is perhaps in this direction, pursuant to the UNCITRAL Model Law 2006.[43] Arbitrations conducted pursuant to unwritten agreements will simply not have the benefit of the New York Convention enforcement obligations,[44] like entirely domestic or non-commercial arbitrations. Section 5 of the Arbitration Act 1996 (UK) appears to require an arbitration agreement to be in writing (albeit interpreting this requirement flexibly); however, oral arbitration agreements may still be enforced pursuant to the common law under section 81(1)(b). In the United States, an arbitration agreement must be in writing to fall within the Federal Arbitration Act, otherwise its effectiveness is a matter of state law.[45]

The issue of substantive validity can encompass a range of concerns. The New York Convention provides limited guidance here by permitting non-enforcement of an arbitration agreement where it is 'null and void' (Art. II). This encompasses traditional considerations which relate to the validity of any contract—challenges which may undermine the genuineness of the (apparent) consent to the agreement, such as those of mistake, misrepresentation, fraudulent inducement, lack of capacity, duress, or undue influence. An arbitration agreement may also be considered to be contrary to public policy—generally such considerations would fall under the heading of subject matter limitations on jurisdiction discussed in section 3.4,[46] but this is not necessarily

[41] Art. II(1) and (2). [42] See e.g. UNCITRAL Model Law 2006, Art. 7.

[43] Compare Options I and II of Art. 7, UNCITRAL Model Law 2006. One example is the French Code of Civil Procedure, Art. 1507 ('An arbitration agreement shall not be subject to any requirements as to its form'), but contrast Art. 1443 for domestic arbitration ('In order to be valid, an arbitration agreement shall be in writing'). See further Born (n. 1), 706–7.

[44] Although the text is unclear, the better view is that the writing requirements in Art. II apply equally to enforcement proceedings under Art. III, IV, and V—see e.g. Born (n. 1), 664–6. But note the UNCITRAL 'recommended interpretation' of Art. II and VII, http://www.uncitral.org/uncitral/en/uncitral_texts/arbitration/2006recommendation.html, which suggests that the scope of the New York Convention may be extended by more favourable national laws.

[45] It is, however, unclear whether the writing requirements under the FAA are the same as those under the New York Convention: see e.g. S. I. Strong, 'What Constitutes an "Agreement in Writing" in International Commercial Arbitration? Conflicts Between the New York Convention and the Federal Arbitration Act', 48 Stanford Journal of International Law 47 (2012). See further e.g. *Sphere Drake Ins v Marine Towing*, 16 F.3d 666 (5th Cir. 1994); *Kahn Lucas Lancaster, Inc. v Lark International Ltd*, 186 F.3d 210 (2nd Cir. 1999).

[46] Like those considerations, public policy challenges to the validity of an arbitration agreement are not concerned with the genuineness of the consent of the parties to arbitration, and so raise distinct issues.

the case. (For example, a racially discriminatory arbitration agreement is likely to be viewed as contrary to public policy even if otherwise valid.) As noted above, pursuant to the doctrine of separability we are only concerned here with challenges which affect the validity of the arbitration agreement, not with those which might invalidate the substantive contract but leave the arbitration agreement itself untouched. The latter would not affect the jurisdiction of the arbitral tribunal, nor would (for similar reasons) a finding that the main contract has been repudiated, frustrated, or otherwise ceased to operate.

For issues of both formal and substantive validity, the most difficult question may be the choice of law question—what legal standards are to be applied to resolve these issues—discussed further in section 3.6.[47] These standards typically depend at least in part on the law governing the arbitration agreement. Another key consequence of the doctrine of separability is that the arbitration agreement may be governed by a different applicable law than that which governs the substantive terms of the contract in which it is found.

3.3.3 Is the arbitration agreement binding on the parties?

A third question which may arise concerning the arbitration agreement is whether it is binding on the relevant parties.[48] The issue may arise particularly in one of three main ways. First, the arbitration agreement may be entered into by a party acting as an agent for another party. Thus, the signatory may bind an (apparent) third party. This is perhaps most common in the context of corporate groups, where a subsidiary may be in reality acting on behalf of a parent company. The principle has sometimes (more controversially)[49] been extended by viewing an arbitration agreement as being entered into on behalf of a corporate group as a whole where there is a (perceived) common intention that any entity in the group is to be bound by (and also entitled to invoke) the arbitration agreement.[50] The issue is not, however, confined to the context of a corporate

[47] See further generally Julian D M Lew, 'The Law Applicable to the Form and Substance of the Arbitration Clause', in Albert Jan van den Berg (ed.), *Improving the Efficiency of Arbitration Agreements and Awards: 40 Years of Application of the New York Convention* (Kluwer Law International, 1999).

[48] See further e.g. Born (n. 1), ch. 10; Blackaby et al. (n. 1), para 2.42; Stavros Brekoulakis, *Third Parties in International Commercial Arbitration* (Oxford University Press, 2011); William Park, 'Non-Signatories and International Arbitration', in Lawrence Newman and Richard Hill (eds), *Leading Arbitrators' Guide to International Arbitration*, 3rd edn (Juris Publishing, 2014); Bernard Hanotiau, 'Non-Signatories in International Arbitration: Lessons from Thirty Years of Case Law', in Albert Jan van den Berg (ed.), *International Arbitration 2006: Back to Basics?* (Kluwer Law International, 2007), 341.

[49] See e.g. *Peterson Farms Inc v C&M Farming Ltd*, [2004] 1 Lloyd's Rep 603.

[50] See e.g. *Dow Chemical* arbitration, ICC Case No. 4131, 9 Yearbook of Commercial Arbitration 131 (1984); Stephan Wilske, Laurence Shore, and Jan-Michael Ahrens, 'The "Group of Companies Doctrine": Where Is It Heading?', 17 American Review of International Arbitration 73 (2006).

group, and may arise in any context in which an agency relationship (or comparable common intention) might be considered to exist or arise.[51]

Second, there are a range of circumstances in which one party may become entitled to assert another party's contractual rights, and may become bound by its contractual obligations. Perhaps most obviously, the rights and obligations of a party under an arbitration agreement may be assigned or novated to a third party.[52] Even without novation, an assignment of rights to a third party may be conditional on their acceptance of the obligations under the contract, including a consent to arbitration—in effect, a new contract containing an arbitration agreement may arise through the assignee's acceptance of the assignment. Another context in which a party may become entitled to assert the contractual rights of another party is subrogation, such as by an insurer of the rights of an insured party. In these cases, a difficult issue may arise as to whether the party asserting its right of subrogation is bound by an arbitration agreement in an underlying contract. This was a key issue in the well-known *West Tankers* litigation saga.[53]

The third scenario in which an arbitration agreement may extend beyond the immediate parties to the contract containing it is where the contract is for the benefit of a third party. Many legal systems allow third parties to enforce contracts entered into in their favour, but the enforcement of such benefits may be made subject to procedural conditions such as an arbitration agreement.[54] In effect, a third party who has taken the benefit of contractual rights may be required to take (or estopped from denying) the burden of the arbitration agreement.[55]

Once again, the choice of law issues, discussed in section 3.6, may be critical to the resolution of each of these questions, because their treatment is likely to be significantly variable in different national legal orders.

3.3.4 What is the scope of the arbitration agreement?

The existence of a valid arbitration agreement binding on the parties does not necessarily imply that the dispute at hand is covered by that agreement—an arbitration clause is generally understood to apply only to a 'defined legal relationship'.[56] Issues may thus arise determining the scope of application of the arbitration agreement, particularly

[51] See e.g. *Dallah Real Estate and Tourism Holding Company v Gov't of Pakistan*, [2010] UKSC 46 (considering whether the government of Pakistan was party to an arbitration agreement entered into by a trust established as a separate legal entity under the law of Pakistan, but finding that this argument did not succeed on the facts); *Egiazaryan v OJSC OEK Finance*, [2015] EWHC 3532 (Comm).

[52] Issues may also arise concerning whether an arbitration agreement survives a merger: see e.g. *John Wiley & Sons, Inc. v Livingston*, 376 U.S. 543 (1964).

[53] See e.g. *Allianz SpA v West Tankers Inc*, [2009] EUECJ C-185/07; *West Tankers Inc v Ras Riunione Adriatica di Sicurta SpA*, [2005] EWHC 454 (Comm).

[54] See e.g. the Contracts (Rights of Third Parties) Act 1999 (UK), s. 8; *Fortress Value Recovery Fund I LLC v Blue Skye Special Opportunities Fund LP (A Firm)*, [2013] EWCA Civ 367.

[55] See e.g. *American Bureau of Shipping v Tencara Shipyard*, 170 F 3d 349 (2nd Cir. 1999).

[56] UNCITRAL Model Law, Art. 7(1).

as to whether it would encompass challenges to the validity rather than just the performance of a contract, and where non-contractual claims arise which may be directly or indirectly related to the performance of the contract.[57] An arbitral tribunal does not have 'general jurisdiction', only the specific jurisdiction derived from the consent of the parties. This question is therefore one of contractual interpretation—determining what range of disputes the parties intended to encompass within their arbitration agreement.

Some courts have traditionally approached this issue as an ordinary question of contractual interpretation, leading to fine distinctions being drawn based on the wording of the arbitration agreement. For example, an arbitration agreement purporting to cover disputes 'arising under' the contract has been interpreted more narrowly than one purporting to cover disputes 'relating to' the contract.[58] In England, this traditional approach was famously rejected by the House of Lords in *Fiona Trust v Privalov*. The Court considered that a 'fresh start' should be made on the issue, and held that:

> the construction of an arbitration clause should start from the assumption that the parties, as rational businessmen, are likely to have intended any dispute arising out of the relationship into which they have entered or purported to enter to be decided by the same tribunal. The clause should be construed in accordance with this presumption unless the language makes it clear that certain questions were intended to be excluded from the arbitrator's jurisdiction.[59]

The Lords noted that this change brought the English courts more in line with the approach in the United States,[60] Germany,[61] and Australia.[62] The new rule is undoubtedly more supportive of arbitration, and means that an arbitral tribunal is to be presumed to have jurisdiction over non-contractual claims relating to the contract containing the arbitration agreement, as well as claims concerning the validity of that contract. This is broadly unobjectionable—perhaps the only query which may be raised is whether it is genuinely reflective of the presumptions of 'rational businessmen' (the court was not relying on empirical evidence for this point), and thus a subjective rule of interpretation based on the presumed intention of the actual parties, or whether it is rather an objective rule adopted as a matter of policy in support of arbitration.[63]

[57] See generally Blackaby et al. (n. 1), para 2.63–2.70; Born (n. 1), ch. 9.

[58] See e.g. *Overseas Union Insurance Ltd v AA Mutual International Insurance Co Ltd*, [1988] 2 Lloyd's Rep 63, 67.

[59] *Fiona Trust v Privalov* (reported as *Premium Nafta Products Ltd v Fili Shipping Company Ltd*), [2007] UKHL 40, [13], per Lord Hoffmann.

[60] *AT&T Technologies Inc v Communications Workers of America*, 475 U.S. 643, 650 (1986); *Threlkeld & Co Inc. v Metallgesellschaft Ltd (London)*, 923 F 2d 245 (2nd Cir. 1991).

[61] Bundesgerichtshof's Decision of 27 February 1970, (1990) 6 Arbitration International 79.

[62] *Comandate Marine Corp v Pan Australia Shipping Pty Ltd*, [2006] FCAFC 192, [165].

[63] There is a whiff of circularity about the decision—it might be thought that well-informed 'businessmen' would expect only that the law, whatever it happened to be, would be applied, and so their 'expectations' would be satisfied by any clearly stated and correctly applied rule of law. If the practice of the courts were to distinguish between the meaning of differently worded arbitration agreements, the adoption of

In the *Fiona Trust* case, the contract was governed by English law and the seat of arbitration was in London, and there was no doubt that the arbitration agreement was itself governed by English law. Although the Court did not focus on the question of applicable law, the ruling of the House of Lords should therefore probably be understood to be a determination only regarding the interpretation of arbitration agreements governed by English law. The interpretation of an arbitration agreement remains a question of contractual interpretation to be determined through application of the law governing the arbitration agreement; *Fiona Trust* simply adds a new rule of contractual interpretation to the canon of interpretative principles in English commercial law. The question of the scope of an arbitration agreement will thus be highly dependent on the applicable law question, discussed further in section 3.6.

3.3.5 Is the arbitration agreement exclusive or non-exclusive?

The interpretation of an arbitration agreement encompasses a further question—whether it is intended that the agreement be exclusive (precluding recourse to courts for any matter falling within the scope of the agreement) or non-exclusive (giving one or both parties the option of initiating arbitration, but not precluding litigation). This issue is unlikely to trouble an arbitral tribunal, because once a tribunal has been established it is generally of no concern to the tribunal whether other means of dispute resolution could have been pursued in the alternative. It is, however, an issue which could readily arise where, despite the existence of an arbitration clause, proceedings are commenced in a court which would ordinarily have jurisdiction over the claim before an arbitration has been initiated—the court should ordinarily stay its proceedings if and only if the clause is exclusive. It might be expected that such clauses would be rare, and in case of ambiguity courts are perhaps unlikely to find that an arbitration clause is non-exclusive because such a provision goes against the legal certainty which commercial parties are generally presumed to desire, although a countervailing presumption may arise that 'clauses depriving a party of the right to litigate should be expected to be clearly worded'.[64] Parties who desire greater flexibility in the available modes of dispute resolution could well intentionally adopt a clause under which the parties 'may', at their option, submit disputes either to arbitration or court proceedings.

Although it is evident that parties will generally not contemplate proceedings arising in both forms in parallel (as part of the *Fiona Trust* principle discussed above),[65]

particular wording by sophisticated parties would arguably indicate their intention better than any broader presumption: see e.g. *Mediterranean Enterprises v Ssangyong Corp.*, 708 F.2d 1458, 1464–65 (9th Cir. 1983).

[64] *Anzen Limited and others (Appellants) v Hermes One Limited (Respondent) (British Virgin Islands)*, [2016] UKPC 1, [13].

[65] See further e.g. *Deutsche Bank Ag v Tongkah Harbour Public Company Ltd*, [2011] EWHC 2251 (Comm).

complex questions may arise regarding the hierarchical relationship between these dispute resolution options. They may operate as genuine alternatives under which the party who initiates proceedings can choose the forum,[66] or alternatively, it might be concluded that the non-exclusive arbitration clause is hierarchically superior, such that the respondent party in court proceedings can force them to be stayed by initiating and/or electing arbitration.[67] If a non-exclusive arbitration agreement is to be adopted, parties would be well advised to deal with these issues expressly.

3.3.6 Is the arbitration agreement enforceable?

The sixth and final question which may be raised concerning the arbitration agreement concerns its enforceability. An arbitration agreement may become unenforceable for a variety of reasons. Some reasons pertain to the party seeking to rely on the arbitration agreement. That party may have waived their rights under the agreement (such as by entering an appearance on the merits in judicial proceedings), or may be estopped by their words or conduct from relying on the arbitration agreement.[68] They may have entered into a settlement agreement, or some other form of dispute resolution clause which renders the arbitration agreement inapplicable, or they may have already arbitrated or litigated their dispute.

The New York Convention provides that an arbitration agreement may be refused enforcement where it is 'inoperative or incapable of being performed' (Art. II). There is some debate concerning what degree of difficulty in performing the arbitration agreement would justify a refusal to enforce it. The mere fact that a party would find it too expensive to arbitrate would not be sufficient.[69] Defects in the arbitration agreement which are capable of being corrected by the courts of the seat of arbitration, by the arbitral institution nominated in the agreement, or by the arbitrators themselves should not be considered to render the arbitration agreement inoperative or incapable of being performed. Thus, if the arbitrator named in an arbitration agreement refuses to act, and the courts of the seat have the power to order a substitute, that power should be exercised. Similarly, a failure to specify the seat of arbitration would not ordinarily prevent the arbitrators from choosing such a seat.

[66] It is an interesting question whether, in such circumstances, a discretionary stay such as that under the *forum non-conveniens* test in the English courts could be used to stay proceedings in favour of an arbitral tribunal (as an available and clearly more appropriate forum to resolve the dispute), pursuant to an optional arbitration agreement.

[67] *Anzen Limited and others (Appellants) v Hermes One Limited (Respondent) (British Virgin Islands)*, [2016] UKPC 1; *Union Marine v Government of Comoros*, [2013] EWHC 5854 (Comm); *NB Three Shipping Ltd v Harebell Shipping Ltd*, [2004] EWHC (Comm) 2001.

[68] See e.g. *Downing v Al Tameer Establishment*, [2002] EWCA Civ 721.

[69] *Paczy v Haendler and Natermann GmbH*, [1981] 1 Lloyd's Rep. 302 (CA).

3.4 Subject Matter Limitations: Arbitrability

The existence of a valid and effective arbitration agreement is not the only consideration in determining whether an arbitral tribunal has jurisdiction. A further issue is whether, in the words of the New York Convention, the dispute concerns 'a subject matter capable of settlement by arbitration'.[70] This is often referred to as the question of 'arbitrability'. The term 'arbitrability' is also sometimes used (particularly in the United States) to refer to the broader question of whether a dispute can be arbitrated, which includes considerations of whether there is a valid and effective arbitration agreement, as well as sometimes issues of admissibility.[71] The narrow sense of arbitrability, adopted here, may then be referred to as 'subject matter arbitrability', or 'objective arbitrability', to be distinguished from questions which essentially concern the validity and effectiveness of the arbitration agreement, including the capacity of a party to enter into such an agreement (sometimes referred to as 'subjective arbitrability').[72] Considerations of subject matter arbitrability are most closely analogous not to questions of jurisdiction in general but to the narrow question of 'justiciability'. In national courts this refers to the issue of whether the dispute is a proper question for a court to deal with, or whether it is, for example, a question that should be left to a foreign court, to politics, or even to the institutions and practices of international law and international relations.[73] The issue here similarly concerns the question of whether there are some disputes with characteristics which render them unsuitable for settlement through arbitration.

Different legal systems take a variety of different approaches to the question of the strengths and weaknesses of arbitration, and thus the appropriate limitations on arbitrability.[74] For this reason, the choice of law question discussed below—*which* legal standards are applied to determine the limits of subject matter arbitrability—can be critical in this context. In general terms, however, it may be stated that disputes are usually considered non-arbitrable for one of two reasons. First, because they involve weaker parties, and it may be considered that, compared with national courts, arbitration might not provide as much procedural protection to such parties, and arbitrators may be less inclined to apply national mandatory rules which protect weaker parties (such as

[70] Art. II(1); see similarly Art. V(2)(a). [71] See e.g. Bermann (n. 33), 10.

[72] For further analysis, see e.g. *Howsam v Dean Witter Reynolds, Inc.*, 537 U.S. 79 (2002); Laurence Shore, 'The United States' Perspective on "Arbitrability"', in Loukas Mistelis and Stavros Brekoulakis (eds), *Arbitrability: International and Comparative Perspectives* (Kluwer Law International, 2009); Louis Fortier, 'Arbitrability of Disputes', in Aksen et al. (n. 20), 269–70.

[73] See generally e.g. Campbell McLachlan, *Foreign Relations Law* (Cambridge University Press, 2014), ch. 6.

[74] See further generally Born (n. 1), ch. 6; Blackaby et al. (n. 1), para 2.124; Ilias Bantekas, 'The Foundations of Arbitrability in International Commercial Arbitration', 27 Australian Year Book of International Law 193 (2008); Mistelis and Brekoulakis (n. 72).

statutes which may invalidate unfair contractual terms). For this reason, some legal systems view consumer, employment, or insurance disputes as non-arbitrable.[75] Other legal systems, however, positively encourage arbitration of at least some such disputes because it is believed that arbitration is more accessible and thus improves access to justice for weaker parties, or otherwise resolves disputes more efficiently (including potentially because of the specialist expertise of arbitrators).[76]

The second reason why disputes may be considered non-arbitrable is because the issues involve significant public interest considerations, or have significant impacts on third parties (who may not be permitted to intervene in arbitral proceedings without the consent of the arbitrating parties, but could potentially do so in court). Criminal and other public law proceedings are, in general, considered non-arbitrable for this reason, as are family law disputes.[77] Art. 2060 of the French Civil Code provides, for example, that '[o]ne may not enter into arbitration agreements in matters of status and capacity of the persons, in those relating to divorce and judicial separation, or on controversies concerning public bodies and institutions and more generally in all matters in which public policy is concerned.' Some disputes which fall within the realm of private law are nevertheless often considered to engage sufficient public interests to be considered non-arbitrable, such as competition law disputes (even those brought through private actions) or intellectual property disputes.[78]

However, the trend is probably toward viewing more disputes as arbitrable.[79] In the US, for example, competition law proceedings were historically viewed as non-arbitrable,[80] but the modern position is that many such disputes can be arbitrated, in part because the courts are likely to have an opportunity to take a 'second look' at any public policy issues in the context of proceedings to set aside or enforce the award.[81] A similar development has taken place in the European Union,[82] including the United

[75] See e.g. Alexandra Wilcke and Isabelle Wildhaber, 'Arbitrating Labor Disputes in Switzerland', 27 Journal of International Arbitration 631 (2010).

[76] See e.g. Thomas Carbonneau, 'Liberal Rules of Arbitrability and the Autonomy of Labor Arbitration in the United States', in Mistelis and Brekoulakis (n. 72), 144; *Circuit City Stores, Inc. v Adams*, 532 U.S. 105 (2001); *AT&T Technologies, Inc. v CWA*, 475 U.S. 643, 650 (1986) (the 'presumption of arbitrability for labor disputes recognizes the greater institutional competence of arbitrators in interpreting collective bargaining agreements'—although note that in this case the court did not distinguish clearly between subjective and objective 'arbitrability'); *Textile Workers v Lincoln Mills*, 353 U.S. 448 (1957).

[77] See e.g. Dragor Hiber and Vladimir Pavić, 'Arbitration and Crime', 25 Journal of International Arbitration 461 (2008).

[78] See generally e.g. William Grantham, 'The Arbitrability of International Intellectual Property Disputes', 14 Berkeley Journal of International Law 173 (1996).

[79] See generally e.g. Bantekas (n. 74).

[80] See e.g. *American Safety Corp v J.P. Maguire & Co.*, 391 F.2d 821 (2nd Cir. 1968).

[81] *Mitsubishi Motors Co v Solar Chrysler-Plymouth*, 473 U.S. 614 (1985); see further e.g. Laurence Smith, 'Determining the Arbitrability of International Antitrust Disputes', 8 Journal of Comparative Business and Capital Market Law 197 (1986); James Bridgeman, 'The Arbitrability of Competition Law Disputes', 19 European Business Law Review 147 (2008).

[82] In *Eco Swiss China Ltd v Benetton International NV*, [1999] ECR I-3055, however, the ECJ held that national courts must set aside an arbitral award as contrary to public policy if it is contrary to certain provisions of EU competition law. Georgios Zekos, 'Antitrust/Competition Arbitration in EU versus

Kingdom,[83] while the position remains contentious in other jurisdictions such as Australia.[84] Intellectual property disputes are also similarly tending to be increasingly viewed as capable of settlement through arbitration.[85] Strictly speaking, the issue of arbitrability should be limited to the question of what types of disputes are considered *legally* suitable for settlement through arbitration, not the question of what types of disputes the *parties* have agreed as suitable for settlement through arbitration (see section 3.3.4), although these two distinct considerations are not always distinguished clearly in practice.[86]

3.5 Who Decides on the Jurisdiction of an Arbitral Tribunal?

This chapter has thus far identified the major issues which can arise concerning the jurisdiction of an arbitral tribunal. There remain two general questions for consideration. This section considers the first, the question of 'who decides' on the jurisdiction of the tribunal, while the following section considers the second, the question of what law or laws govern the jurisdiction of the tribunal.

The question of who should decide on the jurisdiction of an arbitral tribunal is one which raises perennial difficulties.[87] A decision about the jurisdiction of an arbitral tribunal may be made by three different 'actors', each of which is considered in turn below: the parties, an arbitral tribunal, and national courts. As noted above, one key principle which must be observed is that, as a matter of logic, it is unsatisfactory for the arbitral tribunal itself to have the *final* word on its own jurisdiction (as opposed to issues of admissibility), because that goes to the very power of the tribunal. Depending on the

U.S. Law', 25 Journal of International Arbitration 1 (2008); Julian D M Lew, 'Competition Laws: Limits to Arbitrators' Authority', in Mistelis and Brekoulakis (n. 72), 252; Sotiris Dempegiotis, 'EC Competition Law and International Arbitration in the Light of EC Regulation 1/2003', 25 Journal of International Arbitration 365 (2008); Bridgeman (n. 81).

[83] See e.g. *ET Plus SA v Welter*, [2005] EWHC 2115 (Comm).

[84] Colette Downie, 'Will Australia Trust Arbitrators with Antitrust? Examining the Challenges in International Antitrust Arbitrations to Develop a Competition Arbitration Model for Australia', 30 Journal of International Arbitration 221 (2013).

[85] See e.g. *Desputeaux v Éditions Chouette (1987) inc.*, [2003] 1 S.C.R. 178 (in which the Canadian Supreme Court permitted arbitration of a copyright dispute, and more generally favoured a narrow interpretation of arbitrability limitations).

[86] See e.g. *Clough Engineering Limited v Oil & Natural Gas Corporation Ltd*, [2007] FCA 881, [39] and [41]; *ET Plus SA v Welter*, [2005] EWHC 2115 (Comm), [51].

[87] See e.g. Steven Reisberg, 'The Rules Governing Who Decides Jurisdictional Issues: First Options v Kaplan Revisited', 20 American Review of International Arbitration 159 (2009); John Barcelo III, 'International Commercial Arbitration—Who Decides the Arbitrators' Jurisdiction? Separability and Competence-Competence in Transnational Perspective', 36 Vanderbilt Journal of Transnational Law 1115 (2003); William Park, 'Determining Arbitral Jurisdiction: Allocation of Tasks Between Courts and Arbitrators', 9 Arbitration and Dispute Resolution Law Journal 19 (2000).

circumstance, the jurisdiction of the tribunal will thus need to be confirmed either by the parties or by national courts.

3.5.1 Parties

In some situations, the parties will not challenge the validity or effectiveness of their arbitration agreement, but will simply accept that it applies, and participate in the arbitration. This may be the case even if there are reasons why the arbitration agreement may be invalid or ineffective. Both parties may decide that it would nevertheless be convenient to proceed with arbitration—the reasons which led them to agree (or attempt to agree) to arbitration in their contract may still apply when a dispute arises. An arbitral tribunal may formally ask the parties to confirm that they do not contest the jurisdiction of the tribunal, particularly if the arbitrators have some doubt about the validity or effectiveness of the arbitration agreement, and such confirmation can act as a conferral of jurisdiction to the extent that any such concerns actually existed. Even without such formal confirmation, the participation by the parties in the merits of the arbitration without challenging the jurisdiction of the tribunal is likely to constitute submission, which will be viewed itself as providing a foundation for the tribunal's jurisdiction (based on consent, waiver, or estoppel). Leaving aside for the moment questions of arbitrability, if the parties have accepted the jurisdiction of the tribunal in one or more of these ways, the validity of the arbitration agreement is very unlikely to be rejected by the tribunal or by any national court, and so effectively the decision of the parties to accept the validity of the arbitration agreement is determinative.[88]

The more difficult issue concerns what effect a decision by the parties should have on issues which do not concern the validity or effectiveness of their consent, such as those of subject matter arbitrability. If the parties agree to arbitrate a matter which is, under at least one potentially applicable legal order, considered not capable of settlement through arbitration, and neither party objects to the arbitral proceedings, it is not entirely clear what the arbitral tribunal should do. It is clear that the agreement of the parties to arbitrate would not be enforced if the issue were litigated in a court which would apply the law under which the subject matter is non-arbitrable—the arbitration agreement and any arbitral award would simply be invalidated. There is, therefore, an argument that at least in some circumstances an arbitral tribunal should take into account questions of subject matter arbitrability in deciding whether to exercise their jurisdiction, even if these have not been raised by the parties, as part of their duty to render an enforceable award.[89] This is, however, contentious territory—as long as there would be one national court that would view the subject matter of the dispute as arbitrable, it is difficult to say

[88] See e.g. Arbitration Act 1996 (UK), s. 73.

[89] See generally e.g. Martin Platte, 'An Arbitrator's Duty to Render Enforceable Awards', 20 Journal of International Arbitration 307 (2003); Günther Horvath, 'The Duty of the Tribunal to Render an Enforceable Award', 18 Journal of International Arbitration 135 (2001); Blackaby et al. (n. 1), para. 11.11.

that the award would be futile. As a practical matter, if the law governing arbitrability depends on the seat (an issue discussed further below), it would also be open to the parties to agree that an alternative seat be adopted, and this might even be suggested by the tribunal. Indeed, it is possible that the parties might agree to comply voluntarily with the arbitral award (without the need for judicial proceedings), in which case no national court may ever review the determination, and no issues of arbitrability may ever be considered by anyone other than the parties themselves. If, however, the arbitral award is not complied with voluntarily, the decision of the parties that a certain dispute arising between them should be arbitrated clearly cannot itself be determinative when it comes to questions of arbitrability.

In many cases, of course, the party which does not initiate the arbitration *will* contest the proceedings—disputing the validity or effectiveness of the arbitration agreement or the arbitrability of the dispute, or simply refusing to participate in the proceedings. (Non-participation will not, of course, invalidate consent to the arbitration, but it may avoid the risk of submitting to the authority of the tribunal through conduct.) In such circumstances, a decision on the jurisdiction of the tribunal will also therefore need to be made by the arbitral tribunal and potentially by one or more national courts.

3.5.2 Arbitral tribunal

One of the foundational principles of international arbitration is 'competence-competence'.[90] This principle has two fundamentally distinct components. The first component, uniformly adopted in any jurisdiction which accepts arbitration, is the rule of 'positive competence-competence', which simply provides that an arbitral tribunal has the power to rule on its own jurisdiction.[91] In some legal systems (including the United Kingdom[92]) this rule may, however, be departed from by agreement of the parties. The second component is an additional rule of 'negative competence-competence'.[93] The negative aspect of competence-competence does not provide that *only* the arbitral

[90] See generally e.g. Born (n. 1), ch. 7; Blackaby et al. (n. 1), para. 5.105; Collins and Harris (n. 11), para. 16–013; William Park, 'The Arbitrator's Jurisdiction to Determine Jurisdiction', in van den Berg (n. 48), 55; *Ust-Kamenogorsk Hydropower Plant JSC v AES Ust-Kamenogorsk Hydropower Plant LLP*, [2013] UKSC 35; *Dallah Real Estate and Tourism Holding Company v Gov't of Pakistan*, [2010] UKSC 46, [84] ('the principle that a tribunal in an international commercial arbitration has the power to consider its own jurisdiction is no doubt a general principle of law'); UNCITRAL Model Law, Art. 16; Arbitration Act 1996 (UK), s. 30.

[91] See e.g. Arbitration Act 1996 (UK), s. 30.

[92] Arbitration Act 1996 (UK), s. 30(1) ('Unless otherwise agreed by the parties, the arbitral tribunal may rule on its own substantive jurisdiction…').

[93] See generally e.g. Emmanuel Gaillard and Yas Banifatemi, 'Negative Effect of Competence-Competence: The Rule of Priority in Favour of the Arbitrators', in Emmanuel Gaillard and Domenico Di Pietro (eds), *Enforcement of Arbitration Agreements and International Arbitral Awards: The New York Convention in Practice* (Cameron May, 2008).

tribunal has the power to rule on its own jurisdiction[94]—if the tribunal does not have jurisdiction, then no decision made by the tribunal as to its own jurisdiction can be effective to determine that it does. Instead, the effect of the adoption of negative competence-competence is that courts are required (at least in some circumstances) to give the tribunal the *first* opportunity to determine its own jurisdiction. Negative competence-competence is discussed in the next part of this chapter, dealing with the role of the courts in determining the jurisdiction of an arbitral tribunal.

It is generally considered good practice for an arbitral tribunal to rule on its own jurisdiction as a preliminary matter, for the sake of the efficient resolution of the dispute between the parties, although where jurisdictional and merits issues are intertwined this may not be practicable.[95] It is also considered good practice (if possible) for the tribunal's decision on jurisdiction to itself be issued as a preliminary 'award'[96] so that it gains the benefit of the rules on recognition and enforcement under the New York Convention.[97] In unusual cases, arbitral proceedings may be commenced in parallel, and a dispute may arise over which arbitral tribunal has jurisdiction. Since no hierarchy exists between the decisions of the two tribunals, the better view is that the tribunal first seised should generally be given the first opportunity to determine its own jurisdiction, as a matter of 'arbitral comity'.[98] Such considerations would, however, need to be weighed against questions of procedural efficiency and the obligation to enforce the agreement between the parties, and it would potentially be open to a second seised tribunal which views the jurisdiction of the first tribunal as manifestly invalid to adopt a different approach.

3.5.3 Courts

The jurisdiction of an arbitral tribunal may, finally, be a matter determined by a national court. As noted above, the primary principle here is that of separability—the court

[94] This proposition, sometimes described as 'definite' or 'real' competence-competence, was at one time adopted under German law, but has apparently been abandoned: see Born (n. 1), para 7.01. It is sometimes argued that this doctrine, giving the final word on jurisdiction to an arbitral tribunal, forms part of other legal systems, at least if the parties have agreed to it. (See e.g. William Park, 'Determining an Arbitrator's Jurisdiction: Timing and Finality in American Law', 8 Nevada Law Journal 135 (2007).) This proposition suffers, however, from a logical limitation—the agreement that the validity of the arbitration agreement is unreviewable by a court must *itself* be subject to review by a court.

[95] See further John Gotanda, 'An Efficient Method for Determining Jurisdiction in International Arbitrations', 40 Columbia Journal of Transnational Law 11 (2001).

[96] There are different views on whether such a preliminary decision can formally constitute an arbitral award: see further e.g. Lawrence Boo, 'Ruling on Arbitral Jurisdiction: Is that an Award?', 3 Asian International Arbitration Journal 125 (2007).

[97] See e.g. Chartered Institute of Arbitrators (n. 21), 18.

[98] Ibid. See further e.g. Filip De Ly and Audley Sheppard, 'ILA Final Report on *Lis Pendens* and Arbitration', 25 Arbitration International 3 (2009).

(and indeed an arbitral tribunal) should determine the validity and effectiveness of the arbitration agreement as a separate contract.[99] If a challenge to the validity of the contract does not affect the validity of the arbitration agreement, the court should leave consideration of merits questions to the tribunal. As also discussed above, issues which concern the admissibility of the claim, rather than the jurisdiction of the arbitral tribunal, should similarly be left for the tribunal. By contrast, if a challenge goes specifically and directly to the arbitration agreement itself, it is clear that a court may consider the question, although as discussed below courts may nevertheless decide that the arbitral tribunal should be given the first opportunity to address the issues. A further difficult issue is what a court should do if an issue is presented which affects the validity of the contract as a whole, including the arbitration agreement, but is not specifically directed at the arbitration agreement. Practice is somewhat variable, but the better view is that the court should also review the validity question in those circumstances—a challenge to the validity of the arbitration agreement is no less critical because it also affects substantive contractual terms.[100]

The courts of the seat of the arbitration may, in the exercise of their supervisory authority, hear challenges to the jurisdiction of an arbitral tribunal, or be required to consider such issues if asked to appoint an arbitrator or even to make an order restraining the arbitration from being commenced or continued. These issues may, however, equally fall to be decided by *any* court in which substantive proceedings are commenced, where the arbitration agreement may be raised as a jurisdictional 'defence', or by any court in which recognition and enforcement of an arbitral award is pursued, where the invalidity or ineffectiveness of the arbitration agreement may be raised as a defence to enforcement. It is a much debated question whether decisions on arbitral jurisdiction made by the courts of the seat of arbitration should be given greater authority than those of other courts. In practice, arbitrators may decide to continue with an arbitration notwithstanding the finding of a non-seat national court that the tribunal lacks jurisdiction, if the arbitrators take the view that the courts of the seat or the courts of the likely place of enforcement of the arbitral award would disagree. It would be much less likely that arbitrators would continue with an arbitration despite an order from the courts of the seat not to do so. Courts may indeed compel arbitrators not to do so,[101] although the effectiveness of such compulsion is likely to depend on whether the

[99] See e.g. Born (n. 1), ch. 3; Blackaby et al. (n. 1), para 5.100; Arbitration Act 1996 (UK), s. 7; *Fiona Trust v Privalov* (reported as *Premium Nafta Products Ltd v Fili Shipping Company Ltd*), [2007] UKHL 40; *Prima Paint Corp v Flood & Conklin Mfg. Co.*, 388 U.S. 395, 403 (1967); *Buckeye Check Cashing, Inc v Cardegna*, 546 U.S. 440, 445 (2006); French Code of Civil Procedure, Art. 1447; Philippe Leboulanger, 'The Arbitration Agreement: Still Autonomous?' in van den Berg (n. 48), 3; Alan Rau, 'Everything You Really Need to Know About "Separability" in Seventeen Simple Propositions', 14 American Review of International Arbitration 121 (2003).

[100] But see further discussion in Leboulanger (n. 99), 22.

[101] This jurisdiction is now well established in the English courts—see e.g. *Elektrim SA v Vivendi Universal SA (No 2)*, [2007] EWHC 571 (Comm); *Albon v Naza Motor Trading Sdn Bhd*, [2007] EWCA Civ 1124; *Excalibur Ventures LLC v Texas Keystone Inc*, [2011] EWHC 1624 (Comm); *AmTrust Europe Ltd v Trust Risk Group SpA*, [2015] EWHC 1927 (Comm). In *Weissfisch v Julius*, [2006] EWCA Civ 218, the

arbitrators are physically present in the territory because of the territorial limitations on national enforcement jurisdiction—as noted, the venue of an arbitration may (unusually) be distinct from its legal 'seat'. A similar issue may arise after the award has been rendered—an arbitral award set aside by the courts of the seat of arbitration may be viewed by some other national courts as thereby nullified (although the point is highly debated), but the courts of the seat of arbitration are unlikely to view themselves as bound by an equivalent determination by another court.[102]

Another key issue is whether a court should allow full hearing of challenges to the jurisdiction of the arbitral tribunal, or allow the tribunal to determine the issue first, under the doctrine of 'negative competence-competence' (as noted above). Negative competence-competence may be adopted as a rule of national procedural law—under French law it is even a non-derogable procedural law.[103] Alternatively, national law may leave it open to the parties whether such an approach is adopted, by enabling the parties to make use of what is commonly known as a '*Scott v Avery* clause'.[104] Under such clauses, each party agrees not to commence proceedings before a court until the arbitral tribunal has rendered its award (which will of course be after also determining its own jurisdiction). Completion of the arbitral process is thereby made a condition precedent to the jurisdiction of the courts.[105] The effect of such clauses is thus equivalent to the adoption of a strong doctrine of negative competence-competence—the arbitral tribunal is given authority to make the *first* decision regarding its jurisdiction, and to proceed to render an award on the basis of that decision. Careful drafting is necessary if such clauses are to be adopted—some *Scott v Avery* clauses may be interpreted as also precluding application to the court for ancillary relief in support of the arbitration (such as an asset-freezing order), which would risk weakening rather than supporting arbitration.[106]

Negative competence-competence reduces the risk that court proceedings may be used to frustrate the efficient conduct of an arbitration. It also, however, raises the risk that the costs incurred in arbitral proceedings may ultimately be wasted, if national courts disagree with the tribunal's (positive) determination of its own jurisdiction when it comes to recognizing or enforcing an arbitral award. The threshold for the operation

court held that the conduct of an arbitration with a foreign seat should only be restrained in the most exceptional of cases.

[102] See further e.g. *Yukos Capital SARL v OJSC Rosneft Oil Company*, [2012] EWCA Civ 855; Alex Mills, 'The Principled English Ambivalence to Law and Dispute Resolution Beyond the State', in J. C. Betancourt (ed.), *Liber Amicorum for the Chartered Institute of Arbitrators: Selected Topics in International Arbitration* (Oxford University Press, 2016); Albert Jan van den Berg, 'Should the Setting Aside of the Arbitral Award be Abolished?', 29 ICSID Review 263 (2014); Emmanuel Gaillard, 'The Enforcement of Awards Set Aside in the Country of Origin',14 ICSID Review 16 (1999).

[103] French Code of Civil Procedure, Art. 1448.

[104] From *Scott v Avery*, (1856) 10 ER 1121. See generally e.g. Andrew Tweeddale and Keren Tweeddale, '*Scott v Avery* Clauses: O'er Judges' Fingers, Who Straight Dream on Fees', 77 Arbitration 423 (2011).

[105] In *Scott v Avery* itself, the clause went further, providing that no substantive *cause of action* could arise until the arbitrator had given their decision, to avoid falling foul of the 19th-c. rule which prohibited parties from precluding the jurisdiction of the courts. This is, however, not likely to be necessary under modern law.

[106] See e.g. *B v S*, [2011] EWHC 691 (Comm).

of negative competence-competence—whether a court should refer questions to the arbitral tribunal in all cases, or whether it can refuse to do so cases where the arbitration agreement appears invalid or ineffective—is critical in striking the balance between these competing policy considerations.

Perhaps the strongest version of negative competence-competence is provided for in French law.[107] Even if an arbitral tribunal has not yet been established, the French courts must nevertheless refuse to determine the validity of the arbitration agreement unless it is manifestly void or inapplicable[108]—as noted above, this rule cannot even be derogated from by agreement of the parties. (The courts may, however, award provisional or protective relief in support of the prospective arbitral proceedings.)[109] If an arbitral tribunal has been established, the courts are required to submit any dispute concerning the jurisdiction of the tribunal to the tribunal itself for determination. There is no possibility for the court to refuse to do so even if it views the arbitration agreement as manifestly invalid, although it remains open to the court to consider these questions if proceedings are brought to enforce or set aside an award.

In England, the courts have by contrast traditionally tended to insist on a full hearing of questions concerning the validity of the arbitration agreement when deciding whether to stay proceedings,[110] although recent case law emphasizes that the court has the power to stay its own determination of the validity of the arbitration agreement, and in many cases should do so in favour of giving the arbitral tribunal the first opportunity to review this question.[111] The position in the United States is perhaps less clear, although it has been argued that courts in practice adopt a similarly intermediate approach, distinguishing between 'gateway' issues (which ought to be reviewed by the courts if and when they arise) and 'non-gateway' issues (which should at least initially be left to arbitral tribunals). This essentially means applying negative competence-competence selectively depending on the jurisdictional issue which is raised and, perhaps most critically (by contrast with the French approach), whether the intention of the parties was for the jurisdictional issue to itself be arbitrated.[112] The UNCITRAL Model Law leaves the issue open, as it requires a court to refer the parties to arbitration 'unless it finds that the

[107] French Code of Civil Procedure, Art. 1448, 1455, and 1465. See e.g. Gaillard and Banifatemi (n. 93). See also similarly *Shin-Etsu Chemical Co Ltd v Optifibre Ltd*, (2005) Supp (3) S.C.R. 699 (India); *Pacific Int'l Lines (Pte) Ltd v Tsinlien Metals & Minerals Co.*, [1993] 2 H.K.L.R. 249 (Hong Kong).

[108] See e.g. Cour de cassation, 1e civ, 12 Feb. 2014, 13–18.059; Cour de cassation, 1e civ, 18 May 2011, 10–11.008; Cour de cassation, 1e civ, 12 Nov 2009, 09–10.575; Cour de cassation, civ, Chambre commerciale, 25 Nov 2008, 07–21.888; Cour de Cassation, 1e civ, 11 Jul. 2006, 03–11.768; Cour de Cassation, 1e civ, 7 Jun. 2006, 03–12.034.

[109] French Code of Civil Procedure, Art. 1449.

[110] See e.g. *Law Debenture Trust Corporation Plc v Elektrim Finance B*, [2005] EWHC 1412 (Ch). Under English law, a party that has participated in arbitral proceedings may not refer the question of the validity of the arbitration agreement to the courts without the permission of the other party or the tribunal, although they may do so indirectly by commencing substantive proceedings, requiring the court to consider whether the proceedings should be stayed: see Arbitration Act 1996 (UK), ss. 9, 32, and 72(1).

[111] *Fiona Trust v Privalov*, [2007] EWCA Civ 20, [34] ('it will, in general, be right for the arbitrators to be the first tribunal to consider whether they have jurisdiction to determine the dispute').

[112] See e.g. Bermann (n. 33); *Rent-a-Ctr., W., Inc v Jackson*, 130 S. Ct. 2772 (2010).

agreement is null and void, inoperative or incapable of being performed',[113] but does not specify the threshold for making such a finding.

3.6 What law or laws govern questions of jurisdiction?

The analysis above has highlighted a range of different legal questions which may arise for both arbitral tribunals and courts concerning the jurisdiction of an arbitral tribunal. For each of these questions, a decision needs to be made about which law to apply. It would be impossible for this chapter to deal with these issues comprehensively,[114] so the focus will be on two of the most important and typical issues: the validity and interpretation of the arbitration agreement, and the subject matter arbitrability of the dispute.

3.6.1 The law governing the validity and interpretation of the arbitration agreement

Issues concerning the validity and interpretation of an arbitration agreement are generally a matter for its governing law. Pursuant to the doctrine of separability, as noted above, an arbitration agreement is viewed as separate from any contract as part of which it may have been entered into. This also means that the law governing the arbitration agreement has to be determined independently from the law governing the remainder of the contract.[115] If the parties have directly agreed the law which governs the arbitration agreement—through a specific choice of law clause—then all arbitral tribunals and the vast majority of national courts will recognize that choice.[116] The more difficult question is what law to apply where, as is frequently the case, a contract does not have a specific choice of law clause for the arbitration agreement.

Whenever a court is asked to interpret or determine the validity of an arbitration agreement, it faces a choice of law question and must apply the choice of law rules which

[113] UNCITRAL Model Law, Art. 8(1). In the Model Law drafting process, a requirement that courts stay proceedings unless an arbitration agreement is 'manifestly' null and void was proposed but not adopted: UN Doc A/CN.9/233, [77].

[114] For more detailed treatments, see e.g. Horacio Grigera Naón, 'Choice of Law Problems in International Commercial Arbitration', 289 Recueil des Cours de l'Académie de Droit International 9 (2001); Klaus Berger, 'Re-examining the Arbitration Agreement Applicable Law: Consensus or Confusion?' in van den Berg (n. 48), 301; Gary Born, 'The Law Governing International Arbitration Agreements: An International Perspective', 26 Singapore Academy of Law Journal 814 (2014); Born (n. 1), ch. 4; Blackaby et al. (n. 1), ch. 3.

[115] See e.g. Collins and Harris (n. 11), para 16–011.

[116] See e.g. Cindy Buys, 'The Arbitrators' Duty to Respect the Parties' Choice of Law in Commercial Arbitration', 79 St. John's Law Review 59 (2012).

form part of the law of the forum. Those choice of law rules may derive from or be influenced by regional or international rules.[117] The New York Convention provides that the enforcement of an arbitral award may be refused if the arbitration agreement is invalid 'under the law to which the parties have subjected it or, failing any indication thereon, under the law of the country where the award was made'.[118] No such rule is set out for questions of validity which arise before an award has been rendered, although there would be little sense in adopting a different approach. This rule still, however, leaves national legal systems with a considerable degree of latitude in identifying situations in which the parties are considered to have implicitly subjected their arbitration agreement to a particular system of law—this is an issue which must be resolved by national choice of law rules, but practice on the point is variable.

There are two main candidates for the law which should govern an arbitration agreement before national courts. First, the law which governs the substantive obligations between the parties, which is to say (at least generally) the law governing the contract as part of which the arbitration agreement was entered into. Second, the law of the seat of arbitration (the default rule suggested by the New York Convention). Each of these approaches has something to recommend it—it might be argued that parties are likely to assume, unless they clearly indicate otherwise, that their whole contract is governed by a single system of law;[119] but it might also be argued that parties agreeing to arbitrate in a particular place would expect the law of that place to govern all issues concerning the arbitration (not just procedural matters).[120] The approach recently adopted in the English courts in the *Sulamérica* decision is something of an intermediate position. On the one hand, the court found that there is a rebuttable presumption that if the parties have chosen a law to govern their contract they will have made an implied choice of the same law to govern the arbitration agreement: 'In the absence of any indication to the contrary, an express choice of law governing the substantive contract is a strong indication of the parties' intention in relation to the agreement to arbitrate.'[121] On the other hand, the court also held that if the presumption of an implied choice is rebutted,[122] the arbitration agreement 'has its closest and most

[117] It may be noted in passing that arbitration agreements are, however, excluded from the scope of the Rome I Regulation (Regulation (EC) No. 593/2008 of the European Parliament and of the Council of 17 June 2008 on the law applicable to contractual obligations) in the European Union. The choice of law rules are thus to be found in the national law of EU member states, including the common law in England.

[118] Art. V(1)(a).

[119] See e.g. *Arsanovia Ltd v Cruz City 1 Mauritius Holdings*, [2012] EWHC 3702 (Comm).

[120] See e.g. *FirstLink Investments Corp Ltd v GT Payment Pte Ltd*, [2014] SGHCR 12 (Singapore).

[121] *Sulamérica Cia Nacional de Seguros SA v Enesa Engenharia SA*, [2012] EWCA Civ 638, [26]; *Arsanovia Ltd v Cruz City 1 Mauritius Holdings*, [2012] EWHC 3702 (Comm); see further Ardavan Arzandeh, 'The Law Governing Arbitration Agreements in England', Lloyd's Maritime and Commercial Law Quarterly 31 (2013); Sabrina Pearson, 'Sulamérica v Enesa: The Hidden Pro-validation Approach Adopted by the English Courts with Respect to the Proper Law of the Arbitration Agreement', 29 Arbitration International 115 (2013).

[122] In *Sulamérica* the courts found that the presumption was rebutted because the substantive applicable law would have rendered the arbitration agreement unenforceable—essentially adopting a presumption in favour of the effectiveness of the arbitration agreement. As a result, there was no implied choice, and

real connection with the law of the place where the arbitration is to be held and which will exercise the supporting and supervisory jurisdiction necessary to ensure that the procedure is effective'.[123] A similar analysis applies where the parties have not chosen a law to govern their substantive contract—no presumption arises, and the objectively most closely connected law to the arbitration agreement is likely to be the law of the seat of the arbitration[124] (although obvious difficulties arise under this approach if the parties have not chosen a seat and the validity of the arbitration agreement must be determined before the arbitration has been commenced). Some other legal systems do not prioritize either the law of the seat or the law of the substantive contract, but rather the validation of the arbitration agreement, finding that the arbitration agreement only needs to be valid under one potentially applicable law.[125]

When the question of the interpretation or validity of an arbitration agreement arises before an arbitral tribunal, the analysis is significantly different. The arbitral tribunal has no 'law of the forum', and thus no directly applicable choice of law rules. National arbitration laws rarely give the tribunal clear and prescriptive guidance on this point, and arbitral tribunals do not always analyze the issues precisely. A choice of law by the parties which specifically applies to the arbitration agreement will, however, almost always be viewed as binding the tribunal contractually.[126] Because of the doctrine of separability, it is less clear whether a general choice of law clause in a contract should be viewed as governing the arbitration agreement, or only the substantive contractual terms—as noted above, the law of the seat of arbitration may be considered to have a stronger claim because it is the place of performance of the arbitration agreement. An arbitral tribunal may also give effect to a choice by the parties of non-state law to govern their arbitration agreement—such a choice is permitted under the UNCITRAL Model Law.[127] Many national legal systems will not permit a choice of non-state law under their choice of law rules, although it is notable that a different position was adopted in the Hague Principles on Choice of Law in International Commercial Contracts, a model law adopted in 2015, and that arbitral awards based on the application of non-state law are commonly enforced by national courts.[128]

In the absence of a party choice of law for the arbitration agreement, an arbitral tribunal will need some mechanism to determine the governing law—often, to choose between the law of the seat and the law of the substantive contractual terms. Three approaches may be adopted by the tribunal.

the court had to apply the objective choice of law rule, looking to the system of law with which the arbitration agreement had its 'closest and most real connection'.

[123] *Sulamérica Cia Nacional de Seguros SA v Enesa Engenharia SA*, [2012] EWCA Civ 638, [32].

[124] See e.g. *Habas Sinai Ve v VSC Steel Company Ltd*, [2013] EWHC 4071 (Comm).

[125] See e.g. the Swiss Law on Private International Law, Art. 178(2).

[126] This raises a further complex choice of law question which is beyond the scope of this chapter—what law should govern the validity of the choice of law clause itself. See e.g. Art. 10 of the Rome I Regulation. Arbitration agreements, as noted previously, are excluded from the Regulation (Art. 1(2)(e)), but choice of law clauses are not.

[127] Art. 28(1).

[128] See further e.g. Mills (n. 102).

First, it may apply national choice of law rules, most likely those of the seat of the arbitration, in order to determine which national substantive law governs the arbitration agreement. Thus, for example, if the seat of arbitration is England, the tribunal may follow the English case law noted above. The application by an arbitral tribunal of the choice of law rules of the seat was strongly advocated by adherents of the 'territorialist' thesis, such as F. A. Mann (as discussed in section 3.1.3).

Second, the tribunal may apply 'transnational' choice of law rules, which is to say choice of law rules which are not derived from any particular national legal system but from the common practice of arbitration, and use those to determine the governing law for the arbitration agreement.[129] The UNCITRAL Model Law perhaps supports this approach, in directing that '[f]ailing any designation by the parties, the arbitral tribunal shall apply the law determined by the conflict of laws rules which it considers applicable'.[130] The Hague Principles on Choice of Law in International Commercial Contracts, noted above, may serve as such a transnational 'model' law. This approach may be most closely associated with the 'pluralist' thesis on the nature of arbitration (discussed in section 3.1.3), as it acknowledges arbitration's international character but requires the tribunal to identify itself which system of national law should be applied, out of the variety of connected legal orders.

Third, the tribunal may reject the choice of law process altogether, and apply 'transnational' substantive law to govern the arbitration agreement (and perhaps also the substantive contractual obligations between the parties).[131] This approach is evidently most closely associated with those (such as Gaillard) who view arbitration as constituting an autonomous international legal order, as also discussed in section 3.1.3. The rules of substantive law which are applied under this order may be found in the uncodified practice of arbitral tribunals, or in an international codification such as the UNIDROIT Principles of International Commercial Contracts. This third option has, somewhat remarkably, also been adopted as part of French national law—in the absence of a choice of national law by the parties, French courts view arbitration agreements as bound not by any national law but by the rules and principles of 'transnational' arbitration practice.[132]

An arbitral tribunal may also consider a fourth source of national law to be potentially relevant. As noted above, it is commonly considered that arbitrators have a duty to render an enforceable award, and thus should take into account the law that would be applied to the question of the validity of the arbitration agreement by the courts of the predicted place of enforcement of the arbitral award. In cases in which the parties

[129] See generally e.g. Renato Nazzini, 'The Law Applicable to the Arbitration Agreement: Towards Transnational Principles', 65 International and Comparative Law Quarterly 681 (2016).

[130] Art. 28(2)—this provision is not directly concerned with the jurisdiction of the tribunal, but with the merits of the claim. See also e.g. the Arbitration Act 1996 (UK), s. 46(3).

[131] See further e.g. Blackaby et al. (n. 1), para. 3.156; Klaus Berger, *The Creeping Codification of the New Lex Mercatoria*, 2nd edn (Kluwer Law International, 2010).

[132] See e.g. Cour de Cassation, 1e civ, 3 Mar. 1992, 90–17.024; Cour de Cassation, 1e civ, 7 Jun. 2006, 03–12.034.

potentially have assets in multiple jurisdictions, however, that is unlikely to be viewed as a strong justification for the application of any particular law.

3.6.2 The law governing arbitrability

As analysed in section 3.4, the question of subject matter arbitrability presents a distinct issue as compared to other questions of jurisdiction concerning the validity of the arbitration agreement. The law governing the arbitration agreement does not, therefore, necessarily govern the question of arbitrability, although it is one possible law which a court or tribunal could consider. The question of arbitrability could, indeed, also be analysed as an issue relating to the validity of the arbitration agreement—not an issue which goes to the genuineness of the (apparent) consent to the agreement, but one focused on whether the agreement is contrary to public policy. The question is, of course, which 'public policy' should be brought to bear on this issue. As also noted in section 3.4, different national systems take a variety of different approaches as to what types of disputes are capable of settlement through arbitration—for example, permitting or excluding consumer, employment, insurance, or competition law claims—and so the selection of the applicable law may be critical.

A number of different laws could potentially be applied by a court or tribunal to this question.[133] The law of the seat of the arbitration is once again a candidate—it might be argued that an arbitration should not be conducted if the law of the place of the arbitration, which normally provides its procedural law, would not view the subject matter as arbitrable. If a national system excluded consumer or employment claims from arbitration, for example, this might lead it to offer more limited procedural protection for weaker parties in its arbitration law, which could suggest that consumer or employment claims should not be arbitrated under that law. The courts of the seat of arbitration are particularly likely to look to their national law for the applicable limits on arbitrability when they consider challenges to the arbitral award.[134] As noted in section 3.5.3, however, a decision by the courts of the seat of arbitration setting aside an arbitral award may not always be recognized by other national courts, who may instead recognize and enforce the arbitral award if the subject matter of the dispute conforms to their own standards of arbitrability.

Another option is the law governing the arbitration agreement, which might be applied on the basis that it is normally the putative applicable law which governs questions of the validity of a contract.[135] Issues of validity might be viewed as encompassing

[133] See generally e.g. Bernard Hanotiau, 'The Law Applicable to Arbitrability', 26 Singapore Academy of Law Journal 874 (2014); 'The Law Applicable to Arbitrability', in van den Berg (n. 47).

[134] Note UNCITRAL Model Law, Art. 34(2)(b)(i), permitting an award to be set aside if 'the subject-matter of the dispute is not capable of settlement by arbitration under the law of this State' (meaning the law of the seat of arbitration).

[135] See e.g. Art. 10 of the Rome I Regulation.

questions of subject matter arbitrability for an arbitration agreement, although as noted above these may be better viewed as having a distinctive public character.

A third option would be the law governing the merits of the dispute—typically the law governing the substantive contract between the parties, which may (as noted above) be different from the law governing the arbitration agreement. There is at least an argument that the substantive legal order would have the greatest impact on questions of subject matter arbitrability—if, for example, the substantively applicable contract law offers strong protections for consumers or employees, then it might be argued that this limits any concerns about the arbitrability of disputes involving these parties. A complication with this approach is that an arbitration may, however, involve both contractual and non-contractual claims, which may be governed by different systems of law, and it would not be desirable for different legal standards to apply to the question of arbitrability.

A fourth national law which could be applied by a court or arbitral tribunal would be the law of the (likely) place of enforcement of the arbitral award, on the basis that the place of enforcement is unlikely to recognize an arbitral award in respect of subject matter which is viewed within its legal order as incapable of settlement by arbitration. Indeed, Art. V(2)(a) of the New York Convention expressly provides that an award may be refused recognition in a Contracting State if 'the subject matter of the dispute is not capable of settlement by arbitration under the law of that country'.[136] This may, however, be better viewed as a distinct or additional consideration on the basis of public policy rather than arbitrability per se—as Böckstiegel has observed, 'Legal rules restricting arbitrability need not necessarily be part of public policy.'[137] In other words, a state need not refuse enforcement of a foreign arbitral award merely because the subject matter would not be considered arbitrable locally, although there is likely to be a strong mutual influence between the two doctrines.[138] While this rule may be easy for a national court to apply, it may frequently (as noted above) be difficult for arbitrators to determine where an arbitral award is likely to be enforced.

Each of these national legal orders has at least an arguable claim to regulate questions of subject matter arbitrability, but none appears to have a clearly overriding interest, and each may apply widely varying standards. In the face of this complexity, it is no surprise that some arbitral authorities and tribunals prefer (once again) to look to transnational standards rather than any particular national law, applying principles of 'transnational public policy'.[139] While this may appear to simplify the choice of applicable law task for

[136] Note also UNCITRAL Model Law, Art. 36(1)(b)(i), permitting a court to refuse recognition or enforcement of an award on the basis that 'the subject-matter of the dispute is not capable of settlement by arbitration under the law of this State' (meaning the law of the state where recognition or enforcement is sought).

[137] Karl-Heinz Böckstiegel, 'Public Policy and Arbitrability', in Pieter Sanders (ed.), *Comparative Arbitration Practice and Public Policy in Arbitration* (Kluwer Law International, 1986), 182.

[138] See e.g. Abby Smutny and Hansel Pham, 'Enforcing Foreign Arbitral Awards in the United States: The Non-Arbitrable Subject Matter Defense', 25 Journal of International Arbitration 657 (2008).

[139] See e.g. Michael Pryles, 'Reflections on Transnational Public Policy', 24 Journal of International Arbitration 1 (2007); Pierre Lalive, 'Transnational (or Truly International) Public Policy and International Arbitration', in Sanders (n. 137).

the tribunal, the identification of such standards may itself be extremely difficult, particularly as different national legal orders evidently take different approaches.

3.7 Conclusions

The issue of arbitral jurisdiction is foundational to the legitimacy and effectiveness of arbitration, and raises a series of complex concerns. The analysis above should not, however, be taken to suggest that arbitrators commonly consider these issues in great technical depth, or that the practice of arbitrators is consistent or even strongly aims at consistency. This is partly inevitable, partly desirable, and partly problematic.

It is inevitable in the sense that many arbitrations will raise few if any of the issues examined above. The reasons why parties chose arbitration in their contract will often lead them to continue to accept arbitration once a dispute arises,[140] and the reputational and legal costs of challenging an arbitral award on contested grounds may lead parties to accept and comply with arbitral awards. Many disputes will, in addition, centre on the resolution of factual rather than legal issues. Detailed technical analysis of the legal issues may not be necessary or in the interests of the parties, and courts favourably disposed to arbitration are thus unlikely to set aside an arbitral award which does not adopt a legalistic approach.

It is desirable in the sense that one of the traditional attractions of arbitration is that it offers a more flexible and informal mode of dispute resolution than litigation. As long as the arbitrators apply an approach which is principled and pragmatic, many parties are unlikely to have great concerns about whether the approach is analysed in a detailed and technical way which is consistent with general practice. An approach which favours reasonableness and common sense over detailed technical legal analysis may be what parties believe themselves to be contracting into with commercial arbitration.

It is, however, also potentially problematic, because the complexity of these issues and the lack of clarity around the best approach on various points leaves arbitrators with a great deal of discretion as to how issues of arbitral jurisdiction are resolved. Even if arbitrators exercise this discretion in a pragmatic and sensible way, this uncertainty is likely to affect the attractiveness of arbitration itself in two ways. First, even a party who accepts the outcome of the arbitration might find that the approach of the tribunal to determining the validity and scope of its jurisdiction was less than satisfactory, and this may dissuade them from entering into future arbitration agreements. Commercial parties value certainty and predictability as well as practical common sense. Second, a party might challenge the jurisdictional approach of an arbitral tribunal in a court, whether through proceedings to set aside the award or as a defense to enforcement of the award. The approach of national courts to these issues tends to be more technical—with

[140] Although it is not suggested that parties always think carefully and strategically about dispute resolution clauses.

national courts having more clearly defined choice of law rules to determine what law should govern various jurisdictional issues. If a national court rejects the arbitral tribunal's (positive) determination of its own jurisdiction, the time and money invested in the arbitration may effectively be wasted. This is again likely to lead some parties to avoid arbitration in future.

This last point suggests, rightly, that there would be great benefits if national courts and arbitral tribunals had a consistent practice both between themselves and internationally on issues of arbitral jurisdiction. But this is not a realistic prospect in the short term. This is not just because of different national laws and judicial practices and the lack of binding precedent in arbitration. It is also because the different approaches to these issues reflect a number of competing theoretical conceptions of arbitration itself. As Gaillard has argued, 'It is precisely because there are several visions, several competing representations of international arbitration, that the controversies on a number of apparently purely technical topics remain so vivid.'[141]

Those who view arbitrators as exercising power which is delegated by the national legal order in which the arbitration takes place are likely to view the authority of the tribunal as at least principally derived from that legal order, and thereby favour the application of the law of the seat to questions of arbitral jurisdiction. Those who view arbitrators as exercising primarily a contractual authority which may engage with a variety of different national legal orders are more likely to view the jurisdiction of the tribunal as at least principally derived from the legal order establishing that contractual relationship, and thereby favour the application of the law governing the arbitration agreement to questions of jurisdiction, and also favour the determination that this law is (in the absence of a clear choice to the contrary) the law governing the parties' substantive relationship rather than the law of the seat. Finally, those who view arbitration as transnational and autonomous in character, free-floating above or aside national legal orders, are likely to suggest that the answers to the questions regarding arbitral jurisdiction cannot be satisfactorily derived from any national law, but ought to be found in transnational principles and practice. Put simply, the contested issues of arbitral jurisdiction are unlikely to be resolved easily, because they are a reflection in miniature of the major continuing uncertainties surrounding the identity and character of international arbitration as a whole.

141 Gaillard, 'Representations' (n. 7), 272.

CHAPTER 4

APPOINTMENT OF ARBITRATORS

JAN PAULSSON

4.1 Inherent tensions

In its most elementary (and perhaps most noble) form, arbitration is the fruit of an agreement between disputants to ask a trusted person to resolve their dispute. Conflicts are perhaps most likely to be resolved peaceably in this fashion when disputants perceive that their interests are considered with sympathy, and when each of them at all moments is free to abandon the process. In modern parlance, however, 'arbitration' is thought of as a *binding* process; agreements to arbitrate cannot be revoked unilaterally, and arbitral awards must be obeyed even if one of the disputants is unhappy with the outcome. Unless these features of finality are present, the person chosen for the task, whether referred to as a mediator, conciliator, or the like, is in reality a facilitator of negotiation—and negotiations can be broken off unilaterally.

The history of arbitration is confusing unless one is aware of the distinction between binding decision-making and facilitated negotiation. For example, a famous Koranic verse teaches that in cases of marital discord each family should choose a person to resolve the dispute by serving as *hakam*. This is frequently referred to as the origin of an Islamic tradition of arbitration. It is however unclear from the text whether the views of the *hakam* are binding in the absence of acceptance by both sides. Moreover, the recommended process does not indicate the path to a solution if the two nominees ultimately cannot agree. In more recent history, there are recurring examples of processes by which the mandates of so-called arbitrators may be revoked unilaterally at any time (such as the moment a party is disappointed by a procedural initiative, or indeed by the final decision).

In modern usage, arbitration is binding, and anything else created by agreement is some form or another of what might generically be referred to as third-party assisted negotiation. This explains why arbitration contemplates an odd number of arbitrators; indeed, laws regulating arbitration frequently explicitly require it.

It follows that the 'odd' arbitrator, i.e. the one whose voice will be decisive in the event of failure of unanimity, must be appointed jointly, or by a neutral mechanism agreed by the arbitrants. That is simple enough when the process calls for a sole arbitrator, 'one' being the odd number *par excellence*. But if the tribunal is to be composed of three arbitrators, it is often (probably generally) agreed that each side may select anyone it wishes provided they satisfy minimal criteria—such as professional qualifications and the readiness to declare themselves independent and impartial.

What are we to make of this? Are we back to 'third-party assisted negotiation'? What has happened to 'the trusted arbitrator'? After all, the fact that parties have a dispute means that each of them thinks it is right and wishes to prevail, and will act in every instance in such a way to achieve that objective; that objective is also foremost in their minds when they make the unilateral selection of an arbitrator. On that basis, one person whom either party *does not trust* is surely the arbitrator chosen by its adversary. And yet the process is designed to produce a binding result by virtue of the parties' consent to this paradoxical arrangement.

It might be said that the third arbitrator represents common trust, and the opportunity to appoint individual co-arbitrators represents an incentive for each party to adhere to the process in the first place. These two factors create an undeniable tension, which is absent when all three arbitrators are appointed jointly by the parties, or by a neutral institution—since then each arbitrator is trusted as much as a sole arbitrator would be. And yet the common modern practice is to subject each arbitrator to precisely the same duty of independence and impartiality. It would be naïve to deny that this not infrequently generates disbelief in the minds of parties, and hypocrisy on the part of persons named as arbitrators.

In sum, rational discourse about the legitimacy of the process is impeded by a failure to recognize that there is a world of difference between the parties' joint appointment of arbitrators and the opportunity for each party to appoint one arbitrator unilaterally. In each case it might be said that the entire tribunal has been 'appointed by the parties', but that is loose talk.

4.2 Traditional Appointment Methods

The variety of solutions found in bespoke clauses is limited only by the drafters' imagination. It seems safe to say, however, that the arbitration clauses found in most international contracts are not tailor-made, but rather incorporate well-known model texts. It seems likely that the drafters rely on the reputations of the permanent bodies who have developed and refined such model clauses, but are not always aware of the default rules that they entail. For example, the rules of both the ICC and the LCIA provide that there will presumptively be a sole arbitrator, while the UNCITRAL Rules call for three arbitrators. But whereas the ICC and UNCITRAL Rules provide that when there are to be three arbitrators, each of the non-presiding arbitrators will be appointed unilaterally by each of the disputing sides, the LCIA Rules call for three-member tribunals to be entirely appointed by the LCIA itself. In each of these hypotheses, the parties may overcome the default rules by a contrary stipulation, whether in the arbitration clause or indeed by its novation once the dispute has begun.

The merits of the LCIA solution are significant if one thinks it through from a purely practical perspective. When the contract is signed, the parties want performance, not disputation. But differences emerge as a matter of statistical inevitability, and one cannot be certain in advance that one's opponent will conduct itself loyally in that event. If the ambience of the dispute is bitter, it may seem possible that one's adversary would not hesitate to engage in the so-called guerrilla tactics of appointing a fiercely militant arbitrator, who will adamantly take a position on matters of substance as well as procedure, and be a willing accomplice to delaying tactics, for example by threatening to resign or actually doing so and thus causing costly disruption. If so, the party wishing to rely on the arbitral mechanism will be pleased with the LCIA's default rule. In happier circumstances, when both sides are approaching their difference in a more civil fashion, it takes no more than a phone call between opposing counsel to vary the arbitration clause by agreeing (if such is their desire) that each will name its arbitrator with confidence that this opportunity will not be abused.

For its part, the large industry of labour arbitration in the US[1] emerged as a perceived alternative to the option to strike, and has traditionally involved as much negotiation as adjudication, given the decision-makers' focus on 'interest-based' solutions rather than right vs. wrong. It seems no coincidence that 'non-neutral arbitrators' became accepted American figures. As recently as 1962, the law of New York allowed the annulment of awards on the ground of bias only if the offending arbitrator was a 'neutral'; non-neutral arbitrators could be challenged only on the grounds of corruption, fraud, or misconduct.[2] This followed the approach taken by the National Conference of Commissioners when they adopted the Uniform Arbitration Act[3] in 1956. The Chairman of the Commission explained blandly that the double standard recognized the practice that each side could appoint an arbitrator, 'in a loose sense, [to] be his advocate'.[4]

In 1977, the Code of Ethics for Arbitrators in Commercial Disputes adopted jointly by the American Arbitration Association and the American Bar Association set down a presumption to the effect that arbitrators appointed by one party could be 'predisposed' to favour their appointor. This was not reversed until the 2004 revision of the Code—which nevertheless left it possible to opt for the 'non-neutral' model.

[1] In recent years, the American Arbitration Association has administered in excess of 12,000 labor arbitrations annually.

[2] New York Civil Practice Law and Rules, §7511 (b)(1).

[3] A model act for individual states of the US.

[4] Maynard Pirsig, 'The New Uniform Arbitration Act', 11 Business Lawyer 44 (1965), 47.

Persons whose knowledge of arbitration comes from the field of public international law, or from US practice, or indeed from cultures where the closest thing to 'arbitration' is in essence a form of structured negotiation, bring these non-judicial attitudes with them. Yet the modern consensus is that commercial arbitrators should in principle be independent and impartial no matter how they were appointed.[5] It would be simpler if it were universally understood that unilaterally appointed arbitrators in all forms of arbitrations act as special advocates of their appointers, with access to the deliberation room. But this philosophy of candour has not prevailed; most participants in the process strive for a higher ideal than mere simplicity. The result is a blurring of ethical lines, which is resolved only in the hidden recesses of each arbitrator's soul.

The practice of unilateral nominations is an unfortunate expedient, antagonistic to the idea of arbitration. Whatever the qualities of the nominee, the appointing party is focused on winning, not on ensuring the ideal of impartiality. Even a fiercely independent judge and later arbitrator, Pierre Bellet, once *premier président* of the French Court of Cassation and later president of the Iran–US Claims Tribunal in The Hague, once wrote that there were 'degrees of impartiality', and that unilateral nominees needed only to be 'sufficiently impartial' while presiding arbitrators had to be 'particularly neutral'.[6] This may have been realism, but reality is sometimes unacceptable.

There are happy circumstances when any apprehensions the parties may have about a looming case are overcome by the esteem in which they hold the nominees. This is most readily imaginable in small communities, be it an extended family, a religious group, a village, or a network of traders who engage in a multitude of repeat transactions in a specialist business. In such a setting, the disputants may have unquestioning faith in individuals whose decision would be accepted, perhaps with disappointment yet without demur. It may even be unnecessary that the disputants personally *know* the arbitrator because his or her status within the community excludes any doubts as to probity. On a larger scene, any expectation of such mutual confidence in particular persons as individuals may be unrealistic. An Indonesian party is unlikely to have confident knowledge of the community of arbitrators in London; a merchant from Marseilles is unlikely to have any opinion of the leading arbitrators in Valparaíso.

A fundamental question in many arbitrations is whether the co-arbitrators act collegially or follow a hidden agenda of patronage. Does a unilaterally appointed arbitrator keep one wary eye on his fellow arbitrators and the other on the objectives of the nominating party? Or behave like a loyal member of a panel striving impartially toward the collective goal of the best possible award? Or yet again give in to an instinct of competitiveness, using skills of advocacy where they do not belong?

A distaste for hypocrisy causes some practitioners to incline to Bellet's comments, and conclude that one should simply expect that a party-appointed arbitrator will not

[5] William Park, 'Arbitrator Integrity, The Transient and the Permanent', 46 San Diego L. Review 629 (2009), 678. David Branson, to the contrary, considers that the US maintains a different standard; in 'Sympathetic Party-Appointed Arbitrators: Sophisticated Strangers and Governments Demand Them', 25 ICSID Review—Foreign Investment L.J. 367 (2011), 373.

[6] Case note, 1992 Rev. arb. 572.

behave as impartially as one appointed jointly or by a neutral authority. They have a plausible argument. Why do arbitration agreements so often explicitly provide for two unilateral nominations unless each party expects something different from its nominee than from joint or neutral appointees?[7]

True, there are important reasons for desiring the opportunity to name an arbitrator other than seeking a partisan champion. A party knowing that it will be able to ensure that at least one arbitrator is effective and knowledgeable has less reason to fear the spectre of a runaway tribunal (i.e. one that is guilty of procedural ineptness or a preposterous outcome). And from a macroscopic perspective, it seems inevitable that the arbitral process, when it operates on a big stage, nationally or internationally, will less readily be perceived as legitimate when a party is disappointed by an award rendered by three unknown arbitrators. The importance of this factor is enhanced by the fact that appellate review is usually not available.

But nominating parties *also* hope that their nominee will be sympathetic to their position, or indeed defend it. Where does that leave the co-arbitrator, and where does that leave institutions charged with the task of curtailing abuse? What does experience tell us?

Under some circumstances, the pressures on a party-appointed arbitrator are so extreme that any pretence of independent evaluation is an absurdity evident to all. Territorial disputes tend to generate such passions. For example, the award in *Republika Srpska v Federation of Bosnia and Herzegovina* explicitly recited that the context of the arbitration, which arose out of the Dayton Accords and as such was designed to resolve a boundary issue (basically entitlement to the area of Brcko Grad) which had been left aside as intractable by the Accords themselves, made it a 'virtual necessity' to modify the applicable UNCITRAL Rules so that the presiding arbitrator could decide the case alone.[8] Rendered by the presiding arbitrator[9] without the signature of either party-appointed arbitrator, the award stated:

> from the outset the positions of the two parties on the merits have been polar opposites and each party has explicitly refused to compromise. These polar positions and accompanying intense animosities, consistently in evidence from the opening of the Dayton conference onward, made clear from the outset that any party-appointed arbitrator would encounter significant difficulties in conducting himself with the usual degree of detachment and independence. The parties therefore decided to change the rule on decision-making in view of the substantial likelihood that an arbitral resolution could be achieved only by the two parties' agreeing that the rulings of the Presiding Arbitrator will be treated as decisive.[10]

[7] The New York Court of Appeals put it bluntly in *In re Astoria Medical Group*, 11 N.Y. 2d 128, 133 (1962): 'The right to appoint one's own arbitrator... would be of little moment were it to comprehend solely the choice of a neutral. It becomes a valued right, which parties bargain for and litigate over, only if it involves a choice of one believed to be sympathetic to his position or favorably disposed to him.'

[8] Art. 31 of the 1976 UNCITRAL Rules required a majority decision.

[9] Appointed by the President of the International Court of Justice.

[10] *Award of 14 February 1997*, International Legal Materials, 399, 401.

The plain fact remains: unilateral appointments are a usual feature in international arbitration, and they present greater problems than the joint or institutional appointment of presiding arbitrators. Although the modern consensus is that all arbitrators are in principle bound to the same criteria of independence and impartiality, it is naturally more difficult to ensure that they are observed when arbitrators are named by individual arbitrants as opposed to by joint agreement or by an institution. As a result, an important body of hard and soft law—the former principally reflected in national case law and the latter in institutional practices and guidelines by associations such as the International Bar Association—has emerged to regulate such matters as disqualifying factors, *ex parte* communications before and after appointment, and the obligations of disclosure (as well as the consequences of disregarding them). Abuses seem to be rare, but are difficult to police when carried out by unscrupulous and sophisticated actors, and therefore occasionally give rise to notorious miscarriages of arbitral justice. How the frequency of such instances compares with national justice depends of course on what arbitral environments are compared with what court systems.

4.3 The Case Against Unilaterals

The practice of unilateral appointments introduces an adversarial element into the very deliberation of the arbitral tribunal. Disputants tend to be interested in one thing only: a favourable outcome. In arbitration, they exercise any right of unilateral appointment, like everything else, with that overriding objective in view.

The only solution which will be reliable in all circumstances is that any arbitrator, no matter the size of the tribunal, should be chosen jointly or selected by a neutral body. This essential aspect of the process should no longer be misused as a sales argument for arbitration. Confidence enhancement is properly focused on procedural rights (the right to be heard, the opportunity to confront the opponent's case, equality of arms) rather than risking the ineluctable contamination of the ideal—that of an arbitrator trusted by both sides—by a hidden operational code of clientilism.

It may be objected that these animadversions against the practice of unilateral appointments are excessive. The world of arbitration is well used to the phenomenon, and indeed it seems that three-member tribunals generally reach unanimous decisions. Let us accept that this may well be so. There are still reasons for disquiet.

We are not concerned with trouble-free cases that result in unanimous awards. Our model must also work in the difficult cases, which is where any system is tested. One indication of difficulty is a split decision. Is a 2:1 award perceived by the losing party as more legitimate than a decision by a sole arbitrator, because 'three heads are better than one'? That makes no sense—quite the opposite. The losing party in a difficult case is likely to consider that it appointed a 'good' arbitrator, who has somehow been outvoted by a 'bad' arbitrator chosen by an unscrupulous adversary and a feckless president misled by the 'bad' arbitrator. QED: in the eyes of the losing party, the 2:1 decision is *less* legitimate than that of a sole arbitrator in whose selection the opponent would have had no more and no less than an equal say.

In any event, unanimity is not always achieved in principled ways. The practice of unilateral appointments, like it or not, implicitly militates in favour of compromise, and indeed may be said to create an expectation of it. The result penalizes a party whose entitlement would be fully upheld by an objective decision-maker. Moreover, this dynamic toward compromise is likely to contaminate the reasoning of the tribunal, transforming it into something more like a ritual than a record of genuine ratiocination. The practice of unilateral appointments is thus an obstacle to coherent and sincere awards. Since the usual requirement of reasons is intended to serve as a check on arbitrariness, it follows that the subversion of this requirement makes it less likely that awards fulfil their important legitimizing function.

In rarefied environments where sophisticated professionals have ready insights into the way institutions operate, and about the personal reliability of leading individuals, the trouble with unilateral appointments is much attenuated. Lawyers have sufficient knowledge of arbitrators nominated by their opponents, and as for themselves tend to select persons who will be known quantities in the eyes of the presiding arbitrators. But in such an environment, why should not every appointment be joint, or at least made from a list of individuals proposed by a similarly reliable institution? Above all, this attractive model of perfectly informed participants is simply unrealistic with respect to the run-of-the-mill of arbitration. And if arbitration cannot produce run-of-the-mill quality, it may be condemned to function as an enclave of limited relevance.

The two evident solutions are (i) to opt for a sole arbitrator to be chosen, failing agreement, by a highly reputed institution or, (ii) if the true concern is that the case is too important to risk the lapse of even the most outstanding individual person (Homer's nod), three arbitrators appointed in the same way, i.e. eschewing any unilateral nomination. Institutions may experiment with a variety of intermediate solutions, such as 'blind appointments' (i.e. seeking to ensure that nominees do not know who appointed them) or list procedures which have in common the feature that the initial identification of the field of candidates comes from the institution rather than from one party.

An attractive secondary effect of avoiding unilateral appointments is to open the door to a mix of expertise within the arbitral tribunal. International cases often benefit from competence in several disciplines. What happens when three arbitrators have been appointed because of their general acumen in commercial law but the core issue relates to alleged infringement of a patent, or contentions of abuse of dominant position in a complex market, or the understanding of a most-favoured-nation clause in an international treaty? Or when three senior academics are nominated because of their solid reputations in the field of environmental law, but not one of them has any experience in presiding a raucous hearing, or any notion of complex issues of accounting or taxation which would flow from a finding of liability?

Examples could be multiplied. They suggest that this is not only a matter of improving the quality of decision-making, but indeed an issue that relates to ethics: parties who confront a particular constellation of problems cannot *be properly heard* by persons who have accepted the mandate to resolve the dispute without being qualified to assess an essential aspect of it, somewhat like a triathlete who can run and cycle, but swims like a stone. This problem finds a solution in the joint or institutional appointments of the entire tribunal, allowing for a mix of capabilities without concern as to which is predominant (although of course the arbitrants approach such exercises with strategic agenda whereas the institution does not).

Similarly, joint or institutional appointments allow parties to give the opportunity to one talented but inexperienced person to sit next to older hands, thus contributing to replenishment and diversity in the corps of arbitrators. Arbitrants making unilateral appointments do not take such chances.

4.4 Special Considerations When States Are Parties

As seen above, in some types of arbitration, such as those involving states and those that arise in US industrial relations, partisan arbitrators have been tolerated. States are wary of the international legal process, as an external check on their sovereignty, and have traditionally insisted on the unilateral right to appoint at least one arbitrator or judge to international tribunals. This is all the more understandable when one considers the generality and abstraction with which so much of public international law is formulated, the controversies as to their sources and interpretation, and the likely politicization of such disputes.

And so the challenge to the practice of unilateral nominations is unlikely to make much headway in the domain of public international law, due to the political dimensions of most disputes. The very idea of neutrality may be illusory in a nervous world divided by ideology and geopolitical rivalries. The issues that bedevil the jurisprudence of the law of nations are never far from such anxiety, whether they are inherently political, like matters of self-determination and proportional use of force, or inherently flexible, like 'equitable' adjustments in maritime delimitation. Powerful states may fear that they are unpopular, and that adjudicators from jealous, weaker, but more numerous nations will gang up on them. Small states may fear that their own influence is nil, and that they are far less able to resist unfair judgments than, say, the permanent members of the United Nations Security Council.

And so the political context of adjudication under public international law may make it unlikely that disputing states will be able to overcome their insistence on the right to appoint one of the decision-makers unilaterally. Moreover, unilaterally appointed arbitrators in such cases may, given the often political and open-textured nature of the questions raised, have a valuable function of contributing an understanding of the priorities of their appointers, which in turn has the pragmatic and valuable effect of contributing to intelligent decisions likely to be implemented in good faith.

Perhaps in due course we will see a parting of ways in the arbitral ethos, as private parties give up the opportunity of unilateral appointments in return for access to a neutral, incorruptible, and binding system of dispute resolution, reducing legal risk as a parasitic cost of doing business, while states maintain their insistence on appointing 'reliable' arbitrators unilaterally. States are, after all, inherently less law-abiding than private parties; invoking their own conceptions of the public interest as an end that justifies the means, they show themselves with distressing regularity willing to kill in order to impose a solution to conflicts. Private parties can invoke no *casus belli*; they must look to the law and negotiation. Given this disparity, it is perhaps too much to expect states to believe in the possibility of fully neutral arbitration.[11]

But there seems to be no reason why such incredulousness must also prevail in the commercial field. Parties enter into contracts with the objective of relying on them; *ex ante*, this can only be understood as a shared view. That is the premise of the following discussion.

4.5 The pursuit of legitimacy

Recognizing the likelihood that insistence on the 'right' to appoint an arbitrator will not soon go away, one should as a matter of pragmatism take stock of the existing means of preventing the erosion of confidence in tribunals constituted on that premise.

One modest solution involves the restriction of unilateral nominations by specific contractual limitation, such as a requirement that no arbitrator may have the nationality of any party. In the absence of such a restriction, some parties, especially in politically fraught cases, find it impossible *not* to name one of their nationals as arbitrator. That nominee may feel subject to political pressures—whether he or she succumbs to them or fights them. Such restrictions, in other words, are capable of reducing the risk of subversion of arbitral authority.

A more effective mechanism, provided that it is properly conceived, may be an institutional requirement that unilateral appointments be made from a pre-existing list of qualified arbitrators. The danger here is that an arbitral institution ends up skewing the list to favour an 'in-group' operating as an opaque oligopoly. Still, when composed and updated judiciously by a reputable, inclusive, and continually renewed international body, such lists may have undeniable advantages. They might be seen as

[11] Eric Posner and John Yoo have concluded that international tribunals are more effective if they include partisan decision-makers who are attuned to what the powerful disputants will tolerate. See Eric Posner and John Yoo, 'Judicial Independence in International Tribunals', 93 Calif. L. Rev. 1 (2005), 7. Laurence Helfer and Anne-Marie Slaughter, 'Why States Create International Tribunals: A Response to Professors Posner and Yoo', 93 Calif. L. Rev. 899 (2005), criticize their analysis and conclusions, notably by reference to empirical data and state practice—i.e. states' actual preference for independent adjudication. At any rate, it is essential to bear in mind that Posner and Yoo were not studying the far greater number of international tribunals involving private arbitrants.

a useful hybrid of institutional and unilateral appointments; a party may select any of a number of arbitrators, but each of the potential nominees has been vetted by the institution and is less likely to be beholden to the appointing party. This process may be further refined by the practice of 'blind appointments', intended to keep nominees unaware of who appointed them.

The Court of Arbitration for Sport (CAS) in Lausanne, which deals with disputes arising in the context of international sporting competitions, is a pertinent example. Most of its panels comprise three members. Some cases are of international notoriety, involving the disqualification of famous champions or the transfer fees of wealthy professional athletes. Most CAS arbitrations, however, involve far more modest disputes and are resolved after hearings that take less than a full day. Of present importance is that (i) the parties come from all parts of the globe; and (ii) that most of them appear in such proceedings only once in their lives. If they were given the unfettered right to make a unilateral nomination, they would—out of ignorance, fear, or calculation—likely appoint someone unknown to CAS and to their opponent, and therefore as a practical matter shielded from any meaningful verification of suitability. Such an appointee may have little moral standing with the presiding arbitrator beyond what is possible to reveal in a few hours of collaboration—which is not very much. The result might be that the presiding arbitrator would tend to decide alone, thus defeating the purpose of three-member tribunals.

The CAS solution is to require all nominees to be found on a list of qualified arbitrators. It is of importance that this list is lengthy and inclusive, containing nearly 300 names from all over the world. Any party is free to choose the arbitrator it wishes. However selfish its motives, it is restricted to this list of prequalified individuals—and it knows that the same is true for its opponent.

Admirable arbitrators who remain wholly impartial and independent no matter how they are selected may be offended to hear it said that the tradition of unilateral appointments is a menace to arbitration. Yet it is so. The existing checks and balances are too often perceived as inadequate. None of the supposed reasons for this habit stand up to scrutiny, except the plaintive and defeatist assertion that there is no better way.

4.6 Limited Benefits of Disclosure

If for no other reason than to protect the future award against challenges, facts which might raise doubts as to an arbitrator's impartiality and independence should be disclosed. But the infinite variety of circumstances which may be said to give rise to apprehension means that there is great scope for differences in interpreting the duty to disclose. Overemphasis on mechanical disclosure requirements may exclude the honest and do very little to stifle true mischief. There comes a point of diminishing returns where excessive formalism serves only to assist an obstreperous party in fomenting delay and difficulty. As a result, scrupulous arbitrators may be removed from office for trivial reasons, while hypocritical rascals do not even have to break their stride.

That even an extensive duty of disclosure may be ineffective to expose the most errant bias may be demonstrated by a simple example. The blameless arbitrator A presides over one arbitral tribunal involving an oil supply contract and is named as a co-arbitrator to sit on another tribunal dealing with a pharmaceutical licence dispute. The unethical arbitrator B presides the second dispute, and is appointed by a party in the oil contract arbitration. Both have informed all parties of their service on both tribunals and indeed of the identity of the other arbitrators. There are no further facts that B need disclose. Yet he has great sympathy for the party that appointed him in the first case: it is a dominant force in the country where B makes his career; this is a strategically vital case for his appointers; it is in his overwhelming self-interest to be well thought of by that party. So he has a chat with A, saying how pleased he is to have someone with A's great acumen to help him sort out the license case, where B disarmingly admits to very little expertise all the while noting that with respect to the oil case he (B) has vast experience and would be pleased to help A get the right answer if in fact he would be prepared to reciprocate this personal trust. The insidious bargain is implicit but clear; if A were not scrupulous, the process would be fatally corrupted by an arrangement which would surely not be exposed by a questionnaire.

Other scenarios are less appalling but still illustrate why the disclosure mechanism is not a panacea. Consider whether a partner of a very large law firm based in Europe should be excluded from appointment in a case because he discloses that a company affiliated with a party involved in the arbitration instructed one of the firm's office in Asia on an unrelated matter which ended some years ago—irrespective of the fact that the arbitrator has never heard of the company or the transaction, or that the matter generated relatively modest fees. The truth is that any fact disclosed is susceptible to quite different inferences. If one is going to make cynical assumptions, it may be more rational to posit that a lawyer whose firm has worked occasionally for a dominant company in his city would resent that company's not having given the firm more than a trickle of work than to suppose that he would try to make it easier for another lawyer—indeed, a competitor—to win an arbitration for that company. To take the reverse tack, the fact that his firm has never worked for that dominant company may mean that he is not averse to pleasing the potential future client on this occasion. Again, this conceivable bias will not be captured by a box-ticking disclosure exercise.

Lawyer–arbitrator acquaintanceships raise particularly difficult problems. To oblige parties to appoint persons they do not know obviously defeats the very purpose of party-appointed arbitrators. Moreover, any attempt to codify this area by means of detailed reporting requirements (how many meals have you had with X? Lunch or dinner? How many other people were present? What did you discuss? Do you know the names of X's children?) is bound to backfire, once more causing honest people to appear suspect but creating not the slightest problem for the unscrupulous. This is particularly true in the international arena, where geographical and cultural distances may make it impossible to conduct effective investigation of personal networks.

In any event, there is no assurance that arbitrator A, although he has never heard of lawyer X who appointed him, will not see the occasion as one which will allow him to make a new friend. This temptation may be greater than with respect to a true friend, because true friendships are not affected by differences of opinion. In fact, the zest for regulation (as so often) may achieve an entirely undesired effect: to create a climate propitious to the emergence of unsavoury networks of influence or information where A advises B that C is 'reliable' and B returns the favour by telling A about D.

In the 1980s, a controversy arose[12] when the ICC introduced a new standard form of disclosure for arbitrators which called on them to reveal connections not only with parties, but also with their lawyers. The choice of an arbitrator is more often directed by the lawyer than the client. But the notion that personal acquaintance should a priori be considered suspect engendered sharp criticism. The revised form was perceived by its critics as an American initiative which was not only naïve and patronizing, but self-serving, on the premise that the American legal community is vast while in some other countries the opposite situation prevails—with the result that in those places all members of the Bar would be excluded as arbitrators.

Although one may doubt that the American legal community (which may not even be a meaningful concept in the context) had such a conspiratorial intent, there is force in the argument that while an appropriate level of disclosure is indispensable, there is a point of nil if not negative returns. Disclosure is insufficient to cure all ills, and the answer cannot be yet more disclosure. It is an intrinsically limited tool.

4.7 The Unending Need for Innovation and Institutional Reform

There is one single unanswerable objection to the critique of the practice of unilaterals, namely that parties simply do not trust the arbitral institution to appoint impartial and apt arbitrators. Having accepted arbitration as a lesser evil, so the reasoning goes, they do so with severe mental reservations, fearing that the institution will appoint a presiding arbitrator whose case management is poor, and who is moreover too indolent to delve thoroughly into the evidence, too obtuse to understand essential propositions of law, too prone to trust superficial impressions or intuitions, or—worse—biased or unscrupulous. In such circumstances, the one thing a party can do is to insist on the opportunity to appoint one arbitrator whom it can trust to do his or her best to prevent injustice. It might not work; the two others may nonetheless ruin the process. But it is the best we can do, it is said; now do not ask us to accept that this institution appoint all three arbitrators!

[12] Documented in Michael Reisman et al., *International Commercial Arbitration* (Foundation Press, 1997), 572ff.

The bearers of this message of despair need to consider two important responses. They both involve the exhortation not to be passive. The first is the suggestion that parties who sincerely desire a fair and cost-effective process should involve themselves with greater mental energy. A number of ideas may be considered whether or not an arbitral institution has a role in the matter. Once an arbitration has commenced, parties may seek ad hoc agreement between themselves, even if they cannot jointly select the entire tribunal. Thus, to take only a few examples, they might:

- jointly identify the presiding arbitrator, and only thereafter make their unilateral appointments;
- begin with the same joint identification, and then allow the president (i) freely to chose the other arbitrators or (ii) to propose lists to be prioritized by the arbitrants; or
- negotiate with each other a reciprocal right to veto the other's unilateral nominee—perhaps once or twice.

Such approaches may create constructive dynamics and be more plausible than they may seem at first blush. Of course each side is focused solely on the goal of constituting the tribunal most likely to view its case with favour, but that should not mean that it lacks respect for its adversary's intelligence. The achievement of mutual comfort is not impossible. Nothing is lost for trying.

Secondly, this exhortation to active involvement should reasonably include the arbitral institutions. After all, their objective is that the process be smooth and unassailable. So when they take initiatives, like the American Arbitration Association's attempt to devise protocols that seek to engage the arbitrants under its 'Enhanced Neutral Selection Process for Large, Complex Cases', it seems foolish not to take advantage of the opportunity.

Still, if the ultimate stumbling block to eliminating unilateral appointments is distrust, this should be a matter of grave concern to all arbitral institutions. These reflections on one sensitive subject thus lead ineluctably to consideration of another, equally important and delicate matter: the standards and practices of arbitral institutions. Appointing authorities will contribute very little unless they can convince arbitrants and their lawyers that the selection of arbitrators is untainted by improper influence, and to the contrary is exclusively focused on selecting the most qualified individuals, in all senses of the word.

In a complex and transient world, the ideal of personal confidence in the same arbitrator may rarely be attained outside the realm of unusually homogeneous groups. How could individuals with whom the arbitrants have no personal experience fit the bill? It is practically impossible for unilaterally appointed arbitrators to claim such confidence, so trust must ultimately be institutional. Any institution that appoints arbitrators needs to take a hard look at itself and ask whether it is exposed to concerns about (i) poor selections of arbitrators, and even (ii) cronyism and other forms of corruption.

At a time when the ICC exercised a singular dominance on the international scene, it was the focus of attention. Its cosmopolitan membership ensured a widespread familiarity with the way it works, and its ubiquity enabled practitioners on all continents to achieve a certain—if inconstant—comfort level with its track record. The issue of the perceived legitimacy of arbitral institutions is likely to become even more problematic over time because of their growing numbers and diversity. As a handful of other institutions achieved prominence in the final decades of the last century, they were to some extent able to emulate the ICC; they remained relatively few in number, and practitioners became passably familiar with them. But ever more institutions enter the picture, new cohorts of arbitrators emerge, and users of arbitration become more discerning in their appraisal of institutional integrity. The challenge becomes ever greater: how can the process be designed to ensure the perception of acceptable legitimacy?

Although the success of international arbitration is so directly correlated to the absence of a unified international judicial system, the arbitral process has not developed a unified institutional structure either. This point was not lost on the pioneers of international arbitration. In 1961, at the first Congress of what would in due course became known as the International Council for Commercial Arbitration, the second and third topics were 'The Harmonization of the Procedural Rules of Arbitral Institutions' and 'The Creation of an International Agency Empowered to Appoint Arbitrators, Establish Arbitral Procedures, and Register Awards in Order to Facilitate their Execution'.[13] In the course of the ensuing decades, institutions having international ambitions have cooperated extensively and learned much from each other's experience. Indeed they have created the International Federation of Commercial Arbitration Associations for just this purpose. While a useful convergence of practices may thus unquestionably be observed with respect to arbitral procedure, and while institutions continually adapt their rules in light of the developments in the vital interface between national courts and the arbitral process, the same cannot be said with respect to the sensitive functions of appointing, remunerating, and (when necessary) removing arbitrators.

One approach to the problem might have been the creation of a universal institution. Hans Smit, then Director of the Parker School of Foreign and Comparative Law at Columbia University, specifically focused on concerns about the selection of arbitrators when he made a proposal in the form of an article with the self-explanatory title 'The Future of International Commercial Arbitration: A Single Transnational Institution?'[14] He called for 'a single global institution that would make uniformly improved processes and faculties available anywhere in the world'.[15] Existing institutions would be merged into 'branches', and if they declined to do so Professor Smit urged the International Chamber of Commerce to take the initiative alone.[16]

[13] Each topic was the subject of the report of a commission, discussed in the course of the congress and leading to a series of resolutions; see 1961 Rev. arb. 75, 98.

[14] Hans Smit, 'The Future of International Commercial Arbitration: A Single Transnational Institution?' 25 Colum. J. Transnat'l L. 9 (1986).

[15] Ibid. 28. [16] Ibid. 30.

Whether this proposal was ever feasible or desirable is a matter for conjecture; it remained a road not taken. (The objections include cost, bureaucratisation, and monopolistic indolence.) At this stage, the existence of too many other successful institutions makes it implausible that the ICC would even attempt to assert hegemony. The future clearly lies in the emergence of fundamental best practices by which a variety of institutions, while preserving their identities and specific features which users may find attractive,[17] establish a baseline of acceptable practices.

Designing for legitimacy is not about efficiency. All institutions want to be known for good management, and understand that they must constantly seek to improve their practices. This is important, but obvious. The ground is well traversed. Practitioners are aware of the causes of waste, delay, and confusion, and are able to engage in constructive and practical debate about the remedies.

The same cannot be said of institutional legitimacy. It is self-evident as an abstract ideal, but specifics remain obscure. When arbitral institutions fail, it is unlikely to be because the rules of procedure to be applied by arbitrators operating under their aegis are defective. After all, decent rules of that type may readily be acquired by reproducing those of leading institutions. In itself, this is unlikely to ensure the confidence of arbitrants. A putative 'international' institution created in Fantasia is unlikely to build much trust if it is entirely run by Fantasians, or by a small self-perpetrating group; or if it tolerates unprofessional behaviour on the part of arbitrators, or indeed on the part of administrative staff—ranging from sensitive indiscretions to exploring personal professional opportunities when dealing with party representatives.

This is where institutional design comes in. Naturally, poor structures breed distrust. Citizens wonder about the human reality behind the visual props of the judiciary: majestic columns, high benches, august robes. Who chooses the judges? On what basis? How are they motivated? Are they the agents of an all-powerful executive? Are they chosen by popular vote, and do they engage in political campaigns funded by the contributions of the very lawyers who appear before them? Do they have tenure and adequate income, or are they vulnerable to corruption and influence-peddling? Given all these questions, one may well doubt that there are many countries where the citizenry has a comfortable and informed sense of judicial legitimacy.

International tribunals, having no jurisdiction save that bestowed upon them by consent, may be even more vulnerable to rejection by the very parties whose disputes they were designed to judge, because they are in a position, as the saying goes, to vote with their feet.[18]

[17] E.g. some users believe that arbitrator's fees should be computed on an ad valorem basis (the ICC model), while others are convinced of the merits of the time-spent basis (the LCIA model). Both have advantages and disadvantages which may be debated endlessly without proving that either is generally superior.

[18] Two authors called attention to their analysis of voting patterns in the ICJ by publishing an article under the title 'Is the International Court of Justice Biased?' They suggested that judges tended to favour states whose 'wealth level' and—to a somewhat lesser degree—'democracy' level, language, and religion corresponded to that of their own county. Eric Posner and Miguel de Figueiredo, 'Is the International

It is difficult to establish, nurture, and maintain permanent organizations able to supervise the arbitral process in a manner perceived to be legitimate. What they purport to provide is not bricks and mortar, but a pattern of practices that make it acceptable for them to serve as custodians of a process which leads to the binding resolution of disputes. They are quite simply organs of justice. They therefore require the invaluable qualities—the ability to generate consistent processes and organized hierarchies and thus to achieve order, efficiency, and the impartial application of rules—that Max Weber ascribed to sound bureaucracies, essential to successful modern societies. To attain them requires treasure, endurance (including the ability to offer career prospects sufficient to attract incorruptible personnel), and much more: reputation. This is not achieved easily or quickly, especially when set against the constant clamour for less costly processes—and the resourcefulness of arbitrants whose conduct relentlessly add to those costs.

Half a century ago, it was possible for arbitral institutions to present themselves to the international community as purveyors of important innovations of concepts and technique. The very invention of rules that assimilated and catered for the international dimension of dispute resolution was, it seemed, sufficient to justify the creation of such institutions. This is no longer enough. The techniques are now well known. The rules of arbitral institutions are fundamentally similar. The proliferating new entrants have very little new to offer, and are prone to instances of ineptness due to a lack of experience and reliable information. The challenge today is not technique, but human resources and—above all—legitimacy.

To be blunt, only a few arbitral institutions can make credible claims to legitimacy. The naïve announcements of many new entrants fool no one acquainted with the field. That arbitral institutions have 'good rules' is no achievement at all. Anyone sitting at a computer could copy a sterling set of borrowed rules instantly. It does not take much longer for a reasonably resourceful person to establish a purported governing board comprised of individuals happy to lend their names to what might be a useful venture (but will cost them little if it fails).

Soon after a period of naïvely hopeful inactivity, such would-be institutions are likely to become empty edifices waiting only for someone to bother to dismantle them. Another substantial category of institutions simply are not up to the task, or are imbued with features of cronyism which were their *raison d'être* in the first place. Both of these categories create challenges for serious institutions, which run the danger of being

Court of Justice Biased?' U. Chicago Law & Economics, Olin Working Paper No. 234 (2004). The economic jargon did not impress the imposing figure of Rosalyn Higgins, who, in an address to the American Society of International Law, shortly before she assumed the presidency of the ICJ, departed from her customary reserve to deliver some very sharp blows, castigating this approach as showing 'no familiarity with the real issues with which the judge is grappling in the particular cases. For this approach to have any worth, the reader must be sure that the data invoked is correct; that the statistical model is scientifically valid; and that in any event bias *can* be determined in a substantive void, merely by reference to a vote that has been cast. The approach fails on every one of these heads.' See Rosalyn Higgins, *ASIL Proceedings of the 99th Annual Meeting* (2005), 136.

tarred with the same brush. For the decent institutions, the task of reform is work that never stays done. The objectives tend to be constant, but the problems as well as the solutions evolve in reaction to the craftiness of poachers and gamekeepers.[19]

[19] Areas of innovation are suggested and outlined in Jan Paulsson, *The Idea of Arbitration* (Oxford University Press, 2013), 286–97, from which some passages have been reproduced or adapted in this far more succinct contribution.

CHAPTER 5

TRANSNATIONAL PUBLIC POLICY IN INTERNATIONAL ARBITRATION

STAVROS BREKOULAKIS

PUBLIC policy is a key concept for international arbitration, being important for the work of both arbitration practitioners and scholars. It is important for scholars because it has provided the underpinning foundations for the development of theories on transnational autonomy of arbitration. It is important for practitioners because it is enshrined in the 1958 New York Convention for the Recognition and Enforcement of Foreign Arbitral Awards as well as almost all national laws as a ground to resist enforcement of arbitral awards.

It is perhaps because of its theoretical complexity and dynamic nature that the public policy exception 'has been interpreted erratically by the courts and is probably the most misused ground of all [in the New York Convention]'.[1] Equally, arbitration literature on public policy seems to be informed more by conventional wisdom than by critical examination. It is interesting to see that the majority of arbitration literature as well as all the main textbooks in international arbitration offer broadly the same, if equivocal, definition of public policy, as a general principle associated with 'basic notions of morality and justice'.[2] It is also amusing to note that almost no paper on public policy can resist reiterating Burrough J's famous (and by now commonplace) description from almost

[1] Jan Paulsson, 'The New York Convention in International Practice: Problems of Assimilation in the New York Convention of 1958' (ASA, 1996), 100, 113.

[2] Julian Lew, Loukas Mistelis, and Stefan Kroell, *Comparative and International Commercial Arbitration* (Kluwer, 2003), 26–114. See also International Law Association, *Final Report on Public Policy* (New Delhi Conference, 2002).

two centuries ago of public policy as an unruly horse,[3] a phrase which apparently highlights the open-ended, unpredictable and constantly evolving nature of the doctrine.

Has the discussion on public policy in international arbitration settled? I submit not. In fact, I suggest that there are a number of areas related to the doctrine of transnational public policy (or *ordre public international*) that must be revisited, including its very concept, function, and limitations. As explained in the sections below, I submit that the doctrine of transnational public policy which is currently adopted by legal discourse in international arbitration is conceptually and methodologically confusing. There is usually no explanation about how the content and norms of transnational public policy are ascertained, or whether the doctrine functions as a legal principle or a set of legal rules.

The chapter is divided into three sections. After a brief overview of the historical evolution of transnational public policy in section 5.1, section 5.2 examines the legal function of transnational public policy. This section challenges the predominant view in scholarship and in arbitral case law that transnational public policy is a fluid concept that accords arbitrators wide discretion to decide on the basis of non-legal standards such as 'morals', 'values', or 'principles of universal justice'. By contrast, it is suggested, transnational public policy is a legal doctrine which cannot include anything other than *legal* norms, in the form of either legal rules or legal principles.

As is explained, the clear distinction between legal and non-legal conceptions of transnational public policy matters because it has important implications on the judicial function of tribunals in international arbitration. Under a conception of transnational public policy that includes non-legal standards, judicial function is dangerously conflated with legislative function and international arbitrators assume the role of the 'regulators of society', which runs counter to the way our world is politically organized today.

Section 5.3 sets out to identify the rules and principle of transnational public policy. Only a limited number of rules and principles of transnational public policy have developed in relation to some aspects of international commercial and trade law, such as the transnational policy rule prohibiting contracts of bribery and contracts arising out of bribery, and the principle of good faith. The section submits that a transnational rule on public policy can emerge only if a clear policy is evidenced in a wide number of international legal documents, including arbitral awards and court decisions, as well as international conventions and legal instruments promulgated by international or intergovernmental organizations. As is explained, substituting normative views for transnational public policy, as some tribunals have felt empowered to do, is methodologically unjustified and eventually counterproductive.

More generally, the chapter suggests that contrary to what some scholars have suggested,[4] transnational public policy is not a principle that permeates transnational law. In a world where policy contestations persist in a wide number of important areas, such as tax law, environmental law, and even competition law, transnational public

[3] In *Richardson v Mellish*, (1824) 2 Bing. 229, 252.

[4] Catherine Kessedjian, 'Transnational Public Policy', in Albert Jan van den Berg (ed), *International Arbitration 2006: Back to Basics?* (Kluwer Law International, 2007), 857–70.

policy, for better or worse, cannot be used as a legal construct to regulate international business law towards a liberal end.

5.1 Historical Development of Public Policy

Traditionally linked with the broader project of *lex mercatoria*,[5] transnational public policy was the birth child of liberal—mainly continental—arbitration lawyers, such as Professors Fouchard, Goldman, and Lalive. Having lived, studied, and worked in a number of different countries, these international lawyers developed a strong cosmopolitan outlook and a unique appreciation of different legal cultures and traditions. Sustaining a strong belief in the reformist power of international law, transnationalist lawyers conceptualized transnational public policy as the underpinning legal justification for the construction of a transnational legal order, which transcends national boundaries and legal traditions.

According to Pierre Lalive, the arbitration theorist and practitioner, who widely introduced the concept of transnational public policy in the 1980s, 'the international arbitrator does have, and is bound by, a private international law, but…such private international law can only be a "transnational" one, constituted as it is by a number of general principles, either common to all the parties (including States) concerned by a given case, or universal.'[6]

More importantly, perhaps, for many transnationalist arbitration scholars and lawyers, transnational public policy has been used as a moral and normative framework that embeds rules, values, and objectives of a constitutional nature. It has been conceived as the main organizational principle that sustains the integrity of the system of international arbitration, as well as a potent principled defence against claims that arbitration is often employed as the vehicle for powerful corporate interests to escape national regulation.[7] In that sense, transnational public policy provides international tribunals with a legal and moral obligation to refuse to enforce repugnant contracts ex officio, irrespective of whether a contract is illegal under its governing law.[8] Such a constitutional

[5] See Jan Kleinheisterkamp, 'The Myth of Transnational Public Policy' (working paper).

[6] See Pierre Lalive, 'Transnational (or Truly International) Public Policy and International Arbitration', in Pieter Sanders (ed.), *Comparative Arbitration Practice and Public Policy in Arbitration* (Kluwer Law International, 1986), 301. More recently, Emmanuel Gaillard, *Legal Theory of International Arbitration* (Martinus Nijhoff, 2010), further developed the concept of substantive transnational public policy, whereas Julian Lew, in 'Achieving the Dream: Autonomous Arbitration', 22 Arb Int'l 179 (2006), has theorized on transnational procedural public policy.

[7] See A. Claire Cutler, *Private Power and Global Authority: Transnational Merchant Law in the Global Political Economy* (Cambridge University Press, 2003).

[8] See Gaillard (n. 6), 126–30; Lalive (n. 6), 258.

conception of transnational public policy assumes a shift in the duty of international arbitrators from assisting commercial parties in dealing with their dispute to rendering justice, including if necessary taking account of *wider social interests* or *interests of the public*.[9] Thus, transnational public policy has been mainly conceived as a liberal project which allows international lawyers, acting as arbitrators, to complement, or occasionally replace, positive law with their perceptions (which are typically more liberal than those of national judges) of what is good for the public.

Despite its normative purpose, the liberal project of transnational public policy has been met with fierce opposition. For many legal positivists, international law is exclusively structured around the idea of the nation-state, which is seen as the indispensable framework of legal order.[10] Only rules that are derived from a formal source—typically sovereignty—and developed through formal processes are accepted as law.[11] Transnational public policy, therefore, cannot exist because no valid legal norm exists beyond and outside the hierarchy of the state; at best, transnational public policy is nothing more than 'a statement of practical policy', an ideal that we should aspire to.[12]

The objections to transnational law and transnational public policy are well documented in legal literature and there is little point in rehearsing them here, not least because the discussion about transnational law has moved in the last thirty years in particular. Today, the existence of informal legal norms by non-state actors has been increasingly recognized by a number of international law scholars under either analytical jurisprudence[13] or social-legal lines of inquiry.[14] While views favouring formalism and the exclusivity of state law still persist in international legal scholarship,[15] our

9 See Alec Stone Sweet and Florian Grisel, 'The Evolution of International Arbitration: Delegation, Judicialization, Governance', in Walter Mattli and Thomas Dietz (eds), *International Arbitration and Global Governance: Contending Theories and Evidence* (Oxford University Press, 2014), 36.

10 See Paul Lagarde, 'Approach critique de la lex mercatoria', in Philippe Fouchard et al. (eds), *Law of International Economic Relations: A Study Offered to Berthold Goldman* (Litec, 1982).

11 See Francis Mann, 'The UNCITRAL Model Law: Lex Facit Arbitrum', in Pieter Sanders (ed.), *International Arbitration: Liber Amicorum for Martin Domke*; repr. in 2 Arb. Int'l 241 (1986), 241–2 (noting that only recently has arbitration been released from the strictures of formal law).

12 See Lord Justice Mustill, 'The New Lex Mercatoria: The First Twenty-Five Years', 4 Arb. Int'l 86 (1988), 90.

13 See John Linarelli, 'Analytical Jurisprudence and the Concept of Commercial Law', 114 Penn St. L. Rev. 119 (2009), 193 (employing analytical methods to develop a framework for international law); Cralf-Peter Calliess and Peer Zumbansen, *Rough Consensus and Running Code* (Hart, 2010), 56 (relying on the method of 'rough consensus and running code' to develop an analytical framework of transnational law); Ross Cranston, 'Theorizing Transnational Commercial Law', 42 Tex. Int'l L. J. 597 (2007), 602.

14 See here legal pluralism. See Roger Cotterrell, 'Transnational Communities and the Concept of Law', 21 Ratio Juris 1 (2008), 5–6; François Ost and Michel Van de Kerchove, *De la pyramide au réseau? Pour une théorie dialectique du droit* (Publications Fac. St Louis, 2002), 14 (speaking about networks); Robert Wai, 'The Interlegality of Transnational Private Law', 71 L. & Contemp. Probs. 107 (2008), 110.

15 See e.g. Martti Koskenniemi, *The Politics of International Law* (Hart, 2011), 214 (arguing in favour of formalism in international law); Jean d'Aspremont, *Formalism and the Sources of International Law: A Theory of the Ascertainment of Legal Rules* (Oxford University Press, 2011) (arguing that a formal theory of sources remains instrumental in ascertaining rules of international law); Thomas Schultz, 'Some Critical Comments on the Juridicity of Lex Mercatoria', 10 Y.B. of Priv. Int'l L. 667 (2008) (arguing that lex mercatoria lacks the formal requirements which are essential features of a legal system).

understanding of law has irrevocably shifted from the Austinian thesis that law can only be rules backed by threats to a more inclusive and pluralistic concept of law that accepts both state legal rules[16] and a-national or transnational legal standards, in the form of principles, norms and policies—including transnational public policy.[17]

More crucially, it is not only transnational lawyers and scholars who accept that transnational public policy is a valid legal construct rather than an aspiring ideal. A number of national courts, such as the Paris Cour d'appel,[18] the French Cour de cassation,[19] the Swiss Federal Tribunal,[20] and the UK House of Lords, have referred with approval to the concept of transnational public policy.[21]

Today, the main opposition to transnational public policy appears to be more ideological than legal, namely that it reflects a laissez-faire conception of economic liberalism which allows parties to settle their disputes in the shadow of national law.[22] While this discussion is interesting, it goes beyond the scope of this chapter. Accepting the assumption that transnational public policy is a valid legal norm rather than an aspirational ideal, this chapter is mainly concerned with the legal function as well as the content of transnational public policy. Despite the important role that transnational public policy has played in the construction of the concept of international arbitration, both of these questions, especially the former, remain largely under-theorized.

5.2 Nature and Legal Function

Theorists who developed the basic conceptual foundations of transnational public policy and many international arbitration tribunals have always assumed that transnational

[16] See John Austin, *The Province of Jurisprudence Determined* (Weidenfeld & Nicolson, 1954), 13–16.

[17] See Cotterrell (n. 14), 4–5. Even Hart was open to the idea of international law. See H. L. A. Hart, *The Concept of Law*, 2nd edn (Clarendon Press, 1994), 235 (observing that there is no need to search for a basic law (a *Grundnorm*) in international law, and while we can resign ourselves to the idea that international law may not be a system of legal rules, it can well qualify as set of legal rules). There is no need to look for analogies between international law and municipal law in terms of form (because the analogies are too thin), but Hart accepts that there are important analogies in terms of function and content: 'the analogies of content consist in the range of principles, concepts, and methods which are common to both municipal and international law, and make the lawyers' technique freely transferable from the one to the other'.

[18] See *European Gas Turbines SA v Westman International* Ltd, 30 September 1993, (1994) Rev. Arb. 350 note by D. Bureau, and *Fougerolle v Procofrance*, 25 May 1990, (1992) Rev crit. DIP 1990.

[19] See Cour de cassation 1st Civ 23 March 1994, *Société Hilmarton Ltd v société Omnium de traitement et de valorization (OTV)*, JDI 1994, at 701.

[20] See *Emirats Arabes Unis, Royaume d'Arabie Saoudite and others v Westland Helicopters Limited*, 12 ASA Bulletin 52 (1994); *State agency A and State owned bank B v Consultant X*, Tribunal Fédéral, First Civil Chamber, 4P 115/1994, 30 December 1994, in Albert Jan van den Berg (ed.), *XXI Yearbook Commercial Arbitration* (1996), 172–80. Also see Swiss Supreme Court, 4P.278/2005, 8 March 2006, 24 ASA Bulletin 550 (2006).

[21] See *Kuwait Airways Corp v Iraqi Airways Co* (No. 6), [2002] UKHL 19; [2002] 2 A.C. 883 (HL); Adeline Chong, 'Transnational Public Policy in Civil and Commercial Matters', 128 LQR 88 (2012).

[22] See e.g. Cutler (n. 7).

public policy affords arbitrators a wide range of discretion as to how to address a legal question. Under this conception of transnational public policy, international arbitration tribunals can find that a contract is void as against public policy even if it is not illegal under its governing law.

For transnationalist lawyers, transnational public policy is a concept of equitable nature, a statement of predominately moral purpose that includes a number of divergent, if vague, ideas such as 'fundamental rules of natural law', 'principles of universal justice', '*jus cogens*', and 'general principles of morality accepted by what are referred to as "civilized nations"'.[23] The prevailing understanding of transnational public policy in international arbitration is that of a fluid concept whose content is difficult, if not unnecessary, to identify in advance, because it largely depends on the circumstances of the dispute as well as the values of the decision maker. Lalive, for example, refers to transnational public policy as allowing the incorporation in arbitration of 'the *new needs* and *ideas* of the international community',[24] and observes that 'a great deal if not everything' about transnational public policy 'is a question of *personal feeling* or *sensitiveness*'.[25]

However, it is questionable whether this account of transnational public policy *is* or *ought* to be accurate. Guidance from national concepts of public policy may be instructive here. The judicial function of public policy varies in different jurisdictions. The banal generalization about the distinct legal approaches taken by common and civil law jurisdictions applies in full force in relation to public policy. Common law courts, especially in England, have kept public policy confined in certain areas of law and have developed clear and well-defined public policy *rules* to the point that the modern concept of public policy has been criticized as inflexible and unjust.[26]

For example, in the field of illegal contracts English courts have developed the *ex turpi causa* rule of public policy, whereby 'no court will lend its aid to a man who founds his cause of action upon an immoral or an illegal act'.[27] Even under the latest decision of the UK Supreme Court in *Patel v Mirza*,[28] which adopts a more flexible test for illegality on the basis of a number of public policy considerations, arguably allowing some degree of discretion to English judges, the boundaries of the public policy rule are jurisprudentially defined.

[23] Martin Hunter & Gui Conde e Silva, 'Transnational Public Policy and Its Application in Investment Arbitrations', 4(3) Journal of World Investment 367, 370 (2003); International Law Association, 'Report on Public Policy as a Bar to Enforcement of International Arbitral Awards', (2002), Recommendation 1(d) about international public policy and 2(b) about transnational public policy.

[24] See Lalive (n. 6), 316.

[25] Ibid. 310 (emphasis added).

[26] See John Shand, 'Unblinkering the Unruly Horse: Public Policy in the Law of Contract', 30 Cambridge Law Journal 144 (1972), 165: 'for the judges have themselves reacted from the broad and vaporous concept of public policy and reduced it to a set of rules whose operation is predictable and whose application is obligatory and not a matter of discretion.'

[27] See Lord Mansfield's well-known dictum in *Holman v Johnson*, (1775) 1 Cowp. 341, 343: 'The principle of public policy is this; *ex dolo malo non oritur actio*. No court will lend its aid to a man who founds his cause of action upon an immoral or an illegal act.'

[28] See *Patel v Mirza*, [2016] UKSC 42.

By contrast, in most civil law jurisdictions public policy is conceived of as a *legal principle* or *a set of legal principles* which, laid down in civil codes, allow judges discretion to ascertain the content of public policy. In France, for example, principles of public interest, including principles of morality, play a greater part in the courts' decision to refuse to enforce an agreement as contrary to French public policy.[29]

However, while the nature of public policy and judicial function may vary under civil and common law, public policy is a *legal* doctrine under both legal traditions. While non-legal considerations, such as 'morals' or 'values', appear in civil codes and court judgments, the legal nature of public policy does not change. Judges in neither civil nor common law rely on morality, in and of itself, to invalidate contracts as being against public policy. Rather, they rely on legal principles of public policy underpinned by moral and ethical considerations, such as the principle of good faith or the *ex turpi causa*.

Even in civil law jurisdictions, public policy is largely conceived of by reference to fundamental legal and judicial principles. French courts, for example, have defined public policy as including 'the entirety of the *rules*... of fundamental importance which the French legal system requires to be respected even in situations of an international character'.[30]

In Switzerland, the Federal Tribunal has stated:

> The substantive adjudication of a dispute violates public policy only when it disregards some fundamental *legal principles* and consequently becomes completely inconsistent with the important, generally recognized values, which according to dominant opinions in Switzerland should be the basis of any legal order.[31]

In both jurisdictions, public policy encompasses *legal* principles which form part of their legal order, including such principles as *pacta sunt servanda*, the prohibition of abuse of rights, the principle of good faith, the prohibition of expropriation without compensation, the principles of economic freedom, the prohibition of discrimination, the prohibition of corruption, and the protection of personal property.[32]

[29] See Dennis Lloyd, *Public Policy: A Comparative Study in English and French Law* (Gaunt, 1953), 5; also, morals are enshrined in Art. 6 of the French Civil Code which provides that 'statutes relating to public policy and morals may not be derogated from by private agreements'. Art. 1133: 'A cause is unlawful where it is prohibited by legislation, where it is contrary to public morals or to public policy.'

[30] See Paris Court of Appeal, Judgment of 27 October 1994, Rev. Arb. 1994, 709.

[31] 4A_558/20111 Judgment of March 27, 2012 (emphasis added).

[32] See further in Switzerland, Andreas Bucher, 'L'ordre public et le but social des lois en droit international privé', 239 Recueil des cours (1993), 19; Elliott Geisinger and Alexandre Mazuranic, 'Challenge and Revision of the Award', in Elliott Geisinger and Nathalie Voser (eds), *International Arbitration in Switzerland: A Handbook for Practitioners*, 2nd edn (Kluwer Law International, 2013), 249; Gabrielle Kaufmann-Kohler and Antonio Rigozzi, *International Arbitration: Law and Practice in Switzerland*, 3rd edn (Oxford University Press, 2015), 499. The same in Poland: see Johannes Koepp and Agnieszka Ason, 'An Anti-Enforcement Bias? The Application of the Substantive Public Policy Exception in Polish Annulment Proceedings', in *Liber Amicorum Wojciech Popiołek; Polish Court of Civil Procedure*, Art. 1206 §2(2): 'An arbitral award shall also be set aside if the court finds that... the arbitral award is contrary to fundamental principles of the legal order of the Republic of Poland (public order clause).'

The difference, thus, in the judicial function of public policy between civil and common law jurisdictions is a matter of degree, not kind. In other words, while civil and common law jurisdictions allow a different degree of discretion to national courts in ascertaining public policy in the form of a legal rule (in common law) or a legal principle (in civil law), they both require judges to decide a public policy matter on the basis of legal, not extra-legal, considerations. While in non-legal fields, public policy is generally defined as encompassing 'the common sense and common conscience of the citizens as a whole' as well as the 'changing economic needs, social customs, and moral aspirations of the people',[33] the legal concept of public policy, including that of transnational public policy, cannot include anything other than *legal* norms, in the form of either legal rules or legal principles.[34]

The clear distinction between legal and non-legal conceptions of public policy matters because it has important implications on the judicial function of tribunals in international arbitration. Indeed, under a conception of transnational public policy that includes non-legal standards such as 'morals', 'needs', 'ideas', and 'personal feeling or sensitiveness', the judicial function is dangerously conflated with the legislative function. However, transnational public policy should not operate as a gateway for judges and arbitrators to substitute legal reasoning with political expedience and decide on the basis of their personal sense of what they think 'good morals' means for the public. The suggestion of some transnationalist lawyers, such as Kessedjian, that the 'role of the judge or the arbitrator [today is] an essential one for *the regulation of society*' runs counter to fundamental principles of political organization and democratic governance of the majority of states today.

Transnational public policy reflects the fundamental policies of that legal system, and therefore the mandate of international arbitrators is to identify the rules and principles of transnational public policy by reference to legal doctrine rather than principles of moral theory, sociology and political economy. As Reisman observes, for a judge or an arbitrator the 'use of policy is a highly disciplined teleological exercise. [I]t is the policy of the legal system which governs the dispute and not an artifacted policy created by the arbitrators for that particular case.'[35]

The above analysis does not mean that public policy should be equated to the law. The scope of public policy is wider than that of a statute, and courts may render an agreement null and void as being contrary to public policy, even if it is not against

[33] See Jeffrey Lehman and Shirelle Phelps, *West's Encyclopedia of American Law*, 2nd edn (Thomson/Gale, 2005), 173.

[34] See Christopher Gibson, 'Arbitration, Civilization and Public Policy: Seeking Counterpoise between Arbitral Autonomy and the Public Policy Defence in View of Foreign Mandatory Public Law', 113 Penn State Law Review 1227 (2009), 1234, who inaccurately states that 'it is useful to consider the concept of public policy in arbitration as not only reflecting principles fundamental to the dispute resolution method itself, but also as an "interface of exchange" with a larger civilization outside of arbitration.'

[35] See W. Michael Reisman, 'Law, International Public Policy (so-called) and Arbitral Choice in International Commercial Arbitration', in van den Berg (n. 4), 849.

the law.[36] Equally, it does not mean that public policy operates only as a set of inflexible legal rules which allow no discretion. In applying public policy, judges and arbitrators may enjoy some degree of discretion in particular first, when a dispute gives rise to a novel legal issue. In such nowadays rare circumstances, public policy will largely operate as a general principle of law that permits a judge to introduce new legal rules in order to determine whether the novel situation is contrary to the public interest.[37] The determination of a public policy rule and its application to a novel issue, inevitably, necessitates a value judgment by the judge or arbitrator. But this value judgment has defined parameters, and involves a balancing exercise on the basis of existing policies and principles of law. In addressing a novel legal issue, judges are not free to arrive at novel legal policies, or substitute their personal policies for the existing policies of the law in a certain legal system.

However, even when courts are called to exercise discretion under general principles of public policy, judicial function is not unrestrained. Under both common and civil law, national courts have developed certain *tests* to guide, and therefore constrain, the exercise of judicial discretion under public policy. In English law, for example, whether an agreement aiming to restrain trade is contrary to public policy depends on the *test of reasonableness*, which allows English courts to perform a balancing exercise after taking account of the interests of the parties concerned and the interests of the public.[38] Similarly, under Swiss law the test as to whether the power, which a professional association exercises over its members, is against public policy is whether it constitutes an *obvious and grave violation of privacy*, including the right of the member to professional development.[39] While the balancing exercise which the courts have to perform in order to resolve conflicting public interests allows for a value judgment, it does not give national courts unbounded discretion to decide whether public policy is violated on the basis of 'opinions of men of the world'.[40]

Overall, the judicial function under public policy entails that a judge or an arbitrator identifies the public policy rule or ascertains a public policy principle on the basis of 'opinions based on legal learning'.[41] How judges and arbitrators carry out their judicial task and ascertain fundamental policies of the law is not always straightforward, not least because the policy of the law is constantly, albeit slowly, evolving. In all cases, however, they have to rely on legal reasoning and analysis, including review of statutes, judicial

[36] See e.g. in France, René David and Henry De Vries, *The French Legal System: An Introduction To Civil Law Systems* (Oceana, 1958), 134.

[37] See John Bell, *Policy Arguments in Judicial Decisions* (Oxford University Press, 1983), 157.

[38] *Nordenfelt v Maxim Nordenfelt Guns and Ammunition*, [1894] C 535, 565 (per Lord Macnaghten), which remains binding authority.

[39] See Swiss Federal Tribunal Judgment of 27 March 2012, 4A_558/20111 and also judgment 4A_458/2009 of 10 June 2010.

[40] *Rodriguez v Speyer Bros*, [1919] A.C. 59 (Lord Haldane).

[41] Ibid.

precedent, legal doctrine, general principles of law, or even soft law.[42] But the judicial function of judges and arbitrators in ascertaining fundamental policies of the law does not entail surveying the 'changing economic needs, social customs and moral aspirations of the people'.[43] This is the task of the legislator, whose duty is to pass law that reflects contemporary moral standards and social norms.

However, as already mentioned, the prevailing view on transnational public policy in international arbitration betrays confusion about its legal function, with some international arbitral tribunals employing public policy to arrive at decisions on the basis of non-legal considerations.

For example, in ICC Case No. 15300 of 2011, the respondent, a trading company in East Europe, was bidding for a public construction contract in a West Asian state and entered into an agency agreement with the claimant, a company from West Asia, whereby the latter would act as the agent of the former in the procurement process. The respondent won the contract, parts of which were to be performed by a third company. When a dispute arose over the payment of commission under the agency agreement, it became apparent that the parties had in fact entered into two agency agreements. Under the first agreement the parties had agreed on a commission of 4 per cent of the contract price with respect to delivery or service performed in East Europe, and a commission of 3 per cent of the contract price with respect to deliveries or services performed outside East Europe. Under the second agreement, the parties had agreed on a commission of 5 per cent irrespective of where the deliveries or services were performed. The sole arbitrator, siting in Paris, found that the agreement for 5 per cent commission was a scheme for reverse payments ('kick-backs') with the aim of deceiving the third company into paying a commission of 5 per cent to the claimant, which would then pay the excess over the 4 per cent and 3 per cent commission to the respondent. While, as is discussed in section 5.2, bribery and corruption is against transnational public policy, reverse payments are prohibited neither by transnational public policy nor by the public policy of Swiss or French law (the law governing the contract and the law of the seat of the arbitration respectively).[44]

However, the tribunal substituted 'standards of basic morality' for law and public policy, and rendered the parties' agreement void, holding as follows:

[42] See Lloyd (n. 29), 2. Even in France where the concept of *ordre public* is broader than that of public policy in common law countries, allowing courts to depart from strict law to protect social policies by reason of public policy, courts are only able to rely on legal principles of public policy which are derived from written law and general principles of law, and rules which are fundamental to France. See e.g. Jean-Louis Delvové et al., *French Arbitration Law And Practice: A Dynamic Civil Law Approach To International Arbitration*, 2nd edn (Kluwer Law International, 2009), 155–7, 254–60. Also see the U.S. Supreme Court's observation that public policy must be 'well defined and dominant' and based not on 'general considerations of supposed public interests' but on 'laws and legal precedents': *United Paperworkers v Misco, Inc.*, 484 U.S. 29 (1987), 30.

[43] See Lehman and Phelps (n. 33), 173.

[44] See e.g. Swiss Federal Tribunal, 4C.432/2005 of 22 March 2006, BGE/ATF 132 III 460.

> International commercial relationships must meet standards of basic morality in order to be able to claim enforcement of the obligations contracted for. The Sole arbitrator is aware that he is not confronted with issues such as bribery, money laundering, deviation of embargo provisions, violation of competition laws or similar acts for which international treaty instruments would be governing. Nevertheless, the Sole Arbitrator is of the conviction that an international agency agreement which is entered into for the sole purposes to deceive a third party, and thus violates such third party's contractual rights in a manner which is 'particularly offensive', cannot crave for enforcement with the help of the arbitral system, irrespective of whether and under which legal system such act is or would be considered as a criminal offence and without the Sole Arbitrator having to determine the specific legal ramifications of such act in general... In the Sole Arbitrator's conviction, it would not be compatible with fundamental values of international commerce, necessary to allow business being conducted in a loyal surrounding, to lend a helping hand to such agreements.[45]

Similar approaches have been taken by other arbitration tribunals, for example in ICC case No. 3916 of 1982,[46] or in ICC Case No. 3913 of 1981, where the tribunal annulled a consultancy agreement between a French contractor and a British company as being effectively a reverse payment scheme, which, according to the tribunal, was immoral under the 'concept of international public policy as recognised by most nations'.[47]

It is worrying to see that some arbitration tribunals feel empowered under a misplaced concept of transnational public policy to render decisions on the basis of what they consider to be basic standards of morality, no matter how lofty such standards may be. 'Loyalty' (or 'loyal surrounding') is, arguably, a desirable value in international business. However, it is not a fundamental policy protected in law, unlike for example the policy whereby contracting parties ought to be kept to their agreements.[48] Invalidating an agreement, which is not illegal under its governing law or the law of the seat of the arbitration, on the basis that it runs counter to the value of loyalty, is not the kind of legal

[45] Also see ICC Award 6248 of 1990 in Jean-Jacques Arnaldez, Yves Derains, and Dominique Hascher, *Collection of ICC Arbitral Awards 1991–1995* (ICC, 1997), 239; also published in *XIX Yearbook Commercial Arbitration* (1994), 124.

[46] See ICC Case No. 3916 of 1982, in Sigvard Jarvin and Yves Derains (eds), *Collection of ICC Arbitral Awards 1974–1985* (Kluwer Law International, 1994), 51, where the tribunal annulled a consultancy contract, on the basis that the claimant was engaged in activities of exercising influence over public officials of a foreign government (although it was not proved that the intention of the parties was for such purpose), as being against 'a legal principle generally recognized by civilized nations according to which agreement that in serious violation of moral standards or international public policy are null and void or at least cannot be performed'.

[47] See ICC Case No. 3913 of 1981, in Jarvin and Derains (n. 46), 497, where the tribunal annulled a consultancy agreement between a French contractor and a British company as being effectively a reverse payment scheme, which is immoral under the 'concept of international public policy as recognised by most nations'.

[48] See Shand (n. 26), 147; Gerard Brennan, 'Commercial Law and Morality', 17 Melb. U. L. Rev. 100 (1990).

reasoning and judicial function which is expected of arbitrators under the legal doctrine of transnational public policy.

While morals, values, and other non-legal considerations can serve as an underpinning justification of public policy, they cannot be a distinct ground of public policy. Under transnational public policy, arbitration tribunals are constrained in the exercise of their judicial function, and are not generally free to take account of equities. Once an arbitration tribunal identifies a transnational public policy rule, the arbitrator should apply this rule irrespective of whether other overriding moral considerations might suggest that the rule should not apply in the circumstances of the case, or that the application of this rule should be moderated. Conceived as a legal doctrine, transnational public policy does not accord arbitrators discretion to refuse its application in order to give effect to a competing policy, or to correct a harsh outcome or the perceived imbalances of merits between the parties in a particular dispute.[49] Administration of justice is not part of the judicial function of international arbitral tribunals under transnational public policy.

Again, some tribunals have confused the scope of their judicial function, taking equities into consideration under transnational public policy. In the celebrated ICC Case No. 1110 of 1963, for example, a British company engaged an intermediary to secure a public works contract in Argentina in return of a commission of fee amounting to 10 per cent of the value of the contract. When the intermediary brought an arbitration claim, Judge Lagergren, as sole arbitrator, declined jurisdiction to hear the case on the basis that the agreement in question would 'seriously violate *bonos mores* or international public policy' because, as he found *ex officio*, the parties had entered into the contract with an implicit intention of bribing the officials of the Argentinian government.

Judge Lagergren first stated the international public policy rule prohibiting corruption, and he then went on to examine whether the application of this public policy rule might cause injustice in the factual circumstances of the case. Citing 'the interest of due administrating of justice', he observed:

> before invoking good morals and public policy as barring parties from recourse to judicial or arbitral instances in settling their disputes care must be taken to see that one party is not thereby enabled to reap the fruits of his own dishonest conduct by enriching himself at the expense of the other.[50]

Thankfully, not all tribunals confuse their judicial role and function under transnational public policy. In *WDF v Kenya*, the arbitral tribunal carefully reviewed a wide number of international awards and national judgments, as well as international legal instruments, including international conventions and declaration of the General

[49] See *Les Laboratories Servier & Another v Apotex Inc. & Others*, [2014] UKSC 55, 440 (per Lord Sumption).

[50] See ICC Case No. 1110 of 1963, in van den Berg (n. 20), para. 21. Judge Lagergren was eventually satisfied that the application of transnational public policy would not lead to injustice on this occasion, and concluded that he should decline jurisdiction.

Assembly of the United Nations against Corruption and Bribery in International Commercial Transactions, before concluding that a transnational public policy rule against bribery and corruption exists. Avoiding reference to broader non-legal considerations, such as morality, *bonos mores*, or principles of universal justice, the tribunal stated:

> In light of domestic laws and international conventions relating to corruption, and in light of the decisions taken in this matter by courts and arbitral tribunals, this Tribunal is convinced that bribery is contrary to the international public policy or most, if not all, States or, to use another formula, to transnational public policy.[51]

The tribunal also rightly found that the application of a transnational public policy rule is not amenable to equitable corrections.[52] While it acknowledged that the claimant had been solicited to offer a bribe by the Kenyan president himself, and that for that reason the claimant was possibly justified to 'feel strongly the unfairness of the legal case now advanced by Kenya',[53] the tribunal noted that 'as regards public policy . . . the law protects not the litigating parties but the public; or in this case, the mass of taxpayers and other citizens making up one of the poorest countries in the world.'[54]

This observation was echoed by arbitration award in the ICSID Case No. ARB/10/3, where the investment treaty tribunal dismissed the claimant's claims on the basis that the contract under which the claims were made was procured by bribery. While the tribunal acknowledged that the outcome in cases of corruption often appear to challenge perceptions of fairness and justice, it pointed out that the main justification of the public policy defence is to promote 'the rule of law' rather than 'to punish one party at the cost of the other'.[55]

In conclusion, contrary to what transnationalist lawyers seem to believe,[56] transnational public policy is not a legal vehicle to promote liberal values and good morals. It is not a gateway whereby arbitrators can incorporate public discourse on current social, economic, and political affairs into the law.

[51] See *World Duty Free Co Ltd v Republic of Kenya*, ICSID Case No. ARB/00/7, para. 157.

[52] Although note that this was decided before the decision of the English Supreme Court in the case of *Patel v Mirza*, [2016] UKSC 42.

[53] *World Duty Free Co Ltd v Republic of Kenya*, ICSID Case No. ARB/00/7, para. 180.

[54] Ibid. para. 181.

[55] See *Metal-Tech Ltd v Republic of Uzbekistan*, ICSID Case No. ARB/10/3, para. 389: 'While reaching the conclusion that the claims are barred as a result of corruption, the Tribunal is sensitive to the ongoing debate that findings on corruption often come down heavily on claimants, while possibly exonerating defendants that may have themselves been involved in the corrupt acts. It is true that the outcome in cases of corruption often appears unsatisfactory because, at first sight at least, it seems to give an unfair advantage to the defendant party. The idea, however, is not to punish one party at the cost of the other, but rather to ensure the promotion of the rule of law, which entails that a court or tribunal cannot grant assistance to a party that has engaged in a corrupt act.'

[56] See Lalive (n. 6).

Transnational public policy is not a fluid concept allowing arbitrators unbounded judicial discretion either. While originally, in the sixteenth century, public policy was an amorphous and vague idea (a *Weltanschauung*),[57] positive law and jurisprudence became increasingly dense at both national and international level, and have now covered most of the legal ground which was previously occupied by abstract legal concepts such as reason and convenience. As a result, public policy including transnational public policy has nowadays acquired a more precise meaning in the form of legal rules or legal principles.[58]

With these observations on judicial function and nature of transnational public policy in mind, the following sections set out to identify the rules and principles of transnational public policy.

5.3 Content of Transnational Public Policy

5.3.1 Prohibition of bribery and corruption

As already suggested, the identification of rules and principles of transnational public policy involves a disciplined doctrinal exercise that includes review of international legal instruments as well as analysis of arbitral and judicial precedent. While some scholars have suggested that transnational public policy permeates transnational law,[59] a limited number of rules and principles of transnational public policy have developed in relation to only some aspects of international commercial and trade law.

The clearest manifestation of transnational public policy is the prohibition of contract with an illegal subject matter. The illustrative list of illegal contracts offered by transnational theorists typically includes contracts relating to the facilitation or promotion of drug trafficking, terrorist acts, prostitution, child abuse, and slavery.[60] Undoubtedly contracts concerning such kind of reprehensible activities would be contrary to established policies of most, if not all, national laws and international law. In commercial reality, though, the illegality question typically arises in relation to contracts about bribery and corruption.

The public policy rule on prohibition of bribery and corruption is narrower than what some arbitral awards have suggested,[61] and it mainly includes contracts whereby

[57] See Kleinheisterkamp (n. 5), where he traces the intellectual origins of transnational public policy in the development of lex mercatoria.

[58] See Percy Winfield, 'Public Policy in the English Common Law', 42 Harv. L. Rev. 76 (1929).

[59] Kessedjian (n. 4), 857–70.

[60] Lalive (n. 6); International Law Association (n. 23).

[61] See ICC Case No. 15300 of 2011, ICC Dispute Resolution Bulletin (Issue 1, 2016), 81–4.

two parties effectively agree to use illegal means, including illegal payments, in order to assist one of the parties to secure a public contract award. While such agreements may take the form of various contracts such as broker, sponsoring, agency, and consultancy contracts,[62] in essence these contracts are vehicles of bribery and corruption, and therefore the offensive nature and purpose of this type of contracts render them void *ab initio*.[63]

In addition to contracts with a corrupt subject matter (contracts of bribery), transnational public policy prohibits claims arising out of contracts that have been procured by bribery, on the ground of the general principle *ex turpi causa non oritur actio* ('from a dishonourable cause an action does not arise'). Unlike, however, contracts with a corrupt subject matter which are void *ab initio*, contracts procured by corruption are only voidable. Any claim arising out of such contract will be dismissed only if the innocent party elects to avoid the contract. For example, the investment treaty Tribunal in *World Duty Free v The Republic of Kenya*[64] dismissed the claimant's claims in its entirety on the basis that the contract under which the claims were brought was procured by the payment of a cash bribe, in the form of a 'personal donation' to the then president of the Republic of Kenya. The tribunal was satisfied that the respondent had avoided the contract 'unequivocally and timeously.'[65]

The condemnation and prohibition of bribery and corruption is enshrined in a wide number of international conventions.[66] First and foremost, there is the Organisation of Economic Co-operation and Development (OECD) Convention on Combating Bribery of Foreign Public Officials in International Business Transaction,[67] which, as the International Law Association Report on Public Policy observed, reflects 'the mounting international concern about the prevalence of corrupt trading practices' and arguably enshrines 'an international consensus that corruption and bribery are contrary to international public policy'.[68] The OECD convention against bribery has been the catalyst for the development of a number of important international and regional conventions aiming to address issues of bribery and corruption in international transactions, such as the Inter-American Convention against Corruption,[69] the European Union Convention on the Fight Against Corruption Involving Officials

[62] See Richard Kreindler, *Competence-Competence in the Face of Illegality in Contracts and Arbitration Agreements* (Hague Academy of International Law, 2013), 63.

[63] Ibid.

[64] See *World Duty Free Co Ltd v Republic of Kenya*, ICSID Case No. ARB/00/7.

[65] See ibid. para. 183. The same conclusion in *Metal-Tech v Uzbekistan*, ICSID Case No. ARB/10/3.

[66] See more on this in Kreindler (n. 62), 76ff.

[67] Convention on Combating Bribery of Foreign Public Officials in International Business Transactions of 1997, signed on 17 December 1997, and came into effect on 15 February 1999: http://www.oecd.org/daf/anti-bribery/ConvCombatBribery_ENG.pdf.

[68] International Law Association, 'Interim Report on Public Policy as a Bar to Enforcement of International Arbitral Awards' (2000), 22.

[69] Inter-American Convention Against Corruption, signed 29 March 1996: http://www.oas.org/en/sla/dil/docs/inter_american_treaties_B-58_against_Corruption.pdf.

of the European Communities or Officials of Member States,[70] the Council of Europe Criminal Law Convention on Corruption,[71] the Council of Europe Civil Law Convention on Corruption,[72] the African Union Convention on Preventing and Combating Corruption,[73] and the United Nations Convention against Corruption.[74]

All these international and regional conventions prohibit bribery and corruption of public officials in the clearest manner. For example, Art. 15(a) of the UN Convention provides that 'When committed intentionally: (a) The promise, offering or giving to a public official, directly or indirectly, of an undue advantage, for the official himself or herself or another person or entity, on order that the official act or refrain from acting in the exercise of his or her official duties.'[75]

The plethora of international, regional, and national legal instruments on bribery and corruption leave little doubt that a fundamental legal policy transcending national boundaries has developed in the form of a legal rule prohibiting contracts of, and contracts arising out of, bribery and corruption. The existence of a transnational public policy rule against corrupted contracts is widely accepted by commentators,[76] and confirmed by a substantial body of authority, including decisions of national courts[77] and arbitral tribunals.[78]

[70] Convention on the Fight Against Corruption Involving Officials of the European Communities, adopted by the Council of the European Union, Council Act of 26 May 1997, signed on 26 May 1997, and entered into force on 28 September 2005.

[71] Criminal Law Convention on Corruption, adopted by the Committee of Ministers of the Council of Europe, European Treaty Series No. 173, opened for signature on 27 January 1999 and entered into force on 1 July 2002: https://rm.coe.int/CoERMPublicCommonSearchServices/DisplayDCTMContent?documentId=090000168007f3f5.

[72] Civil Law Convention on Corruption, adopted by the Committee of Ministers of the Council of Europe, European Treaty Series No. 174, opened for signature on 4 November 1999, entered into force on 1 November 2003: https://rm.coe.int/CoERMPublicCommonSearchServices/DisplayDCTMContent?documentId=090000168007f3f6.

[73] African Union Convention on Preventing and Combating Corruption (2003), adopted by the Heads of State and Government of the African Union, signed on 11 July 2003: http://www.au.int/en/sites/default/files/treaties/7786-file-african_union_convention_preventing_combating_corruption.pdf.

[74] 24 December 2012, which has 140 signatories and 165 states parties.

[75] See also Art. 1(1) of the OECD Anti-Bribery Convention.

[76] International Law Association (n. 23); Kreindler (n. 62); Bernardo Cremades and David Cairns, 'Trans-national Public Policy in International Arbitral Decisionmaking: The Cases of Bribery, Money Laundering and Fraud', in Andrew Berkeley and Kristine Karsten (eds), *Arbitration: Money Laundering, Corruption and Fraud, Dossiers of the ICC Institute of World Business Law* (Kluwer Law International, 2003), 65–91; Antonio Crivellaro, 'Arbitration Case Law on Bribery: Issues of Arbitrability, Contract Validity, Merits and Evidence', in Berkeley and Karsten, *Arbitration*, 109–47.

[77] For France, see *European Gas Turbines SA v Westman International Ltd*, 30 September 1993, (1994) Rev. Arb. 359, reported in *XX Yearbook Commercial Arbitration* (1995), 198; for England see *Fiona Trust v Yuri Privalov*, [2010] EWHC 3199 (Comm), and *Honeywell International Middle East Ltd v Meydan Group*, [2014] EWHC 1344 (TCC).

[78] See e.g. ICC Case no. 1110 of 1963, award partially published in Julian Lew, *Applicable Law in International Commercial Arbitration* (Oceana, 1978), 553ff. (where the sole arbitrator held that the agreement between a British company and an Argentine intermediary was effectively a vehicle for bribery and corruption. The sole arbitrator rejected jurisdiction on the basis that the contract under which

The majority of the international and regional conventions prohibiting bribery and corruption involve illicit payments to a public official. In recent years, however, there is a noticeable international trend towards prohibition of private commercial bribery ('influence peddling'),[79] which involves a corrupt dealing not with a governmental official, but with agents or employees of prospective commercial partners, typically, to secure an advantage over business competitors.[80] The European Council Criminal Law Convention on Corruption, for example,[81] provides that signatory parties to the Convention shall 'adopt such legislative and other measures as may be necessary to establish as criminal offences under its domestic law the request or receipt by any persons who work for private sector entities'.[82] To the same effect, the 2003 United Nations Convention against Transnational Organised Crime[83] requires that signatory parties shall 'consider establishing non-governmental corruption as a criminal offense'.[84] Similar provisions prohibiting and, under certain circumstances, criminalizing bribery in the private sector can now be found under many national laws, including in the UK[85] and China.[86] Arguably, thus, a public policy against private commercial bribery is currently emerging, as this public policy is further reflected in the decisions of international tribunals and the national law and international instruments of an increasing number of states and intergovernmental organizations.[87]

However, no transnational public policy rule exists for the prohibition of international commercial agreements that fall short of contracts of bribery or contracts arising out of

the claims were made, and therefore the arbitration agreement in that contract, was void ab initio), and the award in ICC Case no 6497 of 1994, in *XXIV Yearbook Commercial Arbitration* (1999), 71, annulling an agreement as being the vehicle for bribery as contrary to Swiss public policy. See also *Westacre v Jugoimport*, ICC Case No. 7047 of 1994, 13 ASA Bulletin 301, 339 (1995), which, while not having found that the contract in question was concluded with an intention to bribe, confirmed the public policy principle that such a contract would be void ab initio. For contracts arising out of bribery, see ICC Case No. 7664, 31 July 1996, 'bribery of public officials for the sale of certain French naval frigates to the Republic of Taiwan by the French Thomson CSF through a Swiss "intermediary"', and also ICC Case No. 3916 of 1982 in Journal Droit International 1984, 930, referred to and translated in ICC Case No. 5622 of 1988, XIX *Yearbook Commercial Arbitration* (1994), 119–20; ICC Case No. 8891 of 1998 published in Journal Droit International 2000, 1076–80; see also ICC case No. 6497 of 1994 in *XXIV Yearbook Commercial Arbitration* (1999), 71, which however on the facts found that bribery was not demonstrated; same in ICC Case No. 7047 of 1994, 13 ASA Bulletin 301 (1995), 301–57; and ICC 6248 of 1990 in Albert Jan van den Berg (ed.), *XIX Yearbook Commercial Arbitration* (1994), 124–40.

[79] Kreindler (n. 62), 63.

[80] *Black's Law Dictionary*, 10th edn (Thomson West, 2014).

[81] See Art. 8 of the Criminal Law Convention on Corruption.

[82] Ibid.

[83] Art. 8 of United Nations Convention Against Transnational Organized Crime and the Protocols Thereto (2003).

[84] See Arts. 15–21 of the United Nations Convention against Corruption (2005), encouraging member states to criminalize both public and private commercial bribery.

[85] The UK Bribery Act of 2010 covers bribery in both the public and private sector; see guidance to the Bribery Act, para. 18: https://www.justice.gov.uk/downloads/legislation/bribery-act-2010-guidance.pdf.

[86] See Art. 8 of the Anti-Unfair Competition Law of the People's Republic of China; Art. 164 of the Criminal Law of the People's Republic of China.

[87] Antonio Argandoña, 'Private-to-Private Corruption', 47 Journal of Business Ethics 253 (2003), 255.

bribery, even if an agreement involves commercial activities which are controversial and prohibited by some national laws.

For example, national laws take notably diverging approaches towards facilitation payments (namely, payments made with the purpose of expediting or facilitating the provision of services or routine government action which an official is normally obliged to perform) and intermediary agreements (namely agreements to attempt to influence the actions, policies or decisions of officials in a government albeit without the use of illegal means such as bribes).[88] While facilitation payments are prohibited under some national laws, notably the UK Bribery Act,[89] they are not specifically prohibited under the OECD Bribery Convention; indeed, under certain conditions they are expressly permitted in some countries, such as Australia, New Zealand, and the United states.[90] Similarly, whereas intermediary or lobbying agreements are expressly prohibited by a number of national laws,[91] they are not illegal or against public policy under other laws, such as US or Swiss law.[92]

In the well-documented ICC Case No. 7047,[93] Westacre, a Panamanian company, and Jugoimport, formerly the Federal Directorate of Supply and Procurement of the Federal Secretariat of National Defence of the Socialist Federal Republic of Yugoslavia (the 'Directorate'), entered into a contract whereby Westacre would provide consultancy services to the directorate for the procurement of contracts for the sale of military equipment to Kuwait. The contract was governed by Swiss law, and provided for settlement of disputes under the ICC Arbitration Rules. The Directorate was awarded the public contract, Westacre claimed the fee under the consultancy contract, and the dispute was referred to arbitration in Geneva. At the arbitration, Jugoimport contended that the intermediary contract with Westacre was against public policy because the consultancy contract was in effect an intermediary agreement that was illegal under Swiss law, as the law governing the contract. Jugoimport further argued that the consultancy contract *was actually performed* by Westacre in a way that was corrupt, including bribing Kuwaiti governmental officials.

[88] See Kreindler (n. 62), 92ff.

[89] Facilitation agreements can trigger the offence under either section 6 of the UK Bribery Act of 2010 or sections 1 and 7. See guidance to the Bribery Act, para. 44: https://www.justice.gov.uk/downloads/legislation/bribery-act-2010-guidance.pdf.

[90] See e.g. s. 105C of the New Zealand Crimes Act of 1961 and 15 USC §78dd-1(b). See in more detail Kreindler (n. 62), 93ff.

[91] See e.g. Egyptian law, which generally prohibits the activity of intermediaries unless the intermediary is a registered consultant firm (Articles 105–8 of the Egyptian Penal Code No. 58 of 1937 (as amended by Law No. 95 of 2003); MENA-OECD Report 'Business Climate Development Strategy, Phase 1 Policy Assessment, Dimension II-1 Anti-Corruption', (2009), 18, 43, 75: https://www.oecd.org/globalrelations/46341460.pdf and Algerian law, Abdulhay Sayed, *Corruption in International Trade and Commercial Arbitration* (Kluwer Law International, 2004), 192–3; ICC Case No. 5622 of 1988, in Albert Jan van den Berg (ed.), *XIX Yearbook Commercial Arbitration* 105 (Kluwer Law International, 1995), 105, paras. 24–26.

[92] See e.g. ICC Case No. 7047 of 1994, 13(2) ASA Bulletin 301 (1995), 301–57; also see ICC Case No. 9333 of 1998, in 19 ASA Bulletin 757 (2001).

[93] See *Westacre v Jugoimport*, ICC Case No. 7047 of 1994, 13(2) ASA Bulletin 301 (1995), 339.

The tribunal found that the bribery allegations had not been established and issued an award in favour of Westacre. As regards Jugoimport's claim that the intermediary agreement was invalid under Swiss law, the tribunal noted:

> Lobbying as such is not an illegal activity. Lobbying by private entities to obtain contracts in third countries is frequently carried on with active support from the state... [Having] good contracts with people making decisions for [Yugoslavia] was probably why [the Directorate] secured Claimant's services.[94]

The Swiss Federal Tribunal and a number of arbitration tribunals have confirmed that unless the parties indented to use the intermediary agreement as a vehicle for bribery and corruption, intermediary agreements under Swiss law are not illegal.[95]

The decisions of arbitration tribunals, giving effect to intermediary contracts, have been criticized by some commentators as 'the ultimate in either naivety or short-sightedness or both', on the basis that intermediary agreements are often corrupt contracts in reality.[96] According to this view, the best course of action for international tribunals would be to refuse to enforce intermediate agreements on the basis that they are against transnational public policy. The problem with this view is that, given the lack of international instruments and the diverging approaches of national laws on intermediary and lobbying agreements, it is rather questionable whether a transnational public policy rule prohibiting such agreements exists.

It might be, indeed, possible that some arbitral awards, giving effect to intermediary contracts, have perhaps naïvely condoned activities which may have lead to bribery,[97] although evidence for bribery in intermediary agreements is typically circumstantial or lacking.[98] However, if the broader question is whether arbitration tribunals can or ought to disregard the clear position of the governing law, which does not include a policy prohibiting intermediary contracts, and render these contracts void on the basis of a *desirable* rather than an existing transnational public policy, the answer must be in the negative.

As explained above, the approach of arbitrators to transnational public policy can only be doctrinal, not normative. Arbitrators cannot substitute positive state law with their views on what *ought* to be against public policy. A transnational rule on public policy can emerge only if a clear policy is enshrined in a wide number of international legal instruments, including international conventions and national laws. If no such international legal instrument exists and the position of national laws on the legality of intermediary contracts varies, transnational public policy will not engage, and the question of whether an intermediate contract is void will depend on the governing municipal law.

[94] See also ICC Case No 4145 of 1984, *XII Yearbook Commercial Arbitration* (1987), para. 48, also discussed in Kreindler (n. 62), 101, which also found that intermediary agreements are valid under Swiss law.

[95] See e.g. ICC Case No. 7047 of 1994, 13(2) ASA Bulletin 301 (1995), 301–57; also see ICC Case No. 9333 of 1998, in 19 ASA Bulletin 757 (2001), and in more detail Kreindler (n. 62), 101.

[96] Ibid. 102. [97] Ibid 101.

[98] See Matthias Scherer, 'Circumstantial Evidence in Corruption Before International Arbitral Tribunals', 5(2) International Arbitration Law Review 29 (2002).

Substituting normative views for transnational public policy is not only unjustified as a matter of methodology; it can also be counterproductive, not least because an award based on a desirable rather than existing public policy rule may eventually be annulled. For example, in ICC Case 5622 of 1988,[99] the parties entered into a brokerage agreement governed by Swiss law whereby the claimant would provide advisory services for the respondent to secure a public contract with Algerian public authorities. The respondent eventually obtained the contract, but it refused to pay the full amount of the agreed commission to the claimant. When the claimant initiated arbitration proceedings, the respondent alleged that the claimant had violated Algerian mandatory law prohibiting the use of intermediaries, and possibly paid bribes to secure the contract for the respondent.

The tribunal found no sufficient evidence of bribery and held that, while trading in influence is prohibited under Algerian mandatory law, such activities are not expressly prohibited under Swiss law. Notwithstanding its finding that trading in influence is legal under Swiss law, the tribunal held that such activity is contrary to transnational conceptions of *bonos mores*, and on that basis it rendered the brokerage agreement null and void. Intriguingly, the tribunal's reasoning that trading in influence under brokerage agreements is contrary to *bonos mores* drew almost exclusively on a number of selective US decisions which had held that trading in influence agreements were void, concluding that rendering the brokerage agreement null and void in this case 'is in keeping with the wish expressed by the US courts to stop activities which are contrary to public policy'.[100] Noting that there is a 'real political will to moralize commercial transactions and to ban traffic in influence from commercial life', the tribunal found that:

> The Law of Algeria does not have the sole aim of serving the interest of Algeria... but it aims at guaranteeing healthy and fair commercial practices and at fighting against corruption in general. In fact, the Law of Algeria lays down a general principle which must be respected by all legal systems wishing to fight corruption.[101]

Unsurprisingly, the award was annulled by the Swiss Federal Tribunal, which held that under Swiss law, trading in influence is neither prohibited by law nor against public policy.[102] The Swiss court stated that the Algerian prohibition of intermediaries, even in the absence of bribes, is 'too broad and protectionist, aimed at guaranteeing a State

[99] See ICC Case No. 5622 of 1988, in Albert Jan van den Berg (ed.), *XIX Yearbook Commercial Arbitration* (1994), 105–23.

[100] The tribunal relied e.g. on the US decisions of *Northrop Corporation v Triad International Marketing SA*, 595 F. Supp. 928 (1984); *Mohamed Habib and Middle East Services v Raytheon Company and Raytheon Services Company*, 616 F.2d 1204 (1980); *Lockheed Aircraft Corporation v Ora E. Gaines*, 645 F.2d 761 (1981). There was no mention or justification by the tribunal of the relevance for US jurisprudence in an arbitration taking place in Switzerland under Swiss law.

[101] See ICC Case No. 5622 of 1988, in Albert Jan van den Berg (ed.), *XIX Yearbook Commercial Arbitration* (1994), 105, paras. 35 and 45.

[102] See *Omnium de Traitement et de Valorisation–OTV v Hilmarton*, Swiss Federal Tribunal, 17 April 1990, in *XIX Yearbook Commercial Arbitration* (1994), 214, 222.

monopoly on foreign trade'. Pointing out to the different hierarchy of policies under Algerian and Swiss law, the court noted that such a provision is a 'serious attack on the parties' contractual freedom and cannot prevail, on the ethical level, over the general and fundamental principles of contractual freedom, in the absence of activities which would also be considered as doubtful under Swiss law'.[103]

It follows that while some commentators and indeed some national laws may condemn intermediary agreements, not all national legal systems do. Crucially, there is no international policy enshrined in international convention or soft law against intermediary agreements and lobbying. Arbitrators thus cannot artificially ascertain policy consensus or ethical common ground in the name of transnational public policy, where such consensus is lacking or where a rule of public policy is enshrined in only some national laws and court decisions.[104]

5.3.2 Abuse of rights or the principle of good faith

Good faith has generally been considered by a number of international arbitration tribunals[105] and commentators,[106] including the Reports of the International Law Association,[107] as a public policy principle of transnational nature.

While it is not part of certain common law legal systems, notably English law, the principle of good faith is a manifestation of the broader legal principle of abuse of rights,[108] recognized in both common and civil law jurisdictions,[109] under different

[103] See ibid. 214, para. 25.

[104] Other tribunals have taken a different approach, holding that the use of intermediaries is not forbidden under Swiss law, notwithstanding the fact that it is prohibited by mandatory laws of the place of performance of the contract, e.g. CCIG award of 23 February 1988; and the same in ad hoc award of 1989, in 9 ASA Bulletin 239 (1991), discussed in Scherer (n. 98).

[105] E.g. see ICC Case No. 10947 of 2002, 22 ASA Bulletin 308 (2004), 308–32; ICC Case No. 6474 of 1992, Partial Award on Jurisdiction and Admissibility, in Albert Jan van den Berg (ed.), *XXV Yearbook Commercial Arbitration* (2000), 279–311.

[106] E.g. see Robert Kolb, 'Principles as Sources of International Law: with Special Reference to Good Faith', 53 Netherlands International Law Review 1 (2006), 13–14; Robert Summers, 'Good Faith in General Contract Law and the Sales Provisions of the Uniform Commercial Code', 54 Virginia Law Review 195 (1968).

[107] See International Law Association (n. 23), Recommendation 1(e).

[108] See Bin Cheng, *General Principles of Law as Applied by International Courts and Tribunals* (Cambridge University Press, 2006), 121; Ahmed El Far, 'Abuse of Rights in International Arbitration' (doctoral thesis, Queen Mary University of London, forthcoming); Gary Born, *International Commercial Arbitration*, 2nd edn (Kluwer Law International, 2014), 1425–6: 'This doctrine rests in part on principles of contract law and good faith, aimed at objectively identifying the parties to a contract, but also on notions akin to estoppel and abuse of right, which operate independently from principles of consent.'

[109] In England, see Roderick Munday, *Agency: Law and Principles* (Oxford University Press, 2010), ch. 4; in France the rule has been established since the 19th c. in the case of the Cour de Cassation, 16 January 1861, *Lizardi v Chaize*, Sirey, Pt I, at 305 (1861); in the US, see Restatement (Third) Agency Section 2.03 (2006). Also Art. 2.2.5(2) of the UNIDROIT Principles of International Commercial Contracts (2004), which provides that 'where the principal causes the third party reasonably to believe

terms and legal constructs, such as *abus de droit*, estoppel, reliance, and *non venire contra factum proprium*.[110]

The public policy justification of the principle of good faith reflects the fundamental equitable proposition that a party in a commercial transaction cannot contradict its previous conduct, especially when its counterparty has justifiably relied on it. Its equitable nature allows the principle of good faith to apply in a variety of factual circumstances in international commercial and trade law. A growing body of arbitration awards, however, suggests that the principle of good faith has acquired a more specific meaning, arguably in the form of an emerging rule of transnational public policy, to deny spurious objections to the jurisdiction of international arbitral tribunals. This emerging rule, akin to the doctrines of competence-competence and separability, has been relied upon by international arbitration tribunals in different circumstances.

For a start, a number of commercial[111] and investment[112] tribunals as well as national courts[113] have prevented a party who signed an arbitration agreement from subsequently relying on *its own municipal law* to avoid arbitration.[114] For example, in ICC Case No. 10947 of 2002,[115] a state relied on its own national law (Ecuador), prohibiting public entities from entering into an arbitration agreement, to argue that an ICC arbitral tribunal sitting in Switzerland had no jurisdiction to determine a dispute between the public entity and a contractor. The tribunal reviewed a number of scholarly writings, decisions of arbitral tribunals, and the law of the seat of arbitration, and found that the arbitration agreement signed by the public entity was valid and binding upon this public entity. It stated that the rule whereby a state is bound by an arbitration agreement it has signed, notwithstanding any contrary provision of its national law, is a 'material rule of

that the agent has authority to act on behalf of the principal and that the agent is acting within the scope of that authority, the principal may not invoke against the third party the lack of authority of the agent'.

110 See the decision of the Swiss Federal Tribunal, BGE 129 III 727 (2003) and 22 ASA Bulletin 364 (2004).

111 See e.g. ICC Case No. 1939, [1973] Rev. Arb. 145; and *Himpurna California Energy Ltd v PT. PLN (Persero)*, ad hoc arbitration under UNCITRAL rules, final award of 4 May 1999, *XXV Yearbook Commercial Arbitration* (2000), 13–108.

112 See e.g. *Millicom and Sentel v Republic of Senegal*, ICSID Case No. ARB-08-20, which states (in para. 103(b)): 'The principle today is firmly established in international arbitration that a State is prohibited from invoking its own domestic law in order to avoid arbitration and its capacity to enter into arbitration clauses. Such an attitude would violate the principles of good faith and of "international public policy".'

113 E.g. *Cour d'Appel de Paris, 1ère chambre*, 17 December 1991; *Cour d'Appel de Paris, 1ère chambre*, 24 February 1994, *Ministère tunisien de l'équipement v société Bec Frères*, [1995] Rev. Arb. 275.

114 See also Andreas Bucher, *Le nouvel arbitrage international en Suisse* (Helbing & Lichtenhahn, 1988), 105–7, points out that the rule of good faith preventing a state entity from raising a defence based on the impossibility to submit to arbitration under its own national law has been upheld consistently enough to have become a principle of transnational public policy; and see Jan Paulsson, 'May a State Invoke its Internal Law to Repudiate Consent to International Commercial Arbitration? Reflections on the Benteler v. Belgium Preliminary Award', 2 Arbitration International 90 (1986).

115 See ICC Case No. 10947 of 2002, 22 ASA Bulletin 308 (2004), 308–32.

international private law' or even a 'new component of international or transnational public policy' or part of the general principle '*venire contra factum proprium*'.[116]

In other cases, arbitral tribunals have prevented a party who signed an arbitration agreement to subsequently rely on *public international law* to avoid arbitration. For example, in the ICC Case 6474 of 1992,[117] a supplier entered into a number of contracts, governed by Swiss law, with the Republic of X. When the supplier initiated arbitration in Zurich, the Republic of X alleged that the arbitral tribunal was lacking jurisdiction because Republic of X was not recognized as a state by the international community, and therefore the arbitration agreement which it had originally signed was invalid. The arbitral tribunal rejected the respondent's jurisdictional objection, stating that the general principle of good faith or the concept of 'estoppel' would prohibit a party from relying on its own non-recognition by the international community in order to avoid or annul its previous undertaking to arbitrate under the contracts.[118] Such a denial of jurisdiction, the tribunal held, 'would be contrary to the clear principle of transnational public policy which is the principle of good faith'.[119]

The underpinning justification for the public policy rule of good faith protecting the jurisdiction of international arbitration tribunals from spurious challenges is twofold. First, the fundamental policy of commercial law that 'protects reasonable expectations'.[120] It is unfair for a party to rely on a contract including an arbitration agreement when it works to the party's advantage, and try to repudiate it when it works to its disadvantage.[121] Second, the policy favouring international arbitration, as a neutral means of disputes arising out of international transactions. The policy favouring international arbitration is enshrined in the 1958 New York Convention for the Recognition and Enforcement of Foreign Arbitral Awards, signed by more than 160 states worldwide, as well as included in the national laws of a wide number of states.[122] Overall, it is generally accepted that promoting international arbitration and protecting reasonable expectations are fundamental policies for the proper functioning of international trade.[123]

[116] ICC Case No. 10947 of 2002, 22 ASA Bulletin 308 (2004), para. 30.

[117] See ICC Case No. 6474 of 1992, *Supplier v Republic of X*, Partial Award on Jurisdiction and Admissibility, in Albert Jan van den Berg (ed.), *XXV Yearbook Commercial Arbitration* 279 (2000).

[118] ICC Case No. 6474 of 1992, *Supplier v Republic of X*, Partial Award on Jurisdiction and Admissibility, in Albert Jan van den Berg (ed.), *XXV Yearbook Commercial Arbitration* (2000), 279, para. 12.

[119] Ibid. para. 36.

[120] See El Far (n. 108); Bernardo Cremades, 'Good Faith in International Arbitration', 27 Am. U. Int'l L. Rev. 761 (2012), 767–8; Lord Steyn, 'Contract Law: Fulfilling the Reasonable Expectations of Honest Men', 113 Law Quarterly Review 433 (1997), 439.

[121] See *American Bankers Insurance Group v. Richard Long, Lillie Long*, 453 F 3d 623 (2006), 627.

[122] Notably in English, French, Swiss, and US law. See Stephen Jagusch and Epaminontas Triantafilou, 'London', in Michael Ostrove, Claudia Salomon, and Bette Shifman (eds), *Choice of Venue in International Arbitration* (Oxford University Press, 2014), 242–3; Carole Malinvaud and Christian Camboulive, 'Paris', in Ostrove et al., *Choice of Venue*, 322–4; Dominique Brown-Berset and Diane Grisel, 'Switzerland', in Ostrove et al., *Choice of Venue*, 418–20; and John Fellas and Hagit Elul, 'United States (New York, Miami, Houston)', in Ostrove et al., *Choice of Venue*, 470–477.

[123] See Lalive (n. 6), 305–6.

5.3.3 Public policy and jurisdiction of investment treaty tribunals

In the context of jurisdiction of international arbitration tribunals, a further wrinkle is the use of international public policy by investment treaty tribunals to both accept and decline jurisdiction.

In some cases, investment treaty tribunals have declined jurisdiction relying on 'considerations of international public policy' in circumstances where the investment was not made in accordance with the host state law,[124] or where the claimant has attempted to circumvent the requirement of nationality under Art. 25 of the ICSID Convention. The underlying public policy here is to prevent parties from abusing the system of investment arbitration.

For example, in *Banko American Resources, Inc. and Société Aurifère du Kivu et du Maniema SARL v Democratic Republic of Congo*,[125] the tribunal declined jurisdiction, on the basis that the original Canadian investor transferred a claim to its US subsidiary, for it to bring an ICSID claim against the Democratic Republic of Congo. Unlike the US, Canada was not at the time a signatory to the ICSID convention. The tribunal stated that international public policy considerations prohibited an investor from abusing the system of investor–state dispute settlement, by seeking to benefit from the 'diplomatic protection by its home State, while another subsidiary of the group possesses the nationality of a Contracting State to the Convention and therefore has standing before an ICSID tribunal'.[126]

In other cases, investment treaty tribunals have employed international public policy to give effect to most favoured nation clauses, which are included in a wide number of bilateral investment treaties (BITs). In *Maffezini v Kingdom of Spain*,[127] the tribunal had to decide whether the most favoured nation clause under the Argentine–Spain BIT extended to the dispute resolution arrangements under the Chile–Spain BIT. The tribunal observed that there are circumstances where 'public policy considerations' would limit the operation of the most favoured nation clause. According to the tribunal, one

[124] See e.g. the *Inceysa Vallisoletana S.L. v Republic of El Salvador*, ICSID Case No. ARB/03/26, para. 248, where the tribunal found that the claimant had obtained the concession by defrauding the state at the public procurement process by misrepresenting its qualifications and submitting false financial statements. The tribunal stated that had it assumed jurisdiction over this dispute, it would have violated international public policy because 'respect for the law is a matter of public policy not only in El Salvador, but in any civilized country'. According to the tribunal, international public policy is a 'meta-positive provision that prohibits attributing effects to an act done illegally', citing the public policy maxim *ex dolo malo non oritur actio*. See also *Phoenix Action v Czech Republic*, ICSID Case No. ARB/06/5, para. 111, citing *Inceysa Vallisoletana, S.L. v Republic of El Salvador*, ICSID Case No. ARB/03/26, Award of 2 August 2006, para. 230, and *Plama Consortium Limited v Bulgaria*, ICSID Case No. ARB/03/24, Award of 27 August 2008, paras. 143–144.

[125] See *Banro American Resources, Inc. and Societe Aurifere du Kivu et du Maniema S.A.R.L. v Democratic Republic of the Congo*, ICSID Case No. ARB/98/7, Award of 1 September 2000.

[126] Ibid. para. 24.

[127] See *Emilio Augustin Maffezini v The Kingdom of Spain*, ICSID Case No. ARB/97/7.

such consideration is the policy of avoiding 'disruptive treaty-shopping that would play havoc with the policy objectives of underlying specific treaty provisions'.[128] On that basis, the tribunal distinguished between dispute resolution provisions in BITs whose underlying purpose is to exclude treaty shopping, such as 'fork in the road' provisions, and those which do not have such purpose. In the former provisions, the tribunal observed, international public policy does not allow the extension of a most favoured nation provision to dispute resolution arrangements in other BITs. By contrast, the tribunal found that the Argentine–Spain BIT did not exclude treaty shopping, and therefore no public policy considerations existed that precluded the extension of the most favoured nation clause in the dispute resolution arrangements under the Chile–Spain BIT to the Argentine–Spain BIT.

While the ruling in *Mafezini* has been followed by other investment treaty tribunals, including for example in *Siemens AG v Argentine Republic*,[129] the use of public policy as a principle of treaty interpretation is not without problems.[130] For a start, as the tribunal in *Plama Consortium* noted, it is unclear what is the origin of these 'public policy considerations' which, according to the *Maffezini* ruling, purport to limit the operation of most favoured nation clauses.[131] The tribunal in *Maffezini* did not explain how it ascertained the policy of avoiding treaty shopping, and which specific BIT policy objectives are undermined by treaty shopping. It is further questionable whether public policy allows a tribunal to read important qualifications and implicit policy objectives in international treaties.[132] Neither Art. 31 nor Art. 32 of the Vienna Convention on the Law of Treaties (VCLT) includes public policy as a primary or supplementary means for interpreting treaties. Was public policy used as the equivalent of the principle of good faith, referred to in Art. 31 of the VCLT to assist the interpretation of a term in accordance with its the ordinary meaning? If yes, the award in *Maffezini* failed to explain.

[128] Ibid. para. 63.

[129] See *Siemens A.G. v The Argentine Republic*, ICSID Case No. ARB/02/8, Decision on Jurisdiction dated 3 August 2004, para. 120: 'there may be public policy considerations that limit the benefits that may be claimed by the operation of an MFN clause, but those pleaded by the Respondent have not been considered by the Tribunal to be applicable in this case.'

[130] See e.g. *Wintershall Aktiengesellschaft v Argentina*, ICSID Case No. ARB/04/14, Award dated 8 December 2008, para. 182, noting that 'the precautions mentioned by the authors of the decision in Maffezini have proved difficult of application, resulting in much uncertainty, as to how to distinguish in a given case between "the legitimate extension of rights and benefits by means of the operation of the MFN clause" on the one hand and how to avoid the use of the MFN clause for purposes plainly of "disruptive treaty shopping" on the other hand'.

[131] See *Plama Consortium Lt v. Republic of Bulgaria*, ICSID Case No. ARB/03/24, Decision on Jurisdiction, dated 8 February 2005, para. 221, referring to Maffezini: 'The present Tribunal was puzzled as to what the origin of these "public policy considerations" is.... It seems that the effect of the "public policy considerations" is that they take away much of the breadth of the preceding observations made by the tribunal in Maffezini.'

[132] See *Telenor Mobile Communications v Republic of Hungary*, ICSID Case ARB/04/15, Award dated 13 September 2006, para. 87, where the award notes Maffezini but questions whether public policy can be the source of such qualifications.

Public policy is not a mode of legal reasoning that allows tribunals to take a purposive interpretation to international or national law rules. As discussed above, public policy functions either as a legal principle or as a legal rule which itself is subject to interpretation and application. Using public policy as a principle of interpretation, rather than as a legal principle or a legal rule, the *Maffezini* ruling has resulted in much uncertainty as regards the function of public policy in assisting investment treaty tribunals to address jurisdictional challenges under most favoured nation clauses.[133]

5.3.4 Public policy as a principle permeating international law?

Transnational public policy is often conceived not only as a moral framework of international law and arbitration but also as a general principle that permeates international law and gives rise to rights and duties in every field of international commercial, trade, and economic law.

Under this normative approach, transnational public policy is often employed by parties to argue that they are entitled to a wide range of rights and remedies that go beyond positive law. For example, in an ICC arbitration seated in Switzerland between two Turkish parties,[134] the arbitrators had to decide a number of procedural issues, including the language of the arbitration. Since the contract was silent on this matter, the respondent felt empowered to argue that international public policy can fill in this gap. Specifically, it argued that the language of the arbitration should be Turkish, as a matter of international public policy which, according to the respondent, mandates that a dispute which arises out of a contract between two Turkish corporations, concluded in Turkey, should be decided in Turkish even if the seat of the arbitration is outside Turkey.

Similarly, tribunals have felt empowered to apply 'public policy' rules to address diverse legal questions in different fields of law. In ICC Case No. 10947 of 2002,[135] the tribunal relied on international public policy to reject the respondent's request to stay its proceedings until a related matter was first decided by Ecuadorian courts. The tribunal stated that staying its proceedings would entail international arbitration being a 'second rank status', which would be against international public policy.[136] Similarly, in ICC Case No. 14053 of 2009,[137] the tribunal decided that, under international public policy, it had the power to unilaterally extend the duration of the arbitration proceedings,

[133] E.g. *Wintershall Aktiengesellschaft v Argentina*, ICSID Case No. ARB/04/14, Award dated 8 December 2008, para. 182, noting that 'the precautions mentioned by the authors of the decision in Maffezini have proved difficult of application, resulting in much uncertainty, as to how to distinguish in a given case between "the legitimate extension of rights and benefits by means of the operation of the MFN clause" on the one hand and how to avoid the use of the MFN clause for purposes plainly of "disruptive treaty shopping" on the other hand'.

[134] ICC Case No. 12575 of 2004, in ICC Dispute Resolution Bulletin (Issue 1, 2016), 76.

[135] See ICC Case No. 10947 of 2002, 22 ASA Bulletin 308, (2004), 308–332.

[136] Ibid. para. 50.

[137] See ICC Case No. 14053 of 2009, ICC Dispute Resolution Bulletin (Issue 1, 2016), 78.

notwithstanding an express provision in the parties' contract providing that an arbitral award shall be issued within three months from the constitution of the tribunal. Other arbitral tribunals and national courts have arrived at the opposite conclusion, ironically also on grounds of international public policy. For example, the French Cour de cassation held that in unilaterally extending the time limits of an arbitration beyond the six-month time-frame agreed upon by the parties, an ad hoc arbitral tribunal did violate a core principle of international public policy, namely party autonomy.[138]

Under the view that transnational public policy is a principle permeating international commercial and trade law, some commentators claim that transnational public policy covers and regulates fields of law, and indeed of human life, as diverse as that of social corporate responsibility, tax evasion, the protection of environment, health, protection of cultural heritage, human dignity, and social justice.[139]

However, there is a fundamental problem with the account of transnational public policy as a ubiquitous principle of international law. As explained above, public policy can assist national courts and tribunals in addressing either existing and well-known legal issues, such as bribery and corruption, or novel legal issues. In both cases, public policy will assist under two conditions. First, if a judge or an arbitrator is unable to identify a rule of positive or customary law to address the legal question before her. Where there is law, policy (even a fundamental one) will not come into play.[140] Second, and more important, if there is a certain degree of policy consensus as to how a legal issue must be addressed. The requirement for policy consensus gives rise to difficult issues. For a start, the required degree of policy consensus is contested. Some authorities have held that for a transnational public policy rule, universal consensus is required,[141] while others have taken a majoritarian approach suggesting that consensus must be found in the 'majority of the states composing the international community'[142] or an elitist, if exclusive, approach suggesting that consensus should be located in the community of 'civilized nations',[143] or 'in the part of the world where the country [which is closely connected with the

[138] Cour de Cassation Civ. 1re, 15 June 1994, *Communauté urbaine de Casablanca v Société Degrémont*, (1995) Rev. Arb. 88, note Gaillard; see also decision of Cour d'Appel de Paris, 22 September 1995, *Société Dubois et Vanderwalle v Boots Frites BV*, with comment by Emmanuel Gaillard, and published in *XXIV Yearbook Commercial Arbitration* (1999), 640–42.

[139] See Kessedjian (n. 4), 869; Frank Hoffmeister and Thomas Kleinlein, 'International Public Order', *Max Planck Encyclopedia of Public International Law* (Oxford University Press), https://opil.ouplaw.com/view/10.1093/law:epil/9780199231690/law-9780199231690-e1430, paras. 13–20, observing that transnational public policy includes peace and security; freedom and equality; economic, social, and cultural development; and respect for nature and shared responsibility.

[140] Unless the public policy reflects peremptory norms of *jus cogens*, a circumstance which raises issues that go beyond the scope of this chapter. See more details in Nartnirun Junngam, 'Public Policy in International Investment Law: The Confluence of the Three Unruly Horses', 51 Tex. Int'l L. J. 45 (2016).

[141] Swiss Federal Supreme Court, 19 April 1994, *Westland Helicopter Ltd*, ATF 120 II 155.

[142] Paris Court of Appeal, 30 September 1993, *European Gas Turbines SA v Westman International Ltd*, (1994) Rev. Arb. 359, note by D. Bureau.

[143] See ICC Case No. 1110 of 1963, Award partially published in Julian Lew (n. 78), 553ff.; Jean-Jacques Arnaldez, Yves Derains, and Dominique Hascher, *Collection of ICC Arbitral Awards 1996–2000* (Kluwer Law International, 2003), 2.

dispute in hand] is located'.[144] More fundamentally, though, policy consensus tends to exist only in very limited areas of law and in relation to very limited questions of law—bribery and corruption being one rare example.

Policy consensus should be understood not in the form of commonplace statements to the effect that public health or the environment ought to be protected or that 'transnational public policy is about human dignity and fundamental principles without which our society would be tantamount to a nightmare'.[145] Such statements are too broad to provide evidence of a concrete cause of policy action, and by extension of the existence of a transnational public policy norm. As explained above, to ascertain policy consensus requires the review of a wide number of international legal documents, including arbitral awards and court decisions, as well as international conventions and legal instruments promulgated by international or intergovernmental organizations.

Even if some form of broad consensus were possible as to which values—social justice, for example—are worth protecting in law, it would still be difficult to identify transnational consensus as to what exactly social justice entails (does it demand equal distribution of social goods or does it involve matching resources with basic needs or merits?), how the demands of social justice should translate in legal rights, or whether it should prevail over other equally worthwhile values such as liberty and party autonomy.[146] Similar difficulties arise if we are looking for evidence of transnational policy consensus that could form the basis of a legal rule with regard to tax evasion, health, and the protection of cultural heritage and the environment.

Even with regard to legal fields, such as competition, where one might expect that policy consensus would be easier to identify nowadays, contestations persist. A number of seminal court decisions, including the decision of the Court of Justice of the European Union,[147] have held that competition law is of mandatory nature.[148] Further, some commentators have remarked that 'a market economy without competition is an oxymoron', and therefore competition law must be considered as part of a universal concept of public policy.[149]

[144] See Swiss Federal Tribunal, 4P.278/2005, 8 March 2006, para. 2.2.2. Also see Gaillard (n. 6), who notes that the content of truly international public policy is to be determined on the basis of a 'comparative law approach and on the existence of international instruments adopted with respect to specific matters and which reflect a broad consensus among the community of states'.

[145] See Kessedjian (n. 4), 868.

[146] See e.g. John Gray, *Gray's Anatomy: Selected Writings* (Penguin, 2010), 34.

[147] See the decision of the Court of Justice of the European Union, 1 June 1999, in the case of *Eco Swiss China Time Ltd v Benetton International NV*, Case C-126/97; Paris Court of Appeal decision in *SA Thales Air Defence v GIE Euromissile and SA EADS France* (1er Ch., sect. C, 18 November 2004); and French Cour de Cassation in *Sté SNF v Sté Cytec Industries BV* (1er Ch. civ., 4 June 2008).

[148] See Decision of the Court of Justice of the European Union in *Eco Swiss China Time Ltd v Benetton International NV*, Case C-126/97; *SA Thales Air Defence v GIE Euromissile and SA EADS France* (1er Ch., sect. C, 18 November 2004).

[149] See Kessedjian (n. 4), 863.

However, while the policy prohibiting agreements or practices that restrict competition between companies is enshrined in the law of a wide number of states[150] whose economies are organized around principles of free market, whether the same conceptions of free market and fair competition are shared in large parts of the world, including for example in China, Russia, the Middle East, Africa and South America, is open to question. Even if one was ready to accept that the general policy to promote market competition was a universal one,[151] it is not clear exactly what rules might ensue from this policy. National and regional competition laws and jurisprudence tend to be detailed, if often complex, to ensure that the law corresponds to sophisticated modern commercial practices purporting to restrict competition. As the Swiss Federal Tribunal stated, in a decision rendered in 2006,[152] 'the differences between the various laws on competition are too acute—especially between Switzerland and the European Union—to allow a finding that a transnational or international rule public policy would have to be found there.'[153]

Overall, contrary to what transnationalist lawyers seem to believe, transnational public policy is not the cure for all malaises and inefficiencies of international law. For better or worse, it is not a tool of global governance, which can regulate international business law towards a liberal end. Transnational public policy can only be understood as a legal concept that is confined to a few legal questions, where concrete evidence of policy consensus exists. Normative accounts of transnational public policy, in which arbitrators can project their moral values onto law, confuse decision-making with legislative function and lack basic democratic legitimacy.

5.4 Conclusion

In the current political environment, where liberal values and traditions are challenged, transnational public policy has been seen (possibly understandably) by transnationalist lawyers as the legal construct to foster liberal causes, including social corporate responsibility, the protection of the environment, and social justice, through international law and international arbitration. Appealing as this normative account of transnational public policy may be, it must be resisted, because it dangerously conflates the judicial function and legislative function, and substitutes political expediency for legal reasoning.

As this chapter suggests, transnational public policy is a legal doctrine which includes legal norms, in the form of either legal rules or legal principles. Non-legal standards such as morals and values may underpin some of the rules and principles of transnational

150 Also see European law: Art. 101(1) of the Treaty of Lisbon which prohibits anti-competitive agreements, including price-fixing, which pursuant to Art. 101(2) are void. Art. 102 prohibits the abuse of dominant position.

151 See Kessedjian (n. 4), 868.

152 See Swiss Supreme Court, 4P.278/2005, 8 March 2006, 24 ASA Bulletin 550 (2006).

153 Ibid. para. 557.

public policy, but they are not distinct public policy grounds. The chapter further suggests that a transnational rule on public policy can emerge only if a clear policy is evidenced in a wide number of international legal documents, including arbitral awards and court decisions, as well as international conventions and legal instruments promulgated by international or intergovernmental organizations.

From this standpoint, transnational public policy does not permeate international law. Rather, only a limited number of rules and principles of transnational public policy can be identified in relation to only some aspects of international commercial and trade law, notably the transnational policy prohibiting contracts of, and arising out of, bribery and the principle of good faith in the form of specific rules to deny spurious objections to the jurisdiction of international tribunals.

CHAPTER 6

HUMAN RIGHTS AND INTERNATIONAL INVESTMENT ARBITRATION

URSULA KRIEBAUM

6.1 Introduction

The treatment of human rights issues by investment tribunals has received increased attention in recent years, especially from the academic world.[1] This is particularly so

[1] See e.g. Pierre-Marie Dupuy and Jorge Viñuales, 'Human Rights and Investment Disciplines: Integration in Progress', in Marc Bungenberg et al. (eds), *International Investment Law* (Hart, 2015), 1739; Ursula Kriebaum (ed.), 'Aligning Human Rights and Investment Protection', TDS 1 (2013); Patrick Dumberry and Gabrielle Dumas-Aubin, 'When and How Allegations of Human Rights Violations can be Raised in Investor–State Arbitration', 13 Journal of World Investment & Trade 349 (2012); Yannick Radi, 'Realizing Human Rights in Investment Treaty Arbitration: A Perspective from Within the International Investment Law Toolbox', 37 North Carolina Journal of International Law and Commercial Regulation 1107 (2012); Megan Sheffer, 'Bilateral Investment Treaties: A Friend or Foe to Human Rights?' 39 Denver Journal of International Law and Policy 483 (2011); Abdullah Faruque, 'Mapping the Relationship Between Investment Protection and Human Rights', 11 Journal of World Investment & Trade 539 (2010); Olivier De Schutter, 'Foreign Direct Investment, Human Development and Human Rights: Framing the Issues', 3(2) Human Rights & International Legal Discourse 137 (2009); Pierre-Marie Dupuy, Francesco Francioni, and Ernst-Ulrich Petersmann (eds), *Human Rights in International Investment Law and Arbitration* (Oxford University Press, 2009); Bruno Simma and Theodore Kill, 'Harmonizing Investment Protection and International Human Rights: First Steps Towards a Methodology', in Christina Binder et al. (eds), *International Investment Law for the 21st Century: Essays in Honour of Christoph Schreuer* (Oxford University Press, 2009), 678; Ursula Kriebaum, 'Human Rights of the Population of the Host State in International Investment Arbitration', 10 Journal of World Investment and Trade 653 (2009); Ursula Kriebaum, *Eigentumsschutz im Völkerrecht: Eine vergleichende Untersuchung zum Internationalen Investitionsrecht sowie zum Menschenrechtsschutz* (Duncker & Humblot, 2008); James Fry, 'International

because tribunals have adopted varying approaches when confronted with human rights-based arguments. Some have responded in a negative way, declining to exercise jurisdiction when human rights were concerned.[2] Others declined to discuss human

Human Rights Law in Investment Arbitration: Evidence of International Law's Unity', 18 Duke Journal of Comparative & International Law 77 (2007); Lahra Liberti, 'Investissement et droits de l'homme', in Philippe Kahn and Thomas Wälde (eds), *Les aspects nouveaux du droit des investissements internationaux* (Brill, 2007), 791; Ursula Kriebaum, 'Privatizing Human Rights: The Interface between International Investment Protection and Human Rights', in August Reinisch and Ursula Kriebaum (eds), *The Law of International Relations: Liber Amicorum Hanspeter Neuhold* (Eleven International, 2007), 165.

[2] See e.g. *Biloune and Marine Drive Complex Ltd v Ghana Investments Centre and the Government of Ghana*, Award on Jurisdiction and Liability, UNCITRAL (1989), (1994) 95 ILR 184, at 203: 'contemporary international law recognizes that all individuals... are entitled to fundamental human rights... which no government may violate. Nevertheless, it does not follow that this Tribunal is competent to pass upon every type of departure from the minimum standard to which foreign nationals are entitled, or that this Tribunal is authorized to deal with allegations of violations of fundamental human rights. This Tribunal's competence is limited to commercial disputes arising under a contract entered into in the context of Ghana's Investment Code. As noted, the Government agreed to arbitrate only disputes "in respect of" foreign investment. Thus, other matters... are outside this Tribunal's jurisdiction... [W]hile the acts alleged to violate the international human rights of Mr. Biloune may be relevant in considering the investment dispute under arbitration, this Tribunal lacks jurisdiction to address, as an independent cause of action, a claim of violation of human rights.' Also see *Rompetrol Group N.V. v Romania*, Award, ICSID Case No. ARB/06/3 (2013), paras. 170–72: 'The Tribunal starts from the elementary proposition that it is not called upon to decide any issue under the ECHR, whether the issue in question lies in the past or is still open. Its function is solely to decide, as between TRG and Romania, "legal dispute[s] arising directly out of an investment" and to do so in accordance with "such rules of law as may be agreed by the parties," which in the present case means essentially the BIT, in application of the appropriate rules for its interpretation. The ECHR has its own system and functioning institutional structure for complaints of breach against States Parties...

(i) The Tribunal is not competent to decide issues as to the application of the ECHR within Romania, either to natural persons or to corporate entities;
(ii) The governing law for the issues which do fall to the Tribunal to decide is the BIT, and notably its requirements for fair and equitable treatment and non-impairment of, and full protection and security for, the investments of investors of one Party in the territory of the other Party;
(iii) The category of materials for the assessment in particular of fair and equitable treatment is not a closed one, and may include, in appropriate circumstances, the consideration of common standards under other international regimes (including those in the area of human rights), if and to the extent that they throw useful light on the content of fair and equitable treatment in particular sets of factual circumstances; the examination is however very specific to the particular circumstances, and defies definition by any general rule.'

For further details, see Ursula Kriebaum, 'The Rompetrol Group N.V. v Romania', 15 JWIT 1020 (2014). Also see *Bernhard von Pezold and Others v Republic of Zimbabwe*, Procedural Order No. 2, ICSID Case No. ARB/10/15 (2012), paras. 57, 58, 60: 'The Arbitral Tribunals agree in this regard with the Claimants that the reference to "such rules of general international law as may be applicable" in the BITs does not incorporate the universe of international law into the BITs or into disputes arising under the BITs. Moreover, neither Party has put the identity and/or treatment of indigenous peoples, or the indigenous communities in particular, under international law, including international human rights law on indigenous peoples, in issue in these proceedings. The Petitioners provided no evidence or support for their assertion that international investment law and international human rights law are interdependent such that any decision of these Arbitral Tribunals which did not consider the content of international human rights norms would be legally incomplete.'

rights arguments, noting that investment protection provisions were more favourable to investors than human rights law.[3] Some, although willing to apply human rights norms in principle, did not pronounce upon them after finding that their violation or incompatibility with investors' rights had not been sufficiently substantiated.[4] Others applied human rights law where it composed part of the applicable law by virtue of the host state being a party to a human rights treaty.[5] And some, when interpreting investment protection treaties, drew inspiration from approaches used by human rights courts, despite the decisive human rights treaty not being in force in the host state in the case at hand.[6]

This chapter briefly reflects upon the requirements for the application of human rights law in investment disputes. It then explores ten different ways that tribunals have dealt with situations where human rights have been invoked or could have been invoked in investment arbitrations.

As we will see, human rights have played a role in various contexts of investment proceedings. One context in which human rights often arise is in respect of purely procedural questions. Yet another, more common context is substantive, where parties invoke human rights to demonstrate the existence or absence of violations of investment protection standards. Human rights have also been relevant to such matters as the assessment of damages or the binding nature of interim measures. In annulment proceedings, one ad hoc committee relied upon human rights considerations to decide whether a fundamental rule of procedure had been violated. Sometimes, it is third parties that introduce such considerations. *Amici* often rely on human rights considerations in order to stress why particular state measures were necessary to protect human rights and should therefore not be deemed to breach investment protection standards.

[3] *Spyridon Roussalis v Romania*, Award, ICSID Case No. ARB/06/1 (2011), paras. 310–12.

[4] *Azurix Corp. v Argentina*, Award, ICSID Case No. ARB/01/12 (2006), para. 261; *Frontier Petroleum v Czech Republic*, Award, UNCITRAL (2010), para. 338.

[5] See e.g. *ADC Affiliate Limited and ADC & ADMC Management Limited v The Republic of Hungary*, Award, ICSID Case No. ARB/03/16 (2006), para. 497; *Ioan Micula, Viorel Micula, S.C. European Food S.A, S.C. Starmill S.R.L. and S.C. Multipack S.R.L. v Romania*, Decision on Jurisdiction, ICSID Case No. ARB/05/20 (2008), para. 88; *Toto Costruzioni Generali S.p.A. v The Republic of Lebanon*, Decision on Jurisdiction, ICSID Case No. ARB/07/12 (2009), paras. 157–160, 167–8; *Hesham T. M. Al Warraq v Republic of Indonesia*, Award, UNCITRAL (2014), paras. 564–5, 621; *Tulip Real Estate and Development Netherlands B.V. v Republic of Turkey*, Decision on Annulment, ICSID Case No. ARB/11/28 (2015), paras. 86–92, 145–53.

[6] See e.g. *Perenco v Ecuador*, Decision on Provisional Measures, ICSID Case No. ARB/08/6 (2009), para. 70; *Total S.A. v The Argentine Republic*, Decision on Liability, ICSID Case No. ARB/04/01 (2010), para. 129; *El Paso v Argentina*, Award, ICSID Case No. ARB/03/15 (2011), para. 598; *Saipem S.p.A. v The People's Republic of Bangladesh*, Decision on Jurisdiction and Recommendation on Provisional Measures, ICSID Case No. ARB/05/07 (2007), para. 130; *Técnicas Medioambientales Tecmed S.A. v Mexico*, Award, ICSID Case No. ARB (AF)/00/2 (2003), paras. 115–17, 122.

6.2 Requirements for the Application of Human Rights Law in an Investment Dispute

Whether an investment tribunal may apply human rights law depends both on the relevant jurisdiction clause and on the applicable law. The wording of compromissory clauses vary across investment protection treaties. In some cases, jurisdiction is restricted to violations of the treaty (most often a Bilateral Investment Treaty (BIT)) containing the applicable jurisdiction clause. Other treaties, however contain broad clauses that provide tribunals with significantly wider jurisdiction. Consider, for example, the Norway–Lithuania BIT which provides for jurisdiction in respect of '[a]ny dispute which may arise between an Investor of one Contracting Party and the other Contracting Party in connection with an investment'.[7] Such a clause would also include disputes involving human rights violations, if and to the extent that they were connected to an investment. It follows that tribunals must decide on a case-by-case basis whether and how far they may look into a particular human rights problem.

It is not only the relevant jurisdictional clause, but also the applicable law which determines if and to what extent an investment tribunal may take human rights law into account. Choice of law clauses typically refer to 'international law', which includes both treaties and customary international law as well as national law.[8] Human rights law may be applicable as a component of international law.[9] This will particularly apply to human rights treaties in force in the investor's host state. Otherwise it must be established that a

[7] Norway–Lithuania BIT (1992), Art. IX.

[8] See e.g. Netherlands–Argentina BIT (1992), Art. 10(7): 'The arbitration tribunal addressed in accordance with paragraph (5) of this Article shall decide on the basis of the law of the Contracting Party which is a party to the dispute (including its rules on the conflict of law), the provisions of the present Agreement, special Agreements concluded in relation to the investment concerned as well as such rules of international law as may be applicable.' See also Tadia Begic, *Applicable Law in International Investment Disputes* (Eleven Publishing, 2005); Christoph Schreuer et al., *The ICSID Convention: A Commentary*, 2nd edn (Cambridge University Press, 2009), Art. 42.

[9] The Report of the Executive Directors on the ICSID Convention, para. 40: 'The term "international law" shall be understood in the sense given to it by Article 38 of the Statute of the International Court of Justice.' This reference to Art. 38 of the Statute of the ICJ shows that ICSID tribunals are to apply the full range of sources of international law. See Schreuer et al. (n. 8), Art. 42, 169–203; Pierre-Marie Dupuy, 'Unification Rather than Fragmentation of International Law? The Case of International Investment Law and Human Rights Law', in Dupuy et al. (n. 1), 56ff.; Emmanuel Gaillard and Yas Banifatemi, 'The Meaning of "and" in Article 42(1), Second Sentence, of the Washington Convention: The Role of International Law in ICSID Choice of Law Process', 18 ICSID Review Foreign Investment Law Journal 348 (2003), 397. See e.g. *Toto Costruzioni Generali S.p.A. v The Republic of Lebanon*, Decision on Jurisdiction, ICSID Case No. ARB/07/12 (2009), paras. 158–60; *Hesham T. M. Al Warraq v Republic of Indonesia*, Award, UNCITRAL (2014), paras. 564–5, 621; *Tulip Real Estate and Development Netherlands B.V. v Republic of Turkey*, Decision on Annulment, ICSID Case No. ARB/11/28 (2015), paras. 86–92, 145–53.

particular human rights norm is customary international law. Finally, human rights obligations may also be applicable as an element of local law.[10]

Furthermore, principles of treaty interpretation as provided for in the Vienna Convention on the Law of Treaties (VCLT) offer the possibility of taking human rights into consideration when deciding whether a violation of investment law has occurred.[11] Art. 31(3)(c) of the VCLT requires that in the interpretation of a treaty there 'shall be taken into account, together with the context:... any relevant rules of international law applicable in the relations between the parties'.[12]

It is disputed whether human rights norms are relevant rules in the context of interpreting investment treaties. Further, it is not entirely clear what the phrase 'applicable in the relations between the parties' means in an investor–state arbitration context.[13] Human rights norms will obviously be relevant to the interpretation of an investment protection treaty if the preamble of the treaty refers to such rules. Furthermore, if both states party to a BIT conferring jurisdiction on the tribunal are also parties to a particular human rights treaty, this requirement will also be satisfied.[14] The situation is more problematic with regard to regional investment protection treaties such as NAFTA or the ECT. In such a context, the additional question arises whether all the parties to the regional treaty must be parties to the human rights treaty relied upon as well. There is, however, no uniform answer to this question.[15]

In any event, human rights norms may influence the meaning of the terms and provisions of an investment treaty through treaty interpretation. They may be of importance, for instance, in determining the meaning of the fair and equitable treatment standard,[16]

[10] Dupuy (n. 9), 59ff. [11] See e.g. Simma and Kill (n. 1).

[12] Vienna Convention on the Law of Treaties, 1155 UNTS 331 (1969), Art. 31(3)(c).

[13] See e.g. Simma and Kill (n. 1); Thomas Wälde, 'Interpreting Investment Treaties: Experiences and Examples', in Binder et al. (n. 1), 772; Richard Gardiner, *Treaty Interpretation* (Oxford University Press, 2008), 260–75; Campbell McLachlan, 'Investment Treaties and General International Law', 57 ICLQ 361 (2008); UN International Law Commission, 'Fragmentation of International Law: Difficulties Arising from the Diversification and Expansion of International Law', UN Doc A/CN.4/L.682 (2006), paras. 410–80; Campbell McLachlan, 'The Principle of Systemic Integration and Article 31(3)(c) of the Vienna Convention', 54 ICLQ 279 (2005). Also see *Oil Platforms Case (Iran v United States of America)*, I.C.J. Reports (2003), para. 41, but also see Separate Opinion of Judge Buergenthal (paras. 22–3) and Separate Opinion of Judge Higgins (paras. 45–6).

[14] UN International Law Commission (n. 13), para. 472. Simma and Kill refer furthermore to the concept of *erga omnes* obligations. See Simma and Kill, (n. 1), 701; Bruno Simma, 'From Bilateralism to Community Interest in International Law', 250 Recueil des Cours 293 (1994).

[15] See e.g. UN International Law Commission (n. 13), paras. 471–2; Joost Pauwelyn, *Conflict of Norms in Public International Law* (Cambridge University Press, 2003), 257–63; McLachlan, 'The Principle of Systemic Integration' (n. 13), 313–15; Mark Villiger, *Commentary on the 1969 Vienna Convention on the Law of Treaties* (Brill, 2009), 433.

[16] See e.g. Stephen Vasciannie, 'The Fair and Equitable Treatment Standard in International Investment Law and Practice', 70 BYIL 99 (1999); Patrick Dumberry, 'The Quest to Define "Fair and Equitable Treatment" for Investors under International Law: The Case of the NAFTA Chapter 11 Pope & Talbot Awards', 3 Journal of World Investment & Trade 657 (2002), 657–91; Christoph Schreuer, 'Fair and Equitable Treatment in Arbitral Practice', 6 Journal of World Investment and Trade 357 (2005); Barnali Choudhury, 'Evolution or Devolution? Defining Fair and Equitable Treatment in International Investment Law', 6 Journal of World Investment & Trade 297 (2005); Rudolf Dolzer and Christoph

or of full protection and security clauses,[17] with regard to decisions on direct or indirect expropriation,[18] or when identifying the international minimum standard.[19] Similarly, human rights considerations can find their way into investment law through the concept of 'legitimate expectations' which plays a role in several protection standards.

For tribunals to be able to make use of human rights law, human rights considerations must be invoked by either the investor or the host state. So far, no state has sued an investor for human rights violations. One reason for this may be that human rights violations often occur in complicity with the host state.[20] The main reason, then, is lack of consent to arbitrate human rights issues. In the case of an investment contract, it depends on the text of the contract whether a state can sue an investor if its actions require an intervention from the state to prevent human rights violations. Where consent is based on a national investment statute or BIT, it will often not be perfected so as to allow arbitration against an investor.[21] States desiring such an effect will thus have to adapt their BITs accordingly. States dispose of their own legal orders to prevent investors from committing acts that would amount to human rights violations, and thus investment arbitration is not necessary for such purposes.

Schreuer, *Principles of International Investment Law*, 2nd edn (Oxford University Press, 2012), 130–60; Ioana Tudor, *The Fair and Equitable Treatment Standard in the International Law of Foreign Investment* (Oxford University Press, 2008).

[17] Dolzer and Schreuer (n. 16), 160–65.

[18] Ibid. 98–129; Campbell McLachlan, Laurence Shore, and Matthew Weininger, *International Investment Arbitration* (Oxford University Press, 2007), 290–97. On indirect expropriation, see e.g. Vaughan Lowe, 'Regulation or Expropriation?', 55 Current Legal Problems 447 (2002); Rudolf Dolzer, 'Indirect Expropriations: New Developments?', 11 NYU Environmental Law Journal 64 (2003); W. Michael Reisman and Robert Sloane, 'Indirect Expropriation and its Valuation in the BIT Generation', 74 British Year Book of International Law 115 (2003); Gary Sampliner, 'Arbitration of Expropriation Cases Under U.S. Investment Treaties: A Threat to Democracy or the Dog That Didn't Bark?' 18 ICSID Review Foreign Investment Law Journal 1 (2003); Jan Paulsson and Zachary Douglas, 'Indirect Expropriation in Investment Treaty Arbitration', in Norbert Horn and Stefan Kröll, *Arbitrating Foreign Investment Disputes: Procedural and Substantive Legal Aspects* (Kluwer Law International, 2004), 145; L. Yves Fortier and Stephan Drymer, 'Indirect Expropriation in the Law of International Investment: I Know It When I See It, or Caveat Investor', 19 ICSID Review Foreign Investment Law Journal 293 (2004); Daniel Clough, 'Regulatory Expropriations and Compensation under NAFTA', 6 Journal of World Investment & Trade 553 (2005); Andrew Newcombe, 'The Boundaries of Regulatory Expropriation in International Law', 20 ICSID Review Foreign Investment Law Journal 1 (2005); Ursula Kriebaum, 'Regulatory Takings: Balancing the Interests of the Investor and the State', 8 Journal of World Investment & Trade 717 (2007); Kriebaum, *Eigentumsschutz im Völkerrecht* (n. 1); Kriebaum, 'Expropriation', in Bungenberg et al. (n. 1), 959.

[19] Alireza Falsafi, 'The International Minimum Standard of Treatment of Foreign Investors' Property: A Contingent Standard', 30 Suffolk Transnational Law Review 317 (2007).

[20] See e.g. African Commission on Human and Peoples' Rights, 'The Social and Economic Rights Action Center and the Center for Economic and Social Rights v. Nigeria': http://www.cohre.org/store/attachments/SERACper cent20andper cent20CE SRper cent20v.per cent20Nigeria.doc.

[21] Often, the BIT clause even restricts jurisdiction to claims by investors and excludes the possibility for the host state to sue the investor. See e.g. Canada-Uruguay BIT (1997), Art. 12: 'Any dispute between one Contracting Party and an investor of the other Contracting Party, relating to a claim by the investor that a measure taken or not taken by the former Contracting Party is in breach of this Agreement, and that the investor has incurred loss or damage by reason of, or arising out of, that breach...'.

As a result, cases where investors have sued states which in turn have responded by invoking human rights as a defence are more common. A further familiar avenue of informing tribunals of human rights implications raised by investment arbitration are *amicus curiae* petitions by civil rights groups and human rights NGOs.[22]

6.3 Ten different ways of dealing with potential human rights issues in investment disputes

It is possible to identify ten ways in which tribunals have reacted to human rights issues. Sections 6.3.1–6.3.4 deal with cases where tribunals did not apply human rights to a particular case, or chose not to employ them for the purpose of interpreting substantive investment protection standards, although one of the parties requested it.

Section 6.3.5 addresses instances where tribunals applied human rights law to an investment dispute in the context of the fair and equitable treatment standard. Sections 6.3.6 and 6.3.7 concern cases where tribunals relied on human rights law to interpret diverse provisions of investment protection treaties. In these cases, the state party to the investment protection treaty was often, but not always, a party to the human rights treaty the tribunal relied upon.

Section 6.3.8 deals with the approach of investment tribunals to human rights abuses committed by investors. Section 6.3.9 reviews cases where human rights issues were at stake but neither the state nor the tribunal relied upon human rights law. Section 6.3.10 considers instances where states invoked human rights as a defence and tribunals took such norms into account, finding them 'not to be inconsistent' with investment treaty obligations.

[22] See e.g. *Aguas del Tunari S.A. v Republic of Bolivia*, NGO Petition to Participate as Amici Curiae, ICSID Case No. ARB/02/3 (2002), paras. 47–8; *Aguas del Tunari S.A. v Republic of Bolivia*, Letter from President of Tribunal Responding to Petition, ICSID Case No. ARB/02/3 (2002); *United Parcel Service of America v Canada*, Decision on Petitions for Intervention and Participation as Amici Curiae, ICSID Case No. UNCT/02/1 (2001), para. 40; *Methanex v United States*, Decision on Amici Curiae, UNCITRAL (2001), paras. 47–9; *Glamis Gold v United States*, Decision on Application and Submission by Quechan Indian Nation, UNCITRAL (2005), para. 10; *Suez, Sociedad General de Aguas de Barcelona, S.A. and Vivendi Universal, S.A. v Argentine Republic*, Order in Response to a Petition for Transparency and Participation as Amicus Curiae, ICSID Case No. ARB/03/19 (2006), paras. 14–19; *Biwater Gauff (Tanzania) Ltd v United Republic of Tanzania*, Petition for Amicus Curiae Status, ICSID Case No. ARB/05/22 (2006), paras. 7–8; *Biwater Gauff (Tanzania) Ltd v United Republic of Tanzania*, Procedural Order No. 5, ICSID Case No. ARB/05/22 (2006), para. 50; *Pietro Foresti, Laura De Carli, and Others v Republic of South Africa*, Petition for Limited Participation as Non-Disputing Parties in Terms of Articles 41(3), 27, 39 and 35 of the Additional Facility Rules, ICSID Case No. ARB(AF)/07/01 (2009), paras. 2.1, 3–4.1. Also see Statement of the North American Free Trade Commission on Non-Disputing Party Participation (USTR 2003): http://www.international.gc.ca/assets/trade-agreements-accords-commerciaux/pdfs/Nondisputing-en.pdf.

It is not suggested that all cases that concern issues of human rights can be neatly categorized within these ten categories. In fact, some cases reflect several of the features described below.

6.3.1 Lack of jurisdiction over human rights issues

In some cases in which investors relied on human rights arguments, tribunals held that they lacked jurisdiction over such issues. Interestingly, tribunals have not used this approach in cases in which states have invoked human rights arguments as a defence.

An early instance of a tribunal adopting such a restrictive approach was *Biloune v Ghana.*[23] In that case, the claimant alleged that his investment had been expropriated and that he had been subjected to a denial of justice and his human rights had been violated by arbitrary detention and deportation.[24] Ghana is obviously not a party to the European Convention on Human Rights (ECHR). At the time it was not yet a party to the African Charter on Human and Peoples' Rights or to the UN Covenant on Civil and Political Rights either. As a result, Mr Biloune did not enjoy access to a separate international forum for the purpose of asserting his human rights.

In an effort to pursue his human rights claims, Mr Biloune turned to arbitration. The jurisdictional clause in Art. 15 of the GIC Agreement (an investment contract) covered '[a]ny dispute between the foreign investor and the Government in respect of an approved enterprise'.[25] The applicable law comprised the investment contract and the national law of Ghana.[26] The investment tribunal, however, held that it lacked jurisdiction to examine the human rights violations allegedly suffered by the investor in the context of an investment dispute. It found that, although international law recognizes that all individuals have human rights, its jurisdiction was limited to commercial disputes arising out of the contract. Specifically, the tribunal held that it had not been authorized to deal with allegations of human rights violations as an independent cause of action:

> [C]ontemporary international law recognizes that all individuals ... are entitled to fundamental human rights ... which no government may violate. Nevertheless, it does not follow that this Tribunal is competent to pass upon every type of departure from the minimum standard to which foreign nationals are entitled, or that this Tribunal is authorized to deal with allegations of violations of fundamental human rights.
>
> This Tribunal's competence is limited to commercial disputes arising under a contract entered into in the context of Ghana's Investment Code. As noted, the Government agreed to arbitrate only disputes "in respect of" foreign investment. Thus, other matters ... are outside this Tribunal's jurisdiction ... [W]hile the acts alleged

[23] *Biloune and Marine Drive Complex Ltd v Ghana Investments Centre and the Government of Ghana*, Award on Jurisdiction and Liability, UNCITRAL (1989), (1994) 95 ILR 184.

[24] Ibid. para. 202. [25] Ibid. [26] Ibid. para. 207.

> to violate the international human rights of Mr. Biloune may be relevant in considering the investment dispute under arbitration, this Tribunal lacks jurisdiction to address, as an independent cause of action, a claim of violation of human rights.[27]

Therefore, the tribunal declined to exercise jurisdiction over the alleged human rights violations as an independent cause of action, but did not exclude possible relevance of human rights violations when considering violations of the investment contract.

In *Rompetrol v Romania*[28] the investor alleged that the manner in which investigations had been conducted by Romanian authorities had breached due process rights, among them Art. 6(3)(a)[29] of the ECHR.[30] One point of controversy between the parties was the relevance of the ECHR for the interpretation of the BIT's standards. The claimant took the position that even if the ECHR had been respected, the BIT could nevertheless have been violated.[31] Pursuant to the argument of the respondent, the ECHR constituted a benchmark for BIT violations, meaning that if the ECHR had been complied with, the requirements of the BIT would also have been satisfied.[32]

The tribunal adopted a restrictive approach towards the relevance of human rights law in the investment context. Despite both parties submitting ECHR-based arguments, the tribunal expressed a general refusal to decide 'any issue under the ECHR whether the issue in question lies in the past or is still open'. In terms of defining the task of the tribunal, it concluded that:

> Its function is solely to decide, as between TRG and Romania, "legal dispute[s] arising directly out of an investment" and to do so in accordance with "such rules of law as may be agreed by the parties", which in the present case means essentially the BIT, in application of the appropriate rules for its interpretation.[33]

The tribunal took this approach although both the home state of the investor (The Netherlands) and the host state (Romania) were parties to the ECHR. The jurisdiction clause in the Netherlands–Romania BIT does not limit the tribunal's jurisdiction to breaches of its standards, but refers to 'solving disputes with respect to investments' in general.[34] This would, arguably, also include disputes arising out of ECHR violations targeting investors.

Art. 42(1) of the ICSID Convention, which governs applicable law, refers to 'such rules of international law as may be applicable', and therefore includes the ECHR if its violation is directly related to a legal dispute arising out of an investment. The mere fact that

[27] Ibid. para. 203.

[28] *Rompetrol Group N.V. v Romania*, Award, ICSID Case No. ARB/06/3 (2013). For more on the award, see Kriebaum (n. 2).

[29] ECHR, Art. 6(3)(a): 'Everyone charged with a criminal offence has the following minimum rights: (a) to be informed promptly, in a language which he understands and in detail, of the nature and cause of the accusation against him.'

[30] *Rompetrol Group N.V. v Romania*, Award, ICSID Case No. ARB/06/3 (2013), para. 54.

[31] Ibid. para. 60. [32] Ibid. para. 169. [33] Ibid. para. 170.

[34] The Netherlands–Romania BIT (1983).

the European Court of Human Rights (ECtHR) is competent to interpret the ECHR does not exclude other organs from identifying ECHR breaches. Despite the tribunal's refusal to issue an opinion on a violation of the ECHR in the context of the investment dispute, it did not rule out the possibility of resorting to the ECHR for interpretative purposes.[35]

A slightly different constellation of facts was prevalent in *Pezold v Zimbabwe*.[36] In that case, a non-disputing party petitioned for leave to submit an *amicus curiae* brief referring in particular to the UN Declaration on the Rights of Indigenous Peoples. The tribunal found that the question of indigenous peoples' rights was not within the scope of the dispute before it.[37] It also held, in this regard, that the BIT:

> does not incorporate the universe of international law into the BITs or into disputes arising under BITs... [and that] [t]he Petitioners provided no evidence or support for their assertion that international investment law and international human rights law are interdependent such that any decision of these Arbitral Tribunals which did not consider the content of international human rights norms would be legally incomplete.[38]

Therefore, the tribunal was of the opinion that issues of human rights were genuinely beyond its competence despite both applicable BITs containing broad jurisdiction clauses. The Zimbabwe–Germany BIT covers 'disputes between a contracting party and a national or company of the other contracting party concerning an investment of such national or company'[39]; and the Switzerland–Zimbabwe BIT provides for jurisdiction with regard to 'solving disputes with respect to investments between a Contracting Party and an investor of the other Contracting Party'.[40]

6.3.2 No interpretation of BITs in light of human rights principles since the legal situation is different under investment protection treaties

At least two cases can be found in which tribunals stated that the legal situation under a human rights treaty was different from that under investment protection treaties, and therefore they did not apply principles established in human rights law to investment law cases. The ECHR was not part of the applicable law in any of these cases where states sought to rely on concepts developed by the ECtHR to justify interferences with investors' rights.

[35] *Rompetrol Group N.V. v Romania*, Award, ICSID Case No. ARB/06/3 (2013), para. 172.

[36] *Bernhard von Pezold and Others v Republic of Zimbabwe*, Procedural Order No. 2, ICSID Case No. ARB/10/15 (2012).

[37] Ibid. paras. 57–60.

[38] Ibid. paras. 57–8.

[39] Zimbabwe–Germany BIT (1995), Art. 11.

[40] Swiss–Zimbabwe BIT (1996), Art. 10.

Siemens v Argentina is an example of such an approach. In this case, Argentina relied on the ECtHR's judgment in *James v United Kingdom* to argue that expropriations do not necessarily require compensation in the amount of full market value.[41] The tribunal observed that the legal situation under the BIT was not comparable to that under human rights law, since 'Article I of the First Protocol to the European Convention on Human Rights permits a margin of appreciation not found in customary international law or the Treaty'.[42] The tribunal did not specify a particular difference between treaty texts. While the ECHR text does not specify the amount of compensation required, the BIT clearly sets out that compensation shall correspond to the value of the investment expropriated.[43]

The tribunal in *Pezold v Zimbabwe* also followed this approach. The case concerned expropriations without compensation of three estates owned by the claimants, including forestry and agricultural businesses. The expropriation occurred in the context of Zimbabwe's land reform programme. The respondent relied on jurisprudence of the ECtHR, arguing that the proportionality doctrine and the doctrine of margin of appreciation would be equally applicable to the case at hand. It submitted that the tribunal should permit a wide margin of appreciation in terms of allowing states to determine whether land reforms were necessary and how they should be achieved.[44] The tribunal, however, rejected this approach. Noting that concepts from other fields of public international law should only be transplanted into investment law with caution, it held:

> As to 'margin of appreciation' and the Respondent's argument that it should be given a wide margin when determining what is in the Zimbabwean public interest, the Tribunal is of the opinion that due caution should be exercised in importing concepts from other legal regimes (in this case European human rights law) without a solid basis for doing so. Balancing competing (and non-absolute) human rights and the need to grant States a margin of appreciation when making those balancing decisions is well established in human rights law, but the Tribunal is not aware that the concept has found much support in international investment law. The Respondent has only referred the Tribunal to European human rights cases in its arguments.
>
> This is a very different situation from that in which margin of appreciation is usually used. Here, the Government has agreed to specific international obligations and there is no 'margin of appreciation' qualification within the BITs at issue. Moreover, the margin of appreciation doctrine has not achieved customary status. Therefore the Tribunal declines to apply this doctrine.[45]

[41] *Siemens A.G. v The Argentine Republic*, Award, ICSID Case No. ARB/02/8 (2007), para. 346.

[42] Ibid. para. 354.

[43] Argentina–Germany BIT (1991), Art. 4(2): 'Die Entschädigung muß dem Wert der enteigneten Kapitalanlage unmittelbar vor dem Zeitpunkt entsprechen... La indemnizacion deberá corresponder al valor de la inversión expropdiada...'

[44] *Bernhard von Pezold and Others v Republic of Zimbabwe*, Award, ICSID Case No. ARB/10/15 (2012), paras. 453–4.

[45] Ibid. paras. 465–6.

Similar to the Germany–Argentina BIT, the Germany–Zimbabwe BIT spells out that compensation 'shall be equivalent to the value of the expropriated investment'. It therefore uses different wording from the ECHR. Additionally, *James v United Kingdom*, which was referred to by Zimbabwe, involved claims of a national rather than a foreign citizen. The ECtHR has specifically emphasized the need to treat foreign citizens differently with respect to compensation.[46]

6.3.3 Investor rights offer a higher and more specific level of protection compared to human rights instruments

Other tribunals have found that investor rights offer a higher and more specific level of protection compared to human rights instruments, and have therefore refused to apply the latter. An example of this approach can be found in *Roussalis v Romania*.[47] There, the claimant relied on the right to a fair trial in the ECHR and on the protection of property in its First Addition Protocol. For this purpose it invoked Art. 10 of the BIT[48] that provided that any more favourable international law obligation for investors existing between the parties to the BIT shall prevail over the provision of the BIT.[49] Jurisdiction under the BIT is limited to 'disputes ... concerning an obligation ... under this Agreement'.[50] Given that Art. 10 of the BIT permits importing more favourable substantive protection standards, the tribunal's jurisdiction also extends to them.

However, this was not discussed in the award. Instead, the tribunal found the protection offered by the BIT to be more specific and favourable than that of the ECHR, thus refusing to apply the latter.[51] However, the tribunal did not exclude the application of

[46] *James and Others v United Kingdom*, (1986) ECHR 2, para. 63: '[T]here may well be good grounds for drawing a distinction between nationals and non-nationals as far as compensation is concerned.' On this issue, see Ursula Kriebaum, 'Nationality and the Protection of Property under the European Convention on Human Rights', in Isabelle Buffard et al. (eds), *International Law Between Universalism and Fragmentation* (Brill, 2008), 649.

[47] *Spyridon Roussalis v Romania*, Award, ICSID Case No. ARB/06/1 (2011).

[48] Greece–Romania BIT (1997), Art. 10 provides that: 'If the provisions of law of either Contracting Party or obligations under international law existing at present or established hereafter between the Contracting Parties in addition to this Agreement, contain a regulation, whether general or specific, entitling investments by investors of the other Contracting Party to a treatment more favourable than is provided for by this Agreement, such regulation shall to the extent that it is more favourable, prevail over this Agreement.' Also see *Spyridon Roussalis v Romania*, Award, ICSID Case No. ARB/06/1 (2011) paras. 117 and 310.

[49] *Spyridon Roussalis v Romania*, Award, ICSID Case No. ARB/06/1 (2011), paras. 117 and 309.

[50] Greece–Romania BIT (1997), Art. 9.

[51] *Spyridon Roussalis v Romania*, Award, ICSID Case No. ARB/06/1 (2011), para. 312: 'The Tribunal does not exclude the possibility that the international obligations of the Contracting States mentioned at Article 10 of the BIT could include obligations deriving from multilateral instruments to which those states are parties, including, possibly, the European Convention of Human Rights and its Additional Protocol No. 1. But the issue is moot in the present case and does not require decision by the Tribunal,

human rights obligations under Art. 10 of the BIT if they are more favourable than obligations under the BIT.[52]

6.3.4 Human rights were not fully argued

In some cases, tribunals appeared willing, in principle, to apply human rights, but refrained from doing so for lack of sufficient substantiation by the parties. In these cases tribunals abstained from in-depth analyses of the compatibility between investor protection and human rights standards.

One such example is the case of *Azurix v Argentina*.[53] The case concerned a concession for the distribution of drinking water and the treatment of sewage in Argentina. Blaming the foreign investor for an algae bloom in a reservoir and water contamination, the government encouraged consumers not to pay their water bills. It also prevented the investor from increasing its rates. As a result, Azurix sought to terminate the concession, but the government of the province where the investment was located initially rejected the request. Finally, the province terminated the concession itself, alleging a failure to provide the agreed services under the concession.

The investor argued that Argentina's measures constituted an indirect expropriation, as well as a violation of the fair and equitable treatment, non-discrimination, and full protection and security standards. In response, Argentina explicitly invoked human rights-based arguments to justify its actions, stating that a hierarchy exists between human rights provisions and investment protection standards. How this argument had been developed by Argentina's expert is unknown, given that neither the legal briefs nor the expert opinions of the case are publicly available.

What has been revealed by the award is Argentina's argument that there was a conflict between its investment obligations and human rights obligations, namely consumers' rights, in which case, it argued, the latter must prevail:

> The Respondent also raises the issue of a conflict between the BIT and human rights treaties that protect consumers' rights. According to Argentina's expert, a conflict between a BIT and human rights treaties must be resolved in favor of human rights because the consumers' public interest must prevail over the private interest of service provider. On this point, the Claimant argues that the user's rights were duly protected by the provisions made in the Concession Agreement and the Province fails to prove how said rights were affected by the termination.[54]

given the higher and more specific level of protection offered by the BIT to the investors compared to the more general protections offered to them by the human rights instruments referred above. Consequently Article 10 of the BIT cannot, in its own terms and in the instant case, serve as a useful instrument for enlarging the protections available to the Claimant from the Romanian State under the BIT.'

[52] Ibid. [53] *Azurix Corp. v Argentina*, Award, ICSID Case No. ARB/01/12 (2006).

[54] Ibid. para. 254.

The tribunal did not enter into an abstract discussion about a possible hierarchy of norms in international law. Instead, it noted that a conflict between human rights and investment protection norms had not been sufficiently advanced and therefore any incompatibility between human rights and the standards of the applicable BIT could not be assessed:

> The Respondent has also raised the issue of the compatibility of the BIT with human rights treaties. The matter has not been fully argued and the Tribunal fails to understand the incompatibility in the specifics of the instant case. The services to consumers continued to be provided without interruption by ABA during five months after the termination notice and through the new provincial utility after the transfer of service.[55]

The tribunal subsequently found that the actions of the province were arbitrary, and constituted a violation of the fair and equitable treatment and full protection and security standards.[56]

The tribunal in *Frontier Petroleum v Czech Republic* adopted a similar approach. In that case, the claimant had referred to Art. 6 of the ECHR. However, neither party had pleaded the case law of the ECtHR or explained why a relevant violation should (or should not) have occurred. The tribunal therefore declined to delve into the issue of applicability and violation of the ECHR:

> With respect to Claimant's argument that by operation of Articles III(3) and III(4) of the BIT, Claimant was entitled to the same right to expeditious proceedings before a court in the Czech Republic as are persons entitled to such treatment under the ECHR, the Tribunal notes that rights under the ECHR accrue to everyone, regardless of nationality. This obviates Claimant's need to rely on the BIT to invoke such rights. The Parties have not pleaded the jurisprudence of the ECHR in these proceedings, therefore this Tribunal makes no finding as to whether any standard set by the ECHR is applicable here and has been breached.[57]

In the cases discussed in this section, human rights were invoked by investors and states alike to influence the application and interpretation of investment protection standards by tribunals. The tribunals did not reject the human rights arguments for reasons of jurisdiction or applicable law, nor did they find it inappropriate in principle to take human rights law into consideration when interpreting investment provision standards in accordance with Art. 31(3)(c) of the VCLT. However, the tribunals did clarify that for a human rights argument to merit consideration in an investment arbitration case, it would have to be fully argued.

[55] Ibid. para. 261. [56] Ibid. paras. 377, 393, 408.

[57] *Frontier Petroleum v Czech Republic*, Award, UNCITRAL (2010), para. 338.

6.3.5 To the extent that human rights are part of the applicable law they will be applied

In another group of cases, tribunals considered human rights norms to be part of the applicable law and applied them side by side with the applicable investment provisions. The result of the human rights analysis was then used as a factor in determining whether obligations under investment law had been violated.

In *Toto Costruzioni Generali S.pA. v Lebanon*[58] the tribunal pointed out that it was not restricted to applying the treaty's standards, but was authorized to rule on any breach of international law in general.[59] For this purpose it referred to the clause on applicable law. Art. 7 of the Italy–Lebanon BIT contains the following provision on applicable law:

> The arbitral tribunal shall decide the dispute in accordance with the provisions of this Agreement and the applicable rules and principles of international law.[60]

The jurisdictional clause in Art. 7 of the BIT is also broad and provides jurisdiction, namely, 'in case of a dispute regarding investments'.

The tribunal carefully distinguished between the ECHR and the UN Covenant on Civil and Political Rights (ICCPR). It declined to rely upon the ECHR, given that it did not constitute part of the applicable law, but found the ICCPR to be applicable. The dispute concerned a highway construction contract. The claimant argued that the long duration of legal proceedings before the Lebanese *Conseil d'État* violated the FET provision in the BIT between Italy and Lebanon. In this context the claimant invoked several judgments of the ECtHR concerning violations of the right to a fair trial (Art. 6 ECHR) as well as the corresponding guarantee in Art. 14 ICCPR.

The ICCPR was part of the applicable law since Lebanon was a party to it, but the ECHR was not. Without explicitly mentioning Art. 7 of the BIT but applying the normative content of Art. 7, the tribunal rejected the submitted references to the judgments of the ECtHR.[61] However, it upheld the invocation of Art. 14 of the ICCPR and took the decisions of the Human Rights Committee into consideration.[62] In the end, the tribunal rejected the claims of the investor for lack of sufficient proof of having had recourse to internal remedies that would have allowed acceleration of the procedure before the *Conseil d'État*.[63]

Al Warraq v Indonesia[64] is a further example of a tribunal applying human rights law in an investment case. That case concerned the bailout of a bank. Indonesian courts

[58] *Toto Costruzioni Generali S.p.A. v The Republic of Lebanon*, Decision on Jurisdiction, ICSID Case No. ARB/07/12 (2009).

[59] Ibid. para. 154.

[60] Italy–Lebanon BIT (1997), Art. 7(3).

[61] *Toto Costruzioni Generali S.p.A. v The Republic of Lebanon*, Decision on Jurisdiction, ICSID Case No. ARB/07/12 (2009), para. 157.

[62] Ibid. paras. 158–60.

[63] Ibid. paras. 167–8.

[64] *Hesham T. M. Al Warraq v Republic of Indonesia*, Award, UNCITRAL (2014), paras. 556–605.

found the investor guilty of contributing to the bank's collapse. They convicted him *in absentia* of corruption and money laundering without providing him with a possibility of participating in the criminal proceedings. In the ensuing investment arbitration, the award was rendered on the basis of an investment protection treaty of the Organisation of the Islamic Conference. Its Art. 13 provides:

> The investor shall be entitled to damages for any injury incurred by him resulting from any of the following acts committed by a Contracting Party…
>
> B) failure to comply with the international obligations and undertakings incumbent on the Contracting Party in favor of the investor pursuant to this Agreement or voluntary or negligent assent to taking the measures necessary for their implementation…[65]

The tribunal applied Art. 14 of the ICCPR, which guarantees a fair trial in criminal proceedings, finding that a denial of justice and a violation of the fair and equitable treatment standard had occurred. It held that Art. 14 was binding upon Indonesia and contains rules that allow deciding whether a denial of justice has occurred through a trial *in absentia*. The tribunal held that:

> all persons charged with a criminal offence have a primary, unrestricted right to be present at the trial to defend themselves…Trials in absentia are not prohibited under Article 14(3) only when the accused person, although informed of the proceeding sufficiently in advance, voluntarily declines to exercise his right to be present.[66]

The tribunal found that Al Warraq had neither been informed correctly of the accusation nor of his conviction, and that he had not been interrogated as a suspect. Furthermore, it found that he had been deprived of the opportunity to nominate a representative for his trial as well as for the appeals proceedings. Therefore, Indonesia had violated the guarantees contained in the ICCPR. This amounted to a denial of justice and hence constituted a violation of the FET standard.[67] The tribunal used the provisions of the ICCPR to decide on the conformity of court proceedings with the FET standard under the BIT.

Both the *Toto* and the *Al Warraq* tribunals used human rights norms as a basis for their legal findings concerning the FET standard under the relevant BITs. They incorporated elements of human rights-based fair trial standards into the FET standard. To be able to do so, both tribunals first found the relevant human rights treaty to be part of the

[65] Author's translation from the original French: 'L'investisseur aura droit à des dommages-intérêts pour tout préjudice subi par lui et résultant de l'un de ces actes suivants commis par une Partie Contractante:…B) non respect des obligations et des engagements internationaux incombant à la Partie Contractante en faveur de l'investisseur conformément au présent Accord ou [a]bstention volontaire ou par négligence de prendre des mesures nécessaires pour leurs exécution…'

[66] *Hesham T. M. Al Warraq v Republic of Indonesia*, Award, UNCITRAL (2014), paras. 564 and 565.

[67] Ibid. para. 621.

applicable law in the case under consideration. In both cases there was no situation of a potential conflict between investment law standards and human rights standards. Rather, the normative relationship between the two was complementary.

The situation was different in *Urbaser v Argentina*.[68] In that case, the host state relied on human rights norms to defend its interference with investor rights. The dispute arose in the context of Argentina's financial crisis in 2001–2. The claimant was a shareholder in a concessionaire that provided water and sewage services in the province of Buenos Aires, Argentina. The investor never invested, to the extent provided for in the concession contract, in the expansion of services to achieve a broader coverage. Urbaser argued that a number of measures adopted by the province of Buenos Aires had made a profitable operation of its concession impossible. Furthermore, it claimed that the province had conducted renegotiations of the concession in a manner that led to its termination in 2006 because of the political desire to return utility concessions to the state. Argentina argued that the investment failed not due to its measures to cope with the financial crises (which included 'pesification' and tariff freezes) but because of the shareholders' deficient management and its failure to fulfil its obligations under the concession agreement.

The tribunal took Argentina's human rights obligations into account when interpreting the FET provision of the Argentina–Spain BIT. With regard to the human right to water, it made several important findings. Concerning the compatibility of human rights and investment law obligations, the tribunal decided that the state has to fulfil both sets of obligations simultaneously:

> its obligations regarding the population's right to water, and its obligations towards international investors. The Argentine Republic can and should fulfil both kinds of obligations simultaneously. In so doing, the obligations resulting from the human right to water do not operate as an obstacle to the fulfilment of its obligations towards the Claimants.[69]

The tribunal held that the province had to guarantee the continuation of basic water supply, and that this universal basic human right was a component of the framework of the claimant's legitimate expectations:[70]

> Respondent rightly recalls that the Province had to guarantee the continuation of the basic water supply to millions of Argentines. The protection of this universal basic human right constitutes the framework within which Claimants should frame their expectations.[71]

Given the major impact of the emergency measures on the investment, the tribunal considered the measures viewed in isolation as a breach of the FET standard.[72] However, since the investment had already been struggling, the tribunal found the emergency

[68] *Urbaser S.A. and Consorcio de Aguas Bilbao Bizkaia, Bilbao Biskaia Ur Partzuergoa v The Argentine Republic*, Award, ICSID Case No. ARB/07/26 (2016).

[69] Ibid. para. 720. [70] Ibid. paras. 623–4. [71] Ibid. para. 624. [72] Ibid. para. 680.

measures were not the cause of the failure to meet the concession's obligations. Therefore, it decided that the emergency measures per se did not cause a violation of the FET standard.[73] Furthermore, it found that the state of necessity defence was available to Argentina. The authorities only breached the FET provision of the BIT by engaging the investor in doomed renegotiations of the concession contract.[74] But since the concession was already deprived of any future due to the failure of the claimants to make the necessary investments, the tribunal did not award any damages.[75]

Argentina also brought a counterclaim, arguing that the concessionaire's failure to provide the necessary investment for the expansion of the network violated the investor's commitments and its obligations under international law based on the human right to water.[76] The tribunal accepted jurisdiction for the counterclaim. With regard to the counterclaim, the Tribunal said *obiter* that investors can violate the human right to water by destroying access to water. Therefore, they have an obligation to abstain from such acts.[77] However, the tribunal held that the claimants' obligation to comply with the negative obligation (to refrain from destroying access to water) was 'not a matter for concern in the instant case'.[78]

The tribunal based this finding of an 'obligation to abstain' contained in Art. 30 of the Universal Declaration of Human Rights[79] and Art. 5 of the Covenant on Economic, Social and Cultural Rights,[80] as well as on Principle 8 of the International Labor Office's Tripartite Declaration of Principles concerning Multilateral Enterprises and Social Policy (1977 as amended 2006).[81,82]

Art. 30 of the Universal Declaration of Human Rights as well as Art. 5 of the Covenant on Economic, Social and Cultural Rights prevents reliance on rights contained in the Universal Declaration of Human Rights or the Covenant respectively to destroy other rights contained in the respective instrument.[83] Thereby, they do not

[73] Ibid. paras. 680–83. [74] Ibid. paras. 843–7. [75] Ibid. paras. 846–7.

[76] Ibid. para. 36. [77] Ibid. para. 1210. [78] Ibid.

[79] Universal Declaration of Human Rights, Art. 30: 'Nothing in this Declaration may be interpreted as implying for any State, group or person any right to engage in any activity or to perform any act aimed at the destruction of any of the rights and freedoms set forth herein.' See UN General Assembly Resolution 217A (1948).

[80] Covenant on Economic, Social and Cultural Rights, Art. 5: '1. Nothing in the present Covenant may be interpreted as implying for any State, group or person any right to engage in any activity or to perform any act aimed at the destruction of any of the rights or freedoms recognized herein, or at their limitation to a greater extent than is provided for in the present Covenant. 2. No restriction upon or derogation from any of the fundamental human rights recognized or existing in any country in virtue of law, conventions, regulations or custom shall be admitted on the pretext that the present Covenant does not recognize such rights or that it recognizes them to a lesser extent.' See UN General Assembly Resolution 2200A (XXI) (1966).

[81] Governing Body of the International Labour Office, 'Tripartite Declaration of Principles concerning Multilateral Enterprises and Social Policy' (adopted 204th session (1977), as amended 279th session (2000), 295th session (2006), and 329th session (2017)).

[82] *Urbaser S.A. and Consorcio de Aguas Bilbao Bizkaia, Bilbao Biskaia Ur Partzuergoa v The Argentine Republic*, Award, ICSID Case No. ARB/07/26 (2016), paras. 1196–9.

[83] Edward Guntrip, 'Urbaser v Argentina: The Origins of a Host State Human Rights Counterclaim in ICSID Arbitration?' (EJIL Talk, 2017), https://www.ejiltalk.org/urbaser-v-argentina-the-origins-of-a-host-state-human-rights-counterclaim-in-icsid-arbitration/. On the Covenant on Economic, Social and

forestall reliance on another treaty. Specifically, they do not prevent an investor from relying on a BIT. The International Labor Office's Tripartite Declaration of Principles concerning Multilateral Enterprises and Social Policy is a soft law document that does not create binding obligations for corporations under international law. Therefore, it is doubtful whether these provisions can be used as a basis to establish a human rights obligation for investors to abstain from interfering with a population's right to water.

With regard to the issue at stake, namely a potential obligation under international law to create water connections and expand the network, the tribunal found that under current international law there was no positive obligation on investors to provide access to water based on international human rights law. The acceptance of the bid and the concession contract could not create such an obligation under international law.[84] Therefore, the counterclaim failed on the merits.

In this case, the tribunal resolved a perceived conflict between investment law and human rights law obligations. It did so by applying international human rights norms to frame the interpretation of what legitimate expectations are under the FET standard of the BIT. In some of the above cases it was investors who invoked human rights, whilst in others it was the state. Nevertheless, in both situations tribunals used the technique of bringing human rights and investment law in line with one another.

6.3.6 Inspiration from the approach of human rights bodies if the host state is a party to the corresponding human rights treaty

In another group of cases, tribunals did not directly base their findings on human rights norms but used them as a means of interpreting investment law standards in accordance with Art. 31(3)(c) of the VCLT. This group of cases distinguishes itself from the former only by the extent to which human rights were used to interpret investment law standards. In the previous subsection, tribunals fully applied human rights standards to the facts of the case to reach a decision on the violation of an investment protection provision, whereas in this subsection, tribunals merely used them as inspiration for the interpretation of the investment protection standard.

An example of such an approach is the *Micula v Romania*[85] case. In that case, the tribunal used a human rights-based argument in its decision on jurisdiction as one of several reasons for upholding the Swedish nationality of the investor. The tribunal had

Cultural Rights, Art. 5(1), see Ben Saul, David Kinley, and Jacqueline Mowbray, *The International Covenant on Economic, Social and Cultural Rights* (Oxford University Press, 2014), 263ff.

[84] *Urbaser S.A. and Consorcio de Aguas Bilbao Bizkaia, Bilbao Biskaia Ur Partzuergoa v The Argentine Republic*, Award, ICSID Case No. ARB/07/26 (2016), para. 1212.

[85] *Ioan Micula, Viorel Micula, S.C. European Food S.A, S.C. Starmill S.R.L. and S.C. Multipack S.R.L. v Romania*, Decision on Jurisdiction, ICSID Case No. ARB/05/20 (2008).

to answer the question whether nationality that was properly obtained can fade away because of the disappearance of an effective link.

The parties disagreed in this context on the role of international law in the interpretation of Art. 1(a) of the Sweden–Romania BIT.[86] The BIT does not contain a provision on applicable law. Therefore, according to Art. 42 of the ICSID Convention, the tribunal was required to apply 'the law of the Contracting State party to the dispute and such rules of international law as may be applicable'. The tribunal mentioned that it would take into account, as provided for by Art. 31(3)(c) of the VCLT, any relevant rules of international law. In this context it held that it would take into consideration the 'right to a nationality' under Art. 15 of the Universal Declaration of Human Rights[87] when deciding on the investor's nationality.[88]

A similar approach was taken in the case of *Rompetrol v Romania*. In that case, the tribunal declined to decide on a violation of human rights norms in its decision on the merits. However, in the context of a challenge to counsel whose participation allegedly created a bias of the tribunal, it referred to the right to a fair trial enshrined in Art. 6 of the ECHR. The tribunal rejected the challenge with reference to Art. 6 of the ECHR, and explained that challenging counsel should not become an alternative to raising a challenge against the tribunal itself.[89] In doing so it relied on the ECHR for interpretative assistance.

The tribunal took the same approach in *obiter* in the merits phase concerning the FET standard. There, it stated that under particular circumstances human rights considerations may be relevant for the interpretation of the FET standard:

> The category of materials for the assessment in particular of fair and equitable treatment is not a closed one, and may include, in appropriate circumstances, the consideration of common standards under other international regimes (including those in the area of human rights), if and to the extent that they throw useful light on the content of fair and equitable treatment in particular sets of factual circumstances; the examination is however very specific to the particular circumstances, and defies definition by any general rule.[90]

In *Lauder v Czech Republic*, the BIT did not contain a definition of expropriation or nationalization. The tribunal in that case held that it is generally accepted that a wide variety of measures can lead to an indirect expropriation, and referred to a description of indirect expropriation by the ECtHR.[91] Unlike the tribunal in *Toto v Lebanon*, the

[86] Ibid. para. 87.

[87] Universal Declaration of Human Rights, Art. 15: 'everyone has a right to a nationality and no one shall be arbitrarily deprived of his nationality...'

[88] *Ioan Micula, Viorel Micula, S.C. European Food S.A, S.C. Starmill S.R.L. and S.C. Multipack S.R.L. v Romania*, Decision on Jurisdiction, ICSID Case No. ARB/05/20 (2008), para. 88.

[89] *Rompetrol Group N.V. v Romania*, Decision of the Tribunal on the Participation of a Counsel, ICSID Case No. ARB/06/3 (2013), para. 20.

[90] *Rompetrol Group N.V. v Romania*, Award, ICSID Case No. ARB/06/3 (2013), para. 172.

[91] *Ronald S. Lauder v The Czech Republic*, Award, UNCITRAL (2001), para. 200: 'It is generally accepted that a wide variety of measure are susceptible to lead to indirect expropriation, and each case is

Lauder v Czech Republic tribunal did not discuss whether the ECHR constituted part of the applicable law. It mentioned the ECtHR's jurisprudence alongside literature and then explained why no indirect expropriation occurred. Yet, importantly, it did not rely specifically on the criteria developed in the ECtHR jurisprudence. In this sense, the tribunal took inspiration from ECHR jurisprudence rather than applying it *stricto sensu*.

In *ADC v Hungary*[92] the tribunal referred to the judgments of a number of courts and tribunals, among them the ECtHR,[93] concerning the applicable standard for the assessment of damages to support the application of the *Chorzów Factory* standard for this purpose.[94]

In *Frontier Petroleum v Czech Republic* the tribunal considered that the criteria applied by the tribunal in *Toto v Lebanon* was useful in deciding whether the duration of a procedure before a domestic court amounted to a violation of the fair and equitable treatment standard. The tribunal in *Toto* had relied on the judgments of the Human Rights Committee. Both Lebanon and the Czech Republic are party to the UN Covenant on Civil and Political Rights. The tribunal in *Frontier Petroleum* held:

In assessing whether the delays at the regional court were such that they constituted a breach of the fair and equitable treatment standard, the tribunal finds the criteria set forth in Toto useful:

> To assess whether court delays are in breach of the requirement of a fair hearing, the ICCPR Commission takes into account the complexity of the matter, whether the Claimants availed themselves of the possibilities of accelerating the proceedings, and whether the Claimants suffered from the delay.[95]

The tribunal in *Frontier Petroleum* was not willing to decide on the applicability and potential violation of Art. 6 ECHR. Nevertheless, it used the criteria developed by the Human Rights Committee on the right to a fair trial that had been applied by the tribunal in *Toto v Lebanon*, to decide whether a violation of the fair and equitable treatment standard had occurred. It inquired whether the case was complex, whether the claimant had availed itself of possibilities of acceleration, and whether it had suffered from the delay, finally denying a violation of the FET standard.[96]

The ad hoc Committee in *Tulip v Turkey* referred to the case law of the ECtHR as a means of interpreting Art. 52 of the ICSID Convention. In that case, the tribunal held that provisions in human rights instruments dealing with fair trial are relevant to the

therefore to be decided on the basis of its attending circumstances... The European Court of Human Rights in *Mellacher and Others v. Austria* (1989 Eur.Ct.H.R. (ser. A, No. 169)), held that a "formal" expropriation is a measure aimed at a "Transfer of property", while a "de facto" expropriation occurs when a State deprives the owner of his "right to use, let or sell (his) property".'

[92] *ADC Affiliate Limited and ADC & ADMC Management Limited v The Republic of Hungary*, Award, ICSID Case No. ARB/03/16 (2006).

[93] Ibid. para. 497. [94] Ibid. para. 499.

[95] *Frontier Petroleum v Czech Republic*, Award, UNCITRAL (2010), para. 328.

[96] Ibid. paras. 329–34.

interpretation of the concept of a violation of a fundamental rule of procedure in Art. 52 of the ICSID Convention:[97]

> Provisions in human rights instruments dealing with the right to a fair trial and any judicial practice thereto are relevant to the interpretation of the concept of a fundamental rule of procedure as used in Article 52(1)(d) of the ICSID Convention. This is not to add obligations extraneous to the ICSID Convention. Rather, resort to authorities stemming from the field of human rights for this purpose is a legitimate method of treaty interpretation.[98]

The ad hoc committee proceeded to apply the criteria established by the ECtHR in the context of equality of arms and the obligation to state reasons.[99]

The obligation for tribunals to give reasons for their decisions arises out of the overriding duty to afford the parties a fair hearing, guaranteed in Article 48(3) of the ICSID Convention and ICSID Arbitration Rule 47(1)(i), and reiterated in numerous decisions of ICSID ad hoc committees. In *Ruiz Torija v Spain*, the ECtHR stated:

> The Court reiterates that Article 6(1) [of the ECHR] obliges the Courts to give reasons for their judgments, but cannot be understood as requiring a detailed answer to every argument. The extent to which this duty to give reasons applies may vary according to the nature of the decision. It is moreover necessary to take into account, inter alia, the diversity of the submissions that a litigant may bring before the Courts and the differences existing in the Contracting States with regard to statutory provisions, customary rules, legal opinion and the presentation and drafting of judgments. That is why the question whether a Court has failed to fulfil the obligation to state reasons, deriving from Article 6 of the Convention, can only be determined in the light of the circumstances of the case.[100]
>
> It is the opinion of the Committee that these broad parameters apply equally to international tribunals constituted under the ICSID Convention. The depth and extent of the duty to give reasons will inevitably vary from one case to another. The duty is contextually sensitive and a tribunal's reasons need not be extensive as long as its decision makes sense and enables the parties to know the strengths and weaknesses of their respective cases.[101]

The ad hoc committee did not discuss whether, in the particular case, the ECHR was part of the applicable law, despite Turkey being a party to the ECHR. However, it made a general statement to the effect that the parameters concerning the obligation to state reasons within the right to a fair trial, as protected by the ECHR, were equally applicable to tribunals constituted under the ICSID Convention.

[97] *Tulip Real Estate and Development Netherlands B.V. v Republic of Turkey*, Decision on Annulment, ICSID Case No. ARB/11/28 (2015), paras. 86–92, 145–53.

[98] Ibid. para. 92.

[99] Ibid. paras. 145–53.

[100] *Ruiz Torija v Spain* (1994) ECHR (18,390/91), Series A/303-A, para. 29.

[101] *Tulip Real Estate and Development Netherlands B.V. v Republic of Turkey*, Decision on Annulment, ICSID Case No. ARB/11/28 (2015), paras. 152–3.

In contrast to the tribunals in section 6.3.5, which directly applied human rights norms to the facts under consideration, for the purpose of deciding upon violations of investment treaty standards, tribunals in this section used human rights norms in a more general way. They did not intend to directly apply a human rights instrument to the case under consideration. This is in line with the fact that they did not deal with the issue of whether a particular treaty was part of the applicable law. Rather, the tribunals in this subsection drew inspiration for their interpretation of various investment treaty provisions from the judgments of human rights organs. They employed it in the context of procedural questions (challenges to counsel), questions of jurisdiction (nationality), and interpretation of treaty standards (FET, indirect expropriation), as well as the interpretation of Art. 52 of the ICSID Convention.

6.3.7 Inspiration from the approach of human rights bodies even if the corresponding human rights treaty is not applicable

In a number of cases, investment tribunals drew inspiration from the analyses of human rights bodies, even though the host state was not a party to the relevant human rights treaty. This was the case, for example, in *Perenco v Ecuador.* The tribunal relied upon, among other sources of inspiration, the ECtHR judgments on the binding nature of interim measures.[102]

Similarly, in *El Paso v Argentina* the tribunal relied upon, among other sources of inspiration, the judgments of the ECtHR regarding Art. 15 of the ECHR to decide whether the phrase 'essential security interest' in Art. XI of the Argentina–US BIT is a self-judging clause. Art. 15 of the ECHR provides for the possibility to derogate from certain rights of the convention under specific circumstances, and has always been interpreted as 'not self-judging' by the ECtHR.[103]

In *Saipem v Bangladesh*, the tribunal also relied on judgments of the ECtHR on Art. 1 of the Additional Protocol on property protection to confirm its finding that immaterial rights, in the particular case an ICC award, can be the object of an expropriation.[104] Furthermore, it referred to ECtHR judgments when it decided that a court decision can amount to expropriation.[105]

The tribunal in *Tecmed v Mexico*[106] also relied extensively on concepts developed by the ECtHR in the context of the right to property to decide on the occurrence of an

[102] *Perenco v Ecuador*, Decision on Provisional Measures, ICSID Case No. ARB/08/6 (2009), para. 70.

[103] *El Paso v Argentina*, Award, ICSID Case No. ARB/03/15 (2011), para. 598.

[104] *Saipem S.p.A. v The People's Republic of Bangladesh*, Decision on Jurisdiction and Recommendation on Provisional Measures, ICSID Case No. ARB/05/07 (2007), para. 130.

[105] Ibid. para. 132. The Tribunal made reference to *Allard v Sweden*, (2003) ECHR (35,179/97), paras. 50–53, 61.

[106] *Técnicas Medioambientales Tecmed S.A. v Mexico*, Award, ICSID Case No. ARB (AF)/00/2 (2003).

indirect expropriation. The case concerned the revocation of a licence for the operation of a landfill site. As a first step, the tribunal established, in accordance with the sole effects doctrine, whether the host state's interference had been severe enough to amount to expropriation. It found that the claimant had been radically deprived of the economic use and enjoyment of its investment, and concluded, 'as far as the effects of such Resolution are concerned, the decision can be treated as an expropriation under Article 5(1) of the Agreement.'[107]

As a second step, it applied the proportionality test developed by the ECtHR to confirm its finding. It balanced the public interest, presumably pursued by the interference, against the burden imposed upon an investor,[108] holding:

> There must be a reasonable relationship of proportionality between the charge or weight imposed to the foreign investor and the aim sought to be realized by any expropriatory measure.[109]

The tribunal used the proportionality test as an additional element to decide whether an expropriation had occurred at all. It did not mention that the ECtHR used the proportionality test for a different purpose—namely to examine whether an expropriation is justified or leads to a violation of the convention.[110] Therefore, the investment tribunal applied the concept of proportionality taken from human rights law to a different context in investment law.[111]

[107] Ibid. paras. 115–17.

[108] The tribunal based its award on the ECtHR's decision in *Matos and Silva*, (1996) ECHR, para. 92. In doing so, it applied a proportionality test and established a relationship between the two criteria 'effect' and 'purpose' of the interference. See *Técnicas Medioambientales Tecmed S.A. v Mexico*, Award, ICSID Case No. ARB (AF)/00/2 (2003), para. 122: '[T]he Arbitral Tribunal will consider, in order to determine if they are to be characterized as expropriatory, whether such actions or measures are proportional to the public interest presumably protected thereby and to the protection legally granted to investments, taking into account that the significance of such impact has a key role upon deciding the proportionality.' In applying this proportionality test the *Tecmed* Tribunal relied on judgments of the ECtHR—namely, *Mellacher v Austria*, (1989) ECHR 25, *Pressos Compania Naviera v Belgium*, (1995) ECHR 471, and *James and Others v United Kingdom*, (1986) ECHR 2–and balanced the public interest of the host state and the investor's interest in having its investment protected.

[109] *Técnicas Medioambientales Tecmed S.A. v Mexico*, Award, ICSID Case No. ARB (AF)/00/2 (2003), para. 122. In the omitted footnote the tribunal referred to *Mellacher v Austria*, (1989) ECHR 25 and *Pressos Compania Naviera v Belgium*, (1995) ECHR 471.

[110] The ECtHR takes the decision that an expropriation has occurred based on a sole effects test. Under the ECHR, any interference with the peaceful enjoyment of property triggers a proportionality test. This test comprises an overall examination of the various interests at stake—one element of the test is the amount of compensation obtained for the expropriated property, if any. If an expropriation had occurred, compensation would, in principle, be full compensation. But there are exceptional circumstances that would allow a lesser amount to be paid. If the interference is of lesser severity than an expropriation, the ECtHR will also apply a proportionality test where, in principle, less than fair market value or no compensation will be required except in exceptional circumstances. The test is whether, taking into consideration all the facts, the state interference with property rights had created an excessive burden for the individual.

[111] For a critical analysis of the use of the proportionality test in investment arbitration, see N. Jansen Calamita, 'The Principle of Proportionality and the Problem of Indeterminacy in International Investment

Like the tribunals in the previous section, tribunals here drew inspiration for their interpretation of various investment treaty provisions (binding nature of interim measures, essential security interest, rights that can be expropriated, etc.) from the case law of human rights organs without any intention of applying human rights norms directly. Direct application would not have been possible since, in contrast to section 6.3.6, in the cases discussed here the respective human rights treaties were not applicable. In such a situation great care must be taken to make sure that the principles developed in human rights law are equally valid in investment law.

6.3.8 A serious human rights violation on the part of the investor will lead to the loss of investment protection

In some cases, tribunals applying a BIT containing a clause that investments must be made 'in accordance with host state law'[112] found that an investment made in serious violation of host state law did not enjoy the protection of the BIT.[113] In other words, they held that human rights abuses by investors that are at the same time in breach of host state law may lead to a loss of investment protection. But it appears that even without a treaty provision of this kind, tribunals will generally refuse to afford protection to investments that are made contrary to host state law.[114]

Treaties', in Andrea Bjorklund (ed.), *Yearbook of International Investment Law and Policy, 2013–2014* (Oxford University Press, 2015), 157–200.

[112] See e.g. Germany–Philippines BIT (1997), Art. 1; Bulgaria–China BIT (1989), Art. 1(1); Bangladesh–Italy BIT (1990), Art. 1(1); Spain–Ecuador BIT (1996), Arts. 2 and 3; Netherlands–Bolivia BIT (1992), Art. 2. On these clauses see e.g. Andrea Carlevaris, 'The Conformity of Investments with the Law of the Host State and the Jurisdiction of International Tribunals', 9 Journal of World Investment & Trade 25 (2008); Christina Knahr, 'Investments in Accordance with Host State Law', 4 TDM 5; Ursula Kriebaum, 'Illegal Investments', in Christian Klausegger et al., *Austrian Arbitration Yearbook 2010* (AAY, 2010), 307; Rahim Moloo and Alex Khachaturian, 'The Compliance with the Law Requirement in International Investment Law', 34 Fordham International Law Journal 1473 (2011).

[113] See e.g. *Fraport AG Frankfurt Airport Services Worldwide v The Republic of the Philippines*, Award, ICSID Case No. ARB/03/25 (2007), para. 401; *Alasdair Ross Anderson et al. v Republic of Costa Rica*, Award, ICSID Case No. ARB(AF)/07/3 (2010), paras. 50, 53, 58, 59; *Gustav F W Hamester GmbH & Co KG v Republic of Ghana*, Award, ICSID Case No. ARB/07/2 (2010), paras. 123–6, 138; *Saba Fakes v Republic of Turkey*, Award, ICSID Case No. ARB/07/20 (2010), para. 115; *Quiborax S.A., Non Metallic Minerals S.A. and Allan Fosk Kaplún v Plurinational State of Bolivia*, Decision on Jurisdiction, ICSID Case No. ARB/06/2 (2012), paras. 255, 282; *Fraport AG Frankfurt Airport Services Worldwide v Republic of the Philippines (No. 2)*, Award, ICSID Case No. ARB/11/12 (2014), para. 328; *Mamidoil Jetoil Greek Petroleum Products Societe S.A. v Republic of Albania*, ICSID Case No. ARB/11/24 (2015).

[114] See e.g. *Plama Consortium Limited v Republic of Bulgaria*, ICSID Case No. ARB/03/24 (2008), para. 138; *Gustav F W Hamester GmbH & Co KG v Republic of Ghana*, Award, ICSID Case No. ARB/07/2 (2010), para. 124; *SAUR International SA v Republic of Argentina*, Award, ICSID Case No. ARB/04/4 (2012), para. 308; *Veteran Petroleum Limited (Cyprus) v The Russian Federation*, Award, UNCITRAL, PCA Case No. AA 228 (2014), paras. 1349–52.

Take, for example, the case of *Phoenix Action v Czech Republic*.[115] The tribunal held:

> To take an extreme example, nobody would suggest that ICSID protection should be granted to investments made in violation of the most fundamental rules of protection of human rights, like investments in pursuance of torture or genocide or in support of slavery or trafficking of human organs.[116]

However, an investment that was made legally but is subsequently conducted in violation of human rights would not be covered by this sanction. To ensure that investments must not only be made but also remain in accordance with human rights throughout their lifetime in order to enjoy investment protection, states could use formulations like the one included in Art. 2(2) of the China–Malta BIT (2009), which provides:

> Investments of either Contracting Party shall be made, and shall, for their whole duration, continuously be in line with the respective domestic laws.

The inclusion of a reference to human rights would further strengthen a provision of this kind.

6.3.9 The tribunal decided in conformity with human rights without mentioning them

There are cases in which a state could have justified interference with an investment with human rights arguments, but the relevant governments did not do so, or referred to human rights only indirectly. Therefore, the tribunals also did not include human rights arguments in their reasoning.

The award in *Biwater Gauff v Tanzania*[117] is an example of such a case. In that case, the investor had failed to take certain promised actions designed to protect indigent consumers. As a reaction, Tanzania terminated the investment contract because of the poor performance of the investor.[118] The investor responded by filing a claim under the auspices of the ICSID. The tribunal held that terminating the investment agreement because of the investor's poor performance was not a breach of contract and did not amount to a violation of the FET standard.[119] *Amici* submitted that the respondent's measure was in line with Tanzania's duty under human rights law to ensure access to water for its citizens.[120]

[115] *Phoenix Action Ltd v The Czech Republic*, Award, ICSID Case No. ARB/06/5 (2009).

[116] Ibid. para. 78.

[117] *Biwater Gauff (Tanzania) Ltd v United Republic of Tanzania*, Award, ICSID Case No. ARB/05/22 (2008).

[118] Ibid. para. 789.

[119] Ibid. paras. 491–2, 605, 814(b).

[120] Amicus Curiae Submission of The Lawyers' Environmental Action Team (LEAT), The Legal and Human Rights Centre (LHRC), The Tanzania Gender Networking Programme (TGNP), The Center for

In the *Biwater Gauff* case, the very purpose of the investment contract was to give effect to the right to water, ensuring the state's compliance with its international human rights obligations by enabling the delivery of water to the public. The respondent's measure, to terminate the lease contract, was in line with Tanzania's duty under human rights law to ensure access to water for its citizens. Therefore, human rights could have served as justification for its interference with the investor's rights.

However, only the *amicus curiae* brief explicitly invoked human rights arguments. Tanzania argued that water and sanitation services are of vital importance, and that it had a right or perhaps even a duty to protect the functioning of these services.[121] But neither the respondent nor the tribunal made any explicit reference to the human right to water. The tribunal considered the termination of the contract not to be a violation of the BIT.[122] Therefore, the tribunal ultimately decided the case in a way that respected the human rights obligations of the state, albeit without mentioning these obligations. However, one cannot reproach the tribunal for not basing its reasoning on the right to water of the population, since the state did not rely on its human rights obligations in the first place.

A similar situation occurred in *Methanex v United States.*[123] The case concerned a Canadian producer and distributor of methanol, the main ingredient in the gasoline additive MTBE. The dispute arose out of a Californian ban of MTBE. While MTBE has a positive effect on air quality, the Californian legislator considered MTBE to pose an environmental and public health risk due to its possible seepage into groundwater, including sources of drinking water, that outweighed its clean air benefits.[124] The investor argued that the ban was tantamount to an expropriation of the company's investment and thus violated Art. 1110 of the NAFTA; that it was enacted in breach of the national treatment obligation in Art. 1102 of the NAFTA; and that it was also in breach of the international minimum standard of treatment under Art. 1105 of NAFTA.[125]

The tribunal found that no violation of the national treatment standard had occurred,[126] and that Art. 1105 of the NAFTA had not been violated by the MTBE ban.[127] With regard to its expropriation claim, the *Methanex* tribunal applied the police powers doctrine, and found that a non-discriminatory measure in the public interest taken in accordance with due process requirements that targets, among others, foreign investors is not an expropriation. Therefore, the United States prevailed with its defence that it legislated to protect its ground and drinking water resources, and the tribunal denied

International Environmental Law (CIEL), The International Institute for Sustainable Development (IISD) in Case No. ARB/05/22 before the International Centre for Settlement of Investment Disputes between *Biwater Gauff (Tanzania) Limited and United Republic of Tanzania* (2007), paras. 7, 11, 68, 69, 95, 96.

[121] *Biwater Gauff (Tanzania) Ltd v United Republic of Tanzania*, Award, ICSID Case No. ARB/05/22 (2008), para. 434.

[122] Ibid. paras. 488, 791.

[123] *Methanex v United States*, Award, UNCITRAL (2005).

[124] MTBE Public Health and Environment Protection Act of 1997, California Senate Bill No. 521, Ch. 816: http://www.leginfo.ca.gov/pub/97-;98/bill/sen/sb_0501-0550/sb_521_bill_19971009_chaptered.html.

[125] *Methanex v United States*, Award, UNCITRAL (2005), Part IV, Ch. A, para. 1.

[126] Ibid. Part IV, Ch. B, para. 38.

[127] Ibid. Part IV, Ch. C, para. 27.

both the occurrence of an expropriation and a violation of FET. A human right to water might have been relevant but was not mentioned.

The same is true for the case of *Glamis Gold Ltd v United States*,[128] where the Quechan Indian Nations' rights in California were at stake. In that case, human rights considerations were addressed only in the *amicus curiae* briefs.[129] Rather than relying on human rights norms, the state relied on federal and state laws that accord protection to sacred tribal sites and other tribal resources.[130] The tribunal ultimately did not find a violation of the NAFTA.

What all these cases have in common is that the states did not invoke human rights as a justification for adverse measures. In all of them, only the *amici* invoked human rights arguments to justify the measures, but the tribunals did not use human rights arguments in their reasoning. In arbitration it is neither common nor necessary to deal with arguments not presented by one of the parties, especially if they do not change the outcome of a case. From this perspective it was perfectly appropriate not to discuss the human rights concerns of the *amici*. From a public international law perspective, it does not create problems if a tribunal decides a case in line with human rights law, even if not explicitly dealing with it. Yet, for the critical observer it is of great interest whether tribunals refer to human rights concerns explicitly.

6.3.10 No inconsistency between human rights and investment treaty obligations

Several tribunals that had to decide cases in the context of public services (e.g. the supply of water or electricity) have pointed out that they had taken human rights considerations into account, and that human rights obligations and investment treaty obligations were not inconsistent.

In *CMS Gas Transmission Company v Argentina*[131] and *Suez v Argentina*,[132] Argentina tried to invoke human rights as a defence in a situation of economic crisis which resulted in widespread unemployment and poverty. It contended that since the economic and social crisis affected human rights, the protections afforded under the respective investment treaties should not prevail.[133] One line of argument by Argentina was that human

[128] *Glamis Gold v United States*, Award, UNCITRAL (2009).

[129] *Glamis Gold v United States*, Decision on Application and Submission by Quechan Indian Nation, UNCITRAL (2005), paras. 7, 9–13; *Glamis Gold v United States*, Decision on Application and Submission by Quechan Indian Nation, UNCITRAL (2005) (Supplemental Submission), paras. 1–7, 9.

[130] See e.g. *Glamis Gold v United States*, Statement of Defense of Respondent United States of America, UNCITRAL (2005), paras. 14, 28.

[131] *CMS Gas Transmission Company v The Republic of Argentina*, Award, ICSID Case No. ARB/01/8 (2005).

[132] *Suez, Sociedad General de Aguas de Barcelona, S.A. and Vivendi Universal, S.A. v Argentine Republic*, Award, ICSID Case No. ARB/03/19 (2010).

[133] *CMS Gas Transmission Company v The Republic of Argentina*, Award, ICSID Case No. ARB/01/8 (2005), para. 114.

rights norms were hierarchically superior to guarantees contained in investment protection treaties. Another argument was that a state of necessity would allow for derogation from investment protection provisions.

In *CMS*,[134] Argentina argued that the economic and social crisis affecting the country compromised basic human rights, and that in such a situation an investment treaty could not prevail since that would constitute a violation of constitutionally recognized rights.[135] The tribunal did not enter into a discussion on the hierarchy of norms, but denied a conflict between human rights and investor rights on the facts of the particular case. It found no question affecting fundamental human rights when considering the issues in dispute:

> In this case, the Tribunal does not find any such collision. First because the Constitution carefully protects the right to property, just as the treaties on human rights do, and secondly because there is no question of affecting fundamental human rights when considering the issues disputed by the parties.[136]

The *Suez*[137] cases concerned foreign shareholders in water and sewage concessions. Argentina prohibited a price increase that was designed to compensate for the precipitous decline in the value of the Argentine peso due to the economic crisis. The tribunal found Argentina liable for breaching the FET obligations of the BIT. In the context of the state of necessity discussion, the tribunal mentioned Argentina's argument that its human rights obligations would trump obligations emanating from the BIT. The tribunal rejected this argument, holding the correct position to be that Argentina must respect both sets of obligations simultaneously:

> Argentina has suggested that its human rights obligations to assure its population the right to water somehow trumps its obligations under the BITs and the existence of the human right to water also implicitly gives Argentina the authority to take actions in disregard of its BIT obligations. The Tribunal does not find a basis for such a conclusion either in the BITs or international law. Argentina is subject to both international obligations, *i.e.* human rights *and* treaty obligations, and must respect both of them. Under the circumstances of this case, Argentina's human rights

[134] Ibid. paras. 114, 121.

[135] Ibid. para. 114: 'In respect of the legal regime of treaties in Argentina, the Respondent argues that while treaties override the law they are not above the Constitution and must accord with constitutional public law. Only some basic treaties on human rights have been recognized by a 1994 constitutional amendment as having constitutional standing and, therefore, in the Respondent's view, stand above ordinary treaties such as investment treaties. It is further argued that, as the economic and social crisis that affected the country compromised basic human rights, no investment treaty could prevail as it would be in violation of such constitutionally recognized rights.'

[136] Ibid. para. 121.

[137] *Suez, Sociedad General de Aguas de Barcelona, S.A. and Vivendi Universal, S.A. v Argentine Republic*, Award, ICSID Case No. ARB/03/19 (2010); *AWG Group Ltd v The Argentine Republic*, Decision on Liability, UNCITRAL (2010); *Suez, Sociedad General de Aguas de Barcelona, S.A. and Vivendi Universal, S.A. v Argentine Republic*, Decision on Liability, ICSID Case No. ARB/03/19 (2010).

> obligations and its investment treaty obligations are not inconsistent, contradictory, or mutually exclusive. Thus, as was discussed above, Argentina could have respected both types of obligations.[138]

The *amici* on the other hand suggested to the tribunal that '[h]uman rights law could displace investment law in two situations examined in this section, namely a situation of conflict of norms and a situation of necessity'.[139] They based their argument on the *jus cogens* status of certain human rights norms such as the right to life. As Diane Desierto has convincingly shown, the hierarchy of norms approach causes more problems than it solves. Not only is it impossible to prove that all human rights invoked would qualify as *jus cogens*, but the results of such a qualification would not be helpful to the state invoking the argument. To fulfil the requirements of Art. 53 of the VCLT, one would have to argue that the investment protection treaty was contrary to *jus cogens* at the time of its conclusion. The consequence of this argument would be that the investment protection treaty would be void *ab initio*. This would lead to an obligation of the host state to eliminate the consequences of any act performed in reliance on the treaty.[140]

The tribunal held that ensuring a right to water to the population and fair and equitable treatment to investors were not mutually exclusive, and could have been achieved by Argentina at the same time.[141] It followed that Argentina was obligated to observe both its human rights and BIT obligations. Argentina could not simply assert human rights obligations to justify setting aside investment obligations altogether. Furthermore, like the *CMS* tribunal, the *Suez* tribunal held that Argentina had contributed to the emergency situation it was facing from 2001 to 2003, and therefore did not fulfil the requirement of Art.25 (2) (b) of the ILC Articles on State Responsibility.[142]

The dispute in *SAUR v Argentina*[143] also arose in the context of the 2002 financial crisis, and the facts resemble, to a certain extent, those of the *Suez* cases. SAUR had invested

[138] *Suez, Sociedad General de Aguas de Barcelona, S.A. and Vivendi Universal, S.A. v Argentine Republic*, Award, ICSID Case No. ARB/03/19 (2010), para. 240. Also see *AWG Group Ltd v The Argentine Republic*, Decision on Liability, UNCITRAL (2010), para. 240; *Suez, Sociedad General de Aguas de Barcelona, S.A. and Vivendi Universal, S.A. v Argentine Republic*, Decision on Liability, ICSID Case No. ARB/03/19 (2010), para. 250.

[139] Centro de Estudios Legales y Sociales (CELS), Asociación Civil por la Igualidad y la Justicia (ACIJ), Consumidores Libres Cooperativa Ltda: De Provisión de Servicios de Acción Comunitaria, Unión de Usuarios y Consumidores, Center for International Environmental law (CIEL), 26: http://www.ciel.org/Publications/SUEZ_Amicus_English_4Apr07.pdf.

[140] Diane Desierto, 'Conflict of Treaties, Interpretation, and Decision-Making on Human Rights and Investment During Economic Crises', TDM (2013), 37ff.

[141] *Suez, Sociedad General de Aguas de Barcelona, S.A. and Vivendi Universal, S.A. v Argentine Republic*, Award, ICSID Case No. ARB/03/19 (2010), para. 240; *AWG Group Ltd v The Argentine Republic*, Decision on Liability, UNCITRAL (2010), para. 262.

[142] *Suez, Sociedad General de Aguas de Barcelona, S.A. and Vivendi Universal, S.A. v Argentine Republic*, Award, ICSID Case No. ARB/03/19 (2010), paras. 241–3; *AWG Group Ltd v The Argentine Republic*, Decision on Liability, UNCITRAL (2010), paras. 263–5; *Suez, Sociedad General de Aguas de Barcelona, S.A. and Vivendi Universal, S.A. v Argentine Republic*, Decision on Liability, ICSID Case No. ARB/03/19 (2010), paras. 263–5.

[143] *SAUR International SA v Republic of Argentina*, Award, ICSID Case No. ARB/04/4 (2012).

in a provincially owned water company that held a concession for drinking water, sanitation, and sewage in the Argentinean province of Mendoza. In the context of the 2002 financial crisis, Argentina froze all water prices charged to consumers and a dispute concerning tariff renegotiations arose. The project ran into financial difficulties and, as a consequence, into problems with the quality and quantity of sewage services, consumer services, and drinking water quality.

In 2003 SAUR turned to arbitration. Argentina argued that it had to terminate and renationalize the concession to ensure service and to protect the public interest in health and the right to water.[144] Further, it invoked the state of necessity defence,[145] claiming that the measures were a legitimate exercise of 'police powers',[146] and asserted that the province had only made use of its contractual rights to terminate the contract due to breaches by the concessionaire.

Before the tribunal entered into the details of the various investment protection standards, it dealt with Argentina's human rights defence. The tribunal recognized that human rights in general and the human right to water in particular had to be taken into consideration. It justified this by the fact that they are represented in the Argentinian constitution and are part of the general principles of international law which are part of the applicable law according to Art.8.4 of the BIT. In this vein, the tribunal held:

> In fact, human rights in general, and the right to water in particular, constitute one of the various sources that the Tribunal will have to take into account in resolving the dispute, since these rights are of great importance within the Argentine legal system as constitutional rights, and, moreover, they form part of the general principles of international law. Access to drinking water constitutes, from the point of view of the State, a basic public service and, from the point of view of the citizen, a fundamental right.[147]
>
> For this reason, concerning this matter, the legal order can and must reserve for the Public Authority legitimate functions of planning, supervision, police, sanction, intervention and even termination, in order to protect the general interest.[148]

Having emphasized the significance of human rights in principle, the tribunal proceeded to state that the obligations under human rights law were compatible with those under investment law:

[144] Ibid. para. 32. [145] Ibid. paras. 451–4. [146] Ibid. paras. 328, 394–5.

[147] Ibid. para. 330: 'En réalité, les droits de l'homme en général, et le droit à l'eau en particulier, constituent l'une des diverses sources que le Tribunal devra prendre en compte pour résoudre le différend car ces droits sont élevés au sein du système juridique argentin au rang de droits constitutionnels, et, de plus, ils font partie des principes généraux du droit international. L'accès à l'eau potable constitue, du point de vue de l'État, un service public de première nécessité et, du point de vue du citoyen, un droit fondamental.'

[148] Ibid. para. 330: 'Pour ce motif, en cette matière, l'ordre juridique peut et doit réserver à l'Autorité publique des fonctions légitimes de planification, de supervision, de police, de sanction, d'intervention et même de résiliation, afin de protéger l'intérêt général.'

> But these prerogatives are compatible with the rights of investors to receive the protection offered by the BIT. The fundamental right to water and the right of the investor to benefit from the protection offered by the BIT operate on different levels: the concessionary company of a basic public service is in a situation of dependency on the public administration, which has special powers to guarantee its enjoyment by virtue of the priority of the fundamental right to water; but the exercise of these powers is not absolute and must be combined with respect for the rights and guarantees granted to the foreign investor under the BIT. If the government decides to expropriate the investment, treat the investor unfairly or inequitably, or deny the promised protection or full security, all this by violating the BIT, the investor will be entitled to be compensated under the terms of the Treaty.
>
> Counterbalancing these two principles will be the task that the Tribunal will have to perform in its analysis of the substantive claims presented by Sauri.[149]

Furthermore, the tribunal denied that there was a sufficient causal link between the declaration of the state of necessity and the measures imposed by the provincial authorities that led to the expropriation.[150] Therefore, the tribunal decided that it did not have to enter into a discussion on the issue of which circumstances might give rise to a genuine conflict between the right of access to water and investment protection norms.

After the general discussion of its approach to Argentina's human rights arguments, the tribunal made no further references to a right to water in its subsequent analyses of substantive treaty violations. In response to the 'police powers' defence invoked by Argentina, it stated that the measures could not be considered a legitimate use of the province's police powers in view of the gravity and deliberateness of the province's failure to abide by a previous settlement.[151]

Ultimately, the tribunal found that an expropriation had occurred. It also held that Argentina had violated the FET standard by a 'financial strangulation' of the concessionaire in order to justify the termination and renationalization of the concession. This conduct was incompatible with the demands of a public administration that is conscientious, impartial, and respectful of the rights of its subjects.[152]

In contrast to the approach of the tribunals mentioned in sections 6.3.5 and 6.3.6, the tribunal in *SAUR* was only prepared to take human rights considerations into account in

[149] Ibid. paras. 331–2: 'Mais ces prérogatives sont compatibles avec les droits des investisseurs à recevoir la protection offerte par l'APRI. Le droit fondamental à l'eau et le droit de l'investisseur à bénéficier de la protection offerte par l'APRI opèrent sur des plans différents: l'entreprise concessionnaire d'un service public de première nécessité se trouve dans une situation de dépendance face à l'administration publique, qui dispose de pouvoirs spéciaux pour en garantir la jouissance en raison de la souveraineté du droit fondamental à l'eau; mais l'exercice de ces pouvoirs ne se fait pas de façon absolue et doit, au contraire, être conjugué avec le respect des droits et des garanties octroyés à l'investisseur étranger en vertu de l'APRI. Si les pouvoirs publics décident d'exproprier l'investissement, de traiter l'investisseur injustement ou de façon non équitable ou de lui refuser la protection ou la pleine sécurité promises, tout ceci en violant l'APRI, l'investisseur aura le droit d'être indemnisé dans les termes que le Traité lui accorde. Contrebalancer ces deux principes sera la tâche que le Tribunal devra effectuer lors de son analyse des prétentions substantives présentées par Sauri.'

[150] Ibid. paras. 461, 463. [151] Ibid. para. 405. [152] Ibid. paras. 505–6.

a very abstract manner. It merely stated that human rights norms were applicable and compatible with the investment protection provisions of the BIT. It did not explicitly deal with human rights considerations when interpreting the expropriation provision in assessing the police powers of the government, nor discuss human rights arguments when interpreting the FET provision.

In a similar manner, and as already set out above, the *Urbaser* tribunal applied human rights law to frame the FET standard, in particular its legitimate expectations element. Like the tribunals just mentioned, it also set out that human rights and investment law obligations are compatible and that states have to fulfil both sets of obligations simultaneously.

6.4 Conclusion

There are multiple ways in which investment tribunals may take international human rights law into account. How much weight a tribunal may give to human rights considerations depends on the jurisdiction clause, the applicable law, and the possibility of considering them via treaty interpretation.

In section 6.3.1, tribunals were asked to apply human rights norms to the facts before them. The tribunals denied to apply human rights norms for lack of jurisdiction. Human rights had been either invoked by claimants or raised by a non-disputing party that petitioned for leave to submit an *amicus curiae* brief. The jurisdictional clauses covered either 'any dispute with respect of an approved enterprise' (*Biloune*) or 'disputes with respect to investments' (*Rompetrol*, *Pezold*). The applicable law was host state law and the contract in *Biloune*, and host state law and international law as provided for in Art. 42 of the ICSID Convention in the other cases. The tribunals declined jurisdiction despite a broad jurisdictional norm that had not limited jurisdiction to disputes arising out of the contract or the BIT.

In section 6.3.2, host states wanted to import concepts developed by the ECtHR into expropriation provisions of BITs. The tribunals declined to do this based on the argument that the legal situation prevailing under the applicable legal instruments was different—i.e. that the legal concepts contained in the property protection clause of the ECHR, that was not part of the applicable law, were not comparable to the expropriation provisions of the applicable BITs.

In section 6.3.3, the claimant had relied on a provision of the BIT that provided for importing more favourable protection provisions from other treaties. The tribunal would have been prepared to apply human rights standards of applicable human rights treaties if only these had offered a higher degree of protection than the applicable investment protection treaty, which the tribunal found not to be the case.

In section 6.3.4, tribunals were confronted with issues of alleged incompatibilities of human rights law and investment law in one case and an alleged human rights violation through state measures in the other. Both cases were similar to the extent that human rights arguments had not been sufficiently substantiated by the party invoking them. This caused both tribunals to declare that they were willing, in principle, to apply human rights law. Yet, they declined to do so in practice because the parties had not sufficiently argued those points. These cases demonstrate that it is essential that human rights are fully argued to receive consideration in investment arbitration cases.

In section 6.3.5, tribunals applied human rights norms to the facts of the cases to determine whether investment law obligations had been violated. They did so after having found that human rights constituted part of the applicable law in the case under consideration. One tribunal even distinguished between the ECHR, which it found not to be applicable, and the UN Covenant on Civil and Political Rights. They applied human rights law independent of whether the investor had relied on human rights or whether the state had relied on them to justify its measures.

In section 6.3.6, tribunals did not deal with the issue whether the particular human rights treaty used for inspiration was part of the applicable law. Tribunals imported concepts from the ECHR where the state parties to these cases were also parties to the ECHR or, in one case, to the Covenant on Civil and Political Rights. But the tribunals in their awards did not mention this. They took inspiration from human rights provisions when interpreting investment treaty provisions in the context of various issues of investment treaty law.

In section 6.3.7, tribunals took inspiration from the jurisprudence of the ECtHR even though the ECHR was not part of the applicable law, since the respondent states were not party to the Convention. In section 6.3.8, a tribunal stated in *obiter* that human rights abuses by investors would lead to a loss of investment protection. In section 6.3.9, tribunals decided cases that raised human rights issues where only the *amici curiae* had mentioned them in their submissions. The respondent states did not rely on possible human rights arguments to defend their causes, and tribunals in these cases decided them in line with human rights law without explicitly basing their decision on human rights norms.

Lastly, section 6.3.10 dealt with cases where human rights had been invoked as a defence by host states to justify measures interfering with investors' rights. The tribunals pointed out that they had taken human rights considerations into account. At the same time they found them not to be inconsistent with investment treaty obligations. Therefore, they came to the conclusion that the state had an obligation to respect both investor rights and human rights simultaneously.

A number of variables determine these diverse groups of cases. For example, human rights issues may be invoked by the investor, the host state, or *amicus curiae*. The applicable treaty may provide the tribunal with jurisdiction over all disputes arising out of an investment, or just over disputes on the alleged violation of the treaty's substantive standards. The law applicable to the dispute may extend to international law in general or may be circumscribed more narrowly. Human rights may have been pleaded as a separate cause of action or merely in support of a particular interpretation of an investment treaty. Human rights may have been pleaded in some detail or may merely have been referred to in passing. Further, the host state may or may not be party to a human rights treaty that is relied upon.

Despite this variety of circumstances, it is possible to draw some general conclusions. The cases show that tribunals are hesitant to get involved in 'stand-alone human rights issues'—i.e. to be transformed into human rights tribunals even if a human rights violation arises directly out of an investment, and human rights obligations were part of the applicable law. So far, no tribunal has found a violation of a stand-alone human rights norm—not even in cases where human rights were part of the applicable law and the tribunal had jurisdiction with regard to any legal dispute arising out of an investment.

With regard to the possibility of transferring ideas and principles from human rights law to investment law, we find a variety of different approaches. A number of tribunals were willing to import concepts developed in the context of human rights law to investment arbitration. Some of them did so even *ex officio*. In other cases, the parties had invoked and discussed those concepts in some detail. This holds true for several principles, including, for example:

- expropriation and the principle of proportionality;
- issues relating to the calculation of damages;
- the fact that immaterial rights can be expropriated; and
- the fact that expropriations can also be performed by courts.

Other matters where tribunals referred to the jurisprudence of human rights courts were the binding nature of interim measures and the issue of the 'non-self-judging nature' of emergency provisions. A third set of cases concerned fair trial issues. Here some tribunals drew inspiration from the ECtHR or the UN Human Rights Committee; others even directly applied human rights provisions, since they were part of the applicable law.

However, we also find tribunals that refuse to import principles found in human rights law. In these cases, the tribunals found that the human rights rules in question were conceptually incompatible with the relevant investment protection principles. Where human rights arguments had not been fully argued, tribunals declined to decide on violations of human rights norms or incompatibilities of human rights obligations with investment law obligations. This occurred independently of whether or not the claimant or respondent had raised the human rights issue. Tribunals also made it clear that investors responsible for human rights abuses would not enjoy investment protection.

It remains an open question how human rights should influence investment protection during periods of economic crises. Tribunals have consistently found there to be no hierarchy of norms between human rights and investment law obligations. None of the tribunals analysed above came to the conclusion that there would be a conflict of norms between investment law and human rights law, and a conclusion as to which set of obligations ought ultimately to prevail. Rather, they chose to systemically integrate human rights law into investment provisions, either by applying human rights provisions directly to reach a decision on the violation of an investment protection standard or by taking inspiration from applicable human rights norms. This approach is in line with the International Law Commission's report on Fragmentation that argues that international law ought to be conceived as one integrated system.[153]

In view of the various critiques that investment tribunals ignore human rights or environmental concerns, it seems to be of importance that international investment tribunals view international law as a coherent system of norms and not as fragmented into various branches. So far, we can see no genuine friction between human rights and investment law in the investment context. Where tribunals have refused to apply human rights concepts in investment law cases, this has never been in a situation of norm conflict between investment law and human rights law. Rather, tribunals that declined to import concepts from human rights treaties into investment protection treaties held that the investment treaty they had to apply contained norms explicitly regulating the problem under consideration but in a different way from human right treaties.

[153] International Law Commission (n. 13), para. 420, Fifty-Fifth Session of the General Assembly, 'Fragmentation of International Law: Difficulties Arising From the Diversification and Expansion of International Law', UN Doc. A/CN.4/L.702 (2006). See also Christoph Schreuer and Ursula Kriebaum, 'From Individual to Community Interest in International Investment Law', in Ulrich Fastenrath et al. (eds), *From Bilateralism to Community Interest: Essays in Honour of Bruno Simma* (Oxford University Press, 2011), 1079; Moshe Hirsch, 'Interactions between Investment and Non-Investment Obligations', in Peter Muchlinski, Federico Ortino, and Chiristoph Schreuer, *Oxford Handbook of International Investment Law* (Oxford University Press, 2008), 154.

CHAPTER 7

ENFORCEMENT

ANDREA K. BJORKLUND

THE ready enforceability of arbitral awards is the single strongest component of the architecture that undergirds international arbitration. Two conventions are the primary mechanisms ensuring that enforceability. The first, the Convention on the Recognition and Enforcement of Foreign Arbitral Awards, was concluded in 1958 and is colloquially known as the New York Convention.[1] As of June 2019, it boasts 160 state parties[2] and can apply in both commercial and investment arbitrations. The second, the Convention on the Settlement of Investment Disputes Between States and Nationals of Other States, colloquially referred to as the ICSID Convention or the Washington Convention, was concluded in 1965.[3] It has 154 state parties as of June 2019 and, as the name suggests, applies to investment disputes.[4] Other regional conventions exist and may apply in the case of certain disputes,[5] but do not rise to the level of prominence or frequency of use of the New York and Washington Conventions.

[1] Convention on the Recognition and Enforcement of Foreign Arbitral Awards (adopted 10 June 1958, entered into force 7 June 1959), 330 UNTS 3 (New York Convention).

[2] See UNCITRAL, *Status: Convention on the Recognition and Enforcement of Foreign Arbitral Awards* (New York, 1958), http://www.uncitral.org/uncitral/en/uncitral_texts/arbitration/NYConvention_status.html, accessed 17 December 2018. The breadth of these parties is particular impressive—as one commentator has noted, they no longer include any 'conspicuous absences': 'In this sense, the Convention in substance has become the universal instrument that its proponents intended it to be': Wei Shen, *Rethinking the New York Convention: A Law and Economics Approach* (Intersentia, 2014), 41.

[3] Convention on the Settlement of Investment Disputes Between States and Nationals of Other States (adopted 18 March 1965, entered into force 14 October 1966), 575 UNTS 159 (ICSID Convention). Investment disputes include arbitrations based on treaties, contracts, and national investment laws.

[4] ICSID, 'List of Contracting States and Other Signatories of the Convention (as of August 27, 2018)', https://icsid.worldbank.org/en/Documents/icsiddocs/Listper cent20ofper cent20Contractingper cent20 Statesper cent20andper cent20Otherper cent20Signatoriesper cent20ofper cent20theper cent20 Conventionper cent20-per cent20Latest.pdf, accessed 17 December 2018.

[5] See e.g. Inter-American Convention on International Commercial Arbitration (adopted 30 January 1975, entered into force 16 June 1976), 1438 UNTS 245; European Convention on International Commercial Arbitration (adopted 21 April 1961, entered into force 7 January 1964), 484 UNTS 349; Arrangements Concerning Mutual Enforcement of Arbitration Awards Between the Mainland and Hong Kong (concluded January 2000, entered into force 1 February 2000), incorporated into Hong Kong law by the Legislative Council in January 2000 through the Arbitration (Amendment) Ordinance 2000 (2 of 2000), becoming effective on 1 February 2000.

In an ideal arbitration the losing party satisfies the award rendered against it voluntarily, and the dispute ends without need for recourse to any coercive means of enforcement. Though many arbitrations are confidential, surveys and anecdotal evidence suggest that the majority of awards in both commercial and investment arbitration are paid without the involvement of formal enforcement mechanisms.[6] Some cases have, however, less satisfactory outcomes. An arbitral tribunal cannot force a judgment debtor to pay the award rendered by the tribunal. The tribunal is *functus officio* and, even if it were not, lacks the coercive mechanisms attendant upon municipal courts—hence the need for international conventions obliging states to lend that coercive authority to the assistance of arbitration, thereby ensuring that a judgment creditor can collect an award in its favour.

Involuntary enforcement of an arbitral award thus inevitably involves an intersection between the international arbitral process and a municipal legal system. One feature of the regime is the portability of awards—they can be enforced in multiple jurisdictions, making it less possible for judgement debtors to avoid payment by moving assets out of a given jurisdiction. This does not mean that a determinedly evasive judgment debtor cannot make enforcement extremely difficult or even impossible, but it does mean that a typical commercial actor would have to avoid many attractive business destinations in order to ensure continued immunity from enforcement.

The regime for enforcement of arbitral awards is based on a structure that prioritizes enforcement so long as awards are rendered pursuant to certain largely procedural safeguards. This approach is an attempt to balance the principle of party autonomy with concern on the part of national courts that they not be co-opted into enforcing awards not consistent with at least rudimentary principles of fair play. Judgment debtors can thus resist enforcement should the arbitration have failed to comport with fundamental notions of due process. In the case of the New York Convention, two other grounds for resisting enforcement have to do with policy considerations in the enforcing state.

As the scope of this book indicates, arbitration has become—perhaps it always was—a complex field. The advent of investment treaty arbitration has made it even more so. Investment arbitration can refer to arbitrations carried out under investment treaties, to arbitrations involving investments that are carried out under contracts, and even to arbitrations based on national investment laws. Some investment arbitrations involve both a treaty and a contract or contracts. Investment arbitrations are enforceable under the ICSID Convention provided that both the home state of the claimant investor and the respondent host state are party to the ICSID Convention, and that other criteria—that there is an investment for purposes of the ICSID Convention, that there is a legal dispute, and that there is consent to ICSID Convention arbitration—are satisfied. Most

[6] Numbers on enforcement, or the lack thereof, are hard to find given the dispersed nature of arbitral awards. A survey published in 2008 by the Queen Mary–University of London School of International Arbitration explains that most corporations have not encountered major difficulties with respect to the recognition and enforcement of arbitration awards, with participants needing to use coercive measures to enforce awards in only 11% of the surveyed cases. See Queen Mary–University of London School of International Arbitration, '2008 Corporate Attitudes: Recognition and Enforcement of Foreign Awards' (2008), available at :http://www.arbitration.qmul.ac.uk/media/arbitration/docs/IAstudy_2008.pdf, accessed 20 March 2019, 10.

other arbitrations, whether they involve investments or not, take place in such a manner as to be enforceable under the New York Convention.[7]

One of the attractions of the field of arbitration is the possibility of creating a dispute resolution process designed specifically for the particulars of the conflict in question—bespoke justice. International arbitration has been successful because of that creativity, but it is also the case that some potential for novelty and innovation is more theoretical than practical. Particularly when it comes to ensuring the enforceability of their awards, parties have tended to be risk-averse. Thus, parties in a commercial dispute tend to ensure that the New York Convention applies when they are crafting their arbitration clause. In an investment dispute they will ensure that either the New York Convention or the Washington Convention applies. This chapter will thus address the enforcement regime under those two conventions, with somewhat more emphasis on the New York Convention. This focus results from differences between the two instruments; the New York Convention permits disputing parties to resist enforcement in national courts, whereas the ICSID Convention requires that all member states treat ICSID Convention awards as if they are final judgments of their own courts.

This chapter first describes the enforcement regime under the New York Convention, It addresses some fundamental New York Convention precepts: (i) the question of territorial linkage, and in particular the role of the 'place' of arbitration; (ii) the requirement of commerciality; (iii) the requirement of 'foreign-ness'; and (iv) the limitation on the number of grounds on which states can deny enforcement. Second, the chapter will briefly describe enforcement under the ICSID Convention, noting some anomalies that persist despite the streamlined enforcement regime. Third, the chapter will describe various hurdles to enforcement under both conventions, notwithstanding the apparently straightforward enforcement obligations each contains.

7.1 The New York Convention's Enforcement Regime

The New York Convention is sometimes described as the most successful international convention in history.[8] This might be hyperbole, but it is not far off the mark. With 160

[7] ICSID has an 'Additional Facility' which is available for arbitrations in which either the investor's home state or the host state is party to the ICSID Convention (ICSID Additional Facility Rules, April 2006), ICSID/11 https://icsid.worldbank.org/en/Documents/resources/AFR_2006per cent20English-final.pdf, accessed 17 December 2018. Additional Facility arbitrations have a place of arbitration and are enforceable under the New York Convention, rather than the ICSID Convention. In its current (2019) round of rules revisions, ICSID is considering opening the Additional Facility further by not requiring that either disputing party have a link to the ICSID Convention; should that extension be adopted, those awards would still be enforceable under the New York Convention. See ICSID Secretariat, 'Proposals for Amendment of the ICSID Rules: Synopsis', vol. 1, 2 August 2018. https://icsid.worldbank.org/en/amendments/Documents/Homepage/Synopsis_English.pdf, accessed 17 December 2018, para. 65.

[8] Pieter Sanders, 'Foreword', in *ICCA's Guide to the Interpretation of the 1958 New York Convention: A Handbook* (ICCA, 2011), v: 'The 1958 New York Convention is the most successful multilateral instrument in the field of international trade law. It is the centrepiece in the mosaic of treaties and arbitration laws

state parties, the New York Convention underpins the arbitration regime because it facilitates the enforcement of awards in national courts. In addition to its other attractions, arbitration is appealing to disputing parties because an arbitration award is more enforceable than most court judgments.[9]

The core obligation in the New York Convention is simple: 'Each Contracting State shall recognize arbitral awards as binding and enforce them in accordance with the rules of procedure of the territory where the award is relied upon, under the conditions laid down in the following articles.'[10] To strengthen the obligation, the drafters provided: 'There shall not be imposed substantially more onerous conditions or higher fees or charges on the recognition or enforcement of arbitral awards to which this Convention applies than are imposed on the recognition or enforcement of domestic arbitral awards.'[11]

The domestic procedures in question encompass, among other matters, 'the identification of the appropriate court in which to seek enforcement, requirements for that court to exercise jurisdiction, limitations periods for seeking enforcement, court assistance with discovering the location of seizable assets, the mechanisms through which attachment of assets occurs, state immunity laws, limitations periods specifying the time within which enforcement must be sought, and the like'.[12] This pragmatic approach permitted avoiding the daunting task of developing uniform rules to apply across a range of jurisdictions.

The drafters of the New York Convention were reacting to years of difficulty resulting from a limited scope of application and onerous procedural requirements, including the double exequatur, found in the Geneva Convention on the Execution of Foreign Awards of 1927[13] and the Geneva Protocol on Arbitration Clauses of 1923,[14] the New York

that ensure acceptance of arbitral awards and arbitration agreements. Courts around the world have been applying and interpreting the Convention for over fifty years, in an increasingly unified and harmonized fashion.'

9 Recent developments in the Hague Conference on Private International Law regarding the formulation of a Judgments Convention mean that this statement might not prove to be true forever. See the discussion at n. 122 and accompanying text. Moreover, the Hague Choice of Courts Convention entered into force 1 October 2015 (Convention on Choice of Court Agreements (adopted 30 June 2005, entered into force 1 October 2015), 44 ILM 1294). Under the Hague Choice of Courts Convention, if parties to a contract designate a court in one of the Convention's member states for the resolution of their dispute, courts in the other member states must enforce the ensuing judgment. To date, however, the only member states are Denmark, the European Union, Mexico, Montenegro and Singapore. See https://www.hcch.net/en/instruments/conventions/status-table/?cid=98, accessed 17 December 2018.

10 New York Convention (n. 1), art III.

11 Ibid. While some delegates had suggested 'national treatment'—the same procedures for the enforcement of foreign awards as domestic awards--that suggestion was rejected. In some cases the procedures were too different and there was little will to bring them together, while in others enforcement of domestic awards required no official action but states were not prepared for foreign awards to be enforced without any kind of review. Albert Jan van den Berg, *The New York Arbitration Convention of 1958* (T. M. C. Asser Institute, 1981), 235–6.

12 Van den Berg (n. 11), 235–6.

13 Convention on the Execution of Foreign Arbitral Awards (adopted 26 September 1927, entered into force 25 July 1929), 92 LNTS 301.

14 Protocol on Arbitration Clauses (adopted 24 September 1923, entered into force 28 July 1924), 27 LNTS 157.

Convention's predecessors. Double exequatur meant that the state in which an arbitration took place had to confirm the award was 'final' before any other jurisdiction acted, a procedure that effectively conferred on one state a veto over enforcement. The Geneva Conventions also required that a judgment creditor prove the award had been rendered in accordance with all applicable procedural requirements, and that it had been made in conformity with the requirements of the law governing the arbitration procedure—a law with which the enforcing court was not necessarily conversant. These obligations placed a heavy burden on the judgment creditor to prove its entitlement to the award rendered in its favour.[15] The New York Convention eliminated these requirements and replaced them with the much more modest obligation to provide authenticated documents.[16] The New York Convention also established a presumption in favour of enforceability; the party resisting enforcement bears the burden of showing that one of the grounds in Article V is met.

This section addresses the concept of the 'place' or 'legal seat' of the arbitration, and how that concept intersects with the New York Convention. It then considers the issues of commerciality and foreignness as requirements for award enforceability under the New York Convention. Finally, it covers the grounds on which member states may deny enforcement under the New York Convention.

7.1.1 A-nationality and the place of arbitration

Arbitration is attractive because it provides a neutral forum in which the parties to a dispute arising from an international transaction can avail themselves of dispute settlement untethered to any national jurisdiction with any attendant disadvantages, including bias, whether real or perceived. The de-nationalized or 'a-national' arbitration is the ideal of the genre—an arbitral tribunal that operates without intersecting with municipal courts.[17]

An arbitration that functions without any need for court intervention approximates this ideal. In the event that the arbitration is not seamless, and some assistance beyond what the arbitrators can provide is necessary, such as the appointment of arbitrators themselves, having a national authority that can support the arbitration is normally seen as beneficial and as necessary to avoid risk.

The New York Convention does not explicitly address the concept of de-nationalized arbitral awards, though given the backdrop against which it was negotiated an implicit rejection of the idea is evident.[18] Furthermore, the language and structure of the Convention presuppose a link between the arbitration and territory. First, the Convention

[15] Van den Berg (n. 11), 7. [16] Ibid. 246; New York Convention (n. 1), Art. IV.

[17] Emmanuel Gaillard, 'L'ordre juridique arbitral: réalité, utilité et spécificité', 55 McGill L. J. 891 (2010).

[18] Van den Berg (n. 11), 34–7.

applies to awards rendered in the territory of another state party to the Convention, which would seem to exclude a-national awards that in theory at least are not made in any particular country.[19] Article V(1)(e) assumes that awards might have been set aside in the place in which they were made; this too suggests a structure that presupposes a place of arbitration. The New York Convention could function without Article V(1)(e), certainly—the enforcing state could still scrutinize the award on the other grounds available for resisting enforcement. Yet the attachment of most jurisdictions to a territorial nexus for arbitration, demonstrated by the reciprocity reservation in which New York Convention states agree to enforce awards rendered in other New York Convention member states, suggests that pure a-nationality is unlikely to prevail any time soon.[20]

7.1.2 Commerciality

The New York Convention permits states to limit their obligations to awards considered commercial under the national law of the state making the declaration.[21] This requirement has given rise to some difficulties, especially in arbitrations involving states or state entities, because of ambiguity about whether certain activities are commercial or sovereign in nature. Arbitrations that might ordinarily be deemed 'commercial'—i.e. they involve a contract between a state or state entity and a private party, municipal law governs the contract, and a commercial arbitration institution is the proposed dispute resolution venue—might also be regarded as non-commercial due to the actors involved and/or the nature or purpose of the activity in question. Some states might have legislation or policies regarding what kinds of activities are properly considered commercial. Just as in the field of sovereign immunity it is difficult to distinguish between sovereign acts and commercial acts, it can be difficult to ascertain whether an arbitration clearly falls on one side of the divide or the other.[22]

[19] Ibid. 37.

[20] See the discussion of arbitration under the ICSID Convention in section 7.2.

[21] New York Convention (n. 1), Art. I(3). 'When signing, ratifying or acceding to this Convention, or notifying extension under article X hereof, any State may on the basis of reciprocity declare that it will apply the Convention to the recognition and enforcement of awards made only in the territory of another Contracting State. *It may also declare that it will apply the Convention only to differences arising out of legal relationships, whether contractual or not, which are considered as commercial under the national law of the State making such declaration*' (emphasis added). Forty-eight states have made this declaration; see UNCITRAL (n. 2).

[22] David P. Stewart, 'The UN Convention on Jurisdictional Immunities of States and Their Property', 99(1) American Journal of International Law 194 (2005), at 199. See also Andrea K. Bjorklund, 'Sovereign Immunity as a Barrier to the Enforcement of Investor-State Arbitral Awards: The Re-Politicization of International Investment Disputes', 21 American Review of International Arbitration 211 (2010), 225–9.

Many if not most bilateral investment treaties permit arbitrations under both the ICSID Convention and the New York Convention. In some instances only the latter is available because the states party to the investment treaty are not both party to the ICSID Convention. While some international investment agreements specify that disputes arising under them are 'commercial' for purposes of the New York Convention,[23] others do not so specify, though such an assumption might be implied, given the desire on the part of the treaty parties to establish a workable arbitration regime and their permitting arbitration under rules other than those provided by the ICSID Convention. One might anticipate that a state resisting enforcement in an investment treaty case could raise the argument that the dispute involved a non-commercial matter, though this does not seem to have happened yet.

7.1.3 The foreign nature of enforceable awards

The New York Convention applies to *foreign* arbitral awards. By its terms the Convention requires state parties to enforce all arbitral awards made in the territory of a state *other than* the state in which enforcement is sought. This broad scope of application would require enforcement of an arbitral award made in a state that has not adopted the New York Convention. In practice, however, 74 states have taken a reservation specifying that their commitment is only to enforce awards made in the territory of another New York Convention state.[24] This reciprocity reservation could have limited the generality of the Convention, but with the large number of state parties it has not impeded the effectiveness of the Convention or the attractiveness of international arbitration. Well-advised parties always site their arbitrations in a New York Convention state in order to ensure the broadest possibility enforceability of an award.[25] At the time of negotiating the place of arbitration (which is usually done in the course of negotiating the broader contract and the dispute resolution provisions that will apply in the event of a dispute arising under that contract), neither party knows who will win or lose any eventual dispute; each thus has the incentive to maximize the enforceability of any eventual award. With the plethora of choices available there is no reason not to choose a New York Convention state as the *situs*. Rare exceptions could involve arbitrations

[23] See e.g. North American Free Trade Agreement (NAFTA) (concluded 17 December 1992, entered into force 1 January 1994) 32 ILM 289, 605, Art. 1136(7); Comprehensive Trade and Economic Agreement between Canada and the European Union (CETA) (signed 30 October 2016, provisionally entered into force), Art. 8.41(5); Agreement Between the Government of Canada and the Government of the Republic of Benin for the Promotion and Reciprocal Protection of Investments (signed 9 January 2013, entered into force 12 May 2014), Art. 38(5); Treaty Between the United States of America and the Oriental Republic of Uruguay Concerning the Encouragement and Reciprocal Protection of Investment (signed 4 November 2005, entered into force 31 October 2006), Art. 34(10).

[24] See UNCITRAL (n. 2).

[25] Gary B. Born, *International Commercial Arbitration*, 2nd edn (Kluwer Law International, 2014), 2056.

with states or state entities whose national laws or policies require that any arbitration occur in that state.[26]

The New York Convention also permits states to enforce awards 'not considered domestic' by the enforcing state. The exact language is: '[The Convention] shall also apply to arbitral awards not considered as domestic awards in the State where their recognition and enforcement are sought.'[27] This rather awkward phraseology was intended to encompass situations permitted particularly by the then-extant arbitral laws of France and Germany under which parties could choose to arbitrate in one country but subject their arbitration to the arbitral law of another country.[28] Thus a contract might call for arbitration in Paris but for German arbitration law to apply. From a French perspective, would the resulting award be considered international? The provision permits a French court to apply the New York Convention in such a case. Also of note is the discretionary nature of the criterion; only if the enforcing court 'considers' the award not to be domestic would it need to enforce it. As Professor van den Berg has pointed out, in most enforcing jurisdictions the fact that the award was made in the territory of another party would alone make the award enforceable under the New York Convention.[29]

The United States has interpreted that language to encompass any arbitration, even one that would ordinarily be considered domestic, if certain conditions are met: 'An agreement or award... which is entirely between citizens of the United States shall be deemed not to fall under the Convention unless that relationship involves property abroad, envisages performance or enforcement abroad, or has some other reasonable relation with one or more foreign States.'[30] In practice, this approach has led to some procedural confusion—an award in an arbitration seated in the United States is apparently simultaneously subject to set-aside under the Federal Arbitration Act *and* enforceable under the New York Convention in U.S. courts. The majority of U.S. jurisdictions treat such awards as subject to confirmation or set-aside under the Federal Arbitration Act; the New York Convention does not apply to them in U.S. courts.[31]

[26] Ibid. 2069 (footnotes omitted): 'In virtually no instances do national laws deny the parties' autonomy to select the arbitral seat. The only arguable exceptions, which are discussed below, involve national laws providing that particular categories of claims may only be resolved in local courts, which are in fact applications of the nonarbitrability doctrine, and judicial decisions applying variations of the *forum non conveniens* doctrine to agreements selecting the arbitral seat, which are in fact (illegitimate) applications of rules relating to unconscionability.'

[27] New York Convention (n. 1), Art I(1).

[28] Van den Berg (n. 11), 22–3. The possibility of this split between the place of arbitration and the *lex arbitri* is also reflected in Art. V(1)(e): 'The award has not yet become binding on the parties, or has been set aside or suspended by a competence authority of the country in which, or under the law of which, that award was made.' See section 7.1.4(5) for a discussion of Art. V(1)(e).

[29] Van den Berg (n. 11), 25.

[30] U.S. Federal Arbitration Act, Pub. L. 68–401, 43 Stat. 883, sec. 202.

[31] The U.S. Restatement on International Commercial Arbitration initially recommended that, contrary to prevailing practice, U.S. Convention awards be subject only to enforcement under the New York Convention; resistance to enforcement would effectively serve as a motion to vacate. See Council Draft No. 3, section 4.1.a (December 2011). In the final version of the Restatement, however, this approach was

The goal of this language was to broaden the reach and power of the Convention; in practice, as the US experience illustrates, a too-broad application of the Convention fits uneasily with the existing architecture of international arbitration, which assumes a sphere of application for municipal law.

7.1.4 Grounds for refusing enforcement

The fact that an award is enforceable in multiple jurisdictions—in every state party to the applicable convention—means that multiple intersections with multiple different laws are possible. It also means that conflicting approaches to, and interpretations of, the various provisions are likely, even inevitable. Some techniques are available for minimizing those disparities. First, according to Albert Jan van den Berg, the grounds for refusing enforcement are meant to be construed narrowly.[32] Second, centralized databases of awards rendered under the New York Convention are available to help those faced with enforcement questions see, and potentially conform to, the approach taken by other tribunals.[33]

Article V of the New York Convention sets out an exhaustive list of the grounds for refusing enforcement. Section 1 includes those grounds on which the judgment debtor bears the burden of proof. Section 1 grounds are largely procedural matters and no review of the award on the merits is permitted. Section 2 grounds are arbitrability of the subject matter of the dispute and public policy of the state of enforcement, each of which may be raised by the parties or by the reviewing court *sua sponte*. The reviewing court has discretion when determining whether or not to refuse enforcement even if one of the grounds is proved: enforcement 'may' (not 'must') be refused. This permissiveness does not mean that courts are expected to enforce even in the presence of the proof of one of the Article V grounds for resisting enforcement, but does give them that option in exceptional circumstances, such as when the debtor might be viewed as estopped from asserting the ground for refusal or when the court views that the public policy counselling against enforcement should fall to a competing public policy that would favour it.[34]

Below is a brief review of the Article V grounds for resisting enforcement.

1. **V(1)(a)—The parties to the agreement referred to in article II were, under the law applicable to them, under some incapacity, or the said agreement is not valid**

jettisoned in favour of subjecting those awards to confirmation or set aside under the Federal Arbitration Act, in keeping with prevailing court practice. See Proposed Final Draft section 4.9.a (April 2019). The draft was approved at the ALI Annual Meeting in May 2019.

[32] Van den Berg (n. 11), 267–8.

[33] UNCITRAL Secretariat, *Guide on the Convention on the Recognition and Enforcement of Foreign Arbitral Awards* (New York, 1958), 2016 edn, http://newyorkconvention1958.org/, accessed 22 March 2019. See also McGill Model Arbitration Law Database, available at https://www.maldb.ca/about-this-site.html, accessed 11 March 2019.

[34] Van den Berg (n. 11), 265–6.

under the law to which the parties have subjected it or, failing any indication thereon, under the law of the country where the award was made.

The focus of Article V(1)(a) is the validity, or invalidity, of the arbitration agreement. The article is complex primarily because of the choice-of-law issues involved.

The first is the question of the applicable law relating to capacity. The provision itself elides the question: are the parties—under the law applicable to them—incapacitated? What choice-of-law rules does a court apply to determine 'the law applicable to them'? Generally the applicable choice-of-law rules are those of the enforcing jurisdiction.[35]

Different questions arise when the contracting party is a state or state entity. Difficult estoppel questions can arise—if the law is clear that the entity does not have the capacity to enter into an arbitration agreement, but someone with apparent authority enters into such an agreement anyway, can the state be estopped from raising incapacity as a defence?[36]

The second choice-of-law question is whether the agreement is valid under the law applicable to it, which is either the law selected by the parties or the law of the country where the award was made. Party autonomy is honoured here. Yet often one still has the question of whether the parties actually selected a law to be applied to the arbitration agreement itself. Sometimes the parties will specify that a law is applicable to the arbitration agreement, but much more likely is a situation in which the container contract—the contracting memorializing the transaction and in which the arbitration clause is embedded—has a choice-of-law clause and the question is whether that choice applies to the arbitration agreement in addition to the rest of the contract.[37] An alternative is that the law of the place of arbitration, assuming a place is selected by the parties, should govern the arbitration agreement. That choice is justified on the ground that the parties have selected a particular jurisdiction to host the arbitration, and the most likely inference is that they intended their entire *arbitral* relationship to be governed by that jurisdiction's law.[38]

A third choice-of-law question is whether the choice of law refers to the 'whole' law of that jurisdiction (thus including the conflict-of-laws rules of that law), or to the substantive law of that jurisdiction. When the question is one of party autonomy, the usual assumption is that reference to a particular applicable law excludes that jurisdiction's choice-of-law rules. The question is less clear when one is under the default rule found in V(1)(a)—does 'the law of the country where the award was made' refer to the

[35] Leonard V. Quigley 'Accession by the United States to the United Nations Convention the Recognition and Enforcement of Foreign Arbitral Awards', 70 Yale L. J. 1049 (1961), 1067.

[36] See Emmanuel Gaillard, 'France: Court of Cassation Decision in Southern Pacific Properties Ltd. et al. v. Arab Republic of Egypt (Appellate Review of Arbitral Awards between States and Private Parties)', 26(4) I.L.M. 1004 (1987), 1004–7.

[37] Alan Redfern and Martin Hunter, *Law and Practice of International Commercial Arbitration*, 4th edn (Sweet & Maxwell, 2004), para. 2–86.

[38] Van den Berg (n. 11), 293.

whole law of that country, thus requiring application of the choice of law rules of that country to ascertain the applicable law? Many have argued yes.[39]

A fourth choice-of-law question relates to a challenge to the very existence of an agreement to arbitrate. The law of the forum in which post-award relief is sought is usually applicable here, on the grounds that any applicable law chosen in the contract or the law of the arbitral seat itself cannot be used to determine whether there was ever any agreement to contract that contains those laws.[40]

Also complex is the interplay between a *court's* consideration of this question and a decision of the arbitral tribunal regarding the validity of an agreement to arbitrate.[41] In most circumstances one would expect the respondent to seek dismissal of the arbitration for lack of consent at the outset of the arbitration. How should a court view an earlier decision of the arbitral tribunal on this question? If the challenge goes to the validity of the container contract as a whole (as opposed to being lodged against the arbitration agreement itself), the decision is often considered to have been entrusted to the arbitrator, based on the principle that the arbitration agreement is separable from the main contract, and the parties likely entrusted the arbitral tribunal with the task of ascertaining the validity of the overarching agreement.[42] If, on the other hand, the challenge is to the very *existence* of the container contract—for example, that any signatures on it purporting to bind one of the parties were forged—then a court will decide the matter.[43] So, too, if the complaint can be lodged against only against the arbitration agreement, a court will likely decide the matter *de novo*, on the ground that arbitrators cannot determine their own jurisdiction if there was never an agreement to arbitrate in the first place.[44]

2. V(1)(b) The party against whom the award is invoked was not given proper notice of the appointment of the arbitrator or of the arbitration proceedings or was otherwise unable to present his case

This provision deals with certain essential due process considerations. It is generally held to encompass 'the fundamental principle of procedure, that of fair hearing and

[39] Ibid. 276–7.

[40] William W. Park, 'The Arbitrator's Jurisdiction to Determine Jurisdiction', in Albert Jan van den Berg (ed.), *International Arbitration 2006: Back to Basics?* (Kluwer Law International, 2007), 130.

[41] See George A. Bermann, 'The "Gateway" Problem in International Commercial Arbitration', 37(1) Yale Journal of International Law 1 (2012).

[42] Alan S. Rau, 'Everything You Really Need to Know about "Separability" in Seventeen Simple Propositions', 14 Am. Rev. Int'l Arb. 1 (2003).

[43] This has been the prevailing position. In the United States there is a circuit split, with the Third and Fifth Circuit determining the matter is for the court, while the Second Circuit would apparently defer to the arbitrator's decision. See e.g. *Will-Drill Resources Inc. v Samson Resources Co*, 352 F.3d 211 (5th Cir. 2003); *China Minmetals Materials Imp. & Exp. Co. v Chi Mei Corp.*, 334 F.3d 290 (3rd Cir. 2003); *Europcar Italia, S.pA. v Maiellano Toursc, Inc.*, 156 F.3d 310, 315 (2nd Cir. 1998). See Born (n. 26), 3216–17. For a discussion of the absurdity of the difference between validity and existence, see Alan S. Rau, 'Separability in the United States Supreme Court', 2006 Stockholm In'tl Arb. Rev. 1, 18–19 (2006).

[44] Rau (n. 42), 119 n. 323.

adversary proceedings, also referred to as *audi et alteram partem*'.[45] Abiding by due process provisions is essential to ensuring the legitimacy of arbitration.

This deceptively simple requirement masks more complicated questions. Against whose standards should due process be judged? The standards of the enforcing court? The standards of the law of the place of arbitration? International standards? If it is the first, there is a concern about parochialism.[46] Related is the concern about which due process standards apply. It would be inappropriate to require that an arbitral tribunal observe the same processes followed in national courts, often under the dictates of a constitution, yet alternatives against which to measure the arbitral process might not be readily available. If it is the second, one has the concern that the enforcing court might not be expert in the standards required in the place of arbitration. The third bears the most promise but is the most amorphous.[47] This is not necessarily disqualifying; measuring due process in an arbitration against too-specific standards could defeat the purpose of the Convention.

The notice requirement is not unduly onerous. Service of process in line with national procedure laws is not required. Even constructive notice can suffice in certain circumstances.[48] Similarly, the requirement that a party be able to present its case does not mean the party has the right to present an unlimited number of witnesses; the arbitrators retain control of the case and can impose reasonable limits on the procedure.

There is potential tension between the due process requirement and the requirement in Article V(1)(d) that the procedure comport with the agreement of the parties. Balancing this tension, and ensuring the legitimacy of the arbitral proceedings, means that party autonomy cannot be invoked to override fundamental due process.[49]

3. V(1)(c) The award deals with a difference not contemplated by or not falling within the terms of the submission to arbitration, or it contains decisions on matters beyond the scope of the submission to arbitration, provided that, if the decisions on matters submitted to arbitration can be separated from those not so submitted, that part of the award which contains decisions on matters submitted to arbitration may be recognized and enforced

This provision permits resistance to enforcement on the ground that the arbitrators have exceeded their authority. It is based on the consensual nature of arbitration; because the tribunal gains its authority, at least in part, from the parties' agreement to arbitrate, its authority is limited to matters encompassed in that agreement. Note that there is a link

[45] Van den Berg (n. 11), 297.

[46] Note that due process could also potentially be viewed as a matter of public policy under Art. V(2)(b) of the New York Convention, which would permit a reviewing court to raise the matter *sua sponte*. In practice this has not been a consideration; parties resisting enforcement will not overlook potential due process grounds for resisting enforcement and thus usually lodge their objections under Art. V(1)(b). Born (n. 25), 3495–6, 3646–95.

[47] Ibid. 3504–7. [48] Ibid. 3510–11.

[49] Van den Berg (n. 11), 301; Julian D. Lew, Loukas A. Mistelis, and Stefan M. Kröll, *Comparative International Commercial Arbitration* (Kluwer Law International, 2003), 711.

to New York Convention Article V(1)(a)—if there is no valid arbitration agreement, then ipso facto the tribunal lacks jurisdiction and any claim under Article V(1)(c) would be moot. Rather, Article V(1)(c) involves cases 'where the arbitration agreement may be valid as such, but the arbitrator has given decisions which are not contemplated by or not falling within the scope of the arbitration agreement and the questions submitted to him by the parties'.[50]

Like Article V(1)(a), this provision does not specify the law applicable to the question of the proper interpretation of the submission to arbitration. The same choice of law considerations canvassed in the discussion of Article V(1)(a) apply here.

This provision is implicated in two common scenarios. The first is when the arbitrators are alleged to have acted beyond the scope of authority granted to them—for example, the arbitration agreement covers disputes arising under the contract in which it is found, but one party claims damages for a tort related to the breach of contract. The second is when an arbitration agreement expressly excludes power from a tribunal—for example, it precludes the tribunal from awarding punitive damages, or specific relief, but the tribunal does not honour the limitation.[51]

4. V(1)(d) The composition of the arbitral authority or the arbitral procedure was not in accordance with the agreement of the parties, or, failing such agreement, was not in accordance with the law of the country where the arbitration took place.

Party autonomy is deliberately at the forefront of this provision. Parties retain control over the choice of the arbitral tribunal as well as over the procedure by which the arbitration will be conducted. The elevation of party autonomy is an attempt to reduce the role of the place of arbitration in response to practice under the Geneva Convention, which prevented enforcement until the award had become final in the place it was made (the so-called 'double exequatur' requirement).[52] Given that parties generally do not comprehensively outline procedures to govern their arbitration, the default rules set out in the applicable arbitral rules and/or in the law of the place of arbitration likely play a role as well, whether they are viewed as the arbitral procedure chosen by the parties (assuming the parties designated the place of arbitration in their contract) or as the residual rules in the absence of party selection.[53] Moreover, the choice of those rules, which

[50] van den Berg (n. 11), 312.

[51] On the question of limiting arbitral authority to award punitive damages, see Alan S. Rau, 'Punitive, Exemplary, "Vindictive", or Edifying Damages of Whatever Nature', in *Liber Amicorum William Laurence Craig* (LexisNexis, 2016).

[52] Geneva Convention on the Execution of Foreign Awards, 26 September 1927, entered into force 25 July 1929, 92 LNTS 301, Art. 1(d): 'the award has become final in the country in which it has been made, in the sense that it will not be considered as such if it is open to opposition, appel or pourvoi en cassation (in the countries where such forms of procedure exist) or if it is proved that any proceedings for the purpose of contesting the validity of the award are pending.' See also van den Berg (n. 11), 323, and the discussion accompanying nn. 13–15.

[53] See Alan S. Rau, 'The New York Convention in American Courts', 7 Am. Rev. Int'l Arb. 213 (1996), 222.

generally grant significant discretion to the arbitral tribunal, is viewed as an endorsement of that exercise of discretion by the parties.

To justify setting aside an award, the departure from the parties' agreement would have to be material, and not a justifiable exercise of arbitral discretion.[54] Objections would also ordinarily have to be made relatively contemporaneously with the arbitral tribunal decision; otherwise a party will be deemed to have waived any objection to the tribunal's departure from the procedure agreed upon by the parties.

This provision can be used to challenge an arbitral tribunal's failure to apply the law selected by the parties.[55] This possibility is not, however, easily invoked. An incorrect application of the law selected by the parties is not justification for a challenge. Thus, parties will have to show the tribunal really did apply a different law, and did not merely misapprehend the law chosen by the parties. Moreover the law applied must be truly different from the parties' choice of law; the tribunal might well justify its application of a different law on various grounds, including that the law chosen by the parties was the 'whole law' of that jurisdiction, such that the applicable choice-of-law rules pointed to another law as the rule of decision for the matter at hand.[56]

One question that is not answered in this provision is the role of mandatory rules. While the arbitration laws of most jurisdictions include few or no mandatory provisions, should they do so, the extent to which party autonomy can override the rules is unclear. Note the potential for 'Scylla and Charybdis' here.[57] What if there are mandatory provisions of law in the country where the arbitration is to take place? If the arbitral tribunal follows the law of the place of arbitration and disregards the agreement of the parties, then the award would be valid in the arbitral venue but potentially unenforceable elsewhere. If, on the other hand, the arbitrators honour the agreement of the parties and disregard mandatory law in the place of arbitration, then the award would be enforceable under V(1)(d) but would be set aside in the courts of the place of arbitration, and thus possibly unenforceable under V(1)(e).

Opinions are mixed as to whether arbitrators should honour mandatory law in the scenario set out above.[58] An argument in favour of presuming that party autonomy triumphs over mandatory law, at least in the first instance, is that it is consistent with the pro-enforcement bent of the New York Convention and reasonable in light of the likely difficulty an arbitral tribunal might have in ascertaining the mandatory nature of a given law. The losing party could challenge the award in the place of arbitration, and the courts in the place of arbitration would assess the validity of the award and the relative strength

[54] See e.g. Born (n. 25), 3560–76.

[55] Stefan Kröll, 'The German Law on the Recognition and Enforcement of Foreign Arbitral Awards', 18(3) Int'l Arb. Rep. 29 (2003), 34; Born (n. 26), 3303–4.

[56] See generally Giuditta Cordero-Moss, 'Can an Arbitral Tribunal Disregard the Choice of Law Made by the Parties?', 1 Stockholm Int'l Arb. Rev. 1 (2005).

[57] Van den Berg (n. 11), 329–30.

[58] See e.g. ibid. 326, and Georgios Petrochilos, *Procedural Law in International Arbitration* (Oxford University Press, 2004), 38–9, 352–9; George A. Bermann and Loukas A. Mistelis (eds), *Mandatory Rules in International Arbitration* (Juris, 2010).

of party autonomy vis-à-vis the mandatory nature of the law in question. An enforcing court would then have the discretion, under Article 5(1)(e), to determine whether or not to honour a vacated award.

5. V(1)(e) The award has not yet become binding on the parties, or has been set aside or suspended by a competent authority of the country in which, or under the law of which, that award was made.

This provision has proved to be of enduring importance and complexity. It implies that only one court (or possibly two) has the authority to set aside or suspend an arbitral award. It also highlights another area of intersection between legal regimes—what should an enforcing court should do when another court has found an arbitral procedure wanting? What, if any, preclusive effect should the latter's judgment be given? On what basis should that determination be made? What about the inverse case, where a set-aside petition has failed? Should the set-aside court's determination be given deference? Finally, how does giving one jurisdiction authority over set-aside relate to the principle of a-nationality of arbitration?

Strictly speaking Article V(1)(e) suggests that two different jurisdictions—the country in which the award is made, *or* the country under the law of which the award is made—could set aside or suspend an award. The disjunctive 'or' suggests that these could theoretically be two different jurisdictions, and that each is a 'competent authority' as described in the Convention, meaning they have the power to set aside the award. The phrase 'or under the law of which, that award was made' was inserted at the instigation of the USSR delegate[59] and addresses the theoretical case of an agreement of the parties that a given arbitration award be governed by a law which is different from the law of the country where the award was made.[60]

In practice those two jurisdictions have functionally merged—the country in which the award is made is the same as the country under whose law the award is made, as the designation of 'place' of arbitration is also deemed to be a selection of the *lex arbitri*. Parties do not gratify the hearts of scholars by engaging in the hypothetically rich possibility of, for example, siting their arbitration in Paris while stipulating that the English Arbitration Act should govern. The *lex arbitri* helps to ensure the efficacy of an arbitration. Why choose a place of arbitration while hampering the applicability of its arbitral law by displacing it with another? Or, to put it another way, if that other arbitral law is more desirable, why not site your arbitration in that locale? Why take the risk that a French court might refuse to apply English arbitral law? Even if the French court attempted to apply English law, why take the risk that it would be unable to do so correctly?

[59] United Nations Conference on International Commercial Arbitration, 'Consideration of Other Possible Measures for Increasing the Effectiveness of Arbitration in the Settlement of Private Law Disputes', E/CONF.26/SR.23, 12 September 1958, 15.

[60] Van den Berg (n. 11), 350. See also the discussion in section 7.1.3.

Article V(1)(e) demonstrates acceptance that the country in which the award is made can set aside the arbitral award; its very existence suggests a rejection of the a-national nature of arbitration and some emphasis on the primacy of the role of the place of arbitration in policing the arbitration. Differences in the English and French text of Article V of the New York Convention led some commentators to question the discretion of national courts to disregard the decision of the place of arbitration about setting aside the award. Whereas the English version of Article V uses the terms 'Recognition and enforcement of the award *may* be refused... only if...', the French version of the same provision provides that 'La reconnaissance et l'exécution de la sentence ne *seront refusées*... que si...'[61]

At present, and notwithstanding the earlier debate, it is fairly widely accepted that an enforcing court has the discretion to honour or to disregard the decision of the place of arbitration about setting aside the award.[62]

Despite having an option, most courts will not enforce an award that has been set aside in the place of arbitration, though practice is not uniform. France, for example, in keeping with its commitment to the a-nationality of arbitral awards, does not give deference to the set-aside decision.[63] The United States ordinarily gives deference to the decision on set-aside, but courts retain discretion to enforce the award if the set-aside decision does not warrant respect.[64]

[61] On this controversy, see e.g. Philippe Fouchard, 'La portée internationale de l'annulation de la sentence arbitrale dans son pays d'origine', 1997(3) Rev. Arb. 329 (1997), 344; Jan Paulsson, 'Enforcing Arbitral Awards Notwithstanding Local Standard Annulments', 6(2) Asia Pacific Law Review 1 (1998), 6, n. 10; Born (n. 25), 3428–33.

[62] Professor van den Berg (n. 11, 355) explains the rationale behind honouring the decision of the court deciding the set-aside petition: 'A losing party must be afforded the right to have the validity of the award finally adjudicated in one jurisdiction. If that were not the case, in the event of a questionable award a losing party could be pursued by a claimant with enforcement actions from country to country until a court is found, if any, which grants the enforcement. A Claimant would obviously refrain from doing this if the award has been set aside in the country of origin and this is a ground for refusal of enforcement in other Contracting States.'

[63] Emmanuel Gaillard and John Savage (eds), *Fouchard, Gaillard, Goldman on International Commercial Arbitration* (Kluwer Law International, 1999), 49, para. 94: 'In the light of th[e] liberalization of international arbitration, in 1981 the French legislature considered the localization of international arbitration superfluous. Enacting rules specific to international arbitration, it decided against defining their territorial sphere of application and therefore also refrained from connecting an arbitration with foreign aspects to a particular country's legal system. The French courts will still sometimes examine which law should govern an arbitration of that kind. However, they now do so only in exceptional cases, encouraged to abandon the choice of law method by the French New Code of Civil Procedure, which contains no choice of law rules. In other words, under French law international arbitration does not need to be characterized, *prima facie*, as being national or foreign.'

[64] In favour of non-enforcement, see e.g. *TermoRio S.A. E.S.P.*, 487 F.3d 928, at 941 (D.C. Cir. 2007); *Baker Marine (Nigeria) Ltd v Chevron (Nigeria) Ltd.*, 191 F.3d 194, 197 (2nd Cir. 1999); cf. *Chromalloy Aeroservices v Arab Republic of Egypt*, 939 F. Supp. 907 (D.D.C. 1996); Restatement of the Law (Third) on International Commercial Arbitration, section 4-16(b) (Council Draft No. 3, 23 December 2011). On the reasons for continuing to have some discretion on this point, see Jennifer Cabrera, Dante Figueroa, and Herfried Wöss, 'The Administrative Contract, Non-arbitrability, and the Recognition and Execution of Awards Annulled in the Country of Origin: The Case of Commisa v. Pemex', 32 Arbitration International 125 (2016).

Retaining at least some discretion to question the bona fides of the judgement of the set-aside court would seem to make sense. For example, if the place of arbitration is in a jurisdiction whose courts might be viewed as likely to favour one side or another, concerns about the neutrality of the court might be heightened.[65] As noted by John Fellas, 'It is important, therefore, that there be some standard for reviewing foreign judgments vacating awards to ensure than any bias that was avoided through arbitration at the merits stage does not creep in at the vacatur stage through a parochial approach by a national court at the arbitral seat.'[66]

If a court has discretion to determine whether or not to honour a set-aside decision, it also has to determine which criteria to use when making that decision. The New York Convention does not contain any standards for set-aside of awards, thus leaving it to individual states to establish set-aside criteria. Without specific guidance from the Convention,[67] several possibilities exist. One is to examine the set-aside decision vis-à-vis the law governing set-aside in the place of arbitration.[68] This approach has the effect of placing the enforcing court in the position of a court of appeal in another jurisdiction.[69] Another approach is to assess whether the arbitral award would pass muster under the arbitral law of the enforcing court.[70] Yet another approach is to shift to the law of judgments, and to decide whether the court decision setting aside the award meets the criteria for enforcement of court judgments.[71] This latter position is appealing intuitively—why should a court decision about arbitration be treated any differently than a court decision about something else? Yet it also has the potential effect of effectively sidestepping the reasons the parties selected arbitration in the first place—to avoid the hazards attendant on the enforcement of judgments.

[65] One response to this problem is that parties should choose only neutral venues as places of arbitration. This pragmatic solution is not always an option in cases where state entities are involved, and state law might require that arbitration be seated in a local jurisdiction.

[66] John Fellas, 'Confirmation of Awards Vacated at the Arbitral Seat', 256(73) New York Law Journal (14 October 2016).

[67] Cf. Born (n. 25), 3168–73 (suggesting that implied limits can be found in the New York Convention).

[68] The European Convention (IX(2)) says that the only when an award has been set aside on one of the grounds in Art. IX(1) (which are substantially similar to V(1)(a)–(d)) can enforcement under the NYC be refused. This excludes the possibility of incorporating particularities in set aside legislation. The country of origin can still set aside on all its grounds; the European Convention simply limits that effect in other countries. See VDB NYC 356–7.

[69] Gary H. Sampliner, 'Enforcement of Nullified Foreign Arbitral Awards', 14(3) Journal of International Arbitration 141 (1997).

[70] Jan Paulsson, 'Rediscovering the N.Y. Convention: Further Reflections on Chromalloy', 12 Mealey's Int'l. Arb. Rep. 20 (1997).

[71] Linda Silberman and Maxi Scherer, 'Forum Shopping and Post-Award Judgments', in Franco Ferrari (ed), *Forum Shopping in the International Commercial Arbitration Context* (Sellier, 2013), 324–9. Cf. van den Berg (n. 11), 346: 'If in the country of origin a leave for enforcement is issued by the court on the award, the leave may constitute a court judgment in that country. Such judgment may furthermore have the effect of absorbing the award into the judgment in that country. If in this case the enforcement is sought in another Contracting State, the question arises whether the award is to be enforced as a foreign award under the Convention or as a foreign judgment on another basis. In other words, does the merger of the award into the judgment in the country of origin have an extra-territorial effect?'

It is also possible for the decision whether to honour the set-aside decision to merge into a question of public policy. For example, in *Pemex v Mexico*, the U.S. Second Circuit, considering whether to give effect to an award vacated by a Mexican court, noted that 'a final judgment obtained through sound procedures in a foreign country is generally conclusive . . . *unless* . . . enforcement of the judgment would offend the public policy of the state in which enforcement is sought'.[72] A judgment offends public policy when it is 'repugnant to fundamental notions of what is decent and just' in the enforcing State.[73]

6. V(2)(a) The subject matter of the difference is not capable of settlement by arbitration under the law of [the enforcing state].

This ground for refusal of enforcement—arbitrability of the subject matter of the dispute—is infrequently considered, particularly as less and less subject matter is viewed as incapable of settlement by arbitration.[74] It can be raised by the party resisting enforcement or raised by the arbitral tribunal *sua sponte*, thereby underscoring its importance, when and if relevant. The idea is that it is not subject to party autonomy but goes to the core of whether an enforcing court should lend its support to a particular arbitral award. Arbitrability limitations frequently relate to specific considerations of public policy—such as in the bankruptcy context, when the rights of third parties need to be considered in conjunction with those of primary litigants.[75] Arbitrability could also relate to the commercial nature (or lack thereof) of a dispute, if a state has adopted the commercial reservation discussed in section 7.1.2.

Another reason for the relative paucity of cases is that subject-matter arbitrability is also a ground for refusal to enforce the agreement to arbitration under New York Convention Article II. Thus, defences to arbitration based on arbitrability are often raised at the beginning of the procedure, rather than at the end.

Article V(2)(a) is concerned with the arbitrability of the dispute in the eyes of the *enforcing* jurisdiction, not the jurisdiction in which the arbitration occurred, or any other jurisdiction whose prescriptive authority might be at issue in the case. Whether or not the dispute was arbitrable under another state's law would usually be evaluated by that state in conjunction with a set-aside application or in a procedure to compel (or resist) arbitration. An enforcing court would thus evaluate arbitrability under another jurisdiction's laws indirectly, either through resistance to enforcement on the ground that the decision had been set aside in another jurisdiction, or in a request to enforce an

[72] *Corporación Mexicana De Mantenimiento Integral, S. De R.L. De C.V. v Pemex-Exploración y Producción*, 2016 WL 4087215 (2nd Cir., 2 August 2016), 27 (citing *Ackermann v Levine*, 788 F.2d 830, 837 (2nd Cir. 1986) (emphasis in original)).

[73] Fellas (n. 66).

[74] See Jean-François Poudret and Sebastien Besson, *Comparative Law of International Arbitration*, 2nd edn (Sweet & Maxwell, 2007), 302–5 (describing certain intangible and tangible property rights that are not viewed as arbitrable in certain jurisdictions); William W. Park, *Arbitration of International Business Disputes: Studies in Law and Practice* (Oxford University Press, 2006), 25–6.

[75] See e.g. Poudret and Besson (n. 74), 303.

agreement to arbitrate. Non-arbitrability in another jurisdiction might also be evaluated on the basis of public policy—would it violate public policy for an enforcing court to honour an award made in contravention of another jurisdiction's laws on arbitrability? Given the emphasis on 'truly international public policy' by enforcing courts, which is explained in more detail below, this theoretical possibility has not been applied in practice.

7. V(2)(b)Recognition or enforcement of the award would be contrary to the public policy of [the enforcing state].

The intriguing concept of public policy has spawned multiple books and articles.[76] As is the case with subject-matter arbitrability, public policy may be invoked by the party resisting enforcing or it may be raised by the enforcing court *sua sponte*. In some ways public policy is something of a catch-all term—each of the above grounds for resisting enforcement could be said to arise from particular public policies—but public policy as used in Article V(2)(b) is limited to occasions when 'enforcement would violate the forum state's most basic notions of morality and justice'.[77] Failure to apply the proper law, or an inaccurate application of law, or using evidentiary practices different from those in the forum state, would not be violations of public policy warranting non-enforcement. In civil law jurisdictions in particular, courts are wont to refer to 'international public policy' (*ordre public international*).[78] The idea is that narrow national interests do not justify failure to enforce a judgment; only those matters triggering global ignominy should warrant a decision not to enforce.[79] Thus, arbitrations that facilitate corruption or terrorist activity would violate public policy.

The clear language of Article V(2)(b) directs consideration of the forum state's public policy, not the public policy of other jurisdictions that might have an interest in the

[76] A partial list includes: W. Michael Reisman, 'Law, International Public Policy (So-Called) and Arbitral Choice in International Commercial Arbitration', in Albert Jan van den Berg (ed.), *International Arbitration 2006: Back to Basics?* (Kluwer Law International, 2007); Catherine Kessedjian, 'Transnational Pubic Policy', in van den Berg, *International Arbitration 2006*; Pierre Lalive, 'Ordre public transnational (ou réellement international) et arbitrage international', (1986) Rev Arb 329, 362–5; Audley Sheppard, 'Public Policy and the Enforcement of Arbitral Awards: Should There Be a Global Standard?' (2004) TDM 1, 2–3; Pierre Lalive, 'L'ordre public transnational et l'arbitre international', in Gabriella Venturini and Stefania Bariatti (eds), *Liber Fausto Pocar: New Instruments of Private International Law* (Giuffrè 2009), 603; International Law Association, *Final Report on Public Policy as a Bar to Enforcement of International Arbitral Awards*, 2002; Pieter Sanders (ed.), *Comparative Arbitration Practice and Public Policy in Arbitration* (Kluwer Law International, 1987).

[77] ILA (n. 76), para. 12 (quoting *Parsons & Whittemore Overseas Co., Inc. v Société Générale de l'Industrie du Papier RAKTA and Bank of America*, 508 F.2d 969, 974 (2nd Cir. 1974).

[78] Ibid. paras. 3–4.

[79] As the U.S. court put it in Parsons and Whittemore (n. 77, 974): 'In equating "national" policy with United States "public" policy, the appellant quite plainly misses the mark. To read the public policy defense as a parochial device protective of national political interests would seriously undermine the Convention's utility.'

dispute. The decision of most courts to focus on international public policy means that they have not looked at public policies of the forum state but on transcendent policy matters in which other states also likely have an interest.

7.2 The ICSID Convention's enforcement regime

The ICSID Convention is self-contained in that the only recourse available against an award is annulment under ICSID Convention Article 52.[80] It also has an enforcement regime should a judgment debtor fail to pay an award: that regime, while also self-contained, provides for recourse to national courts in the event of non-payment of pecuniary obligations by the judgment debtor.

7.2.1 A-nationality

The ICSID Convention is designed to be a-national. The state parties to the Convention created a stand-alone mechanism for the resolution of investment disputes that is formulated not to interact with national courts unless and until a judgment debtor is delinquent in its obligations. If the parties agree to seek the assistance of national courts they can do so, but ordinarily the process is expected to operate independently of them. There is no 'place' of arbitration.[81] The ICSID Convention does have a control mechanism, which is annulment before an ad hoc committee, convened under the Convention, on the grounds found in the Convention.[82] Notably these grounds do not include a challenge based on public policy or arbitrability.

The a-national nature of ICSID gives way to the necessity of enlisting the assistance of national courts for enforcement purposes. Indeed, one of the attractions of the ICSID regime is that the states party to the convention have made robust promises with respect to enforcing judgments rendered by ICSID Convention tribunals.

[80] ICSID Convention (n. 3), Art. 52.

[81] This is true for arbitrations under the ICSID Convention. When there is an arbitration under the ICSID Additional Facility Rules, there is a place of arbitration and the award is not enforceable under the ICSID Convention's rules but under the New York Convention or other applicable treaty mechanism.

[82] See ICSID Convention (n. 3), Art. 52(1): 'Either party may request annulment of the award by an application in writing addressed to the Secretary-General on one or more of the following grounds: (a) that the Tribunal was not properly constituted; (b) that the Tribunal has manifestly exceeded its powers; (c) that there was corruption on the part of a member of the Tribunal; (d) that there has been a serious departure from a fundamental rule of procedure; or (e) that the award has failed to state the reasons on which it is based.'

7.2.2 Enforcement of ICSID awards

The ICSID Convention contains a trio of provisions outlining a compliance mechanism in the host courts of the contracting states. Article 53 requires that each state party enforce pecuniary obligations imposed by awards as if they were final judgments of the courts of that state.[83] ICSID Convention arbitral awards thus avoid any impediments to enforcement found in treaties or domestic laws applicable to the enforcement of foreign judgments or awards.[84] Theoretically, then, ICSID Convention awards are more readily enforceable than awards under the New York Convention.[85]

Article 54(1) refers both to the recognition of awards and to the enforcement of any pecuniary obligations contained therein. Recognition confirms the award as *res judicata* in the confirming jurisdiction and is often a step preliminary to the enforcement of an award (*exequatur*).[86] Article 54(2) outlines the formal procedures that should govern recognition or enforcement in the state's courts. Finally, Article 54(3) provides that execution of the award is to be governed 'by the laws concerning the execution of judgments in force in the State in whose territories such execution is sought'.[87]

In the English version of the text, Articles 54(1) and 54(2) both refer to 'enforcement', while Article 54(3) refers to 'execution'. The equally authentic French and Spanish texts do not change the terms they use in the different sections of Article 54. The leading authority on the ICSID Convention, Professor Christoph Schreuer, has suggested that the appropriate way to reconcile these differences under Article 33(4) of the Vienna Convention on the Law of Treaties is to conclude that the terms 'execution' and 'enforcement' are identical in meaning.[88] The result of that interpretation is that under Article 54 the obligation to *recognize* extends to all awards, whether they order restitution or other remedies, whereas the obligation to *enforce* extends only to pecuniary obligations. This interpretation is also consistent with practical limitations to national courts enforcing non-pecuniary obligations.

Article 55 is the last of the three articles pertaining to the enforcement of ICSID awards. It provides that '[n]othing in Article 54 shall be construed as derogating from the law in force in any contracting State relating to immunity of that State or of any foreign State from execution'.[89] Though it gives the state the opportunity to assert an immunity claim to resist enforcement of the award as against particular assets, Article 55

[83] ICSID Convention (n. 3), Art. 54(1) ('Each Contracting State shall recognize an award rendered pursuant to this Convention as binding and enforce the pecuniary obligations imposed by that award within its territories as if it were a final judgment of a court in that State').

[84] Christoph Schreuer, with Loretta Malintoppi, August Reinisch, and Anthony Sinclair, *The ICSID Convention: A Commentary*, 2nd edn (Cambridge University Press, 2009), 1117–18.

[85] The New York Convention could still apply to an ICSID Convention award when enforcement is sought in a non-ICSID Convention state. Also, as noted earlier, the New York Convention can also apply to awards rendered under the ICSID Additional Facility Rules, which are not Convention awards.

[86] Schreuer, with Malintoppi, Reinisch, and Sinclair (n. 84), 1128–30.

[87] ICSID Convention (n. 3), Art. 54(3).

[88] Schreuer, with Malintoppi, Reinisch, and Sinclair (n. 84), 1134–9.

[89] ICSID Convention (n. 3), Art. 55.

has no bearing on the award's status; states have a compliance obligation under Article 53 regardless of an investor's ability to find assets to seize.[90] If a state fails to honour an award, the home state of the investor, whose ability to exercise diplomatic protection was suspended during the arbitration itself, can reassert itself into the process, including by seeking redress in the International Court of Justice.[91]

The drafters of the ICSID Convention were not especially concerned that Article 55 would prove an impediment for investors to collect monies due to them because they did not expect states to fail to abide by their obligations.[92] In fact, the original motivation for providing an explicit mechanism for the enforcement of awards was to ensure that states would be able to recover against investors who might be loath to pay awards rendered against them. The result is that the holder of an unpaid ICSID Convention award can seek enforcement in the courts of any ICSID Convention country, but its ability to recover against states or state entities will be limited by municipal laws on sovereign immunity.

7.3 Key challenges in enforcement proceedings

The foregoing sections have demonstrated the elaborate mechanisms that facilitate the enforcement of arbitral awards. Overall they have to be deemed successful—one of the primary reasons for arbitration's continued and growing popularity is the enforceability of arbitral awards. Notwithstanding this overall success rate, unresolved questions, both old and new, continue. Section 7.3 will address some of those vexing matters, some of which arise from the pragmatic decision to let states themselves determine the procedures whereby their enforcement obligations will be implemented. Others go to the very nature of what an arbitral award is. One relates to the proposed multilateralization of investment law.

7.3.1 Jurisdiction over judgment debtors and/or their assets

The New York and Washington Conventions are designed to streamline enforcement against the award debtor by effectuating claims against assets. The enforcement obligations

[90] Stanimir Alexandrov, 'Enforcement of ICSID Awards: Articles 53 and 54 of the ICSID Convention', in Christina Binder, Ursula Kriebaum, August Reinisch, and Stephan Wittich (eds), *International Investment Law for the Twenty-First Century: Essays in Honour of Christoph Schreuer* (Oxford University Press, 2009), 322; Schreuer, with Malintoppi, Reinisch, and Sinclair (n. 84), 1106–7.

[91] ICSID Convention (n. 3), Arts. 27(1) and 64.

[92] Schreuer, with Malintoppi, Reinisch, and Sinclair (n. 84), 1107, 1152.

under the Washington Convention extend only to pecuniary awards.[93] Enforcement under the New York Convention can encompass both injunctive relief and pecuniary relief.[94] One question for the enforcing court is how it establishes jurisdiction. Must there be jurisdiction over the person or entity who is an award debtor, or only over the asset? In the case of injunctive relief, the former must be true; in the case of the latter, the presence of assets alone is arguably sufficient.[95] But what if a judgment creditor wants to enforce prophylactically—to obtain an order seizing assets in the event they come in to the jurisdiction? Can this be done only in places where the court would otherwise have jurisdiction over the person of the judgment debtor?[96] Or can it be done in places where the debtor might be likely to have assets at some point in time—in a major commercial centre, such as the United States or the United Kingdom, for example? This is not simply hypothetical. A judgment creditor might want such an order because many jurisdictions have a limitations period (often three years) for enforcing an arbitration award. A judgment debtor might also be doing everything it can to hide its assets; a prophylactic order allows assets even evanescently present to be more readily seized.[97] Other reasons might include seeking the assistance of the court to locate assets, particularly in a jurisdiction (such as the United States) likely to permit broad discovery.[98]

The ICSID Convention treats pecuniary remedies slightly differently from the New York Convention. The ICSID Convention itself does not preclude tribunals from issuing awards for specific relief (certain bilateral investment treaties might limit the ability of tribunals to order non-monetary relief),[99] but limits the enforcement obligations of contracting states party to pecuniary obligations. The losing party would

[93] ICSID Convention (n. 3), Art. 54(1).

[94] Born (n. 25), 3433: 'It is well-settled that the New York Convention applies to awards granting non-monetary relief (*e.g.* declaratory or injunctive relief), as well as awards of monetary sums.'

[95] See e.g. *Frontera Res. Azerbaijan Corp. v State Oil Co. of Azerbaijan Republic*, 582 F.3d 393, 398 (2nd Cir. 2009): '[T]he district court did not err by treating jurisdiction over either SOCAR or SOCAR's property as a prerequisite to the enforcement of Frontera's petition.'

[96] Requiring personal jurisdiction has been the preferred approach in the United States, but in the aftermath of the *Daimler v Chrysler* case, which narrowed the concept of 'general jurisdiction', and two other cases which narrowed the existence of 'specific jurisdiction', asserting jurisdiction over judgment debtors in the United States is harder than it was earlier. *Daimler A.G. v Bauman*, 571 U.S.___(2014); *Bristol-Myers Squibb v Superior Court of California*, 582 U.S.___(2017); *Goodyear Dunlop Tires Operations, S.A. v Brown*, 564 U.S. 915 (2011).

[97] See e.g. *Sonera v Çukurova*, 750 F.3d 221 (2nd Cir. 2014); cf. *Chevron Corporation and Chevron Canada Ltd v Yaiguaje et al.*, (2015 SCC 42) (permitting, in the context of enforcement of a court judgment, the assertion of jurisdiction over the judgment debtor without requiring a substantial presence or the contemporaneous presence of assets in the territory: 'In today's globalized world and electronic age, to require that a judgment creditor wait until the foreign debtor is present or has assets in the province before a court can find that it has jurisdiction in recognition and enforcement proceedings would be to turn a blind eye to current economic reality' (*Chevron*, para. 57). The Canadian court emphasized that the assertion of jurisdiction did not in and of itself imply that the judgment was enforceable; the judgment debtors could still argue against enforcement on the relevant grounds.

[98] *Argentina v. NML Capital Ltd*, 573 U.S.___(2014).

[99] NAFTA (n. 23), Art. 1135. US and Canadian treaties generally follow this approach.

have an international obligation to honour the award, and the prevailing investor's home state could seek relief in the International Court of Justice, but other states party to the ICSID Convention have no obligation to enforce the award. This limitation is an explicit recognition of the public law taboo—the principle that a court will not infringe the public laws of another state.[100] It also reflects a practical limitation—even if a court in one state could be persuaded to order another state's legislature to rescind a law or another state's executive branch to rescind regulations, it would have no way to enforce that order.

7.3.2 Intersection with municipal laws and procedures

Both the New York and ICSID Conventions defer to domestic rules on procedure in the actual implementation of the state's international obligations. This makes sense—crafting a uniform procedural regime that could somehow accommodate deep-seated expectations in multiple jurisdictions would be enormously time-consuming, if it were possible at all. Yet consigning those decisions to national courts gives rise to potentially divergent practices as well as opportunities for judgment debtors to effectively resist enforcement on grounds other than those found in the applicable Conventions.

7.3.2.1 *Forum non conveniens*

The New York Convention says that states party to the convention '*shall* recognize arbitral awards as binding and enforce them in accordance with the rules of procedure of the territory where the award is relied upon'.[101] This requirement can mean that procedural defences, insofar as they are rules of procedure, might also be raised when a judgment creditor seeks to enforce an award. In common law courts, in particular, some judgment debtors have argued that the case should be dismissed on the grounds of *forum non conveniens* because the action would more properly be entertained in an alternative forum. This argument has only rarely been accepted,[102] and is arguably inconsistent with the raison d'être of the New York Convention (and the ICSID Convention, too). The portability of New York Convention awards is one of the hallmarks of the Convention and one of its strengths. It would not make sense if only certain states were 'appropriate' venues in which to seek enforcement.

It is also questionable whether *forum non conveniens* is a procedural rule at all, as it 'does not address *how* litigation shall proceed, but *whether* it shall proceed'.[103] *Forum*

[100] Schreuer, with Malintoppi, Reinisch, and Sinclair (n. 84), 1136–9, paras. 72–80.

[101] New York Convention (n. 1), Art III.

[102] For a U.S. case, see *Monegasque de Reassurances S.A.M. (Monde Re) v Nak Naftogaz of Ukraine*, 311 F3d. 488, 495–6 (2nd Cir. 2002). See also Linda Silberman, 'Civil Procedure Meets International Arbitration: A Tribute to Hans Smit', 23(3–4) American Review of International Arbitration 439 (2012), 446–50.

[103] 'Restatement of the Law, The U.S. Law of International Commercial and Investor–State Arbitration, Proposed Final Draft' (24 April 2019), section 4.27, reporter's note b(ii).

non conveniens is primarily a common law concept; it is largely unknown in civil law jurisdictions. The likelihood that it is the type of procedural rule to which the New York Convention refers is thus unlikely, as it is a defence that would not be available in many jurisdictions. Notwithstanding their lack of success, the reference to domestic procedural rules permits resistant debtors to make such arguments.

7.3.2.2 *ICSID Convention awards as 'final' judgments of member-state courts*

The manner in which ICSID Convention awards are enforced has been the subject of several cases in the United States. The precise processes for enforcing an ICSID Convention award are left to the individual states in which enforcement is sought. The ICSID Convention does not attempt to dictate a uniform procedural system. Seeking recognition in one U.S. court of a judgment from another U.S. court is ordinarily a procedural matter that occurs *ex parte*. Yet the assertion of jurisdiction is rather more than merely procedural. Enforcing an ICSID Convention award requires the effective assertion of jurisdiction over a foreign sovereign in addition to procedurally transforming the ICSID Convention award into a final judgment.

After some divergent opinions, two U.S. Circuit Courts have now held that the assertion of jurisdiction over a foreign sovereign in the ICSID Convention context (as well as in the New York Convention context) must comply with the Foreign Sovereign Immunities Act.[104] This means a plenary procedure in which a sovereign may contest the assertion of jurisdiction, rather than an *ex parte* procedure in which no opportunity for argument is given (arguments about execution immunity would be considered separately). The FSIA recognizes an 'arbitration' exception—if a sovereign has agreed to arbitrate, it ordinarily would be regarded as having consented to the assertion of jurisdiction over it.[105] The fact that there is a plenary procedure, however, gives the state the opportunity to argue that the assertion of jurisdiction is inappropriate, whether or not the argument is ultimately successful. In recent cases under the Energy Charter Treaty, in which Spain has lost investment cases related to its decision to change its regulatory regime regarding solar power, Spain has argued, *inter alia*, that it never consented to arbitrate with investors from other EU member states, thus negating the arbitration exception in the FSIA.[106] While decisions on the Spanish cases had not been made as of

[104] Foreign Sovereign Immunities Act of 1976, PL 94-583, 90 Stat. 2891 (FSIA). *Mobil Cerro Negro Ltd et al. v Bolivarian Republic of Venezuela*, No. 15-707 (2nd Cir. 2017), 16–17.

[105] FSIA (n. 104), 20 U.S.C. §1605(a)(6).

[106] See e.g. *Novenergia II—Energy & Environment (SCA) v Kingdom of Spain*, Civ. Action No. 1:18-cv-1148 (Respondent the Kingdom of Spain's Memorandum of Law in Support of Motion to Dismiss and to Denty Petition to Confirm Foreign Arbitral Award (D.D.C) (16 October 2018); *Eiser Infrastructure Limited and Energia Solar Luxembourg S.à.r.l. v Kingdom of Spain*, Case No. 18-cv-016860-CKK (Memorandum of Points and Authorities in Support of Respondent's Motion to Dismiss for Lack of Jurisdiction under the FSIA) (D.D.C.) (14 December 2018); *Infrastructure Services Luxembourg S.A.R.L. and Energia Termosolar B.V. v Kingdom of Spain*, Civ. Action No. 1:18-cv-1753 (EGS) (Respondent the Kingdom of Spain's Memorandum of Law in Support of Motion to Dismiss Petition to Enforce Arbitral Award) (D.D.C.) (28 December 2018).

July 2019,[107] the fact that Spain has had the opportunity to present the argument shows the importance of the decision about the need to have plenary procedures in order to assert jurisdiction over sovereigns; in an *ex parte* procedure, the assertion of jurisdiction would have been automatic and any dispute would have likely centred only on questions related to execution immunity, and in particular which assets were commercial and thereby available for execution purposes.

7.3.2.3 *Execution immunity*

Section 7.2 discussed the assertion of jurisdiction over a state in enforcement proceedings involving a state as a judgment debtor. It did not address the assertion of jurisdiction over a state's assets, which enjoy an immunity distinct from that of the state. Professor Sompong Sucharitkul, the Special Rapporteur for the International Law Commission's project on the codification of the law of state immunity, described state immunity from execution as 'the last fortress, the last bastion of State immunity.'[108] The New York Convention does not address execution immunity. Claimants seeking enforcement of awards under the New York Convention have argued, with very limited success, that the agreement of a state to arbitrate found in an investment treaty or in a concession contract encompasses an implied waiver of a claim of immunity not only from the jurisdiction of the enforcing court but also from the execution of any resulting award.[109] The implied waiver argument is easier under the New York Convention because it contains no explicit reservation of waiver with respect to execution, such as that found in Article 55 of the ICSID Convention. Article 55 clearly refers to the municipal law on execution immunity in the place in which execution of the award is sought. Thus, actual execution of an award depends on the municipal state immunity law of the jurisdiction in which the assets are located.[110] While most states follow the doctrine of restrictive immunity with respect to execution immunity, successful execution requires identifying the commercial assets of the judgment debtor, which can be quite difficult.

[107] In a May 2019 decision in *Tatneft v Ukraine*, the D.C. Circuit decided, in a *per curiam* opinion, that by signing the New York Convention Ukraine waived its immunity to enforcement of arbitration awards under the Convention. *Tatneft v Ukraine*, No. 18-7057 (28 May 2019). The same logic would presumably apply to the signing of the ICSID Convention.

[108] Sompong Sucharitkul, Commentary to ILC Draft Articles, Art. 18, para. 1, C/AN.4/L/452/Add 3.

[109] Stephen J. Toope, *Mixed International Arbitration* (Cambridge University Press, 1990), 146–8; Albert Jan van den Berg, 'Some Recent Problems in the Practice of Enforcement Under the New York and ICSID Conventions', 2 ICSID Rev. Foreign Investment L. J. 439 (1987), 450; V. O. Orlu Nmehielle, 'Enforcing Arbitration Awards under the International Convention for the Settlement of Investment Disputes (ICSID Convention)', 7(1) Annual Survey of International and Comparative Law 21 (2001), 35.

[110] See section 7.1.2. For a general discussion of this topic, see Andrea K. Bjorklund, 'Sovereign Immunity as a Barrier to the Enforcement of Arbitral Awards', 21 American Review of International Arbitration 211 (2010); 'State Immunity and the Enforcement of Investor–State Arbitral Awards', in Binder et al. (n. 90).

7.3.3 Emergency arbitral awards

A recent enforcement question is whether an emergency arbitrator award is enforceable. Emergency arbitrators are an increasingly frequent phenomenon, as prior to the formation of a tribunal parties seek to preserve the status quo ante, often by means of an order issued on an emergency basis. Should those orders be deemed awards and thus be considered enforceable under the New York Convention? While the practice is in one sense too new to be considered uniform, the provisional answer would seem to be yes. In an SCC case in which Stockholm was the place of arbitration, a Ukrainian court of appeal enforced an award ordering Ukraine to refrain from collecting tax revenues at a higher rate than had earlier been charged (the rise in the rate was one of the issues challenged in the arbitration).[111]

7.3.4 Multilateralization of investment arbitration

Establishing a 'multilateral investment court' (MIC) is one of the hot topics in investment arbitration.[112] For purposes of enforcement, some very specific questions arise. One is whether a MIC will establish its own enforcement mechanisms, or whether MIC judgments would be 'awards' and thus be enforceable under the New York Convention (or the ICSID Convention assuming parties to the MIC are also parties to the ICSID Convention). If a putative MIC feeds into either existing mechanism, there could easily be a third stage of review prior to enforcement. Under likely MIC procedures, a first instance tribunal would render a decision, followed by the appellate body. The appellate body award would then be enforceable under the New York Convention, and judgment debtors could conceivably resist enforcement in municipal courts on New York Convention grounds. A treaty would presumably require that judgment debtors waive their rights to resist enforcement after the award had already withstood appeal, but the question is whether the courts in New York Convention jurisdictions would accept that waiver, or accept that the appeal effectively replaced the vetting process that accompanies enforcement.

In the ICSID Convention scenario, it is not clear whether or how appeal could replace annulment, absent an amendment to the ICSID Convention changing the provision that annulment is the exclusive means of challenging an ICSID Convention award.[113] If the Convention were deemed capable of *inter partes* amendment, such that an annulment/appeal process replaced the current annulment-only process, then those

[111] Yaroslav Petrov, 'JKX vs. Ukraine: An Update on the Enforcement of Emergency Arbitrator's Award', Kluwer Arbitration Blog (12 August 2016). The case is being heard in cassation, so the decision cannot be considered definitive.

[112] For a discussion as to whether the MIC has the attributes of a court, see Andrea K. Bjorklund and Jonathan Brosseau, 'L'accord commercial entre le Canada et l'Union européenne prévoit-il une résolution des différends par arbitrage ou règlement judiciaire ?' 14 Sciences Po Law Review 16 (2018).

[113] ICSID Convention, (n. 3), Art. 53(1).

awards would be subject to enforcement under the ICSID Convention, but only in those states that had accepted the *inter partes* amendment.[114] There might be ways around this obstacle: amending the ICSID Convention is possible but cumbersome.[115] A different possibility, and one that could more readily encompass an appellate mechanism, would be to establish a protocol to which states could adhere; the protocol would govern arbitrations in which the European Union was a party and could also establish an appeals process.

The European Commission, and the Union itself, are increasingly important factors in the investment arbitration landscape. One extant question is whether the European Union will pay all awards against it, or permit its member states to do so, if the award is deemed contrary to principles of EU law. For example, the European Union directed Romania not to pay an award rendered against it in *Micula v Romania* on the grounds that the award constituted an effective payment of the state aid that Romania withdrew from Micula and for which it was ordered to pay compensation.[116] The recent decision of the General Court in the *Micula* case suggests that EU law would not preclude payment.[117]

The Court of Justice of the European Union (CJEU) decided in Case No. 1/17 that the investment court system in the CETA (a likely precursor to a MIC) is consistent with EU law. Still, the question remains whether a judgment that the EC deems to infringe on the autonomy or integrity of EU law might not be enforced, at least in EU courts, on public policy grounds. What are the implications of this view for enforcement of arbitral awards not just in the European Union but more generally? Does not every state have the potential to regard its law as special and deserving of protection on public policy grounds? In fact this is one of the reasons the ICSID Convention does not permit public policy as a ground to resist enforcement.[118]

Even though the CJEU has upheld the compatibility of the CETA investment court with EU law, judgment creditors might still be worried about whether the European Union, or its member states, would pay awards in individual cases. To be sure, the European Union and its member states have pledged to honour any such awards.[119]

[114] August Reinisch, 'Will the EU's Proposal Concerning an Investment Court System for CETA and TTIP Lead to Enforceable Awards? The Limits of Modifying the ICSID Convention and the Nature of Investment Arbitration', 19(4) Journal of International Economic Law 761. Further hurdles to the use of the ICSID Convention are that at present the European Union is not a party to the ICSID Convention and is not able to ratify it. Article 67 of the ICSID Convention (n. 3) specifies that it is open only to states who are members of the World Bank.

[115] If the ICSID Convention were amended, another factor to consider would be ensuring that the European Union itself could become a party to the Convention, given its exercise of competence the foreign direct investment arena. At present ICSID Convention membership is limited to states. ICSID Convention (n. 3), Art. 67.

[116] Commission Decision (EU) 2015/1470 of 30 March 2015 on state aid SA.83517 (2014/C) (ex 2014/NN) implemented by Romania—Arbitral award Micula v. Romania of 11 December 2013 (notified under document C(2015) 2112).

[117] *Micula v European Commission* (ECLI:EU:T:2019:423) (18 June 2019).

[118] Schreuer, with Malintoppi, Reinisch, and Sinclair (n. 84), 1139–41, paras. 82–7.

[119] CETA (n. 23), Art. 8.41(2).

Yet an investor likely wants to know what its avenue for redress is in the event the European Union does not pay voluntarily.

The hurdle of 'execution immunity' is especially notable in this specific context: state assets (and in this context 'state' would include the European Union) are entitled to immunity unless they are used for commercial purposes.[120] This hurdle must be faced against any state respondent, but might be particularly difficult against the European Union. One question is how many commercial assets the European Union holds outside the Union in states party to the New York Convention. Within the European Union itself, no award against the European Union can be enforced unless the CJEU approves the payment: 'The property and assets of the Union shall not be the subject of any administrative or legal measure of constraint without the authorisation of the Court of Justice.'[121]

7.3.5 Competition for enforcement capability

Will arbitration retain its allure if other types of judgments—perhaps court judgments or perhaps judgments from a multilateral investment court—are equally readily enforceable? The latter was discussed in section 7.1.4. Certainly for a long period of time there will still be investment treaty arbitrations that do not feed into a MIC. At present UNCITRAL member states are considering the wisdom of establishing a MIC;[122] should they decide to move forward, the court would have to be designed, procedural mechanisms would have to be worked out, and an enforcement mechanism, if there is a separate one, would have to be created. Then member states would have to take steps to ensure that it was applicable to investment treaty arbitrations. If one is to look at the Mauritius Convention on Transparency in Treaty-Based Investor-State Arbitration[123] as a guide, that process alone will take some little time. The Mauritius Convention, adopted on 10 December 2014, was opened for signature on 17 March 2015 and entered into force on 18 October 2017, about two and a half years later. It currently has 23 signatories, but only five of them have ratified the Convention.[124]

In addition, treaty shopping might become more prevalent if MIC enforcement is seen as more cumbersome or less certain than straightforward ICSID or NYC enforcement.

[120] See generally Andrea K. Bjorklund, 'State Immunity and the Enforcement of Investor-State Arbitral Awards', in Binder et al. (n. 90), 302.

[121] Consolidated version of the Treaty on the Functioning of the European Union, 2008, OJ C/115/47, Protocol (no. 7) on the Privileges and Immunities of the European Union (C/115/266), Art. 1.

[122] See UNCITRAL, 'Working Group III-2017 to present: Investor–State Dispute Settlement Reform', http://www.uncitral.org/uncitral/en/commission/working_groups/3Investor_State.html, accessed 5 July 2019.

[123] United Nations Convention on Transparency in Treaty-Based Investor–State Arbitration, adopted 10 December 2014, entered into force 18 October 2017, www.uncitral.org/uncitral/uncitral_texts/arbitration/2014Transparency_Convention.html, accessed 5 July 2019.

[124] See https://treaties.un.org/pages/ViewDetails.aspx?src=TREATY&mtdsg_no=XXII-3&chapter=22&lang=en, accessed 5 July 2019.

It is possible, too, that states and investors who enter into contracts will select 'commercial' arbitration to enhance the enforceability of ensuing judgments (and perhaps to enhance confidentiality).

Courts are the other likely competing venue. The Hague Choice of Courts Convention has a limited number of adherents now, though those state parties do include the EU member states as well as Mexico. China and the United States have signd but not yet ratified the treaty.[125] The more ambitious Hague Judgments Convention project has been resurrected, and the text was released in July 2019.[126] Courts might thus be seen as reasonable rivals to arbitration, at least in some jurisdictions, should these treaties garner wide adherence such that court judgments have enforcement potential equal to arbitral awards.

7.4 Conclusion

The enforceability of arbitral awards has made international arbitration a robust, sought-after mechanism for the settlement of international disputes in both the commercial and investment law realms. Recent strides have been taken to raise court judgments to the same level, but it will be at best many years before judgment-enforcement conventions have the same breadth of reach as the arbitration conventions. In the area of investment arbitration, some proposals to replace the existing arbitral process with courts nonetheless envisage—at least in some iterations—reliance on one or both arbitral conventions for enforcement, a testimony to their efficacy.

Notwithstanding more than 50 years of practice under each (though the frequency of ICSID Convention arbitrations increased greatly starting in the 1990s) new questions continue to arise. So far they have been answered in ways that do not undermine the functioning of the conventions, even though answers have not been uniform. While some propose amending the New York Convention,[127] others vehemently oppose it.[128] Improvements undoubtedly could be made to both the New York and ICSID Conventions. Yet each has proved stalwart and flexible. As of the early twenty-first century, they still remain the touchstones for enforcement, and the enforceability of awards is the touchstone of international arbitration.

[125] See 'Status Table', https://www.hcch.net/en/instruments/conventions/status-table/?cid=98, accessed 3 July 2019.

[126] Convention on the Recognition and Enforcement of Foreign Judgments in Civil or Commercial Matters, Twenty-Second Session of the Hague Conference on Private International Law, Final Act, 2 July 2019, https://assets.hcch.net/docs/f55fc0a1-1a3c-4368-9199-48e8df11ff3e.pdf, accessed 3 July 2019.

[127] See e.g. A. J. van den Berg, Explanatory Note, in ICCA, *The New York Convention at 50* (Kluwer Law International, 2008), 649.

[128] See e.g. Emmanuel Gaillard, 'The Urgency of Not Revising the New York Convention', in ICCA (n. 127), 689.

CHAPTER 8

INTER-STATE ARBITRATION

†V. V. VEEDER

INTER-STATE arbitration is largely influenced by two different traditions, drawn from diplomacy and commerce under public and private international law respectively. At a time when the legitimacy of many forms of arbitration is encountering increasing difficulties (both substantive and procedural),[1] the historical path taken to reach the present practice of arbitration by states may explain the growing hostility towards arbitration shared across the political spectrum, particularly where a bilateral or multilateral treaty imposes an obligation on states to agree to arbitration in advance of a dispute: i.e. 'obligatory' arbitration and not a form of *compromis*.[2]

As to this first diplomatic tradition, from the earliest times of nation-states, princes, potentates, and popes have resorted, upon request or at their own initiative, to different forms of arbitration to settle peacefully existing disputes between states, including a home state's espousal of its national's claim against a host state. The alternative of conflict between disputing states was regarded generally as unpalatable, if a diplomatic settlement could resolve the particular dispute. For example, in 1493, Pope Alexander IV decided the geographical dispute between Spain and Portugal over the division of their

[1] The USA's blocking of new members to hear disputes by the WTO's Appellate Body, thereby compromising the WTO system as a whole, derives from a contempt for 'unaccountable international tribunals' as recently expressed by the President of the USA to the UN General Assembly (see *Financial Times*, 2 October 2016, 1). Since 2014, similar political views have been repeatedly expressed by the European Commission. E.g. the European Trade Commissioner (Dr Cecilia Malmström) in 2015 rejected investor–state arbitration (ISDS) for the EU's new free trade agreements: 'there is a fundamental and widespread lack of trust in the fairness and impartiality of the old ISDS model'; and, under the EU's proposal for a new international investment court and appellate body, 'It will be judges, not arbitrators, who sit on these cases.' See also Sophie Lemaire, 'Arbitrage d'investissement et Union Européenne', Rev. arb. 1029 (2016), 1034 'elle [EU] propose une révolution du modèle contentieux qui le caractérise.'

[2] The phrase 'obligatory arbitration' is here borrowed from the first Hague Peace Conference, where it signified an agreement by states to arbitrate in advance of any dispute, as distinct from a *compromis* agreed after the outbreak of a dispute.

colonial empires. In modern times, the origin of inter-state arbitration has been attributed to the Jay Treaty of 1796 between the USA and Britain, which provided for arbitration as a quasi-judicial means to end myriad differences outstanding from the American Revolution and the Treaty of Paris of 1783. Its commissions produced more than 500 decisions over five years. These were, however, mixed claims commissions composed of the two states' representatives, not swayed by the appointment of independent arbitrators, a neutral appointing authority, or the use of an established arbitral procedure. It followed an earlier precedent under the Treaty of Münster of 1648 between the Netherland and Spain (as part of the Peace of Westphalia). Moreover, consistent with the historical role of arbitration, the Jay Treaty addressed existing disputes and did not cover future disputes between the two states. If it was arbitration at all, by today's standards, it was arbitration by arbitrators in name only.[3]

The second commercial tradition is older. Transnational arbitration between merchants, before an impartial tribunal of the parties' choosing, under an established procedure, pre-dates the emergence of nation-states. In the nineteenth and twentieth centuries, the increasing use of concession contracts and investment agreements between a host state and a foreign national made use of this commercial tradition in the form of arbitration clauses contractually agreed between the foreigner and the state.[4] Later, when host states established, in their place, nationalized companies or wholly owned foreign trade corporations to contract with foreign nationals (as in the USSR, an example followed by most 'socialist' countries in Europe and China), their arbitration clauses conformed to this second commercial tradition.

The major changes began during the last part of the nineteenth century. The Washington Convention of 1871 between the USA and Britain introduced a significant change to the diplomatic tradition. That treaty primarily addressed existing claims by the USA (for itself and also espousing its nationals' claims) arising from Britain's misconduct as a neutral state during the American Civil War. The USA and Britain there agreed an arbitration tribunal comprising a majority of impartial arbitrators (three), together with the parties' respective representatives (two). It gave rise to the *Alabama Arbitration* in Geneva and its majority award of 1872, thereby precluding a real risk of a third war between these two states. Drawing upon both diplomatic and commercial traditions, the parties and the arbitration tribunal also firmly established the general principle of consensual arbitration as the preferred alternative to armed conflict, even for a major dispute involving matters of honour for both parties.

However, the Washington Convention addressed only existing disputes. By the end of the nineteenth century it was becoming necessary to introduce an arbitration mechanism for future disputes between states, as existed for commercial arbitrations between

[3] As concluded by J. G. Merrills in regard to the Jay Treaty and its progeny: 'These early Anglo-American commissions were not judicial tribunals in the modern sense, but were supposed to blend juridical with diplomatic considerations to produce (in effect) a negotiated settlement.' See *International Dispute Settlement*, 6th edn (Cambridge University Press, 2017), 89.

[4] See Jean Ho, *State Responsibility for Breaches of Investment Contracts* (Cambridge University Press, 2018).

merchants. Such an obligatory arbitration, agreed by states in advance of a dispute, was addressed at length by the Hague Peace Conferences of 1899 and 1907. These two conferences established both the high- and low-water marks for the peaceful settlement by arbitration of disputes between states.

The 1899 Peace Conference was convened by the Russian Empire on 12 August 1898 in a note (or 'rescript') by the Russian Minister of Foreign Affairs addressed to foreign ambassadors in St Petersburg. It called for an international conference between states to ensure a true and stable peace and, above all, to put an end to the progressive development of modern armaments. It was thus to be primarily a peace conference at a time when several European states maintained standing forces measured in millions of soldiers and sailors, absorbing 25 per cent or more of state revenues. For such states, including Russia, these ruinous and ever-increasing costs threatened national security almost as much as armed conflict. The 1899 Conference was also to take place within living memory of Germany's victory in the Franco-Prussian War 1870–71, with France's lost territories in Alsace and Lorraine still unrecovered, the conflict between Chile and Peru in 1882, the Sino-Japanese War of 1894, the war between Greece and Turkey in 1897, the Spanish–American War of 1898 and, as regards incipient armed conflict, the 'Fashoda incident' between France and Britain also in 1898.

The Russian Note came as a surprise to many, not least to the Russian Minister for War and also its principal international jurist, F. F. Martens, acting as legal adviser to the Russian Ministry of Foreign Affairs (but then away from St Petersburg on holiday).[5] The Russian proposal nonetheless proved immediately popular in many countries; as a result, it could not be ignored by the Great Powers notwithstanding deep suspicions in many places as to Russia's true motives. Later, these were partially dispelled by Russia's proposed programme for the Conference, prepared by Martens for the Russian Ministry of Foreign Affairs. His memoranda of 11 October 1898 and 1 March 1899 proposed a universal conference, open to all 'civilised nations', to be held in St Petersburg (later changed to The Hague as a compromise between Paris, Brussels, Bern, and Copenhagen).[6] His

[5] Fedor Fedorovich Martens (1845–1909), born in what is now Estonia and also known as Friedrich Fromhold von Martens or Frédéric de Martens (in German and French), had been an arbitrator in the *Bering Sea Arbitration* between Britain and the USA over pelagic seal fishing by Canada (1892–3); the sole arbitrator in the *Costa Rica Packet Arbitration* between Great Britain and the Netherlands (1895–7); and the presiding arbitrator (or 'umpire') in the *Anglo-Venezuelan (Guiana) Arbitration* (1897–9) held in the Quai d'Orsay in Paris (sitting with Lord Justice Russell and Lord Collins, appointed by Britain, and Justices Fuller and Brewer of the U.S. Supreme Court, appointed by Venezuela). Martens spoke fluent German, French, and English (in addition to, of course, Russian). Martens was later appointed as the first Russian representative to the PCA and an arbitrator in the first two arbitrations brought before the PCA under the 1899 Hague Convention: the *Pious Fund Arbitration* (1902) and the *Venezuela Preferential Claims Arbitration* (1904). He helped to negotiate for Russia the arbitration submission between the USA v Russia in 1900 (the '*Asser Arbitration*'). In 1905, he attended the Portsmouth Peace Conference convoked by President Theodore Roosevelt to bring a peaceful end to the Russo-Japanese War.

[6] Although Martens recorded that the choice of The Hague surprised many, he strongly supported that choice given the Netherlands' historically good relations with Imperial Russia and its status as the home of Hugo Grotius (Huig de Groot): see Frédéric Martens, 'La Conférence de la Paix à la Haye' (Arthur Rousseau, 1900), 10.

memoranda primarily addressed issues of peace and disarmament; but he also proposed the creation of a permanent mechanism for international arbitration for the peaceful settlement of disputes between states. Perceptively, as a practical realist, Martens warned against the creation of an international court binding upon states 'always and in all instances'. That was, in his view, 'utopian'. His proposal excluded compulsory arbitration to prevent a future war or to terminate an existing war, but it included obligatory arbitration for limited categories of future disputes between states.[7]

The first Hague Conference was opened on 6 May 1899, attended by 27 states represented by many well-known international jurists.[8] Its sessions were private, excluding the general public. The conference was closed on 17 July 1899, to broad acclaim as regards its conventions on the laws and customs of war, commissions of inquiry and arbitration.[9] Martens, albeit not the head of the Russian delegation, was regarded as the 'soul' of the conference with his extensive legal, diplomatic and linguistic abilities. For the conference, Martens had submitted a draft outline for a convention on obligatory arbitration of certain categories of dispute 'so far as they do not concern the vital interests nor national honor of the contracting states' (Art. 8 of the Russian proposal). These latter exceptions were explained in an accompanying note: 'no Government would consent in advance to adhere to a decision of an arbitral tribunal which might arise within the

[7] For Martens' comprehensive biography, see Vladimir Pustogarov, *Our Martens*, trans. W. Butler (Kluwer Law International, 1993, 2000); see also 'Frederic de Martens' (Editorial Comment), 3 American Journal of International Law 983 (1909); Thomas Holland, 'Frederic de Martens', 10 Journal of the Society of Comparative Legislation 10 (1909); Hans Wehberg, 'Friedrich v. Martens und die Haager Friedenskonferenzen', 20 Zeitschrift für Internationales Recht 343 (1910); Lauri Mälksoo, 'Friedrich Fromhold von Martens (Fyodor Fydorovich Martens) (1845–1909)' in Bardo Fassbender and Anne Peters (eds), *Oxford Handbook of the History of International Law* (Oxford University Press, 2012); Rein Müllerson, 'F. F. Martens—Man of the Enlightenment: Drawing Parallels between Martens' Times and Today's Problems', 25 European Journal of International Law 831 (2014). Having been forgotten or spurned for so long, even in Russia, Martens is now the subject of many legal histories, of which only a selection are listed here. Very belatedly and dwarfed by the over-large portrait of Tsar Nicholas II, a bust of Martens is now displayed in the Peace Palace's Small Arbitration Room.

[8] Austria-Hungary, Belgium, Bulgaria, China, Denmark, France, Germany, Britain, Greece, Italy, Japan, Luxemburg, Mexico, Montenegro, The Netherlands, Persia, Portugal, Romania, Russia, Serbia, Siam, Spain, Sweden (with Norway), Switzerland, Turkey and the USA. Korea attempted to attend the Conference but was refused admission, being treated as part of Japan. Apart from Mexico, no Latin American state attended the conference, although many were supporters of general arbitration treaties: see e.g. Art. 4 of the Plan of Arbitration agreed by the Pan-American Congress of 1890 (by 16 of 19 American states), and Art. 1 of the Treaty of Arbitration between Argentina and Italy of 23 July 1898. The majority of states taking part in the 1899 Hague Conference were European.

[9] For a full account of the Hague Conferences, see Shabtai Rosenne (ed.), *The Hague Peace Conferences of 1899 and 1907 and International Arbitration: Reports and Documents* (Asser Press, 2001); Arthur Eyffinger, *The 1899 Hague Peace Conference: The Parliament of Man, the Federation of the World* (Kluwer Law International, 1999); Jean Allain, *A Century of International Adjudication: The Rule of Law and its Limits* (Asser Press 2000); Hersch Lauterpacht, *The Function of Law in the International Community* (Oxford University Press, 1933), 27, 184; Hans von Mangoldt, 'Development of Arbitration and Conciliation Treaties and Arbitration and Conciliation Practice since The Hague Conferences of 1899 and 1907', in J. Gills Wetter (ed.), *The International Arbitral Process: Public and Private* (Oceana, 1979), 243.

international domain, if it concerned the national honour of a state, or its highest interests, or its inalienable possessions.'[10]

This left disputes for obligatory arbitration as to two broad classes: (i) pecuniary damages suffered by a state or its nationals as a consequence of international wrongs on the part of another state or its nationals; and (ii) disagreements as to the interpretation or application of treaties between states in four defined fields. The latter comprised: (a) treaties relating to posts and telegraphs,[11] railroads, submarine telegraph cables, regulations preventing collisions between vessels on the high seas, and navigation of international rivers and inter-oceanic canals; (b) treaties concerning the protection of intellectual, literary, and artistic property, money and measures, sanitation, veterinary surgery, and phylloxera; (c) treaties relating to inheritance, exchange of prisoners and reciprocal assistance in the administration of justice; and (d) treaties for marking boundaries, so far as they concerned purely technical and political questions (Art. 10 of the Russian proposal).[12]

In the accompanying note, Martens also explained the necessity for obligatory arbitration, without the need for a *compromis* to be agreed by the parties after their particular dispute had arisen:

> The recognition of the obligatory character of arbitration, were it only within the most restricted limits, would strengthen legal principles in relations between nations, would guarantee them against infractions and encroachments; it would neutralize, so to speak, more or less, large fields of international law. For the states obligatory arbitration would be a convenient means of avoiding the misunderstandings, so numerous, so troublesome, although of little importance, which sometimes fetter diplomatic relations without any reason therefor. Thanks to obligatory arbitration, states could more easily maintain their legitimate claims, and what is more important still, could more easily escape from unjustified demands. Obligatory arbitration would be of invaluable service to the cause of universal peace. It is very evident that the questions of the second class, to which alone this method is applicable, very rarely form a basis for war. Nevertheless, frequent disputes between states, even though with regard only to questions of the second class, while not forming a direct menace to the maintenance of peace, nevertheless disturb the friendly relations between states and create an atmosphere of distrust and hostility in which some incident or other, like a chance spark, may more easily cause war to burst forth. Obligatory arbitration, resulting in absolving the interested states from all responsibility for any solution of the difference existing between them, seems to be fitted to contribute to the maintenance of friendly relations, and in that way to facilitate the peaceful settlement of the most serious conflicts which may arise within the field of their most important interests.[13]

[10] Allain (n. 9), 23; Rosenne (n. 9), 97.

[11] Martens invoked, as the earliest example of obligatory arbitration, Art. 16 of the multilateral Postal Union of 1874, providing for the settlement by arbitration of all disputes between contracting states arising from the interpretation and application of that treaty. This obligation extended to future disputes.

[12] Eyffinger (n. 9), 'The Work of The Third Commission'; Allain (n. 9), 22–3.

[13] Rosenne (n. 9), 97.

The Russian proposal was referred to the conference's third commission, chaired by the French delegate, Léon Bourgeois. It was partly opposed by the USA as regards the inclusion of treaties concerning rivers and canals; but most of all by Germany with its general objections to any form of obligatory arbitration, supported at different times by Austria, Italy, Turkey, and Romania. Their opposition to obligatory arbitration almost wrecked the work of the third commission. During the third commission's second meeting on 26 May 1899, addressing (inter alia) arbitration, Britain's delegate, Sir Julian Pauncefote, adopted Martens' proposal and took it further (with Martens' support):[14]

> If we want to make a step in advance, I believe it is absolutely necessary to organise a permanent international tribunal which can assemble instantly at the request of contesting nations. This idea being established, I believe that we shall not have very much difficulty in coming to an understanding upon the details. The necessity for such a tribunal and the advantages which it would offer, as well as the encouragement and even impetus which it would give to the cause of arbitration have been set forth with vigour and clearness—and equal eloquence—by our distinguished colleague, Mr Descamps, in his interesting 'Essay on Arbitration'...[15]

This British proposal was subsequently reduced to writing, in the form of seven draft articles. Art. 1 provided for the organization of a private tribunal, governed by a code to be agreed at the Conference; Art. 2 provided for a permanent office and secretariat; Art. 3 required each contracting state to nominate two of its respectable jurists as members of the tribunal; Art. 4 provided for the role of the secretariat in receiving notices from disputing parties and transmitting names for the parties' selections as arbitrators (not limited to names submitted by contracting states); and Art. 5 offered recourse to the tribunal to all states, whether or not contracting states. The remaining articles established a 'Permanent Council of Administration' to control the office and addressed the allocation of expenses between the contracting states and disputing parties.

The 'Essay on Arbitration' cited by Pauncefote included a compilation by Baron Descamps of arbitration clauses in treaties concluded by states attending the Hague Conference. Paradoxically, Descamps opposed Martens' proposal; but he now suggested, perhaps mollified by Pauncefote's diplomatic flattery, that the third commission establish a *comité d'examen* to consider the British and Russian proposals, soon joined by a third proposal by the USA providing (inter alia) for a right of appeal from an award

[14] Sir Julian Pauncefote (1828–1902), later Lord Pauncefote, had been a member of the English and Hong Kong Bars. After a distinguished career in the British Colonial and Foreign Services (including stints as Attorney-General of Hong Kong), he was appointed in 1889 the UK's ambassador to the USA. In that capacity, Pauncefote negotiated in 1897 the 'Olney–Pauncefote' treaty between Britain and the USA providing for general arbitration, subject to exceptions (albeit never ratified by the USA) and the USA–UK treaty leading to the Bering Sea Arbitration over Canadian pelagic sealing rights. As a practising lawyer and senior diplomat, Pauncefote was undoubtedly familiar with both state–state and private commercial arbitration. There is no biography of Lord Pauncefote; but see his obituary in *The London Times*, 26 May 1902.

[15] Baron Descamps was the Belgian representative and a member of the third commission.

for 'a substantial error of fact or law'. This committee was to comprise an extraordinary group of international jurists: T. M. C. Asser (Netherlands), Baron d'Etournelles (France), F. W. Holls (USA), H. Lammasch (Austria-Hungary), F. F. Martens (Russia), E. Odier (Switzerland), and P. Zorn (Germany), with Baron Descamps (Belgium) as president.[16] Notably, Pauncefote was missing; apart from Holls, all represented European states. The committee met on seventeen occasions; and the third commission considered its work on nine occasions during May to July 1899.[17]

The third commission's committee laboriously addressed the establishment of a permanent court of arbitration and the binding obligation on states, by treaty, to refer to this new arbitral body certain (but not all) categories of dispute, always excluding disputes touching upon a state's dignity and vitally important interests. These proposals were supported by Russia, the USA, and Britain, but, again, strongly opposed by Germany.[18] Germany eventually moderated its position under the influence of its delegate (Zorn), supported by the USA's delegate (Holls) on their joint consultative visit to Berlin. The committee also considered Martens' proposal for a code of arbitration procedure.

The eventual result was a consensus in the form of The Hague Convention on the Peaceful Settlement of International Disputes, which entered into force on 19 September 1900 (the 1899 Hague Convention). It created the Permanent Court of Arbitration (PCA), which was neither a court nor an arbitration tribunal, still less a permanent court or arbitration tribunal. It was nonetheless a permanent mechanism comprising a secretariat, a registry, and a chamber of senior jurists appointed by the contracting states as potential arbitrators. Its name and functions were, inevitably, a compromise to achieve unanimity. As to the PCA's name, Germany had proposed 'Permanent Organisation for Arbitration', or 'Permanent List of Arbitrators', or 'Permanent Court of Arbitrators' (but not 'Arbitral Court'); when these were all opposed, it proposed 'Permanent Court of Arbitration', which was accepted. This was the high-water mark. As to the PCA's function, Germany (Zorn) adamantly refused to accept any form of obligatory arbitration, supported by Italy (Nigra). Martens, Descamps, and Pauncefote intervened to no avail. As explained by Zorn: 'To hasten this evolution too greatly would be to compromise the very principle of arbitration, towards which we are all sympathetic.' This was, after so much effort by Martens and such an expenditure of goodwill by other states, the low-water mark.

The results of the second 1907 Hague Peace Conference were somewhat disappointing as regards obligatory arbitration. The original proposal for this second conference on peace, the rules of war, and disarmament had come from the USA's President

[16] In addition to Martens and Descamps, these comprised T. M. C. Asser of The Netherlands (1838–1913), Baron d'Estournelles of France, F. W. Holls of the USA, H. Lammasch of Austria-Hungary (1853–1920), E. Odier of Switzerland (formerly IDRC secretary), and P. Zorn of Germany.

[17] See Eyffinger (n. 9) for a detailed account.

[18] See the critical account of Germany's conduct in Sabine Konrad, 'The Asser Arbitration', in Ulf Franke, Annette Magnusson, and Joel Dahlquist (eds), *Arbitrating for Peace* (Wolters Kluwer, 2016), 41–4.

Theodore Roosevelt prior to the Russo-Japanese War in 1905. However, after the Portsmouth Peace Conference putting an end to that war, the USA diplomatically left the formal invitation to Russia and the Netherlands. The groundwork was again prepared by F. F. Martens, at the request of the Russian Ministry of Foreign Affairs. Martens proposed (inter alia) improving the provisions for inter-state arbitration in the 1899 Hague Convention. After an audience with Tsar Nicholas II, Martens (with B. E. Nolde, a former student, as his secretary)[19] visited Berlin (twice), Paris, London, Rome, Vienna, and The Hague for preparatory consultations. In a mark of the respect accorded to him personally, Martens was received by the German Emperor Wilhelm II, the French President (Armand Falkier), King Edward VII and the British Prime Minister and Foreign Secretary (Sir Henry Campbell-Bannerman and Sir Edward Grey), the Queen of the Netherlands, King Victor Emmanuel III (with the Italian Prime Minister), Emperor Franz Josef (with the Austro-Hungarian Minister of Foreign Affairs); and then again by the German Emperor on his return to Russia for a further audience with Nicholas II. For an international jurist and arbitrator (particularly a commoner from a modest background with no aristocratic status in Russia), these consultations were unprecedented.

The second Peace Conference was opened at The Hague on 15 June 1907, attended by 44 states and 232 delegates. It now included several Latin American states. The Conference's work was concluded on 18 October 1907. Its achievements were limited by new rivalries between Britain, France, and Russia on the one side and, on the other, Germany and Austria-Hungary. The Conference led to the replacement of the 1899 Convention with the 1907 Convention for the Pacific Settlement of International Disputes (the 1907 Hague Convention). The issue of obligatory arbitration was again raised by the delegations from the USA and Portugal supported by Martens (Russia) and Léon Bourgeois (France). It was again strongly opposed by Germany. There was to be no permanent international court and no obligatory arbitration.

The Conference nonetheless confirmed the role of inter-state arbitration under Art. 37 of the 1907 Convention, as first recorded in Art. 15 of the 1899 Convention: 'International arbitration has for its object the settlement of disputes between states by judges of their own choice and on the basis of respect for law.' Art. 38 of the 1907 Convention, restating Art. 16 of the 1899 Convention, provided:

> In questions of a legal nature, and especially in the interpretation or application of international Conventions, arbitration is recognised by the Signatory Powers as the

[19] Baron B. E. Nolde (1876–1948) was a jurist, diplomat and Baltic German (born in what is now Latvia). He became in 1914 the legal adviser to the Russian Ministry of Foreign Affairs and was appointed to membership of the PCA by Russia in 1914. In 1921, after the October 1917 Revolution, Nolde and his immediate family escaped from Soviet Russia to settle as permanent exiles in Paris. In 1930, Nolde was a co-arbitrator in the second *Harriman Arbitration* in Paris under the US company's concession agreement agreed with the USSR in 1925: see †V. V. Veeder, 'Looking for Professor B. E. Nolde', in A. I. Muranov et al. (eds), *In Memoriam: V. A. Kabatov and S. N. Lebedev* (Moscow, 2017), 401, revised (in English) in *Jus Gentium* 3(1) (2018), 255.

most effective, and at the same time the most equitable means of settling disputes which diplomacy has failed to settle.

The Conference also maintained, in theory but certainly not in practice, the principle of obligatory inter-state arbitration on the unilateral demand of one state for questions 'which may arise eventually' (i.e. future disputes), subject to the disputing parties' agreement (Art. 39 and 40 of the 1907 Convention). As the German representative commented: 'It is difficult to say less in more words.'[20] The delegates agreed to hold a third Hague Peace Conference in 1915. By the end of this second Conference, Martens was exhausted and seriously ill. As he noted in his diary: 'The Second Peace Conference has ended, and in all likelihood I will not be at the Third.'[21] Martens died in 1909. With the outbreak of the World War in August 1914, there was to be no third Hague Conference in 1915.

The PCA was first housed at Prinsengracht 71, The Hague from 1901 to 1913 and thereafter to the present day at the Peace Palace. Its existence for more than a century marks the development of modern inter-state arbitration.[22] Its work began almost immediately. The first arbitrations under the 1899 Convention were the *Pious Fund Arbitration* (1902) and the *Venezuela Preferential Arbitration* (1904).[23] The first commission of inquiry addressed the dispute between Great Britain and Russia over the *Doggerbank Incident* (1904).[24] The selection of arbitrators was not limited to the individual members of the PCA, as shown by the composition of the tribunal in *Russian Claim for Indemnities*.[25] Between 1899 and 1914, under the 1899 and 1907 Hague Conventions, there were eight references to arbitration before the PCA, together with two commissions of inquiry. There was also a change in the practice of several states agreeing bilateral treaties providing for obligatory arbitration in conformity with the Russian proposal at the first Hague Conference. For example, Art. 1 of the 1911 Franco-Danish treaty provided that future differences of a juridical character shall be submitted to

[20] Baron Marschall von Bieberstein, cited in Lauterpacht (n. 9), 193 (fn. 3).

[21] Pustogarov (n. 7), 327.

[22] See the summaries of arbitration awards under the 1899 and 1907 Hague Conventions in P Hamilton et al. (eds), *The Permanent Court of Arbitration: International Arbitration and Dispute Resolution—Summaries of Awards, Settlement Agreements and Reports* (Kluwer Law International, 1999). See also International Bureau of the Permanent Court of Arbitration, *Analyses des sentences* (PCA, 1934).

[23] *The Pious Fund Arbitration* (USA v Mexico), Award, 14 October 1902 (H. Matzen, E. Fry, F. de Martens, T. M. C. Asser, A. P. de S. Lohman), UNRIAA, 14 October 1902, Vol. IX; *Venezuela Preferential Arbitration* (Germany, Great Britain, Italy v Venezuela), Award, 22 February 1904 (N. V. Mouraviev, H. Lammasch, F. de Martens), UNRIAA, 22 February 1904, Vol IX, 107–10; Hamilton (n. 22), 31–5.

[24] The Doggerbank Incident (1904) brought Britain and Russia to the brink of war when the Russian fleet, on its voyage from the Baltic to the Sea of Japan during the Russo-Japanese War (1904–5) mistook British unarmed fishing-boats for Japanese warships in the North Sea. It was the first Inquiry under the 1899 Hague Convention: see The Dogger Bank Report, 26 February 1905 (Spaun, Fournier, Dombassoff, L. Beaumont, Ch. H. Davise); Hamilton (n. 22), 297.

[25] *Russian Claim for Indemnities* (Russia v Turkey), Award, 11 November 1912 (Ch. E. Lardy, M. de Taube, A. Mandelstam, A. Arbro Bey, A. Réchid Bey); Hamilton (n. 22), 81–7. André Mandelstam was not a member of the PCA.

arbitration provided that 'they do not affect the vital interests, independence or honour of either of the contracting parties nor the interests of third Powers'; and Art. 2 of the treaty excluded from this proviso disputes over pecuniary claims, contractual debts due to nationals of the other party, the interpretation and application of commercial and navigation treaties, and all conventions relating to industrial (intellectual) property, copyrights, posts and telegraphs, etc.

After the 1914–18 World War, there was still no third Hague Conference. There were, however, indirect results from the Hague Conferences: the creation of the Permanent Court of International Justice (1925) and, after the Second World War, the International Court of Justice (1946), with their jurisdictions capable of agreement prior to a dispute under Art. 36 and 36(2) respectively. Although such legal proceedings before the PCIJ and ICJ were not arbitrations, as observed by Professor P. J. Baker in regard to the PCIJ, it was on the doctrine embodied in the Russian proposal at the Hague Conferences 'that all subsequent development, both of theory and practice, was based'.[26] In 1928, the League of Nations sought to establish a universal treaty for inter-state arbitration, the 'Geneva General Act', but it came to nothing, despite attempts by the UN General Assembly to revive it in 1947-1949.[27]

These developments included the continued rejection by states of appellate appeals from the merits of an award, the eventual agreement of many states to different forms of obligatory arbitration, and the participation of non-state actors in arbitrations against states. As to the first, the finality of arbitration awards was an important issue at the first and second Hague Conferences. As already noted, the USA's delegate at the first Hague Conference (Holls) proposed a right of appeal from an adverse award, exercisable within three months, for a substantial error of fact or law (Art. 7 of the USA proposal). The committee rejected this proposal. The Dutch delegate (Asser) proposed a limited form of revision for an award. In a modified form (if agreed by the disputing parties), the committee adopted the latter proposal for revision by a bare majority.

Martens strongly opposed both proposals, particularly the USA's proposal. His address merits citing at length because it remains relevant today:[28]

> ... in what does the importance of this question consist? Is it true that a rehearing of a judicial award based upon error or upon considerations not sufficiently founded is not desirable? Ought we not, on the contrary, to wish to have an error corrected by new documents or new facts which may be discovered after the close of the arbitration? No, gentlemen, it would be most unsatisfactory and unfortunate to have an arbitral award, duly pronounced by an international tribunal, subject to reversal by a new judgment. It would be profoundly regrettable if the arbitral award did not terminate, finally and forever, the dispute between the litigating nations, but should provoke new discussions, inflame the passions anew, and menace once more the peace of the world. A rehearing of the arbitral award, as provided for in Article 55,

[26] P. J. Baker, 'The Obligatory Jurisdiction of the Permanent Court of International Justice', 6 BYIL 68 (1925), 84.

[27] See von Mangoldt (n. 9), 247–50.

[28] Eyffinger (n. 9), 'To the Rescue of Arbitration'.

> must necessarily have a disastrous effect. There should not be left the slightest doubt on this point. The litigating Power against which the arbitral award has been pronounced will not execute it, certainly not during the three months, and it will make every effort imaginable to find new facts or documents. The litigation will not have been ended, but it will be left in suspense for three months with the serious aggravation that the Government and the nation which have been found guilty will be drawn still more into recrimination and dangerous reciprocal accusation. That is the explanation of the significant fact that in the committee of examination Article 54 [*sic*] was adopted by only five votes to four. The end of arbitration is to terminate the controversy absolutely. The great utility of arbitration is in the fact that from the moment when the arbitral judgment is duly pronounced everything is finished, and nothing but bad faith can attack it. Never can an objection be raised against the execution of an arbitral award. Now, if we accept the principle of a hearing, what will be the role of the arbitrators before and after the award? At the present time they are able to end forever an international dispute, and experience has shown that as soon as the award has been rendered, newspapers, legislative chambers, public opinion, all bow in silence to the decision of the arbitrators. If, on the contrary, it is known that the award is suspended for three months, the state against which judgment has been given will do its utmost to find a new document or fact. In the meantime the judgment will be delivered over to the wrangling of public opinion. It will not settle or put an end to the matter. On the contrary, it will raise a storm in the press and parliament. Everything will be attacked—the arbitrators, the hostile Government, and above all the home Government. They will be accused of having held back documents and concealed new facts. For three months the discussion upon the judgment will be open. Never can a judgment given under such conditions have a moral binding force which is the very essence of arbitration…

The USA's proposal for an appeal on the merits was also rejected by the third commission. As a result, the 1899 Hague Convention precluded any appeal from an award.[29] Conversely, the commission accepted the committee's draft on revision, resulting in Art. 55 of the 1899 Hague Convention.[30] The second Hague Conference likewise rejected any appeal from an award.[31] However, it introduced the possibility of referring back to the arbitration tribunal any dispute as to the award's interpretation or execution, as well as re-stating the earlier provision on revision.[32] There is a significant practical difference between an appeal on legal and factual merits from an award

[29] Art. 54 of the 1899 Hague Convention provided: 'The award, duly pronounced and notified to the agents of the parties at variance, puts an end to the dispute definitively and without appeal.' (Art. 81 of the 1907 Hague Convention provided: 'The award, duly pronounced and notified to the agents of the parties, settles the dispute definitively and without appeal.')

[30] Art. 55 of the 1899 Hague Convention provided: 'The parties can reserve in the compromise the right to demand the revision of the award…It can only be made on the ground of the discovery of some new fact calculated to exercise a decisive influence on the award, and which, at the time the discussion was closed, was unknown to the Tribunal and the party demanding the revision…'

[31] Art. 81 of the 1907 Hague Convention restated, in different wording, Art. 54 of the 1899 Hague Convention (see n. 29).

[32] Arts. 82 and 83 of the 1907 Hague Convention.

and other attacks on the finality of an award, whether in the form of interpretation, revision, remission, or even annulment for want of jurisdiction or other significant defect in the arbitral procedure.

The Hague Conferences accepted this difference, as did the International Court of Justice. The court has no general or inherent jurisdiction to adjudicate upon the validity of an arbitral award between states, still less between a state and a non-state party. As regards states, when the PCIJ was being established, a proposal was made to empower it as a court of review for claims of nullity of awards between states on the basis that the PCIJ was to be considered as a higher authority and the guarantor of impartial decisions.[33] In 1929, the Assembly of the League of Nations adopted a resolution inviting the Council to consider the procedure whereby states could refer to the PCIJ a complaint that an international arbitral tribunal had exceeded its jurisdiction.[34] In 1958, a limited jurisdiction to review awards (but not by way of appeal on the merits) was considered in the ILC's Model Rules on Arbitral Procedure.[35] Art. 35 of these Model Rules provided: 'The validity of an award may be challenged by either party on one or more of the following grounds: (a) That the tribunal has exceeded its powers; (b) That there was corruption on the part of a member of the tribunal; (c) That there has been a failure to state the reasons for the award or a serious departure from a fundamental rule of procedure; (d) That the undertaking to arbitrate or the compromis is a nullity.' Seven years later, its terms influenced the drafting of Art. 52 of the ICSID Convention 1965 on the grounds for annulment of an ICSID award under the ICSID Convention.

Art. 36(1) of the ILC's Model Rules also provided: 'If, within three months of the date on which the validity of the award is contested, the parties have not agreed on another tribunal, the International Court of Justice shall be competent to declare the total or partial nullity of the award on the application of either party.' The rationale for this proposal was explained by the Special Rapporteur, Professor George Scale, in his Third Report: 'In our view, intervention by the International Court of Justice must be maintained in this case as the only acceptable solution, since the Court's prestige, as also the exceptional nature of the proceedings, is likely to prove reassuring.'[36]

The Special Rapporteur's Fourth Report proposed that the ICJ should act as a court of cassation: 'Among the precedents for this we may mention a resolution adopted by the Institute of International Law at its session in 1929 held at New York; more particularly, the discussions held in the Council and Assembly of the League of Nations under the chairmanship of Rundstein, the eminent Polish jurist, between 1928 and 1931; and lastly, Art. 67 of the rules of the International Court of Justice.'[37] That proposal also went nowhere, save as regards arbitration awards referred for annulment to the ICJ by the disputing parties' ad hoc consent, as in *Guinea-Bissau v Senegal* (1989) and *Honduras v*

[33] Karin Oellers-Frahm, 'Judicial and Arbitral Decisions, Validity and Nullity', *Max Planck Encyclopaedia of Public International Law*, §20.

[34] Lauterpacht (n. 9), 206 (fn. 2).

[35] ILC Report, A/3859, 83ff.

[36] A/CN.4/109 and Corr. 1, §76.

[37] A/CN.4/113, §26.

Nicaragua (1960).[38] Accordingly, the ICJ's jurisdiction over disputed arbitration awards must still be established ad hoc, by special agreement or submission, or, possibly, through declarations made under Art. 36 of the ICJ's Statute. In short, the disputing state parties must by some means or another consent to the ICJ's reviewing the award.[39] What remains significant is that there was no support in the ILC, PCIJ, ICJ, or ICSID for any appeal on the merits of an award, be it for errors of law or errors of fact.

As to the eventual agreement of many states to different forms of obligatory arbitration, between 1899 and 1999, 33 disputes were referred to the PCA and, from 1999 to 2016, a further 180 disputes. These included many obligatory arbitrations. Even where there exists a permanent international court as an alternative forum, several states have preferred inter-state arbitration under Annex VII of UNCLOS administered by the PCA, to inter-state litigation before ITLOS in Hamburg.[40] The PCA's membership has increased from 71 contracting states in 1970 to 122 contracting states in 2020.

As to disputes involving a state and a foreign national, as already indicated, Martens had proposed at the first Hague Conference obligatory arbitration for future disputes between states relating to 'pecuniary damages suffered by a state or its nationals as a consequence of international wrongs on the part of another state or its nationals'. At first, the PCA would not accept for arbitration a dispute between state and non-state. It did so gradually, beginning in 1935 with *Radio Corporation v China*.[41] In 1962, the PCA changed its arbitration rules, expressly permitting the reference of such disputes under the 1907 Hague Convention.[42] In 1970, the first PCA arbitration between a state and a foreign national took place between Sudan and the English construction company,

[38] *Guinea-Bissau v Senegal*, Award, 31 July 1989, Judgment, [1991] ICJ Reports 53; *Honduras v Nicaragua*, Award, 23 December 1960, Judgment, [1960] ICJ Reports 192. (Art. 64 of the 1965 ICSID Convention provides that any dispute between contracting states concerning the interpretation or application of the convention (but not the finality of an ICSID award) shall be referred to the ICJ unless the concerned states agree otherwise. To date, there has been no such reference.) See, generally, W. Michael Reisman, *Nullity and Revision* (Yale University Press, 1971).

[39] In the absence of any mechanism for the review of an award, the dispute over the award may compound that of the original dispute: see the unresolved controversy over the Final Award of 29 June 2017 in *Arbitration between Croatia and Slovenia* (where the PCA acted as the registry).

[40] E.g., as to obligatory arbitration, *The Barbados v Trinidad and Tobago Arbitration* (2004), *The Guyana v Surinam Arbitration* (2007), *The Bangladesh v India Arbitrations* (2009, 2014), *The Bangladesh v Myanmar Arbitration* (2014), *The Chagos Arbitration between the United Kingdom and Mauritius* (2015), *The Philippines v China Arbitration* (2016), *The Duzgit Integrity Arbitration (Malta v São Tomé and Príncipe)* (2016); *The Ukraine v Russia Arbitration* (2017), and, pending, *The Arctic Sunrise Arbitration (Netherlands v Russia),* and *The 'Enrica Lexie' Incident (Italy v India)*. As to obligatory conciliation, on 11 April 2016, pursuant to Art. 298 and Section 2 of Annex V of UNCLOS, Timor-Leste initiated compulsory conciliation proceedings against Australia (pending).

[41] *Radio Corporation of America v China*, Award, 13 April 1935 (J.A. van Hammel, A. Hubert, R. Farrer), under an arbitration clause in the parties' agreement. Hamilton, (n. 22), 145.

[42] The PCA's 1982 'Rules of Arbitration and Conciliation for Settlement of Investment Disputes between Two Parties of Which Only One is a State; see Wetter (n. 9), 53; Antonio Parra, *The History of ICSID* (Oxford University Press, 2012), 17.

Turiff, under a *compromis* applying to a dispute arising from their construction contract. It led eventually to an award in Turiff's favor.[43] In 1993, the PCA introduced its 'Optional Rules for Arbitrating Disputes Between Two Parties of Which Only One Is a State'.[44] By this date, many states had acceded to the 1965 ICSID Convention providing for the obligatory arbitration of investor-state disputes agreed by states.[45] Collectively, these were massive developments.

The 1965 ICSID Convention did not expressly address treaty-based disputes between investors and contracting states. Such a category of disputes was entirely missing from the Executive Directors' Report on the Convention.[46] The first bilateral investment treaty made between the Federal Republic of Germany and Pakistan in 1959 contained a provision for inter-state arbitration, but no provision for investor–state arbitration. Such an inter-state arbitration provision allowed the home state to espouse against the host state the investor's claim as its national, but the investor was not a party to that inter-state arbitration.

From about 1962 onwards, under bilateral investment treaties and later the ICSID Convention, the investor could initiate an arbitration under the treaty in its own name, thereby suspending diplomatic protection by the home state (as provided by Art. 26(1) of the ICSID Convention). The first investor–state dispute under a bilateral investment treaty was referred to ICSID arbitration in 1987: *AAPL v Sri Lanka*.[47] UNCTAD has since identified more than 1000 treaty-based disputes referred to investor–state arbitration,

[43] *Turiff Construction (Sudan) Limited v Sudan*, Award, 23 April 1970, decided under the law of Sudan; Erades, 17 *N.T.I.R.* 200 (1970); Hamilton (n. 22), 164. The eventual tribunal comprised L. Erades (President), R. J. Parker and K. Bentsi Enchill, respectively a judge from the Netherlands, a QC from England (later a judge in the Court of Appeal of England and Wales), and, as appointed by the President of the ICJ in default of appointment by Sudan, a Ghanaian jurist. The Parties' Counsel included many English specialists in international commercial arbitration, including R. A. MacCrindle QC and (as they became later) Sir Michael Kerr, Lord Mustill, and Lord Saville, with Messrs Redfern, Hunter, and (Geoffrey) Lewis. It was not the first PCA arbitration between a foreign national and a host state: see *Radio Corporation v China* (1935).

[44] The PCA has now several sets of Optional Rules: The most recent, the PCA Arbitration Rules 2012, is a consolidation of four sets of PCA procedural rules which separately remain extant: the Optional Rules for Arbitrating Disputes between Two States (1992); the Optional Rules for Arbitrating Disputes between Two Parties of Which Only One is a State (1993); the Optional Rules for Arbitration Between International Organizations and States (1996); and the Optional Rules for Arbitration Between International Organizations and Private Parties (1996) (see 'PCA Model Clauses and Submission Agreements', available on the PCA's website: <pca-cpa.org>).

[45] The ICSID Convention introduced investor–state arbitration by ICSID to replace an informal role performed by the World Bank in diplomatically resolving investment disputes between states involving one state's national: see Parra (n. 42), 21.

[46] Thus, para 23 of the Executive Directors' Report refers to domestic 'investment promotion legislation', '*compromis*', and an 'investment agreement' between the disputing parties providing for the submission to the Centre of future disputes arising out of that agreement. There is no reference to any bilateral or multilateral investment treaty.

[47] *Asian Agricultural Products Limited v Sri Lanka*; Award, 27 June 1990 (El-Kosheri, Asante and Goldman), ICSID Case No ARB/87/3, 4 ICSID Rep 250; see also Franke et al. (n. 18), 191. (The respondent host state did not contest the ICSID tribunal's jurisdiction.)

producing 444 final awards (up to 2019).[48] Inter-state arbitration reached its apogee with the Iran–US Claims Tribunal, established in 1981 under the Algiers Declaration of 19 January 1981. Its work began at the Peace Palace in the PCA's Japanese Room and Small Arbitration Room; and it remains incomplete after more than 35 years. The principal change, however, has come from the practice of states since 1965 in agreeing bilateral and multilateral investment treaties providing for obligatory investor–state arbitration, including the Energy Charter Treaty, NAFTA, CAFTA, and more than 3,000 bilateral investment treaties.

Such a form of arbitration does not fit easily into the traditional forms of inter-state arbitration or international commercial arbitration. In the *Loewen* award (2003), under NAFTA's Chapter 11, the NAFTA tribunal characterized the right of the investor under a treaty to refer its claim to arbitration against the host state in its own name as deriving from the right of its home state against the host state:

> There is no warrant for transferring rules derived from private law into a field of international law where claimants are permitted *for convenience* to enforce what are in origin the rights of Party states.[49]

Other arbitration tribunals have adopted different analyses. In *Mondev* (2002), the NAFTA tribunal rejected the USA's objection *ratione temporis*:

> Nor do Articles 1105 or 1110 of NAFTA effect a remedial resurrection of claims a Canadian investor might have had for breaches of customary international law occurring before NAFTA entered into force. It is true that both Articles 1105 and 1110 have analogues in customary international law. But there is still a significant difference, substantive and procedural, between a NAFTA claim and a diplomatic protection claim for conduct contrary to customary international law (a claim which Canada has never espoused).[50]

In *Corn Products*, the NAFTA tribunal decided:

> ...when a State claimed for a wrong done to its national it was in reality acting on behalf of that national, rather than asserting a right of its own. The pretence that it was asserting a claim of its own was necessary, because the State alone enjoyed access to international dispute settlement and claims machinery. However, there is no need to continue that fiction in a case in which the individual is vested

[48] UNCTAD, 'World Investment Report 2015: Reforming International Investment Regime', (2015), Ch. IV. UNCTAD, 'World Investment Report 2020' (forthcoming 2020).

[49] *Loewen Group and Loewen v USA*, ICSID Case No. ARB(AF)/98/3, Award, 26 June 2003 (Mason, Mustill, Mikva), para. 233 (emphasis added). State courts have taken different views, e.g. the Court of Appeal of England and Wales: 'The award on this point in Loewen is controversial' in *Occidental v Ecuador* 2005 EWCA (Civil) 116; [2006] QB 432, para 22, dismissing Occidental's appeal from the Commercial Court (Aikens J) (2005) EWHC 774 (Comm).

[50] *Mondev v USA* (N. Stephen, J. Crawford, S. Schwebel), Award, 11 October 2002, ICSID Case No. ARB(AF)/99/2, para. 74.

> with the right to bring claims of its own. In such a case there is no question of the investor claiming on behalf of the State. The State of nationality of the Claimant does not control the conduct of the case. No compensation which is recovered will be paid to the State. The individual may even advance a claim of which the State disapproves or base its case upon a proposition of law with which the State disagrees.[51]

Whichever of these views are correct, it is manifest that investor–state arbitration under a treaty is a form of both inter-state arbitration and international commercial arbitration that is subject to public international law.[52] By and large, that form has worked well for its users. Over the last 20 years, whether fish or fowl or neither of these, investor–state arbitration has been widely supported by many states. As Judge Schwebel has observed, 'What is clear is that investor/State arbitration has proved to be a significant and successful substitute for the gunboat diplomacy of the past. It represents one of the most progressive developments of international law in the whole history of international law.'[53]

In conclusion, the recent history of state–state and also, in part, of investor–state arbitration is the history of the PCA. As intended by the two Hague Conferences more than a century ago, arbitrations under treaties are still marked by the necessity for the parties' consent (including a state's limitation as to the categories of dispute referable to arbitration), a neutral appointing or administering authority, a settled procedure subject to party autonomy, the parties' involvement in the appointment of the tribunal, and the absence of any appeal from an award for an error of law or fact. For inter-state arbitration and (notwithstanding the ICSID and New York Conventions) investor–state arbitration also, the recognition of the award by the losing party is usually made voluntarily. It is the parties' arbitration, the award is the product of their consent, and, accordingly, the award has a moral binding force for the parties often absent from non-consensual mechanisms. So far, Martens would readily recognize today's practice of arbitration by states. It is also probable that he and his colleagues at both Hague Conferences would not be surprised by the current opposition to international mechanisms for the obligatory resolution of disputes. In 1999, Judge Shi Jiuyong (later President of the ICJ), wrote: 'Today, the International Court of Justice and the Permanent Court of Arbitration are complimentary institutions within the community of nations, each having its

[51] *Corn Products v Mexico* (C. Greenwood, A. Lowenfeld, J. Alfonso Serrano de la Vega), Decision on Responsibility, 15 January 2008, ICSID Case No. ARB(AF)/04/01, para. 173.

[52] In *Occidental v Ecuador*, the Court of Appeal acknowledged that 'under English private international law, an agreement to arbitrate may itself be subject to international law rather than the law of a municipal legal system' (paras. 33–4). See also Zachary Douglas, 'The Hybrid Foundations of Investment Treaty Arbitration', 74 BYIL 151 (2003); José Alvarez, 'Are Corporations 'Subjects' of International Law?', 9 Santa Clara Journal of International Law 1 (2011); Johnathan Bonnitcha, Lauge Poulsen, and Michael Waibel, *The Political Economy of the Investment Treaty Regime* (Oxford University Press, 2017), 65–6; Anthea Roberts, 'Triangular Treaties: The Extent and Limits of Investment Treaty Rights', 56 Harvard International Law Journal 353 (2015).

[53] Stephen Schwebel, 'Introduction', in Franke et al. (n. 18), 6.

own unique role to play in the global network of mechanism of third party dispute resolution.'[54] Almost twenty years later, for that role to continue as regards the legitimacy of obligatory arbitration, there is probably a need for a Third Hague Conference on Arbitration attended by states who resort to arbitration in its different forms (whether by themselves or by their nationals), guided by F. F. Martens' historical sense of practical realism.

[54] Hamilton (n. 22), xii.

PART II

ACTORS

CHAPTER 9

THE ETHOS OF ARBITRATION

THOMAS SCHULTZ

IMAGINE two groups of people. The first group is composed of a colourful patchwork of individuals: some young, some old; some wild, some tame; some from the left, some from the right; some chagrined spirits, some solar souls; some cultivating friendship and warmth, some pursuing individuality and jealousy; some free, some revering Calvin, some fearing djinns; some machos and some tiptoeing angels; some male, some female, and some unclear; some enjoying this very text, some already hating it for its indecorousness in the legal academy. The second group is composed almost exclusively of white men aged 50 to 70, properly and somewhat strictly educated in European or North American universities, more possessive than generous, overworked and quite unhappy, rather disillusioned, all dark-suits-and-sober-ties, intellectually somewhat insecure, socially somewhat haughty.

Importantly the individuals in both groups have the same average legal proficiency.

Now imagine you are an individual. You have a dispute with another person. It bothers you greatly; it is the first thing that comes to mind when you wake up every day; it matters to you. One of the two groups—as a *group*—will decide on the outcome of your dispute. Which one do you choose? (Do pause to think.)

Switch hats. Now you are a society, a community. You know that within yourself there will inevitably be many people fighting over more or less anything. There will be disagreements; there will be disputes. These disputes, and how they are resolved, will very much structure what you are, as a society. Again the two groups from above present themselves to offer their services in taking care of these disputes. Which one do you choose?

Switch hats one last time. You have become a big, grey, soulless company. Churning out profits, grinding lives within. A rival company uses an idea close to yours and makes with it even more profit than you do. You see an opportunity to move in for the kill, invoking a patent infringement. Which group of decision-makers is for you?

All right. If you are a normal human being, you probably have a preference between the two groups for each of your successive hat-wearing roles.

If, instead, you are a properly trained lawyer from a proper, upright law school, if you have performed well so far in what remains the dominant way of teaching law and thinking about law, then you should in fact not have a preference at all between the two groups. Remember: the members of the two groups have the same average level of legal proficiency. And as a 'good lawyer', you probably have been led to believe that the same level of interpretive proficiency and legal knowledge will lead them, will lead anyone, to the correct legal solutions with the same likelihood.

If, now, you are a social psychologist, it may well be that you would in fact choose the first group, for all three situations. You might do so regardless what your own values are, what your traditions and political orientations might be, even if you only care about yourself and care nothing about minorities and diversity and equality and representativeness for the sake of representativeness. You might choose the first group because it is likely, as a group, to make better, smarter, more innovative, more adaptive decisions. Diversity makes the group better 'cognitively' as it were.

If you are mostly anyone except the properly trained lawyer from above, you would also understand that choosing between these two groups amounts to choosing between two different universes of justice, two different axiological fields, two different worlds of references. Two groups governed by two different ethea. Two groups governing *through* two different ethea.

This chapter seeks to explain what just happened. And considers how it may play out in arbitration.[1]

The discussion starts with the distinction of two well-known schools of thought regarding how legal decision-makers make decisions, how judges and arbitrators decide cases. The point is simply to anchor the discussion in a recognizable and hopefully helpful theoretical framework. I will be speaking, very briefly, of legal formalism and legal realism, of justification and decision-making, of rules and ethea. The rest of the discussion will then endeavour to itemize credible factors of arbitration decision-making, things that likely determine the decisions arbitrators make. I will group these factors in two categories, corresponding brutally to two approaches in law & economics, of which I will make an entirely rough rendering: rational choice theory and behavioural economics. That distinction, to be clear, is strictly not important for the contents of the discussion: it is just there to put it all into some sort of order, some sort of logical organisation.

[1] This chapter builds on earlier work, some with colleagues, some without: Thomas Schultz and Robert Kovacs, 'The Law Is What the Arbitrator Had for Breakfast: On the Determinants of Arbitrator Behavior', in J. C. Betancourt (ed.), *Defining Issues in International Arbitration: Celebrating 100 Years of the Chartered Institute of Arbitrators* (Oxford University Press, 2016) 238; Thomas Schultz, 'Arbitral Decision-Making: Legal Realism and Law & Economics', (2015) 6 Journal of International Dispute Settlement 231; 'The Three Pursuits of Dispute Settlement', (2014) 1 Czech & Central European Yearbook of Arbitration 227; Thomas Schultz and Robert Kovacs, 'The Rise of a Third Generation of Arbitrators? Fifteen Years after Dezalay and Garth', (2012) 28 Arbitration International 161.

In the end, the argument this chapter makes is a simple one: the ethos of arbitration plays a role in the decisions that arbitration produces, and this ethos is not necessarily one that is suited for all the different types of parties and disputes that arbitration has come to cover. It also may not be one that our political societies will necessarily condone now that they are becoming aware of it. And it probably is even damaging for the arbitration industry in the longer run.

9.1 Legal Formalism v. Legal Realism

The distinction between legal formalism and legal realism is not quite new in legal scholarship. But notice how, in just a few pages, it will make the argument to come rather obvious.

The core idea of legal formalism is simple: judges apply law to facts. This sounds good, straightforward, axiomatic even. But behind this simple statement is the idea that judges apply the law to the facts of the case and, if this is done competently, thus reach the correct answer. *The correct* answer. Generations of law students have been tortured with this idea that their job is to find the correct answer in a wide range of situations. But, indoctrination aside, when we think of it, the idea really is not entirely agreeable that there is one correct answer to a legal question, and that we need to search for it, as we search for something in nature with a magnifying glass; that it is already out there, and that we don't make it.[2] That this happens sometimes, yes, quite possibly, but that this is representative of how things work generally?

(Nothing new here, I know. I am just setting the scene. Bear with me.)

From this a further point follows: the point that legal decisions are correctly inferred from rules and facts through logical deduction, that logics is entirely enough to come to correct legal solutions, that law is all about logical, mechanical deductions of answers from general rules applied to concrete facts. In this understanding, adjudicative decision-making is a rule-based activity with external factors having no bearing on the outcome of cases, having nothing to do in adjudicative decision-making.[3] Judges apply the law deductively and get to the right answer. It's all about matter-of-factly deducing answers from rules applied to facts.[4]

[2] Daniel Bodansky, 'Legal Realism and Its Discontents', (2015) 28 Leiden Journal of International Law 267, 271: 'Policy considerations, morality, ideology, the personal sympathies and assumptions of the judge—none of these factors matter in [adjudicate decision-making], since judges do not make the law, they simply find it.'

[3] Richard Posner, *How Judges Think* (Harvard University Press, 2008), 41; Matthew C. Stephenson, 'Legal Realism for Economists', (2009) 23 Journal of Economic Perspectives 191, 193; Daniel Bodansky, 'Legal Realism and Its Discontents', (2015) 28 Leiden Journal of International Law 267, 271.

[4] Richard Posner, 'The Jurisprudence of Skepticism', (1988) 86 Michigan Law Review 827, 865; William M. Wiecek, *The Lost World of Classical Legal Thought* (Oxford University Press, 2001), 7: judges have 'no more discretion to invent a legal rule on instrumentalist grounds or policy preferences than a chemist ha[s] to dictate the outcome of an experiment'.

This is the approach that Justice Brett Kavanaugh, appointed in 2018 to the US Supreme Court, raised as a shield when he was fighting off accusations of sexual misconduct, in his Opening Statement to the Senate Judiciary Committee:

> A good judge must be an umpire—a neutral and impartial arbiter who favors no litigant or policy. As Justice Kennedy explained…judges do not make decisions to reach a preferred result. Judges make decisions because 'the law and the Constitution, as we see them, compel the result.' Over the past 12 years, I have ruled sometimes for the prosecution and sometimes for criminal defendants, sometimes for workers and sometimes for businesses, sometimes for environmentalists and sometimes for coal miners. In each case, I have followed the law. I don't decide cases based on personal or policy preferences. I am not a pro-plaintiff or pro-defendant judge. I am not a pro-prosecution or pro-defense judge. I am a pro-law judge.[5]

In other words his argument was this: 'Come on, what's all the fuss about my behaviour, the law and the constitution compel the result anyway, so let me do my job and tell you what it is that they compel; my personality is irrelevant; what I do or don't do with defenceless women in my free time is beside the point, has nothing to do with what the law and constitution say.' Rarely, probably, has a star judge been so keen on portraying himself as a powerless, nearly robotic bureaucrat.

Another example: Justice Antonin Scalia, a US Supreme Court judge positively famous for his particularly conservative and nationalistic views, defended his approach to judging with the following statement: interpretation, he said, 'begins and ends with what the text says and fairly implies'.[6] I'm not really conservative, the idea goes, I just read the text better than others.

Regardless of the credibility one accords to such statements, one has to pause wait a minute, how about a judge's sense of justice? Surely judges try to do justice? Surely the function of judges is to render justice? Now do judges really only think about justice as being a good mechanic, a good logician?

If you start to think that way, you are quickly drawn to wondering whether judges really have no ideologies, no political preferences. Or rather that their ideologies and political preferences play out in real life—in how they vote, in the entertainments they pursue, in the people they socialize with, in the cars they drive, in the clothes they wear, in the drinks they drink—but not in the legal decisions they make. Really? Then you might ask, if it's all logical, can't a computer do it? Can't a computer do it better than a human being? You might also think, if you embrace this approach, that there really is no reason for law students to learn about legal philosophy, about values, about history, about symbols in justice. Shakespeare's great plays, for instance, with all their quests for quasi-universal truths about justice, can't possible tell us anything relevant to how

[5] Brett Kavanaugh, Opening Statement to the Senate Judiciary Committee, 4 September 2018.

[6] Antonin Scalia and Bryan A. Garner, *Reading Law: The Interpretation of Legal Texts* (Thomson West, 2012) 16. The full quote is: 'Textualism, in its purest form, begins and ends with what the text says and fairly implies.' Textualism was Scalia's favoured approach.

judges take or should take decisions. You might even think that the fate of women in the US will remain unaffected by Brett Kavanaugh's appointment.

You might even wonder, if you're both really eager and consequential in your thinking, why the curriculum of law studies doesn't involve a heavy dose of formal logics—if really it is all about mechanical, logical deduction.

The sort of discussion I've been conducting so far in this chapter is often disliked by lawyers.

The more candid ones explain that this is the only way they know how, that it is the only thing they were ever taught (at least in law school). In fact, if we don't think that way, we are told we are not good lawyers. Well, quite; it's true that most law schools deliver this sort of message. But what should be clear is that formalism is just one school of thought. Just one. There are other ways to think about how law works, how judges make decisions, what makes a good lawyer, what law is all about.

This implies that law teaching in most law schools, where it is focused on formalism only, makes these law schools akin to schools of divinity, as opposed to faculties of theology. (A faculty of theology—at least for the sake of the argument I'm trying to make here—is a place where you learn about religions, about religion itself, the idea of a religion, what the role of religion is. A school of divinity is a place where you are taught to think as the members of a given religion think, where you are taught a certain religion, a certain faith. You are not free to choose. You are not supposed to think by yourself. You are supposed to learn, remember, and reproduce. Hey (former) law student: these last three verbs sound familiar?) Put yet differently, imposing the view that formalism is the only way to do things with law is a form of anti-intellectualism.

But enough deconstruction. Let me turn to reconstructing something else. This something else is legal realism. Which, of course, is only another school of thought. It is not 'the truth' either. Just another school of thought, which allows us to think differently and therefore see different things.

So the first thing legal realists say is this: formalists have forgotten a key thing about human beings. This key thing is the distinction between decision-making and justification, between how we make decisions and how we justify our decisions.[7] The point is terribly simple. But here are two quick examples, just to make this more concrete. I might say I'm late in completing this chapter for the Handbook because I have too many ongoing academic projects, but in reality my private life took an interesting turn which I'm not supposed to talk about. Or I might say, as a judge, that I decided that the accused got fifteen years in jail because I just applied the law, but in reality the victim reminded me of my own sister, who died very young.

So legal realists said yes, of course, the way judges *justify* how they make decisions is correctly described by the formalists; they got it right on this point. Legal realists and formalists agree that judges justify their decisions by pointing to mechanical deductions

[7] Joseph W. Singer, 'Legal Realism Now', (1988) 76 California Law Review 465, 472. See also Brian Z. Tamanaha, 'Understanding Legal Realism', (2009) 87 Texas Law Review 731, 752; Frederick Schauer, 'Legal Realism Untamed', (2013) 91 Texas Law Review 749, 755–6.

of decisions from general rules applied to concrete facts. But decision-making, legal realists continue, is different. Realists want to be... realistic. They consider judges to be human beings.[8] And as human beings, there is no reason judges would not take the law into consideration when they make decisions, but equally there is no reason why they should not also be influenced by a whole variety of other factors. Such other factors could for instance be their own pursuit of justice, the fact that they want to appear in a positive light when they make a decision, that at least some of them hope for a promotion to a higher court somewhere, that they want to be able to come home and tell their husbands and girlfriends that they took the right decision, etc. And arbitrators, of course, are no different; they simply have different determinants, different constraints and incentives that influence their decision-making. They also make 'mistakes' in their decisions, as any human being from time to time does, and their 'mistakes' may be different from those of judges because other cognitive biases and heuristics colour their thinking.[9]

So what? Well, the point of this chapter will precisely be to show the what. But already now a simple observation might point the way. In his contribution to the Handbook, Moshe Hirsch writes that 'notwithstanding numerous arguments raised by various parties, and few tribunals' general statements regarding the superior status of peremptory human rights, no investment tribunal has discharged a party from its investment obligations or reduced the amount of compensation due to the injured party'.[10] If we take a realist's approach, we would have to acknowledge that the situation may be much better (or worse, depending on the axiological preference) than it looks: the only thing we do know is that no investment tribunal has yet been willing to justify its decision on these points by reference to peremptory human rights norms. Whether the changing ethos in investment arbitration, suggested by the first part of Hirsch's quote, has indeed had an influence on investment obligations and compensation is unknown and would be extremely difficult to ascertain with certainty—but it just appears rather likely. This would further suggest that human rights 'activists' likely are making an impact through their work; they likely are changing the way investment arbitrators make decisions. The counter-argument 'Well, then show me the change', demanding as proof that this change figure in the text of arbitral awards—it misses the point entirely. It misses the point out of what one might be tempted to call 'blinding formalism'.[11] That arbitrators are not yet willing to acknowledge any of this in how they justify their decisions is a different matter, determined by different factors.

[8] Jerome Franck, 'Are Judges Human? Part II', (1931) 80 University of Pennsylvania Law Review 233.

[9] This idea of arbitrators' cognitive biases and heuristics was first explored by Susan D. Franck, Anne van Aaken, James Freda, Chris Guthrie, and Jeffrey J. Rachlinski, 'Inside the Arbitrator's Mind', 66 Emory Law Journal 1115 (2017). See further, in this volume, the excellent discussion in Anne van Aaken and Tomer Broude, 'Arbitration from a Law and Economics Perspective' (Ch. 36) and Christopher Drahozal, 'Empirical Findings on International Arbitration: An Overview' (Ch. 27).

[10] Moshe Hirsch, 'The Sociological Dimension of International Arbitration: The Investment Arbitration Culture', Ch. 30 below.

[11] Jerome Franck, *Law and the Modern Mind* (Transaction, 2009 [originally published 1930]), 53, 165: legal formalism is blind 'legal fundamentalism', blinker-wearing 'rule-fetichism'.

Don't get me wrong, though: yes, there clearly is a relationship between justification and decision-making, in the sense that when judges or arbitrators decide something, they most likely already think of how they will have to justify their decision. And when they justify their decision, they presumably normally try to take into consideration as much as possible of what led them to the decision in the first place. But different likely determinants guide decision-making (which I'll discuss in the balance of this chapter) and justification (elements of socio-professional propriety come to mind, which plainly relate to questions of ethos too, but their difference from decision-making are arguably important enough to deserve a study of their own).

One important point to remember from this discussion is that it is really quite wrong to say that legal realists contend that law has no role to play.[12] Many people accuse realists of this, but this is clearly incorrect, a witless misunderstanding, or a facile straw man. Legal realists simply say that if you want to understand how judges make decisions, if you want to understand judicial decision-making, if you want to understand how law works in practice, if you want to understand the life of the law, you have to look beyond the codes and statutes and cases and all the law on the books. You have to look at people. And if we want to understand arbitral decision-making, we need to look beyond the black letter law rules of arbitration. We have to look at the people, at what credibly makes arbitrators decide the cases the way they do.

(If this sounds boringly obvious to you, do realize that what I'm saying here is still blasphemy in most legal circles.)

To close this discussion of formalism v. realism: as I said, formalists tend to argue that there is a (in principle one) correct answer to a legal question.[13] Realists, on the other hand, would rather contend that there is more than one correct decision. Because, what is a correct decision? It is one that can be justified, in law, and typically there's more than one decision that can be justified in law, with justification being nothing more than a social construct of acceptability. There's typically a range of correct legal decisions for a given legal question. The question that is of interest, then, is which one of the many possibilities within this range will the judge, or the arbitrator, most likely choose? And the answer to this question is what the balance of this chapter ponders. Therein lies its contribution.

9.2 Rational choices

As I said in the introduction to this chapter, I will sort the different likely factors that influence the decisions of arbitrators into two categories, which roughly correspond to

[12] Jakob V. H. Holtermann and Mikael Rask Madsen, 'European New Legal Realism and International Law: How to Make International Law Intelligible', (2015) 28 Leiden Journal of International Law 211: embracing legal realism does not imply discarding the epistemology of internal doctrinal approaches in order to inevitably turn to the empiricist methodologies of the social sciences, falling from one into the other as it were.

[13] I do of course recognize that I am setting up a straw man myself here, but I do not wish to start a discussion of determinacy within the formalist tradition. My point is clearly not to suggest that the formalists are wrong on that particular argument.

two approaches in law & economics: rational choice theory and behavioural economics. But I need to enter this caveat: the chapter does not seek to contribute to the theory of law & economics, to the conceptualization of the different types of factors that influence decision-making. My categories may be sloppy. My arguments may not be fully congruent with law & economics theory. The terminology I use might make economists sigh in irritation. But it doesn't matter. I'm not trying to build a coherent system of thought.[14] I'm merely trying to point to some factors of decision-making. Factors which I believe to be critical if we want to understand how arbitrators are likely to take decisions, now and in the future, now and in reaction to the different changes in the arbitration regimes that inevitably will come, in particular in investment arbitration. This will lead me in the end to an insistence on how important it is to understand the ethos of this field of practice.

Let me start with rational choice theory, with the incentives and constraints that arbitrators should respond to if they were perfectly rational beings.[15] A rational choice, in that sense, is one by which you get the best reward, by which you maximize your utility, your interests. Now, no one, of course, is perfectly rational. But few people are perfectly irrational either. Where exactly a given arbitrator in a given situation and an idealized average arbitrator in an idealized average situation are on this continuum of sorts between rationality and irrationality isn't a possible task for this chapter. My point here is simply to suggest what rational determinants of behaviour arbitrators are likely to respond to; sometimes this will check out in practice, sometimes it won't: my hope is merely that this perspective clarifies more than it muddles our understanding. I aim at nothing close to a computational, algorithmic representation of arbitrator decision-making, at no model offering great predictive accuracy in actual cases.[16]

Over the next pages, I will first briefly elaborate on what rational choice theory means in the current context. Then I will apply this theory to arbitrators' decisions on the merits, to procedural decisions, to 'extreme' arbitration decisions, and finally to decisions which in fact have little to do with the case at hand.

So, the general idea is very simple: it is to consider that every person tends to maximize her self-interest. This is, roughly, the idea of rationality in this context. In theory every person tends to do this, and this includes every decision-maker, and arbitrators too. This means that when arbitrators make decisions, they would have their own interests in mind. Or not actually consciously in mind, but in its translated form of a self-serving bias, in the sense of 'a simple psychological mechanism [leading to] conflate what is fair and what benefits oneself'. (In plain language: I only do what is fair,

[14] For a conceptually cleaner and more sophisticated discussion of the same overall articulation, see Myriam Gicquello, 'The Reform of Investor–State Dispute Settlement: Bringing the Findings of Social Psychology into the Debate', (2019) 10 Journal of International Dispute Settlement 561.

[15] A discussion of rationality can be found in Ch. 36 below.

[16] For a discussion of the methodological objectives of law & economics, see the discussion in Ch. 36.

but what I find fair is unconsciously shaped by what serves my interests.[17]) And why would they not?

To be clear, when I say that arbitrator pursue their own interests, that they maximize their own interests, by 'interests' I mean both what economists call 'self-regarding interests' (such as making yourself richer, even if just a bit), something that benefits only yourself or at least that directly benefits yourself, and also what economists call other-regarding interests: here, the idea is that if I like someone and make that someone better off, that makes me content, and thus better off, too. These are interests that benefit me indirectly, by directly benefiting someone else.[18]

Now, what does the idea that arbitrators pursue their own interests tell us about how they are likely to make decisions on the merits?

I will start with the least controversial bit. Arbitrators have a rational interest in applying the law applicable to the merits in a way that corresponds to the parties' expectations: this implies, for instance, to transnationalize the law applicable to the merits.[19] What this concretely means is that if, say, Turkish law is applicable to the merits of a case, arbitrators are likely to apply it differently than the Turkish courts would. The arbitrators would apply it in a way that better fits the transnational environment of arbitration. Turkish law is made less idiosyncratic, less locally particular, coloured by what would be done elsewhere.[20] (To be clear, my argument does not imply that Turkish law is more idiosyncratic than any other national law.) For instance, let us imagine the exists a particularly idiosyncratic provision on the passing of risk from the seller to the buyer in Turkish law; such a provision would like be interpreted in a manner that brings it closer to transnational norms and practices, possibly as reflected in the UNIDROIT principles.

[17] George Loewenstein, *Exotic Preferences: Behavioral Economics and Human Motivation* (Oxford University Press, 2007), 219.

[18] On self-regarding and other-regarding interests, I am stealing the citations from Aaken and Broude, Ch. 36 below, who discuss these conceptual points far more elegantly than I do: Ernst Fehr and Klaus Schmidt, 'The Economics of Fairness, Reciprocity and Altruism: Experimental Evidence and New Theories', in Serge Kolm and Jean Mercier Ythier (eds), *Handbook of the Economics of Giving, Altruism and Reciprocity* (Elsevier, 2006), vol. 1, s. 2; and Werner Güth, Rolf Schmittberger, and Bernd Schwarze, 'An Experimental Analysis of Ultimatum Bargaining', (1982) 3 Journal of Economic Behavior and Organization 367. Technically, in economic theory, this inclusion of both self-regarding and other-regarding interests is a departure from classic rational choice theory and embraces elements of more recent behavioural economics. But as I said, let's not go there, it doesn't make a difference to my argument.

[19] As arbitrators themselves put this: Gabrielle Kaufmann-Kohler, 'Arbitral Precedent: Dream, Necessity, or Excuse?', (2007) 23(3) Arbitration International 357, 364; 'Le contrat et son droit devant l'arbitre international', in François Bellanger et al. (eds), *Le contrat dans tous ses états* (Stämpfli, 2004), 361. I have discussed this at greater length than I can do here in Thomas Schultz, 'Some Critical Comments on the Juridicity of Lex Mercatoria', (2008) 10 Yearbook of Private International Law 667. See also the discussions of the implications of this practice in Alec Stone Sweet and Florian Grisel, *The Evolution of International Arbitration. Judicialization, Governance, Legitimacy* (Oxford University Press, 2017), 125, and Dolores Bentolila, *Arbitrators as Lawmakers* (Kluwer Law International, 2017), 164.

[20] This can be likened to the so-called 'globalist' mindset of judges, which expresses the degree to which they take foreign law into account when interpreting national law: see e.g. Elaine Mak, *Judicial Decision-Making in a Globalised World: A Comparative Analysis of the Changing Practices of Western Highest Courts* (Hart, 2013), 102–6.

Nothing contentious here. But do notice that we are not in the realm of mechanical inference of decisions from rules.

Let me turn to something more controversial, from which more pungent points follow for our understanding of arbitration as a socio-legal phenomenon and its overall ethos. As an arbitrator, your interests are not advanced much by making good decisions on the merits. By good decisions, I mean decisions whose justifications in law are reasonable, understandable, well-articulated, sophisticated where sophistication is required, thorough in their analysis, precise in their reasoning. Rationally, if you are an arbitrator, you shouldn't care much about decisions on the merits and shouldn't put much effort into them. If your time and energy are limited, rationally you should rather do something else.

Why is this?

First, there is almost no direct sanction for arbitrators making bad decisions on the merits: they are very unlikely to be set aside on this ground. Bad award on the merits? Too bad; nothing much happens, at least formally. From a black letter law perspective, the system of arbitration is built in such a way as to allow the production of arbitrary or nearly arbitrary decisions on the merits with no formal consequence. Why would anyone issue a nearly arbitrary decision? Because it takes less effort. Why would anyone favour what takes less effort over what takes more? Well, that is precisely the point of rationality. 'The system' says that you have done your job as an arbitrator if you render anything but the craziest decision on the merits, one that can actually be set aside on a point of merits.

Very little happens on the informal front too: there's little reputation sanction for poor merits decisions because most awards are confidential. Almost no one beyond the parties will know that an arbitrator messed up on the merits. As an arbitrator you are unlikely to lose future mandates, future appointments, because of bad decisions on the merits, because almost no one will know you did.

Yes, but eventually word of mouth will catch up with you, right? Surely people will know, progressively, that you are reckless on the merits and you will get a kick?

Well, it appears you won't.

A few years ago, I conducted a survey, with a PhD student, of the grounds on which counsel choose arbitrators.[21] 'Does it matter to you, and to your client, that the arbitrator you intend to appoint is a good and committed lawyer on points of substance?' we essentially asked. 'No,' in effect, was their answer. Legal proficiency for merits decisions was not, they said, a criterion for appointment. So even if you build a reputation for bad decisions on the merits, it would appear not to damage your attractiveness as an arbitrator.

In a way, this makes sense. One way to understand arbitration is to see it as a business thing for business people. And business people, one may assume, want to win more than anything else; they want an award in their favour, not (to go into extremes for the sake of the argument) a demonstration of scholarly erudition. If they lose, they are unlikely to be terribly interested in whether it was due to a reasonable, understandable, well-articulated,

[21] Schultz and Kovacs, 'Third Generation of Arbitrators' (n. 1).

sophisticated, thorough, and precise decision, or just because of tough luck. And if they win, why care if the decision made good legal sense? From that perspective, the criterion for selecting an arbitrator would simply be this: how likely will I win with this person? It wouldn't be: 'does this arbitrator draft good awards on the merits?' From that perspective, choosing an arbitrator is not about justice; it is about chances of winning.

Surely, then, things are different for investment arbitration? Because there, many if not most awards are published, and the legal quality of the reasoning is dissected *ad* nauseam by scholars and practitioners alike. So if it becomes widely known that an arbitrator's reasoning in investment awards is, say, manifestly contradictory, inconsistent, or practically nonexistent, then this person's appointments as arbitrator quickly dwindle, right?

Actually no, it appears they don't. In a paper published a few years ago, Federico Ortino identified a number of investment arbitral decisions based on 'egregious failures', produced by arbitral legal reasoning that precisely was 'manifestly contradictory, inconsistent or practically non-existent'.[22] And these arbitrators' appointment rates did... nothing special. Their attractiveness as arbitrator seemed unaffected. (A caveat must be entered: I didn't actually run statistical regressions on these arbitrators' appointments to exclude the significance for appointments of criticism on reasoning, so I have no reliable statistical proof for my argument. But from an insider's informal view, demand for these individuals has not been altered.)

Think for a moment about what's involved here. If there is little incentive to make efforts to produce good decisions on the merits, if the objective of crafting well-articulated, thorough, etc. awards on merits is not an important factor of arbitrator decision-making (technically it would be a meta-factor, but never mind), then one can expect overall lower-quality merits decisions from arbitrators than from judges. Whether this is indeed the case is extremely hard to assess reliably. Then again, if you compare the decisions of, say, the International Court of Justice and the Swiss Supreme Court and the French Cour de Cassation and the UK Supreme Court to the awards of some of the leading investment arbitrators, a noticeable difference does emerge. Few people have seriously argued that decisions of the ICJ and the other courts just mentioned are based on reasoning that is manifestly contradictory, inconsistent, or practically nonexistent. It would seem, then, that in the ethos of arbitration, great lawyering on points of substance is not particularly a virtue—and rationally so. To arbitration insiders, this is boringly commonplace. To outsiders, it may well be somewhat unsettling.

A further point follows: if it doesn't matter to make good decisions on the merits, why not let someone else do it for you? If you are an arbitrator, why not let, say, your first-year junior associate make the decision for you? Which in practice may, for instance, mean that the arbitrator decides who wins and perhaps how much, but then the reasoning justifying this conclusion, the crafting of the decision as it were, is left to someone else—just like any other task which is rationally not really important because it

[22] Federico Ortino, 'Legal Reasoning of International Investment Tribunals: A Typology of Egregious Failures', (2012) 3 Journal of International Dispute Settlement 31, 31.

has little impact if done wrong, is thus not really part of the core of one's job, and should be left to some deuteragonist, should be delegated. All this, I insist, would be rational behaviour.

Now does this actually happen? To be sure, an empirical study would be ideal. (Not of course the sweet sort, as do exist, which ask arbitrators if they themselves do it.) But in the meantime, if a particular practice has a particular name, it is probably fair to assume it is somewhat widespread. The name here is 'the fourth arbitrator'.[23] Some arbitrators do have a clear reputation for using 'fourth arbitrators'—for delegating the actual legal reasoning in part or in whole, if not the decision itself, to the secretary to the tribunal. Again, why not, after all, if rendering bad decisions on the merits doesn't really count in the game? And again, our survey of the grounds on which counsel choose arbitrators showed that a reputation for delegation does not decrease an arbitrator's allure for appointment.[24] So: taking and reasoning the decisions for which you have been appointed does not seem to be a virtue in the current arbitration ethos—quite rationally so. And again: a dull, if somewhat indecorous point to insiders, but one that may be arresting to outsiders.

The story is different for procedural decisions. Arbitrators have much greater rational interest in their decisions on points of procedure.

This is so, first, because of how the system is built. The award may be set aside if it results from defective procedural decisions—the grounds for annulment are normally procedural. As an arbitrator, if you mess up the conduct of a procedure, you may well be formally considered not to have done your job properly, which is the meaning of having your decision annulled. So there are greater direct sanctions for decisions on procedure, which increase their rational importance, their value for arbitrators.

There are also more powerful reputation sanctions at play here: procedural mistakes are more easily discernible by the community, 'derailed' arbitrations easier to identify. When something is wrong procedurally, it is more obvious than when something is off on the merits. Messed-up procedures lead to all sorts of moves by the aggrieved party. A bad decision on the merits provokes little reaction.

It would follow that, if procedural decisions are valuable to arbitrators, this creates an incentive to produce good decisions, and thus overall one can expect fairly high-quality procedures in arbitration. Based on experience, this would seem to be true. A proper study would require reliable markers of procedural quality with sound comparators for other dispute settlement mechanisms—this seems barely feasible.

[23] Simon Maynard, 'Laying the Fourth Arbitrator to Rest: Re-valuating the Regulation of Arbitral Secretaries', (2018) 34 Arbitration International 173; Andrew Williams, 'Tribunal Secretaries: The LCIA Seek to Rein in the "Fourth Arbitrator"', November 2017, www.hfw.com/Tribunal-Secretaries-the-LCIA-seek-to-rein-in-the-Fourth-Arbitrator-November-2017; Lawrence W. Newman and David Zaslowsk, 'The Yukos Case: More on the Fourth Arbitrator', *New York Law Journal*, 28 May 2015; Constantine Partasides, 'The Fourth Arbitrator? The Role of Secretaries to Tribunals in International Arbitration', (2002) 18 Arbitration International 147.

[24] Schultz and Kovacs, 'Third Generation of Arbitrators' (n. 1).

It would also follow that arbitrators would have much less reason to delegate the procedural handling of a case to someone (unless the someone is more competent than they themselves are, but that is a different scenario altogether).

Now notice the irony of what this implies—the sort of irony that only real life can imagine: when you choose an arbitrator, you can expect to get a real 'day in court' with her, to have a good procedure during which you can really make your case and everything is handled well. But this does not necessarily have much of an impact on the substantive outcome.

But let me change tack and look at the goodness of good procedural decisions from a different angle. Arbitrators can make, and have a rational interest in making, procedural decisions which aren't only good for the parties, but good for themselves too (or good for themselves instead).

The point is again terribly simple. The size of the overall arbitration pie is in part defined by procedural decisions that arbitrators themselves make. Some procedural decisions create jobs for arbitration. If an arbitrator asserts jurisdiction over a given dispute, or considers a given claim admissible, he creates a job for himself. If she does that for an entire array of disputes, by contributing to the shape of certain legal doctrines (questions of non-signatories, arbitrability, or thresholds of validity for arbitration agreements come to mind), she creates an entire array of jobs. This aspect of arbitration is in fact at the very heart of what allowed it to become such an industry.

Let's pause for a moment to consider the power, and the temptation, that are involved. Imagine someone offers you a job. You really want the job, for some reason or other, otherwise you wouldn't be in the trade to begin with. You can always take the job, because even if you have too many of them you can delegate much. The only thing required for you to actually get it is a legal condition which needs to be fulfilled. And you are the one who decides whether the condition is fulfilled or not. If you find that, no, the condition is not fulfilled, the job is gone. If you find that, yes, the condition is fulfilled but later a court says you shouldn't have found that, then . . . nothing, really, happens to you. True, your award may get annulled, but essentially you get to keep your fees.

And so, over time, the obstacles to the occurrence of individual arbitrations have progressively decreased, the arbitration industry has grown, the ethos in the community has consolidated. A great number of arbitrations have taken place which wouldn't have but for these mechanisms. This may be for better or worse, but certainly it is for the better as far as concerns arbitrators and the arbitration community at large. If it weren't for this, the whole field would have been smaller, less significant legally, economically, socially; I wouldn't be here writing this; you wouldn't be there reading it; there wouldn't even have been an Oxford Handbook of International Arbitration.

Oscar Wilde points the way to the next observation about arbitrators' rational interest in their own decisions: 'The only thing worse than being talked about is not being talked about.' It is worse not to have a reputation than to have a bad reputation. It is worse not to be known than to be known for making bad decisions.

For what are 'bad' decisions really? For instance, biased decisions on the merits, systematically favouring one type of party, are in fact entirely valuable in stimulating party appointments of wing arbitrators. After all, it is widely believed (rightly or wrongly[25]) that the choice of partisan wing arbitrators by each party is their best option. (Of course, this works only for those types of arbitrations, such as investment arbitration, in which there are discernibly different types of parties; this is not the case for many commercial arbitrations between corporations.) More surprisingly perhaps, even a reputation for making nominally 'bad' procedural decisions may help attract appointments: a tendency to make procedural decision which derail arbitrations may be precisely what certain parties want, in principle respondents. Think of it this way: if a decision needs to be taken on something, on some point of office politics for instance, but you don't want the decision to be taken at all, what better than to entrust the decision to a committee you know will be paralysed by in-fights? I'm not making this up. If you'll allow an anecdote: a few years ago, someone asked me what I thought of a given person as a possible arbitrator on a three-member panel. I winced. And politely explained, my face probably marked by furrows of worry, that the risk of endless complications would be real. My interlocutor gracefully smiled. And said nothing. I suppose partly because it confirmed my interlocutor's hopes and partly because of how naïve I had been in not understanding the strategy. Two years later, the arbitration was making as much progress as a sports car in the sand. (Sadly enough, the arbitrator in question was socially beaming with pride at having been chosen for such an important case.)

Finally, a quick point needs to be made about arbitrators' incentive to source non-arbitrator work. The point, simple as it is, helps understand both the rational determinants of arbitrator decision-making and the overall arbitration ethos. For many arbitrators, interesting as arbitrator work might be, it shouldn't come at the expense of better-paying counsel work, for the arbitrator herself or for her law firm. So long as arbitrators also have revenues, directly or indirectly, from non-arbitrator work for a certain community of clients, the interests of these clients are likely to rationally incentivize or constrain their decision-making. Here's a simple example: if you, an arbitrator, are part of a law firm which advises pharmaceutical companies, for instance, then it would be unwelcome for you to support arbitration decisions against the general interests of the pharmaceutical industry. We all effectively represent the interests that are at stake for us when we participate in collective decisions. For law firms, the most interesting clients are not normally consumers, developing states, NGOs, human rights groups, etc. The most interesting clients are normally corporations; the bigger the better. This issue, generally called the problem of 'double-hatting' of individuals as arbitrators and as counsel, is well known.[26] It simply bore repeating here, in order to offer a more complete picture of the arbitration ethos, which is based in part on the rational choices offered to arbitrators.

[25] Todd Tucker, 'Inside the Black Box: Collegial Patterns on Investment Tribunals', (2016) 7 Journal of International Dispute Settlement 183, suggesting that overly partisan arbitrators may in fact lose persuasive power and thus end up isolated on arbitral tribunals, in the minority.

[26] See e.g. Malcolm Langford, Daniel Behn, and Runar Hilleren Lie, 'The Revolving Door in International Investment Arbitration', (2017) 20 Journal of International Economic Law 301.

9.3 Behavioural economics

As fits my profession (I'm an academic), my perspective is more categorical, more critical, more eerie too, and above all more irritating and unseemly than the representation people typically have of arbitration. But as fits my profession, I'm offering it anyway. I can already hear the reaction: 'It isn't as bad as his discussion suggests. Arbitrators aren't single-mindedly focused on their own interests! Pfftt, academics...'

Quite. But wait.

The reality is indeed not exactly like what I've described above.

One reason is that our actual rationality, so to speak, is imperfect. We, arbitrators or not, don't always make decisions which are good for ourselves, or at least not as good as they ideally, theoretically could be. We are not always rational and rarely entirely rational. We don't always maximize our self-interest, our utility. We are usually rational within limits. Economists might say that our rationality is bounded by information limitation (we don't know everything and make uninformed decisions), by cognitive limitation (we don't understand everything), and by time limitations (we can't wait, essentially).[27] Psychologists, sometimes on a different tack from economists, might suggest that we also make decisions based in part on emotional and identity-based factors, guided as we often are by what we feel in the moment and by how we perceive ourselves, by how we construct our own identity.[28] (Whether emotionally best decisions are, after all, part of our self-interest, and their pursuit thus rational, is a discussion we don't need to have because it makes no difference to the points I'm trying to make.) All these are, in essence, the factors that behavioural economics focus on.[29]

[27] Herbert Simon, *Models of Man, Social and Rational: Mathematical Essays on Rational Human Behavior in a Social Setting* (Wiley, 1957), 198: 'The alternative approach employed in these papers is based on what I shall call the principle of bounded rationality: The capacity of the human mind for formulating and solving complex problems is very small compared with the size of the problems whose solution is required for objectively rational behavior in the real world—or even for a reasonable approximation to such objective rationality.' Herbert Simon, 'Rational Decision Making in Business Organizations', (1979) 69 American Economic Review 493, 502: 'bounded rationality is largely characterized as a residual category—rationality is bounded when it falls short of omniscience. And the failures of omniscience are largely failures of knowing all the alternatives, uncertainty about relevant exogenous events, and inability to calculate consequences.'

[28] See e.g. Roberta Muramatsu and Yaniv Hanoch, 'Emotions as a Mechanism for Boundedly Rational Agents: The Fast and Frugal Way', (2005) 16 Journal of Economic Psychology 201; Gerd Gigerenzer and Peter M. Todd, *Simple Heuristics That Make Us Smart* (Oxford University Press, 2000); Carlos Andres Trujillo, 'The Complementary Role of Affect-Based and Cognitive Heuristics to Make Decisions Under Conditions of Ambivalence and Complexity', (2018) 13(11) PloS ONE.

[29] See e.g. Christine Jolls, Cass Sunstein, and Richard Thaler, 'A Behavioral Approach to Law and Economics', (1998) 50 Stanford Law Review 1471, and van Aaken and Broude, Ch. 36 below. Interesting discussions also take place in Tomer Broude, 'Behavioural International Law', (2015) 163 University of Pennsylvania Law Review 1099 and Lauge N. S. Poulsen, *Bounded Rationality and Economic Diplomacy: The Politics of Investment Treaties in Developing Countries* (Cambridge University Press, 2017).

The point here, brutally simplified, is this: 'All sorts of extraneous factors—emotions, biases, and preferences—can intervene, most of which you can do absolutely nothing about.'[30] (That, by the way, is how Justice Antonin Scalia conceded that his way of thinking doesn't, in fact, entirely begin and end with the text.)

So, what are the extraneous factors likely to influence the decision-making of arbitrators? These are, then, factors beyond the mechanical application of law to facts and beyond the rational responses to interest-maximization discussed above.

More precisely, what are the factors that are specific to arbitrators, as opposed to judges, for instance, or the factors that play out specifically in arbitration? This precision is important because an entire array of factors beyond law and beyond what can be explained by rationality play a role in the decision-making of any legal authority: so it was shown, for instance, that judges are influenced by inadmissible evidence (for example a privileged document, which is displayed in court in breach of the rules of procedure and which a judge cannot, legally, take into accountit: it nevertheless likely influences the judge's decision); by confirmation bias (once an initial idea of guilt or liability takes hold, all subsequent elements of the trial are interpreted in favour of that initial idea); by hindsight bias (for example, when determining liability, behaviour that is obviously reasonable after a fact is considered to have been clearly reasonable before the fact as well); by anchoring (simply mentioning a figure, with regard to liability for instance, in the relevant context tends to 'anchor' representations of what is an appropriate figure); and even by blood glucose levels (hypoglycaemia leading to decisions more likely to uphold the status quo).[31] There is no reason why factors like these don't also play out in arbitration, in just the same way as they do elsewhere; there is no reason for arbitrators not to be subject to the same cognitive biases and heuristics as everyone else. Yes, arbitrators are human beings too. They also experience bouts of anger, have love affairs, trust their own people more than they do others, are seduced by unusually attractive counsel or parties or witnesses, hold all sorts of unconscious prejudices against all sorts of people, have back pain and toothache, cut hearings short because they want to drive up to their chalets in the mountains, are swayed by the advice their friends gave them and the worldviews their parents taught them. But what does this tell us about arbitration as a socio-legal phenomenon? Not very much. Precisely because these factors play out in more or less all socio-legal phenomena in which there are decision-makers. (Obviously, the limited relevance of these factors for the understanding of arbitration as a specific socio-legal phenomenon has nothing to say about their importance for the practice of arbitration or for needs of reform to de-bias arbitrators—but these are separate discussions.[32])

[30] Antonin Scalia and Bryan A. Garner, *Making Your Case: The Art of Persuading Judges* (Thomson, 2008), 'Introduction'.

[31] For a short summary, see Charles D. Ehrlich, 'The Ungoverned Brain: A Wild Card in Arbitral Decision-Making', 2016 1 ARIAS-US Quarterly 7. For longer discussions, see David Klein and Gregory Mitchell (eds), *The Psychology of Judicial Decision Making* (Oxford University Press, 2010).

[32] On this front, see e.g. van Aaken and Broude, Ch. 36 below; Drahozal, Ch. 27 below; Tony Cole (ed.), *The Roles of Psychology in International Arbitration* (Kluwer Law International, 2017); Jan-Philip Elm, 'Behavioural Insights into International Arbitration: An Analysis on How to De-Bias Arbitrators',

Now then, what is there that is specific to arbitration in this context of non-legal, non-rational factors of decision-making? Arguably there is a specific ethos, broadly speaking, in arbitration. A spirit of the arbitration community. A set of attitudes and aspirations. An ethos that is different from the likely ethos of most courts and judiciaries.

Joost Pauwelyn pointed the same way when he said that investment arbitrators are from Mars and WTO panellists from Venus.[33] He meant, brutally simplified here to mark the difference, that investment arbitrators are conceited high-profile experts where trade adjudicators are selfless technocrats from diplomatic circles. A different ethos prevails in each group: for the WTO panellists, 'team play and policy, rather than individualism and honed legal skills, are valued', whereas '[investment] arbitrators generally come from more egocentric, star-driven professions—private law practice, legal academia—where individual performance, reputation, and legal craftsmanship are key factors in advancement'.[34] Arguably the WTO panellists incarnate the rule of law while the investment arbitrators embody the rule of lawyers.[35]

Yet more than that follows from the general point. The specific ethos of arbitration creates a range of specific extra-legal factors of decision-making, specific emotions, axiological and ideological references, all manner of non-rational determinants of arbitrator decision-making.

But let me roll back my explanation a bit. Let me start with who you are.

Suppose I asked you 'Who are you?' Most likely, in telling me who you are, who your 'self' is, you will describe a set of social roles. For instance, you might say, 'I'm a Singaporean citizen, from Pulau Ujong; I'm a Buddhist, a lawyer, I'm middle-class, daughter of so and so, sister of so and so', and so on. 'You' will be that unique nexus amongst these social roles. In other words, who you are is defined by your class, ethnicity, religion, and membership in a tradition and community. Some philosophers call this the 'encumberedness of the self', which essentially means that the 'self' is always encumbered by its social roles, that social roles are constitutive—they constitute, they shape, the self.[36] From a slightly different angle, social psychology might say that people

(2016) 27 American Review of International Arbitration 75; Edna Sussman, 'Arbitrator Decision Making', (2013) 24 American Review of International Arbitration 502, arguing, precisely, that the purpose of her study is to offer 'suggestions to foster a more robust deliberative overlay and improve the quality of decisions by arbitrators. It also provides suggestions for counsel's consideration to aid them in capitalizing on these unconscious influences'; Susan Franck, 'The ICSID Effect? Considering Potential Variations in Arbitration Awards', (2011) 51 Virginia Journal of International Law 825; 'Empiricism and International Law, Insights for Investment Treaty Dispute Resolution', (2008) 48 Virginia Journal of International Law 767; Christopher Drahozal, 'A Behavioral Analysis of Private Judging', (2004) 67 Law & Contemp. Probs. 105.

[33] Joost Pauwelyn, 'The Rule of Law without the Rule of Lawyers? Why Investment Arbitrators are from Mars, Trade Adjudicators are from Venus', (2017) 109 American Journal of International Law 761.

[34] Ibid. 781.

[35] Ibid. 763: 'The WTO manages to have (something of a) rule of law without the rule of lawyers' while 'the world investment regime seems, at present, to have too much rule of lawyers and not enough rule of law'.

[36] Michael J. Sandel, 'The Procedural Republic and the Unencumbered Self', (1984) 12 Political Theory 81.

have both a personal and a social identity,[37] and that they tend to 'incorporate their group membership into their concept of themselves'.[38]

All individuals, then, including judges and arbitrators, are bound up with their various communities, their social class, gender, ethnicity, their family background, their religion if they have one and the norms and values that go with it, and all their other conditions of life. Judges' and arbitrators' selves are encumbered, including in their decision-making, by their multiple social roles and social identities. As Myriam Gicquello explains, it is simply unrealistic, in fact dehumanizing, to think of arbitrators as individuals making decisions in strict isolation of their social environment.[39]

The point is simple: conceptions of the self affect behaviour, including decision-making, and conceptions of the self are in turn partly group-based.[40] Judges and arbitrators aren't really free then, not in the Kantian ideal of the autonomous individual who truly decides for herself, a pure reflective character whose decisions are based only on what philosophers call practical reason[41]—which is 'the general human capacity for resolving, through reflection, the question of what one is to do'.[42] When legal adjudicators decide cases, their identity also diffusely comes in to bear on the outcome, without reflection, and through their identity it is all of their social roles which play a role in determining how and what they decide.[43]

One impact of these social roles on decision-makers is that they tend to favour, often unconsciously, their own group, their own community, their own social class, their own gender, etc., and the perceived norms and values to go with them. The same essential argument has been made throughout the ages (from at least the fifth century BC to today) and across disciplines (philosophy, ethology, biology, literature, psychology, ...): there is a difference in sentiments of justice for those near and like us and for those far and different from us.[44] This is arguably also caused, beyond considerations of social identity as identity, by a 'desire to promote and maintain positive relationships within the group'.[45]

[37] Henry Tajfel and John C. Turner, 'The Social Identity Theory of Intergroup Behaviour', in S. Worchel and W. G. Austin (eds), *Psychology of Intergroup Relations* (Nelson-Hall, 1986).

[38] Wendy L. Martinek, 'Judges as Members of Small Groups', in David E. Klein and Gregory Mitchell (eds), *The Psychology of Judicial Decision Making* (Oxford University Press, 2010), 77.

[39] Gicquello (n. 14).

[40] Roy F. Baumeister, 'The Self', in Daniel T. Gilbert, Susan T. Fiske, and Gardner Lindzey, *The Handbook of Social Psychology*, vol. 1, 4th edn (McGraw-Hill, 1998); Henri Tajfel, *Differentiation between Social Groups: Studies in the Social Psychology of Intergroup Relations* (Academic Press, 1978).

[41] Thomas Hill, 'The Kantian Conception of Autonomy', in John Christman (ed.), *The Inner Citadel: Essays on Individual Autonomy* (Oxford University Press, 1989).

[42] R. Jay Wallace, 'Practical Reason', in Edward N. Zalta (ed.), *The Stanford Encyclopedia of Philosophy* (Spring 2018), https://plato.stanford.edu/archives/spr2018/entries/practical-reason/.

[43] See e.g. Jeffrey Budziak, 'Promotion, Social Identity, and Decision Making in the United States Courts of Appeal', (2016) 4 Journal of Law and Courts 267.

[44] See the review in Stephen C. Neff, *Justice Among Nations* (Harvard University Press, 2014), 1–13.

[45] Marilynn B. Brewer, 'The Psychology of Prejudice: Ingroup Love or Outgroup Hate', (1999) 55 Journal of Social Issues 429, 441–2.

Considerations like these have for instance led to feminist legal theory—a movement in legal scholarship based on the idea that embedded in legal institutions are instruments to maximize the power of men and to minimize the power of women.[46] Men, the idea goes, naturally will tend to favour men, and what represents masculinity in the dominant discourse; women will tend to favour women, and what represents the feminine in the dominant discourse. And so if male judges tend to favour men and values considered 'male', mostly unconsciously, more women are needed in the judiciary to better reflect the overall spread of values in society.

Applied to arbitration, this suggests that arbitrators, as a group, make decisions coloured by the particular characteristics present in the 'group' of arbitrators, in the arbitration community. Arbitrators, simply put, are influenced by the arbitration ethos.

So what is the arbitration community like?

At arbitration conferences twenty years ago, one would hear, occasionally, a lone voice timidly suggesting that the arbitration world was mostly inhabited by the second group I imagined at the beginning of this chapter (not, then, the colourful patchwork of individuals). Or, more precisely, that the arbitration establishment, those who shape the ethos of the community, was made up of old white men, dark suits in appearance, grey and conservative in spirits. Back then, addresses of that nature would typically be followed by awkward and embarrassed silence, sideways glances, polite applause, and hurried passage to the next speaker.

Since then the discourse has changed. Passage to the next speaker is slower, the applause more sustained for those who denounce the state of things. The actual state of things, however, has changed in ways that still require statistical analysis to be noticed.[47] That the arbitration community is 'pale, male, and stale' has progressively become its standard, nearly official description.[48]

'Pale': the idea is that most arbitrators, and certainly those who set the tone, the 'powerbrokers' as they are sometimes called, are of white ethnic background.[49] More specifically, they hail from Western, developed states, from Europe and North America mostly. Even arbitrators formally from other geographical backgrounds, for instance from developing countries, were typically educated in Western universities.

One reason why this matters is that arbitrators are likely to have a certain ideology of justice, a certain idea of what dispute settlement is all about;[50] and there are noticeable differences between ideal dispute resolution in (to take just one example using extremely

[46] See e.g. Nancy Levit, Robert R. M. Verchick, and Martha Minow, *Feminist Legal Theory: A Primer*, 2nd edn (NYU Press, 2016).

[47] See e.g. Fan Yang, 'Opportunities for Young Practitioners in International Arbitration', (2017) 83 *Arbitration* 394.

[48] See the discussion in Susan D. Franck, 'The Diversity Challenge: Exploring the "Invisible College" of International Arbitration', (2015) 53 Columbia Journal of Transnational Law 429.

[49] Sergio Puig, 'Social Capital in the Arbitration Market', (2014) 25 European Journal of International Law 387.

[50] I have suggested a rough typology, just to help structure ideas, in Thomas Schultz, 'The Three Pursuits of Dispute Settlement', (2011) 1 Czech & Central European Yearbook of Arbitration 227.

broad notions) Asian culture as opposed to Western culture.[51] The Western culture or ideology of dispute settlement is for instance understood to be more confrontational than the Asian ideology. (I repeat: these are extremely broad notions, but they are probably illustrative enough to make my point.) Arbitrators, in particular in investment arbitration, are also often blamed for favouring parties from developed states, and the latest statistics seem to support the claim.[52]

And as I've said above, decision-makers tend to favour, often unconsciously, their own. A simple story comes to mind to make us see the concern: When Jay-Z, the rap musician, had a dispute with a company to which he had sold his clothing brand, he had to choose an arbitrator from a roster of the American Arbitration Association. None of the people on the roster were black (Jay-Z, of course, is). An expanded list of 200 names was suggested. But even there only three of the potential arbitrators were black, and one of them had a conflict of interest which ruled him out. A choice of only two possible arbitrators out of several hundred, Jay-Z argued, already showed bias against him; he felt cornered, facing a system of justice that didn't, as he put it, 'reflect his background and life experience'. [53] He turned to the New York Supreme Court. The court had some initial scepticism typical of lawyers: 'what exactly is the legal basis for the discontent?' it effectively first asked, before engaging in a slippery-slope fallacy, reflecting that if the need for representativeness is recognized in arbitration, eventually every party with minority traits could halt their arbitration—as if requiring some representativeness would necessarily end up with a requirement for perfect representativeness.[54] But eventually the court recognized the merits of Jay-Z's claim and stayed the arbitration.[55] (The reactions within the arbitration community to the case were noteworthy too: 'it has never been shown that arbitrators discriminate against people different from them!' was the typical remark. As if what is true for decision-makers other than arbitrators didn't apply to arbitrators. As if lawyers could be content with keeping their knowledge limited to law and legal studies, in this case even more specifically to arbitration studies.[56] Or, as Stavros Brekoulakis put it, if the arbitration community continues to use the legal standard of bias to understand and assess the legal phenomenon of arbitration, dark times are ahead for the profession.[57])

[51] Simon Roberts and Robert Palmer, *Dispute Processes: ADR and the Primary Forms of Decision-Making*, 2nd edn (Cambridge University Press, 2012).

[52] Weijia Rao, 'Development Status and Decision-Making in Investment Treaty Arbitration', (2019) 59 International Review of Law and Economics 1.

[53] Ben Beaumont-Thomas, 'Jay-Z Logo Lawsuit Halted Over Racial Bias in Arbitration Hearing', *The Guardian*, 29 November 2018: www.theguardian.com/music/2018/nov/29/jay-z-logo-lawsuit-racial-bias.

[54] See the public transcript of the hearing in *Carter v Iconix*: <iapps.courts.state.ny.us/fbem/DocumentDisplayServlet?documentId=FdpFn27QhD1AZa4bYamQrw==&system=prod>

[55] Beaumont-Thomas (n. 53).

[56] On the fallacy of the thought that legal phenomena can be explained with legal concepts alone, see Bastien François, 'Une théorie des contraintes juridiques peut-elle n'être que juridique?', in M. Troper, V. Champeil-Desplats, and C. Grzegorczyk (eds), *Théorie des contraintes juridiques* (LGDJ, 2005).

[57] Stavros Brekoulakis, 'Systemic Bias and the Institution of International Arbitration: A New Approach to Arbitral Decision-Making', (2013) 4 Journal of International Dispute Settlement 553.

'Male': the vast majority of arbitrators are men, probably close to 85 per cent overall and even more among those with the greatest influence on the community's ethos.[58] This would lead, based on what I said above, to a tendency to favour men and values typically considered to represent masculinity. What these values exactly are is not something I could comfortably or usefully pinpoint in passing in this chapter; and if it is unhelpful it will be quickly put away. But let me put it this way: given that the dominance of men is stronger in arbitration than in courts generally—in OECD countries 54 per cent of professional judges are women[59] and the worldwide average is a bit below 30 per cent of women judges[60]—then by opting for arbitration the parties opt into the more patriarchal zones of society. (As Thomas Clay flippantly puts it, public justice seems to be for women, private justice for men.[61]) These patriarchal zones of society, at least in many Western states, tend to be backward zones, zones that we tend to fight against, to progressively get away from.

Notice the grim point that follows: by opting for arbitration, the parties opt into an axiologically backward domain of justice. Whether this is good or bad is of course a value judgment, depending on the values one individually holds. But the point, which hopefully becomes increasingly clear, is that arbitration forms a distinguishable domain of human activity, as sociologists Luc Boltanski and Laurent Thévenot put it, with its own 'principles of judgment'—in other words its own ethos, distinguishable from the rest of society.[62]

And then 'stale': the adjective (whose overly derogatory character must be excused because of its brilliant rhetorical quality) is meant to suggest that arbitrators, on average, and in particular leading arbitrators, are predominantly over 50 years old and often over 60—the average age of ICC arbitrators was for instance 56 in 2017.[63]

So what, you might ask? The point is not ageism. Of course, arbitration practitioners acquire experience with age, and experience likely makes them better. And judges in many countries are not necessarily much younger—in England, for instance, 85 per cent of magistrates are aged over 50 and 55 per cent are over 60,[64] though in France the

[58] The International Chamber of Commerce reported: 'In 2017, of all arbitrators…16.7% were women—that is a 1.9% increase compared to 2016': see '2017 ICC Dispute Resolution Statistics', 2018–2 ICC Dispute Resolution Bulletin 59, with a summary and comparison to 2016 available at <iccwbo.org/media-wall/news-speeches/icc-court-releases-full-statistical-report-for-2017>. See further discussions in Yang (n. 47) and Puig (n. 49).

[59] OECD, 'Women in the Judiciary: Working Towards a Legal System Reflective of Society', March 2017, www.oecd.org/gender/data/women-in-the-judiciary-working-towards-a-legal-system-reflective-of-society.htm.

[60] UN Women, 'Progress of the World's Women 2011–2012', 2011 www.unwomen.org/en/digital-library/publications/2011/7/progress-of-the-world-s-women-in-pursuit-of-justice#view, 60, table 2.5.

[61] Thomas Clay, 'L'arbitrage est-il un être normal?', in *L'exigence de justice. Mélanges Robert Badinter* (Dalloz, 2016), 225, 228.

[62] Luc Boltanski and Laurent Thévenot, *On Justification: Economies of Worth* (Princeton University Press, 2006). See also the discussion in François Ost, 'Arbitration and Literature', Ch. 37 below.

[63] '2017 ICC Dispute Resolution Statistics' (n. 58), 59.

[64] Lord Chief Justice of England and Wales and Senior President of Tribunals, 'Judicial Diversity Statistics 2018': https://www.judiciary.uk/publications/judicial-diversity-statistics-2018, 14.

median age of magistrates is 46 for women and 51.5 for men, where women make up 66 per cent of all magistrates in the country.[65] That proficiency in legal decision-making peaks at a much older age than it does in, say, the typical sport is of course a highly plausible hypothesis.

The point is simply that older people are on average more conservative. (Although it is unclear whether it is specifically the current generation of the 'old' that is more conservative than the current generation of the 'young', or whether people generally become more conservative with age—think of the saying: 'If you're not a socialist at 20, you have no heart; if you are not a conservative at 60, you have no brains.' Or as politics scholar James Tilley puts it, 'It is very difficult to tell whether it is getting older, or being born at a certain time, that causes people to have different political preferences.'[66]) At any rate, what's involved here is this: conservative, politically right-wing values are quite strong in the arbitration ethos be it only because of a question of age.

Let me brutally simplify this. The fact (if you'll allow the casual observations of an untrained sociologist of professions, untrained cultural anthropologist, untrained social psychologist to count as fact) is that the arbitration industry is a very conservative, macho community—more than masculine, it is really rather macho. And it is strongly enough so that even many of those who are not technically pale, male, or stale tend to behave as if they were; unsurprisingly—notions of habitual peer pressure come to mind.

Continuing at the same level of casual observation, combined with basic common sense, it is rather obvious that there is a strong ideological attitude in arbitration that arbitration is good, legitimate. There's a clear pro-arbitration ideological stance in arbitration. This makes perfect sense. And recall what I said above: the ideological attitudes of decision-makers always play a role in decision-making. So, predictable as it is, this means that a number of arbitration concepts, or legal thresholds in arbitration, are interpreted in a pro-arbitration way.[67]

Such a positive self-referential attitude may seem commonplace ('we all believe in what we do!'). But it isn't necessarily so: probably many judges believe that it is not in fact a good thing that everything ends up in court. A likely common experience of anyone who's ever set foot in court is that judges are not necessarily happy for you to be there.

A further aspect of the overall arbitration ethos is what one might call a strongly corporate culture, likely fuelled by the heavy involvement of big commercial law firms in the field. The credo of this culture is perhaps best described by this excerpt of the famous speech by Gordon Gecko in the 1987 movie *Wall Street*:

[65] Yoann Demoli and Laurent Willemez, 'Les magistrats: un corps professionnel féminisé et mobile', Ministry of Justice, Infostat Justice no. 161, April 2018: www.justice.gouv.fr/art_pix/stat_Infostat_161.pdf, 1.

[66] James Tilley, 'Hard Evidence: Do We Become More Conservative with Age?', *The Conversation*, 4 October 2015 <theconversation.com/hard-evidence-do-we-become-more-conservative-with-age-47,910>; James Tilley and Geoffrey Evans, 'Ageing and Generational Effects on Vote Choice: Combining Cross-Sectional and Panel Data to Estimate APC Effects', (2014) 33 Electoral Studies 19.

[67] Recall the discussion above on the size of the overall arbitration pie. For examples, see Schultz, 'Arbitral Decision-Making' (n. 1).

> The new law of evolution in corporate America seems to be survival of the unfittest. Well, in my book you either do it right or you get eliminated. In the last seven deals that I've been involved with, there were 2.5 million stockholders who have made a pretax profit of 12 billion dollars. Thank you. I am not a destroyer of companies. I am a liberator of them! The point is, ladies and gentleman, that greed, for lack of a better word, is good. Greed is right, greed works. Greed clarifies, cuts through, and captures the essence of the evolutionary spirit. Greed, in all of its forms; greed for life, for money, for love, for knowledge has marked the upward surge of mankind. And greed, you mark my words, will not only save Teldar Paper, but that other malfunctioning corporation called the USA.

Simply put, arbitration is on the political right. Its political ethos is one of right-wing laissez-faire politics, the sort where greed is good, where being poor is a failure and it's your fault and you are less meritorious.

Now why is that a problem, you might ask? It has always been like that, and there is nothing wrong in itself in being conservative—so what?

Well, the point is simply that as a consumer, as an employee, as a developing state, the dominant political attitude is against you. To illustrate the point by its mirror image, if you are, say, a large bank, would you be pleased to be judged by a system of justice dominated by an ethos of hardcore socialists?

What I've been describing so far isn't only a problem for some parties to arbitration (typically the sort of parties for which arbitration wasn't initially designed). It likely also is, and increasingly will be, a problem for arbitration itself. The problem is called 'groupthink'. The problem is not that the values I've described abound in the arbitration ethos; the problem is that there aren't enough other values. The problem is that the arbitration community looks too much like the second group I've described on the first page of this chapter.

The idea of groupthink theory, drawn from social psychology, is that a group that is too homogeneous in its composition loses out in thinking quality. Heterogeneous groups think better collectively than homogeneous groups. A group whose members are too much alike produces, collectively, less good outputs, and is therefore less able to anticipate and react to problems and backlashes.

The idea, expressed in greater details, is that member homogeneity, combined with insulation of the group from outside and so-called provocative situational context (e.g. importance of high stress and low temporary self-esteem induced by a constantly stressful environment), creates an illusion of invulnerability, closed-mindedness, pressures towards uniformity, an illusion of unanimity, self-censorship, or more concretely incomplete survey of both objectives and alternatives, poor information search, and selective bias in information processing. Put simply, following Irving Janis, 'a deterioration of mental efficiency, reality testing, and moral judgment that results from in-group pressures'.[68] Put yet simpler, suboptimal collective intelligence.[69]

[68] Irving L. Janis, *Victims of Groupthink* (Houghton Mifflin, 1972), 9.

[69] Irving L. Janis and Leon Mann, *Decision Making: A Psychological Analysis of Conflict, Choice, and Commitment* (Free Press, 1977). This was first applied to arbitration by Gicquello (n. 14).

The point is plain, if you think of it: if we all think alike, we'll never challenge one another's ideas, and if we just cling on to established ideas, we still wouldn't have invented the wheel and the iPhone, penicillin and the light bulb, the computer and the world wide web. As Gicquello explains clearly, groupthink is 'a *pathology* affecting group decision-making'.[70] It's bad when it happens.

And arbitration, as a community, probably is and certainly appears to be much more homogeneous than many if not most judicial communities.[71] In most countries, judges are reasonably different one from another, and certainly across countries. Arbitration conferences, by contrast, are marked by a great level of stereotypicality. As Clay puts it, 'the field is conservative and originality, even imaginativeness, are often considered a flaw'.[72] (The somewhat unusual way in which this very chapter is written, as you may have noticed, is precisely part of the response to that need for originality; its very style is part of the effort to rattle the field's conventions, including its aesthetics.)

What this means is that the arbitration community, as a community, probably doesn't think terribly well, certainly less well than it would if there were more diversity, more women, younger people, people truly from non-Western cultures and who have not seriously been contaminated by Western cultures. This affects the arbitration community as a whole and thus the overall output of arbitration as a field, as a system of justice. It also affects individual arbitral tribunals if they are composed of more than a sole arbitrator, as Anne van Aaken and Tomer Broude argue: 'there is a problem with international arbitration: international arbitrators may be more prone to share the same mindset, since their diversity in terms of geography and gender is rather small, which in turn might lessen the de-biasing potential of group adjudication in comparison with courts.'[73]

9.4 Conclusion

At the centre of mostly any lesson about law should be an understanding of people. How people think. How people decide. How people live. Law ultimately is about people, more than it is about rules. If we only take interest in rules, we slowly turn into sociopaths.

The idea that we can really understand arbitration, and form an opinion about it, merely by studying its rules and procedures and cases is one that should be resisted, firmly. The basic point this chapter elaborated on is that it matters very much who decides arbitration cases, what sort of people constitute the arbitration world and what they likely respond to, and how all of this forms the arbitration ethos.

[70] Ibid.

[71] For a similar argument, that arbitrators are part of a 'close-knit community', see Sergio Puig and Anton Strezhnev, 'Affiliation Bias in Arbitration: An Experimental Approach', (2017) 46 Journal of Legal Studies, 371.

[72] Clay (n. 61), 230.

[73] Aaken and Broude, Ch. 36 below.

To take just one example: if one or several international investment courts come to replace investment arbitration, but the judges on these courts are the same as the current investment arbitrators, have the same ethos, how much change can we really expect?[74]

Some people from the arbitration community might read this text and not recognise themselves. They might be shocked that this is how I (and others like me) think of them. But we should remember that my account is a generalization, as any account of an ethos would be. And generalization of course simplify.

I can also hear, as I peck these last words before sending the manuscript off to the publisher, a different sort of reaction: contempt at my idealism, combined with a righteous claim that this is an entirely legitimate way to think, to decide, to live. Business is business. And indeed if arbitration didn't have ever-widening societal consequences this would be quite all right.

[74] A more fine-grained approach is provided by Gicquello (n. 14).

CHAPTER 10

MARGINALS AND ELITES IN INTERNATIONAL ARBITRATION

FLORIAN GRISEL

THIS chapter sheds light on a field that has raised significant interest in recent years: the sociology of individuals who are routinely appointed as international arbitrators to settle the important business disputes that commonly arise in transnational settings.[1] These individuals serve as the private judges of global business law, and their governance functions have grown together with the growth of international arbitration, which is now the preferred method for resolving these disputes.[2] The private nature of these appointments and the creation of a closed group of elite arbitrators (sometimes described as a 'mafia') have raised important concerns within civil society.[3]

This chapter builds upon prior research on the sociological evolution of international commercial arbitration (ICA) and extends it—on the basis of original data—to investor–state arbitration (ISA). The data referred to herein are drawn from an exhaustive

[1] See Yves Dezalay and Bryant Garth, *Dealing in Virtue: International Commercial Arbitration and the Construction of a Transnational Legal Order* (University of Chicago Press, 1996); Emmanuel Gaillard, 'Sociology of International Arbitration', in David D. Caron et al. (eds), *Practising Virtue: Inside International Arbitration* (Oxford University Press, 2015), 187; Malcolm Langford, Daniel Behn, and Runar Lie, 'The Revolving Door in International Investment Arbitration', 20 Journal of International Economic Law 301 (2017); Thomas Schultz and Robert Kovacs, 'The Rise of a Third Generation of Arbitrators? Fifteen Years after Dezalay and Garth', 28 Arbitration International 161 (2012).

[2] See Alec Stone Sweet and Florian Grisel, *The Evolution of International Arbitration* (Oxford University Press, 2017).

[3] See Corporate Europe Observatory and the Transnational Institute, *Profiting from Injustice: How Law Firms, Arbitrators and Financiers are Fueling an Investment Arbitration Boom* (2012). In this chapter, I use the term 'elite' to identify the leading individuals in ISA, which I measure against the number of appointments which they gathered. I leave aside the possibility that other individuals may gather a smaller number of appointments than my 'elite' but might also be considered as an 'elite' group by insiders. I also disregard the debate concerning the possibility that parties might choose 'good' or 'bad' arbitrators (on this subject, see Thomas Schultz's Ch. 9 in this Handbook), and only focus on appointment metrics.

review of the appointments of arbitrators at the International Centre for Settlement of Investment Disputes (ICSID) since 1972. ICSID is arguably the most important global institution operating in ISA. For that reason, it can serve as a basis for illustrating the social dynamics and evolution of ISA.

On the basis of this case study, this chapter shows how the elites of ICA have successfully gained a strong and growing foothold in the burgeoning field of ISA, despite the structural differences between ICA and ISA. This common sociological grounding of arbitrators in ISA and ICA is counterintuitive—one would expect, in light of the public nature of the respondent parties in ISA, to find a larger proportion of individuals who have built local connections with states through a commitment to public service.[4] However, this chapter undertakes to show how the elites of ISA and ICA significantly overlap and have developed similar social strategies to secure legitimacy within the unified field of international arbitration (both ISA and ICA). It will also show how investor-claimants (and the lawyers who represent them) have played a key role in building an ISA elite that shares key characteristics with the ICA elite.

This chapter is organized into two section. Section 10.1 provides a summary of past research carried out on the elite of ICA. This research highlights the emergence of notable figures—which I call the 'secant marginals'[5]—in the period from the 1950s to the 1970s, and their key role in the development of ICA as a fully formed substitute for national courts. It also explains how the current elite of ICA has followed the path blazed by the 'secant marginals' but have gone further in building a new field situated at the intersection of various social systems.[6] Section 10.2 presents the results of exhaustive research carried out on the appointment of arbitrators at ICSID since 1972. It shows the migration of ICA elites towards ISA, and the emergence of a common breed of arbitrator across ICA and ISA. Finally, it shows the important role played by investor-claimants in the emergence of this ISA elite.

10.1 The role of 'secant marginals' in the emergence of an ICA elite

Section 10.1 summarizes past research conducted on the ICA elite based on two data sets: a first data set that compiles all appointments at the International Chamber of Commerce (ICC) between 1922 and 1973, and a second data set based on the 'Who's

[4] An analogy could be drawn in this regard with the constitution of a public international law elite in the 1920s. See Guillaume Sacriste and Antoine Vauchez, 'The Force of International Law: Lawyers' Diplomacy on the International Scene in the 1920s', 32 Law & Social Inquiry 83 (2007).

[5] The term 'secant marginal', coined by Michel Crozier, designates an individual whose legitimacy arises at the intersection of several social systems. Although they are 'marginalized' in these different social systems, these individuals draw social legitimacy from their ability to display special skills in an intersected space where only few people can operate.

[6] My understanding of the term 'social system' is broad. It encompasses, among others, legal systems, cultures, and professions.

Who List of the Most Highly Regarded Individuals in Commercial Arbitration (2015)',[7] which presents important information pertaining to the individuals on the list. The full results of this past research are set out in a separate article;[8] section 10.1 will present these results in summary form. It will explain how the first data set sheds light on a generation of elite arbitrators at the ICC who emerged at the intersection of various social systems in the 1950s and 1960s. These 'secant marginals' played a key role in developing ICA as a cooperative interface between several systems, and as a credible alternative to national courts. The second data set temporally extends the information from the first data set by showing that members of the current ICA elite have reproduced the features of the 'secant marginals' in situating themselves at the intersection of several groups and social systems.

10.1.1 The old generation of 'secant marginals'

On the basis of an exhaustive review of ICC cases decided between 1922 and 1973, I argue that ICA was constructed by 'secant marginals' who operated at the intersection of several social systems without nurturing an exclusive sense of loyalty towards any of them.[9] This conclusion is derived from a review of relevant information about the ten most frequently appointed ICC arbitrators during this period.[10] Through their repeated appointments, these arbitrators were most likely to have exerted influence over the development of ICA. A biographical study of these arbitrators highlights their complex, hybrid profiles, which often derives from their personal histories as migrants. Consider for instance the profiles of the following individuals:

- *Lazare Kopelmanas* was an international civil servant based in Geneva. He was born in Lithuania before moving to France and then Switzerland. Although his main career was at the UN in Geneva, he served frequent stints in law schools all over the world (France, Switzerland, the USA and the Netherlands). His personal and professional history led him to develop an ability to navigate between different legal systems. His professional eclecticism at the juncture of academia and international civil service is a distinctive feature of his career. He also advised the UN throughout the negotiations that led to the European Convention on International Commercial Arbitration (1961).

[7] The Who's Who list appears to be specific to commercial arbitration, although many overlaps can be found with investment arbitration, as shown below in section 10.2.

[8] See Florian Grisel, 'Competition and Cooperation in International Commercial Arbitration: The Birth of a Transnational Legal Profession', 51(4) Law & Society Review 790 (2017).

[9] On this notion of 'secant marginal', see Michel Crozier and Erhard Friedberg, *L'acteur et le système. Les contraintes de l'action collective* (Seuil, 1977), 86.

[10] These individuals are: Ernest Barda, Ottoarndt Glossner, Berthold Goldman, Lazare Kopelmanas, Gunnar Lagergren, Ernst Mezger, Henri Monneray, André Panchaud, Pierre-Jean Pointet, and Paul van Reepinghen.

- *Ernst Mezger* was born in Germany, which he left in order to escape Nazi anti-Semitism in the 1930s. He settled in Paris, where he became an attorney. Similarly to Kopelmanas, Mezger nurtured strong connections with academia in parallel to his legal career. He was, for example, involved with the *Institut de droit comparé* at the University of Paris II (where he ended up teaching) and the *Comité français de droit international privé* (of which he became the vice-president).
- *Berthold Goldman* was born in Romania, and then moved to Paris where he studied law. He became a professor in France, produced important scholarship in various legal fields (competition law, company law, comparative law, and arbitration law) and ended up heading the University of Paris II. Although Goldman shares some features with the French legal elite, he was never fully assimilated into his host country, as evidenced by the campaign of anti-Semitism and racism that accompanied his nomination as president of Paris II.

Each of these individuals was a 'secant marginal' in the sense that they developed layered expertise at the intersection of several social groups and systems. They became skilled brokers between various professions (notably academia and legal practice), and could navigate with ease among various legal systems due to the skills they accumulated through their (often unchosen) travels. These ICA leaders did not fully belong to local elites (contrary to the claim made by Yves Dezalay and Bryant Garth),[11] but existed at the interstices of various systems, where they found space to promote inter-systemic cooperation.

An example of this type of cooperative action is the debate which occurred starting in the 1960s on the *lex mercatoria*. This *lex mercatoria* was described by Dezalay and Garth as an emanation of the 'grand old men' (typically law professors from continental Europe) who sought to maintain dominance over ICA by promoting a semi-equitable system that would favour their set of skills (rather than those displayed by the 'young technocrats').[12] However, the debates on *lex mercatoria* actually resulted from the academic inquiries led by 'secant marginals' such as Berthold Goldman in France and Clive Schmitthoff in the United Kingdom (a Jewish immigrant from Germany who built a career as a law professor in England). These 'secant marginals' were in effect engaging in intensive institutional 'bricolage',[13] borrowing various elements from different legal systems in order to build a cooperative institutional platform on which ICA could thrive.

Another important feature of these 'secant marginals' was their involvement with various arbitral institutions. For instance, Paul van Reepinghen, a Belgian national who garnered the highest number of appointments at the ICC during this period, founded the Belgian Centre for Arbitration and Mediation (CEPANI) in 1969. Similarly,

[11] See Dezalay and Garth (n. 1), ch. 3. [12] Ibid. 39–42.

[13] On the notion of 'bricolage', see Claude Lévi-Strauss, *La pensée sauvage* (Plon, 1962). This term is used here to explain how actors borrow tools from various systems in order to build and maintain their own system.

Ottoarndt Glossner founded the German Institute of Arbitration (DIS) in 1974 after chairing the ICC's Commission on International Commercial Arbitration.

Of course, some individuals in the first data set did not share, at least at first sight, the features of these 'secant marginals'. This was the case, for instance, of Gunnar Lagergren and André Panchaud, both prominent judges, in Sweden and Switzerland respectively. In fact, Lagergren and Panchaud seemed a lot more grounded in the social systems of their country of origin than the other individuals. However, they also displayed an ability to navigate across legal systems and think beyond local peculiarities (as shown for instance by the 1963 award rendered in ICC Case No. 1110, in which Lagergren introduced the notion of 'transnational public policy', a legal concept that would subsequently flourish).[14]

10.1.2 The current elite of ICA

The second data set provides a sociological picture of the current elite in ICA, and allows us to see how this picture may be the same or different from the 'secant marginals'. The information is based on the 'Who's Who List of the Most Highly Regarded Individuals in Commercial Arbitration (2015)', which provides biographical data concerning each of the 25 individuals included on the list.[15] The results of the research on this list are telling: these individuals present consistent sociological features in three particular respects.

First, all of them are barristers or attorneys. This affiliation is sometimes more symbolic than real, but signals the importance of technical skills in ICA. The fact that these individuals are lawyers does not mean that they are not hybrids in the same way as the 'secant marginals'. In fact, the second salient feature concerns their involvement in academia—almost all of them (23 out of 25) have built a portfolio of academic activities. Some of them were originally trained as law professors, while others entered academia at a later stage of their careers through visiting or adjunct professorships. Many of them (seven out of 25) have written reference textbooks or monographs on ICA. For these individuals, academic affiliations appear to serve as a signal to the arbitration market that they are well-equipped to navigate across legal systems. Elite arbitrators often advertise a list of their academic affiliations on their websites, insisting upon the multiplicity and international character of these affiliations. The goal is to burnish their reputations as legal experts who are able to bridge various legal systems and cultures.

Third, these individuals have developed strong connections with leading arbitral institutions, most of them occupying high-level positions in these institutions. One

[14] See *Argentine Engineer v British Company*, Award, ICC Case No. 1110, 3 Arbitration International 282 (1994).

[15] These individuals are: Judith Gill, Bernard Hanotiau, Gary Born, Toby Landau, Audley Sheppard, AJ Van Den Berg, Emmanuel Gaillard, L. Yves Fortier, †V. V. Veeder, David W. Rivkin, Pierre Bienvenu, Gabrielle Kaufmann-Kohler, Alexis Mourre, Stephen Jagusch, Constantine Partasides, Henri Alvarez, Klaus Sachs, Yves Derains, Laurent Lévy, Julian Lew, Donald Donovan, Jan Paulsson, Michael Pryles, Eduardo Silva Romero, and William Rowley.

counts no fewer than one president of the ICC International Court of Arbitration, two presidents of the Singapore International Arbitration Court, three presidents of the London Court of International Arbitration, and one secretary general of the ICC International Court of Arbitration. These affiliations illustrate the emergence of a transnational field anchored in global institutions, within which these transnational legal experts are able to navigate.

In light of the above, it would appear that the current elite of ICA have reproduced the features of the 'secant marginals', having layered various types of expertise (notably the practice of law and legal academia) while operating at a specifically transnational level (as evidenced by their various affiliations with arbitral institutions). A major difference between the old generation of 'secant marginals' and the current elite of ICA concerns the way in which they have acquired the relevant characteristics: while the 'secant marginals' acquired them incidentally and found themselves well-positioned to construct the ICA system, the current elite of ICA appears to have intentionally leveraged existing social capital in order to gain traction within the newly constituted transnational field.[16]

This story concerns individuals who are specialized in the settlement of disputes involving companies and/or private individuals. It does not immediately concern, or concerns only marginally, disputes involving states or state entities. One would expect, for the latter type of disputes, to come across profiles that are more localized and grounded within a national legal elite. It could be expected that public entities would typically nominate individuals who display such a profile, as is evidenced, for instance, by the judges appointed to the International Court of Justice.[17] However, the data presented here contradicts this expectation: the decision-makers in ISA disputes—which always involve public entities—present sociological features that are very close to the elite of ICA. In fact, one can observe many overlaps between these elites, as a successful career in ICA often paves the way to a career in ISA. This line of analysis will be further explored in section 10.2.

10.2 Cross-fertilization between ICA and ISA and the (re)production of arbitration elites

Section 10.2 builds upon the prior analysis of ICA and seeks to extend it to ISA. For that purpose, data has been extracted from an exhaustive review of 624 cases brought to

[16] See Grisel (n. 8).

[17] E.g. the judges appointed by France at the International Court of Justice were all high-level French public officials (3 out of 5 were members of the *Conseil d'Etat* or the Supreme Administrative Court, and the remaining two came from the Ministry of Foreign Affairs). Similarly, the judges appointed by the UK were all prominent professors, barristers, or members of the Foreign Service. Four out of seven had held the prestigious Whewell Professorship at Cambridge University or the Chichele Professorship at Oxford University.

ICSID (and 1,749 appointments made in these cases) since 1972.[18] The methodology consists of identifying the most successful arbitrators at ICSID across time, and further exploring their sociological profiles. The results of this data analysis are presented in three subsections. The first subsection explores the links between the 'secant marginals' at the ICC and the first cases submitted to ICSID. The second subsection shows the emergence of an 'ICSID arbitration club' through the practice of re-appointment (i.e. the appointment of an individual multiple times). The third subsection further explores the identity of 'club' members, and seeks to identify the entry points into the ISA elite. The various contact points between the ISA and ICA elite will be highlighted, as well as the significant influence of investors acting as claimants over the emergence of an ISA elite.

10.2.1 The 'secant marginals' at ICSID

The first phase in ICSID history was characterized by relatively slow growth. The first case at ICSID (*Holiday Inns v Morocco*) was registered in 1972, seven years after the Washington Convention was signed. Only nine arbitration cases were registered in the 1970s, and 15 in the 1980s. Among the arbitrators appointed in these cases were some of the top ICC arbitrators, individuals I include in the group of 'secant marginals'. For example, Gunnar Lagergren was appointed president of the *Holiday Inns v Morocco* tribunal by ICSID. In 1974 André Panchaud was appointed by the parties as president of the *Giardella v Côte d'Ivoire* tribunal. Berthold Goldman was appointed president of the *Amco v Indonesia* tribunal by ICSID, and co-arbitrator by the claimant in the *AAPL v Sri Lanka* case.

Along with these 'secant marginals', there were other individuals who—although not included in my first list of top ICC arbitrators—displayed very similar profiles. For instance, Michael Kerr, a prominent English judge born in Germany, who would later become the first president of the London Court of International Arbitration,[19] was appointed in a series of cases against Jamaica. Similarly, Pieter Sanders, a prominent ICC arbitrator, attorney and law professor from the Netherlands, gathered two ICSID appointments in *Guadalupe v Nigeria* and *Atlantic Triton v Guinea*. Finally, John Foster (a British MP and prominent barrister), who also garnered numerous appointments at the ICC prior to 1972, was appointed by claimants in the *Holiday Inns v Morocco* case (before resigning after his nomination to be a director of one of the claimant companies).[20]

Even when they did not come from the ICA world, prominent individuals in ICSID practice shared the features of the 'secant marginals'. For instance, the general counsel of

[18] This review is exhaustive as of 15 July 2017.

[19] See Michael Kerr, *As Far as I Remember* (Hart, 2006).

[20] Antonio Parra, *The History of ICSID* (Oxford University Press, 2012), 162.

the World Bank (and founder of ICSID), Aron Broches, was a Jewish immigrant, raised and educated in Amsterdam, who left the Netherlands in 1939 for New York, where he earned an LL.B. degree from Fordham University in 1942.[21] He continued to maintain links with his country of origin as a legal adviser to the Netherlands Economic Mission and Netherlands Embassy in New York and Washington, respectively, from 1942 until 1946, before joining the newly created International Bank for Reconstruction and Development.[22] He shared to some extent the features of the 'secant marginals': a lawyer educated in two countries (the Netherlands and the USA) who migrated from his country of origin and learned how to navigate among different social and legal systems.

The above data evidence a link between ICA practice and the development of ICSID, a feature that would remain salient (and even grow) over the course of ICSID history. Although these individuals belonged to the group of 'secant marginals' described above, or shared their characteristics (as evidenced by their professional and personal trajectories), the ICSID group were more visible and established as local elites than the other individuals listed among the top ICC arbitrators.

A combination of factors might explain this small sociological difference between the 'secant marginals' appointed at ICSID and the other 'secant marginals'. First, ICSID might have sought to establish its legitimacy as a system of private justice at the outset of its existence by favouring the appointment of prominent members of the legal profession. Second, the involvement of states in these cases might have prompted the disputing parties (and ICSID) to appoint individuals with a high social standing and particularly strong guarantees of independence. A look at the most frequently appointed arbitrator at ICSID between 1972 and 1982 provides additional support to this interpretation. This individual, who garnered five appointments during this period, all by ICSID, was Jørgen Trolle, a relative unknown on the international scene, but one who had been a member of the Supreme Court of Denmark for 21 years, including four years as its president.[23]

However, as will be seen below, this tendency to appoint 'secant marginals' with local elite traits appears to have faded as a new generation of elite arbitrators with increasingly uniform social features emerged. Members of the new generation did not face the same legitimacy issues as the old generation, as they often leveraged existing social capital (typically acquired domestically) in order to gain expertise that would give them entrance into the transnational legal field.[24] What appears clearly, however, are the wide avenues connecting ICA and ISA, to the point where both practices seem to share a common pool of elite arbitrators.

[21] Antonio Parra, 'Remembering Aron Broches' (Oxford University Press Investment Claims, 2016).
[22] Ibid. [23] Parra (n. 20), 162. [24] See Grisel (n. 8).

10.2.2 The emergence of an ICSID arbitrator club

The first decades of ICSID arbitration were relatively modest in terms of activity, but the number of cases started growing exponentially in the 1990s. As a result, the total number of arbitrator appointments also grew at a very rapid pace. Figure 10.1 summarizes this evolution, and also offers a breakdown of the proportion of first appointments and re-appointments across four time periods (1972–82, 1983–92, 1994–2004, 2005–17).

The growing practice of re-appointment is striking when seen in the light of these temporal divisions. In the first two periods (1972–92), the proportion of re-appointments is significantly smaller than first appointments. However, the situation is reversed in the next two periods (1994–2017): re-appointments account for more than 50 per cent of all appointments in these periods, increasing to 80 per cent of all appointments in the most recent period (2005–17).

ICSID appointments are therefore highly concentrated, with a few individuals garnering the bulk of all appointments. Between 2005 and 2017, the 20 most frequently appointed ICSID arbitrators garnered 406 appointments, or 32.9 per cent of the 1,234 appointments during that time period. A similar evolution can be seen in the appointment practices at the ICC between 1922 and 197,3 albeit with a smaller proportion of re-appointments (less than 50 per cent in the last sub-period between 1963 and 1972).

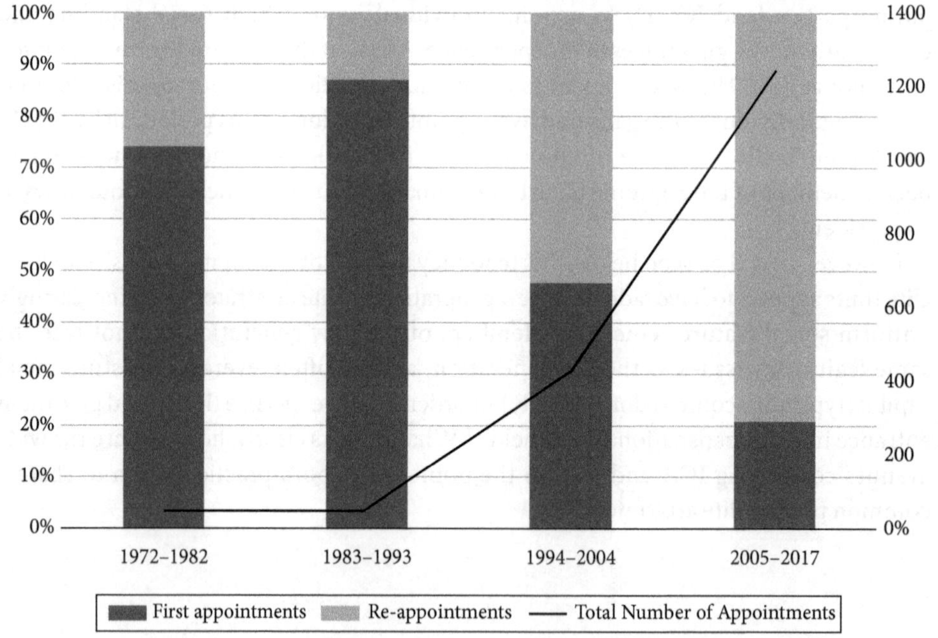

FIGURE 10.1. The emergence of the ICSID arbitration club.

One effect of the practice of re-appointment has been the creation of a club of top arbitrators who share the bulk of the cases, thereby building social capital.[25] A fine-grained analysis of this club of elite arbitrators is crucial in order to fully understand the social dynamics of ISA.

10.2.3 The 'ICSID arbitrator club' and its contacts with ICA

10.2.3.1 *The growing overlap between ISA and ICA elites*

The hypothesis I wish to explore in this section is whether the early involvement of ICA specialists, specifically of the 'secant marginals', in ICSID arbitration has had any impact on the current sociology of ISA arbitrators. In order to test this hypothesis, I have identified the ICSID arbitrators who obtained more than nine appointments between 2005 and 2017. This yielded a sample of 42 individuals, each of whom collected between nine and 57 appointments during this period. I then determined: (1) whether each of these individuals also appears in the 'Who's Who List of the Most-Highly Regarded Individuals in Commercial Arbitration (2015)', and/or (2) whether they have had experience as commercial arbitrators. The results are presented in Table 10.1.

Table 10.1 shows that 41 of the 42 individuals listed fulfil the second condition. The lone individual who does not fulfil the second condition also does not fulfil the first. Fifteen individuals listed in Table 10.1 appear in the 'Who's Who List of the Most Highly Regarded Individuals in Commercial Arbitration (2015)', which indicates that they belong to both the ICA and ISA elites. Twenty-six of these individuals do not appear in the Who's Who List but have had at least some experience as arbitrators in commercial disputes, usually at the ICC. Being an ICC arbitrator is a defining feature shared by most of these 26 individuals. For instance, individuals such as Karl-Heinz Böckstiegel or L. Yves Fortier were first appointed as arbitrators in an ICC case.[26] Although there is fierce competition among the different ICA institutions, the ICC still appears to be the reference institution for elite arbitrators. In fact, three individuals on the list (Pierre Tercier, Alexis Mourre, John Beechey) are former chairmen of the ICC International Court of Arbitration, and two (Yves Derains and Horacio Grigera Naon) were secretaries general of that institution.

Another way of analysing the data is to focus on the lone individual who does not appear to have had any involvement in ICA. This is Vaughan Lowe, an Emeritus Professor at Oxford University, specializing in public international law, who has had a more linear trajectory than most leading arbitrators. The data shows a clear overlap

[25] See Sergio Puig, 'Social Capital in the Arbitration Market', 25 EJIL 387 (2014).

[26] Sebastian Perry, 'Portrait of the Arbitrator' (GAR, 2014); Rachel Bendayan, 'Interview with a Leading International Arbitration: L. Yves Fortier', 18 Arbitration News 16 (2013), 16–17.

Table 10.1 The overlap between ISA and ICA elite arbitrators

Names	No. of ICSID appointments (2005–2017)	Who's Who List of the Most Highly Regarded Individuals in Commercial Arbitration (2015)	Practice in ICA (as arbitrator)
Stern, Brigitte	57	N	Y
Orrego Vicuna, Francisco	25	N	Y
Fortier, L. Yves	23	Y	Y
Alexandrov, Stanimir	21	N	Y
Kaufmann-Kohler, Gabrielle	20	Y	Y
Veeder, V. V.	20	Y	Y
Thomas, J. Christopher	20	N	Y
Douglas, Zachary	20	N	Y
Sands, Philippe	19	N	Y
Grigera Naon, Horacio A.	19	N	Y
Van den Berg, Albert Jan	18	Y	Y
Fernandez-Armesto, Juan	18	N	Y
Hanotiau, Bernard	17	Y	Y
Brower, Charles N.	16	N	Y
Park, William W.	16	N	Y
Williams, David A. R.	16	N	Y
Landau, Toby	16	Y	Y
Paulsson, Jan	15	Y	Y
Tercier, Pierre	15	N	Y
Lalonde, Marc	15	N	Y
Cremades, Bernardo M.	15	N	Y
Lowe, Vaughan	14	N	N
Oreamuno, Rodrigo	14	N	Y
Pryles, Michael C.	13	Y	Y
Mourre, Alexis	13	Y	Y
Beechey, John	13	N	Y
Von Wobeser, Claus	12	N	Y
Born, Gary B.	12	Y	Y
Rowley, J William	11	Y	Y
McLachlan, Campbell A	11	N	Y
Böckstiegel, Karl-Heinz	11	N	Y
Vinuesa, Raul E.	11	N	Y
Griffith, Gavan	10	N	Y
Sachs, Klaus	10	Y	Y
Gaillard, Emmanuel	9	Y	Y
Dupuy, Pierre-Marie	9	N	Y
Derains, Yves	9	Y	Y
Hossain, Kamal	9	N	Y
Bernardini, Piero	9	N	Y
Zuleta, Eduardo	9	N	Y
Lévy, Laurent	9	Y	Y

between the ISA and ICA elites. Being a top commercial arbitrator seems to be a common route (although not the only one) towards becoming a top investment arbitrator. It even seems that the heirs of the 'secant marginals' (those shown in the Who's Who List) have not only been able to succeed as commercial arbitrators but have also translated their legitimacy as elite arbitrators into the world of ISA. Of course, some of them have succeeded in building legitimacy in both fields at the same time; for instance, individuals like Albert Jan van den Berg, Jan Paulsson, and Emmanuel Gaillard have been involved in ICSID proceedings since the early 1980s as counsel or arbitrators, and seem to have developed their profiles as both ISA and ICA experts very early on. The data in Table 10.1 seems to indicate the existence of an overlap, at least of contact points, between ISA and ICA. This hypothesis will be further explored in light of additional data.

10.2.3.2 *The emergence of stable social features across the ISA and ICA elites*

To further explore this hypothesis, I have broken down all the ICSID cases into four equal batches of approximately 154 cases. These four batches of cases are shown in chronological order. The cases in these four batches were registered at ICSID during the following time periods: 1972–2004, 2004–10, 2010–14, and 2014–17.[27] For each batch, the names of the fifteen most frequently appointed arbitrators were selected. In total, 34 individuals have garnered 624 appointments out of a total number of 1,749 appointments (or almost 35.7 per cent of all appointments).[28] The results of this breakdown across the four batches of cases are shown in Table 10.2.

Table 10.2 shows that the elite in ICSID arbitration has remained stable over time. Seventeen individuals (out of 34 shown in Table 10.2) were among the fifteen most frequently appointed arbitrators during at least two periods (or batches of cases).

A key to the analysis is to determine whether the elite of ICSID arbitration shares social features with the ICA elite. In section 10.1, I presented results of past research showing that members of ICA elite share stable social features, namely affiliation with the bar, the pursuit of academic activities,[29] and positions within arbitral institutions.[30] The same analysis was applied to the individuals listed in Table 10.2, with results that are strikingly similar to those obtained for ICA. These results are compiled in Table 10.3.

[27] The data excludes conciliation cases, and cases submitted to ad hoc annulment committees.

[28] Some individuals gathered more total appointments between 1972 and 2017 than the 'top 15' from each period, but these appointments were not sufficient for these individuals to appear in the 'top 15' lists for each of the periods shown in Table 10.2.

[29] I considered several factors to establish the existence of an 'academic activity' that is sufficiently significant, including the number of scientific publications in specialized reviews authored by the individual, as well as affiliations with universities or law schools and memberships in scientific societies.

[30] I considered only individuals who held an official position in one of the leading arbitral institutions (International Chamber of Commerce, London Court of International Arbitration, Stockholm Chamber of Commerce, American Arbitration Association, Dubai International Arbitration Centre, Singapore International Arbitration Centre, Hong Kong International Arbitration Center, and China International Economic and Trade Arbitration Commission).

Table 10.2 The ICSID elite members (1972–2017)

0–155 (1972-2004)		156–310 (2004–2010)		311–465 (2010-2014)		466–624 (2014–2017)	
Name	Appointments	Name	Appointments	Name	Appointments	Name	Appointments
Bernardini Piero	8	Berman, Franklin	7	Alexandrov, Stanimir	6	Alexandrov, Stanimir	11
Böckstiegel, Karl-Heinz	8	Bernardini, Piero	7	Douglas, Zachary	8	Beechey, John	6
Brower, Charles	6	Brower, Charles	12	Fortier, L. Yves	10	Born, Gary	6
Cremades, B. M.	11	Cremades, Bernardo M.	8	Hanotiau, Bernard	7	Douglas, Zachary	14
Fadlallah, Ibrahim	6	Fortier, L. Yves	8	Landau, Toby	7	Fernandez-Armesto, Juan	6
Fortier, L. Yves	11	Grigera Naon, Horacio A	6	McLachlan Campbell	8	Fortier, L. Yves	7
Kaufmann-Kohler, Gabrielle	6	Kaufmann-Kohler, Gabrielle	16	Mourre, Alexis	7	Grigera Naon, Horacio	7
Lalonde, Marc	7	Lalonde, Marc	10	Orrego Vicuna, Francisco	11	Hanotiau, Bernard	7
Lauterpacht, Elihu	10	Lowe, Vaughan	9	Park, William W.	7	Oreamuno, Rodrigo	6
Oreamuno, Rodrigo	7	Orrego Vicuna, Francisco	12	Sands, Philippe	8	Pryles, Michael C	7
Orrego Vicuna, Francisco	10	Paulsson, Jan	8	Stern, Brigitte	23	Reichert, Klaus	7
Paulsson, Jan	7	Sands, Philippe	6	Tercier, Pierre	7	Sands, Philippe	7
Rezek, Francisco	6	Stern, Brigitte	21	Thomas, Christopher	7	Stern, Brigitte	18
Van den Berg, Albert Jan	12	Thomas, Christopher	8	Van Den Berg, Albert Jan	8	Thomas, Christopher	6
Weil, Prosper	6	Veeder, V. V.	8	Veeder, V. V.	10	Van den Berg, Albert Jan	6

Table 10.3 clearly shows that the elite of ICSID arbitration present social features which are similar to the ICA elite in terms of these three criteria.

First, all of the individuals listed in Table 10.3 have pursued significant academic activities during their careers. Some of them are law professors, specializing in public international law (Elihu Lauterpacht, Vaughan Lowe, Philippe Sands), private international law (Gabrielle Kaufmann-Kohler, Bernard Hanotiau), or contract law (Pierre Tercier). Others joined academia at a later stage in their careers as adjunct, visiting, or full professors. For instance, Jan Paulsson began occupying the Michael Klein Distinguished Scholar Chair at the University of Miami School of Law after leaving his position as Freshfields' co-head of the international arbitration and public international law groups.

Even when they do not hold a professorship, all of these individuals commonly engage in academic debates by publishing articles in specialized reviews, participating in conferences, and teaching at universities around the world. Engaging with the academic world seems to be a mark of legal sophistication, and a sign of one's ability to avoid identifying with only one specific legal system and culture. It is also a way to control and shape academic debates about international arbitration. One of these individuals (L. Yves Fortier) has even created (and presumably funded) a chair at McGill University bearing his name, specializing in 'international arbitration and international commercial law'.[31] It is important to note, however, that these individuals have not limited themselves to academic careers; they have also had long-standing involvement with legal practice, among other activities.

Second, all of the individuals listed in Table 10.3 are barristers or attorneys. Some of them are members of a bar even though they do not seem to have had significant involvement in practising law (e.g. Pierre Tercier and Brigitte Stern). However, most of them had successful careers as counsel before (or at the same time as) specializing as arbitrators. This is the case, for example, for Jan Paulsson, †V. V. Veeder, and Toby Landau. In this regard, Langford, Behn, and Lie have evidenced the revolving doors between different roles in international investment arbitration, particularly arbitrator and legal counsel.[32] Barrister chambers often provide these individuals with a platform to develop their activities as arbitrators. These barrister chambers are usually located in London, and have housed many of the individuals listed in Table 10.3.

In particular, eight of the 34 individuals listed in Table 10.3 are affiliated with two barrister chambers in London: Essex Court Chambers[33] and 20 Essex Street.[34] 20 Essex Street has even created a page on its website presenting the 'full-time arbitrators' affiliated with the chamber.[35] Twelve of the 34 are Queen's Counsel (or Senior Counsel), a

[31] See 'Fortier Chair in International Arbitration & International Commercial Law': http://www.mcgill.ca/fortier-chair/.

[32] Langford et al. (n. 1).

[33] Franklin Berman, Vaughan Lowe, Toby Landau, †V. V. Veeder, and Campbell McLachlan.

[34] Charles Brower, L. Yves Fortier, and Francisco Orrego Vicuna.

[35] See: http://www.20essexst.com/members.

Table 10.3 Social features of the ICSID elite (1972–2017)

Name	Gender	Nationality	Academic activities	Position in an arbitral institution	Attorney or barrister
Bernardini, Piero	M	Italian	Y	Y	Y
Böckstiegel, Karl-Heinz	M	German	Y	Y	Y
Brower, Charles	M	American	Y	Y	Y
Cremades, Bernardo M.	M	Spanish	Y	Y	Y
Fadlallah, Ibrahim	M	French/Lebanese	Y	Y	Y
Fortier, L. Yves	M	Canadian	Y	Y	Y
Kaufmann-Kohler, Gabrielle	F	Swiss	Y	Y	Y
Lalonde, Marc	M	Canadian	Y	Y	Y
Lauterpacht, Elihu	M	British	Y	N	Y
Oreamuno, Rodrigo	M	Costa Rican	Y	Y	Y
Orrego Vicuna, Francisco	M	Chilean	Y	Y	Y
Paulsson, Jan	M	French	Y	Y	Y
Rezek, Francisco	M	Brazilian	Y	N	Y
Van den Berg, Albert Jan	M	Dutch	Y	Y	Y
Berman, Franklin	M	British	Y	N	Y
Grigera Naon, Horacio A.	M	Argentinian	Y	Y	Y
Christopher Thomas, J.	M	Canadian	Y	Y	Y
Lowe, Vaughan	M	British	Y	N	Y
Sands, Philippe	M	British	Y	N	Y
Stern, Brigitte	F	French	Y	Y	Y
Veeder, V. V.	M	British	Y	Y	Y
Alexandrov, Stanimir A.	M	Bulgarian	Y	N	Y
Douglas, Zachary	M	Australian	Y	N	Y
Hanotiau, Bernard	M	Belgian	Y	Y	Y
Landau, Toby	M	British	Y	Y	Y
McLachlan, Campbell Alan	M	New Zealander	Y	Y	Y
Mourre, Alexis	M	French	Y	Y	Y
Park, William W.	M	American	Y	Y	Y
Tercier, Pierre	M	Swiss	Y	Y	Y
Beechey, John	M	British	Y	Y	Y
Born, Gary B.	M	American	Y	Y	Y
Fernandez-Armesto, Juan	M	Spanish	Y	Y	Y
Pryles, Michael	M	Australian	Y	Y	Y
Reichert, Klaus	M	Irish/German	Y	Y	Y

mark of excellence for barristers in the common law world.[36] Many individuals have chosen to create their own boutique firm in order to manage the cases in which they act as arbitrators (more rarely as counsel).[37]

Third, another prominent feature of the individuals listed in Table 10.3 is their involvement with arbitral institutions. A significant majority of them (25 out of 34) hold positions on the boards or governing bodies of prominent arbitral institutions (specialized in ICA). It should be noted, however, that this majority is less significant than the one observed in ICA (92 per cent of the individuals appearing in the 'Who's Who List of the Most Highly Regarded Individuals in Commercial Arbitration' displayed such affiliations). The concentration of power is still staggering: one counts four presidents of the London Court of International Arbitration (Karl-Heinz Böckstiegel, Jan Paulsson, William Park, L. Yves Fortier) and three presidents of the ICC International Court of Arbitration (Pierre Tercier, John Beechey, Alexis Mourre) among the individuals listed in Table 10.3. Affiliations with these institutions serve as a transnational anchor which top arbitrators use to maintain strong connections with (and privileged knowledge of) the global market in international arbitration.

Based on the above data, my preliminary conclusion, therefore, confirms the initial hypothesis of this chapter: the elites of ICA and ISA significantly overlap, and share some fundamental social features. This seems to support the argument that an increasingly uniform field of international arbitration has been emerging. A possible explanation for this overlap is offered by Schultz and Kovacs, who documented the importance of 'managerial' profiles among top arbitrators (without distinguishing commercial and investment arbitration).[38] In particular, Schultz and Kovacs highlighted the importance of 'specialization in the law and practice of arbitration' and 'strong management abilities' in parties' selections of a given individual as arbitrator.[39] Thus, the overlap between ISA and ICA might be explained by the 'proceduralization' of arbitration (especially given that ISA procedure is very similar to ICA procedure and, therefore, requires the mobilization of similar skills).

To further explore the hypothesis of ICA/ISA overlap, it is also useful to examine whether the individuals listed in Table 10.3 display local elite backgrounds (a feature that was not salient in the world of ICA). One would expect to see a higher number of such individuals within the ISA world, due to the intrinsic nature and political sensitivity of disputes involving states. The results of my research as shown in Table 10.3 are nuanced. It is true, as noted above, that ICSID and the disputing parties at ICSID initially chose individuals who drew on significant social capital resulting from their local careers (such as Jørgen Trolle). It is noteworthy that some of the individuals in Table 10.3 have

[36] These individuals are: Elihu Lauterpacht, Franklin Berman, Christopher Thomas, Vaughan Lowe, Philippe Sands, †V.V. Veeder, Zachary Douglas, Toby Landau, Campbell McLachlan, Klaus Reichert, Marc Lalonde, and L. Yves Fortier.

[37] This is the case e.g. of L. Yves Fortier, Gabrielle Kaufmann-Kohler, Jan Paulsson, Albert Jan Van Den Berg, Bernard Hanotiau, Pierre Tercier, Juan Fernandez Armesto, and John Beechey.

[38] Schultz and Kovacs (n. 1), 161.

[39] Ibid. 170.

held high political or governmental offices, usually towards the beginning of their careers.

These individuals have often come from the developing world; for example, Francisco Orrego Vicuna was the Chilean Ambassador to the United Kingdom in the early 1980s; Stanimir Alexandrov was Vice Minister of Foreign Affairs of Bulgaria; Rodrigo Oreamuno was the Vice-President of Costa Rica in the 1990s; and Francisco Rezek was the Foreign Minister of Brazil between 1990 and 1992. Arbitrators from the developed world have occasionally taken the same path: L. Yves Fortier was the Canadian Ambassador to the United Nations (1988–92); Marc Lalonde was the Canadian Minister of Finance (1982–4); Pierre Tercier was a member and the chairman of the Swiss Antitrust Commission (1989–98); and Juan Fernandez-Armesto was the chairman of the Spanish Securities and Exchange Commission (1996–2000).

However, governmental activities do not seem to have been a determining factor in these individuals' elite status. Of course, holding high political office can serve as an entry point into ISA, but only when combined with other skills, usually obtained through a career as a practising lawyer and/or law professor. For instance, L. Yves Fortier entered into the arbitration field through his appointment in the landmark ICC case arising from the construction of the Channel Tunnel between France and Great Britain. Fortier described his transition from international diplomacy to arbitration as follows:

> Before I went to New York in the autumn of 1988 as Canada's Ambassador and Permanent Representative to the United Nations (UN), I had practised law for more than 25 years, mainly as a trial lawyer. I knew very little about international arbitration although I had appeared as counsel before some ICC tribunals. Therefore, I was vaguely familiar with the environment. When I came back to Montréal from New York in the spring of 1992 and rejoined my law firm, I decided that, rather than resuming my practice as a trial lawyer, I wanted to become an international adjudicator. I sought counsel and was informed that the large so-called 'magic circle law firms' in London controlled many of the arbitral appointments. Ogilvy Renault had an office in London at that time and I asked my friend and partner of the day in London if he could schedule meetings for me with the arbitration partners of these firms.... That evening, I received a call from my London partner informing me that Alan [Redfern] had enquired whether he could put my name on a short list of candidates to serve as chairman of an ICC tribunal, which was seized of a US$1bn cost overrun claim relating to the construction of the Tunnel.[40]

This extract shows how Fortier was able to leverage his connections as a practising lawyer and his international profile into a first appointment in an ICC case. His hybrid skills—combining a knowledge of common and civil law with a familiarity with international law and diplomacy—were arguably a key to his first appointment. This confirms the difficulty of drawing a sharp distinction between ICA and ISA elite profiles: it

[40] Bendayan (n. 26), 16–17.

would appear that both sets of elites prosper when they are present at the intersection of different legal and social systems.

The main distinction that can be drawn from our research rather concerns the older elite of international arbitration as compared with the current elite: while the current elite has been able to leverage existing social capital (in Fortier's case, broadly typical of this group, an appointment as UN Ambassador and a partnership in a global law firm) in order to gain traction in the transnational space, the old elite often lacked this kind of social capital and instead combined skills gained through their (often unwanted) travels and work experience in a unique way. In both ISA and ICA, roles in local public functions can be a factor in gaining access to the arbitration elite, but they are systematically combined with other qualifications.

10.2.3.3 *The private impetus for ICSID appointments*

Another important aspect of the arbitrators listed in Tables 10.2 and 10.3 concerns the nature of their appointments. Are these top arbitrators nominated by claimants (investors) or respondents (states), or do they act more frequently as presidents (appointed by ICSID or by the parties)? It is possible to sketch a broad picture of these appointments on the basis of information published by ICSID. Table 10.4 presents the arbitrators listed in Table 10.2 and specifies the number of appointments coming from claimants (C), respondents (R), ICSID (I), and/or as president (PR). When an arbitrator is appointed mostly by claimants, the number of appointments is printed in bold; if mostly by respondents, it is printed in italic; and individuals appointed as president are shown in underlined text.

A review of Table 10.4 shows several trends in the appointment of ICSID elite arbitrators. One trend concerns the pre-eminence of claimant appointments among these elite arbitrators. Another trend concerns the evolution over time among the different sources of appointments.

First, it is noteworthy that a majority of the individuals listed in Tables 10.2 and 10.4 were appointed primarily by claimants. For instance, claimants were responsible, by a very large margin, for the majority of the appointments of Horacio Grigera Naon, Charles Brower, Gary Born, Klaus Reichert, Piero Bernardini, Stanimir Alexandrov, and Marc Lalonde. It is also noteworthy that four individuals on this latter list have had close affiliations with global law firms: Grigera Naon is a former special counsel at White & Case; Brower is a former partner at White & Case; Stanimir Alexandrov is a partner at Sidley; and Gary Born is a partner at WilmerHale. These affiliations might explain the origins of their appointments: the client base of these prominent lawyers in top US law firms consists mostly of private entities (although these firms also represent some public entities). It is not surprising that individuals with a preponderance of private connections tend to gather more appointments from investors. Some arbitrators obviously benefit from their close connections with global law firms, which have appointed them in multiple cases (as exemplified further below by Francesco Orrego Vicuna). Brower offered this explanation in a recent interview:

Table 10.4 The ICSID elite: who appoints them? (1972–2017)

0-155 (1972–2004)		156–310 (2004–2010)		311–465 (2010–2014)		466–624 (2014–2017)	
Name	Appointments	Name	Appointments	Name	Appointments	Name	Appointments
Bernardini Piero	**8 (C-5, R-2, PR-1 (I-1))**	Berman, Franklin	7 (C-2, R-2, PR-3 (I-1))	Alexandrov, Stanimir	**6 (C-6)**	Alexandrov, Stanimir	11 (C-10, I-1)
Böckstiegel, Karl-Heinz	8 (C-3, R-1, PR-4 (I-1))	Bernardini, Piero	7 (C-4, PR-3 (I-2))	Douglas, Zachary	*8 (C-2, R-6)*	Beechey, John	6 (C-5, PR-1)
Brower, Charles	**6 (C-5, PR-1)**	Brower, Charles	**12 (C-12)**	Fortier, L Yves	10 (C-6, PR-4 (I-1))	Born, Gary	**6 (C-6)**
Cremades, BernardoM.	11 (C-5, R-2, PR-4 (I-1))	Cremades, Bernardo M	8 (C-2, R-4, PR-2 (I-1))	Hanotiau, Bernard	**7 (C-5, R-1, PR-1 (I-1))**	Douglas, Zachary	*14 (R-12, PR-2)*
Fadlallah, Ibrahim	6 (C-3, R-2, PR-1 (I-1))	Fortier, L Yves	8 (C-4, PR-4 (I-1))	Landau, Toby	*7 (R-6, PR-1)*	Fernandez-Armesto, Juan	6 (PR-6)
Fortier, L. Yves	11 (C-2, R-1, PR-6)	Grigera Naon, Horacio A.	**6 (C-6)**	McLachlan Campbell	8 (R-4, PR-4)	Fortier, L. Yves	**7 (C-6, PR-1)**
Kaufmann-Kohler, Gabrielle	**6 (C-4, R-1, PR-1)**	Kaufmann-Kohler, Gabrielle	16 (C-3, PR-13 (I-2))	Mourre, Alexis	7 (C-2, R-3, PR-2)	Grigera Naon, Horacio	**7 (C-7)**
Lalonde, Marc	**7 (C-7, PR-1)**	Lalonde, Marc	**10 (C-6, R-2, PR-3)**	Orrego Vicuna, Francisco	**11 (C-10, PR-1)**	Hanotiau, Bernard	7 (C-3, R-1, PR-3)
Lauterpacht, Elihu	10 (C-4, R-1, PR-5)	Lowe, Vaughan	9 (C-1, R-2, PR-6 (I-3))	Park, William W.	7 (C-3, PR-4)	Oreamuno, Rodrigo	*6 (R-6)*
Oreamuno, Rodrigo	7 (R-1, PR-6 (I-4))	Orrego Vicuna Francisco	12 (C-6, R-2, PR-4 (I-3))	Sands, Philippe	*8 (R-8)*	Pryles, Michael C	7 (C-5, R-2)

Orrego Vicuna, Francisco	<u>10 (R-1, PR-9 (I-6))</u>	Paulsson, Jan	8 (C-3, R-1, PR-3 (I-2)	Stern, Brigitte	*23 (R-23)*	Reichert, Klaus	7 (C-7)
Paulsson, Jan	7 (C-3, R-1, PR-3 (I-1))	Sands, Philippe	*6 (C-1, R-5)*	Tercier, Pierre	<u>7 (R-1, PR-6 (I-1))</u>	Sands, Philippe	*7 (C-1, R-5, PR-1)*
Rezek, Francisco	6 (R-4, PR-2 (I-1))	Stern, Brigitte	*21 (R-18, I-1, PR-2 (I-1))*	Thomas, Christopher	*7 (R-7)*	Stern, Brigitte	*18 (R-18)*
Van den Berg, Albert Jan	**12 (C-6, R-3, I-1, PR-2 (I-2))**	Thomas, Christopher	*8 (R-8)*	Van den Berg, Albert Jan	8 (C-4, R-1, I-1, PR-2 (I-1))	Thomas, Christopher	*6 (R-6)*
Weil, Prosper	<u>6 (C-1, R-1, PR-4 (I-3))</u>	Veeder, V. V.	<u>8 (PR-8)</u>	Veeder, V. V.	<u>10 (C-1, R-1, PR-8)</u>	Van den Berg, Albert Jan	6 (C-3, R-1, PR-2)

> People get pigeonholed. When you start out as an arbitrator, you get asked by your friends. The people I knew were mostly at large American law firms representing claimants, so that's where the appointments came from.[41]

The influence of global law firms on the arbitration market may, therefore, explain why the private sector seems to be driving the appointment of elite arbitrators. This market structure of international arbitration is also a key to understanding the overlap between ICA and ISA elites: the contact point between both sets of elites may be these global law firms that manage both ISA and ICA cases, and appoint ICA arbitrators in ISA cases (and vice versa).

However, it should be noted that a small number of other individuals in Table 10.4 present the diametrically opposed profile of being mostly appointed by respondents. This is the case, for instance, of individuals like Brigitte Stern, Zachary Douglas, Toby Landau, Philippe Sands, and Christopher Thomas, none of whom are affiliated with global law firms. Three of them are barristers in chambers that have had a long-standing tradition of representing public entities in international law cases (Essex Court Chambers and Matrix Chambers). Three are prominent public international law professors.

These arbitrators typically garner a very high number of appointments. For example, Stern has gathered the highest number of arbitrator appointments in the history of ICSID. This concentration of a large number of cases in the hands of a few arbitrators tends to confirm the above hypothesis of the 'private impetus' for the ICSID elite. Indeed, states are not as well-connected to the global law firms (which control a large portion of the appointments) as investors. As a result, a small number of arbitrators are repeatedly appointed by states, and they tend to garner more appointments than their colleagues who are favoured by foreign investors. Conversely, investors are able to promote a larger number of elite arbitrators (even if these arbitrators do not necessarily gather as many total appointments as the individuals appointed by states).

The effects of this 'private impetus' are unclear. In fact, the existence of a bias against states has not been clearly established in ISA.[42] The dynamics within the arbitral tribunal often come down to an opposition—more or less to be expected—between party-appointed arbitrators, with the final decision made by the president. Such dynamics cannot clearly favour one side or the other unless the president is also biased. It is noteworthy in this regard that very few individuals in Tables 10.2 and 10.4 show any apparent 'bias' based on their distribution of appointments (even though, of course, parties tend to appoint arbitrators who are more likely to favour their position in the arbitration). Two relevant examples are Albert Jan van den Berg and †V. V. Veeder. Van den Berg has been appointed as co-arbitrator by both investors and states, and has also gathered a significant number of appointments as president in an investor to state proportion that is remarkably balanced. Veeder has mostly been appointed as president,

[41] Sebastian Perry, 'A Political Animal', 8 Global Arbitration Review 11 (2013), 11.

[42] See Stone Sweet and Grisel (n. 2), 190.

and his nominations as co-arbitrator do not indicate any apparent bias in favour of either investors or states.

Second, the trajectories of certain individuals in moving from one category to another is also noteworthy. Three individuals present interesting profiles in this respect. Francisco Orrego Vicuna began his ICSID career by being appointed as president by ICSID (six out of ten cases in the first period), but never by investors. The proportion slowly reversed, to the point where he was appointed by investors in ten out of eleven cases in the third period. One reason might be his decisions that were perceived to strongly favour investor interests (such as *Fedax v Venezuela* and *CMS v Argentina*; for both, Orrego Vicuna was president). Even more relevant is the fact that Orrego Vicuna was appointed at least eight times by the same law firm (Freshfields) on behalf of investors between 2008 and 2013.[43] This fact supports the hypothesis that global law firms drive the constitution of ISA elites through repeat appointments on behalf of investors (even though Freshfields has also appeared on behalf of states, including Kenya, Egypt, and Turkey).

Another interesting case is L. Yves Fortier. Fortier was clearly perceived as a neutral arbitrator in his first years of activity: most of his appointments were as president. Over time, however, he was increasingly appointed by claimants; he was appointed by investors in six out of seven cases during the most recent time period (Table 10.4). Again, decisions rendered as president might act as signals to the market that a specific individual leans more towards states or investors—in the case of Fortier, his involvement as president in the Yukos case (in which the investors obtained the largest award of damages in ISA history) might have signalled (rightly or not) a pro-investor bias. Finally, the trajectory of Gabrielle Kaufmann-Kohler follows a trend that is also noteworthy. Kaufmann-Kohler obtained a majority of her appointments from investors during the first time period (Table 10.4), but later gathered an increasing number of appointments as president.

10.3 Conclusion

This chapter analyses the sociological characteristics of the elite of both ICA and ISA. The data strongly support the contention that ICA and ISA elites significantly overlap, with ICA elites migrating towards ISA in the 1970s. In particular, the chapter argues that the 'secant marginals' who built ICA after the Second World War also became involved in the early ICSID cases, and that their hybrid social features were reproduced over time, in both ICA and ISA. Another significant contact point between both ICA and ISA is the global law firms that commonly represent both private parties in ICA and investors

[43] See *Burlington Resources, Inc. v Republic of Ecuador*, Decision on the Proposal for Disqualification of Professor Francisco Orrego Vicuna, ICSID Case No. ARB/08/05 (2013), para. 22. The case of Orrego Vicuna is not an isolated one.

in ISA. As a consequence, elites in ISA and ICA now overlap, and top arbitrators commonly act as commercial and investment arbitrators. While it is difficult to measure the impact of these sociological traits on substantive outcomes in international arbitration, recent attempts by governmental entities such as the European Commission to regulate the profiles of ISA arbitrators[44] show the importance and sensitivity of these questions.

[44] Commission draft text TTIP (2015), Art. 9(4)/10(7).

CHAPTER 11

MEDIATORS IN ARBITRATION

JACQUELINE NOLAN-HALEY

11.1 Introduction

This chapter focuses on mediation in practice and describes mediation's role in contemporary transnational dispute system design. It acknowledges the general trend towards settlement facilitation in international arbitration, and focuses on mediators giving shape and structure to that facilitation. It examines the mediation process, its advantages, commonalities with and differences from arbitration, and the growth of transnational mediation practice. Reflection on the relationship between mediation and justice, equity and fairness, summons up several models of mediator behavior that seek to achieve justice. Special attention is paid to contemporary convergences with arbitration and mediation and the controversial mixture of arbitration and mediation—mediation processes that include aspects of mediation within arbitration and arbitration within mediation. Finally, it offers some cautionary considerations on blending mediation and arbitration and proposes several questions for reflection about the way forward.

11.2 Mediation and arbitration: conceptual understandings

Any discussion of the presence of mediators in the realm of international arbitration requires an understanding of relevant terminology. The meaning of mediation and arbitration is a subject on which there is often a great deal of muddled thinking, for example when mediation is confused with 'meditation' and other therapeutic practices.

Arbitration and mediation involve differentiations in roles and processes. There are also commonalities and more recently, convergences with these processes when mediation assumes many features traditionally associated with arbitration. Thus, before reflecting on the role of mediators in international arbitration, it is useful to be clear on terminology to prevent confusion about meaning from clouding the discussion.

The traditional (western) definitions of arbitration and mediation are straightforward. Arbitration is a consensual, adjudicative process in which disputing parties have the opportunity to present their case to a neutral third party who makes a final decision regarding the outcome of the dispute or disagreement.[1] In comparison, mediation is an interest-based negotiation process facilitated by a neutral third party who has no decision-making authority but who assists disputing parties in reaching a consensual agreement. Important interests of the parties include autonomy and dignity. The core differentiation lies in the presence or absence of adjudicative powers in the neutral. Definitional understandings may vary in different cultures. As one scholar has observed, 'mediation in China is very different from what is called mediation in the ADR literature'. The systems are different enough that 'it would be seriously misleading simply to use the English word without further explanation'.[2] For example, in court-connected mediation, judges in China[3] take on the dual roles of mediator and adjudicator in the same case.

The word 'mediation' is frequently used interchangeably with the term 'conciliation', as in the UNCITRAL Model Law on International Commercial Mediation and International Settlement Agreements Resulting from Mediation.[4] Whether in fact they are the same process appearing under different names is contestable. In some legal cultures, mediation is distinguishable from the more directive conciliation process. There, the neutral third party may be more actively involved in moving disputing parties towards agreement, offering legal information and proposals for settlement.[5] For this reason, some commentators suggest that the conciliation process should be positioned between mediation and arbitration.[6]

11.2.1 The value of mediation and mediators

Mediation is often promoted as being less costly and time-consuming than arbitration (although there is little reliable data on the speed of dispute resolution processes in general.) Compared to litigation, mediation can reduce the economic and emotional

[1] Gary Born, *International Commercial Arbitration* (Kluwer Law International, 2014), 250–56.

[2] Donald Clarke, 'Dispute Resolution in China', in Tahirih Lee (eds), *Contract, Guanxi, and Dispute Resolution in China* (Routledge 1997), 369, 428.

[3] Jeffrey Lee, 'Mediation in Mainland China and Hong Kong: Can They Learn from Each Other?', 16 Asian-Pac. L. & Pol'y J. 101 (2014).

[4] UNCITRAL Model Law on International Commercial Mediation and International Settlement Agreements Resulting from Mediation, 2018 (amending the UNCITRAL Model Law on International Commercial Conciliation (2002).

[5] Nadja Alexander, *International and Comparative Mediation: Legal Perspectives* (Kluwer Law International, 2009), 2.

[6] Laurence Boulle and Miryana Nesic, *Mediation: Principles, Process, Practice* (LexisNexis, 2001), 79.

costs of resolving disputes, and empirical studies show high compliance and user satisfaction rates with mediation.[7] Several years ago Craig McEwen and Thomas Milburn described what they labelled the 'paradox of mediation', namely that when parties in conflict who are reluctant to use mediation are required to mediate, they find the process fair and satisfying and would recommend it to others.[8]

Mediation's benefits flow from the culture of mediation which changes the paradigm in dispute resolution from adversarial, positional bargaining to a more problem-solving approach focused on underlying needs and interests. Not tethered to procedural or evidentiary rules, mediation offers flexibility and informality. It emphasizes cooperative communications between parties who are encouraged to think 'outside the box' and to reach creative solutions. As a general matter, mediation's success depends upon the parties' willingness to participate in good faith in the process.

Mediators as neutral third parties can add value to the parties' negotiations. Research on barriers to negotiation shows that many negotiations fail to result in a consensual agreement because of structural defects and perceptual distortions in the negotiation process.[9] For example, cognitive barriers (thoughts or thought processes that impede settlement) can result in information being distorted. Take the cognitive barrier of 'loss aversion', which refers to the tendency of people to prefer avoiding losses instead of obtaining equivalent gains.[10] Studies show that the intervention of skilled mediators can make a difference in helping parties to overcome this and other barriers to settlement. Even if mediation is unsuccessful in resolving the dispute, mediators can help the parties choose an appropriate dispute resolution process and help them prepare for that process.

11.2.2 Differentiations and commonalities

Thinking about mediators in the world of international arbitration calls for an appreciation of the fundamental differences between the roles of arbitrators and mediators. The critical difference between the two roles lies in the nature of decision-making. Arbitrators decide the outcome of parties' disputes. Mediators help the parties to decide the outcome themselves. This means, as Lon Fuller observed long ago, that the purpose of each of these processes has its own distinct moralities:

> The morality of mediation lies in optimum settlement, a settlement in which each party gives up what he values less, in return for what he values more. The morality of arbitration lies in a decision according to the law of the contract.[11]

[7] See Robert Bush, 'What Do We Need a Mediator For? Mediation's Value-Added for Negotiators', 12 Ohio St. J. on Disp. Res. 1 (1996); Roselle Wissler, 'The Effectiveness of Court-Connected Dispute Resolution in Civil Cases', 22 Conflict Resol Q. 55 (2004), 65, 68.

[8] Craig McEwen and Thomas Milburn, 'Explaining a Paradox of Mediation', 9 Neg. J. 23 (1993).

[9] Kenneth Arrow et al. (eds), *Barriers to Conflict Resolution* (W. W. Norton, 1995).

[10] Daniel Kahneman and Amos Tversky, 'Conflict Resolution: A Cognitive Perspective', in Arrow et al. (n. 9), 54–6.

[11] Lon Fuller, 'Collective Bargaining and the Arbitrator', 3 Wisconsin L. Rev. 3 (1963), 23–4.

Apart from Fuller's vision of 'distinct moralities', there are multiple process differences between arbitration and mediation. Arbitration is a formal process. Parties present proofs and arguments to the arbitrator to influence a decision in their favour. The arbitrator makes the final decision. Mediation is a less formal process: parties simply share their views of the situation with the mediator. Party self-determination is generally understood to be the quintessential principle of mediation. This means quite simply that the parties who are affected by a dispute decide the outcome of the dispute.

Communications with the neutral third party are also treated differently in each process. *Ex parte* communications with the arbitrator are generally not allowed, whereas the mediator may meet frequently in private caucuses with each of the parties in an effort to probe for mutual interests. Both arbitration and mediation are private processes, but mediation has greater confidentiality protections to limit the use in subsequent proceedings of evidence gleaned from the mediation process. The role of law is also different in each process. Arbitrators engaged in decision-making generally focus on the parties' legal rights. Mediators concentrate on the parties' underlying needs and interests when helping them reach an agreement. Law may be one of the values the parties consider in mediation, but it will not necessarily be determinative of the outcome. Finally, with respect to enforcement, mediation has lacked the enforcement regime of internationally agreed treaties, such as the UN Convention on Recognition and Enforcement of Arbitral Awards (New York Convention).[12] That gap may soon be closed. In 2018, the UN approved a convention for the enforcement of mediated settlement agreements, entitled the United Nations Convention on International Settlement Agreements Resulting from Mediation. This convention opened for signatures in August 2019 and will be called the Singapore Convention.[13]

Despite the essential differences between arbitration and mediation, there are significant commonalities. With the exception of mandatory court-connected programs, mediation and arbitration are both presumed to be consensual processes based on party autonomy. Mediation has an added layer of consent in that parties must agree not only to participate in the mediation process but also to accept the substantive outcome of the mediated agreement. Numerous ethical standards, including the Model Standards of Conduct for Mediators and the European Code of Conduct for Mediators, echo this requirement by emphasizing the importance of party self-determination. Both mediation and arbitration are governed by domestic legislation, and in the case of international disputes, both have the benefit of laws to govern in a transnational regime, the UNCITRAL Model Law on International Commercial Mediation and International Settlement Agreements Resulting from Mediation and the UNCITRAL Model Law on International Commercial Arbitration.[14] Finally, the end-game for both processes is the same—to achieve justice with efficiency in the resolution of disputes.

[12] E. A. Deason, 'Enforcement of Settlement Agreements in International Commercial Mediation: A New Legal Framework?', 22 Disp. Resol. Mag. 32 (2015).

[13] There will likely be a transitional period as countries decide whether to adopt the Singapore Convention.

[14] UNCITRAL (n. 4); UNCITRAL Model Law on International Commercial Arbitration (1985 with amendments as adopted in 2006).

11.3 Mediation, justice, and fairness

Scholars have advanced at least three goals of dispute settlement mechanisms. They should maximize party satisfaction, advance the rule of law, and promote substantive social values that are embodied in legal rules.[15] At a more basic level, the point of any dispute resolution system is to achieve justice. Mediation is no exception. Unlike the formal legal system with its multiple regulatory structures, mediation is informal justice which represents an equitable rather than legal regime in which parties design their own individualized justice. This results in customized solutions based on the parties' notions of procedural and substantive fairness.

Procedural justice is a primary goal of the mediation process, and it is directly linked to parties' perceptions of distributive justice. It focuses on parties' perceptions of fairness of the process that produced the outcome in a given case. Studies show that parties perceive consensual processes such as mediation to be fair because they offer a significant amount of process control, and this is true regardless of whether the process leads to a favourable outcome. Parties who believe that they have been treated fairly are more likely to believe that the outcome of the process is fair, that distributive justice has been achieved. They are then more likely to comply with the outcome.[16]

Mediators play a significant role in managing the parties' perceptions of fairness and justice. By providing parties with the opportunity to tell their story (voice), treating them respectfully, in an even-handed way, and with dignity, all characteristics of procedural justice, they enhance the parties' perceptions of fairness.[17] Mediators encourage parties to respect each other's preferences and values, thus giving them control of fairness. The parties decide what is fair as a matter of distributive justice. They do so based on competing considerations of equality, equity, need, or their own moral judgments.[18] These principles may provide them with solutions that are not available with adjudicative decision-making, relief such as apologies, reconciliation, and various forms of peace-making.

11.3.1 Mediation and equity

The presence of mediators in the global dispute resolution regime signals the strong influence of equity as mediation finds its roots in equity jurisprudence. Just as equity

[15] See e.g. Thomas Schultz, 'The Three Pursuits of Dispute Settlement,' 1 Czech (& Central European) Yearbook of Arbitration 227 (2010).

[16] Nancy Welsh, 'Perceptions of Fairness', in Andrea Schneider and Christopher Honeyman (eds), *The Negotiator's Fieldbook* (American Bar Association, 2006), 165, 170.

[17] Ibid. 170.

[18] See Johnathan Hyman, 'Beyond Fairness: The Place of Moral Foundations Theory in Mediation and Negotiation', 15 Nevada Law Journal 959 (2015), 961. See also Morton Deutsch, 'Justice and Conflict', in Morton Deutsch and Peter Coleman (eds), *The Handbook of Conflict Resolution: Theory and Practice*, 3rd edn (Jossey-Bass, 2014), 29.

sought to provide relief not available at common law, mediation promises relief from the rigidity of the courts and other adjudicative decision-making.[19] Of course, equity is not the sole province of mediators. Arbitrators may also apply general concepts of fairness and equity instead of strict adherence to the law when parties authorize them to act *ex aequo et bono* or as *amiable compositeur.* But they do so as adjudicators, and it could well be that an arbitrator's perception of what is equitable and fair may differ from that of the parties. Mediation offers an equity event because the outcome is determined by the parties themselves. It vests broad discretion in the disputing parties to resolve disputes based on their perceptions of individualized justice or what they believe to be fair.

The historic parallels between mediation and equity are relevant in shaping our ideas about justice in transnational dispute resolution. Mediation, like equity, was conceived of as justice without law. It offers the possibility of individualized justice, which may be in tension with strict legal justice. It prevents the law from interfering with 'the need to do justice' in a particular case. Just as equity moderated the rigidity of the common law by integrating fairness and moral values into the judicial process, mediation offers fair alternatives to legal values and judicial and arbitral decision-making. Soft law guidelines in the form of professional codes direct mediators to promote agreements that are fair according to prevailing social standards. The UNCITRAL Model Law on International Commercial Mediation and International Settlement Agreements Resulting from Mediation, Art. 7, provides a clear example with its admonition that 'in conducting the proceedings, the mediator shall seek to maintain fair treatment of the parties and, in so doing, shall take into account the circumstances of the case'. Finally, just as equity offered relief from harsh pleadings and procedural rules that operated to deny disputants justice in the common law courts, mediation offers relief from the rigidity of a rules-bound justice system.

11.3.2 Mediators and justice

Mediation provides the opportunity for individualized justice through the exercise of party self-determination and the expression of dignity. While this may be true in theory, in practice the value of self-determination is dependent on context and culture. The western-influenced Model Standards of Conduct for Mediators emphasize the primacy of party self-determination by ranking it first in its list of ethical standards. Mediators from non-western countries, however, view self-determination in a different light. In China for example, mediators are influenced more by traditional Confucian values of compromise to preserve harmony and personal relationships than they are by the Model Standards' emphasis on party self-determination.[20]

[19] Jacqueline Nolan-Haley, 'Merger of Law and Mediation: Lessons from Equity Jurisprudence and Roscoe Pound', 6 Cardozo J. Conflict Resol. 57 (2005).

[20] Jacqueline Nolan-Haley, Harold Abramson, and Pat Chew, *International Conflict Resolution: Consensual ADR Processes* (Thomson West, 2005), 134.

Most accounts of self-determination in mediation claim that its value lies in its support for autonomy and dignity. In reality, the autonomy narrative often depends upon the mediator's behavioral approach to achieving justice in mediation. How mediators conduct themselves in mediation, the model they choose, is often a function of their definition of and thoughts about mediation in relationship to justice. Mediation literature is replete with core definitional questions: Is mediation simply a settlement process? Is it about empowerment and recognition? Is it about transformation? The pragmatic goal of most mediators is to reduce conflict and resolve it through an agreement. Some mediators may have an alternative agenda that seeks to empower parties, help them improve relationships, or provide greater understanding of each other. Despite the competing definitions of mediation, most commentators agree that the purpose of mediation is to assist disputing parties in reaching a consensual resolution of their dispute. Mediators typically do this by engaging in a variety of behaviours and models that have given rise to a dizzying array of options including: facilitative, evaluative, transformative, narrative, understanding-based, and wisely directive mediation. There are variations within each model, depending on the mediator's style. The core difference among models is how directive the mediator is with respect to shaping the substantive outcome.

The most commonly discussed models of mediator behaviors are the *facilitative* and *evaluative* approaches. The *facilitative* approach represents the traditional understanding of mediation as a relational process, a concept famously expressed in Lon Fuller's description of mediation's 'capacity to reorient the parties towards each other, not by imposing rules on them, but by helping them to achieve a new and shared perception of their relationship, a perception that will redirect their attitudes and dispositions toward one another'.[21] Contemporary mediation discourse engages with additional values from empowerment to efficiency, while the relational story is less prominent. Nevertheless, the relational story remains an enduring reminder of mediation's intrinsic value. *Facilitative* mediators respect the parties' autonomy and their ability to make decisions. They help parties to reach agreement by focusing on their underlying needs and interests, suggesting questions for them to consider, framing and reframing issues. *Evaluative* mediation (often favoured by lawyers) involves the mediator in active engagement by providing the parties with some form of assessment. This mediator offers information that leads parties to settlement, whether it is a legal evaluation on the merits, a mediator's proposal for settlement, or a gentle nudge toward a particular result. The mediator's proposal might look very much like an arbitrator facilitating settlement.

In reality, the dichotomy between *facilitative* and *evaluative* behaviours is a false one. There is no 'pure' facilitation or evaluation, but a range of mediation activities that can be mapped between the extremes of these two poles.[22] When it comes to the behaviour of mediators and parties, a diverse range of expectations exist, all of which are highly

[21] Lon Fuller, 'Mediation: Its Forms and Functions', 44 S. Cal. L. Rev. 305 (1971), 325.

[22] Leonard Riskin, 'Decision-Making in Mediation, The New Old Grid and the New Grid System', 79 Notre Dame L. Rev. 1 (2003).

dependent on context. Even the meaning of the terms *facilitative* and *evaluative* may vary in different countries.

A variation of the *evaluative* approach is the *wisely directive* model found in some Islamic countries and China among other areas. This mediator is a repository of knowledge, and promotes specific solutions based on any number of values derived from law, religion, and culture. The parties expect to receive an evaluation from this mediator who in turn expects the parties to follow it.[23]

Transformative mediation focuses on communications and relationships. Rather than emphasizing settlement through problem-solving as the goal for the parties, the transformative mediator guides the parties to determine their own direction and supports the parties' deliberations and decision-making. The mediator focuses on the parties' communications and interactions, encouraging them to move away from negative behaviours to empowerment and recognizing the perspectives of others.[24]

Narrative mediation, also considered a transformative process, is a story-telling model of mediation. It examines the sociocultural context within which conflict arises. Narrative theory claims that the stories parties tell about themselves and their conflict shape their perceptions and reactions to the conflict. Rather than emphasizing facts, the mediator attempts to help the parties uncover their biases and assumptions in order to create solutions to conflict.[25]

The *understanding-based* model is founded on the premise that when parties have a complete understanding of their own and the other's perspectives, resolution is possible. After gaining a deep understanding of the whole situation, parties are able to craft creative and satisfactory solutions that reflect their multiple interests. A key aspect of this model is collaboration with the mediator, parties, and lawyers (if they are involved), all working together. Thus, there is no place for caucusing or other forms of shuttle diplomacy.[26]

11.4 The Growth of International Mediation

Within the field of ADR, arbitration has long been the preferred mode of resolving international commercial disputes. This preference has given arbitrators a starring role on the international dispute resolution stage, leaving mediators on the sidelines.

[23] Nolan-Haley et al. (n. 20), 132.

[24] Robert Bush and Joseph Folger, *The Promise of Mediation: The Transformative Approach to Conflict*, rev. edn (Jossey-Bass, 2004).

[25] John Winslade and Gearld Monk, *Narrative Mediation: A New Approach to Conflict Resolution* (Jossey-Bass, 2000).

[26] Gary Friedman and Jack Himmelstein, *Challenging Conflict: Mediation Through Understanding* (Jossey-Bass, 2008).

Arbitration's promises of speed, finality, reduced costs, and expertise are all distinct benefits that matter to global businesses. In recent years, however, there has been growing unease with the increasingly adversarial flavour of international arbitration. There is the perception that it has become too much like the American litigation model, with discovery, delay tactics, and the high costs that accompany these practices. All of this can have a negative impact on maintaining long-term commercial relationships and developing cross-border initiatives. With increased litigation over foreign arbitration awards, certainty of enforcing arbitration awards in foreign countries has declined.[27] Lack of judicial independence, corruption, or inability to locate the assets of the award debtor have chipped away at certain enforcement of arbitration awards. In addition to high arbitration costs, there have been costs to business opportunity linked with an adversarial dispute settlement mechanism, and this has also played a role in the growth of mediation. In short, disenchantment with many aspects of international arbitration has opened space for mediation to blossom. The upshot is that mediators are becoming significant actors in transnational dispute resolution practice.[28]

11.4.1 Mediation's growing and visible role in international dispute resolution

In an increasingly competitive global economy, a larger number of international businesses are seeking lower costs and more efficient cross-border dispute resolution mechanisms. These businesses have turned to mediation, which can provide the services of global dispute resolution as part of a large array of approaches to the resolution of disputes. The growing interest in mediation as an international dispute resolution process is reflected in the activities of numerous international and regional organizations, laws, and protocols. Private provider organizations, formerly devoted to arbitration, have expanded their focus and now offer rules and procedures to resolve commercial disputes through mediation. Notable examples include organizations such as the International Centre for Dispute Resolution (ICDR), the World Intellectual Property Organization (WIPO), the London Court of International Arbitration, (LCIA), the CPR International Institute for Conflict Prevention & Resolution, and the International Chamber of Commerce (ICC). The World Bank, working with the International Finance Corporation, is also promoting international commercial mediation, and the World Trade Organization's (WTO) dispute settlement system offers mediation as one method of resolving trade disputes between members.[29]

[27] Carrie Menkel-Meadow, 'Variations in the Uptake of and Resistance to Mediation Outside of the United States', in Arthur Rovine (eds), *Contemporary Issues in International Arbitration and Mediation: The Fordham Papers* (Brill/Nijhoff, 2014), 210--11, n. 78.

[28] See Thomas Stipanowich, 'The International Evolution of Mediation: A Call for Dialogue and Deliberation', 46 VUWLR 1191 (2015).

[29] S. I. Strong, 'Beyond International Commercial Arbitration? The Promise of International Commercial Mediation', 45 Wash. U.J.L. & Pol'y 11 (2014).

Many jurisdictions have adopted separate legislation to govern mediation practice. From the UNCITRAL Model Law on International Commercial Mediation and International Settlement Agreements Resulting from Mediation to the EU Mediation Directive,[30] the landscape is covered with multiple regulatory frameworks on topics such as mediator accreditation, confidentiality, and good-faith participation.[31] Soft law guidelines are also available as evidenced by the International Bar Association's (IBA) approval of rules for investor–state mediation and the ICC Mediation Rules. Similarly, the International Mediation Institute (IMI), established in the Hague, has undertaken numerous efforts to provide standards and quality in mediation practice as well as in the underdeveloped area of mediation advocacy.

Over the last two decades, several countries, notably in the European Union and the United States, have intentionally promoted mediation and other forms of ADR to advance access to justice. They have engaged in this project with a high degree of intensity, funding mediation programs in commercial and public justice areas, mandating mediation in court systems, and issuing directives. The preamble of the EU Mediation Directive simply assumes that mediation provides access to justice. Mediation has also been exported from developed to developing countries, often promoted under the banner of access to justice.[32] Over the years, however, critics have questioned whether mediation has delivered on its promise of providing access to justice, claiming that it offers only a path to escape the vagaries of the adjudication process, that consent is often coerced, and that it amounts to second-class justice for the poor who bargain in the shadow of power imbalances.[33]

11.4.2 Resistance to mediation

A notable feature of modern mediation development is pushback from potential users. European resistance to mediation has been documented in the European Parliament Report, 'Rebooting the Mediation Directive: Assessing the Limited Impact of Its Implementation and Proposing Measures to Increase the Number of Mediations in the EU'.[34] In some emerging democratic African countries, mediation's focus on the goals of settlement and peacemaking has been resisted. For some parties, these goals require too much compromise, posing a threat to their legal and customary rights. Resistance may

[30] See UNCITRAL (n. 4); EU Mediation Directive 2008/52/EC (2008).

[31] Manon Schonewille and Fred Schonewille (eds), *The Variegated Landscape of Mediation: A Comparative Study of Mediation Regulation and Practices in Europe and the World* (Eleven International, 2014), 23.

[32] Jacqueline Nolan-Haley, 'Mediation and Access to Justice in Africa: Perspectives from Ghana', 21 Harv. Neg. L. Rev. 59 (2015), 62.

[33] See e.g. Hazel Genn, *Judging Civil Justice: The Hamlyn Lectures* (Cambridge University Press, 2010), 78–125; Owen Fiss, 'Against Settlement', 93 Yale L.J. 1073 (1984).

[34] 'Rebooting the Mediation Directive: Assessing the Limited Impact of its Implementation and Proposing Measures to Increase the Number of Mediations in the EU' (2014): <http://www.europarl.europa.eu/RegData/etudes/etudes/join/2014/493042/IPOL-JURI_ET(2014)493042_EN.pdf>.

also come from lawyers who resent the involvement of mediators in their clients' business, and who are or choose to be unfamiliar with how mediation operates or how to represent clients in the mediation process.

Resistance to mediation arises from one of the more contested issues in contemporary mediation practice, which is whether courts have the power to compel parties to participate in mediation when they have not consented to do so. Even within the same legal cultural traditions, no consensus on the legitimacy of compulsory mediation exists. Consider two common law cultures, the United States and England. US courts have upheld mandatory mediation programmes so long as parties are not coerced to reach an agreement. Compulsion is viewed as permissible regarding entry into the process but not during the process. English courts, on the other hand, following the lead of *Halsey v Milton Keynes General NHS Trust and Steel v Joy* (2004),[35] do not require unwilling parties to mediate their cases because compulsory referral would violate a litigant's fundamental rights to have access to the courts and would run afoul of Art. 6 of the European Convention on Human Rights. While compulsory referral to mediation is considered unacceptable in England, encouragement to use ADR can be robust. *Halsey* upheld a court's right to impose costs on a party who has unreasonably refused to consent to mediate. This represented a departure from the general English rule on costs.

Focusing on these two common law jurisdictions reveals a story about 'mediation exceptionality', about treating mediation differently from other non-adjudicatory processes in both jurisdictions. One of the primary features of mediation exceptionality is the different manner in which mediation is first promoted and then delivered. In the United States, mediation is, in theory, a voluntary consensual process based on the principle of party self-determination. But in practice, it is frequently delivered as a compulsory process. Many court programmes require that parties participate in mediation as a condition precedent to having a trial. Mediation is also promoted as a consensual process in England, but it is delivered under the shadow of the court's power to penalize parties who resist the court's invitation to mediate. The infusion of non-consensual attributes into mediation, particularly in court-related programmes, is one of the distinct features of mediation not shared by other non-adjudicatory dispute resolution processes.

Another example of exceptionality with regard to other non-adjudicatory processes is mediation's departure from the application of general legal rules. In England, instead of the usual rule that the unsuccessful party will pay the costs of the successful party, mediation presents the exceptional case where costs may be imposed on a successful party whose consent to mediation is deemed to have been withheld unreasonably.[36] In the United States, application of the usual rules of contract law to mediation has been questioned by those scholars who argue that mediated agreements should be treated differently from standard contracts—that laws should provide for

[35] *Halsey v Milton Keynes General NHS Trust and Steel v Joy*, [2004] EWCA (Civ) 576.

[36] Jacqueline Nolan-Haley, 'Mediation Exceptionality', 78 Fordham L. Rev. 1247 (2009).

cooling-off periods before mediated agreements take effect so that parties have the opportunity to exercise a right of rescission.[37]

11.4.3 Legal issues

Paradoxically, mediation, which is both an alternative and a complement to the adversary system of justice, has spurned its own path to litigation, requiring a return to the adversary system to resolve disputes. Based on research conducted in the United States, three areas which have generated substantial mediation litigation are issues related to good faith participation in mediation, breaches of confidentiality, and the enforceability of mediation agreements.[38] Enforceability continues to be a concern in the international arena, both with agreements to mediate and with those which result from a mediation.

With respect to agreements to mediate, it is not uncommon for parties to provide for mediation in a pre-dispute escalation clause. The primary legal issue relates to whether mediation was a condition precedent to the commencement of arbitration or court proceedings. If the language of the clause indicates clearly that mediation must first be commenced within a particular period of time, attempts have been made to vacate arbitral awards in court because the arbitration was commenced prematurely.[39] Courts in Europe and the United States generally enforce multi-tier dispute resolution clauses. A strict approach in considering the parties' obligation to mediate may be adopted, denying costs to a party because of its unreasonable refusal to recognize a request to mediate. Arbitral tribunals, on the other hand, tend to accept jurisdiction and proceed with arbitration even in the face of a clear breach of an agreement to mediate.[40] As a result of this disparity, some scholars have called for an international convention regarding enforcement of parties' agreements to mediate.[41]

The enforcement of mediated settlement agreements raises different challenges, one of which has been the lack of an international regime that supports enforcement. It is not clear whether and to what extent mediated settlement agreements are enforceable under contemporary international dispute resolution because until recently, mediation did not have the benefit of an international enforcement protocol such as the New York Convention which upholds arbitral awards. Enforcement practice varies in different jurisdictions. In some countries mediated settlements are enforced as court judgments.[42] In others, arbitral tribunals are able to convert mediated settlement agreements into

[37] Nancy Welsh, 'The Thinning Vision of Self Determination in Court-Connected Mediation: The Inevitable Price of Institutionalization?', 6 Harv. Neg. L. Rev. 1 (2001), at 86.

[38] See James Coben and Peter Thompson, 'Disputing Irony: A Systematic Look at Litigation about Mediation', 11 Harv. Neg. L. Rev. 43 (2006).

[39] Paul Mason, 'The Arbitrator as Mediator, and Mediator as Arbitrator', 28 J. of Int'l Arb. 41 (2011).

[40] CEDR Commission on Settlement in International Arbitration, 'Final Report' (2009): <http://www.cedr.com/about_us/arbitration_commission/Arbitration_Commission_Doc_Final.pdf>.

[41] Strong (n. 29), 32.

[42] Alexander (n. 5), 307–10.

arbitral awards.[43] In American cases, parties would generally attempt to use contract law to enforce mediated agreements. Going forward, efforts by UNCITRAL should prove helpful in establishing an enforcement regime for mediated settlement agreements. In 2018 the United Nations approved the UN Convention on International Settlement Agreements Resulting from Mediation (Singapore Convention). In addition, UNCITRAL amended its Model Law on International Commercial Conciliation to be consistent with the Convention. It was renamed the UNCITRAL Model Law on International Commercial Mediation and International Settlement Agreements Resulting from Mediation. As countries begin to adopt these instruments, there should be more certainty regarding the enforceability of agreements resulting from mediation.

11.4.4 Convergences: mediation—the new arbitration

Much has been written about international arbitration's drift towards the litigation arena due to the influence of Anglo-American adversarial behaviours[44] as well as mediation's foray into the arbitration arena. At the same time, empirical studies show that mediation and other forms of settlement are becoming common in the course of commercial arbitral proceedings.[45] In recent years, mediation and arbitration practices have gradually converged, blending boundaries with arbitration's push toward settlement and mediation's assumption of aspects of arbitration. In many respects, the roles of arbitrator and mediator are becoming increasingly interconnected. Arbitrators are adopting facilitative approaches, and mediators are leaning towards adjudicatory modes of behaviour.

Mediation's transition to arbitral modes of behavior is due in large measure to the increased presence of lawyers representing parties in mediation or 'legal mediation'. Lawyers' behaviour in international mediation has been described as similar to conduct in a 'mini arbitration'.[46] Lawyers have subtly changed the traditional dynamic in mediation from an interest-based to a rights-based process, a transition consistent with the lawyers' philosophical preference for a distributive adversarial framework. Legal mediation has taken on many of the features traditionally associated with arbitration such as adversarial posturing by attorneys in the name of zealous advocacy, adjudication by neutral third parties, and the practice of attempting to influence the mediator (spinning). The lawyer representing a party in mediation attempts to 'spin' the mediator to be helpful in achieving a desired outcome whether through persuasion, strong evaluations, or mediator proposals. Studies show that lawyers generally control the

[43] Ibid. 310–12.

[44] Klaus Berger, 'Integration of Mediation Elements into Arbitration: "Hybrid" Procedures and "Intuitive" Mediation by International Arbitrators', 19 Arbitration International 387 (2003), 390.

[45] Thomas Stipanowich and Zachary Ulrich, 'Commercial Arbitration and Settlement: Empirical Insights into the Roles Arbitrators Play', 6 Penn St. Y.B. on Arb. & Mediation 1 (2014), 25.

[46] Eric Schwartz, 'International Conciliation and the ICC', 10 ICSID Rev. Foreign Investment L.J. 98 (1995), 112.

mediation process, often preferring evaluative models.[47] With the growth of legal mediation and lawyers' interest in receiving evaluations, mediators are moving toward a decision-making mode, once exclusively the province of arbitrators. It is not surprising, then, that some marketing materials for international arbitration conferences are directed to mediators. While mediators move toward a decision-making mode, arbitrators are moving in the opposite direction of bringing the parties together to reach a solution.

11.5 Mediators, Arbitrators, and Settlement

There is nothing new about combining mediation with arbitration. In ancient civilizations, blending mediation and adjudication was a natural way to achieve harmony and resolve disputes in civil society. Disputing parties sought out a trusted member of the community to help them find a solution. That third party would first seek to have the parties reconcile before imposing any decision.[48]

The pragmatic narrative accounting for this modern development of hybridization might be simply that settlement in arbitration, including mediation, is an idea whose time has come. An equally plausible, albeit more altruistic, account is that mediation's interest-based approach to problem-solving has inspired the work of many arbitrators who seek to achieve efficiency, cost-effectiveness, and just outcomes with dignity. Whether arbitrators have a duty to encourage mediation and other forms of settlement remains unclear.[49] Some scholars believe that arbitrators have a duty to inquire about whether they can assist parties in settlement.[50] Other scholars encourage arbitrators to settle, arguing that the optimal time to resolve an international business dispute is after the commencement of an international arbitration proceeding.[51] Still others argue that in appropriate circumstances, whether as a matter of duty or of good practice, arbitrators should encourage settlement.[52] Theoretically, at least, coupling and uncoupling arbitration and mediation at different points within one process may suggest a function of dispute systems design principles. However far this theory may be carried, the mixture of aspects of mediation within arbitration and arbitration within mediation carries

[47] Jacqueline Nolan-Haley, 'Mediation: The "New Arbitration"', 17 Harv. Neg. L. Rev. 61 (2012).

[48] Christian Buhring-Uhle, Lars Kirchhoff, and Gabriele Scherer, *Arbitration and Mediation in International Business*, 2nd edn (Kluwer Law International, 2006). Dilyara Nigmatullina, *Combining Mediation and Arbitration in International Commercial Dispute Resolution* (Routledge 2019).

[49] Catherine Rogers, *Ethics in International Arbitration* (Oxford University Press, 2014), 96–7.

[50] Henry Brown and Arthur Marriott, *ADR Principles and Practice*, 3rd edn (Sweet & Maxwell, 2012).

[51] Harold Abramson, 'Protocols for International Arbitrators Who Dare to Settle Cases', 10 Am. Rev. Int'l Arb. 1 (1999), 2.

[52] Michael Collins, 'Do International Arbitral Tribunals Have Any Obligation to Encourage Settlement of the Disputes Before Them?', 19 Arbitration International 333 (2003).

practical consequences for the parties, as will become apparent during the development of the themes in this chapter.

It is not clear from the empirical studies the degree to which arbitrator settlement activity is authentic mediation, how much is simply incorporating mediative elements into the arbitral proceedings, how much is raw settlement protocol, and how much is arbitrators simply converting settlement conferences into mediation. To the extent that mediation of some kind is occurring as a result of arbitrators' activities, we have limited information about what happens during the process. The blanket of confidentiality in mediation limits disclosure more than litigation and arbitration do. Case reports are found in anecdotal stories by mediators and in litigated mediation cases. Limited studies based on direct observations of mediation, user surveys, and transcriptions of actual mediation sessions have been available for some time.[53]

11.5.1 Cultural differences: the civil law, common law divide

A variety of different forms of arbitration include notions of compromise, social justice and equity.[54] Similarly, the arbitrator's role in mediation and other forms of settlement also varies, depending upon legal and cultural contexts. In some cases arbitrators simply establish the groundwork for settlement by managing the pre-hearing process, ruling on dispositive motions, etc. In other cases, they actively contribute to bringing about settlement through informal discussions with parties about their legal rights. Alternatively, arbitrators may transition into the role of mediator by engaging in hybrid processes that intentionally combine mediation with arbitration. Such chameleon-like behaviour is not unique to arbitrators. Rather, hybrid combinations correspond to new forms of judicial dispute resolution, which Judith Resnik has characterized 'the privatization of process'. Judges add mediation and other methods of dispute resolution to their adjudicative role in this process.[55]

Scholars believe that arbitrators perceive their role in encouraging mediation and other forms of settlement according to the legal culture with which they are most familiar, such as the manner in which judges perform their adjudicatory functions in that legal culture.[56] In some respects, a civil law/common law divide reflects those respective approaches to judicial dispute resolution—inquisitorial in the civil law and adversarial in the common law. Understanding this relationship helps to explain why an arbitrator from the common law tradition might be unwilling to assist the parties in negotiating a

[53] See e.g. Coben and Thompson (n. 38); Deborah Kolb, *When Talk Works: Profiles of Mediators* (Jossey-Bass, 1994).

[54] See Yuval Sinai, and Michal Alberstein, 'Court Arbitration by Compromise: Rethinking Delaware's State Sponsored Arbitration Case', 13 Cardozo Pub. L. Pol'y & Ethics J. 739 (2015).

[55] Judith Resnik, 'The Privatization of Process: Requiem for and Celebration of the Federal Rules of Civil Procedure at 75', 162 U. Penn L. Rev. 1793 (2014).

[56] Chistpher Koch and Eric Schafer, 'Can It Be Sinful for an Arbitrator Actively to Promote Settlement?', Arbitration and Dispute Resolution Law Journal 147 (1999), 153–4.

mutually acceptable solution, or why his or her counterpart from a civil law jurisdiction might be more disposed to explore the possibilities of settlement.

11.5.2 Combining mediation and arbitration

Mediation now occurring within international arbitration may arise from ad hoc mediation agreements, pre-dispute, or contractual escalation clauses or through a mediation 'window', a concept introduced by the CEDR Commission on Settlement in International Arbitration in 2009. This window provides a deliberate pause in the arbitral proceedings to promote the mediation process. If all the parties request mediation, the arbitrator may adjourn the arbitration proceedings to allow mediation to take place. Finally, mediation may take place in one of the more contested hybrid processes such as arb-med or med-arb. Each process has distinct characteristics.

The arb-med process begins with arbitration and then shifts at some point in the proceeding to mediation. There are a number of variations to this scheme. One model involves a process of completed arbitration, followed by the tribunal's rendering its award without disclosing it to the parties. A mediator (not one of the arbitrators) then helps to facilitate a negotiated settlement with the parties. Either party is free to terminate the mediation and accept the tribunal's award.[57] In another variation, US mediator Kenneth Feinberg begins the process by hearing all parties. He then prepares a written non-binding settlement recommendation and transitions into a private mediation session where, referring to his recommendation, he attempts to persuade parties to minimize their differences.[58] Proponents claim that arb-med champions the value of self-determination by encouraging disputing parties to settle their differences themselves. Critics are concerned with the potential for coercion, arguing that parties may feel pressured to agree during mediation because of a recommendation made by a third party whose arbitration decision lurks somewhere in the background.[59]

In reverse fashion, med-arb, also referred to as intra-arbitral mediation,[60] begins with mediation, and if the mediation is unsuccessful in achieving a settlement, the process changes to arbitration. Some commentators have suggested that there is more talk and commentary than action involving international use of the med-arb process, and the virtues and vices of this hybrid process are still not the subject of a meaningful scholarly consensus.[61] Supporters claim that med-arb advances the values of finality, flexibility,

[57] Michael McIlwrath and John Savage, *International Arbitration and Mediation: A Practical Guide* (Kluwer Law International, 2010).

[58] Kenneth Feinberg, 'Mediation: A Preferred Method of Dispute Resolution', 16 Pepperdine L. Rev. 5 (1989).

[59] William Ross and Donald Conlon, 'Hybrid Forms of Third Party Dispute Resolution: Theoretical Implications of Combining Mediation and Arbitration', 25 Academy of Management Review 416 (2000), 424.

[60] Neil Andrews, *Andrews on Civil Processes*, vol. 2: *Arbitration and Mediation* (Intersentia, 2013), 67.

[61] McIlwrath and Savage (n. 57).

and efficiency and that it will lead to greater perceptions of procedural and distributive justice. To the extent that parties believe they have been treated fairly, the parties are more likely to comply with arbitral rulings.[62]

Critics point to the lack of due process protections for parties during the transition from mediation to arbitration.[63] As parties lose the opportunity to share confidential information with the mediator, a primary benefit of mediation, the process is more accurately a pre-arbitration hearing. Critics also paint a stark picture of the dark side of med-arb by arguing that as arbitration begins to resemble the more expensive litigation, mediation's ascendancy casts a shadow on the economics of private arbitration practice. Thus, far from providing benefits, med-arb is encouraged by arbitrators to enhance the profitability of arbitration by including a mediation segment and 'selling the two processes as one package'.[64]

11.5.2.1 *Ethical issues*

Combining arbitration and mediation raises the serious ethical issue of whether one person should assume the dual roles of mediator and arbitrator in the same case. In addition to legal questions related to the appropriate role of judicial review, there are practical concerns with this duality.[65] The purist wonders how one person can serve in both positions. Very different sets of skills and perspectives are required in each role: the number of individuals qualified to serve in both roles must surely be limited. Beyond the practical concerns, the most common objection to the use of the same neutral party in both the mediation and arbitration process is the threat to mediation's core principles of self-determination, impartiality, and confidentiality. Critics claim that even the parties' informed consent cannot cure defects in the med-arb process. While informed consent may seem in principle to be a solution, the reality is otherwise. Parties may be less willing to share information in the mediation session if they know it will turn into an adjudication process. Those who do disclose information may fear possible bias by the neutral party, now the mediator and later the arbitrator. Finally, med-arb may incentivize adversarial behaviour if attorneys misuse the mediation by turning it into an advocacy process and trying to persuade the neutral to rule in their favour.[66]

As with the practice of arbitrator facilitation of settlement, there are different views shaped by legal culture on the propriety of using the same neutral party in both processes. The dominant view in the United States and many other western countries is that the same individual should not serve in both roles in the same case.[67] This position is

62 Ross and Conlon (n. 59), 424.

63 Brian Kelso, 'Drawing Outside the Lines: Utilizing International Approaches to Resolve Due Process Concerns in Med-Arb' (Mayhew–Hite Report, 20 November 2015): <http://moritzlaw.osu.edu/mayhew-hite-report/2015/11/20/kelso-placeholder/>.

64 Brian Pappas, 'Med-Arb and the Legalization of Alternative Dispute Resolution', 20 Harv. Neg. L. Rev. 157 (2015), 169.

65 Ellen Deason, 'Combinations of Mediation and Arbitration with the Same Neutral: A Framework for Judicial Review', 5 Y.B. on Arb. & Mediation 219 (2013).

66 Pappas (n. 64).

67 Stipanowich and Ulrich (n. 45), 25.

reflected in the UNCITRAL Model Law on International Commercial Mediation and International Settlement Agreements Resulting from Mediation, Art. 13 (2018). In comparison, some eastern cultures do permit the same person to serve as a mediator and arbitrator. In China for example, where amicable dispute resolution is embedded in the legal system, mediation is frequently used in arbitration proceedings. Arbitrators enjoy wide discretion to adopt any method that they consider appropriate in furthering mediation, as long as the parties agree.[68] Recent commentators, giving credence to the critics, have discussed some of the problems which undermine the quality and effectiveness of mediation in mainland China where, as discussed earlier in this chapter, judges exercise the dual roles of mediator and adjudicator. Many parties are unwilling to speak freely in mediation for fear that what they say may be used against them in later legal proceedings.[69]

A frequent objection to the use of the same neutral party in hybrid dispute resolution processes such as med-arb is its debilitating effects on the value of neutrality—a term for which there are multiple and sometimes conflicting definitions. Often equated with impartiality (rightly or wrongly), neutrality is viewed by many as an important and legitimizing aspect of mediation practice for which several countries have created standards to provide guidance. Likewise, international organizations such as the United Nations, ICC, and WTO have all established standards governing neutrality and impartiality in mediation. The U.S. Model Standards of Conduct for Mediators and the European Code of Conduct for Mediators require that mediators act with impartiality towards the parties. Placing more emphasis on fairness, the IMI Code of Professional Conduct requires mediators to 'act in an unbiased manner, treating all parties with fairness, quality and respect'.

But neutrality is not a universally shared or core value of mediation. Some scholars argue that it may be unrealistic for mediators to offer neutrality to the parties. For some, fairness can trump neutrality, a claim illustrated in the famous exchange between Lawrence Susskind and Joshua Stulberg in the 1980s. Susskind argued that mediators had the responsibility to assure that there are fair outcomes in mediation and that they lead to socially desirable outcomes. Stulberg replied that no such responsibility existed and that justice demands mediator neutrality. Almost four decades years later, neither one has changed his position.[70] Others have alluded to the mythical quality of neutrality in mediation, and Roger Fisher of *Getting to Yes* famously once described a neutral mediator as 'a eunuch from Mars, totally powerless'.[71] In the final analysis, neutrality is a relative concept which must therefore be considered in context. In cultures which adhere to the *wisely directive* mediator approach, a neutral mediator would be considered

[68] J. Fei and D. Gu, 'Methods of Facilitating Mediation by Arbitrators in China', New York Dispute Resolution Lawyer 43 (2016), 45.

[69] Lee (n. 3).

[70] Bernie Mayer, 'What We Talk About When We Talk About Neutrality: A Commentary on the Susskind-Stulberg Debate, 2011 Edition', 95 Marq. L. Rev. 859 (2012).

[71] Melissa Katsoris, 'Does Nationality Influence Neutrality? The Ethical Standards and Expectations of International Mediators', 39 Fordham Internat'l L. J. 695 (2016), 700 n. 20.

unhelpful at the very least. Similarly, in the political context of peacekeeping mediation efforts, neutrality has limitations. This is illustrated by former UN Secretary General Kofi Annan's admonition that 'impartiality does not—and must not—mean neutrality in the face of evil'.[72] There is also the risk that one of the party's stance in a mediation process may influence the way the arbitrator will perceive the same party (and its case) at the later stage of arbitration.

Finally, using the same neutral in hybrid processes presents risks to confidentiality, an important feature of the mediation process. Communications made in mediation are protected from disclosure in varying degrees depending upon jurisdiction. Confidentiality protections are also incorporated into ethical guidelines for mediators. Critics argue that by using the same neutral in the med-arb process, confidentiality is essentially lost.[73] Even when two different neutrals are involved, ethical issues arise regarding the permissible limits of communication between two different neutrals in the course of resolving disputes.

11.5.2.2 *Informed consent*

Informed consent is an ethical, moral, and legal concept that is deeply ingrained in many cultures and required in many disparate activities. In transactions requiring informed consent, the legal doctrine defines individual consent as competent, informed about the particular intervention, and voluntary. Informed consent is the foundational moral and ethical principle that promotes respect for individual self-determination and honors human dignity.

In mediation practice, the principle of informed consent is not an end in itself but a means to achieve the fundamental goal of fairness. Fairness requires that parties know what they are doing when they decide to participate in mediation, that they understand all aspects of the decision-making process, and that they understand the outcome in mediation. Toward this end, the principle of informed consent in mediation protects the psychological and legal interests associated with the values of autonomy, human dignity, and efficiency.[74]

Disclosure requirements for mediators are a prevailing feature in the informed consent regime of many mediation statutes and ethical standards. Regulations vary in the amount and type of information that parties receive. Some states have elaborate disclosure provisions while others take a limited approach. At a minimum, most regulations require mediators to provide procedural information about mediation. Beyond basic process information, disclosure requirements may include information about how mediation differs from other forms of conflict resolution, any mediator conflicts of interest, relevant laws, costs, and settlement options.

[72] 'Secretary General Reflects on Promise, Realities of his Role in World Affairs, in Address to Council on Foreign Relations', UN press release SG/SM/6865 (19 Jan. 1999).

[73] Pappas (n. 64), 172–8.

[74] Jacqueline Nolan-Haley, 'Informed Consent in Mediation: A Guiding Principle for Truly Educated Decisionmaking', 74 Notre Dame L. Rev. 775 (1998).

The cloak of informed consent offers protective coverage for party participation in various forms of med-arb and arb-med. Scholars who approve of these hybrids based on the principle of party self-determination and autonomy condition their endorsement on the informed consent of the parties. Many rules of dispute resolution institutions which provide oversight supervision for these hybrid processes also require consent (ICC Rules of Arbitration). Similarly, soft law and other professional guidelines focus on the importance of obtaining the parties' consent (IBA Guidelines on Conflict of Interest). In some jurisdictions written consent signed by the parties may be required for legal efficacy.

Informed consent seems to be the magic wand that serves as an effective waiver of any potential conflicts of interest which might affect the third party acting as a neutral person in a combined mediation and arbitration process. Yet it may be a deceptive magic wand. Some scholars have criticized existing rules and guidelines for the lack of attention paid to the psychological ramifications of shifting from the role of adjudicator to that of facilitator and vice versa. They question whether these rules take into account the complex psychological factors involved in international arbitration.[75] Recent empirical research on arbitrators' decision-making supports this critique. Arbitrators (like judges) can be biased in their decision-making. They tend to make intuitive decisions, and are influenced by cognitive illusions such as anchoring and framing which can be powerful influences on how parties make decisions.[76] Finally, the magic wand of informed consent practices might be ineffective in resolving questions depending on the sufficiency of a mediator's disclosure.

11.6 Challenges Going Forward

This chapter has offered a reality check on the practices of mediation embedded in many ways with arbitration practice and regulated in the international arena. Convergences with arbitration and mediation have produced hybrid processes, now a vibrant part of transnational dispute systems design. This hybridization suggests a growing realization that access to justice might be better achieved not only outside the courtroom but also outside the arbitration process or integrated with the arbitration process. Players in the global dispute resolution arena are becoming more sophisticated. Their conflicts are becoming increasingly complex and may require integrated solutions such as combinations of mediation and arbitration.

Going forward, we should focus on improving the quality and effectiveness of the current transnational dispute resolution regime where arbitrators are accustomed to dealing in a harmonized world with laws and rules while mediators' comfort zones lie

[75] Sophie Nappert and Dieter Flader, 'A Psychological Perspective on the Facilitation of Settlement in International Arbitration: Examining the CEDR Rules', 2 J. Int. Disp Settlement 459 (2011).

[76] Susan Franck et al., 'Inside the Arbitrator's Mind', 66 Emory L.J. 1115 (2017).

with party self-determination and individualized justice. In this regard, a number of questions and challenges are presented. What is the optimal way for mediation and arbitration to work together? What are the limits of consent? What is the proper protocol when parties ask arbitrators to convert a mediated settlement agreement into an arbitration award? How do we manage the tension between the need for flexibility and diversity in designing dispute resolution systems with the need for a predictable framework based on core values? What is the role of lawyers representing parties in mediation and in hybrid processes? In reflecting on these questions there may be an urge to adopt a regulation mindset—drafting more soft law guidelines or encouraging 'best practice' protocols. That instinct should be resisted. Perceptions and approaches differ between cultures and countries. Cultural context matters. Consent matters. Caution and conversation should continue.

CHAPTER 12

CIVIL SOCIETY AND INTERNATIONAL INVESTMENT ARBITRATION

Tracing the evolution of concern

NATHALIE BERNASCONI, MARTIN DIETRICH BRAUCH, AND HOWARD MANN

12.1 Introduction

Civil society engagement with trade and investment agreements is not new. Indeed, civil society organizations (CSOs) led much of the opposition to the North American Free Trade Agreement (NAFTA) in the early 1990s that produced side agreements on the environment and labor. Civil society opposition also played a large role in the demise of the negotiations on the Multilateral Investment Agreement in the Organisation for Economic Co-operation and Development (OECD) in the late 1990s.[1]

But what is at issue in this chapter is civil society engagement with international investment arbitration rather than all the elements of trade and investment treaties. While the two cannot easily be disentangled, we will try to do so here.

International investment arbitration is now on expansion mode. As of 31 July 2019, there were 983 publicly known treaty-based investment arbitrations, 76 of which initiated in 2018, and 31 in the first half of 2019. The average for the ten-year period 2009–2018 is

[1] When the draft treaty went public in 1997, the proposal became a topic of intense public debate as well as a strong opposition campaign led by CSOs in many countries, including Canada-based Council of Canadians, US-based Public Citizen and Friends of the Earth, and Malaysia-based Third World Network. Many of these organizations had already been engaged in the opposition to NAFTA.

62 new treaty-based cases per year, and since 2010 the number of such cases has more than doubled.[2] To compare with other international dispute settlement mechanisms, the number of new treaty-based investment arbitrations initiated between 1995 and 2018 (948 cases) was 2.3 times higher than the total number of contentious cases initiated before the International Court of Justice (ICJ) (76 cases)[3] plus the number of panels established under the World Trade Organization (WTO) Dispute Settlement Body (336 cases)[4] in the same period. At the time of writing, the International Centre for Settlement of Investment Disputes (ICSID) had also registered 120 arbitration cases invoking investor-state contracts.[5]

Much of the civil society focus on international arbitration has been on the Investor–State Dispute Settlement (ISDS) process included in many international investment agreements. While this chapter will focus primarily on this aspect, it may be noted that the historical role of commercial arbitration as the progenitor of investment treaty arbitration, and the procedural and structural links between ISDS and commercial arbitration are important for the discussions on civil society engagement. Civil society recognized early on the problems of using a commercial arbitration model for investment arbitration, which involves public law matters, and concluded that this created a misappropriation of a tool that up to that time had only been used for private commercial purposes or very well-defined state-to-state purposes. The crossing of these purposes and actors to create public law arbitration between investors and states is what created this sense of misappropriation and led to a spotlight being shone on the regime by civil society.

This chapter will look back at the beginnings of civil society engagement with international arbitration through the experience with investment treaties, including the advancement of transparency and the ability to submit *amicus curiae* briefs. It will begin by looking at early civil society engagement on the issue of investment arbitration in the context of NAFTA in the 1990s. It will trace developments in the first investment treaty cases in the early 2000s in which the practice of non-party participation through *amicus* briefs began, and then move on to how civil society spearheaded improvements at ICSID and the United Nations Commission on Trade Law (UNCITRAL) on the transparency of the investment arbitration process.

It will then show that, with these developments and the improved transparency in an area that was traditionally highly opaque, civil society along with states, academia, and the broader public steadily learned more about the nature of international investment arbitration processes. Concerns increased with the growth in the number of ISDS claims, and the use of arbitration as a tool of first threat rather than a tool of last resort

[2] United Nations Conference on Trade and Development (UNCTAD), 'Investment Dispute Settlement Navigator': <https://investmentpolicy.unctad.org/investment-dispute-settlement>.

[3] International Court of Justice, 'List of All Cases' (2020): <http://www.icj-cij.org/en/list-of-all-cases/introduction/desc>.

[4] World Trade Organization, Dispute settlement activity – some figures (2020), ch. 6: <https://www.wto.org/english/tratop_e/dispu_e/dispustats_e.htm>.

[5] International Centre for Settlement of Investment Disputes (ICSID), 'Cases': <https://icsid.worldbank.org/en/Pages/cases/AdvancedSearch.aspx>.

against government measures, as illustrated by the war of big tobacco against anti-smoking laws, even in the smallest of developing countries.[6] This led to wide criticism, provoking health groups to lobby for carve-outs for the tobacco sector from ISDS in investment treaties.[7] More critically, civil society in Europe began to focus on the issue of lack of independence and accountability of arbitrators in investment arbitration, ultimately leading to a proposal by the European Commission to create a 'multilateral investment court system', and to integrate provisions into their bilateral treaties to replace the traditional arbitration regime.

We will then look at how civil society participation and the intervention of affected communities has evolved, and at what would be needed today for a more comprehensive and inclusive investment-related dispute settlement system—one that covers a broader range of investment-related issues (including corporate conduct that harms the environment or violates human rights) and relationships (enhancing access to justice to all stakeholders, including individuals and communities affected by foreign investments).

This chapter uses the term 'civil society' loosely. We will use it to include individuals and organizations who are independent of the government and who are non-business actors. The types of civil society organizations (CSOs) involved in various aspects of the public concern and debate on international investment law and dispute settlement also vary greatly, ranging from think-tanks to more activist organizations and movements.

12.2 Opening Views of Civil Society: From Lack of Awareness to Concern

12.2.1 NAFTA and the early days of international investment law and arbitration

The initial inclusion of arbitration in investment treaties generally went unnoticed. For the purpose of this chapter, let us begin with NAFTA as the baseline for civil society reactions during its completion in 1992. In the backdrop of the emerging trade and environment debate around the predecessor of the WTO, the General Agreement on

[6] This was made famous, or infamous, by comedian John Oliver, who uncovered letters sent by tobacco companies to the Government of Togo threatening international arbitration if the government took then-planned measures to reduce smoking in the country. John Oliver, 'Tobacco: Last Week Tonight with John Oliver (HBO)' (Last Week Tonight, 2015): <https://www.youtube.com/watch?v=6UsHHOCH4q8>.

[7] See e.g. Action on Smoking and Health (ASH), 'Breaking: Tobacco Carve-Out in TPP' (2015): <http://ash.org/breaking-tobacco-carve-out-in-tpp/>; Trans-Pacific Partnership Agreement (TPP) (2016), Ch. 29, Sec. A, Art. 29.5: <https://www.mfat.govt.nz/assets/_securedfiles/trans-pacific-partnership/text/29.-exceptions-and-general-provisions.pdf>.

Tariffs and Trade (GATT), the discussions around NAFTA centred on the potential of the agreement for causing environmental harm and negative impacts on labour, as well as a race to the bottom on related domestic and international standards. These concerns ultimately led to the conclusion of two separate agreements, the North American Agreement on Labor Cooperation and the North American Agreement on Environmental Cooperation. However, neither of these so-called side agreements had any legal impact on NAFTA itself, which contained the disciplines on trade and investment. Thus, the side agreements had no impact whatsoever on the rules governing the investment arbitration provisions or the substantive obligations in the investment chapter that the arbitration processes would come to enforce. Indeed, even during the negotiation of the side agreements, there was no public discussion on the potential impact of the ISDS process included in NAFTA, whose repercussions were then still years from being exposed.[8]

This reflected two things. First, the trade ministers that managed the side agreement process had no intention of allowing the side agreements to impact NAFTA itself. Negotiators of the side agreements for all three parties had much leeway, but that leeway ended at anything that might impact the trade and investment rules in NAFTA.

Second, this result reflected the reality that, to the extent it was known at all, the investment arbitration process was largely seen as directed at Mexico and no impacts on Canada or the US were expected.[9] This assumption, however, lasted less than three years after NAFTA came into force. In 1996 the first notice of intent to arbitrate under NAFTA was issued against Canada,[10] and several more followed against all three NAFTA states within two to three years. Eight of the first ten cases addressed environmental issues.[11] The broader concern over NAFTA's environmental impacts turned out to be justified, but not through the anticipated race to the bottom. Instead, it was the arbitration rights granted to foreign investors that put the environment under siege.

The three North American environment ministers understood this dynamic, and in 1998 the Secretariat of the North American Environment Commission commissioned a first study on the impacts of NAFTA arbitration on environmental regulation. The research was presented in June 1999 at the annual meeting of the Environment

[8] The side agreements were negotiated in 1992–3. The first arbitration under Ch. 11 of NAFTA, *Ethyl Corp v Canada*, was commenced in 1996. (Disclosure: Howard Mann, one the current authors, was a member of the Canadian negotiating team for the environmental side agreement.)

[9] Government of Canada, Department of External Affairs, 'North American Free Trade Agreement: Canadian Statement on Implementation' (1994): <http://www.international.gc.ca/trade-agreements-accords-commerciaux/assets/pdfs/N11_JAN1994.pdf>; United States Congress, 'North American Free Trade Agreement Implementation Act': <https://www.gpo.gov/fdsys/pkg/BILLS-103hr3450enr/pdf/BILLS-103hr3450enr.pdf>.

[10] Ethyl Corporation filed a Notice of Intent to Submit a Claim to Arbitration on 10 September 1996 and submitted a Notice of Arbitration against Canada on 14 April 1997.

[11] For a catalogue and review of the earliest cases, see Howard Mann, 'Private Rights, Public Problems: A Guide to NAFTA's Controversial Chapter on Investor Rights' (IISD, 2001): <http://www.iisd.org/library/private-rights-public-problems-guide-naftas-controversial-chapter-investor-rights>.

Commission.[12] The Investment Chapter of NAFTA and its arbitration provisions were thus recognized as potential sources of impacts on the environment and environmental regulation across the continent.

As public concern was growing over the substance of the international investment rules and the types of cases covered in the first ISDS disputes, especially under NAFTA, concern was also growing over the opaqueness of the arbitration process. In the NAFTA context, this concern became a media issue when the second arbitration against Canada was launched and government officials denied its existence when asked. Challenged later, they argued they had to do so due to the confidentiality provisions in the arbitration rules. The media, however, jumped, led by an editorial in Canada's *Globe and Mail* newspaper entitled 'NAFTA Cone of Silence', raising the issue of transparency for the first time.[13]

12.2.2 From NAFTA's 'Cone of Silence' to transparency: the first *amicus curiae* brief in investment arbitration and other developments

The discussion and concerns about transparency and the environmental issues raised in early cases under NAFTA led five CSOs to take the debate further in 1999. The International Institute for Sustainable Development (IISD), on the one hand, and EarthJustice Legal Defense Fund, as counsel for Communities for a Better Environment, Bluewater Network, and the Center for International Environmental Law (CIEL), on the other hand, initiated a process to have the arbitration tribunal in the *Methanex* case accept *amicus curiae* briefs.[14] The first 'Petition', by IISD, sought permission to submit the brief, access to the pleadings of the parties to date, access to the hearings themselves, and a right to appear at the oral hearings. EarthJustice, CIEL, and the others then followed suit. In effect, three specialized groups with strong legal expertise had decided,

[12] Howard Mann and Konrad von Moltke, 'NAFTA's Chapter 11 and the Environment: Addressing the Impacts of the Investor–State Process on the Environment. Executive Summary' (IISD, 2002): <http://www.iisd.org/library/naftas-chapter-11-and-environment-addressing-impacts-investor-state-process-environment> (presented at the Annual Meeting of the Commission on Environmental Cooperation, 1999).

[13] The Globe and Mail (editorial), 'NAFTA Cone of Silence', *Globe and Mail* (1998). See also Heather Scoffield, 'NAFTA Process Unacceptable', *Globe and Mail* (1998), 4.

[14] *Methanex Corporation v United States of America*, In the Matter of An Arbitration under Chapter 11 of the North American Free Trade Agreement and the UNCITRAL Arbitration Rules, Petition to the Arbitral Tribunal submitted by the International Institute for Sustainable Development, 25 August 2000: <http://www.iisd.org/library/arbitration-under-chapter-11-north-american-free-trade-agreement-and-uncitral-arbitration>; *Methanex Corporation v United States of America*, In the Matter of An Arbitration under Chapter 11 of the North American Free Trade Agreement and the UNCITRAL Arbitration Rules, Amended Petition of Communities for a Better Environment, the Bluewater Network of Earth Island Institute, and the Center For International Environmental Law to Appear Jointly as Amici Curiae, 13 October 2000: <http://www.ciel.org/Publications/Methanex_ICSID_Oct2000.pdf>.

largely independently, to seek to work within the system to 'force' it open, paving the way for similar applications in other arbitrations under NAFTA and other investment treaties. Interestingly, Canada and the US both formally supported the initial petitions for *amicus* status, while Mexico opposed. Canada's decision was finally made minutes before the deadline for Canada to submit its view after being ruled on in the Prime Minister's office following much inter-department debate and lobbying by Methanex for Canada to oppose the petitions.[15]

The tribunal in *Methanex* allowed for the submission of the two *amicus* briefs in a decision issued in January 2001,[16] a decision that was to be followed multiple times over in future cases. It held:[17]

> There is undoubtedly public interest in this arbitration. The substantive issues extend far beyond those raised by the usual transnational arbitration between commercial parties. This is not merely because one of the Disputing Parties is a State... The public interest in this arbitration arises from its subject-matter, as powerfully suggested in the Petitions. There is also a broader argument, as suggested by the Respondent and Canada: the Chapter 11 arbitral process could benefit from being perceived as more open or transparent; or conversely be harmed if seen as unduly secretive. In this regard, the tribunal's willingness to receive amicus submissions might support the process in general and this arbitration in particular, whereas a blanket refusal could do positive harm.

Even so, the tribunal denied access to the pleadings of the parties, access to the hearing, and permission to speak at the hearing. Access to the pleadings was, however, obtained through access to information requests in the US, which the US government granted. In addition, the *Methanex* tribunal, following a second request by IISD that propelled the arbitrating parties to change their own minds,[18] opened the oral hearing to the public in the spring of 2005 through a live video feed at the World Bank headquarters. This led, in fact, to a second submission by IISD, CIEL, EarthJustice, and the others together querying the scope of the US arguments in relation to environmental management issues. The US arguments originally focused on public health issues, but after the second *amicus* submission they expressly included environmental protection within the scope of the police powers rule under customary international law. Although not accepted by

[15] Mark MacKinnon, 'Canada, U.S. Support role for NGO in NAFTA', *Globe and Mail* (2000): <http://www.theglobeandmail.com/report-on-business/canada-us-support-role-for-ngo-in-nafta/article22500360/>.

[16] *Methanex Corporation v United States of America*, 'Decision of the Tribunal on Petitions From Third Persons to Intervene as Amici Curiae' (2001): <http://www.italaw.com/sites/default/files/case-documents/ita0517_0.pdf>.

[17] Ibid. paras. 27, 29.

[18] *Methanex Corporation v United States of America*, Joint Motion to the Tribunal Regarding the Petitions for Amicus Curiae Status by the International Institute for Sustainable Development and Communities for a Better Environment, Bluewater Network and Center for International Environmental Law (2003): <http://www.state.gov/documents/organization/17769.pdf>.

the tribunal, this perceived change in arguments by the US showed that transparency could produce positive results.[19]

At roughly the same time as developments in the *Methanex* case unfolded, governmental action on transparency began, with the three NAFTA parties taking the lead after having their hands forced by civil society actions. In 2003, the three NAFTA states issued a NAFTA Free Trade Commission (FTC) statement implying a recognition in all NAFTA cases of the right of civil society agents to submit *amicus* briefs, subject to approval by the tribunal to accept them.[20] Canada and the US also issued independent but similar statements signalling their commitment to have public proceedings in NAFTA arbitrations.[21] Mexico did not join the statement at the time, but endorsed it in 2004.[22]

Not all CSOs sought to improve the investment treaty regime from within it. Reflecting the divergence of views, several also initiated constitutional law challenges to trade and investment treaties that included ISDS. In March 2001, three CSOs commenced proceedings in Ontario courts challenging the constitutionality of the dispute settlement provisions of NAFTA Chapter 11.[23] The case was ultimately rejected, leaving open the specific question whether the Canadian Constitution is applicable to NAFTA arbitrations at all, but finding that the dispute settlement mechanism set forth by NAFTA would neither violate the Constitution nor violate the principles of judicial independence or the rule of law.[24]

Finally, in an attempt to expand transparency in NAFTA and other investment arbitration cases, in October 2002, IISD launched the Investment Law and Sustainable Development mailing list as a weekly news bulletin, designed to shed light and promote public debate on ongoing investment treaty negotiations and disputes, and rebranded it in 2005 as Investment Treaty News (ITN).[25] This was the first service to allow the public

[19] See e.g. Federico Ortino, 'The Impact of Amicus Curiae Briefs in the Settlement of Trade and Investment Disputes: An Analysis of the Shrimp/Turtle and Methanex Decisions' (2009): <https://ssrn.com/abstract=1,656,844>.

[20] NAFTA Free Trade Commission (FTC), 'Statement of the Free Trade Commission on Non-Disputing Party Participation' (2003): <http://www.state.gov/documents/organization/38791.pdf>.

[21] Howard Mann, 'The Free Trade Commission Statements of October 7, 2003, on NAFTA's Chapter 11: Never-Never Land or Real Progress?' (IISD, 2003): <http://www.iisd.org/pdf/2003/trade_ftc_comment_oct03.pdf>.

[22] NAFTA FTC, 'NAFTA Free Trade Commission Joint Statement: Decade of Achievement' (2004), 2: <http://www.sice.oas.org/TPD/NAFTA/Commission/Statement2004_e.asp>.

[23] *Council of Canadians et al v R*, (2005) CanLII 28,426 (SC).

[24] *Council of Canadians et al v Canada (Attorney General)*, (2006) CanLII 40, 222 (CA). Another, broader challenge was brought in 2013, when a British Colombia First Nation made attempts to challenge the Canada–China Foreign Investment Promotion and Protection Agreement on the basis that Canada failed to consult with the First Nations whose constitutionally protected rights and title may be affected by the agreement. The case was ultimately dismissed by the Federal Court of Appeals in 2015, concluding the lack of 'causal relationship' between the effect of the challenged treaty and rights and interests asserted.

[25] IISD, 'Investment Treaty News': <http://www.iisd.org/itn>. Among the early commercial and non-commercial reporting services were Investment Arbitration Reporter (IAR, set up by Luke Peterson, the first ITN editor) and Global Arbitration Review. The reporting was a necessary addition to the services that began to emerge listing and providing updates on those cases that were public. Todd Weiler, a practitioner who was involved in some of the earlier NAFTA cases, created the NAFTAClaims.com website,

and governments to gain insight into ongoing and concluded investment treaty cases, involving public policy and, often, public interest issues.

12.3 TRANSPARENCY IN REVISED ARBITRATION RULES

12.3.1 The 2006 revision to the ICSID arbitration rules

In April 2006, inspired by developments around NAFTA and pushed by civil society, ICSID implemented a series of changes to all its arbitration rules for the first time since the ICSID Convention came into force in 1966.[26] The revision addressed some of the problems in investment arbitration relating to transparency and public participation. Accordingly, the revised rules included provisions on the publication of awards, access of third parties to proceedings, and written submissions by non-disputing parties.

First, Rule 48, which relates to the publication of the award, was amended 'to facilitate the prompt release of excerpts, by making their early publication mandatory, and clarify the wording of the provision'.[27] The revised Rule 48 provides:

> The Centre shall not publish the award without the consent of the parties. The Centre shall, however, promptly include in its publications excerpts of the legal conclusions of the Tribunal.

As in the past, ICSID would only publish the award as a whole if the parties consented. However, since—in contrast to UNCITRAL Arbitration Rules at the time—ICSID rules have always allowed each of the parties to make the decisions and awards public unilaterally, without consent of the other party, many of the awards were published on non-ICSID websites dedicated to investment treaty arbitration.

Second, Rule 32 on the oral procedure was amended to give more power to the tribunal to decide whether to open the proceedings.[28] The old Rule 32.2 provided that '[t]he Tribunal shall decide, with the consent of the parties, which other persons besides the

and Professor Andrew Newcombe of the University of Victoria, Canada, created the Investment Treaty Arbitration Law (ITALaw) website. These services complement UNCTAD's Investment Policy Hub.

[26] Howard Mann et al., 'Comments on ICSID Discussion Paper, "Possible Improvements of the Framework for ICSID Arbitration"', (IISD 2004): <http://www.iisd.org/library/comments-icsid-discussion-paper-possible-improvements-framework-icsid-arbitration>.

[27] ICSID, 'Proposed Amendments to the ICSID Rules and Regulations', Working Paper (2005), 9: http://icsid.worldbank.org/ICSID/FrontServlet?requestType=CasesRH&actionVal=OpenPage&PageType=AnnouncementsFrame&FromPage=NewsReleases&pageName=Archive_per cent20Announcement25.

[28] Ibid. 10.

parties, their agents, counsel and advocates, witnesses and experts during their testimony, and officers of the Tribunal may attend the hearings'. This was amended as follows:

> Unless either party objects, the Tribunal, after consultation with the Secretary-General, may allow other persons, besides the parties, their agents, counsel and advocates, witnesses and experts during their testimony, and officers of the Tribunal to attend or observe all or part of the hearings, subject to appropriate logistical arrangements. The Tribunal shall for such cases establish procedures for the protection of proprietary or privileged information.

Although the revised ICSID Rules seem slightly more favourable towards public hearings, the *Biwater* Tribunal, as discussed below, would not permit open hearings because the investor had opposed.[29]

Third, the revised ICSID Rules explicitly include a provision relating to the submission of *amicus curiae* briefs. The ICSID Rules were silent with respect to the *amicus curiae* question until the 2006 revisions, although the practice had already emerged for ICSID tribunals to accept briefs of amici. The Tribunal in the *Aguas Argentinas* case was the first ICSID tribunal to deal with *amicus curiae* submissions. In that case, a group of foreign enterprises that held a concession to operate water and waste-water services in Buenos Aires initiated arbitration against Argentina, alleging that the government's legal and regulatory measures in response to the 2001 crisis destroyed the value of their investment. Five CSOs—four based in Argentina (Asociación Civil por la Igualdad y la Justicia [ACIJ], Centro de Estudios Legales y Sociales [CELS], Consumidores Libres Cooperativa Ltda. de Provisión de Servicios de Acción Comunitaria, and Unión de Usuarios y Consumidores), supported by the lawyers of CIEL—filed a petition for transparency and participation, asserting that the case involved public interest matters and fundamental rights of the people living in the affected area, requesting access to the hearings, permission to submit *amicus curiae* briefs, and 'timely, sufficient, and unrestricted access to all of the documents' on record. Responding to the petition, the tribunal denied access to the hearing and the record, but accepted that it had the power to accept *amicus curiae* briefs, and set out a procedure for the CSOs to do so in the case at hand.[30]

[29] *Biwater Gauff (Tanzania) Ltd v United Republic of Tanzania*, ICSID Case No. ARB/05/22, Procedural Order No. 5 (2007), paras. 70–71.

[30] *Suez, Sociedad General de Aguas de Barcelona, S.A. and Vivendi Universal, S.A. v Argentine Republic (formerly Aguas Argentinas, S.A., Suez, Sociedad General de Aguas de Barcelona, S.A. and Vivendi Universal, S.A. v. Argentine Republic)*, ICSID Case No. ARB/03/19, Order in Response to a Petition for Transparency and Participation as *Amicus curiae* (2005); *Suez, Sociedad General de Aguas de Barcelona, S.A. and Vivendi Universal, S.A. v Argentine Republic (formerly Aguas Argentinas, S.A., Suez, Sociedad General de Aguas de Barcelona, S.A. and Vivendi Universal, S.A. v. Argentine Republic)*, ICSID Case No. ARB/03/19, Order in Response to a Petition by Five Non-Governmental Organizations for Permission to Make an Amicus Curiae Submission (2007).

Subsequent to *Aguas Argentinas*, the ICSID Secretariat suggested changes to the ICSID Arbitration Rules to expressly provide for submissions of non-disputing parties. The revised ICSID Rules integrate the *Aguas Argentinas* outcome in an explicit provision, Rule 37.2, allowing tribunals to accept *amicus curiae* briefs, with or without the consent of the parties:

> After consulting both parties, the Tribunal may allow a person or entity that is not a party to the dispute (in this Rule called the 'non-disputing party') to file a written submission with the Tribunal regarding a matter within the scope of the dispute. In determining whether to allow such a filing, the Tribunal shall consider, among other things, the extent to which:
>
> (a) the non-disputing party submission would assist the Tribunal in the determination of a factual or legal issue related to the proceeding by bringing a perspective, particular knowledge or insight that is different from that of the disputing parties;
>
> (b) the non-disputing party submission would address a matter within the scope of the dispute;
>
> (c) the non-disputing party has a significant interest in the proceeding.
>
> The Tribunal shall ensure that the non-disputing party submission does not disrupt the proceeding or unduly burden or unfairly prejudice either party, and that both parties are given an opportunity to present their observations on the non-disputing party submission.

12.3.2 The first amicus curiae submission under the 2006 ICSID arbitration rules: the case of *Biwater v Tanzania*

The case of *Biwater v Tanzania* was the first to apply and test the revised ICSID Rules relating to transparency and public participation. The dispute involved a controversy between the Tanzanian government and a British investor on the provision of water services in Tanzania's capital, Dar es Salaam, from 2003 until 2005. In May 2005, Tanzania announced that it had terminated its contract with the investor because the company had failed to provide clean drinking water to millions of people in its capital. In response, the British investor Biwater sought some US$20 million from an arbitration tribunal for alleged violations of the Tanzania–United Kingdom bilateral investment treaty (BIT).

Although the new ICSID rules according to the *Biwater* tribunal 'clearly reflect an overall trend in th[e] field towards transparency',[31] the tribunal significantly limited the

[31] *Biwater Gauff (Tanzania) Ltd v United Republic of Tanzania*, ICSID Case No. ARB/05/22, Procedural Order No. 3 (2006), para. 122.

public's access to information, arguing that 'other values' related to the dispute settlement process were at risk. Against the will of the government of Tanzania to make all documents public in order to keep its citizens informed, the tribunal sided with the investor, who argued confidentiality was necessary to protect the 'procedural integrity of the process' and assure the 'non-aggravation of the dispute'. Despite its recognition of the clear trend in ICSID towards increased transparency, the importance of permitting governments to share information with its citizens, and the absence of any harm in the present case resulting from the public's access to information about the proceeding, the tribunal determined that transparency was trumped by the threat of potential, future harm to the process.

In November 2006, three Tanzanian and two international CSOs filed a petition for *amicus curiae* status, requesting access to key arbitration documents, open hearings, and the opportunity to reply directly to any questions from the tribunal concerning their submissions in the case of *Biwater v Tanzania*.[32] The petitioners submitted a petition pursuant to Rule 37.2 of the amended Arbitration Rules, which explicitly provides the authority for tribunals to accept *amicus curiae* submissions. The *Biwater* Tribunal granted the five CSOs leave to file a written submission in the proceeding in February 2007, but rejected the request to access key arbitral documents, as well as the petitioners' application that the hearings be open to the public or, at least, that the petitioners be allowed to reply directly to any questions from the tribunal concerning their submissions.[33] Despite these hurdles, the tribunal relied significantly on the legal and factual arguments of the *amici* in the final award.

While there is no requirement under the ICSID Arbitration Rules for a panel to address arguments made in any brief when issuing the final award, this tribunal not only explicitly did so, but stated that the submission provided 'a very useful initial context for the Arbitral Tribunal's enquiry'.[34] Thus, the *amicus* brief contributed substantially to the outcome of this case by shaping the discussion of the final award and providing additional factual and legal information. The tribunal spent twelve pages in the final award discussing the arguments raised in the *amicus* brief, and stated that the 'submissions have informed the analysis of claims ... and where relevant, specific points arising from the *Amici*'s submissions are returned to in that context'.[35]

As the first case under the 2006 rules, the *amicus* submission in the *Biwater* arbitration continued to pave the way for further developments on transparency and public participation.

[32] *Biwater Gauff (Tanzania) Ltd v United Republic of Tanzania*, ICSID Case No. ARB/05/22, Petition for Amicus Curiae Status (2006).

[33] *Biwater Gauff (Tanzania) Ltd v United Republic of Tanzania*, ICSID Case No. ARB/05/22, Procedural Order No. 5 (2007).

[34] *Biwater Gauff (Tanzania) Ltd v United Republic of Tanzania*, ICSID Case No. ARB/05/22, Award, para. 355.

[35] Ibid. para. 392.

12.3.3 How civil society brought transparency to UNCITRAL's agenda

In July 2013, UNCITRAL formally adopted the UNCITRAL Rules on Transparency in Treaty-Based Investor–State Arbitration (Transparency Rules), which came into effect on 1 April 2014. These rules are the result of a process that lasted over six years. IISD and CIEL were instrumental in bringing the issue of transparency to the forefront of UNCITRAL's agenda. The two organizations provided expertise throughout the negotiation process, by intervening in the discussions, preparing analyses of textual options, and proposing content for rules on transparency.[36]

When the UNCITRAL Working Group II on International Arbitration and Conciliation began its work on the revision of the 1976 UNCITRAL Rules in September 2006, transparency and public participation in investor–state arbitration were not on the agenda. For the Working Group's session in February 2007, IISD and CIEL prepared a joint paper that set out why and how the UNCITRAL Rules should be revised to address the public interest needs of state arbitrations.[37] As a result, transparency issues were debated at some length the following year at the February 2008 session.[38] and brought to the UNCITRAL Commission. At its 41st session in June and July 2008, the Commission ordered the working group to take up transparency in investment arbitration immediately after the revision of the rules—a major achievement for the advocates of transparency.

Working group discussions on the transparency rules began in October 2010. No consensus could be established, however, on the form which the 'legal standards' on transparency in investor–state arbitration should take, and how they would apply to future and existing treaties. A compromise started to emerge in the working group in February 2012: it was decided that the transparency rules would automatically apply to future treaties based on the opt-out approach, but for them to apply to *existing* treaties, parties would have to opt-in.[39] To examine the potential mechanisms permitting application to existing treaties, the working group decided that the UNCITRAL

[36] Fiona Marshall and Howard Mann, 'Good Governance and the Rule of Law: Express Rules for Investor-State Arbitrations Required' (IISD, 2006): <http://www.iisd.org/pdf/2006/investment_uncitral_rules_ rrevision.pdf>. See also CIEL, 'UNCITRAL Arbitrations Involving State as a Party – Transparency, Public Participation and Accountability' (CIEL, 2006): <http://ciel.org/Publications/UNCITRAL_Statement_18Sep06.pdf>.

[37] IISD and CIEL, 'Proposed Revisions to the UNCITRAL Rules for Investor–State Arbitrations' (2007): <http://www.iisd.org/pdf/2010/uncitral_proposed_revisions_2010.pdf>.

[38] See IISD and CIEL, 'Revising the UNCITRAL Arbitration Rules to Address Investor–State Arbitrations' (2008): <http://www.iisd.org/pdf/2008/investment_revising_uncitral_arbitration_dec.pdf>.

[39] UNCITRAL, 'Report of Working Group II (Arbitration and Conciliation) on the Work of its Fifty-Sixth Session', (2012), UN Doc A/CN.9/741, paras. 54–5: http://daccess-ods.un.org/access.nsf/Get?OpenAgent& DS=A/cn.9/741&Lang=E.

secretariat should prepare wording for a convention on transparency and a unilateral declaration.[40]

The working group reached consensus on the scope of application and content of the transparency rules and finally adopted them in February 2013.[41] The UNCITRAL Commission formally adopted them in July 2013.[42] The new Transparency Rules,[43] ensuring transparency throughout the treaty-based investor–state arbitrations to which they apply, are an integral part of the UNCITRAL Arbitration Rules, and apply on a default basis to UNCITRAL investor–state arbitrations conducted under investment treaties concluded after 1 April 2014, when the new rules came into effect.[44]

The working group started the preparation of a transparency convention in September 2013,[45] resulting in the United Nations Convention on Transparency in Treaty-Based Investor–State Arbitration, opened for signature in Mauritius in March 2015. The convention facilitates the application of the Transparency Rules to investor–state arbitrations arising under the bulk of investment treaties concluded prior to the Rules' entry into force, including arbitrations under rules other than the UNCITRAL Arbitration Rules. At the time of writing, 23 countries had signed the convention, of which five (Cameroon, Canada, Gambia, Mauritius, and Switzerland) had ratified it.[46] The convention entered into force on 18 October 2017.[47]

The advances in transparency in the UNCITRAL context undeniably would not have occurred without the involvement of specialized civil society groups. Despite strong opposition by some members and observers of the UNCITRAL Working Group and hesitations of the UNCITRAL Secretariat to allow the participation of civil society

[40] Ibid. paras 138 and 141. [41] Ibid.

[42] United Nations Information Service, 'UNCITRAL Adopts Transparency Rules for Treaty-Based Investor–State Arbitration and Amends the UNCITRAL Arbitration Rules', press release (2013): <http://www.unis.unvienna.org/unis/pressrels/2013/unisl186.html>.

[43] United Nations, 'UNCITRAL Rules on Transparency in Treaty-Based Investor–State Arbitration' (2014): <http://www.uncitral.org/pdf/english/texts/arbitration/rules-on-transparency/Rules-on-Transparency-E.pdf>.

[44] Lise Johnson and Nathalie Bernasconi-Osterwalder, 'New UNCITRAL Arbitration Rules on Transparency: Application, Content and Next Steps' (IISD, CIEL, and Vale Columbia Center on Sustainable International Investment, 2013): <http://www.iisd.org/pdf/2013/uncitral_rules_on_transparency_commentary.pdf>. See also Dimitrij Euler et al., *Transparency in International Investment Arbitration: A Guide to the UNCITRAL Rules on Transparency in Treaty-Based Investor–State Arbitration* (Cambridge University Press, 2015).

[45] UNCITRAL, 'Report of Working Group II (Arbitration and Conciliation) on the Work of its Fifty-Eighth Session' (2013), UN Doc A/CN.9/794: <http://daccess-ods.un.org/access.nsf/Get?OpenAgent&DS=a/Cn.9/794&Lang=E>.

[46] UNCITRAL, 'Status United Nations Convention on Transparency in Treaty-Based Investor-State Arbitration' (2014): <https://uncitral.un.org/en/texts/arbitration/conventions/transparency/status>.

[47] UNCITRAL, 'United Nations Convention on Transparency in Treaty-Based Investor–State Arbitration', (2014): <https://www.uncitral.org/pdf/english/texts/arbitration/transparency-convention/Transparency-Convention-e.pdf>.

experts in 2006, the ultimately inclusive UN process allowed for constructive exchanges and outcomes.

12.3.4 The gains of *amici* in peril

The original expectation regarding *amicus curiae* briefs was for the conditions for their acceptance to be interpreted broadly, erring on the side of more inclusiveness than exclusion. Recent tribunal decisions, however, show that this expectation is not being widely met.

In *Eli Lilly v Canada*, the claimant, a US pharmaceutical company, maintains that Canada breached the expropriation and fair and equitable treatment (FET) provisions of NAFTA when Canadian courts applied the 'promise utility' patent law doctrine to invalidate two of Eli Lilly's patents. In February 2016, the tribunal received nine applications for leave to file *amicus curiae* briefs, from academics, research institutions, and private sector associations from Canada and the US, as well as from Mexico, Nepal, South Africa, Switzerland, and the United Kingdom.[48]

In its February 2016 decision regarding the applications, the tribunal seems to have made a general determination that *amici* not resident in a treaty state do not have an interest.[49] It noted that the NAFTA FTC Statement on non-disputing party participation of 7 October 2003 referred to 'a person of a Party, or that has a significant presence in the territory of a Party', and held that 'applications by non-disputing parties who are not a person of, or have no significant presence in the territory of, Canada, Mexico or the United States cannot be entertained'.[50] Accordingly, it denied the application of all academics based in countries other than the three NAFTA state parties 'for lack of standing'.[51] It also denied two other applications—one by Innovative Medicines Canada (IMC) and BIOTECanada (BTC), and another by Pharmaceutical Research and Manufacturers of America (PhRMA), the Mexican Association of the Research Based Pharmaceutical Industry (AMIIF), and Biotechnology Innovation Organization (BIO)—as the submissions 'would not assist the Tribunal in the determination of a factual or legal issue related to the arbitration by bringing a perspective, particular knowledge or insight that is different from that of the disputing parties'.[52]

The approach taken by the *Eli Lilly* tribunal limits the ability of persons and organizations to bring their perspective on issues of global importance, such as patent law. Also, it runs counter to previous decisions, such as *Biwater* (already discussed), which is one of the most important examples of usefulness of an *amicus* brief to a tribunal.[53] Here, the

[48] *Eli Lilly and Company v Government of Canada*, An Arbitration Under Chapter 11 of the NAFTA and the UNCITRAL Arbitration Rules, 1976, Case No. UNCT/14/2, Procedural Order 4 (2016), paras. 2–3.

[49] Ibid. paras. 3–4. [50] Ibid. para. 2. [51] Ibid. paras. 3–4. [52] Ibid.

[53] Farouk El Hosseny, 'The Role of Civil Society in Investment Treaty Arbitration: Status and Prospects' (Leiden University Repository, 2016), 185.

amicus process would not have occurred, as two of the co-*amici* were international think- tanks based outside the treaty parties' territory, providing the expertise to the CSOs based in Tanzania.

In *Infinito Gold v Costa Rica*, a Canadian mining company initiated ICSID arbitration against Costa Rica, complaining against the government's ban on open-pit mining and the cancellation of the company's exploitation concession regarding the Crucitas gold mining project, in an alleged violation of several standards of the Canada–Costa Rica BIT.[54] In September 2014, Asociación Preservacionista de Flora y Fauna Silvestre (APREFLOFAS), a Costa Rican CSO for environmental protection, petitioned the tribunal for *amicus curiae* status, highlighting the public interest concerns with the environmental damage caused by the claimant's activity to water sources and animal and plant life.[55]

In its June 2016 decision on APREFLOFAS's application, the tribunal decided to confer non-disputing party status on it and allow it to make a written submission, noting that its purpose is environmental protection and that its submission would fall within the scope of the dispute and could assist the tribunal in better understanding certain factual and legal aspects of the dispute.[56] At the same time, however, the tribunal noted that APREFLOFAS's requests to access the principal arbitration documents and to attend and participate in oral hearings exceeded the scope of ICSID Arbitration Rule 37(2), which only permits the tribunal to allow written submissions by non-disputing parties.[57] The tribunal only granted APREFLOFAS access to selected portions on the claimant's memorial on the merits and the respondent's memorial on jurisdiction, allowing it to 'use these materials exclusively for the purposes of preparing its written submission'.[58] As to APREFLOFAS's request to attend and participate in hearings, the tribunal straightforwardly denied this in view of Infinito Gold's objection.[59] This approach is slightly more favourable than that of the *Biwater* tribunal in that the *amici* had access to selected portions of the memorials; but overall, the limited access to documents and hearings remains an obstacle to ensuring useful submissions and enhancing third-party participation.

In *Bear Creek v Peru*, initiated in 2014, Canadian mining company Bear Creek Mining Corporation is asking for damages of over US$500 million at ICSID over Peru's alleged breaches of the expropriation, FET, and most-favoured-nation (MFN) clauses of the Canada–Peru Free Trade Agreement (FTA).[60] In 2007 Peru had granted Bear Creek an authorization to develop a silver mining project in the country. However, responding

[54] *Infinito Gold Ltd v Republic of Costa Rica*, ICSID Case No. ARB/14/5, Request for Arbitration (2014).

[55] *Infinito Gold Ltd v Republic of Costa Rica*, ICSID Case No. ARB/14/5, Petition for Amicus Curiae Status (2014).

[56] *Infinito Gold Ltd v Republic of Costa Rica*, ICSID Case No. ARB/14/5, Procedural Order No. 2 (2016), paras. 31–7.

[57] Ibid. para. 29. [58] Ibid. para. 44. [59] ibid, para. 48.

[60] *Bear Creek Mining Corporation v Republic of Peru*, ICSID Case No. ARB/14/21, Claimant's Memorial on the Merits (2015).

to growing concerns and protests by civil society groups regarding the potential environmental damages of the project to Lake Titicaca, the Peruvian government rescinded the authorization in June 2011.[61]

In June 2016, the Columbia Center on Sustainable Investment (CCSI) sought leave from the tribunal to file an *amicus curiae* submission. CCSI argued that it met the four non-exhaustive factors listed in the applicable FTA which the tribunal must consider in determining whether to admit such submissions, including that the submission would assist the tribunal in the determination of a factual or legal issue related to the arbitration.[62]

In July 2016, however, the tribunal rejected CCSI's application. Noting that 'both Parties [were] represented by distinguished international law firms with extensive experience in international investment arbitration' and that 'the Parties [had] filed lengthy and detailed submissions and evidence regarding every aspect of the case', the tribunal was not convinced that, despite its experience in the field, 'CCSI would be able to contribute any further information or arguments that would assist the Tribunal in the determination of a factual or legal issue related to the arbitration by bringing a perspective, particular knowledge or insight that is different from that of the disputing parties'.[63]

These three of several examples show that the relevant language in arbitral rules is not tight enough to prevent tribunals from taking a less open and inclusive approach than that adhered to by some of the earlier tribunals. While the NAFTA FTC statement on non-disputing party participation should be regarded as a positive development, in that it recognizes the right of civil society agents to submit *amicus curiae* briefs in NAFTA cases, the *Eli Lilly* decision evidences that its scope is still limited, as it allows tribunals to dismiss submissions from stakeholders based outside the NAFTA state parties, however useful their submissions may be to the tribunal and however significant their interest may be in the arbitration.

The *Infinito Gold* case, in turn, shows that ICSID Arbitration Rule 37(2), while permitting tribunals to accept *amicus* briefs, falls short of granting *amici* more meaningful opportunities to engage in the arbitration through wider access to the record and to hearings even when either or both of the disputing parties oppose. In *Bear Creek*, the *amicus* did not even request access to the record or hearings; it merely wished to make a written submission to assist the tribunal in matters of international law and public policy. Even so, the tribunal rejected the petition, unconvinced that it could be assisted by a submission from a renowned academic research centre. This case reminds us that it is easy for a tribunal, given the open wording of the existing rules, to shift from the spirit of openness intended to one that is unnecessarily restrictive.

[61] Luke Eric Peterson, 'Canadian Miner Hires Law Firm and Threatens Arbitration over Blocked Mining Project in Peru' (Investment Arbitration Reporter, 2014): <http://tinyurl.com/pj5z7xn>.

[62] *Bear Creek Mining Corporation v Republic of Peru*, ICSID Case No. ARB/14/21, Procedural Order 6 (2016), paras. 11–17.

[63] Ibid. paras. 36–9.

12.4 From Transparency in Investment Arbitration to a Call for Deeper Reform

12.4.1 Transparency exposes flaws and leads to demands for deeper reforms

The engagement of civil society within the system was crucial for advances in transparency, such as the adoption of the UNCITRAL Transparency Rules and the Mauritius Convention, as well as the possibility of civil society gaining some limited access to investor–state arbitration processes. Many of these reforms advanced by civil society were actively opposed by the arbitration Bar. One documented example is the declaration issued by the 'Milan Club', a leading association of arbitrators, which opposed the introduction of transparency in UNCITRAL.[64] Given that much of the critique of the investment arbitration process centred on the lack of transparency, the injection of transparency arguably helped the process regain some credibility, preventing a full backlash.

At the same time, the transparency incrementally brought to the regime through case reporting, the publication of decisions and documents, open hearings, and investigative reporting also revealed to states, civil society, and academia many of the flaws in investor–state arbitration. Raising cogent questions as to its legitimacy, transparency has led to public debate and discussion about a series of issues, including:

- conflicts of interest of arbitrators and lack of independence;
- the lack of diversity among arbitrators;
- the lack of appeals that have led to contradicting decisions on key legal issues; and
- the limited opportunity to review legally wrong decisions and the resulting risk of arbitrator lawmaking, especially to expand the regime.

Think-tanks like IISD pointed to several of these issues as they became evident, including through its regular reporting in ITN,[65] as well as in early submissions during the ICSID and UNCITRAL reform processes,[66] building awareness amongst policy-makers and civil society, and generating different levels of incremental change, depending on

[64] UNCITRAL, 'Report of the Working Group Forty-Eighth Session' (2015), Annex II: <http://www.uncitral.org/uncitral/en/commission/sessions/48th.html>.

[65] IISD, 'Investment Treaty News': <http://www.iisd.org/itn>.

[66] Nathalie Bernasconi-Osterwalder, Lise Johnson, and Fiona Marshall, 'Arbitrator Independence and Impartiality: Examining the Dual Role of Arbitrator and Counsel' (IISD, 2010): <http://www.iisd.org/pdf/2011/dci_2010_arbitrator_independence.pdf>; Fiona Marshall and Howard Mann, 'Revision of the UNCITRAL Arbitration Rules, Good Governance and the Rule of Law: Express Rules of the UNCITRAL Arbitration Rules for Investor-State Arbitrations Required' (IISD, 2006): <http://www.iisd.org/pdf/2006/investment_uncitral_rules_rrevision.pdf>.

the issues.[67] However, the discussions on many of these issues began to intensify when the European Union began trade and investment negotiations including ISDS with Canada and the US. These developments led to a strong mobilization amongst CSOs in Europe, who started asking questions about the investor–state arbitration model—at the time a new debate in Europe. In 2012, two European CSOs—the Corporate Europe Observatory and the Transnational Institute—published a provocative report entitled 'Profiting from Injustice: How Law Firms, Arbitrators and Financiers Are Fueling an Investment Arbitration Boom'. The report exposed many of the issues and concerns listed above. It was widely disseminated and received significant attention in the press.[68] Civil society criticism of the traditional ISDS model would contribute to important developments in EU institutions leading to major ISDS reforms at the European level, as demonstrated in the two following sections.

12.4.2 The European proposal on a new investment court system

As a first reaction to the broad public opposition to ISDS, the European Commission undertook a public consultation on the topic from March to July 2014, in which concerns about investment arbitration were extensively expressed by broader civil society.[69] As a further reaction to the public consultation and to concerns by EU member states and the European Parliament, on 16 September 2015 the European Commission published a proposal on Investment Protection and Resolution of Investment Disputes and Investment Court System (ICS).[70] While aimed primarily at the EU–US TTIP negotiations, the ICS proposal also aimed at replacing the investor–state arbitration process in

[67] Nathalie Bernasconi-Osterwalder and Lise Johnson, 'Submission to Working Group II on International Arbitration: Vienna October 1–5, 2012. Comments on Draft Articles 1, 3, 7 and 8' (IISD, CIEL, and Vale Columbia Center, 2012): <http://www.iisd.org/library/submission-working-group-ii-international-arbitration-vienna-october-1-5-2012-comments-draft>.

[68] Pia Eberhardt and Cecilia Olivet, 'Profiting from Injustice: How Law Firms, Arbitrators and Financiers are Fueling an Investment Arbitration Boom' (Corporate Europe Observatory and the Transnational Institute, 2012): <https://www.tni.org/en/briefing/profiting-injustice>. See also 'Secrets of a Global Supercourt', a more recent investigative news series by BuzzFeed News, exposing how the threat of ISDS intimidates nations against enacting measures in the public interest. In addition, it showed how financial firms have transformed the regime into an engine of profit, and how the US is vulnerable to suits from foreign investors. See Chris Hamby, 'Secrets of a Global Supercourt: A BuzzFeed News Investigation' (BuzzFeed News 2016): <https://www.buzzfeed.com/globalsupercourt>.

[69] European Commission, 'Report of Online Public Consultation on Investment Protection and Investor to State Dispute Settlement (ISDS) in the Transatlantic Trade and Investment Partnership Agreement (TTIP)' (2015): <http://trade.ec.europa.eu/doclib/docs/2015/january/tradoc_153044.pdf>. See also Nathalie Bernasconi, 'Reply to the European Commission's Public Consultation on Investment Protection and Investor to State Dispute Settlement (ISDS) in the Transatlantic Trade and Investment Partnership Agreement (TTIP)' (IISD, 2014): <http://www.iisd.org/library/reply-european-commissions-public-consultation-investment-protection-and-investor-state>.

[70] European Commission, 'Commission Draft Text TTIP: Investment' (2015): <http://trade.ec.europa.eu/doclib/docs/2015/september/tradoc_153807.pdf>.

all ongoing and future EU investment negotiations. When launching the proposal, the EU Trade Commissioner at the time, Cecilia Malmström, expressly recognized that the reform process initiated at the EU level was triggered by civil society concerns:

> From the start of my mandate . . ISDS has been one of the most controversial issues in my brief. I met and listened to many people and organisations, including NGOs, which voiced a number of concerns about the old, traditional system. It's clear to me that all these complaints had one common feature—that there is a fundamental and widespread lack of trust by the public in the fairness and impartiality of the old ISDS model. This has significantly affected the public's acceptance of ISDS and of companies bringing such cases.
>
> We must keep in mind that investment protection is an important part of the EU's investment policy. EU investors are the most frequent users of the existing system, which individual EU countries have developed over time. This means that we, from the EU side, must take our responsibility to reform and modernise it.[71]

The proposed system deals with a number of concerns that had become apparent over the years. Composed of a first-instance tribunal and an appeal tribunal, the proposed system attempts to allow for increased consistency of awards and the possibility of correcting legal errors made at first instance. In an attempt to deal with the perceived lack of independence of arbitrators, it also imposes high qualification requirements for 'judges' who are appointed to a roster, not by the disputing parties but by the state parties to the treaty. The adjudicators may not serve as counsel in parallel investment treaty cases, to avoid conflicts of interest currently left unaddressed in the traditional investment arbitration model. The new mechanism has already been integrated in treaties the EU has negotiated, including with Canada and Vietnam. Both treaties also contain provisions on the possible establishment of a multilateral investment tribunal and appellate mechanism in the future.[72]

In addition to providing for a process on *amicus curiae* submissions by referring to UNCITRAL Rules on Transparency (which includes Art. 4 on 'Submission by a Third Person'), the original EU ICS proposal for the TTIP includes a provision—not incorporated in the agreements with Canada and Vietnam—granted natural or legal persons who can establish a direct and present interest in the result of the dispute the right to intervene as third parties. Art. 23(1) on the intervention by third parties provides that the tribunal *shall* permit such persons to intervene—in contrast to the language used in the *amicus curiae* context, which provides that the tribunal *may* allow the third person to file a submission. While 'limited to supporting, in whole or in part, the award sought by one of the disputing parties', this *right* of intervention would allow civil society groups and individuals to submit statements, attend hearings, or make oral statements,

[71] Cecilia Malmström, 'Proposing an Investment Court System' (2015): <https://ec.europa.eu/commission/commissioners/2014–2019/malmstrom/blog/proposing-investment-court-system_en>.

[72] Comprehensive Economic and Trade Agreement (CETA), 30 October 2016, Art. 8.29; Free Trade Agreement, European Union–Vietnam, 29 May 2015, Ch. II, Sec. 3, Art. 15.

provided they can establish a direct and present interest in the result of the dispute.[73] To our knowledge, this provision has not found its way into any of the treaties negotiated by the EU so far.

12.4.3 Public concern continues as EU proposes the creation of a multilateral investment court

The issue of ISDS in all its forms continues to be at the centre of attention around trade and investment negotiations on both sides of the Atlantic. In Germany, three CSOs in August 2016—Compact, Food-Watch, and More Democracy—together with another 125,000 citizens whose signatures they gathered, filed a class action challenging the legality of the Canada–EU Comprehensive Economic and Trade Agreement (CETA) in the Federal Constitutional Court of Germany. With the final ruling still pending as of December 2016, the court issued an interim decision in October rejecting the claimants' application for a preliminary injunction aimed at preventing the German representative in the Council of the European Union from signing the CETA and agreeing to its provisional application. Even so, the court emphasized in the interim decision that the provisional application should only concern those parts that undoubtedly fall within EU competence—that is, the provisional application of the CETA would not apply to the controversial areas in certain chapters, including the dispute settlement system and portfolio investments (Chapters 8 and 13).[74]

The constitutionality of CETA was also put into question in Canada. In October 2016, three individual Canadian citizens—a member of the Queen's Privy Council and two members of COMER, a Canada-based CSO—launched a constitutional challenge against the CETA in the Federal Court of Canada in Toronto.[75] Among the various unconstitutional content alleged, the plaintiffs challenged the legitimacy, transparency and accountability of the ISDS mechanism included in the treaty.[76] As of the moment of writing, the respondents have not yet filed their responses.[77]

While the EU public consultation and the constitutional challenges launched by civil society are ongoing, it is safe to say that, despite the proposed reforms, the ICS continues to be heavily criticized by the public and certain states for continuing to pursue an approach that circumvents domestic courts and allows only one group of actors to bring

[73] Commission Draft Text TTIP (n. 70), Arts. 23.1 and 23.3.

[74] For a detailed analysis of the case and the interim decision, see Jelena Bäumler, 'Only a Brief Pause for Breath: The Judgment of the German Federal Constitutional Court on CETA', 7(5) Investment Treaty News (ITN) 3 (2016).

[75] *Helleyer et al v Trudeau et al* (2016), Toronto T-1789-16 (FCTD): http://www.canadianbankreformers.ca/wp-content/uploads/2016/10/Court-Document.pdf.

[76] Ibid. Statement of Claim, 20–21.

[77] A record of entries for the proceeding is available at: <http://cas-cdc-www02.cas-satj.gc.ca/IndexingQueries/infp_RE_info_e.php?court_no=T-1789-16&select_court=T>.

claims—only foreign investors, to the exclusion of states or the affected communities.[78] This narrow approach to investment-related dispute settlement is linked to the substantive law applicable to dispute resolution under most investment treaties and chapters today, which creates substantive rights for foreign investors only, without corresponding obligations.

From 21 December 2016 to 15 March 2017, the European Commission conducted another public consultation on the ICS, seeking inputs from stakeholders on the EU policy on investment dispute resolution and possible options for multilateral reform, including the possible establishment of a permanent Multilateral Investment Court.[79] Although concern was expressed that only investors would have the right of action in such a court, and that there was a need to allow affected communities to intervene and defend their rights, no such provisions have been introduced in EU texts so far.

It will be interesting to examine and compare developments at the EU with developments at the regional level, where similar attempts are under way to move away from ad hoc arbitration to more structured and permanent approaches to investment-related dispute settlement, in relation to different substantive investment treaty models—models that incorporate a new repartition of rights and obligations of investors, states and other stakeholders.[80]

12.5 Time to Rethink Dispute Settlement in a New Era of International Law on Globalization

12.5.1 One-sided rights and remedies

The broader civil society concern over the role of international investment treaties remains that, as part of the broader international economic law on globalization, it is uniquely focused on the rights and remedies of one actor, the foreign investor. While

[78] Natacha Cingotti et al., 'Investment Court System Put to the Test: New EU Proposal Will Perpetuate Investors' Attacks on Health and Environment' (Canadian Centre for Policy Alternatives, Corporate Europe Observatory, Friends of the Earth Europe, Forum Umwelt, und Entwicklung (German Forum on Environment and Development), and the Transnational Institute, 2016): <http://www.s2bnetwork.org/wp-content/uploads/2016/04/icstest_web.pdf>. See other criticisms, Seattle To Brussels Network: <http://www.s2bnetwork.org/tag/ics/>.

[79] European Commission, 'Questionnaire on Options for a Multilateral Reform of Investment Dispute Resolution' (2016): <http://trade.ec.europa.eu/consultations/index.cfm?consul_id=233>.

[80] See Makane Mbengue, 'The Quest for a Pan-African Investment Code to Promote Sustainable Development', 5(5) Bridges Africa (2016): <http://www.ictsd.org/bridges-news/bridges-africa/news/the-quest-for-a-pan-african-investment-code-to-promote-sustainable>; Katia Fach Gómez and Catharine Titi, 'UNASUR Centre for the Settlement of Investment Disputes: Comments on the Draft Constitutive Agreement', 7(3) Investment Treaty News 3 (2016).

new models show that this does not have to be the case,[81] this remains the case in recent treaties negotiated, such as the CETA and the TPP.[82] In line with this approach, arbitration provisions found in investment treaties allow only one actor to initiate an arbitration, leaving states, as respondents, to pay damages to investors. While several tribunals have recognized that investors can have obligations under investment treaties and that these obligations can have an impact on the application of investor rights by tribunals, and while new-generation investment treaties and models include provisions on obligations of investors, remedies under investment treaties remain a right of foreign investors only.[83]

Not only is the right to initiate an arbitration limited in the investment treaty context, but the right to intervene is also extremely limited. The ability of non-parties to submit *amicus curiae* briefs is not a right but is subject to the discretion of the tribunal. As a consequence, the mechanism is very limited and, as recent cases show, subject to far-reaching restrictions.

The attempt of civil society to intervene as third parties in *UPS v Canada* was rejected, among other reasons, because the petitioners did not have rights or obligations under NAFTA Chapter 11, which the tribunal was concerned with.[84] Since only foreign investors were granted procedural and substantive rights under the investment chapter of the now replaced NAFTA, the consequence of the *UPS* approach is that there is no avenue for intervening for any other stakeholders. For example, an investment could affect specific property or other rights of an indigenous community, or it could have a direct impact on the lives and the environment of local communities. However, these rights or interests cannot be taken into account for deciding about the intervention of their holders if the reasoning is that these rights or interests must be incorporated in the investment treaty itself.

In treaty-based investment arbitration, therefore, submitting an *amicus* brief is the only avenue for intervening in a case, at the discretion of the tribunal. There is no right to be heard, or a right to take part in proceedings, for affected or harmed communities.[85]

[81] Southern African Development Community (SADC), 'SADC Model Bilateral Investment Treaty Template with Commentary' (SADC 2012): <http://www.iisd.org/itn/wp-content/uploads/2012/10/SADC-Model-BIT-Template-Final.pdf>; Government of the Republic of India, 'Model Text for the Indian Bilateral Investment Treaty' (2015): <http://investmentpolicyhub.unctad.org/Download/TreatyFile/3560>; United Nations Economic Commission for Africa (UNECA) and African Union, 'Ninth Joint Annual Meetings of the African Union Specialized Technical Committee on Finance, Monetary Affairs, Economic Planning and Integration and the Economic Commission for Africa Conference of African Ministers of Finance, Planning and Economic Development, Meeting of the Committee of Experts, "Draft Pan-African Investment Code"' (2016), UN Doc E/ECA/COE/35/18: <http://www.uneca.org/sites/default/files/uploaded-documents/CoM/com2016/e1600511.pdf>.

[82] CETA (n. 72), Ch. 8, Sec. F, Art. 8.18; TPP (n. 7), Ch. 9, Art. 9.1.

[83] Mehmet Toral and Thomas Schultz, 'The State, a Perpetual Respondent in Investment Arbitration? Some Unorthodox Considerations', in Michael Waibel et al. (eds), *The Backlash Against Investment Arbitration: Perceptions and Reality* (Kluwer Law International, 2010), 577–602.

[84] El Hosseny (n. 53), 280; *United Parcel Service of America Inc. v Government of Canada*, Decision of the Tribunal on Petitions for Intervention and Participation as Amicus Curiae (2001).

[85] El Hosseny (n. 53), 293.

The inequality of arms between different economic stakeholders and between different sets of rights and obligations is also an issue in the context of investment contracts. These may have, if well negotiated, a balanced set of rights and obligations for the contracting parties, and both parties would have access to the arbitration process. This typically still excludes other stakeholders who may be affected through the investment operation regulated in the contract. While these stakeholders may well have opportunities to appear before domestic courts or processes, they have only limited opportunities at the international level to intervene in disputes between companies and the government or to bring a claim against a government or a company in case of harm. For example, UNCITRAL Arbitration Rules provides for joinders, but only where requested by a party. The rule also has a very limited scope and gives the arbitrator the discretion to reject.[86] In many cases, the international arbitration under a contract may not even be known to other stakeholders.

12.5.2 New approaches to investment-related dispute settlement

Over the past few years, new forms of investment-related dispute settlement have been and continue to be explored. In 2013, the United Nations Conference on Trade and Development (UNCTAD) outlined five main reform paths for investor-state arbitration: promoting alternative dispute resolution (ADR), tailoring the existing regime through individual treaties, limiting investor access to ISDS, introducing an appeals facility, and creating a standing international investment court.[87] UNCTAD continues to advance ISDS reform in the broader context of reforming investment treaties under a holistic approach (covering their substantive, procedural, and systemic aspects), particularly through the Action Menu and Roadmap for IIA Reform laid out in UNCTAD's 2015 World Investment Report.[88] Attorneys Claes Cronstedt of the Swedish bar and Robert C. Thompson of the California Bar propose an international arbitration tribunal on business and human rights, broadening the reach of international arbitration rules and institutions to include human rights disputes involving multinational enterprises, their business partners, and victims of abuses.[89] At its 50th session, in July 2017, the UNCITRAL Commission entrusted its Working Group III with a broad mandate to work on the possible reform of ISDS. The working group has identified

[86] UNCITRAL, 'UNCITRAL Arbitration Rules' (2013), Art. 17(5).

[87] UNCTAD, 'Reform of Investor–State Dispute Settlement: In Search of a Roadmap', IIA Issues Note No. 2 (2013): <http://unctad.org/en/PublicationsLibrary/webdiaepcb2013d4_en.pdf>.

[88] UNCTAD, 'Chapter IV: Reforming the International Investment Regime: An Action Menu', World Investment Report (UNCTAD 2015): <http://unctad.org/en/PublicationChapters/wir2015ch4_en.pdf>.

[89] Claes Cronstedt and Robert Thompson, 'A Proposal for an International Arbitration Tribunal on Business and Human Rights', 57 Harvard International Law Journal 66 (2016). For the text of the proposal, see Claes Cronstedt and Robert Thompson, 'An International Arbitration Tribunal on Business and Human Rights', Version Five (2015): <http://www.l4bb.org/news/TribunalV5B.pdf>.

concerns regarding ISDS, considered that reform is desirable, and is, at the time of writing, in the process of developing recommendations.[90] The EU's ICS model, as described earlier, has addressed many of the concerns identified in the context of traditional investment arbitration. However, only its proposal in the TTIP context begins to address the role of non-party intervention, which could open the door for stakeholders whose rights or interests might be affected, beyond *amicus curiae* submissions. Overall, the way forward proposed by the EU risks becoming a vehicle for entrenching the law as prevalent in most investment treaties today. If not designed with a broader objective in mind, it might be difficult for the law and related processes to develop toward a more holistic investment treaty model that balances the rights and obligations of different actors and proposes creative ways to resolve conflict.[91]

In 2014, IISD started a process with experts from academia, governments, civil society, and international organizations to discuss what investment-dispute settlement mechanisms could look like were they to be built anew, exploring alternative models to supplement or replace existing mechanisms. One particular concern of the experts was to move investment-related dispute settlement away from the investor–state arbitration paradigm in recognition of the fact that investment-related conflicts are complex, and involve actors beyond investors and states. It was concluded that investment-related dispute settlement should be more solution-oriented and inclusive of actors other than investors and states, such as communities or individuals affected by a foreign investment. The process should also be more open to considering concerns other than business-oriented concerns included in most investment treaties, and should extend to public health, labour rights, environmental protection, and other public interests.[92]

The ongoing process aims at producing a model agreement to create an international dispute settlement agency for trans-boundary and other investments[93] and aims to assist initiatives to create global or regional dispute settlement mechanisms, such as the proposal of the EU to create a multilateral investment court, or different initiatives in Africa and Latin America. Because these initiatives are not related to any specific investment treaty that might incorporate narrow approaches to rights and obligations, there is an opportunity to develop a model that allows for inclusive dispute settlement that can apply to a range of existing or future treaties and other instruments. The desired result of this initiative is to achieve a new global framework on the international law on globalization that is more balanced and equitable, and that provides rights and remedies to a range of stakeholders, not just one group.

[90] UNCITRAL, 'Working Group III: Investor-State Dispute Settlement Reform': <https://uncitral.un.org/en/working_groups/3/investor-state>.

[91] IISD, 'Reply to the European Commission's Public Consultation on a Multilateral Reform of Investment Dispute Resolution': <http://www.iisd.org/library/reply-european-commission-s-public-consultation-multilateral-reform-investment-dispute>.

[92] IISD, 'Investment-Related Dispute Settlement: Reflections on a New beginning' (IISD, 2015): <http://www.iisd.org/library/investment-related-dispute-settlement-reflections-new-beginning>.

[93] IISD, 'Investment-Related Dispute Settlement: Towards a Comprehensive Multilateral Approach' (IISD, 2016): <http://www.iisd.org/library/investment-related-dispute-settlement-towards-inclusive-multilateral-approach>.

CHAPTER 13

THE CONTROL OVER KNOWLEDGE BY INTERNATIONAL COURTS AND ARBITRAL TRIBUNALS

JEAN D'ASPREMONT

THIS chapter constitutes a heuristic exercise meant to reimagine international courts and arbitral tribunals as bureaucratic bodies controlling the social reality created by the definitional categories of international law. Its primarily claim is that, in performing their wide variety of functions, international courts and arbitral tribunals not only make use of the social reality created by international law, but also exert control over it. This control over the social reality created by the definitional categories of international law is approached as a form of control over knowledge and, it is argued, constitutes a feature of bureaucratic processes. In contending that international courts and arbitral tribunals control knowledge in this way, this chapter projects an image of international dispute resolution processes as bureaucratic sites of the exercise of power.

By virtue of this specific representation of international courts and arbitral tribunals as bureaucratic bodies controlling knowledge, this chapter challenges some common representations of international courts and arbitral tribunals as resorting to some pre-existing knowledge, and accordingly sheds light on the extent to which international courts and arbitral tribunals define social reality and the problems which they intervene in. The chapter ultimately aims at providing new perspectives on the power exercised by international courts and arbitral tribunals,[1] while also inviting international lawyers to

[1] On the idea of exercise of public authority by international courts, see generally Armin von Bogdandy and Ingo Venzke, 'In Whose Name? An Investigation of International Courts' Public Authority and its Democratic Justification', 23 European Journal of International Law (2012).

reflect on the extent to which the knowledge they rely on to manage the world is controlled by international courts and arbitral tribunals.[2]

The chapter starts by shedding light on the bureaucratic nature of international courts and arbitral tribunals inherent in their control of knowledge (section 13.1). It then provides some indications as to the type of knowledge that falls within the ambit of the control of international courts and arbitral tribunals understood as bureaucratic bodies (section 13.2). It continues with a presentation of the modes of control used by international courts and arbitral tribunals to control knowledge (section 13.3). The final section grapples with some of the implications of the portrayal of international courts and arbitral tribunals as bureaucratic bodies controlling knowledge in terms of the type of contestation which such an account enables (section13.4).

Before we begin, however, a few preliminary caveats are necessary. First, as already mentioned, the discussion that follows is heuristic.[3] It seeks to project a specific image of international courts and arbitral tribunals with a view to raising awareness about under-explored dimensions of international dispute resolution. Thus, this chapter is not meant to make any grand descriptive claim as to what kind of rationality is at work in international adjudicatory processes. In that sense, the image of international dispute settlement processes that is produced here is not meant to be exclusive of other possible outlooks.[4] Nor does the representation put forward here claim any kind of empirical superiority.[5]

Second, for the sake of the heuristic exercise attempted here, this chapter speaks of 'international courts and arbitral tribunals' without taking pains to distinguish between the great variety of judicial bodies involved in the resolution of international disputes.[6] It is contended here that the generic character of such a category—and the occasional oversimplification that comes with it—is no obstacle to the heuristic exercise attempted here.

[2] The idea of 'managerialism' in international legal thought was coined by Martti Koskenniemi. See Martti Koskenniemi, 'The Politics of International Law: 20 Years Later', 20 European Journal of International Law 7 (2009). On the managerialist posture of contemporary international lawyers, see Jean d'Aspremont, 'Jenks' Ethic of Responsibility for the Disillusioned International Lawyer', 27 European Journal of International Law (2017). According to Jouannet, there has always been an element of 'welfarism' and interventionism in how we think about international law. See Emmanuelle Jouannet, *The Liberal-Welfarist Law of Nations: A History of International Law* (Cambridge University Press, 2012).

[3] For a useful definition of the heuristic method of inquiry in international legal studies, see Cédric Dupont and Thomas Schultz, 'Towards a New Heuristic Model: Investment Arbitration as a Political System', (2016) 7 Journal of International Dispute Settlement 3.

[4] For other heuristic exercises about international courts and arbitral tribunals, see Thomas Schultz, 'Arbitral Decision-Making: Legal Realism and Law & Economics', 6 Journal of International Dispute Settlement 231 (2015); Dupont and Schultz (n. 3).

[5] For a similar attempt to describe legal reasoning and generate readers' imaginative empathy for a certain image of legal reasoning without claiming superiority over others, see Pierre Schlag, 'The Aesthetics of American Law', 115 Harvard Law Review 1049 (2002), 1054.

[6] For a taxonomy of international judicial bodies, see Cesare Romano, Karen Alter, and Yuval Shany, 'Mapping International Adjudicative Bodies, the Issues, and Players', in Cesare Romano, Karen Alter, and Yuval Shany (eds), *The Oxford Handbook of International Adjudication* (Oxford University Press, 2013), 3; see also David D. Caron, 'Towards a Political Theory of International Courts and Tribunals', 24 Berkeley Journal of International Law (2006), 401.

Last but not least, it must be stressed that the discussion that follows is not functional, in that it does not approach control of knowledge as a new 'function' of international courts and arbitral tribunals. Indeed, this discussion is not meant to supplement existing studies[7] which have shed light on the extent to which international courts and arbitral tribunals, besides their traditional roles as dispute settlement bodies,[8] compliance assessors,[9] and law consolidators,[10] also perform a role in norm advancement,[11] regime maintenance,[12] tipping political balances,[13] mobilizing public opinion,[14] recording history,[15] enforcing authority,[16] exercising administrative review authority,[17] exercising constitutional review authority,[18] generating credibility of commitments,[19] stabilizing normative expectations,[20] controlling and legitimizing public authority exercised by others,[21] etc. Said differently, the control over knowledge is not construed here as yet another function of international courts and arbitral tribunals.[22]

[7] See generally Benedict Kingsbury, 'International Courts, Uneven Judicialization in Global Order', in James Crawford and Martti Koskenniemi (eds), *The Cambridge Companion to International Law* (Cambridge University Press, 2012), 203; Jose Alvarez, 'What Are International Judges For?' in Romano et al. (n. 6), 158; Armin von Bogdandy and Ingo Venzke, 'On the Functions of International Courts: An Appraisal in the Light of Their Burgeoning Public Authority', Working Paper No. 2012–10 (Amsterdam Center for International Law, 2012); Karen Alter, 'The Multiple Roles of International Courts and Tribunals: Enforcement, Dispute Settlement, Constitutional and Administrative Review', Buffet Centre for International and Comparative Studies Working Paper No. 12-002 (2012). There are also sophisticated taxonomies of the various roles of the members of the judiciary. See e.g. Susan Franck, 'The Role of International Arbitrator', 12 J. Int'l & Comp. L. 499 (2006). For similar studies on the functions of domestic courts, see Martin Shapiro, *Courts: A Comparative and Political Analysis* (University of Chicago Press, 1981).

[8] For some critical thoughts on the rise and fall of the idea of international courts as peace-maker, see Christian Tams, 'World Courts as Guardians of Peace', Working Paper 15 (Centre for Global Cooperation Research, 2016). See also Yuval Shany, 'No Longer a Weak Department of Power? Reflections on the Emergence of a New International Judiciary', 20 EJIL 73 (2009), 77–8; Inis Claude, *States and the Global System: Politics, Law and Organization* (Macmillan,1988), 160–73.

[9] On this classical role of courts, see Dinah Shelton, 'Form, Function, and the Powers of International Courts', 9 Chicago Journal of International Law 537 (2009).

[10] The idea that international courts contribute to the consolidation and the development of international law is an old one. As early as 1934, Hersch Lauterpacht published a series of papers on *The Development of International Law by the Permanent Court of International Justice*. See also Hersch Lauterpacht, *The Function of Law in the International Community* (Oxford University Press, 2011). For a recent re-examination of this question, see Christopher Tams and Antonios Tzanakopoulos, 'Barcelona Traction at 40: The ICJ as an Agent of Legal Development', 23 Leiden Journal of International Law 781 (2010). On the idea that international arbitration is not necessarily linked to the application of international law, see Stephen Neff, *Justice Among Nations* (Harvard University Press, 2014), 328–9.

[11] Shany (n. 8).

[12] Ibid. See also Kinsbury (n. 7), who speaks of 'routinized adjudication as governance'.

[13] Karen Alter, 'Tipping the Balance: International Courts and the Construction of International and Domestic Politics', 13 Cambridge Yearbook of International Studies 1 (2011).

[14] Tams (n. 8), 25. [15] Ibid.

[16] Shelton (n. 9); Alter (n. 7); Karen Alter, 'Delegating to International Courts: Self-Binding vs. Other-Binding Delegation', 71 Law and Contemporary Problems 37 (2008).

[17] Alter (nn. 7, 16). [18] Ibid. [19] Kingsbury (n. 7), 203.

[20] Von Bogdandy and Venzke (n. 7). [21] Ibid.

[22] It must be acknowledge that the idea of control over knowledge bears resemblance with what Benedict Kingsbury has identified as the management of information by courts. See Kingsbury (n. 7).

In the same vein, this chapter does not seek to contribute to the studies of the capacities in which international courts and arbitral tribunals engage in their adjudicatory functions[23]—that is, whether they act as agents of the parties,[24] agents of the community,[25] trustees,[26] etc. Rather, more modestly, it seeks to provide an image of international courts and arbitral tribunals as bureaucratic bodies exercising control over the social reality created by the definitional categories of international law, and to reflect upon what this means for international lawyers.

13.1 The Nature of the Controllers: International Courts and Arbitral Tribunals as Bureaucratic Bodies

A first series of observations is warranted as to the nature of the controllers discussed here, namely the nature of international courts and arbitral tribunals when they control knowledge. According to the understanding of bureaucracy adopted here, the exercise of control over knowledge is a feature of the bureaucratic process.[27] This means that international courts and arbitral tribunals, when they engage in the control of the social reality created by the definitional categories of international law, act as bureaucratic bodies.

This image of courts as bureaucratic bodies is not new,[28] let alone with respect to international courts and arbitral tribunals.[29] Obviously, such an image depends on one's

For some criticisms of functionalist approaches, see Mikael Madsen, 'Towards a Sociology of International Courts', iCourts Online Working Paper No. 1 (2013), 12.

[23] On this question, see generally von Bogdandy and Venzke (n. 7). See also Alec Stone Sweet and Florian Grisel, 'The Evolution of International Arbitration: Delegation, Judicialization, Governance', in Walter Mattli and Thomas Dietz (eds), *International Arbitration and Global Governance: Contending Theories and Evidence* (Oxford University Press, 2014), 23.

[24] Eric Posner and John Yoo, 'Judicial Independence in International Tribunals', 93 Cal. L. Rev. 1 (2005).

[25] Lauterpacht (n. 10), 5. For the identification of some 'community-originated institutions', see Caron (n. 6).

[26] On the debate between international courts as agents versus international courts as trustees, see Karen Alter, 'Agents or Trustees? International Courts in their Political Context', 14 European Journal of International Relations 33 (2008). See also Kenneth Abbott and Duncan Snidal, 'Why States Act Through Formal International Organizations', 42 Journal of Conflict Resolution 3 (1998).

[27] For Philip Allott, the fact that courts are physically isolated, symbolically distinct, and systematically distinct from the rest of social reality is what allows them to reinvent that social reality. See generally Philip Allott, 'The International Court and the Voice of Justice', in Vaughan Lowe and Malgosia Fitzmaurice (eds), *Fifty Years of the International Court of Justice* (Cambridge University Press, 2016), 17.

[28] See Robert Burns, 'Is Our Legal Order Just Another Bureaucracy?' 48 Loy. U. Chi. L. J. 413 (2016).

[29] Ingo Venzke, 'International Bureaucracies from a Political Science Perspective: Agency, Authority and International Institutional Law', 9 German Law Journal 1401 (2008); Mathilde Cohen, 'Judges or Hostages? The Bureaucratization of the Court of Justice of the European Union and the European Court

account of what constitutes a bureaucratic body. The dominant understanding informing the portrayal of international courts and arbitral tribunals as bureaucratic bodies postulates that they are bureaucratic bodies because of their control over knowledge when exercising their adjudicatory power. This mundane idea that the rational-legal exercise of power through knowledge is a feature of a bureaucratic mode of organization is traditionally traced back to Max Weber, whose work has enjoyed dramatic popularity among international lawyers.[30]

From such a perspective, international courts and arbitral tribunals can be construed as bureaucratic bodies because their power is exercised through knowledge.[31] From that vantage point, the knowledge which international courts and arbitral tribunals deploy is supposedly very wide and includes information as diverse as positive rules and their content (*jura novit curia*),[32] the modes of legal reasoning, the modes of establishing facts, procedures, etc. This image of international courts and arbitral tribunals as bureaucratic bodies as a result of their exercise of power through knowledge is not contradicted by their use of specific knowledge which—like scientific knowledge[33]—they do not have access to and which they must hire from other bureaucratic bodies. In the situation where international courts and arbitral tribunals must hire knowledge from third parties, they continue to exercise power through knowledge according to this common understanding of bureaucracies.

The account of bureaucratic bodies adopted here[34] challenges the traditional Weberian understanding of courts and tribunals as bureaucratic bodies whose powers are allegedly based on the knowledge they use. Rather, it is submitted here that the Weberian approach to the bureaucratic character of international courts and arbitral tribunals obfuscates the extent to which the knowledge that they make use of is

of Human Rights', in Bill Davies and Fernanda Nicola (eds), *European Law Stories* (Cambridge University Press, 2017), 58.

[30] Max Weber, *The Theory of Social and Economic Organization*, trans. A. M. Henderson and Talcott Parsons (Martino, 2012), 330–36. See also Roberto Unger, *Law and the Modern World: Toward a Criticism of Social Theory* (Free Press, 1976), 59.

[31] According to Alasdair MacIntyre, controlling through knowledge is bureaucracy's strongest claim to legitimacy, a claim which arguably fails. See Alasdair MacIntyre, *After Virtue*, 3rd edn (University of Notre Dame Press, 2007), 86.

[32] In that respect, it is noteworthy that the common aphorism underpins this image of international courts and arbitral tribunals as bureaucratic bodies exercising power through knowledge, although the knowledge deployed by such bodies is far wider and more diverse than indicated by the aphorism. On thisaphorism, see Joe Verhoeven, 'Jura Novit Curia et le juge international', in Pierre-Marie Dupuy et al. (eds), *Common Values in international Law: Essays in Honour of Christian Tomuschat* (Engel, 2006), 635. Also see Takane Sugihara, 'The Principle of Jura Novit Curia in the International Court of Justice: With Reference to Recent Decisions', 55 Japanese Yearbook of International Law 77 (2012). For some qualification of this idea, see *Asylum (Colombia/Peru)*, ICJ Rep. (1950), 226–77; *Rights of Nationals of the United States of America in Morocco (France v United States of America)*, ICJ Rep. (1952), 200; *Fisheries Jurisdiction (Federal Republic of Germany v Iceland)*, ICJ Rep. (1974), 181.

[33] Jean d'Aspremont and Makane Mbengue, 'Strategies of Engagement with Scientific Fact-Finding in International Adjudication', 5 Journal of International Dispute Settlement 240 (2014).

[34] For another account of bureaucracy based on the multiplicity of actors, the division of functions or responsibilities among them and the reliance upon a hierarchy as the central device to coordinate their activities, see Owen Fiss, 'The Bureaucratization of the Judiciary', 92 Yale Law Journal 1442 (1983), 1444.

controlled by them. In other words, the account of bureaucracy that is embraced here acknowledges the power of bureaucracies to shape the very problems that they ought to address, and points to the extent to which bureaucracies influence the construction of the social reality in which they intervene.[35] International courts and arbitral tribunals are thus construed as bureaucratic bodies, not by virtue of their power being exercised *through* knowledge but by virtue of their control *over* knowledge. As is explained in the remainder of this chapter, this control amounts to the steering of the definitional categories of the law they deem applicable, allowing them to contribute to the constitution of the social reality which they ought to address.

The remainder of this chapter seeks to elaborate upon the notions both of *knowledge*[36] and of *control*,[37] with a view to shedding light on the extent to which international courts and arbitral tribunals, as bureaucratic bodies, contribute to the constitution of the social reality in which they intervene. Before proceeding with the substantiation of this claim, a final remark on the idea of bureaucracy is warranted. The foregoing should suffice to show that the idea of bureaucracy is not used pejoratively. It is true that bureaucracy often evokes pathological and systemic dysfunctions,[38] rule-based rigidity,[39] an inclination to shy away from engagement and discretionary evaluation,[40] or the dilution of responsibility.[41] Whilst it cannot be excluded that some of these pathologies apply to international courts and arbitral tribunals, it is not the aim of this chapter to reach any diagnostic of that sort. The image of international courts and arbitral tribunals as bureaucratic bodies is projected here solely because it is an integral part of the claim that they control knowledge while performing their wide variety of functions.

13.2 The Object of Control: The Knowledge Controlled by International Courts and Arbitral Tribunals

Section 13.1 put forward a new understanding of bureaucratic bodies that allows one to construe international courts and arbitral tribunals as bureaucratic bodies by virtue of

[35] For a similar understanding of bureaucracy, see Venzke (n. 29), 1414. See also John Ruggie, 'International Responses to Technology: Concepts and Trends', 29 International Organization 557 (1975), 569–70.

[36] See section 13.2. [37] See section 13.3.

[38] This is a traditional charge against the bureaucratization of courts. See Fiss (n. 34), 1444.

[39] Weber (n. 30), 330–6. See contra, Fiss (n. 34), 1452. On this debate, see also Burns (n. 28).

[40] This is a traditional charge against the bureaucratization of courts. See Fiss (n. 34), 1443.

[41] This is the criticism famously voiced by Hannah Arendt, 'On Violence', in *Crises of the Republic* (Houghton Mifflin, 1972), 103, 137–8. For an application of that criticism to the American judiciary, see Fiss (n. 34), 1458; See also Dennis Thompson, 'Moral Responsibility of Public Officials: The Problem of Many Hands', 74 Am. Pol. Science Rev. 905 (1980); André Nollkaemper 'The Problem of Many Hands in International Law', in Alberta Fabricotti (ed.), *The Political Economy of International Law: A European Perspective* (Elgar, 2016), 278.

their control over knowledge rather than their power exercised through knowledge. The very notion of *knowledge* that is controlled by international courts and arbitral tribunals and that of *control* must now be further elaborated upon.

The knowledge that is controlled by international courts and arbitral tribunals for the sake of the claim made in this chapter refers to the social reality constituted by the application of the definitional categories[42] of international law.[43] Such a social reality amounts to knowledge because the claims made about this social reality are held to be universal.[44] And yet, these claims about the known social reality created by the definitional categories of international law are only real to international law,[45] and inevitably co-exist with alternative claims about alternative social realities which may or may not be known by international lawyers.[46]

The idea that (international) law and legal categories create their own social reality is not new.[47] This idea entails that (international) law creates the categories of how

[42] On the idea that legal categories are a creation of law, see Karl Olivecrona, 'Legal Language and Reality', in Ralph Newman (ed.), *Essays in Jurisprudence in Honor of Roscoe Pound* (Bobbs-Merrill, 1962), 151–2: 'Yet it is obvious that the rights and duties as well as the legal properties and powers do not belong to the sensible world, the world of facts. Nobody can directly ascertain their presence in a particular case. If an astronaut from a distant planet were to descend some day on our earth, he would not be able to perceive any rights or duties, legal powers or properties.'

[43] On the distinction between data and knowledge, see Régis Debray, *Transmitting Culture*, trans. Eric Rauth (Colombia University Press 1997), 16.

[44] On the universalizing effect of legal claims, see Pierre Bourdieu, 'The Force of Law: Toward a Sociology of the Juridical Field', 38 Hastings Law Journal 805 (1987), 844. See also Martti Koskenniemi, 'Hegemonic Regimes', in Margaret Young (ed.), *Regime Interaction in International Law* (Cambridge University Press, 2012), 305, 311; Martti Koskenniemi, 'The Mystery of Legal Obligation', 3 International Theory 319 (2011), 324: 'Law's power and attraction lie in its offering what appears a universal point of view, its ability to raise mere opinions onto a status of what is (universally) right. And yet this universal standpoint constantly eludes us. Rules show themselves as mere interpretations, principles are challenged by equally powerful counter principles, etc.' Compare with Jack Balkin, 'The Proliferation of Legal Truth', 26 Harvard Journal of Law and Public Policy 5 (2003), 108: 'What law does, and can do, is proliferate ideas, concepts, institutions and forms of social imagination, which can attach themselves to, reorganize, and even displace existing forms of social understanding, social practice, and social reality.' It has been shown that such universality is constantly eluding us.

[45] See Balkin (n. 44), 106. See also Thomas Schultz, 'Life Cycles of International Law as a Noetic Unity: The Various Times of Law-Thinking', in Luca Pasquet, Klara van der Ploeg, and Leon Jankiewicz (eds), *International Law and Time: Narratives and Techniques* (Springer, 2018).

[46] See Balkin (n. 44), 109.

[47] As far as the definitional power of international law is concerned, see Philip Allott, 'The Idealist's Dilemma: Re-Imagining International Society': http://www.ejiltalk.org/the-idealists-dilemma-re-imagining-international-society/: 'The whole of the law is a vast work of fiction, a masterpiece of the human imagination, creating its own entirely artificial reality. Lawyers—even practising lawyers—are creative writers, re-inventing the story of the law every day.') See also Philip Allott, 'Language, Method and the Nature of International Law', 45 BYBIL 79 (1971), 118; James Crawford, 'International Law as Discipline and Profession', 106 ASIL Proceedings (2012), 16: 'We are collectively part of the makers of that world'); Balkin (n. 44), 104: 'Law has power over people's imaginations and how they think about what is happening in social life'; Paul Bohannan, 'The Differing Realms of the Law', 67 American Anthropologist 33 (1965). Compare with the idea of normative universe (nomos) developed by Robert Cover, 'The Supreme Court 1982 Term. Foreword: Nomos and Narrative', 97 Harvard Law Review 4 (1983), 4–5.

international lawyers experience and see the world.[48] This is the common idea that (international) law is performative of the very reality in which it is meant to intervene.[49] The definitional impact of (international) law has even been recognized as one of the most critical forms of power.[50] This chapter is not the place to revisit the idea that law constitutes the reality to which it applies. Instead, it looks into the control that international courts can wield on the constitution of social reality when they deploy the definitional categories of international law. In other words, for the sake of this discussion, international courts and arbitral tribunals are considered to control knowledge because they *steer* the definitional categories of international law that constitute the social reality to which international law is applied.

The steering of the definitional categories of international law by international courts and arbitral tribunals, and thus the correlative control over the knowledge about the social reality constituted by the definitional categories of international law, can bear a wide range of consequences.[51] For instance, it is uncontested that their control over knowledge can be instrumental in the determination of those rules that qualify as legal rules[52] and the content thereof, the value given to past decisions, the content and effect of

[48] This is what has led some scholars to invite us to look at law from the perspective of the study of culture. See Lawrence Rosen, *Law as Culture: An Invitation* (Princeton University Press, 2006), 4. See also Balkin (n. 44), 104: 'It is a form of cultural software that shapes the way we think about and apprehend the world.'

[49] From the perspective of speech act theory, law can thus be reduced to a series of performative statements. What the speech act theory developed by philosophers of language teaches us is that even such constative statements are performative. Constative statement does not just 'say' something but also perform a certain kind of action. More particularly, the actual utterance of the constative statement and its ostensible meaning performs an action: naming. Once the addressees of a statement understand it, they understand the intention of the author to communicate with them and to name. This is no different in the case of the international legal scholarship. When making scholarly statement, international legal scholars perform an operation of naming. See generally John Austin, *How to Do Things with Words* (Clarendon Press, 1979), 4. See also John Searle, *Speech Acts* (Cambridge University Press, 1969), 1–12.

[50] Bourdieu (n. 44): 'Law is the quintessential form of symbolic power of naming that creates the things names' (838); 'What is at stake in this struggle is monopoly of power to impose a universally recognized principle of knowledge of the social world' (837). On the idea that Bourdieu and Foucault allowed us to better understand how lawyering is connected to knowledge production, see Nikolas Rajkovic, 'Rules, Lawyering, and the Politics of Legality: Critical Sociology and International Law's Rule', 27 Leiden Journal of International Law 331 (2014), 341. This idea is now widely accepted in (international) legal scholarship. See Koskenniemi (n. 2), 11; Balkin (n. 44), 113: 'Law is most powerful when we see the world through its eyes, when its understanding becomes part of our understanding, and when its truth becomes part of our truth.'

[51] See generally Allott (n. 27), 17: 'Like any other social institution, a court is a transformatory structure-system, transforming social reality in particular ways. Itself the product of the past social reality of a particular society, a court makes a specific contribution to the general social reality of a particular society, a court makes a specific contribution to the general social task of forming a given society's future out of that society's past, as it acts in society continuous present.' See also Dupont and Schultz (n. 3), 5.

[52] The ambit of international law is itself a social reality constituted by its own definitional categories. The definitional categories determining the frontiers of international law are found in the doctrine of sources. See generally Jean d'Aspremont, *Formalism and the Sources of International Law* (Oxford University Press, 2011).

domestic law.[53] The use of the definitional categories of international law by international courts and arbitral tribunals also bears upon the reputation of the actors involved, the configuration of movements of capital, the financial situation of the parties, the future behaviour of the parties as well as that of other actors, the extent of individual or collective damage, etc.

The deployment of the definitional categories of international law will also simultaneously contribute to the writing of a particular history of the dispute or that of the relationship between the parties.[54] In doing so, they similarly participate in the delineation of the spheres of controversy[55] and create a specific 'structured space of contestation'.[56] The way in which international courts and arbitral tribunals use such definitional categories can even influence the very terms around which international politics are articulated.[57] Indeed, in exercising such control, international courts and arbitral tribunals contribute to the (re)definition of the definitional categories themselves and that of their content while also impacting on the way future instances of disagreement are debated by establishing 'content-laden reference points that participants in legal discourse can hardly escape'.[58] The cognitive consequences of the control over knowledge by international courts and arbitral tribunals are thus plentiful.

A final remark on the notion of knowledge as it is understood here must be formulated. It must be pointed out that social reality that is created by international courts and tribunals can be constituted through definitional categories of a general and overarching character (e.g. states, disputes, territories, non-compliance, wrongfulness, practice, regimes, damages, use of force) or through definitional categories specific to certain rules or regimes (war crimes, refugee, exclusive economic zone, nationally determined contributions, investment, fair and equitable treatment, etc.).[59] Either way, the knowledge under control here is the knowledge about the social reality constituted by the definitional categories of international law.[60]

[53] This is a point to which Laurence Boisson de Chazournes brought my attention.

[54] This will apply particularly to the case of what David D. Caron has called 'retrospective' dimension of institutions. See Caron (n. 6).

[55] Claude (n. 8), 172. See conversely, on the idea that the language of law is about ordering, Harold Berman, *Law and Language: Effective Symbols of Community* (Cambridge University Press, 2013), 77.

[56] Caron (n. 6), 411.

[57] On the idea that international law is constitutive of politics, see Christian Reus-Smit, 'Introduction', in Christian Reus-Smit (ed.), *The Politics of International Law* (Cambridge University Press, 2004), 1, 5; 'The Politics of International Law', ibid. 14. See also, for an illustration of this constitutive role of international law on politics, Dino Kritsiotis, 'When States Use Armed Force', ibid. 45–79.

[58] Ingo Venzke, 'Understanding the Authority of International Courts and Tribunals: On Delegation and Discursive Construction', 14 Theoretical Inquiries in Law 381 (2013).

[59] The most consequential of these definitional categories is probably the state. In this respect, see Michel Foucault, *Security, Territory, Population: Lectures at the Collège de France 1977–1978* (Picador, 2009), 247: 'It would be absurd to say that the set of institutions we call the state date from this period of 1580 to 1650...After all, big armies had already emerged...Taxation was established before this, and justice even earlier...But what is important...and what is at any rate a real, specific, and incompressible historical phenomenon is the moment this something, the state, really entered into reflected practice.'

[60] In that sense, the account given here is very different from the account of the work of international courts proposed by Hersch Lauterpacht. According to him, the completeness of the rule of law is an a

Indications as to what the notion of *control* in the context of the present discussion actually refers to are now warranted. In light of the understanding of knowledge that is embraced here, the control of international courts and arbitral tribunals refers to the power of shaping and steering the definitional categories which international courts and arbitral tribunals deploy when they adjudicate. Although the performativeness of such control remains contingent on the set of social realities made possible by the definitional categories of international law, it is thus the power to contribute to the constitution of the social reality they are called upon to address.

Importantly, control over knowledge through the use of the definitional categories of international law, as is understood here, is not carried out mechanically. It is inevitably informed by a wide range of constraints, values, and agendas, including awareness of their consequences in terms of distributive justice,[61] normative considerations, conscious or unconscious structural biases,[62] dispute avoidance strategies,[63] endeavours to manage more global problems,[64] quests for greater sophistication of regulatory frameworks,[65] ventures to tame contestation affecting the rules concerned and create consensus,[66] efforts to unify or de-fragment the applicable law,[67] attempts to increase the appeal of the dispute resolution mechanisms and entice actors to use it again,[68] etc. It is not the purpose of this chapter to review the constraints and agendas that inform the way in which international courts and arbitral tribunals use the definitional categories of international law and control knowledge about the social reality created through the definitional categories of international law. Nor is this chapter aimed at unravelling the way power works behind the steering of the definitional categories.[69] The more modest ambition of the remaining part of this chapter is to account for the way in which this control is carried out as well as the implications of such control.

priori assumption of every system of law, and there can thus be no gaps in the legal system as a whole. As a result, international courts have the function of filling gaps by virtue of a wide variety of techniques, including the deployment of general principles of law, which allow them to always unearth a legal solution. See Lauterpacht (n. 10), 113–43.

[61] David Kennedy, *A World of Struggle* (Princeton University Press, 2016), 217: 'the distributive impact of law has rarely been a focal point in mainstream international legal scholarship.'

[62] Ibid. 218–55; Koskenniemi (n. 2), 9.

[63] See Christopher Tams, 'No Dispute About Nuclear Weapons?' (EJIL: *Talk!*, 2016).

[64] This was part of Lauterpacht's idea of courts' function regarding filling gaps for the sake of allowing international law to rule the world. See generally Lauterpacht (n. 10), 113–43.

[65] See the remarks of Kennedy (n. 61), 218–55.

[66] On the idea that courts tip political balances, see Alter (n. 13).

[67] On the idea that fragmentation is sometimes a deliberate policy, see Eyal Benvenisti and George Downs, 'The Empire's New Clothes: Political Economy and the Fragmentation of International Law', 60 Stanford Law Review 595 (2007).

[68] Thomas Schultz, *Transnational Legality: Stateless Law and International Arbitration* (Oxford University Press, 2014), 14; Andrea Bianchi, 'Gazing at the Crystal Ball (Again): State Immunity and *Jus Cogens* beyond Germany v Italy', 4(3) Journal of International Dispute Settlement 457 (2013).

[69] See Michel Foucault, *Discipline and Punishment* (Penguin, 1977), 27: 'There is no power relation without the correlative constitution of a field of knowledge, nor any knowledge that does not presuppose and constitute at the same time power relations.'

13.3 Modes of Control over Knowledge: Constituting and Communicating Social Realities

This section elaborates upon the modes of control over the knowledge of the social realities created by the definitional categories of international law which international courts and arbitral tribunals resort to. It distinguishes between two sets of modes of control. On the one hand, control over knowledge is made possible by the intervention of courts and tribunals in the very constitution of social realities (direct control). On the other hand, control over knowledge is wielded through the way in which information about the social reality created by the definitional categories of international law is communicated by international courts and arbitral tribunals (indirect control).

13.3.1 Control over the constitution of social realities (direct control)

International courts and arbitral tribunals control the knowledge about the social reality created by the definitional categories of international law in multiple ways which are not mutually exclusive.[70] First, and most evidently, they select international law's definitional categories by selecting the rules they apply. Indeed, these definitional categories follow the applicable law as it is delineated by international courts and arbitral tribunals. This means that through the definition of the applicable law—and thus also the definition of the dispute—international courts and arbitral tribunals come to apply certain definitional categories rather than others, and hence allow the creation a certain social reality rather than others.[71] The definition of the dispute and that of the applicable law constitutes the most tangible expression of control over knowledge by international courts and arbitral tribunals.

Second, international courts and arbitral tribunals also exercise direct control over knowledge in (re)defining these definitional categories when applying them.[72] Indeed, international courts and arbitral tribunals constantly act as what Régis Debray has called a 'relay'[73] for these definitional categories, thereby remolding the definitional cat-

[70] On the idea that knowledge is also created by the practice under definitional categories, see Anothony Giddens, *Central Problems in Social Theory: Action, Structure, and Contradiction in Social Analysis* (Macmillan, 1979), 69.

[71] For a recent review of questions of applicable law in international adjudicatory practice, see Sienho Yee, 'Article 38 of the ICJ Statute and Applicable Law: Selected Issues in Recent Cases', 7 Journal of International Dispute Settlement 472 (2016).

[72] Allott (n. 27), 39: 'There is nothing to prevent the Court from reimagining itself as a source of a new legal reality.'

[73] Debray (n. 43), 19–20.

egories of international law in the course of their deployment.[74] This second mode of direct control is not difficult to grasp given that the definitional categories, which are themselves the result of a struggle to impose certain social realities rather than others,[75] remain indeterminate.[76] And in doing so, they simultaneously participate in the (re) definition of the definitional categories of international law themselves, thereby impacting subsequent uses of such definitional categories.[77]

Thirdly, international courts and arbitral tribunals, who have at their disposable a wide range of possible social realities that can potentially be constituted, select and actualize some specific social realities among the range of social realities made possible by the definitional categories of international law. When selecting among the social realities made possible by the definitional categories of international law, they are often called upon to reconcile distinct social realities with which they are confronted within the adjudicatory process. Indeed, international courts and arbitral tribunals often come to apply several definitional categories at the same time, thereby building several social realities and having to reconcile them. In this situation, with a view to performing their adjudicatory function, they are called to squeeze all these social realities into one another and produce a consistent and intelligible picture.[78] While definitional categories are, in themselves, reductionist by nature,[79] international courts and arbitral tribunals are called upon to carry out an extra stereotyping[80] to make all these social realities work together. This exercise of selection and reconciliation of social realities can be construed as a form of direct control over knowledge.

[74] Ibid. 27: 'Transformation by is transformation of. That which is transported is remodeled, refigured, and metabolized by its transit. The receiver finds a different letter from the one its sender placed in the mailbox.'

[75] For an illustration of the idea that definitional categories originates in the struggle to impose certain categories rather than others, see Jean d'Aspremont, 'The Articles on the Responsibility of International Organizations: Magnifying the Fissures in the Law of International Responsibility', 9 International Organizations Law Review 15 (2012). For a radically different understanding of the definitional categories of law as a receptacle of the past, see Berman (n. 55), 76–9.

[76] See also Martti Koskenniemi, 'The Fate of Public International Law: between Technique and Politics', 207 Modern Law Review 1 (2007), 7.

[77] It is noteworthy that the nature of (re-)definition of the definitional categories of international law has been the object of diverging understandings in the international legal thought. For some scholars, this could correspond to a matter of social practice being produced by the social practice of law-applying authorities. See d'Aspremont (n. 52). For others, it is more a matter of interpretation. See Ingo Venzke, *How Interpretation Makes International Law: On Semantic Change and Normative Twists* (Oxford University Press, 2012); Duncan Hollis, 'The Existential Function of Interpretation in International Law', in Andrea Bianchi, Daniel Peat, and Matthew Windsor (eds), *Interpretation in International Law* (Oxford University Press, 2015), 78. For a conciliatory position, see Jean d'Aspremont, 'The Multidimensional Process of Interpretation: Content-Determination and Law-Ascertainment Distinguished', ibid. 111.

[78] The argument has been made regarding American courts by Pierre Schlag, 'Spam Jurisprudence, Air Law and the Rank Anxiety of Nothing Happening', 97 Geo. L. J. 803 (2009), 815.

[79] Ibid. 815–16. In the same vein, see Friedrich Kratochwil, *Rules, Norms, and Decisions* (Cambridge University Press, 1989), 10: '[O]ne of the most important functions of rules and norms in such a world is the reduction in the complexity of the choice-situations in which the actors find themselves. Rules and norms are therefore guidance devices which are designed to simplify choices.'

[80] The expression is from Schlag (n. 78), 828.

13.3.2 Control over the communication of social realities (indirect control)

It is submitted here that there cannot be social reality if it is not communicated to the audience where it appears as real.[81] In that sense, there cannot be knowledge as long as the social reality constituted through the steering of the definitional categories of international law is not communicated by international courts and arbitral tribunals.[82] It is important to stress that communication is not understood here as the question of the medium used to impart the decision reached by international courts and arbitral tribunals. Rather, communication is construed here in a broad sense, and includes the way in which the social reality created by the definitional categories of international law is presented and sold to other professionals.

In that sense, communication, for the sake of the discussion conducted here, is a matter of argumentative packaging. Such argumentative packaging provides the format under which the social reality is judged during the verification process carried out by the professional community to which that social reality is addressed. For the sake of the argument made here, the way in which international courts and arbitral tribunals communicate about the information related to the social realities constituted by the definitional categories of international law constitutes an indirect form of control over knowledge as it is understood here.

International courts and arbitral tribunals communicate about the social reality constituted by the definitional categories of international law—and thus indirectly control knowledge—through a wide variety of tools. Without asserting any type of comprehensiveness, three specific argumentative tools used by international courts and arbitral tribunals when communicating about social realities must be mentioned here: interpretation, techniques of evidence, and precedents. Each of these tools allows international courts and arbitral tribunals to communicate about their use of the definitional categories of international law and their control over knowledge. From the perspective adopted here, interpretation, rules of evidence, and precedents are thus understood, not as definitional categories in themselves, but rather as means to package the social realities constituted by the deployment of the definitional categories of international law.

From the perspective of the discussion conducted here, the doctrine[83] of interpretation is construed as an indirect mode of control over knowledge because it is instrumental to

[81] See Bruno Latour, *Science in Action* (Harvard University Press, 1987), 40–41: 'You may have written a paper that settles a fierce controversy once and for all, but if readers ignore it, it cannot be turned into a fact; it simply cannot. You may protest against the injustice; you may treasure the certitude of being right in your inner heart; but it will never go further than your inner heart; you will never go further in certitude without the help of others. Fact construction is so much a collective process that an isolated person builds only dreams, claims and feelings, not facts.' See also Debray (n. 43); Carl Friedrich, 'Loyalty and Authority', 2 Confluence 307 (1954), 312.

[82] On the idea that communication is the authority's medium for international courts, see Venzke (n. 58).

[83] It seems more appropriate to speak about the 'doctrine' of interpretation rather than rules of interpretation. On this point, see d'Aspremont (n. 77), 111. In this respect, the doubts expressed by some of the

the way in which international courts and tribunals communicate about the social reality—and especially the content of rules—established by the definitional categories of international law.[84] As a mode of communication—and thus indirect modes of control—the doctrine of interpretation has long been the object of some sophisticated formalization.[85] Whether such formalization has actually restricted the interpretive powers of international judges and arbitral tribunals is not a question that ought to be addressed here.[86] The point is that the doctrine of interpretation constitutes an important tool for international courts and arbitral tribunals to communicate information about the social reality constituted by the definitional categories, and especially the content of the rules they apply.

Another mode of indirect control over knowledge by international courts and arbitral tribunals is found in the way in which they communicate about the establishment of the facts of the case. The facts of the case constitutes another social reality constituted on the occasion of the adjudicatory process. The communication about the establishment thereof is meant to be subject to certain techniques of evidence. This means that, for the sake of the discussion carried out here, evidentiary techniques constitute a set of communicative tools about the factual findings made by international courts and arbitral tribunals. In this respect, it is worth recalling that international courts and arbitral tribunals usually organize their communication about their factual findings made by distinguishing between the burden of proof and standards of proof.[87] At each level,[88] international courts and arbitral tribunals enjoy considerable leeway to tailor their communication, especially given the fact that there is no such thing as a ready-made

drafters of the Vienna Convention on the Law of Treaties are worth recalling. E.g. Alfred Verdross raised the question of the nature of the rules of interpretation which the International Law Commission intended to codify, arguing that 'the Commission ought first to decide whether it recognised the existence of such rules' (ILC, 726th Meeting, A/CN.4/167; reproduced in 1 YILC 20 (1964), para. 15). In his view, 'it was highly controversial whether the rules established by the case-law of arbitral tribunals and international courts were general rules of international law or merely technical rules'. In the same vein, Sir Humphrey Waldock conceded that he 'was decidedly lukewarm on rules on interpretation, including them more because he thought this was expected of him than out of genuine expectation that rules on interpretation would be of much use' (cited in Jans Klabbers, 'Virtuous Interpretation', in Malgosia Fitzmaurice et al. (eds), *Treaty Interpretation and the Vienna Convention on the Law of Treaties: 30 Years On* (Martinus Nijhoff, 2010), 17–18.

84 For a similar understanding, see Andrea Bianchi, 'The Game of Interpretation in International Law', in Bianchi et al. (n. 77).

85 See d'Aspremont (n. 77).

86 See generally Venzke (n. 77).

87 On questions of methods of proof, see Marco Roscini, 'Evidentiary Issues in International Disputes Related to State Responsibility for Cyber Operations', 50 Texas International Law Journal 233 (2015).

88 This being said, it must be noted that, at the level of the burden of proof, most judicial bodies will uphold traditional position of *onus incumbit actori* vindicated by the International Court of Justice (*Corfu Channel (United Kingdom v Albania)*, ICJ Rep. 4 (1949), 18). See the remarks of see Andrea Gattini, 'Evidentiary Issues in the ICJ's Genocide Judgment', 5 Journal of International Criminal Justice 899 (2007); Marco Roscini (n. 87), 243–4. This means that in most contentious international proceedings, international courts and arbitral tribunals do not establish the fact themselves but rely on the facts as evidenced by the parties to the dispute. That does not mean, however, that they do not have to communicate about them.

and all-encapsulating 'doctrine' of evidence which applies across the board and which all international courts and arbitral tribunals would be expected to share and apply.[89]

A third mode of indirect control over knowledge is provided by the means through which international courts and arbitral tribunals assign weight—in the present—to past judicial decisions.[90] From the perspective adopted here, past pronouncements and their present significance constitute another type of social reality constituted on the occasion of an adjudicatory process.[91] In this context, the declared absence of a formal doctrine of precedent (*stare decisis*) can be construed as a communicative strategy about the authority of the past in the present, and thus a form of indirect control over knowledge.[92]

[89] The practice denotes the resort to a wide variety of standards: 'indubitable proof' (UK–Venezuela Claims Commission 1903, Reports of International Arbitral Awards, Vol. IX, at 400), 'convincing evidence' (ICJ, Nicaragua, 1986, para. 24, 29 , 62, 109; see also *Congo v. Uganda*, 2005, paras. 72, 91, 136), 'clear evidence' (ICJ, Nicaragua, 1986, para. 24, 29 , 62, 109), 'weighty and convincing' (ICJ, *Congo v. Uganda*, 2005, paras. 72, 91, 136), 'fully conclusive' (ICJ, Genocide, 2007, para. 209 (for claim involving charges of exceptional gravity)), 'beyond any doubt' (See ICJ, Genocide, 2007, para. 422), 'beyond reasonable doubt' (ECHR, Ireland vs United Kingdom, Series A, No. 25, at 65, para. 161), *Cyprus vs Turkey*, ECHR (2001-IV) 36, para. 115. On the standard of proof of the ECHR, see the remarks of Monika Ambrus, 'The European Court of Human Rights and Standards of Proof in Religion Cases', 8 Religion and Human Rights 2 (2013), 107–37), 'preponderance of the evidence'. This also seems to be the standard adopted by the Iran–US Claims Tribunal. See e.g. *Dadras International and PER-AM Construction Corporation v The Islamic Republic of Iran, and Tehran Redevelopment Company*, 31 Iran-US CTR, 127, para. 123, 'prima facie evidence'. For such an interpretation of WTO panels practice, see Petro Mavroidis, 'Development of WTO Dispute Settlement Procedures Through Case-Law', in Federico Ortino and Ernst-Ulrich Petersmann (eds), *The WTO Dispute Settlement System 1995–2003* (Kluwer Law Ionternational, 2004), 153), 'clear and convincing' (*Trail Smelter (US vs Canada)*, 3 RIAA (1963–5), 1905, 1941. See also Eritrea–Ethiopia Claims Commission, 1 July 2003, Prisoners of War (Eritrea's Claim 17), Partial Award, para. 46), 'objective assessment' (Appellate Body Report, EC-Hormones, para. 117), etc. This has been extensively discussed in relation to the ICJ. See Anna Riddell and Brendan Plant, *Evidence before the International Court of Justice* (British Institute of International Law and Comparative Law, 2009), 416; M. Kamto, 'Les moyens de prévue devant la Cour internationale de Justice à la lumière de quelques affaires récentes portées devant elle', 49 German Yearbook of International Law (2006), 259; G. Niyungeko, *La preuve devant les jurisdictions internationales* (Bruylant, 2005); Michelle T. Grando, *Evidence, Proof, and Fact-Finding in WTO Dispute Settlement* (Oxford University Press, 2009), 90–91. Simone Halink, 'All Things Considered: How the International Court of Justice Delegated its Fact-Assessment to the United Nations in the Armed Activities Case', 40 NYU Journal of International Law and Politics 13 (2008), 21–5; M. Kazazi, *Burden of Proof and Related Issues: A Study on Evidence Before International Tribunals* (Nijhoff, 1996); Marco Roscini, 'Evidentiary Issues in International Disputes Related to State Responsibility for Cyber Operations' 50 Texas International Law Journal 233 (2015), 248. For some critical remarks on the quest for common rules on evidence, see S. de Smet, 'Review of Anna Riddell and Brendan Plant, Evidence before the International Court of Justice', 68 Cambridge Law Journal 666 (2009); see also Marco Roscini, 'Evidentiary Issues in International Disputes Related to State Responsibility for Cyber Operations', 50 Texas International Law Journal 233 (2015), 249.

[90] On the question of precedents as a question of how the past is given authority in the present, see Venzke (n. 58).

[91] It is acknowledged that this indirect form of control comes very close to the direct control that manifests itself in the selection and determination of the application law. See section 13.3.1.

[92] Whilst it is uncontested, in both the literature and the case law, that there is no formal rule of *stare decisis* before international adjudicatory bodies, it is similarly uncontested that practice witnesses a general tendency of international courts and arbitral tribunals—sometimes called *de facto stare decisis*—to refer to and rely on one another. On that question in general, see M. Shahabuddeen, *Precedent in the*

After all, the choice to turn down the principle of *stare decisis* and the rejection of a formal doctrine of precedent boils down to a choice for a wide communicative discretion about how the past is used and constituted. In other words, the current state of the practice pertaining to precedents is itself a strategy about how much leeway international courts and arbitral tribunals enjoy when they communicate about the relevance and content they give to the past in the present. From the perspective of the discussion here, this choice is nothing more than an indirect mode of control over knowledge.[93]

13.4 Concluding Remarks: Contestation, Collaboration, and Suspicion

The previous sections have sought to produce an image of international courts and arbitral tribunals as bureaucratic bodies, not by virtue of their power through knowledge but rather through their control over knowledge—that is, the social realities created by the definitional categories of international law. It seems uncontested that control over knowledge constitutes an extreme form of power.[94] In that sense, the heuristic exercise conducted here has provided perspectives on the dramatic power exercised by international courts and arbitral tribunals[95] as well as the type of society they contribute to

World Court (Cambridge University Press, 1996); E. de Brabandere, 'The Use of Precedent and External Case Law by the International Court of Justice and the International Tribunal for the Law of the Sea', 15 Law and Practice of International Courts and Tribunals (2016), 24–55; 'Arbitral Decisions As a Source of International Investment Law', in T. Gazzini and E. de Brabandere (eds), *International Investment Law: The Sources of Rights and Obligations* (Martinus Nijhoff, 2012), 245–88; C. Shreuer, 'Diversity and Harmonization of Treaty Interpretation in Investment Arbitration', 3 Transnational Dispute Management (2006), 14; M. Paparinskis, 'Sources of Law and Arbitral Interpretations of Pari Materia Investment Protection Rules', in O. K. Fauchald and A. Nollkaemper (eds), *Unity or Fragmentation of International Law: The Role of International and Nationals Tribunals* (Hart, 2011), 4; S. Schill, *The Multilateralization of International Investment Law* (Cambridge University Press, 2009), ch. VII.C.; see also G. Kaufmann-Kholer, 'Arbitral Precedent: Dream, Necessity or Excuse', 23 Arbitration International (2007), 368; Stefan Schill, 'System-Building in Investment Treaty Arbitration and Lawmaking', 12 German Law Journal 1083 (2011), esp. 1096–1108.

[93] For another alternative outlooks on the doctrine of precedent, see Harlan Cohen, 'Theorizing Precedent in International Law', in Andrea Bianchi, Daniel Peat, and Matthew Windsor (eds), *Interpretation in International Law* (Oxford University Press, 2014), 268–89.

[94] Foucault. His famous 1975 work, *Surveiller et punir*, has been translated as *Discipline and Punishment* (Penguin, 1977), 27: 'There is no power relation without the correlative constitution of a field of knowledge, nor any knowledge that does not presuppose and constitute at the same time power relations.' Wendy Brown, 'Power After Foucault', in John S. Dryzek, Bonnie Honig, and Anne Phillips (eds), *The Oxford Handbook of Political Theory* (Oxford University Press, 2008). See Yves Dezalay and Bryan Garth, *Dealing in Virtue: International Commercial Arbitration and the Construction of a Transnational Legal Order* (University of Chicago Press, 1996).

[95] On the idea of exercise of public authority by international courts, see generally von Bogdandy and Venzke (n. 1), 1.

shape.[96] This final section reflects on the possibility of a contestation of the powers of these administrative bodies, especially by those professionals without judicial capacity—that is, those that neither compose these international courts and arbitral tribunals nor plead before them.

It is submitted that those professionals without judicial capacity—be they scholars, lecturers, legal advisers, activists, etc.[97]—may well feel an urge to contest the extent to which international courts and arbitral tribunals control knowledge. It is not only that they find themselves competing with international courts and arbitral tribunals because they similarly seek to control the social realities created by the definitional categories of international law. It is also that they may feel that such administrative bodies are overly unbridled, and that the responsibility for steering the definitional categories of international law should be shared more evenly.

It must be acknowledged, however, that the avenues for contestation available to these professionals without judicial capacity are rather limited. First, they commonly engage in the very same constitutive enterprise as the bureaucratic bodies discussed above, although their steering of the definitional categories of international law may not be as authoritative and impactful. Second, they are rarely in a position to formulate objections based on legitimacy and accountability[98] against international law and arbitral tribunals, as the former often cannot prove better credentials than the latter in this respect. Third, to many of these professionals, dismantling the power of these bureaucracies may seem only to postpone problems, for any law-application authoritative processes that would replace the bureaucratic control over knowledge discussed here would bring about a similar control over knowledge. In this context, downright contestation or dismantlement of these bureaucratic bodies, despite some compelling objections against their powers, may not be a posture available to the professionals of international law.[99]

Because contestation and dismantlement of these administrative bodies is usually not an option, professionals of international law with no judicial capacity, more often than not, choose to collaborate with those bureaucracies whose power they cannot seriously contest. They do so with the hope that they will be able to influence the way these bodies steer the definitional categories of international law and contribute to the constitution of the social reality. In other words, most professionals of international law prefer complicity to contestation, let alone dismantlement.

[96] See Madsen (n. 22), 27.

[97] On the various roles in which international lawyers engage with international law, see Jean d'Aspremont, André Nollkaemper, Tarcisio Gazzini, and Wouter Werner (eds), *International Law as a Profession* (Cambridge University Press, 2017).

[98] On the challenge of rehabilitating the legitimacy of international courts and arbitral tribunals, see Romano et al. (n. 6), 158.

[99] The question of contestation and dismantlement would obviously arise in very different terms with respect to those whose professional activities are not directly vested in international legal argumentation. This question is not, however, addressed here.

The inclination of international lawyers to choose to cooperate with those bureaucratic bodies whose power they cannot contest[100] may be where the main epistemological lesson of the heuristic exercise conducted here lies. Thinking of international courts and arbitral tribunals as bureaucratic bodies that control knowledge helps us understand why these are sites of power most international lawyers feel they must conquer. Yet, if complicity is the fate of those professionals who neither compose these bureaucratic bodies nor plead before them, that does not relieve them of their obligation to remain suspicious at all times towards the social realities which these courts and tribunals create.[101]

[100] Compare the idea of complicity developed by Bourdieu (n. 44), 844: 'The specific property of symbolic power is that it can be exercised only through the complicity of those who are dominated by it.'

[101] I have developed elsewhere this call for suspicion in relation to international courts: Jean d'Aspremont, 'International Lawyers and the International Court of Justice: Between Cult and Contempt', in James Crawford, Abdul G. Koroma, Said Mahmoudi, and Alain Pellet (eds), *The International Legal Order: Current Needs and Possible Responses. Essays in Honour of Djamchid Momtaz* (Brill, 2017), 117–30.

PART III

VALUES

CHAPTER 14

EFFICIENCY—WHAT ELSE?

Efficiency as the emerging defining value of international arbitration: between systems theories and party autonomy

LOUKAS MISTELIS

14.1 Introduction and Theoretical Framework

INTERNATIONAL arbitration case numbers are slowly but steadily increasing and arbitration is gaining acceptance in jurisdictions where it was previously under-utilized or not encouraged; at the same time, the subject matters of disputes referred to arbitration are also expanding—to include, for example, financial disputes,[1] and technology, media, and telecommunications disputes.[2] As a corollary, it is an inevitable consequence that

[1] In 2013 the School of International Arbitration surveyed corporate counsel around the world to explore the views of major industry sectors towards arbitration. In addition to the well-established sectors of construction, infrastructure, and energy, financial services have also emerged as an industry sector which has slowly embraced arbitration. See 'Corporate Choices in International Arbitration: An Industry Approach', <http://www.arbitration.qmul.ac.uk/media/arbitration/docs/pwc-international-arbitration-study2013.pdf> (last visited 18 March 2019).

[2] The use of international arbitration in technology, media and telecommunications disputes was surveyed in 2016 by the School of International Arbitration and presented in the executive summary at: http://www.arbitration.qmul.ac.uk/media/arbitration/docs/Fixing_Tech_report_online_singles.pdf (last visited 18 March 2019). See also Queen Mary University of London, '2018 International Arbitration Survey: The Evolution of International Arbitration', available at: <http://www.arbitration.qmul.ac.uk/media/arbitration/docs/2018-International-Arbitration-Survey---The-Evolution-of-International-Arbitration-(2).PDF>.

the level and frequency of scrutiny and criticism towards arbitration is also increasing. One key concern is the extent to which arbitration is (and can be characterized as) an efficient process. For many years, there was a presumption or perhaps a false impression that arbitration was quick and inexpensive.

There is also an interesting tension between party autonomy[3]—arbitration being a creature of the parties—and the desire of various authors (supported nowadays by arbitral institutions) to attribute to arbitration systemic qualities[4] and features of private ordering.[5] The simple reality is that arbitration continues to be the result of party autonomy (the joint intent of parties to resolve their disputes by arbitration) and as such, it is a process designed—whether by disputing parties, arbitral institutions, or arbitral tribunals—to meet the parties' objectives and expectations. The tension between bespoke (or ad hoc) arbitral procedural regulation and more predictable ('systemic') regulation is ongoing. Arguably, the latter seems to win, as more often parties opt for institutional arbitration which provides for a pre-designed regulatory framework for arbitration to be conducted and organized. Most importantly, institutional arbitration also respects and honours party autonomy, and this is confirmed by the most important relevant regulatory sources[6] and all leading arbitration rules.[7]

Against this background, institutional rules relating to arbitration appear to strive for an efficient and economic process and try to moderate the effect of party autonomy.

While, looking back, efficiency did not feature as a typical feature of international arbitration some twenty odd years ago, serious concerns were expressed about the cost and length of proceedings.[8] Paradoxically, at the same time, arbitration has been seen as

[3] See e.g. Franco Ferrari (ed.), *Limits to Party Autonomy in International Commercial Arbitration* (Juris, 2016).

[4] See e.g. Roger Cotterrell, 'Transnational Communities and the Concept of Law', 21 Ratio Juris 1 (2008), 5–6; Gunther Teubner, 'Global Bukowina: Legal Pluralism in the World Society', in Gunther Teubner (ed.), *Global Law Without a State* (Dartsmouth, 1997), 13, 15; Gunther Teubner, 'Global Private Regimes: Neo-spontaneous Law and Dual Constitution of Autonomous Sectors?' in Karl-Heinz Ladeur (ed.), *Public Governance in the Age of Globalization* (Routledge, 2017), 71–87; Stephan W. Schill, 'International Arbitrators as System-Builders', (2012) 106 Proceedings of the Annual Meeting (American Society of International Law) 295; Niklas Luhmann, *Law as a Social System* (Oxford, 2009); Joseph Weiler, 'The Geology of International Law: Governance, Democracy and Legitimacy', 64(3) Zeitschrift für ausländisches öffentliches Recht und Völkerrecht 547 (2004), 549.

[5] See e.g. Stephen Ware, 'Private Ordering and Commercial Arbitration: Lasting Lessons from Mentschikoff', 1 Journal of Dispute Resolution 1–18 (2019); Steven Schwarcz, 'Private Ordering', 97 Northwestern University Law Review 319 (2002).

[6] See Convention on the Recognition and Enforcement of Foreign Arbitral Awards (New York, 1958, entered into force on 7 June 1959) (New York Convention), Article V(1)(d): 'The composition of the arbitral authority or the arbitral procedure was not in accordance with the agreement of the parties, or, failing such agreement, was not in accordance with the law of the country where the arbitration took place.'

[7] See ICC Rules of Arbitration ('ICC Rules') (March 2017), LCIA Arbitration Rules ('LCIA Rules') (October 2014), SIAC Rules of Arbitration ('SIAC Rules') (August 2016), HKIAC Rules, ('HKIAC Rules') (November 2018), AAA-ICDR Arbitration Rules ('AAA-ICDR Rules') (June 2014).

[8] See <http://www.arbitration.qmul.ac.uk/media/arbitration/docs/IAstudy_2006.pdf> (2006), 6, 7, 19 (last visited 18 March 2019), where 50% of the respondents to the survey identified the cost associated with the arbitration as the primary concern about arbitration, with the time needed for the resolution of the dispute as the second main disadvantage. See further, with more analysis, Loukas Mistelis,

a method of dispute resolution which saves money and time for the users.[9] However, in the last ten years, or perhaps a bit longer, there has been a marked awareness of, and indeed demand for, a higher level of efficiency in the arbitral process.[10]

'International Arbitration—Corporate Attitudes and Practices—12 Perceptions Tested: Myths, Data and Analysis Research Report', 15(3–4) Am. Rev. of Int'l Arb. 525 (2004), 545–50.

[9] Richard Naimark and Stephanie Keer, 'International Private Commercial Arbitration: Expectations and Perceptions of Attorneys and Business People', (2002) 30 Int'l Bus. Lawyer 203; 'Dispute Wise Business Management: An American Arbitration Association Sponsored Study' (2003), p. 9, available at: <http://fundacionsignum.org/wp-content/uploads/2016/07/aaa_mediacion-arbitraje-resolucion-conflictos-dispute-wise_study_research_report_2011.pdf> (last visited 10 January 2019).

[10] See Hermann Bietz, 'On the State and Efficiency of International Arbitration: Could the German "Relevance Method" Be Useful or Not?' (2014) 12 30 SchiedsVZ 121; Michael Dunmore, 'Increased Efficiency and Lower Costs in Arbitration: Sole Member Tribunals', (2015) IV(1) Indian J. Arb. L. 27–33; Debevoise & Plimpton LLP Protocol to Promote Efficiency in International Arbitration, at: <http://www.debevoise.com/~/media/files/capabilities/arbitration/protocol_promote_efficiency_intl_arbitration1.pdf> (2010) (last visited 18 March 2019); Diane Desierto, 'Rawlsian Fairness and International Arbitration', (2015) 36(4) U. Pa. J. Int'l L. 939–93; David Earnest, Raul Gallardo, Gardar Vidir Gunnarsson, and Tobiasz Kaczor, 'Four Ways to Sharpen the Sword of Efficiency in International Arbitration', (2013), available at: <http://www.arbitration-icca.org/media/0/13630881906410/four_ways_to_sharpen_the_sword_of_efficiency_yicca_group_paper.pdf> (last visited 18 March 2019); John Fellas, 'A Fair and Efficient International Arbitration Process', PLI Course Handbook, (2007) International Arbitration 10796; Cristina Florescu, 'The Arbitration Agreement and Arbitrability: Towards Achieving Efficiency in International Arbitration', (2015) Austrian Yearbook Int'l Arb. 51–71; Fabricio Fortese and Lotta Hemmi, 'Procedural Fairness and Efficiency in International Arbitration', (2015) 3(1) Groningen J. Int'l L. 110–24; Lucy Greenwood, 'Does Bifurcation Really Promote Efficiency?', (2011) 28(2) J. Int'l Arb. 105–§11; Veijo Heiskanen, 'Key to Efficiency in International Arbitration', (2015) 30 ICSID Review 481–5; ICC Commission on Arbitration and ADR, 'Task Force on Reducing Time and Costs in Arbitration', available at: <http://www.iccwbo.org/Advocacy-Codes-and-Rules/Document-centre/2012/ICC-Arbitration-Commission-Report-on-Techniques-for-Controlling-Time-and-Costs-in-Arbitration/> (last visited 18 March 2019); 'JAMS International Efficiency Guidelines 2011 for the Pre-Hearing Phase of International Arbitrations', at: <http://www.jamsinternational.com/international-arbitration-efficiency-guidelines> (last visited 18 March 2019); Nana Japaridze, 'Fair Enough? Reconciling the Pursuit of Fairness and Justice with Preserving the Nature of International Commercial Arbitration', (2008) 36(4) Hofstra L. Rev. 1415–46; Jennifer Kirby, 'Efficiency in Arbitration: Whose Duty Is It?' (2015) 32(6) J. Int'l Arb. 689-696; Elisabeth Leimbacher, 'Efficiency under the New ICC Rules of Arbitration of 2012: First Glimpse at the New Practice', (2013) 31(2) ASA Bulletin 298–315; Michael McIlwrath, 'Faster, Cheaper: Global Initiatives to Promote Efficiency in International Arbitration', (2010) 76 Arbitration 532–7; Michael Moser, 'The "Pre-Hearing Checklist": A Technique for Enhancing Efficiency in International Arbitral Proceedings', (2013) 30(20 J. Int'l Arb. 155–9; Christopher Newmark, 'Controlling Time and Costs in Arbitration', in Lawrence W. Newman and Richard D. Hill (eds), *The Leading Arbitrators' Guide to International Arbitration*, 3rd edn (Juris, 2008), 81–96; Veit Öhlberger and Jarred Pinkston, 'The Arbitrator and the Arbitration Procedure, Iura Novit Curia and the Non-Passive Arbitrator: A Question of Efficiency, Cultural Blinders and Misplaced Concerns About Impartiality', (2016) Austrian Yearbook Int'l Arb. 101–17; Wilson Pimentel, 'Efficiency and Equilibrium in the Allocation of Costs', (2015) XII Revista Brasiliera de Arbitragem 59–67; Karl Pörnbacher and Alexander Dolgorukow, 'Reconciling Due Process and Efficiency in International Arbitration: The Arbitrator's Task of Achieving the One without Sacrificing the Other', (2013) LXI(3) Annals FLB–Belgrade Law Review 50–62; Andreas Respondek, 'Five Proposals to Further Increase the Efficiency of International Arbitration Proceedings', (2014) 31(4) J. Int'l Arb. 507–13; Jorg Risse, 'Ten Drastic Proposals for Saving Time and Costs in Arbitral Proceedings', (2013) 23(3) Arb. Int'l 5; Paola Sanchez, 'Introducing Efficiency into the 2010 IBA Rules on Evidence: Does this Create a Back Door for Introducing Additional Inefficiencies into the System?' (2011) 1(1) International Commercial

It is unclear, and indeed debatable, whether international arbitration is innately efficient or whether efficiency is what disputing parties seek from arbitration. It is equally unclear what efficiency in international arbitration means. In addition, it is not always clear as to what disputing parties consider as efficiency. The *Oxford English Dictionary* suggests that efficiency is 'the state or quality of being efficient', and identifies the origin of the word in Latin and in the 'late 16th century (in the sense 'the fact of being an efficient cause'): from Latin *efficientia*, from *efficere* accomplish'.[11] Relying on the historical meaning of the word, any arbitration that results in an award would be considered an efficient arbitration. However, perhaps this historical definition does not work well with a modern business-like approach that many parties expect from arbitration. It is not merely a matter of getting an outcome but also getting an outcome in a process which itself appears and perhaps also is efficient.

For many, if not all, arbitration users, efficiency seems to be a relative value: if local court proceedings with an international element last for years and with the possibility of remedies after the decision by the court of first instance, then proceedings in typical arbitration cases (which last for twelve to eighteen months) would be considered to be rather fast. For parties used to fast, efficient local courts, arbitration may appear to be somehow slow. Legal fees are comparable in litigation and arbitration proceedings, but court fees and arbitration fees may differ substantially. At the same time the lack of an appeal mechanism in arbitration also ensures that the outcome of arbitration is final, and the process appears to be more efficient. Consequently, there may be no universal concept of efficiency: parties may have different efficiency expectations depending on their legal background, culture, expectations, and experiences. However, there may also be a 'transnational' or 'international arbitration autonomous' concept of efficiency.

In any event, it is arguable whether efficiency can only be linked to 'quantitative' criteria such as time and cost of arbitration proceedings. Ultimately, arbitration is typically established to ensure a fair resolution of a dispute in a procedure guided and informed by party autonomy (a consensus between the parties to the extent possible) and due process. In most cases tribunals would be prepared to sacrifice efficiency in order to ensure full observance of due process—a phenomenon recently coined as 'due process paranoia'[12]—although tribunals increasingly assume the role of efficient procedural

Arbitration Brief 3–4; Anne-Veronique Schläpfer and Marily Paralika, 'Striking the Right Balance: The Roles of Arbitral Institutions, Parties and Tribunals in Achieving Efficiency in International Arbitration', 2(2) BCDR Int'l Arb. Rev. 329–42 (2015); Albert Jan van den Berg (ed.), *Planning Efficient Arbitration Proceedings: The Law Applicable to International Arbitration* (Kluwer Law International, 1996); George von Mehren and Alana Jochum, 'Is International Arbitration Becoming Too American?' (2011) 2 Global Bus. L. Rev 47–58; Irene Welser, 'Efficiency: Today's Challenge in Arbitration Proceedings', (2014) Austrian Yearbook Int'l Arb. 151–66.

[11] <https://en.oxforddictionaries.com/definition/efficiency> (last visited 18 March 2019).

[12] See the 2015 Queen Mary School of International Arbitration Survey, entitled 'Improvement and Innovations in International Arbitration', which coined the term "due process paranoia" at: <http://www.arbitration.qmul.ac.uk/media/arbitration/docs/2015_International_Arbitration_Survey.pdf>, 5, 10 (last visited 18 March 2019); see also Klaus Peter Berger and Ole Jensen, 'Due Process Paranoia and the Procedural Judgment Rule: A Safe Harbour for Procedural Management Decisions by International Arbitrators', (2016) 32 Arb. Int'l 415–35.

managers. Ideally due process, party autonomy, and efficiency ought to be aligned in perfect harmony, ensuring also that the outcome of the case is correct.[13] One of the key advantages of arbitration is its flexible and adaptable procedure.[14]

This chapter first explores the origins of the quest for efficiency in international arbitration and its establishment as a value of international arbitration (section 14.2) before exploring and assessing the role of the arbitrators (14.3), and arbitral institutions (14.4) in ensuring efficiency. In the concluding remarks (14.5), the efficiency paradigm is presented, as well as an assessment as to whether we have moved to a law & economics approach in international arbitration. The law & economics approach to international arbitration is not new,[15] but it is not well established either.

14.2 Origins of Efficiency and Its Establishment as a Value of International Arbitration

Since arbitration is an alternative to adjudication by a national court in the public sector, funded by the state via the taxpayers and the disputing parties, any departure from national courts would imply additional costs for disputing parties.

To draw a parallel, if national litigation is the equivalent of a public transport system (buses or trains), then arbitration would most likely be a taxi (perhaps equivalent to institutional arbitration) or other private vehicle (perhaps equivalent to ad hoc arbitration) hired by the disputing parties. Public transport is normally available for a small fare; it is generally predictable and familiar but may or may not be suitable for a particular journey; and its use may be intimidating if a party is foreign, does not speak the language of the driver, cannot read the signs, and is unfamiliar with local customs. While public transport is funded by the states and taxpayers, the private car or taxi is something the users will have to pay themselves; in exchange, the parties can also choose the actual car, dictate the route, choose a driver in whom they are confident, and ensure that the service is what they wish for by expressing their choices. And while public transport is almost always available as a default, users may positively opt not to use it because private transport seems more appropriate or convenient for their own purposes.

It seems that users of international arbitration, like users of private car hire, are aware that this is a bespoke and perhaps more expensive service; they also know that the speed

[13] See Fortese and Hemmi (n. 10), 116.

[14] See Julian Lew, Loukas Mistelis, and Stefan Kröll, *Comparative International Commercial Arbitration* (Kluwer Law International, 2013), paras. 1-7, 1-14–1-18.

[15] See Orley Aschenfelter and Radha Iyengar (eds), *Economics of Commercial Arbitration and Dispute Resolution* (Elgar, 2009) (it is worth noting that some of the essays date back to 1961); Alessandra Casella, 'On Market Integration and the Development of Institutions: The Case of International Commercial Arbitration', (1996) 40 European Economic Review 155–86.

of the service is subject to external factors and may or may not be predictable, although the typical expectation is that the service would be quicker than the public one and also more comfortable and accommodating to personal needs of the parties. And indeed, this is what parties choose and pay for: they can always enjoy some privacy and even comfort in using a tailor-made service of their own choice.

It seems that international arbitration may compromise on efficiency but offers other benefits that may significant outweigh the potential risk of lack of efficiency. In cross-border matters, the comfort and convenience of not having to submit to the jurisdiction of the courts of the other party is so significant that any additional cost and complication may be well justified as a business risk.

As we have already seen, in recent years, the quest for efficiency has been clearly expressed and accentuated as corporate users of arbitration wish to receive prompt and better service by the arbitration service providers (arbitral institutions and arbitrators) and 'value for money'.[16] In this section, the origin and justification of the efficiency mandate (14.2.1) and the establishment of efficiency as a value of international arbitration (14.2.2) are explored.

14.2.1 Origins and justification of efficiency mandate

It has been suggested that 'economics and process control have been identified as the main reasons why many companies have moved toward[s] arbitration to resolve disputes'.[17] In a nearly historical context, Mentschikoff, in 1961, suggested relying on a survey because 'the reasons commonly given for arbitration—speed, lower expense, more expert decision, greater privacy—are appealing to all businessmen, and yet not all utilize arbitration'.[18] Moreover, as suggested in 1985 by David,[19] arbitration's purpose was to maintain harmony between 'persons who were destined to live together' in cases where the rules and procedures were too rigid.

In the same way, more than 30 years ago, national courts applauded arbitration as demonstrated by the U.S. Supreme Court in *Mitsubishi v Soler*.[20] In this case, the U.S. Supreme Court, in considering the arbitrability of antitrust claims, took into consideration the characteristics of international arbitrational, and stated that 'adaptability and access to expertise are hallmarks of arbitration'.[21] More interestingly, it stated

[16] See McIlwrath (n. 10); and Loukas Mistelis and Crina Baltag, 'Trends and Challenges in International Arbitration: Two Surveys of Inhouse Counsel of Major Corporations', (2008) 5(2) WAMR—World Arbitration and Mediation Review 83–110.

[17] Orley Aschenfelterand Radha Iyengar, 'Introduction', in Orley Aschenfelter and Radha Iyengar (eds), *Economics of Commercial Arbitration and Dispute Resolution* (Elgar, 2009), p. x.

[18] Soia Mentschikoff, 'Commercial Arbitration', 61 Columbia L. Rev. 846 (1961), 850.

[19] René David, *Arbitration in International Trade* (Kluwer Law International, 1985), p. 29.

[20] *Mitsubishi Motors Corp. v Soler Chrysler-Plymouth, Inc.*, 105 S. Ct. 3346 (1985).

[21] Ibid. 633.

that arbitration flexibility and the expeditious results provided by it would best serve parties' needs.[22]

For these reasons, in the following years, arbitration was considered a successful method for resolving disputes in an international context,[23] and had experienced an exponential growth. This phenomenon was the result of different factors. Of course, the development of international commerce played an important role.[24] However, a number of reasons contributed to the growth of international arbitration. In particular, arbitration was considered to be cheaper, less time-consuming, and more confidential than court proceedings. More importantly, parties could establish their own dispute resolution mechanism by designing every stage of the procedure. Furthermore, the enforcement of the arbitral award was made easier by the New York Convention, the 'single most important pillar on which the edifice of international arbitration rests'. Above all, another factor was neutrality. Parties from different nations could choose a neutral method of settling commercial disputes rather than going before the respective national courts.

In line with these considerations, Rivkin defined the original concept of arbitration as a dispute resolution method involving 'two business people taking their dispute to a wise business person in whom they both trusted, describing their respective claims, and then asking the arbitrator to provide them with the best solution to their dispute'.[25] In principle, arbitration is seen by practitioners and scholars as an efficient method for the resolution of international commercial disputes.

It is in the last fifteen to twenty years that some issues have been raised with respect to international arbitration. In fact, while certain aspects of arbitration have remained the same, others have drastically changed. In particular, costs and duration have been identified as the factors that might endanger the existence of international arbitration itself.[26] Parties started complaining about the duration of arbitration procedures, resulting in legal fees that made up most of the costs.[27] This is true: the 'longer a process takes, the more it is likely to cost'.[28] In 2006, the average duration of an arbitration was two years, while a number of arbitrations concluded within four years.[29] Moreover, the costs involved in the process were surprisingly high. It was also established that the lion's share of the costs, between 85 and 90 per cent, would be costs for legal representation

[22] Ibid.

[23] Philippe Fouchard et al., *Fouchard, Gaillard, Goldman on International Commercial Arbitration* (Kluwer Law International, 1999), 1.

[24] Ibid.

[25] David W Rivkin, 'Towards a New Paradigm in International Arbitration: The Town Elder Model Revisited', (2008) 24 Arbitration International 378.

[26] See Risse (n. 10), 453.

[27] Lucy Greenwood, 'Sketch: The Rise, Fall and Rise of International Arbitration—a View from 2030', (2011) 77(40 Arbitration 437.

[28] Peter Morton, 'Can a World Exist Where Expedited Arbitration Becomes the Default Procedure?' (2010) 26 Arbitration International 103.

[29] Queen Mary University of London, '2006 International Arbitration Study: Corporate Attitudes and Practices' (n. 8), 7.

(counsels' fees), while about 10 to 15 per cent of the costs was representing what was paid for arbitrators, counsel, and institutions.[30] As a consequence, as shown in 2008 by a Queen Mary University survey, 41 per cent of in-house counsel said they were prepared to use transnational litigation to solve international disputes.

The arbitration community tried to address these issues. For example, the ICC issued in 2007 the report (updated in 2012 and 2018) entitled *Techniques for Controlling Time and Costs in Arbitration.*[31] Law firms made efforts as well. For example, Debevoise & Plimpton LLP published a protocol on the promotion of efficiency in international arbitration in 2010,[32] in which they announced their intention to streamline the arbitral process by drafting a detailed statement of claim, or through the request of fast-track schedules.

Since then, the situation has changed quite significantly. For example, the Hong Kong International Arbitration Centre (HKIAC) introduced in its 2018 rules a number of changes aimed at improving the efficiency of the process, such as a procedure for an early determination of points of law or fact.[33] At present, arbitration is the preferred method of dispute resolution.[34] However, there are still concerns relating to the efficiency of arbitration. As shown in the 2018 Queen Mary Survey on International Arbitration,[35] respondents have proposed a plethora of solutions that might be adopted to improve efficiency of the arbitral process. Interestingly enough, they highlighted the importance of an early case management conference. In addition, they pointed out the need for both arbitrators and counsel to 'get creative' so as to design the proceedings according to the needs of the case. In particular, it has been suggested that procedural orders be tailored, rather than using the standardized ones. Moreover, arbitrators should limit the number of rounds of submissions, that might sometimes be too lengthy and not focused on the key disputed issues.[36]

Efficiency has now indisputably taken centre stage as far as disputing parties and arbitration institutions are concerned. Arbitration institutions are expected to safeguard and even deliver the efficiency mandate in cooperation with the disputing parties. Reconciling expectations of disputing parties with the desire for efficiency is not always a simple exercise. Therefore, efforts are still needed to improve arbitration efficiency. Whether these efforts come from arbitral institutions, the arbitration community,[37] or the disputing parties themselves, it is essential that the disputing parties participate in the efficiency discussions and related arbitral procedure design, and are not alienated.

[30] Queen Mary University of London, '2008 Corporate Attitudes and Enforcement of Arbitral Awards', 5, available at: <http://www.arbitration.qmul.ac.uk/media/arbitration/docs/IAstudy_2008.pdf> (last visted 18 March 2019).

[31] ICC Commission on Arbitration and ADR, 'Task Force on Reducing Time and Costs in Arbitration' (n. 10).

[32] Debevoise & Plimpton LLP Protocol to Promote Efficiency in International Arbitration (n. 10), 1–2.

[33] 2018 HKIAC Administered Arbitration Rules.

[34] Queen Mary University of London, '2018 International Arbitration Survey: The Evolution of International Arbitration' (n. 2), 5.

[35] Ibid. 25. [36] Ibid.

[37] Emmanuel Gaillard, 'Sociology of International Arbitration', (2015) 31 Arbitration International 1.

Before exploring how to improve the efficiency of the arbitral process, the wider question would be to understand what efficiency means—or better, to identify the factors falling within the concept of efficiency. In the next section, we look at efficiency as a value in international arbitration, with the purpose of understanding what this concept entails.

14.2.2 Efficiency as a value of international arbitration

As a starting point, it should be noted that there is no definition of efficiency. Arbitration is a product of party autonomy and, as a result, the efficiency of the process itself is the result of the parties' choices according to their own priorities. Thus, it is not possible to give a general definition of efficiency in arbitration. What can be said is that efficiency is a relative concept, and as such has to be assessed by taking into account different factors. In particular, an evaluation has to be made in accordance with the dispute or the main agreement between the parties. It is only by taking into account the underlying dispute that it would be possible to assess the efficiency of the arbitral process.

First of all, a factor to be considered is time. Of course, in general, the shorter the process, the better. However, as suggested by Heiskanen, it is not the duration of an arbitration per se to be taken into account.[38] Indeed, the duration of an arbitration has to be related to the dispute at stake. For example, if a twenty-year oil and gas concession agreement dispute took two years to conclude, the arbitration would be considered efficient, while if the situation were the opposite, the efficiency of the arbitration might be in question. Indeed, considering the potential duration of an arbitral procedure in relation with the agreement underlying the dispute might allow us to understand how efficient the arbitral process is.

Secondly, the efficiency of arbitration proceedings can be assessed by relating the value of the dispute and the cost of the arbitral proceedings.[39] This evaluation might focus also on the value of the transaction underlying the dispute. However, in this case, the problem would be that the value of the dispute is different from that of the underlying agreements generally. Comparing the foreseeable costs of the arbitration with the value of the transaction might give rise to some issues when the amount claimed in the proceedings is considerably less than the value of the transaction between the parties. To the contrary, the relation between the value of the claim and the cost of the proceedings might allow a more realistic picture. Indeed, it allows us to apprehend whether the process would be cost-efficient by measuring the difference between the costs to be borne and the amount to be awarded.

Another factor to take into account is the value of the award itself.[40] The value of arbitral awards is twofold. It is based on the legal framework that allows recognition and

[38] Heiskanen (n. 10), 482. [39] Ibid. 482–3.

[40] Loukas Mistelis, 'Award as an Investment: The Value of an Arbitral Award or the Cost of Non-enforcement', 28 ICSID Review 64 (2013), 71.

enforcement in all the signatory States of the New York Convention. At the same time, arbitral awards maintain an economic value regardless of whether ot not the award has been enforced.

As to compliance and enforcement, it has to be noted that awards are typically voluntarily complied with. As shown by the 2008 survey of the School of International Arbitration,[41] only on a very small number of occasions had enforcement proceedings been initiated to ensure enforcement. Indeed, only in 11 per cent of cases did respondents of the survey need to proceed to courts or other enforcement agencies to enforce an award.[42] Even in such cases, only a small number of respondents reported that they encountered difficulties when seeking recognition and enforcement.[43] In the same survey, in-house lawyers reported that 'the difficulties in enforcing an award often arose because of the circumstances of the award-debtor rather than deficiencies in the arbitral or court proceedings'.[44] As a consequence, the survey indicated that 70 per cent of the difficulties mentioned related to lack of assets and inability to locate the debtor's assets.[45] Furthermore, there might be some concerns as to the effectiveness and the efficiency of the New York Convention.[46] This is why it has been suggested that settlement may present a better option than the attempt to enforce through national courts.

In particular, according to the 2008 survey, counsel stated that enforcement issues are generally connected to the attitude of local bureaucrats and courts; in 10 per cent of cases survey respondents made reference to difficulties arising from corruption at local courts.[47] Notwithstanding such difficulties, it must be pointed out that 84 per cent of respondents reported recovering between 76 and 100 per cent of the awarded sum.[48] This is not to be seen as a defect of arbitration. To the contrary, it should be noted that most awards are the basis for the enforcement of a very substantial percentage of the sum awarded.

More importantly, the value of arbitral awards can be assessed independently of recognition and enforcement. In fact, it is worth mentioning that alternative options to enforcement have been developed. For example, post-awards settlement has been used as a successful means to recover a substantial part of the amount awarded.[49] In the same way, assignment of awards seems to be an increasing practise in order to facilitate the

[41] Loukas Mistelis and Crina Baltag, 'Recognition and Enforcement of Arbitral Awards and Settlement in International Arbitration in Practice: Corporate Attitudes and Practices', 19 Am Rev Intl Arb 319 (2008), 343.

[42] Queen Mary University of London, '2008 Corporate Attitudes and Enforcement of Arbitral Awards' (n. 30), 6.

[43] Mistelis and Baltag (n. 41), 345. [44] Ibid.

[45] Queen Mary University of London, '2008 Corporate Attitudes and Enforcement of Arbitral Awards' (n. 30), 10.

[46] See Stavros Brekoulakis, 'Enforcement of Foreign Arbitral Awards: Observations on the Efficiency of the Current System and the Gradual Development of Alternative Means of Enforcement', (2013) American Review of International Arbitration 415.

[47] Mistelis and Baltag (n. 41), 348–9. [48] Mistelis (n. 40), 72.

[49] See Loukas Mistelis, 'The Settlement-Enforcement Dynamic in International Arbitration', 19 American Review of International Arbitration 377 (2008), 383–7.

enforcement of an award, even though only a small a number of examples is available.[50] For example, it has been reported that the award in *CMS v Argentina*[51] was assigned to a fund, Blue Ridge Investment LLC, which ensured the enforcement by exercising diplomatic pressure.[52]

As the above considerations demonstrate, efficiency in arbitration does not relate to just one particular aspect. It involves the whole arbitral process. Different factors should be taken into account to arrive at a possible definition of efficiency. Moreover, efficiency is a relative concept and its content might vary according to the perspective from which we look at it. What arbitrators could consider efficient might not be considered so by the parties. Thus, in general, it can be said that efficiency might concern different aspects of international arbitration. For this reason, the efficiency of international arbitration should be assessed by looking at the different players involved in the process. It would thus be possible for them to understand what they believe is efficient and, at the same time, what they could do to improve the efficiency of the proceedings.

The following sections will look at the players involved in international arbitrations in order to show how the concept of efficiency might vary through the eyes of different observers. The chapter does not specifically address the role disputing parties may have in ensuring efficiency.

14.3 Role of Arbitrators

There is not doubt that arbitrators can play an essential role in assessing and improving the efficiency of the arbitral proceedings. A particular area for improvement is management of the case. Indeed, efficient management of the proceedings might result in reducing costs substantially. This is the challenge arbitrators face in striving to be effective 'managers' of the arbitral proceedings.[53]

'Management of the case' refers to the procedural decisions of arbitrators, namely those planning, organizing, and structuring the conduct of the process, and those made during the proceeding as a response to requests of the parties.[54] Of course, in rendering such decisions, arbitrators have more or less discretion depending on the type of decision and the rules with which they have to comply (applicable arbitration rules and laws).

[50] See Gregory Lazarev, 'Assignment of Arbitral Awards', available at: <http://arbitrationblog.practicallaw.com/assignment-of-arbitral-awards/>, accessed 11 December 2018.

[51] *CMS Gas Transmission Company v Argentine Republic*, ICSID Case No. ARB/01/8, Award (12 May 2005).

[52] Jorge E. Vinuales and Dolores Bentolila, 'The Use of Alternative (Non-judicial) Means to Enforce Investment Awards', in Laurence Boisson de Chazournes, Marcelo Kohen, and Jorge E. Vinuales (eds), *Diplomatic and Judicial Means of Dispute Settlement: Assessing their Interactions* (Brill, 2012), also in SSRN: SSRN-id2125051, 13.

[53] Alan Redfern, 'The Changing World of Arbitration', in David D. Caron et al. (eds), *Practising Virtue: Inside International Arbitration* (Oxford University Press, 2015), 50.

[54] Berger and Jelsen (n. 12), 417.

In addition, when a degree of discretion can be exercised, the arbitrators have to observe and protect the due process rights of the parties. Indeed, the protection of due process rights, among with the legitimacy of arbitration, is part of the arbitrator's role as a guardian of the system. Therefore, it is within the limits established by the need to protect due process rights that arbitrators have to exercise their discretion in managing the arbitral proccedings.

In this section, we will look, first, at the power and duties of arbitrators (14.3.1) and, secondly, at the need to balance due process with the efficiency and fairness of the process (14.3.2). Furthermore, we will consider which measures the arbitrators might take to improve the efficiency of the system (14.3.3).

14.3.1 Power and duties of arbitrators

To begin with, we need to identify the extent to which arbitrators have the power to streamline the arbitral proceedings. Of course, as mentioned, arbitration is the result of party autonomy. It is for the parties to decide, first, whether they want arbitral proceedings, and secondly, how they want them to be structured and conducted. This is the flexibility that has always been considered one of the essential features of international arbitration.[55] However, as suggested by Berger and Jensen, parties' freedom to design the proceedings more often than not results in 'nothing more than a rough-cut overcoat'.[56] In fact, when the arbitration clause does not provide further procedural specifications or it is an institutional clause, the procedural framework would be quite broad. In particular, arbitral institutional rules as well as national laws allow the arbitral tribunals to execise broad discretion concerning the procedural management of the proceedings.

As to arbitral institutions, for example, Article 14.4 of the LCIA Rules[57] deals with the conduct of the proceedings by providing the general duty to act fairly and impartially as between the parties. Moreover, it provides the duty to adopt procedures depending on the circumstances of the case, with the purpose of avoiding delays and guarantee efficient and expeditious means for the resolution of the dispute. And in doing so, according to Article 14.5, the tribunal will have a wide discretion.

In the same way, Article 22 of the ICC Rules[58] provides that the tribunal and the parties 'shall make any effort to conduct the arbitration in an expeditious and cost effective-manner' by taking into account the complexity and value of the dispute. Moreover, according to Article 25, the tribunal within as short a time as possible shall establish the facts by all appropriate means.

[55] Julian D. M. Lew, Loukas A. Mistelis ,and Stefan M. Kröll, *Comparative International Commercial Arbitration* (Kluwer Law International, 2003), 1-14–1-16.

[56] Berger and Jelsen (n. 12), 419.

[57] LCIA Arbitration Rules ('LCIA Rules') (October 2014).

[58] ICC Rules.

In the HKIAC Rules,[59] similar provisions can be found as to the conduct of arbitration. In particular, Article 13.1 provides that it is for arbitrators to adopt suitable procedures for the conduct of the proceedings in order to avoid unnecessary delay or expense. In discharging such duties, arbitrators have to take into account the complexity, the amount in dispute, and the use of technology, provided that the parties' reasonable opportunity to be heard will be protected. Finally, the UNCITRAL Arbitration Rules in Article 17[60] also provide that the tribunal 'shall conduct the proceedings so as to avoid unnecessary delay and expense and to provide a fair and efficient process for resolving' the dispute.

The situation is not very different if we look at national arbitration laws. For instance, under Section 33 of the English Arbitration Act,[61] the arbitral tribunal shall act fairly and impartially, and adopt procedures suitable to the circumstances of the case. Moreover, as provided by Section 34, the tribunal has the power to deal with all procedural and evidential matters, with the possibility for parties to agree on any matter. As matter of the fact, the English Arbitration Act was one of the first national arbitration legislation to introduce efficiency as a factor for the exercise of discretion by arbitral tribunals.

In the same way, French law allows arbitrators to exercise discretion in the conduct of arbitral proceedings as well. Indeed, unless otherwise agreed by the parties, the tribunal shall define the procedure in accordance with Article 1509 (2) of the CPC.[62] Swiss law has a similar provision. In fact, the Federal Law on Private International Law, under Article 182(1),[63] provides that the parties may determine the procedure either directly or by reference to rules of arbitration. In case the parties have not determined the procedure, under Article 182(2), it is for the tribunal to determine the procedure, and abritrators can do this directly or refer to a statute or to rules of arbitration.

Therefore, arbitral tribunals are generally allowed either by national laws or by institutions' rules to exercise a significant degree of discretion in dealing with the procedural management of the case. It could not be otherwise, given the flexibility of the arbitral proceedings. On the other hand, however, a relevant question remains open. Indeed, it is not clear to what extent arbitrators can exercise such a discretion. In the next section, we will attempt to establish whether arbitrators face any limits in the management of the case.

14.3.2 Balancing due process, fairness, and efficiency: the due process paranoia

Identifying the limits to which arbitral tribunals are subject when dealing with the management of the case is an easy task, at least in theory.

First of all, arbitrators have always to respect expressed agreements between the parties concerning the management of the proceedings. Secondly, they have to respect

[59] HKIAC Rules (n. 7). [60] UNCITRAL Arbitration Rules 2013.

[61] English Arbitration Act 1996. [62] French Civil Procedeural Code.

[63] Private International Law Statute of 18 December 1987.

the parties' rights to present their case and be treated equally. In particular, as pointed out by Berger and Jensen,[64] these are the grounds for annulment or non-enforcement that might be preventing arbitrators from streamlining the proceedings. Further, the violation of the parties' right to present their case is the ground on which the so-called 'due process paranoia' lies.[65]

This phenomenon was defined in the Queen Mary 2015 International Arbitration Survey[66] as the 'reluctance by tribunals to act decisively in certain situations' to avoid challenges based on the violation of the parties' right to present their case. In particular, interviewees made reference to 'situations where deadlines were extended repeatedly, evidence was admitted late in the process, and disruptive behaviour was accepted given the concern that the award would otherwise be vulnerable to challenge'. However, the question remains as to whether this phenomenon is justified or whether (as its name suggests) it is based only on a false perception of reality. The answer seems to be the latter—or seems to be so if we consider the so-called arbitration friendly jurisdictions. Indeed, understanding if such a phenomenon is justified requires looking at how national courts deal with challenges based on the aforementioned behaviour. As to the requests for extension of deadlines, it can be seen that national courts confirmed arbitral awards despite the fact that the Tribunals denied such requests.

In *Triulzi Cesare SRL v Xinyi Group*, the Singapore High Court confirmed the decision of the arbitral tribunal despite the fact that the tribunal did not grant the extension of a deadline.[67] The underlying dispute arose between *Triulzi Cesare SRL*, an Italian company manufacturing and producing washing machines for glass sheets, and *Xinyi Group*, a Hong Kong company selling glass products.[68] During the arbitration proceedings, the tribunal did not grant the extension of a deadline for the submission of an expert's witness statement since it would have been in conflict with the procedural timetable.[69] Moreover, the initial deadline set by the tribunal was extended by ten days even though this period of time was not considered sufficient by the claimant.[70] As a result, the award was challenged before the Singapore High Court on the basis that the tribunal violated the claimant's right to be heard.[71] However, the Singapore High Court confirmed the decision of the tribunal by stating that the claimant was not denied a reasonable opportunity to file the expert witness statement and the tribunal had exercised his case management powers reasonably and properly.[72] Notably, the court relied on a previous case in which an arbitral tribunal was described as 'a master of his own procedure' with wide discretionary powers.[73] Moreover, the court pointed out that even though the exercise of case management is subject to the rules of natural justice, which includes the right to be heard, arbitral tribunals are subject to other competing factors.[74] The court

64 Berger and Jensen (n. 12), 421. 65 Ibid.
66 2015 Queen Mary School of International Arbitration Survey (n. 12), 10.
67 *Triulzi Cesare SRL v XinyiGroup (Glass) Co Ltd*, [2014] SGHC 220.
68 Ibid. para. 1. 69 Ibid. para. 148. 70 Ibid. para. 142.
71 Ibid. para. 17. 72 Ibid. para. 151.
73 Ibid. para. 131; *Soh Beng Tee & Co Pte Ltd v Fairmount Development Pte Ltd*, [2007] 3 SLR(R) 86, 60.
74 *Triulzi Cesare SRL v XinyiGroup (Glass) Co Ltd*, [2014] SGHC 220, para. 131.

mentioned as an example Article 22(1) ICC Rules 2012, according to which the tribunal has to conduct the arbitration in an expeditious and cost-effective manner taking into account the complexity and value of the dispute. It stated that the tribunal has to accord weight to the 'practical realities of the arbitral ecosystem such as promptness and price'.[75] The court went on to analyse the factual circumstances of the case and, in light of them, confirmed the decision of the Arbitral Tribunal.

In case no. 11 Sch 02/08,[76] the Dresden Court of Appeal arrived at a similar conclusion. After a tribunal rendered an award in Norway on 30 October 2007, the respondent commenced an action for annulment of the award before the Dresden Court of Appeal.[77] Among other complaints, it alleged the violation of due process on the basis that it had not received the claimant's response to its statement timely and that the tribunal had not extended the time limit to reply.[78] The court confirmed the decision of the tribunal. In particular, it stated that the tribunal simply had not believed the statement of the respondent according to which the claimant's e-mails and letters containing the claimant's response were not received by the former's attorney.[79] The tribunal's conclusion was supported by the fact that when the response was sent by e-mail in August 2007, the e-mail was allegedly caught in the spam-filter. The court did not consider the award to be in violation of the defendant's right to due process.

In the same way, in case 4A 490/2016,[80] the Swiss Federal Tribunal denied the violation of the right to be be heard, for the tribunal did not grant an extension for the submission of comments on the concept of 'simulated contracts'. The dispute arose out of an agreement between Lybian companies for the construction of a mixed-purpose building.[81] At a preparatory meeting, the parties agreed that the tribunal should first rule on its jurisdiction and the applicable law.[82] Following the receipt of the parties' submissions on jurisdiction, the tribunal asked the parties to submit their comments on the concept of simulated contract.[83] While the claimant submitted such comments in a timely way, the respondent did not do so. The tribunal then issued an interim award confirming its jurisdiction over the matter, and the respondent applied to have the award set aside by the Swiss Federal Tribunal.[84] In particular, the respondent / applicant argued that the tribunal violated its right to be heard for not having granted the extension of time.[85] The Swiss Federal Tribunal did not agree with the respondent-applicant. In particular, it stated that the respondent's request to grant an extension of time due to its counsel's holiday absence was not sufficient to show a violation of the right to be heard.[86] Moreover, the tribunal pointed out that in any case the respondent could not allow the period granted to elapse without any further action. In fact, the respondent did not submit any comments in the period they set, even though it received claimant's comments in a timely manner.

[75] Ibid.

[76] Judgment of 6 August 2008, (2009) XXXIV YB Comm Arb 522 (OLG Dresden 2008).

[77] Ibid. 522. [78] Ibid. 522. [79] Ibid. 524.

[80] Judgment of 6 March 2017, (2017) 35 ASA Bull 428 (Swiss Federal Tribunal 2017), English version available at: <http://www.swissarbitrationdecisions.com/atf-4a-490-2016>.

[81] Ibid. para. A.a. [82] Ibid. para. B.a. [83] Ibid. para. B.a.

[84] Ibid. para. C. [85] Ibid. para. 3.3.3. [86] Ibid.

When it comes to the submission of new arguments or new evidence, it seems that only egregious cases would lead to the annulment of the award.[87] Indeed, the general tendency of national courts is to confirm the decisions of arbitral tribunals unless there has been an egregious violation of the right to be heard on the part of the tribunals.

In case no. 25 Sch 09/08,[88] the Hamm Court of Appeal confirmed the decision of the arbitral tribunal, notwithstanding that the latter ignored a brief which was submitted by the claimant three days before the oral hearing. In this case, the dispute arose out of supply contracts the conclusion of which was provided by a framework contract between the parties.[89] Arbitration proceedings were commenced in Moscow and the tribunal rendered four decisions in favour of the claimant. The latter then sought to enforce the arbitral awards in Germany, where the respondent raised certain defences under Article V(1) of the New York Convention.[90] Among other allegations, the respondent argued that there had been a violation of due process, since it was not given the opportunity to reply to a brief submitted late by the claimant.[91] With respect to this argument, the Hamm Court of Appeal stated that there was no violation of due process, since in the award the tribunal did not take the document into account. At the same time, the tribunal stated that the respondent did not prove the contrary, nor the the fact that the documents contained new factual arguments.[92]

Even considering the submission of documents after a cut-off date, the result does not change. In *Pacific China Holdings Ltd (In Liquidation) v Grand Pacific Holdings Ltd*, the Hong Kong Court of Appeal confirmed the decision of a tribunal to refuse additional authorities.[93] The dispute arose out of a loan agreement concluded by the parties. After the tribunal rendered an award in favour of the respondent, the claimant applied to the Hong Kong Court of First Instance to have the award set aside on the ground that it was not able to present its case and the procedure was not in accordance with the agreement of the parties.[94] The Court of First Instance considered that the refusal on the part of the tribunal to receive and take into account the additional authorities submitted belatedly prevented the claimant from presenting its case.[95] The Hong Kong Court of Appeal did not agree with such a decision. To the contrary, it stated that the Court of First Instance was not entitled to interfere with a case management decision falling within the discretion of the tribunal,[96] and as a result it set aside the order of the Court of First Instance.

However, it should be noted that even the late submission of a statement on the eve of a hearing might be accepted by an arbitral tribunal. The English High Court decided

[87] See e.g. *Société MORS v Société Supermarket Systems*, 1995 Rev arb 887 (Paris Cour d'appel 1991), where the Paris Court of Appeal annulled an arbitral award on the basis that the tribunal relied on evidence that was previously excluded.

[88] Judgment of 28 November 2008, (2009) XXXIV YB Comm Arb 536 (OLG Hamm 2008).

[89] Ibid. 536–7. [90] Ibid. 537.

[91] Ibid. 537. [92] Ibid. 541.

[93] *Pacific China Holdings Ltd (In Liquidation) v Grand Pacific Holdings Ltd*, [2012] 4 HKLRD 1, para. 68 (Hong Kong Court of Appeal 2012).

[94] Ibid. 2. [95] Ibid. para. 68. [96] Ibid.

thus in *Ispat Industries Ltd v Western Bulk Pte Ltd*,[97] a case concerning the cancellation of a charterparty.[98] During the arbitration proceedings, the claimant produced a statement on the eve of the hearing and the tribunal accepted it, arguing that the witness could be cross-examined on the second day of the hearing. Such a conduct was contested by the counterparty.[99] After the award was rendered, the respondent filed an application under sections 68 and 69 of the Arbitration Act 1996.[100] The respondent's application was based on the ground inter alia that the tribunal had breached its duty under section 33 to act fairly and to give the respondent a reasonable opportunity to deal with the claimant's case. In particular, it argued that there was no sufficient time to prepare for cross-examination and that, given the failure of the claimant to disclose relevant documents, it was not possible to prepare an effective cross-examination.[101] The court did not agree with the respondent, since it considered the decision of the tribunal to be a case management decision.[102] In particular, it stated that the tribunal did not fail to consider whether the counsel would have the opportunity to read and take into account the statement produced by the claimant.[103] Moreover, on the disclosure point, it stated that conducting the cross-examination without the relevant documents 'is always and necessarily the case where a party at trial cross-examines a witness about an alleged failure to disclose relevant documents'.[104]

Concerning other hypothetical disruptive conduct, a request for a postponement of a hearing immediately before its commencement is the most prevalent scenario.[105] However, even in this case, it has to be noted that only egregious cases would lead to the annulment of the award.

In *ASM Shipping Ltd of India v TTMI Ltd of England*,[106] the request to postpone a hearing given the absence of one of the parties' lead counsel was denied by the tribunal. The arbitration concerned a disputes related to a charterparty.[107] Following the issue of the award, an application under Section 68 of the English Arbitration Act 1996 was made by the respondent on the grounds that one of the arbitrators should have recused himself, and that the tribunal refused an adjournment following the absence of the respondent's counsel.[108] Notably, as to the refusal to grant an adjournment, the High Court confirmed the decision of the tribunal, and stated that 'the test is whether the decision to refuse an adjournment was 'so far removed from what could reasonably be expected of the arbitral process that it must be rectified'.[109] Moreover, the High Court pointed out that an adjournment would have caused a delay, entailing unnecessary costs.[110]

[97] *Ispat Industries Ltd v. Western Bulk Pte Ltd*, [2011] EWHC 93 (Comm.). On challenges based on section 68 of the English Arbitration Act, see Bruce Harris, Rowan Planterose, Jonathan Tecks, Lord Neuberger, and Garth Stewart, *The Arbitration Act 1996* (Wiley-Blackwell, 2014).

[98] Harris et cl. (n. 9), 2. [99] Ibid. 26. [100] Ibid. 1.

[101] Ibid. 26. [102] Ibid. 27. [103] Ibid.

[104] Ibid. [105] Berger and Jelsen (n. 1), 427.

[106] *ASM Shipping Ltd of India v TTMI Ltd of England*, [2005] EWHC 2238 (Comm), para. 38 (English High Court 2005).

[107] Ibid. para. 2. [108] Ibid. para. 8. [109] Ibid. para. 38. [110] Ibid.

In the same way, the U.S. Southern District Court of New York in *PT Reasuransi Umum Indonesia v Evanston Ins Co*[111] applied a similar test to the decision of an arbitral tribunal concerning a dispute which arose in connection with the parties' obligations under reinsurance contracts.[112] The arbitral tribunal rendered a decision in favour of the respondent, and then the claimant sought to vacate the award on several grounds, among which was the failure of the tribunal to postpone the hearing.[113] On this point the U.S. District Court maintained that when there is a reasonable decision not to grant a postponement, national courts are reluctant to interfere with the award.[114] Moreover, it pointed out that for nine months the respondent had been silent, whereas four days before the hearing it made a request for a postponement. The tribunal communicated with the parties by conference call and decided not to grant the postponement. In light of these circumstances the court considered that the refusal to grant the extension could not fall within the concept of misconduct on the part of arbitral tribunal.

As all these cases demonstrate, so-called due process paranoia is not justified by the approach of national courts. Indeed, our brief review of cases shows that courts are inclined to confirm arbitral awards unless there have been egregious violations of due process. In fact, as long as arbitrators arrive at a reasonable decision, there might be no concern as to whether a case management decision is in violation of due process. This consideration seems consistent with the results of the 2018 Queen Mary University International Arbitration Survey, where the legitimacy of the due process paranoia phenomenon was contested both by counsel and arbitrators.[115] In particular, the argument is that explaining the arbitrator's conduct by referring to the due process paranoia would be misleading. In fact, such a phenomenon would not be justified, given the existence of arbitration-friendly jurisdictions where the courts tend to defer to arbitrators with respect to the conduct of the arbitral proceedings.

14.3.3 Effective and efficient management of the arbitration process

Having ascertained that the due process paranoia would not and should not limit the proactiveness of arbitrators, it is useful to establish what can be done in practice to streamline arbitral proceedings. The following sections consider some proposals are being considered.

To begin with, establishing a limit of pages for the parties' submissions might be an effective solution to save time and costs.[116] Of course, such a rule should be agreed by

[111] *PT Reasuransi Umum Indonesia v Evanston Ins Co*, XIX YB Comm Arb 788, 790 (US District Court, SDNY 1992).

[112] Ibid. 788. [113] Ibid. 788–9. [114] Ibid. 791.

[115] Queen Mary University of London, '2018 International Arbitration Survey: The Evolution of International Arbitration' (n. 2), 27.

[116] Risse (n. 10), 456.

the parties in the terms of reference or in any other similar document setting out procedural directions, and its purpose would be to avoid parties' repetition of arguments. In fact, even though at first glance some might say that this solution would jeopardize the right to be heard and to present the case, the truth is that it would allow parties to focus on good arguments rather than put forward the hopeless ones.[117] Moreover, this seems to be in line with the results of the 2018 Queen Mary University International Arbitration Survey, where a number of both arbitrators and counsel pointed out that on a case-by-case basis arbitrators should limit the number of pages of submissions and the rounds of submissions.[118] On the rounds of exchanges of party submissions, some arbitration operate on the basis of three rounds (Request/Answer, Statement of Claim amd Defence, Reply/Rejoinder), but many have four, five, or even six rounds of submissions (to accommodate document production rounds, skeleton arguments pre-hearing, and post-hearing submissions). Moreover, it should be noted that such a rule of page limit is provided even in contexts other than international arbitration. For example, as pointed out by Risse,[119] the procedure before the European Court of Justice provides for a limit of 50 pages for a party submission.[120]

Another possible solution to be taken into account concerns the identification of the material issues of the case at an early stage. The most relevant issues might be identified gradually during the proceedings. At the preliminary meeting, a first attempt could be made to identify the crucial issues of the case, at least in general terms.[121] Following the parties' submissions and after having discussed this identification with the parties, the tribunal might deliberate and determine which are the most relevant issues of the case and which ones the tribunal would not wish to consider,[122] at least at this stage. This identification (or narrowing) of the issues does not prevent the tribunal from assessing other issues that during the hearing are identified as significant and that the tribunal considers decisive. However, even in such a scenario, a proper early management of the case would still result in saving costs, avoiding delays, and improving the overall efficiency of the arbitral proceedings.

In the same way, the use of sanctions might be considered an effective means to promote the efficiency of the arbitral proceedings. In particular, as pointed out in the 2018 Queen Mary University International Arbitration Survey, interviewees complained about dilatory tactics employed by counsel that are not sanctioned either because arbitrators do not deem appropriate to sanction parties or because arbitrators are not in possession of the appropriate instruments.[123] In particular, over 70 per cent of survey

[117] Ibid.

[118] Queen Mary University of London, '2018 International Arbitration Survey: The Evolution of International Arbitration' (n. 2), 26.

[119] Risse (n. 10), 456.

[120] Practice Directions to Parties before the General Court, L 68/23, 7 Mar. 2010, 5.

[121] Michael E. Schneider, 'Lean Arbitration: Cost Control and Efficiency Through Progressive Identification of Issues and Separate Pricing of Arbitration Services', (1994) 10 Arbitration International, 132.

[122] Risse (n. 10), 461.

[123] Queen Mary University of London, '2018 International Arbitration Survey: The Evolution of International Arbitration' (n. 2), 27.

respondents pointed out that dilatory tactics of the parties and counsel should be sanctioned.[124] In fact, a number of interviewees stated that lengthy submissions and frivolous motions should not be accepted, and that arbitrators should be in a position to address disruptive behaviour. To this end, a solution might be represented by the allocation of costs based not only on the 'the costs follow the event' rule but also on the efficiency of the parties.[125] In the 2017 ICC Arbitral Rules, such mechanism is provided.[126] Specifically, Article 38 Section 5 provides arbitrators with full discretion as to how to allocate the cost based on the efficiency or inefficiency of case management. This mechanism would allow tribunals to take into account attorneys' fees, to determine whether they are proportionate to the arbitration, and to decide whether dilatory tactics or unreasonable arguments have been used by the parties.

Moreover, improving the use of technology in international arbitration might be the key solution in guaranteeing a high standard of efficiency in the arbitral proceedings. This is in line with the results of the 2018 Queen Mary University International Arbitration Survey. Indeed, interviewees stated that the efficiency of the arbitral proceedings might be increased by the use of information technology (IT).[127]

In particular, the most used IT forms are hearing room technologies, videoconferencing, and cloud-based storage, whereas artificial intelligence and virtual hearing rooms are used less. However, with respect to all the forms of IT mentioned (albeit in different percentages), users stated that such forms should be used more often in international arbitration to make the arbitral proceedings more efficient. In fact, they pointed out that the most relevant advantage of using technology is the opportunity to conduct hearings and meetings through means of communicaton that do not require the physical presence of parties and arbitrators.[128] This would result in substantial savings in terms of money and time that would be spent otherwise on reaching a given location for a meeting between parties and arbitrators. Use of technology and, most importantly, the dematerialization of written submissions and exhibits can also contribute to cost saving and more efficient conduct of proceedings: instead of dozens of boxes, parties may be required to submit a tablet or to upload everything onto a cloud system. This is increasingly common, and arbitration tribunals request paperless submissions up to the hearing and occasionally even at the hearing.

Notwithstanding the potential advantages of the use of technology, it has to be noted that a number of counsel questioned the effectivenes of conducting cross-examinations of witnesses or hearings through videoconference. The reason behind this opposition might be represented by the fear that the reactions of the witness would not be clearly understandable.[129] However, it has to be noted that the development of technology

[124] Ibid. 35. [125] Risse (n. 10), 462. [126] Article 38 (5) ICC Rules (n. 7).

[127] Queen Mary University of London, '2018 International Arbitration Survey: The Evolution of International Arbitration' (n. 2), 26–7.

[128] Ibid. 32.

[129] Sophie Nappert and Paul Cohen, 'The Impact of Technology on Arbitral Decision Making:The Practicioner's Perspective', in Christian Aschauer and Piers Maud (eds), *Arbitration in the Digital Age: The Brave New World of Arbitration* (Cambridge University Press, 2017), 133.

provides a high-resolution picture that allows the participants to understand the facial expressions as well as the voice tone and body language of the witness.[130] The immediacy of video-conferencing can therefore no longer be considered an issue. The only remaining objection to this kind of technology is represented by the ineffable component of in-person contact, thanks to which participants might have a better opportunity to assess the veradicity of the witnesses involved.[131]

The launch of the Prague Rules[132] in December 2018 aims also at bringing about a higher degree of efficiency by adopting a more inquisitorial approach. Specifically, Article 2 refers to proactive tribunals, Article 7 to the concept of *jura novit curiae*,[133] and Articles 11 and 12 to adverse inferences a tribunal may draw when a party refuses to cooperate, and allocation of costs in accordance with efficiency and cooperation of disputing parties. Whether an inquisitorial approach is the solution to the lack of efficiency is ultimately a question of legal culture. It may well be argued that arbitration is culturally and by design consensual, and hence that more moderate adversarial processes allowing for party autonomy ought to be preferred over inquisitorial models. However, it is undisputed that the objectives of the rules are positive; practice will confirm whether this soft law codification achieves its objectives.

In this section, we have put forward certain proposals to improve the efficiency of arbitral proceedings. Leaving aside the specific solutions proposed, this section demonstrates that there is room for improvement of efficiency in international arbitration, and that a proactive approach by arbitrators migh result in saving time and costs without jeopardizing due process. Moreover, the use of technology in the proceedings might be of great importance in the future, either to streamline the proceedings or to render more appealing international arbitration to solve disputes of particular sectors.

What remains to consider is the role of arbitral institutions with respect to efficiency of arbitral proceedings efficiency. In the next section we will address the relation between party autonomy and powers of arbitral institution, and the 'judicialization' of the arbitral proceeding.

14.4 The Role of Arbitral Institutions

Nowadays, it appears that most arbitration agreements provide for institutional arbitration. The main consequence of this choice is the administration by the institution of

[130] Ibid. 133. [131] Ibid. 134.

[132] 'Rules on the Efficient Conduct of Proceedings in International Arbitration', available at: <https://praguerules.com/upload/medialibrary/9dc/9dc31ba7799e26473d92961d926948c9.pdf>.

[133] On the topic, see Loukas Mistelis and Metka Potocnik, '*Iura Novit Arbiter*: The English Approach', in Franco Ferrari and Giuditta Cordero Moss (eds), *Jura Novit Curia in International Arbitration* (Juris, 2018), 135–67, and also other chapters included in the book.

several tasks during the arbitration. It follows that the institutional arbitral rules will be applicable to the arbitral proceedings. Thus, arbitral institutions are in in the best position to improve the efficiency of arbitral proceedings. To this end, most institutions have introduced expedited procedures and other provisions with the purpose of streamlining arbitral proceedings. For example, the ICC has introduced an expedited procedure[134] following similar introductions by ICDR,[135] SIAC,[136] the HKIAC,[137] and the 2012 Swiss Chambers' Arbitration Institution.[138]

While the introduction of expedited procedures and other provisions aims at improving the efficiency of the arbitral process, the question would remain whether the institutional rules would prevail over the procedural agreements of the parties. This would lead to what Berger has called in a recent article 'the party autonomy paradox',[139] namely the phenomenon according to which the parties, by agreeing to institutional arbitration, would agree to limit their autonomy as well. Moreover, it would be worth exploring whether the level of formality and sophistication introduced by these procedures would have a negative impact on the efficiency of the arbitral proceedings.

In the following sections we will discuss party autonomy and powers of arbitral insitutions (14.4.1) and so-called 'judicialization' in relation to the efficiency of arbitration (14.4.2).

14.4.1 Party autonomy and powers of arbitral institutions

Arbitration institutions can be considered ancillary entities participating in arbitrations conducted under their administration.[140] Indeed, in institutional arbitrations, certain measures taken by the institutions assume a decisional character. Of course, arbitrators remain the subjects to whom the principal decision-maker role is assigned.[141] However, institutional decisions might assume a material character, since they might influence the outcome of the merits directly or indirectly.[142] In particular, the capacity of institutions to impact the proceedings they administer is clear if one looks at the finality of certain decisions concerning discrete aspects of the dispute. An example might be the decisions in respect of costs.[143] Moreover, the materiality of certain decisions might come from the consequences they have on the framework applicable to the arbitral proceedings. This is the case of decisions concerning the seat of arbitration and the set of arbitral rules. In other cases, the materiality of decisions derives from the fact

[134] Article 30 ICC Rules and Appendix VI (n. 7).
[135] Article 6 ICDR International Arbitration Rules as amended (2014) (n. 7).
[136] Article 5 Singapore International Arbitration Centre Rules of Arbitration (n. 7).
[137] Article 42 HKIAC Rules (n. 7).
[138] Article 42 Swiss Chambers' Arbitration Institution Rules ('Swiss Rules') (June 2012).
[139] Klaus P. Berger, 'Institutional Arbitration: Harmony, Disharmony and the "Party Autonomy Paradox"', 34 Arbitration International 473 (2018), 486.
[140] Rémy Gerbay, *The Functions of Arbitral Institutions* (Kluwer Law International, 2016), 196.
[141] Ibid. 188. [142] Ibid. 189. [143] Ibid. 189.

that they impact the composition of the tribunal either directly—when they nominate arbitrators—or indirectly—when they decide the number of arbitrators.[144] In particular, in order to assess the relation between party autonomy and the powers of arbitral institutions, it would be worth taking into account the latter, namely the decisions concerning the number of arbitrators.

As mentioned above, different institutions have introduced expedited procedures. In fact, in 2017, by introducing the Expedited Procedure Rules, the ICC joined other institutions such as the ICDR, the HKIAC, and the SIAC. All these institutions give preference to the appointment of a sole arbitrator provided that the amount of the dispute is within a certain threshold. The rationale behind this approach is that the involvement of only one arbitrator would likely result in substantial savings in terms of time and costs. However, the provision concerning the appointment of a sole arbitrator varies according to the institution.

Article 41.2(b) of the HKIAC Rules provide that the arbitral institution invites the parties to agree on a sole arbitrator. In case of failure by the parties to agree on the appointment of a sole arbitrator, the parties can agree on a different number of arbitrators. Thus, an agreement providing for three arbitrators will prevail over the provision of the institution. The approach followed by the ICC Rules and the SIAC Rules is different in that it allows arbitral institutions to override parties' agreements providing for a different number of arbitrators. In fact, SIAC Rule 5.2(b) provides that 'the case shall be referred to a sole arbitrator, unless the President determines otherwise'. In the same way, according to Article 2 of Appendix VI of the ICC Rules, 'the Court may, notwithstanding any contrary provision of the arbitration agreement, appoint a sole arbitrator'. This approach raises a question as to whether arbitral institutions can ignore the parties' agreement in light of the discretion their rules grant them.[145]

As it has already been pointed out, efficiency in arbitration is a relative concept depending on the view of the observer. Thus, if the parties have provided in the arbitration agreement that the tribunal will consist of three members, then priority should be given to the parties' intention. In fact, the parties may have considered that a dispute between them would be better decided by three arbitrators rather than a sole arbitrator. Indeed, their perception of efficiency might differ from the one of the arbitral institution. However, it should be noted that national courts dealing with this issue have arrived at different conclusions.

On the one hand, in *Noble Resources International Pte Ltd v Shanghai Good Credit International Trade Co Ltd*,[146] the Shangai No. 1 Intermediate People's Court gave priority to party autonomy.[147] the dispute arose out of a contract for the sale and purchase of iron ore and the arbitration agreement contained in the contract provided for a tribunal

[144] Ibid. 192. [145] Berger (n. 139), 486.

[146] *Noble Resources International Pte Ltd v Shanghai Good Credit International Trade Co Ltd*, 11 August 2017, (2016) Hu 01 Xie Wai Ren No. 1.

[147] See Sacchit Joshi and Brijesh Chhatrola, 'Expedited Procedure Vis-à-Vis Party Autonomy, Enforceable?' (Kluwer Arbitration Blog, May 2018), available at: <http://arbitrationblog.kluwerarbitration.com/2018/05/12/expedited-procedure-vis-vis-party-autonomy-enforceable/>, accessed 22 January 2019.

consisting of three arbitrators.[148] When commencing the arbitration, the claimant requested that the proceedings be conducted under the expedited procedure under the SIAC Rules. Following the claimant's request, the SIAC appointed a sole arbitrator for the case. The respondent contested the application of the expedited procedure as well as the appointment of a sole arbitrator. However, the respondent did not participate in the proceedings, and the tribunal rendered an award against it in its absence.[149] At the recognition and enforcement stage in mainland China, the respondent challenged the award under the New York Convention. In particular, it contested the composition of the tribunal, arguing that it was not in accordance with the parties' agreement as provided by the arbitration clause. The Shanghai Court stated that the interpretation of Article 5.2(b) of the SIAC Rules should not give the President of the SIAC absolute discretion in dealing with the composition of the arbitral tribunal. On the contrary, full consideration should be given to the partie's agreement in light of party autonomy. In fact, the latter should prevail over the powers of arbitral institution. Thus, the appointment of a sole arbitrator by the President of the SIAC was considered to be in violation of the arbitration agreement.[150] Accordingly, the Shangai Court did not recognize and enforce the award.

On the other hand, in *AQZ v ARA*,[151] under similar factual circumstances, the Singapore High Court stated that, given the choice of the parties to submit a dispute under the SIAC Rules providing for the expedited procedure, there was no violation of the arbitration agreement. In this case the dispute concerned the alleged existence of a contract for the sale and purchase of Indonesian non-coking coal.[152] The day after commencing the arbitration proceedings, the claimant requested the application of the expedited procedure under SIAC Rules.[153] Such an application was objected to by the respondent, who contested both the existence of the arbitration agreement and the application of the expedited procedure. The President of the SIAC granted the request and appointed a sole arbitrator, while the respondent reserved all its right to challenge.[154] Following the rendering of the award in favour of the claimant, the respondent applied to set aside the award. Its application was based inter alia on the ground that the composition of the arbitral tribunal and/or the procedure was in breach of the parties' agreement.[155] The Singapore High Court concluded that in light of the parties' express choice of the SIAC Rules containing the expedited procedure, the decision of overriding the agreement providing for a three-member tribunal was consistent with party

[148] James Kwan, 'PRC Court Refuses to Enforce SIAC Arbitral Award Made by One Arbitrator Under Expedited Arbitration Procedures when Arbitration Agreement Provided for Three Arbitrators' (Hogan Lovells, 2017), 2: <https://www.hoganlovells.com/en/publications/prc-court-refuses-to-enforce-siac-arbitral-award-arising-out-of-the-expedited-procedure-where-arbitration-agreement-provided-for-three-arbitrators>, accessed 17 January 2019.

[149] Ibid. 3. [150] Ibid. 4.

[151] *AQZ v ARA*, [2015] SGHC 49. For a discussion on this case, see G. Born and J. Lim, 'AQZ v ARA: Singapore High Court Upholds Award Made under SIAC Expedited Procedure' (Kluwer Arbitration Blog, March 2015): <http://arbitrationblog.kluwerarbitration.com/2015/03/09/aqz-v-ara-singapore-high-court-upholds-award-made-under-siac-expedited-procedure/>, accessed 22 January 2019.

[152] Ibid. 3. [153] Ibid. 4. [154] Ibid. 5. [155] Ibid. 61.

autonomy.[156] Moreover, it pointed out that the SIAC Rules do not exclude from their scope agreements concluded before the expedited procedure came into force. For these reasons, the expedited procedure provisions might override parties' agreement entered even before their introduction. In particular, the court adopted a commercially sensible approach according to which the fact that the parties opted for a three-member tribunal in their agreement was considered as just one of the elements to take into account.[157] The other factors to consider were the complexity of the dispute, the quantum claimed, and when the agreement was concluded.[158] Moreover, the Singapore High Court stated that a 'judicious' exercise of discretion by the president could not constitute a sufficient ground for challenge of the award.

These two decisions are indicative of the tension existing between party autonomy and the powers of arbitrators and arbitral institutions. The approach followed by the Singapore High Court might be justified by the need to ensure that arbitral institutions can exercise their administrative decisions without the risk that eventually the award is going to be challenged and refused recognition and enforcement. This is why, generally, national courts tend to grant arbitral institutions a broad discretion in exercising their function. However, it has to be noted that the decision involving the composition of the tribunal concerns the element to which international arbitration owes its success, namely party autonomy. Leaving the opportunity for an entity other than the parties to decide, with a broad range of discretion, the composition of the tribunal means limiting party autonomy. Moreover, especially when there seems to be no impasse,[159] it is not clear why arbitral institutions should be granted a prerogative that has always belonged to the parties. This is why it might be preferable to choose a solution that would take into consideration the parties' view on the composition of the tribunals. For example, the approach adopted by the HKIAC might be preferable. The case would be referred to a sole arbitrator unless otherwise provided by the arbitration agreement. As a result, the parties would be given the possibility of assessing the efficiency of the arbitral proceedings. Moreover, it would allow a dialogue between the parties and the institution and, in case of disagreement, the intention of the parties in the arbitration agreement would prevail.

14.4.2 'Judicialization' and efficiency of international arbitration

In the 2013 Queen Mary University survey concerning corporate choices of various industries in international arbitration,[160] a number of complaints were expressed as to the increasing 'judicialization' of arbitral proceedings. In particular, these complaints referred to the increased formality of proceedings and the similarities with litigation in terms of costs and delays.

[156] Ibid. 131. [157] Ibid. 132. [158] Berger (n. 139), 489. [159] Ibid. 492.

[160] Queen Mary University International Arbitration Survey, '2013 Corporate Choices in International Arbitration: Industry' (n. 1), 5.

It is undeniable that international arbitration has been changing over the years, and it will keep changing. In particular, it has been submitted that one of the aspects that arbitration would have in common with litigation before the domestic courts would be the increased sophistication in terms of procedures.[161] As a result, arbitrations would be characterized by an increasing use of strict and clearly defined procedural norms.[162] However, the introduction of clear procedural rules have positive effects on international arbitration. Of course, it would depend on the rules. However, this chapter has shown that the introduction of procedural rules, either by arbitrators during the proceedings or in general by institutions, might lead to improvement of the efficiency of arbitrations. Thus, a more sophisticated procedure would not lead necessarily to delays and increasing costs. In the same way, a very strict and inflexible procedural framework may lead to dissatisfaction of the parties and several applications before, during, and after the arbitration.

A selective judicialization might streamline the arbitral proceedings instead of being detrimental to their efficiency.[163] For example, we have discussed the identification at an earlier stage of the material issues of the case. Notwithstanding the fact that it requires more experience and sophistification in terms of procedure on the side of the disputing parties and arbitral tribunals, this approach would result in reducing costs and time. Indeed, the hearing would focus only on the issues considered relevant by the tribunal and the parties. Therefore, the result would be a more streamlined procedure focusing only on the most crucial issues, despite the alleged increased sophistification.

Moreover, some argue that the expansion of arbitral institution rules in terms of length and detail might be considered an indicator of the 'judicialization' phenomenon.[164] There is no doubt that arbitral insitutions are expanding their rules. However, even assuming that this expansion is leading to a more sophisticated procedure, most rules are aimed at improving efficiency in international arbitration. For example, Appendix IV of the 2017 ICC Rules provides techniques that can be used to control time and costs by the arbitral tribunal. At the same time, according to Article 22(1), 'the arbitral tribunal and the parties shall make every effort to conduct the arbitration in an expeditious and cost-effective manner, having regard to the complexity and value of the dispute'. Despite its general character, this provision would allow arbitrators and parties to tailor the proceedings in the most efficient way. Moreover, even considering the expedited procedure rules, the result does not change. Indeed, there is no doubt that the purpose of such rules is to streamline the arbitral proceedings. For instance, one might criticize Article 2 of Appendix VI of the ICC Rules, since it allows the arbitral institution to override the parties' agreement. However, even in this case, such a provision would foster the efficiency of the proceedings in terms of time and costs.

161 Ibid.

162 Rémy Gerbay, 'Is the End Nigh Again? An Empirical Assessment of the "Judicialization" of the International Arbitration', 25 American Journal of International Arbitration 223 (2014), 228.

163 Leon Trakman and Hugh Montgomery, 'The "Judicialization" of International Commercial Arbitration: Pitfall or Virtue?' 30 Leiden Journal of International Law 405 (2017), 408.

164 †V. V. Veeder, 'Strategic Management in Commencing an Arbitration', in Albert Jan van den Berg (ed), *Arbitration Advocacy in Changing Times* (Kluwer Law International, 2011), 27.

14.5 Concluding remarks: the efficiency paradigm

Assessing efficiency in international arbitration is not an easy task. Indeed, it is a relative concept the content of which varies depending on the different parties, actors, and factors involved in the arbitral process. In particular, we have seen how the assessment of various factors may lead to different concepts of efficiency. For example, one approach might be to link the duration of arbitration and the matter disputed. Focusing on the relation between value of the dispute and the costs of the arbitral proceedings might be an effective approach as well. Moreover, the value of the award itself might be taken into consideration. As we have shown, the value of arbitral awards might be assessed independently of recognition and enforcement in light of the high rate of voluntary compliance and the increasing practice of alternatives to traditional enforcement, e.g. by assignment of awards or contract renegotiation on the basis of awards. We have also indicated that efficiency is a rather recent value of the arbitration, as it appears to have acquired prominence only in the last twenty years. This is why we have attributed the adjective 'emerging' to the word 'value'. Regulation of efficiency may be bespoke and 'from within': disputing parties set their objectives and expectations and design the conduct of 'their' arbitration accordingly. Alternatively, regulation of efficiency may be 'from outside': arbitral institutions or other formulating agencies design an arbitral process into which the parties can opt in; they can then partially modify that procedure, to the extent that opting out of the rules is permitted. In the 'from outside' model we attribute systemic qualities arbitration.

As section 14.2 demonstrated, the efficiency of the arbitral process can only be assessed by taking into account different factors. Further, such factors may vary depending on the parties and actors involved in arbitration. In fact, what arbitrators consider efficient might not correspond with parties' idea of efficiency. For this reason, in section 14.3 we tool into account the role of arbitrators in assessing the efficiency of the process.

National laws or institutions generally give arbitral tribunal rules a very significant degree of discretion in dealing with the procedural management of the case. Therefore, arbitrators are in an excellent position to improve the efficiency of the proceedings. In particular, we have explored the so-called 'due process paranoia' phenomenon to answer the question whether it would be justified for tribunals to adopt a more rigorous approach in setting procedural directions. This question has to be answered in the affirmative, especially considering that most jurisdictions that can be considered arbitration-friendly would allow arbitrators to deal with the case management without interfering with it. Further, after having discussed the due process paranoia phenomenon, we have proposed some techniques arbitrators might follow to streamline the arbitral proceedings.We focused on the limitation of pages for the parties' submissions, the identification of the material issues of the case at an early stage, the use of sanctions to avoid dilatory tactics, the use of technology in international arbitration, and a more proactive role in case management which, however, would not amount to the tribunal acting in an inquisitorial fashion. These represent a limited number of proposals, of course. However, they might have beneficial effects on the arbitral proceedings in terms of efficiency. It seems that case management which involves the parties is consensual in nature, and creates a positive and cooperative atmosphere in the arbitration.

After having considered the role of arbitrators, in Section 14.4 we focused on the role of the arbitral institutions. Given the increasing use of institutional arbitrations, institutions have the opportuity (and arguable the means) of addressing the efficiency of arbitral proceedings. This is the reason why most arbitral institutions have introduced expedited procedures. However, it is in respect of the latter procedures that certain issues might arise. In particular, some expedited procedure provisions allow the institution to override the parties' agreement. Concerning this issue, national courts have arrived at different conclusions. It is suggested here that a solution favouring parties' agreement should be preferred.

International arbitration relies on party autonomy and approaches which are consensual and cooperative. Consequently, parties' joint intention should prevail unless the impasse of the arbitral proceedings would require the institution to intervene. At the same time, the introduction of new, clear, strict rules by institutions should be favoured. Despite certain complaints as to the increasing judicialization of arbitral proceedings, this chapter has shown that the introduction of new procedural rules in most cases is aimed at improving the efficiency of arbitration.

It is essential for international arbitration to address and meet parties' procedural expectations and needs/objectives. Arbitration is a process owned by the parties. However, arbitrators and institutions steer the process and have a role in ensuring that the process is not frustrated. To go back to the transport metaphor used earlier: while the parties choose the mode of transport—taxi or private care hire—companies running taxis and car hire services (arbitration institutions), and indeed drivers of such vehicles (arbitrators), have a duty to ensure that the journey is safe for everyone involved. In that sense efficiency (speed and cost saving) is almost never a stand-alone value: it is combined and coexists with rule compliance and fairness values. The vehicle companies (arbitral institutions) and drivers (arbitrators) have to ensure rules compliance (due process) and a safe journey (operating in accordance with the law and rules and existing procedural rules). Where there is no tension in this respect, party autonomy and efficiency can work together. And indeed in such a framework of efficiency, compliance can take a central role.

As arbitration grows, it acquires more frequently than before systemic qualities, and efficiency is part and parcel of those qualities. Parties may design their own efficiency paradigm by exercising their party autonomy and agreeing to a process of their liking. This will typically imply opting for ad hoc arbitration or a 'relative efficiency' within a choice of institutional arbitral rules. However, when the parties cannot reach an agreement, the safeguard of efficiency is in the hands of arbitral institutions and arbitral tribunals.

CHAPTER 15

LEGAL CERTAINTY AND ARBITRATION

FRÉDÉRIC BACHAND AND FABIEN GÉLINAS

15.1 Introduction

In a volume on arbitration, why—the reader may wonder—should there be a chapter devoted to legal certainty, rather than one highlighting its flip side, legal flexibility?[1] After all, arbitration's flexibility has traditionally been viewed not only as one of its distinctive features but also as one of its key advantages.[2] Would it not make more sense, then, to reflect on the everlasting quest for an optimal balance between certainty and flexibility by underscoring the latter's central place among the foundational values of the international arbitration system?

Perhaps not, for the editors' decision to place the emphasis on legal certainty is consistent with a noticeable shift in the balance between certainty and flexibility that will be explored throughout this chapter. While legal flexibility surely continues to deserve a place among the core values of international arbitration, it is legal certainty's stock that has been on the rise in recent years. The shift can be felt throughout the international arbitration system, and it is mainly driven by an increased awareness that too much flexibility can ultimately imperil arbitration's legitimacy.[3] While, in the

[1] Other key concepts that come to mind when one thinks about the flipside of legal certainty include legal indeterminacy (on which, see Ken Kress, 'Legal Indeterminacy', 77 California L Rev 283 (1989)) and legal under-determinacy (on which, see Lawrence Solum, 'On the Indeterminacy Crisis: Critiquing Critical Dogma', 54 U Chicago L Rev 462 (1987)). Legal certainty is taken here as a composite of clarity, publicity, stability, predictability, and consistency.

[2] See e.g. Bernard Hanotiau, 'L'arbitre, garant du respect des valeurs de l'arbitrage', in Gerald Aksen et al. (eds), *Global Reflections on International Law, Commerce and Dispute Resolution: Liber Amicorum in Honour of Robert Briner* (ICC, 2005), 369–70.

[3] The main theme of the 2016 Congress of the International Council for Commercial Arbitration (ICCA) is a clear reflection of this shift: 'The Contribution of International Arbitration to the Rule of Law'.

commercial setting, the shift toward greater certainty is occurring in response to concerns emanating from users of arbitral services (Section 15.2), in the investment context, it rather reflects concerns about the power of arbitrators to shape public international law (Section 15.3).

15.2 The International Commercial Arbitration Context

In the field of international commercial arbitration, the tilting of the balance towards greater certainty, while deplored by some, appears to be an unavoidable—and perhaps even desirable—consequence of the increased diversity and heterogeneity of the international commercial arbitration community.

15.2.1 Certainty and the enforcement of arbitral agreements and awards

To be sure, legal certainty has been a central concern for stakeholders since the inception of the modern international commercial arbitration system. For users of the system, the very decision to include an arbitration clause in a contract is driven—to a significant extent—by a need for clarity as to where and how disputes these users are unable to resolve amicably may be adjudicated. The explanation for this need for clarity is twofold. From an economic standpoint, uncertainty regarding the manner in which disputes arising out of international commercial transactions may be resolved raises the costs of doing business on a global scale; it therefore erects a very real barrier to international trade.[4] From a legal standpoint, significant differences in the rules governing international jurisdiction from one country to another give rise to much uncertainty regarding where, and under which conditions, a legal action can be entertained in a given jurisdiction.[5] As the U.S. Supreme Court famously observed in *The Bremen*, 'The elimination of all such uncertainties by agreeing in advance on a forum acceptable to both parties is an indispensable element in international trade, commerce, and contracting.'[6]

The arbitration clause is, of course, not the only contractual device to which business entities that operate internationally can turn in order to address these uncertainties.

[4] When it agreed to establish the United Nations Commission on International Trade Law (UNCITRAL), the General Assembly of the UN acknowledged that 'divergencies arising from the laws of different states in matters relating to international trade constitute one of the obstacles to the development of world trade' (UNGA Res 2205 (XXI) (1966)).

[5] On these differences, see generally Hélène van Lith, *International Jurisdiction and Commercial Litigation: Uniform Rules for Contract Disputes* (T.M.C. Asser Press, 2009).

[6] *The Bremen v Zapata Off-Shore Co.*, 407 U.S. 1, paras. 13–14 (1972).

However, as arbitration came to be viewed, during the twentieth century, as generally better suited to the needs of international business than litigation before national courts, states seeking to promote the development of international trade focused their efforts on the legal framework governing arbitration clauses and the international circulation of awards, rather than on attempting to harmonize rules relating to forum selection clauses and the international circulation of judicial decisions.[7]

The legal framework governing arbitration required attention because national laws often failed to provide adequate assurance that undertakings to resort to final and binding arbitration would be upheld and acted upon by national courts. While in some jurisdictions, pre-dispute arbitration clauses were invalid,[8] elsewhere the problem rather related to a long-standing reluctance on the courts' part to give full legal effect to arbitration agreements and awards.[9]

The centrepiece of states' initiatives, the enactment of the Convention on the Recognition and Enforcement of Foreign Arbitral Awards of 1958 (the New York Convention)—which has rightly been described as a 'universal constitutional charter for the international arbitral process'[10]—addressed the problem in three crucial respects. First, the convention established, in Art. II(1), that as a general rule, arbitration agreements to which it applies must be recognized as valid by all contracting states. Second, it imposed on the courts of contracting states an obligation to refer to arbitration all international commercial disputes falling within the scope of valid arbitration agreements, with the importance of legal certainty being further underscored by national court decisions correctly holding that Art. II(3) removes any discretion that courts may otherwise have enjoyed to refuse to give effect to an arbitration agreement on grounds of convenience.[11] Third, the enactment of the New York Convention addressed users' need for finality and closure by requiring national courts to recognize and enforce foreign arbitral awards, subject to a limited number of exhaustively enumerated exceptions that clearly established, firstly, that judicial review of the merits is generally off limits and, secondly, that party autonomy deserves to be promoted to the

[7] Initiatives aimed at encouraging states to harmonize rules relating to international jurisdiction have enjoyed relatively little success. Efforts in this regard include the 2005 Convention on Choice of Court Agreement (commonly known as the Hague Choice of Court Convention), only entered into force in 2015 (it is currently binding on Mexico, Singapore, and the members of the European Union) and the Convention of 2 July 2019 on the Recognition of Foreign Judgments in Civil or Commercial Matters (commonly known as the Hague Judgments Convention, not yet entered into force).

[8] E.g. in our home jurisdiction, the Canadian province of Quebec, the validity of pre-dispute arbitration clauses was only firmly recognized at the beginning of the 1980s: see John Brierley, 'Quebec Arbitration Law: A New Era Begins', 40 Arb J 20 (1985).

[9] Examples that come to mind include the common law revocability doctrine, which emerged in the early 17th c. (see Paul Carrington and Paul Castle, 'The Revocability of Contract Provisions Controlling Resolution of Future Disputes Between the Parties', 67 Law & Contemp Probs 207 (2004), 208), as well as the discretion later enjoyed by judges in many common law jurisdictions to refuse to give effect to an otherwise valid and applicable arbitration agreement (on which, see Michael Mustill and Stewart Boyd, *Commercial Arbitration*, 2nd edn (Butterworths, 1989), 24).

[10] Gary Born, *International Commercial Arbitration*, 2nd edn (Kluwer Law International, 2014), 98.

[11] Marike Paulsson, *The 1958 New York Convention in Action* (Kluwer Law International, 2016), 65–6.

greatest extent possible. Here as well, national courts have further reinforced legal certainty by adopting a *when-in-doubt-recognize-and-enforce* approach, reflecting what has often been described as the New York Convention's 'pro-enforcement bias'.[12]

Clearly, then, meeting users' need for legal certainty was central to the post-World War II initiative that led to the adoption of the New York Convention. But as the convention fell well short of a comprehensive legal framework governing all aspects of the international arbitration process, its contribution to legal certainty was fairly narrow in focus. This was not so much a shortcoming of the New York Convention as it was a reflection of a broader reality, which is that the need for comprehensive, clearly ascertainable, and rather rigid rules was—at the time—mostly limited to aspects of international arbitration law governing the relationship between arbitral proceedings and national judicial systems.[13]

15.2.2 Certainty's increased importance in the conduct of arbitral proceedings

With respect to the conduct of international commercial arbitral proceedings, however, the long-standing orthodoxy has been that users' interests are best served by a legal framework that—in sharp contrast to the comprehensive and detailed *ex ante* guidance provided by states' civil justice systems—allows the process to be significantly tailored to the specific circumstances of the case through *ex post* procedural and evidentiary decisions made mostly by arbitrators but also occasionally by the parties themselves or an arbitration institution of their choosing. In other words, the international arbitral process has to offer not only a private form of adjudication but also—and crucially—a truly alternative form of adjudication: a quintessential example of bespoke justice.[14]

The pre-eminence of legal flexibility in this context was enshrined in arbitration rules and national statutes that contained relatively few provisions regulating the conduct of arbitral proceedings and delegated to arbitral tribunals extensive discretionary powers

[12] Andreas Börner, 'Article III', in Herbert Kronke et al. (eds), *Recognition and Enforcement of Foreign Arbitral Awards: A Global Commentary on the New York Convention* (Kluwer Law International, 2010), 116.

[13] See also, in this vein, Art. 5 of the UNCITRAL Model Law on International Commercial Arbitration (UNCITRAL Model Law on International Commercial Arbitration, 1985 (with amendments as adopted in 2006) (UNCITRAL 2008)), which provides that '[i]n matters governed by this Law, no court shall intervene except where so provided in this Law' and which is all about legal certainty: 'Although the provision, due to its categorical wording, may create the impression that court intervention is something negative and to be limited to the utmost, it does not itself take a stand on what is the proper role of courts. It merely requires that any instance of court involvement be listed in the model law. Its effect would, thus, be to exclude any general or residual powers given to the courts in a domestic system which are not listed in the model law. The resulting certainty of the parties and the arbitrators about the instances in which court supervision or assistance is to be expected seems beneficial to international commercial arbitration' (UNCITRAL, 'Analytical Commentary on Draft Text of a Model Law on International Commercial Arbitration: Report of the Secretary-General', A/CN.9/264 (1985), Art. 5, para. 2).

[14] Jan Paulson, *The Idea of Arbitration* (Oxford University Press, 2013), 7.

to deal with procedural and evidentiary matters left unaddressed by the parties. For example, the United Nations Commission on International Trade Law's highly successful UNCITRAL Arbitration Rules of 1976 contained a mere 41 articles, one of which provided that 'Subject to these Rules, the arbitral tribunal may conduct the arbitration in such manner as it considers appropriate, provided the parties are treated with equality and that at any stage of the proceedings each party is given a full opportunity of presenting his case' (Art. 15(1)). The 1985 UNCITRAL Model Law on International Commercial Arbitration adopted a similarly hands-off approach to the regulation of arbitral proceedings, and its functional equivalent to Art. 15(1) of the 1976 Arbitration Rules[15] was described by the UNCITRAL Secretary-General as the 'Magna Carta' of arbitral procedure and 'the most important provision of the model law'.[16]

Writing at the beginning of the 1990s, Howard Holtzmann expressed the view that the balance between certainty and flexibility achieved in the UNCITRAL Arbitration Rules and other leading normative instruments was widely viewed as satisfactory by users of the international arbitration system.[17] He was mindful, however, that the extensive flexibility offered by those rules could prove counterproductive in at least some cases. Judge Holtzmann's preferred solution, which drew on his experience at the Iran–United States Claims Tribunal, was to encourage arbitrators to hold pre-hearing conferences in order to clarify at the outset of the arbitration how the tribunal intended to exercise its extensive procedural and evidentiary powers. He concluded with the observation that 'it would be useful for UNCITRAL or the International Council for Commercial Arbitration (ICCA) to undertake to prepare guidelines for prehearing conferences that would be widely available for use in international cases.'[18]

In truth, however, a movement questioning the received wisdom about the benefits of international arbitration's flexibility had already gathered enough steam to alarm those who treasured it most. Notably, writing in the late 1980s, Philippe Fouchard lamented the fact that the process's flexibility was increasingly seen as a source of arbitrariness rather than a guarantee of efficiency. He warned that efforts aimed at constraining arbitrators' procedural and evidentiary powers would inevitably lead to more formalism, needlessly complex proceedings, and increased costs. He even viewed these efforts as contributing to what he characterized as a 'crisis', which, he hoped, would subside once users of the international arbitration system grew weary of wasting money, time, and energy in endless squabbles.[19]

Unsurprisingly, Fouchard was horrified when, a few years later, UNCITRAL responded positively to Judge Holtzmann's invitation to prepare guidelines for pre-hearing

[15] Art. 19(1) of the UNCITRAL Model Law on International Commercial Arbitration (n. 13) reads as follows: 'Subject to the provisions of this Law, the parties are free to agree on the procedure to be followed by the arbitral tribunal in conducting the proceedings.'

[16] See UNCITRAL (n. 13), Art. 19, para.1.

[17] Howard Holtzmann, 'Balancing the Need for Certainty and Flexibility in International Arbitration Procedures', in Richard Lillich and Charles Brower (eds), *International Arbitration in the 21st Century* (Transnational, 1994).

[18] Ibid. 19. [19] Philippe Fouchard, 'Où va l'arbitrage international?' 34 McGill LJ 435 (1989).

conferences in international arbitration cases.[20] To the great French scholar, UNCITRAL's initiative constituted a grave menace to arbitration's very essence, and was all the more deplorable in that it implicitly advocated an American-inspired approach to the administration of evidence. Not only was international arbitration's flexibility under threat, so was its universality. UNCITRAL's suggested guidelines were nothing less than '*atterrantes*'—'appalling'—and their non-binding nature did little to alleviate Fouchard's concerns.[21]

What UNCITRAL ultimately published—in 1996—were not guidelines per se but rather Notes on Organizing Arbitral Proceedings.[22] The UNCITRAL Notes were not the first instrument designed to increase certainty by providing additional *ex ante* guidance on procedural or evidentiary matters. Previously, the International Bar Association (IBA) had adopted 'Supplementary Rules Governing the Presentation and Reception of Evidence in International Commercial Arbitration' in 1983, but these rules had not proved as successful as their drafters had hoped.[23] The UNCITRAL Notes, however, were the first among a series of normative instruments, adopted in the past twenty years, that proved to have much more influence on the practice of international arbitration.[24] People may reasonably disagree on whether we can go so far as to speak of an 'explosion of soft law'[25] in the field of international arbitration, but it cannot be denied that these developments are among the most significant in recent years.

Despite the fact that many of the recently adopted instruments were explicitly not intended to limit international arbitration's flexibility,[26] most observers will agree that,

[20] UNCITRAL, 'Draft Guidelines for Preparatory Conferences in Arbitral Proceedings: Report of the Secretary-General. Addendum', A/CN.9/396/Add.1 (1994).

[21] Philippe Fouchard, 'Une initiative contestable de la CNUDCI. À propos du projet de directives pour les conférences préparatoires dans le cadre des procédures arbitrales', Rev. Arb 461 (1994).

[22] For an assessment of the UNCITRAL Notes, see Philipp Habegger and Anna von Mühlendahl, 'The UNCITRAL Notes on Organizing Arbitral Proceedings: Time for an Update?' in Stefan Kröll et al. (eds), *International Arbitration and International Commercial Law: Synergy, Convergence and Evolution* (Kluwer Law International, 2011). The UNCITRAL Notes are currently being revised: see UNCITRAL, 'Settlement of Commercial Disputes: Revision of the UNCITRAL Notes on Organizing Arbitral Proceedings. Note by the Secretariat', A/CN.9/WG.II/WP.194 (2015).

[23] Nigel Blackaby et al., *Redfern and Hunter on International Arbitration* (Oxford University Press, 2015), para. 6.95.

[24] See esp. the IBA Rules on the Taking of Evidence in International Commercial Arbitration (1999, revised in 2010 and renamed the IBA Rules on the Taking of Evidence in International Arbitration); the IBA Guidelines on Conflicts of Interest in International Arbitration (2004, revised in 2014); the IBA Guidelines on Party Representation in International Arbitration (2013); as well as ICC, 'ICC Commission Report: Controlling Time and Costs in Arbitration': <http://www.iccwbo.org/Advocacy-Codes-and-Rules/Document-centre/2012/ICC-Arbitration-Commission-Report-on-Techniques-for-Controlling-Time-and-Costs-in-Arbitration/> (2007, revised 2012). The IBA rules and guidelines are available at: <http://www.ibanet.org/Publications/publications_IBA_guides_and_free_materials.aspx#Practice Rules and Guidelines>.

[25] See e.g. Gabrielle Kaufmann-Kohler, 'Soft Law in International Arbitration: Codification and Normativity', 1(2) JIDS 283 (2010), 298.

[26] E.g. the preamble of the 2010 IBA Rules on Evidence (n. 24) mention that they 'are not intended to limit the flexibility that is inherent in, and an advantage of, international arbitration'. The IBA's Guidelines on Party Representation (n. 24) send an even stronger message about international arbitration's flexibility:

as a matter of fact, they do have a fettering effect on arbitrators' discretion. As noted by two experienced arbitrators and leading academics, it is now clear that 'soft law serves as a constraint on arbitral autonomy';[27] it 'exercises a significant influence over the way arbitration proceedings are conducted', which entails that 'even though the law may be soft, flexibility is traded for predictability'.[28] This is particularly true of two instruments developed by the IBA: its guidelines on conflicts of interest[29] and its rules on the taking of evidence.[30] Clearly, the proliferation of highly influential 'soft' instruments provides compelling evidence that, insofar as the conduct of international commercial arbitral proceedings is concerned, the balance between certainty and flexibility is currently shifting toward the former.

Other recent developments point in the same direction. Particularly noteworthy is a significant change in the manner in which a growing number of arbitral institutions deal with arbitrator challenges. Traditionally, leading institutions neither provided reasons nor published any information relating to the decisions on challenges that they were occasionally called upon to make under their rules. Users of the international arbitration system thus had little information about the success rates of challenges or the circumstances under which they were likely to succeed. But over the past ten years or so, as the number of arbitrator challenges has increased significantly, many observers have called for greater transparency in order to address a rising dissatisfaction among users with the lack of institutional guidance in this area.[31] The London Court of International Arbitration (LCIA) led the way in responding to these calls, in May 2006, when it decided that it would henceforth publish its decisions on challenges, in the form of abstracts.[32] Other institutions have since followed suit, and there is now talk of a 'growing trend in the direction of publication by leading arbitral institutions'.[33]

'[They] are not intended to limit the flexibility that is inherent in, and a *considerable* advantage of, international arbitration' (emphasis added).

[27] William Park, 'The Procedural Soft Law of International Arbitration: Non-Governmental Instruments' in Lukas Mistelis and Julian Lew (eds), *Pervasive Problems in International Arbitration* (Kluwer Law International, 2006), 142.

[28] Kaufmann-Kohler (n. 25), 16.

[29] See e.g. Paula Hodges, 'The Arbitrator and the Arbitration Procedure: The Proliferation of "Soft Laws" in International Arbitration. Time to Draw the Line?', Austrian YB Int'l Arb 205 (2015), 209 ('[P]ractically speaking, the Guidelines have acquired considerable force and weight').

[30] See e.g. Born (n. 10), 200, noting that according to a 2012 survey, 'the IBA Rules [on the taking of evidence] are used in 60% of international arbitrations'.

[31] See e.g. Geoff Nicholas and Constantine Partasides, 'LCIA Court Decisions on Challenges to Arbitrators: A Proposal to Publish', 23 Arb Int 1 (2007); Gary Born, 'Institutions Need to Publish Arbitrator Challenge Decisions' (Kluwer Arbitration Blog, 2010): <http://kluwerarbitrationblog.com/2010/05/10/institutions-need-to-publish-arbitrator-challenge-decisions/>; Margaret Moses, 'Reasoned Decisions in Arbitrator Challenges', 3 YB on Int'l Arb 199 (2013).

[32] See Adrian Winstanley, 'Director General's Review of 2006': <http://www.lcia.org/media/Download.aspx?MediaId=43>. So far, abstracts for the 28 challenges that occurred between 1996 and 2010 have been published in LCIA, 'Special Edition on Arbitrator Challenges', 27(3) Arb Int (2011).

[33] See Born (n. 10), 1830. The International Court of Arbitration of the International Chamber of Commerce recently decided that it would provide parties with reasons in support of some of the decisions it may be called upon to make under its rules. The publication of those reasons, however, is not

Another area where calls for greater predictability have been made in recent years is with respect to costs. Under the leading statutes and rules, international arbitral tribunals have traditionally enjoyed broad discretionary powers in allocating costs.[34] But perceived inconsistencies and incoherence in the manner in which those powers are exercised have left many hoping for reforms designed to improve predictability in this area.[35] The International Chamber of Commerce (ICC) Commission on Arbitration and ADR has recently changed the landscape in this area by collating, presenting, and analysing ICC decisions on costs in a published ICC report.[36] The report insists that, given that 'party autonomy and flexibility are central to international arbitration, there is no single, universal approach to the allocation of costs'.[37] Yet, the combination of a requirement that 'discretionary' cost decisions be 'fully reasoned'[38] and the availability of those reasoned decisions clearly fosters the development of best practices and the harmonization of expectations that will soon make guidelines possible. Some authors have already proposed that internationally acceptable guidelines providing a framework for cost awards be developed.[39]

15.2.3 The demand for increased certainty: a plausible explanation

The jury still seems to be out on whether these developments will eventually strengthen or weaken the international commercial arbitration system. Michael Schneider is

contemplated. See ICC, 'Note to Parties and Arbitral Tribunals on the Conduct of the Arbitration under the ICC Rules of Arbitration' (ICC, 2016), paras. 11–13: <http://www.iccwbo.org/products-and-services/arbitration-and-adr/arbitration/practice-notes,-forms,-checklists/>.

[34] See Jeff Waincymer, *Procedure and Evidence in International Arbitration* (Kluwer Law International, 2012), 1191.

[35] See esp. Michael Bühler, 'Awards of Costs in International Commercial Arbitration: An Overview', 22 ASA Bulletin 249 (2004), 249 ('There is indeed an arbitral precedent to support nearly any approach a tribunal may wish to apply to its cost decision. Even cost awards rendered under the same arbitration rules sometimes vary fundamentally without any apparent reason. The bottom line is that it is often impossible to predict with any satisfactory degree of certainty how the costs will be awarded'). See also John Gotanda, 'Bringing Efficiency to the Awarding of Fees and Costs', in Kröll and et al. (n 32), 141 ('In international arbitrations, awarding arbitration costs and attorneys' fees is often an arbitrary and unpredictable decision'); Sundaresh Menon, 'Keynote Address', in Albert Jan van den Berg (ed.), *International Arbitration: The Coming of a New Age?* (Kluwer Law International, 2013), 19.

[36] ICC, 'Decisions on Costs in International Arbitration: An ICC Commission Report', 2 ICC Dispute Resolution Bulletin (ICC, 2015): <http://www.iccwbo.org/Advocacy-Codes-and-Rules/Document-centre/2015/Decisions-on-Costs-in-International-Arbitration-ICC-Arbitration-and-ADR-Commission-Report/>.

[37] Ibid. para. 7.

[38] Ibid. para. 42 ('[T]he tribunal has full discretion to award reasonable costs'), para. 43 ('[An] award must contain reasons for the decision on the allocation of costs'; '[T]o render a fully reasoned decision on costs, arbitrators need to give the parties a full opportunity to be heard on the matter').

[39] See Robert Smit and Tyler Robinson, 'Cost Awards in International Commercial Arbitration: Proposed Guidelines for Promoting Time and Cost Efficiency', 20 Am Rev Int'l Arb 267 (2009); Marc Goldstein, 'Arbitral Cost Allocation Decisions: Should Guidelines Accompany Discretion?' in Stephen Huber and Ben Sheppard Jr (eds), *AAA Yearbook on Arbitration and the Law*, 23rd edn (Juris, 2011).

among those who have most forcefully resisted the 'strong trend in arbitration practice steadily eroding [the] principles [of flexibility and responsiveness to the needs of a specific case] in the name of predictability'.[40] Critics have often pointed out that efficiency is compromised not only by the fact that proceedings are less likely to be well adapted to the circumstances of the dispute, but also because instruments seeking to provide further *ex ante* procedural or evidentiary guidance can lead parties to waste time and money bickering, at the outset of an arbitration, about problems that may never materialize.[41]

It may well be that the contemporary shift toward legal certainty actually hinders, rather than promotes, the efficiency of proceedings. However, a critical assessment of this development cannot be limited to a cost-benefit analysis focusing on whether—on balance—it has a positive or negative impact on the efficiency of the international commercial arbitration system. One must also take into account the real likelihood that, rather than merely being driven by an ill-considered quest for greater efficiency, users' demand for increased certainty may reflect—to a significant extent, if not primarily—understandable concerns about the system's legitimacy.[42]

To grasp why, it may be useful to begin by noting how the extensive procedural and evidentiary discretion that international arbitrators have traditionally enjoyed is, at first glance at least, difficult to reconcile with basic requirements of the rule of law. Adjudicative discretion is, of course, not illegitimate in itself, but it cannot be free of all legal constraints. As Lord Bingham recently put it, 'The rule of law does not require that official or judicial decision-makers should be deprived of all discretion, but it does require that no discretion should be unconstrained so as to be potentially arbitrary. No discretion may be legally unfettered.'[43]

This point, however, holds true generally but not universally. As Park observed twenty years ago, '[t]ightly-knit homogeneous groups often find informal extra-legal adjudication more appropriate than legally binding procedures', as in this context, '[n]otions of fairness may be more important than strict application of rules'.[44] Park's observation is relevant to the present discussion because, in its early days—as it mainly reflected a

[40] Michael Schneider, 'President's Message: The Problem with Predictability', in Domitille Baizeau and Bernd Ehle (eds), *Stories from the Hearing Room: Experience from Arbitral Practice. Essays in Honour of Michael Schneider* (Kluwer Law International, 2015), 261. See also Michael Schneider, 'The Essential Guidelines for the Preparation of Guidelines, Directives, Notes, Protocols and Other Methods Intended to Help International Arbitration Practitioners to Avoid the Need for Independent Thinking and to Promote the Transformation of Errors into "Best Practices"', in Laurent Lévy and Yves Derains (eds), *Liber amicorum en l'honneur de Serge Lazareff* (Pedone, 2011).

[41] See also Ugo Draetta, 'The Transnational Procedural Rules for Arbitration and the Risks of Overregulation and Bureaucratization', 33 ASA Bulletin 327 (2015).

[42] On the legitimacy of international arbitration, see generally Stephan Schill, 'Developing a Framework for the Legitimacy of International Arbitration', in Albert Jan van den Berg (ed.), *Legitimacy: Myths, Realities, Challenges* (Kluwer Law International, 2015).

[43] Tom Bingham, *The Rule of Law* (Penguin, 2010), 54. See also Brian Tamanaha, *On the Rule of Law: History, Politics, Theory* (Cambridge University Press, 2004), 199.

[44] William Park, 'Neutrality, Predictability and Economic Co-operation', 12(4) J Int'l Arb 99 (1995), 105–6.

continental European approach to adjudication[45]—international commercial arbitration was characterized by a certain professional and sociopolitical cohesion that provided reassurance to users that the arbitrators' extensive procedural and evidentiary powers would generally be exercised in a sufficiently principled and predictable—and thus legitimate—manner.[46] In other words, sociopolitical cohesion ensured that shared understandings and common values would place a satisfactory measure of constraint on the exercise of discretion.

Because of arbitration's success in becoming the globally preferred means of resolving international commercial disputes, the field is now much more diverse, heterogeneous, and even polarized.[47] The shared assumptions and trust that historically made it possible, and even preferable, for procedural and evidentiary issues to be left to the arbitrators' discretion have been eroding steadily.[48] And to quote Park again, this time from his 2002 Freshfields Lecture, 'if backgrounds and experiences differ materially, the ad hoc imposition of procedures uncustomary to one side and not announced in advance, risks reducing the perception of arbitration's legitimacy'.[49] Therefore, it seems plausible, at the very least, that the contemporary shift in the balance between certainty and flexibility is nothing more than a natural and predictable, and perhaps in some respects even desirable,[50] consequence of the evolution in the sociocultural make-up of the international commercial arbitration community.[51]

15.3 The Investment Arbitration Context

Investment arbitration calls only in some respects for a distinct analysis, because the investment arbitration community overlaps significantly with the international commercial arbitration community. While the considerations of legal certainty that drove the establishment of the system and the procedural framework governing arbitral proceedings are in part comparable to the developments seen in commercial arbitration, the shift in the balance between certainty and flexibility in the investment context has

[45] Thomas Carbonneau, 'The Ballad of Transborder Arbitration', 56 Miami L Rev 773 (2002), 781.

[46] Fouchard (n. 19), 447.

[47] Emmanuel Gaillard, 'Sociology of International Arbitration', 31 Arb Int 1 (2015), 14, noting 'a clear trend ... towards the evolution of international arbitration from a solidaristic to a polarized model'.

[48] Bruno Oppetit, *Théorie de l'arbitrage* (Presses universitaires de France, 1998), 10: 'En s'universalisant à l'ensemble de la planète, l'arbitrage s'est banalisé, affadi, voire même altéré, en s'éloignant de ses origines.'

[49] William Park, 'The 2002 Freshfields Lecture. Arbitration's Protean Nature: The Value of Rules and the Risk of Discretion', 19 Arb Int 279 (2003), 284.

[50] Ibid. 283, where Park tentatively argues that 'the benefits of arbitrator discretion are overrated; flexibility is not an unalloyed good; and arbitration's malleability often comes at an unjustifiable cost.'

[51] On which, see Susan Franck et al., 'International Arbitration: Demographics, Precision and Justice', in van den Berg (n. 42).

played out most strikingly in the development of substantive investment protections and the role that case law has come to play in that development.[52]

15.3.1 Legal certainty as an objective of investment arbitration

Undeniably, legal certainty has been a central concern in the establishment and growth of the investment arbitration system. Fostering legal certainty in the treatment of international investment disputes was a means to the end of achieving an increased flow of cross-border investment, and thus economic development.[53] Before the system was established, the existing avenues of recourse open to investors were widely considered to lack legal certainty. On one side, the public international law system of espousal of claims in state-to-state procedures, which may have been somewhat effective at a time when cross-border investments were large and few, had become inadequate in a world including an increasing population of international investors. On the other side, 'while such disputes would usually be subject to national legal processes', 'international methods of settlement' were recognized, in the diplomatic language of the Convention on the Settlement of Investment Disputes between States and Nationals of Other States (the Washington, or ICSID Convention), as 'appropriate', at least in certain cases.[54]

Put more bluntly, judicial recourse before the courts and under the laws of the host state was widely viewed as falling short of the expected standards of neutrality and predictability. With respect to both espousal of claims and national legal processes, political factors difficult to square with the concept of an enforceable legal right affected outcomes to a degree seen as incompatible with growing expectations of legal certainty. The movement toward legal certainty in that cross-border context thus started not from a position of legal flexibility but from one in which political expediency played a role deemed too pervasive.

[52] Though this chapter does not focus on the contents of bilateral investment treaties, it must be noted that states' evolving treaty-drafting practices in this area reflect a trend toward giving increased importance to legal certainty. The substantive provisions of bilateral investment treaties are nowadays more detailed and precise than they were a few decades ago: Kathryn Gordon and Joachim Pohl, 'Investment Treaties over Time: Treaty Practice and Interpretation in a Changing World', OECD Working Papers on International Investment 2015/02, 24–5 (despite language in many treaties remaining vague, increase in number of issues covered by investment treaties and greater detail in language clarifying key concepts in more recent treaties); Flavien Jadeau and Fabien Gélinas, 'CETA's Definition of the Fair and Equitable Treatment Standard: Toward a Guided and Constrained Interpretation', 1 Transnational Dispute Management (2016) (connecting greater substantive precision in Canada–EU Comprehensive Economic and Trade Agreement to push toward greater precision in bilateral investment treaties).

[53] Karl-Heinz Böckstiegel, 'Commercial and Investment Arbitration: How Different Are They Today?' 28(4) Arb Int 577 (2012), 587.

[54] Convention on the Settlement of Investment Disputes between States and Nationals of Other States (adopted 1965, entered into force 1966), 575 UNTS 159, preamble (ICSID Convention).

The means by which legal certainty was to be improved were, in good measure, borrowed from the advances already made in the field of international commercial arbitration. Building in part upon the New York Convention and the rules and practices of existing arbitral institutions, states were able to set up, with relative ease, a system that would not only lead to binding results but would also be capable of growing incrementally with each instance of a state giving consent to arbitrate an investment dispute or a category of such disputes.[55]

In this new system, once consent to arbitrate was secured, the resulting award could be enforced under the New York Convention, relying on its expansive network of signatories. In cases falling under the ICSID Rules (as opposed to the Additional Facility Rules), increased guarantees of enforceability, and thus legal certainty, came into play. First, for purposes of enforcement, the award is treated, in a contracting state, like a final court judgment of that jurisdiction,[56] and thus bypasses the vagaries of local rules concerning the enforcement of foreign awards, including any local interpretations of the public policy ground for refusal of enforcement under the New York Convention.[57]

Second, the annulment or setting-aside avenues normally available to challenge an arbitral award at the seat of arbitration are foreclosed, thus eliminating the uncertainties associated with local annulment or setting-aside criteria, which the New York Convention does not harmonize.[58] The local review procedures at both the seat of arbitration and the place of enforcement have thus been replaced by a centralized review system allowing annulment based only on restrictive grounds.[59] Although this centralized review system has probably not brought as much certainty as had been wished,[60] it was clearly intended to increase legal certainty.[61]

Turning now to the rules governing the conduct of investment arbitration proceedings, the rules set out in the ICSID Convention are more detailed than those found in the typical arbitration rules discussed earlier in the context of international commercial arbitration. This is likely indicative of a heightened concern among states for legal certainty, a concern that was already reflected in the slightly more formalized practices

[55] Ibid.: '[M]utual consent by the parties to submit such disputes to conciliation or to arbitration through such facilities constitutes a binding agreement which requires . . . that any arbitral award be complied with'; '[N]o Contracting State shall by the mere fact of its ratification, acceptance or approval of this Convention and without its consent be deemed to be under any obligation to submit any particular dispute to conciliation or arbitration.'

[56] Ibid. Art. 54(1).

[57] Convention on the Recognition and Enforcement of Foreign Arbitral Awards (adopted 1958, entered into force 1959), 330 UNTS 38, Art. V(2)(b).

[58] Ibid. Art. V(1)(e). The convention does not regulate the treatment of the award at the seat but does recognize the annulment or setting aside of the award at the seat as a valid ground for refusing enforcement.

[59] ICSID Convention (n. 54), 52.

[60] See generally Gaëtan Verhoosel, 'Annulment and Enforcement Review of Treaty Awards: To ICSID or Not to ICSID', 23(1) ICSID Rev 119 (2008).

[61] Christoph Schreurer, *The ICSID Convention: A Commentary* (Cambridge University Press, 2009), 903.

of state-to-state dispute settlement.[62] For example, the ICSID 'Rules of Procedure for Arbitration Proceedings' (ICSID Rules) contain detailed provisions about sessions, sittings, and deliberations of the tribunal,[63] all subjects upon which the sets of rules typically used in commercial arbitration are mostly silent.

Similarly, the ICSID Rules provide details of the written procedure[64] and rules for the taking of evidence that are not normally found in the arbitration rules used in international commercial matters.[65] Nevertheless, the investment arbitration system as a whole has been anchored, from its inception, in the procedural practices established and evolving in the fast-growing field of international commercial arbitration.[66] The arbitrators called upon to decide the early cases were, as they are today, often steeped in the practice of commercial arbitration, and recourse is still made in the investment context to sets of rules, such as the UNCITRAL 'Arbitration Rules' (UNCITRAL Rules) and the 'Rules of Arbitration of the International Chamber of Commerce' (ICC Rules), that were originally intended for, and are widely used in, international commercial settings.[67] Conversely, amendments intended at least in part to better accommodate investment arbitration have been brought to both the UNCITRAL Rules (e.g. scope of application[68]) and the ICC Rules (e.g. applicable law in the absence of a contract[69]), and reflect the current reality of the broad overlap in procedural practices.

This overlap means that the normative shift toward greater legal certainty in procedure observed in commercial settings and described earlier in this chapter has also taken place in the practice of investment arbitration. The considerable efforts deployed by the IBA with regard to the harmonization of practices and expectations in the areas of evidence and conflicts of interest are apt examples. The 'soft' instruments that are the results of those efforts have shown their relevance and gained traction in both commercial and investment arbitration. The highly successful evidence rules of 1999, originally intended for international *commercial* arbitration, thus became, in 2010, the IBA 'Rules on the Taking of Evidence in International Arbitration'. The word 'commercial' was

[62] J. G. Merrills, *International Dispute Settlement* (Cambridge University Press, 2005), 98. Also see James Crawford, 'Continuity and Discontinuity in International Dispute Settlement: An Inaugural Lecture', 1(1) JIDS 1 (2010), 9–10.

[63] See ICSID, 'Rules of Procedure for Arbitration Proceedings', Rules 13–15: <https://icsid.worldbank.org/ICSID/StaticFiles/basicdoc/partF.htm>.

[64] Ibid. Rule 31. [65] Ibid. Rules 33–7.

[66] This is not to say that international commercial arbitration practice did not borrow, historically, from the practice of state-to-state arbitration: Crawford (n. 62), 13.

[67] Andrea Bjorklund, 'The Emerging Civilization of Investment Arbitration', 113(4) Penn State Law Rev 1269 (2009), 1271.

[68] UNCITRAL, 'UNCITRAL Arbitration Rules' (as revised in 2010), Art. 1(1): <http://www.uncitral.org/pdf/english/texts/arbitration/arb-rules-revised/arb-rules-revised-2010-e.pdf>.

[69] ICC Rules of Arbitration, Art. 21: <http://www.iccwbo.org/products-and-services/arbitration-and-adr/arbitration/icc-rules-of-arbitration/>. See more generally ICC, 'States, State Entities, and ICC Arbitration: Report of the ICC Commission on Arbitration and ADR' (ICC, 2012): <http://www.iccwbo.org/Advocacy-Codes-and-Rules/Document-centre/2012/ICC-Arbitration-Commission-Report-on-Arbitration-Involving-States-and-State-Entities-under-the-ICC-Rules-of-Arbitration/>.

removed from the title to acknowledge the fact not only that the rules may be used, but also that they were being used, in investment arbitration.[70]

As for the IBA Guidelines on Conflicts of Interest in International Arbitration, the first version of the rules, brought out in 2004, was 'originally intended to apply to both commercial and investment arbitration'. For a time, a measure of uncertainty might have 'lingered as to their application to investment arbitration',[71] but this was put to rest in the 2014 version.[72] Finally, calls for greater consistency and predictability in the allocation of costs, outlined above in the context of commercial arbitration, have been echoed in investment arbitration, where a traditional state-to-state, no-recovery position has not been reliably followed and space has been created for a costs-follow-the-event element.[73]

15.3.2 Legal certainty and the law that is common to investment agreements

What is distinctive about the movement toward greater legal certainty in investment arbitration is that it has largely been driven by the perceived role of arbitrators in interpreting and developing substantive law. To be sure, users of international commercial arbitration also display a preference for clear and detailed substantive legal norms. First, they systematically refrain from giving arbitrators the power to decide as *amiables compositeurs* or *ex aequo et bono*[74]—an option that is generally not available in litigation and is sometimes presented as an advantage of arbitration.[75] Second, in a large majority of cases, users of international commercial arbitration still subject their disputes to a national law even if they have the option—which is, again, generally not available in

[70] See 1999 IBA Working Party & 2010 IBA Rules of Evidence Review Subcommittee, 'Commentary on the Revised Text of the 2010 IBA Rules on the Taking of Evidence in International Arbitration' (IBA, 1999–2010), 2: <www.ibanet.org/Publications/publications_IBA_guides_and_free_materials.aspx> ('The word "commercial" was deleted from the title of the Rules to acknowledge the fact that the IBA Rules of Evidence may be and are used both in commercial and investment arbitration.')

[71] Preface to the IBA Guidelines on Conflicts of Interest in International Arbitration (n. 24), 2.

[72] Ibid. para. 5.

[73] See David Smith, 'Shifting Sands: Cost and Fee Allocation in International Investment Arbitration', 51 Va J Int'l L 749 (2011); Judith Gill, James Freeman, and Tomasz Hara, 'Investment Treaty Tribunals' Divergent Approaches to Costs: Reflections Following Decisions in Two Cases Commenced Against the Republic of Turkey', Turkish Commercial Law Review 5 (2015); Academic Forum on ISDS, 'Excessive Costs & Insufficient Recoverability of Cost Awards' (Working Group 1: Catharine Titi, Julien Chaisse, Marko Jovanovic, Facundi Pérez Aznar and Gabriel Bottini), 14 March 2019, 6.

[74] The ICC statistics are revealing in this respect. While Art. 21(3) of the ICC Rules clearly allows for it, in the cases received in 2018, the parties gave arbitrators such powers only once (in that case the power to decide *ex aequo et bono*): The ICC, '2018 ICC Dispute Resolution Statistics', 1 ICC Dispute Resolution Bulletin 12 (2019).

[75] See Simon Greenberg, Christopher Kee, and J. Romesh Weeramantry, *International Commercial Arbitration: An Asia-Pacific Perspective* (Cambridge University Press, 2011), 138. See generally Laurence Kiffer, 'Amiable Composition and ICC Arbitration', 18(1) ICC Int'l Ct Arb Bull 51 (2007); Florian Grisel, 'Droit et non-droit dans les sentences arbitrales CCI. Une perspective historique', 25(2) ICC Int'l Ct Arb Bull 13 (2014).

litigation[76]—to refer instead to a set of transnational rules of law.[77] Presumably they do this, at least in part, because national law affords them greater legal certainty.[78] The widely exercised freedom to designate the governing rules of law, in turn, have prevented the predictability of substantive law from becoming a systemic issue that could raise serious legitimacy questions.[79] This cannot be asserted with the same confidence with respect to investment arbitration.

International investment law could hardly have been described as a fully developed body of substantive law when the system of investment arbitration began to grow. The only serious attempt at codifying the principles and rules of international investment law, the Multilateral Agreement on Investment, ultimately failed at a key juncture in the push toward globalization.[80] At that juncture, the failed multilateral agreement had been the world's only hope to prevent the staggering explosion in the number of bilateral agreements on investment that ultimately resulted. What the world ended up with instead was a patchwork of approximately 3,000 bilateral investment treaties with broadly similar, but not identical, provisions, compounded by an uncertain connection to customary law and to case law. The debate that ensued about fragmentation and unity in investment law, and about arbitral lawmaking and precedent more particularly, was inevitable.[81] Few would now deny that investment arbitrators have displayed a tendency to 'multilateralize' bilateral investment treaties, and to reason in a way that implies the existence of an overarching body of international investment law.[82] Also, no one can

[76] Greenberg et al. (n. 75). On the evolution of mainstream thinking about the use of non-state law as governing law by national courts, see Geneviève Saumier, 'The Hague Principles and the Choice of Non-State "Rules of Law" to Govern an International Commercial Contract', 40(1) Brooklyn Journal of International Law 1 (2013).

[77] ICC (n. 74): in 2018, only in 2% of the contracts did the parties choose a set of transnational rules of law. It should be noted, however, that these statistics only account for cases where the contract between the parties contains a choice of law clause (i.e. in 87% of the total number of cases referred to ICC arbitration in 2018).

[78] The view that the application of national law to international transactions affords more predictability than transnational alternatives, however, is not unanimous. See notably Marc Blessing, 'Regulations in Arbitration Rules on Choice of Law', in Albert Jan van den Berg (ed.), *ICCA Congress Series No. 7* (Kluwer Law International, 1996), 439.

[79] Although the so-called *lex mercatoria* debate, in its various forms and iterations, has generated and still generates a considerable amount of scholarly output and can be described as 'existential', it has never significantly affected, let alone threatened, the mainstream practice of international commercial arbitration.

[80] Organisation for Economic Co-operation and Development (OECD) Negotiating Group on the Multilateral Agreement on Investment (MAI), 'The Multilateral Agreement on Investment Draft Consolidated Text', DAFFE/MAI(98)7/REV1 (1998). For context, see Sol Picciotto, 'Linkages in International Investment Regulations: The Anatomies of the Draft Multilateral Agreement on Investment', 19 U Pa J Int'l Econ L 731 (1998).

[81] Andreas Lowenfeld, 'Investment Agreements and International Law', 42 Colum J Transnat'l L 123 (2003); Andreas Lowenfeld, 'Public Policy and Private Arbitrators: Who Elected Us and What Are We Supposed to Do?' (2005): <https://www.mcgill.ca/pjrl/files/pjrl/john_e._c._brierley_memorial_lecture_andreas_f._lowenfeld.pdf>. See generally Andrés Rigo Sureda, *Investment Treaty Arbitration: Judging under Uncertainty* (Cambridge University Press, 2012).

[82] Stephan Schill, *The Multilateralization of International Investment Law* (Cambridge University Press, 2009).

deny that some form of precedent has taken hold in the system.[83] However, the extent to which this practice is appropriate and justified and, if so, on what basis and according to what parameters, remains controversial today.

Consistency and coherence make the law predictable and enhance legal certainty. As such, they are worthy of being pursued as a core aspect of the rule of law.[84] Since the practice of precedent has been, up until now, the only realistic means of fostering consistency and coherence in investment law, a sense that it is in some form desirable has emerged. Legal theorists known for their work on the rule of law have often emphasized that following precedent goes hand in hand with the fostering of consistency.[85] Arbitrators have thus accepted the relevance of prior decisions; they have done so, importantly, at the instigation of parties, including state parties, that have presented arguments before them and have cited to precedents.

Yet reminders that arbitrators should focus their attention on the language of the particular treaty provisions they are applying are not uncommon. 'Let us respect the text, apply that text, and not try to develop theories of text that go beyond its own terms,' James Crawford has warned.[86] One is also commonly reminded of the fact that no arbitral award can be considered binding beyond the parties and the particular case it decides. The situation is the same, essentially, as that described at Article 59 of the Statute of the International Court of Justice (ICJ Statute): 'The decision has no binding force except between the parties and in respect of that particular case.'[87] Building on the analogy, according to Article 38(d) of the ICJ Statute, judicial decisions are a 'subsidiary means for the determination of rules of law'. This means, according to Gilbert Guillaume, that a judge 'is not compelled to follow the same solution that justified the decision he had previously made'.[88]

This also means, however, that the judge 'will be inclined to do so [i.e. to follow the same solution] in order to ensure legal certainty'.[89] While the notion that an arbitral

[83] Of note on this topic is the empirical work of Jeffrey Commission, 'Precedents in Investment Treaty Arbitration: A Citation Analysis of a Developing Jurisprudence', 24 J Int'l Arb 129 (2007). See also Gabrielle Kaufmann-Kohler, 'Arbitral Precedent: Dream, Necessity or Excuse? The 2006 Freshfields Lecture', 23 Arb Int'l 357 (2007); Christoph Schreuer and Matthew Weiniger, 'A Doctrine of Precedent?' in Peter Muchlinsky, Federico Ortino, and Christoph Schreuer (eds), *The Oxford Handbook on International Investment Law* (Oxford University Press, 2008); Andrea Bjorklund, 'Investment Treaty Arbitral Decisions as Jurisprudence Constante', in Colin Picker, Isabella Bunn, and Douglas Amer (eds), *International Economic Law: The State and Future of the Discipline* (Bloomsbury, 2008); Yas Banifatemi (ed.), *Precedent in International Arbitration* (Juris, 2008); Jan Paulsson, 'International Arbitration and the Generation of Legal Norms', in Albert Jan van den Berg (ed.), *International Arbitration 2006: Back to Basics?* (Kluwer Law International, 2007; Academic Forum on ISDS, 'Lack of Consistency and Coherence in the Interpretation of Legal Issues' (Working Group 3: Julian Arato, Yas Banifatemi, Chester Brown, Diane Desierto, Fabien Gélinas, Csongor Istvan Nagy and Federico Ortino), 30 January 2019, paras. 4–6).

[84] See generally Lon Fuller, *The Morality of Law* (Yale University Press, 1969), 33, 38–9.

[85] See e.g. ibid. 42–3; Tamanaha (n. 43), 122–6.

[86] James Crawford, 'Similarity of Issues in Disputes Arising under the Same or Similarly Drafted Investment Treaties', in Banifatemi (n. 83), 100.

[87] On precedent under the ICJ Statute, see Mahamed Shahaduddeen, *Precedent in the World Court* (Cambridge University Press, 1996).

[88] Gilbert Guillaume, 'Can Arbitral Award Constitute a Source of International Law under Article 38 of the Statute of the International Court of Justice?' in Banifatemi (n. 83), 107.

[89] Ibid. Among the decisions of the International Court of Justice, see notably the Joint Declaration of Vice-President Ranjeva, Judges Guillaume, Higgins, Kooijmans, Al-Khasawneh, Buergenthal, and Elaraby

award can be viewed as 'binding' within the meaning of the strict English doctrine of *stare decisis* is of course generally rejected, several commentators and arbitrators have put forward the notion of settled jurisprudence (*jurisprudence constante* or *ständige Rechtsprechung*) as an appropriate comparator for international arbitration.[90] *Jurisprudence constante* is thought by some to evoke a degree of 'bindingness' that is quite stringent. According to Thomas Wälde, for example, 'Such jurisprudence constitutes the applicable "law" and deviation is only possible in rare circumstances, *e.g.* "distinction", possibly sanctionable as "manifest excess of powers"—perhaps under ICSID annulment practice—or "manifest error of law" if this is available under national arbitral award challenge rules.'[91]

If that is the case, the main difference between the English notion of precedent and *jurisprudence constante* is that the binding rule in the first case comes from a single decision of a hierarchically superior authority, while in the second, it seemingly comes from a series of consistent decisions made by possibly equal adjudicatory authorities. Given the absence, up to now, of a hierarchy of adjudicatory authorities in investment arbitration (i.e. the absence of an appeal mechanism), the concept of *jurisprudence constante* seems like a better fit than a strict English-style doctrine of precedent. A third possibility, however, would be to explain the practice in terms of a soft doctrine of precedent, persuasive precedent, according to which arbitrators have a discursive duty to engage with or to consider relevant like cases, and possibly to provide reasons for departures.[92]

In the 'horizontal' context of investment arbitration, precedent obviously has its limits. As Jan Paulsson once put it, one may hope that, in the long run, 'good awards will chase the bad',[93] although there remains a risk that 'fundamental disagreements' will persist.[94] This is not the place to pursue this line of enquiry, or go into a detailed analysis of how following precedent may play out on specific issues. To keep focus on the fundamental issue of legal certainty, however, a general objection to precedent in investment arbitration that has been levelled recently may usefully be addressed within the space constraints of this volume.

15.3.3 The value of precedent as legal certainty

One of the editors of this volume, Thomas Schultz, has argued elsewhere that following precedent should not be considered a 'moral positive' unless the substantive law that it

in the cases concerning *Legality and the Use of Force* (Preliminary Objections), [2004] ICJ Report 330, paras. 476, 621, 766, 912, 1061, 1208, 1353.

[90] Gabrielle Kaufmann-Kohler, 'Is Consistency a Myth?' in Banifatemi (n. 83), 147.

[91] Thomas Wälde, 'Confidential Awards as Precedent in Arbitration: Dynamics and Implication of Award Publication', in Banifatemi (n. 83), 115.

[92] This is, roughly, the situation that prevails in English law in respect of decisions that are not strictly binding: Rupert Cross and J. W. Harris, *Precedent in English Law*, 4th edn (Clarendon Press, 1991), 4, 27.

[93] Paulsson (n. 83), 889.

[94] Kaufmann-Kohler (n. 90), 145.

makes consistent is itself a moral positive.[95] The argument he makes is rather elaborate and cannot be rendered here in all of its nuances, but the crux is as follows. The argument first adopts a widespread understanding of the rule of law: 'the type of rule of law sought to be advanced when the virtues of consistency and predictability are extolled... is agnostic to the actual contents of the set of rules it characterizes'.[96] Thus, 'law may reinforce the benignity or evilness of a regime', since law is necessary to carry out both morally worthy and iniquitous long-term projects effectively.[97] Therefore, the pursuit of consistency through following precedent is morally neutral. It is, in and of itself, 'neither good nor bad'; it has no value independent from the substantive law being made consistent.[98] In other words, '[a] bad rule applied consistently, in a predictable way, in highly regularized patterns, may do more harm than the same rule applied inconsistently, occasionally, in an unpredictable way.'[99]

It follows that arbitrators 'should seek consistency only when doing so furthers a benign, desirable regime'.[100] Assuming, *arguendo*, that the substantive law of the investment regime is bad on policy grounds, the argument concludes that arbitrators should focus on their basic job: 'to decide cases, not to make general rules'.[101] Although there may be a lesson in the argument, three points should suffice to dispel the doubts it may have raised in the reader's mind about the independent value of legal certainty and, more narrowly, the value of the practice consisting in following precedent.

First, from the fact that rule-of-law methods can be used to carry out evil or iniquitous designs more effectively, it does not follow that consistency has no independent value. To assume that it does would be to misunderstand a central value fostered by legal certainty. The reason, ultimately, why legal certainty is perceived as a universally recognized good[102] is that it creates the necessary space for human agency and thus human dignity to flourish. It provides, in the famous words of Lon Fuller, 'dependable guideposts for self-directed action'.[103] It allows people to plan their lives and their affairs within a relatively stable framework of rules and principles. Incidentally and more prosaically, closer to the subject of investment, legal certainty stimulates enterprise and exchange through the reliable enforcement of *ex ante* expectations. Consistency and predictability in the application of bad substantive law is generally better than the arbitrary application of the same law, because it allows people to better plan their affairs. This has value independent of the content of substantive law. The fact that the value in question may be outweighed by other values in particular situations does not work to negate the 'moral positive' that is legal certainty.[104]

[95] Thomas Schultz, 'Against Consistency in Investment Arbitration', in Zachary Douglas, Joost Pauwelyn, and Jorge Viñuales (eds), *The Foundations of International Investment Law: Bringing Theory into Practice* (Oxford University Press, 2014).

[96] Ibid. 312. [97] Ibid. 312. [98] Ibid. 313.

[99] Ibid. [100] Ibid. [101] Ibid.

[102] Tamanaha (n. 43), 'Introduction'.

[103] Fuller (n. 84), 229. These very words appear in the paper presenting the argument. Schultz (n. 95), 310.

[104] This may be the case e.g. if the substantive law required the prosecution and hanging of all men who do not have blue eyes. See Schultz (n. 95), 311. Even in this case, one can see that knowing the rule in advance would have great value for all involved.

Second, the argument drastically underplays a fundamental aspect of the arbitral mandate in the investment context. Unless investment arbitrators are given a different mandate in particular settings, their 'basic job' is not just 'to decide cases' but to decide them 'according to law'.[105] The meaning of this requirement is complex and its ramifications in terms of the practice of precedent are not always fully apparent. When the law is unclear, arbitrators still have to decide according to law. They still have to provide reasons for their decisions,[106] and those reasons have to be legal reasons. The reasons must show, in other words, that claimants had a right, or no right, to what they were claiming. Lon Fuller explains this as follows:

> This problem can be approached somewhat obliquely from a different direction by asking what is implied by 'a right' or by 'a claim of right'. If I say to someone, 'Give me that!' I do not necessarily assert a right. I may be begging for an act of charity, or I may be threatening to take by force something to which I admittedly have no right. On the other hand, if I say, 'Give that to me, I have a right to it', I necessarily assert the existence of some principle or standard by which my 'right' can be tested.
>
> To be sure, this principle or standard may not have antedated my claim... At the same time, this claim does necessarily imply a principle which can give meaning to the demand that like cases be given like treatment.[107]

In other words, in order to be made 'according to law', a decision must necessarily reach beyond itself by referring to a principle of decision that can potentially apply to future cases that are relevantly alike.[108] Hence the unseverable connection between the requirement that investment arbitrators decide according to law and the prudential practice, in that context, of engaging with precedent. The duty imposed on arbitrators is both forward- and backward-looking.

Third and last, thinking in terms of the age-old desideratum that like cases be treated alike may shed light on the actual duty that arbitrators should feel bound to fulfil. The argument against consistency appears to assume a fairly constraining form of following precedent. Yet the desideratum that like cases be treated alike does not necessarily imply a strict duty to follow past decisions. In a horizontal setting, with no hierarchy between tribunals, such a duty obviously raises issues of path dependence that can become

[105] See e.g. ICSID Convention (n. 54), Art. 42, which as a general rule requires tribunals to decide disputes in accordance with 'such rules of law as may be agreed by the parties' or, in the absence of such an agreement, in accordance with the law of the contracting state party and any rule of international law that may be applicable. As an exception to the requirement for decisions according to law, Art. 42 permits a tribunal to decide a dispute *ex aequo et bono*, upon agreement of the parties.

[106] See e.g. ibid. Art. 48(3).

[107] Lon Fuller, 'The Forms and Limits of Adjudication', 92 Harvard L Rev 352 (1978), 363. This paper was published posthumously. It should be noted that Fuller was apparently never satisfied that it was ready to be brought out. The published version dates back to 1959.

[108] It has been argued that this requirement provides arbitration with a kind of legitimacy that is peculiar to legal forms of adjudication: Fabien Gélinas, 'Arbitration as Transnational Governance by Contract', 7(2) Transnational Legal Theory 1 (2016).

problematic.[109] The desideratum, as observed historically,[110] seems compatible with a practice of persuasive precedent as highlighted above. The practice of following precedent can of course evolve and adjust, over time, to the needs of the regime in question.[111] That is because the right balance between the formal justice sought through legal certainty and the substantive justice pursued by means of substantive rules is not static.[112] Is it more important that a rule be settled than that it be settled right?[113] No, not necessarily: it is often neither more nor less important. Therein lies the lesson in the argument against consistency: while the pursuit of legal certainty is to be encouraged, it is often in tension with the equally important value of substantive justice.

15.4 Conclusion

The movement toward greater legal certainty in arbitration outlined in this chapter is hardly surprising given the 'triumph'[114] of the rule of law as one of the few political and legal ideas that have ever gained, at least on the surface, universal appeal.[115]

In international commercial arbitration, this movement has been witnessed most strikingly in the multiplication of soft instruments outlining best procedural practices, which have had the effect of constraining the discretionary powers of arbitrators and institutions. This movement is likely a result of the sociocultural changes attendant on the growth and diversification observed in the commercial arbitration community. The previously shared expectations and informal understandings of a close-knit community have been shaken and obscured by an increasingly large and diverse community in need of more explicit guidance. Whether this shift is making international commercial arbitration more efficient is unclear; it is, however, responding to a seemingly growing suspicion of discretionary power, even where exercised benevolently, and a heightened expectation of legal certainty.

109 Alex Stone Sweet, 'Path Dependence, Precedent, and Judicial Power', in Martin Shapiro and Alex Stone Sweet (eds), *On Law, Politics, and Judicialization* (Oxford University Press, 2002).

110 See e.g. R. W. M. Dias, *Jurisprudence*, 4th edn (Butterworths, 1985), 56.

111 See Norberto Bobbio, 'Nouvelles réflexions sur les normes primaires et secondaires', in Chaïm Perelman (ed.), *La règle de droit* (Bruylant, 1971), 120. The treatment of precedent is quite possibly a secondary rule of customary law, based not only on the actions and beliefs of arbitrators but also on those of users.

112 It is also useful to pay attention to the flip side of the desideratum: that different cases should not be treated alike. This can shed light on how complex regime overlaps may be approached from an adjudicatory standpoint: e.g. cases governed by different treaties may be comparable in some respects and not in others.

113 The saying according to which it is more important that a rule be settled than that it be settled right (*Burnet v Coronado Oil & Gas Co.*, (1932) 285 U.S. 393, at 406 (Brandeis J., dissenting)) is the leitmotiv in the argument being discussed here. See Schulz (n. 95), 298, 303, 307, 311.

114 Jerold Auerbach, *Justice Without Law?* (Oxford University Press, 1983), 14.

115 See Tamahana (n. 43), 1.

In investment arbitration, the movement toward greater certainty has played out most specifically around the means of developing substantive investment protections and the role that case law has come to play in that development. The explosion in the number of bilateral treaties pursuing very similar objectives through similar but non-identical provisions set the stage for a debate about the role of arbitrators in developing an overarching investment law. While the debate rages on about the role of arbitrators, a loosely defined practice of precedent has taken hold.

To the extent that a sufficient number of awards were going to be published, the practice of precedent, in some form, was entirely predictable. The practice promotes consistency and predictability, and therefore legal certainty as a rule of law value—one that is generally worth pursuing irrespective of the value of the substantive rules whose consistent application it promotes. The practice is also tied to the requirement that arbitrators decide according to law. However, doctrines of precedent that aim to 'bind' arbitrators in a horizontal structure should be entertained only with great care. Softer, discursive versions of precedent relying on persuasion rather than bindingness are likely more appropriate to the stage of development of investment law today.

Across the entire field of international arbitration, legal certainty seems to have gained in importance. This has many advantages that are universally recognized. It may be an appropriate time, however, to recall that formal justice is always in tension with substantive justice. The more predictable the law is, the less flexible it becomes in both its application and its evolution.

CHAPTER 16

INTERNATIONAL ARBITRATION AS PRIVATE AND PUBLIC GOOD

RALF MICHAELS

16.1 Introduction

INTERNATIONAL arbitration is often characterized as an exclusively private dispute resolution mechanism, sharply distinguished from litigation, which is viewed as public, because it is provided by the state. This is clearest for commercial arbitration.[1] Commercial arbitration is initiated on the basis of a private arrangement: a party cannot be subjected to arbitration unless they agreed to it previously. The arbitrator is appointed not by the state but by, or on the basis of, an agreement by the parties. The applicable procedures are determined by party agreements, as is the question whether the arbitrator should decide on the basis of law, and if so, on which law. Investment arbitration is a little more difficult to categorize, given its emergence from public international law, its involvement of states as parties, and the frequency with which it deals with public law measures.[2] Indeed, significant differences exist between commercial and investment

[1] William Park, 'Private Adjudicators and the Public Interest: The Expanding Scope of International Arbitration', 12 Brook. J. Int'l L. 629 (1986); Peer Zumbansen, 'Piercing the Legal Veil: Commercial Arbitration and Transnational Law', 8 Eur. L.J. 400 (2002); A. Claire Cutler, *Private Power and Global Authority: Transnational Merchant Law in the Global Political Economy* (Cambridge University Press, 2003); Moritz Renner, 'Private Justice, Public Policy: The Constitutionalization of International Commercial Arbitration', in Walter Mattli and Thomas Dietz (eds), *International Arbitration and Global Governance: Contending Theories and Evidence* (Oxford University Press, 2014), 117. See also Ralf Michaels, 'Roles and Role Perceptions of International Arbitrators', ibid. 47, 68–72.

[2] Gus van Harten, 'The Public–Private Distinction in the International Arbitration of Individual Claims Against the State', 56 ICLQ 371 (2007); Alex Mills, 'Antinomies of Public and Private at the

arbitration.[3] Nonetheless, it too is characterized as a private dispute resolution mechanism at least in the sense that it is resolved by institutions other than state courts.

This dichotomy between arbitration and adjudication is unsatisfactory. It cannot account for the many parallels that exist between both mechanisms. And it cannot account for the degree to which arbitration itself displays both public and private elements, much less how these elements relate to each other.

This chapter approaches the private and public nature of international arbitration in a manner different from the usual one. It asks not whether arbitration is private or public law, which remains a problematic categorical distinction, but instead whether it is a private or public good. The distinction between private goods and public goods, developed in economics, promises new insights for an assessment of arbitration, too. The chapter first introduces that economic distinction between private and public goods. It then demonstrates the ways in which adjudication by courts combines elements of private and public goods, before finding a parallel combination of private and public good aspects in international arbitration. The discussion will concern mainly commercial arbitration, though investment arbitration will also be considered to some extent as well. The chapter ends by laying out some implications.

16.2 Arbitration between Public and Private

The suggestion that enforcing privately created arbitration agreements is automatically consistent with the public interest has always been subject to criticism. In 1944, Heinrich Kronstein launched a fundamental attack on arbitration that can still be heard, with slight changes, today:

> Few commercial transactions affect only the interested parties; the simplest contract may give rise to unexpected repercussions. And with this expanding sphere of influence has come the opportunity for dominant interests to weigh down the balance in their favor. Arbitration, viewed as a social instrument, has moved from the sphere

Foundations of International Investment Law and Arbitration', 14 J. Int'l Econ. Law 469 (2011); Anthea Roberts, 'Clash of Paradigms: Actors and Analogies Shaping the Investment Treaty System', 107 American Journal of International Law 45 (2013); Julie Maupin, 'Public and Private in International Investment Law: An Integrated Systems Approach', 54 Va. J. Int'l L. 367 (2014); José Alvarez, 'Is Investor–State Arbitration "Public"?', 7 J. Int'l Disp. Resol. 534 (2016).

[3] See Karl-Heinz Böckstiegel, 'Commercial and Investment Arbitration: How Different Are They Today?', 28 Arb. Int'l. 577 (2012); Piero Bernardini, 'International Commercial Arbitration and Investment Treaty Arbitration: Analogies and Differences', in David D. Caron et al. (eds), *Practising Virtue: Inside International Arbitration* (Oxford University Press, 2016), 52.

of isolated individual transactions into a realm where its significance in the light of public interest may be overlooked no longer.[4]

Similar criticism is voiced against international commercial arbitration. By privatizing what should be public regulation, and by putting investors on an equal footing with sovereign states instead of subjecting them to sovereign power, democracy, so it is argued, is undermined, and as a consequence public interests are, not sufficiently considered.[5] These types of arguments have special force against institutionalized arbitration in NAFTA, and they came to the fore fully in the opposition against the Transpacific Trade and Investment Partnership (TTIP).[6]

This critique of arbitration goes to the heart of the institution of arbitration. It rests, essentially, on two assumptions. The first is that arbitration is essentially not a private matter but is so deeply linked with society that it must be viewed as performing a social function. (Not surprisingly, Kronstein's attack came not long after the legal realist attack on the public/private distinction). The second assumption is that this social function is better handled by courts than by arbitrators.

We can identify responses to both assumptions. As against the first assumption—that arbitration performs more than a mere private function—two related arguments are made. The first response points to subject-matter limitations of commercial arbitration. Certain matters that necessarily concern society at large are typically not arbitrable; this is especially still the case for many matters of regulatory law. Secondly, however, it is argued that even where matters of social concern like antitrust law are arbitrated, the effects of arbitration remain confined to the parties and thus yield no negative externalities.[7]

As against the argument from the comparative competence of judges, it is argued that arbitrators are as capable as judges of dealing with matters of public concern.[8] Moreover, judges can review, *ex post*, whether arbitrators applied regulatory law properly (though the very limited grounds of review in the enforcement of arbitral awards in Art. V of the New York Convention puts this latter argument in doubt.)[9] Indeed, it is sometimes sug-

[4] Heinrich Kronstein, 'Business Arbitration: Instrument of Private Government', 54 Yale L.J. 36 (1944), 39. For some comparable contemporary arguments, see e.g. Cutler (n. 1).

[5] From the burgeoning literature, see only Amr Shalakany, 'Arbitration and the Third World: Bias under the Scepter of Neo-Liberalism', 41 Harv. Int'l L.J. 419 (2000); Barnali Choudhury, 'Recapturing Public Power: Is Investment Arbitration's Engagement of the Public Interest Contributing to the Democratic Deficit?', 41 Vand. J. Int'l L. 775 (2008).

[6] See e.g. Patricia Garcia-Duran and Leif Eliasson, 'The Public Debate over Transatlantic Trade and Investment Partnership and Its Underlying Assumptions', 51 Journal of World Trade 23 (2017).

[7] Jan Paulsson, *The Idea of Arbitration* (Clarendon Press, 2013), 118–20.

[8] Catherine Rogers, 'International Arbitration's Public Realm', in Arthur Rovine (ed), *Contemporary Issues in International Arbitration and Mediation: The Fordham Papers 2010* (Brill, 2012), 169–70. This is one of the grounds on which the US Supreme Court allowed matters of antitrust law to go to arbitration in its famous Mitsubishi decision. *Mitsubishi Motors Corp v Soler Chrysler–Plymouth Inc.*, 473 U.S. 614 (1985). The court extended arbitrability to securities fraud claims in *Shearson/American Express Inc v McMahon*, 482 U.S. 220 (1987) and *Rodriguez de Quijas v Shearson/American Express Inc*, 490 U.S. 477 (1989).

[9] E.g. Luca Radicati di Brozolo, 'L'illicéité qui crève les yeux: critère de contrôle des sentences au regard de l'ordre public international (à propos de l'arrêt Thalès de la Cour d'appel de Paris)', Rev. arb.

gested that arbitrators are often even more capable than state courts of giving proper regard to matters of social concern.[10] First, the interest of international commerce in an effective dispute resolution mechanism is thought to outweigh the interest of states in their own public policies.[11] Second, state courts are thought to have their own bias, because they, as national institutions, are likely to overestimate the importance of their own mandatory laws, and possibly underestimate the importance of other laws' mandatory norms. In this perspective, only arbitrators can properly assess matters of social concern in their entirety. Indeed, it is argued that international arbitration often takes on cases that could not or would not be brought in courts.[12] This is true for commercial arbitration, which often needs a neutral forum that only arbitration can provide, but it is especially true for investment arbitration, which is often justified as being necessary in order to spur investment in the first place (though the evidence for this claim is actually shaky).[13]

This tension between the private nature of arbitration and public concerns is well known and often discussed. A problem in the debate is that the concepts 'private' and 'public' themselves are not fully clear, nor is the distinction between them. This analytical problem of the public/private distinction, discussed in western law since the early twentieth century, has a direct impact on discussions of international arbitration that have not yet been fully explored. International arbitration is not purely private; it exists as a mixture of private and public laws.[14] But the exact configuration of this mix remains unclear.

What would be needed is a distinction between public and private that is less normatively laden and has more analytical sharpness. Both are promised by the theory of public goods. The distinction between public and private goods, developed in the discipline of economics, is at heart technical not ideological. It therefore promises a potentially better analytical framework for the question of public and private in international arbitration. It cannot substitute for the important normative questions underlying the legitimacy of international arbitration, but it can help provide a foundation for these questions.

(2005), 529; Richard Buxbaum, 'Public Policy, Ordre Public and Arbitration: A Procedural Scenario and a Suggestion', in Peter Hay et al. (eds), *Resolving International Conflicts: Liber Amicorum Tibor Várady* (Central European University Press, 2009), 91.

[10] Catherine Rogers, 'The Vocation of the International Arbitrator', 20 Am. U. Int'l L. Rev. 957 (2005), 995–6; Rogers (n. 8), 169–70.

[11] Park (n. 1), 664.

[12] Paulsson (n. 7).

[13] See only UNCTAD, 'The Role of International Investment Agreements in Attracting Foreign Direct Investment to Developing Countries' (UNCTAD 2009): <http://unctad.org/en/Docs/diaeia20095_en.pdf>; UNCTAD, 'The Impact of International Investment Agreements on Foreign Direct Investment: An Overview of Empirical Studies 1998–2014': <http://investmentpolicyhub.unctad.org/Upload/Documents/unctad-web-diae-pcb-2014-Sep%2024.pdf>; Jason Webb Yackee, 'Do BITs "Work"? Empirical Evidence from France', 7 J Int Disp Settlement 55 (2016).

[14] Christopher Drahozal, 'Private Ordering and International Commercial Arbitration', 113 Penn St. L. Rev. 1031 (2009). See also Robert Wai, 'Transnational Liftoff and Juridical Touchdown: The Regulatory Function of Private International Law in an Era of Globalization', 40 Colum. J. Transnat'l L. 209 (2002).

16.3 Public and Private Goods

The idea of distinguishing public and private goods emerges from economics. Here, the meaning of a public good is not that sometimes used in legal discourse, where it describes, often unspecifically, something of public concern, equivalent to a public interest.[15] It is, at least in principle, descriptive. There is no intrinsic normative superiority of one type of good or another. There are, however, implications. The determination of whether a certain good is private or public is valuable information for the question of how it should best be provided—through markets, through regulation, or in other ways.

16.3.1 The definition of public goods

In economics, public goods have a relatively clear definition that can be traced back to the introduction of the concept by Samuelson in 1954 and Musgrave in 1959.[16] Public goods are defined by two criteria. The first is *non-rivalry*: if one person consumes the good, this does not exclude another person from consuming the good as well. The second criterion is *non-excludability*: it is impossible to provide the good to one person (or a defined set of persons) while at the same time excluding others. A standard example is the light of a lighthouse. It is non-rivalrous in consumption: the fact that one ship benefits from the light does not deprive other ships from consumption. And its consumption is non-excludable: the light necessarily shines for all ships, pirate ships included. A second standard example is national defence: if a state's military defends a territory, then each citizen is protected, and one citizen's protection does not diminish that of another. In this, public goods differ from private goods. An apple can serve as example: it creates rivalry in consumption (if I eat it you can no longer eat it), and it is excludable (the store owner can decide not to give you the apple).

Non-rivalry and non-excludability are related, but they are not similar. It is possible to have goods that are non-rivalrous in consumption but nonetheless enable exclusion. Such goods were long called 'club goods', after the introduction of the concept by Hardin and Buchanan in 1965;[17] a preferable contemporary term is 'toll goods'. Toll bridges are an example. At least as long as such bridges are not congested, their consumption is non-rivalrous: one driver's use of the bridge does not deprive another driver from using the

[15] Thus the use e.g. in Ioannis Glinavos, 'Public Interests, Private Disputes: Investment Arbitration and the Public Good', 13 Manchester Journal of International Economic Law 50 (2016).

[16] Paul Samuelson, 'The Pure Theory of Public Expenditure', 36 Review of Economics and Statistics 387 (1954); Paul Musgrave, *The Theory of Public Finance* (McGraw-Hill, 1959). For an introduction, see Richard Cornes and Todd Sandler (eds), *The Theory of Externalities, Public Goods, and Club Goods*, 2nd edn (Cambridge University Press, 1996).

[17] James Buchanan. 'An Economic Theory of Clubs', Economica 32 (1965), 1–14; Todd Sandler, 'Buchanan Clubs', 24 Constitutional Political Economy 265 (2013).

Table 16.1 Ostrom's typology of goods

		Subtractability of use (rivalrousness)	
Difficulty of excluding potential beneficiaries		*Low*	*High*
	Low	Toll (club) goods	Private goods
	High	Public goods	Common-pool resources

After Elinor Ostrom, *Understanding Institutional Diversity* 24 (2005), 24.

bridge at the same time. Nevertheless, there is excludability: drivers are excluded from using the bridge unless they pay the required toll.

On the other hand, it is also possible to have goods that are rivalrous but not excludable and which are called, after Elinor Ostrom, common-pool resources.[18] The historical commons is an example: it was a grazing meadow open to all citizens (non-exclusive) that could eventually be overgrazed (rivalry).[19] The resulting concepts are summarized in Table 16.1.

Two further clarifications are required. First, the distinctions between private and public goods are not hard and fast. Rather, excludability and rivalry are continua: there may be more or less of each of them, meaning that public and private goods are mere endpoints on a spectrum. Second, goods may change their nature. Television programs, for example, were once thought of as public goods; now that providers are able to scramble content and make its availability dependent on payment of a fee, they are more properly characterized as toll goods. To some extent, whether a good is private or public becomes a function of available technology, but also of the applicable legal framework.

16.3.2 The provision of public goods

Discussion of public goods emerged in close connection with questions of efficient provision of goods. Both non-rivalrousness and non-excludability, thus the assumption, hamper the efficient provision of such goods by markets, because they require the producer of such goods to internalize all costs without enabling them to charge for the benefits to third parties. Private individuals therefore typically lack the correct incentives to produce public goods. As a consequence, public goods are traditionally closely linked to their provision by the state, sometimes so much so that the two are equated: a public good, according to some, is a good provided (or at least subsidized) by the state. On the

[18] Vincent Ostrom and Elinor Ostrom, 'Public Goods and Public Choices', in Daniel Cole and Michael McGinnis (eds), *Elinor Ostrom and the Bloomington School of Political Economy*, vol. 2: *Resource Governance* (Lexington Books, 2015), 3–35. The text was originally published in Emanuel Savas (ed), *Alternatives to Delivering Public Services: Toward Improved Performance* (Westview Press, 1977), 7–49.

[19] Garrett Hardin, 'The Tragedy of the Commons', 162 Science 1243 (1968).

other side of the divide, private goods are sometimes defined as those goods that are provided through market mechanisms.

But the traditional definition of a public good does not imply who provides it. On the one hand, it is possible for public goods to be provided by private persons. As long as the benefits to the creator of the public good are greater than her costs, she will have an incentive to create the good, even though it benefits others for free. For example, an owner of many ships may find it worthwhile to invest in a lighthouse, even though she cannot exclude others from its use or charge them for it.[20]

On the other hand, although there are severe impediments to the provision of public goods through the market, their provision through the state also faces problems. Some of these are problems of information. Thus, for example, it could be possible, at least in theory, to determine the optimal provision of public goods as a function of the aggregation of individual preferences. That optimal state is called a Lindahl equilibrium; it emerges when the total per-unit price paid by each member of a society equals the total per-unit cost of the public good.[21] However, a big problem for the state is its difficulty in assessing individual preferences. Majority voting is only a very incomplete substitute, for a variety of reasons. In addition, public choice literature has identified reasons why state institutions often will not provide optimal solutions: state agents act on the basis of incentives that are not always optimally congruent with public or common interests.[22]

Additional challenges emerge from globalization. The idea that public goods are best provided by the state presumes one state and one public. But under conditions of globalization, the good's benefits often transcend the individual state (think of the environment, but also of global trade). In addition, states stand in competition with each other in the provision of goods. These problems are central to the emerging discussion of so-called global public goods and the question how these can be provided in a world of states.[23] It is viewed as a core task of international law to regulate and enable the production of public goods in a world without a central decision-making authority.[24]

[20] See Ronald Coase, 'The Lighthouse in Economics', 17 J. Law & Econ. 357 (1974), repr. in Ronald Coase, *The Firm, the Market and the Law* (University of Chicago Press, 1988), 187. See also David Van Zandt, 'The Lessons of the Lighthouse: "Government" or 'Private' Provision of Goods', 22 J. Legal Stud. 47 (1993).

[21] Leif Johansen, 'Some Notes on the Lindahl Theory of Determination of Public Expenditures', 4 Int'l Econ. Rev. 346 (1963), based on Erik Lindahl, *Die Gerechtigkeit der Besteuerung* (Hakan Ohlssons Buchdruckerei, 1919).

[22] See e.g. Gordon Tullock, 'Public Decisions as Public Goods', 79 J. of Pol. Econ. 913 (1971).

[23] E.g. Charles Kindleberger, 'International Public Goods Without International Government', 76 American Economic Review 1 (1986); Inge Kaul, Isabelle Grunberg, and Marc Stern (eds), *Global Public Goods: International Cooperation in the 21st Century* (Oxford University Press, 1999); Inge Kaul et al. (eds), *Providing Global Public Goods: Managing Globalization* (Oxford University Press, 2003); Scott Barrett, *Why Cooperate? The Incentive to Supply Global Public Goods* (Oxford University Press, 2007); Adrienne Héritier (ed.), *Common Goods: Reinventing European and International Governance* (Rowman & Littlefield, 2002).

[24] Dan Bodansky, 'What's in a Concept? Global Public Goods, International Law, and Legitimacy', 23 Eur. J. Int'l L. 651 (2012); Gregory Shaffer, 'International Law and Global Public Goods in a Legal Pluralist World', 23 Eur. J. Int'l L. 669 (2012), 683–93; Nico Krisch, 'The Decay of Consent: International Law in an Age of Global Public Goods', 108 American Journal of International Law 1 (2014).

It is in this context that the relation between international arbitration and public goods becomes relevant. On the one hand, we may ask whether arbitration as a private mechanism in fact represents such a transformation of what was once considered a public good (law) into a private good. On the other hand, we may ask whether arbitration in fact does represent such a public good itself, albeit one that is provided by other means than the state. In that case, the question arises how it can be optimally provided.

16.4 Adjudication as comparison

In order to assess these questions, it is helpful to start, for the purpose of comparison, with adjudication by state courts. Law is widely viewed as a public good.[25] So is adjudication as a part of law,[26] though often in a rather unspecific way that requires further analysis. Landes and Posner were the first to point out that this traditional view of adjudication as purely public is incomplete because it lumps together different functions of adjudication, especially those of dispute resolution on the one hand and rule production on the other.[27]

16.4.1 Adjudication as a private good

Landes' and Posner's main argument is that the core aspect of litigation, namely the resolution of disputes, is a private not a public good. A market for dispute resolution is conceivable: adjudicators could compete for business based on quality and price, and parties could choose the adjudicator they deem best. Although they do not argue from the definition of public and private goods introduced above, we can see that dispute resolution fulfils these criteria too. First, resolution of a dispute allows exclusion: third parties cannot, without the consent of the litigants or a decision by the court, join an existing adjudication; the *res judicata* effect is limited to the parties. The fact that courts can and do charge fees demonstrates the excludability of adjudication. Second, resolution of a dispute is, at least to some extent, rivalrous. As long as an adjudicator is occupied with the resolution of one dispute, she cannot at the same time resolve another. This aspect is eased a little in the public adjudication system. The right of access to court makes courts less rivalrous: in principle, one person's litigation does not preclude

[25] See Tyler Cowen, 'Law as a Public Good: The Economics of Anarchy', 8 Econ. & Phil. 249 (1992); Paul Rubin, 'Public Goods and the Evolution of Altruism: The Case of Law', 26 Politics and the Life Sciences 26 (2007), 29. A separate discussion (in which arbitration is central) is whether this implies that law must be provided by the state; see, most recently, Gillian Hadfield, *Rules for a Flat World: Why Humans Invented Law and How to Reinvent it for a Complex Global Economy* (Oxford University Press, 2016).

[26] E.g. Deborah Rhode, 'Access to Justice', 69 Fordham L. Rev. 1785 (2001); Ruth Bader Ginsburg, 'In Pursuit of the Public Good: Access to Justice in the United States', 7 Wash. U.J.L. & Policy 1 (2001).

[27] William Landes and Richard Posner, 'Adjudication as a Private Good', 8 J. Leg. Stud. 235 (1979).

another's. However, this aspect comes under pressure given the limited resources of the adjudicatory system.[28]

To be sure, it does not follow that adjudication is purely private. To be effective, dispute resolution depends on enforcement by the state. The state must force parties to answer claims in court, the state may have to force parties to disclose evidence they possess, and the state may be called upon to enforce a resulting judgment. None of this, however, refutes the idea of dispute resolution as a private good. It is characteristic of private goods in general that they need to be enforced.

16.4.2 Adjudication as a public good

Dispute resolution is not, however, the only function of adjudication. In various other ways, adjudication serves as a public good.[29] One of these is the *production of law*. Judicial opinions create law not only for the parties, but also—as precedent—for the legal system at large. This makes the judicial production of legal rules a positive externality. Rules are a public good in that they increase legal certainty, predictability, and consistency.[30] This is so regardless of whether precedent is formally binding (as in common law systems) or merely persuasive (as in other legal systems)—a distinction that has in reality lost much of its practical importance. In either case, legal decisions increase the material of experience on which legal actors—judges, but also attorneys—and the public in general can rely. In providing legal security and fostering the rule of law, adjudication is of crucial importance.

Now rule production, unlike dispute resolution, is a public good.[31] Rule production is non-rivalrous, and it is non-exclusive. The rule from a case (other than the actual verdict) cannot be confined to the litigants themselves; it must, at least in principle, claim general applicability. Moreover, rule production is necessarily non-exclusive: unless judgments are rendered with written reasons and published and thereby made publicly available, no rules are produced. This helps specify: adjudication becomes a public good of law production insofar as its decisions are written down and promulgated.

Adjudication is a public good in a second way: it *creates public information*. A court file contains significant information about a dispute and its background. Especially (but not exclusively) in a system like the US legal system, with its extensive pre-trial discovery, the creation and divulgence of such information is of considerable importance (and its

[28] Limitations stemming from limited resources have led some to question the public character of adjudication: Rex Lee, 'The American Courts as Public Goods: Who Should Pay the Costs of Litigation?', 34 Cath. U. L. Rev. 267 (1985). This is called, by economists, 'rationing by waiting': Yoram Barzel, 'A Theory of Rationing by Waiting', 17 J. Law & Econ. 73 (1974).

[29] See also, now, Joshua Paine, 'International Adjudication as a Global Public Good?', EJIL 29 (2018), 1223.

[30] This aspect is irrespective of the substantive quality of the law; see e.g. Frédéric Sourgens, 'The Virtue of Path Dependence in the Law', 56 Santa Clara L. Rev. 303 (2016).

[31] Landes and Posner (n. 27), 238–40; Richard McAdams, 'The Expressive Power of Adjudication', U. of Ill. L. Rev. 1043 (2005), 1114.

avoidance is a significant incentive for defendants to settle).[32] Insofar as the results of such discovery become public, they represent public goods: (publicized) knowledge is non-rivalrous and non-exclusive.[33] Much important knowledge has been created through litigation—the strategies of tobacco-producing companies to conceal the health effects of their products is just one of many examples. Indeed, in some types of litigation, human rights litigation for example, production and divulgence of information is often the prime purpose of plaintiffs: a conviction with subsequent enforcement is often viewed as less important than the provision of a public forum and the inquiry into what happened.

There is a third way in which private litigation qualifies as a public good, and it is what I call here, untechnically, *public interest litigation*. Under public interest litigation I understand such litigation in which the parties, broadly speaking, litigate matters that in turn concern public goods. This includes litigation over public law rules like environmental law or antitrust law, which are, typically, mandatory, meaning they are not under the disposition of the parties. It includes cases in which plaintiffs act as so-called 'private attorney generals' who litigate in the interest of the public.[34] Insofar as litigation thereby partakes in the enforcement of law, it qualifies as a public good because law enforcement is also, in principle, a public good.[35]

A final 'soft' public good aspect of adjudication is the way in which it enhances both the *quality and the reputation of the legal system*.[36] Published judicial rulings are a good as 'reasoned elaboration and visible expression of public values'.[37] When judges gain expertise through adjudication, this qualifies as a public good, or at least a club good because that expertise also benefits future litigants. The same can be said, to some extent, for the experience gained by attorneys.[38] Even though the service that they provide is a private good, the quality of their work contributes to the functioning of the legal system at large.

16.4.3 The provision of adjudication

Adjudication is, thus part private good, part public good. This has consequences for the optimal way in which it can be provided. The traditional theory suggests that public goods should, typically, be produced by the state. Adjudication, however, even insofar as it is a public good, cannot be created by the state without participation by private parties.

[32] David Luban, 'Settlements and the Erosion of the Public Realm', 83 Geo L.J. 2619 (1995), 2625. Luban argues that secret settlements may be public bads and should therefore not be allowed (pp. 2626, 2647).

[33] See the discussion in Joseph Stiglitz, 'Knowledge as a Global Public Good', in Kaul et al. (n. 23), 308–10.

[34] Jeremy Rabkin, 'The Secret Life of the Private Attorney General', 61 L. & Contemp. Probs. 179 (1998); Hannah Buxbaum, 'The Private Attorney General in a Global Age: Public Interests in Private International Antitrust Litigation', 26 Yale J. Int'l L. 219 (2001).

[35] See Gordon Tullock, 'Public Decisions as Public Goods', 79 J. Pol. Econ. 913 (1971).

[36] Luban (n. 31), 2623–6. [37] Ibid. 2626. [38] Ibid. 2623–4.

Adjudication cannot take place unless a suit is brought, and it cannot proceed to completion if the plaintiff decides to withdraw her claim, or if the parties settle. This has consequences for costs and for settlements.

As concerns incentives to bring suits, the mix between private and public good aspects of litigation justifies a mixed cost structure. If parties had to bear the entirety of the costs of litigation, while not receiving all the benefits, they might lack incentives to litigate and the public good would not be provided.[39] If, on the other hand, litigation were free, parties might overuse the court system. From this perspective, therefore, partial subsidization of litigation by the state is justified.[40] With regard to 'private attorney generals,' punitive damages fulfill a similar function: they enhance the incentive for a plaintiff to bring suit in the public interest.

Likewise, settlements prevent the production of public goods that adjudication would produce.[41] Settlement prevents the creation of new law because it prevents a judgment. Moreover, where settlement is secret, it also prevents the production of information. This effect is unavoidable insofar as adjudication over private rights cannot be taken out of the disposition of the parties who hold these rights. It can be prevented, however, insofar as some public good aspects are compatible with private disposition. Thus, it is possible to subject settlements with third-party aspects to judicial approval (as is done with class action settlements in the United States). And it is at least imaginable that the factual findings of public interest litigation be disclosed even though the litigation itself is settled.

16.5 International arbitration

16.5.1 International arbitration as a private good

What follows for the law of international arbitration? Is international arbitration a private good? At least as concerns international commercial arbitration, the answer seems at first to be undoubtedly yes. Commercial arbitration represents the actualization of Landes and Posner's hypothetical market for judges.[42] In principle, arbitration is a

[39] See Steven Shavell, 'The Social versus the Private Incentive to Bring Suit in a Costly Legal System', 11 J. Legal Stud. 333 (1982).

[40] E.g. Louis Kaplow, 'Private versus Social Costs in Bringing Suit', 15 J. Legal Stud. 371 (1986). See also Bruce Fein, 'Citizen Suit Attorney Fee Shifting Awards: A Critical Examination of Government-"Subsidized" Litigation', 47 L. & Contemp. Probs. 211 (1984). Contrariwise, insofar as arbitration produces only private goods, it should not be subsidized: Steven Shavell, 'Alternative Dispute Resolution: An Economic Analysis', 24 J. Legal Stud. 1 (1995) 8; Stephen Ware, 'Is Adjudication a Public Good? "Overcrowded Courts" and the Private Sector Alternative of Arbitration', 14 Cardozo J. of Conflict Resolution 899 (2013).

[41] Jules Coleman and Charles Silver, 'Justice in Settlements', 4 Soc. Phil. & Pol'y 102 (1986), 114–9.

[42] See also, now, Richard Posner, 'What Do Arbitrators Maximize?' in Peter Nobel, Katrin Krehan, and Philipp von Ins (eds), *Law and Economics of International Arbitration* (Schulthess, 2014), 123.

private good that is completely subject to contract and market forces. Arbitrators compete for appointments; parties appoint them based on a combination of price and, more importantly, reputation and expected return.[43] The result is, indeed, dispute resolution as a private good, at least insofar as each individual arbitral proceeding is viewed. Individual proceedings are exclusive: the parties pay for the arbitrator and exclude others from the proceedings. Or, put differently, the arbitrator provides her services exclusively to the parties who pay for it. Moreover, insofar at least as the individual arbitrator is concerned, arbitration is rivalrous.

Traditionally, arbitration has been exclusively a private good. Resolving disputes by doing justice in the individual case was once their only function. Arbitrators were not required to apply law strictly if doing so was in the way of justice between the parties. Arbitrators were not bound by precedent, certainly not by arbitral precedent. Nor were arbitrators themselves expected to produce awards that would have any relevance beyond the parties.

16.5.2 International arbitration as a public good

This reality of arbitration as a purely private good no longer exists, however, if it ever did. It is worth analysing to what extent arbitration today qualifies as a public good in ways comparable to adjudication.

16.5.2.1 *Law production*

The first public good aspect of adjudication discussed above is *law production*. Traditionally, arbitration does not partake in law production, but this is no longer fully true. Arbitral awards with important reasoning are sometimes published, at least in part with regard to legal reasoning; many call for more extensive publication.[44] In that respect, care is taken to make awards non-recognizable to protect private interests and publish only those parts that are of general interest.[45] As a consequence, they can serve as precedent at least in a weak sense—even if arbitral precedent is not binding, it can

[43] Whether the resulting market is perfect is a different question; see Catherine Rogers, *Ethics in International Arbitration* (Oxford University Press, 2014), 72.

[44] Julian Lew, 'The Case for the Publication of Arbitration Awards', in Jan Schultsz and Albert Jan van den Berg, *The Art of Arbitration* (Kluwer, 1982), 223. For broad discussion, see Valériane König, *Präzedenzwirkung internationaler Schiedssprüche* (de Gruyter, 2013), 39–71; Alberto Malatesta and Rinaldo Sali (eds), *The Rise of Transparency in International Arbitration* (Juris, 2013); Elina Zlatanska, 'To Publish or Not to Publish Arbitral Awards: That is the Question…', 81 Arbitration 25 (2015); Alec Stone Sweet and Florian Grisel, *The Evolution of International Arbitration* (Oxford University Press, 2017), 119.

[45] See e.g. Joshua Karton, 'A Conflict of Interests: Seeking a Way Forward on Publication of International Arbitral Awards', 28 Arb. Int'l 447 (2012). For a practical example, see the Guidelines for the Anonymous Publication of Arbitral Awards of the Milan Chamber of Arbitration: <http://www.camera-arbitrale.it/Documenti/guidelines-anonymous-publication-arbitral-awards.pdf>.

provide guidance for future arbitrators (and also, occasionally, courts) and for future potential litigants and participants in the market.[46]

In commercial arbitration, the role of precedent remains quite limited,[47] perhaps because it is not necessary: substantive national law is already developed by state courts. In specialized areas like sports and domain name arbitration, by contrast, the role of precedent is indeed quite significant. Insofar, arbitrators do create law and thereby create public goods.[48] Much of the law they produce is procedural. Some of it is also substantive: the alleged new *lex mercatoria* rests at least in part in the holdings of arbitrators.

In investment arbitration, precedent plays a greater role.[49] Case law is a source of international law, albeit a subsidiary one (Art. 38(1)(c) ICJ Statute). Although the ICSID Convention provides, in its Art. 48(5), that awards shall not be published without the consent of the parties, ICSID does at least provide general information about each of its decisions.[50] Many investment arbitration decisions are now published, at least in abbreviated form. As a consequence, there emerges a wealth of case law that often serves, effectively, as weak precedent, even though there is no doctrine of *stare decisis* and even though decisions often concern different investment treaties.[51] This is not always viewed positively: arbitrators, it is sometimes said, are asked to provide justice in the individual case and enforce a specific contract, not create law for future disputants.[52]

Is the result a public good? There is the concern that arbitrators will develop law that deviates from what would be optimal, a law that favors, disproportionately, one set of interests. Kronstein (again) formulated this concern as follows:

> In the name of freedom of contract courts have given arbitrators the power to determine the legality of a contract, and in addition have conferred on them the power to develop and systematize new "rules," outside of and uncontrolled by courts, yet applicable in entire fields of business. This, in turn, has led to a recasting of judicial rules pertaining to enforcement of foreign and domestic awards designed to protect the coordinated national and international systems of arbitration rather than the concept of law.[53]

[46] See Gabrielle Kaufmann-Kohler, 'Arbitral Precedent: Dream, Necessity or Excuse?', 23 Arb. Int'l 357 (2007); Emmanuel Gaillard and Yas Banifatemi (eds), *Precedent in International Arbitration* (Juris 2008); König (n. 43), 91.

[47] See the statistics in Kaufmann-Kohler (n. 45); König (n. 43).

[48] Rogers (n. 10), 999–1005.

[49] Alec Stone Sweet, Michael Chung, and Adam Saltzman, 'Arbitral Lawmaking and State Power: An Empirical Analysis of Investment Arbitration', 8 Journal of International Dispute Settlement 579 (2017).

[50] See, in more detail, Meg Kinnear, Eloïse Obadia, and Michael Gagain, 'The ICSID Approach to Publication of Information in Investor–State Arbitration', in Malatesta and Sali (n. 43), 107.

[51] For empirical studies, see Jeffery Commission, 'Precedent in Investment Treaty Arbitration: A Citation Analysis of a Developing Jurisprudence', 24(2) Journal International Arbitration 129 (2007); König (n. 43), 160–245.

[52] Irene Cate, 'The Costs of Consistency: Precedent in Investment Treaty Arbitration', 51 Colum. J. Transnat'l L. 418 (2013); Thomas Schultz, 'Against Consistency in Investment Arbitration', in Zachary Douglas, Joost Pauwelyn, and Jorge Viñuales (eds), *The Foundations of International Investment Law: Bringing Theory into Practice* (Oxford University Press, 2014), 297–316.

[53] Heinrich Kronstein, 'Arbitration is Power', 38 N.Y.U.L. Rev. 661 (1963), 667. See also Schultz (n. 50), 311.

Empirical studies do not appear to support this concern, at least in commercial arbitration.[54] Arbitrators in commercial arbitration, by and large, appear to follow the law as it is laid down by courts, and develop new law only in areas specific to arbitration. We do not see a preference for arbitral over judicial precedent, much less (at least systematically) different legal assessments between arbitrators and judges.

It may still be the case that results in arbitration differ, on average, from those in adjudication (though such a difference would be hard to measure for a variety of reasons). This in itself would not take away from the public good character of arbitration. Whether these results are inferior to those of state courts is a complex question that is beyond this chapter (though it will be addressed, briefly, in the conclusion).

16.5.2.2 *Information production*

The legal reasoning in arbitral decisions is thus in many cases no longer private. By contrast, confidentiality remains important with regard to factual findings. Confidentiality can be important to parties: they often have an interest in maintaining information private. At the same time, information can be a public good and create positive externalities. Once information is made public, it becomes both non-rivalrous and non-excludable, and can create positive externalities. In at least some cases, non-publication of information prevents the creation of a public good.[55]

This tension between a private interest in confidentiality and a public interest in factual disclosure is an issue particularly in mixed arbitration (between private parties and the state). Insofar as investment arbitration challenges state regulations, its findings are regularly of public interest. Where what is at stake are public concerns, like whether certain fuel additives are detrimental to health, or whether advertisement has an impact on smoking, a public interest in information is hard to deny.[56] In the area of investment arbitration, this has been recognized. For example, the 2014 UNCITRAL Rules on Transparency in Treaty-based Investor-State Arbitration, which the Mauritius Convention on Transparency makes applicable for signatory states,[57] provides for far-reaching publication of party statements and even of expert reports and witness statements; it also requires hearings to be open.[58]

[54] Christopher Drahozal, 'Is Arbitration Lawless?', 40 Loy. L.A. L. Rev. 187 (2006); Stone Sweet et al. (n. 46).

[55] E.g. Cindy Buys, 'The Tension Between Confidentiality and Transparency in International Arbitration', 14 Am. Rev. Int'l Arb. 121 (2003), 137; A. Claire Cutler, 'The Privatization of Global Governance and Modern Law Merchant', in Héritier (n. 23), 127, 140.

[56] *Methanex Corp v United States*, Final Award of the Tribunal on Jurisdiction and Merits, 44 I.L.M. 1345 (2005); *Phillip Morris Asia Ltd v Commonwealth of Australia*, Award on Jurisdiction and Admissibility, PCA Case No. 2012-12 (2015).

[57] United Nations Convention on Transparency in Treaty-based Investor-State Arbitration (2015).

[58] UNCITRAL, 'The UNCITRAL Rules on Transparency in Treaty-based Investor-State Arbitration', Annex I to the report of UNCITRAL on the work of its 46th session (A/68/17): <http://www.uncitral.org/uncitral/en/uncitral_texts/arbitration/2014Transparency.html>. For commentary, see Julia Salasky and Corinne Montineri, 'UNCITRAL Rules on Transparency in Treaty-Based Investor-State Arbitration', 31 ASA-Bulletin 774 (2013). More generally, see William Kenny, 'Transparency in Investor State Arbitration', 33 J. Int'l Arb. 470 (2016).

Outside of investment arbitration, transparency is less wide, but it exists, too. Beyond the general discussion whether confidentiality is a norm or must be specifically agreed upon by the parties, some laws that accept a principle of confidentiality include a 'public interest exception'.[59] In Esso/BHP, the Australian High Court declared that the state was entitled to inform the public about the arbitration, as a limitation to its confidentiality obligation. The holding was based explicitly on considerations of public interest and externalities from the arbitration, emphasizing the public good aspect of this information:

> Why should the consumers and the public of Victoria be denied knowledge of what happens in these arbitrations, the outcome of which will affect, in all probability, the prices chargeable to consumers by the Public Utilities?[60]

Such an exception is mostly admitted in particular where the government, or a state-owned corporation, is a party, as was the case in Esso/BHP.[61] Governments have specific duties of disclosure to the public. However, the argument from public interest is not linked to the character of the parties but to the nature of the dispute matter, meaning that a public interest exception to confidentiality could be justified also in arbitration between private parties, insofar as matters of public concern are at stake.[62] This is so especially with regard to public duties of information. Publicly traded companies, for example, may have a duty to disclose the existence of arbitral proceedings.[63]

16.5.2.3 *Public interest arbitration*

These cases, in which the knowledge created in the arbitration is of general interest, lead to a related area: arbitration that is in the public interest. Such public interest arbitration is traditionally somewhat limited in commercial arbitration, due to the private and contractual nature of arbitration. The enforcement of public interests in arbitration is often difficult outside the realm of contractual relations. It is, by contrast, frequently implicated in mixed arbitration (between private parties and states), insofar as regulations by the

[59] Andrew Tweeddale, 'Confidentiality in Arbitration and the Public Interest Expectation', 21 Arb. Int'l 59 (2005); Stavros Brekoulakis and Margaret Devaney, 'Public–Private Arbitration and the Public Interest under English Law', 80 Modern Law Review 22 (2017). See also, Alex Stone Sweet and Florian Grisel, The Evolution of International Arbitration: Judicialization, Governance, Legitimacy (Oxford University Press, 2017), 238–40.

[60] *Esso Australia Ltd v Plowman* (High Ct. Australia), 21 Yb. Commercial Arbitration 132 (1996), 152.

[61] *Commonwealth of Australia v Cockatoo Dockyard Pty* (1995), No. 95/014, XXI Yearbook Commercial Arbitration 137 (1996), 153; *Television New Zealand Ltd v Langley Productions*, [2000] 2 N.Z.L.R. 250. See also, Law Commission of New Zealand, *Improving the Arbitration Act 1996* (Law Commission, 2003), 22.

[62] Joyiyoti Misra and Roman Jordans, 'Confidentiality in International Arbitration', 23 Arb. Int'l 39 (2006), 45–7; Fan Kun, 'Expansion of Arbitral Subject Matter: New Topics and New Areas of Law', in Stavros Brekoulakis, Julian Lew, and Loukas Mistelis (eds), *The Evolution and Future of International Arbitration* (Kluwer Law International, 2016), 299, 314.

[63] Valéry Denoix de Saint Marc, 'Confidentiality of Arbitration and the Obligation to Disclose Information on Listed Companies or During Due Diligence Investigations', 20 Journal of International Arbitration 211 (2003); Gu Weixia, 'Confidentiality Revisited: Blessing or Curse in International Commercial Arbitration?', 15 Am. Rev. Int'l Arb. 607 (2006), 627.

state are implemented that concern broader interests. Insofar as the public interest concerns a public good, arbitration over it has public good implications, too.

The first area in which such public interest arbitration exists concerns relations between the government and private parties, in which government regulation is involved. The clearest application is in investment arbitration, though even outside the area of investment, governments and private parties can agree to settle potential disputes through arbitration instead of litigation.[64] In some ways, this is the flipside of public interest litigation: the investor does not bring a claim in the interest of the public on the basis of a state's public law, but he brings a claim against a state's public law. Typically, this happens in his own private interest, though that alone does not necessarily mean that what is created is a private good. The potential effect of such arbitration is what is called 'regulatory chill': governments may, from fear of being sued, refrain from regulation that which they would otherwise have undertaken.[65]

Whether regulatory chill represents a public good (positive externalities), a public bad (negative externalities), or something else is hard to say in the abstract. One concern about investment treaties and investment arbitration is that they produce negative externalities: in restricting regulations in favour of individual investors, the arbitrator creates negative externalities for those who would otherwise have benefited from the regulation; it undermines public regulation. Insofar as investment arbitration deals with inefficient regulations, it can actually have positive spillover effects. To the extent that the investor succeeds and the affected state retracts a regulation that was inefficient, the benefits are felt not only by the investor who was a claimant but also by others similarly affected. It is somewhat unlikely that investment arbitrators have the tools and abilities to assess such questions of public goods.

A second area of at least potential public interest arbitration exists as class, mass, and collective arbitration.[66] Such large-scale arbitration concerns cases in which a large number of individuals suffer injuries that are largely or even entirely identical. As a consequence, legal systems have developed different ways of accounting for the shared interests of these individuals by grouping them together in the arbitration and extending the legal force of a resulting award to all victims. Large-scale arbitration exists, so far, mostly in the domestic realm (particularly in the United States); its use in international commercial arbitration is still relatively rare. The U.S. Supreme Court raised the question whether class arbitration is still arbitration, but comparison demonstrates it is in many ways not so different from multi-party arbitration.[67] What makes it different is that it can be a case of public interest arbitration. Although focused specifically on

[64] See Gary Born, 'A New Generation of International Adjudication', 61 Duke L.J. 775 (2010), 826–31.

[65] Kyla Tienhaara, 'Regulatory Chill and the Threat of Arbitration: A View from Political Science', in Chester Brown and Kate Miles (eds), *Evolution in Investment Treaty Law and Arbitration* (Cambridge University Press, 2011), 606–27.

[66] S. I. Strong, *Class, Mass, and Collective Arbitration in National and International Law* (Oxford University Press, 2013).

[67] S. I. Strong, 'Does Class Arbitration Change the Nature of Arbitration? Stolt-Nielsen, AT&T, and a Return to First Principles', 17 Harv. Negot. L. Rev. 1 (2012).

compensation, large-scale arbitration has an unavoidable regulatory component to it, turning it more into a public good.[68]

Finally, to some extent one can speak of public interest arbitration whenever an arbitration involves claims aimed at the enforcement of public law.[69] Much public law creates public goods: antitrust law enables market structures that benefit all consumers, for example. Public law can, as we know, be enforced also through litigation; it can therefore theoretically also be enforced through arbitration. Whether arbitration is particularly good at this is disputable. Even where public laws appear in arbitration, their effects are typically confined to the parties.[70] Proponents often point to the ban on corruption as an internal norm of international arbitration: arbitrators refuse to enforce contracts based on corruption and thereby create, or at least protect, a public good. A detailed study makes this doubtful: arbitrators not only lack the required tools, especially as concerns evidence; they often also lack sufficient incentive.[71]

16.5.2.4 *Quality and reputation of the arbitral system*

Finally, another arguable public good produced through arbitral awards is the quality and reputation of the arbitral system.[72] Just like judges and attorneys, arbitrators and counsel in arbitration gain experience and expertise. This expertise serves, first and foremost, their own business interests. It can, however, turn in part into a public good insofar as it benefits the arbitral system at large. This is so because arbitration, in order to be a functioning system altogether, requires a degree of expertise from all its participants.[73]

In addition, the frequent use of the international arbitration system, together with the publication of ensuing decisions, can enhance its perceived legitimacy, both among participants and in society in general.[74] Again, this serves in part the private interest of arbitration participants—arbitrators, attorneys, arbitral institutions. And again, the enhanced legitimacy of the arbitral system can in turn have positive spillover effects for other potential users of arbitral justice.

Quality and reputation, thus, have positive externalities. The question remains whether this makes them public goods. Catherine Rogers has argued for understanding them as club (or toll) goods because, although they are available to all, they must be paid for.[75] Indeed, if one focuses only on the direct impact of quality gains on future parties, then there is a remnant of excludability: access requires the paying of significant entry

[68] *Abaclat et al v Argentine*, ICSID Case No. ARB/07/5, Decision on Jurisdiction and Admissibility (2011), esp. the dissenting opinion of Abi-Saab.

[69] See Dora Marta Gruner, 'Note. Accounting for the Public Interest in International Arbitration: The Need for Procedural and Structural Reform', 41 Colum. J. Transnat'l L. 923 (2003).

[70] Paulsson (n. 7).

[71] Cecily Rose, 'Questioning the Role of International Arbitration in the Fight against Corruption', 31 J. Int'l Arb. 183 (2014).

[72] Rogers (n. 10), 1005–7. [73] Paulsson (n. 7), 147.

[74] See e.g. Fabien Gélinas, 'Arbitration as Transnational Governance by Contract', 7 Transnat'l Legal Theory 181 (2016), 190; Stephan Schill, 'Conceptions of Legitimacy of International Arbitration', in Caron et al. (n. 3), 106, 118.

[75] Rogers (n. 42), 362–3.

fees. Directly, the quality of participants in arbitration benefits only participants. Indirectly, however, insofar as the enhanced quality of the arbitral system is viewed as foundational of the transnational rule of law and the stability of international trade, it is non-excludable. This would characterize it as a public good, albeit one produced through private investment. Insofar as transnational law is a public good, and insofar as international arbitration is where this transnational law is administered, the quality of arbitration itself at least contributes to the public good of transnational law.

A potential challenge remains. Insofar as parties take their disputes to arbitration, they take them away from the courts.[76] In addition, arbitration may even take lawyers away from becoming judges because arbitration is more lucrative.[77] To the extent that adjudication is better than arbitration at producing public goods, the flight into arbitration reduces the production of public goods. But it seems plausible that arbitration and adjudication are only in partial competition. Arguably, both may draw on different types of disputes, and courts and arbitration may often work in tandem rather than in competition. International arbitration, it is often said, deals with those cases for which courts are not well equipped. If this is so, the relation between arbitration and adjudication is said to become one of symbiosis rather than competition.[78] Whether this is actually true is a matter of empirics that is beyond this chapter.

16.5.3 The provision of international arbitration

This leaves a problem, discussed earlier in the context of courts. We saw that even the public good of adjudication cannot be brought about without the participation of private parties who initiate litigation and do not settle it. This is even more true for arbitration. Arbitration requires consent from both parties, rather than just a decision by the plaintiff to file suit at a competent court, as is the case for litigation. Moreover, in principle at least the parties control the procedure all the way through. They may, therefore, have insufficient incentive to invest in the production of public goods; often they even have an interest in avoiding such externalities, expressed in a common interest in confidentiality.[79] Arbitrators, on the other hand, have little independent incentive to make law beyond the case before them,[80] though they could, at least in theory, have an interest in publication of their awards as a way to market their qualities.

[76] Luban (n. 31), 2625; Posner (n. 41), 126; Lord Thomas of Cwmgiedd, 'Developing Commercial Law through the Courts: Rebalancing the Relationship between the Courts and Arbitration' (Bailii Lecture, 2016).

[77] Posner (n. 41), 126–7.

[78] Paulsson (n. 7), 259.

[79] Buys (n. 53), 122–3. Whether there is an intrinsic duty of confidentiality, or whether confidentiality must be agreed on, remains a matter of much discussion. See e.g. ICC Bulletin, 'Confidentiality in Arbitration' (ICC, 2009); Ileana Smeureanu, *Confidentiality in International Commercial Arbitration* (Kluwer Law International, 2011).

[80] Anne van Aaken and Tomer Broude, Ch. 36 in this volume, sect. 36.3. See already Robert Cooper, 'The Objectives of Private and Public Judges', 41 Public Choice 107 (1983); McAdams (n. 30), 1116.

There are three especially important mechanisms for the provision of public goods: enforcement, publicity, and public participation. The first one, enforcement, is relatively ineffective. As for state enforcement, there are very few requirements for arbitral awards to be enforced. Enforcement still focuses largely on the private good aspects of an award. Even the refusal of enforcement on the grounds of lack of arbitrability or of public policy violations (Art. V(2) New York Convention) is only a very weak incentive, given how narrowly it is interpreted. Moreover, states have an incentive only to provide national, not global public goods. States are not immediately interested in creating or incentivizing positive externalities beyond their own borders (beyond their interest in participation in international trade).

Outside of enforcement by state courts, the production of public goods is therefore mostly guaranteed through supervisory institutions in the realm of institutional arbitration. However, qualitative control is largely absent. The ICC in particular, through its court, aims to ensure a high quality of arbitral awards and proceedings and in this sense supports at least to some extent the production of public goods. Other institutions have less intrusive vetting mechanisms.

In the end, the onus is on the ethical conduct of the arbitrator, which would give her a dual role between private service provider and guardian of the public good.[81] Whether she will have sufficient incentives to do so is a different question. The arbitrator who refuses to arbitrate in the face of corruption is often named as a model, but corruption is also something of an exception in this regard.

If enforcement is relatively ineffective, it is through publicity, by contrast, that most of the public good aspects of arbitration are produced. Publication of awards helps create law. Publicness of proceedings helps create public information, and thereby makes use of the often considerable costs that contribute to the creation of this knowledge in arbitration. And publicness increases both quality and legitimacy of enforcement.

The most important mechanism here is the publication of arbitral awards, as discussed before. There is no general duty under national laws that every international award be published; indeed, although such a duty is sometimes advocated,[82] this seems both hard to justify and also unnecessarily intrusive. However, at least some institutions contribute to public goods by publishing arbitral awards. Although their incentive is to increase the legitimacy and reputation of their respective institutions, the effect is a public one. In addition, enforcement by states helps create public goods in another way, albeit arguably unintentionally. Insofar as arbitral awards are presented for enforcement, their content must necessarily be made public, at least to some extent, and gets publicized insofar as the judicial proceedings are public.[83]

[81] Rogers (n. 42), 42.

[82] Paul Comrie-Thomson, 'A Statement of Arbitral Jurisprudence: The Case for a National Law Obligation to Publish International Commercial Arbitral Awards', 34(2) Journal of International Arbitration 275 (2017).

[83] This is true in legal systems where a right to access to judgments exists. This is not the case in every state.

Finally, public participation can contribute to the provision of public goods, because it shifts the incentives of the actors involved. Arguably, the greatest deficit in international arbitration insofar as it affects society at large is the lack of public participation. *Amicus curiae* participation could help a little.[84] Greater public interest in international arbitration might increase the public goods aspects, but it might also, for that reason, disincentivize participation in arbitration, or incentivize settlement in order to avoid publication.[85]

16.6 Implications

Implications from this overview must be tentative, but they may not be without relevance.

16.6.1 From private good to mixed good

A first insight concerns the evolution of arbitration. There is much talk about the juridification of international arbitration, a tendency of arbitration to become more and more like litigation.[86] This chapter has shown how this tendency of approximation exists with regard to the relation between private and public goods, too. Arbitration started out as a purely private good. It has since adopted more and more aspects of a public good, in tune with litigation. Just as litigation is not a mere public good, arbitration is not a mere private good: both mechanisms combine both elements.

Although therefore international arbitration comes today as a mix of public and private arbitration, the mix is not the same for each arbitration. On the one side of a continuum stands big investment arbitration, like the one concerning tobacco packaging in Australia.[87] Such arbitration regularly has significant externalities. It is therefore rarely properly characterized as a private good. On the other side of the continuum stands the standard case of commercial arbitration, where the private aspect outweighs the public aspect. Run-of-the-mill arbitration contributes little to the development of law (less, arguably, than decisions of first instance courts), and does not deal with facts or laws of public interest.

[84] Choudhury (n. 5), 814; Katia Fach Gómez, 'Rethinking the Role of Amicus Curiae in International Investment Arbitration: How to Draw the Line Favorably for the Public Interest', 35 Fordham Int'l L.J. 510 (2011); Eugenia Levine, 'Amicus Curiae in International Investment Arbitration: The Implications of an Increase in Third Party Participation', 29 Berkeley J. Int'l L. 200 (2011).

[85] Emilie Hafner-Burton and David Victor, 'Secrecy in International Investment Arbitration: An Empirical Analysis', 7 J Int Disp Settlement 161 (2016).

[86] Stone Sweet and Grisel (n. 43).

[87] *Philip Morris Asia Limited v The Commonwealth of Australia*, UNCITRAL, PCA Case No. 2012–12.

Insofar as law at large is viewed as a public good, it seems clear now that international arbitration can contribute to its production. Choudhury argues that investment arbitration has become such a global public good because it fulfils the two requirements: it is non-rivalrous because use by one state does not exclude others, and it is non-exclusive because by now investment law has become a general system of law.[88] Similar arguments could be made for international commercial arbitration. Underlying these ideas is the presumption that arbitration fills a niche which domestic litigation cannot fill.[89] This is the case most strongly, arguably, for investment arbitration. Here it is argued, with some plausibility, that domestic courts are not sufficiently independent to deal with investors' claims. A similar argument is often made for international commercial arbitration, even though it has somewhat less strength here, because international commercial dispute resolution has a possible venue—national courts.

16.6.2 Normative basis

The move from private good to mixed good has implications for the normative basis of international arbitration. Unlike investment arbitration, which is based on treaty, commercial arbitration still rests on a contract. Now, contract is a proper basis for the provision of private goods; indeed, private goods are a core concern of contracts. But contract becomes a problematic basis once the mixed character of arbitration is recognized. Of course, public goods can emerge from contract (though with difficulty).[90] But commercial contracts, especially exchange contracts, are focused on private, not public goods. Parties have no interest in the production of public goods, even if they would benefit from others producing such goods: they would prefer to free-ride. The contractual basis of arbitration thus continues to stand in tension with its character as a partly public good.

In a way, then, the realization of arbitration as a mixed private/public good invites the consideration of a mixed private law/public law foundation. In investment arbitration, such a foundation is convincing. Investment arbitration often combines public international law and private contracts. The exact combination, however, remains disputed. Julie Maupin's proposal of an integrated systems approach seems best able to capture the way in which public and private are interwoven.[91]

[88] Barnali Choudhury, 'International Investment Law as a Global Public Good', 17 Lewis & Clark L. Rev. 481 (2012).

[89] Paulsson (n. 7), 174.

[90] For one model, see David Schmidtz, 'Contracts and Public Goods', 10 Harv. J.L. & Pub. Pol'y 475 (1987); Alexander Tabarrok, 'The Private Provision of Public Goods via Dominant Assurance Contracts', 96 Public Choice 345 (1998).

[91] Maupin (n. 2). The systems approach is adopted in Joost Pauwelyn, 'At the Edge of Chaos? Foreign Investment Law as a Complex Adaptive System: How It Emerged and How It Can Be Reformed', 29 ICSID Review 372 (2014).

Something similar seems appropriate for commercial arbitration. A traditional analysis would be to suggest that freedom of contract is limited: parties are free to create private goods as among themselves, but the law restricts their freedom in favour of the production of public goods. According to such an analysis, arbitration would be characterized by a combination of private ordering through contract, on the one hand, and public law as administered and adjudicated by states on the other. But such an analysis cannot explain why the move in arbitration towards a public good emerges much more from inside than from outside the arbitration system—it is more a non-state than a state development. Arbitration practitioners and arbitral institutions contribute more to the publicization of arbitration than to state institutions.

A better normative conceptualization of investment and commercial arbitration therefore lies in new ideas about the self-constitutionalization of international arbitration. Gunther Teubner suggested in 1996 that the new *lex mercatoria* was based not on the individual contract but on contract as an institution.[92] Such ideas have been taken up both for investment arbitration[93] and for commercial arbitration.[94] The idea is, essentially, that the arbitral system itself builds its own constitutional system, which provides both its functional foundations and its basis of legitimacy. Within this idea, the public/private distinction is no longer one of the actors involved (private parties vs state).

16.6.3 The proper regulation

Finally, although an analysis of public and private goods is mostly descriptive, there are normative implications. The provision and protection of private and of public goods follow different mechanisms, even if it is too simple to merely allocate one with private parties and the other with the state.

In order to design optimal regulation, it helps first to remember that the mix between public and private good looks different for different types of arbitration. The biggest difference here exists between investment arbitration on the one hand, with a strong public good aspect, and commercial arbitration on the other, where the public good aspect is more remote. If this is correct, then it justifies the sometimes criticized different treatment of investment arbitration on the one hand and of commercial arbitration on the other. In commercial arbitration, the assumption is now of treating arbitration as a public good and thus of opening it for publication and for intrusion of public values. Limitations must be specifically justified. In commercial arbitration, by contrast, the

[92] Gunther Teubner, '"Global Bukowina": Legal Pluralism in the World Society', in Gunther Teubner (ed), *Global Law Without a State* (Dartmouth, 1997), 3.

[93] Alec Stone Sweet and Florian Grisel, 'Transnational Investment Arbitration: From Delegation to Constitutionalization?' in Pierre-Marie Dupuy et al. (eds), *Human Rights in International Investment Law and Arbitration* (Oxford University Press, 2009); id./id. (n. 57). David Schneiderman, 'Legitimacy and Reflexivity in International Investment Arbitration: A New Self-Restraint?', 2 J. Int'l Disp. Settlement 471 (2011).

[94] Renner (n. 1). See also Zumbansen (n. 1).

assumption is that of a private good. Here, it is the treatment as a public that requires special justification.

In addition, there are different ways in which arbitration becomes a public good, and they receive different regulatory treatment. First, law production through the publication of the legal analysis part of awards generally contributes to the creation of public goods, without great interference with private interests. The costs of publication are not very high, which means parties are not asked to pay much for something that benefits others. A partial subsidization, as in court proceedings, is not possible in arbitration, but it does not seem necessary. The current tendency already goes towards greater levels of publication. The reasons are not fully clear; they may include a greater common need of the arbitration industry in producing common knowledge, combined with a need for greater legitimacy. At least from a public goods perspective, the widespread publication of awards should be encouraged.

Matters are somewhat different as concerns the publication of factual findings. Here, the existing division between investment and commercial arbitration reflects differences in the public good character. Investment arbitration, which regularly affects public interest, is open to such publication. Commercial arbitration, by contrast, is often not. It remains to be seen to what extent a public interest exception could be justified in this area, too. Generally, greater levels of publication of factual findings may take away many parties' incentives to use arbitration in the first place.

Public interest arbitration is too complex and manifold to discuss here in sufficient details. It is worth pointing out, however, that we are observing the rise of a transnational public policy that may have the potential of transcending national public policies as a generator of public interest.[95] This is a direct consequence, and sign, of the constitutionalization of arbitration. Such transnational public policy will not, and should not, replace the consideration of national public policy in arbitration, because national legislation continues to be an expression of public goods; it comes as an addition.

[95] Renner (n. 1).

CHAPTER 17

INVESTMENT ARBITRATION AS CONSTITUTIONAL LAW

Constitutional analogies, linkages, and absences

DAVID SCHNEIDERMAN

17.1 Introduction

The virtues of the good arbitrator are similar to those of a good judge, insists Jan Paulsson.[1] What is sought in arbitration is 'civilized closure' via 'a fair hearing'.[2] The arbitrator, furthermore, is 'omnipotent'. 'She becomes someone with greater authority than the most excellent trial judge, or the most eminent intermediate court of appeal. Her award is as final as a judgment of the supreme court of the nation,' Paulsson declares.[3] Are there reasons, beyond appeals to fair processes and judicial finality, that justify investment arbitrators portraying themselves as equivalent to apex national courts? This chapter advances one set of reasons: that investment arbitration serves functions analogous to those of high courts when interpreting constitutional text. It is the performance of constitution-like functions that gives rise to normative concerns that continue to trouble the field.

As in the case of high courts issuing authoritative interpretations of constitutional texts, arbitrators are tasked with determining the propriety of state action with reference to open-ended obligations that states owe to foreign investors and their investments. In so doing, investment arbitrators have the power to determine the propriety of state

[1] Jan Paulsson, *The Idea of Arbitration* (Oxford University Press, 2013), 9.

[2] Ibid. 13; Marc Lalonde similarly describes the arbitral function as acting 'like a judge' in Julius Melnitzer, 'The New Peacekeepers', 28(8) Canadian Lawyer 18 (2004), 21.

[3] Paulsson (n. 1), 16.

action, a task Kelsen declares, 'not infrequently undertaken by positive law constitutions, in that they prescribe or preclude certain content'.[4] Viewed from this angle, investment arbitration can be likened to the performance of judicial review under national constitutions. This is a proposition that will be resisted by many investment lawyers and arbitrators. Analogizing to constitutional rules and institutions will be seen as contributing to a 'legitimacy crisis' presently confronting investor–state dispute settlement (ISDS).[5] Legitimation problems have arisen because legitimacy requires more than merely following correct legal processes. There is expected to be some value beyond mere legality served by the power of coercive law.[6]

Some will have recourse to constitutional analogies in order to shore up legitimacy concerns that have arisen in respect of the system's model of dispute settlement.[7] It takes time, it is said, for consensus on constitutional matters in jurisdictions like the United States to materialize.[8] In which case, it also takes time for investment law to secure the requisite legitimacy that is accorded to constitutional regimes. Others look to the analogy in order to highlight the constitution-like functions served by the system's standards of protection and dispute settlement mechanism. This mode of analysis highlights the constitutional deficiencies exhibited by investment law. Rather than promoting the project of global constitutional law, this approach has a more critical punch. In either case, the thought experiment is often viewed among investment lawyers as controversial. As the system is perceived as falling short of a fully constitutionalized regime, Vadi eschews such analogies for fear that it 'risks harming international investment law rather than fixing it'.[9] Constitutionalism as critique is less interested in buttressing legitimacy than in deepening investment arbitration's self-understandings.

The object of this chapter is to draw out the implications of the constitutional analogy from both a functional and normative point of view. I turn first to 'Constitutional analogizing' (Section 17.2). Two modes of analogizing are identified, as I have just described

[4] Hans Kelsen, *Introduction to the Problems of Legal Theory*, trans. Bonnie Paulson and Stanley Paulson (Clarendon Press, 1992), 64.

[5] United Nations Conference on Trade and Development (UNCTAD), *World Investment Report 2015: Reforming International Investment Governance* (UNCTAD, 2015), 128. Analogizing investment arbitration to judicial models, Stone Sweet and Grisel write, pits them in an 'increasingly intense, real-world struggle against those wedded to representing arbitration in terms provided by the [private] contractual model': Alec Stone Sweet and Florian Grisel, *The Evolution of Investment Arbitration: Judicialization, Governance, Legitimacy* (Oxford University Press, 2017), 33.

[6] Jürgen Habermas, *Legitimation Crisis*, trans. Thomas McCarthy (Beacon Press, 1975), 98. I address variable understandings of legal legitimacy in David Schneiderman, 'International Investment Law's Unending Legitimation Project', 49 Loyola University of Chicago Law Journal 229 (2017).

[7] International lawyers have long had recourse to constitutional law in order to understand developments within their field. See Richard Collins, 'Constitutionalism as Liberal-Juridical Consciousness: Echoes From International Law's Past', 22 Leiden Journal of International Law 251 (2009), 254.

[8] Remarks of Mark Kantor as reported in Andrea Bjorklund, 'Improving the International Law and Policy System: Report of the Special Rapporteur', in José Alvarez and Karl Sauvant (eds), *The Evolving International Investment Regime: Expectations, Realities, Options* (Oxford University Press, 2011), 218.

[9] Valentina Vadi, *Analogies in International Investment Law and Arbitration* (Cambridge University Press, 2016), 195.

them: one that is intended to restore legitimacy to investment arbitration and the other that heightens legitimacy concerns. These two modes are offered as heuristics for understanding the constitution-like functions performed by investment arbitrators in the course of interpreting substantive treaty protections. Adopting a critical mode reveals numerous problems that investment arbitration chooses to remain silent about, including a version of the separation of powers that is difficult to defend from a constitutional angle. I then turn to 'Constitutional linkages' (Section 17.3), which evaluates the performance of investment arbitrators in a few instances where tribunals have directly engaged with national constitutional law in the course of issuing reasons. The focus in this section is on how tribunals handle interpretation of constitutional texts and high court rulings as law applicable or relevant to an investment dispute. These exercises in constitutional engagement, I argue, turn out to be less than satisfactory.[10] Finally, in 'Constitutional absence' (Section 17.4), I confront a significant defect in constitutional analogizing: that the 'people' are absent from its account. The suggestion that international courts, and investment arbitration in particular, serve as constituent authority in the absence of a polity is examined and critically assessed. The chapter concludes by arguing that investment arbitration will continue to be of doubtful legitimacy so long as investment arbitration is characterized as performing constitution-like functions. It is, as a consequence, likely to attract more, not less, political heat.

17.2 Constitutional Analogies

Anthea Roberts has observed that 'analogical reasoning is rife' in the investment law field. The quest for analogies is to be expected in a field that is 'novel and hybridized',[11] an area of 'uncharted law, not yet fully registered in any of our established maps of legal authority,' she writes.[12] In such an unstable environment, we can expect scholars to be less methodological and more territorial, either stretching their own preferred canvas onto the global frame or rejecting analogies altogether. It should come as no surprise, then, to learn that some have had recourse to the analogy between investment law and constitutional law and, relatedly, as between investment arbitration and high court adjudication. It has been said that constitutional analogizing in investment law is 'not

[10] On the posture of engagement, see Vicki Jackson, *Constitutional Engagement in a Transnational Era* (Oxford University Press, 2010), 9.

[11] Anthea Roberts, 'Clash of Paradigms: Actors and Analogies Shaping the Investment Treaty System', 107 Am. J. of Int'l L. 45 (2013), 50. See also Oliver Diggelmann and Tilmann Altwicker, 'Is There Something Like a Constitution of International Law? A Critical Analysis of the Debate on World Constitutionalism', 68 Zeitschrift für ausländisches öffentliches Recht und Völkerrecht 623 (2008); Vadi (n. 9).

[12] Neil Walker, *Intimations of Global Law* (Cambridge University Press, 2015), 151. It has also been said that investment law's constituent elements 'flow from entirely unremarkable and well-known law making techniques of international law'. See Martins Paparinskis, 'Analogies and Other Regimes of International Law', in Zachary Douglas, Joost Pauwelyn, and Jorge Viñuales (eds), *The Foundations of International Investment Law: Bringing Theory into Practice* (Oxford University Press, 2014), 73.

normative' but descriptive.[13] This, I argue, is not the case—constitutional analogizing typically is in the service of one of two related normative ends.[14]

17.2.1 Project mode

The first normative goal envisages investment arbitration as contributing to the construction of a transnational legal order analogous to the constitutional law of capital-exporting states.[15] The project is about enhancing the legitimacy of investment treaty and arbitration law. Officials in the U.S. State Department, for instance, regularly characterized investment disciplines in the postwar period as reflecting 'enlightened' constitutional principles, namely, those found in the U.S. Constitution.[16] During debates over whether to confer trade promotion authority upon President Obama, the U.S. Trade Representative (USTR) declared that investment 'obligations and U.S. investment agreements are based on the same legal principles available under the U.S. Constitution and the US legal system.'[17] This was echoed by a group of some 50 law professors, in an open letter to congressional leadership, who claimed that many of the rights conferred upon investors 'are similar to those guaranteed by the U.S. Constitution, but [which] ... might not be guaranteed in foreign countries.'[18]

Stephan Schill has made notable contributions in this regard by maintaining that investment arbitration enforces norms analogous to those found within the public law of national states.[19] Schill maintains that investment arbitration is 'functionally analogous' to the administrative and constitutional law of national legal systems.[20] Arbitrators

[13] Vadi (n. 9), 225, 259. At the same time, Vadi acknowledges (p. 260) that analogizing can enhance the perception of legitimacy, in which case it does serve normative, and not merely descriptive, ends.

[14] I have elsewhere contrasted these modes of imagining constitutional law 'beyond the state' in David Schneiderman, 'A New Global Constitutional Order?' in Tom Ginsburg and Rosalind Dixon (eds), *Research Handbook on Comparative Constitutional Law* (Edward Elgar, 2010), 190–5. Also see David Kennedy, 'The Mystery of Global Governance', in Jeffrey Dunoff and Joel Trachtman (eds), *Ruling the World? Constitutionalism, International Law and Global Governance* (Cambridge University Press, 2009), 61; Walker (n. 12), 149.

[15] I do not here consider a 'societal-constitutionalist' (or systems-theoretic) account of arbitral functions. For such an analysis, see David Schneiderman, 'Legitimacy and Reflexivity in International Investment Arbitration: A New Self-Restraint?' 2 Int'l J. of Dispute Management 471 (2011).

[16] Kenneth Vandevelde, *The First Bilateral Investment Treaties: U.S. Postwar Friendship, Commerce, and Navigation Treaties* (Oxford University Press, 2017), 24–5.

[17] United States Trade Representative, 'The Facts on Investor–State Dispute Settlement', in 'Tradewinds: The Official Blog of the United States Trade Representative' (USTR, 2014): <https://ustr.gov/aboutus/policyoffices/pressoffice/blog/2014/March/Facts-InvestorState%20Dispute-Settlement-SafeguardingPublic-Interest-Protecting-Investors>.

[18] Payam Akhavam et al., 'An Open Letter about Investor–State Dispute Settlement' (2015): <https://www.mcgill.ca/fortier-chair/isds-open-letter>.

[19] A more elaborate discussion can be found in David Schneiderman, 'The Global Regime of Investor Rights: Return to the Standards of Civilised Justice?' 5 Transnational L. Theory 60 (2014).

[20] Stephan Schill, 'International Investment Law and Comparative Public Law: An Introduction', in Stephan Schill (ed.), *International Investment Law and Comparative Public Law* (Oxford University Press, 2010), 15.

should, therefore, have recourse to the public law of leading capital exporting states. These will be the 'representative legal systems' of the common law and civil law world, rather than their idiosyncratic transplants elsewhere in the world.[21] These leading legal systems, after all, are 'more advanced public law systems'[22] and will have 'influenced the public law systems of many other countries'.[23]

This analogizing is in the service of establishing a legal order with the authority and legitimacy to frame public law on a global scale. It seems improper, from this vantage point, to have recourse to different constitutional projects, such as the one in South Africa, where property rights are discordant with standards of protection promoted by investment treaty arbitration.[24] As if to underscore the constitutional analogy, the Republic of South Africa has adopted a course of terminating all of its BITs with a view to relying, instead, upon constitutional protections for foreign investors (and others), in addition to a new Protection of Investment Act, in the service of its post-apartheid socio-economic project.[25]

A tendency toward 'constitutionalism-as-project' mode is also present in proposals that investment arbitrators adopt proportionality analysis in the course of issuing reasons.[26] In light of the legitimacy problems that continue to dog investment arbitration, scholars have called for the adoption of a mode of reasoning common to high courts in many parts of the world. A focus on means–ends scrutiny is a seemingly 'tailor-made solution for dealing with intra-constitutional tensions', argue Stone Sweet and Matthews.[27] It would be 'suicidal' for arbitrators to proceed otherwise, with 'a heavy thumb pressed permanently down on the investors' side of the scales in cases with very high political stakes'.[28] Tribunals thereby will have adopted standards 'congruent with an emerging set of public law principles for global regulatory governance'.[29] This is a revealing admission, as high courts world-wide have had recourse to proportionality as

[21] Ibid. 29.

[22] Stephan Schill, 'Enhancing International Investment Law's Legitimacy: Conceptual and Methodological Foundations of a New Public Law Approach', 52 Va. J. Int'l L. 57 (2011), 60.

[23] Schill (n. 20), 29.

[24] David Schneiderman, 'Investment Rules and the New Constitutionalism: Interlinkages and Disciplinary Effects', 25 L. & Social Inquiry 757 (2000).

[25] South Africa, Protection of Investment Act, Act No. 22 of 2015, and Xavier Carim, 'International Investment Agreements and Africa's Structural Transformation: A Perspective from South Africa', in Kavalit Singh and Burghard Ilge (eds), *Rethinking Bilateral Investment Treaties: Critical Issues and Policy Choices* (Both Ends, 2016), 61–2.

[26] For a more detailed discussion, see David Schneiderman, 'Global Constitutionalism and its Legitimacy Problems: Human Rights, Proportionality, and the Future of International Investment Law', *12 Journal of Law & Ethics of Human Rights* 251 (2018).

[27] Alec Stone Sweet and Jud Matthews, 'Proportionality and Balancing in Global Constitutionalism', 47 Columbia J. of Transnational L. 72 (2008), 89.

[28] Alec Stone Sweet, 'Investor–State Arbitration: Proportionality's New Frontier', 4 L. & Ethics of Human Rights 47 (2010), 75.

[29] Benedict Kingsbury and Stephan Schill, 'Investor–State Arbitration as Governance: Fair and Equitable Treatment, Proportionality and the Emerging Global Administrative Law', in Benedict Kingsbury et al. (eds), *El nuevo derecho administrativo global en América latina. Desafíos para las inversiones extranjeras, la regulación nacional y el financiamiento para el desarrollo* (RPA, 2009), 275–6.

a means of lending legitimacy to the exercise of judicial review in circumstances where there is a great deal of controversy over the meaning of constitutional fundamentals.[30] A further illustration of project constitutionalism is taken up in more detail in Section 17.4.

17.2.2 Critical mode

Critical constitutionalists also take up national constitutional analogies in order to frame their critiques, as in the case of 220 professors of law and of economics who called upon the U.S. Congress to reject ISDS in the Trans-Pacific Partnership (TPP). While acknowledging that private companies can enforce constitutional rights in U.S. courts, investment arbitration circumvents a 'democratically responsive legal framework', threatening 'to dilute constitutional protections, weaken[ing] the judicial branch, and outsource[ing] our domestic legal system to a system of private arbitration that is isolated from essential checks and balances'.[31]

One could characterize Gus Van Harten's work as falling between project and critical constitutional modes of inquiry. Van Harten draws out the implications of the constitutional analogy by likening investment arbitration to a 'unique form of public law adjudication'.[32] As it concerns the scope of regulatory capacity of sovereign authority—regulating the 'relationship between those who govern and those who are governed'—investment arbitration resembles 'the domestic adjudication of individual claims against the state under administrative or constitutional law'.[33] Investment arbitration, however, lacks the 'basic hallmarks of judicial accountability, openness, and independence' associated with public law adjudication.[34] It is 'the courts *and only the courts*,' Van Harten maintains, 'who should have the final authority to interpret the law that binds sovereign power'.[35] In order to solve this institutional dilemma, Van Harten calls for an 'independent judiciary' to adjudicate investment claims.[36] His views, however, appear to be evolving toward a more radical restructuring of the regime.[37]

I have, in my own work, been thinking in a critical constitutional mode, invoking constitutional law and practice in order to frame and critically evaluate investment arbitration outcomes.[38] The argument has not been that investment treaties serve as

[30] The circumstances giving rise to the spread of proportionality in national high courts is discussed further in David Schneiderman, 'Judging in Secular Times: Max Weber and the Rise of Proportionality', 63 Supreme Court L. Rev. (2d) 557 (2013).

[31] Citzen.org, '220+ Law and Economics Professors Urge Congress to Reject the TPP and Other Prospective Deals that Include Investor-State Dispute Settlement (ISDS)' (2016): <http://www.citizen.org/documents/isds-law-economics-professors-letter-Sept-2016.pdf>

[32] Gus Van Harten, *Investment Treaty Arbitration and Public Law* (Oxford University Press, 2007), 10.

[33] Ibid. 70–71. [34] Ibid. 5. [35] Ibid. 11. [36] Ibid. 183.

[37] Gus Van Harten, 'Reforming the System of International Investment Dispute Settlement', in C. L. Lim (ed.), *Alternative Visions of the International Law on Foreign Investment: Essays in Honour of Muthucumaraswamy Sornarajah* (Cambridge University Press, 2016), 105.

[38] See e.g. David Schneiderman, *Constitutionalizing Economic Globalization: Investment Rules and Democracy's Promise* (Cambridge University Press, 2008); 'Global Constitutionalism and International

'supraconstitution' or are part of constitutionalism beyond the state that takes 'precedence' or 'prevails' over host state national law.[39] This is not to say that constitutionalism cannot be envisaged at levels beyond national states, only that we should enter this terrain cautiously, armed with empirical evidence and suitable conceptual tools at hand.[40] To this end, I have emphasized the regime's 'constitution-like features'. This has the advantage of not insisting upon exaggerated claims about a 'full-blown' constitution while enabling the identification of linkages between national constitutional orders and transnational legal ones. It also aids in making more transparent how candidates for global public law emerge out of privileged (namely, capital-exporting) national legal discourses. While there is little doubt that there are massive pressures emanating from many capital-exporting states and international financial institutions to 'lock in' developing states to investment treaty commitments, and not to deviate from the legal norms expressed by this so-called 'supraconstitution,' we should be hesitant to describe it in such exalted terms.

There are three distinct strands to this version of 'constitutionalism as critique'. The first is the claim that standards of protection mimic rights protections found in constitutional orders of most capital-exporting, in addition to many capital-importing, states. These include non-discrimination guarantees (national treatment), rights to property (expropriation and nationalization and full protection and security), contractual rights (legitimate expectations doctrine), and due process rights, both procedural and substantive (non-arbitrariness and fair and equitable treatment). Admittedly, these constitutional analogies do not encompass all standards of protection found in the modern investment treaty system, but they include an important number of them. Moreover, to repeat, the argument is that investment rules are constitution-like, not that they mimic constitutional rights in every respect.

Standards of protection do not merely outline the rules of engagement when state policy outcomes impact negatively on private interests (e.g. as might a version of procedural due process). Rather, these opaque standards require the declaration of winners and losers, in which case, certain interests will be accorded priority over other considerations. That is, investment treaty arbitration serves distributive functions. The aim is that of encouraging foreign investment and extending and intensifying economic relations by promoting the free movement of capital across borders.[41] These outcomes are secured, as Weber declared, by having recourse to what he called formally rational law:

Economic Law: The Case of International Investment Law', 7 European Yearbook of Int'l Economic L. 23 (2016).

[39] The position taken in Stephen Clarkson and Stepan Wood, *A Perilous Imbalance: The Globalization of Canadian Law and Governance* (UBC Press, 2009), 55.

[40] Walker, for instance, has been tracing the constitutional outlines of the European project along a number of dimensions, including institutionalizing juridical and political-institutional order and, collective self-authorship, together with elements of social integration and discursive practices associated with constitutionalism. See Neil Walker, 'Taking Constitutionalism Beyond the State', 56 Political Studies 519 (2008), 526 and, generally, Walker (n. 12).

[41] *Saluka Investments BV v Czech Republic*, Partial Award, UNCITRAL/Permanent Court of Arbitration (2006), para. 300.

calculable and predictable rules that facilitate the spread of markets. Law is to be emptied of its 'substantive' elements—laws, for instance, that promote values associated with social justice and human dignity—that will wreak havoc on markets.[42] Investor confidence thereby is preserved and changes in government policy, associated with the idea of 'political risk', mitigated.[43]

In which case, democratic government is expected to get out of the way of the pursuit of profit. Yet one of the principal virtues of democratic government is an ability to experiment and even to change course. As Tocqueville observed, it was an ability to make '*faux réparables*' (repairable mistakes) that distinguishes democracy from other forms of government.[44] The investment rules regime is intended to dampen such policy shifts. Transparent and fair procedures that enable the revision of societal goals are to be cabined.[45] Of course, investors do not, and cannot, always win. States would have reason to withdraw and the system would then collapse.

Second, most standards of protection, like rights in constitutional systems, are deliberately underspecified.[46] Arbitration tribunals are granted a wide interpretive ambit not unlike that available to national high courts in constitutional states. According to Douglas, investment treaty standards are 'uncertain' just like fundamental freedoms in 'a constitutional text'.[47] Arbitrators seize upon the opportunity to be as creative as they like, even devising 'ideas that none of the parties presented'.[48] As Richard Posner has observed, in interpreting constitutional rights, a high court's freedom of action can be as capacious as that of a legislature's.[49] Arbitrators, like judges, can be understood to be doing more than merely applying law—they are, in politically salient disputes, as likely

[42] Max Weber, *Economy and Society: An Outline of Interpretive Sociology* (University of California Press 1978), 655–7.

[43] This is the 'important contribution' made by investor–state arbitration, according to the series editors of Oxford Monographs in International Law in their preface to Martins Paparinskis, *The International Minimum Standard and Fair and Equitable Treatment* (Oxford University Press, 2013), vii.

[44] Alexis de Tocqueville, *De la démocratie en Amérique* (Gallimard, 1961), 339; *Democracy in America*, trans. Harvey Mansfield and Delba Winthrop (University of Chicago Press, 2000), 216. A Tocquevillian critique of investment law can be found in David Schneiderman, 'Against Constitutional Excess: Tocquevillian Reflections on International Investment Law', (2018) 85 University of Chicago Law Review 585–608.

[45] Christoph Möllers, *The Three Branches: A Comparative Model of Separation of Powers* (Oxford University Press, 2013), 52.

[46] N. Jansen Calamita, 'International Human Rights and the Interpretation of International Investment Treaties: Constitutional Considerations', in Freya Baetens (ed.), *Investment Law within International Law: Integrationist Perspectives* (Cambridge University Press, 2013), 171. Admittedly, not all standards of protection lack precision, just as in the case of provisions in national constitutions (e.g. 'No person . . . shall be eligible to the Office of the President . . . who shall not have attained to the age of 35 years'). Many of the controversial standards in both systems, however, lack precision.

[47] Zachary Douglas, *The International Law of Investment Claims* (Cambridge University Press, 2009), 84–5.

[48] Brigitte Stern, 'The Future of International Investment Law: A Balance Between the Protection of Investors and the States' Capacity to Regulate', in José Alvarez and Karl Sauvant (eds), *The Evolving International Investment Regime: Expectations, Realities, Options* (Oxford University Press, 2011), 186.

[49] Richard Posner, *How Judges Think* (Harvard University Press, 2008), 82.

to be acting strategically, given the multiple audiences (investors, states, NGOs, journalists, public opinion) for their awards.[50]

Investment arbitrators, admittedly, perform fact-finding functions not typically associated with appellate review. But arbitrators, like apex courts, usually have the last word: there is no overriding judicial power that can invalidate their interpretations, short of treaty revision (akin to constitutional amendment).[51] Even though the power of investment arbitrators, like judges on high courts, is a 'negative' one—they can only tell governments what not to do, not direct them to do it—they, practically speaking, can direct governments to behave in specific ways by recommending conduct that will not run afoul of investment treaty standards (e.g. the improbably high standards set out under fair and equitable treatment).[52] There also are occasions when governments will choose not to adopt a course of action because of a threatened or pending investment dispute (associated with the 'chilling effect').[53]

The design of the investment treaty system gives rise to a third feature: a professional class of investment arbitrators who interpret and apply its vague guarantees. Rather than allowing these protections to be worked out within national courts or inter-state fora, tribunal members (two of them party appointed) are tasked with the responsibility of filling in the content of treaty standards of protection. In this way, investment tribunals serve functions similar to high courts, while bypassing them,[54] yet without the accompanying institutional guarantees of judicial independence and impartiality—an absence upon which Van Harten has laid emphasis. This brings to the surface a related feature having constitutional implications that I discuss next, namely, the system's problematic separation of powers.

17.2.3 Separation of powers

In its classic formulation, the separation of legislative, executive, and judicial powers enhances liberty. Montesquieu is credited with having popularized this understanding

[50] See David Schneiderman, 'Judicial Politics and International Investment Arbitration: Seeking an Explanation for Conflicting Outcomes' 30 Nw. J. Int'l L. & Bus. 383 (2010); *Loewen Group Inc and Loewen v United States*, Award, ICSID Case No. ARB(AF)/98/3 (2003).

[51] Aside from ICSID Annulment proceedings and limited grounds for judicial review guided by the New York Convention. See Eric de Brabandere, *Investment Treaty Arbitration as Public International Law: Procedural Aspects and Limitations* (Cambridge University Press, 2014), 53–4.

[52] *Técnicas Medioambientales Tecmed SA v Mexico*, Award, ICSID Case No. ARB(AF)/00/2 (2003). For a critique, see Zachary Douglas, 'Nothing if Not Critical for Investment Treaty Arbitration: Occidental, Eureko and Methanex', 22 Arbitration International 27 (2006), 28 (Tecmed offers 'a description of perfect public regulation in a perfect world, to which all states should aspire but very few (if any) will ever attain').

[53] Gus Van Harten and Dayna Nadine Scott, 'Investment Treaties and the Internal Vetting of Regulatory Proposals: A Case Study from Canada', 7 Journal of International Dispute Settlement 92 (2016).

[54] Tom Ginsburg, 'International Substitutes for Domestic Institutions: Bilateral Investment Treaties and Governance', 25 Int'l Rev. of L. and Economics 107 (2005), 119.

of the mid-eighteenth-century English constitution, even though it did not capture well the idea of the 'balanced' or 'mixed' constitution that was then in operation.[55] Montesquieu warned that if the legislative and executive were united in the same person, there would be no liberty; and if the judicial power were not separated out from the other two, despotism would ensue.[56] Tracing the career of the concept is beyond the scope of this discussion,[57] but it famously was taken up in the U.S. Constitution of 1787 and has been adapted, in varying degrees, in other constitutional orders.

The object of the separation, as Montesquieu puts it, is to check the other branches by use of the power of refusal.[58] He goes on to say: 'These three powers should naturally form a state of repose or inaction. But as there is necessity for movement in the course of human affairs, they are forced to move, but still to move in concert.'[59] Given the difficulty of coordination as between the branches, under Montesquieu's system, 'divided power results in citizens being less governed'.[60] The separation of powers serves, in other words, as a potential veto on movement on the part of the other two branches. According to Tsebelis's game-theoretic account, constitutional courts are 'veto players' insofar as they block legislative change and 'cannot be overruled by the political system'.[61] This is in contrast to circumstances where the legislative branch can overrule judicial interpretation, as might happen when courts interpret statutes in ways that legislators find objectionable. By narrowing the 'winset' of agreement required to upset the status quo to three branches, constitutional systems enhance policy stability, Tsebelis writes.[62] Recall Paulsson's claim that arbitrators are 'omnipotent' because they cannot be easily overruled.[63] This renders investment arbitrators, practically speaking, veto players in the functioning of host state constitutional systems.

Tsebelis is less concerned with the judicial veto in operative democratic systems because of the method for high court judicial appointment. In the USA, for instance, appointments require nomination by the President together with the advice and consent of the Senate. This facilitates some degree of consensus among the political branches that 'eliminate[s] extreme positions, and practically guarantee[s] that the median of the

[55] It was better conceived as balanced as between the monarch, the lords, and the commons. See W. B. Gwyn, *The Meaning of the Separation of Powers: An Analysis of the Doctrine from its Origin to the Adoption of the United States Constitution* (Martinus Nijhoff, 1965), 108; M. J. C. Vile, *Constitutionalism and the Separation of Powers*, 2nd edn (Liberty Fund, 1998), 93.

[56] Baron de Montesquieu, *The Spirit of the Laws*, trans. Thomas Nugent (Hafner Press, 1949), bk 11, ch. 6; Bernard Manin, 'Montesquieu', in François Furet and Mona Ozouf (eds), *The Critical Dictionary of the French Revolution*, trans. Arthur Goldhammer (Belknap Press, 1989), 734.

[57] A short version of the separation of powers' intellectual history is taken up in David Schneiderman, *Red, White and Kind of Blue? The Conservatives and the Americanization of Canadian Constitutional Culture* (University of Toronto Press, 2015), ch. 3. For a more robust history, see Gwyn (n. 55), and Vile (n. 55).

[58] Montesquieu (n. 56), 160. [59] Ibid.

[60] Pierre Manent, trans. Rebecca Balinski, *An Intellectual History of Liberalism* (Princeton University Press, 1995), 62.

[61] George Tsebelis, *Veto Players: How Political Institutions Work* (Princeton University Press, 2002), 226.

[62] Ibid. 21. [63] Paulsson (n. 1), 16.

court will be centrally located in the policy space'.[64] In other words, consensus-seeking methods of judicial selection will ensure that judges are not ideological outliers but rather are 'absorbed' (or embedded) within the host state policy arena.

This is not the case for a majority, if not for all, of the members of an investment arbitration tribunal. If, in the usual case, nominees appointed by state parties will be expected to be more 'sympathetic' to the respondent's point of view,[65] this will not always (and, to many, should not) be the case.[66] State appointees may not be ideologically aligned with host state national politics—indeed, in the case of ICSID appointment, no tribunal member is permitted to be a national of either party, unless agreed otherwise.[67] Nor should we expect tribunals to be 'centrally located' in host state policy space. Tsebelis' account may help to explain why apex courts in operative democracies do not stray too far from the centre of gravity of national politics. It does not, however, generate solace for those concerned with the unchecked expansion of investment arbitration.

There are, of course, some checks available to states and citizens. They include drafting new language that can be negotiated in future treaty text, issuing interpretive directives, or renegotiating old text along new lines.[68] States, in short, have some mechanisms of control to redirect investment arbitration along alternative pathways.[69] There are limits to this capacity for control, however. The NAFTA Free Trade Commission, for instance, has the power to issue directives that are 'binding on a tribunal' (Art. 1131), yet its 31 July 2001 'Note of Interpretation' was not very successful in containing arbitral interpretation of NAFTA's minimum standard of treatment.[70] As arbitrators exhibit less restraint than have national high courts in similar circumstances,[71] it is unrealistic to expect arbitrators to exercise much prudence (outside of politically salient disputes and disputes launched against the United States). There is nothing, in sum, analogous to an

[64] Tsebelis (n. 61), 227.

[65] Doak Bishop and Lucy Reed, 'Practical Guidelines for Interviewing, Selecting and Challenging Party-Appointed Arbitrators in international Commercial Arbitration', 14 Arbitration Int'l 395 (1998), 405.

[66] Charles Brower and Charles Rosenberg, 'The Death of the Two-Headed Nightingale: Why the Paulsson–van den Berg Presumption that Party-Appointed Arbitrators are Untrustworthy is Wrongheaded', 29 Arbitration Int'l 7 (2013), 15.

[67] International Centre for Settlement of Investment Disputes, 'ICSID Convention, Regulations and Rules', (ICSID 2006), Rule 1.3.

[68] The proposal for a so-called 'investment court' is not taken up here as it purports to be a significant departure from investment arbitration, even as it calls upon investment lawyers and arbitrators to serve as adjudicators. For my assessment of the proposal, as revealed in recent EU treaties with Canada and Vietnam, see David Schneiderman, 'Investment Law's Unending Legitimacy Project', 49 Loyola University of Chicago Law Journal 229 (2017), 249–53.

[69] Anthea Roberts, 'Power and Persuasion in Investment Treaty Interpretation: The Dual Role of States', 104 Am. J. of Int'l L. 179 (2008); Jason Webb Yackee, 'Controlling the International Investment Law Agency', 53 Harvard J. of Int'l L. 391 (2012).

[70] E.g. *Mondev International Ltd v United States*, Award, ICSID Case No. ARB (AF)/99/2 (2002). But see *Glamis Gold Ltd v United States*, Award, Ad hoc--UNCITRAL Arbitration Rules (2009).

[71] Gus Van Harten, *Sovereign Choices and Sovereign Restraints: Judicial Restraint in Investment Treaty Arbitration* (Oxford University Press, 2013), 159.

elected legislature that can serve as a corrective to arbitral misinterpretation.[72] Finally, there is the option of exiting entirely from the system. Exit, however, is considered a perilous path for states desirous of signaling their openness to foreign investment. Other means of promoting inward investment—in South Africa, via sectoral charters, or in Brazil, via new cooperation and investment facilitation agreements—may serve to promote economic development, more effectively, perhaps, than investment treaties have done to date.[73] The threat of investor flight, however theoretical in reality, continues to discourage the exit option.[74]

Having explored the constitution-like functions served by investment arbitration and accompanying normative concerns, in the next section I turn to examples where, in the course of issuing reasons, investment tribunals have had occasion to interpret national constitutional text.

In addition to other cases, I closely examine one such dispute, *Teco v Guatemala*. The discussion is meant to underscore the constitution-like functions served by investment arbitration in the course of issuing reasons, and the problematic interpretive tilt that is often exhibited.

17.3 Constitutional Linkages

Investment tribunals will engage with a variety of host state laws including, on occasion, constitutional law. Host-state laws may be applicable or relevant to a dispute, for instance, in determining whether investors have cognizable legal rights or whether investment treaty standards have been violated.[75] When such opportunities arise, a tribunal might interpret constitutional text or consider appellate review of the constitution. The worry is that, on such occasions, a tribunal will misconstrue what the constitution, in fact, requires.

This lamentably turns out to have been the case in *Metalclad v Mexico*.[76] The tribunal took the dispute as an opportunity to ascertain the constitutional capacity of the municipality of Guadalcazar to issue a building permit for remediation of a hazardous waste facility site. The site previously was shut down by order of the Mexican federal government because of the leaching of chemicals into the local water supply. Rehabilitation of

[72] Möllers (n. 45), 158.

[73] Jason Webb Yackee, 'Bilateral Investment Treaties, Credible Commitment, and the Rule of (International) Law: Do BITs Promote Foreign Direct Investment?', 42 L. & Society Rev. 805 (2008); Christian Bellak, 'Economic Impact of Investment Agreements', Working Paper No. 200 (Vienna University of Economics and Business 2015): <https://epub.wu.ac.at/4625/1/wp200.pdf>.

[74] Penelope Simons and Audrey Macklin, *The Governance Gap: Extractive Industries, Human Rights, and the Home State Advantage* (Routledge, 2014), 350. Simons and Macklin argue that the worry about investor flight is overstated and 'losing its potency'.

[75] This distinction is emphasized by Douglas (n. 52), 41.

[76] *Metalclad Corp v Mexico*, Award, Ad hoc—ICSID Additional Facility Rules, ICSID Case No. ARB(AF)/97/1 (2000). This aspect of the dispute is discussed in more detail in Schneiderman (n. 38), 82–4.

the site, now under new ownership and with, the initial encouragement of governments at federal and state levels, was not welcomed by the local city council. The company refused, initially, to engage with the municipality, denying that there was any requirement to procure a municipal construction permit, even though the previous owner had done just this. The investor eventually did apply at the urging of the federal government in order to maintain 'amicable' relations.[77]

As a consequence of the municipality unanimously refusing to grant the permit, the tribunal concluded that there was a denial of NAFTA's minimum standard of treatment under international law. In addition to fairness concerns, this was also because the municipality had no authority to deny the construction permit on environmental grounds. Rather, the municipality's authority was confined to a determination of whether 'appropriate construction considerations' had been satisfied, namely, 'physical construction or defects in that site'.[78] In other words, the tribunal was of the opinion that the city did not have constitutional authority to take into account environmental concerns when determining whether to issue a municipal construction permit. The government of Mexico proffered expert evidence from three constitutional experts, including two former jurists on the Mexican Supreme Court, opining that it was entirely within the constitutional authority of the municipality to consider environmental effects. Without explanation, the tribunal preferred the evidence of the claimant's expert, an American national who was pursuing a master of laws at the University of Monterey.[79]

In *CMS v Argentina*, the tribunal took sides in an interpretive dispute over the meaning of the Argentinian constitutional right to property.[80] The context was the 2001 collapse of the Argentinian economy and the de-linking of the peso with the U.S. dollar, resulting in massive losses to foreign investors who had bought into the privatization wave of the 1990s. CMS, owning about 30 per cent of the shares in a gas transportation company, sought damages in the wake of the Argentine government's measures. Those measures had the effect of investors sharing, along with locals, in the burden of economic loss. The tribunal rejected the argument that the Argentine government was respectful of constitutional commitments to property. After all, the tribunal observed, the constitution 'carefully protects the right to property'.[81] In its construction of Argentina's constitutional text, the tribunal preferred an aberrant interpretation of the constitutional property clause by the Argentinian high court, one declaring the government's emergency measures a 'flagrant violation' of constitutional property rights.[82] Both prior and subsequent to that ruling, the Argentine Supreme Court permitted all variety of intrusions into private property realms. The tribunal weighed in on the

[77] *Metalclad Corp v Mexico* (n. 76), para. 41. [78] Ibid. paras. 68, 86.

[79] *The United Mexican States v Metalclad Corp*, Petitioner's Outline of Argument, Supreme Court of British Columbia No. L002904 (2001), paras. 423–6.

[80] This aspect of the dispute is discussed in more detail in David Schneiderman, *Resisting Economic Globalization: Critical Theory and International Investment Law* (Palgrave Macmillan, 2013), 46–7.

[81] *CMS Gas Transmission Company v Argentina*, Award, ICSID Case No. ARB/01/8 (2005), para. 121.

[82] Horacio Spector, 'Constitutional Transplants and the Mutation Effect', 83 Chicago-Kent L. Rev. 129 (2008), 140.

controversy by preferring one side over the other—the one that had, for a time, resurrected the discredited late nineteenth-century doctrine associated with vested rights.[83]

The linkages between constitutional law and international investment law were plainly on display in the dispute between Florida-based Teco and the Republic of Guatemala. The tribunal emerged as a constitutional arbiter, of a sort, practically over-ruling opinions of the Guatemalan Constitutional Court. At issue was the ambit of authority granted to the Guatemalan National Electricity Commission (the 'regulator') to set electricity rates. The statutory regime contemplated that the regulator would consult an expert commission in order to minimize the influence of 'politics' on rate-setting. The commission was expected to recommend rates that would offset the costs of a model 'efficient' company.[84] In this instance, the regulator dissolved the expert commission after receiving its report, and relied instead upon another independent assessment when setting electricity rates. Having set rates without relying upon the expert commission, the regulator had deprived the investor of its expected rate of return, and thereby had denied it fair and equitable treatment under the Free Trade Agreement between the Dominican Republic, the United States, and Central America (CAFTA-DR).[85] No reasonable investor, it was claimed, would have invested in Guatemala's electricity sector without this 'independent check' on the 'Government's rate-setting power'.[86]

The investor's local operator separately pursued *amparo* proceedings in Guatemalan courts, seeking to vindicate its constitutional rights.[87] These claims were initially accepted in lower court rulings, describing the regulator's actions as offending 'due process' rights under the constitution in addition to violating the relevant statutory regime.[88] The Guatemalan Constitutional Court reversed these rulings in 2009 and 2010. The Electricity Commission, the court concluded in its May 2009 decision, was not legally bound to follow the advice of the independent expert commission; rather, the regulator solely had the power to set tariffs. The constitution 'forbids the delegation of duties, unless authorized by law,' the court declared.[89] No such delegation of power was available here. Conferring such a power on an expert 'assistant', the court ruled, breached

[83] Ibid.; *CMS Gas Transmission Company v Argentina*, Award, ICSID Case No. ARB/01/8 (2005), para. 141.

[84] *Teco Guatemala Holdings LLC v The Republic of Guatemala*, Memorial on Objections to Jurisdiction and Admissibility and Counter-Memorial on the Merits (2012), para. 146.

[85] The investor claimed that the legal regime expected to guarantee a real rate of return of 7–13%, adjusted for inflation in *Teco Guatemala Holdings LLC v The Republic of Guatemala*, Claimant's Memorial (2011), para. 261.

[86] Ibid. para. 260.

[87] The relevant part of Art. 12 of the Guatemalan Constitution provides: 'No one may be sentenced or deprived from his [or her] rights, without being summoned, heard and defeated in a legal process before a competent and pre-established judge and tribunal.'

[88] *Teco Guatemala Holdings LLC v The Republic of Guatemala*, Claimant's Memorial (2011), para. 274.

[89] *Teco Guatemala Holdings LLC v The Republic of Guatemala*, Award, ICSID Case No. ARB/10/17 (2013), para. 234; *Case File No. 1836-1846-2009*, Constitutional Court of Guatemala, 31 (18 November 2009). Art. 154 of the Guatemalan Constitution provides, in part: 'The public function may not be delegated, except in the cases specified by the law, and it may not be exercised without a previous oath of loyalty to the Constitution.'

the principle of legality that was characteristic of the rule of law.[90] It was these passages in the court's opinion that the tribunal relied upon in finding for the investor. The tribunal insisted that the Constitutional Court had not addressed the question of procedural abuse under the constitution, leaving room for the tribunal to find a violation of due process.

However, the court did outline the contents of what due process rights under the constitution entailed. 'The right to due process acknowledged in the Political Constitution of the Republic,' the majority of the Court declared:

> allows an individual or legal entity to have access to the judicial or administrative proceedings established by law, whereby such persons and entities may be permitted to exercise their freedom to begin a proceeding, to appear before the competent authorities, to follow the relevant procedures and steps, submit and object to evidence, plead their interests and to obtain a resolution based on the law. It also provides the possibility of challenging the decision and abiding by the conclusiveness of the proceedings.[91]

Applying these considerations, the court concluded that the right of due process 'has been respected in all its phases'.[92] The regulator had the power 'to resolve the matter; thereby forming its own judgment based on the facts or information gained from exercising competence and other aspects that contribute to a determination of the facts', and did so in accordance with due process.[93]

In taking jurisdiction, the tribunal admitted it would be obliged to consider Guatemalan constitutional law, but denied that it would be acting as an appellate court. Instead, the tribunal maintained that it would apply only international law, all the while deferring to the findings of the Constitutional Court.[94] It was international treaty law and not Guatemalan constitutional law that was applicable law—the tribunal was considering a 'different dispute' based on 'different legal rules'.[95] As a consequence, the court's rulings were not 'binding'. It is noteworthy that, in an investment dispute launched by a majority shareholder in the same local company, Madrid-based Iberdrola, arising out of the same set of facts, another tribunal declined to take jurisdiction. According to the *Iberdrola* tribunal, the claimant's arguments amounted to 'no more than a discussion of local law, which it [the tribunal] is not competent to take up and resolve again as if it were a court of appeal'.[96]

[90] *Teco Guatemala Holdings LLC v The Republic of Guatemala* (n. 89), para. 235; Case File No. 1836-1846-2009 (n. 89), 29 (18 November 2009).

[91] Ibid. 24 (18 November 2009).

[92] Ibid. 32.

[93] *Teco Guatemala Holdings LLC v The Republic of Guatemala*, Memorial on Objections to Jurisdiction and Admissibility and Counter-Memorial on the Merits (2012), para. 212; *Case File No. 1836-1846-2009*, Constitutional Court of Guatemala, at 26 (18 November 2009).

[94] *Teco Guatemala Holdings LLC v The Republic of Guatemala*, Award, ICSID Case No. ARB/10/17 (2013), para. 477.

[95] Ibid. para. 517.

[96] *Iberdrola Energía S.A. v The Republic of Guatemala*, Award, ICSID Case No. ARB/09/05 (2012), para. 349. The tribunal accepted jurisdiction in respect of Iberdrola's denial of justice claim which, at

By contrast, the *Teco* tribunal was prepared to entertain the claim. In the course of explaining why the Teco claim could proceed, the tribunal relied upon a passage in the Constitutional Court ruling indicating that the court had refrained from addressing the 'rationality' of the tariff.[97] This could be understood in one of two ways, observed the tribunal. The court could have been referring either to the 'content of the tariff' or to the 'process leading to its establishment'.[98] Because the Constitutional Court addressed the question of whether an expert commission could bind the regulator, which the tribunal interpreted as having to do with content of the tariff, the question of process deliberately was left open. The court's ruling did not, the tribunal concluded, preclude consideration of the regulator's procedural conduct.

Yet, as mentioned, the Constitutional Court in its May 2009 judgment directly addressed the question of process. The court concluded that the 'right to due process invoked in the amparo action herein has been respected in all its phases'.[99] The court declined to review the 'rationality of the tariff' and, instead, responded to the 'only damage reported... based on the concept of legal due process'.[100] The Constitutional Court's ruling of 18 November 2009 was explicit that it had not reviewed the 'rationality of the tariff' but 'only focused on the concept of due legal process'.[101] The tribunal in *Iberdrola* accepted that the court had declined, in this passage, to rule on the 'reasonableness of the tariffs'.[102] The *Teco* tribunal, by contrast, took up an interpretation that was in direct conflict with the court's own clearly stated declarations.

By ignoring material parts of the constitutional ruling, the tribunal could then find a violation of the international minimum standard of treatment.[103] The Electricity Commission had a 'duty, under the regulatory framework, to give them [the Expert Commission] serious consideration and to provide valid reasons in case it decided to depart from them'.[104] To do otherwise amounted to arbitrariness, violating both the Guatemalan legal framework and the minimum standard of treatment.[105] The regulator, in other words, did not have unlimited discretion to set rates but, instead, was expected to follow a certain process mandated by national and international law.

In ICSID annulment proceedings, Guatemala alleged that the tribunal manifestly exceeded its powers by taking up a dispute already litigated under Guatemalan courts.

bottom, amounted to a mere 'disagreement' with the Guatemalan Constitutional Court (para. 491). At the time of writing, the claimant has launched a new dispute, presumably on the grounds accepted by the *Teco* tribunal, at the Permanent Court of Arbitration. See *Iberdrola Energía, S.A. v Republic of Guatemala*, Case No. 2-17-42: https://pca-cpa.org/en/cases/162/.

[97] *Case File No. 1836-1846-2009*, Constitutional Court of Guatemala, at 33 (18 November 2009).

[98] *Teco Guatemala Holdings LLC v The Republic of Guatemala*, Award, ICSID Case No. ARB/10/17 (2013), para. 563.

[99] *Case File No. 1836-1846-2009*, Constitutional Court of Guatemala, 32 (18 November 2009).

[100] Ibid. 33. [101] Ibid.

[102] This passage in the 18 November 2009 Constitutional Court decision is quoted in *Iberdrola Energía S.A. v The Republic of Guatemala*, Award, ICSID Case No. ARB/09/05 (2012), para. 469.

[103] *Teco Guatemala Holdings LLC v The Republic of Guatemala*, Award, ICSID Case No. ARB/10/17 (2013), paras. 490–92.

[104] Ibid. para. 562. [105] Ibid. paras. 680–82.

Investment tribunals are not meant to undertake administrative review to ensure compliance with local law, it was argued.[106] The Annulment Committee, operating under its restrictive terms of reference,[107] concluded that the tribunal's decision was 'tenable as a matter of law'.[108] The tribunal had interpreted the Constitutional Court ruling as not precluding a finding that the regulator was obliged to 'seriously consider' the expert report and 'provide reasons' why it chose to depart from its recommendations. The regulator, in the words of the Annulment Committee, 'did not enjoy unlimited discretion'.[109] The tribunal acted properly in respecting the Constitutional Court's rulings, the Annulment Committee declared, while answering questions left open—matters upon which it had 'not pronounced itself'.[110]

As I have argued, the Constitutional Court directly addressed the charge that there were procedural defects, and found none. Indeed, the court laid down a number of features associated with the constitutional guarantee of due process—matters, in the common law world, associated with the idea of 'natural justice'—and found that they were not violated. In the words of the court, the regulator could 'form its own judgment' so long as this was done in accordance with constitutional due process rights.[111] The tribunal chose not to 'defer' to this part of the court's opinion and, instead, pretty much ignored it. In proceeding in this fashion, the tribunal diverged substantially from the court's ruling, and granted greater rights to the investor than those available under the Guatemalan constitution. The tribunal award, in this way, looks like a form of 'informal' constitutional rule that upsets and supersedes, practically speaking, host state constitutional law.[112]

It is not often that investment arbitration tribunals address national constitutional law in the course of issuing reasons. On the few occasions when they do, as highlighted in this section, tribunals have not performed so well. National constitutional law is sometimes distorted in order to suit the imperatives of international investment law, tilting in favour of investor protection and the mitigation of political risk. One wishes

[106] *Teco Guatemala Holdings LLC v The Republic of Guatemala*, Decision on Annulment, ICSID Case No. ARB/10/23 (2016), para. 205. Guatemala, at the initial hearing and in the annulment proceedings, alleged that the investor's only complaint under international treaty was a 'denial of justice' claim, which it chose not to pursue. The tribunal, thereby, 'put itself in the shoes of an international appellate court'. The Annulment Committee disagreed (see paras. 265, 291).

[107] Christoph Schreuer, *The ICSID Convention: A Commentary*, 2nd edn (Cambridge University Press, 2009), 900–04.

[108] *Teco Guatemala Holdings LLC v The Republic of Guatemala*, Decision on Annulment, ICSID Case No. ARB/10/23 (2016), para. 222.

[109] Ibid. para. 290. [110] Ibid. para. 291.

[111] *Case File No. 1836-1846-2009*, Constitutional Court of Guatemala, 26 (18 November 2009).

[112] James Tully, 'On Local and Global Citizenship: An Apprenticeship Manual', in *Public Philosophy in a New Key*, vol. 2: *Imperialism and Civic Freedom* (Cambridge University Press, 2008), 260. It is noteworthy that there were two dissenting justices to the Constitutional Court's May 2009 reasons. The dissenting justices concluded, as did the tribunal, that the regulator's conduct ran afoul of Guatemalan law. That the tribunal's conclusions may have echoed those of the justices was 'irrelevant', the Annulment Committee concluded. What mattered was the Constitutional Court's majority decision, which, in the opinion of the tribunal, left an opening to find arbitrariness. See *Teco Guatemala Holdings LLC v The Republic of Guatemala*, Decision on Annulment, ICSID Case No ARB/10/23 (2016), para. 299.

that tribunals would approach this task a little more carefully, as did the *Iberdrola* tribunal, with a measure of deference and an appreciation for the constitutional values at stake.

17.4 Constitutional Absence?

Is this unappealable form of judicial review—one that might distort national constitutional principles—justifiable? One of the difficulties of 'stretching' the constitutional analogy beyond the nation state is the absence of global *demos*[113]—a political community having the constituent authority to establish a new constitutional order. If not among the people of the world, where might that source of constituent authority reside? Investment law scholars have not shown much interest in this question. Scholarship in global constitutional law, by contrast, has been seeking out sources of constituent authority. For some, the source with which to legitimate new transnational legal orders are national political ones that have authored systems of global law. This is how Habermas explains away legitimacy problems associated with the rise of the WTO. The mechanisms of opinion and will formation within states, he writes, generate 'chains of legitimation' with which transnational legal institutions can produce binding law.[114]

Others aim to relocate constituent authority from the self-governing people to the judicial branches. This is how sociologist Christopher Thornhill theorizes the establishment of an emergent constitutional order on a global scale.[115] This scholarly innovation, which privileges judicial functions, bears a striking resemblance to a strand of investment law scholarship that seeks to justify the assignment of authority to investment tribunals in the interests of promoting the 'rule of law'.[116] In this section, I examine the argument that investment tribunals stand in for the constituent authority of the people.

[113] Walker (n. 40), 521. Bogdandy and Venzke write that a constitutionalist argument 'does not convince', in Armin von Bogdandy and Ingo Venzke, 'In Whose Name? An Investigation of International Court's Public Authority and Its Democratic Justification', 23 European Journal of International Law 7 (2012), 22.

[114] Jürgen Habermas, 'The Constitutionalization of International Law and the Legitimation Problems of a Constitution for World Society', 15 Constellations 444 (2008), 447; Jürgen Habermas, 'Euroskepticism, Market Europe, or a Europe of (World) Citizens', in Jürgen Habermas, *Time of Transitions*. trans. Ciarin Cronin and Max Pensky (Polity Press, 2006), 81; Jürgen Habermas, 'The European Nation-State and the Pressures of Globalization', in Pablo de Greiff and Ciran Cronin (eds), *Global Justice and Transnational Politics* (MIT Press, 2002), 224.

[115] Chris Thornhill, *A Sociology of Transnational Constitutions: Social Foundations of the Post-National Legal Structure* (Cambridge University Press, 2016).

[116] E.g. Thomas Walde, 'Renegotiating Acquired Rights in the Oil and Gas Industries: Industry and Political Cycles Meet the Rule of Law', 1 Journal of World Energy Law & Business 55 (2008), 57, n. 11; Stephan Schill, '"Fair and Equitable Treatment" as an Embodiment of the Rule of Law', in Rainer Hofmann and Christian Tams (eds), *The International Convention On The Settlement Of Investment Disputes (ICSID): Taking Stock After 40 Years* (Nomos, 2007), 31.

While Thornhill's project is to render global constitutional law more legitimate, my hope is that readers will see the advantages of proceeding in a critical constitutional mode.

If, according to classical democratic accounts, the people were considered the proper constituent authority,[117] the judiciary now serves as their proxy. Thornhill asserts that '[e]ffective constitutent power is freely accorded to judicial institutions applying transnational norms'.[118] The judiciary are accorded this authority because they shield political systems from themselves—from pressures for inclusion that confront states but which they are incapable of satisfying.[119] By inclusion, Thornhill refers to the inability of national states to fully absorb, and thereby govern, their internally differentiated and pluralistic polities. Incorporating international human rights norms within national constitutional structures renders states better able to respond to these neglected constituencies, and better equipped to absorb the excluded within existing political institutions. Thornhill designates as inclusion failures the inability of national legal orders to respond to human rights claims, refugee rights, minority rights, or the rights of citizens in combat zones. Each group of rights claimants would have remained excluded were it not for international human rights norms and institutions acting as a backstop.[120] With such reciprocal arrangements in place, states can transfer some responsibility upwards to international institutions while incorporating international human rights norms downwards, into local legislation via a process of 'inner-legal construction'.[121]

It is commitment to these and other human rights norms that the judiciary further anchors within national legal orders. Demands for inclusion, Thornhill insists, could not otherwise 'be sustained by national laws alone'.[122] The reciprocal movement between global and local has the beneficial effect of enhancing the legitimacy of states, Thornhill maintains, by insulating them from 'destabilizing pressures'.[123] It is upon this ground that the European Union, for instance, has constructed its 'emergent transnational constitution'.[124] Other regional and international courts perform similar functions, articulating principles that are often internalized by national courts into 'norms with effective or near-constitutional force... forming a many-tiered supranational constitution'.[125] With judges exercising norm-making authority, 'few laws can be seen

[117] Emmanuel Joseph Sieyès, 'What Is the Third Estate?' in *Political Writings*, trans. Michael Sonenscher (Hackett, 2003), 133. Thornhill persuasively argues in later work that the ideal has hardly touched ground with the real. There are, he maintains, few European examples of constituent authority being exercised by the people. There even were 'few Member States', he writes, that 'were formed as fully evolved democracies before their integration into the EU': Chris Thornhill, 'A Tale of Two Constitutions: Whose Legitimacy? Whose Crisis?' in William Outhwaite (ed.), *Brexit: Sociological Responses* (Anthem, 2017), 77, 82.

[118] Chris Thornhill, 'Contemporary Constitutionalism and the Dialectic of Constituent Power', 1 Global Constitutionalism 369 (2012), 371.

[119] Thornhill appears to be following Luhmann, who describes the binary inclusion–exclusion as a 'kind of meta-code' in Niklas Luhmann, *Law as a Social System*, trans. Klaus A. Ziegert (Oxford University Press, 2004), 489. See Thornhill (n. 125), 9, n. 5. As he put it in a jointly authored book on Luhmann, inclusivity 'in short is both the reality and the precondition of modern democracy': Michael King and Chris Thornhill, *Niklas Luhmann's Theory of Politics and Law* (Palgrave, 2003), 83.

[120] Thornhill (n. 115), 106–16. [121] Ibid. 128, 384. [122] Ibid. 25. [123] Ibid. 23, 25, 26.

[124] Thornhill (n. 118), 371. [125] Ibid. 372.

clearly to originate in primary constituent acts'. Instead, that function has migrated to 'numerous institutions, but mainly constituted judicial bodies located between national polities and supranational legal domains, [which] assume powers of constitution making'.[126] Constituent power is now 'intrinsically juridified',[127] giving rise to a 'distinct transnational constitution'.[128]

Thornhill's sociological account is compelling insofar as he understands transnational legal processes as intertwined with national legal ones. Nation-states do not disappear, but are assimilated into larger processes in which they remain significant actors. Each sphere 'dialectically interpenetrate[s]' the other, and they are 'reciprocally formative', he declares.[129] This account is congenial with Kjaer's account of 'modern statehood' and transnational legal ordering as emerging 'hand in hand'.[130] It also is congenial with Macklem, who ascribes to international human rights law the role of mitigating the adverse effects of the international law's recognition of state sovereignty. Human rights, for Macklem, 'operate in international law to secure a measure of legitimacy for the role that sovereignty plays in constituting the structure of the international legal order'.[131] International human rights thereby serve the end of correcting pathologies of international law's own making. For Thornhill, transnational law similarly operates to insulate states from inclusion failures, thereby enhancing the legitimacy of the sovereignty accorded to states under international law.

Though he prefers to base his account on human rights courts, Thornhill's argument also is congenial with narratives embraced by investment lawyers and arbitrators: that an international judiciary saves states from themselves. The investment law bar claims that host state political and legal processes are defective, even biased, against foreign investors, whose interests are not well taken into account.[132] The investment bar articulates unspecified worries about 'institutionalized bias' in favour of local nationals and a lack of neutrality in local courts.[133] As the Clayton tribunal self-servingly put it, resolving disputes before investment tribunals offers 'independence and detachment from domestic pressures' that are not available to local courts.[134] International adjudication is meant to remedy defects by defending norms that, it is hoped, will become internalized within host state legal orders.[135]

[126] Ibid. 374. [127] Ibid. [128] Thornhill (n. 115), 8. [129] Thornhill n. 117, 24.

[130] Poul Kjaer, *Constitutionalism in the Global Realm: A Sociological Approach* (Routledge, 2014), 17.

[131] Patrick Macklem, *The Sovereignty of Human Rights* (Oxford University Press, 2015), 40.

[132] *Técnicas Medioambientales Tecmed SA v Mexico*, Award, ICSID Case No ARB(AF)/00/2 (2003), para. 122.

[133] Won-Mog Choi, 'The Present and Future of the Investor-State Dispute Settlement Paradigm', 10 J. of Int'l Economic L. 725 (2007), 735.

[134] *Clayton v Canada*, Award on Jurisdiction and Liability, Permanent Court of Arbitration, Case No. 2009-04 (2015), para. 439.

[135] See e.g. Keneth Vandevelde, 'The Political Economy of a Bilateral Investment Treaty', 92 American Journal of International Law 621 (1998), 639; Michael Hart and William Dymond, 'NAFTA Chapter 11: Precedents, Principles, and Prospects', in Laura Dawson (ed.), *Whose Rights? The NAFTA Chapter 11 Debate* (Centre for Trade Policy and Law, 2002), 128, 168.

There are many difficulties with this judicialized account of constitutional formation. They flow, in part, from Thornhill's drawing out of hard-to-sustain generalizations from the transnational legal scene. As I argued in Section 17.2, it seems methodologically perilous to engage in grand theorizing about a global constitutional order. There are, in addition, normative implications to this sociological account that are worth highlighting.[136] I turn to these descriptive and normative deficiencies in the discussion that follows.

17.4.1 Voice

Thornhill insists that pressures for inclusion cannot be accommodated by 'national laws alone'.[137] In the investment arbitration context, one hears similar complaints about the failure of local law to include foreign investors.[138] Even if not well substantiated,[139] the claim is that investors are not taken into account in the production of host state law and policy. Instead, investors (and states) are able to rely upon international adjudication that acts as a backstop to national constitutional orders falling short of a general minimum standard of treatment abroad that purport to mimic national constitutional experiences.[140]

To this end, investment arbitration serves the purposes that Madison's design served in the 1787 U.S. Constitution: as a means of checking the influence of pluralist competition on self-governing majorities.[141] The analogy is not that far-fetched. The USTR insists, as mentioned, that investment treaty norms mirror rights available to U.S. citizens under the U.S. constitution. This helps to explain why the U.S. has not yet lost a NAFTA dispute, USTR argues. As a consequence, the executive branch insists that the U.S. must 'continue to write the rules' for the global economy.[142] It may be more accurate to say that investment treaty standards of protection exceed protections

[136] Thornhill purports to be making a contribution to normative political inquiry. See Chris Thornhill, 'Towards a Historical Sociology of Constitutional Legitimacy', 37 Theor. Soc. (2008), 168.

[137] Thornhill (n. 115), 25.

[138] E.g. *Técnicas Medioambientales Tecmed SA v Mexico*, Award, ICSID Case No. ARB(AF)/00/2 (2003), para. 122.

[139] See e.g. Emma Aisbett and Lauge Poulsen, 'Relative Treatment of Aliens: Firm-Level Evidence from Developing Countries', Working Paper 122 (2016): <http://www.geg.ox.ac.uk/geg-wp-2016122-relative-treatment-aliens-firm-level-evidence-developing-countries>.

[140] Harnack House Reflections, 'Essentials of a Modern Investment Protection Regime: Objectives and Recommendations for Action' (2015): <http://www.jura.fu-berlin.de/fachbereich/einrichtungen/oeffentliches-recht/lehrende/hindelangs/Harnack-House/Harnack-House-Reflections-Investment-Protection-ENG.pdf>.

[141] Thomas Wälde and Abba Kolo, 'Environmental Regulation, Investment Protection and "Regulatory Taking" in International Law', 50 International and Comparative Law Quarterly 811 (2001), 847.

[142] United States Trade Representative, 'The Facts on Investor–State Dispute Settlement' *Tradewinds: The Official Blog of the United States Trade Representative* (USTR 2014): <https://ustr.gov/about-us/policy-offices/press-office/blog/2014/March/Facts-Investor-State%20Dispute-Settlement-Safeguarding-Public-Interest-Protecting-Investors>.

available to citizens in most developed states.[143] In which case, it is correct to say these are demands that are not satisfied by national laws alone.[144]

But why should foreign investors be granted such privileged access to legal processes that offer the highest standards of protection known to international and municipal law? As Jeremy Waldron observes, 'no such certainty is available in any other realm of economic activity'. Waldron cautions that 'honest jurists working with the notion of the Rule of Law should have nothing to do with cynical uses of the ideal that are designed to do nothing more than underwrite the investor-profits of predatory and extractive enterprises'.[145]

Might investor concerns be better addressed by the adoption of different national legal processes rather than excessive ones out of proportion to expressed needs? A commitment to the common law principle of *audi alteram partem* ('listening to the other side') on the part of host states could address investor complaints that arise as a result of not being 'taken into account'.[146] What could be sought out are practices that best accommodate the inclusion of those that otherwise are overlooked—whether they be foreign nationals or affected communities. It is not that such processes are likely to produce consensus—dissatisfaction and disagreement are as likely to result—but they can help to sway, even shape, national policy outcomes. Admittedly only a procedural remedy, it could serve to ameliorate conditions giving rise to investment disputes in the first place.

17.4.2 Human rights

Another source of difficulty is the overdrawn claim that the content of transnational law originates out of international human rights norms. It is in these origins that an international judiciary gains the requisite legitimacy to assume constituent authority. Human rights provide an 'underpinning', Thornhill writes, for constituent power of judicial interpretation 'without recourse to primary political acts'.[147] I argued above that investment treaty protections channel some of the language and norms that can be found in national constitutional texts of capital-exporting states. Yet it appears to be the case that arbitrators operate some distance removed from the fields of human rights,

143 See David Schneiderman, '"Writing the Rules of the Global Economy": How America Defines the Contours of International Investment Law', London Review of International Law 6 London Review of International Law 255 (2018).

144 Armand de Mestral and Robin Morgan, 'Does Canadian Law Provide Remedies Equivalent to NAFTA Chapter 11 Arbitration?' in Armand de Mestral (ed.), *Second Thoughts: Investor–State Arbitration Between Developed Democracies* (CIGI, 2017); Lise Johnston and Oleksander Volkov, 'Investor–State Contracts, Host-State "Commitments" and the Myth of Stability in International Law', 24 Am. Rev. of Int'l Arbitration 361 (2013).

145 Jeremy Waldron, *The Rule of Law and the Measure of Property* (Cambridge University Press, 2012), 73.

146 David Schneiderman, 'Listening to Investors (and Others): *Audi Alteram Partem* and the Future of International Investment Law', in de Mestral (n. 144), 131.

147 Thornhill (n. 115), 368.

national or international.[148] References to human rights in investment arbitration are described as 'sparse and infrequent'[149]—its norms treated as 'non-significant.'[150] One could safely say that there has been some resistance to the incorporation of human rights into investment law's domains.[151]

There is no question that investment treaty standards encompass a robust form of property right, but even investors are disinclined to frame their claims in these terms. Why would they, when they can take advantage of broadly framed market participation rights that are given wide interpretation by arbitrators?[152] These are precisely the type of 'trade-related, market friendly human rights' that empower the already powerful.[153] Rather than merging human rights considerations into investment law's domains, never mind having those rights prevail in cases of conflict, investment lawyers and arbitrators prefer to manage, and thereby contain, their influence. Human rights, in other words, will continue to operate at a safe distance from investment treaty arbitration.[154] That this is the case may help to explain some of the legitimacy problems that have arisen in the field of investment arbitration.

Though he does not consider investment arbitration, Thornhill does consider the cognate field of trade law. WTO panels, he acknowledges, exhibit 'certain constitutional features'. At times, WTO rulings refer to general international law and 'even to international human rights'. In their functional areas of jurisdiction, the panels serve to 'fortify rights' held by individuals.[155] Thornhill admits that the WTO is not the ideal constitutional model for promoting inclusion, as its rights 'manifestly contradict some entrenched rights, especially social rights and rights of labour protection'.[156] Drawing an analogy between the rights of traders and international human rights is more contentious than Thornhill lets on. Alston argues that such an approach 'fundamentally redefine[s]' the 'contours' of international human rights law, twisting

[148] David Schneiderman, 'At the Borders of International Investment Arbitration and Human Rights', in Tsvi Kahana and Anat Scolnicov (eds), *Boundaries of States, Boundaries of Rights: Human Rights, Private Actors and Positive Obligations* (Cambridge University Press, 2016). For a more sanguine view of investment tribunal engagement with human rights, see Ursula Kriebaum, 'Human Rights and International Investment Arbitration', Ch. 6 in this volume.

[149] Clara Reiner and Christoph Schreuer, 'Human Rights and International Investment Arbitration', in Pierre-Marie Dupuy et al. (eds), *Human Rights In International Investment Law And Arbitration* (Oxford University Press, 2009), 82.

[150] Moshe Hirsch, *Invitation to the Sociology of International Law* (Oxford University Press, 2015), 129.

[151] Given this strategy of avoidance, Kriebaum can conclude that there has been 'no friction' or 'norm conflict' between human rights and investment arbitration. See Kriebaum, Ch. 6 this volume.

[152] Ernst-Ulrich Petersmann, 'International Rule of Law and Constitutional Justice in International Investment Law and Arbitration', 16 Indiana J. of Global L. Studies 513 (2009), 524.

[153] Upendra Baxi, *The Future of Human Rights*, 2nd edn (Oxford University Press, 2006), 258.

[154] The argument is more elaborately made, from a systems-theoretic perspective, in Schneiderman (n. 148).

[155] Thornhill (n. 115), 370–71. Thornhill admits that these rights also can be in tension with other rights enforced within national constitutional law. He might also have added, in tension with other international human rights instruments.

[156] Ibid. 371.

them into the service of Hayekian libertarianism.[157] Insofar as Thornhill can claim that the WTO system 'derives constitutional power from rights', it serves as a weak illustration of how judicial constitutionalization is justifiable with reference to human rights enforcement.

17.4.3 Enhancing power

There is also the problematic claim that the transnational constitution, authored by international adjudicators, enhances and reinforces the power of national states. Thornhill means by this that transnational constitutional law serves to reinforce the interests of national states by legitimating their authority, enabling them to function 'more autonomously and effectively'.[158] He admits that it would be absurd to claim that there is no 'curtail[ing of] certain competences of national states'. It is undeniable, he writes, that there exists a 'tension between international law and state sovereignty'.[159]

In the case of investment law, this is no mere tension: diminishing state authority is its *raison d'être*. Investment treaties inhibit state regulatory space in a wide range of policy domains. It is expected that treaty protections will be enforced by investment tribunals or, preferably, that states will internalize these limitations on their capacity for action as part of their learning about 'good governance'.[160] It is for this reason that the United Nations Conference for Trade and Development (UNCTAD) has declared the system is suffering from a 'legitimacy crisis', requiring reforms which 'ensure that states retain their right to regulate for pursuing public policy interests'.[161] Thornhill recognizes that some features of transnational constitutional law undermine state capacity by 'stabiliz[ing] neoliberal legal forms'.[162] He insists, nevertheless, that it will generally prop it up by prompting states to avoid inclusivity failures. Investment law does so, however, only by denuding states of their authority, removing capacities that otherwise were available to capital-exporting states as they were in the throes of developing their own economies.[163]

If investment law serves as a warrant, of sorts, to investors that their capital will be protected from diminution in value when states engage in conduct that runs afoul of treaty standards, we can connect that assurance with damage awards that enhance state indebtedness. Debt, for Lazzarato, is about 'stifling our possibilities for action'.[164] Investment arbitration, for this reason, turns out to be not only a mechanism for

[157] Philip Alston, 'Resisting the Merger and Acquisition of Human Rights by Trade Law: A Reply to Petersmann', 13 European Journal of International Law 815 (2002), 816.

[158] Thornhill (n. 115), 19. [159] Ibid. 23.

[160] Santiago Montt, *State Liability in Investment Treaty Arbitration: Global Constitutional and Administrative Law in the BIT Generation* (Hart, 2009), 74.

[161] UNCTAD (n. 5), 128. [162] Thornhill (n. 115), 21.

[163] Ha-Joon Chang, *Kicking Away the Ladder: Development Strategy in Historical Perspective* (Anthem Press, 2002).

[164] Maurizio Lazzarato, *The Making of the Indebted Man: An Essay on the Neoliberal Condition*, trans. Joshua Jordan (Semiotext(e), 2011), 71.

swelling indebtedness, but also one of domination.[165] Large damage awards serve to ensure that states do less. Instead, they are expected to do no more than generate the conditions for investor confidence, acting as 'debt collection agencies on behalf of a global oligarchy of investors'.[166] This serves to stifle the possibilities for political action. It is a form of domination insofar as it inhibits present possibilities while projecting constraints 'into the future'.[167]

17.4.4 Ascendance of experts

Ascribing to judges the task of constituting authority for a transnational constitutional order gestures toward the rise of experts and the demise of publicly accountable government. According to Beck's account, expert governance makes sense in a 'risk society' that no longer has the ability to control, through the usual techniques, the 'hazards and insecurities induced and introduced by modernization itself'.[168] In this new phase, professional knowledge elites—the mass media and scientific and legal professionals—emerge as key figures in defining risks and conceiving of ways of responding to them.[169] From this perspective, maintaining investor confidence, by lowering political risk and mitigating the effects of democratic politics, is a project of intensifying significance.[170] As Weber predicted, the increasing rationalization of law requires 'specialized' experts who can 'by technical means' resolve controversies.[171] Investment arbitration, as investment law's dispute settlement apparatus, ostensibly serves the purpose of fortifying investor confidence by preferring expert knowledge to generalist (and allegedly biased) judges presiding in national courts.

Beck was hopeful that the rise of a risk 'technocracy' would generate demands for publicity and openings for more political action.[172] Thornhill's account gives us less cause for such optimism. The turn to governing by professional knowledge elites means that important pronouncements about how we should live—'above all, to decide on how to allocate scarce resources'[173]—are made by a small cadre of experts. Yet determinations about the relation between states and markets are highly contestable judgments.[174]

165 Ibid. 115, 123.

166 Wolfgang Streeck, 'The Crises of Democratic Capitalism', 71 New Left Rev. 5 (2011), 28.

167 Lazzarato (n. 164), at 71.

168 Ulrich Beck, *Risk Society: Towards a New Modernity* (Sage, 1992), 21.

169 Ibid. 23.

170 Streeck (n. 166), 60. Reducing political risk is important because, '[g]iven the dynamics of economic nationalism . . . foreign corporations in the long run, to paraphrase Keynes, are all dead': Theodore Moran, *Multinational Corporations and the Politics of Dependence: Copper in Chile* (Princeton University Press, 1974), 224.

171 Weber (n. 42), 775, 875.

172 Ulrich Beck, *What is Globalization?* (Polity Press, 2000), 42.

173 Martti Koskenniemi, 'The Fate of Public International Law: Between Technique and Politics', 70 Modern L. Rev. 1 (2007), 4.

174 'As long as capitalism has not yet managed to dissolve popular concepts of social justice into efficiency-theoretical notions of market justice, capitalism and democracy, or markets and politics, will not cease interfering with each other': Wolfgang Streeck, 'How to Study Contemporary Capitalism', 53 European J. of Sociology 1 (2012), 14.

Disciplining the future of public life by arbitral rule is to 'master time',[175] contributing to the further separation of the economy from self-rule and the ability of citizens to protect themselves from the deleterious effects of markets.[176]

17.5 Conclusion

Coming to grips with novel transnational legal processes requires creativity, a multi-disciplinary disposition, and attention to 'phenomena that are endlessly contradictory and complex'.[177] It will, as a matter of course, generate analogies with processes already ongoing within national states. In the case of investment arbitration, this prompts envisaging investment arbitration as performing functions that can be likened to those performed by high courts when interpreting constitutional texts. The analogy, to be sure, is not perfect, but has the advantage of shedding light on a complex regime.

The object of this chapter has not been to operate in 'constitutional project' mode so as to generate innovations by which the regime's legitimacy can be improved. Instead, it has offered a constitutional lens through which to uncover constitution-like functions performed by investment arbitration tribunals and, in so doing, clarify the ways in which this form of arbitration falls well short of constitutional prototypes. It turns out that investment arbitration exhibits a partial view. It aims to 'depoliticize' investment disputes when, as a matter of course, such functions fall within the realm of what is ordinarily branded as political. Because investment arbitration implicates the capacity of public authority to act in a wide variety of regulatory contexts, the separation of law from politics is hard to credibly maintain. This is not to deny that investment arbitration is a specialized form of legal argumentation distinct from political forms. Rather, it is to say that investor–state disputes are embedded within regimes of political discourse and political power.[178]

As a consequence more, not fewer, actors are likely to pay closer attention to the work of investment arbitration tribunals. To the extent that tribunals appear to be exercising authority similar to that of national high court judges—that is, to the extent that they look like they are performing functions that can be likened to the interpretation of national constitutional texts—they will attract increasing public scrutiny.[179] It is not that high courts everywhere raise similar concerns. As suggested above, to the extent that

[175] François Ewald, 'Insurance and Risk', in Graham Burchell, Colin Gordon, and Peter Miller (eds), *The Foucault Effect: Studies in Governmentality with Two Lectures by and an Interview with Michel Foucault* (University of Chicago Press, 1991), 207.

[176] This was a question that preoccupied Karl Polanyi. See e.g. Karl Polanyi, *For a New West: Essays 1919–1958* (Polity, 2014), 218.

[177] James Rosenau, 'Supraterritoriality and Interdisciplinarity', 3 Int'l Studies Rev. 115 (2011), 115.

[178] David Schneiderman, 'Revisiting the Depoliticization of Investment Disputes', Yearbook on International Investment Law and Policy, 2010–11 (Oxford University Press, 2012).

[179] Michael Zürn, Martin Binder, and Matthias Ecker-Ehrhardt, 'International Authority and its Politicization', 4 Int'l Theory 69 (2012).

tribunals are viewed as 'centrally located' in host state 'policy space', there is likely to be less controversy, in the ordinary course, over the performance of judicial review functions.[180] Judicial institutions situated within extant constitutional settings are more likely to attract the sort of loyalty (what is called 'diffuse support') commonly enjoyed by high courts in operative democracies.[181] Investment tribunals do not pretend to be 'centrally located' in host state policy space.[182] Nor are they likely to generate the loyalty that is common to high courts in constitutional democracies, given that their function is to vindicate the interests of the privileged few. Until such time as they can gain such loyalty, it will be the case that many national publics will be as distrustful of investment arbitration as investment arbitrators are of national publics.

Nor should those functions be accepted as analogous to constituent power exercised by self-governing polities. The proposal that an international judiciary, of which investment arbitrators are a representative part, should have ascribed to them authority to generate and render legitimate a transnational constitutional order is disquieting. Moreover, the grounds offered in support of this authority in the investment arbitration context appear shaky. Rather than generating support for a new constitutional order, the proposal invites a 'post-constituent constitutionalism' that is without the people.[183]

If this chapter has been successful in drawing out constitutional analogies, it will have the effect of attracting more, not less, scrutiny to investment arbitration. As Bogdandy and Venzke observe, international courts (and they include investment arbitration in their discussion) 'need to be understood as part of the overall framework of democratic politics'. Transnational legal spaces, in their view, need to be places where 'actors can engage in meaningful political contestation'.[184] Though rules for third party intervention in some arbitration facilities have been relaxed, this will not likely be sufficient to stem demands to further politicize the field.[185] Determining who gets to frame the narrative going forward—what analogies emerge as most suitable for understanding this phenomenon—will help determine the future direction of investment arbitration.

[180] Tsebelis (n. 61), 227.

[181] James Gibson, 'The Legitimacy of the U.S. Supreme Court in a Polarized Polity', 4 J. Empirical Legal Stud. 507 (2007), 512.

[182] Though it could be said that they are centrally located within an idealized version of capital exporting state policy space.

[183] Neil Walker, 'Post-Constituent Constitutionalism? The Case of the European Union', in Martin Loughlin and Neil Walker, *The Paradox of Constitutionalism: Constituent Power and Constitutional Form* (Oxford University Press, 2007), 247, 252.

[184] Bogdandy and Venzke (n. 113), 30. On contestation as a prerequisite for legitimate transnational legal orders, see Schneiderman (n. 6).

[185] For further discussion, see Nathalie Bernasconi, Martin Dietrich Brauch, and Howard Mann, 'Civil Society and International Investment Arbitration: Tracing the Evolution of Concern', Ch. 12 this volume.

CHAPTER 18

THE ENVIRONMENT AND INVESTMENT ARBITRATION

MAKANE MOÏSE MBENGUE AND DEEPAK RAJU

THE relationship between investment arbitration and the environment has been the subject of several works of scholarship.[1] Most view investment arbitration as a threat to environmental regulation, and examine whether sufficient safeguards have been built into treaty texts and arbitral practice to preserve regulatory space for states to advance environmental objectives.

Investment arbitration provides a mechanism to enforce rights[2] of the investor against the host state. Such enforcement would, presumably, be required only in instances where the host state's interests[3] diverge from those of the investor. If one were

[1] Jorge Vinuales, 'Foreign Investment and the Environment in International Law: An Ambiguous Relationship', 80 British Yearbook of International Law 224 (2010); *Foreign Investment and the Environment in International Law* (Cambridge University Press, 2012); Rudiger Tscherning, 'Indirect Expropriation of Carbon-Intensive Investments and the Fair and Equitable Treatment Standard in International Investment Arbitration: A Commentary on the Pending Vattenfall v Federal Republic of Germany Dispute' (working paper); Asa Romson, *Environmental Policy Space and International Investment Law* (Stockholmiensis, 2012); David Gantz, 'Potential Conflicts Between Investor Rights and Environmental Regulation Under NAFTA's Chapter 11', 33 Geo. Wash. Int'l L. Rev. 651 (2001), 719–20; Daniel Loritz, 'Corporate Predators Attack Environmental Regulations: It's Time to Arbitrate Claims Filed Under NAFTA's Chapter 11', 22 Loy. L.A. Int'l & Comp. L. Rev. 533 (2000), 548; Susan Franck, 'The Legitimacy Crisis in Investment Treaty Arbitration: Privatizing Public International Law Through Inconsistent Decisions', 73 Fordham Law Review 1521 (2005).

[2] While there is some debate on whether investors are direct holders of 'rights' under IIAs, or only holders of 'interests', that distinction is not relevant for the purposes of this chapter. For a discussion on the matter, see Zachary Douglas, 'The Hybrid Foundations of Investment Treaty Arbitration', 74 (1) British Yearbook of International Law 151 (2003).

[3] The authors recognize that within a host state, there may be several interest groups with conflicting interests. For the purposes of this chapter, we assume that the 'interests of the host state' are those interests that are expressed, prioritized, or pursued by the government of the host state.

to accept that host states are always more interested in environment protection than the investors are, and that the need for investment arbitration arises only where the investor seeks to enforce an interest adverse to that of the host state, it would be a foregone conclusion that investment arbitration poses threats to the environment, and the only remaining point of enquiry would be whether investment treaties have sufficient substantive and procedural safeguards to ensure that environmental concerns do not always make way for investors' interests.

However, states are at liberty to choose the objectives that they pursue and set their own priorities between various competing objectives. There is no reason to assume that host states always accord the highest priority to environmental objectives. In some instances, they may be keen to pursue economic or other objectives at the cost of the environment.[4]

As for investors, the debate surrounding the effects of foreign investment on the environment is not new. While some authors focus on 'technology transfer', arguing that foreign investors bring with them innovative technologies that reduce the environmental impact of commercial activities,[5] others believe that investors pick out destinations with lax environmental regulation, incentivizing a 'race to the bottom'.[6] The truth perhaps lies somewhere in between. Investors in some sectors—e.g. renewable energy—would find some or all of the host state's measures for environment protection commercially profitable. On the other hand, there would be sectors where investors would stand to lose from environmental measures. Thus, whether a foreign investor's interests align with a host state's interest to protect its environment depends on a number of factors, including the sector of investment and the nature of the environmental measure.

Thus, while a search for safeguards against 'private' interests of the investors trumping the 'public' interest of environment protection is an integral part of the enquiry into the

[4] As discussed below, the draft Pan-African Investment Code foresees the possibility of states seeking to attract investments through lax regulation. It expressly provides that 'Member States shall not encourage investment by relaxing or waiving compliance with domestic environmental legislation'. See African Union Commission Economic Affairs Department, Draft Pan-African Investment Code, Art. 37(1).

[5] See Ronald Findlay, 'Relative Backwardness, Direct Foreign Investment, and the Transfer of Technology: a Simple Dynamic Model', 92(1) Quarterly Journal of Economics 1 (1978); Ralf Krüger, 'Attracting Foreign Direct Investment into Renewable Energy' (Second International Energy Efficiency Forum, Dushanbe, Tajikistan, 2011): <http://www.unece.org/fileadmin/DAM/energy/se/pp/eneff/IEEForumDushanbeSept2011/1.2.2_Krueger.pdf>; Bento Cerdeira and João Paulo, 'The Role of Foreign Direct Investment in the Renewable Electricity Generation and Economic Growth Nexus in Portugal: a Cointegration and Causality Analysis' (2012): <http://mpra.ub.uni-muenchen.de/41533/1/MPRA_paper_41533.pdf>; OCO Insight, 'FDI in Renewable Energy: A Promising Decade Ahead' (2012): <http://www.ocoglobal.com/uploads/default/files//FDI_in_Renewable_Energy_A_promising_decade_ahead.pdf>. See also Michael Hübler and Andreas Keller, 'Energy Savings via FDI? Empirical Evidence from Developing Countries', 15(1) Environment and Development Economics 59 (2010), 59–80; Brian Aitken Ann Harrison, 'Do Domestic Firms Benefit from Direct Foreign Investment? Evidence from Venezuela', 89 American Economic Review 605 (1999), 605–18.

[6] See Kirsten Engel, 'State Environmental Standard-Setting: Is There a Race and Is It to the Bottom?', 48 Hastings Law Journal 271 (1997); Yuquing Xing and Charles Kolstad, 'Do Lax Environmental Regulations Attract Foreign Investment?' 21(1) Environmental and Resource Economics 1 (2002).

relationship between the environment and investment arbitration, the enquiry cannot end there. One also needs to account for the possibility of environmental protection being actively sought by a claimant in an investment dispute. In this chapter, the authors enquire how investment arbitrators have acted, and are likely to act, when faced with issues related to the protection of the environment. We divide this enquiry into three broad sections.

Section 18.1 discusses the manner in which some 'classic' Bilateral Investment Treaty (BIT) provisions have been interpreted and applied in environmental contexts. These are not provisions specifically dealing with environmental concerns, but general BIT provisions which, given the fact pattern presented in a dispute, have been applied in an environmental context. In other words, the interaction of these provisions with environmental objectives has been shaped mostly by arbitral tribunals, rather than treaty negotiators. These provisions have already received much attention in the literature, including previous work by the present authors.[7]

Section 18.2 examines certain recent drafting innovations that states have adopted, with a view to specifically negotiating and accommodating environmental concerns in treaties. These provisions often coexist with the more 'classic' BIT provisions, and seek to modify the outcome that would normally result from the operation of those provisions, when certain fact patterns arise. While most of these provisions have yet to find application before arbitral tribunals—and many of them are yet to be incorporated into binding treaties—we believe an examination of those provisions can be of assistance in predicting how investment arbitrators of the future may approach environmental issues.

In section 18.3, we depart from our discussion of treaty texts to undertake a more conceptual discussion on the approach of investment arbitrators to environmental concerns, specifically dealing with questions relating to scientific evidence, margin of appreciation, and precautionary action.

18.1 'Classic' BIT provisions

According to some counts, the current number of International Investment Agreements (IIAs)—including BITs, regional agreements, and investment protection provisions in free trade agreements—stands at over 3,000.[8] Yet most of these treaties have a large number of commonalities in their texts. Most offer protection against direct and

[7] Makane Mbengue and Deepak Raju, 'Energy, Environment and Foreign Investment', in Eric De Brabandere and Tarcisio Gazzini (eds), *Foreign Investment in the Energy Sector: Balancing Private and Public Interests* (Brill, 2014).

[8] According to UNCTAD, there are currently 2.953 BITs (of which 2.322 are in force) and 363 other treaties with investment provisions (of which 294 are in force). See UNCTAD, International Investment Agreements Navigator, <http://investmentpolicyhub.unctad.org/IIA>.

indirect expropriation, a guarantee of fair and equitable treatment, and protection against discrimination. None of these provisions were specifically designed to deal with environmental concerns. Yet arbitral tribunals have been called upon to interpret and apply these provisions in environmental contexts.[9] Below, we discuss these, and other provisions, that appear commonly in BITs, and have found application in environmental contexts.

18.1.1 Preambular recitals

Several IIAs make references to environmental objectives in their preambles. One of the preambular recitals in the US Model BIT states: 'Desiring to achieve these objectives in a manner consistent with the protection of health, safety, and the environment, and the promotion of internationally recognized labor rights.'[10] The preamble of the Australia–Chile FTA (2008) similarly requires the parties to 'implement this Agreement in a manner consistent with sustainable development and environmental protection and conservation'.

Preambular texts in IIAs are not enforceable. Thus, no matter how strongly they express the concerns of the parties for the environment, they do not create or mitigate rights or obligations for the state parties or the investors. Yet, as is well accepted in customary international law, the preamble of a treaty is a relevant tool for interpretation of the text.[11] Where the accurate meaning of a substantive provision is in dispute, the preambular text may be helpful in lending support to the more environment friendly solution.[12] In this regard, one may draw an analogy with the reliance, by the WTO Appellate Body, on the preambular language relating to sustainable development, while interpreting the meaning and scope of the Article XX exception to GATT commitments.[13]

[9] See e.g. *Saar Papier Vertriebs GmbH v Poland,* UNCITRAL Awards, 16 October 1995 (not public); *Metalclad Corporation v United Mexican States,* ICSID ARB(AF)97/1, Award, 30 August 2000; *S.D. Myers Inc. v Government of Canada,* Award, 13 November 2000; *Tecnicas Medioambientales SA (Tecmed) v United Mexican States,* ICSID ARB(AF)00/2, Award, 29 May 2003; *MTD Equity Sdn Bhd. & MTD Chile S.A. v The Republic of Chile,* ICSID ARB/07/7, Award, 25 May 2004.

[10] See US–Uruguay BIT (2005) and US–Rwanda BIT (2008): 'Desiring to achieve these objectives in a manner consistent with the protection of health, safety, and the environment, and the promotion of internationally recognized labor rights.'

[11] Vienna Convention on the Law of Treaties, Art. 31: '1. A treaty shall be interpreted in good faith in accordance with the ordinary meaning to be given to the terms of the treaty in their context and in the light of its object and purpose. 2. The context for the purpose of the interpretation of a treaty shall comprise, in addition to the text, including its preamble and annexes.'

[12] See Makane Mbengue, 'The Notion of Preamble', in Rüdiger Wolfrum (ed.), *Max Planck Encyclopedia of Public International Law* (Oxford University Press, 2012).

[13] 'United States - Import Prohibition of Certain Shrimp and Shrimp Products', WT/DS58/AB/R, para. 129.

18.1.2 Investment 'in accordance with' environmental law

Several IIAs require, as a precondition to the protections set out in them, that investments be made 'in accordance with' the laws of the host state.[14] On several occasions, arbitral tribunals have held that the provision barred them from exercising jurisdiction where the investment in question was made in contravention of the host state's domestic law.[15]

These provisions do not typically enumerate the areas of law that the investment should 'accord' with. While they would include specific restrictions on foreign investment—e.g. sectoral caps or prior-approval requirements for foreign investment—their wording is usually broad enough to cover the entire legal system of the host state.[16] Notably, a violation of general domestic laws against corruption has been held to be within the coverage of this provision.[17] While not yet tested, an investment made in contravention of environmental laws would presumably be within the reach of this provision and would be denied the protection of the IIA, including access to arbitration.

It is important to note that the provision refers to 'making' the investments in accordance with domestic law. That is, it concerns itself with the legality of the investment at the time it was made. It does not cover subsequent violations of environmental (or other) laws by the investor, or a subsequent change in laws which renders the investor's conduct illegal.

18.1.3 Non-discrimination provisions

Most IIAs contain 'national treatment' clauses that prohibit treating investors protected by IIAs less favourably than domestic investors of the host state, and 'most favoured nation' clauses which prohibit treating investors protected by IIA less favourably than investors of third countries. These may also find application in environmental contexts.

[14] See e.g. Ukraine–Lithuania BIT, Art. 1(1); Agreement between the Federal Republic of Germany and the Republic of the Philippines for the Promotion and Reciprocal Protection of Investments, Art. 1, 18 April 1997; Agreement between the Islamic Republic of Pakistan and the Republic of Turkey Concerning the Reciprocal Promotion and Protection of Investments Art. 2, 16 March 1995; Treaty Between United States of America and the Argentine Republic Concerning the Reciprocal Encouragement and Protection of Investment, 14 November 1991; Agreement on Encouragement and Reciprocal Protection of Investments between the Kingdom of the Netherlands and the Czech and Slovak Federal Republic, 29 April 1991. Also see Christina Knahr, 'Investments "in Accordance with Host State Law"', in August Reinisch and Christina Knahr (eds), *International Investment Law In Context* (Eleven Publishing, 2008), 27; Rahim Moloo and Alex Khachaturian, 'The Compliance with the Law Requirement in International Investment Law', 34(6) Fordham International Law Journal 1473 (2011).

[15] *Fraport AG Frankfurt Airport Serv. Worldwide v Republic of the Philippines*, ICSID Case No. ARl/03/25, Award, 16 August 2006, para. 394; *Tokios Tokeles v Ukraine*, ICSID Case No. ARB/02/18, Decision on jurisdiction, 29 April 2004, para. 84; *Desert Line Projects LLC v Republic of Yemen*, ICSID Case No. ARB/05/17, Award, 6 February 2008, paras. 104–5.

[16] See Knahr (n. 14); Moloo and Khachaturian (n. 14).

[17] *Gustav F W Hamester GmbH & Co KG v Republic of Ghana*, ICSID Case No. ARB/07/24, Award, 18 June 18 2010, para. 123.

On the one hand, non-discrimination provisions may come in the way of rewarding domestic or foreign investors for their environment friendly practices and punishing those not following such practices. In the investment context, there exists no cogent jurisprudence as to whether investments and investors not similarly placed in terms of environmental impact are to be accorded equal treatment. For instance, a feed-in tariff programme that pays a higher price for electricity generated from renewable sources, in comparison to electricity generated from conventional sources, may come under attack as *de facto* discrimination against a foreign investor engaged in the generation of conventional electricity. Under such a circumstance, it is unclear whether arbitral tribunals will hold that the foreign investor was not in similar circumstances as the investors in renewable energy, and therefore not entitled to equal treatment.

One may recall the WTO Appellate Body's ruling in *EC - Asbestos*[18] which held that the health effects of products could be relevant in determining whether they are 'like products', for the purposes of claims of discrimination. The same logic, by extension, could also apply to environmental effects. However, that ruling was based on the fact that consumer tastes and preferences are relevant in determining 'likeness of goods' in the trade context. There is no parallel jurisprudence in the investment context to indicate that perceptions of the consumers or the public are relevant in determining whether two investors are in 'like circumstances'.[19]

Non-discrimination provisions may, on the other hand, serve to prohibit arbitrary promotion of environmentally inferior investments to serve vested or parochial interests. If the markets are structured in such a way that they reward environmentally friendly products, the non-discrimination provisions will help them access a level playing field. In such a market, the non-discrimination provisions will ensure that the governments do not create artificial barriers to clean technology or create advantages for environmentally inferior alternatives, based on protectionist considerations.

An example of this may be seen in the domestic content requirements that some countries impose in relation to their renewable energy programmes, and in how the non-discrimination provisions in WTO law have been employed by other countries to

[18] *European Communities - Measures Affecting Asbestos and Asbestos-Containing Products*, WT/DS 135/AB/R, para. 122: 'In this case especially, we are also persuaded that evidence relating to consumers' tastes and habits would establish that the health risks associated with chrysotile asbestos fibres influence consumers' behaviour with respect to the different fibres at issue.'

[19] In fact, the case law on 'like circumstances' appears to suggest that the test is less demanding than the 'like products' test in WTO. See *Marvin Roy Feldman Karpa v United Mexican States*, ICSID Case No. ARB(AF)/99/1, Award, 16 December 2002, paras. 171–2 (holding that the 'universe' of firms in 'like circumstances' are all the firms that are in the business of reselling/exporting cigarettes); *S.D. Myers, Inc. v Government of Canada*, UNCITRAL, Partial Award, 13 November 2000, para. 251 (finding that the claimant and the domestic firms were in like circumstances because they carried on the same economic activity); *Methanex Corporation v United States of America*, UNCITRAL, Final Award, 3 August 2005, paras. 17–19 (ruling that *identical* comparators, where available, are to be considered to be in 'like circumstances'; where there are no identical comparators, less 'like' comparators could be considered. The tribunal recalled the 'flexibility' afforded by the provision); *Merrill & Ring Forestry L. P. v Government of Canada*, UNCITRAL, ICSID Administrated, Award, 31 March 2010 (finding that the appropriate comparator was investors subject to the same regulatory measure under the same jurisdictional authority).

challenge these requirements.[20] While the non-discrimination provisions strike at the domestic content requirements, they leave the renewable energy programmes intact, ensuring that energy suppliers are free to base their procurement decisions on effectiveness and cost considerations rather than the geographical origins of the components.[21] A domestic content requirement in such a programme could skew the market for renewable energy, and creates inefficiencies. While the non-discrimination provisions in IIAs are yet to be invoked in relation to such requirements, it is likely that they may be able to bring about the same effect, if invoked.

18.1.4 Fair and equitable treatment

The fair and equitable treatment (FET) standard is one of the most litigated provisions in IIAs, and it has been interpreted very broadly by investment arbitral tribunals. The exact meaning and scope of the commitment depends on the actual wording of the agreement at hand.[22] According to Muchlinsky:

> the concept of fair and equitable treatment is not precisely defined. It offers a general point of departure in formulating an argument that the foreign investor has not been well treated by reason of discriminatory or other unfair measures being taken against its interests. It is, therefore, a concept that depends on the interpretation of specific facts for its content. At most, it can be said that the concept connotes the principle of non-discrimination and proportionality in the treatment of foreign investors.[23]

The fluidity of the FET standard has led some commentators to call it the 'catch all' provision in IIAs.[24] The FET standard has, inter alia, been held to include the protection of legitimate expectations.[25]

[20] *Canada - Certain Measures Affecting The Renewable Energy Generation Sector*, WT/DS412/AB/R; *Canada - Measures Relating To The Feed-In Tariff Program*, WT/DS426/AB/R; *India - Certain Measures Relating to Solar Cells and Solar Modules*, WT/DS 456/AB/R; *United States - Certain Measures Relating to the Renewable Energy Sector*, WT/DS 510.

[21] See *Panel Report, India - Certain Measures Relating to Solar Cells and Solar Modules*, para. 7.19: 'Our analysis of the DCR measures proceeds on the understanding that it is the WTO consistency of those measures, and not the legitimacy of the policy objectives pursued through the National Solar Mission, that is in dispute in this case.' See also Prabhash Ranjan and Deepak Raju, 'What the WTO Panel did not Decide on Solar Panels', *Financial Express*, 16 March 2016: <http://www.financialexpress.com/fe-columnist/what-the-wto-panel-did-not-decide-on-solar-panels/226070/>.

[22] OECD, 'Fair and Equitable Treatment Standard in International Investment Law', Working Papers on International Investment No. 2004/3: <http://www.oecd.org/daf/inv/internationalinvestmentagreements/33776498.pdf>.

[23] Peter Muchlinski, *Multinational Enterprises and the Law*, 2nd edn (Oxford University Press, 2007), 625.

[24] Nathalie. Bernasconi, 'Background Paper on Vattenfall v Germany Arbitration', International Institute for Sustainable Development (2009): <http://www.iisd.org/pdf/2009/background_vattenfall_vs_germany.pdf>.

[25] *International Thunderbird Gaming Corporation v The United Mexican States*, UNCITRAL, Separate Opinion of Professor Thomas Walde, December 2005, para. 37; *Saluka Investments BV v Czech Republic*,

The jurisprudence on FET clause has sought to strike a balance between the expectations of the investor and the regulatory freedom of the host state. For instance, the *Saluka* tribunal held that the FET standard 'requires a weighing of the Claimant's legitimate and reasonable expectations on the one hand and the Respondent's legitimate regulatory interests on the other'.[26]

While the right to impose environmental regulation is undisputedly recognized, the FET standard may strike at the manner and the context in which the regulation is imposed. For instance, in *Metalclad*, the denial of a building permit violated FET standard because the permit 'was denied at a meeting of the Municipal Town Council of which Metalclad received no notice, to which it received no invitation, and at which it was given no opportunity to appear'.[27] In *Tecmed*, the lack of prior notice to the investor about the non-renewal of the landfill operating license, and the social and political pressure on the authority to relocate the landfill which provided the background to the decision, were crucial in sustaining a finding of violation of the FET standard.[28]

While the FET standard protects legitimate expectations, the jurisprudence is clear that absent a stabilization clause, the investors cannot legitimately expect that the regulatory framework will remain static.[29] For instance, the *Saluka* tribunal held that 'in order to determine whether frustration of the foreign investor's expectations was justified and reasonable, the host state's legitimate right subsequently to regulate domestic matters in the public interest must be taken into consideration as well',[30] and highlighted the 'high measure of deference that international law generally extends to the right of domestic authorities to regulate matters within their own borders'.[31]

Thus, the FET standard does not necessarily frustrate non-discriminatory, reasonable, transparent regulatory measures for the protection of the environment even when the measure imposes additional costs on the investor. In fact, it is conceivable that in certain circumstances, investors may use the FET standard to force the host state to adhere to certain levels of environmental protection that they previously committed to.

Additionally, investors and environmental activists converge in the call for strong, fair, transparent, and predictable institutions with well-defined mandates. While investment protection may require one course of action by these institutions and the protection of the environment may require a completely different course of action, the broad defining characteristics of the institutional framework sought by both types of interests largely converge. For instance arbitrariness and selective enforcement of environmental

UNCITRAL, Partial Award, 17 March 2006, para. 306; Abhijit Pandya and Andy Moody, 'Legitimate Expectations in Investment Treaty Arbitration: An Unclear Future', 15 Tilburg Law Review 93 (2011), 105.

[26] *Saluka Investments BV v Czech Republic*, UNCITRAL, Partial Award, 17 March 2006, para. 306.

[27] *Metalclad Corporation v United Mexican States*, ICSID ARB(AF)97/1, Award, 30 August 2000, para. 91.

[28] *Tecnicas Medioambientales SA (Tecmed) v United Mexican States*, ICSID ARB(AF)00/2, Award, 29 May 2003.

[29] *Saluka Investments BV v Czech Republic*, UNCITRAL, Award, 17 March 2006, para. 442.

[30] Ibid. [31] Ibid.

standards, or delayed adjudication of environment-related objections to investment projects, are likely to hurt both investors and the environment.

18.1.5 Protection against expropriation

The guarantee against expropriation was, in the initial phases of international investment law, the most important guarantee sought by investors. Today, expropriation clauses have evolved to cover not merely the classic cases of direct expropriation but also indirect expropriation irrespective of the form it takes.[32] Indirect expropriation has been defined broadly to include any government action that deprives the investor of the use or enjoyment of the assets or unduly delays the use or enjoyment of such assets.[33]

There has been a consensus among international lawyers that not all taking of property by the government amounts to expropriation. Brownlie reflects on this position by stating:

> state measures, prima facie a lawful exercise of powers of governments, may affect foreign interests considerably without amounting to expropriation. Thus, foreign assets and their use may be subjected to taxation, trade restrictions involving licenses and quotas, or measures of devaluation. While special facts may alter cases, in principle such measures are not unlawful and do not constitute expropriation.[34]

Sornarajah categorizes non-discriminatory measures for the protection of environment as 'non-compensable takings', along with measures relating to anti-trust, consumer protection, securities, and land planning.[35]

In practice, what separates expropriation from non-expropriatory regulation appears to be: 'i) the degree of interference with the property right, ii) the character of governmental measures, i.e. the purpose and the context of the governmental measure, and iii) the interference of the measure with reasonable and investment-backed expectations'.[36] In *Pope & Talbot*, the NAFTA tribunal observed, 'mere interference is

[32] Robert Sloane and W. Michael Reisman, 'Indirect Expropriation and its Valuation in the BIT Generation', 74 British Yearbook of International Law 115 (2004); Caroline Henckels, 'Indirect Expropriation and the Right to Regulate: Revisiting Proportionality Analysis and the Standard of Review in Investor-State Arbitration', 15(1) J Int'l Economic Law 223 (2012); See e.g. US–Bangladesh BIT (1986), Art. III:1: 'No investment or any Part of an investment of a national or a company of either Party shall be expropriated or nationalized by the other Party or subjected to any other measure or series of measures, direct or indirect tantamount to expropriation (including the levying of taxation, the compulsory sale of all or part of an investment, or the impairment or deprivation of its management, control or economic value), all such actions hereinafter referred to as "expropriation", unless the expropriation...'

[33] See references in the previous footnote.

[34] Ian Brownlie, *Principles of Public International Law*, 6th edn (Oxford University Press, 2003), 509.

[35] Muthucumaraswamy Sornarajah, *The International Law on Foreign Investment* (Cambridge University Press, 1994), 283.

[36] OECD, '"Indirect Expropriation" and the "Right to Regulate" in International Investment Law', Working Paper No. 2004/4 (2004); see also Simon Baughen, 'Expropriation and Environmental

not expropriation; rather, a significant degree of deprivation of fundamental rights of ownership is required'.[37] While some actions falling within the 'police powers' of the state may not be characterized as expropriation at all, 'public purpose' may act as the first prong of justification of certain measures even if they amount to expropriation.

Termination of concessions or other measures calling for termination of the whole or a part of the operations of the investors may be argued to be expropriation. It would be for the investor to demonstrate that the measure has had the effect of interfering with the ownership, control, or enjoyment of the investment. The state would be able to avoid liability by demonstrating that (i) there is no deprivation of property; (ii) the deprivation is in exercise of the police powers; (iii) the deprivation is a permissible expropriation complying with the requirements of the IIA; or (iv) the conduct is exempted from the applicability of the IIA commitments by operation of the exceptions specifically provided for in the IIA.

There may also be a situation, though it is yet to arise, where an investor whose operations depend on the existence of a minimum environmental standard may allege an indirect expropriation against the government for not maintaining the said standard and thereby causing economic prejudice to the investor.

18.2 Some recent drafting innovations

As mentioned earlier, the interaction between the traditional BIT provisions and the environment has mostly been driven by arbitral tribunals, rather than by conscious drafting choices and negotiated outcomes. In other words, the discussion focused on how arbitral tribunals have applied, and may apply, generally worded treaty provisions in environmental contexts. Recently however, there have been a number of attempts to place environmental concerns on the negotiating agenda for IIAs, and to specifically design language aimed at balancing environmental objectives with investment protection. In this section, we analyse some of these IIA provisions specifically designed to protect the environment.

Unlike the provisions discussed above, the drafting innovations considered here are mostly yet to be tested before arbitral tribunals. Some of the examples we consider are derived from model BITs, and are yet to be accorded binding force by incorporation in a BITs. Hence, our analysis of these provisions is necessarily predictive in nature.

Regulation the Lessons of NAFTA Chapter Eleven', 18(2) Journal of Environmental Law 207 (2006), 207–28.

[37] *Pope & Talbot Inc. v The Government of Canada*, UNCITRAL, Interim Award, 2000, para. 99.

18.2.1 A GATT-style general exception for the environment

The 1999 Argentina–New Zealand BIT sets out a general exception in the following terms:

> The provisions of this Agreement shall in no way limit the right of either Contracting Party to take any measures (including the destruction of plants and animals, confiscation of property or the imposition of restrictions on stock movement) necessary for the protection of natural and physical resources or human health, provided such measures are not applied in a manner which would constitute a means of arbitrary or unjustified discrimination.[38]

Similarly, the Canada–Egypt BIT stipulates:

> Provided that such measures are not applied in a discriminatory or arbitrary manner or do not constitute a disguised restriction on foreign investment, nothing in this Agreement shall be construed to prevent a Contracting Party from adopting measures to maintain public order, or to protect public health and safety, including environmental measures necessary to protect human, animal or plant life.[39]

The most recent version of the Indian model BIT comes with a set of 'General Exceptions'. The text of the provision reads:

> Nothing in this Treaty shall be construed to prevent the adoption or enforcement by a Party of measures of general applicability applied on a nondiscriminatory basis that are necessary to: (i) protect public morals or maintaining public order; (ii) protect human, animal or plant life or health; (iii) ensure compliance with law and regulations that are not inconsistent with the provisions of this Agreement; (iv) protect and conserve the environment, including all living and nonliving natural resources; (v) protect national treasures or monuments of artistic, cultural, historic or archaeological value.[40]

In the Indian model BIT, the word 'necessary' is accompanied by a footnote which seeks to clarify its meaning: 'In considering whether a measure is "necessary", the Tribunal shall take into account whether there was no less restrictive alternative measure reasonably available to a Party.'[41]

[38] Agreement Between the Government of the Argentine Republic and the Government of New Zealand for the Promotion and Reciprocal Protection of Investments, 27 August 1999, Art. 5(3).

[39] Agreement Between the Government of Canada and the Government of the Arab Republic of Egypt for the Promotion and Protection of Investments, 13 November 1996, Art. XVII(3).

[40] Government of India, Ministry of Finance, 'Model Text for the Indian Bilateral Investment Treaty': <http://finmin.nic.in/the_ministry/dept_eco_affairs/investment_division/ModelBIT_Annex.pdf, Article 32>.

[41] Ibid. n. 6.

The scheme of these provisions is clearly inspired by the General Exceptions set out in Article XX of GATT. In the context of various sub-paragraphs of Article XX that exempt measures 'necessary' to achieve some similarly enumerated objectives (and similarly, in the context of the Agreement on Technical Barriers to Trade), WTO jurisprudence has evolved to focus on the concept of 'less trade restrictive alternatives'.[42] Simply put, where a measure is asserted to be 'necessary' to secure a defined objective, a WTO panel would first determine the degree of contribution made by that measure to the attainment of the objective, and then assess whether a reasonably available 'less trade restrictive alternative' could have made a similar degree of contribution to the objective.

If the question is answered in the affirmative, the measure is held to be not 'necessary' for the achievement of the objective. On the other hand, where the question is answered in the negative, the measure passes the necessity test. Footnote 6 to the Indian model BIT attempts to incorporate this 'necessity test'. While the other examples above do not expressly set out an interpretation for the word 'necessary', it is likely that tribunals interpreting them may be tempted to refer to WTO jurisprudence on the necessity test when called upon to undertake this interpretive exercise.

Creation of GATT-style general exceptions in BITs would indeed go a long way to preserve regulatory space for the host states to achieve their environmental objectives. Yet a few uncertainties do remain, when transposing trade concepts into the investment context. Specifically, concerns arise in the context of the 'necessity test' and its notion of 'restrictiveness'.

The trade disciplines are multilateral, and the WTO dispute settlement system is tasked with preserving the 'proper balance of rights and obligations' among members.[43] The notion of trade distortion, therefore, is necessarily multilateral. In other words, if a complaining member identifies an alternative measure that would have been less restrictive to its own trade, but would have restricted the trade of other WTO members more than the measure actually adopted by the responding member, a WTO panel is unlikely to accept that measure as a less trade-restrictive alternative. Trade restrictiveness of a measure, and of proposed alternatives, is assessed from its impact on multilateral trade, not its impact on the trade of the complaining member alone.

Investment obligations, however, are mostly bilateral and only rarely multilateral. Nothing requires an investment arbitral tribunal to take into account the rights and interests of investors other than the claimant before it. Conceptually, therefore, an investment arbitral tribunal is more likely to approach 'investment restrictiveness' from the perspective of how much impact the measure at issue and proposed alternatives have on the rights of the particular investor before it, or at most, on the rights of all the investors protected by the BIT from which the tribunal derives its jurisdiction. This would mean that in each case, to succeed on the 'necessity' test, the state would need to

[42] Appellate Body Report, *US - Tuna II (Mexico)*, para. 320; Appellate Body Report, *US - COOL*, para. 376; Appellate Body Report, *Brazil - Retreaded Tyres*, paras. 150–51; Appellate Body Report, *EC - Seals*, para. 5.261; Appellate Body Report, *Korea - Various Measures on Beef*, para. 166.

[43] Understanding on Rules and Procedures Governing the Settlement of Disputes, Art. 3.3.

rebut the availability of alternatives which are less restrictive from the perspective of the particular investor concerned (or from the perspective of all the investors covered by the particular BIT). This absence of multilateralism in the approach to restrictiveness makes it very difficult, or at times even impossible, for the state to actually design environmental measures that would fit into the exceptions in its BITs. Instead of undertaking a generalized consideration of the availability of alternatives that can preserve the interests of all its treaty parties (as is the case with GATT),[44] the state will need to now engage in a search for alternatives that is treaty-specific or investor-specific.

[44] See Deepak Raju, 'General Exceptions in the Indian Model BIT: Is the "Necessity" Test Workable?' 7(2) Jindal Global Law Review 227 (2016), 227–43: While the Appellate Body of the WTO has placed the notion of 'trade restrictiveness' at the centre of its necessity analysis, it has never defined the concept. An important question that remains unanswered is from whose perspective trade restrictiveness of a measure and the proposed alternatives need to be assessed. Assessing the trade restrictiveness of a measure solely from the perspective of the complaining member may yield a markedly different result from assessing it from the collective perspective of all trading partners of the responding member.

This can be best illustrated by an example. WTO Member A imposes an additional duty of 10% on the import of 'widgets' which are admittedly harmful to human health. Member A has no domestic production of 'widgets', and it is anticipated that the additional duty would decrease the consumption of 'widgets' in country A by 20% a year. Country B claims that the overall import duty on 'widgets' now exceeds the bound tariff scheduled by Country A in its schedule of concessions and alleges a violation of Article II of GATT. Country A accepts that the measure violates Article II, but claims justification under Article XX(b), asserting that the measure is 'necessary to' protect public health. In the context of the necessity test, Member B would likely identify a number of alternatives that arguably could achieve a 20% reduction in the annual consumption of 'widgets'. Say, Member B argues that placing warning signs on packages of 'widgets' or educating the public about the ill-effects of 'widgets' could result in this result. These alternative would be 'less restrictive' not only for imports of 'widgets' into country A from a single exporter, or from country B. These alternatives are 'less restrictive' from the perspective of other trading partners of country A as well. On the other hand, if country B were to argue that a 20% reduction in the consumption of 'widgets' could be achieved by placing an additional duty of 20% on the imports of 'widgets' from country C, while exempting country B's imports from any additional duty, this would be 'less trade restrictive' from country B's perspective, but not from country C's perspective or from a multilateral perspective.

While neither the text of Article XX nor the jurisprudence of the Appellate Body is explicit on which of these vantage points the restrictiveness of measures and alternatives is to be assessed from, it is inconceivable that a panel would accept an alternative which is 'less trade restrictive' only for the trade of the complaining member, while more restrictive from a multilateral perspective, as a proper 'less trade restrictive alternative'. This is because of the multilateral nature of WTO rights and obligations. The dispute settlement system is charged, under Article 3.3 of the DSU, to preserve the 'proper balance between rights and obligations' of the members under the covered agreements. Were WTO panels to approach trade restrictiveness of measures and alternatives solely from the perspective of the complaining member, they would be disturbing this balance.

Additionally, were a member to adopt a 'less trade restrictive' alternative to one of its assailed measures, which is less restrictive only from the perspective of one complaining member, it would be engaging in discrimination between that member and its other trading partners. Article I of GATT—and the relevant MFN provisions in other WTO agreements—would make such an alternative measure WTO-inconsistent. Since the illegality of such alternative measures arises from provisions that are part of the applicable law in WTO dispute settlement, a WTO panel faced with such a proposal for an alternative could rule that the proposed alternative is not 'reasonably available' to the complaining member.

Procedurally, third-party participation in WTO disputes would provide an avenue for any WTO member other than the parties to the dispute an opportunity to comment on the trade restrictiveness of the measure from its perspective.'

Irrespective of whether investment restrictiveness is understood from a bilateral or a multilateral perspective, there exists another conceptual difficulty in operationalizing such provisions. GATT concerns the trade in goods. What is protected under that agreement is the competitive opportunity[45] for goods originating in one member state to enter the territory of another member state, and after such entry, to be distributed on the domestic market of the latter member state. Thus, while the various provisions in GATT (and other goods agreements) add levels of detail to the discipline, it is possible to conceptually reduce the disciplines, at their most fundamental level, to be a protection of competitive opportunity to sell goods.[46] This, in turn, allows one to conceptualize 'trade restrictiveness' as the degree of interference with the competitive opportunity to sell goods.[47]

In practice, panels assess the restrictiveness of a measure from the design, structure, and operation of the measure.[48] On the other hand, investment commitments do not allow any such simplification. While one may argue that at a basic level investment commitments protect the competitive opportunity of investors to derive a profit from their investment, this would be unhelpful. A comparison of how much two different environmental measures may impact an investor's (or all investors') opportunity to derive profits would be way more complex an endeavour than comparing the impact of two different environmental measures on the collective ability of exporters to sell goods. This once again prejudices the ability of states to actively seek out *ex ante* environmental measures that would pass the 'necessity' test under this exception.

[45] Panel Report, *Korea - Alcoholic Beverages*, para. 10.81; Appellate Body Report, *Canada - Periodicals*, 18; Panel Report, *Argentina - Hides and Leather*, paras. 11.182–11.184; Appellate Body Report, *EC - Asbestos*, para. 103.

[46] We note that while the Appellate Body has never defined the concept of 'trade-restrictiveness' in any detail, it observed, in the context of the TBT Agreement, that the expression would mean 'something having a limiting effect on trade'. See Appellate Body Report, *US - Tuna II (Mexico)*, para. 319. See also Panel Report, *US - Tuna II (Mexico)*, para. 7.455: 'Turning first to the question of what constitutes "trade-restrictiveness" in this context, we note that Mexico argues that measures that are 'trade-restrictive' include those that impose any form of limitation of imports, discriminate against imports or deny competitive opportunities to imports and that the United States agrees with Mexico that a measure that imposes limits on imports or discriminates against them would meet the definition of a measure that is "trade-restrictive". We also agree.'

[47] A general exception, on the lines of Article XX of GATT, also exists in Article XIV of the General Agreement on Trade in Services. For the sake of brevity and clarity, the arguments in this chapter focus on the general exceptions and the accompanying concepts of 'necessity' and 'trade restrictiveness' in the goods context. The same arguments could equally be made with reference to the general exceptions in the GATS, in the sense that 'trade restrictiveness' can be simplified to be understood as the degree of interference with the competitive opportunity to sell services.

[48] See e.g. Appellate Body Report, *Japan - Alcoholic Beverages II*, 29; Appellate Body Report, *Canada - Periodicals*, 30–32; Appellate Body Report, *Thailand - Cigarettes (Philippines)*, para. 130; Appellate Body Report, *Chile - Price Band System (Article 21.5—Argentina)*, para. 202; Appellate Body Report, *US - Offset Act (Byrd Amendment)*, paras. 254 and 257; Appellate Body Report, *China - Auto Parts*, para. 171; Appellate Body Report, *China - Publications and Audiovisual Products*, para. 230; Appellate Body Report, *US - Clove Cigarettes*, paras. 182, 206, 215; Appellate Body Report, *US - Tuna II (Mexico)*, para. 225; Appellate Body Report, *US - COOL*, paras. 269, 271, 373; Appellate Body Report, *US - Tuna II (Mexico)*, para. 317.

Thus, while GATT-style general exception clauses represents an active accommodation of environmental concerns in the treaty text, the necessity test set out therein may be unworkable. In view of these difficulties associated with a necessity test, one may consider some drafting alternatives which create the relevant exception without reliance on the concepts of necessity or investment restrictiveness.

18.2.2 Clarifications and carve-outs

Recently, drafters of IIAs have experimented with adding clarificatory language or carve-outs that limit the operation of certain specific IIA obligations in environmental contexts. Unlike general exceptions discussed above, these provisions relate to a specific obligation alone.

The Trans-Pacific Partnership's provisions on expropriation are accompanied by a clarification:

> Non-discriminatory regulatory actions by a Party that are designed and applied to protect legitimate public welfare objectives, such as public health, safety and the environment, do not constitute indirect expropriations, except in rare circumstances.[49]

Similar provisions appear in the current draft of the Pan-African Investment Code (PAIC).[50] First, while the PAIC, like current BITs, guarantees protection against discrimination, in the form of MFN and national treatment, it has provisions to ensure that distinction on environmental grounds is protected. Both MFN and national treatment are guaranteed where the foreign investor is in 'like circumstances' compared to domestic investors or investors of a third state. Both the guarantees are accompanied by a list of considerations that must be taken into account in determining whether investors are in 'like circumstances'. Among these considerations is 'effects on the local, regional or national environment, the health of the populations, or on the global commons'. Additionally, both guarantees are accompanied by a set of exceptions to the guarantee against discrimination. Among these is a clarification that '[a]ny regulatory measure taken by a Member State that is designed and applied to protect or enhance legitimate pub-

[49] Trans-Pacific Partnership: <https://ustr.gov/sites/default/files/TPP-Final-Text-Investment.pdf, Annex 9-B>.

[50] The African Union is currently working on a Pan-African Investment Code. While discussions are still ongoing as to the exact legal status that the final product will enjoy—whether it will be a multilateral treaty on investment binding on African Union members, or a common model BIT that the members can use in their negotiations with third parties—the draft reflects the current state of thinking, on the part of the African states, on the course that future investment treaties should take. The current draft has some unique environmental provisions that may have far-reaching implications. For instance, specifically addressing the concerns about states competing to attract investments at the cost of environmental objectives and engaging in a 'race to the bottom', the Code provides that 'Member States shall not encourage investment by relaxing or waiving compliance with domestic environmental legislation'. Where a member state considers that another member state has engaged in such behaviour, it may seek consultations.

lic welfare objectives, such as public health, safety and the environment' does not constitute a breach of the non-discrimination obligations.

Similarly, the guarantee against expropriation is accompanied by a clarification that a 'non-discriminatory measure of a Member State that is designed and applied to protect or enhance legitimate public welfare objectives, such as public health, safety and the environment, does not constitute an indirect expropriation.'

18.2.3 Investor obligations

Though there is some discussion on allowing claims and counterclaims by the host state before investment arbitration tribunals,[51] traditionally, the state has been the perpetual respondent and the investor the perpetual claimant in investment arbitration. This is hardly surprising, since 'investment disputes', which are the subject matter of investment arbitration, are typically defined to mean disputes about alleged non-conformity with obligations assumed under the IIA. Traditionally, IIAs set out obligations for the states parties to them, and not for the investors. Hence, 'investment disputes' typically involve the adjudication of alleged violations of their obligations by the states.

The confinement of the investor's role to that of a claimant and the state's role to that of a defendant has traditionally made it nearly impossible to address environmental violations by the investor, except as a justification for a government action challenged by the investor, or, in some exceptional situations, as counterclaims with a view to offsetting any compensation payable to the investor. This severely narrows the scope of environment related claims that can be placed before the arbitral tribunal.

The notion that investors may have certain obligations towards the host state is not unprecedented. However, traditionally these obligations have been located within the domestic laws of the host state, enforceable before domestic judicial fora[52] or, in some exceptional cases, the laws of the home state of the investor, enforceable before the domestic courts of the home State.[53] There have also been multiple efforts to codify 'principles' of 'corporate social responsibility' (CSR) and 'socially responsible investment' (CRI), which usually fail to have legal consequences.[54]

[51] *Spyridon Roussalis v Romania*, ICSID Case No. ARB/06/1, Award, 7 December 2011; *Goetz v Burundi*, ICSID Case No. ARB/01/2, Award, 21 June 2012; Gustavo Laborde, 'The Case for Host State Claims in Investment Arbitration', 1(1) Journal of International Dispute Settlement 97 (2010); Yaraslau Kryvoi, 'Counterclaims in Investor–State Arbitration', LSE Law, Society and Economy Working Papers 8/2011: <http://www.lse.ac.uk/collections/law/wps/WPS2011-08_Kryvoi.pdf>; Jean Kalicki, 'Counterclaims by States in Investment Arbitration', Investment Treaty News, 14 January 2013: <http://www.iisd.org/itn/2013/01/14/counterclaims-by-states-in-investment-arbitration-2>.

[52] One may recall that the BIT litigation between Ecuador and Chevron originally arose from Ecuadorian authorities imposing damages on Chevron, purportedly under domestic law provisions.

[53] For instance, in the aftermath of the Bhopal gas tragedy of 1984, both the government of India and several victims of the gas leak initiated legal action against Union Carbide before US domestic courts.

[54] OECD, Guidelines for Multinational Enterprises, Annex I to the Declaration on International Investment and Multinational Enterprises, 25 May 2011; UN Global Compact: <www.globalcompact.org>; UN Global Compact Office, 'United Nations Guide to the Global Compact: A Practical Understanding

A recent innovation in this regard is the inclusion of binding obligations for the investors, in the text of IIAs. Some of the initial efforts in this direction took the form of references, in preambles or other provisions of IIAs, to the 'principles' of CSR, or requiring states parties to 'encourage' investors to abide by these principles.[55] While these provisions allowed the location of the 'sources' of some form of investors' obligations within the IIAs, they did not go as far as creating directly enforceable obligations for the investors, which an arbitral tribunal could enforce.

Perhaps a more ambitious iterations of the concept of investor obligations appears in the draft PAIC. These include that investors 'shall contribute to the economic, social and environmental progress with a view to achieving sustainable development of host states'. Another such provision obligates investors 'in performing their activities, [to] protect the environment and where such activity causes damages to the environment, take reasonable steps to restore it as far as possible'. Where an investor breaches these obligations, the host state may seek damages or other remedies for that breach, through counterclaims in an investment arbitration.

Thus, even in the most ambitious iteration of investor obligations currently available, those obligations act as a shield for the host state when a claim is brought against it before an arbitral tribunal by the investor. Those obligations do not allow the state to initiate investment arbitration in respect of environmental harm on its own accord and have those claims adjudicated. This may indeed be on account of a preference, on the part of the host states, to have their environmental claims against investors adjudicated by their own domestic courts under their own municipal laws.

18.2.4 Transparency

One of the criticisms often levelled against investment arbitration is that it lacks the transparency afforded by court proceedings. A few recent drafting innovations aim at added transparency in investment arbitration, that should permit heightened public scrutiny of disputes involving public interests, including environmental concerns.

of the Vision and the Nine Principles' (2003); Betty King, 'The UN Global Compact: Responsibility for Human Rights, Labour Relations, and the Environment in Developing Nations', 34 Cornell International Law Journal 481 (2001).

[55] See Canada–Peru FTA (2009), Art. 810: 'Each Party should encourage enterprises operating within its territory or subject to its jurisdiction to voluntarily incorporate internationally recognized standards of corporate social responsibility in their internal policies, such as statements of principle that have been endorsed or are supported by the Parties. These principles address issues such as labor, the environment, human rights, community relations and anti-corruption. The Parties therefore remind those enterprises of the importance of incorporating such corporate social responsibility standards in their internal policies'; Trans-Pacific Partnership, Art. 9.17: 'The Parties reaffirm the importance of each Party encouraging enterprises operating within its territory or subject to its jurisdiction to voluntarily incorporate into their internal policies those internationally recognised standards, guidelines and principles of corporate social responsibility that have been endorsed or are supported by that Party.'

The most notable initiative in this regard is the UNCITRAL Rules on Transparency in Treaty-based Investor–State Arbitration, which came into effect in 2014.[56] The Rules apply to any investor–state arbitration initiated under the UNCITRAL Arbitration Rules, pursuant to an investment treaty concluded on or after 1 April 2014, unless the parties to the treaty agree to the contrary.

The Rules create a repository, which receives the notice of arbitration, as soon as the claimant serves it on the respondent. The repository is required to make the notice of arbitration and the identity of the parties public, upon the receipt of the notice of arbitration. This permits public scrutiny of, and public engagement with, the arbitral process from the very beginning. The Rules also provide for publication of an extensive list of documents relating to the dispute, including statements and submissions of the parties, witness statements, and a table listing all the exhibits. The tribunal has discretion as to whether the exhibits themselves should be made public. The Rules also provide for public hearings and there are limited exceptions for confidential information.

Interestingly, the Rules appear to have found acceptance with the negotiators of some of the recent IIAs. The investment chapter of EU–Canada Comprehensive Economic and Trade Agreement (CETA) specifies that the transparency rules will apply.[57] CETA actually goes one step further in requiring that the exhibits themselves be published.[58] In addition, it provides for publication of the documents on a website, and for hearings to be open.[59] Similar proposals were also made in the EU informal proposal for TTIP and the final draft of the TPP.

18.2.5 Non-disputing party and interested third parties

With a view to safeguarding systemic interests in investment arbitration, some recent IIAs provide for participation by parties other than the claimant and the respondent.

CETA provides for participation by the 'non-disputing Party', meaning a CETA party, who is not directly involved in the dispute, with a view to making arguments on the interpretation of the treaty. Also, the rules of procedures permit the tribunal to receive unsolicited *amicus curiae* submissions from 'non-governmental persons established in a Party'.[60] Similar provisions were also included in the draft texts for TTIP and TPP.

The participation of non-disputing parties and interested third parties would presumably allow the tribunals to receive valuable perspectives on public interests involved in the dispute, even if neither of the disputing parties is interested in raising or pursuing those interests. This could be of particular value in environmental disputes.

[56] UNCITRAL Rules on Transparency in Treaty-based Investor–State Arbitration: <http://www.uncitral.org/pdf/english/texts/arbitration/rules-on-transparency/Rules-on-Transparency-E.pdf>.

[57] CETA, Art 8.36. [58] CETA, Art. 8.36.3. [59] CETA, Art. 8.36.5.

[60] CETA, Annex 29-A, paras. 43–6.

18.3 Scientific Uncertainty and Margin of Appreciation in Environmental Context

Environmental regulation often involves states undertaking complex scientific enquiries, and acting even where those enquiries are not entirely conclusive on the existence of the risks in question or the efficacy of the course of action under consideration. Were an investment arbitral tribunal called upon to review the state's action—say, in the context of an environmental exception like the ones discussed above—the standard of review that the tribunal adopts would likely have consequences on the outcome of the dispute.

The tribunal could look into the scientific evidence that was considered (or ought to have been considered) by the national authorities, and decide for itself *de novo* whether an environmental risk of the nature described by the host state actually existed, and whether the host state's response to that risk was appropriate. On the other hand, the tribunal could look into the scientific nature of the *process* and reasoning adopted by the host state, rather than the scientific accuracy of the outcome. In the former scenario, the possibility of the tribunal disagreeing with the state's assessment of the scientific evidence, and consequently finding the measure at issue to be not a genuine piece of environmental regulation, would be higher than that in the latter scenario.

While the WTO Appellate Body has repeatedly rejected the assertion that panels owe responding Members 'deference' in assessment of certain factual matters, some of the WTO agreements have mechanisms built into them that ensure that States do enjoy the ability to act in the face of uncertainty, and do enjoy some discretion where scientific questions cannot be answered with absolute certainty. For instance, Art. 5.7 of the Agreement on Sanitary and Phytosanitary Measures allows States to act against certain risks 'in cases where relevant scientific evidence is insufficient.' Also, interpreting Art. 5.1 of the SPS Agreement, the WTO Appellate Body has clarified that members are entitled to base measures covered by that agreement 'on divergent or minority views provided they are from a respected and qualified source.'[61] In that context, the adjudicatory role of a WTO panel examining whether a member's measures against an alleged risk lack scientific basis would be to (i) examine whether the scientific basis of the risk assessment comes from a respected and qualified source and can accordingly be considered 'legitimate science' according to the standards of the relevant scientific community; and (ii) examine whether the reasoning of the risk assessor is objective and coherent and that, therefore, its conclusions find sufficient support in the underlying scientific basis.[62]

IIAs do not typically contain language instructing arbitral tribunals how to react to situations like this. Each tribunal is somewhat at liberty to choose its own approach to such problems, informed by the practice of tribunals before them. However, some

[61] Appellate Body Reports, *US/Canada - Continued Suspension*, para. 677.

[62] Appellate Body Report, *Australia - Apples*, para. 220.

recent awards indicate that arbitral practice may lean towards the course adopted by the WTO, rather than towards *de novo* review. For instance, in *Methanex Corp* and *Glamis Gold Ltd*, the tribunal held:

> Having considered all the expert evidence adduced in these proceedings by both Disputing Parties, the Tribunal accepts the UC Report as reflecting a serious, objective and scientific approach to a complex problem in California. Whilst it is possible for other scientists and researchers to disagree in good faith with certain of its methodologies, analyses and conclusions, the fact of such disagreement, even if correct, does not warrant this Tribunal in treating the UC Report as part of a political sham by California. In particular, the UC Report was subjected at the time to public hearings, testimony and peer-review; and its emergence as a serious scientific work from such an open and informed debate is the best evidence that it was not the product of a political sham engineered by California, leading subsequently to the two measures impugned by Methanex in these arbitration proceedings. Moreover, in all material respects, the Tribunal is not persuaded that the UC Report was scientifically incorrect: the Tribunal was much impressed by the scientific expert witnesses presented by the USA and tested under crossexamination by Methanex; and the Tribunal accepts without reservation these experts' conclusions.[63]

While the tribunal does express a view of whether the evidence was 'scientifically incorrect', its main concern appears to have been whether the evidence before it represented a 'serious, objective and scientific approach'.

Recently, a number of other tribunals have sought to arrive at the same outcome through reliance on the concept of 'margin of appreciation'[64] originally developed by the European Court of Human Rights.[65] The doctrine is not without controversy, and has been rejected by some other tribunals and commentators as lacking applicability in the context of investment arbitration.[66]

[63] *Methanex Corp. v United States*, Final Award of the Tribunal on Jurisdiction and Merits, Part II, Ch. D.

[64] *Handyside v United Kingdom*, 24 ECtHR (ser. A) (1976), para. 48: 'By reason of their direct and continuous contact with the vital forces of their countries, state authorities are in principle in a better position than the international judge to give an opinion on the exact content of {the contents of a limitation clause} as well as on the necessity of a restriction or limitation intended to meet them.'

[65] *Electrabel S.A. v Republic of Hungary*, ICSID Case No. ARB/07/19, Decision on Jurisdiction, Applicable Law and Liability, 30 November 2012; *Cont'l Cas. Co. v Argentine Republic*, ICSID Case No. ARB/03/9, Award, 5 September 2008, para. 181 and n. 270; *Frontier Petroleum Servs. Ltd v Czech Republic*, UNCITRAL, Final Award, 12 November 2010, para. 527; *Micula v Romania*, ICSID Case No. ARB/05/20, Decision on Jurisdiction and Admissibility, 24 September 2008; William Burke-White and Andreas von Staden, 'Private Litigation in a Public Law Sphere: The Standard of Review in Investor-State Arbitrations', 35 Yale Journal of International Law 283 (2010); Barnali Choudhury, 'Recapturing Public Power: Is Investment Arbitration's Engagement of the Public Interest Contributing to the Democratic Deficit?' 41 Vanderbilt Journal of Transnational Law 775 (2008); Anna Katselas, 'Do Investment Treaties Prescribe a Deferential Standard of Review?' 34(1) Michigan Journal of International Law 87 (2012); Yuval Shany, 'Toward a General Margin of Appreciation Doctrine in International Law?' 16 European Journal of International Law 907 (2005); Jean-Pierre Cot, 'The Margin of Appreciation', in Wolfrum (n. 12).

[66] *Siemens A.G. v Argentine Republic*, ICSID Case No. ARB/02/8, Award, para. 354; Julian Arato, 'The Margin of Appreciation in International Investment Law', 54(3) Virginia Journal of International Law 545 (2014).

18.4 Conclusions

The foregoing discussion intends to introduce the readers to some aspects of the complex interactions between investment protection and the environment. In section 18.1, we reviewed the more 'classic' BIT provisions, and how they have been interpreted and applied in environmental contexts. As many authors have said before us, our enquiry in that section reveals a mixed bag of conclusions. There are instances where these classic provisions have been interpreted and applied to curtail states' ability to meaningfully pursue environmental regulation. In a number of instances, however, what may initially appear to be an attack on environmental regulation turns out, upon closer examination, to be aimed at the *manner* in which environmental regulation is undertaken—arbitrariness, discrimination, or protectionism. We have also identified the potential for these clauses, in certain circumstances, to be used by investors to demand a higher level of environmental protection than what the state is prepared to deliver. The only conclusion that one may derive about the relationship between these 'classic' BIT provisions and environmental objectives is that the outcome will depend on the specific treaty, the specific tribunal, and the fact pattern involved in each case.

Having concluded our discussion on 'classic' BIT provisions, we moved on to certain recent drafting innovations that appear to be promising, in that they seek to modify the operation of the 'classic' provisions in a manner more friendly towards the environment. While these provisions do signal how negotiators and drafters view the ideal interaction between the environment and investment protection, many obstacles need to be overcome before these provisions can be fully operationalized. Some of these provisions—like GATT-style general exceptions—while ambitious in their environmental objectives, are uncertain in their functional value. Also, since many of our examples in this discussion were derived from model BITs, it remains to be seen whether political consensus can be built around these provisions, so as to accord them a place in binding treaty texts.

Finally, departing from our examination of treaty texts—be they 'classic' or 'innovative'—we addressed a more systemic issue relating to whether investment tribunals can preserve the ability of states to act in a precautionary manner on environmental concerns, even where scientific evidence on the risks, and on the proposed solution, is not entirely conclusive. While we find that arbitral practice on that question is still evolving, we have found some indication that the tribunals may be accommodating in that regard. However, the precise legal basis on which they may choose that course of action remains uncertain.

Finally, if we were to offer one conclusion derived from the entirety of the discussion above, it would be that international investment law appears to be fast reinventing its relationship with the environment. Both negotiators and arbitrators appear to be moving towards finding balanced solutions. Thus, it would be unfair, at present, to judge international investment law's relationship with the environment entirely with reference to 'classic' BIT provisions and the historical baggage that comes with those provisions. While forces for a more balanced set of disciplines appear to be hard at work, it remains to be seen what the final outcome of this evolution will be.

CHAPTER 19

THE MULTIPLE FORMS OF TRANSPARENCY IN INTERNATIONAL INVESTMENT ARBITRATION

Their implications, and their limits

ESMÉ SHIRLOW AND †DAVID D. CARON[1]

In 1897, Australia's *Daily Telegraph* newspaper reported that renewed 'negotiations for an arbitration treaty between England and America... shows that there is a growing power of public opinion at the back of the arbitration movement'.[2] Some four years later, in 1901, the same newspaper predicted in reaction to the establishment of the Permanent Court of Arbitration that:

> [p]ublic interest in the institution will perhaps be stimulated a little when some nation invokes the court, and its inutility is shown by the other party refusing to have anything to do with arbitration...[3]

These diverging perspectives on the role of international arbitration, and on the levels of public interest in international arbitral proceedings, resonate in modern debates about

[1] David passed away before the completion of this chapter. I am grateful to David's family for trusting me to carry it forward to completion, and to the editors for their agreement to retain the chapter in this volume. David and I had many enjoyable and challenging discussions about transparency over the years that I knew him, and I am grateful to have had the opportunity to reflect the content of some of these conversations in this chapter. I gratefully acknowledge the contributions of Daniel Litwin for his research assistance in preparing this chapter.

[2] *The Daily Telegraph* (Sydney, Australia), 8 November 1897, 4.

[3] Ibid. 16 April 1901, 4.

state–state, individual–state, and international commercial arbitration.[4] This has particularly been the case for international investment arbitration, which involves claims filed by investors against states. In this field, there has been a particularly concerted campaign for the publication of awards and other arbitral documents, for the opening of arbitral hearings to the public, and for the participation of a more diverse group of stakeholders in arbitral proceedings.[5]

In isolation, each of these strands of the campaign for greater transparency in international investment arbitration might be characterized as a reform effort focused on a series of technical changes to aspects of the international arbitral process. They could alternatively, however, be viewed from a broader angle, insofar as collectively they articulate and are driven by more fundamental concerns about international investment arbitration. Seen from this broader perspective, the campaign for greater transparency in international investment arbitration is underpinned by differing perspectives on the structure of transparency, its role in the international arbitral

[4] Both state–state and individual–state arbitration differ from international commercial arbitration insofar as they involve at least one state as a disputing party, whereas international commercial arbitration takes place between private (non-state) parties. Despite their differences, these forms of arbitration are collectively referred to as 'international arbitration' in this chapter. Scholars have long debated the features that render an arbitral proceeding 'international' in character. Relevant factors suggested include whether the tribunal derives its mandate from a treaty; is empowered to determine disputes involving state/s; and/or uses international law as the applicable law. See e.g. Cesare Romano, Karen Alter, and Yuval Shany, 'Mapping International Adjudicative Bodies, the Issues, and Players', in Cesare Romano, Karen Alter, and Chrisanthi Avgerou (eds), *The Oxford Handbook of International Adjudication* (Oxford University Press, 2014) 6; Robert Kolb, *The International Court of Justice* (Hart, 2013) 72; Hege Elisabeth Kjos, *Applicable Law in Investor–State Arbitration: The Interplay between National and International Law* (Oxford University Press, 2013) 44. The present chapter does not seek to resolve these debates. It instead focuses on investment arbitration to highlight themes that may hold relevance to other forms of international arbitration, noting that structural differences may inform the salience of these themes in different contexts. See, further: †David D. Caron, 'Framing Political Theory of International Courts and Tribunals: Reflections at the Centennial', (2006) 100 Proceedings of the Annual Meeting 55 (American Society of International Law), 56.

[5] The literature on developments concerning transparency in investment arbitration is extensive. See e.g. David D. Caron, 'Regulating Opacity: Shaping How Tribunals Think', in David D. Caron et al. (eds), *Practising Virtue: Inside International Arbitration* (Oxford University Press, 2015); Esmé Shirlow, 'Dawn of a New Era? The UNCITRAL Rules and UN Convention on Transparency in Treaty-Based Investor–State Arbitration', (2016) 31 ICSID Review 622; João Ribeiro and Michael Douglas, 'Transparency in Investor–State Arbitration: The Way Forward', (2015) 11 Asian International Arbitration Journal 49; Emilie M. Hafner-Burton and David G. Victor, 'Secrecy in International Investment Arbitration: An Empirical Analysis', [2016] 7(1) Journal of International Dispute Settlement 161; Gabriele Ruscalla, 'Transparency in International Arbitration: Any (Concrete) Need to Codify the Standard?' (2015) 3 Groningen Journal of International Law 1; N. Jansen Calamita, 'Dispute Settlement Transparency in Europe's Evolving Investment Treaty Policy: Adopting the UNCITRAL Transparency Rules Approach', (2014) 15 Journal of World Investment and Trade 645; Julie Maupin, 'Transparency in International Investment Law: The Good, the Bad and the Murky', in Andrea Bianchi and Anne Peters (eds), *Transparency in International Law* (Cambridge University Press, 2013). There have also been calls for increased transparency during the negotiation of the instruments under which these arbitrations occur. This topic is outside the scope of this chapter, but is considered in: Esmé Shirlow, 'Three Manifestations of Transparency in International Investment Law: A Story of Sources, Stakeholders and Structures', (2017) 8 Goettingen Journal of International Law 73.

process, and the subjects and stakeholders which transparency might benefit. Reforms to transparency in international investment arbitration are thus 'both technically narrow and strategically broad'.[6]

This chapter considers the reforms sought through campaigns for greater procedural transparency in investment arbitration, and the concerns and motivations underlying such reforms. It proceeds in three parts. Section 19.1 tackles the question of what 'transparency' means. It draws out the differences between the concepts of 'availability', 'access', and 'participation' to identify three distinct types of 'transparency'. With these concepts as its backdrop, Section 19.2 examines the emergence of procedural transparency in international investment arbitration to explore how 'transparency' has been envisaged and articulated in that setting. Section 19.3 considers the key objectives said to underlie reforms to procedural transparency in investment arbitration. It connects those objectives to the three types of transparency identified in Section 19.1 to consider whether the types of reforms pursued thus far are adapted to achieving their stated purposes. A final section concludes.

This chapter uses procedural transparency in international investment arbitration as a case study to explore broader themes with relevance to other forms of international arbitration, including state–state and international commercial arbitration. Different types of international arbitration are procedurally unique and implicate a range of differing interests and stakeholders. Each type of international arbitration has nevertheless come under increased scrutiny and pressure to reform. This chapter highlights that campaigns for reform involve more than just technical dimensions. To understand reform movements in any field, it is necessary to consider *what* is being sought through reform, *why* it is being sought, and whether proposed reforms are *adapted* and *sufficient* to achieve those goals. By focusing on these issues as they arise in relation to transparency reforms in international investment arbitration, the chapter sets forth a framework that can be deployed to analyse the promises and pitfalls of other reform options in other fields of international dispute settlement.

19.1 The Multiple Forms of Transparency

Transparency is a concept that is 'difficult to grasp in terms of content'.[7] It holds a multitude of possible meanings, even where invoked within a single field of law.[8] References to 'transparency' in international arbitration might, for example, refer to the public

[6] Caron (n. 5), 379.

[7] Andrea Bianchi, 'On Power and Illusion: The Concept of Transparency in International Law', in Bianchi and Peters (n. 5), 7.

[8] See, generally: ibid.; Anne Peters, 'Towards Transparency as a Global Norm', in Bianchi and Peters (n. 5), 534–5; Maupin (n. 5), 142, 160.

availability of information about the activities of the participants or institutions involved in international arbitrations, the norms applied to determine disputes, or the extent to which individual proceedings are publicly accessible or documents produced in those proceedings made publicly available.[9] It could alternatively refer to the capacity of third parties to view or participate in the creation of applicable norms or in specific arbitration proceedings.[10] The meaning and purpose of 'transparency' will therefore differ according to the specific context in which it is invoked.[11] In this chapter, the term 'transparency' is used to designate the availability and accessibility of information about arbitral proceedings, as well as the capacity to participate in those proceedings.[12] This has been termed 'procedural' transparency in the existing literature.[13] The distinction between availability, accessibility, and participation in this definition of transparency is important, because it signifies that there can be qualitatively different forms of 'transparency' in international arbitration.

Where it is used to designate the 'availability' of information, 'transparency' becomes an information-centric concept.[14] From this perspective, entities might be considered to be 'transparent' where they 'increase the amount of information available to the public about their activities, intentions and decision-making processes'.[15] Arbitral proceedings might thus be classified as 'transparent' to the extent, for example, that information about their existence or substance is made publicly available.[16] Transparency-as-availability entails the disclosure of information. The scope of such transparency will depend upon *how much* information is made available about arbitral proceedings. At its most limited, it might describe the availability of information about the disputing parties to an arbitral proceeding, or even the very existence of that proceeding. It could otherwise refer to the disclosure of a range of documents generated in the arbitral process or to the opening of arbitral hearings to public view.

Transparency-as-accessibility requires something more than the mere release of information about arbitral proceedings. It entails that information released about arbitral proceedings be of a certain *quality* that makes it comprehendible—and so accessible—to its target(s).[17] This is a more 'user-centric' notion of transparency.[18] Whereas

[9] Shirlow, 'Dawn of a New Era?' (n. 5), 624. [10] Ibid. 624–5. [11] Bianchi (n. 7), 8.

[12] This definition builds on Shirlow, 'Three Manifestations of Transparency' (n. 5), 74.

[13] Joachim Delaney and Daniel Magraw, 'Procedural Transparency', in Peter Muchlinski, Federico Ortino, and Christoph Schreuer (eds), *The Oxford Handbook of International Investment Law* (Oxford University Press, 2008).

[14] Maupin (n. 5), 150.

[15] Daniel R. McCarthy and Matthew Fluck, 'The Concept of Transparency in International Relations: Towards a Critical Approach', (2017) 23 European Journal of International Relations 416, 421.

[16] Some basic information about international arbitration—even if not about specific disputes—has always been available for public view. See generally Maupin (n. 5), 151.

[17] This has been referred to as 'transparency as information' in other fields: McCarthy and Fluck (n. 15).

[18] Jenifer Shkabatur, 'Transparency With(out) Accountability: Open Government in the United States', 31 Yale Law & Policy Review 79 (2012), 127.

'transparency-as-availability' focuses on the release of information *from* a regime *to* a target, 'transparency-as-accessibility' focuses on the receipt of that information *by* the target.[19] In this model of transparency, disclosures of information will only achieve 'transparency' insofar as they are sufficient to allow the target to understand something about the information that has been released.[20] This form of transparency empowers the target of the transparency measures to 'readily grasp, compare, and evaluate' released information.[21] The disclosure of information will thus achieve 'transparency-as-accessibility' where it generates 'clarity around decision-making processes'[22] such as to support the ability of the target to 'understand' and 'make use of the information'.[23]

Finally, rather than referring to the capacity of a target to observe or understand an arbitral proceeding, 'transparency' might entail a capacity of that target to actively take part in that arbitral proceeding. 'Transparency-as-participation' focuses upon there being a 'dialogue' between arbitral tribunals and the target(s) of transparency measures.[24] This form of transparency focuses neither on the transfer of information ('availability') nor on understanding of that information ('accessibility'), but rather on the ability of the target to participate in the process by which information is constructed ('participation'). Transparency-as-participation may differ in degree depending upon the 'quality, quantity and diversity of input' afforded to the target.[25] It might entail, for example, a capacity for non-disputing parties to file written submissions to a tribunal about a dispute, a requirement for the tribunal to engage with those written submissions, or even procedural equality between the disputing parties and certain non-disputing parties who are nonetheless stakeholders in the outcome of a dispute.

As Figure 19.1 illustrates, these three types of transparency build upon one another and are interlinked. Transparency-as-availability is a 'foundational' form of transparency.[26]

[19] See, similarly, on the one- versus two-way interactions implied in differing accounts of transparency: McCarthy and Fluck (n. 15), 421. See, for discussion of how release of information might *undermine* transparency as accessibility, Marilyn Strathern, 'The Tyranny of Transparency', 26 British Educational Research Journal 309 (2000), 313 (suggesting that the release of 'more information' might lead to 'less understanding').

[20] McCarthy and Fluck (n. 15), 419–20; William Mock, 'On the Centrality of Information Law: A Rational Choice Discussion Law and Transparency', 17 John Marshall Journal of Computer and Information Law 1069 (1999), 1081.

[21] Shkabatur (n. 18), 127. See, similarly, Anoeska Buijze, 'The Six Faces of Transparency', 9 Utrecht Law Review 3 (2013), 9.

[22] McCarthy and Fluck (n. 15), 421. [23] Mock (n. 20), 1081.

[24] McCarthy and Fluck (n. 15), 422.

[25] Elizabeth Figueroa, 'Transparency in Administrative Courts: From the Outside Looking In', 35 Journal of the National Association of Administrative Law Judiciary 1 (2015), 8.

[26] Anne Peters, 'The Transparency Turn of International Law', 1 Chinese Journal of Global Governance 3 (2015), 3. See, similarly, Cristoffer Nyegaard Mollestad, 'See No Evil? Procedural Transparency in International Investment Law and Dispute Settlement', 79, and Johannes Koepp and Cameron Sim, 'The Application of Transparency', 65, in Dimitrij Euler et al. (eds), *Transparency in International Investment*

Participation	• procedural equality between third parties and disputing parties • requirement for disputing parties or the arbitral tribunal to respond to third party submissions • capacity for third parties to make oral submissions • capacity for third parties to make written submissions	Active transparency ↑
Accessibility	• public outreach activities, including trainings • tours of facilities for the media, the public, etc. • written or webcast summaries of arbitral decisions • use of press releases to issue information about arbitral proceedings, institutions, or rules	
Availability	• holding of open hearings (physical, webcast) • release of documents from arbitral proceedings • release of basic information about arbitral proceedings, institutions, or rules	Passive transparency

FIGURE 19.1 The Different Dimensions of Transparency

It is foundational because a target of transparency can neither comprehend nor participate in arbitral proceedings without having access to at least some relevant information about them. Despite being foundational, transparency-as-availability is the most passive form of transparency. It may be present without any act of comprehension or interaction on the part of the target with the available information.

Transparency-as-accessibility builds upon transparency-as-availability because it entails that available information be released for a particular purpose and be adapted to achieve that purpose. It might not be sufficient to achieve transparency-as-accessibility, for example, for an arbitral institution to release hundreds of pages of arbitral documents if the stakeholders intended to benefit from the release of those documents are unable to process and understand the information contained within them. 'Accessibility' renders 'availability' meaningful, and 'participation' possible. Transparency-as-participation entails the most active form of transparency, according to which information is made available and accessible in order to support the interaction of the target of transparency with the process through which the available or accessible information was generated. Section 19.2 introduces the campaign for increased procedural transparency in international investment arbitration by reference to these differing understandings of transparency.[27]

Arbitration: A Guide to the UNICTRAL Rules on Transparency in Treaty-Based Investor–State Arbitration (Cambridge University Press, 2015); UNCITRAL, 'Report of Working Group II (Arbitration and Conciliation) on the Work of Its Fifty-Third Session (Vienna, 4–8 October 2010)', (2010) UN Doc. A/CN.9/712 32.

[27] Efforts to achieve greater transparency in the negotiation of investment treaties could also be analysed according to these differing understandings of transparency. This topic is, however, outside the scope of this chapter.

19.2 Procedural Transparency in International Investment Arbitration: From Absence, to Availability, and Participation

The investment treaties and contracts under which many early investment arbitrations were conducted were largely silent on the issue of procedural transparency.[28] The absence of provisions favouring transparency in treaties, contracts, and institutional rules meant that issues of transparency for many early investment arbitrations were regulated by tribunals and disputing parties on a case-by-case basis.[29] Whilst most tribunals accepted that there was no presumption of confidentiality in investment arbitration,[30] the ad hoc resolution of transparency issues caused procedural unpredictability as to what—if any—information might be disclosed for each case.[31] This situation kindled criticisms of investment arbitration, which came to be perceived as a 'secret' form of dispute settlement.[32] Such criticisms ultimately prompted states and arbitral institutions to initiate reforms to the procedures associated with international investment arbitration. This included reforms designed to make publicly available more information about arbitral proceedings and to provide greater participatory rights for non-disputing parties. This section introduces key reforms to investment treaties and institutional rules to show how they have promoted transparency as both 'availability' and 'participation' in investment arbitration proceedings.

[28] See, generally, Nyegaard Mollestad (n. 26), 38; Shirlow, 'Dawn of a New Era?' (n. 5), 625; David Gaukrodger and Kathryn Gordon, 'Investor–State Dispute Settlement: A Scoping Paper for the Investment Policy Community', [2012] OECD Working Papers on International Investment, Paper No. 2012/364.

[29] See, generally, Gary B. Born and Ethan G. Shenkman, 'Confidentiality and Transparency in Commercial and Investor–State International Arbitration', in Catherine A. Rogers and Roger P. Alford (eds), *The Future of Investment Arbitration* (Oxford University Press, 2009), 32. Compare e.g. *Methanex*, Decision of the Tribunal on Petitions from Third Persons to Intervene as 'Amici Curiae', 15-Jan-2001; *United Parcel Service of America Inc v Canada*, UNCITRAL, Decision of the Tribunal on Petitions for Intervention and Participation as *Amici Curiae* (17 October 2001); *Glamis Gold v United States of America*, UNCITRAL, Decision on Application and Submission by Quechan Indian Nation (16 September 2005).

[30] See e.g. *Biwater Gauff (Tanzania) Limited v United Republic of Tanzania*, ICSID Case No. ARB/05/22, Procedural Order No. 3 (29 September 2006), para. 121.

[31] See e.g. the approaches adopted in: *United Parcel Service of America Inc v Canada*, UNCITRAL, Decision of the Tribunal on Petitions for Intervention and Participation as *Amici Curiae* (17 October 2001) (n. 29); *Methanex Corporation v United States of America*, UNCITRAL, Decision of the Tribunal on Petitions for Persons to Intervene as *Amici Curiae* (15 January 2001); *Glamis Gold v United States of America*, UNCITRAL, Decision on Application and Submission by Quechan Indian Nation (16 September 2005) (n. 29).

[32] See e.g. Ruth Teitelbaum, 'A Look At the Public Interest in Investment Arbitration: Is It Unique? What Should We Do About It?' (2010) 5 Publicist 54.

19.2.1 Treaty practice

Most early investment treaties did not contain detailed rules related to procedural transparency. Over time, however, states modified their treaty-drafting practice to ensure that more information about investment arbitrations would be publicly available. An early example of an investment treaty addressing issues of transparency was the 1994 North American Free Trade Agreement (NAFTA) between Canada, Mexico, and the United States (US).[33] That treaty incorporated a number of positive disclosure obligations providing for a framework of transparency-as-availability.[34] Article 1127 of NAFTA, for example, required responding states to provide to the other NAFTA states any notices of arbitration they received under NAFTA, as well as 'copies of all pleadings filed in the arbitration'.[35] NAFTA also incorporated transparency provisions designed to benefit the public more broadly. Article 1137, for example, addressed the public release of arbitral awards.[36]

As the NAFTA experience shows, transparency-as-availability may be directed towards the public at large, but narrower classes of beneficiaries for transparency measures are also possible. Indeed, in 2001, the NAFTA parties expanded their existing disclosure obligations to target a wider class of beneficiaries than just themselves, recording their agreement 'to make public in a timely manner all documents submitted to, or issued by' NAFTA investor–state arbitral tribunals.[37] In 2003, the US and Canada expanded the scope of information to be made publicly available, recording their agreement to the opening of arbitral hearings to the public.[38] The NAFTA parties also in that year addressed the issue of transparency-as-participation by issuing a statement on non-disputing party participation in NAFTA investor–state proceedings.[39] The statement provided for the filing of written submissions by certain non-disputing parties with leave from the tribunal.[40] It thus shifted the emphasis from

[33] North American Free Trade Agreement between the Government of Canada, the Government of the United Mexican States, and the Government of the United States of America (1992/1994).

[34] Ibid. On the leadership of NAFTA states on this issue, see generally: Jack J. Coe, 'Transparency in the Resolution of Investor–State Disputes: Adoption, Adaptation, and NAFTA Leadership', 54 University of Kansas Law Review 1339 (2006), 1339–40; Nyegaard Mollestad (n. 26); Calamita (n. 5), 645.

[35] North American Free Trade Agreement between the Government of Canada, the Government of the United Mexican States, and the Government of the United States of America (1992/1994), Art. 1127.

[36] Ibid. 1137. Under Annex 1137.4, where either Canada or the US is the respondent party, that state or the claimant investor may make the arbitral award public; where Mexico is the respondent party, the applicable arbitration rules apply to the publication of an award.

[37] NAFTA Free Trade Commission, 'Notes of Interpretation of Certain Chapter 11 Provisions', 31 July 2001, para. A(2)(b).

[38] Statement of the Free Trade Commission on Non-disputing Party Participation, 7 October 2003 (2004 16 WTAM 167); United States and Canada, Statement on Open Hearings in NAFTA Chapter Eleven Arbitrations, 7 October 2003.

[39] Ibid.

[40] Statement of the Free Trade Commission on Non-disputing Party Participation, 7 October 2003; United States and Canada, Statement on Open Hearings in NAFTA Chapter Eleven Arbitrations, 7 October 2003.

transparency-as-availability of arbitral materials towards a view of transparency encompassing limited opportunities for participation by non-disputing parties in arbitral proceedings.

Following these NAFTA developments, the US and Canada revised their model investment treaties to incorporate similar transparency frameworks. The 2004 US model investment treaty, for example, incorporated provisions requiring the disclosure by the responding state of materials produced during arbitral proceedings, including its pleadings.[41] It further provided for the publication of arbitral awards, orders, and hearing transcripts, as well as open hearings.[42] The model thus sought to transition from the (absent) transparency regime applicable under existing US investment treaties towards a regime of 'availability'. The model treaty also addressed the issue of participation, envisaging scope for arbitral tribunals to accept *amicus curiae* submissions from non-disputing third parties.[43] Canada's 2004 model treaty similarly provided for the publication of all documents submitted to and issued by the arbitral tribunal, open hearings, and the filing of *amicus* submissions.[44] The model clarified, however, that any tribunal granting leave for the filing of *amicus* submissions was 'not required to address the submission at any point in the arbitration'.[45]

Subsequent treaty practice from 2005 onwards has reflected these expanding conceptions of transparency. Treaties have provided, inter alia, for the public release of documents[46] and open hearings[47] as well as the filing of written submissions by non-disputing third parties.[48] Treaty-drafting practice has thus shifted from silence on the issue of transparency, towards transparency regimes providing for greater availability of information about arbitral proceedings and some limited opportunities for non-disputing parties to participate in those proceedings. These reforms suggest that—at least in some respects—'[i]nvestor–state treaty arbitration ceased to be hidden from public view long ago'.[49]

[41] United States Model Investment Treaty (2004), Art. 29(1).

[42] Ibid. Arts. 29(1)(d) and (e), 29(2).

[43] Ibid. Art. 28(3).

[44] Canada Model Investment Treaty (2004), Arts. 38(1) (open hearings), 38(3) (publication of documents), 38(4) (publication of award), 39 (*amicus* submissions).

[45] Ibid. Art. 39(7).

[46] See, for an early example, Agreement between the United Mexican States and the Republic of Panama for the Promotion and Reciprocal Protection of Investments (2005), Art. 20(4) ('El laudo arbitral será público, a menos que las partes contendientes acuerden lo contrario').

[47] See, for an early example, Treaty between the United States of America and the Oriental Republic of Uruguay concerning the Encouragement and Reciprocal Protection of Investment (2005), Art. 29(2) ('The tribunal shall conduct hearings open to the public and shall determine, in consultation with the disputing parties, the appropriate logistical arrangements').

[48] See ibid. Art. 28(3) ('The tribunal shall have the authority to accept and consider amicus curiae submissions from a person or entity that is not a disputing party').

[49] Charles N. Brower and Sadie Blanchard, 'What's in a Meme? The Truth about Investor–State Arbitration: Why It Need Not, and Must Not, Be Repossessed by States', 52 Columbia Journal of Transnational Law 689 (2013), 717.

19.2.2 Institutional reforms

Changes to treaty-drafting practice occurred in parallel with amendments to institutional procedural rules. Until the mid-2000s, institutional procedural rules were either silent as to procedural transparency or provided for transparency on an opt-in basis (i.e. with the consent of both disputing parties). The 1976 Arbitration Rules of the United Nations Commission on International Trade Law ('UNCITRAL Rules') provided, for example, that arbitral awards could only be published or proceedings opened with the consent of the disputing parties.[50] The Arbitration Rules of the International Centre for Settlement of Investment Disputes ('ICSID Rules') similarly required party consent for the attendance of third parties at hearings (until 2006),[51] though were more permissive in providing for the publication of basic information about arbitral proceedings registered in the ICSID framework.[52] The ICSID Rules also provided (from 1984) for the publication of excerpts of legal reasoning from ICSID arbitration awards.[53] Such institutional rules nevertheless on the whole reflected a view that confidentiality was a principal advantage of international arbitration.[54] Beginning in the mid-2000s, however, arbitral institutions came under increasing pressure to provide for greater procedural transparency. This led to reform movements in both the ICSID (2004–6 and 2018–) and UNCITRAL (2007–14 and 2017–) frameworks. The following subsections provide a brief chronological overview of these reform processes.

19.2.2.1 *ICSID transparency reforms, 2004–2006*

In 2004, the ICSID Secretariat published a working paper setting out possible amendments to ICSID procedures.[55] The paper proposed amendments to the ICSID Rules to provide for greater availability of information about ICSID proceedings, and to support the participation of non-disputing third parties in such proceedings.[56] In 2005, a follow-up paper was published by the Secretariat, proposing text to implement the reforms discussed in the

[50] See e.g. Arbitration Rules of the United Nations Commission on International Trade Law (1976), UNGA Res. 31/98 Art. 25(4) ('Hearings shall be held in camera unless the parties agree otherwise'); Art. 32(5) ('The award may be made public only with the consent of both parties').

[51] ICSID Rules of Procedure for Arbitration Proceedings Rules 32(2), 37(2).

[52] Convention on the Settlement of Investment Disputes between States and Nationals of Other States (1965/1966) 575 UNTS 159 Art. 48(5); ICSID Rules of Procedure for Arbitration Proceedings Rules 6(2), 48(4); ICSID Administrative and Financial Regulations Reg. 22(1).

[53] ICSID Rules of Procedure for Arbitration Proceedings (1984), Rule 48(4).

[54] See further: L. Yves Fortier, 'The Occasionally Unwarranted Assumption of Confidentiality', 15 Arbitration International 131 (1999), 130; Leon E. Trakman, 'Confidentiality in International Commercial Arbitration', 18 Arbitration International 1 (2002), 1; Born and Shenkman (n. 29), 21.

[55] ICSID Secretariat, 'Possible Improvements of the Framework for ICSID Arbitration' (2004), 7–11: <https://icsid.worldbank.org/apps/ICSIDWEB/resources/Documents/Possible%20Improvements%20of%20the%20Framework%20of%20ICSID%20Arbitration.pdf>.

[56] Ibid.

2004 paper.[57] These amendments were adopted in 2006,[58] revising the ICSID Rules to provide for the publication of arbitral documents,[59] the filing of *amicus curiae* submissions,[60] and the holding of open hearings.[61] The publication of arbitral documents, as well as the holding of open hearings, remained subject to party consent under these amendments. Despite these reforms, disputing party preferences meant that written and oral proceedings in ICSID arbitrations frequently remained closed to public view. An empirical study has even suggested that parties involved in arbitrations initiated subsequent to these reforms are 'more likely to conceal the outcome of arbitration than are the parties to disputes that took place prior to ICSID's intensive efforts to increase transparency'.[62]

19.2.2.2 *UNCITRAL transparency reforms, 2007–2014*

The UNCITRAL Rules were developed by a Working Group of the United Nations Commission on International Trade Law. The Working Group first raised the issue of transparency in investment arbitration as a possible topic for revised rules in 2000.[63] It was only in 2007, however, that the possibility of providing for greater transparency in UNCITRAL arbitral procedures gained real traction.[64] In 2008, UNCITRAL tasked the Working Group with a mandate to develop reforms to recognize the importance of transparency in investment arbitration.[65] In 2009, the Working Group indicated that it was ready to consider the matter of transparency in treaty-based arbitration 'as a matter of priority'.[66] Ultimately, this led to the development, and adoption in 2014, of Rules on Transparency in Treaty-based Investor–State Arbitration ('Transparency Rules').[67]

[57] ICSID Secretariat, 'Suggested Changes to the ICSID Rules and Regulations' (2005), 3–4: <https://icsid.worldbank.org/apps/ICSIDWEB/resources/Documents/Suggested%20Changes%20to%20the%20ICSID%20Rules%20and%20Regulations.pdf>.

[58] Rules of Arbitration of the International Centre for Settlement of Investment Disputes (2006), Rules 32 and 37; ICSID Additional Facility Arbitration Rules, Arts. 39 and 41.

[59] ICSID Rules of Procedure for Arbitration Proceedings, Rule 48(4).

[60] Ibid. Rule 37(2).

[61] Ibid. Rule 32(2).

[62] Emilie M. Hafner-Burton, Zachary C. Steinert-Threlkeld, and David G. Victor, 'Predictability versus Flexibility: Secrecy in International Investment Arbitration', 68 World Politics 413 (2016), 436.

[63] UNCITRAL, 'Report of the Working Group on Arbitration on the Work of Its Thirty-Second Session (Vienna, 20–31 March 2000)' (2000) A/CN.9/468 paras 6(f), 107(f). See, for a detailed overview of discussions of transparency in this forum: Shirlow, 'Dawn of a New Era?' (n. 5).

[64] UNCITRAL, 'Report of the Working Group on Arbitration and Conciliation on the Work of Its Forty-Sixth Session (New York, 5–9 February 2007)' (2007), para. 61.

[65] UNCITRAL, 'Report of the United Nations Commission on International Trade Law, Forty-First Session (16 June–3 July 2008)' (2008) A/6317, para. 314.

[66] UNCITRAL, 'Report of Working Group II (Arbitration and Conciliation) on the Work of Its Fiftieth Session (New York, 9–13 February 2009)' (2009) UN Doc. A/CN.9/669, para. 121.

[67] United Nations General Assembly, 'United Nations Commission on International Trade Law Rules on Transparency in Treaty-Based Investor–State Arbitration and Arbitration Rules (as revised in 2010, with New Article 1, Paragraph 4, as Adopted in 2013)', Resolution adopted by the General Assembly on 16 December 2013, 68/09.

The Transparency Rules 'reverse the presumptions of confidentiality and privacy in investment treaty arbitration in favour of a presumption of openness'.[68] The Rules provide for the public release of documents generated during arbitral proceedings.[69] They also permit non-disputing parties to attend oral hearings[70] and to participate in proceedings by filing written submissions.[71] The Rules thus enhance the public availability of information about arbitral proceedings and the scope for participation by non-disputing parties. The Rules apply to arbitrations filed under treaties concluded after 1 April 2014, or to arbitrations under earlier treaties where the disputing parties consent to their application.[72] To broaden the applicability of the Rules, a Convention on Transparency in Investor–State Treaty-Based Arbitration was adopted by UNCITRAL in 2014.[73] The Convention provides a mechanism for states to consent to the application of the Transparency Rules to arbitral proceedings filed under treaties already in force on 1 April 2014, whether or not initiated under the UNCITRAL Rules.[74] The Transparency Convention entered into force on 18 October 2017.[75]

19.2.2.3 *UNCITRAL transparency reforms, 2017–*

In 2017, UNCITRAL resolved to move the question of possible further reforms to investment arbitration to a different Working Group for consideration.[76] That Working Group met towards the end of 2017 to address possible reforms through a three-step process.[77] In a first stage—completed in 2018[78]—the Working Group sought 'to identify and consider concerns' about investment arbitration.[79] In a second stage, now also completed, the Working Group 'consider[ed] whether reform [was] desirable in light of any identified concerns'.[80] Now in the third stage, the Working Group is 'develop[ing] any relevant solutions to be recommended to the Commission'.[81]

[68] Stephan W. Schill, 'Transparency as a Global Norm in International Investment Law' (*Kluwer Arbitration Blog*, 15 September 2014): <www.kluwerarbitrationblog.com/2014/09/15/transparency-as-a-global-norm-in-international-investment-law/>.

[69] United Nations General Assembly (n. 67), Arts. 2 (information about the commencement of arbitral proceedings) and 3 (documents generated in the proceedings).

[70] Ibid. Art. 6. [71] Ibid. Art. 4. [72] Ibid. Art. 1(2).

[73] United Nations General Assembly, Resolution 69/116 ('United Nations Convention on Transparency in Treaty-based Investor–State Arbitration'), UN Doc. No. A/Res/69/116 (18 December 2014).

[74] Ibid. Art. 2.

[75] See UNCITRAL, 'Status: United Nations Convention on Transparency in Treaty-based Investor–State Arbitration (New York, 2014)': <www.uncitral.org/uncitral/en/uncitral_texts/arbitration/2014Transparency_Convention_status.html>.

[76] United Nations General Assembly, 'Report of the United Nations Commission on International Trade Law Fiftieth Session (3–21 July 2017)', UN Doc A/72/17, para. 264.

[77] See, generally: UNCITRAL, 'Report of Working Group III (Investor–State Dispute Settlement Reform) on the Work of Its Thirty-Fourth Session (Vienna, 27 November–1 December 2017)' (2017), A/CN.9/930/Rev.1.

[78] UNCITRAL, 'Report of Working Group III (Investor–State Dispute Settlement Reform) on the Work of Its Thirty-Sixth Session, Part I' (2018) A/CN.9/964.

[79] UNCITRAL (n. 77), para. 19. [80] Ibid. para. 19. [81] Ibid. para. 19.

Transparency has featured as a central part of these discussions. In its first meeting under the new reform mandate, the Working Group emphasized 'the importance of transparency in ISDS [investor–state dispute settlement]', with delegates noting that:

> transparency was a key element of the rule of law, and of access to justice as well as the legitimacy of the ISDS system. In that light, it was said that transparency was important for shedding light on ISDS, thus providing states the necessary information to respond to general criticisms of ISDS.[82]

In completing the first part of its mandate, the Working Group identified 'two potential areas of work' to enhance procedural transparency in investment arbitration.[83] The Working Group first encouraged 'the implementation and promotion of the transparency standards' in the Rules and Convention, as a means of enhancing 'public understanding of ISDS' and addressing 'the perceived lack of legitimacy of the system'.[84] The Working Group further identified aspects of arbitral proceedings to which transparency requirements could be extended, including arbitrator appointment processes[85] and third-party funding.[86]

19.2.2.4 *ICSID transparency reforms: 2018–*

A further reform process was initiated by the ICSID Secretariat in 2018. Amongst other proposed reforms, the Secretariat has suggested reforms to enhance transparency in ICSID proceedings. These amendments would provide for the publication of arbitral decisions and orders within 60 days if neither party objects to such publication within that time period.[87] The suggested reforms further provide for open hearings and the publication of hearing transcripts absent objection by the disputing parties.[88] The envisaged amendments retain the capacity for non-disputing parties to apply to make written submissions as part of arbitral proceedings.[89] In developing these reforms, the Secretariat has specifically acknowledged the connection between transparency-as-availability and transparency-as-participation. It has noted, for example, that comments received from states and other stakeholders indicate that non-disputing parties should 'be given greater access to case documents and hearings', and that decisions on non-disputing party participation should be publicly released 'so third parties and states could better understand how the criteria in the Rules are applied'.[90]

[82] Ibid. para 80. [83] Ibid. para 87. [84] ibid. para 87.

[85] UNCITRAL, 'Report of Working Group III (Investor–State Dispute Settlement Reform) on the Work of Its Thirty-Fifth Session (New York, 23–7 April 2018)' (2018) A/CN.9/935, paras. 76–7; UNCITRAL, 'Report of Working Group III (Investor–State Dispute Settlement Reform) on the Work of Its Thirty-Sixth Session, Part I', paras. 102–3.

[86] UNCITRAL, 'Report of Working Group III (Investor–State Dispute Settlement Reform) on the Work of Its Thirty-Fifth Session (New York, 23–27 April 2018)', paras. 90–92.

[87] ICSID Secretariat, 'Proposals for Amendment of the ICSID Rules: Synopsis, Volume 1' (2018), para. 45 (the reforms deem there to be party consent to the publication of awards if the parties do not object to such publication in writing within that time period: para. 44).

[88] Ibid. para. 47. [89] Ibid. para. 48.

[90] ICSID Secretariat, 'Proposals for Amendment of the ICSID Rules: Working Paper, Volume 3' (2018), 892.

19.2.3 Conclusions

This section has outlined the various approaches that have been taken to date to address and increase procedural transparency in investor–state arbitration. It outlined key changes to state treaty practice and institutional rules to consider what new aspects of investment arbitration have been opened to view and interaction. From this brief overview, it is clear that states and arbitral institutions have effected multiple changes to the transparency regimes applicable in investment arbitrations.[91] As a result, investment arbitration has moved closer and in some aspects even beyond the transparency regimes applicable in other international,[92] and domestic,[93] settings. In their reform efforts, states and arbitral institutions have, however, emphasized particular types of transparency over others. Reform has focussed on increasing both the availability of information about international arbitral proceedings, and the capacity for a greater range of stakeholders to participate in those proceedings. As Figure 19.2 highlights, matters of accessibility have yet to be squarely addressed, and issues of participation have only been addressed at the margins.

Participation	~	procedural equality between third parties and disputing parties	Active transparency
	~	requirement for disputing parties or the arbitral tribunal to respond to third party submissions	
	~	capacity for third parties to make oral submissions	
	✓	capacity for third parties to make written submissions	
Accessibility	~	public outreach activities, including trainings	
	~	tours of facilities for the media, the public, etc.	
	~	written or webcast summaries of arbitral decisions	
	~	use of press releases to issue information about arbitral proceedings, institutions, or rules	
Availability	~	holding of open hearings (physical, webcast)	
	✓	release of documents from arbitral proceedings	
	✓	release of basic information about arbitral proceedings, institutions, or rules	Passive transparency

FIGURE 19.2 The Different Dimensions of Procedural Transparency in Investment Arbitration

[91] On these and other reforms, see further David D. Caron and Esmé Shirlow, 'Dissecting Backlash: The Unarticulated Causes of Backlash and Its Unintended Consequences', in Geir Ulfstein and Andreas Føllesdal (eds), *The Judicialization of International Law: A Mixed Blessing?* (Oxford University Press, 2018).

[92] For an overview of approaches to transparency in other international adjudicative contexts, see Thore Neumann and Bruno Simma, 'Transparency in International Adjudication', in Bianchi and Peters (n. 5), 449.

[93] European Parliament Directorate-General for External Policies, *The Investment Chapters of the EU's International Trade and Investment Agreements in a Comparative Perspective* (2015), 74: <www.europarl.europa.eu/thinktank/en/document.html?reference=EXPO_STU%282015%29534998>.

19.3 The Implications of Different Forms of Transparency in International Arbitration: Being Transparent about the Goals and Limits of Transparency

States and arbitral institutions have cited a range of concerns to which transparency reforms have purportedly been addressed. Increased transparency has, for example, been favoured as a means of keeping arbitral tribunals accountable, of enhancing the consistency and predictability of case outcomes, of improving the quality of arbitral awards, and of enhancing the legitimacy of international arbitration.[94] Transparency thus operates as 'a placeholder for multiple anxieties' about international arbitration.[95] It is nevertheless important to identify the precise goals to which reforms to transparency are addressed, because such goals should inform the types of transparency which are sought. This section introduces two of the key objectives stated to underlie reforms to procedural transparency in international investment arbitration. It connects those objectives to the types of transparency introduced in Section 19.1. This analysis demonstrates how the achievement of reform objectives will depend upon the presence of certain types of transparency, as well as on an awareness of their limitations.

19.3.1 Transparency as a means of enhancing accountability

Proponents of increased procedural transparency in investment arbitration commonly suggest that transparency offers a means of enhancing the accountability of arbitral

[94] See e.g. ICSID Secretariat (n. 90), 857. Transparency may also be sought for non-instrumental reasons. It is frequently justified as intrinsically valuable, for example, because it is linked to other values, including equality, autonomy, participation, trust, the rule of law, or fairness. See further: Claudia Reith, 'Enhancing Greater Transparency in the UNCITRAL Arbitration Rules: A Futile Attempt', 2 Yearbook on International Arbitration 297 (2012), 300; Geir Ulfstein, '*Transparency in International Law*, edited by Andrea Bianchi and Anne Peters', 109 American Journal of International Law 448 (2015), 448; Avinash Poorooye and Ronan Feehily, 'Confidentiality and Transparency in International Commercial Arbitration: Finding the Right Balance', 22 Harvard Negotiation Law Review 275 (2017), 286. The discussion in this chapter focuses upon instrumental goals for transparency, rather than its intrinsic qualities. Where transparency is valued as a good in itself, this may reflect broader values in a regime. See, generally, Shirlow, 'Three Manifestations of Transparency' (n. 5), 93–4.

[95] Elizabeth Fisher, 'Transparency and Administrative Law: A Critical Evaluation', 63 Current Legal Problems 272 (2010), 277.

tribunals, arbitral institutions, and the regime of investment arbitration more broadly.[96] The UNCITRAL Working Group engaging in the most recent (2017–) reform process, for example, acknowledged in its 2018 deliberations:

> There were also calls for arbitral institutions to play a greater role in the selection of arbitrators, and to establish more transparent procedures regarding the appointment of arbitrators. It was pointed out that little information about selection methods resulted in limited accountability in the system. It was suggested that the selection criteria should be published along with explanation of the selections.[97]

Transparency can enhance accountability by shifting power from arbitral tribunals or institutions to other stakeholders.[98] Increased transparency offers a means of empowering these stakeholders to monitor and even control the conduct of arbitral tribunals and institutions.[99]

Effective monitoring of tribunals depends upon the availability of at least some information about arbitral proceedings.[100] Transparency-as-availability therefore provides a basic platform for achieving accountability because it 'provides the public with a better understanding of whom to blame when problems arise'.[101] To achieve accountability, transparency-as-availability reforms should focus upon the release of materials which will support the monitoring of the actors for which accountability is sought. A transparency reform designed to achieve accountability of arbitral tribunals might, for instance, target the release of documents related to the identity or qualities of arbitrators. This could include, for instance, documents relating to arbitrator challenges or conflicts of interest.[102] The capacity to monitor arbitral proceedings will further be

[96] See e.g. Ulfstein (n. 94), 448; Poorooye and Feehily (n. 94), 282; Cindy Buys, 'The Tensions between Confidentiality and Transparency in International Arbitration', 14 American Review of International Arbitration 121 (2003), 134; Krista Nadakavukaren Schefer, 'Article 1: Scope of Application', in Euler et al. (n. 26), 33.

[97] UNCITRAL (n. 85), para. 66.

[98] Peters (n. 8) 554 (transparency as a 'promoter of shifts in power').

[99] Jonathan Fox, 'The Uncertain Relationship between Transparency and Accountability', 17 Development in Practice 663 (2007), 665, 668. See similarly: Shkabatur (n. 18), 82–3; Andreas Schedler, 'Conceptualising Accountability', in Andreas Schedler, Larry Diamond, and Marc F. Plattner (eds), *The Self-Restraining State: Power and Accountability in New Democracies* (Lynne Rienner, 1999), 14–17; Thomas N. Hale, 'Transparency, Accountability and Global Governance', 14 Global Governance 73 (2008), 74.

[100] On the required conditions for 'monitoring', see: McCarthy and Fluck (n. 15), 421; Alexandru Grigorescu, 'Transparency of Intergovernmental Organizations: The Roles of Member States, International Bureaucracies and Nongovernmental Organizations', (2007) 51 International Studies Quarterly 625.

[101] Figueroa (n. 25), 8.

[102] This matter was raised before the Working Group, but did not receive support for inclusion in the Rules: UNCITRAL, 'Report of Working Group II (Arbitration and Conciliation) on the Work of Its Fifty-Fourth Session (New York, 7–11 February 2011)' (2011) UN Doc. A/CN.9/717, para. 153. See, for further information about the EU proposal: Ingo Venzke, 'Investor–State Dispute Settlement in TTIP from the Perspective of a Public Law Theory of International Adjudication', [2016] Amsterdam Law School, Legal Studies Research Paper Series, Paper No. 2016–11.

enhanced by other forms of transparency, particularly transparency-as-accessibility. As Shkabatur emphasizes, 'information should be released in a form that allows multiple stakeholders—and not only the most professional public interest groups—to share, process, and publicise information that is pertinent to . . . public accountability'.[103] Reforms achieving transparency-as-accessibility support effective monitoring because they require tribunals or institutions not only to 'inform' stakeholders of their activities but also to 'explain' them.[104]

For accountability to be meaningful, 'monitoring' must be coupled with some possibility to 'sanction' the monitored actor in reaction to information about its performance. Sanctioning makes accountability actionable.[105] Instead of merely opening up arbitral tribunals and institutions to increased public scrutiny, accountability depends upon stakeholders being accorded some *capacity* or even *right* to demand answers or change from the purportedly accountable entity.[106] To achieve accountability, then, 'it is necessary not only to know what [a tribunal is] doing, but also to have some way to make [it] do something else'.[107] Whereas 'monitoring' might be supported by 'passive' forms of transparency, 'sanctioning' requires more 'active' transparency.[108] It therefore depends upon something more than just transparency-as-availability.[109] In fact, even soft forms of sanctioning—including complaints to the media or to local officials—will rely upon at least transparency-as-accessibility. Stakeholders need to be not only informed, but also *engaged*, before they can seek to sanction tribunals to hold them accountable.[110] More coercive forms of sanctioning will be predicated upon transparency-as-participation. Reforms to transparency might therefore only achieve accountability, for example, where they extend sanctioning powers beyond the disputing parties and arbitral institutions to groups of selected stakeholders, or even the public generally. Such participatory capacities are necessary to connect the knowing (monitoring) and doing (sanctioning) of accountability.

[103] Shkabatur (n. 18), 119–20.

[104] Lindsay Stirton and Martin Lodge, 'Transparency Mechanisms: Building Publicness into Public Services', 28 Journal of Law & Society 471 (2001), 475.

[105] Wim Voermans, 'Judicial Transparency Furthering Public Accountability for New Judiciaries', 3 Utrecht Law Review 148 (2007), 150.

[106] Strathern (n. 19), 313; McCarthy and Fluck (n. 15), 421.

[107] Thomas N. Hale and Anne-Marie Slaughter, 'Transparency: Possibilities and Limitations', 30 Fletcher Forum of World Affairs 153 (2006), 154. See similarly: Stirton and Lodge (n. 104), 475.

[108] McCarthy and Fluck (n. 15), 421.

[109] Stirton and Lodge (n. 104), 475; Hale and Slaughter (n. 107), 154; Figueroa (n. 25), 56. Although see Reith (n. 94), 300 ('transparency increases accountability because, when parties to arbitration are aware that their conduct will be the subject of public scrutiny, they will be less inclined to behave improperly. The same is true for the arbitral tribunal itself because, if arbitrators know that the proceedings and the final awards will become public knowledge, they will investigate more thoroughly and make a more accurate decision').

[110] Hale (n. 99), 76. As Hale and Slaughter point out, such soft-form accountability relies upon particular circumstances for success including e.g. a degree of organization amongst stakeholders in order to have traction and influence: Hale and Slaughter (n. 107), 162–3.

19.3.2 Transparency to alleviate suspicion, improve understanding, and enhance legitimacy

Transparency reforms have also been touted as integral to the legitimacy of investment arbitration.[111] The UNCITRAL Working Group which developed the Transparency Rules observed in 2010, for example, that increasing procedural transparency in investment arbitration offered 'an important step to respond to the increasing challenges regarding the legitimacy of international investment law and arbitration as such.'[112] The Working Group considered that increasing the public availability of information about arbitral proceedings and providing for greater participation by non-disputing parties could enhance 'public understanding'[113] and overcome public 'suspicion' of investment arbitration.[114] The ICSID amendment process (2018–) similarly embraces a view that '[i]ncreased transparency enhances the public legitimacy of ISDS', including because 'access to documents, hearings, decisions and Awards enhances public understanding and confidence in ISDS.'[115]

Transparency could conceivably enhance the perceived legitimacy of investment arbitration by improving the arbitral decision-making process (input legitimacy) and/or arbitral decisions themselves (output legitimacy).[116] Transparency might offer input legitimacy by, for example, ensuring that arbitral tribunals conduct decision-making processes which are 'informed by, and responsive to, a wide range of interests.'[117] Transparency may also enhance output legitimacy by improving the quality of the decisions rendered by tribunals.[118] Access to *amicus curiae* submissions might, for example, prompt more informed and thorough decision-making on the factual and legal issues implicated in investment disputes.[119] The increased availability of materials from

[111] See e.g. Reith (n. 94), 300 ('transparency promotes the legitimacy of the arbitral proceedings. The more the civil society is informed about the proceedings, the more it will lead to increased acceptance and trust in the process among the public'); Stephan W. Schill, 'Editorial: Five Times Transparency in International Investment Law', (2014) 15 Journal of World Investment & Trade 363; Poorooye and Feehily (n. 94), 286 ('Transparency can lead to a higher degree of trust and acceptance of the arbitral process'); Peters (n. 8), 557–8.

[112] UNCITRAL (n. 26), paras. 16, 17, 46, 62. See, similarly: UNCITRAL (n. 102), para. 112. See also detailed discussion in Shirlow, 'Dawn of a New Era?' (n. 5), 647.

[113] UNCITRAL, 'Report of the Working Group on Arbitration and Conciliation on the Work of Its Forty-Eighth Session (New York, 4–8 February 2008)' (2008) UN Doc. A/CN.9/646, para. 57; UNCITRAL (n. 26), paras. 17, 53.

[114] Ibid. paras 16, 17, 46, 62, 63; UNCITRAL (n. 102), para. 116.

[115] ICSID Secretariat (n. 90), 857.

[116] On sources of legitimacy, see generally Stephan W. Schill, 'Conceptions of Legitimacy of International Arbitration', in Caron et al. (n. 5).

[117] Tomoko Ishikawa, 'Third Party Participation in Investment Treaty Arbitration', 59 International & Comparative Law Quarterly 373 (2010), 409.

[118] Peters (n. 8), 561.

[119] See, generally, discussion in: Eugenia Levine, 'Amicus Curiae in International Investment Arbitration: The Implications of an Increase in Third-Party Participation', 29 Berkeley Journal of International Law 200 (2011), 217; Patrick Wieland, 'Why the Amicus Curia Institution Is Ill-Suited to

investment arbitration might also allow tribunals to benefit from higher-quality disputing party submissions on which to base their decisions. Publicly available information about previous proceedings could, for instance, 'assist parties to develop their case by allowing them to refer to previous disputes raising similar factual issues or analogous legal norms',[120] or to commentary on such materials prepared by academics, practitioners, and civil society.[121]

Transparency, legitimacy, and acceptability are relational concepts.[122] It is therefore important to consider *whose* perspectives on the legitimacy and acceptability of investment arbitration matter.[123] The legitimacy or acceptability of investment arbitration might be judged by a range of actors, be they non-governmental organizations, civil society, stakeholders in specific disputes, the treaty parties, third states, government officials, the media, academics, lawyers and other practitioners, or even arbitrators.[124] Arbitral institutions and states have, however, thus far not sought to direct transparency reforms to specifically engage any of these particular subgroups. They have instead targeted transparency reforms to a nebulous 'public' or 'civil society'.[125] This has meant that reform efforts have not specifically addressed how transparency measures might be targeted to influence how these various groups view and engage with investment arbitration.

To tailor transparency reforms to achieve the goals of enhanced legitimacy and acceptability, it is necessary to identify the intended beneficiaries of transparency. This is because the accessibility of released materials to each of the above subgroups will differ depending upon a range of factors, including for example their familiarity with investment law or arbitral procedure.[126] It is of course possible that a greater availability of information in itself will enhance the legitimacy of investment arbitration by showing that tribunals do not have 'anything to hide'.[127] Domestic studies overwhelmingly indicate, however, that the public is unlikely to learn much about adjudicative systems through direct observation of proceedings or perusal of case files.[128] Instead, the media

Address Indigenous Peoples' Rights before Investor–State Arbitration Tribunals: Glamis Gold and the Right of Intervention', (3 Trade, Law and Development 334 (2011), 335, 340; Ishikawa (n. 117), 402.

[120] See e.g. ICSID Secretariat (n. 90), 857 ('Increased transparency allows disputing parties to better comprehend the ISDS process and more effectively prepare litigation: parties can assess the procedural and substantive arguments available to them by referring to past cases. Parties can also make more informed decisions about arbitrator selection if they have access to prior orders, decisions and Awards').

[121] Nyegaard Mollestad (n. 26), 13; Daniel Barstow Magraw Jr. and Niranjali Manel Amerasinghe, 'Transparency and Public Participation in Investor–State Arbitration', 15 ILSA Journal of International & Comparative Law (2008), 337, 345.

[122] Grigorescu (n. 100), 627. [123] Ibid. [124] Shirlow, 'Dawn of a New Era?' (n. 5), 652.

[125] UNCITRAL (n. 26), paras. 60, 65, 127; UNCITRAL (n. 102), para. 50; UNCITRAL, 'Report of the Working Group on Arbitration and Conciliation on the Work of Its Fifty-Fifth Session (Vienna, 3–7 October 2011)' (2011) A/CN.9/736, paras. 33, 48; UNCITRAL, 'Report of Working Group II (Arbitration and Conciliation) on the Work of Its Fifty-Sixth Session (New York, 6–10 February 2012)' (2012) UN Doc. A/CN.9/741, para. 61.

[126] Shirlow, 'Dawn of a New Era?' (n. 5), 652–3.

[127] Coe (n. 34), 1361. See similarly Schill (n. 111), 364.

[128] Leslie J. Moran, 'Every Picture Speaks a Thousand Words: Visualizing Judicial Authority in the Press', in Priska Gisler et al. (eds), *Intersections of Law and Culture* (Palgrave Macmillan, 2012), 31.

or third parties may need to perform intermediary functions to translate legal proceedings to mass audiences.[129]

Increased legitimacy and public understanding of investment arbitration may therefore depend upon the *creation*—and not just release—of information about arbitral proceedings.[130] This was acknowledged by the UNCITRAL Working Group in the development of the Transparency Rules. That Group observed that mere publication of information 'would not necessarily be sufficient to achieve the desirable level of public awareness and that information might need to be made available in other forms'.[131] There has thus far, however, been little appetite for reforms targeting transparency-as-accessibility. Reforms have, for example, taken a broad view of the types of information that should be made publicly available about arbitral proceedings.[132] They have nevertheless not addressed whether such released information is *accessible* to the various possible targets of transparency measures. Transparency reforms have therefore focused upon types of transparency which are on their own ill-adapted to achieving the objectives of increased acceptability and legitimacy.

19.3.3 Adapting transparency to achieve reform objectives

Particular types of transparency will be better adapted to achieving particular reform goals than others. It is therefore necessary to approach reforms to investment arbitration from an analytical, rather than normative, perspective.[133] Instead of assuming that increased transparency will enhance the accountability and legitimacy of investment arbitration, it is necessary to determine which kinds of transparency will promote those goals, and in which circumstances. The objectives of any reform should inform the types of transparency that are sought. As Shkabatur notes, these questions should play a 'vital role' in the design of transparency measures, but 'have long been ignored by the architects of transparency policies'.[134] So too in investment arbitration, reforms to procedural transparency have thus far not engaged meaningfully with *how* transparency might be adapted to achieve the specific goals of a particular reform process.

The campaign for greater transparency in international investment arbitration has focused predominantly upon *what* is being disclosed, and *how much* will be open to view. It has also to a more limited extent engaged with the question of *who* should be able to participate in arbitral proceedings. Reforms have thus focused predominantly on

[129] Shirlow, 'Three Manifestations of Transparency' (n. 5), 92. See similarly: Figueroa (n. 25), 26.

[130] Some investor–state tribunals recognize as much, preparing an 'executive summary' of their decisions in order to bolster 'governmental and public faith in the integrity of the process of arbitration' and/or to 'communicate its conclusions succinctly to the various branches of government or public involved': *Glamis*, Award, 8-Jun-2009 (UNCITRAL), 4–5.

[131] UNCITRAL (n. 26), para. 38.

[132] E.g. in considering the public release of arbitral documents, the UNCITRAL Working Group concluded that 'the public might have an interest in any or all of them': ibid. para. 65.

[133] See similarly Fox (n. 99), 665.

[134] Shkabatur (n. 18), 81.

increasing the quantity of information released about arbitral proceedings and on expanding the scope of third party participation. Such reforms have principally privileged views of transparency-as-availability. They have also endorsed a passive (one-way) view of transparency-as-participation. Such reforms are not sufficient in themselves, however, to guarantee accountability or legitimacy.

The near-myopic focus on passive forms of transparency has meant that transparency reforms have to date largely been ill-adapted to achieving their identified objectives. Transparency reforms will be particularly ill-suited to achieving accountability or legitimacy where disclosed information is not accessible or relevant (transparency-as-accessibility) or used and impactful (transparency-as-participation).[135] Reforms that fail to address transparency-as-accessibility, or which provide for thin forms of transparency-as-participation, may even compound the issues to which reform efforts are directed. The release of dense and quantitatively numerous documents from arbitral proceedings might, for example, 'inhibit the ability of a broad array of individuals and civil society groups to effectively access and understand the released information'.[136] Such releases might simply privilege those stakeholders with the 'resources to collect, analyze and interpret' such materials.[137] They may therefore empower specific—already 'internal'—stakeholders like states, lawyers, and arbitrators, and disempower other—'external'—actors.[138] As Figueroa notes, transparency reforms will only be successful 'if they give users the information they need, when they need it, and in the form they need it for making an effective decision'.[139]

The disconnect between the objectives sought through reform efforts and the types of transparency introduced through such reforms perhaps explains the sustained sense amongst states and civil society that reforms to investor–state arbitration have failed to generate a 'transparent' regime. Depending upon the ultimate goals underpinning reform, future additional reforms may therefore be necessary.[140] Transparency reforms may increasingly, for example, need to address active, rather than just passive, forms of transparency to generate the desired levels of accountability and legitimacy for investment arbitration.[141] There may also be measures available in addition to transparency to achieve desired reform objectives.[142] Transparency must come to be viewed as 'a conduit to regulation, not as regulation itself'.[143] Recognizing that investment arbitration requires greater accountability or legitimacy leaves open the question of whether transparency is better or worse, all things considered, than *other* forms of regulation for achieving those goals.[144] The overwhelming focus on transparency, however, can lead to the value of other mechanisms being overlooked.[145] This is particularly troubling in

135 Peters (n. 8), 535. 136 Shkabatur (n. 18), 118–19. 137 Peters (n. 8), 555.

138 See further Shirlow, 'Dawn of a New Era?' (n. 5). 139 Figueroa (n. 25), 56.

140 Shirlow, 'Three Manifestations of Transparency' (n. 5), 92.

141 Ibid. 142 Peters (n. 8), 579. 143 Hale (n. 99), 162–3.

144 See generally Caron (n. 5), 395; Frederick Schauer, 'Transparency in Three Dimensions', 2011 University of Illinois Law Review 1339 (2011), 1348.

145 Caron (n. 5), 397.

circumstances in which there has been little empirical analysis of the limits, and potential risks, of transparency reforms in investment arbitration.

19.4 Conclusion

This chapter has sought to take the complexity of transparency seriously. It has traced the development of procedural transparency in international investment arbitration to tease apart different types of transparency, whilst also considering their objectives and consequences. The analysis set out here indicates that the meaning, promise, and limits of transparency will differ for different stakeholders and different reform objectives. What emerges is an understanding of transparency that is closely connected to the development of, and hopes for, international investment arbitration. Transparency has emerged as a key means of improving international investment arbitration, including making it more accountable and more legitimate. An agenda that seeks to identify and enact effective reforms to reach this promise must take into account the types of transparency best adapted to achieve these goals. In considering transparency in international investment arbitration, then, it is vital that states, arbitral institutions, and other stakeholders confront the assumptions and motivations underpinning suggested reforms in order to best adapt those reforms to achieve their stated objectives.

While the unique features of investment arbitration have prompted these debates about transparency to attain particular salience in that field, the contours of the discussion in this chapter hold importance for reform agendas in other fields of international arbitration. The chapter has, in particular, emphasised the importance of appraising reform agendas critically. It has highlighted the importance of clarifying *what* is being proposed, what is being *excluded* from that discussion, and how these understandings influence the concrete outcomes of reform efforts as well as the appraisal of their success by disparate stakeholders. The chapter has thus emphasised the importance of pursuing reform agendas that promise only what they can deliver. This is necessary to avoid the pitfalls associated with reform efforts that are ill-adapted to achieve their stated purposes, and to better adapt reform efforts to achieve desired reform objectives.

CHAPTER 20

ARBITRATION AND OFFSHORE RESOURCES IN DISPUTED MARITIME AREAS

TIBISAY MORGANDI*

20.1 INTRODUCTION

IT is an observable fact that disputes over maritime boundaries are mostly caused by competing desires of states to exploit offshore natural resources, in particular oil and gas deposits. Indeed, it is well known that the law on maritime boundaries was developed precisely in order to allocate rights over offshore natural resources.[1] It has also however long been observed that the law on maritime boundary delimitation, as developed by international tribunals, ostensibly pays only scant regard to this underlying basis of the disputes at issue. Rather, the law purports to base itself on other principles, most importantly an equidistance principle. In particular, the unilateral activities of states are consistently rejected as being 'relevant circumstances' relevant to a boundary delimitation.[2] And, at least when they leave an irreversible mark on the continental

* The author is grateful to Lorand Bartels for comments.

[1] In *North Sea Continental Shelf*, Judgment [1969] ICJ Rep 3, para. 97, the ICJ noted that '[the] natural resources of the subsoil of the sea in those parts which consist of continental shelf are the very object of the legal regime established subsequent to the Truman Proclamation'.

[2] Malcolm Evans, 'Relevant Circumstances', in Alex Elferink, Tore Henriksen, and Signe Veierud Busch (eds), *Maritime Boundary Delimitation: The Case Law* (Cambridge University Press, 2018), 255.

shelf, unilateral activities in disputed areas pending a delimitation have also traditionally been seen as strongly discouraged, even prohibited.[3]

However, if one looks at what tribunals do, contrary to what they say they do, they invariably choose a delimitation line, ostensibly based on equidistance, that follows oil companies' drilling activities—so long as these activities have not taken place beyond a 'plausible' equidistance line.[4] Interestingly, it appears that oil companies take a conservative approach, following such a plausible equidistance line, even when the concessions granted to them by coastal states would allow them to drill beyond that line. Moreover, again contrary to what they say, tribunals do not condemn states for authorizing drilling activities in disputed areas, provided that these activities have not taken place beyond a plausible equidistance line. What is more, tribunals are also extremely reluctant to draw a delimitation line through already drilled deposits, which would make them a shared resource. This has occurred in some cases, but these are best seen as anomalous cases, at least one of which is the result of a cartographical error.[5] In short, states, oil companies and tribunals are engaged in a game in which, so long as certain basic rules are respected, those who drill first will win.

20.2 It's all about the oil . . . or is it?

The law on maritime boundary delimitation can be dated to the 1945 Truman Proclamation, in which the United States claimed jurisdiction over all resources in its continental shelf, which was followed two years later by an offshore drilling platform.[6] These events sparked an international effort to establish a regime governing states' activities in the sea, which culminated in the 1982 United Nations Convention on the Law of the Sea (UNCLOS).[7] Its critical provision is Article 77 which, reflecting customary international law, grants a coastal state exclusive rights to explore its continental shelf and exploit its resources.[8]

[3] See e.g. Nicholas Ioannides, 'The Legal Framework Governing Hydrocarbon Activities in Undelimited Maritime Areas', 68 ICLQ 345 (2019), 365.

[4] Until determined by a tribunal, an equidistance line can only be predicted with a degree of probability since a tribunal might adjust it on the basis of so-called 'relevant circumstances' and proportionality. As described in Section 20.2, these adjusting factors do not formally include oil concessions or drilling activities.

[5] Clive Schofield and Chris Carleton, 'Technical Considerations in Law of the Sea Dispute Resolution', in Alex Elferink and Donald Rothwell (eds), *Oceans Management in the 21st Century* (Leiden: Brill, 2004), Chapter 12.

[6] Elizabeth Nyman, 'Offshore Oil Development and Maritime Conflict in the 20th Century: A Statistical Analysis of International Trends', 6 Energy Research & Social Science 1 (2015), 2.

[7] United Nations Convention on the Law of the Sea, 10 December 1982, 1833 UNTS 397, in force 16 November 1994.

[8] UNCLOS Arts. 77(1) and 77(2). The rights accruing to a coastal state in the continental shelf are inherent and exist *ipso facto* and *ab initio*; *North Sea Continental Shelf* (n. 1), para. 19.

The practical effect of these legal developments was to place a premium on sovereign rights to a continental shelf, which in turn depends on maritime boundaries. It is therefore not surprising that maritime boundaries have been the subject of an increasing number of inter-state disputes, especially in areas known to be rich in natural resources. A recent quantitative study finds: 'A lack of maritime boundaries does not necessarily produce conflict, but when combined with a growth in the profitability in maritime resources such as offshore petroleum, it seems likely to increase the likelihood of international disputes.'[9] In addition, disputes are exacerbated when states act unilaterally in authorizing drilling and even unilateral exploration[10] in disputed maritime areas.

When disputing parties are not able to reach a delimitation agreement on their maritime boundary providing for an 'equitable' result, as Article 83(1) of UNCLOS requires, they sometimes outsource the delimitation of a maritime boundary between them to tribunals in accordance with Article 83(2). Beyond this, UNCLOS offers little guidance as to how a tribunal should delimit a continental shelf maritime boundary.[11] In particular, it does not specify that tribunals should adopt any method for delimiting the continental shelf, so long as the result is 'equitable' (or, strictly speaking, what the parties might have considered 'equitable').[12] Nonetheless, it is now established practice that delimitation should follow three steps: the adoption of a provisional equidistance line, which can then be adjusted on the basis of 'relevant circumstances' and, in some cases, on the basis of proportionality.[13] It is a matter of some note, however, that tribunals insist that this exercise should be—and is—conducted without taking into consideration where offshore hydrocarbons might be located, or where states might have issued licences for the exploration or exploitation of these resources. As the ICJ said in *Cameroon v Nigeria* of the 'relevant circumstances' element of the analysis:

> Overall, it follows from the jurisprudence that, although the existence of an express or tacit agreement between the parties on the siting of their respective oil concessions

[9] Nyman (n. 6), 2.

[10] This is because a state may acquire confidential information on the presence (or absence) of deposits which may affect the bargaining position of a neighbouring state with an interest in those deposits. See *Delimitation of the Maritime Boundary between Ghana and Côte d'Ivoire*, Provisional Measures, ITLOS Case No. 23, Order of 25 April 2015, paras. 92–5. See also Yoshifumi Tanaka, 'Unilateral Exploration and Exploitation of Natural Resources in Disputed Areas: A Note on the Ghana/Côte d'Ivoire Order of 25 April 2015 before the Special Chamber of ITLOS', (2015) 46 Ocean Development & International Law 315, 316.

[11] It is different for the territorial sea for which Art. 15 of UNCLOS establishes a specific method of delimitation, the so-called 'triple rule': (a) the delimitation has to be effected by agreement between the coastal States; (b) failing agreement between the parties, the delimitation has to be effected in accordance with the principle of equidistance; (c) where special circumstances exist, the median line has to be corrected in light of these circumstances. See Yoshifumi Tanaka, *The International Law of the Sea* (Cambridge University Press, 2012), 200.

[12] However, as Tanaka argues—in a study that has become a seminal work on this topic—international courts have interpreted Art. 83(1) as providing for the application of the equidistance method to the delimitation of the continental shelf. See Tanaka (n. 11), 201.

[13] Massimo Lando, *Maritime Delimitation as a Judicial Process* (Cambridge University Press, 2019).

> may indicate a consensus on the maritime areas to which they are entitled, oil concessions and oil wells are not in themselves to be considered as relevant circumstances justifying the adjustment or shifting of the provisional delimitation line. Only if they are based on express or tacit agreement between the parties may they be taken into account.[14]

Likewise, in *Guyana v Suriname*, the arbitral tribunal said that a survey of pertinent case law showed 'a marked reluctance of international courts and tribunals to accord significance to the oil practice of the parties in the determination of the delimitation line'.[15]

20.3 Back to Black

Many authors have considered it strange that tribunals applying the law on maritime boundary delimitation should ignore its primary rationale. Evans even calls it 'paradoxical, to say the least, since the entire point of the continental shelf regime was to facilitate orderly exploration and exploitation of its natural resources'.[16] There are, however, various reasons that this makes sense.

First of all, there are practical problems inherent in determining boundaries based on oil and gas deposits. Most importantly, it is often unclear what the extent and value is of these resources until they have been extensively explored,[17] and that, in turn, depends on investments that will only be made when it is clear which state (or states) have rights to the resources, and on activities that, according to what tribunals have said, should not even take place until the boundaries have been delimited. Second, as a matter of logic the allocation of any resource has to follow a principle that is independent of that resource. That principle could be of any type, ranging from an allocation of shares according to a fixed principle, such as equality, which has been rejected by tribunals,[18] or the proximity of a state to the resource, which is essentially the basis of the law as it

[14] *Case Concerning the Land and Maritime Boundary Between Cameroon and Nigeria (Cameroon v Nigeria; Equatorial Guinea intervening)*, Judgment [2002] ICJ Rep 303, para. 304. Admittedly, in *Continental Shelf (Tunisia/Libyan Arab Jamahiriya)*, Judgment [1982] ICJ Rep 18, paras. 118 and 133(B)(4), the ICJ considered the granting of oil concessions a relevant circumstance. This was however in an unusual case, namely when a mutual practice of granting concessions was considered to have established a modus vivendi regarded as equitable by the parties and which reflected an express or tacit agreement between them. This was an unusual case, because the practice was inherited from the former colonial powers of the states in dispute (i.e. France and Italy).

[15] *Award in the Arbitration regarding the Delimitation of the Maritime Boundary between Guyana and Suriname*, 17 September 2007, 30 RIAA 130, para. 390.

[16] Evans (n. 2), 254.

[17] Even if the location of relevant offshore resources were known, a separate question concerns their recoverability and, most importantly, their profitability. Some deposits turn out to be dry, and drilling technology and prices are constantly developing, for reasons including policies driven by climate change.

[18] In *Continental Shelf (Libyan Arab Jamahiriya/Malta)*, Judgment [1985] ICJ Rep 13, para. 46, the ICJ referred to 'the principle that although all States are equal before the law and are entitled to equal treatment, "equity does not necessarily imply equality", nor does it seek to make equal what nature has made unequal; and the principle that there can be no question of distributive justice'.

currently stands. But what is clear is that the principle cannot itself be based on a factor to which it is to be applied, namely, the location or size or potential of the resource itself, without an exogenous element. That would result in circular reasoning. So the paradox is not, on closer inspection, a paradox at all, but rather the inevitable result of legal logic. Given this set of circularities involved in any allocating shares of unexplored resources based on factors related to those resources themselves, it is perhaps truer to say that, far from it being 'paradoxical' that tribunals ignore resources when determining maritime boundaries, this is the most logically and practically sensible approach.

On the other hand, if one looks at what tribunals do, and not just at what they say they do, it appears that they do, in fact, give weight to the drilling activities of oil companies as authorized by coastal states. This is against the background of another phenomenon, which is that, regardless of the areas that states claim in maritime boundary disputes, they typically act quite conservatively in granting concessions[19] on the basis of either historical boundaries (supported by a treaty) or some plausible equidistance line.[20] Also important is that tribunals do not condemn states for authorizing drilling in disputed areas pending delimitation. Put simply, wherever possible, tribunals recognize the status quo in relation to deposits already drilled. All of this leads to the conclusion that states are effectively permitted to authorize unilateral exploratory and production activities, including drilling that has an irreversible effect, provided that they do so on the basis of an at least plausible maritime boundary.

That tribunals recognize and endorse unilateral drilling is especially surprising because it also contradicts the notion that states should refrain from engaging in any unilateral practice in a disputed area which violates Article 83(3) of UNCLOS[21] or which prejudices the rights of the other party, and it is clear that drilling is an activity of this type. In *Guyana v Suriname*, the tribunal said, in the context of unilateral exploratory

[19] *Cameroon v Nigeria* (n. 14), is an exception for reasons that are explained below.

[20] In *Dispute Concerning Delimitation of the Maritime Boundary Between Ghana and Côte d'Ivoire in the Atlantic Ocean*, ITLOS Case No. 23, Judgment of 23 September 2017, para. 132, the Special Chamber said: 'States often offer and award oil concessions in an area yet to be delimited. It is not unusual for States to align their concession blocks with those of their neighbouring States so that no areas of overlap arise. They obviously do so for different reasons, but not least out of caution and prudence to avoid any conflict and to maintain friendly relations with their neighbours.' It continued by saying that '[t]o equate oil concession limits with a maritime boundary would be equivalent to penalizing a State for exercising such caution and prudence.' (ibid). However, this was essentially the line adopted by the Special Chamber in any case.

[21] Article 83(3) reads: 'Pending agreement as provided for in paragraph 1, the States concerned, in a spirit of understanding and cooperation, shall make every effort to enter into provisional arrangements of a practical nature and, during this transitional period, not to jeopardize or hamper the reaching of the final agreement. Such arrangements shall be without prejudice to the final delimitation.' This provision contains two distinct but related obligations. First, states are under a best efforts obligation of conduct to 'enter into provisional arrangements of a practical nature', including apportioning the hydrocarbon deposit located in the area subject to overlapping claims. Second, states are under an 'obligation of mutual restraint' to refrain from actions likely to 'hamper or jeopardize' the final delimitation of their maritime boundaries. Both obligations are reinforced by the good faith required of States in the performance of their obligations arising under UNCLOS. See 'Report on the Obligations of States under Art. 74(3) and 83(3) of UNCLOS in respect of Undelimited Maritime Areas', *BIICL*, London, 2016.

drilling by Guyana in a disputed area, that 'unilateral acts that cause a physical change to the marine environment will generally be comprised in a class of activities that should be undertaken only jointly or by agreement between the parties'.[22] This was because these activities 'may jeopardise or hamper the reaching of a final delimitation agreement as a result of the perceived changes of the status quo that they would engender' and thus violate the second limb of Article 83(3).[23] Similarly, in its Order for Provisional Measures in *Ghana/Côte d'Ivoire*, the ITLOS Special Chamber said that 'the ongoing exploration and exploitation activities [including drilling] conducted by Ghana in the disputed area will result in a modification of the physical characteristics of the continental shelf' and that in such a situation 'there is a risk of irreparable prejudice'.[24] In this case, as Côte d'Ivoire had requested provisional measures, the prejudice in question was to the potential rights of Côte d'Ivoire, namely, 'to decide when, how and under what conditions the exploitation of these resources would take place, and even whether it should take place'.[25] And yet, even in these cases, the tribunals have ended up endorsing these practices; moreover, they have done so, where possible, by drawing a maritime boundary that places the drilled deposits entirely within the maritime area of the state authorizing the drilling activities.

20.4 Three Disputes *De Facto* Recognizing Unilateral Drilling Practices

The following illustrates these observations by reference to three key disputes involving unilateral drilling of oil resources in undelimited areas: *Cameroon v Nigeria*, before the International Court of Justice, *Guyana v Suriname*, before the Permanent Court of Arbitration and *Ghana/Côte d'Ivoire*, referred initially to an arbitral tribunal and then by Special Agreement to a Special Chamber of ITLOS.

20.4.1 *Cameroon v Nigeria* (2002)

The relatively conservative approach of states to the authorization of unilateral drilling in undelimited areas is well illustrated in *Cameroon v Nigeria*. Here, Nigeria originally claimed a large maritime area based on its claimed rights over the Bakassi peninsula by issuing oil concessions partially encroaching upon Cameroon's concessions (see crosshatched areas in Figure 20.1 showing the area of overlap between Nigeria's and Cameroon's concessions).

[22] *Guyana v Suriname* (n. 15), para. 480. Tribunals have not regarded unilateral activities such as granting pre-drilling concessions and seismic surveys to violate Art. 83(3).

[23] Ibid. [24] *Ghana/Côte d'Ivoire*, Provisional Measures (n. 10), paras. 88 and 89.

[25] Ibid. para. 77 (quoting Côte d'Ivoire).

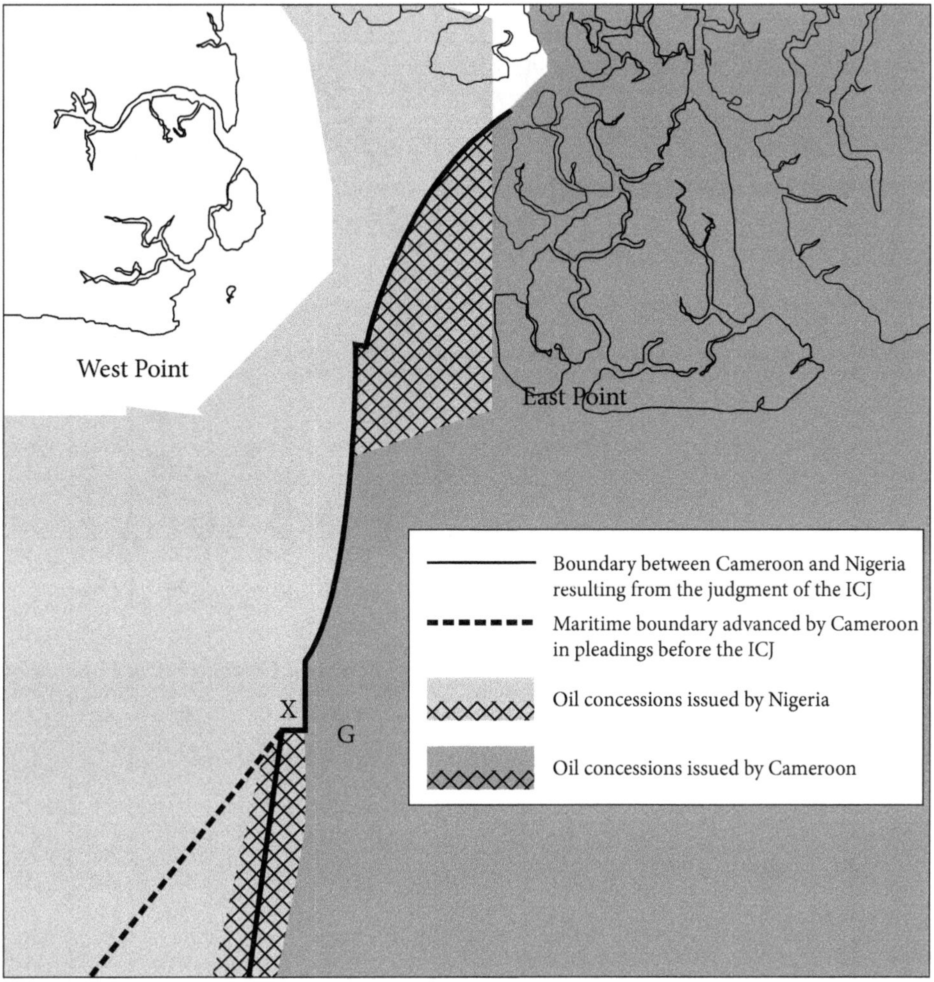

FIGURE 20.1 The Location of Cameroon and Nigeria Oil Concessions and the Delimited Maritime Boundary

Source: Schofield and Carleton

It is therefore notable that Nigerian authorized drilling activity (marked in light grey in Figure 20.2) did not extend to the entirety of the area claimed but was confined to its side of the line relied upon by Cameroon, namely the line agreed by the parties in the 1971 Yaoundé II Declaration, which they later extended in the 1975 Maroua Declaration.[26]

[26] *Cameroon v Nigeria* (n. 14), para. 214. The line from the mouth of the Akwayafe River to point G was established in two steps. The 1971 Yaoundé II Declaration established a line from the Bakassi Point and the King Point down to point 12, and the 1975 Maroua Declaration extended this line from point A (adjacent to point 12) to point G. See Figure 20.2.

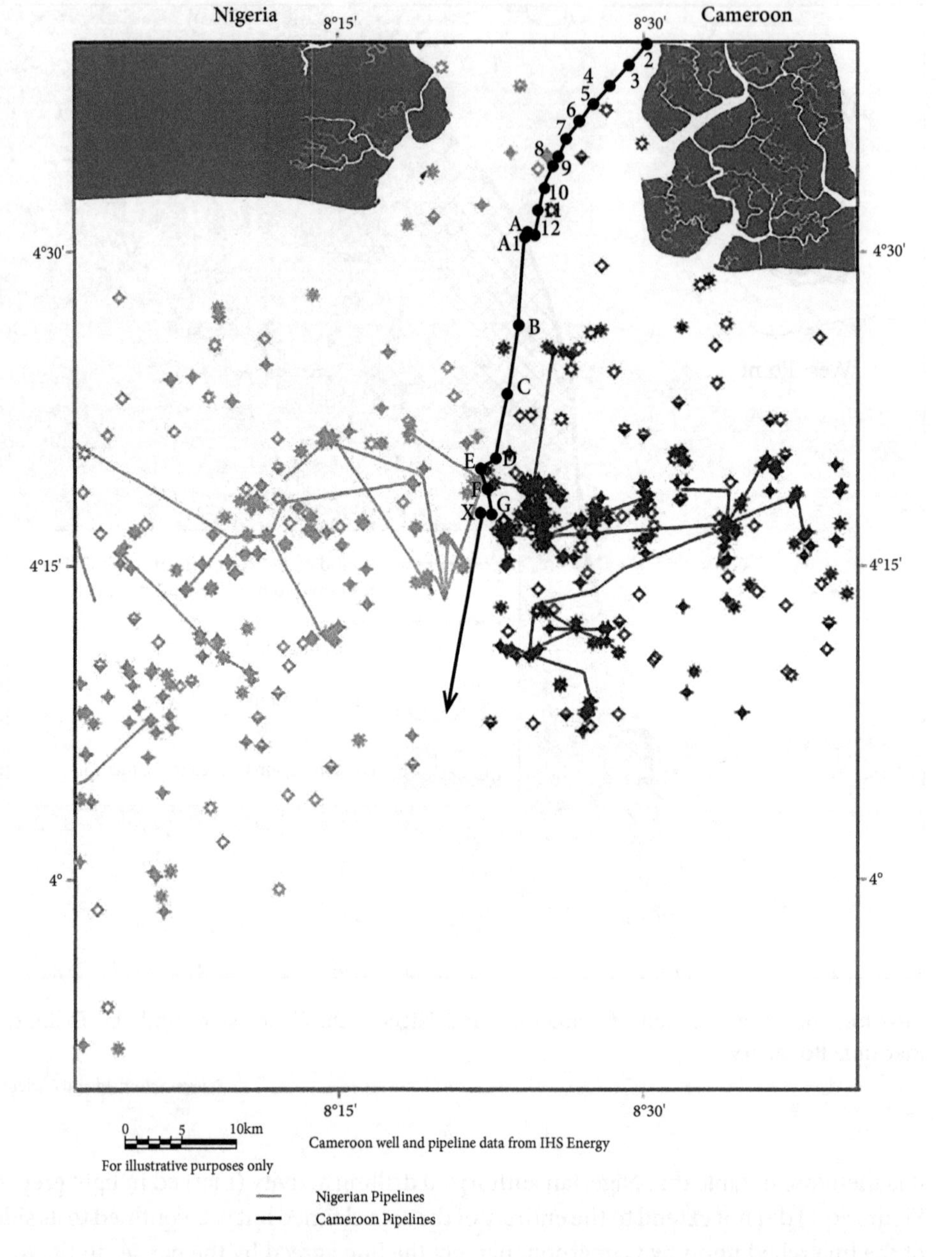

FIGURE 20.2 The Location of Wells Drilled Pursuant to Cameroon and Nigeria Concessions and the Delimited Maritime Boundary

Source: adapted from *Cameroon v Nigeria (Merits)*, Maritime Boundary Map, at 449 and Rejoinder of Nigeria, Figure 10.4

Perhaps less surprisingly, Cameroonian authorized drilling activity (marked in dark grey in Figure 20.2) remained on its side of this line.[27]

The court accepted this line[28] but had to decide on the line from Point G, where the 1975 Maroua line ran out. The court drew a short line from Point G directly westwards to Point X, which it said reflected equidistance, and then drew a line southwards also on the basis of equidistance (see Figure 20.3). This southward line also came with an unexpected problem, in that it ended up awarding a deposit drilled by Nigeria to Cameroon (see Bogi Field in Figure 20.3). It has been pointed out that the court made a series of technical mistakes in drawing the line,[29] and, according to one of the lawyers

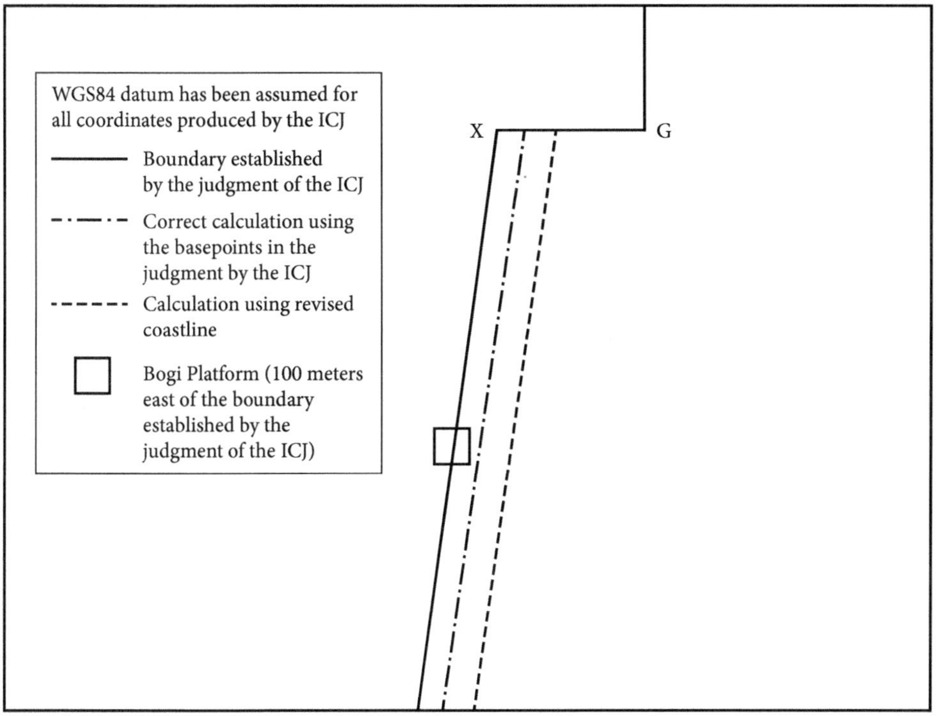

FIGURE 20.3 The Bogi Field and the Delimited Maritime Boundary between Cameroon and Nigeria

Source: Schofield and Carleton

[27] One of Cameroon's wells is on Nigeria's side of the line (see dark grey point beyond the line from point A to point G (i.e. the Maroua line) in Figure 20.2), but this can be explained by the fact that it was drilled in 1972 and thus predates the 1975 Maroua line.

[28] *Cameroon v Nigeria* (n. 14), para. 268.

[29] There was a transcription error in the coordinates, the coastline no longer corresponded to the map used as a reference, and the court was unclear as to the 'datum' to be used in drawing the line. See Schofield and Carleton (n. 5), 243–9; also James Devaney, *Fact-Finding before the International Court of Justice* (Cambridge University Press, 2016), 85.

involved in these proceedings, this was contrary to the court's intention.[30] Indeed, the parties themselves established a mixed commission to determine where the line should lie, and what to do about deposits straddling that line.

20.4.2 *Guyana v Suriname* (2007)

In *Guyana v Suriname*, Guyana had granted concessions based on an equidistance line. Interestingly, despite formally claiming a line based on a bisector method,[31] at the time of the proceedings Suriname granted a concession to Repsol and other private companies on its side following the equidistance line claimed by Guyana (see Figure 20.4).[32]

As in *Cameroon v Nigeria*, the tribunal adopted a very similar equidistance line,[33] and, as in that case (ignoring errors), this ended up protecting Guyana's already drilled deposits in the disputed area (Shell's Abary 1 field drilled in the 1970, Total's Arapaima 1 drilled in 1990 and CGX's Horseshoe West 1 drilled in 2000: see Figure 20.5). That this was not any real surprise is evidenced by the reaction to the award of CGX, the company to which Guyana had granted a licence to conduct exploratory drilling in the undelimited area before the dispute arose.[34] CGX's CEO stated: 'we finally got the border resolution we wanted... the CGX team is excited to going back to work.'[35]

Aside from the result, this dispute had other features favouring unilateral drilling. Guyana had authorized CGX to drill in a disputed area, but despite various statements that Guyana's conduct had violated Article 83(3) of UNCLOS, in particular by failing to inform Suriname in advance, the tribunal declined to make any specific findings that Guyana's authorization of drilling was a violation of this provision.[36] Also, the tribunal considered whether the injury suffered by Guyana as a result of Suriname's forceful eviction of the CGX oil rig from the disputed area might have been compensable. The tribunal said that it was not, but this was only because the injury had been 'sufficiently addressed' since Guyana, as a result of the delimitation, had 'undisputed title to the area'

[30] Tim Daniel, 'Expert Evidence before the ICJ', paper presented at the Third Bi-Annual Conference of ABLOS (2003), 5.

[31] *Guyana v Suriname* (n. 15), para. 221.

[32] Ibid. para. 231.

[33] The tribunal adopted an adjusted equidistance line to delimit the territorial sea and an unadjusted equidistance line to delimit the continental shelf and the exclusive economic zone (EEZ). *Guyana v Suriname* (n. 15), paras. 323–5 (delimitation of the territorial sea) and 392 (delimitation of the continental shelf and EEZ).

[34] CGX is a Canadian oil and gas exploration company that was operating in the undelimited area at the time when the dispute arose. Guyana started proceedings against Suriname in reaction to Suriname's expulsion of the CGX's exploratory rig from the undelimited maritime area the day before CGX was scheduled to commence drilling on the Eagle field.

[35] CGX Energy, press release, 20 September 2007.

[36] *Guyana v Suriname* (n. 15), para. 486.

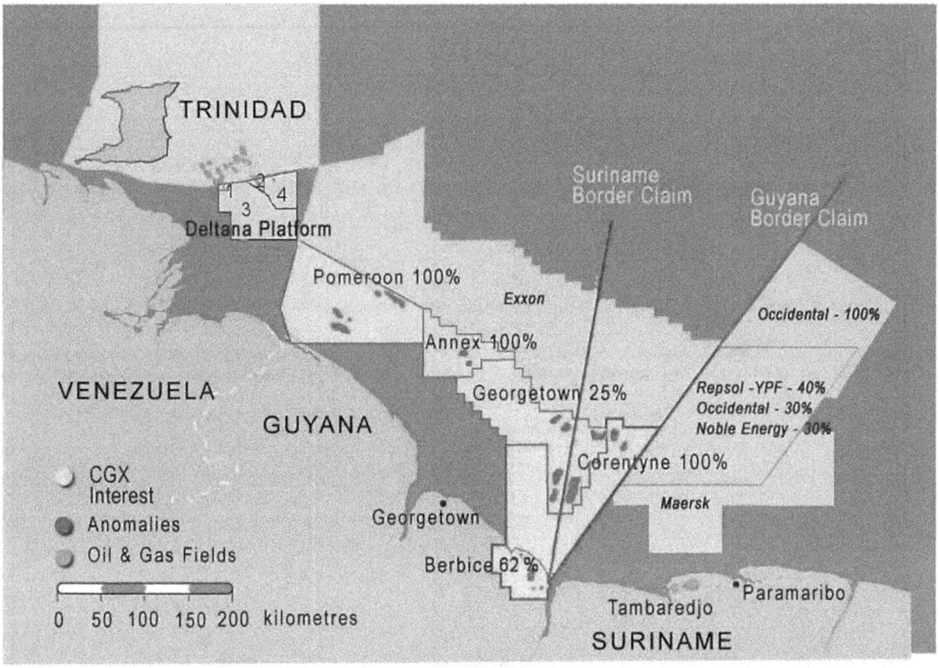

FIGURE 20.4 The Location of Concessions Granted by Guyana and Suriname and their Maritime Claims

Source: CGX Energy

at issue.[37] This is very far from the condemnation of activities in disputed areas that one might have expected from an application of Article 83(3) of UNCLOS.

20.4.3 *Ghana/Côte d'Ivoire* (2017)

In *Ghana/Côte d'Ivoire*, Ghana had authorized drilling in an area disputed with Côte d'Ivoire based on what Ghana claimed was a 'customary' equidistance line. This drilling had been conducted prior to the commencement of dispute settlement proceedings, on four oilfields: the Tano West 1 Field (1999 and 2002), the Ebony 1 Field (2008), the 'TEN' Field (made of the Tweneboa, Enyenra and Ntomme deposits, 2009) and the Wawa 1 Field (2012). All of these fields fell well within Côte d'Ivoire's claimed area (see Figure 20.6).

Ghana also argued that Côte d'Ivoire, while claiming a larger area based on a bisector line,[38] had in fact authorized drilling exclusively on Côte d'Ivoire's side of the customary

[37] Ibid. para. 450.

[38] Counter-Memorial of Côte d'Ivoire, Vol I, 4 April 2016, 132–162.

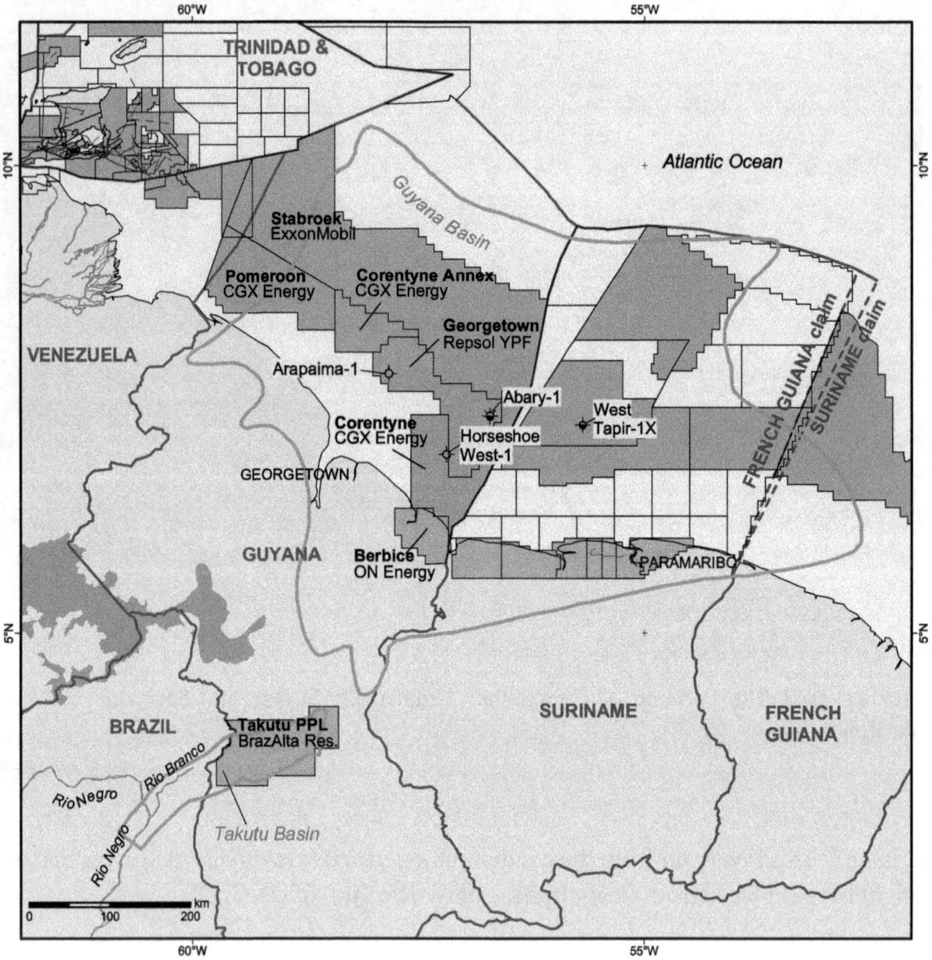

FIGURE 20.5 The Location of Drilled Deposits in Guyana and the Delimited Maritime Boundary between Guyana and Suriname

Source: Wood Mackenzie

equidistance line (see Figure 20.7).[39,40] Ghana also authorized drilling exclusively up to the claimed customary equidistance line (See Figure 20.7).[41]

In the end, the tribunal while formally rejecting Ghana's 'customary' equidistance line, drew a very similar equidistance line, finding no relevant circumstances that would

[39] Côte d'Ivoire's drilling activity is marked in dark grey.

[40] *Ghana/Côte d'Ivoire*, Judgment (n. 20), para. 132. See also Youri van Logchem, 'The Rights and Obligations of States in Disputed Maritime Areas: What Lessons Can Be Learned from the Maritime Boundary Dispute between Ghana and Côte d'Ivoire?' 52 Vanderbilt Journal of Transnational Law 121(2019), 154.

[41] Ghana's drilling activities are marked in light grey.

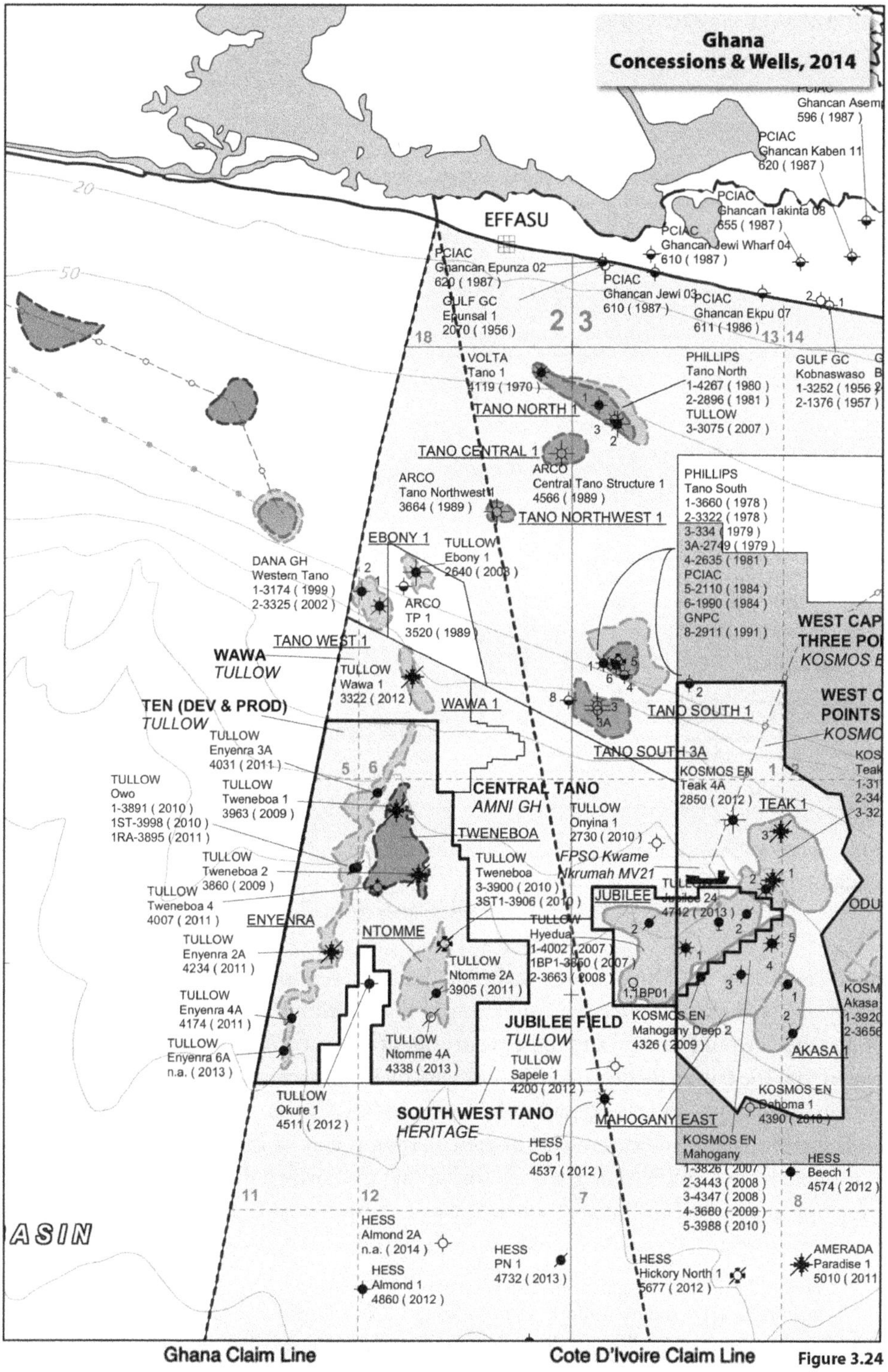

FIGURE 20.6 The Location of Ghana Concessions and Drilled Deposits and the Maritime Border Claims of Ghana and Côte d'Ivoire

Source: Memorial of Ghana, *Ghana/Côte d'Ivoire (Merits)*, Figure 3.24

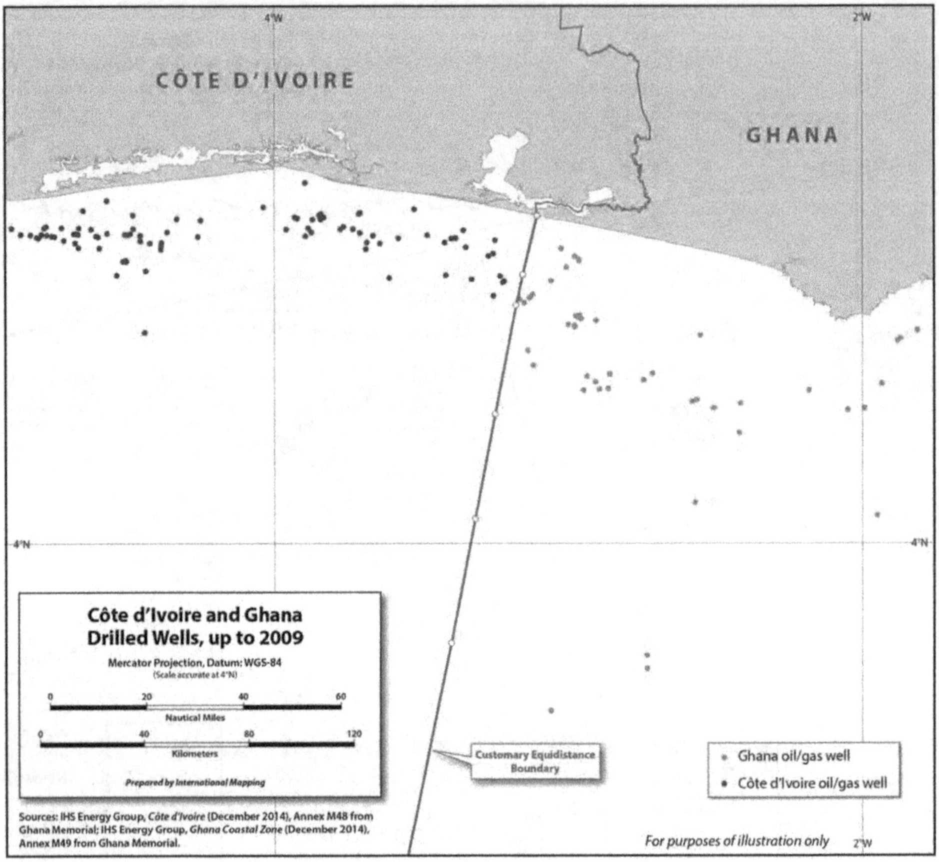

FIGURE 20.7 The Location of Deposits Drilled by Ghana and Côte d'Ivoire and the Customary Equidistance Line Claimed by Ghana

Source: Reply of Ghana, *Ghana/Côte d'Ivoire (Merits)*, Figure 2.22

justify adjusting it.[42] Once again, the drilled deposits were allocated entirely to Ghana, a result welcomed by the companies operating in the undelimited area. Tullow, for example, stated that it would resume and increase production of the TEN field,[43] and Erin Energy stated that the tribunal's decision did 'not negatively impact any of the discovered fields on the Company's Expanded Shallow Water Tano (ESWT) block'.[44]

The tribunal in this case also pursued the approach of the tribunal in *Guyana v Suriname* by not condemning Ghana for having authorized drilling and (in this case even) producing oil in the area when it was in dispute. At the provisional measures

[42] *Ghana/Côte d'Ivoire*, Judgment (n. 20), para. 480.

[43] Offshore Energy Today, 'Tullow Set to Resume TEN Drilling After Maritime Dispute Ruling' (25 September 2017), available at https://www.offshore-energy.biz/tullow-set-to-resume-ten-drilling-after-maritime-dispute-ruling/.

[44] Offshore Energy Today, 'Erin Energy Gearing Up for 3D Seismic after Ghana-Ivory Coast Border Ruling' (26 September 2017), available at https://www.offshore-energy.biz/erin-energy-gearing-up-for-3d-seismic-after-ghana-ivory-coast-border-ruling/.

stage, Côte d'Ivoire requested that all ongoing oil activities in the disputed area be suspended.[45] However, the ITLOS Special Chamber allowed Ghana to pursue ongoing production from the wells already drilled, considering the potential environmental and financial damage that such suspension would have caused to Ghana.[46] It merely ordered Ghana not to authorize any *new* drilling in the disputed area.

At the merits stage, the ITLOS Special Chamber considered once more the unilateral activities that Ghana had authorized in the disputed area, including both those that had been completed and those that it had not ordered Ghana to cease at the provisional measures stage. It decided that Ghana had not breached Côte d'Ivoire's sovereign rights as it had conducted its activities in good faith,[47] but it went further, saying that Ghana's drilling activities in the disputed area did not 'constitute a violation of the sovereign rights of Côte d'Ivoire [...] even assuming that some of those activities took place in areas attributed to Côte d'Ivoire by the present Judgment'.[48] The ITLOS Special Chamber also held that Ghana had not violated Article 83(3) of UNCLOS because it had 'undertaken hydrocarbon activities only in an area attributed to it', even though this area was disputed at the time.[49] This provoked Judge Paik to say in his separate opinion: 'To condone the unilateral activities of such a scale in the circumstances of the present case would certainly send a wrong signal to States pondering over their next move in a disputed maritime area elsewhere. I regret that the Special Chamber has just done that.'[50]

Whether the signal being sent is right or wrong is open to debate.[51] However, it is certainly true that the three cases mentioned here have the result of encouraging states to authorize unilateral exploration and exploitation activities in disputed areas pending delimitation.

20.5 Conclusion

It has been argued in this chapter that, when they have a discretion to do so, tribunals reward states with rights to drilled deposits, provided that this is done according to a plausible boundary line. If this argument is correct, it is also appropriate to consider why this might be the case. One possibility is that states are not being rewarded, but are simply enjoying the fruits of an accurate prediction of the boundary line. This may indeed

[45] *Ghana/Côte d'Ivoire*, Provisional Measures (n. 10), para. 81.

[46] The tribunal's rationale was that such suspension 'would entail the risk of considerable financial loss to Ghana and its concessionaires and could also pose a serious danger to the marine environment resulting, in particular, from the deterioration of the equipment': *Ghana/Côte d'Ivoire*, Provisional Measures (n. 10), para. 99.

[47] *Ghana/Côte d'Ivoire*, Judgment (n. 20), para. 592. See also Van Logchem (n. 40), 165.

[48] *Ghana/Côte d'Ivoire*, Judgment (n. 20), para. 594.

[49] Ibid. para. 633. See also Van Logchem (n. 40), 163–4.

[50] *Ghana/Côte d'Ivoire*, Judgment (n. 20), Separate Opinion of Judge Paik, para. 19.

[51] Van Logchem (n. 40), 176, says that 'the reasoning of the Special Chamber cannot but have negative effects'.

be a partial explanation, but it also overstates the predictability of maritime boundary delimitation. Another explanation might be that tribunals do not wish to interfere with the exploration and exploitation of energy resources per se, particularly given the large investments that are necessary for these activities to take place. This might account for the reluctance of the ITLOS Special Chamber to expose Ghana to large financial losses by ordering the shutting down of all activities in the disputed area, even if these risked causing irreparable damage to the rights of Côte d'Ivoire.

Alongside these explanations, there may well be others, quite possibly involving the interests of the oil companies. In addition, there is a piece that is difficult to fit into this puzzle, which is the extreme reluctance of tribunals not only to create shared deposits by drawing lines through known deposits (although this may be unavoidable or done by mistake) but even to address the ways in which shared deposits might be handled by the disputing parties. In the early history of maritime boundary delimitation, it appeared that some rules on allocating shared deposits might be developed. The ICJ, in *North Sea Continental Shelf*, outlined the problem of deposits lying across a delimited boundary:

> [I]t frequently occurs that the same deposit lies on both sides of the line dividing a continental shelf between two States, and since it is possible to exploit such a deposit from either side, a problem immediately arises on account of the risk of prejudicial or wasteful exploitation by one or other of the States concerned.[52]

The court recognized that state practice had dealt with this problem in the form of joint development agreements, which it considered 'particularly appropriate' to 'preserv[e] the unity of the deposit'.[53] However, it did not consider that the 'unity of the deposit constitutes anything more than a factual element which it is reasonable to take into consideration in the course of the negotiations for a delimitation',[54] indicating that unitization is an idea to be considered by the parties (both before and after delimitation) rather than conduct to be ordered by tribunals. Thirty years later, there was still little progress. In 1999, the tribunal in *Eritrea/Yemen* said merely that the parties 'should give every consideration to the shared or joint or unitised exploitation' of oil and gas resources discovered to be straddling the maritime boundary in the future.[55] Eight years after that, in 2007, the *Guyana v Suriname* arbitral tribunal did not even mention the fact that a deposit would become shared as a result of its delimitation (see Figure 20.8). This was remarkable in light of the fact that the deposit in question, Wishbone, had already been identified by CGX in its exploration studies and drilling was due to take place under a concession granted by Guyana before the award,[56] meaning that activities on this deposit would be prohibited unless both parties were in agreement.

[52] *North Sea Continental Shelf* (n. 1), para. 97.

[53] Ibid. para. 99.

[54] Ibid. para. 97.

[55] *Second Stage of the Proceedings between Eritrea and Yemen (Maritime Delimitation)*, 17 December 1999, 22 RIAA 335, para. 86.

[56] Memorial of Guyana, Vol III, 22 February 2005, Annexes 156–159.

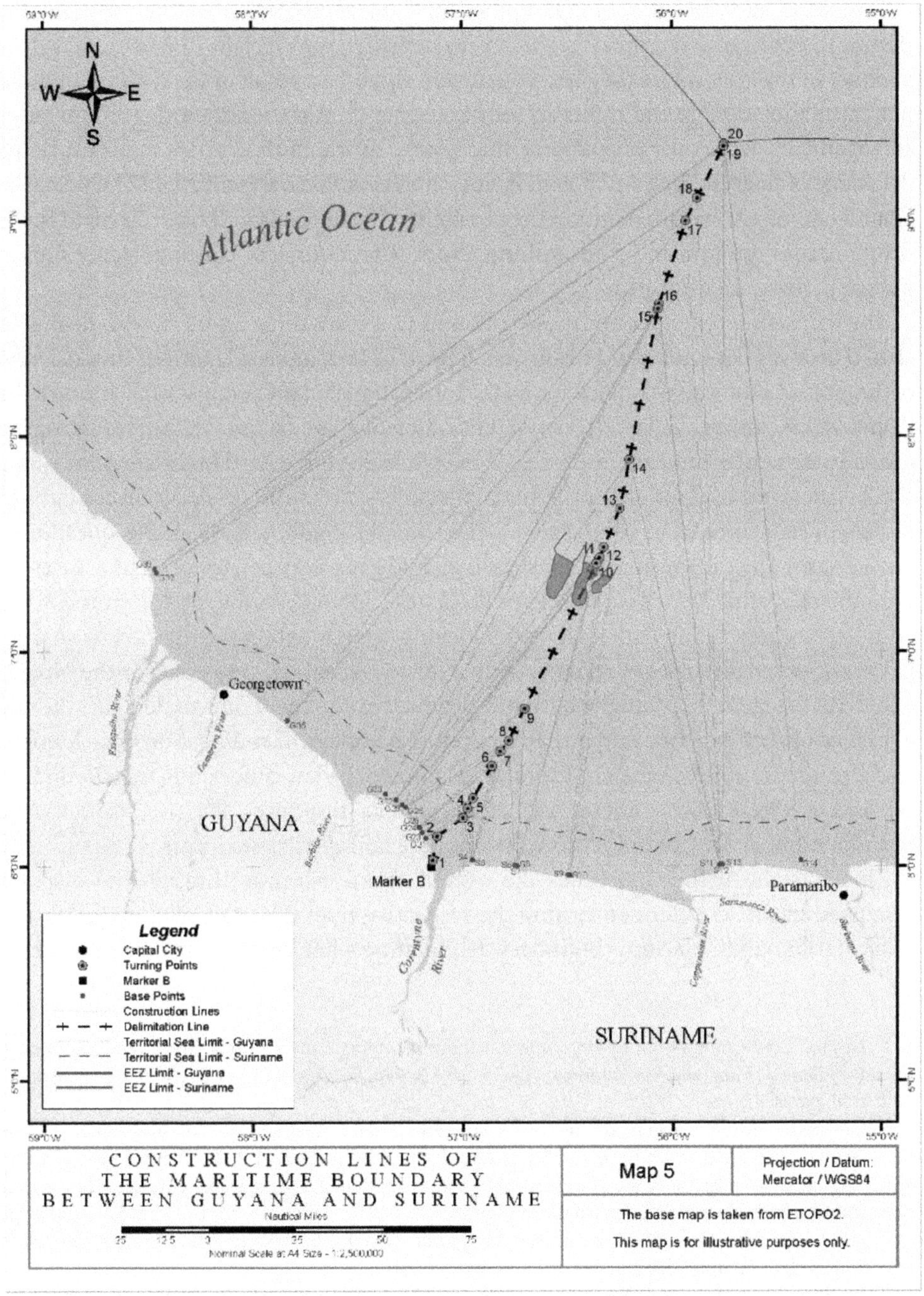

FIGURE 20.8 The Location of the Wishbone Deposit Straddling the Delimited Maritime Boundary

Source: CGX Energy

Five years later, in 2012, ITLOS opined in *Bangladesh/Myanmar* that 'it is for the Parties to determine the measures that they consider appropriate' to ensure that their conduct in the area where they had concurrent rights as a result of the delimitation did not cause prejudice to the rights of the other party.[57] Also, it added that 'cooperative arrangements' were only one among 'many ways in which the parties may ensure the discharge of their obligations'.[58] And in 2017, in *Ghana/Côte d'Ivoire*, the ITLOS Special Chamber omitted even to mention the possibility that deposits may be discovered in the future across the line and said nothing about what course of conduct states should pursue in these circumstances.[59]

The increasing reluctance of these tribunals to say anything about how to deal with shared deposits does not exist in isolation. It must be seen alongside the effective deletion of the topic as a subject of codification by the International Law Commission.[60] In 2002, the Commission commenced work on the codification of 'shared natural resources' (covering groundwater and oil and gas resources),[61] but while this project led to the adoption of the Draft Articles on the Law of Transboundary Aquifers,[62] its work on shared hydrocarbons faced stiff resistance from several states. The United Kingdom, for example, questioned 'the need for any universal rules on shared oil and gas resources, or for draft articles on the subject', stating that it was a matter for states (rather than for the Commission) to address, by cooperating with a view to achieving 'agreement on the division or sharing of cross-border oil and gas fields',[63] while Norway, speaking on behalf of the Nordic countries, suggested: 'It might be more productive for the Commission to note the existence of such practice rather than to attempt a process of codification, which might lead to more complexity and confusion in relation to the law concerning transboundary oil and gas reserves.'[64] These and other similar responses led, in 2010, to the abandonment of the Commission's work on shared oil and gas resources.

This episode further illustrates the overall theme running through the disputes discussed in this chapter concerning the respective roles of states, oil companies and arbitral tribunals in maritime boundary delimitation when rights to offshore oil and gas

[57] *Dispute Concerning Delimitation of the Maritime Boundary between Bangladesh and Myanmar in the Bay of Bengal (Bangladesh/Myanmar)*, ITLOS Case No. 16, Judgment of 14 March 2012, para. 475.

[58] Ibid. paras. 472–6.

[59] On the shared deposits created by the delimited boundary, see Pieter Bekker and Robert van de Poll, 'Ghana and Côte d'Ivoire Receive a Strict-Equidistance Boundary', 21 ASIL Insights 11, 13 October 2017: available at https://www.asil.org/insights/volume/21/issue/11/ghana-and-cote-divoire-receive-strict-equidistance-boundary-boundary.

[60] For a comprehensive review see Tibisay Morgandi, *Bilateral Energy Governance: State Practice in International Law* (Cambridge University Press, forthcoming).

[61] Working Paper on Shared Natural Resources: feasibility of future work on oil and gas, prepared by Special Rapporteur Shinya Murase, 9 March 2010, UN Doc A/CN.4/621, at 1–2.

[62] Resolution adopted by the General Assembly on the Report of the Sixth Committee (A/63/439), The law of transboundary aquifers, 11 December 2008, UN Doc A/RES/63/124.

[63] United Kingdom, Official Records of the General Assembly, Sixty-Third Session, Sixth Committee, Summary record of the 16th meeting (New York, 27 October 2008), UN Doc A/C.6/63/SR.16, para. 58.

[64] Norway (on behalf of Denmark, Finland, Iceland, Norway and Sweden), Official Records of the General Assembly, Sixty-Third Session, Sixth Committee, Summary record of the 16th meeting (New York, 27 October 2008), UN Doc A/C.6/63/SR.16, para. 30.

deposits are at stake. As has been shown, arbitral tribunals have various incentives to draw lines around drilled deposits, where possible, rather than through them. As such, they are not simply the mouthpieces of an impartial law, but rather players in a larger game, and, despite what they say, they appear to be conscious of this fact, in particular by not straying too far into areas that states reserve for themselves. But states (and, behind the scenes, oil companies) also have a use for tribunals in resolving disputes between themselves, in particular if this is to endorse their practices, provided that these practices take place according to broadly established expectations. Perhaps the best way to understand the dynamic—which may be taken as a paradigm of arbitration—is as a game in which states, tribunals, and private companies play interdependent roles according to broadly agreed rules leading to more or less predictable outcomes.

List of Figures with Sources

Figure 20.1: Clive Schofield and Chris Carleton, 'Technical Considerations in Law of the Sea Dispute Resolution' in Alex Elferink and Donald Rothwell (eds), *Oceans Management in the 21st Century* (Leiden: Brill, 2004), 242

Figure 20.2: adapted from *Cameroon v Nigeria*, Judgment [2002] ICJ Rep 303, at 449 and Rejoinder of Nigeria, *Cameroon v Nigeria (Merits)*, 4 January 2001, Figure 10.4

Figure 20.3: Clive Schofield and Chris Carleton, 'Technical Considerations in Law of the Sea Dispute Resolution' in Alex Elferink and Donald Rothwell (eds), *Oceans Management in the 21st Century* (Leiden: Brill, 2004), 249

Figure 20.4: CGX Energy, Consolidated Financial Statements for the Year ended December 31, 2006—Management's Discussion and Analysis (Update 2006), at 2, available at http://cgxenergy.ca/cmsAssets/docs/financials/AnnualMeetingPackage-UpdateandFinancials.pdf

Figure 20.5: Wood Mackenzie, Guyana: On the Brink of Exploration Success? Upstream Insight Latin America (2008), at 6, available at http://cgxenergy.ca/cmsAssets/docs/analysts/Wood%20Mackenzie/WoodMacKenzie-Nov08.pdf

Figure 20.6: Memorial of Ghana, *Ghana/Côte d'Ivoire (Merits)*, Vol I, 4 September 2015, Figure 3.24

Figure 20.7: Reply of Ghana, *Ghana/Côte d'Ivoire (Merits)*, Vol I, 25 July 2016, Figure 2.22

Figure 20.8: CGX Energy, Maritime Border Resolution—Boundary Award Map, available at http://cgxenergy.ca/cmsAssets/images/CGXOffshoreAward.PNG

PART IV

PARADIGMS

CHAPTER 21

INTERNATIONAL ARBITRATION

A critical private international law perspective

HORATIA MUIR WATT

THE contemporary rise of arbitration as a significant—and, increasingly, predominant—mode of dispute resolution in the context of international trade and investment has been remarkably unhampered by negative appraisals of its political economy, institutional structures, and substantive impact. Yet, throughout the last quarter of the twentieth century, such critique has been severe. Sociological studies have revealed the ways in which a handful of 'dealers in virtue', functioning as a closed club, managed to lay the foundations of a highly lucrative industry.[1] Third world critics denounce the distinctly Western and pro-capital flavour of the growing body of awards purportedly constitutive of a new *lex mercatoria*.[2] Growing unease with the world-wide investment regime

[1] Growing criticism draws attention to a broad range of issues relating to the functioning of arbitration as an institution (the scourge of conflicts of interest, old-boy networks, sexism, excessive stipends), which threaten its legitimacy, along with the credibility of professional arbitrators, within the international community. See esp. Yves Dezalay and Bryant Garth, *Dealing in Virtue: International Commercial Arbitration and the Construction of a Transnational Legal Order* (Chicago University Press, 1996).

[2] The new *lex mercatoria* represents a body of norms issuing from the 'community of merchants' in the form of commercial custom or practice, arbitral awards, and principles enshrined in various soft-law texts. It raises an interesting theoretical debate, which raged in the 1970s at the time international commercial arbitration began to soar, as to whether these norms qualify as 'law' or not. Arbitration figures prominently in this debate: it provides the requisite organic dimension for the *lex mercatoria* to become a legal system—meaning that even if the existing set of rules is incomplete, it can be supplemented by authorized interpreters (see, by its most active proponent, Berthold Goldman, *Frontières du droit et 'lex mercatoria'* (Archives de Philosophie du Droit, 1964), 177). Today, the debate is rather whether the *lex mercatoria* can properly be codified (as the Unidroit principles for international commercial contracts purport to do) and whether parties can choose it as the governing law before state courts. It is generally recognized as an acceptable choice, on the other hand, in international arbitration. See Emmanuel Gaillard, 'Trente ans de *lex mercatoria*. Pour une application sélective de la méthode des principes généraux du droit', 122 Journal du Droit International 5 (1995).

targeted arbitration as compounding its perceived pro-investor bias.[3] A political economy perspective furthermore underscores the ways in which various legal systems, particularly those involved in competition to attract the arbitration industry, have progressively facilitated the recognition and enforcement of arbitral awards.[4]

Arbitration has continued to soar notwithstanding in a growing number of areas, with the explicit support of courts and governments alike, right across the geopolitical board.[5] It has absorbed the toolbox of proportionality so as to better exercise judicial review over host country regulation of investment,[6] is repeatedly represented as the natural venue for cross-border commercial conflicts,[7] and has become an accepted source of post-national rule-making in the wider context of global economic governance.[8] This remarkable immunity to critique may be due to the essentially 'external' nature of the objections thus raised.[9] Indeed, it is only recently, in the context of the Transatlantic Trade and Investment Partnership (TTIP) negotiations, that political concerns about the relationship of arbitration and the public policies of host countries have been voiced in any effective way—largely amplified by social media.[10] However, the very same context has also shown the remarkable strength of the arbitration lobby. It may even be that current proposals for a permanent investment court, ostensibly designed to respond to

[3] Muthucumaraswamy Sornarajah, *The International Law on Foreign Investment*, 3rd edn (Cambridge University Press, 2010).

[4] See below. On the ways in which public policy considerations are 'deactivated' by the combined operation of choice of court agreements and liberal enforcement provisions, see Horatia Muir Watt, 'Party Autonomy in International Contracts: From the Makings of a Myth to the Requirements of Global Governance', 6 European Review of Contract Law 250 (2010).

[5] Interestingly, international arbitration has become a worldwide phenomenon, not limited to Western Europe and the United States, where it flourished initially, but spreading to Asia, Latin America, and the Arab world. Arguably, it is the apanage of late capitalist expansion. Indeed, the worldwide foreign investment regime has amplified its importance as the 'natural' forum for trade and investment disputes.

[6] Alec Stone Sweet and Florian Grisel, 'The Evolution of International Arbitration: Delegation, Judicialization, Governance', in Walter Mattli and Thomas Dietz, *International Arbitration and Global Governance: Contending Theories and Evidence* (Oxford University Press, 2014), emphasizing that the introduction of proportionality reasoning in investment arbitration signals a turn away from the private law model of adjudication.

[7] The success of arbitration in the global economy is linked to the fact that it has arguably become the natural or default forum in the case of commercial disputes (Gilles Cuniberti, 'Beyond Contract: The Case for Default Arbitration in International Commercial Disputes', 32 Fordham International Law Journal 417 (2009)) and is moreover the mandatory mode of dispute resolution in the direct investment context.

[8] On private post-national rule-making, see e.g. Nico Krisch, 'Conceptualising Postnational Rule-Making', Working Paper (2011); Nico Krisch, Roger Cotterrell and Maksymillian del Mar, *Authority in Transnational Legal Theory: Theorising Across Disciplines* (Edward Elgar, 2016).

[9] Meaning that criticism is addressed from outside the legal institution (e.g. from an economic perspective) and does not focus on its legal niceties (concepts, logic, coherence…). From an internal perspective (i.e. from within the law), distributional consequences are of little import when freedom of contract, or consent, are at stake.

[10] It could also be that transnational civil society was still in its infancy when arbitration began to embody charismatic authority beyond the state, in an environment that favoured expert knowledge in all its forms.

cure arbitration's legitimacy deficit in the context of investment treaties, represent the ultimate albeit paradoxical triumph of privatized dispute resolution.[11]

Be that as it may, it is clear that when distributional issues in arbitration are neatly cloaked in the vocabulary of transnational justice, or embedded in such venerable constructions as freedom of contract, it is difficult to challenge its outcomes or processes, or to dislodge the widespread understanding that, in all events, no acceptable alternatives exist to privatized or expert-based modes of dispute resolution for transnational economic disputes involving non-state actors.[12] At the same time, undeniably, arbitration as a legal institution per se—detached from the investment context and independently of distributional issues affecting the law applicable to markets—has a venerable pedigree[13] and moreover much to recommend it in appropriate contexts; transnational commerce has provided a particularly propitious setting for its expansion, for reasons which are no doubt perfectly sound when applied to equal, professional parties. It would certainly be excessive to reject it outright, as much as it is equally problematic to accept its current forms and functions indiscriminately.

This contribution envisages international arbitration as a crucial part of the legal framework that has progressively enabled the contemporary neo-liberal orientation of global governance.[14] As such, it presents the perspective of critical private international law.[15] If the latter discipline constitutes a significant viewpoint in this respect, it is precisely because it provided the foundational legal tools and discourse by means of which international arbitration attained such astounding success as a cornerstone of cross-border trade and investment regimes.[16] The specific contention here is that in sanctifying freedom of contract to an unprecedented degree, including unrestricted party choice of law and forum, it has deactivated the regulatory constraints to which private actors are subject in a domestic setting and, involuntarily thereby, sealed the 'loss of control' by nation-states of various crucial aspects of the global economy.

[11] See e.g. Muthucumaraswamy Sornarajah, who claims that 'an Investment Court would not cure such illegitimacy. A Court would become a device for neoliberal rules of investment protection with even greater authority': 'An International Investment Court: Panacea or Purgatory?' Columbia FDI Perspectives 180 (2016).

[12] When both parties are state actors, the WTO regime steps in. But of course, the state/non-state divide is blurry, as state intervention is often designed to protect the interests of private actors who are national 'champions'.

[13] On arbitration's pre-modern pedigree, see the historical account in Charles Jarrosson, *La notion d'arbitrage* (LGDJ, 1987).

[14] For a more general study of the role played by private international law in the creation or maintenance of blind spots in global governance, see Horatia Muir Watt, 'Private International law Beyond the Schism', 2 Transnational Legal Theory 347 (2011).

[15] The critical strand within private international law focuses on the historical contribution by this discipline to the subordination of the public to the private in the steering of the world economy. In this respect, it shows how private international law has been complicit in shielding private power from accountability, responsibility, and public scrutiny, and encouraging the pursuit of profit to the detriment of competing values, beyond control.

[16] Paradoxically, moreover, the discipline turns a blind eye to the very phenomena which it might have appeared to be specifically equipped to govern, thereby reinforcing the hiatus between the reach of state regulation and the global processes of production and markets.

In the vein of such critique, this contribution is organized in three sections, as follows. Section 21.1 will revisit the libertarian idea of contract as untrammelled 'party autonomy',[17] on the basis of which international arbitration achieved its initial success in a commercial context, before migrating to the public international world of investment law at the turn of the twentieth century. This venerable principle of private law has been the single most significant enabling factor in the transition from liberalism to neo-liberalism,[18] which has seen sovereign states relinquish political control,[19] individually and collectively, in respect of significant dimensions of global governance (Section 21.1).

The stage is thus set for an exploration of the grievances generally addressed to arbitration as emblematic of the privatization of global governance, understood alternatively as a confiscation of power in the hands of a happy few individuals or as the subordination of public concerns to private interests. Section 21.2 will set out this 'privatization critique'.[20] But are there any other conceivable avenues worth exploring? Even given current turbulence within the investment regime, arbitration has become so embedded as a mode of transnational dispute resolution that most feasible avenues of reform are, if not purely cosmetic, at least designed to improve the institution rather than to displace or replace it. While concrete proposals for an independent (court-like) structure have been made in the context of the TTIP negotiations, this contribution pursues a very different path, suggesting that seeing arbitration in terms of networks might herald an epistemological and political change based on the sociological reality which generally lies at the heart of its critique (Section 21.3).

21.1 The Neo-Liberal Turn: Foundational Legal Tools

21.1.1 Overview: arbitration in context

Arguably the most significant principle of contemporary private international law, 'party autonomy'—or more simply, contractual freedom of choice of the governing

[17] As explained below, the principle of party autonomy in private international law is so unquestioned as to have attained mythical status.

[18] For the difference between classical and neo-liberalism, see Michel Foucault, *La naissance de la biopolitique. Cours au Collège de France, 1978–1979* (Seuil, 2004).

[19] Its operation illustrates Saskia Sassen's astute observation that globalization processes which undermine state sovereignty (and state law) and lead to the perception of a loss of control originate in, and are encouraged by, decisions made within these states themselves: *Losing Control? Sovereignty in an Age of Globalization* (Columbia University Press, 1996). In enabling capital to accede to 'regulatory lift-off' with the help of private international law, states have laid the foundations of autonomous private ordering from more public or collective concerns. Similarly, moreover, they have enabled competing forms of authority, which arbitrate, enforce, and legitimize such private structures, thereby serving the free global market for legal products and services.

[20] Paraphrasing W. Mark C. Weidemaier, 'Arbitration and the Individuation Critique', 49 Ariz. L. Rev. 69 (2007).

law—fulfils a key function within the political economy of private ordering. It empowers private actors to harness state legislation—that of any, freely chosen, nation-state—to the needs of their cross-border transaction. Between its first intimations at the turn of the twentieth century and its later widespread success in the context of post-war international trade, free contractual choice of law had to overcome the concern that a '*contrat sans loi*' might encourage market actors to opt out of the requirements of the rule of law.[21] Hence, the idea (formally enshrined in many of the legal instruments which promote party choice of law today)[22] that party freedom to substitute one legal system for another is necessarily conditional on two factors which, together, ensure the benign oversight of the community of liberal states.[23]

Firstly, such freedom is triggered by a requirement of internationality (there must be an international contract in order to benefit from free choice of law), designed to prevent domestic contracts from circumventing local public policy. The idea here is that private ordering is supreme by default only: no state has an exclusive claim to regulate a case which has cross-border elements, nor are its policies likely to be affected to the same degree when its connection with the contract is diluted. Secondly, the chosen law must be that of a nation-state or at least effectively in force in (any) given country, so as to prevent parties from 'cherry-picking' from the laws of different countries and inventing their own, self-fashioned, private regime: this excludes soft-law instruments, supposed general principles of international contract law, or the *lex mercatoria*. Such requirements aim to safeguard the purportedly common public interest, encouraging private enterprise within limits analogous to those that each state imposes domestically (i.e. within its own sphere of sovereignty) on its own markets.

The idea of party autonomy migrated later to the field of international jurisdiction,[24] where it was seen as promoting, more pragmatically, procedural economy and ease of risk management.[25] Freedom to choose the applicable law was therefore followed by an equally gradual acceptance of free choice of forum in cross-border litigation. But in order to be effective, a contractual choice of forum and the judgment to which it gave rise needed to be widely enforceable, which led to a liberalization of the conditions for the cross-border movement of foreign decisions. Such movement was initially justified by the needs of international commerce; a more contemporary reading referred to the

[21] For details, see Muir Watt (n. 4).

[22] See e.g., enshrined in the EU context, Regulation EC No. 593/2008 on the law applicable to contractual obligations (Rome I), Art. 3.

[23] See Ralf Michaels and Nils Jansen, 'Private Law Beyond the State? Europeanization, Globalization, Privatization', 54 Am. J. Comp. L. 843 (2006).

[24] In the US, the landmark cases are *The Bremen et al. v Zapata Off-Shore Co.*, 407 U.S. 1 (1972) and *Mitsubishi v Soler Chrysler-Plymouth*, 473 U.S. 614 (1985). In the EU, see Regulation EC No. 44/01 (Brussels I), now 'recast' as Regulation EU No. 1215/2012 (2012) on jurisdiction and the recognition and enforcement of judgments in civil and commercial matters. See also the Hague Convention on Choice of Court Agreements (2005).

[25] The substitution of the pragmatic quest for efficiency for the philosophical foundations of contract law mark the decline, towards the middle of the 20th c., of the influence of continental legal theory in comparative private international law, which focused on the determination of the applicable law, in favour of the predominantly jurisdictional concerns of the common lawyers.

enhancement of global jurisdictional competition, which would supposedly reap benefits in terms of the improvement of the quality of judicial services worldwide.[26] Finally, once choice of court was allowed, there was little reason to prevent parties from opting out of the formal legal system altogether and resorting to private or contractual dispute resolution.

Reputedly more flexible (if not cheaper), international commercial arbitration presented all the advantages of forum selection clauses, with the added attraction of confidentiality. Furthermore, when political stakes were high (such as in state investment contracts), it could claim to rise above the partisan politics of local legal systems; it was progressively endowed with 'autonomy' in respect of local procedural and substantive constraints in the name of its greater neutrality. Increasingly commonplace in practice, arbitration agreements thrived both in commercial and investment contexts as initial doubts as to the desirability of allowing private actors to forego access to state courts have dwindled. Its widespread recognition as an institution of global governance was quickly enhanced by rapid and competitive legalization within, across and between nation-states.[27]

While this move towards more efficient and less regulated dispute resolution appeared (or was made to appear)[28] inexorable and moreover highly desirable, it induced less visible changes in the liberal balance between market and regulation, collective and individual interests, or public and private ordering, attained during the first part of the twentieth century. In this respect, it heralded a neo-liberal articulation of the relationship between private will and public law, in which the first is not subordinate to the authority of the second but stands in its very stead.[29] Private actors can exit any legal system—meaning they can opt out of constraints imposed by any specific legal system—through the combined effect of choice of forum, choice of law, and free movement of decisions or awards. This is in effect to authorize jurisdictional 'barrier-crossing',[30] through which, in a move well-rehearsed in the field of regulatory competition, (public) law becomes (private) commodity. The market for laws comes about when free choice of law is accompanied by an arbitration agreement and liberalized conditions of enforcement of the ensuing award; competition though private arbitrage pushes down the cost of local regulation in the form of social, environmental, or human rights standards.

[26] Jens Dammann and Henry Hansmann, 'Globalizing Commercial Litigation', 94 Cornell L. Rev. 1 (2008).

[27] Legalization took the form of national legislation, bilateral and multilateral treaties, and the creation of transnational institutions (on the model of the Paris International Chamber of Commerce).

[28] The current success of international arbitration owes much to the role of the 'epistemic community of arbitrators', often exercising academic authority, in shaping discourse.

[29] This point is made very forcibly by Michel Foucault (n. 18).

[30] Horatia Muir Watt and Luca Radicati di Brozolo, 'Party Autonomy and Mandatory Rules in a Global World', 6 Int'l L. F. D Int'l 90 (2004). For the concept and references, see Horatia Muir Watt, 'Aspects économiques du droit international privé', 305 Recueil des cours de l'Académie de la Haye 1 (2004), 219.

In other words, private actors can attain 'regulatory lift-off'[31] because the liberal state has renounced—or has been constrained by competitive economic forces to give up—the means to ensure the primacy of its own (or another's) public policy regulation over 'private legislation'. By allowing parties to cross jurisdictional barriers unhindered, the principle of free choice inverts the relationship between public law and private choice and generates a competitive market for legal products and judicial services in which the common good (however defined by any state with a plausible claim to govern) is always likely to lose out to a libertarian vision of the world. The market for corporate charters (as within the US or the EU) is a classic example of the temptation to 'shop' around from one jurisdiction to another, in order to circumvent any legal constraints which stand in the way of profit maximization; in the international sphere, a similar phenomenon explains why capital invests in jurisdictions where the cost of social or environmental regulation is low (and where, for example, the levels of reparation likely to be awarded in cases of industrial accidents remain lower than the overall return from investments).

A theorization of this state of affairs has been provided by economic accounts of inter-jurisdictional competition through free party choice, that could purportedly induce a globally optimal result across the board. Empowerment of economic actors to navigate various domestic laws through similar regulatory arbitrage is at the heart of global financial markets,[32] and illustrates more generally the ways in which the law can facilitate accumulation by dispossession[33] on a global level.

21.1.2 Specifics: the expansion of arbitration

The first sign of the transformation described above is linked to the expanded scope of arbitration ('arbitrability'),[34] which allows parties to renounce the jurisdiction of the courts (any national court) in disputes involving issues of public regulation or policy (such as competition law). Substituting private for public dispute resolution is of course to confer normative authority on arbitrators, who, in deciding such disputes, inevitably create norms. The self-description of the arbitrator as akin to the sports umpire who merely declares the winner at the end of the game has little purchase today, particularly since the rise of investment arbitration and the recourse by arbitrators to the legal tools of constitutional courts.[35] But as long as such authority is exercised in respect of issues

[31] Robert Wai, 'Transnational Liftoff and Juridical Touchdown: The Regulatory Function of Private International Law in a Global Age', 40 Columbia Journal of Transnational Law 209 (2002).

[32] Katharina Pistor, 'A Legal Theory of Finance', 41 Journal of Comparative Economics 315 (2013).

[33] David Harvey, *A Brief History of Neoliberalism* (Oxford University Press, 2005).

[34] Comparative legal vocabulary differs here, as do the respective conceptions of the proper role of the courts in arbitration supervision: see George Bermann, 'Les questions liminaires en arbitrage commercial international', Trav.com.fr. DIP (2012), 81. Here, arbitrability is taken in the European sense to mean the range of substantive legal issues that can validly be subjected to arbitration and, more specifically, the extent to which a dispute involving public regulatory law or public policy can be so subjected.

[35] See the analysis of the jurisdictionalization of arbitration by Stone Sweet (n. 6).

that might broadly be described as of private interest, insofar as they could be definitively decided by contract, the legitimacy and utility of arbitration can hardly be contested.

There is no reason indeed why private actors should not, in lieu of negotiated agreement, submit to the decision of a chosen third party. Moreover, given minimal (anonymous) publicity, or even the inevitable (though longer term) diffusion of practices through capillarity within a given professional community, the repeated interventions of a body of competent experts on technical issues can contribute positively to the creation of a pool of common knowledge; applied to recurring legal issues in contract law, this may lead to channelling or fine-tuning standards of behaviour. The main challenges here are to ensure procedural impartiality and transparency, and to avoid involving weaker (uninformed or poor) actors in a process that is likely to surpass their means and deprive them of otherwise available access to the substantive protection of the law, or the redistributive action of the courts. This is why, for example, arbitration in consumer disputes needs to be closely monitored.[36]

However, the balance between public and private interests becomes more fragile when parties are allowed to elect private dispute resolution in fields in which at least one legal system with a credible claim to regulate pursues a restrictive public policy that purports to uphold a collective interest (such as the protection of weaker parties). But since it is obviously unrealistic to expect arbitrators (for economic reasons)[37] or foreign courts (for political reasons) to implement such policies in the same way as would national courts, the principal means of preventing the violation of crucial mandatory laws of any concerned state is by imposing a 'second look', *ex post*, at the judgments or awards issuing from the chosen forum.[38]

However, the second sign of the transformation is that this *ex post* control is gradually shrivelling. At the outset, it is often either impracticable (when no enforcement is required, the parties having settled, for instance), or problematic (when the supervising court is not better equipped than the arbitrator to make an assessment on the merits of the dispute),[39] or indeed practically excluded through deference to the chosen forum (as in cases as notorious as the Lloyd's litigation, where, through a strategic choice of

[36] Case C-168/05, *Mostaza Claro v Centro Móvil* (2006), ruling that a national court seised of an action for the annulment of an arbitration award must determine whether the arbitration agreement is void and annul the award where the arbitration agreement contains an unfair term even when the consumer has not raised the issue of unfairness in the arbitration proceedings. See, more generally, Maud Piers, 'Consumer Arbitration in the EU: A Forced Marriage with Incompatible Expectations', 2 Journal of International Dispute Settlement 209 (2011).

[37] William Landes and Richard Posner, 'Adjudication as a Private Good', 8 Journal of Legal Studies 235 (1979).

[38] For the idea of the 'second look', designed to prevent circumvention of regulatory policy by the combined use of choice of law and forum, see *Mitsubishi v Soler Chrysler-Plymouth*, 473 U.S. 614 (1985): 'in the event that choice-of-law forum and the choice-of-law clauses operated in tandem to as prospective waiver of a party's right to pursue statutory remedies…for antitrust violations, we would have little hesitation in condemning the agreement as against public policy.'

[39] E.g. when the dispute involves issues of economic assessment in competition law. See Luca Radicati di Brozolo, 'Antitrust: A Paradigm of the Relations between Mandatory Rules and Arbitration. A Fresh Look at the Second Look', 7(1) International Arbitration Law Review 23 (2004).

English forum, American investors specifically recruited to cover the impending asbestos-linked deficit were unable to resist claims by Lloyds, despite lack of prior information as to the extent of the risks involved, which would have led to the termination of the contract under US Securities regulation).[40]

But a further, powerful economic incentive for states deliberately to renounce their 'second look' has been competition for arbitration business—whether or not in the form of instituting a declared free zone for arbitration.[41] The real problem, therefore, lies in the fact that when court access is thus privatized, there is a correlative absence of judicial (or arbitral) consideration of interests beyond those of the parties to the dispute.[42] Moreover, in this context, national regulation can be described as being 'on offer', or available for party choice, but cannot properly be said to 'govern' private conduct.

Furthermore, this confiscation of the public sphere by the private signifies that there are no remaining tools with which to connect the (undoubtedly desirable) freedom involved in choice to correlative responsibility or accountability towards third parties, affected communities, or more widely, the world at large. Indeed, there are three reasons to doubt that arbitration does not implicate interests beyond those that are directly implicated in the dispute. In the first place, courts extend the binding effect of arbitration agreements to unsuspecting non-signatories in various situations, which, while variable from system to system, nevertheless derogate from the privacy of contract (in cases of bills of lading; chains of sales contracts; corporate statutes; various instances of subcontracting…).

Secondly, although each arbitration procedure is theoretically discrete, it is clear that something resembling an arbitral case law, including cross-references between awards, has been building up for a long time. Indeed, an important component of the *lex mercatoria* is supposedly based on the common principles applied by commercial courts and arbitrators, so that the mass of available awards is undoubtedly normative and arguably law-like. Moreover, it is common practice for arbitrators in investment practice to cite previous decisions of other tribunals.[43]

Lastly, as seen above, the extent of 'arbitrability' has expanded to such an extent over disputes involving public regulatory law that only family law matters or, in some juris-

[40] See *Roby v Corporation of Lloyd's*, 996 F 2d 1353 (2nd Cir 1993); *Bonny v Society of Lloyd's*, 3 F 3d 156 (7th Cir 1993).

[41] Bahrain was the first country to establish an arbitration 'free zone' in 2010. Since then, the idea has proliferated. See e.g. the China (Shanghai) Pilot Free Trade Zone (FTZ) launched in September 2013, where the Shanghai International Economic and Trade Arbitration Commission (also known as the Shanghai International Arbitration Centre, SHIAC) has facilitated the resolution of FTZ-related disputes in a commercially attractive manner by establishing under its auspices the FTZ Court of Arbitration in October 2013. Now, SHIAC has promulgated new arbitration rules with a modern suite of mechanisms for the conduct of international arbitration in the FTZ.

[42] See again Landes and Posner (n. 37).

[43] An interesting question is of course whether any real influence attaches to such cited cases, or whether, independent of their content, they represent as it were a conventional reference which signals the membership of the author of the citation in an epistemological community. On this point (which is not limited to arbitrators), see the research memorial by Damien Charlotin, 'Of Islands and Bridges: an Empirical Study of Citations between World Courts', Working Paper (2016) (on file with the author).

dictions, disputes involving unequal parties, are still subject to a monopoly of the courts. It is hardly surprising, therefore, that this particular model of privatized adjudication has spread to the field of investment. Here, the external impact of arbitration is the most obvious, since arbitral awards bind the state party, affect its regulatory choices, and are enforced on public finance.

The development of investment arbitration, which took place relatively unchallenged or unnoticed within the framework of ICSID,[44] has become highly controversial. The ongoing debate about the appropriate mechanism for dispute resolution in the TTIP negotiations demonstrate that the enforcement of private contractual rights under international law has begun to raise serious concerns about the legitimacy of arbitral awards affecting the common good and the lack of public accountability of arbitrators.[45] This not necessarily because of a widespread subjective arbitral bias in favour of investor interests (although this cannot be excluded), but more by reason of the structural effects of a contractual mode of dispute resolution in areas where public interests are involved, but where the investment treaties themselves are inherently biased in favour of investor interests. In other words, a contractual or private mode of dispute resolution is geared, by definition, to the reproduction of the content (or bias) of the convention on which it is based and which it is designed precisely to uphold. Thus, investor assets are protected from the restrictive effects of regulation within the host state—expropriations, nationalizations, local public policies—through the liberal principles governing private bargains.

Such liberal principles are truncated from, or unencumbered by, more social developments or regulatory trends detectable in comparative domestic contract law (such as consumer protection, and restrictions on the use of various clauses deemed to be 'unconscionable'). This supremacy of the basic tenet of liberal contract law, according to which contractual promises once legally formed are binding (or *pacta sunt servanda*), notwithstanding common trends towards a more social model in domestic law, is ensured by virtue of a wondrous legal doctrine known as the *Grundlegung*.

This doctrine distinguishes two types of claims: those which are based on the violation of a treaty between two states (the host state and the investor's home state) and those which result from a breach of the (private) contract between the investor and a public or

[44] The International Centre for Settlement of Investment Disputes (ICSID), created on the initiative of the World Bank, is, according to its own description, 'an autonomous international institution established under the Convention on the Settlement of Investment Disputes between States and Nationals of Other States, with over one hundred and forty member States... The primary purpose of ICSID is to provide facilities for conciliation and arbitration of international investment disputes.' Its Administrative Council is chaired by the President of the World Bank. It has fostered the proliferation of Bilateral Investment Treaties (BITs), which contain advance consents by governments to submit investment disputes to ICSID arbitration.

[45] The arbitral enforcement of BITs contributes to intensify private accumulation of public goods (land, water, fiscal revenues) in favour of foreign investors, and to the detriment of land or tax policies targeting existing inequalities within the host country. As Tomaso Ferrando puts it, 'the post-colonial International Investment Regime (IIR) is shaped around the imperial system of asymmetrical relationships between core and peripheral countries and has been crucial in frustrating any attempt by peripheral countries to redefine the global political economy': *Law and Territory in Global Production: A Critical Legal Chain Analysis* (Sciences Po, 2015).

private entity within the host state. The former, being a treaty, is governed by public international law; the latter, being merely a contract, is governed by the law chosen by the parties (or, if it is an administrative contract with a public body, by local domestic law). When claims are characterized as 'treaty claims' because they are based on the violation of a bilateral treaty rather than on breach of private contract, they are thereby hoisted into the more hospitable[46] atmosphere of customary international law. The hoisting—a re-characterization of private contractual claims as treaty claims—can be done through the use of different clauses in the bilateral treaty (such as the notorious 'umbrella clause', or the fair and equitable treatment clause) which transforms a breach of the private contract into a breach of the guarantee of fair treatment by the host state. Common principles of arbitral case law then emerge, on the basis of this truncated version of contract law.

21.1.3 Theorizing the critique

The wider critical-theoretical point here is that the rise of the international commercial arbitration regime by virtue of the largely unchallenged idea of party autonomy, as understood in private international law, and the migration of the same model to the field of public regulatory law and investment disputes illustrates, emblematically, the invisible effects of private law in the constitution of global governance. One of these effects is to channel considerable power through the arbitration process.[47] In this respect, a significant impact of the public/private divide in classical liberal thought has been to divert attention away from the ways in which private law structures and justifies power, outside the remit of constitutional or administrative law. The same split within the law between its public and private spheres also means that the classical theorization of private law as apolitical or 'merely technical'[48] has lent credence to the idea that it is unconcerned by issues of power. However, as David Kennedy forcefully points out, it is usual to think of law as *regulating* the basic elements of global political and economic life, or providing 'the sinews of a constituted order' but not as involved in the very *creation* of markets, or money, or debt.[49] This means that law is usually perceived by those

[46] Domestic systems of contract law usually contain exceptions or adjustments to the rule that bargains must be upheld at all times and at all costs, which have not necessarily found their way into international public (treaty) law, which still seems to retain the classical legal model established at the turn of the 20th c. This is not to say that the principles commonly applied in the latter context have not evolved at all in 100 years; but the upholding of bargains as such, whatever the respective strengths of the parties and the historical context of the negotiation, remains a mainstay.

[47] Although, on this point, see Ch. 28 by Thomas Dietz in this Handbook making the point that arbitration has quite a bit less power than chest-beating arbitration people would usually have it!

[48] Duncan Kennedy, 'The Political Stakes in "Merely Technical" Issues of Contract Law', 1 European Review of Private Law 7 (2001), 19, 14, 25.

[49] Ibid. 11, depicting the 'world of struggle' over law and expert knowledge which shapes the global political economy: 'the basic elements of global economic and political life—capital, labour, money and liquidity, as well as power and right—are creatures of law.'

outside the discipline through its more visible expressions, which are mostly 'public' or 'regulatory' law: constitutional, criminal, tax, or perhaps even environmental law; and in the economic field, competition (antitrust), or financial regulation. However, these expressions of the law presuppose the existence of underlying structures (markets, money, debt) which are actually constructs of private law (contracts, obligations, property). Private law puts into place the infrastructure needed for the whole economic system to exist (prior to regulation in one direction or another). In this respect, it works to a large extent invisibly, as if its constructions were perfectly natural.

As shown by critical comparative legal studies, of which the de-naturalization of the apparently natural is now largely the focus,[50] deconstruction of legal discourse is important so as to open up alternatives that might otherwise have remained invisible, or not even been looked for. It does not mean, however, that practices resulting from such beliefs are necessarily to be rejected. Nor does it mean that the myths and fictions which the law uses all the time, and of which party autonomy is certainly part, should be discarded. Revealing them as such merely shows that, when a given institution (such as contract, or its theoretical foundation, party autonomy) is used to justify undesirable effects, there is nothing inevitable about those institutions—despite the invocation of tradition or indeed anthropology—and that even the most embedded of legal constructs is only and precisely that.

Contract, for instance—or its private international version, contractual choice of law—is not intrinsically 'bad' per se, even when—as is recurrent in private international law[51] and as will be seen below in the case of investment arbitration—it has been used to legitimize extreme unfairness. Its effects can be changed, given the appropriate political will or the right social conditions. The question here is therefore what type of social consequences the myth of party autonomy has induced. The perception of unfairness and lack of legitimacy associated with international arbitration in different settings needs to be explored further, and the specific grievances examined.

21.2 The Privatization Grievance

In such a context, what might be termed the 'privatization critique'[52] articulates a series of grievances linked to the inversion, described above, of the classical liberal relationship between public authority and private ordering. These concerns are of course more significant in the context of investment arbitration, although they are also relevant to commercial arbitration, notably in cases of asymmetrical contracts, where the parties have widely unequal bargaining power. Such concerns have been voiced, if not fully

[50] See e.g. Pierre Legrand, 'The Same and the Different', in Pierre Legrand and Roderick Munday, *Comparative Legal Studies: Traditions and Transitions* (Cambridge University Press, 2003), 240.

[51] For some notorious examples, see Muir Watt (n. 14).

[52] See Weidemeier (n. 20).

theorized, in the current debate on the desirability of maintaining investment arbitration within the proposed and highly contested TTIP. There is greater awareness on both sides of the Atlantic of the relationship between the spread of arbitration and, more particularly, arbitral review of political measures and the correlative disempowerment of judicial institutions. According to this perspective, arbitration is seen as a confiscation of power in the name of a few and to the benefit of private interests.

This is seen to raise multiple problems—many of which, of course, are not specific to private international law. In particular, some are essentially about process—lack of the usual judicial guarantees of impartiality linked to the methods of selection of arbitrators; lack of transparency as to the reasons for a given decision. Others, originating in social critique, target structural bias in arbitration due to the cultural or social background of the community of arbitrators, as seen above. Further critique is about the supremacy of expert knowledge in global governance or the construction of discourse.[53] However interesting or significant, these will be set aside here in favour of those which are of special concern to private international law—either because this discipline is peculiarly well-placed to apprehend the phenomena in question, or because the legal governance of international arbitration is precisely part of the problems affecting current practice in the field and the focus of critique. Four sets of problems are emblematic in this respect.

21.2.1 Arbitration and external interests

The contractual nature of arbitration means that it is structurally unable or at least ill-equipped to take account of negative externalities—the interests of affected constituencies, whether these are individuals, communities, or indeed a less defined public interest such as the global environment. Third parties do not have a voice within the arbitral procedure itself (except, marginally, in the form of *amicus* briefs), while their interests do not weigh into the decision-making process. Indeed, treaties generally lack any specific procedure whereby communities or individuals whose interests are unaligned with those of the host state may be heard.[54]

Moreover, host country consent, the cornerstone of the entire regime, purports to legitimate any perceived infringement of its sovereignty.[55] The 'individuation critique' points out that the contractual paradigm excludes, by definition, as an effect of privity of

[53] See David Kennedy, *A World of Struggle: How Power, Law, and Expertise Shape Global Political Economy* (Princeton University Press, 2016).

[54] On civil society participation in investment arbitration, see Ch. 12 in this Handbook by Nathalie Bernasconi, Martin Dietrich Brauch, and Howard Mann.

[55] On the power of consent in this respect, see Shotara Hamamoto, 'Requiem for Indirect Expropriation: On the Theoretical and Practical Uselessness of a Contested Concept', PILAGG e-series (2012). However, when consent is the result of an unequal economic system, the sovereignty of consent is a circular argument.

contract, the voices or interests of third parties.[56] Similarly, Landes' and Posner's famous economic analysis of the incentive structure of arbitration, evoked above,[57] underscores the fact that as long as arbitrators are paid by the parties to the dispute and designated by them in the light of preceding outcomes, they have no economic incentives to ensure that wider interests are considered. True, there have been valiant efforts to invest the arbitrator with a duty to protect the transnational public interest as a corollary of its new privilege as 'natural forum' for transnational disputes. But these are bound to remain a matter of marginal practice or culture as long as the basic incentive structure of the arbitration process is not basically changed.

Prospects for such change are in turn doubtful, as long as states themselves participate in a vast global market for judicial services, in which arbitration—and judicial commercial dispute resolution on an arbitral model—plays a crucial part. The interests of affected communities as expressed in local mandatory legislation have little chance of prevailing as long as free choice of governing law allows regulatory arbitrage between laws of various content, pursuing dissimilar goals.[58] Yet there is nothing extraordinary in the claim that private ordering requires balancing out with other values associated with the public—such as responsibility, accountability, and collective good—in the direction of efforts undertaken by the international community towards responsible management of natural resources, reduction of poverty and economic inequalities, or involvement of local constituencies in global decision-making. Indeed, the global context underscores the absence of the forces that, in various domestic legal orders, have pushed private law to accommodate a modicum of balance between the expansion of markets and other collective values.

21.2.2 Arbitration and autonomous regimes

The privatization of transnational dispute resolution in the field of international trade and investment can be seen as part of an identifiable sequence[59] which lays down the self-supporting foundations of a global neo-liberal market order.[60] Of course, some would claim that this is in itself a mature regulatory choice and desirable outcome.[61] Yet,

[56] See Weidemeier (n. 20). [57] See Landes and Posner (n. 37).

[58] See Muir Watt (n. 30), 273.

[59] The same sequence leads to other phenomena linked to the globalizing economy, such as the impunity of corporate groups in respect of offshore conduct and inadequate attention to the distributional consequences of global value chains.

[60] See Gunther Teubner, *Constitutional Fragments: Societal Constitutionalism and Globalization* (Oxford University Press, 2011), developing the insights of Niklas Luhman on the functional differentiation of social spheres. This book is emphatically not a theory of global constitutionalism involving the search for an all-encompassing set of shared principles of world governance, but a pluralist perspective in which there could only be one common approach, that of 'collision law', which each node (or forum, in more traditional vocabulary) would define for itself.

[61] For a critical discussion of economic approaches and specifically the omission to regulate as a form of regulation, see Muir Watt (n. 30).

one might equally argue that such an outcome is as much the result of the want of a pilot in the global legal cockpit and short-sighted policy-making as it is due to informed political processes. Systems theory as recently applied to the field of transnational dispute resolution can be helpful here.[62] It offers two complementary perspectives.

The first identifies the self-expanding tendencies of autonomous regimes or rationalities, present in late modernity.[63] In short, a sociological perspective sees as the central evolution of late modernity (i.e. emerging within the modern state and accentuated by globalization), the multiplication of areas of autonomous action in society, each developing its own formal rationality, in mutual indifference to each other. Like the nation-state emerging in early modernity, these social sub-systems are self-referential, establishing themselves through processes by which, *ex nihilo*, they constitute their own autonomy. Such spheres concern culture, science, the economy, or law, but also more specialized sub-spheres:[64] among these, the *lex mercatoria*, which is generally represented as spontaneous private commercial ordering, linked organically to arbitration.[65]

Such sub-systems tend to develop a compulsive growth dynamic: according to Gunter Teubner, pathological, self-destructive tendencies[66] can thus be seen in the politicization, economization, juridification, mediatization, and medicalization of the world.[67] Teubner himself gives the example of the (contemporary) *lex mercatoria* to illustrate the ominous expansion of an autonomous regime. The fact that its success rests largely on international commercial arbitration goes to confirm the aptitude of this analysis. As has been seen, state control over arbitrability and the enforcement of arbitral awards has diminished significantly in the collective competition for the arbitration industry, inducing the 'loss of control' described above.[68]

[62] Teubner (n. 60). Social systems theory claims a post-structualist pedigree to the extent that it was Foucault who first identified, as Teubner puts it, 'radically de-personalizing power phenomena and identifying today's micro-power relations in society's capillaries in the discourses/practices of "disciplines"'.

[63] Ibid. These processes describe and explain the crisis of politics in the modern state. It is no longer possible for any authority to represent the whole of society. The political constitution of the state can no longer channel 'the collective energies of the whole society, founding the nation's unity. In modernity, the collective potential is no longer available as a whole, but has been dispersed into numerous social potentials, energies, powers.' This is due to the narrow specialization of the 'communicative media' of each social sphere—power, money, knowledge, law.'

[64] Such as finance, ecology, human rights, or indeed the *lex mercatoria*—which is precisely the rationality developed in and around international commercial arbitration.

[65] See above.

[66] Teubner calls this 'turbo-autopoiesis'.

[67] The analysis is applicable to law itself. See Teubner (n. 60), 80: 'In the case of law, we can clearly see that law not only resolves conflicts and returns to a position of rest. Rather, its own regulations actually generate conflicts, which then call for further regulation. Through its regulatory intervention in daily life, law itself produces the situations which then give rise to conflicts. And, at the same time, each norm generates problems of interpretation, which themselves generate further conflicts. Finally, the sheer mass of legal rules produces rule-conflicts which call for the production of yet more rules. It appears that the high autonomy of law enhances the number of conflicts.'

[68] The normative conclusion is that external political interventions as limits or breaks on these compulsive dynamics as necessary, therefore, to avoid chaos: constitutions (understood as foundational principles governing a specific sphere) serve this very function.

The second, connected phenomenon is the 'escalated differentiation, pluralization and reciprocal compartmentalization of separate spheres'.[69] The propensity of all autonomous orders to expand induces a hiatus paradoxical, so that while they are likely to collide in mutual indifference to the focus and concerns of each other, they do not work (as in the more orderly context of the nation-state) to balance each other out. This generally results in screening off the most powerful of these expanding rationalities from any countervailing move towards liability and accountability. Examples can be found in the various industries (such as the extraction of natural resources or agribusiness) where contractual arrangements between private corporate investors and host countries are enabled by international treaties and enforced thereunder by investment arbitration.[70] Arbitral jurisdiction is linked to issues which arise under the relevant contract or treaty, while the governing law is restricted either to the set of rules chosen by the parties or to the liberal tenets of contract law as described above.

In such cases, the contractual regime is disconnected from taxation, trade, environment, or human rights, which may well be a significant part of the picture; an investor might be claiming the benefit of a contract and all the while be violating human rights and, conversely, the host country might be violating a contractual term while upholding environmental standards.[71] In very concrete terms, the resulting 'compartmentalization' means that a state (home country) which has encouraged (through a bilateral investment agreement) its own citizens or corporations to take up the opportunities made available in the host country under the terms of such an agreement is not held accountable, in return, for corporate misconduct in this context.[72] This is surely wrong.

[69] Teubner (n. 60), 39.

[70] These often comprise lending arrangements which give rise to a cycle of indebtedness on the part of the host state: J. C. Lippert, 'Vulture Funds: The Reason Why Congolese Debt May Force a Revision of the Foreign Sovereign Immunities Act', 21 New York International Law Review 1 (2008).

[71] It might be objected that the investor may be called to respond for its human rights violations (in a different forum). However, to date, this is very rarely so. International law is called upon here to support the 'territorial' reach of jurisdiction.

[72] For example (in a context similar to that of the *Kiobel* case), indigenous river-dwellers who show that the industrial activities of the corporate defendant have despoiled them of their environment or livelihood cannot argue that the defendant's home state, which encouraged it to invest locally with a view to creating a flow of commercial or fiscal revenues, should also have provided correlative control over such activities and ensured that human rights were not violated in the process. A large part of the problem is that the courts of the investor's home state are unready to exercise jurisdiction over the wrongs committed by investors abroad, in the name of the principle of territoriality, supposedly derived from public international law. The same is still true for the reach of human rights obligations incumbent on the home state, which do not reach to foreign territory (e.g. territory beyond that of the contracting states of the European Convention on Human Rights). Thus, the compartmentalization described above has so far prevented the very existence of the international investment regime from providing the legal basis for a state to be held responsible for the extra-territorial conduct of private corporate investors from which it derives fiscal revenue (and to which it serves as 'home' by providing a corporate charter or a domicile, and access to the benefits of the local market).

21.2.3 Arbitration as informal authority

A third set of concerns is linked to the fact that, over time, the mass of individual awards is assembling into a body (or two: one for commercial arbitration and one for investment) of case law with *de facto* persuasive authority,[73] providing a parallel legal framework for the conduct of private transnational trade and investment. The *lex mercatoria* thesis rests on the claim that this case law, intermingled with international public and private soft law, forms an organic legal system administered—albeit diffusely—by arbitrators.

Indisputably, arbitrators create norms, even if formal representations of arbitration see it as a discrete process or liken it to the work of an umpire, or again, when applied to law, as a form of merely technical expertise in the field of commercial custom or conventional practice. Additionally, the discourse secreted by the (still largely academic) arbitral community (self-styled as such) is no doubt more powerful still in promoting arbitration as a normative system endowed with virtues unattainable by the collective efforts of state legal systems. However, arbitration—like all the other overlapping claims to authority by 'unauthorized' actors of the 'second' modernity[74] (such as standard-making by non-state entities, also, unaccountable mafia-like private authority, repressive religious practices, or indicators sponsored by the very entities being assessed)—raises a legitimacy conundrum: in this respect, is arbitration an acceptable source of law-making authority?

Contemporary pluralists attempt to respond to the question of the foundations of transnational authority[75] within the 'global legal paradigm'.[76] Explanations of authority which were marginal within the doctrinal context of nation-state—such as Weber's category of 'charismatic' authority (deriving from the charismatic personality of the holder rather than from law or tradition)—have risen to overriding importance in a global context, where expert knowledge, the power of image, rating agencies, and other spin doctors all flourish.[77] The jurisprudential challenge is to grasp the features of law-likeness without the support of the formal theory of sources of law.

When confronted with global law's eery 'intimations', the question is usually whether such phenomena are sufficiently law-like to be considered as law, albeit beyond the state.[78] Political theory has in turn to accept that statehood can no longer serve as an

[73] Diego Fernández Arroyo, 'Private Adjudication Without Precedent?' in Horatia Muir Watt and Diego Fernández Arroyo (eds), *Private International Law and Global Governance* (Oxford University Press, 2014).

[74] Ulrich Beck, *Risk Society: Towards a New Modernity* (Sage, 1992).

[75] Krisch et al. (n. 8), 2015.

[76] Ralf Michaels, 'Globalisation and Law: Law Beyond the State', in Reza Banakar and Max Travers (eds), *Law and Social Theory*, 2nd edn (Hart, 2013), 287.

[77] Krisch et al. (n. 8). This does not mean of course that there is anything more rational about modern law than about the 'intimations' of the global—'Were we ever Modern?', asks Bruno Latour (*Nous n'avons jamais été modernes* (La Découverte, 1991)—but that rationality is part of the 'mythodology' of modern law with which we are now willing to part.

[78] Neil Walker, *Intimations of Global Law* (Cambridge University Press, 2015), 196, sees a common denominator of ratio and volontas in the various conceptualizations of global law. In other terms, the

exclusive criterion for assessing the legitimacy of the norms that claim to belong within the 'community of laws'.[79] But if the substitute is acceptance by the communities involved, then it is highly doubtful that arbitration would really qualify. In the investment context, state consent is usually invoked to justify the effect of awards rendered on issues of regulatory purport. But there is no consent when it is that of a hostage to the global market for capital, or to the lending policies of international financial institutions.

21.2.4 Arbitration and global distribution

The last set of concerns, the most controversial within civil society since the beginning of the TTIP negotiations, are the ways in which arbitration tends to consolidate the negative distributional consequences of the international investment regime. In other words, arbitration—specifically investment arbitration—is taken as part of the wider problem of investor bias within the quasi-world-wide foreign investment regime. While development economics still posits that the inflow of capital is vital to ensure the needs of host country populations in terms of access to essential public infrastructures and services, the distribution of rights and obligations within the treaty regime, along with the accompanying arbitration process which upholds it, is stigmatized as imbalanced to the detriment of the host state, in favour of the private foreign investor.[80]

This results in the confiscation of local regulatory sovereignty, in fields as sensitive as taxation, public health, and environment; if public interest is persistently sidelined, it is no doubt because the negotiation of such treaties and the accompanying contractual regime takes place outside the public sphere.[81] Such inequalities as denounced within

renewed description of intermingling, hybrid jurisdictional assertions as a new state of global affairs does not appear to modify the legal consciousness into which such claims will have to fit.

[79] This expression is famously Friedrich von Savigny's (*System des heutigen römischen Rechts* (Veit, 1849)). In von Savigny's initial formulation of 'multilateralist' methodology, only the communities (at the time, German princedoms) belonging to a closed 'community of laws', cemented by shared cultural (religious, linguistic, and legal) tradition, were considered as participants in the common allocation of prescriptive authority.

[80] This perception may of course have much to do with switching trends in global capital flows and the new awareness of states which were formerly home to private investors, that under the terms of BITs, their own regulatory powers in respect of local consumers or environment are now seriously curtailed in favour of incoming foreign capital. Sornarajah emphasizes the contemporary reversal under which Western States, previously exporters of capital and now the largest recipients of foreign investment, are becoming wary of the legal arguments and tools developed within 20th-c. investment law (Sornarajah (n. 3), 25, citing examples of contestation, in the context of arbitration or multilateral dispute resolution, by Canada and the US, of facets of foreign investment regimes which they had initially crafted, particularly those which hamper the regulatory power of the host state).

[81] See Lauge Poulsen's Ch. 31 in this Handbook, in particular the part where he describes how many BITs have been negotiated (i.e. barely at all or carelessly, because at least some of the negotiators could not care less, so that the negotiation would not only take place outside the rationality of the public sphere, but outside of any rationality whatsoever). The 'participation deficit' critique is thus formulated by Marc Jacob, 'International Investment Agreements and Human Rights', INEF Research Paper (2010), 2.4.2: '[A] potential concern is the fact that, despite the ultimately far-reaching impact of major international

the substantive investment regime are seen to be perpetuated through arbitration, which is designed to implement the very regime that contains them.[82]

Indeed, a specific set of complaints target the arbitration mechanism consubstantial to these bilateral arrangements. The compulsory offer of arbitration by the host state, and the correlative privilege of the private investor to trigger the arbitration process—once touted as the *nec plus ultra* of impartial international dispute resolution—is now often perceived as exemplifying a lack of mutuality, through which is then ensured the intangibility of the contractual *acquis* in favour of foreign capital. Whether such concerns touch upon the substantive content of the investment treaties or the specific dispute resolution mechanism designed to enforce the commitments of the host state, they are frequently couched in human rights language. Indeed, an increasing number of claims before investment arbitrators[83] tend to show that the whole investment regime is now facing what might be termed a 'human rights ordeal'.

This development is of course, to some extent, a paradox, since the entire regime sprang from the supposed impotence of the private investor vis-à-vis the unbridled power of the local sovereign. In turn, the initial context explains why the substantive guarantees provided for incoming capital flows in bilateral investment treaties tellingly constitute a commitment on the part of the host country both to non-discrimination and to fair and equitable treatment of the investor.[84] In stark contrast to the initial quest to safeguard investor interests by means of a liberal private law framework of individual property rights, contemporary critics therefore denounce the inherent dissymmetry of such a framework, and seek to open the investment regime to collective social and economic rights, variously termed 'third generation' or capability-building rights—framed or not under the ambivalent heading of 'development'—such as access to food or water,

investments (e.g. power plants, water and sewage infrastructure, landfills, mining pits etc.), the BITs providing the basic legal framework for such large-scale projects have traditionally been negotiated and concluded outside the public sphere. This acute participation deficit of concerned sectors of society and NGOs is of course not uncommon when it comes to international treaties. One curt answer to this is that the citizens' consent can be indirectly derived from their respective governments' participation in the treaty-making process. This places a potentially unwarranted degree of faith in national governments' ambitions to promote and protect human rights, which some states will unhesitatingly subordinate to economic development. Another reply furtively questions the wisdom of even having the public participate in all aspects of what is essentially a highly specialised technocratic exercise... [I]t is important to note that public awareness and participation, and therefore ultimately democracy and legitimacy, have traditionally been sidelined in erecting the fundamental tenets of the current investment regime.'

[82] See e.g. a series of excellent studies approaching the intersection between the investment regime and human rights through analysis of arbitration cases: Luke Peterson and Kevin Gray, 'International Human Rights in Bilateral Investment Treaties and in Investment Treaty Arbitration', IISD Research Paper (2003); Jacobs (n. 81); Ursula Kriebaum, 'Privatizing Human Rights: The Interface between International Investment Protection and Human Rights', in August Reinisch and Ursula Kriebaum (eds), *The Law of International Relations: Liber Amicorum Hanspeter Neuhold* (Eleven International, 2007), 165.

[83] For an overview of the cases, see ibid. 167. Joseph Saei, 'Amicus Curious: Structure and Play in Investor-State Arbitration', 8(3) Transnational Legal Theory 247 (2017).

[84] An investor who moves quickly serves as a parameter for the assessment of discrimination and thereby secures a first-mover advantage in the context of the struggle for capital in which the host is inevitably engaged.

or the need for clean environment or inviolate habitat.[85] However, the contractual or treaty-based nature of arbitration, as seen above, has raised (hitherto) insuperable hurdles to such an enterprise.

21.3 A Renewed Legal Framework: From Contracts to Networks

The idea here is that networks might provide a novel way both of conceptualizing arbitration within the governance debate and of ensuring a stricter regulation in the common good. In this respect, it is important to point out that networks provide both an epistemological model and a legal tool.

In the first respect they are complex, evolving, multipartite, cooperative, reflexive, and responsive to both the collective interest of its members and the requirements of the public good.[86] Law itself has been theorized in these very terms.[87] The consequences are far-reaching. In public law, networks provide an alternative to a hierarchical vision of the legal system. In private law, they involve setting aside methodological individualism and taxonomies based on the essence or nature of legal concepts, in favour of more reflexive and unstable approaches. As a powerful example, the 'organizational contract', characterized as a network, has been advanced as an alternative to the traditional, unsatisfactory binary contracts/corporations.[88]

In the second respect, networks constitute a way of linking up disconnected units and treating them as interrelated. In other words, network theory provides the basis on which to impose a form of mutuality—meaning a balanced distribution of benefits and responsibilities—between the participants. It also implies that the network as a whole responds to its own environment, taking due account of the changes within it and its specific claims and needs.

[85] An analogous evolution can be observed within other specialized international regimes such as the WTO, which is similarly seen to be weighted against the interests of the poorest local populations and unaccountable to their hunger. On the possible use of WTO law to provide a legal foundation for the duty of those states which are home to corporate agribusinesses to ensure the protection of access to food by the populations of the third world, see Olivier de Schutter and Kaitlin Cordes, *Accounting for Hunger* (Hart, 2011).

[86] These features are sufficient here. They are of course an immense simplification of the highly sophisticated theories of networks. See e.g. Marc Amstutz, 'The Nemesis of European Private Law: Contractual Nexus as a Legislative Conundrum', in Stefan Grundman, Fabrizio Cafaggi, and Giuseppe Vettori (eds), *The Organisational Contract* (Ashgate, 2013), 306.

[87] Francois Ost and Michel van de Kerchove, *De la pyramide au réseau? Pour une théorie dialectique du droit* (Facultés universitaires Saint-Louis, 2002); Charles Sabel and Oliver Gerstenberg, 'Constitutionalising an Overlapping Consensus: The ECJ and the Emergence of a Coordinate Constitutional Order', 16 European Law Journal 511 (2010).

[88] Grundman et al. (n. 86).

Certainly, the issue of determining the contours of the network raises a first 'diabolical' difficulty.[89] Under what standard can interconnectivity be considered as sufficient to warrant a single system of decision-making, risk allocation, distribution of profits, and responsibility towards third parties? Moreover, without identifying the density required of a network, it is difficult to design an appropriate common regime. In this respect, the methodology to be followed is itself problematic, given that the network must provide the same regulatory reflexivity as its object (this is the 'double reflexive loop').[90] The precise governance implications of such a move would need considerable further elaboration.

Here, it is merely suggested that the pattern formed by the network might conceivably be helpful in apprehending the increasingly powerful system of informal justice and law-making which has developed so spectacularly under late capitalism. Seeing arbitration as a network would therefore have a descriptive dimension. In this respect, it would mean accepting that each discrete arbitrator or arbitration proceedings is part of a wider whole; this might make it easier to explain, for instance, why discrete cases contribute to make a body of law, collectively. But the same move would also have a normative dimension, making it easier, in turn, to respond to the growing legitimacy concerns to which such a system gives rise. Thus, it would mean that any one arbitration must take account of its interactions with its environment, comprising not only the other units in the network but also its wider ecology. This suggestion is once again to be replaced in a specific critical approach to private international law.

21.3.1 Private international law and networks: a short explanatory detour

At first glance, networks would seem to sit easily with familiar modes of reasoning within the conflict of laws. Indeed, private international law takes a systemic view of the law, which rests largely upon the interconnections between specific institutions and larger ensembles. Moreover, its preferred contemporary methodological approach, functionalism—the consideration of the policy objectives of any set of rules so as to determine their scope[91]—plays a significant role in articulating each institution with its wider context.[92] Nevertheless, the encounter between the conflict of laws and the concept of a network also has to deal with severe epistemological difficulties. This is due to the fact that the conflict of laws still reflects the properties of the classic legal model in

[89] Gunther Teubner, 'And if I by Beelzebub Cast out Devils…: An Essay on the Diabolics of Network Failure', in Grundman et al. (n. 86), 110; Amstutz (n. 86).

[90] Yet to be supplied.

[91] Functionalism in the conflict of laws, refers to a legal-realist doctrine in the conflict of laws which has been largely influential in the US. See Symeon Symeonides, 'The American Revolution and the European Evolution in Choice of Law: Reciprocal Lessons', 82(5) Tulane Law Review 1741 (2008).

[92] These features are also part of the interpretive grid specific to a regulatory model of private law. See Hans Micklitz, 'European Regulatory Private Law Project', ERPL (2015).

apprehending the market; it still tends to ignore the dynamics of complex interconnected systems and will work as often as not to fragment a network rather than support it. Examples can be found in the field of multinational corporate groups or in cases of transnational chains of contracts, where the conflict of laws divides up the various connected economic units of a wider assemblage rather than approaching them as a whole.[93] Here, inconsistencies and unfairness ensue from a refusal to recognize the underlying interdependencies between actors or economic transactions which do not 'fit' into the binary categorization of contracts/corporations.

By contrast, this traditionally individuated or compartmentalized perspective is reversed when a deliberately regulatory approach has been adopted in the field of substantive private law, as in the field of consumer legislation or competition in the European Union. Here, the conflict of laws apprehends wider categories of actors and integrates the presence of the market into its modes of reasoning. Might it be made, more generally, to respond to the characteristics of the transnational network and in particular its reflexivity, autonomy, and needs in terms of cooperation? In some cases, the conflict of laws can undoubtedly adapt and enhance the economy of the network. For example, when the latter requires a form of mutuality—meaning a balanced distribution of benefits and responsibilities—between the participants, it is quite easy to find fitting responses, without making any revolutionary move.[94]

[93] For discussion of some concrete examples in the case law of the European Court of Justice, in which it might have been possible either to institute a shared responsibility between a parent undertaking for the conduct of a subsidiary, or again to organize the distribution of risk among the actors in a transnational chain of contracts correlatively to the share of profits, see: Horatia Muir Watt, 'Governing Networks: A Global Challenge for Private International Law', 22(3) Maastricht Journal of European and Comparative Law 353 (2015).

[94] Thus, for instance, regardless of the nature and legal effect of the individual contracts that constitute it, a supply chain may require the existence of reciprocal actions among participants in order to induce or enhance cooperation. Put simply, the conflict rule would need to ensure the application of a single law in the relation between actors at the two ends of the chain; this could easily be engineered, even in the context of existing legal tools. This could perfectly well be attained by means of the method and approach implemented by the 1973 Hague Convention on the law applicable to product liability, now replaced by the Rome II Regulation, Art. 5. The text of Art. 5 of the Rome II Regulation reads as follows:

'1. Without prejudice to Article 4(2), the law applicable to a non-contractual obligation arising out of damage caused by a product shall be: (a) the law of the country in which the person sustaining the damage had his or her habitual residence when the damage occurred, if the product was marketed in that country; or, failing that, (b) the law of the country in which the product was acquired, if the product was marketed in that country; or, failing that, (c) the law of the country in which the damage occurred, if the product was marketed in that country. However, the law applicable shall be the law of the country in which the person claimed to be liable is habitually resident if he or she could not reasonably foresee the marketing of the product, or a product of the same type, in the country the law of which is applicable under (a), (b) or (c).

2. Where it is clear from all the circumstances of the case that the tort/delict is manifestly more closely connected with a country other than that indicated in paragraph 1, the law of that other country shall apply. A manifestly closer connection with another country might be based in particular on a pre-existing relationship between the parties, such as a contract, that is closely connected with the tort/delict in question.'

This approach is particularly fitting because an essential element of the network is that it mandates not to distinguish between contractual and non-contractual relationships among participants, and encourages

The European context is of course the easiest in which to deal with the endemic problem of legal circularity that besets the conflict of laws (what happens when the categories used by the law of the forum assume the existence of a network that the applicable law does not recognize?). It would suffice to pose the network as an autonomous concept through which to apprehend interconnected relationships whenever a regulatory purpose linked to the utility or social purpose of the network so mandates (e.g. ensuring the redistribution of profits along the chain).[95]

Nevertheless, the conflict of laws encounters its own inherent limits here. However innovative its own categories, outcomes are ultimately dependent upon the content of the applicable law. Hence another, highly novel idea, explored in comparative legal scholarship in the field of 'organizational contracts': this would be a reciprocal nesting of networks and conflict of laws reasoning. According to this line of thought, the method of conflict of laws is proposed as a model for network regulation.[96] But the limits of this approach[97] lie in its greater suitability to (quasi-contractual) relationships among participants in a network rather than those of the various members of the group with third parties. In other worlds, the ecology of the network—its sustainable relationship to its environment—would still need to be protected.

Therefore, it is likely that the only suitable method is to design a set of substantive principles to govern both the mutual relationships between participants and the interaction between the network and its environment. However, the question of design remains. A promising approach, again mooted by Gunter Teubner, would be to attempt not an aprioristic definition of applicable rules but a response to the most recurrent *network failures*.[98] Conceivably, the appropriate model might include, firstly, a duty of loyalty towards the network, designed to regulate conflicts of interest or opportunistic behaviour; secondly, a principle of solidarity or risk sharing in respect of third parties; and thirdly, a principle of distribution of profits and sharing of information among participants.

In each instance, this general framework would be adaptable, just like a multi-party relational contract. Access of new participants would look more like adhesion, or risk

their equal treatment in terms of access to rights and allocation of duties. Another case in which the law already provides categories which can be used to enhance a network is the relationship between a group of companies and third parties—creditors or victims of harm. The category of quasi-contracts is available in such contexts in order to circumvent the artificial screen of legal personality that works, on the contrary, to fragment the network.

95 Although this is not, as yet, the path chosen by the Court of Justice within the framework of European instruments: for a critical appraisal of the case law from this perspective, see Muir Watt (n. 93).

96 Amstutz (n. 86). As such, it would be part of the constitution of private network governance. Reversing the process of seeking the law applicable to the various relationships within a network, the idea is to extend the contractual regime attached to the master agreement (master contract) identified as the network's 'center of gravity'. To understand this idea, it is useful to think of the conflict of laws methodology used in the context of chains of contracts: the law governing the original contract determines that contract's own scope—the applicability of its provisions to all participants downstream. The network approach differs, however, because the benchmark contract could be located downstream if necessary.

97 Identified as the difficulty of identifying the master contract.

98 Teubner (n. 89). Although each network type has specific needs, or can be the instrument of a specific regulatory policy, this approach suggests that a general framework might be workable.

acceptance, or a form of quasi-contract, rather than requiring mutual consent according to the liberal model of contract. Interpretation would be dictated according to its own objective (economic), but also to the collective interest of its members and the wider public good. Above all, the individual interests of its participants should not weigh more strongly than those of the entire network, while in the relationship between the network and its environment, the horizon of the common good should always be kept in mind.

21.3.2 Network design and arbitration

There does not seem to be any good reason why the multifarious, discrete arbitrations which take place all the time in the commercial and investment world should not be conceptualized as a network, with similar consequences. The various actor-arbitrators might well be seen as participating in an interconnected enterprise—after all, they were famously characterized as being part of a club or an old-boys' network by Dezalay and Garth![99]—in which solidarity, communication, reflexivity should prevail, as opposed to a picture of fragmented decision-making carried out in ignorance of the wider environment.

Of course, such an idea goes wholly against the grain of the current libertarian, contractual, or consent-based model of arbitration. Risk and profit-sharing, communication, attention to negative externalities are inevitably sore points. Moreover, working out the detailed application of the prototype regime suggested above would be uphill and long-term work. However, such an effort might be the very move required to stem the 'self-destructive tendencies' of this particular autonomous regime. In other words, taking on board the grievances of which it is increasingly the target might just prevent the current inflation in the arbitration industry from escalating out of control (or the bubble from bursting?), with disastrous consequences for all concerned.

[99] Dezalay and Garth (n. 1).

CHAPTER 22

INTERNATIONAL ARBITRATION

A Feminist Perspective

HÉLÈNE RUIZ FABRI AND EDOARDO STOPPIONI

22.1 Introduction: Setting the Scene[1]

As the French phenomenological philosopher Maurice Merleau-Ponty used to say, '*pour voir le monde et le saisir comme paradoxe, il faut rompre avec notre familiarité avec lui*'.[2] Studying an object requires us to take enough distance to grasp its internal mechanism or contradictions, and to highlight its functioning philosophy or discrepancies. This is in a way the logic underlying feminist approaches, whose aim is to uncover the silence of international law, and to show its structural biases and false neutrality.[3] As such, such approaches can help to deconstruct a problem and make it thinkable.[4] However, the aim of this chapter is not to propose a feminist theory of international arbitration. It is instead to use some of the methodological elements of feminist approaches to international law[5] to rethink international arbitration and the current 'crisis' that at least investor-state arbitration faces, so as to question the meaning of this particular situation.

[1] This chapter borrows from the keynote speech given at the opening of the biennial conference of the Society of International Economic Law held on 12–14 July 2018 in Washington, DC on the theme 'International Economic Law in Unsettling Times', which was prepared with the help of Edoardo Stoppioni and is published as H. Ruiz Fabri, 'Understanding International Economic Law in Unsettling Times: A Feminist Approach', 20 Journal of World Investment & Trade 20 (2019), 3–14.

[2] Marcel Merleau-Ponty, *Phénoménologie de la perception* (Gallimard, 1945), viii.

[3] Hilary Charlesworth, Christine Chinkin, and Shelley Wright, 'Feminist Approaches to International Law', (1991) 85 AJIL 613–45.

[4] Hilary Charlesworth and Christine Chinkin, *The Boundaries of International Law: A Feminist Analysis* (Manchester University Press, 2000).

[5] Hilary Charlesworth, 'Feminist Methods in International Law', (1999) 93 AJIL 379–94.

22.1.1 A critical context

If one looks at the macro-tendencies that have structured the evolution of international arbitration in modern times, the rise of international arbitration in economic matters is a fundamental component, and one which has triggered searing critiques. It is a rather recent phenomenon compared to 'old' inter-state arbitration, although the latter remains a historical pattern and a mechanism partially in vogue today (most notably in law of the sea matters). The rise of international commercial arbitration came first, mostly from the decades 1970–1980, when its workload in one decade more than doubled in one decade compared to what it had been during the sic previous decades. These are the years of Goldman's scholarship and of the construction of the idea of *lex mercatoria*, the years of the construction of a community that structures a professional guild encapsulating a whole generation.[6]

When, towards the end of the 1990s, the rise of investment disputes occurred, the same guild of international commercial arbitrators, albeit another generation, took on the settlement of this kind of disputes.[7] As oil arbitrations had triggered the mutation of international commercial arbitration, the Argentinian crisis marked not only the exponential quantitative development of investment arbitration but also the beginning of the recurring theme of discussion of the backlash against investment arbitration.[8]

At first, contestation came mainly from South American states, like Ecuador, which framed a political discourse denouncing the fallacies encountered during their experience with the International Centre for Settlement of Investment Disputes (ICSID) or with United Nations Commission on International Trade Law (UNCITRAL) procedures. They eventually proposed to substitute them with a Unión de Naciones Suramericanas (UNASUR) alternative. Thereafter came another kind of discourse held in and by the European Union (EU). The concerns here were expressed less in political terms and more in terms of conflict of norms with the EU constitutional system. The *Achmea* case adjudicated by the Court of Justice of the European Union was a clear warning, killing (at least prospectively) intra-EU investment arbitration on the basis of its contrariety with EU procedural law (articles 267 and 344 TFEU) and with the principle of autonomy.[9] The Opinion about the Comprehensive Economic and Trade Agreement (CETA) has not been the mortal blow some feared, but a clear acceptance of investor–state dispute

[6] Bryant G. Garth, 'Transnational Arbitral Community', *Max Planck Encyclopedia of International Procedural Law* (Oxford University Press, 2019).

[7] Yves Dezalay and Bryan G. Garth, *Dealing in Virtue: International Commercial Arbitration and the Construction of a Transnational Legal Order* (University of Chicago Press, 1996).

[8] Michael Waibel (ed.), *The Backlash Against Investment Arbitration: Perceptions and Reality* (Kluwer Law International, 2010); David D. Caron and Esmé Shirlow, 'Dissecting Backlash: The Unarticulated Causes of Backlash and its Unintended Consequences', King's College London Law School Research Paper No. 2016-37: <https://papers.ssrn.com/sol3/papers.cfm?abstract_id=2834000##>.

[9] See CJEU, C-284/16, 2018, *Achmea*, ECLI:EU:C:2018:158.

settlement (ISDS) mechanisms in free trade agreements.[10] However, Opinion 1/17 supports the idea that in-depth reform of the system is needed, the outcome of which is not necessarily arbitration. As a reflex action which has some homeostatic features, the main providers of arbitration rules (ICSID and UNCITRAL) have undertaken a thorough reform of their arbitration rules,[11] eventually involving academia, from which sprung praise but also heavy criticism. Some scholars had long voiced their concerns regarding a system which, in their view, disregards public policies due to the 'commercial arbitration bias' of those practising in the area.[12] The doctrinal discourse went as far as total rejection of the imperialist or colonial feature embedded in the mixed arbitration mechanism.[13] Civil society has also been very active in criticizing the system. Third parties, like non-governmental organizations (NGOs), have forced their way into the system. *Amicus curiae* briefs have expressed concerns regarding the importance of human rights or the risks for environmental protection, questioning the system's ability to take these legitimate concerns into consideration.[14] The same path is used by the European Commission to plead for the absence of any jurisdiction of intra-EU treaty-based tribunals, challenging the very existence of the system. At the same time, denouncement of the so-called 'private arbitral tribunals' contributes to the growing rejection of agreements such as the CETA.

22.1.2 Feminist perspective on the meaning of this situation

And yet, the amount of scholarship analysing international arbitration from a feminist perspective is rather sparse, especially if compared to the quantity of feminist studies of international criminal justice and international human rights adjudication. Feminist scholars are apparently less interested in inter-state arbitration and even less in 'economic' arbitration (be it international commercial arbitration or investment arbitration). This blind spot is all the more striking when one considers the quantitative importance

[10] See Opinion of the Court (Full Court) of 30 April 2019, ECLI:EU:C:2019:341; Edoardo Stoppioni, 'L'audience dans l'avis 1/17 sur le CETA' (*blogdroiteuropéen*, 29 June 2018): https://blogdroiteuropeen.com/2018/06/29/laudience-dans-lavis-1-17-sur-le-ceta-par-edoardo-stoppioni/, accessed 2 October 2018.

[11] See, for the most recent proposals for amendment of the rules at ICSID: <https://icsid.worldbank.org/en/Documents/Vol_1.pdf>; and the reflection of Working Group III at UNCITRAL: <http://www.uncitral.org/uncitral/en/commission/working_groups/3Investor_State.html>.

[12] In 2010, a number of international law professors published a 'Public Statement on the International Investment Regime', in which they made recommendations recalling that 'States have a fundamental right to regulate on behalf of the public welfare and this right must not be subordinated to the interests of investors where the right to regulate is exercised in good faith and for a legitimate purpose'. See 'Public Statement on the International Investment Regime' (31 August 2010): <www.osgoode.yorku.ca/public-statement-international-investment-regime-31-august-2010/>, accessed 9 October 2018.

[13] Muthucumaraswamy Sornarajah, *The International Law on Foreign Investment* (Cambridge University Press, 2017); Kate Miles, *The Origins of International Investment Law: Empire, Environment and the Safeguarding of Capital* (Cambridge University Press, 2013).

[14] Hervé Ascensio, 'L'*amicus curiae* devant les juridictions internationales', (2001) 105 Revue générale de droit international public 897–929.

of arbitration in contemporary international law. A feminist reading of international economic law in general,[15] and of international arbitration concerning economic matters more specifically, would therefore fill a gap in contemporary international law doctrine. Moreover, the instruments of the feminist theory of international law can teach us much more than what has been done so far, i.e. almost exclusively focusing on the role and place of female arbitrators. Thus, transferring to international arbitration some of the analysis developed regarding more generally international law and dispute settlement helps to deconstruct the categories commonly used to describe international arbitration, and to identify at least three claims. These problems form part of a crescendo that starts from some solvable structural problems and grows to intrinsic ontological contestations, the first claim being based on the critique of the mechanisms of domination,[16] the second on the critique of biases, the third on the critique of injustice.

22.2 First claim: the mechanisms of domination

A traditional claim of feminist scholars is that it is almost exclusively men who occupy positions of power in international law. The issue can be tackled in more general terms to ask if there is a dominating group in the structure of international law and/or governance, a community that occupies most of the positions of power. Focused on international arbitration, this question leads to the identification of several structures of domination which are (partially) intertwined.

The most obvious starting point is the existence of the so-called 'transnational arbitral community' (TAC),[17] i.e. the group to which one has to belong or by which one has to be acknowledged in order to develop an arbitral practice which is known to be highly rewarding. This is so because party autonomy leads to the appointment of arbitrators in each case, on an *ad hoc* basis. 'The accepted wisdom is that it is essential to appoint someone from inside the arbitration community in order to be taken seriously by the other two arbitrators in the tribunal… the same logic favouring insiders has led to the

[15] For an inspiring analysis, see Sundhya Pahuja, 'Trading Spaces: Locating Sites for Challenge Within International Trade Law', (2000) 14 Australian Feminist Law Journal, 38–54; Anne Orford, 'Feminism, Imperialism and the Mission of International Law', (2002) 71 Nordic Journal of International Law 275–96.

[16] Alison Jaggar, 'Is Globalization Good for Women?' (2001) 53(4) Comparative Literature 298–314.

[17] Bryant G. Garth, 'Transnational Arbitral Community', *Max Planck Encyclopedia of International Procedural Law* (Oxford University Press, 2019); Florian Grisel, 'Competition and Cooperation In International Commercial Arbitration: The Birth of Transnational Legal Profession', (2017) 51 Law and Society Review 790–824; Sara Dezalay and Yves Dezalay, 'Professionals of International Justice: From the Shadow of State Diplomacy to the Pull of the Market for Commercial Arbitration', in André Nollkaemper, Jean d'Aspremont, Wouter Werner, and Tarcizio Gazzini (eds), *International Law as a Profession* (Cambridge University Press, 2017), 311–37.

migration of the leading international commercial arbitrators into international investment arbitration.'[18] The TAC is an inbuilt community. To belong to it requires the individual to go through a complex process involving mentorship, old school ties, generally related to education preferably in an elite university, membership of learned societies or professional associations, links to arbitral institutions and law firms handling arbitrations, scholarly writing promoting both the author and the field with moderate propositions for change, professional rankings, etc. Many elements which resemble the components of a rite of passage also characterize an elite, all the more so as the size of the core of this arbitration community is small.[19]

As is well known, this community is subject to heavy criticisms, recent debates reproaching it for bringing about a fundamental bias in a system which would have become more interested in reproducing itself than in rendering justice,[20] for being a 'little incestuous world,'[21] through practices of 'double-hatting', moonlighting, and revolving doors.[22] Two fronts especially invite a feminist analysis. One is the domination of commercial arbitrators, which is linked to a bias in favour of multinational corporations and against host states, and their competition with public international lawyers. The other is the paucity of female arbitrators. Starting from these critiques, feminist methods provide paths to analyse the functioning of arbitration from a different perspective.

22.2.1 A feminist deconstruction of established categories

First, a feminist analysis leads to the deconstruction of some categories of international arbitration, which is today a multi-faceted and complex phenomenon. It can oppose states (in the public international law tradition) or private individuals (in the commercial law tradition), or can be a mixed mechanism opposing an individual/a private entity to a state. The related categories—inter-state arbitration, international commercial arbitration, international investment arbitration—cannot be considered waterproof. On the contrary, opposing them in a binary way (commercial arbitration vs. investment arbitration, inter-state vs. mixed arbitration) pertains to a vision of international

[18] Bryant G. Garth, 'Transnational Arbitral Community', in *Max Planck Encyclopedia of International Procedural Law* (Oxford University Press, 2019), para. 14.

[19] Sergio Puig, 'Social Capital in the Arbitration Market', (2014) 25(2) EJIL 387–424.

[20] Cecilia Olivet and Pia Eberhardt, 'Profiting from Injustice: How Law Firms, Arbitrators and Financiers Are Fuelling an Investment Arbitration Boom' (2012): <www.tni.org/files/download/profitingfrominjustice.pdf>, accessed 3 August 2019.

[21] Rob Howse, 'What ICSID Does When a Human Rights Victim Tries to Get Justice There: Victor Pey Casado and the Allende Foundation v Chile': <http://worldtradelaw.typepad.com/ielpblog/2017/03/what-icsid-does-when-a-human-rights-victim-tries-to-get-justice-there-victor-pey-casado-and-the-alle.html>, acccessed 2 October 2018.

[22] Malcolm Langford, Daniel Behn, and Runar Lie, 'The Revolving Door in International Investment Arbitration', (2017) 20(2) JIEL 301–32.

adjudication that is too restrictive to grasp the general complexity of the scene and multiplication of grey zones. There is a plethora of commercial arbitration cases where the defendant is a state entity, as witnessed by the proliferation of parallel proceedings and the need to find procedural tools to adjust to this complex reality.[23] Moreover, the divide between mixed claims and inter-state proceedings is to be nuanced in today's international investment arbitration, as shown in some inter-state investment claims such as *Italy v. Cuba*.[24]

Pushing forward this deconstruction of the language of international law, one sees that arbitration comes from the Latin *an-betěre*, conveying the idea of 'one who comes to assist', the person coming to listen and solve a dispute between parties. The term is charged with the idea of an individual having a jurisdictional function. If what lies at the heart of international arbitration is the judicial function, the understanding of such a concept is far from unanimous. One can identify two different components: a private and a public element.[25]

The first component focuses on the consensual instrument allowing the settlement of a dispute opposing some parties (the idea of arbitration being *la chose des parties*). The second component focuses on the idea that the identification of the law applicable to that particular case will have implications beyond the sphere of the parties, and that *iuris dicere* always implies a larger dimension of general interest. The first model explains the need for rapidity and confidentiality, the second explains the need for transparency, and for openness to the legal context and to systemic reasoning. Depending on the sociological origins and on the epistemic community to which the arbitrator belongs, one aspect will tend to prevail. And this may have very strong and technical implications. A good example is the debate on the jurisdictional impact of most-favoured-nation (MFN) clauses in investment arbitration.[26] Oversimplifying the issue, public international lawyers' analysis would generally tend to see international investment law as a branch of their field of expertise, underlining the importance of the sovereign state as a defendant in the arbitration. On the other hand, academics coming from the commercial arbitration field would be less responsive to public international legal problems, and to the fact that the respondent embodies public interest. A broad correlation seems to exist between the rejection of MFN clauses' procedural effects and the public international law analysis of state consent. It ought to be remarked that the large majority of dissenting

[23] See *Ampal-American Israel Corporation and others v. Arab Republic of Egypt*, ICSID Case No. ARB/12/11, Decision on Liability and Heads of Loss, 21 February 2017, para. 258 (on the use of *res iudicata* theories for the management of parallel proceedings of this kinds), and *Lao Holdings NV and Sanum Investments Limited v Lao People's Democratic Republic*, ICSID Case No. ARB(AF)/16/2 and ADHOC/17/1, Procedural Order No. 2, 23 October 2017, para. 34 (on the use of bifurcation to handle these parallel proceedings).

[24] *Italian Republic v. Republic of Cuba*, ad hoc state–state arbitration, 1 January 2008.

[25] Gleider Hernandez, *The International Court of Justice and the Judicial Function* (Oxford University Press, 2014), 93.

[26] Edoardo Stoppioni, 'Jurisdictional Impact of Most-Favoured-Nation Clause', in *Max Planck Encyclopedia of International Procedural Law* (Oxford University Press, 2019).

opinions opposing the jurisdictional impact comes from either public international law professors[27] or practitioners who have previously worked in other public international law adjudicatory bodies.[28] The intellectual influence of ICJ case law on state consent shapes the argumentation in all these cases, especially in dissenting opinions, where it is found abundantly quoted. The same holds true for numerous awards having stood against the procedural function of MFN clauses, whose presidents were public international lawyers.[29]

22.2.2 A feminist assessment of the gender structure of arbitration

Second, many studies have demonstrated the paucity or absence of women in international adjudicative bodies,[30] and from all sides, affecting not only the bench but also the legal teams appearing before international courts and tribunals.[31] Scholars have denounced the opaque nature of appointment procedures that allow resistance to the greater involvement of women in adjudicative bodies,[32] or the strong reactions against those rules established in international courts—like the European Court of Human Rights—to ensure gender diversity.[33] International arbitration is a remarkable example of the scarcity of women's participation to the international bench, with an extremely imbalanced ratio of nominations of 93 per cent male to 7 per cent female at the beginning of the 2010s.[34] And yet, as Gus Van Harten underlined in one of the first articles on the topic, 'The story is also almost entirely that of two women, Gabrielle Kaufmann-Kohler and Brigitte Stern, who together captured 75% of appointments of women. In contrast, the two most frequently appointed men accounted for 5% of the 593 appointments

[27] Brigitte Stern in *Impregilo*, Laurence Boisson de Chazournes in *Garanti Koza*, Marcelo Kohen in *Venezuela US s.r.l.*, Santiago Torres Bernardez in *Ambiente Ufficio*, who has been several times ad hoc judge at the ICJ.

[28] Kamal Hossain in *Teinver*, who has worked several times as UNCLOS annex VII arbitrator.

[29] Gilbert Guillaume was the president of the *Salini v Jordan* tribunal, Pierre Marie Dupuy of the *ICS*, and *Daimler* tribunals, and Brigitte Stern of the *ST-AD* tribunal.

[30] Cecilia M. Bailliet, 'Gender Imbalance in International Courts', *PluriCourts Blog*, 22 September 2015: <https://www.jus.uio.no/pluricourts/english/blog/cecilia-m-bailliet/2015.09.22.bailliet.gender-imbalance-in-courts.html>.

[31] Shashank P. Kumar, and Cecily Rose, 'A Study of Lawyers Appearing Before the International Court of Justice, 1999–2012', (2014) 25(3) European Journal of International Law 893–917.

[32] Nienke Grossman, 'Shattering the Glass Ceiling in International Adjudication', (2016) 56 Va. J. Int'l L. 56 339.

[33] Stéphanie Hennette Vauchez, 'Gender Balance in International Adjudicatory Bodies', in *Max Planck Encyclopedia of International Procedural Law* (Oxford University Press, 2019); 'More Women—But Which Women? The Rule and the Politics of Gender Balance at the European Court of Human Rights', (2015) 26(1) EJIL 195–221.

[34] Sergio Puig, 'Social Capital in the Arbitration Market', (2014) 25 EJIL 387–424, 403.

of male arbitrators.'[35] Looking at 2017 data, Nienke Grossman pointed out that only 16.7 per cent of the arbitrators in proceedings at the International Chamber of Commerce were women, 18 per cent at the Stockholm Chamber of Commerce appointments, 18.2 per cent at the Court of Arbitration of the Singapore International Arbitration Centre, 14 per cent of the total number of appointments to ICSID tribunals or ad hoc committees. The figures become even more striking if put in a historical perspective: between 1966 and 2017, women appointments at ICSID counted for only 9 per cent of 2,200 arbitrator nominations. In addition, it is worth underlining that the slight improvement in the women appointments comes from the policy of arbitral institutions, trying to foster diversity with their direct nominations, while investors and co-arbitrators tend to perpetuate the status quo of a male environment.[36]

In all cases, these challenges to the current structures of domination involve the legitimacy of international arbitration. The usual discourse is that 'legitimacy of international arbitration depends in large part on confidence in the individuals who serve as arbitrators'.[37] However, the fact that this legitimacy is heavily questioned triggers the need for change, a claim of which the TAC is aware. Although it has a homeostatic reflex which likewise proved itself during a generational clash in the 1980s,[38] the current contestation of the various dominations goes further. Scholars like Nienke Grossman have shown that enhancing the presence of women in the international judiciary may contribute to its perceived legitimacy.[39] More generally, there is a claim of necessary diversity. The same concern for perceived legitimacy lies at the heart of the proposals for reform of the ISDS system into a more judicial mechanism, with reinforced impartiality

[35] Gus Van Harten, 'The (Lack of) Women Arbitrators in Investment Treaty Arbitration', FDI Perspectives, February 2012: SSRN: <https://ssrn.com/abstract=2005336>.

[36] Nienke Grossman, 'Feminist Approaches to International Adjudication', in *Max Planck Encyclopedia of International Procedural Law* (Oxford University Press, 2019), noting: 'For example, in 2018, in the London Court of International Arbitration, where women were appointed as arbitrators, the LCIA Court selected the arbitrators in 71% of the cases, while the parties did so only in 13% of the cases, and co-arbitrators did so in 17% of the cases. In 2017, the Stockholm Chamber of Commerce's appointments were 37% women, while women accounted for only 8% of party appointments, and 0% of co-arbitrator appointments. In ICSID, while only 14% of the total number of appointments went to women in 2017, ICISD and the Respondent/State each appointed 43.5% of them, 13% were made jointly by the parties in the underlying arbitration, and no women were appointed by the Claimant/Investor individually or by the co-arbitrators.'

[37] Garth (n. 6), para. 3, referring to J. Crawford, 'The Ideal Arbitrator: Does One Size Fit All?' (2017) 32 American University International Law Review 1003–22.

[38] J. Paulsson, 'Introduction', (1985) 1 Arbitration International 2–5; 'Third World Participation in International Commercial Arbitration', (1987) 2 FILJ 19–65.

[39] Nienke Grossman, 'Legitimacy and International Adjudicative Bodies', (2009) 41 Geo Wash Int'l L Rev. 107; 'Sex on the Bench: Do Women Judges Matter to the Legitimacy of International Courts?', (2011) 12 Chi. J. Int'l L. 647.

and independence guarantees.[40] What is at stake is the alleged neutrality of the pre-existing arbitration community and, with it, of arbitration itself.

22.3 Second claim: biases

One of the main tenets of feminist approaches to international law is the idea of gender bias,[41] and the claim that some international law rules are gender-biased.[42] 'International law is not only made up of men, in the sense that they occupy most of the positions of power and visibility. It is also a law made by men for men only. Women are not subjects in their own right, and their voice is hardly ever heard.'[43] In fact, this claim of gender bias is a good starting point to show that the claim of bias is multifaceted and complex. Indeed, the claim for gender balance opens the door to a more general claim for rebalancing the whole system of arbitration. One can only wonder whether the required changes would not be to the point of changing its nature.

22.3.1 Gender bias

The main point put forward in feminist literature on international arbitration is the idea of gender balance, a subject that has so far captured all the attention and silenced other possible feminist perspectives on international arbitration. Two different discourses have to be identified in relation to gender balance. From an internal point of view, gender balance is an instrument to increase the legitimacy of international arbitration by increasing the role that women play within it. From an external point of view, the gender balance argument is deflecting attention from the general lack of balance of the system: the feminist argument reaches the apex of its disruptiveness. In all cases, the most interesting are the explanations provided for the current gender imbalance, as they also tend to predetermine the possible remedies.

From an internal perspective, the argument based on gender balance aims at increasing the visibility of women in international arbitration. Besides the propositions of mandatory rosters and the voluntaristic policy of arbitral institutions to appoint women as mentioned above, other arguments, which have an essentialist flavour, underline that

[40] Marco Bronckers, 'Is Investor–State Dispute Settlement (ISDS) Superior to Litigation Before Domestic Courts? An EU View on Bilateral Trade Agreements', (2015) 18(3) JIEL 655–77.

[41] Alison Jaggar, 'The Philosophical Challenges of Global Gender Justice', (2009) 37(2) Philosophical Topics, 1–15.

[42] E.g. the definition of sexual assault in international humanitarian law; see 'Rape and Gender Violence: From Impunity to Accountability in International Law', (2003) 2(10) Human Rights Dialogue: <www.carnegiecouncil.org/publications/archive/dialogue/2_10/articles/1052>, accessed 3 August 2019.

[43] Andrea Bianchi, *International Law Theories: An Inquiry into Different Ways of Thinking* (Oxford University Press, 2016), 186.

this lack of women in international arbitration is due to their low tendency to adopt the self-promotion attitudes which play a major role in the TAC. This is somehow a market approach. Therefore, women, although not only them, are encouraged to change their attitude in the investment arbitration community, as the Pledge for Equal Representation in Arbitration initiatives suggest.[44] The Pledge is, in this regard, rather different from GQUAL, which has a broader scope and employs multiple tools to change the selection processes of international adjudicators.[45] The Pledge is considered to have a snowball effect by 'increasing the visibility of talented female lawyers: it reminds them to promote themselves, and it calls upon organisations, law firms, and arbitral institutions to actually offer them opportunities to do so.'[46] This argument feeds the homeostatic tendency: international arbitration preserves its *basic status quo* while renewing itself with increased participation of women. All components of the usual discourse are present, especially the idea that promoting women should not (and does not) involve a trade-off regarding what a good arbitrator is—a requirement which echoes some resistance towards positive actions to increase gender balance.[47] As psychologists demonstrate, this sort of discourse has a dark side,[48] and can be read as encouraging the adoption of male behaviour. However, international arbitration has, more than other adjudicatory fields, the ability to resist or slow down and frame any evolution. Indeed, the 'wind of

[44] 'The Pledge seeks to increase, on an equal-opportunity basis, the number of women appointed as arbitrators in order to achieve a fair representation as soon practically possible, with the ultimate goal of full parity': <http://www.arbitrationpledge.com/about-the-pledge>; Philippe Mirèze, 'Redressing the Balance: The Path Ahead for Gender and Generational Diversity on Arbitral Tribunals', 31 October 2016: <http://arbitrationblog.kluwerarbitration.com/2016/10/31/redressing-the-balance-the-path-ahead-for-gender-and-generational-diversity-on-arbitral-tribunals/>. There were previous initiatives in domestic such as ArbitralWomen, created in 1993 in the US, a non-governmental organization that promotes women in dispute resolution through events, social gatherings, mentoring, and sponsoring to assist women law students to participate in moot courts. See Manel Chibane, 'Brief Observations on Feminism and International Arbitration', (2017) Young Arbitration Review 39.

[45] GQUAL develops 'a global campaign that seeks to promote gender parity in international tribunals and monitoring bodies': <http://www.gqualcampaign.org/about-gqual/>.

[46] Victoria Pernt, 'Women Arbitrators on the Rise', 6 April 2017: <http://arbitrationblog.kluwerarbitration.com/2017/06/04/women-arbitration-rise/>.

[47] See, for a very soft way, Art. 2.2. of the Burgh House Principles on the Independence of the International Judiciary, drawn up in 2004 by a Study Group of the International Law Association, states that 'while procedures for nomination, election and appointment should consider fair representation of different geographic regions and the principal legal systems, as appropriate, as well as of female and male judges, appropriate personal and professional qualifications must be the overriding consideration in the nomination, election and appointment of judges'. In its Resolution of 2011 on the position of international judge, the Institut de droit international expressed the view that selection procedures 'should be such as to ensure the selection of candidates having the required moral character, competence, and experience, without any discrimination, in particular on the grounds of sex, origin, or beliefs': <http://www.idi-iil.org/en/sessions/rhodes-2011/?post_type=publication>. The preparatory report by Judge Gilbert Guillaume underlined that 'high moral status and competence must remain the first criteria of choice... This requirement must be paramount and outweigh all consideration of sex, ethnic origin or religion.'

[48] Laurie A. Rudman, 'Self-Promotion as a Risk Factor for Women: The Costs and Benefits of Counterstereotypical Impression Management', (1998) 74(3) Journal of Personality and Social Psychology 629.

change' in international adjudication comes from 'the increased standardization, transparency and codification of the procedures that govern contemporary selection of international judges', whereas 'appointment to the world of international adjudicatory bodies has historically and routinely operated on the basis of mostly unwritten rules, "polite understandings" that amounted to "gentlemen's agreements" and effectively served to preserve the "boys' club" nature of the world of international adjudication.'[49] Party autonomy regarding appointments of international arbitrators can only prevent such an evolution to an extent, as is confirmed by the fact that the ratio of female appointees among party-appointed arbitrators is especially low.

An external perspective is useful at this point of the analysis, as it allows us to identify the ambiguities of the gender balance argument. More particularly the question is: Why should there be more women in international arbitration? From a normative standpoint, several reasons and rationales can be imported from the general debate about gender balance. 'Some draw on standpoint theories and argue that more diversity brings more experience to the judicial bench; others claim that women and other under-represented groups are simply entitled to serving in the judiciary, on the basis of principles of justice and equality; and others still seek to reformulate theories of representation and claim that true democratic representation ought to be paritary.'[50] Not all these claims equally well match the reality of international adjudication, especially of arbitration. Thus, whereas the rationale of democratic representation could be considered as mirrored in the requirement of representativeness of international benches, no such requirement exists for arbitration, and the reflection should instead focus on the two other proposed rationales: the specifics of women's voices and non-discrimination.

The rationale of the specifics of women's voice relies either on 'the claim that women lawyers tend to be less adversarial and use different modes of legal reasoning (typically, more attention to the context and consequences of fact at hand)' or on the claim that 'the inclusion of women on the bench ensures that a whole new range of life experiences is brought to bear on judicial decision-making, thus enriching and in fact enhancing the quality of the justice delivered'.[51] As Stéphanie Hennette Vauchez explains, 'this view has stemmed from the powerful feminist critique of law's purported objectivity and its insistence on the fact that numerous legal concepts, institutions and modes of operation were in fact male-centered.'[52] Indeed, in their seminal publication on 'Feminist Approaches to International Law',[53] Hilary Charlesworth, Christine Chinkin, and Shelley Wright refer briefly to international dispute settlement. They explained that, drawing on the works of the feminist American psychologist Carol Gilligan, some scholars transposed to dispute resolution the view that a masculine approach tends to rely on an 'ethics of rights', whereas a feminine perspective embraces an 'ethics of care'.[54]

[49] Vauchez (n. 33), para. 37. [50] Ibid. para. 18.
[51] Ibid. para. 19. [52] Ibid. para. 19. [53] Charlesworth et al. (n. 3).
[54] C. Gilligan, *In a Different Voice: Psychological Theory and Women's Development* (Harvard University Press, 1982), 164–74.

Feminist scholars had already defended this very same idea concerning alternative dispute resolution (ADR) mechanisms in national law.[55] Negotiation and mediation would be 'female' methods of approaching disputes, focusing on a *relationship*, whereas arbitration and judicial settlement would mirror a 'male' way of settling disputes, focusing on *rights* and on adjudication's binary analysis of reality based on a dichotomy between a party that is right and a party that is wrong. As a result, feminist scholars essentially analysed international dispute settlement under such a prism: 'alternative, non-litigious, dispute resolution and nonconfrontational negotiation techniques are sometimes proposed as examples of such an approach.'[56] In their later monograph, *The Boundaries of International Law: A Feminist Analysis*, Hilary Charlesworth and Christine Chinkin emphasized that ADR mechanisms are more 'feminine' in their essence and therefore particularly beneficial for women. The core argument is a prolongation of the one previously developed: 'the non-confrontational nature of problem-solving techniques are especially advantageous for women in that they provide the space for women's voices to be heard and their interests to be identified.'[57] This goes well with an approach to dispute settlement from a wider viewpoint than simply international adjudication,[58] overcoming the judicial bias of international practice and scholarship. This bias is clearly denounced:

> although settlement of most international disputes is attempted through negotiation processes, adjudication before the ICJ is consistently given greater attention by international law scholars. This emphasis reflects the primacy accorded to the rule of law upheld through adjudicative processes in Western legal thought, but distorts the reality of international dispute settlement.[59]

It is true that friendly settlements or out-of-court settlements attracts far less attention. Of course, there is always the argument of confidentiality, especially in arbitration. But although the common wisdom is that an out-of-court settlement is always better than going to court, international lawyers remain as a whole fascinated by the intriguing beauty of judicial decision-making, implying a not-so-implicit hierarchy between adjudication and ADR—a hierarchy which also conveys the idea of nobility and authority.

However, although feminist scholarship might have a point in this regard, 'the notion of a feminine voice is problematic when grounded in biology or any fixed understanding of identity', due to its essentialist flavour as well as the absence of conclusive empirical data, but 'it is less easily discarded when grounded in sociological experience'.[60] Indeed, if it is believed that women's presence and experience make a difference, they

[55] Hilary Astor and Christine Chinkin, *Dispute Resolution in Australia*, 2nd edn (LexisNexis Butterworths, 2002), 92ff.; Janet Rifkin, 'Mediation from a Feminist Perspective: Promise and Problems', (1984) 2 Law & Ineq. 21.

[56] Charlesworth et al. (n. 3), 615.

[57] Charlesworth and Chinkin (n. 4), 289.

[58] Feminist approaches on these other topics are very rich. See e.g. A. Orford, 'Muscular Humanitarianism: Reading the Narratives of the New Interventionism', (1999) 10(4) EJIL 679–711.

[59] Charlesworth and Chinkin (n. 4), 288.

[60] Vauchez (n. 33), para. 21.

should be taken into account. Nevertheless, 'if the correct focus ought to be on experiences rather than on gender, then outcome-oriented rationales hardly support an increased proportion of women on judicial benches', except if the increase is done 'for either a more general and even potentially comprehensive understanding of diversity as valuable to courts' composition or for an increased presence of feminist judges—irrespective of their sex.'[61] This brings us back to the question of why there should be more female arbitrators.

Another rationale is non-discrimination, starting with the mere assessment that women represent half of humanity. It would seem logical, if only by evoking the ideas of equality and fairness, that half of the arbitrators and/or other participants in arbitral proceedings are women. But the argument can go much further. As underlined by Stéphanie Hennette Vauchez, scholars[62] have evidenced that 'calling women's underrepresentation "discrimination" allows to call for a reversal of the burden of proof: what if those who claim that gender balance in courts is either irrelevant or inappropriate were the ones that had to justify the status quo of clear gender imbalance as congruent with the qualities of fairness and impartiality?'[63] The argument has an enormous subversive potential. Of course, it could be enough to consider that 'representation of women is important, not because women would necessarily make different choices than men, but because arbitrators who make decisions of public importance should reflect the make-up of those affected by their decisions.'[64] However, even in this case, it is assumed that an increase in the numbers of women would change the field.

In fact, both rationales challenge what the field of arbitration was always considered to be, i.e. neutral, impartial, and objective, and thereby 'the very meaning of many of the principles and values the international elite of (arbitration) has historically prided itself of embodying'.[65] In other words, behind the gender bias lies a value bias.

22.3.2 Value bias

Both rationales of the specifics of women's voices and of non-discrimination encourage to challenge the very dogma of judicial dispute settlement which also pervades international arbitration. The whole idea of procedure can be presented as a ritualization of the principle of equality, in order to establish a level playing field where the power struggles of the parties are not transposed: equality of arms, *audi et alteram partem* are fundamental principles that depict this image of judicial procedures. Through a feminist lens, adjudication becomes a Manichean scheme that tends to silence the different nuances of a more complex reality. Proceduralization implies here rigidifying the

[61] Ibid. para. 22.

[62] Like Anne Phillips, 'Democracy and Representation: Or, Why Should It Matter Who Our Representatives Are?' in Anne Phillips (ed.), *Feminism and Politics* (Oxford University Press, 1998), 224.

[63] Vauchez (n. 33), para. 29.

[64] Van Harten (n. 35).

[65] Vauchez (n. 33), 'para. 18.

dispute settlement approach, and this approach risks silencing different voices. Adjudicative procedure can risk entertaining the power inequalities existing in the international legal order,[66] as demonstrated by the recent much-criticized *Marshall Island* case.[67] At the same time, 'formal legal argument can emphasise the need for a fair procedural treatment and the public articulation of legal rights and duties can protect less powerful litigants from excessive or abusive exercise of power by their opponents. These safeguards may be less rigorously observed in private negotiatory procedures.'[68] Therefore, feminist scholarship highlights the importance of taking power imbalance seriously in international adjudication, and of interpreting procedure in a way that empowers the powerless rather than marginalizing them.

But the value bias has another dimension, especially in economic matters, where a long-lasting debate denounces the neo-liberal bias of international economic rules,[69] on account of its blindness to non-trade values and the way it favours the already powerful. From a structural perspective, this neo-liberal bias is denounced but also reproduced. Thus, the Washington consensus is substituted by the Geneva consensus, supposed to be more open to the role of developing states. Nevertheless, the architecture of the system remains untouched while appearing to be further justified.[70] From a systemic perspective, this looks very much like homeostasis. From a normative perspective, the said neo-liberal bias summarizes the denouncement of the orientation of international economic law rules in order to make market concerns prevail over all other values, like environmental protection or human rights protection.[71] These contestations all thrive on the idea that international economic law would be 'solipsistic and hegemonic',[72] not taking seriously environmental or health or human rights concerns, and asserting its own superiority at the expenses of these other concerns.[73]

It is one of the merits of the debates on constitutionalization of international economic law, as developed for example by Deborah Cass, that they show the need to take into account a plurality of values within the normative space of international economic

[66] Edoardo Stoppioni, 'Decentring the ICJ: A Critical Analysis of the Marshall Islands Judgments', QIL, Zoom-out 45 (2017), 65–75.

[67] *Obligations concerning Negotiations relating to Cessation of the Nuclear Arms Race and to Nuclear Disarmament (Marshall Islands v United Kingdom, Marshall Islands v India, Marshall Islands v Pakistan)* (Preliminary Objections), ICJ Judgment 5 October 2016.

[68] Charlesworth and Chinkin (n. 4), 305.

[69] Andrew Lang, *World Trade Law After Neoliberalism: Reimagining the Global Economic Order* (Oxford University Press, 2011).

[70] Arancha González and Marion Jansen, 'Women Shaping Global Economic Governance' (Intracen, 2019): <http://www.intracen.org/uploadedFiles/intracenorg/Content/Publications/Women%20Shaping%20Global%20Economic%20Governance-WEB.pdf>.

[71] Quinn Slobodian, *Globalists: The End of Empire and the Birth of Neoliberalism* (Harvard University Press, 2018).

[72] Martti Koskenniemi, 'Hegemonic Regimes', in Margaret Young (ed.), *Regime Interaction in International Law: Facing Fragmentation* (Cambridge University Press, 2012), 305–24.

[73] Anne Orford, 'Beyond Harmonization: Trade, Human Rights and the Economy of Sacrifice', (2005) 18(2) Leiden JIL 179–213.

law.[74] The debate has pervaded investment arbitration by putting forth its public dimension and the specificities of states as parties, and underlining that investment arbitrators have all the necessary tools to take seriously states' policy space and right to regulate. The ICSID award in the *Urbaser* case, where the tribunal laid the foundations for investor responsibility under international law by allowing counterclaims, could be a landmark case,[75] just as Philippe Sands' opinion in the *Bear Creek* case demonstrates how an ICSID tribunal can take indigenous communities' rights seriously.[76] At the end of the day, this is also a claim of diversity and pluralism; it shows a need for a more open understanding of the frontiers of law to be applied by arbitral tribunals. It is all the more important when considering the third claim, of injustice, which is the logical prospect of the feminist claim against the very functioning of arbitration and its homeostatic reflex.

22.4 Third claim: injustice

The biases of arbitration entail the 'danger that attention to process can become a substitute for dealing with the underlying issues. Dispute resolution processes do not rectify the structural reasons for disagreement within the international arena.'[77] This reasoning is part of the more general reflection, conducted by feminist scholars, on the problems linked to the injustice permeating the international legal order. Because of its structural biases, everything about international law, from its fundamental structures to its intellectual categories and parlance, makes women invisible and their voice inaudible. This implies a blatant injustice of the system.[78] In international economic law, this debate has translated into the denouncement of global economic injustice. A fundamental claim of feminist perspectives on globalization denounces the dominance and exploitation of weak nations and classes by dominant ones, even if economic power has spread and new powerful actors have emerged, composing a multipolar world.[79] Most of the radical voices denounce this injustice as a corollary of the very structure of international economic law.[80] Echoing this idea that the international legal order would be irremediably

[74] Deborah Cass, 'The "Constitutionalization" of International Trade Law: Judicial Norm-Generation as the Engine of Constitutional Development in International Trade', (2001) 12(1) EJIL 39–75.

[75] *Urbaser SA and Consorcio de Aguas Bilbao Bizkaia, Bilbao Biskaia Ur Partzuergoa v The Argentine Republic*, ICSID Case No. ARB/07/26, Award (8 December 2016), para. 1195.

[76] *Bear Creek Mining Corporation v Republic of Peru*, ICSID Case No. ARB/14/2, Partial Dissenting Opinion of Prof. Philippe Sands (12 September 2017).

[77] Charlesworth and Chinkin (n. 4), 307.

[78] Ann Ferguson, 'Feminist Paradigms of Solidarity and Justice', (2009) 37(2) Philosophical Topics 161–77.

[79] Lea Ypi, 'Capitalism Will Not Give Us the Will to Fight Capitalism: What We Need Is a New International': <http://blogs.lse.ac.uk/politicsandpolicy/capitalism-will-not-give-us-the-will-to-fight-capitalism/>, accessed 2 October 2018.

[80] Bhupinder Chimni, 'A Just World Under Law: A View from the South', (2007) 22(2) American University International Law Review 199–220: <https://digitalcommons.wcl.american.edu/auilr/vol22/iss2/1/>, accessed 3 August 2019.

flawed because of consubstantial biases,[81] the claim of injustice queries whether the fate of international arbitration is structurally and irremediably to produce unjust output.

The answer is undeniably positive, according to the most radical views, because international arbitration consolidates structural injustice instead of correcting it. It is a set of unjustified and unfair outcomes that can be traced back to flawed and unjustified laws and structures,[82] perpetuating inequalities stemming from global imperialism.[83] The contention is that western-designed international economic law institutions are unable to meet the basic needs of poor countries.[84] Others argue that international investment law would systematically skew public policies to the profit of powerful investors, because of its colonial roots and biases.[85] Some feminist scholars have even begun to reflect upon the ways in which writing about processes like globalization in fact contribute to producing a world in which globalization appears irresistible. Thus, postcolonial feminists denounce openly the problems related to normalizing the discourse of economic globalization and of its inequalities, which particularly damage women and benefit all-powerful actors. This goes together with a critique addressed to a more ancient feminist analysis of international law that mostly focuses on gender, and is reproached for being an imperial feminism in that it does not analyse the subtleties of the effects of international economic law on women in the economic 'South'.[86] Therefore, it reinforces the depoliticization of the notion of 'difference'. Thus, Spivak has argued that it is 'particularly unfortunate [if] the emergent perspective of feminist criticism simply reproduces the axioms of imperialism'.[87]

This perspective is important to bear in mind, especially for its commitment to social justice. But the reaction is very often painted with a rather broad brush. A more discerning and constructive feminist analysis tends to highlight the importance of dealing with the situation in a modulated way, pinpointing where injustice is and where structural improvements are needed. This more nuanced approach reflects the ideas of the first generation of feminist engagement, seen as joining the humanitarian mission of international law, with its 'transnational political activism of women supporting peace through international institutions' and their 'unfaltering faith in the international legal system'.[88]

[81] Catherine O'Rourke, 'Feminist Strategy in International Law: Understanding Its Legal, Normative and Political Dimensions', (2017) 28(4) EJIL 1019–45.

[82] Gayatri Spivak, 'Can the Subaltern Speak?' in Cary Nelson and Lawrence Grossberg (eds), *Marxism and the Interpretation of Culture* (University of Illinois Press, 1988), 271–313.

[83] Ranjoo Herr, 'Reclaiming Third World Feminism: Or Why Transnational Feminism Needs Third World Feminism', (2014) 12(1) Meridians: Feminism, Race, Transnationalism 1–30.

[84] Nancy Fraser, *Scales of Justice: Reimagining Political Space in a Globalizing World* (Columbia University Press, 2009).

[85] Lora Verheecke, Pia Eberhardt, Cecilia Olivet, and Sam Cossar-Gilbert, 'Red Carpet Courts: 10 Stories of How the Rich and Powerful Hijacked Justice', 2019: <https://corporateeurope.org/sites/default/files/2019-06/Red%20Carpet%20Courts_1.pdf>.

[86] Anne Orford, 'Contesting Globalization: A Feminist Perspective on the Future of Human Rights', (1998) 8 Transnat'l L & Contemp Probs 171.

[87] Gayatri Spivak, 'Three Women's Texts and a Critique of Imperialism', (1985) 12(1) Critical Inquiry 243.

[88] Andrea Bianchi, *International Law Theories: An Inquiry into Different Ways of Thinking* (Oxford University Press, 2016), 183.

22.5 Conclusion

The central question that a feminist prism encourages appears to be: is international arbitration subjugated by patriarchal domination structures, bias, and injustice, thus mirroring and even reinforcing the idiosyncrasies if international law, especially international economic law? Probably, one could answer *yes* to all these questions, and this is essentially why the legitimacy of international arbitration is so much at stake. However, the absence of such a dispute settlement system would not necessarily lead to a better situation for international economic regulation: 'if international law did not regulate resources at all, the international order would be that much more unjust.'[89] The absence of rules and of dispute settlement resolution would make way for the law of the strongest.

A feminist deconstruction shows the need for clear, transparent, and well-balanced rules and dispute settlement resolution systems, and not their absence. This direction is the one progressively taken by projects of reform. A good example is the new Indian bilateral investment treaty model, specifying what international protection standards entail and balancing the asymmetrical structure of international investment law. This aspiration to a better quality aims to strengthen the rule of law in international economic law[90]—'rule of law' in the meaning used by Joseph Raz, the summary of all legal qualities that a legal system should aspire to in order to adhere to an idea of justice.[91] In this regard, enhancing diversity, be it based on gender, language, culture, or socio-economics, would not only enhance the perceived legitimacy of the field but would improve the quality of the decision-making process. Whatever insiders think of the inappropriateness of these feminist criticisms, they cannot—and the homeostatic reflex shows they do not—ignore the issue of perceived legitimacy. However, the issue will probably not be overcome by filling tribunals with women. The fact that some institutional proposals for reform of the investor–state dispute settlement system focus on a more judicial mechanism, with reinforced impartiality and independence guarantees, shows that the question of whether international arbitration is an irremediably flawed system remains open.

[89] James R. Crawford, 'Change, Order, Change: the Course of International Law', (2013) 365 Collected Courses 369.

[90] Martha Nussbaum, *Women and Human Development: The Capabilities Approach* (Cambridge University Press, 2001).

[91] Joseph Raz, 'The Rule of Law and Its Virtue', (1977) 93 Law Quarterly Review 195–6.

CHAPTER 23

THE ARBITRAL LEGAL ORDER

Evolution and recognition

EMMANUEL GAILLARD

23.1 Introduction

Rivers of ink have been poured out to discuss and analyse different aspects of international arbitration: the arbitration agreement, the role and powers of arbitral tribunals and of domestic courts, the law applicable to the arbitral procedure and to the merits of the dispute, and the effects of an arbitral award. Several disagreements still exist among commentators discussing these and other technical aspects of international arbitration. Rather than a matter of pure methodology, the source of these conflicting views is to be found at a deeper and more abstract level. Those disagreements may be explained by the different visions—or representations—of international arbitration.

The term 'representation of international arbitration' refers to a model that purports to encompass the entirety of the phenomenon of international arbitration, including its sources, objectives, and structure.[1] In other words, a representation offers a comprehensive mental construct of the fundamental relationship between a national legal system and international arbitration which serves as a source of legitimacy and validity of international arbitration.

There are three representations of international arbitration, which attempt to explain which state, or states, provides the relevant source of legitimacy and validity for the arbitration agreement, the arbitral process, and the ensuing award. Under the first representation, the source of legitimacy and validity of arbitration lies in a single national order,

[1] For an analysis of the notion and characteristics of a representation of international arbitration, see Emmanuel Gaillard, 'The Representations of International Arbitration', (2010) 1 Journal of International Dispute Settlement 271, at 273–6.

that of the seat of the arbitration. The second representation anchors international arbitration in a plurality of national legal orders where recognition or enforcement of an award is sought. Finally, the third representation recognizes an autonomous character to international arbitration, viewed as having generated an authentic and independent legal order: the arbitral legal order.

Each one of the three representations is in a position to respond to any and all questions that may arise in the field, be it in connection with the arbitrators' power to adjudicate, the entire arbitral process, or the fate of the ensuing award. As such, the representations cannot be qualified as right or wrong. Moreover, there are no objective criteria that may allow one to choose between each of these models: the choice of one over the other is ultimately a matter of belief and not of scientific view. However, the analysis of these representations also allows a better understanding of the trends that characterize international arbitration law at a given point in time, and to assess the course of its evolution.

This chapter will first explain the basic principles underlying each of the three representations of international arbitration, as well as the consequences of each. Then it will analyse the evolution of the rules governing the conduct of the arbitral proceeding and the rules applicable to the merits of the dispute, from a monolocal view to a transnational view. Finally, it will show that despite attemps to deny the existence or convenience of an arbitral legal order, its existence as a transnational legal order—autonoumous from all national legal orders—is being increasingly acknowledged.

23.2 The Three Representations of International Arbitration

The three representations of international arbitration attempt to explain the relationship between international arbitration and the national legal systems. Each representation carries significant practical consequences for all the players in the field of arbitration, including the arbitrators, the parties, and national judges.

23.2.1 The monolocal vision

In the first representation, international arbitration is exclusively anchored in a single national legal order, that of the state of the seat of arbitration. The seat is viewed as the arbitrator's forum, and the award's legal force stems exclusively from the law of that state. The arbitrator is assimilated to a local judge within such legal order and the award is considered to have a nationality: that of the seat of the arbitration. Although this representation dates back to the early days of international arbitration, it is still valid and present in contemporary thinking.

This representation has been based on two different views: the objectivist and the subjectivist. On the objectivist's viewpoint, the powers of an arbitrator are based on the notion of state sovereignty, pursuant to which the state where the arbitration takes place has an inherent right to regulate the activities on its territory, including the arbitral function assigned to the arbitrators. Pursuant to the subjectivist view, it is the intention of the parties when choosing the seat of the arbitration (or, in the absence of such agreement, the choice of the arbitral institution or the arbitrators themselves) that accords legitimacy to an arbitral tribunal acting under the exclusive control of that state's legal order.

Following this representation, an arbitrator would apply the law of the seat, including its procedural law, laws applicable to the merits of the dispute, including the choice of law rules, and public policy rules (as well as those applicable according to the private international law of the seat). Any decision made by a local judge in the country of the seat of the arbitration would be binding upon the arbitrators, the parties, and the local judges of third states. As a result, any anti-suit injunction ordered by the national courts of the seat of the arbitration would bind the arbitrators.[2] Moreover, a final decision in setting aside proceedings before the courts of the seat of the arbitration—either to set aside or to confirm the award—would be binding upon any third state where recognition or enforcement of the award may be sought. Therefore, while a national court in any third state would be prevented from enforcing an award set aside at the seat of arbitration, it would be compelled to enforce an award which has been confirmed by the courts of the seat.

23.2.2 The Westphalian model

In the second representation, international arbitration is anchored in a plurality of legal orders, namely those of the states where the effectiveness of an award will, under certain circumstances, be recognized. This multilocal model[3] operated a Copernican revolution vis-à-vis the monolocal representation, as it relegates the importance of the seat of the arbitration and instead focuses on the place or places of enforcement of the award as the source of validity of such award and the arbitral process leading to it. Thus, when an award is recognized and/or enforced in a certain jurisdiction, the legal order of the place of enforcement legitimizes a posteriori the whole arbitral process. The arbitrator is not compared to a local judge, he has no specific forum, but the world is his forum. The award has no nationality and its legal force does not stem from the legal order of the seat,

[2] For an analysis of the consequences of anti-suit injunctions under each representation, see Emmanuel Gaillard, 'Transcending National Legal Orders for International Arbitration', in Albert Jan van den Berg (ed.), *International Arbitration: The Coming of a New Age?* (ICCA, 2013).

[3] The reference to 'Westphalian' is inspired by the world model which followed the 1648 Peace of Westphalia, which was based on a juxtaposition of sovereign powers. Similarly, under this second representation each state has an equally legitimate title to decide for itself the conditions under which it will consider an arbitration process and the ensuing award as valid and worthy of enforcement.

but rather from the legal orders that are willing to recognize its effectiveness. This does not mean that the law of all the states where recognition or enforcement are sought should be applied cumulatively, but rather that each state has a title to impose its conception of what constitutes an arbitration worthy of legal protection within the confines of its own legal order. The legal force of an award would, thus, be relative to each legal system, and would in no way transcend the national legal order of any such state.

Under this representation, a number of states have an equal title to impose their views on the arbitral process—both with regards to the conduct of the arbitration or the law applicable to the merits of the dispute. Therefore, arbitrators would not mechanically abide by the decisions rendered by the courts of any jurisdiction, including those of the seat of arbitration. On the contrary, they are free to choose the applicable law, including the procedural law and the law applicable to the merits, as well as the mandatory rules of any given jurisdiction having connections with the dispute. Moreover, national courts of the place where recognition or enforcement are sought are free to make their own determination as to the validity and binding character of an arbitration agreement or an award, irrespective of the determination made on the same issues in any other legal system, including by the courts of the seat of the arbitration.

23.2.3 A transnational legal order

While it is undeniable that national legal orders play an important role in arbitration proceedings, the first two representations are insufficient to fully explain the phenomenon of international arbitration. The idea that a single legal system—that of the seat—can govern the binding force of international arbitration is increasingly anachronistic in a world in which international transactions are common and where, as a result, there are ever more states in which enforcement of arbitral awards may be sought. The Westphalian representation is equally inadequate to justify the source of legitimacy of international arbitration, as it requires the arbitrators to make a determination on the basis of considerations given by a plurality of legal orders—those of the places of enforcement, which are often conflicting on issues relevant to a specific arbitration.[4]

In the third representation, the juridicity of international arbitration is rooted in a transnational legal order, distinct and autonomous from any national legal order: the arbitral legal order. Thus, contrary to the first two representations, in which the legal force of an award stems from one or more national legal orders individually, be it that of

[4] Notably, both the seat and the place or places of enforcement are circumstantial factors which cannot determine the legitimacy of international arbitration. In fact, parties often give little or no thought to the choice of a seat, or are presented with a choice of a seat that is non-negotiable. This often last-minute decision cannot be interpreted as acceptance that the courts of that state should have the last word on any given dispute. Similarly, the place of enforcement is rarely freely chosen by a party, but rather defined by the states where the losing party holds assets. Thus, while the courts of such states will need to review the arbitral award to determine its validity or enforceability under its national legal order, neither of these can be regarded as the ultimate source of validity and legitimacy of such awards.

the country of the seat or that of the place or places of enforcement, the third representation contemplates the states collectively. As such, the validity and legitimacy of international arbitration is based on the consensus existing among states rather than on the will of any individual state to accept the effects of international arbitration. In other words, it is the vast number of states prepared to recognize an award that meets certain criteria that gives to that award and the underlying arbitration proceeding its validity and legitimacy. The arbitrator is not deemed to administer justice on behalf of any state, but rather plays a judicial role for the benefit of the international community. The award has no nationality; it is a decision of international justice, just as would be a decision rendered by a permanent international court established by the international community.

This representation has developed into two different trends: the jusnaturalist and the positivist. While the jusnaturalists justify the sources of arbitration in the higher values that result from the nature of things or society, the positivist model grasps the phenomenon on the basis of the normative activity of the states taken collectively. In other words, for the positivists the arbitrators' power to adjudicate rests on the ultimate recognition of their awards by states, which in practice broadly agree on the conditions that an arbitration must meet in order for it to be considered a binding method of dispute resolution.

Arbitrators acting in a transnational legal order may apply transnational rules, including procedural, choice of law, substantive, and public policy rules. Given that national courts and arbitration tribunals operate in different legal orders, arbitrators will not be bound by the decisions rendered by any national court. Similarly, national courts of third states will not be bound by the decisions rendered by the national courts of any other state, including the seat of the arbitration. Accordingly, an award set aside at the seat would only be deprived of legal effects within that jurisdiction, but will not be rendered invalid or inexistent, so it may be recognized and enforced by the national courts of states other than the seat.

The existence of an arbitral legal order does not imply that national legal orders play no role in international arbitration. In fact, the existence of an arbitral legal order relies on the notion that the laws of various states, when considered collectively, make up the common rules of arbitration law in which the source of the arbitrators' power to adjudicate is rooted.[5] Moreover, the arbitral legal order is in constant interaction with national legal orders, for example when courts of the seat or of a jurisdiction where enforcement is sought review an arbitral award, or for the formation of transnational rules.

[5] This does not necessarily mean that all the rules of the arbitral legal order have been endorsed by all existing national legal orders. Rather, the suggested method—known as the 'transnational rules method'—consists in ascertaining the prevailing trend within national laws at a certain time. As such, the arbitral legal order is a dynamic system which takes into account the evolution of national laws.

23.3 The evolution towards an arbitral legal order

In the practice of international arbitration, the three representations coexist. However, a progressive yet clear evolution towards a full operation of the arbitral legal order may be seen, in particular with regards to the emancipation of the arbitral procedure from the provisions found in the legal order of the seat of the arbitration and the arbitrators' freedom to move away from the choice of law rules of the seat.

23.3.1 The conduct of the arbitral proceedings

In 1923, the Geneva Protocol on Arbitration Clauses adopted the first representation of international arbitration. In particular, Article 2 of the Geneva Protocol provides that:

> The arbitral procedure, including the constitution of the arbitral tribunal, shall be governed by the will of the parties and by the law of the country in whose territory the arbitration takes place.[6]

This representation was further confirmed by the Institute of International Law in the Amsterdam Resolution of 1957, which noted the predominant role of the law of the seat in procedural matters. In particular, Article 9 of the Resolution allowed parties to disregard the restrictions prevailing in the law of the seat only if that law itself so permitted:

> The law of the place of the seat of the arbitral tribunal shall determine whether the procedure to be followed by the arbitrators may be freely established by the parties, and whether, failing agreement on this subject between the contracting parties, it may be settled by the arbitrators or should be replaced by the provisions applicable to procedure before the ordinary courts.[7]

The text adopted by the Institute of International Law in 1957 reflects the drafters' conviction that arbitrators could be assimilated to national judges of the seat of the arbitration.

Since the 1957 Resolution, which was severely criticized by legal scholars, almost all sources of international arbitration law have acknowledged the arbitrators' increased freedom to conduct the arbitral proceedings as they consider appropriate in light of the specific characteristics of each particular dispute. For example, the New York

[6] Protocol on Arbitration Clauses Signed at a Meeting of the Assembly of The League of Nations ("Treaty Series Vol. XVII, published in 1924 (even though the protocol is of 24 September 1923)". The relevant protocol was registered with No. 678. See https://treaties.un.org/Pages/LONViewDetails.aspx?src=LON&id=548&chapter=30&clang=_en), 158.

[7] Institute of International Law, 'Resolution concerning Arbitration in Private International Law', Session of Amsterdam, (1957) It is in Vol. 47, Part II of the Yearbook (at p. 495). See http://www.idi-iil.org/app/uploads/2017/05/4025-47B-OCR-min.pdf, Art. 9.

Convention on the Recognition and Enforcement of Foreign Arbitral Awards of 10 June 1958 clearly departed from the idea that the national legal order of the seat of arbitration is the only source of the award's legal source, and instead adopted a Westphalian view. In particular, the New York Convention considerably minimizes the importance of the role of the seat and, while it recognizes the freedom of the state of the seat to control arbitrations carried out in its territory as it sees fit, it shifts the focus on the conditions of recognition of awards in the national legal order where enforcement is sought.[8]

The 1961 European Convention on International Commercial Arbitration moved even further away from the monolocal representation and provided that, in the absence of an express intent of the parties, arbitrators are entitled to establish 'directly or by reference to the rules and statutes of a permanent arbitral institution', the rules of procedure to be followed by the arbitrators.[9] The 1961 European Convention does not refer to the law of the seat.

In 1989, the Institute of International Law itself recognized that the 1957 Amsterdam Resolution no longer reflected the dominant view:

> These propositions no longer enjoy unanimous support. Many now argue that the arbitration process need not be attached to any national law; the parties can establish a process with agreed-upon characteristics whose lacunae will be filled out either by further party agreement or by the arbitrators.[10]

Instead, the Institute of International Law acknowledged the parties' full autonomy to determine the procedural rules applicable, independently from the law of the seat:

> The parties have full autonomy to determine the procedural . . . rules and principles that are to apply in the arbitration. In particular, . . . these rules and principles may be derived from different national legal systems as well as from non-national sources such as principles of international law, general principles of law, and the usages of international commerce.[11]

Nowadays, most modern arbitration laws currently accept that '[t]he former doctrine pursuant to which the law of civil procedure . . . in force at the place of the seat of the arbitration was binding on the arbitrators in the absence of procedural agreements of the

[8] Emmanuel Gaillard, *Legal Theory of International Arbitration* (Martinus Nijhoff, 2010), para. 33.

[9] European Convention on International Commercial Arbitration, 484 UNTS 349 (adopted 21 April 1961, entered into force 7 January 1964), Art. IV(4)(d).

[10] Institute of International Law, Report by Arthur von Mehren, Session of Santiago de Compostela (1989), 63 Yearbook of the Institute of International Law, Part I, at 44, § 27.

[11] Institute of International Law, 'Arbitration Between States, State Enterprises, or State Entities, and Foreign Enterprises', Session of Santiago de Compostela, (1989) 63 Yearbook of the Institute of International Law, Part II, Art. 6, 330. On the significance of the Resolution, see also Arthur von Mehren, 'Arbitration Between States and Foreign Enterprises: The Significance of the Institute of International Law's Santiago de Compostela Resolution', (1990) 5 ICSID Rev. 54, von Mehren summarizes the evolution in the following manner (p. 57): 'In Santiago, the seat is replaced by party autonomy; the arbitration agreement displaces the law of the seat.'

parties is no longer followed'.[12] For example, the French Code of Civil Procedure provides that:

> An arbitration agreement may define the procedure to be followed in the arbitral proceedings, directly or by reference to arbitration rules or to procedural rules.
>
> In case the arbitration agreement does not define a procedure, the arbitral tribunal shall define the procedure as required, either directly or by reference to arbitration rules or to procedural rules.
>
> Irrespective of the procedure adopted, the arbitral tribunal shall ensure that the parties are treated equally and that the principle of due process is respected.[13]

Moreover, most major arbitration rules give arbitrators broad discretion to conduct the arbitral proceedings. As early as 1975, the ICC Arbitration Rules recognized that arbitrators did not even have to refer to a 'municipal procedural law' in order to address procedural issues that may arise. The provision, which remained essentially unchanged since then, currently provides that:

> The proceedings before the arbitral tribunal shall be governed by the Rules and, where the Rules are silent, by any rules which the parties or, failing them, the arbitral tribunal may settle on, whether or not reference is thereby made to the rules of procedure of a national law to be applied to the arbitration.[14]

Similarly, the 2010 UNCITRAL Rules, often chosen by states to govern arbitrations under international investment agreements, also give arbitrators free reign in the conduct of arbitral proceedings:

> Subject to these Rules, the arbitral tribunal may conduct the arbitration in such manner as it considers appropriate, provided that the parties are treated with equality and that at an appropriate stage of the proceedings each party is given a reasonable opportunity of presenting its case. The arbitral tribunal, in exercising its discretion, shall conduct the proceedings so as to avoid unnecessary delay and expense and to provide a fair and efficient process for resolving the parties' dispute.[15]

Against this background, it must be noted that in general arbitrators do not select in the abstract and at the beginning of the arbitral proceedings a law that would govern the entire procedure, but rather opt to address procedural issues concretely as they arise.

[12] Jean-François Poudret and Sebastien Besson, *Comparative Law of International Arbitration*, 2nd edn (Sweet & Maxwell, 2007), §532. Nevertheless, the standardization of the laws on arbitration towards increased liberalization of procedural issues is not uniform. See Gaillard (n. 8), para 97.

[13] French Code of Civil Procedure (2011), Arts. 1509–10 (author's translation).

[14] ICC Rules of Arbitration (2017), Art. 19.

[15] UNCITRAL Arbitration Rules (2010), Art. 17(1). All other modern arbitration rules are similarly liberal. See e.g. LCIA Arbitration Rules (2014), Art. 14(5); SCC Arbitration Rules (2017), Art. 23; AAA/ICDR International Arbitration Rules (2014), Art. 20(1).

As a result, it is less and less often that arbitrators decide procedural questions by reference to a predetermined law.[16]

In any event, the application of procedural rules by arbitrators will necessarily be influenced by the conception of international arbitration they adhere to. As such, arbitrators who are convinced that their powers exclusively derive from the law of the seat will, in the absence of an agreement between the parties, naturally turn to the rules of procedure applicable before the courts of the seat. By contrast, arbitrators who adhere to the third representation will not necessarily look into the procedural rules of any given national order, including that of the seat, but rather apply their own judgment as to what is required to conduct fair and efficient proceedings in each particular case.

23.3.2 The rules applicable to the merits of the dispute

The evolution of the regime concerning the determination of the law applicable to the merits of a dispute has followed a remarkably parallel path to that of the rules applicable to the conduct of the proceedings described above. In fact, as was the case with procedural rules, the old conception pursuant to which arbitrators should resort to the choice of law rules of the seat to select the law applicable to the merits has increasingly given way to the recognition of the freedom of the parties and, in the absence of such agreement, the freedom of the arbitrators to select the rules of law applicable to the merits of a dispute.

In 1957, the Amsterdam Resolution of the Institute of International Arbitration aligned with the first representation. Article 11 of the Resolution provides that:

> The rules of choice of law in force in the state of the seat of the arbitral tribunal must be followed to settle the law applicable to the substance of the difference.
>
> Within the limits of such law, arbitrators shall apply the law chosen by the parties or, in default of any express indication by them, shall determine what is the will of the parties in this respect having regard to all the circumstances of the case.[17]

The idea which underlies the Amsterdam Resolution—that international arbitration is just one mean through which the legal order of the seat administers justice, irrespective

[16] Arbitrators do, however, often refer to 'soft law' instruments aimed at providing guidelines to arbitrators and parties through various aspects of international arbitration, including in connection with written submissions, production of evidence, and conduct of hearings. These instruments are usually a blend of best practices from legal systems across the world, with the aim of facilitating the arbitral process. See e.g. the IBA Rules on the Taking of Evidence in International Arbitration (2010), the UNCITRAL Notes on Organizing Arbitral Proceedings (2012), the ALI/UNIDROIT Principles of Transnational Civil Procedure (2004), as well as procedural guidelines published by arbitral institutions, such as the ICC Notes to Parties and Arbitral Tribunals on the Conduct of the Arbitration under the ICC Rules of Arbitration (2016), LCIA's Notes for Arbitrators (2015), and SCC's Arbitrator's Guidelines (2014).

[17] Institute of International Law, 'Resolution concerning Arbitration in Private International Law', Session of Amsterdam (1957) Yearbook of the Institute of International Law, Vol. 47, Part II, Art. 11.

of the intent of the parties—has been severely criticized. For example, in 1963 Berthold Goldman dedicated most of his course at The Hague Academy to the justification of a system of determination of the law applicable to the merits wholly autonomous from the law of the seat.[18]

In 1989, the Institute of International Law itself rejected the monolocal conception reflected in its 1957 Resolution and recognized the full freedom of the parties, and alternatively of the arbitrators, to determine the law applicable to the merits of the dispute. In particular, Article 6 of the 1989 Resolution reads:

> The parties have full autonomy to determine the... substantive rules and principles that are to apply in the arbitration. In particular,... these rules and principles may be derived from different national legal systems as well as from non-national sources such as principles of international law, general principles of law, and the usages of international commerce.[19]

Moreover, the 1989 Resolution provides that whenever the parties have left open issues, 'the tribunal shall supply the necessary rules and principles drawing on' the law chosen by the parties, the law indicated by the system of private international law stipulated by the parties, general principles of public or private international law, general principles of international arbitration, or the law that would be applied by the courts of the seat.[20] Thus, the law of the seat is only one of many laws to which the arbitrators may refer in the absence of agreement among the parties.

This view has been adopted by most modern arbitration laws, which acknowledge that the arbitrators' primary duty is to respect the intention of the parties as regards the determination of the applicable rules of law and that, where the parties have remained silent, arbitrators enjoy great freedom in such determination. For example, the French Code of Civil Procedure provides that:

> The arbitral tribunal shall decide the dispute in accordance with the rules of law chosen by the parties or, where no such choice has been made, in accordance with the rules of law it considers appropriate. In any case, the arbitral tribunal shall take trade usages into account.[21]

[18] Berthold Goldman, 'Les conflits de lois dans l'arbitrage international de droit privé', (1963) 109 Recueil des cours 347, at 374–5. Other scholars followed Goldman on the issue. See e.g. Lazare Kopelmanas, *The Sources of the Law of International Trade* (Stevens & Sons, 1964), 272; Philippe Fouchard, *L'arbitrage commercial international* (Dalloz, 1965), §§546ff.; Pierre Lalive, 'Problèmes relatifs à l'arbitrage commercial international', (1967) 120 Recueil des cours 568, at 613 ff.

[19] Institute of International Law, 'Resolution concerning Arbitration Between States, State Enterprises, or State Entities, and Foreign Enterprises', Session of Santiago de Compostela (1989) Yearbook of the Institute of International Law, Vol. 63, Part II, Art. 6.

[20] Ibid. Arts. 4 and 6.

[21] French Code of Civil Procedure (2011), Art. 1511 (author's translation). See similarly, Dutch Code of Civil Procedure (2011), Art. 1054(2); Panamanian Arbitration Law (2013), Art. 56.

Similarly, most major arbitration rules acknowledge the arbitrators' total freedom in the determination of the rules of law applicable to the merits of the dispute. For example, the ICC Arbitration Rules provide that:

> The parties shall be free to agree upon the rules of law to be applied by the arbitral tribunal to the merits of the dispute. In the absence of any such agreement, the arbitral tribunal shall apply the rules of law which it determines to be appropriate.
>
> The arbitral tribunal shall take account of the provisions of the contract, if any, between the parties and of any relevant trade usages.[22]

Using the broad freedom to determine the rules applicable to the merits of the dispute, arbitrators may consider that the rules which are best suited in light of the specific characteristics of a dispute are those created within a specific national legal order, from where their normative value stems. Alternatively, arbitrators may opt to apply transnational rules, characterized, as far as their formation is concerned, by the systematic use of comparative law resources known as the transnational rules method. This method consists on establishing whether a certain rule is generally accepted by states or, to the contrary, is isolated or generally rejected.

The transnational rules applied by arbitrators are not isolated; they constitute an autonomous normative system, in which norms at different degrees of generality operate in an interrelated manner. As such, very general rules, such as contractual good faith, give rise to more specific rules, such as good faith in the conclusion, interpretation, and performance of contracts. Even more specific rules are drawn from these, such as the *contra proferentem* rule, pursuant to which a document is to be interpreted against the party who unilaterally drafted it. Arbitrators also apply widely accepted rules such as the duty to mitigate damages, the validation of contracts that mandate parties to negotiate in good faith, or the condemnation of corruption, without the need to refer to a specific national legal order. More importantly, while these rules are based on the states' normative activity, they do not belong exclusively to any state. These are truly transnational rules.

As with arbitral procedure, when choosing the law to apply to the merits of a dispute, arbitrators will be naturally guided by the representation to which they adhere. Thus, an arbitrator who conceives his role by analogy with that of the judge of the state of the seat will readily resort to the choice of law rules of that country to determine the law applicable to the merits, whereas an arbitrator who adheres to the Westphalian representation will be more sensitive to the diversity of legal systems potentially relevant to the dispute and the parties, and will be inclined to apply the choice of law rules which he considers appropriate. On the contrary, an arbitrator who adheres to the transnational view will be more likely to turn to transnational choice of law rules, as opposed to national law.

[22] ICC Arbitration Rules (2017), Art. 21(1) and (2). See also e.g. UNCITRAL Arbitration Rules (2010), Art. 35(1), AAA/ICDR International Arbitration Rules (2014), Art. 31(1).

23.4 The recognition of the existence of an arbitral legal order

While some commentators have sought to reject it, the existence of an arbitral legal order as an autonoumous legal order—independent from all other national legal orders—is gradually being acknowledged by national legal orders and by arbitrators themselves.

23.4.1 States' recognition of the arbitral legal order

The international community has implicitly granted arbitration true autonomy by conferring on the arbitrators the power to adjudicate international disputes, and by recognizing the result of the arbitral process, i.e. the award, without reviewing the merits of the dispute.[23] Moreover, national legal orders are gradually moving towards a more explicit recognition of the existence of an arbitral legal order, with arbitrators acting as 'international judges' and applying transnational rules.

For example, national courts have acknowledged that arbitral awards are not integrated into the national legal order of the seat of arbitration. Along these lines, the French Court of Cassation held that an award rendered in Switzerland 'is an international award which is not integrated into the legal system of that state, so it remains in existence even if set aside'. Accordingly, 'its recognition in France is not contrary to international public policy'.[24] The Paris Court of Appeal confirmed that 'arbitrators are not an integral part of the legal organization of the state of the seat'.[25] This principle has been consistently applied and developed by French courts.

The Court of Cassation went further, to recognize that arbitral awards are international decisions of international justice rendered by international judges. For example, in *Putrabali* it stated in particularly forceful terms that '[a]n international arbitral award, which is not anchored in any national legal order, is a decision of international justice whose validity must be ascertained with regard to the rules applicable in the country where its recognition and enforcement are sought'.[26] More recently, the same court

[23] Convention on the Recognition and Enforcement of Foreign Arbitral Awards, 330 UNTS 3 (adopted 10 June 1958, entered into force 7 June 1959), Art. III.

[24] *Hilmarton Ltd v Sté Omnium de traitement et de valorization (OTV)*, Cour de Cassation—Première Chambre Civile (23 March 1994) (author's translation).

[25] *La Société S.A. Lesbats et fils v. Monsieur Volker le Docteur Grub*, Paris Court of Appeal (18 January 2007) (author's translation). See, similarly, *Arab Republic of Egypt v Chromalloy Aero Services*, Paris Court of Appeal (14 January 1997); *Bargues Agro Industries v Young Pecan Company*, Paris Court of Appeal (10 June 2004).

[26] *PT Putrabali Adyamulia v Rena Holding*, Cour de Cassation—Première Chambre Civile (29 June 2007) (author's translation). See also *Société ivorienne de raffinage v Société Teekay Shipping Norway et autres*, Paris Court of Appeal (31 January 2008).

described an arbitral award issued by a tribunal with seat in London as 'an international award which is not attached to any national legal order' but is rather a 'decision of international justice which regularity must be examined with regard to the rules applicable in the state where recognition and enforcement are sought'.[27]

National courts have also acknowledged the existence of transnational rules which are applicable by arbitrators. Thus, for example, the Paris Court of Appeal referred to 'truly international and universally applicable' public policy rules.[28] A few years later, the same court referred to the 'ethics of international business as understood by the majority of states composing the international community'.[29] Similarly, the Swiss Federal Tribunal held that when reviewing an award, Swiss courts should take into account 'transnational or universal public policy including fundamental principles of law which are to be complied with irrespective of the connections between the dispute and a given country'.[30]

States have also enacted legislation which reflects their acknowledgment of the existence of a separate arbitral legal order. As such, several states have introduced legislation allowing the parties to an arbitration to waive their right to request the setting aside of an award at the seat of the arbitration in situations where the only connection of the parties with the state is precisely the seat of their arbitration. Thus, in the Private International Law Statute of 1987, Switzerland allowed the parties to waive, partially or totally, their right to request the setting aside of an award at the seat in situations where they do not have their domicile, habitual residence, or business establishment in Switzerland.[31]

What is more, states themselves regularly enter into arbitration agreements pursuant to which they subject themselves to the arbitrators' authority, participate in arbitration proceedings as both claimants and respondents, and comply with arbitral awards rendered against them, failing which they can be subject to enforcement proceedings against them.

Thus, while states have kept the monopoly of the enforcement of arbitral awards, national legal orders have acknowledged the autonomy of the arbitrators' judicial function and of the legal order in which they operate.

[27] *Ryanair Ltd & Airport Marketing Services Ltd v Syndicat mixte des aéroports de Charente*, Cour de Cassation—Première Chambre Civile (8 July 2015) (author's translation).

[28] *Fougerolle v Procofrance*, Paris Court of Appeal (25 May 1990) (author's translation).

[29] *European Gas Turbines SA v Westman International Ltd*, Paris Court of Appeal (30 September 1993) (author's translation).

[30] *Westland Helicopters Ltd v The Arab British Helicopter Company*, Swiss Federal Supreme Court (19 April 1994) (author's translation).

[31] Swiss Private International Law Statute 1987, Art. 192 ('Where none of the parties has its domicile, its habitual residence, or a business establishment in Switzerland, they may, by an express statement in the arbitration agreement or by a subsequent agreement in writing, exclude all setting aside proceedings or they may limit such proceedings…'). Similar legislation has been enacted, among others, in Tunisia (see Tunisian Arbitration Code 1993, Art. 78(6)), Belgium (see Belgian Judicial Code 2013, Art. 1718), Sweden (see Swedish Arbitration Act 1999, Section 51), Peru (see Peruvian Arbitration Act 2008, Art. 63(8)), and Abu Dhabi (see Abu Dhabi Arbitration Regulations 2015, Art. 54).

23.4.2 Arbitrators' recognition of the arbitral legal order

Arbitrators themselves have acknowledged the very premise of the existence of an arbitral legal order, i.e. that the source of the juridicity of international arbitration is not to be found, at least not exclusively, in the legal order of the seat of the arbitration. As such, they have often considered themselves not to be bound by the decisions rendered by the courts of the seat of the arbitration and have refused to comply with orders aimed at interfering with their functions.

For example, in *Salini v Ethiopia* an ICC tribunal analysed whether it needed to 'defer to a judicial order to halt the arbitral proceedings where that order has been issued in the country in which the parties have agreed to hold their arbitration' and ultimately refused to stay the arbitral proceedings, despite an injunction issued by the court of Addis Ababa, the seat of arbitration:

> An international arbitral tribunal is not an organ of the state in which it has its seat in the same way that a court of the seat would be. The primary source of the Tribunal's power is the parties' agreement to arbitrate. An important consequence of this is that the Tribunal has a duty vis-à-vis the parties to ensure that their arbitration agreement is not frustrated. In certain circumstances, it may be necessary to decline to comply with an order issued by a court of the seat, in the fulfilment of the Tribunal's larger duty to the parties.
>
> Of course, this is not to say that a contract, including an arbitration agreement, has a validity that is independent of any legal order. Indeed, a contract derives its binding force from its recognition by one or more legal orders. However, an agreement to submit disputes to international arbitration is not anchored exclusively in the legal order of the seat of the arbitration. Such agreements are validated by a range of international sources and norms extending beyond the domestic seat itself.[32]

The *Salini* tribunal tried to reach a balance between its duty towards the parties (i.e. 'to ensure that their agreement to submit disputes to international arbitration is rendered effective even where that creates a conflict with the courts of the seat of the arbitration')[33] and its duty 'to ensure that any award it renders is enforceable at law'.[34] As a result, it considered that a tribunal 'should [not] simply abdicate to the courts of the seat the tribunal's own judgment about what is fair and right in the arbitral proceedings'.[35] Instead, 'the tribunal must follow its own judgment, even if that requires non-compliance with a court order'.[36]

Similarly, in *Saipem v Petrobangla* an ICC tribunal disregarded several court decisions of the Bangladeshi courts restraining Saipem from proceeding with the arbitration on the ground that 'the revocation of the authority of the ICC Arbitral Tribunal by the

[32] *Salini Costruttori S.P.A. v The Federal Democratic Republic of Ethiopia, Addis Ababa Water and Sewage Authority*, Award Regarding the Suspension of the Proceedings and Jurisdiction, ICC Arbitration Case No. 10623/AER/ACS (2001), paras. 128–9.

[33] Ibid. para. 138. [34] Ibid. para. 140. [35] Ibid. para. 142. [36] Ibid.

Bangladeshi courts was contrary to the general principles governing international arbitration'.[37] After the arbitral tribunal issued a final award finding the Bangladeshi state-owned company Petrobangla liable and ordering it to pay compensation to Saipem, Petrobangla filed a request to set aside the award before the Supreme Court of Bangladesh. The court held that since the tribunal did not have authority to entertain Saipem's claims on the first place, there was no award to set aside. In the Bangladeshi court's words: 'A non-existent award can neither be set aside nor can it be enforced.'[38] Following the Bangladeshi courts' refusal to grant legal effect to the arbitration agreement freely entered into by the state-owned company, Saipem initiated an ICSID arbitration against Bangladesh. The investment treaty tribunal found that Bangladesh had acted contrary to international law and expropriated Saipem's 'right to arbitrate the dispute in Bangladesh under the ICC Arbitration Rules', and ordered Bangladesh to pay Saipem the value of the ICC award.[39]

23.5 Conclusion

Despite attempts to deny the existence or convenience of an arbitral legal order as a distinct legal order, critics have not been able to explain the entirety of the international arbitration phenomenon absent a transnational element. After all, the question of whether an arbitral legal order is desirable or not may be debated and is subject to endless paralegal considerations.

Theoretical debate aside, the fact is that in the last century arbitration has evolved from a system primarily based on the law of the seat to one where the only rule consists, in the end, in the recognition of the parties' freedom and the arbitrators' discretion to determine the contours of the arbitral proceedings and the law applicable to the merits of a dispute as they see fit, subject to compliance with the fundamental principles of procedural equality and due process. In addition, it is a fact that the existence of an arbitral legal order is widely recognized by national legal orders, arbitral institutions, and arbitrators themselves. It cannot be denied, therefore, that the arbitral order exists not only as a mental representation, but as a system of law.

[37] *Saipem S.p.A. v The People's Republic of Bangladesh*, Decision on Jurisdiction and Recommendation on Provisional Measures, ICSID Case No. ARB/05/07 (2007), para. 31 (referring to the decision of the ICC Tribunal in ICC Arbitration Case No. 7934/CK/AER/ACS/MS (unpublished)).

[38] Ibid. para 36. See also *Saipem S.p.A. v The People's Republic of Bangladesh*, Award, ICSID Case No. ARB/05/07 (2009), paras. 171–3.

[39] Ibid. para 204.

CHAPTER 24

EPISTEMIC COMMUNITIES IN INTERNATIONAL ARBITRATION

ANDREA BIANCHI

24.1 Why bother?

It is a legitimate question to ask why international arbitration lawyers should bother about concepts, such as that of 'epistemic communities', which might be widely perceived as fundamentally alien to their area of practice.[1] I reckon that many would swiftly respond that they should not, and should instead get on with their business. Arguably, this would be a very simplistic stance to take on the matter for several reasons. First, to presuppose that practice should be unhindered by theoretical reflection is tantamount to saying that practice and theory can be neatly distinguished and separately dealt with. This is at best a misrepresentation of reality. In fact, any practice requires a theory to be understood and justified. Conversely, any theory needs a practice to be tested and evaluated in terms of being able to provide a persuasive explanation of the processes it claims to account for.

The widely held idea that practitioners get the work done on the ground, while academics worry about petty academic disputes concerning insignificant or irrelevant issues, is misleading.[2] Practitioners—regardless of whether or not they are conscious of it—always act on the basis of a 'theory' or 'method', i.e. a set of presuppositions and beliefs that provide the necessary background to the exercise of their practical skills.

[1] For the purposes of the chapter I take international arbitration to cover both commercial arbitration and investment arbitration (unless otherwise indicated in the text).

[2] Andrea Bianchi, *International Law Theories: An Inquiry into Different Ways of Thinking* (OUP, 2016), 7–9.

Theorists, in turn, cannot afford to neglect the practical import of the social practices that they set out to investigate. The ultimate test for the credibility of legal theory is its capacity to account for the social practice which we call law. If academics indulge in what I call 'armchair theorizing'—by which I mean the disturbing tendency to elaborate complex theoretical constructs that are far removed from the realities they purport to explain—they fail in their mission and jeopardize the credibility of their discipline.[3] In fact, theory and practice are closely intertwined.

Second, intellectual curiosity should always be encouraged regardless of one's profession and personal predisposition. The not too flattering view once put forward by Fitzmaurice that 'the real fault of lawyers... is that they have not, as lawyers, been single-minded enough and have not resisted the temptation to stray into other fields'[4] should not be taken as a standard of reference for contemporary legal theory and practice. Quite the contrary: the capacity to stick one's nose into other disciplines and areas of knowledge can produce interesting insights that can be put to good use in one's academic discipline or area of practice. Even the well-known adage 'Curiosity killed the cat' is often accompanied by the qualifying clause 'but satisfaction brought him back'. Even in popular culture the value of self-restraint in curiosity is offset by the advantages that its actual exercise can bring about!

Ultimately, and perhaps most importantly, international arbitration scholarship appears to make increasing use of the expression 'epistemic communities', often without expounding on its meaning or conceptual underpinnings, but simply taking for granted that people understand the meaning and use of such an expression. Epistemic communities become an explanatory key to classifying and understanding the behaviour of different groups of professionals operating in this area of the law.[5] They are used to understand how ideas and their underlying values are formed and circulated in the field of international arbitration, and to show how the boundaries of this legal regime are designed,[6] how knowledge is formed within the field,[7] and how the varying perception by their members of their role as arbitrators may affect their practice.[8] Epistemic communities may provide a new lens through which one can productively look at the operation of international dispute settlement mechanisms, and may even help determine why different types of adjudicators seem to come from different planets.[9]

[3] Andrea Bianchi, 'The International Legal Regulation of the Use of Force: The Politics of Interpretive Method', 22 Leiden Journal of International Law 651 (2009), 653.

[4] Sir Gerald Fitzmaurice, 'The United Nations and the Rule of Law', 38 Transactions of the Grotius Society 42 (1953).

[5] Anthea Roberts, 'Clash of Paradigms: Actors and Analogies Shaping the Investment Treaty System', 107 American Journal of International Law 45 (2013).

[6] Katherine Lynch, *The Forces of Economic Globalization: Challenges to the Regime of International Commercial Arbitration* (Kluwer, 2003), 94–104.

[7] Kate Miles, *The Origins of International Investment Law: Empire, Environment and the Safeguarding of Capital* (CUP, 2013), 342–3.

[8] Ralph Michaels, 'Roles and Role Perceptions of International Arbitrators', in Walter Mattli and Thomas Dietz (eds), *International Arbitration and Global Governance* (OUP 2014), 47.

[9] Joost Pauwelyn, 'The Rule of Law Without the Rule of Lawyers? Why Investment Arbitrators are from Mars, Trade Adjudicators from Venus', 109 American Journal of International Law 761 (2015).

International arbitrators should take no offence at epistemic communities having become a common way of looking at them as a group. After all, it seems definitely more edifying to be identified as members of an 'epistemic community' rather than 'as a "mafia" or a "club".'[10] If not the ultimate evidence of moral probity, membership in an 'epistemic community' certainly attests to a higher degree of respectability and acceptance by contemporary social standards.

24.2 Whence does it come?

'Epistemic community' is primarily a concept.[11] Concepts are the tools by which disciplines apprehend reality and try to understand the world. They are intellectual constructs that allow for the drawing of boundaries, classifying, orientating, and creating meaning. We use concepts as categories to fit the realities surrounding us, to account for and justify them or, if need be, to contest them and advocate change.[12] Despite their inherent vocation for bringing order by way of theoretical abstraction and systematization, concepts may be volatile. Despite the fixity and 'boundedness' that disciplines tend to attach to them, oftentimes the contours of concepts can be porous. Furthermore, concepts may travel across disciplines and adjust to different cultures and scientific paradigms. A journey almost inevitably changes the traveller, and it should not come as a surprise that this is also the case with concepts. Once they are used in contexts different from the one in which they were originally designed and meant to operate, concepts may take up different connotations and discharge different functions. The concept of 'epistemic communities' is a very good example of such versatility.

Nearly all writings and scholarly contributions dealing with the concept of epistemic communities make reference to the seminal work of political scientist Peter M. Haas.[13] This is fairly revealing about two things. First, the concept finds its origin in a discipline other than international law. Second, the reason why certain ideas or concepts 'stick' or 'fly' or both does not depend on who makes use of them first.[14] Arguably, constructivist

[10] Yves Dezalay and Bryant Garth, *Dealing In Virtue: International Commercial Arbitration and the Construction of a Transnational Legal Order* (University of Chicago Press, 1996), 10, 50.

[11] The intellectual framework used for this chapter has been originally laid down in Andrea Bianchi, 'Epistemic Communities', in Jean d'Aspremont and Sahid Singh (eds), *Concepts for International Law: Contributions to Disciplinary Thought* (Edward Elgar, 2019), 251.

[12] Recently, I have been particularly intrigued by the multifaceted concept of transparency: see Andrea Bianchi, 'On Power and Illusion: The Concept of Transparency in International Law', in Andrea Bianchi and Anne Peters (eds), *Transparency in International Law* (CUP, 2013), 1.

[13] See Peter Haas, 'Introduction: Epistemic Communities and International Policy Coordination', 46 International Organization 1 (1992); 'Epistemic Communities', in Daniel Bodansky, Jutta Brunnée, and Hellen Hey (eds), *The Oxford Handbook of International Environmental Law* (OUP, 2012), 792; 'Ideas, Experts and Governance', in Monika Ambrus et al. (eds), *The Role of Experts in International and European Decision-Making Processes: Advisors, Decision Makers or Irrelevant Actors?* (CUP, 2014), 19.

[14] I still do not know why, but I found it intriguing to read Chip Heath and Dan Heath, *Made to Stick: Why Some Ideas Survive and Others Die* (Random House, 2010).

international relations theorists originally developed the notion, and the term 'epistemic communities' appears in international relations scholarship[15] well before Haas' well-known essay on epistemic communities and international policy coordination. It is the latter, however, that has come to be known and cited as the reference work on epistemic communities.

Indeed, Haas puts forward a notion of epistemic communities that is, in his own words, at a low level of abstraction.[16] By 'epistemic community', he refers to a 'network of professionals with recognized expertise and competence in a particular domain and an authoritative claim to policy-relevant knowledge within that domain or issue-area.'[17] These networks, often of a transnational character, are made of experts 'with professional training who enjoy social authority based on their reputation for impartial expertise.'[18] Depending on the subject or issue-area covered by their expertise, such experts may be scientists and engineers, as is the case primarily with the environmental domain, or economists, for economic issues.

Although they may belong to different disciplines and work in different institutions, they share a number of common features. The latter would include:

> (1) a shared set of normative and principled beliefs, which provide a value-based rationale for the social action of community members; (2) shared causal beliefs, which are derived from their analysis of practices leading or contributing to a central set of problems in their domain and which then serve as the basis for elucidating the multiple linkages between possible policy actions and desired outcomes; (3) shared notions of validity—that is, intersubjective, internally defined criteria for weighing and validating knowledge in the domain of their expertise; and (4) a common policy enterprise—that is, a set of common practices associated with a set of problems to which their professional competence is directed, presumably out of the conviction that human welfare will be enhanced as a consequence.[19]

This grid allows Haas to differentiate other groups of individuals and experts involved in policy-making mechanism. In particular, the 'socialized truth tests and common causal beliefs' would provide the distinctive traits of epistemic communities.[20] These social groups—according to Haas—play an important role 'in shaping patterns of international policy cooperation.'[21] By developing and spreading 'causal ideas and associated normative beliefs', epistemic communities help decision-makers identify their policy options and preferences in any given area for which a particular expertise is required.[22] In this respect, it should be noticed that by bringing up an issue—most of the time of an allegedly technical or scientific character—and by designing an approach to deal with it in order to achieve certain outcomes, epistemic communities shape policies themselves,

[15] See John Ruggie, 'International Responses to Technology: Concepts and Trends', 29 International Organizations 557 (1975).

[16] Haas (n. 13), 'Introduction', 27. [17] Ibid. 3. [18] Ibid., 'Epistemic Communities', 792–3.

[19] Ibid. 792–4; 'Introduction', 3; 'Ideas, Experts, Governance', 29–30.

[20] Ibid., 'Epistemic Communities', 794. [21] Ibid., 'Introduction', 35.

[22] Ibid., 'Epistemic Communities', 792.

as decision-makers and politicians would hardly ever go against what is perceived as 'expert opinion'.

Relevant examples of these epistemic communities would include the so-called 'ecological epistemic community', which is often used as a case study to illustrate the concept.[23] Scientists and experts working within that community help stakeholders and decision-makers shape their policy options and preferred outcomes. The Intergovernmental Panel on Climate Change (ICPP) is often referred to as a paradigmatic example of an epistemic community in the field of environmental protection. The ecological epistemic community, often working with the UN specialized agency UNEP, has been fundamental in the design and implementation of multilateral environmental regimes in the fields of marine pollution, acid rain, stratospheric ozone layer protection, the protection of wetlands, the protection of migratory species, and so on.[24] Occasionally, epistemic communities have failed to fulfil their function and to achieve their goals, as in the case of desertification and whaling.[25]

It would be reductive to limit the illustrations of epistemic communities to the area of environmental protection. Haas identifies other fields in which epistemic communities would be at work, including the European Union, whose multilateral structures and policies are particularly prone to be influenced by them.[26] By definition, epistemic communities share causal beliefs and normative convictions. They create concepts and ideas that are developed and circulated transnationally with a view to shaping patterns of international policy cooperation. Their action appears to be particularly relevant, and their role all the more conspicuous, in policy areas of global concern characterized by complexity and technical uncertainty.

Indeed, scientific uncertainty and complexity appear to be decisive factors (in Haas' view) in explaining the development and the steady consolidation of epistemic communities' role in shaping patterns of international cooperation, particularly through the endorsement of their ideas by powerful countries and international institutions.[27] The social acceptance of and unconditional deference to expert knowledge prompt recourse to epistemic communities' advice by decision-makers. The fact that technical or scientific advice is regarded as 'politically untainted' makes it more likely to work in practice.[28]

This goes hand in hand with contemporary cultural trends that clearly tend to give priority to whatever is perceived to be in conformity with scientific method and technical standards. As noted by others in a different context, there has been a shift from normative to cognitive expectations that has greatly facilitated the emergence of a cultural paradigm based on scientific rationality.[29] To other commentators, the 'transfer of wider

[23] Ibid. 798–802. [24] Ibid. [25] Ibid., 'Ideas, Experts, Governance', 43.
[26] Ibid. 38. [27] Ibid. 35. [28] Ibid. 33.
[29] See Niklas Luhmann, *Social Systems*, trans. John Bednarz Jr. and Dirk Baecker (Stanford University Press, 1995); Andreas Fischer-Lescano and Gunther Teubner, 'Regime-Collisions: The Vain Search for Legal Unity in the Fragmentation of Global Law', 25 Michigan Journal of International Law 999 (2003), 1000: 'In 1971, while theorizing on the concept of world society, Luhmann allowed himself the "speculative hypothesis" that global law would experience a radical fragmentation, not along territorial, but along social sectoral lines. The reason for this would be a transformation from normative (politics, morality,

and wider areas of public policy from politics to expertise' characterizes the history of social progress in the twentieth century.[30] Yet, as aptly noted by Haas, '[d]espite the veneer of objectivity and value neutrality achieved by pointing to the input of scientists, policy choices remain highly political in their allocative consequences.'[31]

The concept of epistemic communities is generally used to explain how certain policy-relevant ideas are selected, and how and by whom they are brought to bear on political behaviour.[32] According to Haas, experts forming epistemic communities are agents of decision-makers.[33] The latter delegate authority to the former in policy areas of which they have no or limited understanding. The agency relationship takes place in a fairly pre-determined setting. States are decision-makers. Epistemic communities are networks made of professionals who provide scientific expertise in complex and highly technical contexts. The fact that its members share causal beliefs and normative commitments, and constitute a fairly cohesive social group, distinguishes epistemic communities from other actors and groups that try to influence policy-making. Haas maintains that whereas epistemic communities operate in the realm of brute and hybrid facts, where science 'reigns', norm entrepreneurs operate in the field of social facts.[34] Ultimately the function of epistemic communities lies in achieving consensual knowledge in any given domain of expertise that is later diffused and used in policy contexts by other actors.

Interestingly, some international relations constructivist scholars had already used the concept of epistemic communities, but—unlike Haas—they did not emphasize the principal-agent dimension. John Ruggie, for example, while describing the collective response by states to new collective situations prompted by science and technology, makes reference to a much broader notion of 'epistemic communities' as 'interrelated roles which grow up around an *episteme*; they delimit, for their members, *the* proper construction of social reality.'[35] Drawing inspiration from Foucault, Ruggie defines '*episteme*' as 'a dominant way of looking at social reality, a set of shared symbols and references, mutual expectations, and a mutual predictability of intention.'[36] While keeping a strict focus on institutionalization, Ruggie holds that by providing a certain vision of reality, epistemic communities 'provide the assumptions from which policies follow and

law) to cognitive expectations (economy, science, technology); a transformation that would be effected during the transition from nationally organized societies to a global society.'

[30] See Harvey Brooks, 'Scientific Concepts and Cultural Change', 9 Daedalus 66 (1965), 71.

[31] Haas (n. 13), 'Introduction', 11 (footnote omitted). Jacqueline Peel, *Science and Risk Regulation in International Law* (CUP, 2013), 77: 'representation of the work of epistemic communities as technical in nature is belied in practice by the intervention of political factors that are often necessary to give scientific assessments broader legitimacy and policy salience.'

[32] See Haas (n. 13), 'Introduction', 4; 'Ideas, Experts, Governance', 20. [33] Ibid. 21.

[34] See ibid. 26. Also see Andy Olson, 'An Empire of the Scholars: Transnational Lawyers and the Rule of Opinio Juris', 29 Perspectives on Political Science 23 (2000): 'In many respects, the community of international lawyers provides a model example of Haas's definition of an epistemic community of elites. This community views itself as a guild of accredited specialists engaged in the formation of society's rules and uniquely qualified to interpret international law.'

[35] Ruggie (n. 15), 570 (emphasis in the original, footnote omitted). [36] Ibid.

shape the pattern of politics in the long run',[37] and, ultimately, the lens through which 'political relationships are visualized'.[38]

Haas denies that international lawyers may constitute an epistemic community on the basis that they would possess neither the consensual knowledge nor the shared normative commitment that characteristically define such social groups.[39] International lawyers would lack also 'the social authority or legitimacy of the technical authority commanded by epistemic communities'.[40] Even in the area of international environmental law, the professional knowledge of lawyers would be 'insufficiently institutionalized to generate common truth tests and a tight sociological network'.[41] Against this background, international environmental lawyers have played a role only in translating into law the ideas elaborated by the ecological epistemic community.

This appears to be a very narrow view of both epistemic communities and international law(yers). Some international law scholars, however, have adhered rather passively to this stance, by accepting that epistemic communities made of scientists and experts, in particular areas such as environmental protection and nuclear non-proliferation, may influence state behaviour.[42] While generally subscribing to the view that international lawyers are not an 'epistemic community', for the reasons expounded by Haas, Werner recognizes that 'it is still possible to form coalitions of like-minded lawyers and influence policy on the basis of knowledge-based claims that go beyond mere advocacy',[43] particularly when international lawyers act as members of Schachter's invisible college of scholars.[44]

International arbitration scholarship seems rather more inclined to conceive of international arbitrators as an epistemic community. This is done in a variety of different ways, though. Some commentators consider only 'arbitrators' as such to be an epistemic community,[45] while others use a wider net and speak of an epistemic community made of all those professionals coming from different disciplines and professional backgrounds, such as 'lawyers, accountants, engineers, contractors, business people etc',[46] who are concerned by this particular practice of dispute settlement.

Nuances are numerous, and sometimes the very understanding of the constitution and operation of epistemic communities differs from one author to another. Dezalay

[37] As defined by Haas (n. 13), 'Introduction', 26. [38] Ruggie (n. 15), 569.

[39] Haas (n. 13), 'Introduction', 19, maintaining that 'members of a given profession or discipline may share a set of causal approaches or orientations and have a consensual knowledge base, [but] they lack the shared normative commitments of members of an epistemic community.' See also Haas (n. 13), 'Epistemic Communities', 802.

[40] Ibid.; Haas (n. 13), 'Ideas, Experts, Governance', 28.

[41] Haas (n. 13), 'Epistemic Communities', 805: International lawyers, however, contribute to disseminating the ideas developed by the ecological epistemic community to states and other international actors.

[42] See Carlo Focarelli, *International Law as Social Construct* (OUP, 2012), 311.

[43] Wouter Werner, 'The Politics of Expertise: Applying Paradoxes of Scientific Expertise to International Law' in Monika Ambrus et al. (eds), *The Role of 'Experts' in International and European Decision-Making Processes: Advisors, Decision Makers or Irrelevant Actors?* (CUP, 2014), 44–62, 60–62.

[44] Oscar Schachter, 'The Invisible College of International Lawyers', 72 Nw U L Rev 217 (1978).

[45] Miles (n. 7), 342. [46] Lynch (n. 6), 95.

and Garth in their seminal work had already characterized international commercial arbitration as 'an epistemic community or issue network organized around certain beliefs in an ideal of international private justice',[47] operating in 'an extremely competitive market involving big business and megalawyering'.[48] Famously described as a small community divided along generational lines, in which a first pioneering group of 'grand old men of arbitration' would later yield control of the field to a new generation of 'technocrats', emphasizing technical skills and specialization, the epistemic community of commercial arbitrators has become a common reference in arbitration scholarship.[49]

More recently, Miles has argued that the fundamental tenets of Dezalay and Garth's thesis hold true also for the community of investment arbitrators.[50] Michaels subscribes to the view that international arbitration in its different components 'fulfils all the criteria traditionally listed for an epistemic community'.[51] For Michaels, the criteria are those provided by Haas, and consist, inter alia, of a shared set of normative and principled beliefs in an ideal of private justice, shared notions of validity, and a common policy enterprise.[52] Likewise, Lynch, with a specific focus on international commercial arbitration, relies on Haas's criteria to emphasize the epistemic community's capacity to influence the international arbitration regime and to direct policy debates, almost invariably favouring certain shared values and enhancing the reputation and prestige of its members, whose expertise 'accorded them access to the political and decision-making authority and served to legitimize their activities'.[53]

24.3 What is it?

To have traced the genealogy of the concept may help us contextualize its original use. I do not believe, however, that this should constrain our ability to define it and make use of it differently. After all, concepts are tools for understanding, and their contours and scope of application may be adjusted to different methods of inquiry and areas of investigation.

I take the concept of '*episteme*' to refer to the 'knowledge' we have of a given field, to the way in which we come to apprehend it theoretically, to use it practically and to explain its operation. In other words, I mean to refer to the set of collective shared beliefs and presuppositions that characterize the field of international arbitration, understood both as a scientific field of theoretical inquiry and as a practice. The ensemble of the actors involved in the dynamic processes whereby our knowledge of international arbitration—i.e. the understanding of what international arbitration is and how it works—is formed and shaped can be properly qualified as an 'epistemic community'. Having thus laid down the basic concept, several qualifications are now in order.

[47] Dezalay and Garth (n. 10), 16. [48] Ibid. 16. [49] Ibid. 34–7.
[50] Miles (n. 7), 342. [51] Michaels (n. 8), 21. [52] Ibid. 52–3. [53] Lynch (n. 6), 95.

First, it should be noticed that the above sketching out of the concept seems oblivious to the philosophical debate underlying the distinctions (to name just a few) between *episteme* on the one hand and *doxa* or *techne* on the other.[54] While traditionally, episteme is contrasted to doxa—understood as opinion or common belief—and to techne—referred to as craft or practice—to me the very notion of episteme tends to include also aspects of the latter terms. I personally do not attribute to the term 'episteme' the connotation of some sort of scientific knowledge or truth claim as opposed to some inferior social beliefs or collective representation of reality that would not be founded on any reliable theoretical framework. I tend to look at episteme as a set of beliefs and presuppositions collectively shared that inform the way in which we understand reality. In some sense, therefore, the dialectics between episteme and doxa do not allow representing the two as juxtaposed concepts.

Along similar lines, I believe that techne—that I take to mean craft or the practical capacity to do things—is also based on some episteme of sorts, as the 'how to do' part of any craft necessarily presupposes a form of acquisition of knowledge and the interiorization of intellectual schemata. In many ways, the latter distinction is reminiscent of the distinction between theory and practice that characterizes many debates in practically all disciplines and branches of knowledge. Be that as it may, I believe that both the theoretical discourse on law and the social practice of law presuppose an episteme and, therefore, an epistemic community that shapes the discourse and sets the boundaries for what is accepted and/or acceptable in the scholarly discourse and in the practice of international arbitration.[55]

Another important aspect is that the concept of epistemic community is a modular one and allows for different degrees of generality. One may think of the complex and broad epistemic community that shapes international arbitration. In turn, one can also think of distinct epistemic communities that constitute the episteme of international arbitration as an academic discipline or a professional practice. Moreover, several epistemic communities can be thought to exist that exercise an influence in the various areas of international arbitration and that are subject-matter-specific. One can have an epistemic commercial arbitration or investment arbitration community.[56] One could look only at arbitrators in both commercial and investment arbitrations—or, rather, include also all the other actors that are involved in or concerned by the process, such as law firms and individual counsel, business entities, academics dealing specifically with such issues. One can also break down the epistemic community of (let's say) international investment

[54] For a cursory and yet accurate overview of the debate, see Richard Parry, 'Episteme and Techne', in *The Stanford Encyclopaedia of Philosophy* (Stanford University, 2014) at: <http://plato.stanford.edu/archives/fall2014/entries/episteme-techne>. See also Anthony Preus, *Historical Dictionary of Ancient Greek Philosophy*, 2nd edn (Rowman & Littlefield, 2015), 138 (doxa); 150–151 (episteme); 380–381 (techne).

[55] On the distinction between law as theoretical discourse and social phenomenon, see Andrea Bianchi, 'Reflexive Butterfly Catching: Insights from a Situated Catcher', in Joost Pauwelyn et al. (eds), *Informal International Lawmaking* (OUP, 2012), 200.

[56] See e.g. Miles (n. 7), 342–3.

arbitrators, and distinguish between those who come to it from a public international law or commercial law background.[57]

Several epistemic communities can be at work at the same time. I am using the concept of modularity precisely in this sense. Modularity, in and of itself, is a concept that travels across disciplines, taking up different connotations.[58] Generally, the notion of modularity has to do with the way in which the components of a system assemble or separate out. In complex networks theory, however, modularity helps determine the existence of community structures and clusters, including connections between them.[59] Recourse to algorithms for finding community structures in scattered clusters of different networks goes well beyond the capacity of this writer! Arguably, it is not even necessary to reconstruct with precision the exact contours and the membership of the different epistemic communities operating in international law for the purpose of this enquiry. No such abstract mapping could do justice to the varying coming together of such communities, and to their constant shifting. What matters is to be aware of their existence with a view to identifying their approximate composition, the mechanisms of social interaction (both internal and external), and their strategies and goals.

Although the aesthetics of law tends to favor 'impersonal *personae*' such as the state, the court, the judge, the lawmaker and similar, the concept of epistemic communities should help us think of all those immaterial entities in terms of individual human beings and social groups. These are communities of individuals that tend to behave as collectives. The interplay between the individual and the collective dimension is fundamental to understanding the dynamics of epistemic communities. Even if some individual members may come to acquire a prominent position, it is by way of interaction amongst the members of the group that the episteme of the field is produced. The vision of the world propounded by an epistemic community is invariably an 'inter-subjective enterprise'.[60]

The way in which I have spoken so far of 'epistemic communities' and the considerations I have just expressed bear a resemblance—although they are not really analogous—to two concepts expounded upon by Foucault. The first one is the concept of *discourse*.[61] One of the most often used and yet highly heterogeneous concepts ever used by the

[57] Incidentally, this distinction is frequently used in international arbitration scholarship to describe the different cultures and mindsets that arbitrators coming from either background carry with them in their work. See Roberts (n. 5).

[58] Just to provide an example in different areas of knowledge, see Gerhard Schlosser and Günter Wagner (eds), *Modularity in Development and Evolution* (University of Chicago Press, 2004); Peter Carruthers and Andrew Chamberlain (eds), *Evolution and the Human Mind: Modularity, Language and Meta-Cognition* (CUP, 2000); Jerry Fodor, *The Modularity of Mind* (MIT Press, 1983).

[59] 'Intuitively, community is a cohesive group of nodes that are connected "more densely" to each other than other nodes in other communities.' See Mason Porter, Jukka-Pakka Onnela, and Peter Mucha, 'Communities in Networks', 56 Notices of the Amer. Math Soc. 1082 (2009), 1086.

[60] In the same sense, although in relation to 'interpretive communities', see Ian Johnstone, 'The Power of Interpretive Communities', in Michael Barnett and Raymond Duvall (eds), *Power in Global Governance* (CUP, 2004), 185.

[61] See esp. Michel Foucault, 'The Order of Discourse', in R. Young (ed.), *Untying the Text: A Post-Structuralist Reader* (Routledge, 1981), 48; *The Archaeology of Knowledge*, trans. A. M. Sheridan Smith (Routledge, 2002).

French philosopher, 'discourse'—unlike its English semantic connotation—is more taken up with such notions as institutions, practices, and ultimately power. Discourse is what causes certain practices and procedures to stay in circulation and others to be excluded. It is about unwritten rules and structures that produce particular utterances and statements that, in turn, generate patterns of practice. Discursive policies, elaborated by social groups of professionals and grounded in power structures, shape what we mean by international arbitration, and set the boundaries of what is or is not a permissible argument within the field, be it the discipline or the social practice of international arbitration.[62]

The second relevant concept is that of episteme, elaborated particularly in the *Archaeology of Knowledge* and in *The Order of Things*.[63] As is well known, Foucault refers to episteme as the 'epistemological unconscious' of a given era:[64] the set of presuppositions and historical conditions that make knowledge possible at any given time and that determine the very boundaries of what is considered as knowledge. Episteme is not a grand theory of sorts that explains the underlying structure of reality. It concerns ways of thinking that inform an epoch and regroup different ensembles of discourses that are in circulation at a given time. In that respect, the concept of episteme is much wider in scope than that of discourse.[65] The role played by 'resemblance' until the end of the sixteenth century,[66] or by what Foucault calls the 'will to know' in the nineteenth century,[67] are apt examples of an episteme of a particular period. One might venture to speculate that 'expertise', or 'rationality', could qualify as a contemporary episteme of sorts. The episteme is so entrenched that most of the time it is invisible to those who move within its boundaries. The latter remark clearly applies also to the episteme created by the epistemic communities that are at work in international arbitration.

As is often the case, different perspectives on similar phenomena can be disconcertingly close to one another if only one is ready to compare the uncomparable. The above concepts echo Thomas Kuhn's concept of paradigms, used to describe the set of beliefs, assumptions, practices, and procedures that characterize the structure of a scientific discipline and, in many ways, 'normal science'.[68] The importance of paradigms in any given

[62] '[I]n every society the production of discourse is at once controlled, selected, organised and redistributed by a certain number of procedures' (see Foucault (n. 61), 'The Order of Discourse', 52), and one of the 'procedures for controlling and delimiting discourse' (p. 56) is precisely the culture of discipline (p. 61).

[63] See Foucault (n. 61), 'The Archaeology of Knowledge', 21; and *The Order of Things: an Archaeology of the Human Sciences* (Routledge, 2002).

[64] See the Preface in Foucault (n. 63), xxiii–xxiv.

[65] Gary Wickham, 'Foucault and Law', in Reza Banakar and Max Travers (eds), *Law and Social Theory*, 2nd edn (OUP, 2013), 217, 225: 'The simplest way to understand this notion—and this is simple without being simplistic— is to think of an episteme as a large, loose collection of discourses built over time and space. Epistemes are not in any way determinate of discourses, rather the term is used by Foucault to allow us to occasionally consider the vaguely co-ordinated (co-ordinated without a co-ordinator, of course) operation of discourses over certain time periods and certain spaces.'

[66] Foucault (n. 63), 19. [67] See Foucault (n. 61), 'The Order of Discourse', 55.

[68] The paradigm provides all the relevant players 'with the rules of the game, describes the pieces with which it must be played, and indicates the nature of the required outcome'. See Thomas Kuhn, 'The Function of Dogma in Scientific Research', in Alistair C. Crombie (ed.), *Scientific Change: Historical Studies*

discipline can hardly be underestimated, as they are the tools by which reality is constructed.

The way in which questions are asked, data is interpreted, and solutions given provides a discipline with its own identity. To know and to share the paradigms of any scientific community is the determinant factor to accept new members of the community. Understandably, the latter will tend to reproduce the research tradition and methods that have favoured their co-optation within the group and that legitimize their standing and power in the scientific community to which they belong.

Setting aside the other interesting aspects for which Kuhn's work has acquired prominence and recognition, particularly the notion of 'paradigm shift' and 'scientific revolution', it seems to me that two elements of his work are worth underlining for the purpose of this chapter.[69] The first is that Kuhn's theses are not confined to the realms of exact sciences but, in his own words, 'are undoubtedly of wide applicability'.[70] Furthermore, in his 1969 Postscript, Kuhn makes a more general point about the need to study 'the special characteristics of the groups that create and use' scientific knowledge that 'like language, is intrinsically the common property of a group or else nothing at all'.[71] Amongst the questions that Kuhn maintains ought to be raised and investigated in relation to any scientific community, one could mention the following:

> How does one elect and how is one elected to membership in a particular community, scientific or not? What is the process and what are the stages of socialization to the group? What does the group collectively see as its goals; what deviations, individual or collective, will it tolerate; and how does it control the impermissible aberration?[72]

It can hardly be denied that a similar line of inquiry should be followed to find out more about the social groups that I characterize as 'epistemic communities' operating in the field of international arbitration.

24.4 What is it not?

Sometimes concepts whose exact contours are difficult to understand can be better apprehended by way of negative definition. By understanding what a concept is not, one hopefully sharpens the focus on what the concept actually is. This reasoning is slightly reminiscent of Derrida's notion of *différance*. The reader may rest reassured. I am not

in the Intellectual, Social and Technical Conditions for Scientific Discovery and Technical Invention, from Antiquity to the Present (Heinemann, 1963), 362. See also Thomas Kuhn, *The Structure of Scientific Revolutions*, 3rd edn (University of Chicago Press, 1996), 113: 'a paradigm is prerequisite to perception itself. What a man sees depends both upon what he looks at and also upon what his previous visual-conceptual experience has taught him to see.'

[69] See, generally, Kuhn (n. 68). [70] Ibid. 208. [71] Ibid. 210. [72] Ibid. 209.

going to venture into a complicated lucubration about the production of textual meaning, or the relationship between signifier and signified. In fact, the reference to Derrida's concept of *différance* is only a playful way to convey a fundamental intuition, namely that the meaning of an expression is better grasped by referring to other words or terms from which the expression itself differs.[73]

Certainly, the concept of 'interpretive communities',[74] which has now acquired common currency in international arbitration scholarship, is the most suitable example of a notion that presents some proximity to that of 'epistemic communities'. So much so that some authors use both expressions interchangeably to connote the role (and power) of distinct social groups in the process of legal interpretation.[75] As is well known, literary critic Stanley Fish developed the notion of 'interpretive community' in connection with literary studies, to explain the question of the source of interpretive authority.[76] The meaning of a text, rather than being determined by the text itself via some intrinsic characteristics of the latter, or by the reader, is determined by the 'cultural assumptions' of an interpretive community in which both are situated. Fish describes an interpretive community as:

> not so much a group of individuals who shared a point of view, but a point of view or way of organizing experience that shared individuals in the sense that its assumed distinctions, categories of understanding, and stipulations of relevance and irrelevance were the content of the consciousness of community members who were therefore no longer individuals, but, insofar as they were embedded in the community's enterprise, community property. It followed that such community-constituted interpreters would, in their turn, constitute, more or less in agreement, the same text, although the sameness would not be attributable to the self-identity of the text, but to the communal nature of the interpretive act.[77]

The concept has been highly controversial and has given rise to heated debate in legal scholarship. It suffices to remember the use of the concept by Owen Fiss in the context of domestic judicial interpretation.[78] In international law, it has been introduced only recently, and it has been primarily used to explain the interaction of different actors in the

[73] See Jacques Derrida's essay on 'Différance', published in English as *Margins of Philosophy*, trans. Alan Bass (University of Chicago Press, 1982), 3. On 'Différance', see David Wood and Robert Bernasconi, *Derrida and Différance* (Northwestern University Press, 1988).

[74] On the concept of 'interpretive communities', see Stanley Fish, *Is There a Text in This Class? The Authority of Interpretive Communities* (Harvard University Press, 1980); *Doing What Comes Naturally: Change, Rhetoric, and the Practice of Theory in Literary and Legal Studies* (Duke University Press, 1989).

[75] See Michael Waibel, 'Demistifying the Art of Interpretation', 22 Europ. J Int'l L 571 (2011).

[76] See Fish, *Doing What Comes Naturally* (n. 74), 141.

[77] Ibid.

[78] See Owen Fiss, 'Objectivity and Interpretation', 34 Stan L Rev 739 (1982); 'Conventionalism', 58 S Cal L Rev 177 (1985), for whom the authority of the interpretive community of domestic judges is external to the process of interpretation and derives from the authority vested in them by the legal system, or, to use Fiss' words, 'by virtue of their office' (p. 746). As regards interpretation, Fiss argues that a 'bounded objectivity', whereby 'disciplining rules' agreed upon and recognized as authoritative by an interpretive community, is possible. See, conversely, Stanley Fish, 'Fish v Fiss', 36 Stan L Rev 1325 (1985).

field of treaty interpretation and, more generally, to account for the activity of interpretation in international law.[79] According to Ian Johnston, interpretive communities 'emerge from discursive interaction in the international legal system, and they help to define the rules and norms that become embedded in institutions'.[80] They 'set the parameters of acceptable argumentation—the terms in which positions are explained, defended and justified to others in what is fundamentally an intersubjective enterprise'.[81] Simply put, interpretive communities direct what can legitimately be said about (international) law.

On an approach to interpretation where meaning is presented as primarily a social construct,[82] which is produced by a complex web of social relations, including the context, the conventional use of words in any given society—as well as the cognitive frames that influence perception and determine outcomes, the role of interpretive communities, and the strategies deployed by them to attribute meaning—is crucial. The lack of consensus on 'categories of understanding' within an interpretive community may have dire consequences. As I have argued elsewhere, the absence of consensus in the interpretive community in charge of shaping the contours of the regulation of the use of force is the most plausible explanation for the current uncertainty about such an important international legal regime.[83]

The notion of 'communities of practice' could also be considered to be akin to—yet different from—that of epistemic communities. While the notion of 'communities of practice' is traced back to social learning theorists and international relations constructivists,[84] it has recently been used by Jutta Brunnée and Stephen Toope to account for the formation of shared understandings that constitute the underpinnings of international law.[85] The central idea is that '[p]eople's understandings of the world, and of themselves, are produced and reproduced through continuous interactions and negotiation of meaning.'[86] This is the reason why, and the process whereby, shared understandings come to underpin the international legal system.

[79] See Ian Johnstone, 'Treaty Interpretation: The Authority of Interpretive Communities', 12 Mich J Int'l L 371 (1991); Johnstone (n. 60), 185; Detlev Vagts, 'Treaty Interpretation and the New American Ways of Law Reading', 4 Eur J Int'l L 472 (1993); Michael Waibel, 'Interpretive Communities in International Law', in Andrea Bianchi, Daniel Peat, and Matthew Windsor (eds), *Interpretation in International Law* (OUP, 2015), 147.

[80] Johnstone (n. 60), 186. [81] Ibid.

[82] I made this point in 'Textual Interpretation and (International) Law Reading: The Myth of (In) determinacy and the Genealogy of Meaning', in Pieter Bekker, Rudolf Dolzer, and Michael Waibel (eds), *Making International Law Work in the Global Economy: Essays in Honour of Detlev Vagts* (CUP, 2010), 54.

[83] Bianchi, (n. 3).

[84] See Jean Lave and Etienne Wenger, *Situated Learning: Legitimate Peripheral Participation* (CUP, 1991); Etienne Wenger, *Communities of Practice: Learning, Meaning, and Identity* (CUP, 1998); Emanuel Adler, *Communitarian International Relations: The Epistemic Foundations of International Relations* (Routledge, 2005).

[85] Jutta Brunnée and Stephen Toope, *Legitimacy and Legality in International Law: An Interactional Account* (CUP, 2010).

[86] Ibid. 62.

The production and maintenance of collective meanings and understandings can only take place in the practice of a community. The accent on social communication and the constitutive power of its members to shape collective beliefs and understandings for the community differs from the agency-centred analysis of Haas's epistemic communities, although it may be thought to spring from a similar strand of constructivist scholarship in international relations. Once they are established, such collective understandings formed through social interaction become 'background knowledge' and 'structure' to the community that, in turn, shape the perception of the world of its members and the way in which they act, evaluate other groups' worldviews, and set their priorities.[87]

Even Bruno Latour's identification of 'modes of existence' that spell out social life in its countless forms can be deemed to be a similar way of looking at reality.[88] The way in which actors assemble in networks and generate continuous relationships and interactions that sustain themselves has proved a very interesting area of study to all of those who are interested in examining the dynamics of societal relations in whatever context they may take place. Although, initially, his work addressed the world of sciences, in particular the analysis of neuroendocrinology in *Laboratory Life*,[89] later Bruno Latour came to be known also by legal scholars for his ethnographical study on the French *Conseil d'État*, aptly titled in the original French *La fabrique du droit*,[90] and later translated into English as *The Making of Law*.[91] The description of how the law comes to life in this particular social network, the importance of the files and the transformations they go through in different phases before eventually producing law, are powerful illustrations of how the law is a distinct 'way of being'.

Although I would not go as far as Derrida in holding that 'the signified concept'—in our case the concept of epistemic communities—'is never present in and of itself',[92] I would nonetheless accept that deferral to other concepts such as those we have explored in this section help us to have a firmer grip on the rather slippery concept of epistemic communities. At the same time, it is hard to resist the temptation of thinking of the relationship between the signifier and the signified as one without a centre of gravity, with no fixed structure. To think that the meaning of 'epistemic communities', like any other meaning, is situational and contingent, shaped by distinctions and negations, is an attempt at shaking up the somewhat simplistic certainty that the lawyerly world invariably affects when it comes to interpretation and to definitions.

87 Ibid. 64–5.

88 See Bruno Latour, *Enquête sur les modes d'existence. Une anthropologie des modernes* (La Découverte, 2012). For an introduction to Latour's work, see Frédéric Audren and Cédric Moreau de Bellaing, 'Bruno Latour's Legal Anthropology', in Banakar and Travers (n. 65), 181.

89 Bruno Latour and Steve Woolgar, *Laboratory Life: The Social Construction of Scientific Facts* (Princeton University Press, 1979).

90 Bruno Latour, *La fabrique du droit. Une ethnographie du Conseil d'État* (La Découverte, 2002).

91 Bruno Latour, *The Making of Law: An Ethnography of the* Conseil d'État, trans. Marina Brilman and Alain Pottage (Polity Press, 2002).

92 Derrida (n. 73), 11.

24.5 What is it for?

At this juncture it might be worth asking what exactly are the functions that epistemic communities perform, and what interest there is for international arbitration lawyers to understand what such communities are made of and how they work. First and foremost, epistemic communities fix the terms of the discourse and shape the way in which we look at international arbitration. A good illustration is provided by the widely held view that arbitration is based on party autonomy and consent.[93] It suffices to look at the majority of international arbitration books or—even better—to ask any international arbitration student to realize how the conviction that arbitration rests on the consent of the parties has become entrenched.[94] This is what most people in legal education first, and later in the practice of international arbitration, have been trained to believe. In fact, the idea that arbitration is purely based on consent is increasingly called into question, and may be a fairly simplistic view to hold in the contemporary world of national and international arbitration.[95] And yet no one would even dream of penalizing a student for saying that arbitration's main feature is that it is based on the consent of the parties. The fundamental role of consent is indeed a good illustration of the general epistemic community of international arbitration producing an intellectual construct that is now part and parcel of the collective imagery of international arbitration lawyers.

Epistemic communities produce a worldview that determines the visual parameters by which we relate to that particular world.[96] They tend to be insular if not completely self-referential, and they often ignore what is going on in other areas, as they tend to believe 'that the only meaningful practice or the very core business of international law is their own specialization'.[97] They are carriers of 'distinct normative visions' that they advocate more or less overtly in order to gain or consolidate control of any given field,[98] be it the whole of international law or one of the substantive areas in which they operate.

[93] Bernard Hanotiau, 'Consent to Arbitration: Do We Share a Common View?', 27 Arbitration International 539 (2011): 'Consent has always been presented as a kind of dogma, the foundation of any arbitration.'

[94] For an overview, see Andrea Steingruber, *Consent in International Arbitration* (OUP, 2012); Christoph Schreuer, 'Consent to Arbitration', in Peter Muchlinsky, Federico Ortino, and Christoph Schreuer (eds), *The Oxford Handbook of International Investment Law* (OUP, 2008), 831.

[95] See Margaret Moses, 'Challenges for the Future: The Diminishing Role of Consent in Arbitration', 4 Y.B. Int'l Arb. 19 (2015). See also Jan Paulsson, 'Arbitration Without Privity', 10 ICSID Review 232 (1995), and, with a more domestic law focus, Jeffrey Stempel, 'Bootstrapping and Slouching Toward Gomorrah: Arbitral Infatuation and the Decline of Consent', 62 Brooklyn Law Review 1381 (1996).

[96] Lynch (n. 6), 97. The worldview is contingent and may vary over time: see Stephan Schill, 'W(h)ither Fragmentation? On the Literature and Sociology of International Investment Law', 22 European Journal of International Law (2011), 875.

[97] Andrea Bianchi, 'Gazing at the Crystal Ball (Again): State Immunity and *Jus Cogens* Beyond *Germany v Italy*', 4 Journal of Int'l Dispute Settlement 457 (2013), 464.

[98] The expression is used with reference to 'interpretive communities' by Waibel (n. 79), 160.

Such communities also produce distinct cultures.[99] Moshe Hirsch analyses, from a sociological perspective, the relationship between international investment law and human rights law to observe that the two communities have different heritages and narratives, with members of each community holding 'different views regarding the role of law and tribunals'.[100]

The fact that international arbitration specialists may bring with them their own cultural background, institutional bias, and professional mindset is hardly surprising, although their collective interaction eventually determines the emergence of prevailing 'paradigms' that may have an influence on the very understanding and functioning of the international arbitration regime.[101] With specific regard to international investment arbitration, the divide between arbitrators who come from different legal backgrounds (commercial law, trade law, public law, and public international law) could be put forward as an example of contending epistemic communities.[102] This may have a bearing on how individual arbitrators or arbitral tribunals develop their arguments and select their sources of authority.[103] For example, public international lawyers tend to intersperse their arguments with frequent references to the case law of the International Court of Justice.[104] Likewise, in the *Continental* case, the presidency of the tribunal by a member of the WTO Appellate Body was probably a cause for the tribunal to make extensive reference to the practice of interpretation of Art. XX of the GATT 1947, in particular as regards the test of necessity to establish whether the measures taken by Argentina were necessary to preserve public order and to protect essential security interests of the country.[105]

The arbitrators' background is hardly a matter of style and argumentation techniques. In fact, it may be a determinant for the perception and treatment of legal issues as

[99] On the concept of legal culture, see David Nelken, 'Using the Concept of Legal Culture', 29 Australian Journal of Legal Philosophy 1 (2004).

[100] Moshe Hirsch, 'The Interaction between International Investment Law and Human Rights Treaties: A Sociological Perspective', in Yuval Shany et al. (eds), *Multi-Sourced Equivalent Norms* (Hart, 2001), 222.

[101] Roberts (n. 5), 49.

[102] Ibid. 45. This is by no means peculiar to the field of international arbitration. Just as well: the competing visions of the 'three tribes'—criminal lawyers, human rights lawyers, and international lawyers—engaged in the shaping of the discourse in international criminal law may be seen as instances of a fragmented episteme leading to a different perception of the very same legal issues (Andrew Clapham, 'Concluding Remarks: Three Tribes in the Future of International Criminal Law', 9 J Int'l Criminal Justice 689 (2011)).

[103] Schill (n. 96), 889.

[104] See *ICS Inspection Control Services Limited (United Kingdom) v The Republic of Argentina*, Award, UNCITRAL, PCA Case No. 2010-9 (2012) (Members of the Tribunal: P.-M. Dupuy, President; S. Torres Bernárdez, Arbitrator; M. Lalonde, Arbitrator); *Garanti Koza LLP v Turkmenistan*, Decision on the Objection to Jurisdiction for Lack of Consent, ICSIID Case No. ARB/11/20 (2013) (Laurence Boisson de Chazournes' Statement of Dissent); *Venezuela US, S.R.L. (Barbados) v Bolivarian Republic of Venezuela*, Award, PCA Case No. 2013-34 (2016) (Marcelo Kohen's Statement of Dissent).

[105] See *Continental Casualty Company (Claimant) and The Argentine Republic (Respondent)*, Award, ICSID Case No. ARB/03/09 (2008) (Members of the Tribunal: Giorgio Sacerdoti, President; †V V Veeder, Arbitrator; Michelle Nader, Arbitrator), para. 192.

important as the notion of jurisdiction. Classical international lawyers tend to look at international jurisdiction as something exceptional based on clearly expressed state consent. In the *Daimler* arbitration, the fact that the President of the tribunal was a public international lawyer most likely caused the tribunal to place a particular emphasis on the need not to presume but to establish consent to the tribunal's jurisdiction.[106] Other tribunals made up of and/or chaired by professionals other than international lawyers are less rigorous in establishing state consent as the indispensable requisite for the exercise of jurisdiction. In the *Planet Mining* case, for instance, the Tribunal departed from the position taken by other arbitral tribunals 'that the expression of consent to ICSID arbitration must be clear and unambiguous', or that consent must be proven through 'affirmative evidence'.[107] Hence, the Tribunal decided to 'assess consent pursuant to the general rules on treaty interpretation'. The tribunal held that '[e]xcept for calling for a writing, the ICSID Convention contains no particular requirement of clarity or otherwise'.[108] Along similar lines, international lawyers are generally opposed to using the MFN clause to establish or expand jurisdiction,[109] whereas others see no obstacle to doing so.[110]

The fact that some arbitrators come from a public international law background may make them particularly sensitive to states' interests, and as such states may appoint them more often than others in investment arbitration proceedings. Conversely, commercial or corporate lawyers are more likely to favor private investors over their state counterparts. This is not due to any particular ideological bias, but rather to the professional 'mindset' that each category of lawyers inevitably carries with it. To someone who has been trained to think of states as the alpha and omega of the international legal system, it would seem natural to accord a somewhat privileged position to them, as opposed to

[106] *Daimler Financial Services AG (Claimant) v Argentine Republic (Respondent)*, Award, ICSID Case No. ARB/05/01 (2012) (Members of the Tribunal: Pierre-Marie Dupuy, President; Charles N. Brower, Arbitrator; Domingo Bello Janeiro, Arbitrator), para. 175: '[I]t is not possible to presume that consent has been given by a state. Rather, the existence of consent must be established. This may be accomplished either through an express declaration of consent to an international tribunal's jurisdiction or on the basis of acts "conclusively establishing" such consent… Non-consent is the default rule; consent is the exception. Establishing consent therefore requires affirmative evidence. But the impossibility of basing a state's consent on a mere presumption should not be taken as a "strict" or "restrictive" approach in terms of interpretation of dispute resolution clauses. It is simply the result of respect for the rule according to which state consent is the incontrovertible requisite for any kind of international settlement procedure.'

[107] *Planet Mining Pty Ltd v Republic of Indonesia*, Decision on Jurisdiction, ICSID Case No. ARB/12/24 and 12/40 (2014) (Members of the Tribunal: G. Kaufmann-Kohler, President; M. Hwang, Arbitrator; A. J. van den Berg, Arbitrator), para. 146.

[108] Ibid.

[109] See *ICS Inspection Control Services Limited (United Kingdom) v The Republic of Argentina*, Award, UNCITRAL, PCA Case No. 2010–9 (2012), para. 274–317; *Impreglio SpA v Argentina*, Award, ICSID Case No. ARB/07/17 (2011) (Brigitte Stern's Concurring and Dissenting Opinion).

[110] See *National Grid plc v The Argentine Republic*, Decision on Jurisdiction, UNCITRAL (2006) (Members of the Tribunal: A. Rigo Sureda, President; E. Whitney Debevoise, Arbitrator; A. Garro, Arbitrator), para. 79–93; *Daimler Financial Services AG (Claimant) v Argentine Republic (Respondent)*, Award, ICSID Case No. ARB/05/01 (2012) (Charles N. Brower's Dissenting Opinion).

private entities. Likewise, to those lawyers who have spent their careers dealing with private parties whose rights and liabilities are equal before the law, it would appear odd indeed to presuppose some sort of ontological priority of one party over the other.[111] Ask anyone in the business of international investment arbitration, and they will know exactly who amongst arbitrators enjoys the reputation of being state-friendly or investor-friendly.

Yet another example in which the arbitrators' background may dictate a different approach to the very same legal issue is the attitude of commercial lawyers and public international lawyers, respectively, vis-à-vis the object and purpose test in treaty interpretation. Whereas the former tend to identify the object and purpose of investment treaties with the promotion and protection of investments, the latter are more prone to weigh the different interests involved, particularly the legitimate interest of the host state. Apt illustrations of such different approaches might be the *SGS* case and the *El Paso* case, respectively, where two ICSID tribunals analyse in fairly different terms the object and purpose of the investment treaty underlying the dispute.[112]

In *SGS* the tribunal adopts an effective interpretation of the relevant treaty provision, emphasizing that the object and purpose of the BIT is to promote and reciprocally protect investments.[113] In *El Paso* the tribunal puts forward the need to provide 'a balanced interpretation' of the BIT in which the private interests of foreign investors are weighed against state sovereignty and the host state's interests.[114] Also Georges Abi Saab's dissenting opinion in *Abaclat* well epitomizes the reluctance of public international lawyers to yield to the view that the object and purpose of an investment treaty can only be that of providing a maximum protection to the investment.[115]

[111] Thomas Wälde, 'Equality of Arms in Investment Arbitration: Procedural Challenges', in Katia Yannaca-Small (ed.), *Arbitration under International Investment Agreements: A Guide to the Key Issues* (OUP, 2010), 161.

[112] See *SGS Société Générale de Surveillance S.A. v Republic of the Philippines*, Decision of the Tribunal on Objections to Jurisdiction, ICSID Case No. ARB/02/6 (2004) (Members of the Tribunal: A. S. El-Kosheri, President; J. Crawford, Arbitrator; A. Crivellaro, Arbitrator); *El Paso Energy International Company v The Argentine Republic*, Decision on Jurisdiction, ICSID Case No ARB/03/15 (2006) (Members of the Tribunal: L. Caflisch, President; B. Stern, Arbitrator; P. Bernardini, Arbitrator).

[113] *SGS* (n. 112), para. 116: 'The object and purpose of the BIT supports an effective interpretation of Article X(2). The BIT is a treaty for the promotion and reciprocal protection of investments. According to the preamble it is intended "to create and maintain favourable conditions for investments by investors of one Contracting Party in the territory of the other". It is legitimate to resolve uncertainties in its interpretation so as to favour the protection of covered investments.'

[114] *El Paso* (n. 112), para. 70: 'This tribunal considers that a balanced interpretation is needed, taking into account both State sovereignty and the State's responsibility to create an adapted and evolutionary framework for the development of economic activities, and the necessity to protect foreign investment and its continuous flow.'

[115] *Abaclat and others v Argentina*, Decision on Jurisdiction and Admissibility, ICSID Case No. ARB/07/5 (2011) (Members of the Tribunal: P. Tercier, President; G. Abi-Saab, Arbitrator; A. J. van den Berg, Arbitrator) (Abi-Saab's Dissenting Opinion), para. 272: 'Finally, the third policy consideration is a cautionary one. It is to caution against the tendency of certain ICSID tribunals to consider any limitation on their jurisdiction—whether inherent in the adjudicative function or carefully negotiated and stipulated in the ICSID Convention or the BITs, to protect the legitimate interests of State parties—as an obstacle

A focus on epistemic communities—that is, social groups of professionals and academics that shape the discursive policies of international arbitration—should not be taken as merely an exercise in some sort of sociological enquiry about membership in the group. Although the latter is a good starting point to understanding the nature of the enterprise, what matters most is to analyse the processes whereby such policies are produced, the strategies deployed, and, more generally, how these communities are structured and how they function. Opening up the social life of these communities makes it possible to better understand how law as a social field or as a 'form of life' operates.[116]

Knowledge is produced and put to use in practice by epistemic communities. This process could be the object of a multi-faceted inquiry that aims to unveil what theoretical and intellectual frameworks, what techniques, methodological tools, and both express and unsaid presuppositions are used within the field, and the way in which they are represented to the outside world. The way in which international arbitration is thought of and practised is pretty much the making of epistemic communities that shape our knowledge of international arbitration at the theoretical and practical level. To conceive of international arbitration as some sort of 'internationalized judicial review'[117]—or at least as a process inspired and governed by public law models,[118] to which public law principles such as transparency, proportionality, and standards of review may apply—is not the same as conceiving of it as merely a confidential dispute settlement mechanism, geared towards protecting private interests, party autonomy, legitimate expectations, and equality of arms.[119]

Ultimately, epistemic communities are also in charge of the social identity of the discipline and the profession.[120] They discharge important communal functions insofar as they represent shared beliefs and interests. By putting forward a common vision of the world, epistemic communities shape the perception of social agents and determine the fundamental tenets of the discourse. If, nowadays, there seem to be different views about what functions international arbitration actually performs and how it works, this is due to the decreasing homogeneity of the episteme that no longer allows representing the

in the way of achieving the object and purpose of these treaties, which they interpret as being exclusively to afford maximum protection to investment, notwithstanding the legitimate interests of the host State.'

[116] Law is also a form of social knowledge in the sense expounded by Charles Camic, Neil Gross, and Michèle Lamont (eds), *Social Knowledge in the Making* (University of Chicago Press, 2011). See their definition of social knowledge at p. 3.

[117] Roberts (n. 5), 47.

[118] As is well known, public law approaches to international investment law have recently gained momentum. For an overview see: Schill (n. 96). See also Gus van Harten, *Investment Treaty Arbitration and Public Law* (OUP, 2007); David Schniederman, *Constitutionalizing Economic Globalization: Investment Rules and Democracy's Promise* (CUP, 2008); Santiago Montt, *State Liability in Investment Treaty Arbitration: Global Constitutional and Administrative Law in the BIT Generation* (Hart, 2012).

[119] Ibid. 48.

[120] See Jean d'Aspremont, 'Wording in International Law', 25 Leiden J Int'l L 577 (2012).

discipline and the practice of international arbitration to be a unitary phenomenon.[121] This plurality of visions quite obviously entails a struggle between different social groups that attempt to impose their own view as the most authoritative and legitimate one.[122] To determine who is entitled to speak authoritatively about international arbitration is certainly a stake that most members of the different epistemic communities at play would consider worth fighting for.[123]

24.6 Why all these questions?

At this point the reader might legitimately ask why it is that all the section titles of this chapter are formulated as questions. In fact, one could reasonably expect that it is precisely the task of books such as this to provide answers and not to raise questions. Yet asking (good) questions is the primary vocation of theoretical studies, and arguably, one of the most useful reflexes to spur reflexivity in the field.[124] Particularly in a field where practitioners most of the time are also those who write about international arbitration, 'conflicts between academic analysis, political appraisal, professional interests, and arbitral independence are undoubtedly numerous'.[125] This may be prejudicial to independent academic inquiry and represent a major obstacle to reflexive analysis.

In a similar vein, Anthea Roberts argues that by spotting the relevant paradigms at work in the field, one may enhance the awareness of the underlying theories and methodologies and foster the analytical skills required to look critically at the investment arbitration system.[126] In a relatively recent and under-theorized field such as international arbitration, the choice of paradigms, frameworks, and analogies to be drawn from other legal fields may determine normative outcomes.[127] Vested interests and strategic postures by all actors involved potentially represent further objects of intellectual investigation.

To problematize issues and to ask questions may be an appropriate way to engage with the said and the unsaid of the world of international arbitration. Furthermore, to raise questions may serve as antidote to the illusion that international arbitration is only

[121] Although see Schill (n. 96), 893, arguing that 'the community of international investment lawyers is sufficiently close-knit and held together by common institutions despite the sometimes different approaches of those with a public international law background and those with a commercial arbitration background.'

[122] I have dealt with this aspect in Bianchi (n. 55).

[123] On the struggle between competing claims to expertise and scientific authority in the field of investment arbitration, see Roberts (n. 5), 57.

[124] Andrea Bianchi, 'On Asking Questions', in Andrea Bianchi (ed.), *Theory and Philosophy of International Law* (Edward Elgar, 2017).

[125] Schill (n. 96), 894. Schill goes on to explain that 'many writers are either limited by rules of professional ethics in taking a stance on certain issues, or at least exercise prudence in making more principled statements, which may cast their independence and impartiality in actual proceedings into doubt, or may negatively affect future appointments.'

[126] Roberts (n. 5), 94. [127] Ibid. 46–7.

about providing answers to legal queries on the basis of technical legal expertise. The disempowerment of the notion of arbitration law as merely objective expertise, and the reconnection of international arbitration with normative and political questions, should eventually lead to a new empowerment of international arbitration scholarship,[128] characterized by more awareness of the social fabric in which international arbitration is embedded, as well as of the political and moral consequences of choices made by decision-makers and justified under the law.[129]

The concept of 'epistemic communities' is only now acquiring common currency in the parlance of international arbitration. Its potential for becoming the lens through which we look at different social groups competing for speaking authoritatively about international arbitration is huge. It is a fair speculation that in the future the academic debate over epistemic communities will intensify. The increasing propensity of younger generations of international arbitration scholars to look elsewhere and to be inspired by concepts and intellectual categories borrowed from other disciplines make this both a likely development and an exciting intellectual prospect.

At the same time, the increasing awareness of the mechanisms and processes whereby knowledge is being formed and used will most likely lead to the development of more sophisticated strategies to acquire control of the field. As I have argued in another context, '[t]hose who create and shape knowledge at all possible levels possess power', and discursive strategies elaborated by knowledge-wielding bodies or groups are controlling.[130] It is epistemic communities that delimit the field of inquiry,[131] set the discursive policy of the discipline, shape institutions,[132] and create knowledge of the field.[133] To fix the boundaries of what international arbitration is and to set the parameters for what is or is not an acceptable argument is no less than making the law. This is where the real stakes lie and what the questions are about.

[128] I take the call for the 're-politicization of international investment law' made by Schill (n. 96, p. 905) to go in the same direction.

[129] Critical studies and insights become more and more common in the field. For an example as regards commercial arbitration, see Horatia Muir Watt's Ch. 21 in this Handbook; and as regards investment arbitration, see Gus van Harten, 'A Critique of Investment Treaties and Investor–State Arbitration', Juridikum 338 (2013). See also Pia Eberhardt and Cecilia Olivet, *Profiting from Injustice: How Law Firms, Arbitrators and Financiers are Fuelling an Investment Arbitration Boom* (Corporate Europe Observatory and Transnational Institute, 2012), and Cédric Dupont and Thomas Schultz, 'Towards a New Heuristic Model: Investment Arbitration as a Political System', 7 Journal of International Dispute Settlement 3 (2016) (taking stock with empirical studies on international investment arbitration, including those that point to the shortcomings of the regime).

[130] Bianchi, (n. 12), 18.

[131] Michaels (n. 8), 48.

[132] Pauwelyn (n. 9), 800, quoting Dezalay and Garth (n. 10), 16–17.

[133] Miles (n. 7), 342.

CHAPTER 25

ARTIFICIAL INTELLIGENCE IN INTERNATIONAL ARBITRATION

MYRIAM GICQUELLO

25.1 Introduction

International arbitration has now become the default mechanism by which to resolve commercial and investment disputes, providing that the involved disputants preliminary consented to give jurisdiction to the arbitral tribunal. This success of international arbitration is undoubtedly due to the benefits it purported to bring; yet some of those initial promises have now eroded.

Indeed, as an alternative to litigation in domestic courts (for commercial disputes) and to diplomatic protection (for investment ones), international arbitration was initially presented as offering—at the same time—the advantages of neutrality, expertise, a final and binding award, confidentiality, and efficiency.[1] Neutrality was ensured, with an arbitral seat remote from the disputants' territories but also with the selection of arbitrators through party appointment—arbitrators, who should normally demonstrate expertise in a particular domain (business, law, etc.).[2] The final and binding award was also one of the main reasons for the popularity of international arbitration. Owing to international agreements widely ratified by the international community (i.e. the 1958 New York Convention and the 1965 International Convention for the Settlement of

[1] For a definition of international arbitration encompassing those characteristics, see Gary Born, *International Commercial Arbitration* (Kluwer Law International, 2014), 291: 'process by which parties consensually submit a dispute to a non-governmental decision maker, selected by or for the parties, who renders a binding decision finally resolving the dispute in accordance with neutral, adjudicative procedures affording the parties an opportunity to be heard.'

[2] E.g. International Convention for the Settlement of Investment Disputes (ICSID), Art. 14.

Investment Disputes), arbitral awards are in fact given a presumption of recognition and enforcement in courts, rendering the arbitration regime more efficient than litigation—the judgments of which are not as easily recognized and enforced.[3] Furthermore, this pro-enforcement presumption is a strong one, as the finality of the arbitral outcome is guaranteed through a lack of an appeal mechanism to review the case on its merits. Besides, the grounds for review or for challenge of the award before a domestic court, or for its annulment before an ad hoc appellate committee, are limited, as they mainly touch upon the integrity of the proceedings and public policy issues—and not on the substantive legal issues (i.e. merits) of the case.[4] Finally, one of the core claims of international arbitration was its efficiency—being initially presented as cheaper and quicker than litigation.

Yet, due to the explosion of cases submitted to arbitral tribunals—both in its commercial and investment branches—international arbitration is now facing rising criticisms as it falls short of those ideals. This backlash is even 'louder' in the international investment regime.[5] Indeed, compared to its commercial counterpart, which only involves private parties (as a result of a contractual agreement between them) and does not affect domestic law, investment arbitration does, touching upon issues of public interest impacting the host state's domestic laws and policies.[6] In a nutshell, it is contended that international arbitration fails to satisfy its goal of efficiency, as it can be more expensive than litigation.[7] In a survey, the cost and duration of the proceedings were even identified as two disadvantages.[8] The impartiality or fairness of the system is also questioned, as it involves a tight community of private arbitrators non-democratically elected who might be driven by considerations other than purely legal ones.[9] In turn, this criticism feeds

[3] Ibid. Art. 54. New York Convention, Art. III. Note though that the recognition and enforcement of judgments rendered by EU member states in other members states is facilitated by (EU) Regulation No 1215/2012 of the European Parliament and of the Council of 12 December 2012 on jurisdiction and the recognition and enforcement of judgments in civil and commercial matters (Brussels Regulations II).

[4] ICSID, Art. 52. New York Convention, Art. V.

[5] See Gabrielle Kaufmann-Kohler and Michele Potestà, 'Can the Mauritius Convention Serve as a Model for the Reform of Investor–State Arbitration in Connection with the Introduction of a Permanent Investment Tribunal or an Appeal Mechanism?': <https://www.uncitral.org/pdf/english/CIDS_Research_Paper_Mauritius.pdf>, accessed 22 July 2019.

[6] This is why there are no legitimacy issues in international commercial arbitration, while there are some in international investment arbitration: see Sect. 25.4.

[7] Jean-Claude Najar, 'Inside Out: A User's Perspective on Challenges in International Arbitration', (2009) 25(4) Arbitration International 515. On judicialization of international arbitration, see Fabricio Fortese and Lotta Hemmi, 'Procedural Fairness and Efficiency in International Arbitration', (2015) 3(1) Groningen Journal of International Law 110.

[8] Queen Mary, University of London, School of International Arbitration and PwC, report: *International Arbitration Survey 2013: Corporate Choices in International Arbitration: Industry Perspectives* (2013): <https://www.pwc.com/gx/en/arbitration-dispute-resolution/assets/pwc-international-arbitration-study.pdf>, accessed 22 July 2019.

[9] See Thomas Schultz and Robert Kovacs, 'The Law Is What the Arbitrator Had for Breakfast: How Income, Reputation, Justice, and Reprimand Act as Determinants of Arbitrator Behaviour', in Julio César Betancourt (ed.), *Defining Issues in International Arbitration: Celebrating 100 Years of the Chartered Institute of Arbitrators* (Open University Press, 2016). For more details, see Sect. 25.2.

that related to the absence of an appeal mechanism or substantive review of the decision, which opens the door for errors of law to sustain or inconsistencies to settle.[10]

Despite those concerns, it is important to safeguard international arbitration so as to avoid a return to domestic courts or to diplomatic protection, which are both far from ideal. Plus, the negative concerns formulated against this system should not make us forget the exclusive benefits it provides—benefits which are in fact missing in the aforementioned alternatives—hence making the preservation of international arbitration an even more important matter. In that context, it was asserted that international arbitration is 'broken', and needs to be repaired.[11] This repair is needed not only because of the specific properties of the system that makes it advantageous, but also because of broader considerations of justice and international adjudication. It is a well-accepted fact that justice needs not only to be done but to be seen to be done.[12] Nonetheless, the resentment against international arbitration necessarily leads us to question whether this perception is present in arbitration—having regard to the concerns about the alleged lack of independence and impartiality of the decision-makers, for example. Furthermore, considering the functions of international adjudication (i.e. dispute settlement, fact-finding, law-making, and governance),[13] we can fairly assert that international arbitration responds those to some extent—either in its investment or commercial branches, or both. The dispute settlement function encompasses three pursuits: maximization of the satisfaction of the parties, furthering the rule of law, and promotion of substantive societal values.[14] The first two are of interest here, as it has already been claimed and proved that international arbitration does (or did) indeed achieve those functions to some extent.[15] And it was also claimed that international arbitration needs to be retained in order to continue the development of the international rule of law.[16]

This chapter hence advocates for the introduction of artificial intelligence in international arbitration. Indeed, the contention is that it would not only reinstate confidence in the arbitral system (from the perspective of the parties and the general public) and

[10] Though the lack of consistency is not a concern in international commercial arbitration, it is in investment arbitration. Yet only unjustified inconsistencies (occurring within the same treaty) are problematic, as we cannot possibly achieve absolute consistency due to the fragmentation of the investment treaty regime.

[11] Najar (n. 7), 517.

[12] *R. v Sussex Justices; Ex parte McCarthy*, (1924) 1 KB 256.

[13] José E. Alvarez, 'What Are International Judges For? The Main Functions of International Adjudication', in Cesare P. R. Romano, Karen J. Alter, and Yuval Shany (eds), *The Oxford Handbook of International Adjudication* (Oxford University Press, 2013). See also on the primary function of resolving disputes: Nienke Grossman, 'Legitimacy and International Adjudicative Bodies', (2009) 41 George Washington International Law Review 107, 111: 'Specifically, they (international fora) must find facts, identify and interpret relevant legal rules or "law," use secondary principles to fill legal gaps and ambiguities, and apply the relevant law to the facts at hand for the purposes of issuing a ruling.'

[14] Thomas Schultz, 'The Three Pursuits of Dispute Settlement', (2010) 1 Czech (& Central European) Yearbook of Arbitration 227.

[15] David W. Rivkin, 'The Impact of International Arbitration on the Rule of Law', (2013) 29(3) Arbitration International 327. See also Thomas Schultz and Cédric Dupont, 'Investment Arbitration: Promoting the Rule of Law or Over-Empowering Investors? A Quantitative Empirical Study', (2015) 25(4) European Journal of International Law 1147. On the maximization of the satisfaction of the parties, see Queen Mary, University of London, School of International Arbitration and PwC (n. 8).

[16] Rivkin (n. 15).

participate in the development of the rule of law, but also engage with broader systemic considerations in enhancing its legitimacy, fairness, and efficiency.[17] Yet, before addressing the why, what, and how of this proposition, a definition of artificial intelligence is warranted. At the onset, it should be noted that this concept has a variety of meanings. Nonetheless, starting with the basics, the online *Oxford Dictionary* defines the term as follows:

> The theory and development of computer systems able to perform tasks normally requiring human intelligence, such as visual perception, speech recognition, decision-making, and translation between languages.[18]

Despite the lack of consensus on its meaning, this chapter will thus use artificial intelligence as encompassing both semi-autonomous and autonomous computer systems (i.e. algorithms) dedicated to assisting or replacing human beings in decision-making tasks.[19] The former consist in supervised algorithms pre-programmed, instructed, by humans for which the same input will always produce the same output, whereas the latter offer 'some learning capabilities'.[20]

I will start with a brief review of the literature to make the point that legal adjudicators (i.e. judges and arbitrators) are far from Montesquieu's ideal of the 'mouth of the law',[21] but are instead subjected to a number of extra-legal considerations, especially behavioural ones. I will then present the conclusions of two extensive research programmes respectively dealing with the performance of statistical (i.e. mechanical) models and naturalistic (i.e. expert) decision-making. From that behavioural analysis, the introduction of artificial intelligence in international arbitration will be discussed within the framework of general considerations of international adjudication (mentioned above) and specific goals pertaining to international arbitration (in its commercial and/or investment branches). I will show that artificial intelligence participates in achieving these goals, while it may still present some limitations—though these are outweighed by its advantages. I will end with practical insights on how it could be realistically implemented.

25.2 The Law is More than What is Found in the Books

This affirmation clearly contradicts the now unrealistic assumption formulated by legal formalists claiming that the law—as embedded in legal texts, status, and

[17] Note that efficiency here is concerned with the length and costs of the proceedings and legitimacy is a concern exclusive to investment arbitration: see Sect. 25.4.

[18] See <https://www.lexico.com/en/definition/artificial_intelligence>, accessed 22 July 2019.

[19] For more details on those, see Sect. 25.5.

[20] Spyros Makridakis, 'The Forthcoming Artificial Intelligence (AI) revolution: Its Impact on Society and Firms', (2017) 90 Futures 46, 49.

[21] Montesquieu, *De l'esprit des lois*, bk XI, ch. VI (1748): 'Les juges de la nation ne sont que la bouche qui prononce les paroles de la loi, des êtres inanimés, qui n'en peuvent modérer ni la force ni la rigueur.'

precedent—provides determinate answer to legal issues; so that the exercise of judges only consists in the application of the law to the facts at hand.[22] Yet this mechanical view of judging as being deprived of any extralegal influences was then challenged by legal realism explicitly recognizing the role of those latter (alongside legal considerations) in judicial decision-making.[23] It was thus contended that judges first reach an outcome and then try to rationalize it in providing legal explanations: a phenomenon known as originalism or textualism-originalism.[24] Such a backward inference runs contrary to the syllogistic exercise characteristic of legal formalism.

The question that necessarily follows this acknowledgement is: what could those extralegal factors be? Attempts were first made to answer this question applying the assumptions of rational choice theory to law; hence giving rise to law & economics. Nevertheless, although quite simple and parsimonious, this literature failed to generate accurate predictions.[25] This failure was due to the fact that the premises of rational choice theory—considering human beings as unbounded in rationality in that they had unlimited capabilities and could not possibly be the subject of personal or social influences—were far from matching reality.[26]

This unverifiable (and unrealistic) picture was questioned by Herbert Simon, who theorized that humans are actually bounded in rationality. Using the metaphors of a pair of scissors, he came to the conclusion that this bound is due to two aspects: the cognitive limitations of an individual and the structure of his/her environment.[27] Compared to its predecessor, this concept has the advantage of being empirically testable—a task that a number of researchers took into their own hands, leading to the furthering of psychology, especially in its cognitive and social elements. Uncontestably, the main contributors to this research programme are Daniel Kahneman and Amos Tversky with their prospect theory (challenging the expected utility model at the core of the rational choice theory/economics methodology) and the identification of rules of thumbs (heuristics) leading to systematic errors (biases) used by decision-makers to cope with their limited cognitive abilities.[28]

[22] See Matthew C. Stephenson, 'Legal Realism for Economists', (2009) 23 Journal of Economic Perspectives 191.

[23] For more details on this distinction between legal formalism (i.e. law in books) and legal realism (i.e. law in action), see Ch. 9 by Thomas Schultz in this volume, nicely presenting those schools of thought.

[24] Richard A. Posner, *How Judges Think* (Harvard University Press, 2008).

[25] Cass R. Sunstein, Christine Jolls, and Richard H. Thaler, 'A Behavioral Approach to Law and Economics', (1998) 50 Stanford Law Review 1471.

[26] Gerd Gigerenzer and Peter M. Todd, 'Fast and Frugal Heuristics: The Adaptive Toolbox', in Gerd Gigerenzer, Peter M. Todd, and ABC Research Group (eds), *Simple Heuristics That Make Us Smart* (Oxford University Press, 2000), 5: 'Many models of rational inference view the mind as if it were a supernatural being possessing demonic powers of reason, boundless knowledge, and all of eternity with which to make decisions.'

[27] Herbert A. Simon, 'A Behavioural Model of Rational Choice', (1955) 69 Quarterly Journal of Economics 99. Also: Herbert A. Simon, 'Invariants of Human Behavior', (1990) 41 Annual Review of Psychology 1, 7: 'Human rational behaviour is shaped by a scissors whose two blades are the structure of task environments and the computational capabilities of the actor.'

[28] Daniel Kahneman and Amos Tversky, 'Prospect Theory: An Analysis of Decision under Risk', (1979) 47 Econometrica 263. Amos Tversky and Daniel Kahneman, 'Judgment under Uncertainty: Heuristics and Biases', (1974) 185 Science 1124.

Hence, in the 1970s, the picture of human beings as super-organisms was abandoned to be replaced by a more realistic view endorsing their bounds. Indeed, not only was their rationality bounded, but also their self-interest and willpower—those limitations being the three pillars of the behavioural economics methodology.[29] This shift—or improvement—of the paradigm (from economics to behavioural economics) was then applied to real-world situations, thus contributing to the development of behavioural law & economics (on the domestic and international planes).[30] This importation of behavioural, psychological findings in a legal context was an explicit recognition that:

> [w]hile computers function solely on logic, human beings do not. All sorts of extraneous factors—emotions, biases, preferences—can intervene, most of which you can do absolutely nothing about (except play upon them, if you happen to know what they are).[31]

To reiterate, as this point is equally relevant in our arbitral context, by this statement Supreme Court Justice Scalia confirmed that legal adjudicators are subjected to those influences as well. This point has even been empirically proved, with a number of studies focusing on the bounded rationality of judges or arbitrators.[32] It was thus found that judges and arbitrators are both subjected to the following cognitive illusions when completing their decision-making task: anchoring, confirmation bias, egocentrism, framing, hindsight bias, and representativeness.[33] Plus considering the second blade of Herbert Simon's scissors, it was also demonstrated that adjudicators are socially influenced by their colleagues on the bench through panel effects for example.[34] It should be noted that this literature is in fact a mere confirmation that experience, expertise, and cognitive abilities (intelligence) are no protection against biased decision-making.[35] Therefore, in light of those fallacies affecting decision-makers—novices or experts to the task; adjudicators having tenure or party-appointed—we might wonder whether it

[29] See e.g. Sunstein et al. (n 25). Tomer Broude, 'Behavioral International Law', (2015) 163 University of Pennsylvania Law Review 1099. Anne van Aaken, 'Behavioral International Law and Economics', (2014) 55 Harvard International Law Journal 421.

[30] Ibid. See also Ch. 36 in this volume by Anne van Aaken and Tomer Broude, presenting both movements: law & economics and behavioural economics.

[31] Bryan A. Garner and Antonin Scalia, *Making Your Case: The Art of Persuading Judges* (Thomson West, Aspatore Books 2008), 'Introduction'.

[32] For a detailed review, see Myriam Gicquello, 'The Reform of Investor–State Dispute Settlement: Bringing the Insights of Social Psychology into the Debate' (2019) 10 Journal of International Dispute Settlement 561.

[33] On see e.g. Chris P. Guthrie, Jeffrey J. Rachlinski, and Andrew J. Wistrich, 'Inside the Judicial Mind', (2001) 86 Cornell Law Review 777. On arbitrators: Edna Sussman, 'Arbitrator Decision-Making: Unconscious Psychological Influences and What You Can Do About Them', (2015) 4 Yearbook of International Arbitration 69; Susan D. Franck, Anne van Aaken, James Freda, Chris Guthrie, and Jeffrey J. Rachlinski, 'Inside the Arbitrator's Mind', (2017) 66 Emory Law Journal 1115.

[34] Pauline T. Kim, 'Deliberation and Strategy on the United States Courts of Appeals: An Empirical Exploration of Panel Effects', (2009) 157 University of Pennsylvania Law Review 1319.

[35] See Sect. 25.3.2 on expertise. On cognitive abilities: Keith E. Stanovich, *What Intelligence Tests Miss: The Psychology of Rational Thought* (Yale University Press, 2010).

would not be wise to introduce artificial intelligence in international arbitration to tackle them.

25.3 Humans versus Machines: Who Wins?

25.3.1 Artificially intelligent decision-making

This proposition is supported by extensive research that consisted in the comparison of mechanical versus clinical decision-making. Those methods differing as:

> By mechanical (or statistical), I mean that the prediction is arrived at by some straightforward application of an equation or table to the data . . . The defining property is that no juggling or inferring or weighting is done by a skilled clinician.[36]

As a number of studies have since been conducted, the terminologies employed have expanded—while still conveying the same idea. The distinction between mechanical and clinical decision-making was reflected in the debates concerning mechanical and non-mechanical, objective and subjective, actuarial and case study, quantitative and qualitative methods.[37] Furthermore, since decision-making is not a unitary task but involves two activities (i.e. collection and interpretation of data), it is worth noting that most of the research evaluating those methods is concerned with their accuracy in the combination (i.e. interpretation) of previously collected data (either statistically or clinically).[38] This point should not be missed, as the conclusions on the accuracy of these methods for each aspect are not uniform. And it is relevant within our arbitral framework, as tribunals are only entrusted with the interpretation of legal provisions and limited by the submission of the parties (i.e. cannot introduce new arguments).

[36] Paul E. Meehl, *Clinical vs. Statistical Prediction: A Theoretical Analysis and a Review of the Evidence* (University of Minnesota Press, 1954), 15–16. See also Robyn M. Dawes, David Faust, and Paul E. Meehl, 'Clinical Versus Actuarial Judgment', (1989) 243 Science, 1668: 'In the clinical method, the decision-maker combines or processes information in his or her head. In the actuarial or statistical method, the human judge is eliminated and conclusions rest solely on empirically established relations between data and the condition or event of interest.'

[37] Jack Sawyer, 'Measurement and Prediction, Clinical and Statistical', (1966) 66 Psychological Bulletin 178. For the sake of consistency and simplicity, this chapter will employ the terms 'statistical' and 'clinical'.

[38] Harrison Gough, 'Clinical vs. Statistical Prediction in Psychology', in L. Postman (ed.), *Psychology in the Making* (Knopf, 1962), 530: 'The defining distinction between clinical and actuarial methods is instead to be found in the way in which the data, once specified, are combined for use in making the prediction.'

After setting the picture right with those preliminary remarks, it is time to address what has been found over the last six decades and what those results entail. The father of this research programme is Paul Meehl, who in 1954 published a 'disturbing little book' entitled *Clinical Versus Statistical Prediction.*[39] Relying on 20 studies, he found that overall (except in one case) the statistical predictions 'were either approximately equal or superior to' the clinical ones.[40] This finding was then reiterated by other researchers: in 1966, Jack Sawyer equally found—using 45 studies—that the statistical combination of data was 'always equal or superior to the clinical mode', adding that 'whatever the data, clinical combination never surpasses mechanical combination'.[41] Thirty years later, William Grove and Paul Meehl reached (again) the same conclusion in an even bigger meta-analysis—using 136 studies—finding that in 64 cases, statistical combination generated better results than its clinical counterpart, in 64 they were equal, and in only 8 the clinical method was better.[42] Those consistent findings on the superior or equal accuracy of statistical models against clinicians are not limited to a specific context or set of conditions but rather apply to 'a wide range of circumstances' involving any 'judgment task, type of judges, judges' amount of experience, or types of data being combined'.[43] Reflecting on his initial findings and the subsequent proliferation of studies on that matter, Paul Meehl concluded in 1986:

> There is no controversy in social science that shows such a large body of qualitatively diverse studies coming out so uniformly in the same direction as this one (the relative validity of statistical versus clinical prediction). When you are pushing ninety investigations, predicting everything from the outcome of football games to the diagnosis of liver disease and when you can hardly come up with a half dozen studies showing even a weak tendency in favour of the clinician, it is time to draw a practical conclusion, whatever theoretical differences may still be disputed.[44]

One such conclusion was first reached by Robyn Dawes and his colleagues, who urged people to focus not on the improvement of clinical methods (as is usually the case)

[39] Paul E. Meehl, 'Causes and Effects of My Disturbing Little Book', (1986) 50 Journal of Personality Assessment 370; Meehl (n. 36).

[40] Ibid. 119. [41] Sawyer (n. 37), 192–3.

[42] William M. Grove and Paul E. Meehl, 'Comparative Efficiency of Informal (Subjective, Impressionistic) and Formal (Mechanical, Algorithmic) Prediction Procedures: The Clinical-Statistical Controversy', (1996) 2 Psychology, Public Policy, and Law 293, 298 (Those latter could be discarded, however, as: 'According to the logicians' "total evidence rule", the most plausible explanation of these deviant studies is that they arose by a combination of random sampling errors (eight deviant out of one hundred and thirty-six) and the clinicians' informational advantage in being provided with more data than the actuarial formula.' Indeed, according to Paul Meehl, for such comparisons to be valid they should rely on identical data provided to the statistical model and the clinician and they should also avoid contexts that could favour the accuracy of the statistical method.)

[43] William M. Grove, David H. Zald, Boyd S. Lebow, Beth E. Snitz, and Chad Nelson, 'Clinical vs Mechanical Prediction: A Meta-Analysis', (2000) 12 Psychological Assessment, 19.

[44] Meehl (n. 39), 373–4.

but rather on the amelioration of statistical models.[45] Dawes and Reid Hastie offered radical advice: 'whenever possible, human judges should be replaced by simple linear models.'[46]

One should wonder what effects the introduction of artificial intelligence in decision-making could possibly entail (in general, and more specifically in the arbitral context). To begin with, it is fair to assume that it will undoubtedly provide an opportunity to comply with the requirements of rational choice theory—something impossible as long as clinicians are involved, due to their bounded rationality. In turn, this focus on deliberation—as opposed to intuition—will enhance the predictability of the arbitral system, as statistical models will always produce the same result (i.e. output) for the same set of data (i.e. input), while the same cannot be said with a clinician.[47] Indeed, whereas humans are inevitably subjected to a number of influences—with or without conscious awareness—on their decision-making behaviour; artificially intelligent systems are free from those.[48] Furthermore, identifying the factors contributing to the superiority of statistical models, Robyn Dawes and his colleagues mentioned fatigue, recency, framing effects, and motivational changes, as well as the general tendency for individuals to be subjected to a confirmation bias in the interpretation of information—data which is only a skewed sample of evidence, and thus not representative.[49] Additionally, a statistical model is cheaper and less time-consuming than a clinical one relying on an individual or a group—hence promoting efficiency—but also relies on explicit procedures, and not on suspicions concerning what could or has happened in the clinicians' minds.[50] Finally, the lack of feedback and an irregular decision-making environment contribute to the superiority of statistical models.[51] It suffices here to say that international arbitration seems to be currently lacking those factors.[52]

Accordingly, the introduction of artificial intelligence in international arbitration could have a number of benefits.[53] Not only could it allow a return to legal formalism (i.e. 'law in the books')—if that ever existed—tackling (behavioural) extra-legal factors in applying the law mechanically to the facts of the case. Plus, we could expect that

[45] Robyn M. Dawes, David Faust, and Paul E. Meehl, 'Statistical Prediction versus Clinical Prediction: Improving What Works', in Gideon Keren and Charles Lewis (eds), *A Handbook for Data Analysis in the Behavioral Sciences: Methodological Issues* (Lawrence Erlbaum, 1993).

[46] Reid Hastie and Robyn M. Dawes, *Rational Choice in an Uncertain World: The Psychology of Judgment and Decision Making* (SAGE, 2009). 60. (Note that this latter conclusion is not unanimously accepted in the literature, as others consider that clinical decision-making should be favoured, or that both statistical and clinical methods should be combined: see below).

[47] Grove and Meehl (n. 42), 315: 'Humans simply cannot assign optimal weights to variables, and they are not consistent in applying their own weights.'

[48] Jörg Rieskamp and Ulrich Hoffrage, 'When Do People Use Simple Heuristics, and How Can We Tell?' in Gigerenzer (et al.) (n. 26),165: 'The main individual characteristics that are reported to influence decision strategies are knowledge and experience, emotional and motivational factors, cognitive abilities, and gender.'

[49] Dawes et al. (n. 36) (on the 'self-fulfilling prophecies' of clinicians and their overconfidence).

[50] Ibid.

[51] Daniel Kahneman, *Thinking, Fast and Slow*, repr. edn (Penguin, 2012). See also below on expertise.

[52] See Sect. 25.3.2 on expertise and Sect. 25.4.

[53] Ibid.

overall this proposition would further the rule of law (notably in bringing certainty and predictability, as the same combination of law and facts will always give the same outcome), enhance both the legitimacy of and compliance with the system, and promote its fairness (as the requirements of independence and impartiality will be automatically restored) and efficiency (through a reduction of costs and duration). Furthermore, it would dispense with the need for an appeal mechanism (concerned with the correctness of the decision) or a review mechanism (dealing with the integrity of the proceedings) that would compromise the finality of the arbitral award.

Given all those positive effects, one might wonder why this option has not already been considered. To be fair, this omission is not exclusive to the legal or arbitral contexts; it is in fact pervasive in a wide range of decision-making situations. Indeed, although it has been extensively demonstrated that statistical combination of data was more accurate (or equal) to clinical interpretation of that same data, the former method is seldom implemented.[54] Reflecting on the effects of his 'disturbing little book', Paul Meehl identified personal factors that might lead to this reluctance,[55] to which Robyn Dawes added some cognitive ones.[56] Although those certainly contribute to the lack of enthusiasm towards the use of statistical models in decision-making, they might not be the main determinants. Indeed, while the literature—over the last six decades and using over 100 studies—is fairly uniform in its conclusions, the practical implications to be given to those latter are far from settled. We could even divide the different schools of thought into three camps: one advocating for the total replacement of clinician decision-making with statistical models, one favouring the reverse (i.e. expert decision-making only), and a third defending their combination. The latter option was advocated by Robert Holt in the very infancy of the research comparing clinical and statistical predictions:

> The real issue is not to find the proper sphere of activity for clinical predictive methods and for statistical ones, conceived in ideal terms as antithetical. Rather we should try to find the optimal combination of actuarially controlled methods and sensitive clinical judgment for any particular enterprise.[57]

Recognizing this third possibility of judgment strategy (adding to the purely statistical or purely clinical approaches), it remained to settle on the form this combination should take. Here, it is necessary to recall the distinction between collection and interpretation of data which could be both clinical and/or statistical. While there could be a combination of clinical and statistical in the collection phase, this should not be the case

[54] Grove and Meehl (n. 42), 319 (interpreting this behaviour as an instance of 'resistance to scientific discovery' or of 'Mencken's dictum that most people believe what they want to believe').

[55] Meehl (n. 39) (i.e. sheer ignorance, the threat of technological unemployment, self-concept, theoretical identifications, dehumanizing flavour, mistaken conception of ethics, computer phobia).

[56] Dawes et al. (n. 45) (e.g. the belief in the rigidity of the statistical models, the failure to modify those latter with post-decision feedback).

[57] Robert R. Holt, 'Clinical and Statistical Prediction: A Reformulation and Some New Data', (1958) 56 Journal of Abnormal and Social Psychology 1, 12. Malcolm Gladwell, *Blink: The Power of Thinking Without Thinking*, repr. edn (Penguin, 2006).

in interpretation.[58] As the research—on the overall superiority of statistical methods—was principally concerned with the interpretive component, it would be wise to let a pure statistical model interpret the data previously collected by clinician(s) or by both methods. For the proponents of a clinical-statistical mix, this method is the most popular, due to the specificities of each component. Indeed, while 'the human brain is a relatively inefficient device for noticing, selecting, categorising, recording, retaining, retrieving, and manipulating information *for inferential purposes*',[59] things are different for data collection, as experts have access to some 'inside information' that models cannot pretend.[60] Furthermore, the reverse combination (i.e. statistical in collection and clinical in interpretation) has already been tested in a number of contexts, where it did worse than a pure statistical method.[61]

25.3.2 Expert decision-making

Human decision-making being flawed in some respects, and bearing in mind the conclusions of the statistical versus clinical research programme, retaining clinicians to make decisions (either exclusively or in combination with statistical models) seems quite paradoxical. Yet, after consideration of the literature dealing with intuitive, naturalistic, expert decision-making, this might not be the case after all. Indeed, while Daniel Kahneman and Amos Tversky depicted intuition as disruptive to rational decision-making (i.e. heuristics and biases research programme),[62] others adopted the opposite view, conceiving of it as helpful. This point was illustrated by Antonio Damasio and his colleagues, who studied the decision-making abilities of brain-damaged patients presenting intact cognitive processes but impaired emotional ones. Although they presented the ability to be fully rational, their decision-making abilities were negatively affected. This led the researchers to develop the somatic marker hypothesis, according to which 'emotion could assist the reasoning process rather than necessarily disturb it',[63] and a '*reduction in emotion may constitute an equally important source of irrational behaviour*'.[64] Therefore, as intuition could be helpful in certain circumstances, it has been claimed that it should be blended with deliberative, logical, statistical, decision-making rather than completely eliminated.[65]

[58] Dawes et al. (n. 36), 1668: 'If clinical and actuarial interpretations agree, there is no need to combine them. If they disagree, one must choose one or the other.'

[59] Grove and Meehl (n. 42), 316 (emphasis added).

[60] Dawes et al. (n. 45), 5, quoting Robert C. Blattberg and Stephen J. Hoch, 'Database Model and Managerial Intuition: 50% Model + 50% Manager', (1990) 36 Management Science 887: 'We have elected to label this inside information as intuition and see it as a valuable decision input.' See also Sawyer (n. 37), 181: 'There is good reason to think that incorporating a clinician into data collection might improve prediction', as he could catch information (e.g. from observation) that a statistical model would miss.

[61] Dawes et al. (n. 45)

[62] Tversky and Kahneman (n. 28).

[63] Antonio Damasio, *Descartes' Error: Emotion, Reason and the Human Brain* (Vintage, 2006), 'Preface'.

[64] Ibid. 53.

[65] Gary A. Klein, *Streetlights and Shadows: Searching for the Keys to Adaptive Decision Making* (MIT Press, 2011).

This alternative view on intuition—dubbed the 'learning perspective' by Robin Hogarth[66]—depicts the process as built 'on mental representations that reflect the entire stream of prior experiences'.[67] This importance of experience (or of expertise, if sufficiently developed) constitutes the focus of the naturalistic decision-making research tradition. This latter consists in the study of the decision-making of individuals in 'real-contexts that are meaningful and familiar to them'.[68] From that approach, this type of intuition was labelled as a source of power and source of knowledge that should not be dismissed in favour of statistical models.[69] To support this claim, it was found that intuitive decision-making could outperform deliberative models providing certain conditions were in place.[70] What could those be? They have to do with the decision-makers and their surrounding environment. The individual needs to be an expert—as distinct from being experienced.[71] How does one become an expert? First of all, expertise building upon experience, it is well accepted that the concerned individual must have 'a sufficient opportunity to practice'.[72] Yet this repetition of behaviour does not render an expert omniscient; on the contrary, the ensuing expertise will be limited to the particular skill, domain, or task in question.[73] Another necessary condition to develop expertise—and not only experience—lies in reliability, meaning that decision-makers should be consistent across their own behaviours (intra-consistency) but also between them (inter-consistency).[74] This latter condition is in fact a mere manifestation

[66] Robin M. Hogarth, 'On the Learning of Intuition', in Henning Plessner, Cornelia Betsch, and Tilmann Betsch (eds), *Intuition in Judgment and Decision Making* (Routledge, 2014).

[67] Henning Plessner, Cornelia Betsch, and Tilmann Betsch (eds), *Intuition in Judgment and Decision Making* (Routledge, 2014), 9. For a more detailed definition, see also: Tilmann Betsch, 'The Nature of Intuition and Its Neglect in Research on Judgment and Decision Making', in Plessner et al., *Intuition in Judgment and Decision Making*, 4: 'Intuition is a process of thinking. The input of this process is mostly provided by knowledge stored in long-term memory that has been primarily acquired via associative learning. The input is processed automatically and without conscious awareness. The output of the process is a feeling that can serve as a basis for judgments and decisions.' Hastie and Dawes (n. 46), 2: 'Choosing wisely is a learned *skill*, which, like any other skill, can be improved with experience.'

[68] Raanan Lipshitz, Gary Klein, Judith Orasanu, and Eduardo Salas, 'Taking Stock of Naturalistic Decision-Making', (2001) 14 Journal of Behavioral Decision Making 331, 332. Gary A. Klein, *Sources of Power: How People Make Decisions*, 20th anniversary edn (MIT Press, 2017), 1 (defining it as 'the study of how people use their experience to make decisions in field settings').

[69] Betsch (n. 67); Klein (n. 68).

[70] T. D. Wilson, *Strangers to Ourselves: Discovering the Adaptive Unconscious* (Harvard University Press, 2002).

[71] Hogarth (n. 66). Note that while expertise is built on past experiences (through prolonged practice), the latter do not necessarily entail the former.

[72] Kahneman (n. 51), 241. See also K. Anders Ericsson, 'Deliberate Practice and Acquisition of Expert Performance: A General Overview', (2008) 15 Academic Emergency Medicine 988.

[73] Barbara A. Spellman, 'Judges, Expertise, and Analogy', in David E. Klein and Gregory Mitchell (eds), *The Psychology of Judicial Decision Making* (Oxford University Press, 2010), 152: 'Due to *study, training, and practice*—often in addition to *talent and motivation* —experts are better than non-experts in some domains of performance. One clear characteristic of expertise is that it is quite limited in domain' (emphasis added).

[74] Hillel J. Einhorn, 'Expert Judgment: Some Necessary Conditions and an Example', (1974) 59 Journal of Applied Psychology 562.

of the requirement of regularity of the environment, as a lack of consistency (as seen in international investment arbitration in particular) greatly hinders predictability.[75] Besides, failure to meet those conditions could render intuition detrimental instead of helpful in the decision-making process.[76] Finally, the development of expertise—through the learning of those regularities with repeated practice—is also dependent on feedback (especially on its speed and quality).[77] This last feature is particularly relevant in the legal context, as it provides low-fidelity feedback which contributes to poor performance.[78]

Assuming that someone does actually become an expert in a particular domain, what would that entail on his/her decision-making abilities? First, it will imply a departure from rational choice theory (as relying on an intuitive component), and thus could not possibly be captured by pure statistical models.[79] This departure notably results from the fact that experts rely on decision-making strategies that are not comprehensive either in the search for information or in its evaluation.[80] This point is in fact illustrated by the Recognition Primed Decision (RPD) model uncovered by Gary Klein after an investigation of the behaviour of nurses and firefighters. This framework aimed to describe how expert decision-makers use their acquired knowledge to arrive at a judgment or decision. It theorized that experts combine both intuitive and deliberative thought processes to reach an outcome (as opposed to relying exclusively on one or the other). This association is inherent in the RPD model, consisting in two subsequent processes—pattern recognition (i.e. the intuitive component) and simulation (i.e. the deliberative part).[81] The impossibility of capturing the insights brought by expertise in procedures or statistical models is due to the fact that expertise permits one to 'see the invisible'.[82] This ability is in turn due to the development of tacit knowledge—as distinct from explicit knowledge that can easily be implemented and communicated—consisting in 'being able to do things without being able to explain how... tacit knowledge is the basis for our skills and the reflection of our experience.'[83] Additionally, not only this

[75] Kahneman (n. 51), 240: 'The two basic conditions for acquiring a skill (being) an environment that is sufficiently regular to be predictable and an opportunity to learn these regularities through prolonged practice.'

[76] Ibid. 241: 'Intuition cannot be trusted in the absence of stable regularities in the environment.'

[77] Ibid.

[78] James Shanteau and Ward Edwards, 'Decision Making by Experts: Influence of Five Key Psychologists', in Evan A. Wilhelms and Valerie F. Reyna (eds), *Neuroeconomics, Judgment, and Decision Making* (Psychology Press, 2014).

[79] Klein (n. 65) (explaining the discrepancies in performance between the two methods).

[80] Jennifer K. Phillips, Gary Klein, and Winston R. Sieck, 'Expertise in Judgment and Decision-Making: A Case for Training Intuitive Skills', in Derek J. Koehler and Nigel Harvey (eds), *Blackwell Handbook of Judgment and Decision-Making* (Wiley-Blackwell, 2004), 305: 'An important attribute of expert decision-makers is that they seek a course of action that is workable, but not necessarily the best or optimal decision. Human decision-making is qualitatively different from normative theories, and this is so among experts as well as novices.'

[81] Klein (n. 65). Klein (n. 68), 24: 'The recognition-primed decision model fuses two processes: the way decision-makers size up the situation to recognise which course of action makes sense, and the way they evaluate that course of action by imagining it.'

[82] Ibid. [83] Ibid. 35.

expanded knowledge-base differentiates experts from novices in their area of expertise,[84] it is also responsible for a number of phenomena:

> Within their domain of expertise, experts tend to be faster and more accurate than novices, tend to have superior short-term and long-term memory for information, see deeper relations in the structure of information, use less cognitive effort, and have more accurate monitoring skills.[85]

Finally, experts also present inherent characteristics contributing to those advantages, those being consistency (i.e. reliability), narrowness (i.e. domain-specificity), validity, and discrimination.[86] In the latter, although an expert tends to rely on 'relatively little information' compared to a layperson, it is his/her ability to discriminate between relevant and irrelevant information which is crucial—a skill novices are lacking, as those are prone to use both types.[87]

Yet the disadvantages of expertise should not be forgotten either—hence the call for combining statistical and clinical methods (with clinicians being experts, not novices). Indeed, relying on experts can be far from ideal under certain circumstances (e.g. in the absence of a predictable, regular environment). Furthermore, expertise is no inoculation against biases—even though experts might be subject to those cognitive errors to a lesser extent than a layperson.[88] This limitation of expert decision-making is nicely illustrated by Amos Tversky: 'Whenever there is a simple error that most laymen fall for, there is always a slightly more sophisticated version of the same problem that experts fall for';[89] equally, judicial and arbitral decision-making literature has proved that judges, jurors, and arbitrators are subjected to heuristics and biases.[90] Finally, experts are also suffering from overconfidence, as 'a person acquiring more knowledge develops enhanced illusion of her skill'.[91] This feeling is problematic since, being uncorrelated to accuracy, it engenders an illusion of validity.

Consequently, the answer to the question 'Humans versus machines: who wins?' is not straightforward. Indeed, both present limitations; yet, purely clinical decision-making should still be avoided whenever possible due to the number of influences such decisions might be subjected to—something not likely to happen with a statistical model.[92] And, although arbitrators are undoubtedly competent due to the skills required

[84] Phillips et al. (n. 80), 299: 'The primary distinction that separates experts from novices appears to be the breadth and depth of their domain specific knowledge. Competence is inherent in the definition of expertise.'

[85] Spellman (n. 73), 152.

[86] David J. Weiss and James Shanteau, 'Who's the Best? A Relativistic View of Expertise', (2014) 28(4) Applied Cognitive Psychology 447.

[87] Shanteau and Edwards (n. 78), 12.

[88] The literature is not in agreement on that point; for a review, see Hastie and Dawes (n. 46).

[89] Quoted in Shanteau and Edwards (n. 78), 14.

[90] See Sect. 25.2.

[91] Kahneman (n. 51), 219.

[92] See Klein (n. 65), 296–7: 'Experience-based thinking is different from analysis-based thinking. The two are not opposed to each other; they are complementary, like daytime vision and night vision.'

of them in exercising this role, they might not necessarily rise to the level of expertise as defined above. The ideal alternative would be to introduce artificial intelligence so as to counteract human decision-makers' limitations.

25.4 Artificial intelligence in international arbitration: so, what?

Proposing a new model based on psychological findings is one thing, assessing its purported benefits is another. Yet, before addressing those and potential disadvantages, some preliminary remarks are in order. Combining statistical and clinical methods seems like a reasonable alternative to begin with, due to the features of international arbitration that hinders the development of expertise. Besides, reliance on a pure clinical model—as in the current system—has already shown its defects in light of the backlash we are now witnessing. Yet, although the superiority of statistical models—compared to clinicians—has been extensively demonstrated, the literature is still divided as to the implications of this finding (does that mean that we should get rid of any sort of human input in decision-making?). Furthermore, the complete elimination of arbitrators—and their replacement by a statistical model—could be highly controversial, not only because of this unsettled literature but also because it might be a change—handing over their fate to machines—that people are not ready to accept yet.[93] To encourage the welcoming of this introduction of artificial intelligence in international arbitration, it would be undoubtedly better to proceed progressively, by first using artificially intelligent models to assist the arbitral community (the former being concerned with data interpretation and collection, the latter with data collection only, i.e. feeding it to the computer program). An outcome generated by a statistical model (even partially) will always be more accurate than, or equal to, the one strictly based on clinicians.[94] Once this mechanism implemented—and, it is hoped, praised by its users and the general public—we could consider the replacement of the clinical part by artificial intelligence (thus leading to a pure statistical model), but only as a last resort (i.e. if it would present additional advantages). Accordingly, the combination—as the prime alternative—will be discussed.[95]

[93] See e.g. Edwina L. Rissland 'Artificial Intelligence and Law: Stepping Stones to a Model of Legal Reasoning', (1990) 99 Yale Law Journal 1957, 1980: 'There will always be a need for human lawyers and judges. The goal is to assist, not to replace.'

[94] See Katz's equation for legal prediction tasks: Daniel Martin Katz, 'Quantitative Legal Prediction—or—How I Learned to Stop Worrying and Start Preparing for the Data-Driven Future of the Legal Service Industry', (2013) 62 Emory Law Journal 909, 929: 'Humans + Machines > Humans or Machines'.

[95] Note that this proposition is in accordance with Milgram's advice in the criminal justice framework to design algorithms to assist judges so as to bring more informed and more objective decisions: Angèle Christin, 'Algorithms in Practice: Comparing Web Journalism and Criminal Justice', (2017) 4(2) Big Data & Society 1, 6, citing Anne Milgram: 'Judges have the best intentions when they make these decisions about risks, but they are making them subjectively. They are like the baseball scouts 20 years ago who

25.4.1 A beneficial approach...

The argument here is that the introduction of artificial intelligence in the interpretive phase of the decision-making process will be highly beneficial to international arbitration, as it will enhance the (perception of) legitimacy, fairness, and efficiency, while also promoting the rule of law. Furthermore, as this proposition will contribute to fulfilling the initial goals of international arbitration, it should also restore the confidence of its users and the public.

Concerning the legitimacy of international arbitration, it should be first emphasized that this is a concern exclusive to international investment arbitration. In international commercial arbitration resulting from a private contractual agreement, the award that follows has an effect only on the parties, and hence cannot possibly impact domestic laws and policies—whereas an investment arbitral award might do so. This impact on the states' regulatory power is one of the reasons why investment arbitration is allegedly confronted by a legitimacy crisis, in addition to the fact that those public laws and policies are in fact challenged by non-democratically elected individuals (party-appointed arbitrators).[96] It is contended that, to be legitimate, international adjudicative bodies should present decision-makers accountable to the general public.[97] Those criticisms of a lack of legitimacy and of accountability in investment arbitration have even been ironically paraphrased by one arbitrator, Johnny Veeder:

> The concept...that an arbitrator is a super-judge, that an arbitral tribunal can operate above any international law with a discretion not given to state courts, a lack of accountability for its conduct and an absence of transparency not afforded to any comparable professional activity in the world, except, possibly secret policemen.[98]

But what is legitimacy and why should we be concerned about it or its perception in international (investment) arbitration? Despite the lack of consensus on the meaning of this concept and the variety of its 'jobs',[99] it has been recognized that the legitimacy

were using their instinct and their experience to try to decide what risk someone poses. They are being subjective, and we know what happens with subjective decision-making, which is that we are often wrong. What we need in this space are strong data and analytics.'

[96] See Rivkin (n. 15), 354: 'Many have described a "backlash" against investor-state arbitration, viewing it as an illegitimate process through which laws and policies are made and unmade, threatening the rule of law by imposing norms, allocating public funds, and constraining the actions of those bestowed with a direct democratic mandate, through a procedure that is beyond public scrutiny and in which the public has no say.'

[97] Mark L. Movsesian, 'International Commercial Arbitration and International Courts', (2008) 18 Duke Journal of Comparative and International Law 424.

[98] Johnny Veeder, 'Due Process—Balancing Fairness and Efficiency—The Harmonising Chord', IBA 12th International Arbitration Day, Due Process in International Arbitration, Transcripts. <https://www.ibanet.org/Search/Taxonomy.aspx?Taxonomy=transcripts&TaxonomyUid=ac31c928-2386-44e0-bd67-fb3b8f87c059>, accessed 22 July 2019.

[99] Thomas Schultz, 'Legitimacy Pragmatism in International Arbitration: A Framework for Analysis', in J. Kalicki and M. Abdel Raouf (eds), *Evolution and Adaptation: The Future of International Arbitration* (Wolters Kluwer, 2018).

crises that international courts and tribunals might face should not be ignored, but instead carefully analysed.[100] More specifically, in the arbitral context, this was illustrated by Thomas Schultz, who highlighted that the use of this concept allows us 'to understand the stability of a regime; its likelihood of change; the direction; velocity, extent, drivers of that change; its implications too'.[101] In this chapter, legitimacy is taken as a justification of the authority of an institution, as emphasized by Tom Tyler, providing that 'legitimacy is psychological property of an authority, institution, or social arrangement that leads those connected to it to believe that it is appropriate, proper, and just'.[102] In turn, this means that if the arbitral regime is perceived as legitimate, compliance by the parties should be enhanced and the general feeling towards it should be rather positive. It is contended that the introduction of artificial intelligence in that framework will achieve this, as it will promote the three factors conferring legitimacy on an international adjudicative body: '(1) fair and unbiased; (2) interpreting and applying norms consistent with what states believe the law is or should be; and (3) transparent and infused with democratic norms.'[103] Since statistical models rely on explicit procedures—and not on vague assumptions of what could be happening in the clinicians' heads—this will enhance the transparency (but also consistency) of the system, as the parties will have access to the whole interpretive process. Consistency in interpretation will also facilitate acceptance of the system by states and stakeholders.[104] Similarly, this reliance on statistical models will emphasize the fair and unbiased nature of the institution.[105]

Also related to legitimacy is the concept of the rule of law, as a system failing to enhance the latter will lose the former.[106] But what is the rule of law? Like legitimacy, it has a great variety of meanings.[107] In this chapter, this concept is taken in the sense of formal legality that requires a certain threshold of predictability in the application and interpretation of rules, which 'implies, for instance, that rules... be applied *coherently, consistently, competently, and impartially*'.[108] Lack of those properties would in turn lead to a state of uncertainty for the disputants (as already witnessed in international investment arbitration), and hence prevent them from adjusting their conduct

[100] See Grossman (n. 13), 109: 'Attempting to define, identify, and analyse legitimacy challenges that international courts and tribunals face is useful to those seeking to expose and remedy their flaws and deepens our understanding of how these institutions should function.'

[101] Schultz (n. 99).

[102] Tom Tyler, 'Psychological Perspectives on Legitimacy and Legitimation', (2006) 57 Annual Review of Psychology 375. See also Daniel Bodansky, 'The Legitimacy of International Governance: A Coming Challenge for International Environmental Law?' (1999) 93 American Journal of International Law 596, 600: 'A quality that leads people (or states) to accept the authority—independent of coercion, self-interest, or rational persuasion—because of a general sense that the authority is justified.'

[103] Grossman (n. 13), 115.

[104] Ibid.: The legal soundness of the decision influencing the support to the concerned institution.

[105] For more details, see below on the promotion of fairness, procedural due process, independence, and impartiality of arbitrators.

[106] Rivkin (n. 15).

[107] Simon Chesterman, 'An International Rule of Law?' (2008) 56 American Journal of Comparative Law 331.

[108] Schultz and Dupont (n. 15), 1164 (emphasis added).

appropriately.[109] It is thus argued that introducing artificial intelligence in the interpretive phase of the decision-making process would contribute to the development of the rule of law, as it would *automatically* bring the properties mentioned. Indeed, coherence and consistency in application and interpretation—resulting in predictability, stability, and certainty—will be ensured: a statistical model will always provide the same output providing that it is presented with the same input, hence also implementing a de facto doctrine of precedent.[110] In addition, owing to this lack of regularity, arbitrators (though undeniably experienced decision-makers) might not have the chance to develop expertise—hence the need for a statistical model to assist them first by taking over the task of data interpretation. Finally, this proposition will also enhance the (perception of) impartiality of international arbitration by providing an objective means of interpreting data, a means which is not driven by personal considerations external to the decision-making task.[111] It should also be noted that it is incumbent on the arbitral community working on improvements of the system to ensure that international arbitration still promotes the rule of law, as it has been proved that arbitration has already contributed to the growth of the rule of law—both domestically and internationally.[112] As David Rivkin emphasized, a return to diplomatic protection or to domestic courts would not achieve that goal, as neither of them 'are conducive to the creation of an international rule of law'.[113]

Procedural fairness (or due process)—one element of the rule of law, a goal of arbitration,[114] as well as an obligation bearing on arbitrators[115]—will also be enhanced with artificial intelligence. But, before explaining how, what is procedural fairness and what does it entail for international arbitration? According to Fabricio Fortese and Lotta Hemmi:

> The core guarantees of procedural due process comprise the arbitrator's duty to treat the parties equally, fairly and *impartially*, and to ensure that each party has an opportunity to present its case and deal with that of its opponent.[116]

Those requirements of procedural fairness are particularly important in international arbitration, as a failure to comply with them will result in the non-recognition or

[109] See Schultz (n. 14), 240, citing Lon L. Fuller, 'A Reply to Professors Cohen and Dworkin', (1965) 10 Villanova Law Review 655, 657 (law's essential function being: 'to subject... people's conduct to the guidance of general rules by which they may themselves orient their behaviour').

[110] Properties currently missing in investment arbitration pervaded with unjustified inconsistencies. There is a caveat, though, as it would not be such a milestone in commercial arbitration due to the confidentiality of the arbitral awards.

[111] See below on fairness. [112] See n. 15. [113] Rivkin (n. 15), 354.

[114] David W. Rivkin, 'Towards a New Paradigm in International Arbitration: The Town Elder Model Revisited', (2008) 24(3) Arbitration International 375, 377: '(i) a fair and neutral process, (ii) conducted by intelligent and experienced arbitrators, (iii) resulting in a timely and well-reasoned decision, and (iv) benefiting from an effective enforcement mechanism.'

[115] William W. Park, 'Arbitration in Autumn', (2011) 2(2) Journal of International Dispute Settlement 287 (alongside the duties to render an accurate, efficient (time- and cost-wise), enforceable award).

[116] Fortese and Hemmi (n. 7), 112 (emphasis added).

non-enforcement of the arbitral award[117]—the enforceability of an award being one goal of international arbitration and one obligation incumbent on arbitrators.[118] Accordingly, the combination (statistical model for data interpretation with experts for data collection) will respond to those requirements. Indeed, it will bring an objective, unbounded, rational decision-maker in the arbitral context—a feature that is currently lacking due to the number of influences (behavioural, motivational, cognitive, social, etc.) human beings might be subjected to. This bounded rationality means it is no surprise that investment arbitrators are often considered to lack independence and impartiality. The design of the current system: (party-appointed arbitrators, who are thus dependent for their reputation and income on their ability to secure such appointments, and the possibility of "double-hatting", thus potentially generating conflicts of interests) undoubtedly contributes in this general opinion.[119] Although the selection of adjudicators by the disputants is criticized, it is also of value, as it furthers the latter's confidence and acceptance of the system's ability to provide them with (the idea of) a neutral forum to solve their disputes. This is why the combination will not undermine this aspect, as parties will still have to appoint someone or some people to collect the data (i.e. through written submissions and oral hearings) to be fed to the artificially intelligent model. This proposition therefore offers the convenience of tackling the alleged partiality and dependence of adjudicators while keeping the parties involved in their appointment, and in still providing parties with the opportunity to present their case and respond to their opponent—hence answering to the above requirements of procedural fairness.

The proposition will also allow the reconciliation of fairness and efficiency (in terms of costs and duration). These factors have often been portrayed as conflicting with each other, following the argument that some trade-off had to be found between the two, since they could not be satisfied at the same time.[120] This balancing exercise was revealed problematic in some circumstances, however, as it prevented arbitral tribunals from fulfilling their obligation to render an enforceable award.[121] Nevertheless, in its infancy, the efficiency of international arbitration was advanced as a reason why it should be favoured over litigation. This picture has now changed, however, with some claiming that this 'foundation of efficiency has begun to dissolve',[122] and others that the costs and length (notably due to a judicialization) of the process are dangerous.[123] How could the introduction of artificial intelligence help in this case? First, it will exempt us from the creation of a second layer of control mechanisms. Such an optimal device for interpretation will render redundant a review or annulment mechanism (mainly concerned with the integrity of the proceedings), hence limiting the costs and duration of the proceedings as well. Equally, there will be no need for an appeal mechanism to control the correctness of the decision, as the latter will necessarily be rightly (in the sense of objectively, optimally, mechanically) produced by the computerized model. Furthermore, this reform option

[117] Park (n. 115). [118] Ibid. [119] Schultz and Kovacs (n. 9).

[120] Fortese and Hemmi (n. 7). As an illustration, they applied Dr Joerg Risse's dilemma of the 'magic triangle' to international arbitration.

[121] Ibid. [122] Najar (n. 7), 517.

[123] Queen Mary, University of London, School of International Arbitration and PwC (n. 8).

exhibits a number of inherent positive cost- and efficiency-related effects. Indeed, statistical models—not relying on groups or committees for interpretation—will inevitably be less time-consuming and more economical (i.e. no deliberations or remuneration of the people participating in such deliberations). It is true that the design and implementation of this proposition will inevitably entail costs. Yet those initial expenses will then be compensated by the fact that, once properly installed, artificially intelligent systems do not incur costs each time they are used—or surely not as significant as the ones we are now witnessing with group decision-making—as additional costs will only be engaged sporadically in order to adapt the model to feedback.[124] It is worth noting that such an adjustment is impossible in the current legal decision-making context, although it is a necessary condition to develop expertise.[125]

25.4.2 ... yet not immune to potential drawbacks

Despite its purported advantages, artificial intelligence also presents limitations. Conflicting feelings toward this new technology are nicely illustrated by Stephen Hawking's comment that 'the rise of powerful artificial intelligence will be either the best or the worst thing ever to happen to humanity. We do not yet know which.'[126] Those concerns about artificial intelligence could be classified into three categories: some consisting in general statements, others being more specific to the legal system as expressed by lawyers, and some relying on the actual working of an artificially intelligent system of decision-making.

Among the opponents to the introduction of such a system, the 'pessimists' fear that humans could become 'computers' pets'.[127] Indeed, they consider that if machines do make better decisions than humans, this task will simply be delegated to the former, with the latter only watching.[128] Others see artificial intelligent systems as competitors to humans—a sentiment shared by the legal profession, with Daniel Katz asserting that the number of legal professionals needed will decline as a result of this combination.[129] This scepticism on the part of the legal profession towards the introduction of algorithms to assist them in their decision-making has already been demonstrated by Angèle Christin in the criminal justice context.[130] Analysing how machines are already used in that legal area, she observed that this scepticism is due to the actors' confidence in their legal judgment, in turn fed by the fact that access to the legal profession involves 'a long training process and high barriers to entry', and to their resistance

[124] Dawes et al. (n. 36); Grove et al. (n. 43).

[125] See above and especially in international arbitration due to the dissolution of the tribunal after the resolution of the dispute and the absence of control mechanisms.

[126] Transcript of Professor Stephen Hawking's speech at the launch of the Leverhulme Centre for the Future of Intelligence, October 19, 2016: <https://www.cam.ac.uk/research/news/the-best-or-worst-thing-to-happen-to-humanity-stephen-hawking-launches-centre-for-the-future-of>, accessed 22 July 2019.

[127] Makridakis (n. 20), 50. [128] Ibid. [129] Katz (n. 94). [130] Christin (n. 95).

towards technological innovation.[131] Others assert that the properties of the legal system (i.e. 'open-textured' concepts—dynamic, and without a 'right answer') make it particularly challenging to welcome the introduction of artificial intelligence.[132] Alongside those rather abstract concerns, however, others are more practice-oriented in that they have regard to the actual functioning of artificially intelligent systems. Examples are concerns about current ethical[133] and liability issues,[134] as well as the lack of accountability[135] and transparency.[136] Briefly, it is claimed that machines do not respond to this ideal of objectiveness, as they are notably influenced by the values and interests of their designers.[137] It is equally asserted that they are opaque, in that transparency requires both accessibility and comprehensibility of information, qualities that are missing in algorithmic decision-making.[138]

Notwithstanding those limitations, it is argued that artificial intelligence should still be introduced in international arbitration, as its alleged benefits will outweigh those alleged limitations. This 'pragmatic' view is justified as there will be an artificial intelligence revolution in any event—like the industrial and digital ones we have already experienced—and therefore, 'the rational alternative is to identify the risks involved and devise effective actions to avoid their negative consequences'.[139] This identification having already begun—as illustrated by the aforementioned concerns—a number of *ex ante* or *ex post* approaches have been thought of[140] or effective regulations implemented.[141]

[131] Ibid. 11.

[132] L. Thorne McCarty, 'Artificial Intelligence and Law: How to Get There from Here', (1990) 3(2) Ratio Juris 189. Though this challenge is not an obstacle—see Sect. 25.5.

[133] Brent Daniel Mittelstadt, Patrick Allo, Mariarosaria Taddeo, Sandra Wachter, and Luciano Floridi, 'The Ethics of Algorithms: Mapping the Debate', (2016) 3(2) Big Data & Society 1 (highlighting six ethical issues algorithms might be confronted with).

[134] David C. Vladeck, 'Machines Without Principals: Liability Rules and Artificial Intelligence', (2014) 89 Washington Law Review 117.

[135] Joshua A. Kroll, Joanna Huey, Solon Barocas, Edward W. Felten, Joel R. Reidenberg, David G. Robinson, and Harlan Yu, 'Accountable Algorithms', (2017) 165 University of Pennsylvania Law Review 633.

[136] Ibid. Mittelstadt et al. (n. 133).

[137] Ibid. See also Batya Friedman and Helen Nissenbaum, 'Bias in Computer Systems', (1996) 14(3) ACM Transactions on Information Systems 330 (identifying three categories of bias in computer systems: pre-existing, technical, and emergent).

[138] Mittelstadt et al. (n. 133). The functionality of algorithms sometimes being kept secret, and if not, their specificities are often incomprehensible to a layperson.

[139] Makridakis (n. 20), 59. Similarly, Rissland (n. 93), 1981: 'Successful projects require not only thorough knowledge of both artificial intelligence and the law, but also a willingness to try new approaches without knowing exactly where they will lead, or whether or not they will achieve exactly the desired result. In short, work in artificial intelligence and the law is no different from work in other fields; you cannot get anywhere without trying; and one invariably learns from trying.'

[140] Kroll et al. (n. 135).

[141] For a review: Lilian Edwards and Michael Veale, 'Enslaving the Algorithm: From a "Right to an Explanation" to a "Right to Better Decisions"?' (2018) 16(3) IEEE Security & Privacy 46–54.

25.5 Practical Insights

If the combination of statistical and clinical methods is favoured in the first place, two aspects need to be addressed: the furthering of expertise in the arbitral framework, and the design of the statistical model that would take on both the collection of data (alongside experts) and its interpretation (exclusively in this task).

On the intuitive (or clinical) component of the combination, it was previously demonstrated that intuition can be useful when it relies on past experiences rising to the level of expertise—as opposed to being based on heuristics. Indeed, this power of intuition derives from the experts' ability to 'see the invisible', in turn allowing them to discriminate between relevant and irrelevant information. It is specifically on account of that latter property that clinicians should not be suppressed in any decision-making context (legal, medical, business, etc.). Instead, the data should be collected building on those competences (in association with a statistical model as well), data subsequently to be fed to the statistical model for its interpretation. Consequently, this requires us to answer the following question: How could the members of the arbitral community develop expertise in this domain?

The conditions of expertise—detailed above—would certainly be a good starting point; and proponents of this intuitive-deliberative combination also suggested guidelines in this respect. To understand those, we must first recall that, according to Gary Klein and Daniel Kahneman, one of the necessary conditions to develop reliable intuitions is that people must have opportunities to learn.[142] This, in turn, happens in two ways, through deliberate practice associated with feedback.[143] The enhancement of expertise will inevitably deal with those, and K. Anders Ericsson, after a review of the literature, observed:

> Significant improvements in performance were realized when individuals were 1) given a task with a well-defined goal, 2) motivated to improve, 3) provided with feedback, and 4) provided with ample opportunities for repetition and gradual refinements of their performance.[144]

Those features should be worked on, therefore, and introduced into international arbitration. Indeed, we could assert that it already presents the first characteristic—the goal being the resolution of the dispute at hand—despite being based on quite vague provisions and unsettled jurisprudence on some interpretive issues (in investment arbitration). As

[142] Kahneman (n. 51); Klein (n. 65).

[143] Note that in this case outcome feedback is quite useless, and thus should be on the process: ibid.

[144] Ericsson (n. 72), 991. See also Gary Klein positing four similar techniques favouring the learning of expertise: Phillips et al. (n. 80), 306: '1. Engaging in deliberate practice and setting specific goals and evaluation criteria; 2. Compiling extensive experience banks; 3. Obtaining feedback that is accurate, diagnostic, and reasonably timely; and 4. Enriching their experiences by reviewing prior experiences to derive new insights and lessons from mistakes.'

to the existence of the second factor, it could be questionable. Ideally, arbitrators should be motivated to ameliorate their decisions; yet, as demonstrated by Thomas Schultz, this might not be the case.[145] The third requirement is missing as well as the fourth, owing to discrepancies in the appointment rates of arbitrators—some being repeatedly appointed, others not.

Should the combination of clinical and statistical methods be considered, however, the development of expertise would influence the people entrusted with feeding the algorithms with the data relevant to resolve the dispute. This information is now dealt with by arbitrators through written submissions and oral hearings preceding the deliberations and outcome of the tribunal. The question is: on whom should this responsibility to provide inputs to the statistical model be conferred? The logical answer would be to hand this task to party-appointed arbitrators, since it will provide the disputants with confidence in the system. For this clinical-statistical method to be optimal, however, we might prefer to use independent legal experts instead.

On the deliberative (or statistical) component of the combination, several questions arise pertaining to its form and the people entrusted with its design. The answers to those are far from being straightforward due to the lack of adoption of this method across a wide range of contexts (despite extensive literature setting out the numerous benefits). Yet rarity does not equal nonexistence: some models have already been used, and could thus be borrowed and adapted to international arbitration.[146] Furthermore, the artificial intelligence and law movement is not new, with some computer systems already designed in areas touching upon criminal justice,[147] taxation law,[148] legal predictions,[149] and legal reasoning.[150] Indeed, this approach was meant to fulfil two motivations: one (theoretical) concerned with the understanding of legal reasoning and argumentation, and another (practical) focusing on 'building computational tools useful for legal practice, teaching, or research'.[151] While law is a challenging area for the introduction of artificial intelligence due to its specific characteristics (e.g. open-textured concepts, dynamic, 'no right answer'), efforts towards its successful integration are deemed worth continuing due to the numerous 'desiderata' it could bring to law.[152] The design of those programmes in the legal system is not an easy thing, and requires a number of preliminary steps. In the context of international arbitration, those would include

[145] Thomas Schultz, 'Arbitral Decision-Making: Legal Realism and Law & Economics', (2015) 6 Journal of International Dispute Settlement 21.

[146] Note that to be able to compare statistical and clinical decision-making in the myriad of studies (already mentioned), statistical models have already been developed and applied.

[147] Christin (n. 95).

[148] On TAXMAN, see e.g. L. Thorne McCarthy, 'Reflections on Taxman: An Experiment in Artificial Intelligence and Legal Reasoning', (1977) 90(5) Harvard Law Review 837.

[149] Katz (n. 94).

[150] Rissland (n. 93), presenting the HYPO project reasoning with cases and hypotheticals.

[151] Ibid. 1960. McCarty (n. 132).

[152] For the lists of law's particular characteristics and of desiderata for artificial intelligence and law, see Rissland (n. 93).

mapping arbitral reasoning, representing the knowledge of the field, and designing methods (i.e. rules) to use this knowledge.[153]

Once those steps are accomplished, the form of the algorithmic model used to assist arbitrators in their decision-making should then be settled on. Will it take the form of a conventional computer system or of machine learning? For the time being the former might be favoured, as the latter is still in its infancy. Indeed, conventional computer systems only rely on pre-programmed instructions—hence presenting no autonomy whatsoever, as compared to a machine learning program—in the form of 'logic, if-then rules, and decision trees', and are equally able to deal with difficult decisions involving a lot of data that human decision-makers (e.g. arbitrators) could not realistically apprehend due to their cognitive limitations.[154]

Nevertheless, the use of machine learning algorithms in international arbitration will definitely be an option to consider—albeit at a later point in time—as it was forecast in 2017 that the artificial intelligence revolution will happen within the next 20 years, with an impact even greater than that of the industrial and digital revolutions.[155] Machine learning systems present a number of additional advantages[156] currently missing from conventional algorithms (computer systems), such as: autonomous improvement of performance over time, as they are learning from experience, detection of patterns as the data is presented (patterns that could be missed by humans due to their limitations), and development of heuristic rules—all to allow automated predictions or decisions.[157] Although it would present limitations, notably pertaining to liability, transparency, and accountability but also accuracy, adaptability, and over-generalization, the usefulness of this technology in law would still be preserved provided that those limitations are properly dealt with.[158] One area of law in which machine learning is deemed to be particularly useful is in the prediction of future legal outcomes:

> The goal of using machine learning is to analyse past data to develop rules that are generalisable going forward. (...) Such a learned model is thus only useful to the extent that the heuristic inferred from past cases can be extrapolated to predict novel cases.[159]

[153] Richard E. Susskind, 'Expert Systems in Law: A Jurisprudential Approach to Artificial Intelligence and Legal Reasoning', (1986) 49(2) Modern Law Review 168, 185: 'Knowledge representation being 'the central issue of the study of legal knowledge engineering.' Similarly: McCarthy (n. 132).

[154] Makridakis (n. 20), 49. [155] Ibid.

[156] Harry Surden, 'Machine Learning and Law', (2014) 89 Washington Law Review 87, 95: 'The focus in machine learning is upon computer algorithms that are expressly designed to be dynamic and capable of changing and adapting to new and different circumstances as the data environment shifts.'

[157] Ibid. 107: 'Machine learning techniques are also useful for discovering hidden relationships in existing data that may otherwise be difficult to detect.' Note that it is true that conventional algorithms can adjust to feedback as mentioned earlier, but this needs some human intervention.

[158] Liability issues being even more problematic, since those machine learning programs lack a principal as they are autonomous and unsupervised: Vladeck (n. 134).

[159] Surden (n. 156), 105. This predictive function being already undertaken by machine learning systems outside law: Katz (n. 94).

If such a programme can already forecast the outcome of a case, there is equally a potential for prescription: deciding the outcome of the case after that same data analysis.

On the last question—responsibility of designing the programme—the task will necessarily fall to a computer scientist, undoubtedly with the assistance of the arbitral community (e.g. arbitral institutions) to properly integrate the subtleties of the legal system, and particularly of international arbitration.[160]

25.6 Conclusion

This chapter has considered the introduction of artificial intelligence in international arbitration in order to restore the initial goals that made it popular in the first place. Since this mode of dispute resolution—an alternative to domestic litigation or diplomatic protection—is now arguably 'broken', it could benefit from such innovation. Furthermore, it has been demonstrated not only that the materialization of this proposition would contribute to the fulfilment of international arbitration ideals but also that it would equally engage with broader considerations of international adjudication such as the promotion of the rule of law (both domestically and internationally), as well as the enhancement of legitimacy, efficiency, and fairness of the system.

The implementation of computerized decision-making in international arbitration is warranted, first, by the psychological literature experimentally proving that human decision-makers are bounded in rationality, and second, by the extensive research programme comparing statistical to clinical methods of interpretation. Furthermore, those findings have been already proved relevant in the legal context—which makes the matter all the more interesting, as those decision-makers are normally appointed for their purported expertise. Hence the question: why has this alternative not been considered earlier? After all, there already exists literature on artificial intelligence and the law, the last few decades have witnessed a number of technological innovations expanding our possibilities, and artificial intelligence is increasingly becoming a 'hot topic'—some even arguing that we will witness a revolution soon. The answer might be that this is due to a scepticism concerning machines accompanied by the praise of expert decision-making. Hence the idea to combine both methods, as decision-making entails two different phases—collection and interpretation of data. Clinicians have been quite good at the former aspect but rather bad in the latter. While this introduction of artificial intelligence into arbitral decision-making could also present limitations, adopting a pragmatic approach—as the benefits are thought to outweigh the disadvantages—it was asserted that those limitations could be appropriately dealt with.

160 Bruce G. Buchanan and Thomas E. Headrick, 'Some Speculation About Artificial Intelligence and Legal Reasoning', (1970) 23 Stanford Law Review, 40: 'the time has come for serious interdisciplinary work between lawyers and computer scientists to explore the computer's potential in law.'

Moving on to the practicalities of this proposition, the combination of expertise with artificial intelligence entails that both need to be developed in international arbitration. It is doubtful that arbitrators could be labelled 'experts' from a psychological perspective, the arbitral context lacking the conditions to acquire this status. Of particular interest here is the form of the computerized system to be adopted: will it be semi-autonomous or autonomous? Whichever program is developed by a computer scientist with the help of the arbitral community, the introduction of even the simplest program (i.e. supervised by human hands, semi-autonomous), appropriately designed to address the specificities, will be highly beneficial to international arbitration. But the scarcity of applications and the existence of productive objections means there is more work to do on both the promotion and implications of this proposition.

CHAPTER 26

INVESTMENT TREATY ARBITRATION*

A justice bubble for the privileged

ANIL YILMAZ VASTARDIS

> There is the old idea, which has withstood the passage of time, that dominant social forces in society maintain their domination not through the use of force but through having their worldview accepted as natural by those over whom domination is exercised.[1]

HISTORICALLY, the use of international arbitration to resolve foreign investment disputes was advocated to prevent discrimination against foreign investors on the basis of their nationality, and avoid violation of their due process rights by so-called abusive governments with weak judiciaries. For this reason, the use of international investment arbitration, particularly investment treaty arbitration (ITA), which arguably has the strongest rights enforcement mechanism existing in international law,[2] has been perceived as facilitating access to justice for foreign investors at the international level. Despite ITA's popularity with investors, this system of dispute settlement has been criticized by state actors, legal scholars, and civil society activists alike for flaws such as lack of consistency, transparency, excessive costs, impartiality, and independence of arbitrators. Ironically, ITA has been promoted to uphold rule of law in host state relationships with foreign investors, but it has been diagnosed with a rule of law deficit itself. In response, several formal initiatives have been launched to reform the existing model of investment

* This is a revised version of an essay originally published as A. Yilmaz Vastardis, 'Justice Bubbles for the Privileged: A Critique of the Investor–State Dispute Settlement Proposals for the EU's Investment Agreements', (2018) 6(2) London Review of International Law 279.

[1] B. S. Chimni, 'Third World Approaches to International Law: A Manifesto', (2006) 8 International Community Law Review 3, 15.

[2] B. A. Simmons, 'Bargaining over BITS, Arbitrating Awards: The Regime for Protection and Promotion of International Investment', (2014) 66 World Politics 12, 17.

arbitration to inject rule of law into ITA.[3] The most ambitious model is promoted by the European Union (EU), and establishes a permanent investment court system (ICS) to replace the current investment treaty arbitration model in EU's new investment treaties.[4] Other key reform initiatives, progressing under the auspices of UNCITRAL and ICSID, are taking a more incremental approach to remedy the flaws in the existing model of arbitration.[5]

While many of ITA's flaws may be remedied by robust reforms responding to critiques, in this chapter I challenge investment treaty arbitration at its core by questioning the validity of insistence on special routes for access to justice reserved to remediate the grievances of a class of privileged investors, which I refer to here as 'justice bubbles'. Despite the potential of the ongoing reform initiatives to genuinely improve the existing investment treaty arbitration model, salvaging and strengthening these justice bubbles that serve the needs of the privileged few sustains and even makes permanent the prioritization of institutions of justice for foreign investors over the improvement of local institutions that could provide justice for members across society, including foreign investors. I recognize that no institutional process used or proposed for settling international investment law (IIL) disputes is perfect, and each process is 'imperfect in different ways given the dynamics of participation within them'.[6] The challenge here is directed towards the singling out of high-value investment disputes as deserving special treatment above and beyond any institutional options available to any other private party aggrieved by governmental abuse.

Two caveats are in order. First, reforming ITA and improvements to local institutions of justice are not necessarily competing agendas amounting to a zero-sum game. Some states could properly resource both the improvement of local institutions and special modes of dispute settlement for foreign investors. That said, if local institutions of justice are strong, the question arises as to why states would need to promote special modes

[3] International Centre for Settlement of Investment Disputes (ICSID), 'Backgrounder on Proposals for the Amendment of the ICSID Rules': <https://icsid.worldbank.org/en/Documents/Amendment_Backgrounder.pdf>, accessed 29 August 2019; UNCITRAL, *Report of Working Group III (Investor–State Dispute Settlement Reform) on the Work of its Thirty-Fourth Session (Vienna, 27 November–1 December 2017)*, UN Doc. No. A/CN.9/930 (19 December 2017); Council of the European Union, 'Negotiating Directive Giving the European Commission a Mandate to Negotiate a Treaty Establishing a Multilateral Court for the Settlement of Investment Disputes', 12,981/17 ADD 1: <http://data.consilium.europa.eu/doc/document/ST-12981-2017-ADD-1-DCL-1/en/pdf>, accessed 29 August 2019.

[4] Council of the European Union (n. 3). China also supports an international court system model to settle investment disputes with foreign investors: N. Chandran, 'China's Plans for Creating New International Courts are Raising Fears of Bias', CNBC, 1 February 2018: <https://www.cnbc.com/2018/02/01/china-to-create-international-courts-for-belt-and-road-disputes.html>, accessed 29 August 2019; A. Roberts and T. St John, 'UNCITRAL and ISDS Reform: China's Proposal', EJIL:*Talk!* 5 August 2019: <https://www.ejiltalk.org/uncitral-and-isds-reform-chinas-proposal/>, accessed 29 August 2019.

[5] There is a possibility that the UNCITRAL Working Group III may become the forum for negotiating a multilateral investment court, but it is as yet in the exploratory phase of identifying main areas of concern and reform.

[6] S. Puig and G. Shaffer, 'Imperfect Alternatives: Institutional Choice and the Reform of Investment Law', (2018) 112(3) American Journal of International Law 361, 362.

of dispute settlement serving only foreign investors. After all, substantial financial and human resources are needed to set up, maintain, and adjudicate disputes before these special modes of dispute settlement on an ongoing or permanent basis in parallel to the existing local justice mechanisms.[7] Where states prioritize allocating resources to the creation and maintenance of justice bubbles for the privileged, they are inevitably taking away valuable resources and attention which could have been used, had the political will existed, to improve the effectiveness of local judicial and non-judicial protection mechanisms that serve all members of society. This kind of internationalization also shields qualifying investors from the challenging realities in the host state, at least as far as dispute settlement is concerned. These challenges have to be shouldered by the rest of the society, while the investor pursues its claim entirely outside the host state and obtains a remedy that the host state must compensate as a matter of priority over any other harm suffered within the host state in connection to the investment.

The second caveat is to make it clear that the objection raised in this chapter is not to the ad hoc use of international arbitration in settling investor–state disputes based on mutual consent of the investor and the host state given in an investment contract. Rather, it is to the efforts to validate the idea that investment treaty 'arbitration without privity'[8] should be the default and most appropriate mode of resolving investor–state disputes. While the critique presented here is relevant beyond the EU's ICS model, the latter deserves particular attention, since its adoption would in all likelihood entrench ever greater prioritization—on a global scale—of the commercial interests of the wealthiest few over wider societal interests by (amongst other things) making justice bubbles for investors more permanent. Introducing a standing court system is likely to lock a relatively large number of states into this mode of dispute settlement for decades, and potentially define the new ISDS system as a template of good governance.

I begin by critically analysing the imposition of ITA as the most appropriate method for resolving investor–state disputes. A brief overview of the recent and increasing backlash against ITA, and the responses this attracted in the form of proposals for a permanent court of investment arbitration, is then examined. The final section argues that the

[7] International courts of similar standing have the following budgets. |The 2019 budget for the Court of the Justice of the European Union is €429.5 million: Court of Justice of the European Union, *The Court in Figures*: <https://curia.europa.eu/jcms/jcms/P_80908/en/>, accessed 29 August 2019. The European Court of Human Rights budget for 2019 amounts to €69,997,500. This covers judges' remuneration, staff salaries, and operational expenditure (information technology, official journeys, translation, interpretation, publications, representational expenditure, legal aid, fact-finding missions, etc.). It does not include expenditure on the building and infrastructure (telephone, cabling, etc.): European Court of Human Rights, *ECHR Budget*: <https://www.echr.coe.int/Documents/Budget_ENG.pdf>, accessed 29 August 2019. The budget for the International Court of Justice for 2017–18 was $47,792,500, United Nations, *Report of the International Court of Justice 1 August 2017–31 July 2018*, Seventy-Third Session, Supplement No. 4 UN Doc. No. A/73/4* (28 September 2018): <https://www.icj-cij.org/files/annual-reports/2017-2018-en.pdf>, accessed 29 August 2019.

[8] J. Paulsson, 'Arbitration Without Privity', (1995) 10 ICSID Review–Foreign Investment Law Journal 232, 232: '[The] new world of arbitration is one where the claimant need not have a contractual relationship with the defendant and where the tables could not be turned: the defendant could not have initiated the arbitration, nor is it certain of being able to even bring a counter-claim.'

establishment of a permanent investment court is a short-sighted solution to deficiencies in local access to justice which is likely to undermine domestic legal developments. What is needed is a rejection of the outsourcing of the settlement of investment disputes on a permanent basis. If this were achieved, it would constitute a paradigmatic shift in approaches to access to justice.

26.1 The Imposition of ITA as the Most Appropriate ISDS Method

Investor–state disputes can be resolved in various fora. ISDS can encompass judicial proceedings, conciliation, mediation, negotiation, and arbitration.[9] Arbitration has been and continues to be advocated as the most appropriate way of settling disputes between international investors and host states.[10] Investment treaty arbitration, particularly, is the most frequently invoked international dispute settlement method to resolve foreign investment disputes for well-resourced investors.[11] An investment treaty is not the only place where arbitration is used. International and local commercial disputes, investment contract disputes, as well as inter-state disputes, are also frequently resolved through arbitration. This can be a legitimate method for resolving disputes, founded on the principles of consent and party autonomy.[12]

In most cases, private parties mutually agree, in a contract, to submit their disputes to arbitration, rather than resorting to national courts. They do so for a variety of reasons—for example, concerns over confidentiality or greater trust in arbitrators' expertise. In these instances, the decision to submit to arbitration is made ad hoc; the parties do not submit all future disputes between themselves to arbitration, but only those that relate to the specific legal relationship referred to in the arbitration agreement. With the reach

[9] Investment disputes may also be brought before the courts of the regional human rights systems. See *Velikovi v Bulgaria*, ECHR App No. 43278/98, (2007) 48 EHRR 27.

[10] See T. St John, *The Rise of Investor–State Arbitration: Politics, Law, and Unintended Consequences* (Oxford University Press, 2018), 184, 198–209 (traces the promotion of investment arbitration as the most appropriate method of ISDS back to the role played by the legal officials in the World Bank who were drafters of the ICSID Convention and who 'disseminated [ICSID arbitration clauses] widely and brokered ISDS clauses into existence in hundreds of contracts and treaties'). See also World Bank Group, *Legal Framework for the Treatment of Foreign Investment*, vol. 2: *Guidelines*, Report No. 11415, paras. 50–52: <http://documents.worldbank.org/curated/en/955221468766167766/pdf/multi-page.pdf>, accessed 29 August 2019. The reform initiatives led by UNCITRAL and the EU start from the presumption that ITA is the most appropriate method but needs to be improved by significant reforms: UNCITRAL, 'Possible Future Work in the Field of Dispute Settlement: Reforms of Investor–State Dispute Settlement (ISDS)', Note by the Secretariat, Fiftieth Session, Vienna, 3–21 July 2017, A/CN.9/917, paras. 9–11.

[11] ICSID, *ICSID Caseload: Statistics* (Issue 2019–1), 10: shows that in 75% of the cases registered with ICSID, the basis of consent invoked by the investor was a treaty.

[12] N. Blackaby, C. Partasides, A. Redfern, and M. Hunter, *Redfern and Hunter on International Arbitration*, 6th edn (Oxford University Press, 2015), 71.

and impact of the agreement strictly limited to the contract and its signatories, arbitration on an ad hoc basis normally does not constitute a large-scale transfer of judicial authority.

In contrast, due to an extensive web of investment treaties including direct consent to arbitration, investment treaty arbitration's personal and material reach is so wide that it does entail such a large-scale transfer. The source of most contemporary investment arbitration, investment treaties negotiated between states, sees a state making a standing offer to arbitrate to an indeterminate number of investors from the other state party.[13] This offer can be accepted by any qualifying investor through the initiation of arbitral proceedings. The host state may not even be aware of the existence of a dispute until it receives the notice of arbitration. The investor which resorts to this mechanism does not need to have negotiated an arbitration agreement for a defined legal relationship. Instead, it can just claim the 'right to arbitrate' which its state has negotiated for its benefit and that of other qualifying investors. Additionally, investment treaty consent can survive a decade or longer after termination of an investment treaty.

I argue in this chapter that a move towards a multilateral investment court system would further entrench the large-scale transfer of judicial authority effectuated by the existing model of investment treaty arbitration. This is not to say that contract-based investor–state arbitration does not give rise to the same concerns raised by treaty-based arbitration, in terms of costs, transparency, legal certainty, arbitrator ethics, etc. However, due to its ad hoc nature explained above, it does not amount to a large-scale transfer of judicial authority, and gives host states more room to change course in their future investment contracts as well as giving them a full opportunity to negotiate an arbitration clause with individual investors directly and more conscientiously.[14] In the following section, I explore the main arguments justifying ITA as the most appropriate method for settling foreign investment disputes.

26.1.1 Justifications of promoting ITA

Two main arguments are often advanced to justify the use of ITA as the most appropriate method of ISDS, as opposed to resolving disputes through the usual route of national courts of the host state and at the international level through diplomatic protection.[15]

[13] Paulsson (n. 8).

[14] For a detailed analysis of how far the scale and gravity of investment treaty arbitration claims were anticipated by states when signing investment treaties, see L. N. Skovgaard Poulsen, *Bounded Rationality and Economic Diplomacy: The Politics of Investment Treaties in Developing Countries* (Cambridge University Press, 2015); see also J. Bonnitcha, L. N. Skovgaard Poulsen, and M Waibel, *The Political Economy of the Investment Treaty Regime* (Oxford University Press, 2017), 70–71.

[15] As an alternative to diplomatic protection, investment arbitration is viewed as a means to depoliticize investment disputes; see I. F. I. Shihata, *Towards a Greater Depoliticization of Investment Disputes: The Roles of ICSID and MIGA (English)* (World Bank, 1992): <http://documents.worldbank.org/curated/en/335931468315286974/Towards-a-greater-depoliticization-of-investment-disputes-the-roles-of-ICSID-and-MIGA>, accessed 29 August 2019.

The first is that it improves access to justice for foreign investors,[16] the second that it contributes to the development of the rule of law through the application of agreed minimal standards in host states[17] as well as internationally.[18] These two arguments are clearly related, given that access to justice is a vital component of the rule of law. While the first justification is narrower in scope, the second one is a broader and bolder assumption. The end goal of both of these justifications is that procedural guarantees offered by ITA enhances investor trust and therefore increases investment contributing to the economic development of the receiving state and overall wellbeing of its citizens.[19] I will explore the access to justice and rule of law justifications in turn.

The use of arbitration to resolve foreign investment disputes was advocated in the postcolonial era to prevent discrimination against foreign investors and avoid denial of justice, leading to a diminution of investment value,[20] by governments which it was feared would be abusive and/or would only have weak judiciaries.[21] Distrust of the local judiciary as corrupt or biased against foreign investors was perceived as a factor which could have deterred investors from entering the host state market.[22] The solution found was to internationalize the resolution of foreign investment disputes. Amid worries that protectionist policies of host states would harm the liberalization of global investment, it was argued that international rules and dispute settlement would help to depoliticize disputes.[23] With its declared aim of empowering foreign investors to access justice, ITA soon became presented as a necessity for any state wishing to attract foreign investment.[24] The idea was accepted that the substantive rights of investors anywhere in the world need to be backed up by procedural means capable of enforcing those rights.

[16] F. Francioni, 'Access to Justice, Denial of Justice and International Investment Law', (2009) 20 European Journal of International Law 729.

[17] S. Franck, 'Foreign Direct Investment, Investment Treaty Arbitration and the Rule of Law', (2007) 19 McGeorge Global Business and Development Law Journal 337; B. K. Guthrie, 'Beyond Investment Protection: An Examination of the Potential Influence of Investment Treaties on Domestic Rule of Law', (2013) 45 NYU Journal of International Law and Politics 1151; J Paulsson, 'Enclaves of Justice', University of Miami Legal Studies Research Paper No. 2010–29: <http://ssrn.com/abstract=1707504>, accessed 29 August 2019.

[18] B. Kingsbury and S. Schill, 'Investor–State Arbitration as Governance: Fair and Equitable Treatment, Proportionality and the Emerging Global Administrative Law', (2009) New York University Public Law and Legal Theory Working Papers 146: <https://lsr.nellco.org/cgi/viewcontent.cgi?referer=https://www.google.com/&httpsredir=1&article=1146&context=nyu_plltwp>, accessed 29 August 2019.

[19] The impact of foreign investment on host state development and the impact of investment treaty commitments on the flows of inward investment are empirically contested questions. For an overview and analysis of the literature on these impacts, see Bonnitcha et al. (n. 14), 155–80.

[20] D. Schneiderman, 'Investing in Democracy? Political Process and International Investment Law', (2010) 60 University of Toronto Law Journal 909, 911.

[21] M.-B. Dembour and N. Stammers, 'Free Trade, Protectionism, Neoliberalism: Tensions and Continuities', (2018) 6(2) London Review of International Law 169; G. Van Harten, 'Five Justifications for Investment Treaties: A Critical Discussion', (2010) 2 Trade, Law and Development 19, 33; J. Alvarez, *The Public International Law Regime Governing International Investment* (Martinus Nijhoff, 2011), 113.

[22] Bonnitcha et al. (n. 14), 86.

[23] N. Tzouvala, 'The Ordo-Liberal Origins of Modern International Investment Law: Constructing Competition on a Global Scale' in JD Haskell and A Rasulov (eds), *European Yearbook of International Economic Law Special Issue: New Voices and New Perspectives in International Economic Law* (Switzerland, Springer 2020) page 38.

[24] Bonnitcha et al. (n. 14), 209–10.

Mainstream thinking on investment arbitration accepts that releasing foreign investors from the necessity of exhausting domestic remedies prior to initiating international arbitration is needed in order to prevent discrimination against, and give voice to, foreign investors who are unrepresented in the host state's political process.[25] This has the effect of prioritizing international solutions which, in turn, reinforces the common perception that domestic institutions, actors, and cultures undermine democracy and human rights, whilst international law promotes them.[26] The view of investment arbitration as the impartial guardian of foreign investors' rights epitomizes the sanctity of the international and the distrust of the local. Interestingly, it also serves to underpin the argument that arbitration stands to improve host states' poor records in terms of the rule of law.[27] What the rule of law means is admittedly elusive.[28] However, in IIL debates, it tends to encompass democratic governance, limitation of government authority by law, legal certainty, protection of basic rights, and (most importantly in the context of this chapter) access to justice.

An argument often made by proponents of investment liberalization is that compelling host states to comply with international investment standards through recourse to an external enforcement mechanism has a positive effect on the local rule of law in the host state.[29] It is argued that this happens in two ways. First, decisions of ITA tribunals act as checks on arbitrary government behaviour contrary to rule of law principles, and compel host states to comply with an external and a more just standard of treatment vis-à-vis foreign investors.[30] Second, by leaving the final word to impartial and independent arbitration tribunals, an increase in the levels of investment protection and legal certainty is achieved, in turn leading to economic and social development in the host state funded by the resources generated from the investment trickling down to improving local judicial and executive capacities. Thus, for ardent proponents of the rule of law function of ITA such as Benedict Kingsbury and Stephan Schill, ITA is a tool capable of fostering 'democratic accountability and participation......good and orderly state

[25] Hence the link made between access to justice and the 'minimum standard of treatment of aliens': see Francioni (n. 16), 731. See also *Técnicas Medioambientales Tecmed SA v United Mexican States* (Award), ICSID Case No ARB (AF)/00/2, 29 May 2003, [122] (*Tecmed v Mexico Award*).

[26] M Koskenniemi, 'It's Not the Cases, It's the System', (2017) 18 Journal of World Investment and Trade 343, 352–3; A. Orford, 'Locating the International: Military and Monetary Interventions after the Cold War', (1997) 38 Harvard International Law Journal 444, 484. See also M.-B. Dembour and T Kelly, 'Introduction: The Social Lives of International Justice', in M.-B. Dembour and T. Kelly (eds), *Paths to International Justice: Social and Legal Perspectives* (Oxford University Press, 2007) 1, 13.

[27] S W Schill, 'International Investment Law and the Rule of Law', in J. Lowell, J. C. Thomas, and J. van Zyl Smit (eds), *Rule of Law Symposium 2014: The Importance of the Rule of Law in Promoting Development* (Academy Publishing, 2015), 81–102; Amsterdam Law School Research Paper No. 2017-18; Amsterdam Center for International Law No. 2017-15: <https://ssrn.com/abstract=2932153>, accessed 29 August 2019; Franck (n.16).

[28] As Brian Tamanaha has observed, the rule of law 'stands in the peculiar state of being *the* preeminent legitimating political ideal in the world today, without agreement upon precisely what it means': B. Z.Tamanaha, *On the Rule of Law: History, Politics, Theory* (Cambridge University Press, 2004), 4 (emphasis in original).

[29] Schill (n. 26); Franck (n. 16). [30] Ibid. 367.

administration and the protection of rights and other deserving interests'.[31] In a similar vein, Susan Franck presents investment treaty arbitration as a contributing factor to the development of the rule of law in host states with a weak rule of law. She argues that 'investment treaty arbitration may create incentives for foreign investment by fostering the development of the rule of law'.[32]

Studies which have attempted to measure the impact of IIL commitments on the volume of inward investment are inconclusive.[33] On rule of law effects, a recent socio-legal study by Mavluda Sattorova demonstrates that 'host states do not necessarily respond to their encounter with investment treaty law by becoming more risk-averse and compliant with good governance norms'.[34] Interviews with relevant government officials, judges, and civil servants have shown that there was limited internalization of the good governance standards found in investment treaties and investment treaty claims have not generally led to noteworthy changes in the standards followed by officials in future dealings with foreign investors.[35] Her study has further found that in some instances, host states '[r]ather than embarking on comprehensive and systemic reforms of governance institutions and practices, some host governments—in particular in developing countries—appear to opt for short-term and localised solutions aimed solely at safeguarding the special treatment of foreign investors and optimising the defence of state interests in investment arbitration disputes'.[36] She concludes that some host states may follow good governance standards in dealings with foreign investors while failing to achieve 'good governance for all'.[37] It is increasingly acknowledged that IIL commitments are not a panacea for remedying rule of law deficiencies in host states.[38]

Neither is there sufficient empirical support for the idea that procedural guarantees contained in IIL make a positive contribution to improving deficiencies in the domestic rule of law.[39] A recent empirical study on the functions of investment arbitration which explores its relationship with the rule of law found that it 'creates at best a weak rule of law effect in countries with a poor record of respect for the rule of law'.[40] On the contrary,

[31] Kingsbury and Schill (n. 18), 8. [32] Franck (n. 16), 340.

[33] Skovgaard Poulsen (n. 14), 7–8.

[34] M. Sattorova, *The Impact of Investment Treaty Law on Host States: Enabling Good Governance?* (Hart, 2018), 196.

[35] Ibid. 65–75. [36] Ibid. 85. [37] Ibid. 196.

[38] Bonnitcha et al. (n. 14), 170–71. See also R Dolzer, 'The Impact of International Investment Treaties on Domestic Administrative Law', (2005) 37 NYU Journal of International Law and Politics 952; T. Ginsburg, 'International Substitutes for Domestic Institutions: Bilateral Investment Treaties and Governance', (2005) International Review of Law and Economics 25, 107–23.

[39] T. Schultz and C. Dupont, 'Investment Arbitration: Promoting the Rule of Law of Over-Empowering Investors? A Quantitative Empirical Study', (2015) 25 European Journal of International Law 1147. Even in states with more robust rule of law, increased use of arbitration might hamper the consistent development of the law by courts. The Lord Chief Justice of England and Wales has argued that the development of the common law by courts in England and Wales was hampered in areas of law where arbitration is increasingly used: Lord Thomas of Cwmgiedd, 'Developing Commercial Law through the Courts: Rebalancing the Relationship between the Courts and Arbitration', 9 March 2016: <https://www.judiciary.gov.uk/wp-content/uploads/2016/03/lcj-speech-bailli-lecture-20160309.pdf>, accessed 29 August 2019.

[40] Schultz and Dupont (n. 39), 1163.

it is argued in this chapter that the large-scale outsourcing of judicial authority under investment treaty law can undermine the evolution of local institutions of justice. In this respect, David Schneiderman warns against the creation of legal enclaves for foreign investors on the grounds that this might deprive 'the investor voice from the enterprise of creating good and generalised rule of law institutions in the host country'.[41] These findings and arguments should prompt us to seriously question the proposition that ITA produces positive rule of law effects in host states.

26.2 The Backlash against ITA and the Move towards a Permanent Court of Investment Arbitration

There has been an intense backlash against ITA from various actors, including states, civil society, and scholars. Critiques of the current system vary from arguing for outright rejection[42] to offering suggestions for remedying its flawed features.[43] Critics particularly refer to a rule of law deficit in the current ITA model: the proceedings' lack of transparency and inclusiveness; the high costs associated with the arbitral procedure and legal representation; the absence of an appeals process; and the inconsistency of decisions on issues involving public interest. They also question the impartiality of arbitrators by pointing to concerns over general conflicts of interest, elitism, and specific vested financial interests in certain outcomes.[44] At a more substantive level, the way ITA serves to

[41] Schneiderman (n. 20), 937; see also Ginsburg (n. 38); S. Mazumder, 'Can I Stay a BIT Longer? The Effect of Bilateral Investment Treaties on Political Survival', (2016) 11 Review of International Organizations 477–521.

[42] Schneiderman (n. 20); OHCHR, 'Investor–State Dispute Settlement Undermines Rule of Law and Democracy, UN Expert Tells Council of Europe', 19 April 2016: <http://www.ohchr.org/EN/NewsEvents/Pages/DisplayNews.aspx?NewsID=19839&LangID=E>, accessed 29 August 2019; D. Davitti, K. Greenman, and N. Tzouvala, 'Crowd-Drafting: Designing a Human Rights-Compatible International Investment Agreement' (2018): <https://portal.research.lu.se/portal/files/55021365/Crowd_Drafting.pdf>, accessed 29 August 2019.

[43] See e.g. G. Van Harten, *Sovereign Choices and Sovereign Constraints: Judicial Restraint in Investment Treaty Arbitration* (Oxford University Press, 2013); S. Schill, 'Enhancing International Investment Law's Legitimacy: Conceptual and Methodological Foundations of a New Public Law Approach', (2011) 52 Vanderbilt Journal of International Law 57.

[44] P Sands, 'Conflict and Conflicts in Investment Treaty Arbitration: Ethical Standards for Counsel', in A Rovine (ed.), *Contemporary Issues in International Arbitration and Meditation: The Fordham Papers* (Brill, 2012), 28–49; J. Linarelli, M. E. Salomon, and M. Sornarajah, *The Misery of International Law: Confrontations with Injustice in the Global Economy* (Oxford University Press, 2018), 163. For empirical studies unpacking these claims, see Sergio Puig, 'Social Capital in the Arbitration Market', (2014) 25 European Journal of International Law 387; M. Langford, D. Behn, and R. Hilleren Lie, 'The Revolving Door in International Investment Arbitration', (2017) 20 Journal of International Economic Law 301.

advance neoliberal policies around the globe, in particular imposing such policies on developing states, has been criticized.[45]

The potentially detrimental effect of ITA on democratic governance merits particular consideration. It has been convincingly argued that broad and inconsistent interpretations by arbitral tribunals of the substantive rights afforded to investors under the IIL regime have a shrinking effect on the policy space of elected governments.[46] Indeed, host states have not always been successful in defending their actions even when explaining they had to interfere with investments in order to fulfil their human rights obligations under international law and domestic constitutions.[47] In response to this unforeseen encroachmnent of investment treaty awards into the regulatory initiatives in the public interest, investment treaty practice is evolving to explicitly reserve public policy space for governments to limit the interpretive discretion of arbitral tribunals regarding the impact of social and environmental regulations on foreign investments.[48] The interpretation of such treaty clauses in arbitral practice is yet to be seen. Particular features of investment treaty arbitration also prompt suspicions of a built-in bias in favour of investors, for example the facts that the process can only be initiated by investors under BITs and that investors are endowed with substantive rights, but without incurring reciprocal obligations.

Solutions offered to rectify these defects have included: enhancing transparency of proceedings and arbitral decisions; increasing third party participation in the procedure via *amicus curiae* interventions; setting up an appeals mechanism; introducing codes of conduct for arbitrators; and limiting the interpretive radius of substantive protections in treaty provisions by listing legitimate policy grounds that can be invoked by host states. Most importantly, in September 2015, the EU proposed the creation of an Investment Court System 'to replace the old ISDS model in all [EU]'s ongoing and future trade negotiations'.[49] This was in response to the negative reactions from around Europe to the

[45] M. Sornarajah, 'Toward Normlessness: The Ravage and Retreat of Neo-Liberalism in International Investment Law', (2010) 2 Yearbook of International Investment Law and Policy 595. See also D. Schneiderman, *Resisting Economic Globalization: Critical Theory and International Investment Law* (Palgrave Macmillan, 2013); Tzouvala (n. 23).

[46] Schneiderman (n. 20); Van Harten (n. 43).

[47] *Tecmed v Mexico Award* (2003); *Suez, Sociedad General de Aguas de Barcelona, SA and Vivendi Universal SA v Argentine Republic* (Decision on Liability), ICSID Case No. ARB/03/19, 30 July 2010; *Urbaser SA and Consorcio de Aguas Bilbao Bizkaia, Bilbao Biskaia Ur Partzuergoa v Argentine Republic* (Award), ICSID Case No. ARB/07/26, 8 December 2016.

[48] See e.g. Comprehensive Economic and Trade Agreement (CETA) between Canada, of the one part, and the European Union and its Member States, of the other part, Art. 8.9; Netherlands Model Investment Agreement (22 March 2019), Art. 2(2): <https://www.rijksoverheid.nl/ministeries/ministerie-van-buitenlandse-zaken/documenten/publicaties/2019/03/22/nieuwe-modeltekst-investeringsakkoorden>, accessed 29 August 2019; Agreement between The Slovak Republic and The Islamic Republic of Iran for the Promotion and Reciprocal Protection of Investments, signed 19.01.2016 and entered into force 30.08.2017, Art. 10.

[49] C. Malmström, 'Proposing an Investment Court System', 16 September 2015: <https://ec.europa.eu/commission/2014–2019/malmstrom/blog/proposing-investment-court-system_en>, accessed 29 August 2019.

initial plans to incorporate ITA into the Transatlantic Trade and Investment Partnership. The proposal immediately became the flagship innovation of the EU's infant investment policy. ICS has been incorporated into CETA, and it is also now found in the EU–Vietnam free trade agreement as the investment tribunal system.[50] The EU's Trade Commissioner has presented the proposal as revolutionary, claiming that it expresses the EU's aspiration to lead the way globally in reforming the current ITA model.[51] The ultimate objective of the EU is to create a multilateral permanent court of investment arbitration modelled around ICS. With China recently expressing its preference for a permanent appellate body to reform the current model of ITA, it has been observed by Anthea Roberts and Taylor St John that 'two of the world's three biggest economies have now signalled support for significant reform of ISDS, including the possible creation of a permanent appellate body'.[52]

The ICS model is the most advanced and complete proposal made so far, and it offers a reformed version of the current ITA system, attempting to address the concerns raised. In the words of the CETA negotiators, the proposed rules aim to institutionalize a fairer and more transparent version of ITA.[53] The key innovation of the ICS is the establishment of a permanent arbitration mechanism consisting of a first instance tribunal and an appeals tribunal operating under full transparency.[54] With this, the EU aims to achieve consistency and transparency in decision-making; overcome the ethical challenges to arbitrator appointments and conduct;[55] and increase third party participation in the proceedings.[56] Other notable provisions of the proposal include sections on interpretation,[57] on restricting parallel claims and claims by investors who acquired the investment for purposes of submitting a dispute against the host state,[58] and on limiting mass claims by an unidentified number of claimants.[59]

To justify maintaining an international dispute settlement mechanism in its investment treaties, the Commission refers to the potential lack of impartiality of domestic courts in claims against host states, state immunity from suit, the unavailability of certain remedies in domestic courts, and—most unconvincingly—the existence of 'different applicable rules which cannot be invoked before domestic courts'.[60] None of these justifications are substantiated. States do not have full immunity from suit in any of the EU jurisdictions

[50] Free Trade Agreement Between the European Union and the Socialist Republic of Vietnam, ch. II, Art. 12: <http://trade.ec.europa.eu/doclib/press/index.cfm?id=1437>, accessed 29 August 2019. (The text of the agreement was published on 1 February 2016, though it has not yet entered into force.)

[51] Malmström (n. 49). [52] Roberts and St John (n. 4).

[53] 'Joint Statement: Canada–EU Comprehensive Economic and Trade Agreement (CETA)', 29 February 2016: <http://europa.eu/rapid/press-release_STATEMENT-16-446_en.htm>, accessed 29 August 2019.

[54] See the ICS draft proposal text for TTIP, 'Transatlantic Trade and Investment Partnership: Trade in Services, Investment and E-Commerce, Chapter II, Investment', Arts. 9, 10, and 18: <http://trade.ec.europa.eu/doclib/docs/2015/september/tradoc_153807.pdf>, accessed 29 August 2019.

[55] Ibid. Art. 11. [56] Ibid. Arts. 22, 23. [57] Ibid. Art. 13(5). [58] Ibid. Arts 14, 15.

[59] Ibid. Art. 6(5).

[60] 'Public Consultation on Modalities for Investment Protection and ISDS in TTIP': <http://trade.ec.europa.eu/doclib/docs/2014/march/tradoc_152280.pdf>, accessed 29 August 2019.

or in Canada. They routinely act as defendants in judicial review claims by private parties. Courts can effectively grant a more diverse set of remedies than arbitral tribunals, which typically grant monetary compensation. Lack of impartiality can be a problem in both arbitration and litigation. The document does not clarify what exactly the obstacle would be for domestic courts to apply international treaty protections to cases before them, where these rules govern the substance of the dispute.[61] There is ample evidence showing application of a wide variety of international law norms by domestic courts, ranging from treaties on human rights to environmental protection.[62]

The Commission's proposal received mixed reactions from critical commentators. These can be divided into five main groups.[63] The first group are arbitration loyalists that object to the court model as an alternative to the current model of ITA on the grounds that the model proposed would politicize and undermine investor protection, primarily due to states appointing the ICS judges.[64] This group argues for the maintenance of the status quo, only with the addition of minor reforms to improve the efficiency of the system, such as increased transparency and increased diversity of arbitrators. The second group consists of those objecting to the adoption of international dispute settlement for investment disputes between liberal constitutional democracies, on the grounds that the negotiating parties have some of the most developed legal systems.[65] For this group, ITA or ICS only makes sense for agreements with countries that do not provide adequate domestic legal protection. Joseph Weiler has labelled this double-standard approach 'European hypocrisy' (in comments that predate the Commission's ICS proposal).[66] In an approach representative of the third group, Weiler wants to see ITA's most egregious defects corrected so that the system can be transformed into a more permanent mechanism for all international investment disputes. In this respect, the ICS is a positive development, with the recognition within this group that there is still some way to go to

[61] The direct applicability of such rules will depend on the constitutional tradition of each contracting state. Even in states that follow a dualist model, treaty protections can be transposed into the domestic legal order via legislation.

[62] D. Shelton, 'Normative Evolution in Corporate Liability for Violations of Human Rights and Humanitarian Law', (2010) 15 Austrian Review of International and European Law 45, 48–51.

[63] Anthea Roberts maps the positions and reactions of states in relation to the reforms being proposed in various avenues in A. Roberts, 'Incremental, Systemic, and Paradigmatic Reform of Investor–State Arbitration', (2018) 112 (3) American Journal of International Law 410.

[64] C. N. Brower and S. Blanchard, 'What's in a Meme? The Truth about Investor–State Arbitration: Why It Need Not, and Must Not, Be Repossessed by States', (2014) 52 Columbia Journal of Transnational Law 689; Judge Stephen Schwebel, Remarks at Sidley Austin (May 17, 2016): <http://isdsblog.com/wp-content/uploads/sites/2/2016/05/THEPROPOSALSOFTHEEUROPEANCOMMISSION.pdf>, accessed 29 August 2019; EFILA Task Force Paper Regarding the proposed International Court System, 1 February 2016: <https://efila.org/wp-content/uploads/2016/02/EFILA_TASK_FORCE_on_ICS_proposal_1-2-2016.pdf>, accessed 29 August 2019.

[65] See e.g. E.-U. Petersmann, 'Transformative Transatlantic Free Trade Agreements without Rights and Remedies of Citizens?' (2015) 18 Journal of International Economic Law 579, 600; M. Kumm, 'An Empire of Capital? Transatlantic Investment Protection as the Institutionalisation of Unjustified Privilege', 25 May 2015, 4(3) ESIL Reflections: <http://www.esil-sedi.eu/node/944>, accessed 29 August 2019.

[66] J. Weiler, 'European Hypocrisy: TTIP and ISDS', *EJIL: Talk!*, 21 January 2015: <http://www.ejiltalk.org/european-hypocrisy-ttip-and-isds/>, accessed 29 August 2019.

achieve a good model of ISDS.[67] Schill argues that as long as the ICS is used on a bilateral basis, the inconsistent interpretations problem in the investment treaty regime as a whole will persist. Second, he argues that the proposal treats national courts and ICS as mutually exclusive options, and therefore undermines the role of 'domestic courts in settling investor–state disputes and ensur[ing] compliance with international law'.[68] The fourth group of reactions views the proposal as making only limited improvements to ITA, with ICS 'mainly a re-branding exercise for ISDS'.[69] This group identifies the following main flaws: the ICS claims can only be initiated by the foreign investors; other relevant rights holders such as community members do not have standing; adjudicators will continue to receive lucrative remunarations when acting as members of the ICS tribunals; and the lack of a requirement to exhaust local remedies undermines domestic institutions.[70] For the final group, whatever improvements the ICS proposal brings to the existing model, foreign investors will still be unjustifiably advantaged compared to other members of society. These critics argue that ICS should be abandoned.[71] This chapter aligns primarily with the final group, but also appreciates, as the fourth group does, the value of an international mechanism being available as a last resort to remediate denials of justice.

26.3 Mind the Justice Bubbles

What justifies treating certain investors as a category of claimants who should be automatically insulated from the access to justice mechanisms which exist at local, including

[67] See e.g. R. Quick, 'Why TTIP Should Have an Investment Chapter Including ISDS', (2015) 49 Journal of World Trade 199; B. Choudhury, '2015: The Year of Reorienting International Investment Law', 20(3) ASIL Insights (2016): <https://www.asil.org/insights/volume/20/issue/3/2015-year-reorienting-international-investment-law>, accessed 29 August 2019; S. W. Schill, 'The European Commission's Proposal of an "Investment Court System" for TTIP: Stepping Stone or Stumbling Block for Multilateralizing International Investment Law?' 20(9) ASIL Insights (2016): <https://www.asil.org/insights/volume/20/issue/9/european-commissions-proposal-investment-court-system-ttip-stepping>, accessed 29 August 2019; C. Titi, 'The European Union's Proposal for an International Investment Court: Significance, Innovations and Challenges Ahead', (2017) 1 Transnational Dispute Management: <https://www.transnational-dispute-management.com/article.asp?key=2427>, accessed 29 August 2019. See also R. Howse, 'Counting the Critics of Investor–State Dispute Settlement: the EU Proposal for a Judicial System for Investment Disputes': <https://cdn-media.web-view.net/i/fjj3t288ah/Courting_the_Criticsdraft1.pdf>, accessed 29 August 2019.

[68] Schill (n. 67).

[69] G. Van Harten, 'Key Flaws in the European Commission's Proposals for Foreign Investor Protection in TTIP', Osgoode Legal Studies Research Paper No. 16/2016 (2016), 12: <http://digitalcommons.osgoode.yorku.ca/olsrps/139/>, accessed 29 August 2019.

[70] See e.g. G. Van Harten, 'ISDS in the Revised CETA: Positive Steps, But Is It the "Gold Standard"?' (20 May 2016) Centre for International and Governance Innovation Investor–State Arbitration Commentary Series No. 6: <https://www.cigionline.org/publications/isds-revised-ceta-positive-steps-it-gold-standard>, accessed 29 August 2019.

[71] Schneiderman (n. 20); OHCHR, 'Investor–State Dispute Settlement Undermines Rule of Law and Democracy' (n. 42).

national, level? Why should they be entitled to a purportedly more robust method of dispute settlement than any other member of society? I argue there is no good reason for this. The special treatment received by international investment disputes is unwarranted, and introduction of a permanent court of investment arbitration is a move in the wrong direction, as it would further entrench the special treatment afforded to certain investors. A permanent court of investment arbitration is a short-sighted solution to the purported rule of law defects within domestic legal systems which can undermine access to justice not only for foreign investors but for any other groups in the society.

Thousands of investment treaties which contain substantive and procedural provisions constitute an unprecedented international legal protection regime with private beneficiaries. The most precious aspect of this regime is its procedural component. The procedural empowerment of investors via ITA has been described as the 'most effective means of resolving investor-state disputes'[72]—a 'real innovation'[73] in the investment treaty regime. What makes the ITA system a justice bubble is not whether the outcomes of these cases overall tend to favour investors—although such an empirical finding would certainly be another indicator of the privileging nature of ITA.[74] Rather, the main problem is the design and operation of this special system of dispute settlement de facto available only to wealthier investors to secure investment interests above and beyond the fora and remedies available to the other members of society in domestic legal systems. I will discuss in two steps the particularly privileging features of investment treaty arbitration leading me to describe it as a 'justice bubble'.

The first step involves identifying the relevant features of investment treaty arbitration's design, and considering the impact of this design on the operationalisation of substantive IIL obligations. Investment treaty arbitration operates in an international legal vacuum in the absence of appropriate checks and balances that would be present in judiciaries compliant with rule of law principles.[75] Investment arbitration was described by one leading arbitration practitioner as the 'wild, wild west of international practice'.[76] This is particularly problematic in ITA, as most investment treaties neither require exhaustion of local remedies nor provide grounds for meaningfully reviewing ITA

[72] C. Reiner and C. Schreuer, 'Human Rights and International Investment Arbitration', in P. M. Dupuy, E.-U. Petersmann, and F. Francioni (eds), *Human Rights in International Investment Law and Arbitration* (Oxford University Press, 2009), 82.

[73] Franck (n. 16), 343; D. Collins, *An Introduction to International Investment Law* (Cambridge University Press, 2017), 214.

[74] The data available on outcomes has been interpreted in different ways by scholars: see e.g. Schultz and Dupont (n. 39), 15–17; S. Franck, 'Development and Outcomes of Investment Treaty Arbitration', (2009) 50 Harvard International Law Journal 435; G. Van Harten, 'The Use of Quantitative Methods to Examine Possible Bias in Investment Arbitration', [2010–2011] Yearbook on International Investment Law and Policy 859.

[75] Such as having binding standards of conduct for members of the judiciary and legal counsel, legal standards for taking evidence, and various levels within the court system with possibilities of appeals at more than one level.

[76] G. Kahale III, Inaugural Brooklyn Lecture on International Business Law: 'ISDS: The Wild, Wild West of International Law and Arbitration', (2018) 44 Brooklyn Journal of International Law 1.

awards. Within this institutional design, arbitral tribunals institute a monopoly over the interpretation of the bilateral investment treaty (BIT) provisions, which are typically 'relatively brief and [written] at a fairly high level of generality'.[77] Because of this, ITA rulings cannot but impact the practice of states regarding their IIL obligations[78] and draw shifting and uncertain boundaries to the regulatory space of host states. This is most problematic when these interpretations made in a legal vacuum impact states' non-investment obligations,[79] such as those under international human rights law or environmental law.[80] In addition to the uncertainty created by the wide interpretive radius within which ITA tribunals operate, tribunals have typically treated their mandate to be limited strictly to the investment claim at hand in isolation from any non-investment obligations of the host states that are intrinsically linked to the investment dispute. This way, an investor claim does not get tangled with any of the other legal rights and interests affected by the investment or by the host state's action or inaction vis-à-vis the investment. Third parties whose rights are affected cannot join as parties, and in most cases not even as interveners, to claim their rights or voice their position. In some cases, third parties may never even find out whether an investment claim exists or has been resolved via ITA. Inevitably, the succinct and abstract formulation of substantive protections, coupled with the absence of a rule of binding precedent, the lack of an appeals mechanism, and the lack of interested third party input, gives ITA tribunals considerable interpretive discretion that can seriously undermine social and environmental protections which stand in the way of investors' rights and interests.

Approaching the investor–state relationship and the disputes from a privity lens, one observes that IIL tends to take a narrow view of the nature and impact of the dispute. However, the way a dispute—concerning, for example, a water concession or the construction of a pipeline—is resolved can have serious effects beyond the immediate parties to the dispute, the more so since an ITA tribunal might hesitate to take public impacts into consideration, given that its mandate is limited by the investment treaty to deal only with investment interests.[81] Since the objective of investment treaties is to promote and protect investments, tribunals generally interpret the abstract rules in a manner compatible with those objectives. Such a narrow and asymmetrical mandate would be unthinkable for a national court. A national court does not have a mandate limited to an investment treaty, and as such does not have legal grounds to refuse to take into consideration the relevant non-investment obligations of the host state. Furthermore, third

[77] S. Ratner, *The Thin Justice of International Law* (Oxford University Press, 2015), 350, 371.

[78] Ibid. 371.

[79] See e.g. *EDF International S.A., SAUR International S.A. and Leon Participaciones Argentinas S.A. v Argentine Republic*, ICSID Case No. ARB/03/23, Award, 11 June 2012, [192]; *Bear Creek Mining Corporation v Republic of Peru*, ICSID Case No. ARB/14/2, Award (30 November 2017); *Vattenfall AB and others v Federal Republic of Germany*, ICSID Case No. ARB/12/12; *Clayton and Bilcon of Delaware et al v Government of Canada*, PCA Case No. 2009–04, Award on Damages (10 January 2019).

[80] C. Titi, *The Right to Regulate in International Investment Law* (Nomos/Hart, 2014).

[81] W. M. Reisman, '"Case Specific Mandates" versus "Systemic Implications": How Should Investment Tribunals Decide?' (2013) 29 Arbitration International 131.

party joinder, intervention as *amicus*, and transparency are all possible in domestic court alternatives of ITA (administrative courts and judicial review). The features described in the preceding paragraphs show that as the ITA system stands, it provides a level of legal protection for investors unseen elsewhere. A permanent court of international arbitration is promising to dial down on some of these special features but, as Van Harten points out,[82] does not really address issues of third party standing and of asymmetrical protection provided only to investors (unlike in the case of contract based arbitration where both parties can initiate arbitration), and provides no clear jurisdictional basis for the serious consideration of non-investment obligations by the ICS tribunals.

The second step to demonstrating the privileging nature of ITA relates to the costs associated with it. Investors able to mount claims against host states through this mechanism are typically wealthy enough the cover the huge costs of ITA or have a large enough investment claim to attract third party funding.[83] Small businesses are less likely to have access to the necessary funds to be able to resort to this mechanism. An OECD survey showed that 'costs for the parties in recent ISDS cases have averaged over USD 8 million with costs exceeding USD 30 million in some cases.'[84] Costs of legal counsel constitute the largest proportion of ITA costs, with claimants and respondents being often represented by large law firms within the same circle.[85] Costs of litigating large-scale commercial disputes before domestic courts can also climb as high as ITA costs, particularly, in North America and Western Europe, due to expensive legal representation often provided by large law firms at similar representation fees charged for ITA claims. Yet, as highlighted in a recent report submitted to the UNCITRAL Working Group III, for many of the investment disputes submitted to investment arbitration, the average costs for the parties would have been significantly less if the disputes were litigated before national courts of the host state.[86] In the latter scenario, court fees are significantly lower

[82] Van Harten (n. 70).

[83] B. Guven and L. Johnson, 'Policy Implications of Third-Party Funding in Investor–State Dispute Settlement', May 2019, CCSI Working Paper 2019, 6: <http://ccsi.columbia.edu/files/2017/11/The-Policy-Implications-of-Third-Party-Funding-in-Investor-State-Disptue-Settlement-FINAL.pdf>, accessed 29 August 2019: 'On average, financing a claim costs US$ 5 million per side. The economics of the investment require a potential award somewhere around a 5×–6× multiplier of costs, meaning the minimum value of a claim that would be attractive to a funder would be somewhere around US$ 30 million.'

[84] OECD, 'Investor–State Dispute Settlement Public Consultation: 16 May–9 July 2012': <http://www.oecd.org/daf/inv/internationalinvestmentagreements/50291642.pdf>, accessed 29 August 2019. A more recent study has shown that the average investment treaty arbitration cost is just short of US$10 million: M. Hodgson, 'Costs in Investment Treaty Arbitration: The Case for Reform'. in J. E. Kalicki and A. Joubin-Bret (eds). *Reshaping the Investor–State Dispute Settlement System: Journeys for the 21st Century* (Brill, 2015), 749.

[85] M. Hodgson, 'Costs in Investment Treaty Arbitration: The Case for Reform', in Kalicki and Joubin-Bret (n. 84), 749; see also D. Rosert, 'The Stakes Are High: A Review of the Financial Costs of Investment Treaty Arbitration' (IISD, 2014): <https://www.iisd.org/sites/default/files/publications/stakes-are-high-review-financial-costs-investment-treaty-arbitration.pdf>, accessed 29 August 2019; Academic Forum on ISDS Working Group 1, 'Excessive Costs and Insufficient Recoverability of Cost Awards' (15 March 2019): <https://www.cids.ch/images/Documents/Academic-Forum/1_Costs_-_WG1.pdf>, accessed 29 August 2019.

[86] Academic Forum on ISDS Working Group 1 (n. 85).

than tribunal costs, and legal representation options are not limited to the world's most expensive law firms. Defendants and claimants in ITA may often find themselves compelled to seek legal representation from the 'experienced' large law firms who are central players in the arbitration industry to increase their chances of success. The magnitude of ITA costs are also obvious even when compared with disputes heard by other international courts. The permanent court model of the EU proposes for the contracting state parties to finance the court, and this could mean a reduction from the arbitrator costs.[87] But it is unlikely that there will be a reduction in the costs of legal representation, which is the largest cost item involved in ITA claims. In fact, CETA Article 8.39(5) requires the unsuccessful party to bear the costs of the proceedings, including the winning party's legal counsel fees, unless the tribunal finds such apportionment unreasonable. This can place additional burden on losing host states, who will likely pay for the high fees charged by leading arbitration law firms representing the investors.

The *Yukos* dispute, which involved a series of claims against Russia by Yukos investors seeking compensation for the violation of their property and due process rights, can serve to illustrate the extent of protections under the current ITA model compared to protection under a regional human rights protection framework. One set of proceedings took place before the European Court of Human Rights (ECtHR),[88] a second set before an ITA tribunal. Both disputes essentially arose from the damage suffered by the energy company Yukos and its shareholders resulting from the same series of host state abuse. A significant difference between these claims was that the first claim was based on the rights guaranteed under human rights law, particularly on the right to a fair trial and the right to property as interpreted and applied pursuant to the ECtHR jurisprudence. The ITA claim was based on broad investment treaty standards (in this instance the Energy Charter Treaty) of expropriation, and fair and equitable treatment. Although both sets of rights broadly cover the same ground and protect the same interests, there is a stark difference between the two dispute resolution processes in terms of their valuation of damages. The ECtHR ordered Russia to pay the claimants €1.87 billion in just satisfaction under the European Convention on Human Rights. This was the largest compensation this court had ever awarded. Still, it was dwarfed by the $50billion awarded by the ITA tribunal for essentially the same dispute under the Energy Charter Treaty.[89]

[87] European Commission 'Factsheet on the Multilateral Investment Court': <https://trade.ec.europa.eu/doclib/docs/2017/september/tradoc_156042.pdf>, accessed 29 August 2019.

[88] *OAO Neftyanaya Kompaniya Yukos v Russia*, ECtHR, Application No. 14902/04), 20 September 2011: <http://hudoc.echr.coe.int/eng?i=001-106308>, accessed 29 August 2019.

[89] *Yukos Universal Limited (Isle of Man) v Russian Federation*, UNCITRAL, PCA Case No. AA 227. Later, the ITA award was set aside by domestic courts at the seat of arbitration (The Hague) on the grounds that the ITA tribunal did not have jurisdiction. An English translation of the judgment is available at: http://www.italaw.com/sites/default/files/case-documents/italaw7258.pdf>, accessed 29 August 2019. The Yukos claimants may still be able to enforce the ITA award, despite the Hague court's decision. See B. Knowles, K. Moyee, and N. Lamprou, 'The US$50 Billion Yukos Award Overturned Enforcement Becomes a Game of Russian Roulette', *Kluwer Arbitration Blog*, 13 May 2016: <http://kluwerarbitrationblog.com/2016/05/13/the-us50-billion-yukos-award-overturned-enforcement-becomes-a-game-of-russian-roulette/>, accessed 29 August 2019.

While both claims resulted in findings of host state violations, the massive difference between the awarded compensation for essentially the same violations speaks to the privileging nature of ITA.

From the perspective of investors, the only obvious disadvantage of ITA, as opposed to using domestic courts and international human rights mechanisms after exhausting local remedies, is the costs of using ITA. In the *Yukos* case, the costs awarded to the claimant in the ITA proceedings reached up to $60 million, while the ECtHR awarded €300,000 in costs—again an unprecedented amount for the ECtHR. Nonetheless, the high costs of using and maintaining ITA actually adds to its privileged nature, since they limit its use to the few privileged investors who can afford it.

When the underlying assumption is that investor–state disputes are most effectively settled internationally, then moving towards an international court of investment arbitration is a genuine attempt to respond to some of the weakenesses identified by the backlash against ITA. If, however, domestic judiciaries respecting the rule of law are the gold standard for access to justice, why move away further from that goal by establishing a permanent arbitration court? If international dispute settlement for foreign investment disputes is a response to a genuine concern about defects in domestic access to justice and rule of law, would it not be ideal to channel efforts to improve the local remedy systems? Admittedly, both of these options are 'imperfect choices', and the international option provides a quicker solution for governments and international organizations to offer investment protection than attempting to improve local justice mechanisms around the globe within host states presenting all sorts of complex challenges. With the two of the world's biggest economies pushing for further internationalization of ISDS and moving away from local solutions, the justice bubble for the few is likely to become more normalized and institutionalized.

26.3.1 No valid justification for prioritizing investor interests

The premise of the argument for transferring settlement of investor–state disputes to international tribunals or courts is that international dispute settlement promises more effective legal protection for foreign investors. It is claimed that foreign investors could be at a disadvantage if they have to challenge host state acts in host state courts, due to possible bias and discrimination against them on the basis of their nationality.[90] In response to this alleged problem, policy-makers have taken the necessary steps to secure due process rights of investors as a matter of priority, in order to help investment flow without undue burden. However, even if it could be assumed that domestic courts and judges may in particular circumstances be biased against foreign investors, the observation has to be made that investors do not form the only group against which domestic courts might carry perceived biases. So, the question arises: what makes IIL disputes more important than other kinds of disputes, such that the creation of such a special and

[90] Francioni (n. 16).

powerful dispute settlement mechanism is warranted for them alone? Would all disputes not deserve to be settled by impartial and efficient courts?

The adoption of the ICS model in CETA exposes that ITA is no longer merely an access to justice solution. Rather, ITA and its institutionalization by a permanent arbitration court is a symptom of the prioritization of capital interests over broader societal interests. It is clear that the EU, its member states, and Canada do not fail to grant effective judicial protection to investors. In the EU, access to effective judicial protection is guaranteed for everyone, regardless of the nationality of the parties, in member state constitutions, under the ECHR to which all EU member states have acceded, and in the EU Charter of Fundamental Rights. In Canada, due process rights are guaranteed by the constitution of the country. In both jurisdictions, the abstract rights guaranteed in these core documents are brought to life by relatively strong national judiciaries. In the EU, a further level of protection is provided at the regional level also through the ECtHR and the Court of Justice of the European Union. The right to a fair trial and access to remedy are among the few human rights granted to corporations, including corporate investors, on a par with individuals (as the *Yukos* case illustrates). Given this, attempts to institutionalize ITA by reference to access to justice and rule of law arguments ring hollow. With this observation, I do not intend to join the 'European hypocrisy' observed by Weiler. Rather, what I wish to stress is the double standard promoted by policy-makers who prioritize safeguarding investor interests while neglecting the effects of potential domestic rule of law flaws on the rest of the society.

If we look at the issue from a legal and procedural empowerment perspective, concerns about access to effective remedies within developed and developing jurisdictions are not unjustified. Focusing on the CETA countries, there is no evidence to suggest that EU member states and the EU legal system and Canada fail to provide effective remedies to foreign investors. Rather, flaws in access to justice primarily affect members of low-income and vulnerable groups in these jurisdictions,[91] and these 'groups most in need of legal assistance have the least access to political leverage that could secure it'.[92] Proponents of ITA often consider foreign investors legally and politically vulnerable against the state apparatus, including its judiciary, because of their nationality and the fact that they do not have the right to vote to elect representatives who will determine the policies affecting their investment.[93] Yet the type of investor likely to use the ITA or ICS mechanisms has far more political leverage to secure its interests within the domestic legal system than many other portions of the society, particularly the poorest and most vulnerable.[94] It is, at best, questionable to reduce democratic representation and political leverage to the act of voting and then to conclude that the ability to vote guarantees that the laws enacted by the legislature will equally guard the interests of all voters.

[91] The term 'vulnerable groups' is used to include, but is not limited to, indigenous peoples, minority groups, single parents, homeless people, children, migrants and refugees, and the disabled.

[92] D. L. Rhode, *Access to Justice* (Oxford University Press, 2004), 3.

[93] *Tecmed v Mexico* Award (2003); C Schreuer, 'Do We Need Investment Arbitration?', in Kalicki and Joubin-Bret (n. 84), 879.

[94] Schneiderman (n. 45), 131.

Moreover, not having the ability to vote does not mean that one's interests will not be protected by legislation. Legal persons such as companies cannot participate in the democratic process through voting, but they can exercise very strong influence, via lobbying, to promote legislation and reforms to judiciary that safeguards their interests.[95] At domestic and international governance levels, large corporate actors and business interests (i.e. international investors) have the leverage to push their agenda forward much more forcefully than other actors, including the disadvantaged communities and civil society organizations that represent their interests.[96]

There is no evidence to show that foreign investors are more vulnerable than any other group to negative bias in domestic courts. Even relative to the treatment of domestic investors, foreign investors are not necessarily more vulnerable to political risk than their domestic counterparts.[97] Indeed, they might receive better treatment before local courts than some domestic investors due to the economic power they have to secure better business outcomes.[98] In addition, regardless of whether a corporation would commonly be classifed as domestic, with sufficient resources it will easily sidestep national law by careful corporate planning which allows the corporation to pose as 'foreign', thus benefiting from favourable investment treaty provisions that national courts are bound to uphold.[99]

Wealthy investors are more likely to possess the expertise and resources to safeguard their rights, even in times of political crises that may adversely affect their investment. This is not to say that they will not suffer from time to time from the whims of capricious governments and biased judiciaries, but it is to say that they remain better placed and equipped to both enforce and defend their rights. Flaws in access to justice are a much more acute problem for the weakest segments of society. The UN Commission on the Legal Empowerment of the Poor has estimated that 'at least four billion people are excluded from the rule of law'.[100] In its work, the UN Commission documented the systemic inequalities for access to justice for the poor and vulnerable.[101] Even in the most

[95] Ibid. 137; E. Aisbett and C. McAusland, 'Firm Characteristics and Influence on Government Rule-Making: Theory and Evidence', (2013) 29 European Journal of Political Economy 214.

[96] Chimni (n. 1), 13; E. Aisbett and L. Skovgaard Poulsen, 'Relative Treatment of Aliens: Firm-Level Evidence from Developing Countries', GEG Working Paper No. 2016/122, December 2016, 5: <https://www.geg.ox.ac.uk/publication/geg-wp-2016122-relative-treatment-aliens-firm-level-evidence-developing-countries>, accessed 29 August 2019.

[97] Aisbett and Poulsen (n. 96). [98] Ibid.

[99] See e.g. *Yukos Universal Limited (Isle of Man) v Russian Federation*, UNCITRAL, PCA Case No. AA 227, and *Libananco Holdings Co Ltd v Republic of Turkey*, ICSID Case No. ARB/06/8. Both saw the applicants arguing that they were foreign investors because they had used corporate entities incorporated in offshore jurisdictions to roundtrip their investments.

[100] UN Commission on Legal Empowerment of the Poor, *Making the Law Work for Everyone*, vol. 1: *Report of the Commission on Legal Empowerment of the Poor* (2008), 3: <https://www.un.org/ruleoflaw/files/Making_the_Law_Work_for_Everyone.pdf>, accessed 29 August 2019; *Report of the Secretary-General on Legal Empowerment of the Poor and Eradication of Poverty*, 13 July 2009, UN Doc A/64/133: <https://www.un.org/ruleoflaw/files/N0940207.pdf>, accessed 29 August 2019.

[101] UN Commission on Legal Empowerment of the Poor, *Making the Law Work for Everyone*, vol. 2: *Working Group Reports* (2008): <https://www.un.org/ruleoflaw/files/making_the_law_work_II.pdf>, accessed 29 August 2019.

developed countries, access to courts and legal representation remains a challenge for low-income and vulnerable individuals due to lack of financial resources, inaccessibility of the law, excessive formalism, geographical distance, and lack of faith in the judiciary.[102] Increasingly limited access to legal aid only serves to exacerbate this challenge.[103]

The inequalities prevalent in all societies disproportionately affect access to justice for the poor and vulnerable, making them suffer more than any other group from flaws in access to justice.[104] All this shows is that the weakest segments of the society are in greater need of legal empowerment than international investors. Yet, states continue to prioritize better and more advanced solutions for remediating investor grievances that operate outside of the local justice mechanisms, instead of prioritizing the needs of the groups that need empowerment more urgently. The legal empowerment rationale behind granting investors direct access to international dispute resolution simply cannot be explained as anything other than being a justice bubble for the privileged.

26.3.2 Justice bubbles undermine development goals

A slightly different but equally powerful argument against the entrenchment of a justice bubble for privileged investors in the direction of a permanent court of investment arbitration is that it is likely to have a fragmenting effect on local legal development,[105] and thus on the development process as a whole. This is not to say that investment arbitration must bear all the blame for the complex process of development. But ITA has often been championed as a tool for economic and social development due to its encouragement of more inward investment into host states. I have already stated that studies show little to no correlation between signing up to ITA and increased levels of investment.[106] On the contrary, the contribution of having direct recourse to an international tribunal or court for resolving investor–state disputes towards development goals is debatable for at least two reasons. Firstly, outsourcing IIL disputes to international tribunals without the prerequisite of exhausting local remedies could be expected to have a chilling effect on the development of local capacity and expertise in important areas of law.[107] Additionally, Mavluda Sattorova explains in her book that imposition of external standards

[102] J. T. Johnsen, *Vulnerable Groups at the Legal Services Market, in Access to Justice and the Judiciary: Towards New European Standards of Affordability, Quality and Efficiency of Civil Adjudication* (Intersentia, 2009); A. Currie, 'A National Survey of the Civil Justice Problems of Low- and Moderate-Income Canadians: Incidence and Patterns', (2006) 13 International Journal of the Legal Profession 217 (presenting examples from Norway and Canada).

[103] Johnsen (n. 102), 33.

[104] M. R. Anderson, 'Access to Justice and Legal Process: Making Legal Institutions Responsive to Poor People in LDCs', IDS Working Paper No. 178, February 2003, 3: <https://www.ids.ac.uk/publication/access-to-justice-and-legal-process-making-legal-institutions-responsive-to-poor-people-in-ldcs>, accessed 29 August 2019.

[105] Ginsburg (n. 38), 119–22.

[106] Bonnitcha et al. (n. 14), 155–80.

[107] Ginsburg (n. 38), 121.

on host states via IIL and ITA can constrain successful internalization of reforms.[108] States may introduce speedy reforms in the aftermath of large monetary awards granted for breach of their IIL obligations, but this type of 'legal transformation does not facilitate the emergence of "nationally felt" legal rules but instead tends to result a widespread criticism and at times suspicion over the desirability of the proposed reforms for the host country'.[109]

Secondly, there is the very high cost of international ISDS; the hugely expensive process cannot but absorb funds from the public purse that many would prefer to see allocated to improving local means for access to justice or to the progressive realization of economic, social, and cultural rights. In other words, the cost of ITA can give rise to the 'gains of economic liberalisation... to be lost to its beneficiaries'.[110] For example, resources to be allocated to the creation and maintainance of the ICS within the EU and its investment treaty partner states could instead be allocated to improvement of legal aid schemes or the improvement of judicial capacities. The channelling of funds to international dispute settlement with investors is particularly detrimental in times of crises: under the current design of ISDS, compensation of international investors that suffered harms in Argentina, Egypt, and Venezuela during or in the aftermath of financial, political, and security crises as a result of host state conduct falling below investment treaty standards is demanded as a matter of priority,[111] even if the countries are struggling or failing to provide most basic needs of their citizens during the same periods.

The former Special Rapporteur on Extreme Poverty and Human Rights has urged states to include the elimination of inequality in access to justice within their post-2015 development goals, viewing it as 'a vital feature of human-centred social and economic development'.[112] Public resources and the attention of policy-makers should not be dedicated to maintaining expensive paths to justice for a privileged few, but to remedying the flaws and inequalities that exist at the local level. Amartya Sen has demonstrated that legal development is an integral part of the process of development, contributing economically, politically, and socially.[113] Improving local access to justice, even from a utilitarian point of view, would have broader positive effects on the investment climate

[108] Sattorova (n. 34), 111–12, 124. [109] Ibid. 111.

[110] C. Tan, 'The New Disciplinary Framework: Conditionality, New Aid Architecture and Global Economic Governance', in C. Tan and J. Faundez (eds), *International Economic Law, Globalization and Developing Countries* (Edward Elgar, 2010), 122.

[111] See e.g. the huge claims in *Ampal-American Israel Corporation and others v Arab Republic of Egypt*, ICSID Case No. ARB/12/11 (Decision on Liability and Heads of Loss), 21 February 2017; *Compañiá de Aguas del Aconquija S.A. and Vivendi Universal S.A. v Argentine Republic*, ICSID Case No. ARB/97/3 (Award), 20 August 2007; *ConocoPhillips Petrozuata B.V., ConocoPhillips Hamaca B.V., and ConocoPhillips Gulf of Paria B.V. v The Bolivarian Republic of Venezuela*, ICSID Case No. ARB/07/30 (Award), 8 March 2019.

[112] M. Sepúlveda, 'Equality and Access to Justice in the Post-2015 Development Agenda', <http://www.ohchr.org/Documents/Issues/Poverty/LivingPoverty/AccessJusticePost2015.pdf>, accessed 29 August 2019.

[113] A. Sen, 'What Is the Role of Legal and Judicial Reform in the Development Process?' paper presented at the World Bank Legal Conference on the Role of Legal and Judicial Reform in Development, 5 June 2000, 13–14: <http://siteresources.worldbank.org/INTLAWJUSTINST/Resources/legalandjudicial.pdf>, accessed 29 August 2019.

beyond legal protection, including the political, economic, and social climate in the host states. Investor–state disputes are only one of the many types of disputes that an investor would have whilst operating in the host state. A well-functioning local legal system would benefit the investor in all its relationships with other parties, including other businesses and its employees.

Improving the local rule of law as a constituent element of, and a catalyst for, development has been on the agenda of inter-governmental organisations, national development agencies, and development banks for decades, particularly with regard to developing countries and countries in transition. The point here is not to re-state that desideratum. The message is instead that, regardless of the development level of a country, improving access to justice for all segments of society would lead to more meaningful development outcomes than providing special justice paths to a privileged few.

26.4 Conclusion

The EU's inclusion of an adapted form of investment treaty arbitration in its investment relationship with Canada, despite lack of evidence to suggest that these countries fail to grant effective legal protection to investors, shows that the prioritization of interests is not necessarily between developing and developed states, but rather—in all states—a division between the economically powerful and the disadvantaged. Within both developing and developed states, the interests of powerful business interests, local or foreign, take priority and are granted 'the highest possible protection'.[114] While investment treaty arbitration may empower investors from developed countries to challenge certain developing state policies, in the same way they empower investors to challenge the policies of developed states that constrain economic gains.

In this chapter, I aimed to shift the focus of discussion from concentrating on how to reform ITA to paying closer attention to whether there are valid justifications for further normalizing and entrenching special justice mechanisms for a group of wealthy investors. I drew attention to how, within states at all levels of development, disadvantaged groups in society are much more seriously and disproportionately affected by weak rule of law compared to international investors. While investors may suffer from arbitrary government interference with their investments, they are better placed to fight back than disadvantaged groups. Outsourcing the resolution of investment disputes to specialized tribunals outside the domestic systems creates a justice bubble for powerful actors who already have significant capacity to effect change in host states. These justice bubbles absorb resources away from the improvement of local institutions of justice and their accessibility by the most vulnerable segments of society. The aim here is not to propose a complete rejection of international paths, arbitration or otherwise, for

[114] D Schneiderman, *Constitutionalizing Economic Globalization: Investment Rules and Democracy's Promise* (Cambridge University Press, 2008), 4.

resolving investment disputes. As with all other types of voluntary alternative dispute settlement, investment arbitration should be available if the parties agree to submit disputes to arbitration in their investment contract. Mandatory recourse to international dispute settlement could also be introduced, subject to the exhaustion of local remedies. However, having investment treaty arbitration as the default, permanent, and direct method of dispute settlement is objectionable. The proposals for permanent courts of investment arbitration take the ad hoc justice bubbles created by a large web of investment treaties one step further by attempting to make ISDS outsourcing permanent. It is a short-sighted plan that is likely to have detrimental effects on access to justice for all.

PART V

EMPIRICAL EVIDENCE

CHAPTER 27

EMPIRICAL FINDINGS ON INTERNATIONAL ARBITRATION

An overview

CHRISTOPHER R. DRAHOZAL

RESEARCH on international arbitration, like research on international law more generally, has taken an 'empirical turn'.[1] As recently as 2005, almost all of the published quantitative studies on international arbitration could be reprinted in one, relatively thin volume.[2] But today, not only are arbitration institutions themselves releasing more data about their caseloads,[3] but scholars and commentators are increasingly incorporating empirical analyses into their research.[4]

[1] Gregory Shaffer and Tom Ginsburg, 'The Empirical Turn in International Legal Scholarship', 106 Am. J. Int'l L. 1 (2012), 1.

[2] Christopher Drahozal and Richard Naimark (eds), *Towards a Science of International Arbitration: Collected Empirical Research* (Kluwer Law International, 2005).

[3] The ICC has provided aggregate data on various aspects of its caseload for years (see e.g. ICC, '2015 ICC Dispute Resolution Statistics', 1 ICC Disp. Resol. Bull. (2016), 9), which have been used in a number of empirical studies. In addition to studies cited elsewhere in this chapter, see e.g. Gilles Cuniberti, 'The International Market for Contracts: The Most Attractive Contract Laws', 34 Nw. J. Int'l L. & Bus. 455 (2014); Stefan Voigt, 'Are International Merchants Stupid? Their Choice of Law Sheds Doubt on the Legal Origin Theory', 5 J. Emp. Legal Stud. 1 (2008). Other institutions are increasingly providing data (to varying degrees) on their caseloads as well. See e.g. American Arbitration Association/International Centre for Dispute Resolution, 'B2B Dispute Resolution Impact Report: 2015 Key Statistics': <http://info.adr.org/2015-key-statistics/>; China International Economic and Trade Arbitration Commission, 'Statistics' (2016): <http://www.cietac.org/index.php?m=Page&a=index&id=40&l=en>; DIS (German Institution of Arbitration), 'DIS Statistics 2015': <http://www.dis-arb.de/upload/statistics/DIS-Statistiken%202015.pdf>; Hong Kong International Arbitration Centre, '2015 Case Statistics': http://hkiac.org/about-us/statistics>; LCIA, 'Registrar's Report 2015': <http://www.lcia.org//media/download.aspx?MediaId=500>; Singapore International Arbitration Centre, 'Statistics' (2016): <http://www.siac.org.sg/2014-11-03-13-33-43/facts-figures/statistics>; Arbitration Institute of the Stockholm Chamber of Commerce, 'SCC Statistics 2015': <www.sccinstitute.com/statistics/>; Swiss Chambers' Arbitration Institution, 'Commented Statistics 2015': <https://www.swissarbitration.org/files/515/Statistics/Commented%20Statistics%202015%20final%2020160810.pdf>; Vienna International Arbitration Centre, 'VIAC Statistics 2015': <http://www.viac.eu/en/service/statistics/89-service/statistiken/293-viac-statistics-2015>.

[4] For a partial list, see PluriCourts, 'Empirical Studies on Legitimacy in International Investment Law' (2014): <https://www.jus.uio.no/pluricourts/english/topics/investment/documents/1-2014-bibliography-

The best-known empirical study of international arbitration is a qualitative study rather than a quantitative one, *Dealing in Virtue* by Yves Dezalay and Bryant Garth.[5] Surveys are a commonly used quantitative methodology, with periodic surveys by the School of International Arbitration at Queen Mary (and others) being the most prominent[6] (although the College of Commercial Arbitrators/Straus Institute for Dispute Resolution Survey on Arbitration Practice[7] and the Survey on the Law and Practice of Arbitration in the European Union by the Brunel Centre for the Study of Arbitration and Cross-Border Investment[8] are also worthy of note). But empirical studies on international arbitration employ a wide array of other methodologies as well, such as observational studies, citation analyses, and simulations and experiments.

This chapter surveys the existing empirical literature on international arbitration as of 2016. It seeks to be thorough but does not claim to be comprehensive. It focuses on quantitative rather than qualitative empirical studies, and covers studies both of

isds-empirical.pdf> (listing 60 empirical studies on investment arbitration and 25 empirical studies on international commercial arbitration).

5 Yves Dezalay and Bryant Garth, *Dealing in Virtue: International Commercial Arbitration and the Construction of a Transnational Legal Order* (University of Chicago Press, 1996).

6 See Queen Mary and Pinsent Masons, *2016 International Dispute Resolution Survey: Pre-empting and Resolving Technology, Media and Telecoms Disputes*; Queen Mary and White & Case, *2015 International Arbitration Survey: Improvements and Innovations in International Arbitration*; Queen Mary and PwC, *2013 International Arbitration Survey: Corporate Choices in International Arbitration: Industry Perspectives*; Queen Mary and White & Case, *2012 International Arbitration Survey: Current and Preferred Practices in the Arbitral Process*; Queen Mary and White & Case, *2010 International Arbitration Survey: Choices in International Arbitration*; Queen Mary and PwC, *International Arbitration: Corporate Attitudes and Practices 2008*; Queen Mary and PwC, *International Arbitration: Corporate Attitudes and Practices 2006*. See also Loukas Mistelis and Crina Baltag, 'Trends and Challenges in International Arbitration: Two Surveys of In-House Counsel of Major Corporations', 2(5) World Arb. & Med. Rev. 83 (2008) (discussing 2006 and 2008 surveys); Stavros Brekoulakis, 'Enforcement of Foreign Arbitral Awards: Observations on the Efficiency of the Current System and the Gradual Development of Alternative Means of Enforcement', 19 Am. Rev. Int'l Arb. 415 (2008) (discussing 2008 survey); Loukas Mistelis, 'International Arbitration: Corporate Attitudes and Practices. 12 Perceptions Tested: Myths, Data and Analysis Research Report', 15 Am Rev. Int'l Arb. 525 (2004) (published in 2006 and discussing 2006 survey); Loukas Mistelis and Crina Baltag, 'Recognition and Enforcement of Arbitral Awards and Settlement in International Arbitration: Corporate Attitudes and Practices', 19 Am. Rev. Int'l Arb. 319 (2008) (discussing 2008 survey); Emilia Onyema, 'Empirically Determined Factors in Appointing Arbitrators in International Commercial Arbitration', 73 Arb. 199 (2007) (discussing 2006 survey).

7 See Thomas Stipanowich, 'Reflections on the State and Future of Commercial Arbitration: Challenges, Opportunities, Proposals', 25 Am. Rev. Int'l Arb. 297 (2014) (focusing principally on US domestic arbitration); Thomas Stipanowich and Zachary Ulrich, 'Arbitration in Evolution: Current Practices and Perspectives of Experienced Commercial Arbitrators', 25 Am. Rev. Int'l Arb. 395 (2014); 'Commercial Arbitration and Settlement: Empirical Insights into the Roles Arbitrators Play', 6 Yb. on Arb. & Med. 1 (2014).

8 See Tony Cole et al., *Legal Instruments and Practice of Arbitration in the EU* (European Parliament, 2014); 'Arbitration in Southern Europe: Insights from a Large-Scale Empirical Study', 26 Am. Rev. Int'l Arb. 187 (2015) (with subsequent articles to examine arbitration in Western Europe, Scandinavia and the Baltic States, and Eastern Europe). The survey data is available on Transnational Dispute Management, 'Data: Survey on the Law & Practice of Arbitration in the European Union' (2015): <http://www.trans-national-dispute-management.com/news.asp?key=568>.

international commercial arbitration and of international investment arbitration. Section 27.1 describes empirical research on the use of arbitration to resolve transnational disputes—in particular, the extent to which parties use arbitration clauses in international contracts, why they do so, and the frequency of international commercial and investment arbitration proceedings. Section 27.2 examines arbitral procedures, and section 27.3 considers the applicable law in international commercial arbitration. Section 27.4 looks at the demographics of international arbitrators, with emphasis on their diversity (or lack thereof), and arbitrator decision-making, in particular potential biases of party-appointed arbitrators, whether arbitrators make compromise awards, and the psychological aspects of arbitrator decision-making. Section 27.5 looks at the controversy over studies of outcomes in investment arbitrations. Finally, section 27.6 examines empirical studies of compliance with and enforcement of international arbitration awards, while section 27.7 considers their precedential effect, if any.

As with all empirical studies, particularly those involving dispute resolution, the empirical studies surveyed here are subject to important limitations. First, the sample studied—of survey respondents, contracts, arbitration proceedings, or court cases—must be representative of the population as a whole. If not, one cannot extrapolate from the results of the study to draw inferences about the entire population. Second, studies of dispute resolution processes—including both litigation and arbitration—face serious potential issues of selection bias. Parties choose whether to litigate or arbitrate,[9] and settle cases non-randomly,[10] which can bias the observed outcomes. Third, important data—in particular, data on the strength or weakness of the merits of the case—are missing from studies of outcomes of arbitration proceedings, which makes it difficult to evaluate whether the claimant's win rate is too high or too low.[11] At a minimum, however, the empirical studies discussed in this chapter provide a picture of international arbitration—both commercial and investment—that is more systematic than the one gleaned from war stories and anecdotal case reports.

[9] See Stephen Ware, 'The Effects of Gilmer: Empirical and Other Approaches to the Study of Employment Arbitration', 16 Ohio St. J. on Disp. Resol. 735 (2001), 755–6: 'Empirical studies can tell us the relative levels of awards and process costs in arbitration and litigation, but that does not mean they can tell us the relative levels of awards and process costs in arbitration and litigation *in comparable cases*. The probative value we give to empirical studies should turn on our level of confidence that the studied cases going to arbitration are comparable to the studied cases going to litigation. And, in reality, nobody knows whether the cases going to arbitration are comparable to the cases going to litigation.'

[10] See George Priest and Benjamin Klein, 'The Selection of Disputes for Litigation', 13 J. Legal Stud. 1 (1984). Compare Daniel Klerman and Yoon-Ho Lee, 'Inferences from Litigated Cases', 43 J. Legal Stud. 209 (2014), 214 ('suggest[ing] that plaintiff trial win rates can provide useful information about the law.'); Jonah Gelbach, 'The Reduced Form of Litigation Models and the Plaintiff's Win Rate' (2016), SSRN, 3 ('assuming Klerman & Lee's conditions appears little different from simply assuming that selection effects are not problematic in the first place').

[11] See Sect. 27.5.

27.1 The Use of Arbitration to Resolve Transnational Disputes

This section discusses empirical studies addressing the use of arbitration to resolve transnational disputes, including (1) how often arbitration clauses are used in international contracts; (2) why parties agree to arbitrate; and (3) the frequency of international arbitration proceedings.

27.1.1 Use of arbitration clauses in international contracts

Commentators often describe arbitration as the 'predominant' (or even the 'only') method of resolving transnational disputes.[12] Survey data support such an assertion. For example, the 2015 Queen Mary/White & Case survey reported that '90% of respondents said that international arbitration is their preferred dispute resolution mechanism, either as a stand-alone method (56%) or together with other ADR (34%)'.[13]

Data on the use of arbitration clauses in international contracts, however, provides a more nuanced picture. In a sample of contracts with at least one non-US party, filed with the US Securities and Exchange Commission (SEC) in 2002, Theodore Eisenberg and Geoffrey P. Miller found a 'surprisingly... low absolute rate of arbitration clauses: only about 20% of international contracts contain them.'[14] Table 27.1 provides a breakdown of the types of contracts in their sample, and the use of arbitration clauses in each type of contract. While 63.6 per cent of international licensing agreements included arbitration clauses, for example, only 18.6 per cent of international merger agreements, 18.2 per cent of international securities purchase agreements, and 5.0 per cent of international credit commitments did so.

[12] See e.g. Sundaresh Menon, 'The Transnational Protection of Private Rights: Issues, Challenges, and Possible Solutions', 108 Am. Soc'y Int'l L. Proc. 219 (2014), 234 ('[A]rbitration is likely to remain the predominant method for the resolution of transnational commercial disputes'); W. Laurence Craig, 'The Arbitrator's Mission and the Application of Law in International Commercial Arbitration', 21 Am. Rev. Int'l Arb. 243 (2010), 251 ('Whatever the benefits on the domestic scene of comparing the merits of arbitration with those of litigation, the comparison is neither interesting nor realistic on the international scene where arbitration is not only the *accepted* but realistically the *only* method of dispute resolution...').

[13] 2015 Queen Mary/White & Case survey (n. 6), 5; 2013 Queen Mary/PwC survey (n. 6), 6 (52% of responding corporations favoured arbitration, while 28% favoured court litigation); Cole et al., *Arbitration in the EU* (n. 8), vol. 2, pt D, 2 (22.5% of respondents estimated that 76–100% of contracts with 'foreign commercial entit[ies]' included an arbitration clause).

[14] See Theodore Eisenberg and Geoffrey Miller, 'The Flight from Arbitration: An Empirical Study of Ex Ante Arbitration Clauses in the Contracts of Publicly Held Companies', 56 DePaul L. Rev. 335 (2007), 350–52; Ya-Wei Lit, 'Dispute Resolution Clauses in International Contracts: An Empirical Study', 39 Cornell Int'l L.J. 789 (2006), 799–800 (finding 14.6% of international merger agreements in SEC filings between 1 January 2002 and 31 March 2003 included an arbitration clause).

Table 27.1 Arbitration clause use in contracts with at least one non-US party

Type of contract	% with arbitration clause	n
Mergers	18.6%	43
Bond indentures	0.0%	4
Settlements	25.0%	12
Securities purchase	18.2%	77
Employment contracts	20.0%	5
Licensing	63.6%	11
Asset sale purchase	30.4%	46
Credit commitments	5.0%	20
Underwriting	7.1%	14
Pooling and servicing	0.0%	3
Security agreements	0.0%	1
Other	16.7%	36
Total	20.2%	272

Source: Eisenberg and Miller (n. 14), 353.

The Eisenberg and Miller findings suggest that arbitration is not the 'predominant' method of dispute resolution for certain types of international contracts. But some commentators have taken the findings too far to the other extreme, concluding that '[i]n practice, arbitration does not seem to compete strongly with well-functioning public courts',[15] and that, 'given their choice, most businesses that negotiate contracts would prefer a judicial dispute resolution system over arbitration'.[16] Both of those assertions ignore important limitations of the Eisenberg and Miller findings.

First, the findings are limited to contracts with at least one party subject to the US securities laws—and hence with an obligation to make disclosures required by those laws. As a result, the Eisenberg and Miller findings provide little information about the use of arbitration clauses in other parts of the world.

Second, the findings are limited to 'material contracts', the only contracts required to be disclosed by SEC rules. The SEC defines a material contract as one 'not made in the ordinary course of business which is material to the registrant'.[17] As the regulation explains: 'If the contract is such as ordinarily accompanies the kind of business

[15] Jens Dammann and Henry Hansmann, 'Globalizing Commercial Litigation', 94 Cornell L. Rev. 1 (2008), 31.

[16] William Woodward Jr, 'Saving the Hague Choice of Court Convention', 29 U. Pa. J. Int'l L. 657 (2008), 669.

[17] 17 C.F.R. §229.601(b)(10)(i). In addition, the SEC has long objected to the inclusion of arbitration clauses in public offering documents. See e.g. Karan Singh Tyagi, 'Carlyle Leaves Out Mandatory Arbitration Clause in IPO' (Kluwer Arbitration Blog, 2012): <http://kluwerarbitrationblog.com/2012/02/07/carlyle-leaves-out-mandatory-arbitration-clause-in-ipo/>. To the extent the contracts in the Eisenberg and Miller sample were parts of public offerings, the SEC policy would provide another reason for the low use of arbitration clauses in those contracts.

conducted by the registrant and its subsidiaries, it will be deemed to have been made in the ordinary course of business and need not be filed unless it falls within [a specified exception].'[18] This limitation to material contracts results in the sample including contracts that are particularly unlikely to have arbitration clauses (such as merger agreements and credit commitments) and excluding contracts that are particularly likely to have arbitration clauses (such as construction, sale of goods, and joint venture agreements).[19]

So while the Eisenberg and Miller findings warn against overstating the use of arbitration clauses in transnational contracts, the limitations on those findings counsel against going too far to the other extreme as well. As Gary Born concludes: 'It is probably true that, in negotiated commercial (not financial) transactions, where parties devote attention to the issue of dispute resolution, and where the parties possess comparable bargaining power, arbitration clauses are more likely than not to be encountered... [B]ut more ambitious statistical claims are unproven.'[20]

27.1.2 Why parties agree to arbitrate

The survey data present a fairly consistent picture of why parties agree to arbitrate transnational disputes. The 2015 Queen Mary/White & Case survey identified the 'enforceability of awards' (65 per cent of respondents) and 'avoiding specific legal systems/national courts' (64 per cent) as the 'most valuable characteristics of international arbitration'.[21] 'Flexibility' and 'selection of arbitrators' (both 38 per cent) were chosen less frequently. By comparison, the least desirable characteristics of arbitration were its 'cost' (68 per cent of respondents), the 'lack of effective sanctions during the arbitral process' (46 per cent), 'lack of insight into arbitrators' efficiency' (39 per cent), and arbitration's 'lack of speed' (36 per cent).[22] An older survey by Christian Bühring-Uhle had similar findings.[23]

[18] 17 C.F.R. §229.601(b)(10)(ii).

[19] Christopher Drahozal and Stephen Ware, 'Why Do Businesses Use (or Not Use) Arbitration Clauses?' 25 Ohio St. J. on Disp. Resol. 433 (2010), 460–66.

[20] See Gary Born, *International Commercial Arbitration*, 2nd edn (Kluwer Law International, 2014), 95.

[21] 2015 Queen Mary/White & Case survey (n. 6), 6 (respondents were asked 'What are the three most valuable characteristics of international arbitration?').

[22] Ibid. 7 (respondents were asked, 'What are the three worst characteristics of international arbitration?').

[23] See Christian Bühring-Uhle, *Arbitration and Mediation in International Business* (Kluwer Law International, 1996), 136; repr. in Drahozal and Naimark (n. 2), 25 (listing 'most significant advantages' of arbitration as the 'neutrality of the forum' and the 'international enforcement of awards'). See also Richard Naimark and Stephanie Keer, 'International Private Commercial Arbitration: Expectations and Perceptions of Attorneys and Business People. A Forced-Rank Analysis', 30(5) Int'l Bus. Lawyer 203 (2002); repr. in Drahozal and Naimark (n. 2), 43 (parties listed 'fair and just result' as the most important issue in the resolution of a particular international arbitration before the AAA); Shahla Ali, 'Approaching the Global Arbitration Table: Comparing the Advantages of Arbitration as Seen by Practitioners in East Asia and the West', 28 Rev. Litig. 791 (2009), 833 (comparing advantages of international arbitration by region of practice; listing neutrality of forum and enforceability of awards as 'areas of convergence' across regions).

But data on the use of arbitration clauses (like the Eisenberg and Miller data discussed in the previous subsection) suggest that party preferences for arbitration may vary systematically by type of contract. Examining characteristics of contracts that commonly do not use arbitration clauses may help explain why parties to those contracts preferred litigation to arbitration. For example, relatively few international merger agreements (18.6 per cent) in the Eisenberg and Miller data included arbitration clauses, which is consistent with the view that parties tend to prefer litigation for bet-the-company cases that may require emergency relief (like those involving corporate mergers).[24]

Similarly, only 5.0 per cent of international credit commitment agreements studied by Eisenberg and Miller used arbitration clauses, presumably because the law applicable to disputes under those agreements tends to be clear and because special foreclosure procedures are available in court.[25] Finally, Erin O'Hara O'Connor and Christopher R. Drahozal found that arbitration clauses commonly carved out (i.e. excluded from their scope) disputes involving preliminary relief or other matters important to protecting intellectual property rights, suggesting that parties may prefer courts to arbitration for protecting rights to innovation (with some evidence suggesting that the preference may be contingent 'on the quality of the court system').[26]

27.1.3 Frequency of international arbitration proceedings

The number of international arbitration cases filed each year continues to grow, as shown in Table 27.2. Most of the institutions listed show some growth between 2012 and 2015, although most of the growth in the total caseload is due to an increase in cases administered by CIETAC. Figure 27.1 illustrates the change over a longer period of time, albeit using a smaller subset of institutions. The total number of cases filed with the six institutions included in Figure 27.1 increased from just over 1,000 in 1993 to over 4,500 in 2015.

The data on the number of arbitration filings are both incomplete and over-inclusive, however. They are incomplete because they do not include all types of international arbitrations,[27] all arbitration institutions,[28] or ad hoc (non-administered) arbitrations.[29]

[24] Drahozal and Ware (n. 20), 462.

[25] Ibid. 460–62; 2013 Queen Mary/PwC survey (n. 6), 7 (82% of respondents in the financial services industry favoured court litigation over arbitration).

[26] Erin O'Hara O'Connor and Christopher Drahozal, 'The Essential Role of Courts for Supporting Innovation', 92 Tex. L. Rev. 2177 (2014), 2189, 2210; Christopher Drahozal and Erin O'Hara O'Connor, 'Unbundling Procedure: Carve-Outs from Arbitration Clauses', 66 Fla. L. Rev. 1945 (2014), 1975–80.

[27] Fig. 27.1 does not include maritime arbitration, for example, which is a frequently used but specialized form of arbitration. See Maritime London, 'Why Choose the UK's Maritime Services' (2016): <http://www.maritimelondon.com/why-choose-uk-maritime-services> ('2,966 maritime disputes were referred to arbitration in London in 2013').

[28] Compare e.g. Table 27.2 with Fig. 27.1.

[29] Richard Naimark, 'Building a Fact-Based Global Database: The Countdown', 20 J. Int'l Arb. 105 (2003), 106 (describing uncertainty over frequency of ad hoc arbitration proceedings); 2008 Queen Mary/PwC survey (n. 6), 15 (concluding based on survey responses that '86% of awards that were rendered

Table 27.2 New cases filed with selected arbitration institutions, by year

	2012	2013	2014	2015
AAA/ICDR	996	1,165	1,052	1,063
CIETAC	1,060	1,256	1,610	1,968
DIS (German Inst'n of Arb)	121	121	132	134
Hong Kong Int'l Arb Centre	293	260	252	271
ICC	759	767	791	801
LCIA	277	301	296	326
Singapore Int'l Arb Centre	235	259	222	271
Stockholm Chamber	177	203	183	181
Swiss Chamber	92	68	105	100
Vienna Int'l Arb Center	70	56	56	40
Total	4,080	4,456	4,699	5,155

Source: The data are collected in Markus Altenkirch and Jan Frohloff, 'Global Arbitration Cases Still Rise: Arbitral Institutions' Caseload Statistics for 2015', Global Arb. News (2016): <http://globalarbitrationnews.com/global-arbitration-cases-still-rise-arbitral-institutions-caseload-statistics-2015/>.

They are over-inclusive because some of the arbitrations included in Figure 27.1 are domestic.[30]

Moreover, evaluating whether the absolute number of international arbitrations shown is large or small requires some sort of baseline for comparison. The number of international arbitrations filed each year is larger than the number of cases filed in U.S. federal court on the basis of alienage jurisdiction—i.e. cases between a citizen of a US state and a citizen of another country—which is 'an indicator of minimum transnational litigation rates in the United States'.[31] But it is relatively small compared to the number of contracts cases filed in US federal court (roughly 25,000),[32] much less as compared to the

over the last ten years were under the rules of an arbitration institution, while 14% were under ad hoc arbitrations').

30 See Markus Altenkirch and Nicolas Gremminger, 'Parties' Preferences in International Arbitration: The Latest Statistics of the Leading Arbitral Institutions', Global Arb. News (2015): <http://globalarbitrationnews.com/parties-preferences-in-international-arbitration-the-latest-statistics-of-the-leading-arbitral-institutions-20150805/> (explaining that percentage of international cases in reported data ranges from 24% for DIS to 100% for the ICC and ICDR). But see 2015 ICC Dispute Resolution Statistics (n. 3), 12 ('75% of the cases received [by the ICC] in 2015 involved parties from different countries... However, ICC also handles many cases involving parties from the same country (domestic cases).).

31 See Christopher Whytock, 'The Arbitration–Litigation Relationship in Transnational Dispute Resolution: Empirical Results from the U.S. Federal Courts', 2(5) World Arb. & Med. Rev. 39 (2008), 46, 51–52; Christopher Whytock, 'The Evolving Forum Shopping System', 96 Cornell L. Rev. 481 (2011), 515 (table 4) (finding roughly 2,000 alienage cases pending in US federal court per year from 2005 to 2008).

32 United States Courts, 'Statistical Tables for the Federal Judiciary' (2015), table C-2: <www.uscourts.gov/file/20032/download> ('Contract Actions, Total': 2015: 25,737).

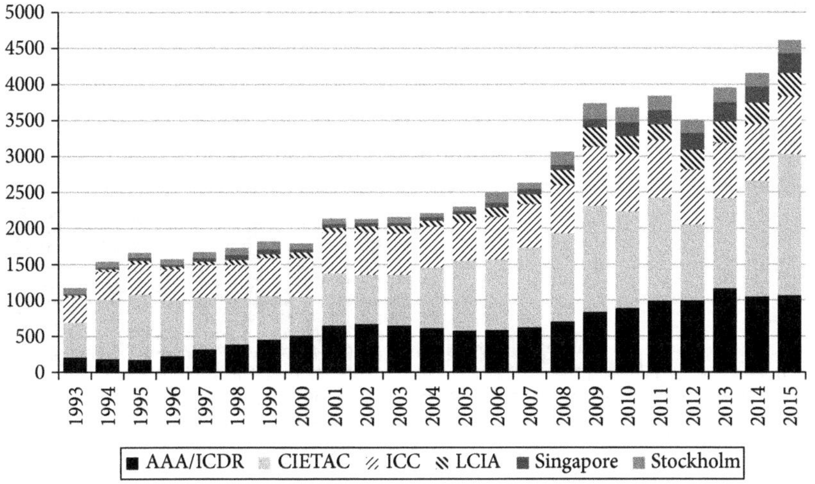

FIGURE 27.1 New Case Filings with Selected Arbitration Institutions, by Year.

Source: Data for 2012-2015 are from Markus Altenkirch and Jan Frohloff, 'Global Arbitration Cases Still Rise: Arbitral Institutions' Caseload Statistics for 2015', Global Arb. News (2016): <http://globalarbitrationnews.com/global-arbitration-cases-still-rise-arbitral-institutions-caseload-statistics-2015/>. Data for 1993-2011 are from Gary Born, *International Commercial Arbitration*, 2nd edn (Kluwer Law International, 2014), 92. Institutions shown are ones for which consistent data are available from these sources for the entire period 1993-2015.

millions of contracts cases filed in US state courts each year.[33] That said, the amount at stake in international arbitrations is much larger on average than the amount at stake in state court contract cases[34] (and likely federal court contract cases as well). Indeed, the average amount at stake in the ICC arbitrations filed in 2015 was $84 million, and the total amount at stake in pending ICC arbitrations was $286 billion.[35]

The growth in investment arbitration cases has been even more pronounced, given the small starting point. Figure 27.2 shows the number of publicly known investment arbitrations filed from 1990 through to 2015, including both investment arbitrations subject to the ICSID Convention (the black portion of the bar) and investment arbitrations not subject to the ICSID Convention (the shaded portion of the bar). Only two known investment arbitration were filed in 1992, while in 2015 at least 72 investment arbitrations were filed. Again, however, the data is incomplete: investment arbitrations not subject to the ICSID Convention may not become publicly known for years after filing, if ever.[36] Moreover, the number of investment arbitrations filed per year is small,

[33] Court Statistics Project, 'Examining the Work of State Courts: An Analysis of 2010 State Court Caseloads' (2012), 10–11 (stating that contracts cases make up 61% of sample of state court filings, and listing total number of state court filings by state in 2010).

[34] See e.g. National Center for State Courts, 'The Landscape of Civil Litigation in State Courts' (2015), 24 (reporting average judgment in sample of state court contracts cases of $9,428).

[35] 2015 ICC Dispute Resolution Statistics (n. 3), 17.

[36] See Luke Peterson, 'Why It's Important to Read Between the Lines of UNCTAD's Annual Review of Investor–State Dispute Settlement Cases', IA Reporter (2014) (explaining that 'claims initiated under the UNCITRAL, ICC, Stockholm or some other rules can be initiated without similar publicity, and may not become "known" to the public for months, years or perhaps ever').

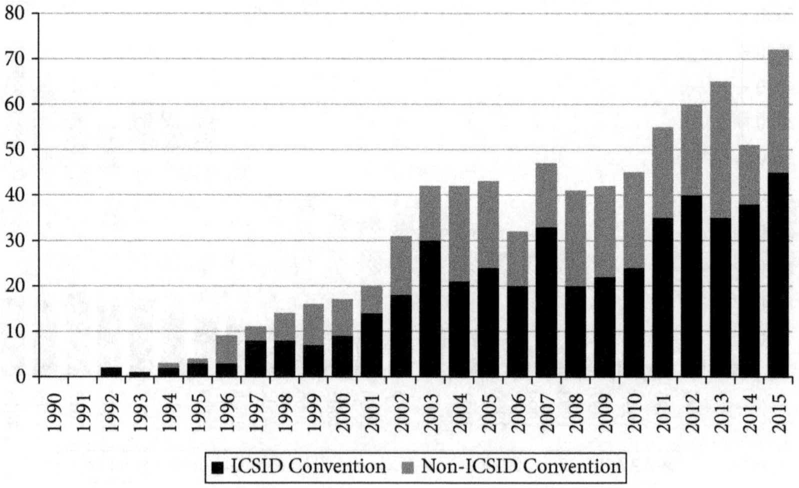

FIGURE 27.2 New Investment Arbitration Filings, by Year.

Source: The data comprise all publicly known investment arbitrations filed from 1990-2015, but not those filed prior to 1990. The dataset is that used in Rachel L. Wellhausen, 'Recent Trends in Investor-State Dispute Settlement', 7 J. Int'l Disp. Settlement 117 (2016), 119-20 (describing data collection), with additional data added; see also Rachel Wellhausen, ISDS Data—2016 Release—Wellhausen.csv, www.rwellhausen.com/data.html (dataset); Rachel Wellhausen, Investor-State Dispute Settlement Codebook (2016), http://www.rwellhausen.com/uploads/6/9/0/0/6900193/isds_codebook_-_wellhausen.pdf. For additional descriptive information about the investment arbitrations in the sample (for the years 1990-2014), see Wellhausen, 'Recent Trends', 123-28 (industry and national origin of investor claimants and characteristics of host state respondents); see also UNCTAD, 'Investor-State Dispute Settlement: Review of Developments in 2015', IIA Issues Note (June 2016), at 2 figure 1 (reporting a total of 696 known investment arbitration cases).

by pretty much any baseline (at most just over 70 cases), although the amount at stake in such cases can be quite large.

27.2 Arbitral procedures

Empirical studies have examined an array of topics about the procedures in international arbitration. The empirical evidence typically is from surveys or observational studies of commercial and investment arbitration proceedings.[37] This section describes empirical insights on selected topics such as the cost and length of arbitration proceedings, the size of arbitral tribunals, interim measures (including emergency arbitrators), multi-party disputes, challenges to arbitrators, the role of tribunal secretaries, and the use of mediation.[38]

[37] There is little recent empirical evidence on the provisions in international arbitration agreements dealing with arbitral procedures. For a good but dated study, see Stephen Bond, 'How to Draft an Arbitration Clause (Revisited)', 1(2) ICC Int'l Ct. Arb. Bull. 14 (1990); repr. in Drahozal and Naimark (n. 2), 65; Drahozal and Naimark (n. 2), 58 ('Information on more recent clauses would be of interest').

[38] There remains limited empirical evidence on some topics, such as document production and witness testimony. Drahozal and Naimark (n. 2), 90–92 (suggesting possible research questions). For an exception,

In addition to providing information about what goes on in international arbitration proceedings, these studies at times also touch on broader themes. First, the data help in evaluating whether international arbitration is becoming more 'judicialized'—i.e. more like court litigation.[39] Second, the data may also be relevant to the extent to which jurisdictions compete to attract arbitration business, and to the effects of that competition.[40] For example, the number of ICC arbitration proceedings held in a country increased following the country's adoption of a revised international arbitration statute, as did the number of arbitrators selected from that country in ICC arbitrations.[41]

27.2.1 Cost of arbitration proceedings

Based on a sample of 221 ICC awards from 2012, the ICC has reported that '[p]arty costs (including lawyers' fees and expenses, expenses related to witness and expert evidence, and other costs incurred by the parties for the arbitration) make up the bulk (83 per cent on average) of the overall costs of the proceedings', while '[a]rbitrators' fees [15 per cent] and case administration [2 per cent] account for a much smaller proportion of the overall costs'.[42] Attorneys' fees and the like appear to make up a higher percentage of investment

see 2012 Queen Mary/White & Case survey (n. 6), 20–31 (survey data on document production and fact and expert witnesses); Mathematica Policy Research, Inc, Recent Practice/Future Possibilities: A Survey of Practitioners in International Commercial Arbitration: Final Report (2005), 35: <https://www.mathematica-mpr.com/-/media/publications/pdfs/recentpractice.pdf> (survey respondents reported that proceedings over previous five years commonly involved 'multiple arbitrators' (80%) and 'counsel from different traditions' (72.5%); less commonly 'interim measures granted' (20%), 'independent experts appointed' (5%), 'jurisdictional or arbitrator challenges' (27.5%), 'more than two parties' (25%), 'discovery/disclosure' (35%)); Cole et al., *Arbitration in the EU* (n. 8), vol 2, pt 1 (responses to survey questions on arbitral procedure).

[39] Christopher Drahozal, 'Disenchanted? Business Satisfaction with International Arbitration', 2(5) World Arb. & Med. Rev. 1 (2008), 3–9 ('The available empirical evidence—both from the ICC and survey respondents—supports the perception that international arbitration is becoming more judicialized'); Rémy Gerbay, 'Is the End Nigh Again? An Empirical Assessment of the "Judicialization" of International Arbitration', 25 Am. Rev. Int'l Arb. 223 (2014), 226 ('[E]mpirical evidence does not support the assumption that international arbitration has recently become more judicialized').

[40] See e.g. 2015 Queen Mary/White & Case survey (n. 6), 12–13 (listing most frequently used arbitral seats over the preceding five years and identifying '[r]eputation and recognition of the seat' as reason why seats were selected most often); Sophie Pouget, 'Arbitrating and Mediating Disputes: Benchmarking Arbitration and Mediation Regimes for Commercial Disputes Related to Foreign Direct Investment', Working Paper 6632 (World Bank, 2013), 12 (rating countries based on restrictions on arbitrators and foreign attorneys and restrictions on arbitral procedures); Charles River Associates, 'Arbitration in Toronto: An Economic Study' (2012), 4 ('From the survey, we estimate that approximately 425 arbitrations [both domestic and international] will occur in Toronto in 2012. On average, survey respondents reported that each arbitration is associated with total expenditures by the parties of approximately $600,000 leading to an estimated total direct expenditure of $256.3 million in 2012').

[41] Christopher Drahozal, 'Regulatory Competition and the Location of International Arbitration Proceedings', 24 Int'l Rev. L. & Econ. 371 (2004); repr. in Drahozal and Naimark (n. 2), 111; Christopher Drahozal, 'Arbitrator Selection and Regulatory Competition in International Arbitration Law', in Drahozal and Naimark (n. 2), 167.

[42] ICC Commission on Arbitration & ADR, Task Force on Decisions as to Costs, 'Decisions on Costs in International Arbitration', 2 ICC Disp. Resol. Bull. 1 (2015), 3; Klaus Sachs, 'Time and Money: Cost

arbitration costs, with one study finding average claimant costs of $4,437,000, average respondent costs of $4,559,000, and average tribunal costs of $746,000 (or 7.7 per cent of the total).[43]

27.2.2 Length of arbitration proceedings

Not surprisingly, on average investment arbitration proceedings take much longer (to final award) than commercial arbitration proceedings. Jeffrey Commission reports that on average an ICSID arbitration takes 1,381 days between filing and award (with the award being issued on average 379 days after the last hearing day), and that on average an investment arbitration under the UNCITRAL Arbitration Rules takes 1,446 days (with the award also being issued on average 379 days after the last hearing day).[44] By comparison, the LCIA reports an average of 20 months (608 days) from filing to award, while the Singapore International Arbitration Centre reports an average of 13.8 months (420 days).[45]

Control and Effective Case Management', in Loukas Mistelis and Julian Lew (eds), *Pervasive Problems in International Arbitration* (Kluwer Law International, 2006), 112 ('[A]ccording to a study undertaken by a well-known Swiss arbitrator, in ICC practice, the share of the tribunal's cost of the total cost of the proceeding nowadays is in the range of 10%. What is particularly interesting in this study is that still 10 years ago such share was two times higher, *i.e.* 20%....'); Celeste Quero, 'Costs of Arbitration and Apportionment of Costs under the SCC Rules', (SCC 2016), 6: <http://www.sccinstitute.com/media/93440/costs-of-arbitration_scc-report_2016.pdf> ('Out of the total costs spent in an arbitration, a median percentage of 81% was paid for costs for legal representation, with the remaining 19% devoted to pay the costs of arbitration'). For data on arbitrator and administrative fees for particular tribunals, see LCIA, 'LCIA Releases Costs and Duration Data' (2015): <http://www.lcia.org/News/lcia-releases-costs-and-duration-data.aspx> (based on all LCIA arbitrations between 1 January 2013 and 15 June 2015 that resulted in a final award) ('The mean costs of an LCIA arbitration is US$192,000. The median costs of an LCIA arbitration is US$99,000'); Singapore International Arbitration Centre, 'SIAC Releases Costs and Duration Study' (2016): <http://www.siac.org.sg/images/stories/press_release/SIAC%20Releases%20Costs%20and%20Duration%20Study_10%20Oct%202016.pdf> (based on sample of 98 SIAC cases from 1 April 2013 to 31 July 2016 in which a final award was issued) (mean cost for arbitrators' fees and administrative fees for all tribunals of $80,337, with mean for sole arbitrator tribunal of $39,207 and for three-member tribunal of $154,371).

[43] See Matthew Hodgson, 'Counting the Costs of Investment Treaty Arbitration', Global Arb. Rev. News (2014) (based on sample of publicly available investment arbitration awards as of 31 December 2012) (noting that '[t]he average tribunal costs in ICSID claims are 10 per cent lower than in an UNCITRAL claim').

[44] Jeffrey Commission, 'How Long Is Too Long to Wait for an Award?', Global Arb. Rev. News (2016); Suha Jubran Ballan, 'Investment Treaty Arbitration and Institutional Backgrounds: An Empirical Study', 34 Wis. Int'l L.J. 31 (2016), 71–2 (finding that the duration of ICSID proceedings 'on average was 1643 days', the 'duration of NAFTA proceedings was on average 1566 days, while [New York Convention] arbitrations were significantly shorter, with an average of 1137 days').

[45] LCIA Cost & Duration Study (n. 42) (reporting mean duration for all tribunals of 20 months, for a sole arbitrator of 18.5 months, and for a 3-arbitrator tribunal of 21 months); SIAC Cost & Duration Study (n. 42) (mean duration for all tribunals of 13.8 months, with mean for sole arbitrator tribunal of 13.0 months and for 3-member tribunal of 15.3 months); see also Quero (n. 42), 8 (reporting mean duration of Stockholm Chamber cases to be 16.2 months, with sole arbitrator cases resolved on average in 10.9

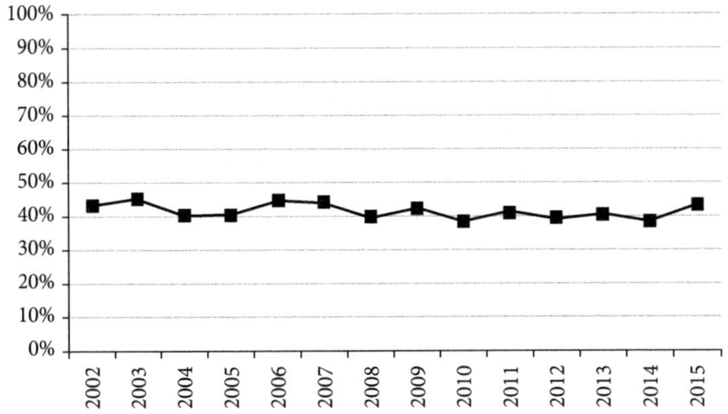

FIGURE 27.3 Percent of ICC Cases with Sole Arbitrators, by Year.

Source: Christopher R. Drahozal, 'Diversity and Uniformity in International Arbitration Law', 31 Emory Int'l L.J. 393 (2017) (describing data sources and methodology); see also LCIA, 'Registrar's Report 2015', 3: <http://www.lcia.org//media/download.aspx?MediaId=500> ('Contrary to the previous year, the appointments made in 2015 reflect a preference for sole arbitrators (52%) as compared to three-member Tribunals (48%). By way of comparison, in 2009, the ratio was two thirds three-member tribunals to one third sole arbitrator; in 2010, the ratio was almost precisely 50/50; in 2011, the ratio tipped back slightly in favour of three-member panels; in 2012, it swung back to 54% in favour of sole arbitrators; in 2013 and 2014, it again reverted in favour of three-member tribunals with a preference of 54% and 62%, respectively.'); Swiss Chambers' Arbitration Institution, 'Commented Statistics 2015', 6: <https://www.swissarbitration.org/files/515/Statistics/Commented%20Statistics%202015%20final%2020160810.pdf> ('Reflecting the increasing number of expedited procedures, almost 2/3 of the cases were submitted to a Sole Arbitrator in 2015').

27.2.3 Size of arbitral tribunals

Roughly half of all international commercial arbitrations involve a sole arbitrator, and the rest involve a three-arbitrator tribunal, with the proportion varying depending on the amount at stake and the institution. As shown in Figure 27.3, in ICC arbitrations, the percentage is closer to 40 per cent of arbitrations with sole arbitrators.

27.2.4 Multi-party proceedings

A sizeable proportion of international arbitration cases involve multiple parties. For example, 34 per cent of ICC arbitrations filed in 2015 involved multiple parties, up from 20 per cent in the 1990s (although the percentage has not changed much for the past decade or so).[46]

months and cases with 3-arbitrator tribunals resolved on average in 19.0 months); Pouget (n. 44), 13 (estimating an '[a]verage length of arbitration proceedings by region' based on hypothetical case, ranging from 36 weeks in Eastern Europe and Central Asia to 65 weeks in Sub Saharan Africa').

46 2015 ICC Dispute Resolution Statistics (n. 3), 10 ('The average number of parties in multiparty cases was 4. However, 14% of multiparty cases involved over 5, and one as many as 31 parties'); Gerbay (n. 39), 242 ('The ICC's data show a significant increase in arbitrations involving more than two parties in recent times. In the period 1982–1992, approximately 20% of ICC arbitrations involved more than two parties. In 2012, the proportion had increased to one-third of all ICC arbitrations. Recent LCIA's statistics show

27.2.5 Interim measures and emergency arbitrators

Arbitrators have the authority to order interim measures in support of the arbitration proceeding, although empirical data suggest that requests for such relief are relatively infrequent. According to the 2012 Queen Mary/White & Case survey, for example, '77% of respondents said they had experience with such requests [for interim measures] in only one-quarter or less of their arbitrations.'[47] The use of emergency arbitrators to rule on requests for interim measures has increased in recent years as the procedure has become more available, with the ICDR registering 67 requests for emergency arbitrators through June 2016, Singapore registering 50, and the ICC registering 34.[48] However, many parties still seem to prefer national courts.[49]

27.2.6 Challenges to arbitrators

Some commentators have expressed concern that adoption of the IBA Guidelines on Conflicts of Interest in International Arbitration has led to an increase in arbitrator challenges.[50] Catherine Rogers offers—and finds mixed empirical support for—an

a similar increase'); HKIAC 2015 Case Statistics (n. 3), ('A quarter of the new arbitration cases submitted to HKIAC involved multiple parties or contracts'); LCIA Registrar's Report 2015 (n. 3), 5 (reporting '18 applications for consolidation under the new provisions in the 2014 Rules involving 77 arbitrations', with 13 applications involving 52 arbitrations 'granted by the relevant Tribunal').

[47] See 2012 Queen Mary/White & Case survey (n. 6), 16–17. Ali Yeşilirmak found 22 cases with a request for interim relief out of 613 AAA/ICDR arbitrations from late 1997 through 2000; in 6 cases the request was granted, in 4 it was denied, and in 12 cases the request was withdrawn or the case ended. See Ali Yeşilirmak, *Provisional Measures in International Commercial Arbitration* (Kluwer Law International, 2005), 165–6. He reported a 'clear increase in the requests for provisional measures in ICC arbitration' over roughly the same period, finding 'nearly 75 awards dealing with provisional measures' in ICC files 'between the mid-eighties and 1998' and 30 awards in English concerning provisional measures during 1999 (p. 166); Richard Naimark and Stephanie Keer, 'Analysis of UNCITRAL Questionnaires on Interim Relief', 16 Mealey's Int'l Arb. Rep. 23 (2001); repr. in Drahozal and Naimark (n. 2), 129 (reporting results of survey on experience with interim measures).

[48] See e.g. Michelle Grando, 'The Coming of Age of Interim Relief in International Arbitration: A Report from the 28th Annual ITA Workshop' (Kluwer Arbitration Blog, 2016): <http://kluwerarbitrationblog.com/2016/07/20/the-coming-of-age-of-interim-relief-in-international-arbitration-a-report-from-the-28th-annual-ita-workshop/> (reporting research by Patricia Shaughnessy finding 'that as of June 2016, ICDR registered 67 emergency arbitrator requests, SIAC 50, ICC 34, SCC 23, and HKIAC 6 requests'); Sarah Zagata Vasani, 'The Emergency Arbitrator: Doubling as an Effective Option for Urgent Relief and an Early Settlement Tool' (King & Spalding Energy Newsletter, 2015): <http://www.kslaw.com/library/newsletters/EnergyNewsletter/2015/May/article8.html> (reporting data on requests for interim measures before emergency arbitrators in cases administered by the ICDR, ICC, SIAC, and Stockholm Chamber).

[49] 2015 Queen Mary/White & Case survey (n. 6), 27 (46% favour '[r]ecourse to relevant domestic courts; 29% prefer '[r]ecourse to an emergency arbitrator').

[50] Born (n. 20), 1896:('Thus, the average annual rate of challenges per pending ICC case in the eleven years prior to adoption of the IBA Guidelines (1993–2003) was 2.10%, while the rate of challenges per pending case in the nine years since 2004 (2004–2012) has been 3.23%—an increase of more than 50%.'

alternative hypothesis: 'of a peak of challenge activity at the time of enactment followed by a reduction' as uncertainty about application of the Guidelines gets resolved.[51]

27.2.7 Tribunal secretaries

Several surveys have examined the use of secretaries by arbitral tribunals, generally finding that '[t]he duties of the secretaries are primarily of an administrative nature' (e.g. 14 of 22 interviewed international arbitrators and practitioners (63.6 per cent)), although commonly the secretary may draft 'non-substantive' parts of the award (11 of 22 interviewees (50.0 per cent)) and, much less commonly, produce a first draft of the award (3 of 22 interviewees (13.6 per cent)).[52]

27.2.8 Mediation

Empirical studies have found that (1) Chinese arbitrators are more willing to mediate in a case in which they are sitting as arbitrator than arbitrators generally;[53] and (2) arbitrators from a civil law background (and German arbitrators in particular) are more willing to employ various techniques to encourage settlement than arbitrators from a common law background (and US arbitrators in particular).[54]

For data on arbitrator challenges in investment arbitration, see e.g. Georgios Dimitropoulos, 'Constructing the Independence of International Investment Arbitrators: Past, Present and Future', 36 Nw. J. Int'l L. & Bus. 371 (2016), 402–3.

[51] See Catherine Rogers and Idil Tumer, 'Arbitrator Challenges: Too Many or Not Enough?' in Arthur Rovine (ed.), *Contemporary Issues in International Arbitration and Mediation: The Fordham Papers 2014* (Brill, 2015), 128, 132–5; 2015 ICC Dispute Resolution Statistics (n. 3), 14: '[T]he number of challenges in the course of the proceedings fell by over half in 2015, compared with 2014. Of the 28 challenges made during the year only 3 were accepted by the Court.'

[52] Joint Report of the International Commercial Disputes Committee & the Committee on Arbitration of the New York City Bar Association, 'Secretaries to International Arbitral Tribunals', 17 Am. Rev. Int'l Arb. 575 (2006), 585; International Council for Commercial Arbitration, Young ICCA Guide on Arbitral Secretaries (ICCA 2014), 62; 2015 Queen Mary/White & Case survey (n. 6), 43, 11–12.

[53] Compare Fan Kun, 'An Empirical Study of Arbitrators Acting as Mediators in China', 15 Cardozo J. on Conflict Resol. 777 (2014), 790 ('The Chinese arbitrators generally consider that it is appropriate for the arbitrators to suggest the use of mediation to the parties at the arbitrators' own initiative (91.7% of the respondents'); Gabrielle Kaufmann-Kohler and Fan Kun, 'Integrating Mediation into Arbitration: Why It Works in China', 25 J. Int'l Arb. 479 (2008), 487 ('In practice, although not obligated to do so by law, Chinese arbitrators systematically take the initiative to ask the parties if they wish the tribunal to assist them in reaching an amicable solution'); Edna Sussman, 'The Arbitrator Survey: Practices, Preferences and Changes on the Horizon', 26 Am. Rev. Int'l Arb. 517 (2015), 537 (51.9% of respondents reported that they were willing to mediate in a case in which they were sitting as arbitrator, as long as the parties gave their informed consent).

[54] Christian Bühring-Uhle et al., 'The Arbitrator as Mediator: Some Recent Empirical Insights', 20 J. Int'l Arb. 81 (2003); repr. in Drahozal and Naimark (n. 2), 135.

27.3 Applicable Law in International Commercial Arbitration

In addition to addressing the means of dispute resolution (arbitration or litigation), international contracts often also specify the law applicable to resolving disputes. Between 80 and 90 per cent of contracts giving rise to ICC arbitrations, for example, specify the law to be applied in resolving disputes arising under the contract.[55] In 2015, 'English law and the laws of the USA were the most frequent choices, between them accounting for a quarter of all contracts', while the laws of other European countries (Switzerland, France, and Germany) were also commonly chosen.[56] Contracts choosing other arbitration institutions surely have different distributions of applicable law, depending at least in part on the nationalities of the parties to those contracts.[57]

A frequently debated topic is the role of the *lex mercatoria* (or Law Merchant) in international commercial arbitration. The term *lex mercatoria* is ambiguous, potentially referring simply to usages of trade that supplement national law, at one end of the spectrum, or to 'an autonomous legal order, created spontaneously by parties involved in international economic relations and existing independently of national legal orders', at the other.[58] Certainly international arbitration rules and statutes provide for usages of trade to be used to resolve parties' disputes in international commercial arbitration.[59] But some commentators assert that international arbitration will lead to the creation of an autonomous legal order, for better[60] or for worse.[61]

[55] See Table 27.3. For a description of a number of studies on choice of applicable law, see Stefan Vogenauer, 'Regulatory Competition Through Choice of Contract Law and Choice of Forum in Europe: Theory and Evidence', in Horst Eidenmüller (ed.), *Regulatory Competition in Contract Law and Dispute Resolution* (C. H. Beck, 2013), 227, 244–592; Joshua Karton, *The Culture of International Arbitration and the Evolution of Contract Law* (Oxford University Press, 2013), 232 (concluding, based on sample of published arbitration awards, that '[i]n all but three of those [39] cases, the tribunal employed an interpretative method consistent with the applicable law'; but noting that all three of those awards were 'applying the law of a common law jurisdiction').

[56] 2015 ICC Dispute Resolution Statistics (n. 3), 17.

[57] See e.g. HKIAC 2015 Case Statistics (n. 3) ('Hong Kong law was the top choice for governing substantive contracts, followed by English law and Chinese law'); Swiss Chambers Commented Statistics 2015 (n. 3), 6 (in 75% of all cases from 2004–15, parties chose Swiss law).

[58] W. Laurence Craig et al., *International Chamber of Commerce Arbitration*, 3rd edn (Oxford University Press, 2000), 623.

[59] Christopher Drahozal, 'Commercial Norms, Commercial Codes, and International Commercial Arbitration', 33 Vand. J. Transnat'l L. 79 (2000), 111–21; repr. in Drahozal and Naimark (n. 2), 233.

[60] E.g. Bruce Benson, 'The Spontaneous Evolution of Commercial Law', 55 S. Econ. J. 644 (1989), 661 (describing the *lex mercatoria* as customary law that is superior to government-made law because '[p]olitically dictated rules are not designed to support the market process; in fact government made law is likely to do precisely the opposite').

[61] Thomas Carbonneau and François Janson, 'Cartesian Logic and Frontier Politics: French and American Concepts of Arbitrability', 2 Tul. J. Int'l & Comp. L. 193 (1994), 221–2 ('At the end of the day, transborder adjudication will be guided by the dictates of the marketplace and the international commercial

But empirical studies to date provide little evidence that parties often want their disputes resolved using the *lex mercatoria*. A survey conducted in 1999 by Klaus Peter Berger and co-authors reported that '[a]bout one third [of respondents] indicated that they were aware of the use of transnational commercial law in international contract negotiations and choice of law clauses', but provided no evidence on the relative frequency of its use.[62] Meanwhile, as shown in Table 27.3, only a very small percentage of contracts giving rise to ICC arbitrations choose to have some sort of a-national or non-national rules of decision govern their dispute (most choose a particular national law, as noted above). And even those small numbers may overstate the extent to which parties select a-national rules in their contracts because the ICC includes as a-national law the Convention on Contracts for the International Sale of Goods, which is an international treaty rather than a-national legal rules.[63]

Felix Dasser similarly has stated that reviewing published arbitral awards from 'more than 50 years yielded just about a dozen cases—or about one case every five years' in which 'the parties [to private contracts] chose a non-national standard... that may qualify as a *lex mercatoria*'; and another 'one pertinent decision every other year' in which the arbitral tribunal relied on an a-national standard when the parties had not so specified in

Table 27.3 Applicable law in ICC arbitration clauses (%), by year

	2012	2013	2014	2015
National or state law	85.4	87.3	82.3	84.1
A-national rules	2.6	2.7	1.7	0.9
None specified	12.0	10.0	16.0	15.0

Source: The data are from the statistical reports published by the ICC for the years 2012–15. See also Swiss Chambers Statistics 2015 (n. 3), 6 (reporting that in 3% of cases administered by SCAI from 2004–2015 parties chose 'international trade law' as applicable law).

community and completely exempt from the reach of sovereign national authority. Law will be generated within the confines of a fully privatized system that is unaccountable to any public organization or process').

[62] Klaus Berger et al., 'The CENTRAL Enquiry on the Use of Transnational Law in International Contract Law and Arbitration', in Klaus Berger (ed.), *The Practice of Transnational Law* (Kluwer Law International, 2001), 91; repr. in Drahozal and Naimark (n. 2), 207. See also 2010 Queen Mary/White & Case survey (n. 6), 15 (examining the extent to which survey respondents 'have used a number of international laws, transnational rules or principles to govern their disputes').

[63] 2015 ICC Dispute Resolution Statistics (n. 3), 17 ('In just 7 contracts, parties chose rules or principles other than national laws. These included the UN Convention on Contracts for the International Sale of Goods (4 contracts), the UNIDROIT Principles of International Commercial Contracts (2 contracts), and equity (1 contract)').

their contract.[64] And a study by Ralf Michaels reported some (but not extensive) use of the UNIDROIT Principles of International Commercial Contracts in international commercial arbitration, typically in connection with other laws, and that use of the Principles as a comprehensive alternative system of law 'is rare and rarely successful'.[65]

27.4 Arbitrator Demographics and Decision-Making

An array of studies of international commercial and investment arbitration have looked at the arbitrators themselves. This section first discusses studies of the demographics of international arbitrators, especially their lack of diversity. It then examines studies of how arbitrators make decisions, with particular emphasis on party-appointed arbitrators, whether arbitrators make compromise awards, and psychological aspects of arbitrator decision-making.[66]

27.4.1 Arbitrator demographics and diversity

Investment arbitrators are the more common subject of empirical research here, at least in part because of the greater availability of data. Commentators have used a number of methods of identifying leading investment arbitrators, with similar results.[67] Todd Tucker

[64] Felix Dasser, 'Mouse or Monster? Some Facts and Figures on the *Lex Mercatoria*', in Reinhard Zimmermann (ed.), *Globalisierung und Entstaatlichung des Rechts, Teilband II: Nichtstaatliches Privatrecht: Geltung und Genese* (Mohr Siebeck, 2008), 129, 142–5 (although noting somewhat greater frequency in contracts with state parties). See also Felix Dasser, 'That Rare Bird: Non-National Legal Standards as Applicable Law in International Commercial Arbitration', 5 World Arb. & Med. Rev. 143 (2011).

[65] Ralf Michaels, 'The UNIDROIT Principles as Global Background Law', 19 Unif. L. Rev. 643 (2014), 643–54 (finding, based on cases in UNILEX database, that '[p]arties rarely choose the PICC'; '[a]djudicators use the PICC even when they have not been chosen'; 'their use as a system is rare and rarely successful'; and '[m]ost use is made of individual provisions, and in connection with other laws'); Eleonora Finazzi Agrò, 'The Impact of the UNIDROIT Principles in International Dispute Resolution in Figures', 16 Unif. L. Rev. 719 (2011), 720 (providing statistical data on the use of the UNIDROIT Principles in international arbitration and court cases, and admitting that 'seventeen years after the publication of the first edition of the UNIDROIT Principles, these figures may appear not too impressive'). See also Giuditta Cordero-Moss and Daniel Behn, 'The Relevance of the UNIDROIT Principles in Investment Arbitration', 19 Unif. L. Rev. 570 (2014), 572 ('The comprehensive set of investment arbitration cases referencing the PICC show that they have been used as "rules of law" applicable to the dispute in one case, as a source of international law in one case, as a corroboration of international law in three cases, and as a corroboration of national law in five cases').

[66] See also e.g. Sussman (n. 58), 527–35 (survey asking arbitrators various questions about deliberations and decision-making).

[67] See e.g. Rishab Gupta and Katrina Limond, 'Who Is the Most Influential Arbitrator in the World?', Global Arb. Rev. (2016), table 7 (calculating 'Arbitrator Influence Index', defined as follows: 'an arbitrator has an AI index of *n* if *n* of his or her decisions issued in investment treaty arbitrations have at least *n*

has described 'eight ideal types of arbitrators' of investment disputes (which might apply as well to arbitrators of commercial disputes), which he divides equally between chair (manager, socialite, dictator, and weak) and wing arbitrators (followers, neutrals, partisans, and turncoats).[68] Robert Kovacs and Alex Fawke found that '[t]he vast majority (88 per cent) [of ISDS arbitrators] have had careers which span some combination of commercial law firms, academia, government and the judiciary'.[69] Sergio Puig has mapped the network of arbitrator appointments in ICSID arbitration, concluding that (1) 'the arbitrator network is dominated by a small, dense and interconnected group, where members at the core are unlikely to escape the observation of other members of the core, but may remain insulated from outside influence'; and (2) 'the arbitrator network is dominated by arbitrators from Europe as well as Anglo-American professionals; however, Latin-American arbitrators trained in Europe, the UK and the US play a fundamental role in the social structure.'[70]

For commercial arbitrators, Yves Dezalay and Bryant Garth, in their book *Dealing in Virtue*, described how 'technocrats' came to replace 'grand old men' in international arbitration.[71] A 2012 survey by Thomas Schultz and Robert Kovacs highlighted the importance of managerial skills for arbitrators today, leading them to suggest the possibility of 'a new generation of arbitrators as managers of dispute resolution processes'.[72]

citations', excluding self-citations and averaging three AI indexes based on 'whether his or her appointment was by an investor, a state or a neutral appointment'); Daphna Kapeliuk, 'The Repeat Appointment Factor: Exploring Decision Patterns of Elite Investment Arbitrators', 96 Cornell L. Rev. 47 (2010), 72 (defining 'those arbitrators who received appointments at least four times to cases registered and concluded during the period under analysis as elite arbitrators'); Ajay Sharma, 'A Study on the Arbitrators Appointed in the ICSID Cases Commencing Since 2011', SSRN, 2 (defining the 18 arbitrators with the most appointments as 'leading arbitrators'); Robert Kovacs and Alex Fawke, 'An Empirical Analysis of Diversity in Investment Arbitration: the Good, the Bad and the Ugly', 12(4) Transnat'l Disp. Mgmt. (2015), 9 (using dataset of '52 individuals with ten or more appointments').

68 Todd Tucker, 'Inside the Black Box: Collegial Patterns on Investment Tribunals', 7 J. Int'l Disp. Settlement 183 (2016), 187–95.

69 Kovacs and Fawke (n. 67), 21–2 (adding that '[f]ew of the most appointed ISDS arbitrators currently work at major international commercial firms', likely to avoid conflict of interest concerns). See also Joost Pauwelyn, 'The Rule of Law Without the Rule Of Lawyers? Why Investment Arbitrators Are from Mars, Trade Adjudicators from Venus', 109 Am. J. Int'l L. 761 (2015), 783 (table 6) (comparing ICSID arbitrators to World Trade Organization panellists); José Costa, 'Comparing WTO Panelists and ICSID Arbitrators: The Creation of International Legal Fields', 1(4) Oñati Socio-Legal Series (2011). For a critique of Pauwelyn's broader thesis, see Catherine Rogers, 'Apparent Dichotomies, Covert Similarities: A Response to Joost Pauwelyn', AJIL Unbound (2016): <https://www.asil.org/blogs/apparent-dichotomies-covert-similarities-response-joost-pauwelyn>.

70 Sergio Puig, 'Social Capital in the Arbitration Market', 25 Eur. J. Int'l L. 387 (2014), 410–13, 419. See also Cai Congyan, 'Structure of Arbitrators and Its Implications Towards ICSID Mechanism: An Empirical Analysis', 9 J. World Inv. & Trade 333 (2008), 340 (table 1) and 343 (table 2) (describing nationality of ICSID arbitrators); Susan Franck, 'Empirically Evaluating Claims About Investment Treaty Arbitration', 86 N.C. L. Rev. 1 (2007), 78 ('109 arbitrators (75% of the population) came from OECD countries.').

71 Dezalay & Garth (n. 5), 34–41.

72 Thomas Schultz and Robert Kovacs, 'The Rise of a Third Generation of Arbitrators? Fifteen Years after Dezalay and Garth', 28 Arb. Int'l 161 (2012), 162. See also 2013 Queen Mary/PwC survey (n. 6), 22 (ranking important factors in company's choice of arbitrator).

Arbitration institutions often publish data on the nationality of the arbitrators they appoint or confirm,[73] and at least one survey provides evidence of the importance of nationality to parties selecting arbitrators.[74]

Numerous commentators have highlighted the limited diversity of international arbitrators—focusing mostly on the lack of gender diversity, but also on the lack of diversity as to racial and other minorities.[75] Empirical studies have highlighted the small percentage of women appointed as arbitrators in investment arbitrations[76] and commercial arbitration (roughly 6–7 per cent female).[77] Women and other minorities are under-represented in international arbitration relative to international courts, national

[73] See e.g. 2015 ICC Dispute Resolution Statistics (n. 3), 14–15 (reporting that 'arbitrators from North and West Europe continued to be the most frequently appointed', although noting an 'increase in the number of appointments and confirmations of arbitrators from Latin America').

[74] Ilhyung Lee, 'Practice and Predicament: The Nationality of the International Arbitrator (with Survey Results)', 31 Fordham Int'l L.J. 603 (2008), 628–9 (results from survey of 19 Korean lawyers with law firms in Seoul who had experience in international arbitration; reporting that respondents (1) 'were nearly unanimous in indicating serious concern of the independence or impartiality of a Japanese arbitrator, with Japanese citizenship, who lives in Japan'; (2) 'also indicated concern of an arbitrator with U.S. citizenship and residence, but born in Japan to Japanese parents'; (3) also expressed concern at 'only slight lower' numbers 'for an arbitrator with U.S. citizenship, born in the U.S. to Japanese parents'; and (4) 'expressed concern (though less serious in degree) for the American arbitrator living in Japan, as well as the American arbitrator living in the United States, or who has a Japanese spouse').

[75] Tony Cole and Pietro Ortolani, 'Diversity in Arbitration in Europe: Insights from a Large Scale Empirical Study', 12(4) Transnat'l Disp. Mgmt. (2015), 10 ('The Survey results evidence a dramatic lack of ethnic diversity in the arbitration field throughout the whole continent: only 30 of 871 Survey respondents described their ethnicity as other than "White"...'); Benjamin Davis, 'American Diversity in International Arbitration 2003–2013', 25 Am. Rev. Int'l Arb. 255 (2014), 260-62 (reporting survey results of respondents' experience with American minorities, women, lawyers with disabilities, and LGBTQ lawyers); Benjamin Davis, 'The Color Line in International Commercial Arbitration: An American Perspective', 14 Am. Rev. Int'l Arb. 461 (2003), 489 ('Over 80 percent of the U.S. Nationals [responding to survey] state they have participated with a U.S. minority in an international commercial arbitration. At the same time over two-thirds of the Other Nationals state that they have not'). See also Susan Franck et al., 'The Diversity Challenge: Exploring the "Invisible College" of International Arbitration', 53 Colum. J. Transnat'l L. 429 (2015), 446–465 (providing demographic information on attendees at the 2014 meeting of the International Congress of Commercial Arbitration (ICCA) in Miami).

[76] E.g. Puig (n. 70), 404–5 ('[A]round 93 per cent of all the appointments are of male arbitrators, suggesting an extreme gender imbalance. It gets even worse: only two women, Professors Stern and Kaufmann-Kohler combined, held three-quarters of all female appointments, pushing the male–female composition of arbitrators in the network to an embarrassing 95 per cent to 5 per cent proportion'); Gus Van Harten, 'The (Lack of) Women Arbitrators in Investment Treaty Arbitration', Colum. FDI Persp. (2012), 1: <http://ccsi.columbia.edu/files/2014/01/FDI_59.pdf> (reporting that in known investment treaty arbitrations prior to May 2010, only 4% of arbitrators were women and only 6.5% of arbitrator appointments went to women); Franck (n. 70), 81–2 ('Women were a tiny fraction of arbitrators in investment treaty arbitration. There were five women (3.5%) in the population of 145 investment treaty arbitrators... In total, the five women appeared in only nine cases and were present in 11% of all awards'); Kovacs and Fawke (n. 67), 12 ('Out of the entire dataset of 499 arbitrators, only 25 are women').

[77] Lucy Greenwood and C. Mark Baker, 'Getting a Better Balance on International Arbitration Tribunals', 28 Arb. Int'l 653 (2012), 655–6 ('[I]t appears that the best estimate of the percentage of women appointed to international commercial arbitration tribunals is around 6%'); Cole and Ortolani (n. 75), 8 ('there is also evidence that non-Male arbitrators may on average receive less prestigious appointments').

courts, corporate boards, and law firm partnerships (20–25 per cent female or more).[78] Institutions (at least in recent years) have tended to do at least somewhat better at appointing diverse arbitrators than parties, but even so, most still have a long way to go.[79]

27.4.2 Party-appointed arbitrators

As noted above, three-arbitrator tribunals are appointed in a substantial proportion of international arbitrations.[80] And the default way to appoint such a tribunal is for each party to appoint one arbitrator and then for the two party-appointed arbitrators together to appoint the chair.[81] Even though the party-appointed arbitrators are appointed unilaterally by one party, with no input by the other, in international arbitrations they nevertheless must meet the same standards of neutrality as the chair.[82]

But there are several reasons why one might expect a party-appointed arbitrator to tend to vote differently from the chair. First, parties unilaterally appointing an arbitrator might pick an arbitrator they perceive likely to rule in their favour, what might be called 'selection bias'. As Martin Hunter famously has said: '[W]hen I am representing a client in an arbitration, what I am really looking for in a party nominated arbitrator is someone with maximum predisposition towards my client, but with the minimum appearance

[78] Greenwood and Baker (n. 77), 658 ('The best estimates of 6% of women appointed as arbitrators on international arbitration tribunals is just over half the 11% figure for female partners on international arbitration teams.'); Kovacs and Fawke (n. 67), 12 ('Around a quarter of partners in UK firms are women.'); Ben Hancock, 'ADR Business Wakes Up to Glaring Deficit of Diversity', Nat'l L.J. (2016) (reporting that 51% of US Circuit Court judges, 52% of US District Court judges, and 74% of U.S. law firm partners are white men); Erika Fry, 'Here's How Many Fortune 500 Board Seats Women Will Hold in 2016', Fortune (2015): <http://fortune.com/2015/11/19/fortune-500-women-board-seats-2016-prediction/> (20% of board seats in Fortune 500 companies were held by women, and 'nearly one-third of new Fortune 500 directors appointed in 2014 were women').

[79] Swiss Chambers Commented Statistics 2015 (n. 3), 1, 9 ('In 2015, 47% of the arbitrators appointed by the SCAI Arbitration Court were women', while 'only 5% of the arbitrators appointed by the parties or the co-arbitrators (as co-arbitrator or chair) were women'); LCIA Registrar's Report 2015 (n. 3), 4 ('in 2015: of the 195 appointees selected by the LCIA Court, 28.2% were women; of the 204 appointees selected by the parties, 6.9% were women; and of the 50 appointees selected by the nominees, 4% were women'); 2015 ICC Dispute Resolution Statistics (n. 3), 15 ('A higher proportion of women were appointed by the Court (54%) than nominated by parties or co-arbitrators (46%), which contrasts with a breakdown of 29% appointments/71% nominations when men and women are taken together'). See also Mirèze Philippe, 'Speeding Up the Path for Gender Equality', TDM 1 (2017), www.transnational-dispute-management.com forthcoming, 3 (providing historical data on appointments of women by the ICC Court and concluding that 'no large disparity exists between the number of women nominated collectively by the parties and the co-arbitrator and the number of women appointed by the Court'—although acknowledging that '75% of the arbitrators are nominated by the parties').

[80] See Sect. 27.2.

[81] E.g. UNCITRAL Arbitration Rules, Art. 9(1).

[82] Ibid. Art. 12(1). In US domestic arbitration, although the default rule now is that party-appointed arbitrators must be neutral and independent, the parties can agree to have non-neutral party-appointed arbitrators (although the chair must be neutral). American Arbitration Association, 'Code of Ethics for Arbitrators in Commercial Disputes, Note on Neutrality' (ABA, 2004).

of bias.'[83] Second, the fact of party appointment might give the arbitrator an incentive to vote in favour of the appointing party—what might be called 'incentive bias'. The arbitrator might want to repay the party for selecting him or her, or curry favour with the appointing party to increase the chances of appointment in a future case.[84]

Commentators have suggested looking at dissenting opinions by arbitrators for evidence that party-appointed arbitrators tend to favour the party that appointed them.[85] Dissenting opinions are relatively rare in international arbitration (although the degree of rarity depends on the baseline for comparison used).[86] The ICC reported that 44 of the 263 (16.7 per cent) partial and final awards issued in 2015 included a dissenting opinion.[87] Albert Jan van den Berg found that roughly 22 per cent of a sample of 150 investment arbitration awards included a dissenting opinion.[88] By comparison, 62 per cent of US Supreme Court opinions include a dissent, while only 2.6 per cent of US court of appeals opinions (but 7.8 per cent of published court of appeals opinions) include a dissent.[89]

If party-appointed arbitrators consistently vote to decide cases the same way as other arbitrators, one would expect dissents to be randomly distributed among arbitrators—e.g. a party-appointed arbitrator would be as likely to dissent to a ruling in favor of the appointing party as one against. But that is not the observed pattern. Of the 34 dissenting opinions in the sample of investment arbitration awards studied by van den Berg, 'nearly all ... were issued by the arbitrator appointed by the party that lost the case in whole or in part'.[90] According to van den Berg: 'That nearly 100 percent of the dissents favor the party that appointed the dissenter raises concerns about neutrality.'[91] That said, the fact that most international arbitration awards are unanimous means that in most cases one of the party-appointed arbitrators voted against the party that appointed him or her (although unanimous awards certainly might mask disagreement among arbitrators in making the award).[92]

[83] Martin Hunter, 'Ethics of the International Arbitrator', 53 Arb. 219 (1987), 223.

[84] Richard Mosk and Tom Ginsburg, 'Dissenting Opinions in International Arbitration', in Matti Tupamäki (ed.), *Liber Amicorum Bengt Broms* (Finnish Branch of the International Law Association, 1999), 259, 275 ('Although party-appointed arbitrators are supposed to be impartial and independent in international arbitrations, some believe that with the availability of dissent, arbitrators may feel pressure to support the party that appointed them and to disclose that support').

[85] See e.g. Drahozal and Naimark (n. 2), 260.

[86] Moreover, focusing solely on dissenting opinions likely understates the extent of disagreement among arbitrators in a three-arbitrator tribunal.

[87] 2015 ICC Dispute Resolution Statistics (n. 3), 18 (another four awards indicated that the case was decided by a majority of the tribunal 'without identifying the dissenting arbitrator').

[88] Albert Jan van den Berg, 'Dissenting Opinions by Party-Appointed Arbitrators in Investment Arbitration', in Mahnoush Arsanjani et al. (eds), *Looking to the Future: Essays on International Law in Honor of W. Michael Reisman* (Martinus Nijhoff, 2011), 821, 824.

[89] Lee Epstein et al., 'Why (and When) Judges Dissent: A Theoretical and Empirical Analysis', 3 J. Legal Analysis 101 (2011), 106 and n. 9. Of course, the likelihood of dissent is greater with a greater number of decision-makers.

[90] Van den Berg (n. 88), 824. [91] Ibid. 825.

[92] Catherine Rogers, 'The Politics of International Investment Arbitrators', 12 Santa Clara J. Int'l L. 223 (2013), 245.

There is no way to tell whether the results reported by van den Berg are due to selection bias or incentive bias or both.[93] Sergio Puig and Anton Strezhnev sought to test for the presence of bias in a setting without selection bias. By using an experimental design, in which respondents were assigned as arbitrators rather than selected by parties, they eliminated the possibility of selection bias (the trade-off, of course, is concerns about whether their experimental results apply in the real world). Their experimental scenario required arbitrators to allocate costs in an investment arbitration proceeding in which the tribunal had ruled in favour of the claimant. In their sample of respondents, they found: 'An arbitrator who is appointed by the loser has only a 36 per cent chance of assigning all of the costs to the losing party. This jumps to about 55 per cent when the arbitrator is appointed by the winner—an increase of roughly 19 percentage points.'[94] Their results thus provide some evidence of bias other than selection bias in party-appointed arbitrators, at least in an experimental setting.

An alternative to party appointment is what is called 'blinded' or 'screened' appointment: a party continues to appoint its arbitrator unilaterally, but the arbitrators do not know which party appointed them (i.e. they are blinded to or screened from the identity of the appointing party). Such an appointment method, it is argued, reduces incentive bias or affiliation bias (although not selection bias) while preserving the benefits of party appointment. The domestic non-administered arbitration rules of the International Institute for Conflict Prevention & Resolution (CPR) have authorized screened appointments for a number of years, and in December 2014 CPR adopted such a procedure in its international rules as well.[95] No empirical data are yet available on how the CPR screened appointment process works in practice, however.[96]

27.4.3 Compromise awards

A common criticism of arbitration, both in the United States and internationally, is that arbitrators make compromise awards—colloquially, that they 'split the baby'. For

[93] Ibid. 246. After examining data on outcomes in investment arbitration, Sergio Puig concludes that '[t]he party-appointing system has an effect in great part because of *selection effect*', although 'there is no reason not to believe that, at some level, affiliation effect is also affecting arbitration'. See Sergio Puig, 'Blinding International Justice', 56 Va. J. Int'l L. 647 (2016).

[94] Sergio Puig and Anton Strezhnev, 'Affiliation Bias in Arbitration: An Experimental Approach', 46 Journal of Legal Studies 371 (2017).

[95] See CPR Non-Administered Arbitration Rules, Rule 5.4 (2007); CPR Rules for Administered Arbitration of International Disputes, Rule 5.4 (2014). According to CPR, more than 15% of its 2015 caseload of three-arbitrator tribunals used the screened selection process, to the evident satisfaction of parties and arbitrators involved.

[96] In their experimental study, Puig and Strezhnev reported that arbitrators appointed by what they characterized as a blinded process tended to make similar decisions to those of arbitrators told they were appointed by the parties jointly. Puig and Strezhnev (n. 94), 25. But what they labeled a 'blinded' process was simply not mentioning arbitrator selection in the experimental scenario. So how a blinded selection would work, even in an experimental setting, remains an open empirical question.

example, a RAND Institute survey of US corporate counsel found that the respondents were 'overwhelmingly of the belief that arbitrators tend to split or compromise the award rather than ruling strongly for one party'.[97] One asserted explanation is that arbitrators have 'an incentive to render compromised judgments that do not badly offend either party' to enhance their chances of being appointed again in a future dispute.[98]

But studies have failed to find patterns of arbitration awards consistent with the view that arbitrators frequently make compromise awards. The leading study is by Stephanie Keer and Richard Naimark, who examined a sample of AAA international awards from 1995 through 2000. They reported that the claimants' mean recovery as a percentage of the amount claimed was 50.5 per cent, and the median was 46.7 per cent, which seems to suggest widespread compromise awards. But the distribution of the awards was u-shaped, with 31 per cent awarding 0 per cent of the amount claimed and 35 per cent awarding 100 per cent of the amount claimed, suggesting that 'arbitrators, as a rule, make decisive awards and do not "split the baby"'.[99] Studies of investment arbitration awards[100] and JAMS arbitration awards,[101] as well as an updated study of AAA/ICDR awards,[102] have reached similar conclusions.

A limitation of studies of award outcomes is that outcomes are difficult to evaluate without knowing the strength of the underlying claims. Thus, an award of 10 per cent of the amount claimed would not appear to be a compromise award. But if the most the claimant realistically could expect to recover was 20 per cent of the amount claimed, then an award of 10 per cent (half that amount) might in fact be a compromise award.[103]

[97] Rand Institute for Civil Justice, 'Business-to-Business Arbitration in the United States: Perceptions of Corporate Counsel', (2011), 7 and 12: <http://www.rand.org/content/dam/rand/pubs/technical_reports/2011/RAND_TR781.pdf> ('over 70 percent of respondents agreed, and only 14 percent disagreed'). See also 2012 Queen Mary/White & Case survey (n. 6), 38 ('in-house counsel and private practitioners believe tribunals have unnecessarily 'split the baby' (i.e. courts in the same dispute would not likely have done so) in 18% and 20% of their cases, respectively').

[98] Dammann and Hansmann (n. 15), 34.

[99] Stephanie Keer and Richard Naimark, 'Arbitrators Do Not "Split the Baby": Empirical Evidence from International Business Arbitrations', 18 J. Int'l Arb. 573 (2001); repr. in Drahozal and Naimark (n. 2), 311.

[100] Kapeliuk (n. 67), 81 ('Of the 43 publicly available [ICSID] awards, 26 (60.5%) denied the claimant any recovery and 3 (7%) awarded the claimant 100% of the amount claimed. The claimant received some monetary award in the remaining 14 awards. Interestingly, only one award split the difference by awarding the claimant a sum ranging between 40% and 60% of the claimed amount. The results thus show that arbitration tribunals involving elite arbitrators do not have a tendency to render compromise awards').

[101] Carter Greenbaum, 'Putting the Baby to Rest: Dispelling a Common Arbitration Myth', 26 Am. Rev. Int'l Arb. 101 (2015), 121 ('the majority of [JAMS] awards were rendered within the 0%-20% and 80%-100% of total claim buckets. This study confirms that arbitrators do not have a significant propensity to split claims. In fact, 85.6% of all claims fell into these two buckets. This indicates that compromise judgments are the exception rather than the rule').

[102] American Arbitration Association, 'Splitting the Baby: A New AAA Study' (2007): <https://www.adr.org/aaa/ShowPDF?doc=ADRSTG_014040> (sample of 111 ICDR awards from 2005) (finding u-shaped graph with '[o]nly 7% (8 cases)...awarded in the midrange (41-60% of their filed claim amount)' and '93%...awarded outside the claim midrange').

[103] Another possibility is that repeat arbitrators may alternate ruling for and against the same party, not making compromise awards in any individual case but doing so in the aggregate.

Existing observational studies are unable to control for this possibility, so the most that can be said is that these findings are not consistent with arbitrators making compromise awards, not that they disprove it.[104]

27.4.4 Psychological aspects of arbitrator decision-making

Commentators have shown increasing interest in the application of behavioural psychology (also known as behavioural law and economics), which identifies systematic, non-rational biases in human decision-making, to how arbitrators make decisions.[105] Reflecting this interest, a pair of recent studies have used an experimental methodology to test for an array of cognitive biases in arbitrator decision-making.[106] Both studies administered a series of hypothetical problems to arbitrators attending professional conferences: Susan Franck et al. reported results for a sample of 262 individuals who self-identified as having served as an international arbitrator (in either a commercial or investment case) and who attended the 2014 ICCA Congress,[107] while Rebecca Helm et al. studied a sample of 94 members of the College of Commercial Arbitrators (largely domestic US arbitrators) attending its annual conference in 2013.[108]

[104] In the experimental study described in the next subsection, Susan Franck et al. found that '[w]hile the data did not demonstrate arbitrators never "split the baby"—arbitrators sometimes did precisely that—it casts doubt on the universality of such a narrative.' See Susan Franck et al., 'Inside the Arbitrator's Mind', 66 Emory L.J. 1115 (2017).

[105] For a more detailed discussion of the topic, see Ch. 36 in this Handbook by Anne van Aaken and Tomer Broude. See also Christopher Drahozal, 'A Behavioral Analysis of Private Judging', 67 Law & Contemp. Probs. 105 (2004); repr. in modified form in Drahozal and Naimark (n. 2), 319; Tony Cole (ed), *The Roles of Psychology in International Arbitration* (Kluwer Law International, 2017); Lucy Reed, 'The Kaplan Lecture 2012. Arbitral Decision-Making: Art, Science or Sport?' (2012): <http://www.arbitration-icca.org/media/1/13581569903770/reed_tribunal_decision-making.pdf>; Doak Bishop, 'The Quality of Arbitral Decision Making and Justification', 6 World Arb. & Med. Rev. 801 (2012); Shari Diamond, 'Psychological Aspects of Dispute Resolution: Issues for International Arbitration', in Albert Jan van den Berg (ed.), *International Commercial Arbitration: Important Contemporary Questions* (Kluwer Law International, 2003), 327, 336.

[106] For other examples of experimental studies with arbitrators as subjects, see Dieter Flader et al., *The Psychological/Communicative Preconditions for the International Arbitral Process: Initial Findings of a Research Project and its Methodology* (ISPSW, 2012); Ray Friedman et al., 'Causal Attribution for Interfirm Contract Violation: A Comparative Study of Chinese and American Commercial Arbitrators', 92 J. App. Psych. 856 (2007), 862 (finding Chinese arbitrators 'more likely [than American arbitrators] to make internal attributions for the organizational behaviors that they judged'); Sergio Puig and Anton Strezhnev, 'The David Effect: Underdogs and Investment Arbitrators', SSRN (2016), 3–4 (based on experimental scenario, finding that 'arbitrators more often sympathize with claimants of middle-income states than with claimants from high-income states' and that 'low-income respondent states get a "compensation bump" over middle-income respondent states'). See also Edna Sussman, 'Arbitrator Decision-Making: Unconscious Psychological Influences and What You Can Do About Them', 24 Am. Rev. Int'l Arb. 487 (2013) (comparing results of a survey of arbitrators to results of simulation studies done with judges).

[107] Franck et al. (n. 104).

[108] Rebecca Helm et al., 'Are Arbitrators Human?', 13 J. Emp. Legal Stud. 666 (2016).

To the extent the studies overlapped in what they were examining, they obtained similar results. Both studies examined the performance of the arbitrators on the Cognitive Reflection Test, a three-question test designed to measure the extent to which respondents rely on intuition (incorrectly) in making decisions.[109] The arbitrators tested by Franck et al. answered an average of 1.47 questions correctly, while those tested by Helm et al. answered an average of 1.51 questions correctly.[110] Both samples of arbitrators scored higher than Florida state court judges but similarly to North American lawyers and US administrative law judges. Similarly, both studies found some (albeit in the case of Franck et al. weak) evidence of a framing effect in which 'arbitrators . . . place[d] greater emphasis on losses than gains—a phenomenon often referred to as loss aversion'.[111] In varying settings, arbitrators were more likely to rescind a contract when the buyer sought rescission (after having suffered an out-of-pocket loss) than when the seller sought rescission (after having suffered foregone gains).

As for other possible cognitive biases, Franck et al. found that arbitrators, like other decision-makers, are subject to an anchoring effect, in which providing information about large damages awarded in an irrelevant case tended to increase arbitrator damages awards in a different, unrelated case. Arbitrators performed better than judges and other decision-makers in looking to base rates using 'rational, deductive thought' in evaluating possible negligence rather than 'intuitive, representative thinking'.[112] But arbitrators, like pretty much everyone, suffer from some degree of egocentrism, with 76.6–92 per cent of responding arbitrators stating they were better than the median arbitrator responding at assessing the credibility of witnesses, efficiently administering cases, and 'making accurate and impartial decisions'.[113] Meanwhile, Helm et al. found that almost all arbitrators (92 per cent) committed the conjunction fallacy—failing to recognize that the likelihood of a single event can be no smaller (and likely is larger) than the likelihood of two conjoined events.[114] But arbitrators 'were not frequently subject to confirmation bias in the traditional sense'—they tended to require more evidence than the minimum necessary to resolve a problem, but did not seek out only evidence that would confirm their prior view.[115]

One limitation of both of these studies, of course, is that they were done in experimental settings rather than in the real world. A potentially important difference between arbitrators and judges is that arbitrators face competition in getting selected to serve, which may give them different incentives from judges in deciding cases—incentives that the experiments do not replicate.[116]

[109] See Shane Frederick, 'Cognitive Reflection and Decision Making', 19 J. Econ. Persp. 25 (2005), 27.

[110] Franck et al. (n. 104), supra note 110; Helm et al. (n. 108), 672.

[111] Ibid. 678; Franck et al. (n. 104). [112] Ibid. 110. [113] Ibid.

[114] E.g. Helm et al. (n. 108), 676 ('Option four ("The agency actively recruited a diverse workforce but also unlawfully discriminated against Dina based on her Islamic beliefs") is the conjunction of option one ("The agency unlawfully discriminated against Dina based on her Islamic religious beliefs") and option two ("The agency actively recruited a diverse workforce"). Hence, option four is, as a matter of deductive logic, less likely than either option one or option two').

[115] Ibid. 685. [116] Drahozal (n. 105), 126–8.

27.5 Outcomes of Investment Arbitrations

The most hotly contested empirical issue in international arbitration in recent years has been whether the outcomes of investment arbitrations unduly favour investors at the expense of host countries. This section describes the findings and criticisms of those studies, which necessarily are based only on publicly available data on investment arbitrations.

In addition, and importantly, the studies also are subject to the limitations of studies of litigation outcomes more generally. First, many disputes are settled,[117] and selection bias due to non-random settlement makes outcome data difficult to interpret. Second, win rates and other data on outcomes cannot be evaluated in the abstract but must be understood in light of some baseline.[118] Often, commentators assume, implicitly at least, that a baseline win rate of 50 per cent (claimant wins half the time, respondent wins half the time) both shows a fair process and is the only win rate that shows a fair process. Neither assumption necessarily is correct.

The baseline win rate depends on the strength or weakness of the underlying case, which is not something that empirical researchers typically can observe. If the underlying case is very strong, a high win rate for claimants would be the expected result of a fair process. If the underlying case is very weak, a low win rate for claimants would be the expected result of a fair process. In the former case, a claimant win rate of 50 per cent could in fact show that the process is unfair to claimants, while in the latter case, a claimant win rate of 50 per cent could show that the process is unfair to respondents.

Selection bias from settlement complicates this analysis, but does not change the conclusion. While some models of settlement behaviour predict a 50 per cent claimant win rate, others predict a much higher or much lower claimant win rate, depending on various assumptions.[119] As a result, evaluating outcome data requires a stated and justified baseline expectation of what the win rate in a fair process should be. Mere departures from a 50 per cent win rate (in either direction) do not necessarily show that the process is unfair. Likewise, the finding of a 50 per cent win rate does not itself show that the process is fair. The most that can be said in such a case is that the empirical evidence does not show that the process is unfair (on the explicit or implicit assumption of a 50 per cent baseline win rate).

[117] See e.g. Rachel L. Wellhausen, 'Recent Trends in Investor-State Dispute Settlement', 7 J. Int'l Disp. Settlement 117 (2016), 128 (fig. 3) (finding that 33.1% of investment arbitrations resolved from 1990–2014 were resolved by settlement).

[118] Win rates in court cases for comparable cases might provide such a baseline. But it is very difficult to identify truly comparable cases in court and arbitration, and no set of comparable court cases is available for investment arbitrations.

[119] See supra note 10.

Subject to these limitations, then, what does the data show about outcomes in investment arbitrations?[120] Based on a dataset of publicly available awards as of 1 May 2016, Daniel Behn at al. found that states won in 175 cases (of 330, or 53.0 per cent), while investors won in 155 (of 330, or 47.0 per cent).[121] An additional 49 cases had been discontinued and 116 settled. Of the 175 wins by a state, the state won on jurisdiction in 81 cases and on the merits in 94. Prior studies found similar state and investor win rates, albeit with older or less complete data.[122] Assuming a 50 per cent win rate as the baseline, these empirical results do not show that investment arbitration produces unfair results to host states (but, again, they do not show that it is fair, either).[123]

[120] For studies examining the award of costs in international investment arbitrations, see Hodgson (n. 43) ('A slight majority of arbitration tribunals (56 per cent) have required each party to bear its own costs, that is, an unadjusted costs order. Just 10 per cent of tribunals made a fully adjusted costs order [i.e. ordered one party to pay the other side's party and tribunal costs in full] and 34 per cent a partially adjusted costs order [i.e. ordered one party to pay the other side's party and tribunal costs in part]'); Susan Franck, 'Rationalizing Costs in Investment Treaty Arbitration', 88 Wash. U.L. Rev. 769 (2011), 777 (finding that 'the overall experiences of investors and states were relatively equivalent, with (1) parties often responsible for equal costs, or (2) rough parity between investors and states when tribunals did shift costs'); Thomas Webster, 'Efficiency in Investment Arbitration: Recent Decisions on Preliminary and Costs Issues', 25 Arb. Int'l 469 (2009), 493–4 ('Prior to 2005, it was accepted by many that costs did not follow the event, whether with respect to arbitration costs or legal costs... [F]rom 2005 to 2009... the "costs follow the event" principle was apparently followed in more than half of the awards (64 per cent)'). For studies examining the award of costs in international commercial arbitration, see 2012 Queen Mary/White & Case survey (n. 6), 40–41 (survey data on cost allocation); John Gotanda, 'Yin and Yang: A Comparison of Monetary Remedies in International Investment and Transnational Commercial Disputes', in Ingeborg Schwenzer and Lisa Spagnolo (eds), Towards Uniformity: The 2nd Annual MAA Schlechtriem CISG Conference 49 (Eleven International Publishing 2011), 61 ('CIETAC–CISG... claimants recovered parties' costs at low frequencies. In CIETAC–CISG disputes, attorneys' fees were awarded in 28% of all cases in the current study'); Webster (n. 120), 493 and 513 (table 2) (based on random sample of 100 ICC awards from 2006 to 2008) (finding that 'the principle that the "costs follow the event" was generally applied, although with considerable adaptation to the circumstances); Quero (n. 42), 11 (45% of Stockholm Chamber awards from 2007 to 2014 ordered one party to bear all arbitration costs and attorneys' fees; 34% allocated arbitration costs and attorneys' fees based on relative success on the merits; 21% ordered parties to share arbitration costs equally and bear own attorneys' fees).

[121] Daniel Behn et al., 'Poor States or Poor Governance? Explaining Outcomes in Investment Treaty Arbitration', SSRN (2016), 23–25.

[122] See e.g. Wellhausen (n. 117), 129 (sample of publicly available awards as of 31 December 2015) ('Of the 461 concluded arbitrations, the parties reached a settlement in 153, the investor won in 134, and the state won in 174', with an investor win defined to mean any case in which a state was found to have acted wrongfully); Daniel Behn, 'Legitimacy, Evolution, and Growth in Investment Treaty Arbitration: Empirically Evaluating the State-of-the-Art', 46 Geo. J. Int'l L. 363 (2015), 372 (sample of 147 cases fully or partially resolved from September 2011 to September 2014) (finding investor won on the merits in 43%, lost on jurisdiction in 33%, and lost on the merits in 24%); Susan Franck and Lindsey Wylie, 'Predicting Outcomes in Investment Treaty Arbitration', 65 Duke L.J. 459 (2015), 489–90 (sample of publicly available awards as of 1 January 2012) ('For the 144 awards finally resolving treaty disputes, fifty-seven cases (39.6%) were investor wins. By contrast, there were eight-seven cases (60.4%) where respondents won with no state liability'); Franck (n. 120), 49 (sample of publicly available awards as of 1 June 2006) ('Out of the fifty-two awards finally resolving treaty claims, there were twenty awards (38.5%) where investors won and tribunals awarded damages. By contrast, there were thirty awards (57.7%) where governments paid investors nothing. There were also two awards embodying settlement agreements').

[123] Krzysztof Pelc argues that the 'legal merit' of investment arbitration claims 'has declined precipitously over time, and that this decline is concentrated in indirect expropriation cases', with investors

Behn et al. further broke down the 155 investor wins into 80 'full' wins and 75 'partial' wins, defining a full win as one in which 'the investor is made whole by the outcome—even if there is not success on all claims or that the valuation of damages is less than what the claimant-investor asked for'.[124] Susan Frank and Lindsey Wylie found (from a more limited sample of awards) that 'the mean amounts claimed were approximately US$660 million (US$100 million median), which reflects a nontrivial risk of loss of fiscal resources for both investors and states, particularly for small investors and developing states', but that investors that were awarded damages 'obtained a mean award of US$45.6 million (US$10.9 million median) and an average success rate of 35 per cent (29 per cent median)'.[125]

Howard Mann has argued that investors 'have actually won most of the time: 72 per cent of the decisions on jurisdiction, and 60 per cent of cases decided on the merits.'[126] But the question most studies are examining is not whether investors win too many decisions but whether they win (i.e. are awarded damages on) too many claims. Because investors have to get past multiple hurdles (i.e. jurisdiction, merits, and damages) to recover on a claim, counting wins on each separate hurdle double (or triple) counts investor wins. Of course, cases in which investors win on jurisdiction and lose on the merits certainly may be relevant on policy grounds. Presumably legal fees and other costs are likely to be higher and the investor's settlement leverage is likely to be greater in a case in which the tribunal has found it has jurisdiction. But that is not the central question in most of the studies of investment arbitration outcomes.

Gus Van Harten has attempted a 'workaround' to the inability of empirical studies to 'control for the correct outcome'[127] by coding the content of awards by investment arbitration tribunals as taking an 'expansive' or a 'restrictive' approach to jurisdictional and

winning 'only 21% of indirect expropriation disputes in the last decade'—although it is an overstatement to call the cases 'frivolous' based on the evidence presented. See Krzysztof Pelc, 'Does the International Investment Regime Induce Frivolous Litigation?' SSRN (2016), 32.

[124] Behn et al. (n. 121), 23–4. See also Thomas Schultz and Cédric Dupont, 'Investment Arbitration: Promoting the Rule of Law or Over-Empowering Investors? A Quantitative Empirical Study', 25 Eur. J. Int'l L. 1147 (2014), 1158 (suggesting 'legal-economic definition of a success' for an investor as 'an arbitral decision awarding it 25 per cent or more of the figure it has claimed').

[125] Franck and Wylie (n. 122), 467 (sample of investment arbitration awards publicly available as of 1 January 2012); Franck (n. 120), 58–9 ('The average amount of damages awarded by tribunals was approximately US$10.4 million' and '[t]he difference between the average amounts claimed and awarded was approximately US$333 million'); PwC, 2015 International Arbitration Damages Research (2015), 6: <https://www.pwc.com/sg/en/publications/assets/international-arbitation-damages-research-2015.pdf> (sample of 95 publicly available international arbitration awards over the past 25 years, of which 74% were ICSID investment arbitrations) ('The amount awarded by Tribunals was, on average, 37% of the amount claimed'); Gus Van Harten, 'Who Has Benefited Financially from Investment Treaty Arbitration? An Evaluation of the Size and Wealth of Claimants' (2016), 1: <http://digitalcommons.osgoode.yorku.ca/cgi/viewcontent.cgi?article=1136&context=olsrps> (finding that 'the beneficiaries of ISDS-ordered financial transfers, in the aggregate, have overwhelmingly been companies with more than USD1 billion in annual revenue—especially extra-large companies with more than USD10 billion—and individuals who have over USD100 million in net wealth').

[126] Howard Mann, 'ISDS: Who Wins More, Investors or States?', Inv. Treaty News (June 2015).

[127] Rogers (n. 92), 234.

substantive issues. In part 1 of the study, he found that investment awards show a 'strong tendency in favour of an expansive approach' to arbitral jurisdiction, one that is particularly pronounced for investors from the US, UK, and France.[128] (These findings are consistent with other data finding that arbitrators tend to make decisions in favor of broader arbitral jurisdiction.)[129] In part 2 of the study, examining arbitrator rulings on substantive issues, Van Harten reported 'a strong tendency toward resolutions that enhanced the compensatory promise of investment treaty arbitration for foreign investors and its financial risks for states', with the exception of cases brought against the United States, which Van Harten says benefited from restrictive rather than expansive interpretations.[130] Although Van Harten acknowledges that this evidence does not prove bias (because of possible alternative explanations for the findings), he states that 'the observed variations in resolutions seem unlikely to be explained by some untested factors that may drive case outcomes, such as factual differences among cases'.[131] His findings, however, do not exclude the possibility that the expansive interpretations are the 'correct legal outcome'.[132]

An ongoing debate in the empirical literature is over the relationship between development status of state respondents and their likelihood of success in investment arbitrations. An early study by Susan Franck found that 'irrespective of the definition of development status, there was no statistically significant relationship among the development status of the respondent, the development status of the presiding arbitrator, and

[128] Gus Van Harten, 'Arbitrator Behavior in Asymmetrical Adjudication: An Empirical Study of Investment Treaty Arbitration', 50 Osgoode Hall L.J. 211 (2012), 237–42. For other studies examining jurisdictional decisions in investment arbitrations, see Kathleen McArthur and Pablo Ormachea, 'International Investor–State Arbitration: An Empirical Analysis of ICSID Decisions on Jurisdiction', 28 Rev. Litig. 559 (2009); Ole Fauchald, 'The Legal Reasoning of ICSID Tribunals: An Empirical Analysis', 19 Eur. J. Int'l. L. 301 (2008).

[129] E.g. Christopher Drahozal and Peter Rutledge, 'Contract and Procedure', 94 Marquette L. Rev. 1103 (2011), 1141 ('Arbitrators had issued 135 clause construction awards: 95 (70%) holding that the arbitration clause permitted class arbitration; 7 (5%) holding that the arbitration clause did not permit class arbitration; and 33 (24%) in which the parties stipulated that the arbitration clause permitted class arbitration').

[130] Gus Van Harten, 'Arbitrator Behavior in Asymmetrical Adjudication (Part Two): An Examination of Hypotheses of Bias in Investment Treaty Arbitration', 53 Osgoode Hall L.J. 540 (2016), 546. See also Gus Van Harten, *Sovereign Choices and Sovereign Constraints* (Oxford University Press, 2013), 15–17 ('no evidence emerged that the arbitrators in any case discussed the relative accountability of a legislature as a possible reason for restraint in the review of legislative decisions... there was a lack of evidence of restraint based on the relative capacity of governments... there was limited evidence of arbitrator restraint due to the role of another adjudicative forum... These findings indicate that arbitrators adopted an unrestrained approach relative to what one might expect from courts').

[131] Van Harten, 'Arbitrator Behavior' (n. 130), 215 and 239 (recognizing that his findings 'do not establish the truth of any theoretical expectation of systemic bias').

[132] Rogers (n. 92), 235 ('These outcomes appear to be more expansive than those preferred by individuals whose policy preferences are for narrower investment arbitration jurisdiction. They do not, however, represent a finding that investment arbitrators' "expansive" jurisdictional findings are somehow an improper deviation from the "correct" legal outcome').

outcome. This held true for both (1) winning or losing an investment treaty arbitration and (2) the amounts tribunals awarded'.[133] Gus Van Harten criticized the study for 'equating OECD membership with developed status' and thereby 'includ[ing] in this category a number of countries that are reasonably classified as developing or transition rather than developed countries (e.g. Mexico, Turkey, and former East Bloc countries)'.[134] But Franck's results were unchanged when she re-estimated the models in response to the criticism.[135] A subsequent study by Franck had similar results, concluding, 'When controlling for democracy levels, none of the twenty-one models analyzed could identify a reliable link between outcome and respondent development status.'[136]

The most recent study is by Daniel Behn and colleagues. Using an expanded sample, they found 'a strong and consistent correlation between development status and investment treaty arbitration outcomes', even with 'the identification of higher quality matching indicators to measure executive constraints, bureaucratic quality, judicial independence and corruption levels'.[137] According to the authors: 'The statistical picture remains clear: states with higher levels of economic development are less likely to lose investment treaty arbitration cases; and the inverse applies to states with lower levels of economic development.'[138] But, again, the study cannot exclude the possibility that the reason claims against states with lower levels of economic development are more likely to succeed is that the claims are stronger on the merits (and vice versa).

[133] Susan Franck, 'Development and Outcomes of Investment Treaty Arbitration', 50 Harv. Int'l L.J. 435 (2009), 473. See also Susan Franck, 'The ICSID Effect? Considering Potential Variations in Arbitration Awards', 51 Va. J. Int'l L. 825 (2011), 898 (sample of publicly available awards as of 1 June 2006) (finding 'no general differences between ICSID and non-ICSID cases in amounts claimed and outcomes' and 'no reliable relationship for either amounts claimed or outcome, as a function of Development Status and all ICSID awards').

[134] Gus Van Harten, 'The Use of Quantitative Methods to Examine Possible Bias in Investment Arbitration', Yb. on Int'l Inv. L. & Pol'y 859 (2011), 867–9.

[135] Susan Franck et al., 'Response: Through the Looking Glass: Understanding Social Science Norms for Analyzing International Investment Law', Yb. on Int'l Inv. L. & Pol'y 883 (2011), 893–5. See also Gus Van Harten, 'Reply', Yb. on Int'l Inv. L. & Pol'y 917 (2011); Susan Franck et al., 'Rejoinder', Yb. on Int'l Inv. L. & Pol'y 939 (2011).

[136] Susan Franck, 'Conflating Politics and Development? Examining Investment Treaty Arbitration Outcomes', 55 Va. J. Int'l L.13 (2014), 60.

[137] Behn et al. (n. 121), 34. See also Behn (n. 122), 410–11 ('respondent states with a very high [Human Development Index] score are more likely to successfully defend an investment treaty claim than respondent states with lower HDI scores. In fact... the lower the respondent state's HDI score, the more likely that respondent state will lose an investment treaty case'); Schultz and Dupont (n. 124), 1167 ('In the full period surveyed (1972–2010)... low income countries won 50 percent of the claims that were won by one of the parties... while high income countries were successful in 69 per cent of such cases').

[138] Behn et al. (n. 121), 34. Some studies have found other factors, such as attorney representation and arbitrator characteristics, to be correlated with outcomes in investment arbitrations as well. E.g. Franck and Wylie (n. 122), 520–21 (sample of investment arbitration awards publicly available as of 1 January 2012) ('case-related and hybrid models demonstrated that ITA outcomes exhibited a degree of predictability, and the results were not completely random. The variables most likely to predict outcomes were arguably case selection effects, including investor identity and the presence of experienced counsel').

27.6 Enforcement of International Arbitral Awards

Claimants ordinarily are not satisfied with simply obtaining a favourable award. They also must collect on the award. Estimates are that 90% of ICC arbitration awards are complied with voluntarily,[139] but few empirical studies have examined the issue. In a recent survey by the Institute for Transnational Arbitration, 'Forty-four percent of participants answered that "very few" (10 percent or less) of their commercial arbitration awards were subject to judicial enforcement, while 27 percent answered that "some" (10 to 40 percent) were.'[140] By comparison, in a study published in 2005, Richard Naimark and Stephanie Keer followed up on AAA/ICDR arbitration awards to see what happened after the award was made. Their sample consisted of 153 arbitrations, of which the respondent won in 18 and lost in the other 135. Of the 135 losing respondents, 100 complied with the award at least in part (with 22 renegotiating the amount post-award), while 35 failed to comply.

In addition, '[t]he data also show that 67 of the awards were confirmed by a court and one was confirmed with some alteration of the terms of the award', although only one court set aside an award.[141] Unfortunately, the Naimark and Keer sample was not a random one, so that their results cannot be generalized to AAA or international arbitrations more generally. More recently, Judith Gill and Matthew Hodgson surveyed parties that had been awarded costs in investment arbitrations, and found that 37% of successful respondents and 19% of successful claimants 'were paid nothing at all', while '[o]nly 40 per cent of claimants and 38 per cent of respondents paid costs awards against them voluntarily'.[142]

More studies are available on court enforcement of international arbitration awards. Using a sample of court decisions reported in the ICCA Yearbook Commercial Arbitration, Albert Jan van den Berg has reported: 'In approximately 10% of the reported cases involving the New York Convention, a court has refused enforcement of a foreign

[139] Pierre Lalive, 'Enforcing Awards' in *The ICC, 60 Years of ICC Arbitration: A Look at the Future* (ICC, 1984), 315, 318–19 ('[T]he great majority of awards are recognized and enforced "spontaneously"—over 90% as far as ICC arbitrations are concerned').

[140] See Crystal Robles, 'The 2014 Survey: How Well Are Arbitral Awards Enforced in Practice?' 29(2) News & Notes from the Institute for Transnational Arbitration 5 (2014) (survey respondents were 'practitioners with experience in over 2,000 arbitrations resulting in awards in over 35 jurisdictions'). See also 2008 Queen Mary/PwC survey (n. 6), 8 ('84% of respondents indicated that the opposing party had honoured the award in full in more than 76% of cases').

[141] Richard Naimark and Stephanie Keer, 'Post-Award Experience in International Commercial Arbitration' in Drahozal and Naimark (n. 2), 269, 270–71.

[142] Judith Gill and Matthew Hodgson, 'Costs Awards: Who Pays?', Global Arb. Rev. (15 September 2015).

arbitral award.[143] Country-specific studies of award enforcement are set out in the following subsections.[144]

27.6.1 United States

Christopher Whytock studied published US court opinions (from 1970 through 2008) and found that in '23.1 percent of decisions (19.3 percent in the U.S. District Courts, 33.3 percent in the U.S. Court of Appeals), the court decided that the award should not be enforced'.[145]

27.6.2 China

Relying on a non-random sample of award enforcement cases in China from 1991 to 1999, Randall Peerenboom reported that courts enforced 52 per cent of foreign awards and 47% of CIETAC awards, and that 'investors can expect to recover 75–50% of the award amount in 34% of the cases and half of the award at least 40% of the time'.[146]

[143] Albert Jan Van den Berg, 'Refusals of Enforcement Under the New York Convention of 1958: The Unfortunate Few', 10 ICC Int'l Ct. Arb. Bull. 75 (1999), 75. See also Pouget (n.44), 14 (estimating '[a]verage length of recognition/enforcement proceedings by region' based on hypothetical case, ranging from 39 weeks in East Asia and the Pacific to 386 weeks in South Asia).

[144] In addition, see Ahmed Almutawa and A. F. M. Maniruzzaman, 'Problems of Enforcement of Foreign Arbitral Awards in the Gulf Cooperation Council States and the Prospect of a Uniform GCC Arbitration Law: An Empirical Study', 12(2) Transnat'l Disp. Mgmt. (2015), 24–5 (reporting survey results (based on 41 respondents, of whom 87.5% 'had experience in the field of arbitration in one of more of the GCC states'), that '[o]f the six GCC states, Bahrain and the UAE were viewed as the friendliest', while Saudi Arabia 'was still viewed as the least friendly toward enforcement of foreign arbitral awards').

[145] Christopher Whytock, 'The Arbitration-Litigation Relationship in Transnational Dispute Resolution: Empirical Insights from the US. Federal Courts', 2 World Arb. & Med. Rev. 39 (2008), 74. See also Vera Korzun and Thomas Lee, 'An Empirical Survey of International Commercial Arbitration Cases in the US District Court for the Southern District of New York, 1970–2014', 39 Fordham Int'l L.J. 307 (2015), 343–4 (identifying 122 cases seeking recognition or enforcement and 25 cases seeking *vacatur* of international arbitral awards in the U.S. District Court for the Southern District of New York from 1970 to 2014, although not indicating the outcome of those cases).

[146] Randall Peerenboom, 'Seek Truth from Facts: An Empirical Study of Enforcement of Arbitral Awards in the PRC', 49 Am. J. Comp. L. 249 (2001), 254; repr. in Drahozal and Naimark (n. 2), 285. See also Corinne Tay, 'Enforcement of Arbitral Awards in the People's Republic of China', 26(2) Int'l Constr. L. Rev. 207 (2009), 243 (survey of 53 lawyers based in the People's Republic of China; 32% agreed or strongly agreed, 36% disagreed or strongly disagreed, and 32% were neutral toward the statement that '[t]he award can be easily converted into cash terms within the PRC'). Compare Wang Sheng Chang, 'Enforcement of Foreign Arbitral Awards in the People's Republic of China', in Albert Jan van den Berg (ed.), *Improving the Efficiency of Arbitration Agreements and Awards: 40 Years of Application of the New York Convention* (Kluwer Law International, 1999), 461; repr. in Drahozal and Naimark (n. 2), 277 (finding that Chinese courts 'have recognized and enforced more than 87.7% of awards (as against the non-enforcement of 12.2% of CIETAC awards and 7.14% of foreign awards', although acknowledging that the results were 'incomplete' because 'the responding courts were only a small proportion of those questioned').

27.6.3 Switzerland

Felix Dasser has found that 6.5 per cent of the decisions of the Swiss Federal Supreme Court addressing the merits of a challenge to an international arbitral award resulted in the award being completely or partially set aside, and that, as of 2009, 'the Federal Court typically takes just four months to dispose of a challenge against an arbitral award'.[147]

27.6.4 Italy

Laura Barison reported that the Italian Courts of Appeals of Brescia, Genoa, Turin, and Milan set aside only four of 99 awards (or 4.0 per cent) from the beginning of January 2007 to 30 June 2014.[148]

27.6.5 Sweden

The Committee on the Review of Swedish Arbitration examined all challenges to arbitration awards in the Swedish Courts of Appeals (including both domestic and international arbitrations) from the beginning of 2004 to 31 May 2014, and found that the court annulled an arbitral award in 'almost six percent of all challenges' (including challenges withdrawn or otherwise dismissed by the court).[149]

27.6.6 Australia

Diana Hu and Luke Nottage found an increase in actions for enforcement of foreign arbitral awards in Australia in recent years, but did not report data on the outcomes of the cases.[150]

[147] Felix Dasser, 'International Arbitration and Setting Aside Proceedings in Switzerland: An Updated Statistical Analysis', 28 ASA Bull. 82 (2010), 85 and 92. See also Felix Dasser, 'International Arbitration and Setting Aside Proceedings in Switzerland: A Statistical Analysis', 25 ASA Bull. 444 (2007), 452 (finding that 7% of cases in the Swiss Federal Supreme Court from 1989 to 2005 'led to a complete or partial setting aside of the award').

[148] Alison Ross, 'Italian Judges Tend to Uphold Awards, Research Shows', Global Arb. Rev. (2016) (summarizing study prepared in Italian and available at: <http://res.cloudinary.com/lbresearch/image/upload/v1473350245/indagine_statistica_sull_impugnazione_del_lodo_arbitrale_nazionale_88116_1657.pdf>).

[149] Johan Munck and Helga Hullmann, 'Challenge of Arbitral Awards Before Courts of Appeals', Svensk Juristtidning 1 (2015), 13.

[150] Diana Hu and Luke Nottage, 'The International Arbitration Act Matters in Australia: Where to Litigate and Why (Not)?', SSRN (2017), 2–3. See also Albert Monichino et al., 'International Arbitration in Australia: Selected Case Notes and Trends', 19 Australian J. Int'l L. 181 (2012), 184–5.

27.6.7 Conclusion

All of the studies of court enforcement have important limitations. First, and most obviously, they do not consider voluntary compliance with the award, either before an action is filed in court or after (i.e. through settlement). Second, to the extent the studies rely on published court opinions, they likely understate the extent of court enforcement.[151] In the United States, for example, not all court opinions are published, and published decisions are more likely to address controversial or unsettled issues. An opinion in a routine case enforcing an international arbitral award is less likely to be published than an opinion refusing to enforce an award.[152]

27.7 International Arbitral Awards as Precedent

Unlike court judgments in a common law system, arbitration awards do not serve as binding precedent. No standing appellate arbitral body exists to reverse awards that do not comply with existing law, and arbitral tribunals are not otherwise bound to follow a prior award, even if it is directly on point to an issue in the case. But that does not necessarily mean that no system of precedent exists in international arbitration. Even if awards do not have binding precedential effect on subsequent arbitral tribunals, they may have persuasive precedential effect, convincing subsequent tribunals that the approach taken by the prior tribunal was the correct or proper one.

One possible way to identify whether a prior arbitral award has influenced or persuaded a subsequent tribunal is to see if the subsequent tribunal cited it.[153] Of course, the fact that a tribunal cited a prior award does not necessarily mean that it was influenced by the award. To take an extreme case, the tribunal might have cited a prior award to explain why it thought the award was wrongly decided. That said, the extent to which international arbitral awards in the aggregate cite prior awards would provide some evidence of whether a system of (persuasive) precedent might be developing in international arbitration.

Because investment arbitration awards are more likely to be publicly available than commercial awards, most studies have focused on citation patterns in investment

[151] By comparison, note that the studies by Felix Dasser about enforcement practices of Swiss courts include both published and unpublished court decisions. See Dasser, 'Statistical Analysis' (n. 147), 450.

[152] Drahozal and Naimark (n. 2), 264 ('courts would seem much less likely to report decisions enforcing awards than decisions denying enforcement (because enforcement generally is routine)—although that assertion could be verified empirically').

[153] Richard Posner, 'An Economic Analysis of the Use of Citations in the Law', 2 Am. L. & Econ. Rev. 381 (2000), 382 (stating that citation analysis is 'a well-established method of empirical research in law, economics, sociology (especially the sociology of science), and academic administration').

awards.[154] In his study of investment arbitration awards and decision from 1990 to 2006, Jeffrey Commission found that investment arbitration tribunals were increasingly citing prior ICSID awards, such that, in his view, '[t]he role that precedent has come to play in investment treaty arbitration today resembles the common law doctrine of *stare decisis* absent certain of the associated values advanced in a common law system of precedent'.[155] Citation practices seem to vary depending on the institutional setting of the arbitration. According to a study by Suha Jubran Ballan, ICSID merits awards (issued between 2001 and 2011) cited an average of 9.97 prior awards and NAFTA awards cited an average of 9.25 prior awards (mostly other NAFTA awards), while other investment arbitration awards subject to the New York Convention cited an average of only 5.29 prior awards.[156] In a study of citations by investment arbitration tribunals to Iran–US Claims Tribunal awards, Christopher S. Gibson and Christopher R. Drahozal found that, based on a subsample of NAFTA awards, '[i]n every case in which the ICSID tribunal cited an Iran-United States Claims Tribunal precedent in its decision or award, the parties previously cited that Tribunal precedent in one of their submissions', highlighting the potential importance of party citation practices for studies of arbitral precedent.[157]

Finally, in a less systematic but broader survey of citation practices in arbitral awards, Gabrielle Kaufmann-Kohler reported that (1) only six of 100 arbitral awards in a sample of cases applying the Convention on Contracts for the International Sale of Goods cited prior awards; (2) 15 per cent of ICC arbitral awards (out of a sample of 190 published awards) cited prior awards, 'mostly... with regard to matters of jurisdiction and procedure' rather than substantive law; (3) prior to 2003 only one-sixth of published decisions by the Court of Arbitration for Sports cited prior awards, while after 2003 'nearly every award contains one or more references to earlier CAS awards'; and (4) 'Out of 110 [domain name arbitration] awards issued in the fall of 2006, 540 citations to prior domain name decisions were made in 85 cases.'[158]

[154] The availability of awards is relevant both for purposes of the study itself (to have awards to examine for citations) and for the development of a system of precedent (it is difficult to cite awards as precedent if awards are not publicly available).

[155] Jeffrey Commission, 'Precedent in Investment Treaty Arbitration: A Citation Analysis of a Developing Jurisprudence', 24 J. Int'l Arb. 129 (2007), 149–51, 158.

[156] Ballan (n. 44), 82 (excluding outliers).

[157] Christopher Gibson and Christopher Drahozal, 'Iran–United States Claims Tribunal Precedent in Investor–State Arbitration', 23 J. Int'l Arb. 521 (2006), 540, 543–4.

[158] Gabrielle Kaufmann-Kohler, 'Arbitral Precedent: Dream, Necessity or Excuse? The 2006 Freshfields Lecture', 23 Arb. Int'l 357 (2007), 362–7.

CHAPTER 28

THE RULE OF LAW EFFECTS OF COMMERCIAL ARBITRATION FROM A SOCIO-LEGAL PERSPECTIVE

THOMAS DIETZ

28.1 Standard Narratives and a Socio-Legal Approach to International Commercial Arbitration

Recent years have seen the rise of a now vibrant debate on the role of international commercial arbitration (ICA) on contractual behaviour in international commerce that has not peaked yet. To date, not only are lawyers of private international law dealing with the distinctive legal features of ICA, but also an interdisciplinary community of scholars (including, but not limited to, legal theorists, political scientists, and economists) is discussing ICA as part and parcel of an emerging global legal order.[1] However, although the scholarly debate on ICA has become quite broad recently, it is striking that large parts of the literature continue to corroborate a rather small number of standard narratives on ICA and its various rule of law effects.

[1] For an overview, see Walter Mattli and Thomas Dietz, *International Arbitration and Global Governance* (Oxford University Press, 2014). See also Gregory Shaffer, 'Theorizing Transnational Legal Ordering', 12 Annual Review of Law & Social Science (2016), 231–53.

One often-repeated narrative refers to the functional rise of ICA. It holds that in the absence of a workable state-provided legal forum, ICA has evolved into the most important mechanism of dispute resolution and contract enforcement in global commerce.[2] The contractual parties prefer arbitration over litigation in state courts in terms of neutrality, flexibility, time, and costs. Further, due to the existence of international conventions such as the New York Convention on the Recognition and Enforcement of Foreign Arbitral Awards, arbitral awards are widely considered to be reliably enforceable in almost every state on earth.[3] In order to demonstrate this development of ICA into a pivotal institution in international commerce, pundits of ICA routinely refer to the fact that the caseload handled by major arbitration institutions has been rapidly rising in the wake of globalization over the last three decades.[4]

A second powerful narrative—proposed by scholars who explicitly or implicitly draw on a law and economics framework—highlights the economic efficiency of ICA. By integrating arbitration clauses into their contracts, international parties are free to choose whatever procedural and substantial laws they deem best for their case, including non-national *lex mercatoria* norms. The contractual parties thoroughly compare the different legal options at their disposal and then choose the most efficient laws in order to minimize transaction costs. As a result of these rational design processes, an efficient and beneficial global legal order emerges that promotes global trade and economic growth.[5]

Whereas scholars of law and economics focus on efficiency, legal theorists are concerned with the justice function of ICA; and also in this area we see the emergence of a narrative that has gained more and more ground over the last few years. The core argument is that ICA, despite its largely private character, presents a judicial mechanism that is capable of transcending the parties' wills and that binds private contracts to an overarching set of norms. In doing so, ICA has developed into a more comprehensive legal institution than just an effective dispute resolution mechanism at the disposal of private parties. Rather, it takes over important public policy functions. When arbitrators decide on a case, they do not only resolve the dispute between the parties; as a side effect, they also create the rules that guide contractual behaviour in the global business community and align it to central transnational public policy goals.[6]

[2] See e.g. Gary Born, *International Commercial Arbitration* (Kluwer Law International, 2009); Alan Redfern, Martin Hunter, and Nigel Blackaby, *Law and Practice of International Commercial Arbitration* 5th edn (Sweet & Maxwell, 2009); John Uff, 'The Evolution of Arbitration', in Geoffrey Hartwell (ed.), *The Commercial Way to Justice: The 1996 International Conference of the Chartered Institute of Arbitrators* (Kluwer Law International, 1997), 15–23.

[3] Uff (n. 2).

[4] Yves Dezalay and Bryant Garth, *Dealing in Virtue: International Commercial Arbitration and the Construction of a Transnational Legal Order* (Oxford University Press, 1996), 6, n. 4; Walter Mattli, 'Private Justice in a Global Economy: From Litigation to Arbitration', 55(4) IO 919 (2001), 920; Alec Stone Sweet, 'The New Lex Mercatoria and Transnational Governance', 13(5) J. Eur. Public Policy 627 (2006), 636.

[5] Bruce Benson, 'The Spontaneous Evolution of Commercial Law', 55(3) South. Econ. J. 644 (1989); Erin O'Hara and Larry Ribstein, *The Law Market* (Oxford University Press, 2009).

[6] Fabien Gélinas, 'Arbitration as Transnational Governance: Legitimacy beyond Contract', in A. Claire Cutler and Thomas Dietz (eds), *The Politics of Private Transnational Governance by Contract* (Routledge 2017); Moritz Renner, 'Private Justice, Public Policy: The Constitutionalisation of International Commercial Arbitration', in Dietz and Mattli (n. 1), 117; Alec Stone Sweet and Florian Grisel, 'The Evolution

However, despite the tremendous growth of scholarship on ICA over recent years, these three bold assumptions about the nature and impact of ICA on contractual behaviour in international commerce have rarely been investigated, let alone empirically proven. It is thus still largely unclear to what extent these standard narratives on ICA, repeated over and over again by the pertinent literature, actually present an accurate description of the institution in operation. Even critical legal scholars, who would dismiss most of these views as made up by powerful global elites to back their narrow vested interests, have so far failed to provide a comprehensive analysis of how ICA works in practice.[7]

This chapter seeks to remedy this deficiency by developing a socio-legal perspective on ICA that is rooted in the empirical view of contract as developed in a long line of law and society scholarship[8] most prominently associated with Steward Macaulay.[9] As the key feature, such a socio-legal approach to ICA adopts a law-in-action rather than a law-in-books perspective.[10] In this sense, individual actors and organizations do not simply follow the law, but may alter, reinforce, manipulate, or even ignore the law in their daily courses of action. Law is thus assumed to be a living institution embedded in societal structures, rather than an accumulation of formal rules.[11]

Using a law-in-action approach in his classic work on contractual relations among Wisconsin firms, Steward Macaulay asked: 'What good is contract law?' His research suggested that its role might be much more limited than generally expected. Formal contract laws, he found, only indirectly affected business relations. Contracting partners largely failed to plan their exchange relationships completely, and rarely used formal sanctions to resolve disputes or enforce contractual agreements. Legal planning and legal sanctions were instead found to have negative consequences for the exchange relation. The contracting partners therefore preferred 'handshake agreements', and worked together on the basis of informal local norms. Since Macaulay's path-breaking work, many further empirical studies on contract law have repeated the finding that business-people tend to avoid formal laws in favour of routinely applied social norms and informal conflict resolution strategies. Close inter-actor bonds promote cooperation because

of International Arbitration: Delegation, Judicialization, Governance', in Dietz and Mattli (n. 1), 22; Joshua Karton, *The Culture of International Arbitration and the Evolution of Contract Law* (Oxford University Press, 2013).

[7] A. Claire Cutler, 'International Commercial Arbitration, Transnational Governance, and the New Constitutionalism', in Dietz and Mattli (n. 1), 140; A. Claire Cutler, *Private Power and Global Authority: Transnational Merchant Law in the Global Political Economy* (Cambridge University Press, 2003).

[8] Eugen Ehrlich, *The Fundamental Principles of Sociology of Law*, 4th edn (Transaction, 2002).

[9] Stewart Macaulay et al., *Contracts: Law in Action*, 3rd edn (Carolina Academic Press, 2010); Stewart Macaulay, 'Non-contractual Relations in Business: A Preliminary Study', 28 Am. Soc. Re. 55 (1963), 55–67; 'Elegant Models, Empirical Pictures, and the Complexities of Contract', 11 Law & Society Rev. 507 (1977).

[10] Roscoe Pound, 'Law in Books and Law in Action', 44(3) Am. L. Rev. 12 (1910).

[11] Eugen Ehrlich defined the term as follows: 'The living law is the law which dominates life itself even though it has not been posited in legal propositions. The source of our knowledge of this law is, first, the modern legal document; secondly, direct observation of life, of commerce, of customs and usages and of all associations, not only those that the law has recognized but also of those that it has overlooked and passed by, indeed even of those that it has disapproved.' See Ehrlich (n. 8), 493. See also Mark Suchman and Lauren Edelman, 'Legal Rational Myths: The New Institutionalism and the Law and Society Tradition', 21(4) Law & Soc. Inq. 903 (1996).

actors know that opportunistic behaviour yields undesired outcomes such as the loss of a long-term business partner or, even worse, exclusion from important social and business communities. Macaulay therefore stated that the effects of law on private behaviour are at best 'indirect, subtle, and ambiguous',[12] and concluded that 'academic contract law is not now and never was an accurate description of the institution in operation'.[13]

I will argue in this chapter that the literature on ICA has up to now largely ignored these central insights by law and society scholars. Much current scholarship on ICA has thus fallen into a conceptual trap that Suchman and Edelman defined as 'naïve legal formalism'.[14] ICA is misunderstood as a clear-cut, authoritative, and coercive legal mechanism that directly guides individual behaviour in cross-border contractual relations, without taking into account that the relation between legal institutions and human behaviour are in fact much more diffuse, and shaped by various individual interests, non-legal institutions, and civil power. As a consequence of this naïve legal understanding, existing approaches to ICA tend to perpetuate a number of misleading images about ICA's role in global commerce that will be critically assessed in the remainder of this chapter.

In detail, section 28.2 will assess the caseload of major international arbitration institutions. ICA pundits routinely refer to the increasing numbers of cases filed at international arbitration institutions to demonstrate the rising significance of ICA as an important mechanism of cross-border conflict resolution. However, when this caseload, instead of being looked at in isolation, is put in the context of economic globalization, it becomes clear that, compared to the vast volumes of global trade, the number of annual cases handled by major arbitration houses appears rather small. It will therefore be argued in this chapter that the role of ICA in the governance of cross-border contracts really is much more confined than assumed by large parts of the pertinent literature in the field.

Section 28.3 scrutinizes the claim that arbitral awards are enforceable on an almost worldwide basis. Most importantly, it will be argued here that it is one thing for a country to sign an international convention like the New York Convention and another thing to make it work in practice. In many countries with a strong rule of law tradition, arbitral awards can be reliably enforced. However, in many other countries that today play pivotal roles in global trade, such as Russia, China, Brazil, or India, this is not the case. In these countries, the local courts and law enforcement authorities are often found to work poorly when required to carry out the enforcement of an arbitral award to the end, which in turn delays or even prevents an effective enforcement of arbitral awards. Given this, it seems more accurate to conceptualize ICA as a fragmented legal order that works most effectively in territories with functional rule-of-law-based court systems but less effectively in countries in which such legal traditions are missing.

Section 28.4 critically discusses the efficiency claim associated with ICA. Most importantly, it will be argued that the real behaviour of the parties engaged in international contracts fundamentally deviates from the behaviour that is assumed by standard

[12] Stewart Macaulay, 'Law and the Behavioral Sciences: Is There Any There There?', 6(2) Law Policy 149 (1984), 155.

[13] Stewart Macaulay, 'An Empirical View of Contract', Wis. L. Rev. (1985), 466.

[14] Suchman and Edelman (n. 11), 905.

law and economic approaches. The contractual parties neither thoroughly compare the different legal options at their disposal nor choose the governing laws based on efficiency criteria. Instead, real choice of law practices are driven by bargaining power, and it is usually the party with the greater bargaining power that succeeds in imposing its home laws on the weaker party. Familiarity with a legal system thus plays a far more fundamental role than does efficiency in choosing the governing laws. Consequently, the economic benefits associated with the rise of ICA may be largely overplayed.

Last but not least, section 28.5 discusses the narrative that ICA gives rise to a just global legal order that is capable of fulfilling important public policy functions. In this area we find a variety of elaborate scholarly pieces that convincingly show how in practice arbitral tribunals do not unconditionally enforce the parties' wills as stipulated in the contract, but take overarching public policy norms into account when they decide a case. ICA is thus assumed to have developed a real potential to create a legitimate global legal order. However, legal theorists who advance this view usually fail to take into account that although the internal legal procedures work well, ICA lacks external relevance. The large majority of parties involved in international commerce cannot afford the financial means to get access to arbitration. Most conflicts will therefore never reach the just harbour of ICA, but will be resolved in an informal way based on economic power. ICA thus produces a legal order, but only for big multinational firms that possess the means to use this mechanism. The weaker parties in global chains are largely excluded from using ICA. ICA thus limits access to justice and, in doing so, tends to reinforce existing power relations in global commerce, instead of creating a level legal playing field which guarantees all actors participating in global trade a similar access to the arbitral justice system.

Given all the limitation of ICA, section 28.6 turns to alternative institutions that contractual parties can use to enforce their contracts across borders. The focus is now moved away from ICA towards informal mechanisms that seem to play a far greater role in the governance of international contractual relations than widely assumed. Of course, for scholars of law and society this finding is not surprising at all. It only confirms in large parts their standard view of how contractual relations work in practice. ICA presents only one legal institution within a plurality of formal and informal laws governing cross-border exchange. The chapter will close with a statement on the perspectives of ICA in the light of the major arguments developed throughout the chapter.

28.2 The Caseload of Major Arbitration Houses

In order to reinforce the standard story that ICA has been evolving into a crucial legal institution of global commerce, scholars routinely point to the increasing number of cases filed at major international arbitration institutions.[15] Table 28.1, which provides a

[15] Dezalay and Garth (n. 4), 6; Mattli (n. 4), 920; Stone Sweet (n. 4), 636.

Table 28.1 Caseload of major arbitration houses

Year	ICC	LCIA	SCC	AAA/ICDR	HKIAC	CIETAC	Total
2003	580	99	82	646	287	422	*2,116*
2004	561	83	50	614	280	462	*2,050*
2005	521	110	56	580	281	427	*1,975*
2006	593	130	74	586	394	442	*2,219*
2007	599	127	87	622	448	429	*2,312*
2008	663	163	85	703	602	548	*2,764*
2009	817	272	96	836	429	559	*3,009*
2010	793	246	91	888	291	418	*2,727*
2011	796	224	96	994	275	470	*2,855*
2012	759	265	92	996	293	331	*2,736*
2013	767	290	86	1,165	260	375	*2,943*
2014	791	296	94	1,063[a]	252	387	*2,883*
2015	801	326	103	1,063	252[b]	437	*2,730*

[a] In 2015, total international case filings for the year held steady at 1,063, consistent with 2014 figures.

[b] Estimated.

Source: These numbers are taken from the websites of the respective arbitration houses.

detailed overview of the cases of major arbitration houses between 2003 and 2015, confirms this view. Between 2003 and 2013 the total caseload of ICA has increased by more than one third, from 2,166 cases filed in 2003 to 2,883 cases in 2014. The table also shows that the caseload peaked in 2009 (3,009 total cases) but since then has stagnated at around 3,000 cases. ICA seems thus not to have grown further over the past six years. However, the question that remains largely unconsidered in the pertinent literature on ICA is what these numbers actually mean. Does the number of around 3,000 annual cases filed at major arbitration houses really prove that ICA plays a vibrant legal role in the facilitation of global commerce? Do international business really rely on this mechanism to resolve disputes and to organize their contracts? Answering this question requires more than just looking at pure caseload numbers. Rather, the caseload needs to be put in context.

The first context is provided by a qualitative empirical study on contracts in the global software industry that was conducted by the author in different phases between 2005 and 2012. In this study, interviews with 51 software companies from India, Germany, Bulgaria and Romania were conducted on how these companies organize and enforce their contractual relations across borders.[16] Software development contracts provide an interesting case through which to study the role of ICA because formal contracts have been found to play crucial roles in the governance of such innovation-oriented business

[16] Thomas Dietz, *Global Order Beyond Law* (Hart, 2014).

relations due to the absence of long-established informal industry rules that tend to govern contracts in less innovative business relations.[17]

The results of the study indeed confirm that companies make wide use of formal contracts to organize their business transactions. These contracts also often included arbitration clauses. However, similar to what Bozovic and Hadfield have found in their recent study on contracting practices among innovation-orientated businesses in California,[18] the results also show that when conflicts arise, the parties do not proceed to arbitration but rather rely on informal mechanisms to enforce their contracts. In the first place, formal contracts served the parties as communication documents that made their mutual obligations explicit, but contracts were not used for litigation or arbitration purposes.[19]

Of course, these findings based on a small sample of qualitative interviews do not allow for general conclusions about the role of ICA in global commerce. However, it is possible to triangulate the study with further data to test the plausibility of these findings. One way of doing so is to take a closer look at the caseload data and to put it in the context of economic globalization.

Some arbitration institutions, for example the ICC in Paris, not only display the total annual caseload but also show the country of origin of the parties involved in arbitration. For 2005, the year when the empirical data on German and Indian software companies was gathered, the caseload statistics show a total of 102 German parties and 42 Indian parties were involved in an ICC arbitration.[20] Let us now consider that there exist probably tens of thousands of firms in Germany and India that are engaged in cross-border transactions worth millions of dollars every day. Due to the overall nature of business transactions, it seems fair to assume that most of these companies will eventually experience a contractual relation that turns sour or ends in conflict. Conflicts are part of the business world. But how are all these conflicts resolved? Some are referred to arbitration, but the very small numbers above indicate that the vast majority do not.

The following example relating to the USA makes this point even clearer. In 2009 the US Department of Commerce published a study on the external relations of the US economy and identified that there were 285,843 US firms exporting goods or services to countries outside the USA.[21] On the basis of the ICA caseload statistics (see Table 28.1), it can be assumed in the same year (2009) that around 3,000 US parties were involved in an arbitration case (although it is very likely that this number is too high). If again, we set these two numbers in relation to each other—285,843 exporting firms on the one hand and 3,000 cases involving a US party on the other—it becomes clear that out of the

[17] Iva Bozovic and Gillian Hadfield, 'Scaffolding: Using Formal Contracts to Build Informal Relations in Support of Innovation', USC CLASS Research Paper No. C12-3 (2015).

[18] Ibid. [19] Dietz (n. 16), 142.

[20] ICC, Arbitration Statistics (2005): <http://www.iccwbo.org/Products-and-Services/Arbitration-and-ADR/Arbitration/Introduction-to-ICC-Arbitration/Statistics>.

[21] See U.S. Census Bureau, Department of Commerce, 'A Profile of U.S. Importing and Exporting Companies, 2008–2009' (2011): <http://www.census.gov/foreign-trade/Press-Release/edb/2009/edbrel.pdf>.

number of exporting US firms only a very tiny proportion (less than 1.1 per cent) were involved in an arbitration case. Put differently, almost 99 per cent of all US firms engaged in cross-border trade did not refer a conflict to ICA in 2009. Note, that for most other major players in the global economy, as for example China or Japan, these numbers will be even smaller. Compared to the huge volumes of international trade and the hundreds of thousands of firms worldwide engaged in cross-border business relations, the caseload of ICA appears rather marginal.

In this context, it is also interesting to compare the caseload of ICA with the caseload of domestic courts dealing with domestic commercial cases. Take for example the German commercial courts (*Kammern für Handelssachen*). Even though their caseload has been rapidly decreasing over the past 20 years, the German commercial courts still deal with more than 30,000 cases yearly.[22] Similarly, the case statistics for US Federal District Courts show that these courts alone handle more than 27,000 contract cases per annum.[23] Another interesting figure is provided by Gary Born, who states in his widely cited textbook on ICA that the American Arbitration Association under its domestic commercial rules handles an annual caseload of around 12,000 domestic cases.[24] Again, the scarcity of data does not allow for statistical analysis; however, since there is no reason to assume that conflicts between business partners arise more often in domestic transactions than in cross-border transactions, these numbers seem to indicate that businesses involved in domestic contractual relations proportionally use the courts much more frequently than businesses involved in cross-border contracts would use ICA.

Of course, more quantitative research is needed to fully understand the role of ICA in international commerce. However, the various data sources used in this section point in the same direction: if put into context, the caseload of major arbitration institutions suggests a limited rather than a pivotal role of ICA in the governance of cross-border contracts.

28.3 Worldwide Enforcement of Arbitral Awards

The literature on ICA is full of statements, similar to the one below taken from a widely read textbook on ICA, that assume the effective worldwide enforcement of arbitral awards. Indeed, the enforceability of arbitral awards is widely regarded as one of the key success factors for the rise of ICA:

[22] Statistisches Bundesamt, 'Justizstatistik der Zivilgerichte 2009', Fachserie 10 Reihe 2.1 (2010). Also see Hermann Hoffmann and Andreas Maurer, 'Entstaatlichung der Justiz. Empirische Belege zum Bedeutungsverlust staatlicher Gerichte für internationale Wirtschaftsstreitigkeiten', 31(2) Zs. f. Rechtssoz. 279 (2010).

[23] U.S. Federal District Courts: <https://dockets.justia.com/>.

[24] Born (n. 2), 162.

> Why has arbitration become accepted worldwide as the principal method of resolving international disputes? There are two main reasons. The first is neutrality; the second is enforcement... As to 'enforcement', an international arbitration, if carried through to the end, leads to a decision which is enforceable against the losing party not only in the place where it is made but also internationally, under the provisions of such treaties as the New York Convention.[25]

The arbitration literature highlights a number of multilateral conventions that facilitate the recognition and enforcement of foreign arbitral awards, among which the so-called New York Convention. to which more than 150 states are signatories, is the most important. It is true that that due to these international conventions ICA awards have a far better chance of being enforced than judgments rendered by state courts, since (at least outside of the European Union), a similar multilateral legal framework for the recognition and enforcement of foreign court judgements is absent. However, what practical behaviour really follows from the existence of these international conventions? In the following section we will see that if one takes on a law-in-action perspective with respect to the enforcement of arbitral awards, the picture about the worldwide enforceability of arbitral awards becomes far less clear than the prevailing law-in-books perspective suggests.

Most importantly, the current literature on the enforcement of arbitration awards tends to blend the many legal interconnected layers that are involved in the enforcement of foreign arbitral awards. International conventions, such as the New York Convention, present only one legal layer of enforcement. At the lower levels of enforcement, national courts need to implement foreign arbitral awards and in the case that an arbitration award really is carried out to the end, national law enforcement institutions have to execute the award against the will and tactical legal manoeuvres of the losing party. As Jan Paulsson, one of the most eminent professionals of ICA, notes, it is exactly at this point, when national legal systems come into play in the enforcement of an arbitral award, that enforcement procedures may become problematic:

> [T]he New York Convention stands as an invaluable instance of international cooperation. Still, one must view it without illusion. Its experience has been uneven. Although 150 states are parties to the Convention, anyone familiar with a representative sample of national systems will not realistically expect it to be properly and loyally applied by even half of the signatories. Proclamation of adherence to a text is not enough; institutional development must be up to the task of applying it. Sweet words about building confidence in the reliability of international exchanges are part of an exercise in public relations; what counts is not what politicians say, but what the courts do. Some of the largest countries in the world have signed the New York Convention but are incapable of demonstrating an acceptable record of judicial compliance with its terms. The enforcement of foreign arbitral awards may

[25] Redfern et al. (n. 2), 131.

> be described as routine only in countries that have well-established institutional traditions, including mature legal orders…
>
> Why is it that the places where public justice has the weakest grip also tend to be those where arbitration is most fiercely resisted by the courts? The plausible answers are dismaying—incompetence, xenophobia, corruption—and should warn us that arbitration cannot flourish when the courts are substandard.[26]

A 2008 study again from Queen Mary University of London supports this view. When asked about the recognition and enforcement of foreign arbitral awards, companies reported a range of difficulties. Unsurprisingly, the main difficulty (46 per cent) was hostility to foreign arbitral awards in the place of enforcement. When asked what kind of difficulties they had experienced at the place of enforcement, 56 per cent of company lawyers cited local recognition and enforcement procedures or execution procedures. The majority of company lawyers linked both of these problems with the attitudes of local bureaucrats and courts. Ten per cent of the interviewees cited difficulties with corruption at local courts. When asked about particular countries, the most-mentioned regions, where difficulties are likely to appear in enforcement or execution proceedings, were Central America, South America (including Brazil), and Africa. China was the country mentioned most often, with India and Russia also considered potentially problematic territories.[27]

These results show that despite the New York Convention, international commercial arbitration in its universal form lacks an efficacious worldwide enforcement system. Foreign arbitral awards cannot reliably be enforced in many parts of the world, which are today deeply integrated into the world market, and these limitations again severely constrain the capacity of international commercial arbitration courts to provide a universally viable global legal order for global exchange. It seems thus more accurate to conceptualize ICA as a fragmented legal order that works most effectively in territories with functional rule-of-law-based court systems reliably implementing the enforcement of foreign arbitral awards.

28.4 ICA Providing an Efficient Global Legal Order

There is no doubt that freedom of contract and party autonomy are foundational to ICA. As a binding dispute resolution mechanism, ICA is not imposed on contractual parties but is based on explicit agreements between them. Typically, such agreements do not only include arbitration clauses but also define the contract laws governing the contract.

[26] Jan Paulsson, 'Why Good Arbitration Cannot Compensate for Bad Courts', 30(4) Journal of International Arbitration 345 (2013), 350–51.

[27] See Queen Mary University of London, '2008 International Arbitration Study' (2008), 10–12: <http://www.arbitration.qmul.ac.uk/docs/123294.pdf>.

Once the contractual parties have decided on an arbitrational clause in the contract, these governing laws can be any national or international law or even a-national *lex mercatoria* norms and transnational law codifications such as the UNIDROIT Principles of International Commercial Courts. Essentially, with ICA the parties are free to choose whatever procedural and substantial rules they consider most suitable to their case.

One of the most powerful narratives about ICA states that the parties when engaging in international contracts make extensive use of these wide choices of law options given in ICA. In order to optimize their contractual designs, the parties would first thoroughly compare different contract laws and then choose those contract laws that minimized the costs and risks of transactions in global markets.[28] Non-national *lex mercatoria* norms—norms that are not established through state legislation but evolve over time as bottom-up processes within business communities—are considered to be particularly well adapted to the legal needs of global businesses. Many scholars of arbitration have therefore predicted that for efficiency reasons, international business actors when given the choice in ICA will increasingly choose privately developed *lex mercatoria* norms over state-made contract laws to govern their cross-border contracts.[29]

So far we have addressed the theory, but what can be said about practice? When in 2005 Christopher R. Drahozal summarized the then available data on choice of law practices in international commerce he came to the following conclusion. In fact, the parties to international contracts very rarely use the possibility of referring to transnational private codifications or *lex mercatoria* norms but almost exclusively chose national laws to govern their contracts.[30] In 2010 this picture was confirmed by another study at Queen Mary University of London. The study was based on online questionnaires, with 78 questions that were completed by 136 respondents from February to August 2010. The respondents were mostly legal counsels or heads of legal departments of medium-sized or large international companies from all different kinds of industries and regions. A further 68 qualitative interviews were conducted with the same group of interviewees. Overall, the study included questions about the use of four different forms of a-national commercial laws: 'first, unwritten international principles (e.g. broad concepts of fairness and equity, determination *ex aequo et bono*); second, international treaties and conventions (e.g. the United Nations Convention on Contracts for the International Sale of Goods (CISG); third, commercial law rules relating to trade and international contracts (e.g. UNIDROIT Principles of International Commercial Contracts 2004 (UNIDROIT Principles) and INCOTERMS); fourth, other international rules (e.g. Uniform Customs and Practice for Documentary Credits (UCP).'[31]

[28] Mattli (n. 4).

[29] Klaus Peter Berger, 'The New Law Merchant and the Global Marketplace: A 21st Century View of Transnational Commercial Law', 3 International Arbitration Law Review 91 (2000), 91–102; Benson (n. 5), 644–61; O'Hara and Ribstein (n. 5).

[30] See Ch. 27 by Christopher Drahozal in this Handbook.

[31] Queen Mary University of London, '2010 International Arbitration Survey: Choices in International Arbitration' (2010): <http://www.arbitrationonline.org/docs/2010_International Arbitration Survey Report.pdf>.

The results of the study are clear: different from the assumption that privately made *lex mercatoria* will play an increasingly important role in the organization of global business contracts, the vast majority of international business actors stated that they never or only sometimes use one of the four mentioned forms of a-national commercial law, but routinely choose national law to govern their contracts.

Moreover, the study shows that the decision on which national contract law to choose is less driven by mutual interests in an efficient contract design—as assumed by the standard narrative—than by blunt bargaining power. In most cases the actors do not even engage in a comprehensive legal analysis about the pros and cons of different legal systems, but aim at imposing their familiar home laws on their contractual partner. Only under the condition that bargaining power is distributed equally among the contractual parties do they tend to agree on a governing law that is perceived as 'neutral' (not 'efficient')—typically, according to the study, this applies to English, New York, or Swiss law.

> How is the choice of governing law finally arrived at? Interviewees described how in contractual negotiations each party normally proposes its national law as the governing law of the contract, or one party puts forward its national law in its standard terms and conditions. When the bargaining power of the parties is equally matched, the 'home' law will normally be rejected and the parties will find a mutually acceptable solution, taking into account the factors indicated above. In such a case a 'neutral' law will be chosen.[32]

Overall, these results make it clear that the actual behaviour of the contractual parties largely deviates from the behaviour assumed by the standard narrative within ICA. It is therefore misleading to think of ICA as an institution that gives rise to efficient contractual practices across borders. Under certain conditions, when two equally powerful multinational companies engage in a contractual relation, it might well be that their legal departments negotiate a legal framework that neutrally supports both sides of the transactions. However, such conditions are absent in many (if not most) global business relations when one powerful multinational company has contracts with a multitude of foreign suppliers along global value chains. When there is a huge power gap between the parties, the party with greater bargaining power has no interest in creating a level legal playing field between the contractual parties, but will try to impose its preferred contract laws on the weaker party. According to what we know, this will generally be the home law of the company.

The problem of power in business relations has been widely raised by law and society scholarship many times before. Former legal realists, such as Robert Hale, challenged the principles of party autonomy and formalism in contract law, which they regarded as empowering those who were already the most powerful and thus entrenching existing asymmetries in power.[33] When in international commerce the stronger party takes

[32] Ibid. 14.

[33] Robert Hale, 'Bargaining, Duress and Economic Liberty', 43(5) Columbia Law Review 603 (1943).

advantage of the given wide choice of law options to impose its home law or another law in its interest on the other party, it shifts the risks and transaction costs to the weaker party, which has to accept these risks and costs if it wants to stay in business. The stronger party performs its contractual obligations in a familiar legal environment of its choice. Due to its experience in doing business under this law, it is better informed about the legal consequences of its behaviour, and can rely on its established network of local advisers to clarify specific issues.

The weaker party, on the other hand, finds itself in a much more uncomfortable position. It has to perform its contractual obligations in an unfamiliar legal environment. Lacking experience in doing business under foreign law, it faces higher uncertainties about the legal consequences of its behaviour. For legal advice on foreign law, the weaker party will very likely need to depend on lawyers outside its local network, who are likely to charge considerably higher legal fees which may very quickly become prohibitive. ICA thus does not present a neutral and authoritative legal mechanism that stands above the parties and gives rise to efficient legal practices in global commerce. Rather, it is shaped by extra-legal forces among which bargaining power is the most crucial. ICA does not efficiently reduce transaction costs, but tends to support an uneven legal playing field in which transaction costs are shifted to weaker parties.

28.5 ICA PROVIDING A GLOBAL LEGAL ORDER

However, efficiency is not the only criterion used by scholars to assess ICA. A broader normative debate concerns the public policy functions of ICA, arguing that ICA, despite its private, non-democratic character, gives rise to a legitimate global legal order. One very basic narrative is embedded in the voluntary, consensual view of contracts. This view states that those who are governed by ICA have voluntarily agreed on this legal mechanism in the first place. It is therefore the parties themselves who reach a consensus on the laws and procedures governing their contractual relations. In such a voluntary agreement, any form of coercion is absent. The decision to have disputes governed by ICA therefore represents a meeting of the minds of the contractual parties and can therefore be considered as just.[34]

More nuanced legal theories of ICA object at this point that unlimited party autonomy can hardly give rise to a just and legitimate global legal order. On the one hand, these theories agree that as part of a just global legal order, private contracts should be reliably enforced. On the other hand, there must also be a limit to contract enforcement.

[34] For a general account of freedom of contract in ICA, see Clive Schmitthoff, *International Commercial Arbitration* (Oceana, 1983); Ulrich Drobnig, 'Assessing Arbitral Autonomy in European Statutory Law', in Thomas Carbonneau (ed.), *Lex Mercatoria and Arbitration: A Discussion of the New Law Merchant* (Juris, 1998).

Put simply, courts or arbitral tribunals should enforce contracts, but they should hardly enforce all contracts.[35] In the domestic realm, private contracts are governed by mandatory laws that courts are obliged to follow when deciding a contract case. These mandatory laws aim to align private interests with public policy considerations. From a doctrinal perspective, arbitral tribunals must also consider mandatory laws. However, the procedural rules in arbitration provide very few details regarding how this should happen. Arbitrators therefore have greater leeway than state court judges to manoeuvre around the application of mandatory laws.[36] Given this, some scholars even argue that in arbitration, mandatory laws are in practice largely irrelevant in guiding the decisions of arbitrators.[37]

According to a growing number of legal theorists, ICA can overcome this legal deficiency and develop a public policy function in its own right. Indeed, in recent years, legal scholars have begun to argue that ICA presents more than a mere dispute resolution mechanism at the parties' disposal, but also stands at the centre of an emerging global legal order that produces its own practice of linking arbitral decisions to broader public policy concerns.[38] Many facets of arbitral procedure are directly determined by the contractual parties. However, international arbitration also involves substantial and procedural rules that are established and controlled by third parties. Such rules may be produced by the epistemic community of arbitrators,[39] who implicitly agree on common standards in ICA. These rules may be inherent to legal procedures when arbitrators are forced to give reasons for their awards,[40] or they may functionally evolve to adapt ICA to an ever more complex global economy[41] This is to name only a few possibilities that are mentioned in the pertinent literature of how ICA might produce its own set of 'quasi-mandatory' laws that are not subjected to party autonomy but give rise to an overarching normative order that guides both the behaviour of arbitrators as well as contractual parties.

Indeed, this literature shows that much of the concern regarding the biases of private judges towards economically powerful contractual parties seems unjustified. Like public judges, private arbitrators do not simply enforce private contracts, but base their decisions on broader 'quasi-mandatory' transnational norms of justice, thus giving rise to an emergent system of transitional mandatory laws beyond the nation-state. In this view, arbitration institutions can perform a public policy function, even when they are not democratically legitimized. These insights are crucial, and they are not easily derived from bold theoretical assumptions but are based in part on thorough empirical investigations on how arbitrators behave in practice.[42]

However, theories that view ICA as part and parcel of an emerging global legal order are defective in another sense. They draw far-reaching conclusions about the wide

[35] Gélinas (n. 6).

[36] Moritz Renner, *Zwingendes Transnationales Recht. Zur Struktur der Wirtschaftsverfassung Jenseits des Staates* (Nomos, 2011).

[37] Renner (n. 6). [38] Renner (n. 36). [39] Karton (n. 6). [40] Gélinas (n. 6).

[41] Renner (n. 36). [42] Ibid.; Karton (n. 6).

impact of ICA on contractual behaviour in international commerce by only analysing the internal operations of ICA, without taking into account the outside relevance of these legal mechanisms. In fact, in the real world of contracting, many if not most conflicts will never reach the just harbour of courts. This socio-legal insight also applies to arbitration. The above-mentioned power gaps between contractual parties may be one reason for this. To illustrate this point, see the following example taken from my study on cross-border software development contracts:

> A French company took my developers. And what they did is this: they were supposed to pay me after two months. And it was more than two months that they should pay me. So, they delayed. And they said: we will pay you only when we receive a little paper that you accept the modification of the contract. The modification was that the French company can hire my developers. The contract was drafted under French law. To do something against them was too difficult. And I was too stressed about money and paying people. So, it was something on the limit.[43]

This quotation illustrates two important points. First, stronger parties evidently have at their disposal a large arsenal of non-legal governance mechanisms to impose their will on weaker parties, including delayed payments, ending the business relationship, or spreading a bad reputation about weaker parties in the wider business community. Under these conditions stronger parties can avoid the costs and time-consuming procedures of bringing a case to ICA. These informal means of contractual governance are often much more effective in resolving a conflict in their favour. Weaker parties, on the other hand, will in most cases have to adapt their expectations to the will of stronger parties in order to avoid an immediate cash-flow crisis. Even if it expects an arbitral award in its favour, in many cases the weaker party will lack the knowledge, time, and financial resources to make ICA work.

Access to justice as a further central criterion of defining a legitimate legal order seems to be severely limited in ICA. Again, limited access to justice also constrains the justice function of national legal systems. Socio-legal scholars have emphasized this point many times before.[44] However, due to its private character and enormous costs it may have an even stronger effect on ICA. In ICA, stronger parties have more leverage to use their bargaining power to design the legal conditions of ICA up-front in a way that in practice excludes weaker parties from using this legal mechanism. Hence, ICA—even when its internal operations largely meet the standards of a rule of law based judicial mechanism—does not provide a legal order that works equally for all contractual parties in global commerce.

Rather, ICA tends to reinforce existing power relations in that it enables access to justice predominantly for economically powerful parties while tending to exclude economically weaker parties. ICA thus does not provide an equal legal playing field in which all

[43] Dietz (n. 16), 101

[44] Deborah Rhode, 'Access to Justice', 69 Fordham L. Rev 1785 (2001).

parties would ideally enjoy the same access to justice. Overall, it seems therefore to be more accurate to conceive of ICA as an exclusive legal order driven by large international law firms to govern large-scale transactions between equally powerful international businesses. The average sum at stake in arbitration, which reaches well beyond US$30 million per case (e.g. in ICC arbitrations), adds to this view.

Smaller and weaker parties, who are engaged in hundreds of thousands of cross-border transactions with lower volumes, seem to not take part in ICA.[45] This is to say that the evolution of a just and legitimate transnational legal order based on ICA requires more than due processes and the application of transnational substantial laws beyond the parties' will. Whereas the internal judicial operations present in ICA might well meet the criteria of a just legal system that is able to promote wider public policy functions, the system turns out to be incapable of a broader reach. Access to justice remains limited.

28.6 Legal pluralism

If ICA is less pivotal to the organization of global commerce than often assumed, how are cross-border contracts then governed? Law and society scholars have pointed out on a recurrent basis that when disputes arise and contracts need to be enforced, there is no guarantee that the procedures and rules to solve disputes and to enforce contracts will be formal law.[46] As Macaulay has noted, companies often fail to plan transactions thoroughly and rarely use legal sanctions to enforce contracts. Formal contracts, he continues, are often highly standardized documents that are not worth the paper they are written on once drafted by the legal department, and then seldom referred to when disputes arise. Macaulay's classical insights still rank among the most highly cited in the legal literature and far beyond.

Indeed, Macaulay's findings spurred the development of a scholarly subfield across the disciplines of law, economics, and sociology that is preoccupied with the question of how contractual commitments can be secured if not through courts and legal sanctions.[47]

45 Hermann Hoffmann, 'Transnational Access to Court for Commercial Contract Claims: The Shortcomings of International Commercial Arbitration and Litigation', ZenTra Working Paper in Transnational Studies No. 37 (2014), 12.

46 Macaulay, 'Non-contractual Relations' (n. 9); Robert Ellickson, *Order Without Law* (Harvard University Press, 1991); Lisa Bernstein, 'Opting out of the Legal System: Extralegal Contractual Relations in the Diamond Industry', 21 J. Legal Stud. 115 (1992); David Charny, 'Nonlegal Sanctions in Commercial Relationships', 104 Harv. Law Rev. 373 (1990).

47 Prominent works in the field include: Oliver Williamson, *The Mechanisms of Governance* (Oxford University Press, 1996); Avinash Dixit, *Lawlessness and Economics: Alternative Modes of Governance* (Princeton University Press, 2004); Avner Greif, 'Commitment, Coercion, and Markets: the Nature and Dynamics of Institutions Supporting Exchange', in Claude Mènard and Mary Shirley (eds), *Handbook of New Institutional Economics* (Springer, 2005), 727; Armen Alchian and Harold Demsetz, 'Production, Information Costs, and Economic Organization', 62(5) Am. Econ. Review 777.

Among the many central insights developed by this literature, two aspects stand out: first, the problem of complex and incomplete contracting which leads to both increased uncertainties and costs of litigation, and second, the important role played by non-legal enforcement mechanisms such as reputational networks and self-enforcing contracts based on enduring business relationships.

The relational view of contract conceptualizes economic exchange as embedded in direct social ties between economic actors.[48] In such types of inter-actor constellations, norms of reciprocity, rather than formal contracts and abstract legal rules, create the glue for economic cooperation. As a central function, socially embedded ties and norms address the risk of opportunism by facilitating high-trust relationships. Close inter-actor bonds promote cooperation, as actors know that opportunistic behaviour yields undesired outcomes such as the loss of a long-term business partner or, even worse, exclusion from important social and business communities.[49]

The problem of complex and incomplete contracting characterizes international contracts to the same extent as it characterizes domestic contracts, to say the least. In addition, the legal institutions governing international commerce show considerable signs of dysfunctionality which has only partly been resolved through the rise of ICA. Under these conditions it comes as no surprise that non-legal contract enforcement mechanisms have been found to play a significant role also in the world of international contracting.[50]

Scholars of law and society have pointed out repeatedly that social life is governed by a plurality of formal and informal norms and orders. ICA is only one institution in the total picture of institutions governing contractual behaviour in international commerce. Some conflicts will end up in arbitration. However, given the hundreds of thousands of cross-border transactions taking place every day, most of them will not. It seems to apply to international commerce to an even greater extent than to domestic commerce that formal contract laws only indirectly affect business relations. Also, in international commerce the contracting partners rarely use legal sanctions—including ICA—to resolve disputes or enforce contractual agreements, but instead rely on informal norms and sanctions to govern their contractual relations. Seeing these results, it seems misleading to present ICA as the single most important mechanism of dispute resolution and contract enforcement in international commerce, and one that gives rise to an efficient, just, and effective global legal order beyond the nation-state. In fact, in a world characterized by legal pluralism including formal and informal laws, ICA's role is much more limited than is widely assumed.

[48] Ian Macneil, *Cases and Materials on Contracts: Exchange Transactions and Relationships* (Foundation Press, 1971); Mark Granovetter, 'The Strength of Weak Ties', 78 Am. J. Sociol. 1360 (1973); 'Economic Action and Social Structure: The Problem of Embeddedness', 91(3) Am. J. Sociol. 481 (1985); Brian Uzzi, 'The Sources and Consequences of Embeddedness for Economic Performance of Organizations: The Network Effect', 61(4) American Sociol. Review 674 (1996).

[49] Dixit (n. 47); Granovetter, 'Economic Action' (n. 28).

[50] Dietz (n. 16).

28.7 Perspectives

Let us not get carried away with this less than clear-cut picture of ICA. Given the widely debated constraints of state legal systems to enforce contracts across-borders,[51] ICA remains the only credible legal mechanism with real potential to provide a workable formal legal framework for global commerce. Such a formal legal system may become important as a last resort if contractual relations really turn sour.[52] Further, taking a longer-term perspective, it is even imaginable that ICA will expand its legal functions by enforcing extra-contractual, social, or environmental norms which at present are becoming more and more part of global value chain contracts. With the support of ICA, private contracts might even be turned into effective vehicles of global public regulation.

However, at present, ICA has not reached that stage. There is considerable room for improvement. Access to justice is limited, choice-of-law options tend to reinforce existing power gaps between contractual parties, and substandard national courts in many countries hinder the effective enforcement of arbitral awards. The polished image perpetuated by a significant amount of the existing literature that still determines our perception of ICA obscures these institutional shortcomings and stand in the way of an improved system of ICA. This chapter might be considered merely as a first step to developing a more realistic image of ICA's role in our global economy—one that allows crucial stakeholders from both the public and private sector to confront ICA's institutional shortcomings and improve its long-term legal performance.

[51] Ibid.

[52] For the role of the legal system as a last resort, see: Stewart Macaulay, 'The Real and the Paper Deal: Empirical Pictures of Relationships, Complexity and the Urge for Transparent Legal Rules', in John Campbell, Hugh Collins, and John Wightman (eds), *Implicit Dimensions of Contract: Discrete, Relational, and Network Contracts* (Hart, 2003), 51.

CHAPTER 29

INVESTMENT ARBITRATION AND POLITICAL SYSTEMS THEORY

CÉDRIC DUPONT, THOMAS SCHULTZ, AND JASON WEBB YACKEE

In this chapter we present a vision of investment treaty arbitration filtered through the lens of political systems theory.[1] Political systems theory was developed in the 1950s and 1960s by David Easton, an eminent political scientist.[2] The core idea of Easton's theory, which we describe in more detail below, is that political systems can be understood as consisting of inputs from various actors that are aggregated and transformed into outputs, where outputs, as Easton puts it, consist of the authoritative allocation of values. The import, or impact, of those outputs feed back into the system as actors react to them, by (for example) changing the content or intensity of their level of support for the system as a whole.

Admittedly, Easton's theory was the subject of significant criticism in the 1970s,[3] and today his work is rarely cited by political scientists. He had the misfortune to make unwarranted grandiose claims about his theory's potential to revolutionize the discipline by transforming it into an actual 'science', which would have been conducted under

The authors would like to thank Dr Merih Angin for her contributions to the dataset of investment arbitration claims on which this chapter partly relies.

[1] This chapter builds upon earlier work by Dupont and Schultz: Cédric Dupont and Thomas Schultz, 'Towards a New Heuristic Model: Investment Arbitration as a Political System' 7 Journal of International Dispute Settlement 3 (2016).

[2] David Easton, *A Systems Analysis of Political Life* (Wiley, 1965); *The Political System: An Inquiry into the State of Political Science* (Knopf, 1968); *A Framework for Political Analysis* (Prentice-Hall, 1969).

[3] See e.g. John D. Astin, 'Easton I and Easton II', 25(4) Western Political Quarterly (Dec. 1972), 726–37.

a unified, all-encompassing theoretical framework.[4] Political scientists have almost uniformly rejected these claims, and his theory clearly has failed in that regard. However, if we put this overreach aside, we think that his theory provides a valuable heuristic through which to better and more easily understand the complicated interactions that produce international investment law as we know it today. It eventually helps highlight the sources of stress that seem to be leading the system's actors to rethink whether the system should be modified or even abandoned.

Easton's model, as we present and apply it, is simple, and its vocabulary at least subconsciously familiar. But that does not mean that it is not able to show something new. As Ludwig Wittgenstein put it, 'The aspects of things that are most important for us are hidden because of their simplicity and familiarity. (One is unable to notice something—because it is always before one's eyes.)' The point of a heuristic model is to make familiar things unfamiliar, and thereby make them differently noticeable.

One of the main values of adopting an Eastonian heuristic in the present context is that it serves to correct currently dominant and unduly narrow neo-functionalist understandings of international investment law. Those understandings tend to view the investment law system either through an economic or a legal lens. The first understands the system to be an inevitable 'equilibrium' to a prisoner's-dilemma-like game, the function of which is to resolve otherwise irresolvable problems of 'obsolescing bargain' and 'credible commitment'. The second views the system as an inherently desirable attempt to impose the 'rule of law' on investor–state relations. Either of these views can be useful in their own right, but they also suffer from limitations.

One important limitation of the first is that it exaggerates the stability of current arrangements. An important limitation of the second is that it conceals the sometimes vigorous contestation over what the 'rule of law' in this context should mean or how it should be applied. And a shared limitation of both approaches is a tendency to ignore the multiplicity of actors who actually influence (or agitate to influence) the system's outputs.

As we describe below, a political-systems approach encourages us to move beyond overly reductionist visions of international investment law as a quasi-inevitable product of state–investor interactions, or as the quasi-autonomous and teleological identification and imposition by tribunals of necessarily sensible or correct rules of state behaviour.

To summarize, our key claim is that one way to make better sense of the fragmented understanding we have today of investment arbitration is to view it as a political system: one that transforms the input of key actors into output, with feedback loops from the latter to the former. We contend that seeing investment arbitration as political system allows us to bring out elements of its workings with greater clarity. We claim that,

[4] Henrik P. Bang, 'David Easton's Postmodern Images', 26(3) Political Theory (June 1998), 281–316. There are further controversies around Easton's work, but they do not concern us here. They are largely intra-disciplinary struggles over particular visions of political science's goals and methods, or debates about whether 'political' systems were distinctive from other kinds of social system—again, issues that make no difference to the usefulness of his theories for our purposes.

altogether, this helps us get a better sense of some of the key dynamics of investment arbitration.

In Section 29.1, we explain the idea of a political systems, what this means for investment arbitration at the modelling level, and briefly introduce the main actors of the system. In Section 29.2, we draw on Easton's theory to highlight sources of and reactions to systemic 'stress', a key Eastonian concept. We then briefly conclude in Section 29.3.

29.1 International Investment Law as a Political System

The basic contours of Easton's framework are easy to specify, at least informally:

> The political system is an aspect of the social system. It is an open, transformational system, which functions so as to turn inputs of demands and support into outputs of policies and allocations, the consequences of which then feed back into the inputs. Owing to an inherent scarcity of many valued resources (not least of which is time) there is a propensity to overload or stress, which, if unchecked, could lead to the failure of the system to perform its characteristic function: the allocation of valued goods in an authoritative way. Political systems have the capacity, however, to respond to stress through changes in both system structure and system states; but a system may fail to make such adjustments and therefore fail to persist through time.[5]

Figure 29.1 illustrates the basic approach.[6]

In the simplified model, various actors (whom we identify and discuss further below) provide inputs to the system, in the form of what Easton calls 'demands' and 'support'. He defines demands as 'expressions of opinion that an authoritative allocation with

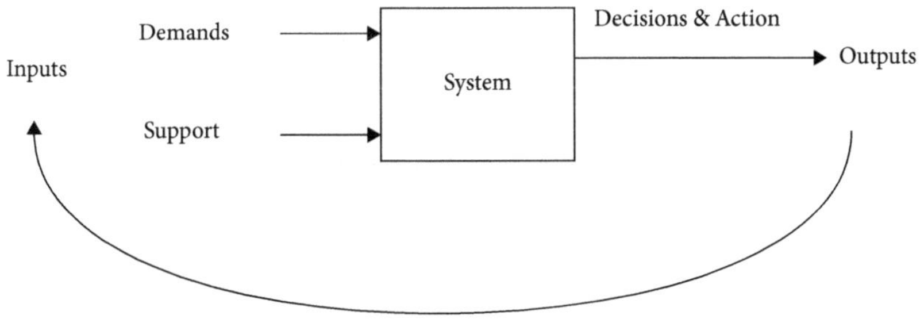

FIGURE 29.1 Simplified Eastonian Model.

[5] Leslie Green, 'Support for the System', 15(2) British Journal of Political Science (Apr. 1985), 131–2.

[6] Adapted from Easton, *A Systems Analysis* (n. 2), 32.

regard to a particular subject matter should or should not be made by those responsible for doing so'.[7] Demands are distinguished from, but may reflect, an actor's 'expectations, opinions, expressions of motivations, ideologies, interests and statements of preference'.[8] To offer a concrete example, a state (or some sub-unit, such as the ministry of foreign affairs) may prefer that international investment law reflect an understanding of the fair and equitable treatment (FET) standard that mirrors the standard enunciated in the famous *Neer* decision.[9] The state makes a 'demand' of the international investment law system when it argues to an investment arbitration tribunal (in a memorandum, at a hearing) that the tribunal's ultimate decision should articulate, as an authoritative statement and application of the law, that same understanding. The award is the 'output' of the system, and it consists of the decision of the tribunal to articulate a certain understanding of FET, and to act by publishing that decision as an award. The system itself can be viewed as the locus of interactions between the system's various actors; it consists of the processes through which their various demands are aggregated into the system's outputs.

'Support', for Easton, consists of actions and attitudes that promote the maintenance and functioning of the system.[10] In the case of the international investment law system, the decision of a state's representative at the World Bank to vote to increase funding to the International Centre for the Settlement of Investment Disputes (ICSID) can be viewed as 'support'. The support doesn't *demand* anything from the system, but it does signal the state's continued willingness to see the system continue to function as it has been. Other kinds of support are easy to identify. If law firms are actors relevant to the system, their decisions to promote the use of ICSID to their clients can be analysed as support. The willingness of businesses to insert ICSID clauses in their investment contracts is support for the system. And so on.

A key aspect of Easton's model is the familiar concept of the feedback loop, illustrated in Figure 29.1 by the curved arrow running from outputs to inputs. The idea here is that the system's actors experience the system's outputs, and that in response to those outputs they adjust the character and quality of the demands that they place on and the support that they provide the system in later rounds. As an example, imagine that the arbitral tribunal rejects the state's demand that its articulation of FET reflects the *Neer* standard. The state is disappointed that the output—the award—articulates a more expansive standard, and, because of that disappointment, the state refuses to vote to fund ICSID the next time the question is presented to the bank's board of directors. Here we see a withdrawal of support that was caused by the system's prior output. Likewise, demands may be modified in reaction to outputs. In the next investment treaty arbitration to which it is a party, the state may abandon its previous demand that the system adopt the *Neer* standard (recognizing the question as having been authoritatively settled that it does not), but will now demand that the correct standard is one that reflects only

[7] Ibid. 38. [8] Ibid. 47.

[9] On the *Neer* decision, see Stephen M. Schwebel, 'Is Neer Far from Fair and Equitable?', 27(4) Arbitration International (December 2011), 555–62.

[10] Easton, *A Systems Analysis* (n. 2), 159–70.

an incremental advance beyond *Neer*. Here the character of the demand has changed because of the earlier output.

One of Easton's major analytic concerns is the possibility—or indeed the likelihood—of 'continuing disequilibrium' in political systems subject to what he calls 'stress'. Stress results from the quantity and quality of demands placed upon the system, which can impede the system from providing authoritative allocations that actors in the system desire. A domestic legal example illustrates one version of the problem.[11] Federal district courts in the United States face large volumes of 'demands' for 'outputs' (high-quality adjudications of civil and criminal matters), but the numbers of federal judges, and their budgets, are highly constrained. The result is systemic 'stress' in which the ability of the courts to produce the desired output (adjudications) is impeded, as the courts—because of the volume of demands and their limited resources—are forced to resort to the suboptimal use of expedited procedures that dispose of cases without a trial, leading to criticisms of (and in a sense, a decline in support for) the courts.

Easton also suggests that stress can occur because of the content (quality) of demands. Actors may make complex demands that the system can process only with great difficulty, or actors may make competing and inconsistent demands that the system cannot easily aggregate. In either case, Easton's concern is that such stresses can impact the quality of system outputs, and that as output quality declines, system actors may reduce their support for, or even abandon, the system. The system may adapt to reductions in support or (threats of) abandonment. Or it may cease to exist, to be replaced by some other system. Easton thus identifies the dynamics and discontinuities that political systems experience as they react, sometimes successfully and sometimes not, to the stresses that actors and their demands place upon them.[12] And this is precisely what is of interest to us in this chapter: the mechanisms and dynamics and stresses of the system are the centre of attention and structure our thinking, putting the focus on how the object of study is changing and adapting.

We have repeatedly used, and will keep using, the word 'system' throughout this chapter. One might wonder, then, whether the word is really apposite: is the investment arbitration system really a system? Is it an actual (or perhaps real, or 'natural') political *system*, in the sense that the human body, for example, is a real, existing, naturally demarcated biological *system*? Easton's answer was to insist that it does not matter: he was only positing the analytic utility of treating a given political system *as if* it were indeed a system.[13] On the one hand, that is largely our approach as well: treating investment arbitration as if it were a 'political system' for analytic purposes can identify interesting and important questions about the potential stability and direction of current rules and institutional arrangements for generating authoritative rules of international investment law. Wearing the 'systems glasses', as it were, encourages us to concentrate on

[11] Our example is based upon Daniel J. Knudsen, 'Institutional Stress and the Federal District Courts: Judicial Emergencies, Vertical Norms, and Pretrial Dismissals', 187 Utah L. Rev. (2014).

[12] For a convincing articulation of this point, see Bang (n. 4).

[13] This move can be criticized. See Green (n. 5), 128–9, who argues that once we accept political systems as purely analytical constructs, notions of persistence and dynamism can have no meaning.

identifying the main actors who seek to shape and influence those rules, as well as the incentive structures in which they operate as they both influence rule creation and experience the consequences of the rules that they help to create.

Then again, it is not such a great jump into heuristic fiction. There is in investment arbitration something naturally demarcatable, and something arguably system-like in a quite objectively determinable sense. The primary products of the system—arbitral awards—are concrete and identifiable; they self-consciously articulate values that claim the status of binding authority; and the primary actors who seek to influence their creation (and who experience their impacts), as well as those actors' sites and patterns of interaction, are relatively easily identified. Quite possibly the Eastonian model does not work for every situation. In some instances, its application might bring to mind Green's memorable *reductio ad absurdum* of a 'political system' consisting of 'this paper, the moon, [and] Whitehall'[14]—which would admittedly be purely analytical, and in the end arbitrary. But there is something more 'real' about the regime of investment arbitration understood as a system in the Eastonian sense.

Figure 29.2 presents a less generic version of Easton's basic model, depicting the international investment law system in the pre-investment-treaty era. Before discussing the model, we should point out one departure from Easton's original formulation. He articulated an analytic distinction between the 'environment' in which a political system

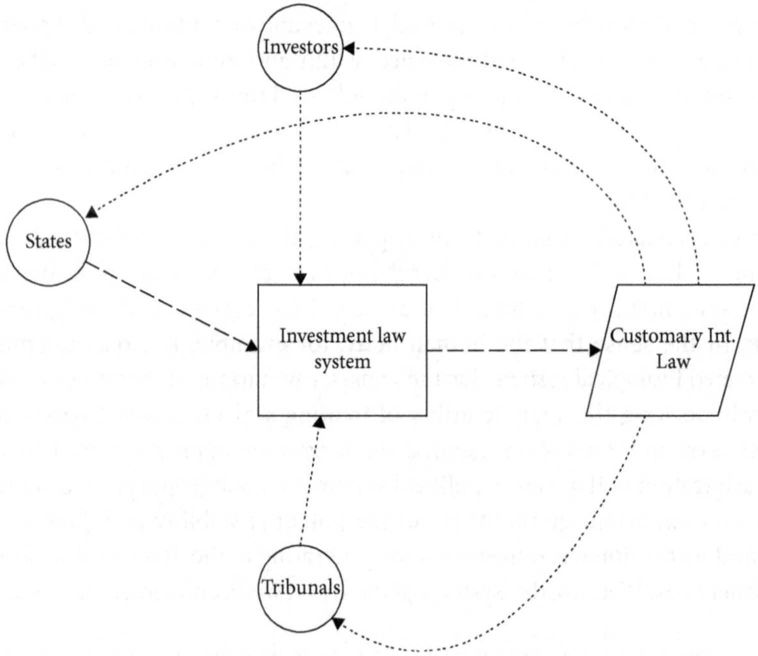

FIGURE 29.2 The International Investment Law System Before BITs.

[14] Ibid. 129.

operated, and those actors who were 'within' the system and able to influence it directly. Actors in the environment (e.g. the voting public) provide 'inputs', while those actors within the system (e.g. politicians) provided what Easton called 'withinputs'. We ignore this complicating distinction (one that has been criticized elsewhere)[15] in order to present a simpler model that, in our view, does not lose analytic or suggestive utility. In our model, then, and even though Easton himself might have characterized states and the other actors as being 'within' the international investment law system, we present them as if they were outside of it, in the 'environment'. In our conception, then, the 'system' contains not the actors themselves, but their modes and patterns of joint interaction in the production of international investment law.

In the pre-BIT era, the main actors who experienced investment law (as outputs) and who actively sought to influence it (through inputs) were states, investors, and tribunals. However, the influence of investment law on investors and tribunals was rather weak, as suggested by the lightly dotted lines. Tribunals came into existence only rarely, on an ad hoc basis, and the rules of custom were so few and vague as to have little real constraining impact on the occasional arbitral decision. Likewise, investors had few opportunities to directly experience international investment law, as custom did not (and does not) allow investors, as private actors, to activate the system through arbitration. Investors largely experienced international investment law only indirectly, when they could persuade their foreign ministries to exercise diplomatic protection on their behalf, which itself functioned as a mix of diplomacy and law.

Figure 29.2 also illustrates (again through lightly dotted lines) that the ability of investors and tribunals to directly place demands on the system was quite weak, or even, for analytic purposes, largely non-existent. Tribunals, as temporary, infrequent, ad hoc affairs, were not sufficiently organized or long-lived enough to formulate and present demands on the system. A robust norm of confidentiality further weakened the ability of tribunals to place demands on the system, as their work product—the natural vehicle for demands—was often secret. And while foreign investment was alive and well in the pre-BIT era, investors rarely had direct access to the adjudicatory fora that today provide their best and most effective means of trying to shape system output. When they did, it was through occasional arbitration clauses in investment contracts that would result in ad hoc and largely secret adjudications.

Instead, we see states as the primary source of demands on and reactors to the system. This privileged role is built into the conceptual apparatus of customary international law itself, which is said to emerge exclusively from the practice of states, and to depend on the sense in which states understand their practice (*opinio juris*). At the same time, the collective nature of custom generation means that states' ability to actively 'demand' certain outputs was quite limited (reflected in a dashed rather than solid line), and that the system correspondingly was able to produce only limited quantities of custom in response. The nature of that custom—rare, vague, incomplete—and the absence of a robust system of international adjudication that would authoritatively

[15] Astin (n. 3), 731 n. 30.

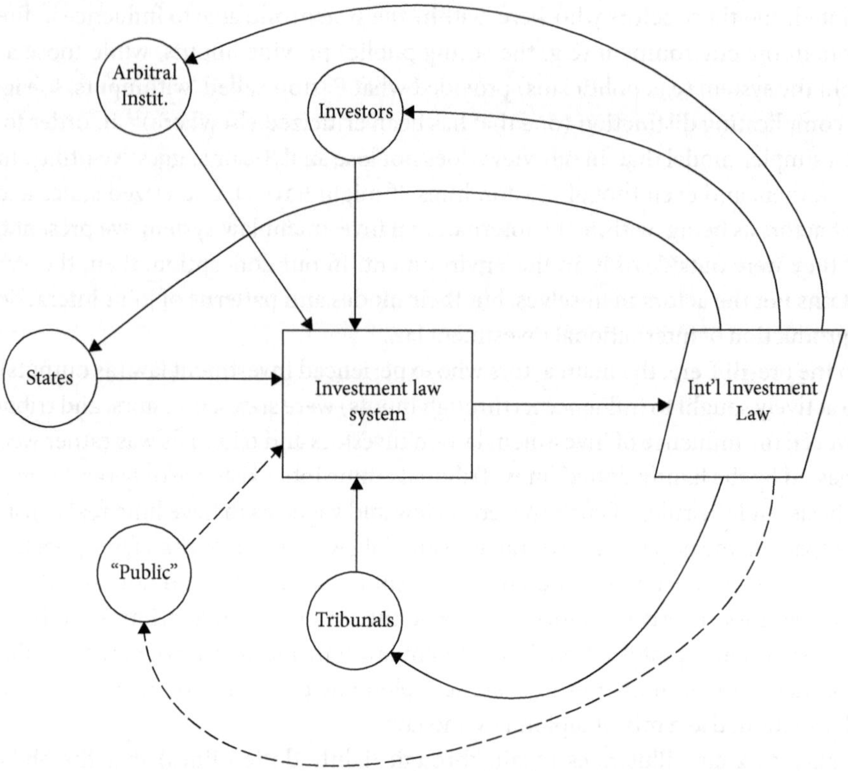

FIGURE 29.3 The Modern International Investment Law System.

interpret, develop, and apply it meant that whatever custom the system did generate was felt only weakly by states (just as it was felt perhaps even more weakly by investors and the occasional tribunal).

Figure 29.3 presents an Eastonian model of the modern international investment law system.

We include five sets of actors as involved in the operation of the modern version of the system: (1) states; (2) investors; (3) arbitral tribunals; (4) arbitral institutions; and (5) the 'public', which we mean as shorthand for the NGOs (and occasionally, individual private citizens) who are increasingly obtaining the right to participate directly in the system's functioning. States are obviously key actors in the modern system, be it only because their consent to investment arbitration is a necessary requirement for the system to operate. Their input, in general terms, revolves around the ways in which they express that consent and how they frame international investment law substantively, through state practice, treaty-making, contracts with foreign investors, and domestic legislative actions, such as consent to investment arbitration in a national 'investment code'. Another type of states' input relates to their behaviour during arbitration procedures. Yet another is their role in choosing arbitrators for institutional lists.

Investors are key too, as they activate the system by filing claims. They are principally corporations but may also be individuals. Their input, again in general terms, revolves around the claims they file or threaten to file, the procedural rules or institution that they use, and the framing of their arguments and claims.

The third category of key actors comprises arbitrators, who sit as tribunals and whose actions and decisions are the most proximate 'cause' of the system's outputs. They are the direct producers of awards, crafted and issued within the framework, guideposts, and constraints set by states and investors. Arbitrators' inputs consist largely but not exclusively in the drafting of their awards, though they may also seek to influence the system through other activities, such as public scholarship.

The fourth category of key actors consists of arbitral institutions, such as ICSID or the ICC, and quasi-arbitral institutions, such as UNCITRAL, because of their role in drafting their own procedural rules and their residual capacity in appointing arbitrators. Their input revolves mainly around the ways in which they exercise this role and this residual capacity, but also extends to their own efforts in exhibiting a successful caseload.

The fifth actor is the 'public'. By 'the public', we do not mean individual citizens at large, the vast majority of whom know nothing about international investment law and make no attempts, and have little or no capacity, to influence the system. Rather, we are referring to the typically organized and specialized segments of civil society (primarily NGOs) who have lobbied for, obtained, and taken advantage of opportunities to participate directly in the system, often through *amicus curiae*-type provisions in arbitration rules. This is not to deny that the larger public has some theoretical capacity to influence the system when, or if, particular investment law issues become highly salient. However, those kinds of mass public inputs will usually be presented to other system actors, such as states, and are best viewed as indirect inputs.

We consider the system's primary output to be the arbitral awards, taken in the aggregate, and including all their variegated effects, from the determination of rights, to their precedential value, to their actual financial implications on all actors involved, to their impact on the reputation of all actors involved, and including all forms of legal, economic, social, and political dimensions. This output has feedback effects on the key actors of the system, who react to it, either by adjusting their input so as to maximize the realization of their own preferences and perceived interests, or by adjusting their actions without seeking to alter the system itself, for instance by simply complying with it or by exiting it. These reactions create the system's dynamics.

We think it important to emphasize that our graphical implementation of Easton's political systems model is just one possible way of summarizing, in a heuristic figure, the kinds and quantities of actors and interactions that produce international investment law broadly construed. It is a choice that puts ease of understanding over exhaustiveness: undoubtedly the graphical representation could be made much more comprehensive. For instance, it would be possible to incorporate into Figure 29.3 the observation that the various actors may try to influence the system's output indirectly, by placing demands directly on other actors. For example, certain segments of the public regularly attempt to influence international investment law by lobbying national governments on investment treaty practice. It would also be possible to further disaggregate our five actors, out of recognition that collectivities such as 'the state' are in reality made up of constituent units (and, ultimately, of individuals) who may have varied interests in the operation of the international investment law system, and different pathways of influence over it. For example, investment treaty litigators in the state's foreign ministry may have very different ideas about the values that the system should be providing than those of government employees in the ministries whose actions are being challenged. We could also disaggregate the system's outputs into customary, treaty, and arbitral law, as different actors may have different kinds and degrees of influence over different forms of international investment law. We ultimately think that something like Figure 29.3 strikes the proper balance between too much fidelity to the complications of reality and too little. Perhaps we err on the side of too little. But the ability of simplifying models, like Easton's, to usefully structure our thinking about complex socio-legal phenomena depends on simplicity.

29.2 Stress in the System?

In this section we use the Eastonian heuristic developed above to frame a discussion of sources of stress in the system. We discuss volume-related stress first, and then content-related stress. Our discussion of the latter focuses most extensively on the system's evolution toward greater transparency and participation rights.

29.2.1 Volume-related stress

At a general level, a comparison between Figures 29.2 and 29.3 illustrates that the system has expanded in terms of the number of actors who place demands upon it and in the system's capacity to produce outputs that have meaningful feedback potential. This expansion is due in large part, of course, to the massive increase in the numbers of investment treaties in force that contain state pre-consents to investor-initiated, binding arbitration. Volume is likely to continue to expand, and perhaps dramatically so, as the system is extended to cover foreign investment between highly developed economies. It is also likely to expand as investment treaty litigation financing grows more institutionalized and becomes more available.

One important implication that we can derive from Easton's framework is that the expanded, modern system is potentially more likely to suffer from 'stress' than was the more primitive system illustrated in Figure 29.2. This is because the modern system is characterized by a much greater number of actors capable of placing demands into the system (volume stress) and by the potential for much greater conflict between demands, as an increasingly heterogeneous set of actors brings different interests and perspectives to bear on the question of what the system should produce (content stress).

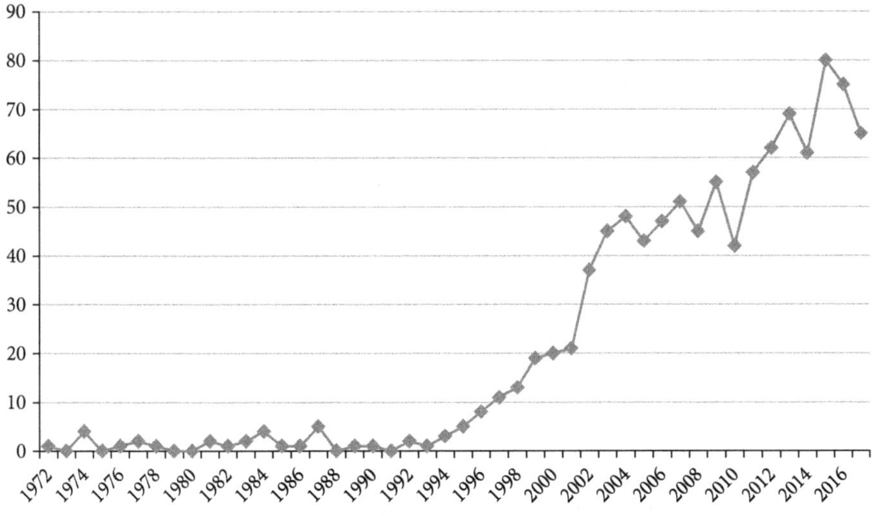

FIGURE 29.4 Annual number of new investment arbitrations.

Figure 29.4 shows the increase in volume of demands in the system, pictured as the annual number of known investment arbitrations filed. Clearly, investors are 'demanding' much more from the international investment law system today than they did just thirty years before: according to our own data, over the last five years (2013–17), investors have initiated 350 new investment arbitrations; during the same five-year span thirty years ago (1983–87), there were only 13. This is a 2,692 per cent, or 27-fold, increase. Over the last three decades, the average growth rate of investment arbitration has been 608 per cent per decade: each new decade, investors have on average filed more than six times more investment claims than they did the decade before.[16] This has brought the number of claims the system has dealt with to a total of 1,012 so far. And as approximately half of these claims have resulted in an award, tribunals are having much more say over what the content of international investment law is and means. In short, demand for the production of investment-related 'authoritative allocations of value' has increased dramatically; the role of investors in making those demands has increased dramatically; and the role of tribunals in providing system outputs has increased dramatically as well.

To what extent has the geometric growth of system activity, illustrated in Figure 29.4, caused stress on the system? To what extent has the system managed to adapt to increased volumes of demands? Dramatic as the figure reported above may be, the likely answers to these two questions are 'not much' and 'almost entirely'.

Most *domestic* adjudicatory systems would have enormous trouble coping with such a tremendous increase in demands. This is because domestic systems typically face static budgets and rosters of judges and a fixed judicial infrastructure. The result is a chronic

[16] In 1988–97, 32 claims were filed; in 1998–2007, that number jumped to 344, which means a growth rate of 1,075%; in 2008–17, the number rose more modestly to 611, which is still a 178% increase compared to the decade before.

inability to adapt to massive increases in demand for outputs.[17] Some international courts, such as the European Court of Human Rights[18] or the Inter-American Court of Human Rights, may face a similar dynamic.[19]

In contrast, the investment law system is, to a great degree, inherently scalable. This is because the system is set up as an ad hoc one that automatically shrinks or expands in response to changes in demand. For example, the system doesn't depend on a budget fixed externally through a cumbersome political process; the main direct costs of adjudication are borne by the parties themselves. Arbitrators earn fees—not a salary—which reflects their work on a particular dispute, and which is paid for by the parties to that dispute. If there is an institution serving to support the arbitration, the parties will pay those fees as well. The main institutions providing such services in principle operate so as to cover their actual costs through fees. In contrast, public courts are often set up so that individual users do not fully cover the costs of their demands for litigation. Judges are salaried, their salaries are paid by the state through tax revenue, and the costs of providing such things as a courthouse are either not charged pro rata to litigants at all or are charged at a highly discounted rate.

The investment law system also doesn't suffer from a supply of qualified adjudicators limited by anything else than the market—individuals good enough and willing enough to do the job. Domestic legal systems tend to strictly limit the number of lawyers who are allowed to serve as judges. For example, the US federal court system has consisted of just 179 appellate judges since 1992, a number set in statute and increased only with great difficulty.[20] In contrast, virtually anyone can serve as an arbitrator in the investment law system. The parties are the only real gatekeepers to arbitral service, and they can—within limits which don't limit—choose anyone they like.[21] Most arbitrators will have

[17] For discussions of caseload crises and the difficulties in alleviating them, see William M. Richman and William L. Reynolds, *Injustice On Appeal: The United States Courts of Appeals in Crisis* (Oxford University Press, 2013); Richard A. Posner, *The Federal Courts: Challenge and Reform*, rev. edn (Harvard University Press, 1999); Andrew B. Coan, 'Judicial Capacity and the Substance of Constitutional Law', 122 Yale Law Journal 314 (2012).

[18] The ECHR's size is fixed by Art. 20 of the European Convention on Human Rights at just one judge per state party (for a total of 47). Yet while the number of judges is ossified by treaty, the court's caseload volume has exploded in recent years, with nearly 90,000 pending applications in 2017, or almost 2,000 cases per judge. The result, according to some observers, is a 'case-overload' that has led to unacceptable delays in decisions. European Law Institute, 'Statement on Case-Overload at the European Court of Human Rights' (July 6, 2012): <https://www.europeanlawinstitute.eu/publications/eli-publications/>.

[19] See e.g. Cesare P. R. Romano, 'The Price of International Justice', 4 Law & Prac. Int'l Cts. & Tribunals 281 (2005), 291–5 (describing how the Inter-American Court of Human Rights' budget 'has become hostage to politics' and suggesting that the IACHR is, as a result, 'on the brink of asphyxiation').

[20] The US court system is hardly the only one in the world to suffer from perceived problems of congestion and inefficiency due to limited numbers of judges and expanding caseloads. Such problems are also endemic in the developing world, and in other developed economies, such as France. For a comparative perspective, see Maria Dakolias, 'Court Performance Around the World: A Comparative Perspective', 2 Yale Human Rights & Development Journal 1 (1999).

[21] The ICSID Convention (Art. 14) does require that arbitrators 'be persons of high moral character and recognized competence'. But the requirement is too vague to have much bite, and we are not aware of any successful challenges to a party-selected arbitrator under it.

expertise in international law and/or international litigation, but the global pool of such expertise is large and growing at a rapid clip.

And finally, the investment law system doesn't depend on a fixed quantity of marble-clad courtrooms or other physical infrastructure. Investment law arbitrations can and do take place anywhere in the world, the possibilities limited only by the lawyers' willingness to take a connecting flight or to stay in four-star rather than five-star hotels.

That said, we may admittedly see some volume-related stress at the margins of the system's operations. In the short term, the supply of highly sought-after arbitrators may be relatively inelastic. The result, arguably, is that a small core of usual suspects is finding itself increasingly stretched thin, as more and more parties demand their services.[22] However, the rewards of participating in the system as an arbitrator are easily great enough that there is a ready supply of individuals willing and able to meet this increased demand. Those rewards are undoubtedly at least partly psychological, but they are clearly monetary as well. Investment law arbitrators can make many hundreds of dollars an hour, and unlike salaried judges, their income climbs as they take on more work. Just as importantly, they can use their service as arbitrators to help win other, more lucrative legal business, serving as counsel or experts in other disputes.[23] Supply, then, certainly isn't a problem in the longer run. And on the demand side, at some stage the mimetic desire (I want what you want because you want it) that appears to drive appointments (I choose a well-known arbitrator because he is well known because he is often chosen) is likely to yield to more efficiency-based considerations, thus reducing the strain on the small core of key go-to individuals. In sum, it isn't a plausible proposition that there will be serious volume-related stress in the form of a want of available and competent investment arbitrators, almost regardless of the heights the system's caseload may reach.

If we flip the perspective, there are two points of worry, however. First, it is possible that volume-related stress may arise as to particular host states subject to mass claims in the face of serious political and/or economic crises. For example, Argentina notoriously suffered through numerous high-value investment law claims in the wake of the 2002 peso crisis, and continues to resist honouring certain awards. Post-Qaddafi Libya, with a barely functioning economic and political system and severe internal and external security problems, is currently facing numerous diverse claims which, if successful, may seriously hobble the country's long-term prospects for stability. And Venezuela lurks in the background as a worst-case scenario—a populous, starving country likely soon to be beset by mass investment treaty claims brought by disappointed sovereign debt-holders. These are all situations of major stress for the host states, which do translate into degree of stress for the system as a whole.

Second, proposed changes to the current system, if implemented, threaten to create volume-related stress in specific parts of the system—in the investment law system as a

[22] Sergio Puig, 'Social Capital in the Arbitration Market', 25 European Journal of International Law 387 (2014).

[23] Malcolm Langford, Daniel Behn, and Runar Lie, 'The Revolving Door in International Investment Arbitration', 20 Journal of International Economic Law 301 (2017).

whole, not specifically in investment arbitration. The European Union's 'investment court' proposal would replace the current ad hoc system of arbitration by establishing a permanent court staffed by a fixed roster of appointed judges. The court's jurisdiction is likely to cover a large volume of foreign investment, and the court's docket would, accordingly, likely be quite active. Depending on the numbers of cases brought, it is easy to envision the court's meagre roster of permanent judges easily overwhelmed. That court, part of the broader system of investor–state dispute settlement, would almost certainly face volume-related stress.

29.2.2 Content-related stress

Putting aside the investment court proposal, content-related stress is a great deal more likely than volume-related stress to be a serious issue in the modern system. This is because the modern system, while scalable in terms of its judicial infrastructure, is also characterized by a diverse set of key actors who input conflicting and sometimes complex demands, the aggregation of which into coherent output of widespread acceptability is increasingly difficult.[24] The problem with content-related stress is that if it crystallizes into the wrong form, the entire system may be abandoned by those actors who feel let down by it. Simply put, if the system's contents go too far in promoting the interests of one key actor at the expense of another key actor, the latter is likely, if rational, to simply walk away.

In the customary international law system, states were the primary actor; moreover, those states that mattered tended to be rich capital-exporting states, relatively few in number, and primarily concerned, in common, with ensuring that the international investment law system produced outputs that strongly protected their foreign investments. Given how customary international law is made, the disadvantaged actors in that system could barely simply walk away from it if they decided they didn't like the normative contents it produced. The modern system is different in four main ways, which make it more prone to content-related stress, to instability, and to eventual rejection.[25]

First, the number of states who actively participate in the system's activities has greatly expanded, and now includes many developing countries: at least 181 countries, and 210 of the world's 234 economies, have signed at least one international investment

[24] Trakman makes a similar observation, noting that one of the system's major challenges is providing host states with 'the capacity to identify, explore, and verify complex socio-economic data to defend against the claims of investors from wealthy states'. Leon E. Trakman, 'The ICISD under Siege', 45 Cornell Int'l L.J. 603 (2013), 616. This means that tribunals themselves must also be capable, or made capable, of understanding and applying such 'complex... data' in a desirable way. There is little reason to think that tribunals as currently staffed have any special expertise in this area, however.

[25] For an application of the same overall model to aspects of stability based on perceptions of legitimacy by key actors, see Thomas Schultz, 'Legitimacy Pragmatism and Political Systems in International Arbitration Lawmaking: A Framework for Analysis', in Jean Kalicki and Mohamed Abdel Raouf (eds), *Evolution and Adaptation: The Future of International Arbitration* (Wolters Kluwer, 2019).

agreement.[26] Governments of these countries should, rationally, favour systemic outputs that preserve a greater degree of policy sovereignty, since they tend to be capital-importers rather than exporters. Their interests in the system thus diverge from those of the world's great capital-exporters. If the old system was arguably imperialistic, in that those dominating countries that exported their capital also exported their norms about when and how such capital was protected, the modern system is at least formally somewhat more inclusive. To be sure, the content-related stress created by the diversity of demands now placed on the system, though technically indeed a stress, is to be welcomed the same way it is welcome that a domestic democratic system exhibits more political colours than just one.

But, regrettably, one may doubt how much exactly the demands of developing countries and capital importers—or perhaps rather the demands that these countries should rationally make—have so far fed into the system: renegotiated BITs typically do not make room for more policy sovereignty than before.[27] Path dependency may explain much of this underreaction by the system to the newly understood interests of capital-importing states: it seems likely that treaty negotiators find it difficult to break free from a certain way of thinking inherited from the most powerful players of the past.[28] Those who shaped the system in the early stages largely locked it into a given intellectual universe: the modern system isn't so different from the old intellectually, in regard to 'the right way to do things'. This would explain why current inputs into the system are so suboptimal from the perspective of the system's new participants.

Second, the system's most important actors—the major capital-exporting states, such as the United States, Canada, and Germany—have begun in recent years to experience the system's outputs *as capital-importers*. This experience—of being sued by foreign investors under international investment law—seems to have caused those countries to begin to rethink whether the system's outputs should reflect such a pro-investor orientation: generally speaking, governments seem to only really question the benefits and

[26] See UNCTAD, International Investment Agreement Navigator: <http://investmentpolicyhub.unctad.org/IIA/IiasByCountry#iiaInnerMenu and Mapping BITs, http://mappinginvestmenttreaties.com/country>.

[27] Tomer Broude, Yoram Haftel, and Alexander Thompson, 'Legitimation Through Renegotiation: Do States Seek More Regulatory Space in Their BITs?' in D. Behn, O. K. Fauchald, and M. Langford (eds), *The Legitimacy of Investment Arbitration: Empirical Perspectives* (Cambridge University Press, forthcoming): 'Based on an original data set comprised of 161 renegotiated agreements, we find that states have not made a systematic effort over the years to recalibrate their BITs for the purpose of preserving more regulatory space.' See also Alec Stone Sweet, Michael Yunsuck Chung, and Adam Saltzman, 'Arbitral Lawmaking and State Power: An Empirical Analysis of Investor–State Arbitration', 8 Journal of International Dispute Settlement 579 (2017).

[28] Wolfgang Alschner, 'Locked in Language: Historical Sociology and the Path Dependency of Investment Treaty Design', in Moshe Hirsch and Andrew Lang (eds), *Research Handbook on the Sociology of International Law* (Edward Elgar, forthcoming): 'path dependency [caused by efficiency considerations, sociological forces and cognitive biases] has prevented adaptations of superior treaty design alternatives and instead geared negotiators into reproducing or refining the [usual standards]. Differently put, negotiators have become locked in language.' It is, of course, not in language per se that they are locked, but in the ideas and intellectual horizons that language expresses.

legitimacy of investment treaties and their contents, or indeed even their legal and political consequences, when they have been bitten by an investment arbitration.[29]

Then again, some traditionally capital-importing countries, and China in particular, now seem quite content with the status quo, as they are becoming ever more capital-exporting countries: the greater the rise of their FDI outflows, the more they insist on maintaining the current state of affairs.[30] In other words, as states realize what the consequences of the investment regime are for them, they tend (or should tend) to change their input into the system, unless their own interests happen to evolve and become more aligned with the system's output: some governments, bowing to the then major capital-exporting states, probably signed investment agreements which did not further their interest much at the time of signing, not realizing what they were doing,[31] but now insist on keeping them as the treaties turn out to be in their new, current interests. Roughly simplified, the targets of the imperialism of old are now the protectors of the system it produced.

Third, investors have increasingly used the system to make complex claims of mistreatment that raise sensitive political questions. In the earlier era, investment arbitration was primarily contract-based, and often involved blatant, expropriatory violations of the basic principle of *pacta sunt servanda*. While disputes over state breaches of contract can obviously raise important issues of public policy (such as the extent to which obligations might survive transitions from autocracy to democracy; or the extent to which obligations might be readjusted in light of other radically changed circumstances), expropriatory breaches of contract are often successfully and uncontroversially resolved by application of the relatively simple principle that formal and specific state promises should almost always be kept.[32]

In contrast, in the modern era investors have begun to use the investment law system to demand protections that go well beyond damages for breach of contract; in particular, they have demanded, and often obtained, the recognition of expansive conceptions of fair and equitable treatment and indirect expropriation—the two key vehicles of investor-right agendas—that would allow them to challenge public-interested government policies that fail to live up to high standards of substantive and procedural due process.[33]

[29] Yoram Haftel and Alexander Thompson, 'When Do States Renegotiate Investment Agreements? The Impact of Arbitration', 13 Review of International Organizations 25 (2018): 'states renegotiate when they learn new information about the legal and political consequences of their treaty commitments, and... such learning is most likely to take place when states are involved in investor–state dispute settlement cases.'

[30] Yoram Haftel, 'BRICS and the Global Investment Regime', in Soo Yeon Kim (ed.), *BRICs and the Global Economy* (World Scientific, forthcoming).

[31] Lauge N. Skovgaard Poulsen and Emma Aisbett, 'Diplomats Want Treaties: Diplomatic Agendas and Perks in the Investment Regime', 7 Journal of International Dispute Settlement 72 (2016).

[32] Jason Webb Yackee, 'Pacta Sunt Servanda in the Era before Bilateral Investment Treaties: Myth and Reality', 32 Fordham Int'l L.J. 1550 (2009).

[33] See e.g. M. Sornarajah, *Resistance and Change in the International Law on Foreign Investment* (Cambridge University Press, 2015), 191ff., 246ff.; Benedict Kingsbury and Stephan Schill, 'Investor–State Arbitration as Governance: Fair and Equitable Treatment, Proportionality, and the Emerging Global Administrative Law', in *ICCA Congress Series 14* (Kluwer Law International, 2009), 5.

Investors making these kinds of demands have used the investment law system to challenge anti-smoking measures,[34] the phase-out of nuclear energy production,[35] and the reversal of controversial public water utility privatizations.[36] These demands effectively ask the system—and particularly its tribunals—to play a role that looks suspiciously political and public, rather than purely legal and private. Tribunals are tasked not with quietly settling discrete, self-contained disputes on the basis of generally uncontested legal principles, but of deciding in a public forum, and on the basis of vague standards and balancing tests, matters of international political economy, limits of state sovereignty, the admissibility of a wide array of public policies, and all manner of policy-tinged disputes that legitimately interest society at large.

Fourth, as the system's outputs have become more politically salient, actors formally outside of the traditional system have fought to obtain a seat at the system's table. That fight has been partially successful, on two main fronts: transparency and participation.

On the first (i.e. transparency), system practice and system rules increasingly allow outsiders to attend tribunal proceedings and to have access to tribunal awards.[37] What was previously a 'secret' (or at least confidential) process now largely takes place in the open. Moreover, NGOs highly critical of international investment law's pro-investment orientation have succeeded in gaining the right to participate in investment treaty litigation through the submission of *amicus curiae*-type memoranda. In the sense of Easton's model, they have successfully challenged the 'gatekeeping' function of the system's traditional actors (primarily, states and investors) who insisted that only they should have the right to formally input demands into the system by virtue of their status as parties to essentially private legal disputes.[38]

The right to participate means that the 'public'—as represented by NGOs, and, occasionally, by motivated individuals—is now in a position to directly place demands (in the form of legal arguments) before an investment treaty tribunal. Those demands are likely to complicate the tribunal's task by presenting demands that the parties proper—the host state government and the investor—have failed to present and may not want presented. The NGO's point of view may diverge from state and investor preferences as to how a particular dispute should be resolved, and may thus add another 'interest' that the tribunal must try to balance and address, complicating the tribunal's tasks. Moreover, NGOs are likely to urge tribunals to take into consideration the larger social

[34] Sergio Puig, 'Tobacco Litigation in International Courts', 57 Harv. Int'l L.J. 383 (2016).

[35] Valentina Vadi, 'Energy Security v. Public Health: Nuclear Energy in International Investment Law and Arbitration', 47 Geo. J. Int'l L. 1069 (2016).

[36] Julien Chaisse and Marine Polo, 'Globalization of Water Privatization: Ramifications of Investor–State Disputes in the Blue Gold Economy', 38 B.C. Int'l & Comp. L. Rev. 1 (2015).

[37] On this move toward greater transparency, see Stephan W. Schill, 'Five Times Transparency in International Investment Law', 15 J. World Investment & Trade 363 (2014).

[38] In Easton's theory, some measure of successful gatekeeping is essential to preventing excess demands from being placed upon the system: Easton, *A Systems Analysis* (n. 2), 90. Note however that NGOs do not have an absolute right to participate as friends of the court. Rather, tribunals have been given the discretion to allow non-party submissions if the tribunal views such submissions as likely to be helpful.

implications of their decisions, further pushing tribunals away from pure law-based adjudication (if there is such a thing) into the more sensitive arena of policy-making.

NGO success in prying open the tribunal process has also been accompanied by successful moves to open up the *investment treaty-making process* itself to public participation.[39] While the treaties are still largely negotiated in secret by close-lipped diplomats, the EU administered a novel 'public consultation' on its nascent investment treaty policy, inviting the public at large to submit written comments in response to a set of questions concerning a proposed EU approach to investment protection.[40] The result was a deluge of comments (nearly 150,000, almost all submitted collectively through NGOs) indicating deep divisions in public opinion about the proper contours of the EU investment law agenda. The extent to which the consultation process has impacted the evolution of EU policy is unclear, but the point for our purposes is that this type of public consultation risks even further complexifying the set of demands placed upon the international investment law system, as it presents the system with a multitude of unfiltered and disaggregated views as to what values the system should produce, and of how it should produce them. While such public comments are obviously not *direct* inputs into the system, they have the possibility of filtering into the system through states, whose own demands on the system will increasingly need to balance as best they can the competing demands of 'the public' for a system that outputs pro-policy-space rules and of business interests for a system that prioritizes 'protection' in the form of restrictions on policy space.

Greater transparency and participation are often presented in the investment law literature as reforms of obvious good effect, serving both to build support for the system (by showing that international investment law is not the product of an evil, scheming cabal) and also to hold those who create it accountable to the *demos*. In that vision, transparency and participation promote system outputs that are, or will be, an equilibrated and widely tolerated set of international investment rules that reflects and maintains an acceptable balance between investor rights to property and state rights to regulate.

But a political-systems approach suggests an offsetting if not opposite view of greater transparency and participation as potentially serving to augment, rather than to mitigate, system stress. We have suggested above that as more and more actors win the right to have a say (i.e. to place demands in the system), the basic task of the system—to filter, aggregate, reject, and reconcile those conflicting demands into acceptable outputs—risks becoming significantly more difficult. Increased transparency is surely driving demands by actors formerly outside the system to be allowed to play a more insider role: the more 'the public' is aware of ability of the system to authoritatively allocate investment-related values, the more it sees an interest in having a seat at the table.

[39] Esmé Shirlow, 'Three Manifestations of Transparency in International Investment Law: A Story of Sources, Stakeholders and Structures', 73 Goettingen Journal of International Law 73 (2017).

[40] European Commission Staff Working Document, 'Report: Online Public Consultation on Investment Protection and Investor-to-State Dispute Settlement (ISDS) in the Transatlantic Trade and Investment Partnership Agreement (TTIP)', 13 Jan. 2015.

Somewhat differently, though also problematically, increased transparency may actually rigidify the system, making it *less* responsive to demands for change, and making the stakes involved in single allocative decisions especially high. As Stephan Schill puts it,

> Transparency not only serves to control the governance function of investor-state arbitration, but reinforces it. Transparency is not only a condition for allowing better accountability of treaty-makers and dispute-resolvers and hence an instrument to constrain the exercise of public authority in international investment relations. It also is an instrument that furthers the governance function of investment treaty arbitration. After all, more transparent arbitral decisions mean more precedent and more impact of those decisions on future behavior of arbitral tribunals, states and investors.[41]

Greater transparency of system outputs transforms those outputs even more, from discrete acts resolving particular disputes into authoritative allocations not just of the case of the day, but of future cases. Once awards are made public, they are more likely to be of public significance, precisely because they enunciate a general rule that claims the authority, even implicitly, to restrict the bounds of how similar disputes must be resolved in the future. Transparency thus serves not simply to make what's at stake in international investment law more obvious; it serves to make what's at stake in each discrete investment arbitration even more important.

In that way, greater transparency may worsen system stress both by giving various factions a focal point around which to challenge and defend the system's outputs and also by making the outcomes of those struggles much more worth fighting about. And once those struggles are 'won' by a particular faction, the victory may become ossified, embedded as it is in a difficult-to-change regime of multilateral treaty text and arbitral jurisprudence that, once unleashed, is difficult to recall.

If that admittedly and perhaps unrealistically pessimistic vision comes to pass, the result is likely to be the abandonment of the system, perhaps akin to what Laurence Helfer calls 'regime shift',[42] and characterized by, in Eastonian terms, a withdrawal of support. What may prevent the current system from going off the rails is, in a sense, precisely that threat of exit. The system continues to depend on the willingness of states to consent to be bound by its outputs, and on the willingness of investors to initiate disputes to be resolved under its rules. Just as it takes two to dance, it takes two to arbitrate. If one of these two actors is dissatisfied for too long with the normative contents produced by the system, which would be a possible result of poorly equilibrated inputs into the system by its many actors, the dance will end. As the investment arbitration industry continues to promote transparency, thereby making the system's normative contents more readily identifiable, it may be preparing its own demise.

[41] Schill (n. 37), 364 n. 5.

[42] Laurence R. Helfer, 'Regime Shifting: The TRIPS Agreement and New Dynamics of International Intellectual Property Lawmaking', 29 Yale J. Int'l L. 1 (2004).

In this regard, what the Eastonian model suggests is that, in the long run, the investment arbitration system will either adapt its output to the interests of its key players, or it will lose support and be replaced by something new. Given path dependencies and the ossification of multilateral treaty texts and arbitral jurisprudence, it is not obvious that adaptation is indeed the system's most likely future.

29.3 Conclusion

Will the international investment law system, understood as a political system, evolve in such a way that investment treaty arbitration of the future continues to exist in a form much as it exists today? Or will the system evolve, or devolve, into something quite different? Easton's theory is far from specific enough to allow us to make a confident prediction. On the other hand, the theory is useful for at least highlighting the potential for significant dynamism. Far from being a system in equilibrium—the stable solution to an iterated Prisoner's Dilemma, in Andrew Guzman's law-&-economic telling[43]—or a system in the midst of a teleological march toward an idealized rule of international law, the international investment law system can be viewed as a *political* system, subject to demands and stresses as actors react and respond to the system's outputs.

Our discussion has highlighted some of the ways in which an Eastonian approach can frame the analysis of international investment law in useful and interesting ways. As we have shown, Easton's model encourages us to examine the potential sources of stress on the system—an exercise that can lead to surprising conclusions, such as our sense that expanding transparency and participation rights may pose largely unappreciated dangers of content stress, or that the EU investment court proposal risks suffering from serious volume-related stress. But Easton's underlying theory is more complex and nuanced than we have presented, and it is capable of more than we have demonstrated. For example, in the present chapter we have not used the theory to focus on the reactions of actors to systemic feedback. There is a rich story to tell there too, but in the interest of space we save it for a future publication.

[43] Andrew T. Guzman, 'Why LDCs Sign Treaties That Hurt Them? Explaining the Popularity of Bilateral Investment Treaties', 38 Va. J. Int'l L. 639 (1998).

CHAPTER 30

THE SOCIOLOGICAL DIMENSION OF INTERNATIONAL ARBITRATION

The investment arbitration culture

MOSHE HIRSCH

30.1 The sociological dimension of international arbitration

Various developments in international arbitration may be explained by research tools borrowed from economic, political, sociological, and other disciplines. These different methodological analyses are not exclusionary but instead complementary. Significant developments in the real life of international arbitration are complex and multi-faceted; involving actors influenced by different mixtures of variables associated with more than one discipline. Arbitrators, for example, are influenced by a combination of economic and cultural factors. In addition, some significant factors influencing international arbitration (such as 'reputation') may be explained by both rational-choice and sociological tools.[1] Thus, while sociological analysis provides a set of valuable tools for inquiry into various international arbitration issues, this study does not aim to substitute rational choice, or political or other modes of analysis, but rather to cast a light on the sociological dimension of international arbitration.

Sociological analysis of international arbitration begins from the premise that individuals' behaviour and normative choices are significantly affected by sociocultural

[1] On the importance of reputation for international arbitrators, see Sections 30.3.3 and 30.4.4.

factors and processes.[2] Since international arbitration reflects and aims to influence patterns of social interactions, Émile Durkheim's famous statement is of vital importance for international arbitration scholars: society is more than the individuals who compose it; society has a life of its own that stretches beyond our personal experience.[3] Thus, the fundamental idea that reverberates in countless sociological studies is that the social whole of a group is greater than the sum of its parts, and knowledge about social relations cannot be derived solely from knowledge about the individuals who compose the group. The sociological core assumptions regarding the influential role of social factors on individual behaviour are extended to the economic realm by economic sociology. Sociologists exploring economic behaviour attack the 'under-socialized' concept of persons that characterizes the economists' analysis.[4] From this perspective, international economic activity does not constitute an exception to numerous social interactions, and trade and foreign investment, for example, are conceived of as specific types of social interaction.[5]

The behaviour of actors participating in international arbitration is not isolated from its social context; it is instead deeply embedded in various sociological factors and processes (such as norms, socialization, or social control). The first stage in the sociological analysis of international law requires identification of the social group, followed by the delineation of its sociocultural features, and concluding with the exploration of the interactions between the group's sociocultural characteristics and legal rules or normative behaviour undertaken by its actors.

This chapter is primarily focused on the investment arbitration community; analysing the interactions between the social features of this community and two significant issues in investment arbitration: (i) the application of human rights law by investment arbitrators; and (ii) the constraining nature of norms regarding side arbitrator impartiality. While the first issue concerns the particular features of the investment arbitration community and its interactions with another social group (the human rights community), the second issue regarding arbitrators' impartiality is explored by employing several theoretical perspectives relating to the structure–agency debate in sociological literature.

Section 30.2 briefly sketches out the features of the investment arbitration community. Sections 30.3 and 30.4 illustrate the scholarly and practical value of the sociological

[2] On this general assumption in sociological literature, see e.g. Richard Schaefer, *Sociology Matters*, 5th edn (McGraw-Hill, 2011), 2–3; John Macionis, *Sociology*, 14th edn (Pearson, 2012), 2–3; Anthony Giddens and Philip Sutton, *Sociology*, 7th edn (Polity, 2013), 7–8; Reza Banakar and Max Travers, 'Introduction', in Reza Banakar and Max Travers (eds), *An Introduction to Social Theory* (Hart, 2002), 1, 3; Shaun Heap et al., *The Theory of Choice: A Critical Guide* (Blackwell, 1992), 63–4.

[3] Emile Durkheim, *Sociology and Philosophy* (Free Press, 1953), 54–5.

[4] Mark Granovetter, 'Economic Action and Social Structure: The Problem of Embeddedness', in Richard Swedberg (ed.), *Economic Sociology* (Edward Elgar, 1996), 239, 245. See also Frank Dobbin, 'The Sociological View of the Economy', in Frank Dobbin (ed.), *The New Economic Sociology: A Reader* (Princeton University Press, 2004), 5.

[5] On sociological analysis of international economic law, see Moshe Hirsch, *Invitation to the Sociology of International Law* (Oxford University Press, 2015), 20ff.

perspective by analysing two prominent issues in contemporary international investment law. Section 30.3 presents a sociological analysis of the sociocultural interactions between the investment arbitration and human rights communities, and their impacts on the limited application of international human rights law by investment tribunals. Section 30.4 addresses one of the fundamental questions in sociological literature in the (limited) sphere of the investment arbitration community: to what extent and how do cultural patterns influence arbitrators? To answer this question, this section succinctly employs three sociological theoretical lenses (the structural-functional, symbolic-interactionist, and Swidler's approaches) to examine some recent empirical results regarding investment arbitrators' impartiality. Section 30.5 briefly recaps the main conclusions drawn from the preceding sections and offers some directions regarding future research work in this field.

30.2 The Investment Arbitration Community

The social features of the community in which international investment legal rules emerge and are implemented, as well as its social relations with other communities, influence the normative behaviour of investment arbitrators in various spheres.[6] The investment arbitration community[7] comprises lawyers, arbitrators, arbitral institutions, and scholars specializing in investment arbitration.[8] This is a sub-group of the larger international arbitration community, with certain features of the two communities overlapping. Thus, for example, the members of both groups share some basic norms, including the principal duties of arbitrators (such as neutrality, fairness, confidentiality, expertise, and efficiency).[9] Members of both communities participate in some common

[6] Some parts of this section substantially draw on section III of: Moshe Hirsch, 'The Sociology of International Investment Law', in Zachary Douglas, Joost Pauwelyn, and Jorge Viñuales (eds), *The Foundations of International Investment Law: Bringing Theory into Practice* (Oxford University Press, 2014), 143, 146–8.

[7] This section does not aim to provide a comprehensive analysis of the investment arbitration community. For a comprehensive (and insightful) sociological analysis of the international commercial arbitration community until 1996, see Yves Dezalay and Bryant Garth, *Dealing in Virtue: International Commercial Arbitration and the Construction of a Transnational Legal Order* (University of Chicago Press, 1996).

[8] For a longer list and detailed discussion of the actors of the international arbitration community, see Emanuel Gaillard, 'Sociology of International Arbitration', 31 Arbitration International 1 (2015), 3–9. On the 'epistemic community' of international investment lawyers and scholars, see Jeswald Salacuse, 'The Emerging Global Regime for Investment', 51 Harvard International Law Journal 427 (2010), 465–6.

[9] See e.g. William Park, 'Arbitration in Autumn', 2 Journal of International Dispute Settlement 289 (2011); Catherine Rogers, 'Between Cultural Boundaries and Legal Traditions: Ethics in International Commercial Arbitration', Stanford/Yale Jr. Faculty Forum Paper No. 01-14, 23–59; Working Paper No. 01–14 (2006), 23–59; Dezalay and Garth (n. 7), 8.

rituals,[10] are concerned about the opinions and respect of their colleagues, and peer pressure[11] exerted by other members occasionally operates to enforce the group's norms.[12] Unlike judges in permanent international courts, many members of the international arbitration community have mixed roles, with many arbitrators contemporaneously working as lawyers.[13]

The *investment* arbitration community presents some distinctive characteristics which differentiate it from the larger international commercial arbitration community. These differences are discernible from, for example, patterns of management of arbitral proceedings[14] or growing polarization.[15] Notwithstanding certain internal divisions and stratification (addressed later in this chapter), this group is considered a fairly close-knit community.[16] Members of the group often use the term 'investment arbitration community' in investment arbitration discussion lists, international legal blogs, conferences, investment awards,[17] and literature.[18] A significant portion of the writing is done by authors involved in investment treaty arbitrations.

Investment arbitrators play a prestigious role in the investment arbitration community. Empirical studies[19] reveal that most arbitrators (69 per cent) originate from Western

[10] On rituals in international arbitration (such as those related to arbitral hearing, prizes and periodic mass meetings), see Gaillard (n. 8), 10–13. On the significance of prizes for the members of the international arbitration community, see e.g. Charles Brower, Michael Pulos, and Charles Rosenberg, 'So Is There Anything Really Wrong with International Arbitration As We Know It?' in Arthur Rovine (ed.), *Contemporary Issues in International Arbitration and Mediation: The Fordham Papers 2012* (Martinus Nijhoff, 2013), 3–4.

[11] On the role of informal social control mechanisms in the investment arbitration community, see Sections 30.4.1 and 30.4.3. On the role of social control mechanism in general international law, see Hirsch (n. 5), 163ff.

[12] See e.g. William Park, 'Arbitrator Integrity: The Transient and the Permanent', 46 San Diego Law Review 629 (2009), 653, 658.

[13] On the 'mixing of roles' of arbitrators and lawyers, see Dezalay and Garth (n. 7), 49–51; Catherine Rogers, *Ethics in International Arbitration* (Oxford University Press, 2014), 318–19.

[14] Bockstiegel highlights certain differences between the management of commercial and investment arbitral proceedings, including the involvement of the parties and their lawyers, formality of the proceedings, and the collection and production of evidence. See Karl-Heinz Böckstiegel, 'Commercial and Investment Arbitration: How Different are they Today?' 8 Arbitration International 577 (2012), 585–6.

[15] On ideological polarization in the investment arbitration community, see further below.

[16] Stephan Schill, 'W(h)ither Fragmentation? On the Literature and Sociology of International Investment Law', 22 EJIL 875 (2011), 877; Joshua Karton, *The Culture of International Arbitration and the Evolution of Contract Law* (Oxford University Press, 2013), 2; Michael Waibel and Yanhui Wu, 'Are Arbitrators Political?' (2001): https://www.researchgate.net/publication/256023521_Are_Arbitrators_Political, 18; Daphna Kapeliuk, 'The Repeat Appointment Factor: Exploring Decision Patterns of Elite Investment Arbitrators', 96 Cornell Law Review 47 (2010), 77–8; Sergio Puig, 'Social Capital in the Arbitration Market', 25 EJIL 387 (2014), 400.

[17] See e.g. *Phoenix Action Ltd v Czech Republic*, Award, ICSID Case No. ARB/06/5 (2009), para. 34.

[18] See e.g. August Reinisch, 'The Proliferation of International Dispute Settlement Mechanisms: The Threat of Fragmentation vs. the Promise of a More Effective System?' in Isabelle Buffard et al. (eds), *International Law between Universalism and Fragmentation: Festschrift in Honour of Gerhard Hafner* (Martinus Nijhoff, 2008), 107, 119.

[19] These studies (mentioned below) have largely examined ICSID investment arbitrators. ICSID is the most important forum in international investment arbitration.

Europe and North America,[20] and approximately 75 per cent come from OECD countries.[21] The lack of gender balance among investment arbitrators is striking: more than 90 per cent of all ICSID appointments are male arbitrators.[22] In ICSID, two women (Brigitte Stern and Gabrielle Kaufmann-Kohler) attracted three-quarters of all female appointments.[23] Women have been much better represented in other international judiciaries.[24]

A relatively small group of frequently appointed arbitrators constitutes the core group exerting significant influence on the investment arbitration community. The repeated nomination of the same person to serve as arbitrator is widespread in investment tribunals[25] (far more common than among WTO panels).[26] Thus, an OECD study notes that 'a group of only 12 arbitrators have been involved (typically as one or more of three arbitrators) in 60 per cent of a large sample of ICSID cases'.[27] This elite group exercises considerable influence in the international legal profession,[28] and since they are present in 60 per cent of the tribunals, their group 'spreads their influence not only on a quarter of tribunals, but well over half of them'.[29] Kapeliuk observes in her study on frequent arbitrators: 'arbitrators appointed at least four times represent 14.9% of the arbitrator population. While this percentage seems low, these arbitrators' presence in the total number of concluded cases is impressive: at least one elite arbitrator was present in 80.2 per cent of the concluded cases.'[30]

The investment arbitration community comprises two sub-groups of specialists with commercial law and public international law background. These two sub-legal cultures

[20] Joost Pauwelyn, 'The Rule of Law without the Rule of Lawyers? Why Investment Arbitrators are from Mars, Trade Adjudicators from Venus', 109 AJIL 761 (2015), 770, and references therein.

[21] David Gaukrodger and Kathryn Gordon, 'Investor–State Dispute Settlement: A Scoping Paper for the Investment Policy Community', OECD Working Paper 2012/03 (2012), 44; OECD, 'Investment Division Investor–State Dispute Settlement', Public Consultation Paper (2012), para. 119: <http://www.oecd.org/dataoecd/61/29/50291642.pdf>; ICSID, 'The ICSID Caseload Statistics (Issue 2016-2)' (2016), 18: <https://icsid.worldbank.org/apps/ICSIDWEB/resources/Documents/ICSIDper cent20Webpercent20Statspercent202016–2percent20(English)percent20Final.pdf>.

[22] Pauwelyn (n. 20), 777; Gaukrodger and Gordon (n. 21), 44. See also Puig (n. 16), 403–4, 419. In contrast, three of the seven members of the WTO Appellate Body are female. See Kapeliuk (n. 16), 78–9.

[23] Pauwelyn (n. 20), 777–8.

[24] Ibid. 778–9; Gus Van Harten, 'The (Lack of) Women Arbitrators in Investment Treaty Arbitration', 59 Columbia FDI Perspectives (2012): <http://ccsi.columbia.edu/files/2014/01/FDI_59.pdf>.

[25] See e.g. Puig (n. 16), 407, 418. For data regarding ICSID repeated appointments during the period 2011–15, see Ajay Sharma, 'A Study on the Arbitrators Appointed in the ICSID Cases Commencing Since 2011', SSRN (2015).

[26] Pauwelyn (n. 20), 775–6; Jose Costa, 'Comparing WTO Panelists and ICSID Arbitrators: The Creation of International Legal Fields', 1 Oñati SocioLegal Series 1 (2011).

[27] OECD (n. 21), para. 120. For additional data on the most frequent arbitrators, see e.g. Kapeliuk (n. 16), 78; Jeffery Commission, 'A Snapshot of ICSID Arbitrators in Pending Cases' (Kluwer Arbitration Blog 2009): <http://kluwerarbitrationblog.com/blog/2009/09/04/a-snapshot-of-icsid-arbitrators-in-pending-cases/>.

[28] Kapeliuk (n. 16), 68–9; Catherine Rogers, 'Emerging Dilemmas in International Economic Arbitration: The Vocation of the International Arbitrator', 20 American University International Law Review 957 (2005), 967. See also Dezalay and Garth (n. 7), 8.

[29] Costa (n. 26), 12. See also Gaukrodger and Gordon (n. 21), 45.

[30] Kapeliuk (n. 16), 73.

present several (occasionally significant) different characteristics.[31] For example, Wälde emphasized the difference between these approaches regarding the underlying relationships between the parties to investment arbitration. While the commercial arbitration tradition tends to underline the principle of 'equality of arms', and not granting states certain privileges, the public international law tradition is marked by pervasive deference to the state.[32] The present-day investment arbitration community (including investment tribunals) is dominated by the commercial arbitration paradigm.[33]

Members of the investment arbitration community are connected by various channels of communication facilitating the transmission of information and exchange. In addition to numerous professional conferences and meetings which provide a means of socializing new members into the existing legal culture,[34] the community is significantly influenced by electronic methods of communication.[35] The electronic means include the Investment Treaty News,[36] Investment Arbitration Reporter,[37] Kluwer Arbitration Blog,[38] and UNCTAD reports as well its Investment Policy Blog.[39] Prominently, the OGEMID[40] subscription-based discussion list includes virtually everybody in the community of investment lawyers, hosting frequent discussions on new developments in investment law and practice.[41] This discussion group publishes annually the OGEMID Awards which are granted, inter alia, to the most influential award of the year as well as the most controversial or surprising arbitration decision of the year (following votes by members of the OGEMID community).[42]

[31] On the differences between the approaches of these two groups, see Thomas Wälde, 'The Present State of Research Carried Out by the English-Speaking Section of the Centre for Studies and Research', in *Hague Academy Report on International Investment Law* (2007), 68ff.; 'Procedural Challenges in Investment Arbitration under the Shadow of the Dual Role of the State: Asymmetries and Tribunals Duty to Ensure, Pro-actively, the Equality of Arms', 26 Arbitration International 3 (2010), 4–5. See also Schill (n. 16), 887–9; Anthea Roberts, 'Clash of Paradigms: Actors and Analogies Shaping the Investment Treaty System', 107 AJIL 45 (2013), 54–5; Böckstiegel (n. 14).

[32] Wälde (n. 31) (Procedural Challenges), 5–8. See also Roberts (n. 31), 55.

[33] Wälde, 'Procedural Challenges' (n. 31), 5. See also Wälde, 'The Present State of Research' (n. 31), 75–6; Schill (n. 16), 888; Roberts (n. 31), 87; Gus Van Harten, *Investment Treaty Arbitration and Public Law* (Oxford University Press, 2007), 5–6, 58; Julie Maupin, 'Public and Private in International Investment Law: An Integrated Systems Approach', 54 Virginia Journal of International Law 367 (2014), 394. On the importance of the equality of the parties in investment arbitration, see e.g. *Malicorp v Egypt*, Decision on the Application for Annulment, ICSID Case No. ARB/08/18 (2013), para. 36. On investment arbitration as a hybrid between public and private law, see e.g. José Alvarez, 'Is Investor–State Arbitration "Public"?', SSRN (2016).

[34] See e.g. Schill (n. 16), 886. See also Karton (n. 16), 7.

[35] Schill (n. 16), 886. [36] Investment Treaty News: <http://www.iisd.org/itn/>.

[37] Investment Arbitration Reporter: <http://www.iareporter.com/>.

[38] Kluwer Arbitration Blog: <http://kluwerarbitrationblog.com/>.

[39] On UNCTAD various reports and publications, see UNCTAD, International Investment Agreements (IIAs) Division on Investment and Enterprise: <http://unctad.org/sections/diae_dir/docs/diae_sectiondescription_en.pdf>.

[40] Oil, Gas, Energy, Mining, and Investment Disputes. On the aims of this electronic discussion forum see also: <http://www.transnational-dispute-management.com/news.asp?key=4>.

[41] Schill (n. 16), 886–7. See also Campbell McLachlan, Laurence Shore, and Matthew Weiniger, *International Investment Arbitration: Substantive Principles* (Oxford University Press, 2007), 19.

[42] As the editors explain: 'It is not designed to be a contest, does not purport to be scientific. This is just informal recognition among colleagues and a little bit of fun to start the new year.' See OGEMID Awards: <http://www.transnational-dispute-management.com/ogemidawards/>.

One of the distinctive trends undertaken in the investment arbitration community is ideological polarization, with many actors (prominently arbitrators and law firms) developing a reputation as either 'pro-investor' or 'pro-state' defenders.[43] This role is often performed throughout the activities of those actors (e.g. academic writing, party-appointed arbitrator).[44] Consequently, parties and their counsels often tend to select arbitrators who have been appointed frequently by either foreign investors or hosting states.[45]

The above features of the investment arbitration community (and additional ones addressed below) shed light on investment tribunals' approach towards human rights law as well as on the constraining force of the norm regarding arbitrators' impartiality.[46]

30.3 Social and Legal Fragmentation: The Investment Arbitration and Human Rights Communities

30.3.1 International investment law and human rights protection

The ongoing proliferation of international investment agreements, growing flow of foreign investment, increasing number of treaties in other branches of international law, and considerable growth of investor–state arbitration enhances the prospects for overlaps between obligations included in investment and non-investment instruments.[47] Consequently, arguments regarding the relationships between rules arising from investment and non-investment instruments (e.g. environmental treaties)[48] are increasingly being brought forth at the different stages of international investment litigation (including during discussions regarding liability[49] and remedies).[50] 'Fragmentation' issues are

[43] See e.g. Pauwelyn (n. 20), 781–2, and references therein.

[44] Gaillard (n. 8), 14.

[45] Bockstiegel (n. 14), 582.

[46] On the links between the practice of 'precedent' in investment arbitration and sociological factors, see Hirsch (n. 6), 158–67. On additional actors of the international arbitration community, see Gaillard (n. 8).

[47] This section substantially draws on ch. 5, section IV(b) of Hirsch (n. 5), 146–53.

[48] For a comprehensive analysis of the interactions between environmental protection and international investment law, see Jorge Viñuales, *Foreign Investment and the Environment in International Law* (Cambridge University Press, 2012), 18–22, 83ff.

[49] See e.g. *S.D. Myers v Canada*, Partial Award, UNCITRAL (2000), para. 150 (with regard to the interaction between NAFTA's investment obligations and the Basel Convention on the Control of Transboundary Movement of Hazardous Wastes and their Disposal). See also *SPP (ME) v Egypt*, Award, ICSID Case No. ARB/84/3 (1992), para. 78 (with regard to the relationship between the UNESCO World Heritage Convention and investment obligations).

[50] See e.g. *Santa Elena v Costa Rica*, Award, ICSID Case No. ARB/96/1 (2000), para. 71 (with regard to the interaction between international environmental law and investment obligations).

particularly controversial with regard to the links between international investment law and human rights instruments, and investment scholars are increasingly studying the interactions between these two spheres of international law.[51] It is noteworthy that international human rights law and investment law grew from the law of state responsibility for injuries to aliens,[52] and that these two branches of international law address an asymmetric legal structure between sovereign states and individuals or companies.[53]

30.3.2 Investment tribunals' jurisprudence

An analysis of investment awards reveals that while these tribunals often incorporate rules of general international law[54] (particularly the Vienna Convention on the Law of Treaties and the ILC Rules on State Responsibility), they adopt a quite consistent approach with regard to the *non*-significant role of international human rights law in investment disputes.[55] With few exceptions (such as the *Mondev* award in 2002 and

[51] See e.g. Pierre-Marie Dupuy, Francesco Francioni and Ernst-Ulrich Petersmann (eds), *Human Rights, International Investment Law and Investor–State Arbitration* (Oxford University Press, 2009); Eric De Brabandere, 'Human Rights Considerations in International Investment Arbitration', in Malgosia Fitzmaurice and Panos Merkouris (eds), *The Interpretation and Application of the European Convention of Human Rights: Legal and Practical Implications* (Martinus Nijhoff, 2013), 183; UNCTAD, 'Selected Recent Developments in IIA Arbitration and Human Rights: International Investment Agreements: IIA Monitor No. 2' (UNCTAD, 2009); Cordula Meckenstock, *Investment Protection and Human Rights Regulation* (Nomos, 2010); Bruno Simma, 'Foreign Investment Arbitration: A Place for Human Rights?' 60 International & Comparative Law Quarterly 573 (2011).

[52] For a detailed account of the historical developments in this sphere, see Pierre-Marie Dupuy and Jorge Viñuales, 'Human Rights and Investment Disciplines: Integration in Progress', in Mark Bungenberg et al. (eds), *International Investment Law* (Nomos, 2015), 1739.

[53] See e.g. Moshe Hirsch, 'Interactions between Investment and Non-Investment Obligations', in Peter Muchlinski, Federico Ortino, and Christoph Schreuer (eds), *The Oxford Handbook of International Law on Foreign Investment* (Oxford University Press, 2008), 154, 179.

[54] For an application of postal treaties in investment proceedings, see *United Parcel Service v Canada*, Award, UNCITRAL (2007), paras. 118–19. For an application of general international law regarding bribery in investment proceedings, see *World Duty Free v Kenya*, ICSID Case No. ARB/00/7 (2006) (invoking international public policy); *Inceysa Vallisoletana S.L. v Republic of El Salvador*, ICSID Case No. ARB/03/26 (2006) (invoking general principles of law).

[55] See e.g. Moshe Hirsch, 'Investment Tribunals and Human Rights: Divergent Paths', in Pierre-Marie Dupuy, Francesco Francioni, and Ernst-Ulrich Petersmann (eds), *Human Rights in International Investment Law and Arbitration* (Oxford University Press, 2008), 97, 106–7; Clara Reiner and Christoph Schreuer, 'Human Rights and International Investment Arbitration', in Dupuy et al., *Human Rights*, 82, 90; Vivian Kube and Ernst-Ulrich Petersmann, 'Human Rights Law in International Investment Arbitration', 11 Asian Journal of WTO & International Health Law and Policy 65 (2016), 69, 86; Barnaly Choudhury, 'Democratic Implications Arising from the Intersection of Investment Arbitration and Human Rights', 46 Alberta Law Review 983 (2009), 988–90. See also Brabandere (n. 51), 191, 208; Tamar Meshel, 'Human Rights in Investor–State Arbitration: The Human Right to Water and Beyond', 6 Journal of International Dispute Settlement 277 (2015).

Urbaser in 2016),[56] investment tribunals have declined to grant significant weight to provisions of international human rights instruments invoked by the parties.[57]

Thus far, notwithstanding numerous arguments raised by various parties, and a few tribunals' general statements regarding the superior status of peremptory human rights,[58] no investment tribunal has discharged a party from its investment obligations or reduced the amount of compensation due to the injured party. And although investment tribunals are generally reluctant to integrate human rights, they are more open towards human rights arguments for the sake of clarifying principles of procedural fairness (such as due process of law), legal methodology (e.g. proportionality), and the right to property.[59]

Several investment tribunals were ready to examine the impact of European human rights law on investment disputes. For instance, the *Tecmed* and *Azurix* tribunals cited case law by the European Court of Human Rights (ECtHR) (the *James* case)[60] in order to emphasize the vulnerability of investors in foreign countries.[61] A later attempt by Argentina to apply the same ECtHR judgment was dismissed by the *Siemens* tribunal, emphasizing the inconsistency between the European Convention's rules regarding the 'margin of appreciation' and international investment law.[62] A more balanced analysis of the case law of the ECtHR was undertaken by the *Mondev*[63] and *Saipem*[64] tribunals.

[56] *Mondev International Ltd v United States of America*, Award, ICSID Case No. ARB(AF)/99/2 (2002), paras. 143–4; *Urbaser SA and Consorcio de Aguas Bilbao Bizkaia v Argentina*, Award, ICSID Case No. ARB/07/26 (2016), paras. 1193–1220.

[57] The interim decision rendered in the *Von Pezold v Zimbabwe* conjoined cases well illustrates investment tribunals' reserved approach regarding the application of human rights in investment disputes. See *Von Pezold and others v Zimbabwe*, Procedural Order No. 2, ICSID Case No. ARB/10/15 (2012), paras. 61, 64.

[58] The *Methanex* tribunal stated that 'as a matter of international constitutional law a tribunal has an independent duty to apply imperative principles of law or jus cogens and not to give effect to parties' choices of law that are inconsistent with such principles'. See *Methanex v USA*, Award, UNCITRAL (2005), Part IV, Chapter C, para. 24. In addition, the *Phoenix* Tribunal explained: 'To take an extreme example, nobody would suggest that ICSID protection should be granted to investments made in violation of the most fundamental rules of protection of human rights, like investments made in pursuance of torture or genocide or in support of slavery or trafficking of human organs.' See *Phoenix Action Ltd v Czech Republic*, Award, ICSID Case No. ARB/06/5 (2009), para. 78. See also *EDF International v Argentine Republic*, Award, ICSID Case No. ARB/03/23 (2012), paras. 912–14.

[59] Kube and Petersmann (n. 55), 68–9, 93. With regard to 'fair trial', see *Tulip v Turkey*, Decision on Annulment, ICSID Case No. ARB/11/28 (2015), paras. 86–92.

[60] *James and Others v The United Kingdom*, No. 8793/79, [1986] ECHR 2, para. 50.

[61] *Técnicas Medioambientales Tecmed S.A. v United Mexican States*, Award, ICSID Case No. ARB(AF)/00/2 (2003), para. 122; *Azurix Corporation v Argentine Republic*, Award, ICSID Case No. ARB/01/12 (2006), para. 311.

[62] *Siemens A.G. v Argentine Republic*, Award, ICSID Case No. ARB./02/08 (2007), para. 354.

[63] *Mondev International Ltd v United States of America*, Award, ICSID Case No. ARB(AF)/99/2 (2002), paras. 143–4.

[64] *Saipem SpA v Bangladesh*, Decision on Jurisdiction and Recommendation on Provisional Measures, ICSID Case No. ARB/05/07 (2007), paras. 130, 132.

In all these cases dealing with the interaction between investment and human rights instruments, no investment tribunal has absolved a party from its investment obligations or reduced the amount of compensation due to human rights instruments.

30.3.3 The sociocultural features of the investment arbitration community and human rights protection

The generally unenthusiastic approach displayed by almost all investment tribunals towards granting significant weight to provisions of international human rights instruments may be explained by various factors, and this section focuses on the sociocultural features of the particular communities in which the relevant rules are formed and implemented, as well as on the inter-relationships between the two communities. The principal argument here is that legal interactions between international investment law and human rights law may be analysed as *social interactions* between the relevant communities. Thus, the *sociocultural distance* between these international legal settings affects the inclination of investment arbitrators to incorporate or reject legal rules developed in international human rights law. The term 'sociocultural distance' refers here to two central elements: (i) the extent of sociolegal difference/commonality between the particular branches and communities; and (ii) the sociocultural inter-relationships between the two communities.

The social settings in which international investment and human rights laws emerge and are interpreted are very different. Members of the two communities pursue extremely different career paths.[65] While most human rights lawyers work in the legal divisions of NGOs,[66] inter-governmental institutions, or governmental ministries, investment lawyers and arbitrators are predominantly lawyers-practitioners, legal scholars, or former judges affiliated with commercial law firms.[67] These divergent career paths indicate that the members of the two communities undergo starkly different socialization processes. For instance, while investment lawyers are inclined to emphasize the importance of the unimpeded flow of capital, legal predictability,[68] and market

[65] On the influence of judges' professional background on judicial behaviour, see Erik Voeten, 'International Judicial Behaviour', in Cesare Romano, Karen Alter, and Yuval Shany (eds), *The Oxford Handbook of International Adjudication* (Oxford University Press, 2014), 550, 565.

[66] On the role of NGOs in the human rights community, see e.g. George Edwards, 'Assessing the Effectiveness of Human Rights Non-Governmental Organizations (NGOs) From the Birth of the United Nations to the 21st Century', 18 Michigan State Journal of International Law 165 (2009).

[67] Waibel and Wu observe that more than 60% of arbitrators are in full-time private practice. See Waibel and Wu (n. 16), 28. See also Pauwelyn (n. 20), 773.

[68] On the importance of legal predictability in international investment law (and Max Weber's theoretical writing), see e.g. *Suez v Argentina*, Decision on Liability, ICSID Case No. ARB/03/17 (2010), para. 203. On the protection of legal predictability in the context of the fair and equitable clause in international investment law, see Moshe Hirsch 'Between Fair and Equitable Treatment and Stabilization Clause', 12 Journal of World Investment and Trade 783 (2011), 783. On some opposition to consistency in investment tribunals' decision-making, see Thomas Schultz, 'Against Consistency in Investment Arbitration', in Zachary Douglas, Joost Pauwelyn, and Jorge Viñuales (eds), *The Foundations of International Investment Law* (Oxford University Press, 2014), 297.

economy ideology;[69] human rights lawyers are more concerned with universal values and underline the primacy of human rights over other international legal rules[70] (including international investment law).[71]

In addition, while human rights lawyers are often linked to a certain social movement and are determined to take sides in political or moral struggles,[72] most investment lawyers are anxious to maintain a neutral position.[73] Each community has a distinct heritage and collective narratives to it.[74] For example, while 'the great petroleum arbitrations' during the 1960s and 1970s 'occupy a quasi-mythical position' in international investment law,[75] the adoption of the Universal Declaration of Human Rights constitutes a central collective narrative for human rights lawyers.[76] Human Rights Day is annually observed worldwide on 10 December, marking the anniversary of the UN General Assembly's proclamation of the Universal Declaration.[77]

Members of each community employ different terminologies. Thus, while human rights lawyers frequently refer to 'the Covenants', 'CAT', or 'CERD', many of them hardly recognize terms like 'FET', 'umbrella clause', or 'fork in the road clause'. Similarly, most investment lawyers are unfamiliar with this human rights jargon. While these different

[69] On the close links between liberal economic ideology and international investment law, see e.g. Kenneth Vandevelde, 'Sustainable Liberalism and the International Investment Regime', 19 Michigan Journal of International Law 373 (1997), 395; Suzanne Spears, 'The Quest for Policy Space in a New Generation of International Investment Agreements', 13 Journal of International Economic Law 1037 (2010), 1045–7.

[70] On the peremptory nature of fundamental human rights, see e.g. Teraya Koji, 'Emerging Hierarchy in International Human Rights and Beyond', 12 EJIL 917 (2001).

[71] See e.g. European Center for Constitutional and Human Rights (ECCHR), 'Human Rights Inapplicable in International Investment Arbitration? A Commentary on the Non-Admission of ECCHR and Indigenous Communities as Amici Curiae before the ICSID Tribunal' (2012), 4: <http://www.ecchr.de/worldbank.html?file=tl_files/Dokumente/Wirtschaftpercent20undpercent20Menschenrechte/ICSIDpercent20tribunalpercent20-percent20Humanpercent20Rightspercent20Inapplicable_Apercent20Commentary.pdf>.

[72] On the opposition of human rights activists to 'the image of the traditional scales of justice—calm, detached, neutral—in favour of a more prophetic image of law as a turbulent struggle', see Deena Hurwitz, 'Lawyering for Justice and the Inevitability of International Human Rights Clinics', 28 YJIL 505 (2003), 512. On 'cause lawyers' (or 'public interest') and their determination to take sides in political and moral struggles, see Corey Shdaimah, 'What's in a Name? Cause Lawyers as Conceptual Category', Working Paper 903 (2006): <https://papers.ssrn.com/sol3/papers.cfm?abstract_id=870441>.

[73] On the importance of neutrality as an element of the 'virtue' of arbitrators, see Dezalay and Garth (n. 7), 8, 83; Karton (n. 7), 114–17. See also Section 30.4.1 of this chapter. On the significance of being distant from politics, see Dezalay and Garth (n. 7), 45, 98.

[74] On collective narratives in the international investment law, see Andreas Kulick, 'Narrating Narratives of International Investment Law: History and Epistemic Forces', in Rainer Hofmann, Christian Tams, and Stephan Schill (eds), *International Investment Law and History* (Edward Elgar, 2016).

[75] See e.g. Dezalay and Garth (n. 7), 74.

[76] Joseph Slaughter, *Human Rights, Inc: The World Novel, Narrative Form, and International Law* (Fordham University Press, 2007), 1–2, 15, 64, 70, 81. On the importance of collective narratives in the sphere of human rights, see Audrey Osler and Juanjuan Zhu, 'Narratives in Teaching and Research for Justice and Human Rights, Education', 6 Citizenship and Social Justice 223 (2011).

[77] See UNGA Res 423 (V) (1950), inviting all states and international organizations to observe this day to celebrate the proclamation of the Universal Declaration on 10 December 1948.

vocabularies do not constitute an insurmountable language barrier, they do underline fundamental conceptual differences between these spheres of international law.[78]

Human rights and investment communities have developed dissimilar legal cultures. Though numerous studies identify legal culture with the nation state, patterns of legal culture can (and must) also be sought at both the sub-national and the transnational level.[79] The different legal cultures prevailing in human rights and investment laws assign different social roles to adjudicators. Generally, international tribunals fulfil two principal functions in the international legal system: settling disputes between the particular rival parties and developing legal rules to guide future behaviour. Tribunals' inclinations in that regard often influence the normative content of their decisions. Thus, tribunals granting significant weight to their law-making role are more likely to take into account wider public policy considerations and seek a due balance between the competing interests. On the other hand, tribunals emphasizing their role in settling the dispute between the specific parties are less prone to granting significant weight to the broader policy issues involved in the disputes. Most investment tribunals are inclined to adopt the *inter partes* model (which is prevalent in commercial arbitration) and grant precedence to their role as settlers of disputes between the particular parties.[80] In light of this prevalent role-perception, most investment arbitrators are inclined to view investor–state disputes as commercial disputes, thus focusing on the particular facts of the dispute and downplaying the weight of public interest issues, including human rights protection.

This inclination to follow the private mode of adjudicating disputes is also illustrated in the prevalent confidential features[81] of most investment arbitral proceedings. Generally,[82] investment arbitration proceedings are not open to the public, tribunals do

[78] On the significance of the language of law, see e.g. Lawrence Friedman, *Law and Society: An Introduction* (Prentice Hall, 1977), 89.

[79] David Nelken, 'Using the Concept of Legal Culture', 29 Australian Journal of Legal Philosophy 1 (2004), 3. On the concept of legal culture, see also Roger Cotterrell, *Law, Culture and Society: Legal Ideas in the Mirror of Social Theory* (Ashgate, 2006), 81–96. On the elements of legal culture, see David Nelken, 'Towards a Sociology of Legal Adaptation', in David Nelken and Johannes Feest (eds), *Adapting Legal Cultures* (Hart, 2001), 3, 25–6. On legal culture as a methodological approach in international economic law scholarship, see Colin Picker, 'Comparative Legal Cultural Analyses of International Economic Law: A New Methodological Approach', 1 Chinese Journal of Comparative Law 21 (2013).

[80] See e.g. *Romak v Uzbekistan*, Award, PCA Case No AA280 (2009), para. 171; *Glamis Gold v The United States of America*, Award, UNCITRAL (2009), para. 3; Wälde, 'The Present State of Research' (n. 31), 75–6; Barnali Choudhury, 'Democratic Implications Arising from the Intersection of Investment Arbitration and Human Rights', 46 Alberta Law Review 983 (2009), 988–99; Van Harten (n. 33), 5–6, 58.

[81] On confidentiality as a core principle of international commercial arbitration and its fundamental link to the principle of party autonomy, see Karton (n. 16), 96–8.

[82] On the recent UNCITRAL rules regarding transparency in treaty investment arbitration (which came into effect on 1 April 2014), see UNCITRAL, 'UNCITRAL Rules on Transparency in Treaty-Based Investor–State Arbitration' (2014): <http://www.uncitral.org/pdf/english/texts/arbitration/rules-on-transparency/Rules-on-Transparency-E.pdf>. See also the UN Convention on Transparency in Treaty-Based Investor–State Arbitration, adopted via UNGA Res 69/116, UN Doc A/RES/69/116 (2014): <http://www.un.org/ga/search/view_doc.asp?symbol=A/RES/69/116&Lang=E>. On the significance of these new rules, see Rogers (n. 13), 315–17; Esmé Shirlow, 'A Step Toward Greater Transparency: The UN Transparency Convention' (Kluwer Arbitration Blog, 2015): <http://kluwerarbitrationblog.com/blog/2015/03/30/a-step-toward-greater-transparency-the-un-transparency-convention/>.

not disclose copies of written pleading and other documents, and oral hearings are closed to the public.[83]

One of the most significant factors affecting the reserved approach of investment tribunals towards human rights law relates to the interactions between the two communities. The relationships between the investment arbitration and human rights communities are often characterized by mistrust and antagonism.[84] These hostile relationships[85] were prominent during the attempts to establish the comprehensive Multilateral Agreement on Investment (MAI) that failed in 1998,[86] as well as during the failed negotiations to formulate an additional WTO agreement on investment (1996–2004).[87] Indeed, one of the significant factors leading to these negotiation failures relates to the opposition of human rights and environmental NGOs.[88]

In light of the considerable *sociocultural distance* between investment and human rights laws, and the deep-rooted tensions between the relevant communities, it is not surprising that investment tribunals are generally reluctant to accord significant weight to human rights treaties in international investment law. The substantial sociocultural

[83] For a comparison between the relevant rules of international arbitration institutions, see Christina Knahr and August Reinisch, 'Transparency versus Confidentiality in International Investment Arbitration', 6 International Courts and Tribunals 97 (2007), 98–103. See also Spears (n. 69), 1073.

[84] See e.g. Corporate Europe Observatory (CEO), 'Profiting from Injustice: How Law Firms, Arbitrators and Financiers are Fuelling an Investment Arbitration Boom' (2012): <http://corporateeurope.org/sites/default/files/publications/profiting-from-injustice.pdf>; Charles Brower and Sadie Blanchard, 'From "Dealing in Virtue" to "Profiting from Injustice": The Case Against "Re-Statification" of Investment Dispute Settlement', 54 Harvard International Law Journal 45 (2014); Network for Justice in Global Investment, 'World Bank Approves Mining Company Suit against El Salvador' (2010): <http://justinvestment.org/2010/08/world-bank-approves-mining-company-suit-against-el-salvador/>.

[85] Gaillard e.g. notes that 'NGOs have penetrated the field of international arbitration... Through amicus curiae briefs, participation in the works of international organizations, numerous publications and aggressive press campaigns, NGOs have promoted values such as the defence of human rights...' See Gaillard (n. 8), 8. The Corporate Europe Observatory states: 'Investment lawyers have become aggressive promoters of a skewed and unjust system on which their six- or seven-digit salaries depend.' See, Corporate Europe Observatory (CEO), 'Conclusion and Recommendations: Investment Arbitration: A Lucrative Industry Built on Illusions of Neutrality' (2012): <http://corporateeurope.org/trade/2012/11/chapter-7-conclusion-recommendations-investment-arbitration-lucrative-industry-built>.

[86] On the MAI and its failure, see Michael Trebilcock, Robert Howse, and Antonia Eliason, *The Regulation of International Trade*, 4th edn (Routledge, 2013), 459–60; Americo Zampetti and Pierre Sauve, 'International Investment', in Andrew Guzman and Alan Sykes (eds), *Research Handbook in International Economic Law* (Edward Elgar, 2007), 211, 249–51.

[87] See WTO, 'Doha Work Programme: Decision Adopted by the General Council on 1 August 2004', WT/L/579 (2004), Art. G: <http://www.wto.org/english/tratop_e/dda_e/ddadraft_31jul04_e.pdf>. See also Trebilcock et al. (n. 86), 589–90.

[88] See e.g. Katia Tieleman, *The Failure of the Multilateral Agreement on Investment (MAI) and the Absence of Global Public Policy Network: Case Study for the UN Vision Project on Global Public Policy Networks* (European University Institute Firenze and Harvard University, 2000), 10–16. On the NGO campaign against the WTO investment agreement, see e.g. Hannah Murphy, 'NGOs, Agenda-Setting and the WTO', Australasian Political Studies Association Conference (2007), 10–13: <http://www.researchgate.net/publication/241103056_NGOs_Agenda-Setting_and_the_WTO>; Trade News, 'WTO: Members Decide On Way Forward In Doha Round', 7(43) Bridges Weekly Trade News Digest 1 (2003), 1.

distance between these sociocultural settings parallels the normative distance between these branches of international law.

30.4 Arbitrators' Impartiality and the Structure–Agency Debate

30.4.1 The structure–agency debate

One of the central debates in sociological literature revolves around the effect of social patterns (such as norms, roles, or identity) on individuals—i.e. to what extent and how does the social structure constrain people in society?[89] This section addresses a parallel question relating to the question: to what extent and how does investment arbitration culture influence arbitrators with regard to the norm of arbitrators' impartiality? To answer this question, we briefly review the structure–agency debate and employ three sociological theoretical lenses (the structural-functional approach, symbolic-interactionist perspective, and Swidler's approach) to analyse a recent empirical study on investment arbitrators' strategies regarding impartiality.

Agency-oriented approaches[90] emphasize the active and creative aspects of human behaviour, while *structure*-oriented approaches underline the constraining nature of uniform social structures on individuals.[91] Proponents of structure-oriented streams (such as the structural-functional approach)[92] emphasize some social processes, such as socialization and social control, influencing most people to conform to their community's norms and roles.[93] Newcomers to a society learn and generally come to accept the basic elements of culture through the process of socialization.[94] Individuals who successfully undergo this process learn to become members of society both by

[89] On the structure–agency debate and international law, see Moshe Hirsch, 'The Sociology of International Law', 55 University of Toronto Law Journal 891 (2005), 916–17, 924–5.

[90] On the symbolic–interactionist approach, see Section 30.4.4.

[91] On the structure–agency debate, see George Ritzer and Jeffrey Stepnisky, *Sociological Theory*, 9th edn (McGraw-Hill, 2013), 510; George Ritzer, *Introduction to Sociology*, 2nd edn (Sage, 2015), 24–5, 86, 488–9; Giddens and Sutton (n. 2), 86–7; James Fulcher and John Scott, *Sociology*, 4th edn (Oxford University Press, 2011), 53; Banakar and Travers (n. 2), 4–5; Sharon Hays, 'Structure and Agency and the Sticky Problem of Culture', 12 Sociological Theory 57 (1994).

[92] On the structural-functional approach, see Section 30.4.3.

[93] The term 'role' refers to socially defined expectations that a person generally follows in a particular social position (e.g. 'parent' or 'employee'); see 'Role (Social Role, Role Theory)', in John Scott (ed.), *Oxford Dictionary of Sociology*, 4th edn (Oxford University Press, 2014), 652. See also 'Role', in Nicholas Abercombie et al. (eds), *Penguin Dictionary of Sociology*, 4th edn (Penguin 2000), 301.

[94] Ritzer (n. 91), 154; Eleanor Maccoby, 'Historical Overview of Socialization Research and Theory', in Joan Grusec and Paul Hasting (eds), *Handbook of Socialization* (Guilford Press, 2007), 13; Macionis (n. 2), 102.

internalizing the values and norms of their social group and by learning to perform their social roles.[95]

Every society deploys diverse social control mechanisms—i.e. means to encourage and enforce conformity with societal norms (including addressing norm violation).[96] Social control involves a myriad of disciplinary mechanisms, both formal authorized by the criminal justice system (e.g. police, courts, and prison officials) and less organized informal ones (including expressions of praise or social disapproval, contempt, ridicule, or isolation).[97] From this perspective, law constitutes one aspect of social control.[98] The next discussion, on arbitrators' impartiality, is followed by an analysis of the practice in this field from three sociological perspectives.

30.4.2 Party-appointed arbitrators and concerns of impartiality

One of the central norms linked to the role of the arbitrator relates to the duty of impartiality. The term *norm* refers in sociological literature to shared expectations about appropriate behaviour in a given situation.[99] Like numerous other international norms overlapping with legal rules,[100] the norm of arbitrator's impartiality is reflected in domestic and international legal rules[101] (prominently the rules of arbitral institutions).[102] This norm is enforced through certain legal procedures (such as ICSID procedure for

[95] See e.g. 'Socialization', in Scott (n. 93), 714; Macionis (n. 2), 102–3.

[96] Erich Goode, *Deviant Behavior*, 9th edn (Prentice Hall, 2011), 49–50; Erich Goode, 'Deviance', in George Ritzer and J. Michael Ryan (eds), *The Concise Encyclopedia of Sociology* (Wiley, 2011), 135; Mathieu Deflem, *Sociology of Law: Visions of a Scholarly Tradition* (Cambridge University Press, 2008), 227ff.

[97] Goode, 'Deviance' (n. 96), 136; *Deviant Behavior* (n. 96), 50–52; Robert Agnew, 'Control and Social Disorganizational Theory', in Clifton Bryant (ed.), *The Routledge Handbook of Deviant Behaviour* (Routledge, 2011), 114, 115–16.

[98] See e.g. Talcott Parsons, 'The Law and Social Control', in William Evan (ed.), *The Sociology of Law: A Social-Structural Perspective* (Free Press, 1980), 60.

[99] 'Norm', in Scott (n. 93), 519; 'Norm', in Abercombie et al. (n. 93), 243. See also Macionis (n. 2), 62; Ritzer (n. 91), 112.

[100] On various interactions between international norms and international legal rules, see Hirsch (n. 5), 165–6. On interactions between domestic laws and norms, see e.g. Saul Levmore, 'Norms as Supplements', 86 Virginia Law Review 1989 (2000).

[101] On the legal obligation of international arbitrators regarding impartiality, see e.g. Loretta Malintoppi, 'Independence, Impartiality, and Duty of Disclosure of Arbitrators', in Muchlinski et al. (n. 53), 789.

[102] See e.g. Arts. 14(1) and 57 of the Convention on the Settlement of Investment Disputes between States and Nationals of other States (adopted 18 March 1965, entered into force 14 October 1966), 575 UNTS 159 ('ICSID Convention'). On the interpretation of these provisions regarding impartiality, see e.g. Peter Horn, 'A Matter of Appearances: Arbitrator Independence and Impartiality in ICSID Arbitration', 11 NYU J. of L. & Bus. 349 (2014), 355 etc.; *Blue Bank v Venezuela*, Decision on the Parties' Proposals to Disqualify a Majority of the Tribunal, ICSID Case No. ARB/12/20 (2013), paras. 55–9.

disqualifying arbitrators)[103] and, as elaborated in the following text, also by certain social mechanisms.

Investment arbitration tribunals commonly include a chairperson who presides over the tribunal and two arbitrators appointed by the respective parties. The nomination of 'side arbitrators' is inherited from international commercial arbitration,[104] and it is linked to the fundamental principles of arbitration regarding party autonomy and the parties' control over arbitral proceedings.[105] The appointment of these arbitrators aims to address some perceived cultural divisions in the international commercial sphere.[106] Parties from diverse legal cultures and languages are interested in appointing an arbitrator who fully understands the legal culture that informed the parties' contractual meaning (which might have led to the dispute) and would assist in explaining issues that might mystify someone from a different legal background.[107] As to the significance of side arbitrators in *investment* tribunals (though this is not the only explanation), Matthews explains: 'The need to cross legal cultures is every bit as great in the field of investment arbitration, particularly when those cultures implicate complicated and conflicting social policies, often impacting the rights of millions of citizens.'[108]

The *formal* duties applied to chairs and party-nominated arbitrators regarding impartiality are virtually the same in most arbitral institutions.[109] Some experts, however, have raised significant concerns that the appointing parties' expectations and tactics, as well as arbitrators' desire to be nominated again to the prestigious role of investment arbitrator, have led many side arbitrators to be loyal to the appointing parties and to favour their interests.[110] 'Pre-interviews' initiated by the disputing parties in investment arbitration constitute a common tactic used by parties 'who ply potential appointees

[103] Art. 57 of the ICSID Convention. See also Arts. 14(1) and 40(2) of ICSID Convention. On ICSID tribunals' jurisprudence, see Malintoppi (n. 101), 793–807; Baiju Vasani and Shaun Palmer, 'Challenge and Disqualification of Arbitrators at ICSID: A New Dawn?' 30 ICSID Review 194 (2014).

[104] Joseph Matthews, 'Difficult Transitions Do Not Always Require Major Adjustment: It's Not Time to Abandon Party-Nominated Arbitrators in Investment Arbitration', 25 ICSID Review 351 (2010), 358–9. On the tradition of party-appointed arbitrators in US labour law, see Ch. 4 by Jan Paulsson in this Handbook.

[105] On the parties' control over the investment arbitral proceedings, see e.g. Park (n. 9), 297. See also Karton (n. 16), 79–85; *Aguas del Tunari S.A. v Bolivia*, Letter from President of Tribunal Responding to Petition by NGOs to Participate as *Amici Curiae*, ICSID Case No. ARB/02/3 (2003); Brower et al. (n. 10), 6ff.

[106] On additional possible motivations for party-appointed arbitrators, see Jan Paulsson, 'Moral Hazard in International Dispute Resolution', 25 ICSID Review 339 (2010), 349–50; Alexis Mourre, 'Are Unilateral Appointments Defensible? On Jan Paulsson's Moral Hazard in International Arbitration' (Kluwer Arbitration Blog, 2010): <http://kluwerarbitrationblog.com/2010/10/05/are-unilateral-appointments-defensible-on-jan-paulssons-moral-hazard-in-international-arbitration/>; Chiara Giorgetti, 'Who Decides Who Decides in International Investment Arbitration?', 35 Univ. Penn. J. Int'l L. 431 (2014), 442–3.

[107] Matthews (n. 104), 359, 362. [108] Ibid. 362.

[109] See e.g. Albert Jan van den Berg, 'Dissenting Opinions by Party-Appointed Arbitrators in Investment Arbitration', in Mahnoush Arsanjani et al. (eds), *Looking to The Future: Essays on International Law in Honor of W. Michael Reisman* (Martinus Nijhoff, 2010), 821, 825; James Carter, 'The Culture of Arbitration and the Defence of Arbitral Legitimacy', in David D. Caron et al. (eds), *Practicing Virtue: Inside International Arbitration* (Oxford University Press, 2015), 97; Matthews (n. 104), 363–5.

[110] See e.g. Mourre (n. 106); Hans Smit, 'The Pernicious Institution of the Party-Appointed Arbitrator', Columbia FDI Perspectives No. 33 (2010); Giorgetti (n. 106), 456–8 and references therein.

with facts from the case in the hope of seeing what their gut reaction would be"[111] Van den Berg's study of investment awards reveals that dissenting opinions are almost universally issued in favour of the party that appointed the dissenter.[112]

30.4.3 Structure-oriented approaches and arbitrators' impartiality

Encountering such concerns regarding the impartiality of party-appointed arbitrators, some well-known experts have offered certain proposals meant to substantially curtail the parties' freedom to unilaterally nominate side arbitrators.[113] Some experienced arbitrators resisted these proposed reforms,[114] and Carter argued that the *cultural* features of the present international arbitration system generally restrain side arbitrators from significantly deviating from the norm of impartiality. He explains that in the international arbitration community 'whose members follow one another's comings, goings and doings, often on a daily basis',[115] reputation concerns pressure arbitrators to conform to the norm of impartiality.[116] According to Carter, if party-nominated arbitrators are not impartial, their reputation is likely to be damaged, which would also reduce their influence within the tribunal.[117]

Carter's defence of the current system of party-appointed arbitrators effectively assumes that arbitrators' reputation functions as a significant social control mechanism,[118] and that arbitrators generally follow their community's norm regarding the duty of impartiality. This explanation echoes *structure-oriented approaches* (and particularly the structural-functional approach) regarding the constraining nature of the social structure on individuals in society. Following a brief (and partial) discussion on the structural-functional approach and its relevance to Carter's analysis, I will succinctly introduce the competing symbolic-interactionist perspective and Swidler's approach. Informed by these sociological approaches, I will assess the constraining force of the norm of impartiality in the practice of investment arbitration.

[111] Todd Tucker, 'Inside the Black Box: Collegial Patterns on Investment Tribunals', 7 Journal of International Dispute Settlement 1 (2016), 10.

[112] Van den Berg (n. 109), 824–5.

[113] See e.g. Paulsson (n. 106), 352–3; Smit (n. 110).

[114] See e.g. Charles Brower and Charles Rosenberg, 'The Death of the Two-Headed Nightingale: Why the Paulsson–van den Berg Presumption that Party-Appointed Arbitrators are Untrustworthy is Wrongheaded', 29 Arbitration International 7 (2013). See also Albert Jan van den Berg, 'Charles Brower's Problem with 100 per cent-Dissenting Opinions by Party-Appointed Arbitrators in Investment Arbitration', 31 Arbitration International 381 (2015).

[115] Carter (n. 109), 110.

[116] Though Carter is of the view that the challenge to legitimacy of investment arbitration is somewhat different (based more on arguments regarding impartiality in favour of investors), the threat of damaging investors' reputation 'serves essentially the same function as a check on bias'. See Carter (n. 109), 104–5.

[117] Ibid. 100.

[118] On social control mechanisms in sociological literature, see Section 30.4.1.

Structural-functionalism was for many years the dominant sociological theory. However, in recent decades its importance has declined dramatically. The two broad theories under the heading of the structural-functional approach are structural-functionalism, which looks at both social structures and their functions, and structuralism, which concerns itself with social structures. While structural-functionalism focuses on visible structures, structuralism is more focused on the social impact of hidden or underlying structures. This perspective emphasizes the interdependence of the various components of society and society's ensuing tendency to enhance integration, and it attaches particular significance to social stability and equilibrium. It highlights the constraining power of social patterns (perceived as external to people) on individual choices. The capacity of individuals to change these 'social facts' is limited. The approach also probes the functions of social structures, i.e. the consequences of any social pattern for the operation of society as a whole.[119] Carter's discussion resonates with some prominent elements of the structural-functional approach. This link is prominent with regard to the 'function' of the norm of impartiality and the role of reputation—with both protecting the interests of the larger arbitration community. Similarly, Carter considers arbitrators' reputation as an important instrument for disciplining arbitrators in this community.[120] Such structural-functional echoes also arise from the conveyed aspiration for enhancing social consensus, and concerns that the less socialized members of the community (inexperienced arbitrators) are more likely to deviate from accepted standards of behaviour regarding impartiality.[121]

Scholars associated with these *agency*-oriented approaches (such as the symbolic-interactionist perspective) do not share the above assumptions of the structural-functional approach, casting doubt whether social norms are uniformly followed by most members of a social group. As elaborated in the following text, a recent empirical study of investment arbitrators undertaken by Tucker[122] reveals a picture closer to the symbolic-interactionist approach, and particularly to Swidler's analysis of cultural patterns.

30.4.4 Agency-oriented approaches and arbitrators' impartiality

The *symbolic-interactionist* approach[123] emphasizes the role of individuals in society, and its point of departure is that social structures emerge and are maintained 'from

[119] See e.g. Emile Durkheim, *The Rules of Sociological Method*, 3rd edn (Free Press, 1962,), 1–13; Ritzer and Stepnisky (n. 91), 239–47; Jonathan Turner, *Contemporary Social Theory* (Sage, 2013), 49–63; Macionis (n. 2), 12–13; Giddens and Sutton (n. 2), 18–21, 55–8; Ritzer (n. 91), 49–53.

[120] See Carter (n. 109), 102. [121] Ibid. 102–5.

[122] Tucker's study is based on personal interviews with 44 investment arbitrators who served in over 90% of the over 260 cases from 1990 through to mid-2015. See Tucker (n. 111), 4.

[123] On the symbolic-interactionist approach to regional trade agreements, see Moshe Hirsch, 'The Sociology of International Economic Law: Sociological Analysis of the Regulation of Regional Agreements in the World Trading System', 19 EJIL 277 (2008), 295ff.

below', through a complex process of interaction among individuals.[124] From this perspective, human beings are not viewed as the products (or victims) of the social system, but rather as active agents capable of resisting, challenging, and changing social structures. The proponents of this approach are generally critical of 'sociological determinism', in which the social action of people is treated as an outward flow or expression of forces playing on them rather than as acts which are built up by people through their interactions.[125]

Ann Swidler's influential approach is closer to the symbolic-interactionist perspective,[126] and presents a more nuanced analysis of the interaction between individuals and culture. This approach better captures the results of the empirical study of investment arbitrators regarding the norm of impartiality. While Swidler agrees that culture is omnipresent in people's daily life, she criticizes the view that culture represents a unified worldview.[127] There is a range of patterned interactions between people and culture, and in reality, culture is often ambiguous and multiple, and includes incoherent understandings.[128]

One of the emblematic features of Swidler's approach is the concept of *repertoire*, which includes habits, skills, and styles, from which people construct strategies of action. Regularly (in 'settled life'), social structures do not only constrain individuals but also constitute 'cultural resources' relied upon by individuals when coping with various situations.[129] Thus, usually people 'do not simply express perspectives or values instilled in them by their culture. Instead, they draw from a multiform repertoire of meanings to frame and reframe experience in an open-ended way.'[130] This repertoire does often not prescribe a specific action; instead, it makes some behaviour more likely to be enacted. Thus, 'that influence is *facilitative* rather than determinative'.[131] In addition, culture provides individuals with certain capacities which enable them to adopt particular courses of action. These 'cultured capacities' include 'time consciousness', skills for evaluating the social world, or the ability to evaluate the character of others.[132] Swidler also asserts that cultural patterns are often *not* uniformly translated into behaviour, and that the

[124] See e.g. Turner (n. 119), 315–17; Ritzer and Stepnisky (n. 91), 347–8, 352–4; Giddens and Sutton (n. 2), 22–3; Macionis (n. 2), 16; Malcolm Waters, *Modern Sociological Theory* (Sage, 1994), 15.

[125] See e.g. Herbert Blumer, *Symbolic Interactionism: Perspective and Method* (Prentice Hall, 1969), 1; Turner (n. 119), 315–17; Giddens and Sutton (n. 2), 22–3; Macionis (n. 2), 16–17. See also Ritzer and Stepnisky (n. 91), 348–53.

[126] Thus e.g. Swidler criticizes Geertz's emphasis of cultural coherence (see Ann Swidler, *Talk of Love: How Culture Matters* (University of Chicago Press, 2001), 2122, 75, 79); individuals are perceived as active agents with significant freedom of action to formulate strategies of action in different circumstances (see e.g. ibid. 40, 79–80, 104–5); and the influence of people's 'repertoires' is facilitative rather than determinative (ibid. 105). On the concept of 'repertoire', see further below. See also David Brinkerhoff, Suzanne Ortega, and Rose Weitz, *Essentials of Sociology*, 9th edn (Wadsworth, 2013), 31; Isaac Reed, '*Talk of Love: How Culture Matters* by Ann Swidler', 31 Theory and Society 785 (2002), 785.

[127] Swidler (n. 126), 75, 169.

[128] Ibid. 24, 69, 75, 160, 169.

[129] Ibid. 104–5. See also ibid. 25, 82–83, 86, 104–17.

[130] Ibid. 40. See also ibid. 82–83, 104–5.

[131] Ibid. 104–5.

[132] Ibid. 73–5. See also ibid. 105–6 on 'cultural equipment'.

constraining effect of culture depends on a broad range of factors, prominently, semiotic codes,[133] context,[134] and institutions.[135]

Sociological analysis aims, inter alia, to identify the sociological perspective which best explains certain social activity (which may occasionally suggest some legal strategy). The picture emerging from Tucker's empirical study of investment arbitrators is better explained by the symbolic-interactionist approach, and particularly by Swidler's account of culture (rather than by the structural-functional approach and Carter's analysis). Tucker's interviews with investment arbitrators confirm that reputation is of major importance to arbitrators, and influences their behaviour.[136] The investment arbitration community revealed from this and other studies includes a set of complex and occasionally inconsistent norms and practices. Thus, along the central norm of arbitrators' impartiality, there are some indications that many side arbitrators sense that they are not expected to be impartial as the tribunal's chairperson, and do not hesitate to quietly assist 'their' party.[137] In addition, some pressure for 'mandatory dissent' seems to exist among party-appointed arbitrators (under which they are expected to dissent if the party that appointed them has lost the case).[138]

As to the constraining force of the norm of impartiality, Tucker's analysis indicates that this norm is not uniformly applied; and that the investment arbitration culture essentially provides arbitrators with a 'repertoire' from which they may construct alternative strategies of action. These multiple strategies relate to various actions, including 'internal' behaviour during deliberation among the arbitrators and 'external' decisions relating to dissenting opinion. Regarding party-nominated arbitrators, Tucker identified three types of arbitrators: the 'followers', the 'neutrals', and the 'partisans'. 'Followers' are characterized by passive behaviour (e.g. they do not read the materials)[139] and are expected to follow the chair's lead.[140] 'Neutrals' do not favour the party that has appointed them, and their main commitments vis-à-vis this party is that the latter's perspective gets a full and fair hearing.[141] 'Partisans' are expected to tilt towards their appointers (at least with regard to the significantly disputed issues). If the latter strategy leaves 'partisans' without allies or influence in the tribunal, they are expected to write a dissenting opinion.[142]

[133] The term 'semiotic code' focuses on the meaning attributed by other people to one's behaviour (e.g. signifying belonging to a distinctive group), and it often leads to external pressure and conformity. See ibid. 162–7, 169.

[134] Culture's influence varies also according to the context and generally, the constraining force of this factor is intensified in settings characterized by polarization, uncertainty and exposure to the public. See ibid. 169–75.

[135] Institutions may also promote behavioral consistency by creating the basis for a shared culture. See ibid. 176–9.

[136] Tucker (n. 111), 7, 19.

[137] Paulsson (n. 106), 344. On the parties' expectation that the side arbitrator 'will take a benign, sympathetic look at the position of the nominating party', see Matthews (n. 104), 362.

[138] Van den Berg (n. 109), 830.

[139] Tucker (n. 111), 10. [140] Ibid. 15. [141] Ibid. 10.

[142] Ibid. 10–12. The latter group of 'neutrals' includes several sub-types.

Chairpersons of investment tribunals are less vulnerable to the above pressures regarding impartiality; but also have a 'repertoire' of several alternative strategies with regard to collegial relations vis-à-vis side arbitrators as well as dissenting opinions. Tucker identified three principal types of effective chairpersons: the 'social', the 'managerial', and the 'dictatorial' chair. 'Social' chairpersons work to create camaraderie (e.g. through shared meals, coffee, and drinks) in order to forge a consensus. Such chairpersons are highly dissent-averse, and are likely to adopt extensive actions to avoid dissenting opinions.[143] 'Managerial' chairs do not socialize or discuss their views of the case until the very end, and they 'run hearings and deliberations as if they were board meetings, following a strict agenda... avoid[ing] any favoritism between the wingmen'.[144] Such chairpersons are first and foremost concerned with establishing the facts and exercising judicial economy; and though they are less dissent-averse than the 'social' chairs, they are likely to take some actions to avoid dissenting opinions.[145] Once 'dictatorial' chairpersons make up their mind on the merits of a case, they are likely to announce their position or circulate a finalized award without having engaged in any meaningful deliberation with side arbitrators. Such chairpersons assume that whichever party they favour, there will be at least one side arbitrator to join them.[146] Tucker's study implicitly suggests that 'dictatorial' chairs are the least averse to dissenting opinions.

30.4.5 Arbitrators' cultural resources and arbitration strategies of action

Comparing the above three approaches to the structure–agency debate, Swidler's approach best captures the investment arbitration culture revealed from Tucker's interviews. This culture is complex and occasionally comprises incoherent norms. Thus, for example, side arbitrators may well encounter inconsistent expectations regarding their duties towards the tribunal (impartiality) and vis-à-vis the appointing parties (quietly assisting the latter and 'mandatory dissenting').[147] Unlike the structural functional worldview, the investment arbitration community does not present arbitrators with a coherent set of normative prescriptions and then pressure them to conform. As noted, both party-nominated arbitrators and chairs have a 'repertoire' of alternative strategies from which they construct their own approaches in a given tribunal. This conclusion is incompatible with the above conclusion of Carter regarding the constraining force of the cultural features of the international arbitrations system (mainly through reputation) on side arbitrators, and the expectation that side arbitrators will generally follow the norm regarding impartiality. Analysis of the practice of side arbitrators revealed from Tucker's empirical study (regarding inconsistent norms) suggests that existing cultural features are often not sufficient to restrain side arbitrators from significantly deviating from the norm of impartiality, and that some reforms should not be ruled out.

[143] Ibid. 5–6. [144] Ibid. 6. [145] Ibid. 7–8. [146] Ibid. 8–9.
[147] On such expectations, see Section 30.4.4.

From Swidler's perspective, an arbitrator's choice of a particular strategy also depends on her/his 'cultured capacities'. For example, a decision by a side arbitrator whether to pursue a strategy of a 'follower', 'neutral', or 'partisan' is significantly influenced by the cultural resources available to the particular arbitrator (e.g. 'partisan' strategies require the capacity to negotiate with co-arbitrators and convince them). Similarly, a decision by a chairperson regarding the question of whether to adopt a 'social' or a 'managerial' strategy also depends on her/his cultural skills regarding social and managerial habits. In this sense, the above repertoire of alternative strategies and the toolkit of cultural resources available to arbitrators are more *facilitative* than determinative. The alternative strategies offered by the community to arbitrators and different sets of 'cultural equipment' do not suggest that the impact of investment arbitration culture is insignificant, but rather that the set of strategies and arbitrators cultural resources is limited.[148]

An analysis of different norms prevailing in a particular society may lead to different conclusions regarding the constraining force of each norm. The pluralistic view of the norms regarding party-appointed arbitrators' impartiality is associated with the heterogeneous character of the investment arbitration community which includes arbitrators (and other actors) from diversified societies and different legal backgrounds (but it does not necessarily apply to other norms in the investment arbitration community). It seems that some basic norms are more uniformly applied in the investment arbitration community. This applies, for example, with regard to the prohibition of permanent and substantial business relationships between an arbitrator and one of the disputing parties.[149]

30.5 Concluding Remarks

A sociological analysis of international arbitration begins from the premise that the normative behaviour and choices of individuals participating in the international arbitration system are significantly affected by sociocultural factors and processes (such as norms, socialization, or social control). The preceding sections demonstrate that the sociological perspective broadens our understanding of the social factors involved in the creation and implementation of international investment law, and that it may occasionally have implications for policy-making as well. While sociological analysis provides a set of valuable tools for inquiring into various issues in international arbitration, this study does not aim to substitute rational choice, or political or other modes of analysis, but rather to cast a light on the sociological dimension of international arbitration.

The discussion on the interaction between investment tribunals and human rights law (in Section 30.3) presents the argument that interrelationships between these two

[148] See e.g. Swidler (n. 126), 106–7.

[149] See e.g. Christoph Schreuer, *The ICSID Convention: A Commentary* (Cambridge University Press, 2009), 513; William Park, 'Arbitrator Integrity', in Michael Waibel et al. (eds), *The Backlash Against Investment Arbitration: Perceptions and Reality* (Kluwer Law International, 2010), 189, 199–200, 235.

branches of international law can be analysed as social interactions between the relevant communities and their respective legal cultures. Such an analysis of the interactions between the relevant social groups suggests that the considerable sociocultural distance between investment and human right laws, as well as the deep-rooted tension between these communities, affects the disinclination of investment tribunals to accord significant weight to human rights instruments in international investment law.

The discussion on the norm of investment arbitrators' impartiality brings to the fore the fundamental question regarding the constraining effect of the investment arbitration culture on arbitrators (here with regard to the norm of impartiality). The combination of Tucker's recent empirical study on investment arbitrators and Swidler's sociological approach leads to the conclusions that the arbitration investment culture is complex, its norms regarding side arbitrators' impartiality are often not uniformly applied, and arbitrators occasionally encounter a 'repertoire' of alternative strategies from which they may draw strategies of action (the selected strategy is influenced also by the 'cultural resources' available to each arbitrator). The above analysis of the practice of side arbitrators (regarding inconsistent norms and existing repertoires) suggests that existing cultural features are often not sufficient to restrain side arbitrators from significantly deviating from the norm of impartiality, and that some reforms should not be ruled out. Beside the norm of arbitrators' impartiality, other norms (unexplored in this chapter) are apparently more uniformly enforced in the investment arbitration community. It seems that the constraining nature of the investment arbitration culture is not uniform, with different norms differently applied in this community.

Future studies in this field may explore additional sociocultural patterns in the investment arbitration community (norms, rituals, or identity) or examine the sociological features of additional arbitration communities (e.g. international sport or maritime arbitration). Such studies may examine the interactions between such communities' characteristics and trends in awards delivered by these tribunals or new institutional norms (e.g. regarding dissenting opinions). Further studies may also analyse social interactions between certain arbitration tribunals and some other actors (such as the International Court of Justice or environmental groups), and the influence of these social interactions on the normative behaviour of arbitrators belonging to these tribunals.

CHAPTER 31

THE POLITICS OF INVESTMENT TREATY ARBITRATION

LAUGE N. SKOVGAARD POULSEN

AT 4.30 p.m. on 30 April 2015, the London offices of King & Spalding were the target of a staged 'exorcism' of corporate power conducted by a group of NGO activists led by Reverend Billy.[1] The Reverend and his followers asked the firm and its lawyers to repent of their cardinal sin: engaging in investment treaty arbitration. Although perhaps the most entertaining, this was but one of a growing number of protests against investment treaty arbitration in Western capitals in recent years.

Until the late 1990s, investment treaty arbitration was an obscure and little-used corner of international economic law. That has changed drastically in recent years. Based on more than 3,000 investment protection treaties—most of which are bilateral—foreign investors have increasingly resorted to investment treaty arbitration when resolving disputes with host states. By 2020, about 1,000 claims had been brought against more than 100 countries, and the vast majority has been filed in the preceding decade. Claims have been in a large number of sectors and covered a very wide range of public policies.[2] Some claims are about outright expropriation, but typically the broad and vaguely drafted treaties have been used to seek compensation for less intrusive forms of government behaviour that would often be subject to broad judicial deference in domestic courts.[3] Most claims have been against developing countries, but developed countries have also been respondents—particularly in recent years. Investors have won or settled more than half of all known claims, including some claims against states with advanced

[1] The event can be seen here: <www.youtube.com/watch?v=-tAztBns9jg>.

[2] Zoe Williams, 'Risky Business or Risky Politics: What Explains Investor–state Disputes?' (PhD dissertation, Hertie School of Governance, 2016).

[3] Toby Landau, 'Saving Investment Arbitration from Itself', Freshfields Bruckhaus Deringer Arbitration Lecture (2011).

legal systems and property right protections. Awards have occasionally been substantial, with several exceeding billions of dollars.

The regulatory reach and financial implications of investment treaty arbitration has made it one of the most potent areas of international dispute settlement. Unsurprisingly, it has also become highly controversial. A leading arbitrator has lamented: 'the more [people] find out what we do and what we say, and how we say it, the more appalled they are.'[4] This includes not just opponents of globalization—like Reverend Billy—but also supporters of international trade and investment.[5] And apart from civil society groups mobilizing against the regime,[6] officials and politicians in some government offices have also begun to question the legitimacy of using a small clique of international arbitrators—often commercial lawyers—to settle public law disputes.

The chapter will discuss the politics of investment treaty arbitration. The chapter is both limited, by honing in on a few core debates, and broad, by using a wide-ranging understanding of 'politics', encompassing the domestic and international political drivers, effects, and justifications of investment treaty arbitration as well as the political reactions to the regime by relevant stakeholders. The chapter starts with focusing on two core political justifications for investment treaty arbitration.[7] The first relates to home-state politics and diplomacy: the ability of investment treaty arbitration to depoliticize investor–state disputes. The second justification relates to host-state politics and institutions: the ability of investment treaty arbitration to convince certain types of foreign investors to commit capital into certain types of jurisdictions due to its effects on host-state governments. On this basis, the chapter will discuss the politics of investment treaty arbitration in recent years, particularly surrounding the unintended consequences of the investment treaty regime as well as the controversy about investment arbitrators themselves.

31.1 Political Justification: Home State Politics and Diplomacy

31.1.1 The theory of depoliticization

A core political justification for investment arbitration is that it provides an avenue for investor–state dispute settlement independent of inter-state politics. This is often

[4] Comments by Johnny Veeder QC at Wilmer Hale seminar on International Arbitration (2014).

[5] E.g. Simon Lester, 'Reforming the International Investment Law System', 30 Md. J. Int'l L. 30 (2015).

[6] E.g. Cecile Olivier and Pia Eberhardt, *Profiting from Injustice: How Law Firms, Arbitrators and Financiers are Fueling an Investment Arbitration Boom* (TNI, 2012).

[7] In addition to investment protection treaties, consent to investor–state arbitration can also be given on an ad hoc basis or in investor–state contracts and domestic laws. Yet while some of the observations in this chapter will also apply to investor–state arbitration more broadly, the focus is the politics of investment treaty arbitration.

referred to as the depoliticization thesis: by reducing home state involvement, the resolution of investor–state disputes is taken out of the realm of diplomacy and into the realm of law.[8] This theory provides a justification for resolving investment disputes through arbitration, regardless of whether the host state's consent to arbitration is contained in investor–state contracts, investment laws, or investment treaties—but in line with the focus of the chapter, this section will focus on investment treaty arbitration.

Article 27 of the ICSID Convention provides that:

> (1) No Contracting state shall give diplomatic protection, or bring an international claim, in respect of a dispute which one of its nationals and another Contracting state shall have consented to submit or shall have submitted to arbitration under this Convention, unless such other Contracting state shall have failed to abide by and comply with the award rendered in such dispute.
> (2) Diplomatic protection, for the purposes of paragraph (1), shall not include informal diplomatic exchanges for the sole purpose of facilitating a settlement of the dispute.

Unlike the ICSID Convention, only few investment protection treaties exclude diplomatic protection explicitly. Yet some investment protection treaties go even further than Article 27(2): unless there is no ICSID jurisdiction or the host state fails to abide with arbitral awards, some model BITs prohibit the pursuit of disputes 'through diplomatic channels'.[9] This language may prohibit even informal diplomatic exchanges, which—if followed—would entirely insulate investment disputes from inter-state relations.

Although the depoliticization thesis has been subject to little rigorous empirical testing (see below), many international lawyers are of the view that it is one of the main benefits of investment treaty arbitration. According to Reisman, for instance, the 'central achievement' of investment treaty arbitration is the isolation of investor–state disputes from 'the caprice of sovereign-to-sovereign politics.'[10] Equally, Lowenfeld is worth quoting at length:

> the essential feature of investor-[s]tate arbitration, as it has developed since the ICSID Convention . . . is that controversies between foreign investors and host states are insulated from political and diplomatic relations between states. In return for

[8] Sergio Puig, 'Social Capital in the Arbitration Market', 25(5) European Journal of International Law 387 (2014). The depoliticization argument often suffers from conceptual confusion. For a critique of its use in contemporary debates, see Martin Paparinskis, 'The Limits of Depoliticization in Contemporary Investor–state Arbitration', in James Crawford and Sara Nouwen (eds), *Select Proceedings of the European Society of International Law* (Hart, 2010)

[9] Ben Juratowitch, 'The Relationship between Diplomatic Protection and Investment Treaties', 2(1) ICSID Review 10 (2008), 16–22.

[10] *Ecuador v United States*, Expert Opinion of Professor W. Michael Reisman, Permanent Court of Arbitration (2012), paras. 20–21.

> agreeing to independent international arbitration, the host state is assured that the state of the investor's nationality (as defined) will not espouse the investor's claim or otherwise intervene in the controversy between an investor and a host state, for instance by denying foreign assistance or attempting to pressure the host state into some kind of settlement. Correspondingly, the state of the investor's nationality is relieved of the pressure of having its relations with the host state disturbed or distorted by a controversy between its national and the host state...The paradigm in investor-state disputes...is a dispute between the first party (nearly always the investor) as plaintiff, and the second party (nearly always the host state or state agency) as respondent. There is no third party.[11]

Figure 31.1 below provides an illustration of this theory. Here, a foreign investment (I) has been expropriated by a host state. To obtain compensation, the investor asks the executive of its home state (E) to impose sanctions against the host state. The use of force for the purpose of diplomatic protection ('gunboat diplomacy') was made illegal after the Second World War, but the executive of the home state could use trade sanctions, reduce aid flows, or employ other non-military means. Yet the executive would prefer to avoid sanctions, when this conflicts with broader security and foreign policy goals. By contrast, the legislature or other core domestic constituents are keen on protecting private corporate interests, which means the executive will face domestic policy costs if it refuses to intervene. When these domestic policy costs are greater than the foreign policy costs of pursuing sanctions (as in this illustration), the home state will proceed with sanctioning the host state until it pays the investor compensation.

The use of sanctions benefits the investor but harms the home state. It is therefore in the interest of the home state to negotiate an investment treaty with the host state providing direct recourse to investor–state arbitration. This gives the executive branch a justification to domestic constituencies for refusing to involve itself in investment disputes abroad. Once investment treaty arbitration is available, the investor can obtain full compensation without the home state incurring foreign policy costs. Note also from Figure 31.1 that if the depoliticization thesis holds true, investment treaty arbitration may be particularly beneficial for host states. For while investment treaty claims can result in costs for host states these may be smaller than the cost of diplomatic sanctions. In this sense, investment treaty arbitration acts as a solution to a 'game of chicken', where both states have an interest in consenting to investment treaty arbitration so as to avoid escalation of the investment dispute to diplomatic conflict.[12]

Three questions arise from this theory. First, the assumption in Figure 31.1 is that the home state is bound to get dragged into the dispute to protect the foreign investor. Yet we know from empirical literature on trade disputes that a 'government filter' makes

[11] *Corn Products Int'l, Inc. v Mexico*, Separate Opinion of Andreas Lowenfeld, ICSID Case No. ARB(AF)/04/01 (2008), paras. 1–4.

[12] Jonathan Bonnitcha, Lauge Poulsen, and Michael Waibel, *The Political Economy of the Investment Treaty Regime* (Oxford University Press, 2017), ch. 7.

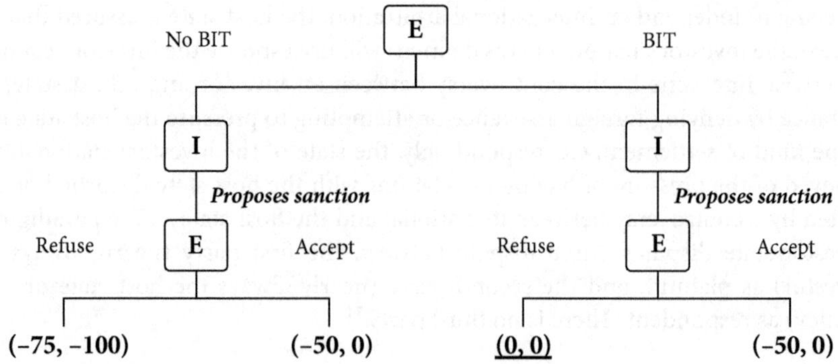

FIGURE 31.1 Investment treaty arbitration as depoliticization.

(*Source*: Jonathan Bonnitcha, Lauge Poulsen, and Michael Waibel, *The Political Economy of the Investment Treaty Regime* (Oxford University Press, 2017), fig. 7.1.)

political considerations important when states consider which disputes are worth scarce political capital.[13] One thing is that formal *diplomatic protection*—i.e. espousal—may be rare in the modern investment regime, but to what extent have home states used their wider range of diplomatic tools to resolve investment disputes in the absence of investment treaty arbitration? And if they have, was depoliticization an important factor among the architects of the investment treaty regime? Finally, has investment treaty arbitration depoliticized investment disputes in practice? Given the short supply of empirical evidence, there are no easy answers to these questions, but as a starting point it is useful to briefly consider the historical context of the investment treaty regime.

31.1.2 Depoliticization as a partial driver of investment treaty adoption

During the colonial era, foreign investment protection was generally in the hands of home states. Disputes with governments outside of formal imperial control were occasionally settled through political and military means.[14] An extreme example was the so-called 'Pastry War' between Mexico and France. Relations between the two governments were sour at the time, so when a French pastry shop in Mexico City was looted in 1838, the French government used it as an excuse to block, bomb, and seize Mexican ports and cities until compensation was paid in full.[15] Although this is an extreme

[13] Christina Davis, *Why Adjudicate? Enforcing Trade Rules in the WTO* (Princeton University Press, 2012).

[14] Charles Lipson, *Standing Guard: Protecting Foreign Capital in the Nineteenth and Twentieth Centuries* (University of California Press, 1985).

[15] William Robertson, 'French Intervention in Mexico in 1838', 24(2) Hispanic American Historical Review 222 (1944).

example, other investment disputes also resulted in inter-state conflicts during the nineteenth century.[16]

During the twentieth century too, investment disputes often spilled over into diplomatic relations. Before focusing on the role of home states, let us first consider the role of the World Bank, as depoliticization was an important factor for setting up the ICSID Convention. During the 1950s and 1960s, the World Bank kept getting dragged into investment disputes as a mediator—much to the frustration of its leadership.[17] One of the most notable instances was when Iran nationalized the oil industry and cancelled concession agreements of the Anglo-Iranian Oil Company. Subsequent to the overthrow of Mosaddegh in 1953, the Bank was called upon as an intermediary in an attempt to find a settlement between the parties. A few years later, the Bank became involved in yet another prominent dispute, trying to facilitate a settlement between the Egyptian government and French and British shareholders of the nationalized Suez Canal Company. One of the core reasons for this part of the Bank's work was that a significant share of its financial resources came from private capital markets, and the Bank would risk higher lending rates if its funds went to governments that failed to settle expropriation disputes (or debt defaults). As a result, the Bank developed a policy of withholding aid from developing countries not providing foreign investors adequate compensation for expropriation. The policy was implemented in practice on several occasions.[18]

This involvement in investment disputes detracted from the broader mission of the World Bank. Since it was already under pressure from developed countries to assist with a safer international investment climate, the management sought to address the issue of dispute resolution.[19] The end result was the ICSID Convention. As noted in the *travaux préparatoires* of the ICSID Convention, one of the key purposes of the ICSID system was 'to remove disputes from the realm of diplomacy and bring them back to the realm of law'.[20] Similarly, the World Bank's General Counsel, who chaired the ICSID Convention

[16] By contrast, Tomz shows convincingly that, in contrast to widely held beliefs, neither gunboat diplomacy nor trade sanctions were important for sovereign debt collection. See Michael Tomz, *Reputation and International Cooperation: Sovereign Debt across Three Centuries* (Princeton University Press, 2007), chs 6, 7.

[17] Antonio Parra, *The History of ICSID* (Oxford University Press, 2012), 21–4; Taylor St John, *ICSID and the Rise of Investor-state Arbitration* (Oxford University Press, 2018). More precisely, it was the International Bank for Reconstruction and Development (IBRD), here merely referred to as the Bank.

[18] Edward Mason and Robert Asher, *The World Bank Since Bretton Woods* (Brookings Institution, 1973), ch. 11. In other cases, however, the Bank was unable to credibly commit to its policy. The International Association for the Promotion and Protection of Private Foreign Investment complained about continued lending to a number of countries, which had expropriated foreign capital without providing compensation. The then President of the Bank, Robert McNamara, replied that while this was unfortunate, there was little the Bank could do, when the home states of the aggrieved investors did not seek to block the loans through their representatives on the Bank's Executive Board. See FCO 59/941.

[19] Aaron Broches, 'Foreign Investment and the Settlement of Disputes with Particular Reference to ICSID', in *Selected Essays: World Bank, ICSID, and Other Subjects of Public and Private International Law* (Martinus Nijhoff, 1995).

[20] International Centre for the Settlement of Investment Disputes (ICSID), *History of the ICSID Convention: Documents Concerning the Origin and the Formulation of the Convention on the Settlement of Investment Disputes between states and Nationals of Other states* (ICSID, 1968), vol. II-1, 273. See also Consultative Meeting of Legal Experts, 'Summary Record of Proceedings', in ibid, 242.

meetings, Aron Broches, argued that ICSID would 'remove disputes from the atmosphere of inter-state relations'.[21] Depoliticization was not the only driver of the ICSID Convention, but for the World Bank it was an important one.

For Western states themselves there is little literature on the politicization of investment disputes. An exception is Maurer, who shows how the American government repeatedly intervened on behalf of American investors during the nineteenth and twentieth centuries.[22] The executive branch, particularly the State Department and the CIA, opposed this practice, as diplomatic protection often came at the expense of broader foreign policy goals. Yet American companies managed to convince Congress to fight for their interests, and Congress in turn twisted the arm of shifting American administrations. After revolutionary Cuba initiated land reforms in 1959, for instance, American sugar firms lobbied Eisenhower to cut Cuba's sugar quota. He hesitated, as State Department officials warned that 'keeping Cuba out of the Sino-Soviet orbit' was 'more important than salvaging of the U.S. investment in Cuba to the complete satisfaction of the U.S. business community"[23] Yet, after a series of subsequent expropriations, Congress decided otherwise and retaliated by blocking the entry of Cuban sugar into the United States—a move which further pushed Castro into Soviet arms.[24] A few years later, in 1962, the story repeated itself. An expropriation in Brazil prompted a number of major American companies to lobby Congress to cut off all American aid to countries expropriating American capital. The Kennedy administration objected, but to no avail. Congress passed the Hickenlooper amendment to the Foreign Assistance Act, requiring the executive to cut all foreign assistance to governments expropriating American capital.

Over the coming decades, American presidents managed to (mostly) stay clear of invoking the Hickenlooper amendment. But the only way possible was to reduce American aid to expropriating nations and threaten economic sanctions. The end-result was a success for expropriated American firms, who almost always managed to receive compensation at fair value, but a failure for American foreign policy, as ardent protection of American corporate interests often contradicted broader strategic considerations.

According to Maurer, this was a key reason the United States supported ICSID and the initiation of its BIT programme: investor–state arbitration gave the executive a credible excuse to say no to American investors asking for diplomatic aid. Some negotiators of US investment treaties have made the same argument. Kenneth Vandevelde, a former US negotiator, notes:

> the situation in which an investor's remedies are *dependent* on upon the United states government is an unsatisfactory one both for the investor and for the government. From the perspective of the United states government, the situation is unsatisfactory

[21] ICSID (n. 22), 527.
[22] Noel Maurer, *The Empire Trap: The Rise and Fall of US Intervention to Protect American Property Overseas, 1893–2013* (Princeton University Press, 2013).
[23] Quoted ibid. 322. [24] Ibid. 328.

> because it may complicate or even impede the conduct of foreign policy in the broad national interest.[25]

A US negotiator of NAFTA's investment chapter equally notes that investor–state arbitration allows 'the investor's sovereign to distance itself from the dispute'.[26] Today, as well, US federal agencies argue that one of the main benefits of investment treaty arbitration is to 'resolve investment conflicts without creating state-to-state conflict'.[27]

Compared to other aims of the US BIT program, however, depoliticization rarely took centre stage. With respect to the US adoption of the ICSID Convention, St John shows that, except for a brief statement by Senator Morse on the depoliticizing promise of the Convention, the main concerns were about promoting and protecting American capital.[28] And with respect to Washington's choice of investment treaty partners, empirical evidence suggests that depoliticization has not been a particularly important driver either. Instead, American investment treaties were used primarily for the protection of American capital and cementing diplomatic relations with politically important countries.[29]

Depoliticization appears to have played an even smaller role in European investment treaty programs. In the case of the UK, sanctions were used after the Suez Crisis in Egypt, Libya's nationalization of BP, and other instances. The overthrow of the Iranian regime was linked to the expropriation of the Anglo-US concession, already mentioned, in which British security forces played an instrumental role. Unlike the US government, however, the British executive branch was more successful in saying no to British firms wanting to escalate investment disputes. The Foreign and Commonwealth Office refused to use aid flows as an instrument of investment diplomacy during the latter part of the Cold War, partly because of the negative experiences with this policy across the Atlantic.[30] Perhaps for this reason, depoliticization was not used by Britain to justify the adoption of the ICSID Convention or the initiation of the British BIT program in the early 1970s.[31]

Depoliticization was not important for the initiation of German BIT programme either. This should come as no surprise, as the German government had no significant tools of diplomatic pressure in the early Cold War period. Interestingly, however,

[25] Kenneth Vandevelde, 'U.S. Bilateral Investment Treaties: The Second Wave', 14(4) Michigan Journal of International Law 621 (1993), 22–3.

[26] Daniel Price, 'Some Observations on Chapter Eleven of NAFTA', 23 Hastings Int'l & Comp. L. Rev 427 (2000).

[27] Office of the United states Trade Representative, 'Fact Sheet: Investor–state Dispute Settlement' (2015): <https://ustr.gov/about-us/policy-offices/press-office/fact-sheets/2015/march/investor-state-dispute-settlement-isds>.

[28] St John (n. 19).

[29] Adam Chilton, 'The Political Motivations of the United states' Bilateral Investment Treaty Program', 23 Review of International Political Economy 614 (2016).

[30] Lauge Poulsen, *Bounded Rationality and Economic Diplomacy: The Politics of Investment Treaties in Developing Countries* (Cambridge University Press, 2015), ch. 3.

[31] Eileen Denza and Shelagh Brooks, 'Investment Protection Treaties: The British Experience', 36 International and Comparative Law Quarterly 908 (1987); Poulsen (n. 32).

German officials initially rejected the inclusion of investment treaty arbitration in early German BITs, as they feared that it 'could turn every case of expropriation into an international litigation with political relevance'.[32] Allowing investors direct recourse to arbitration could drag the German government into disputes it would have preferred to stay clear of—the opposite scenario of the depoliticization thesis. There is little evidence on other European investment treaty programmes, but the evidence available does not point to depoliticization being a crucial driver either.[33]

Similarly, depoliticization was hardly ever a core justification for consenting to investment treaty arbitration for developing countries. An exception is Costa Rica. In the early 1990s, a multilateral loan from the Inter-American Development Bank had been delayed until an (unrelated) investment dispute involving an American investor in Costa Rica was referred to arbitration.[34] A foreign policy advisor to Senator Helms, who intervened on the company's behalf, noted in 1993 that this 'will scare the living daylights out of them'.[35] It did. Costa Rica ratified ICSID that year, and subsequently consented to the arbitration in order to stop American pressure. Yet Costa Rica was an outlier in this respect. Archival records and interviews with core policy-makers suggest that few other developing countries appear to have found depoliticization a crucial justification for investment treaty arbitration.[36]

31.1.3 Depoliticization as a result of investment treaty arbitration?

Irrespective of the intent of treaty drafters, the investment treaty regime may have depoliticized investment disputes, nevertheless. In the *Diallo* case, the International Court of Justice noted that because of investment treaties, 'the role of diplomatic protection has somewhat faded, as in practice recourse is only made to it in rare cases where treaty regimes do not exist or have proved inoperative'.[37] The ICJ here had in mind espousal through diplomatic protection, which is of course not the same as informal diplomatic exchanges or threats of sanctions. Politicization is not a binary variable. But again, notable

[32] Lauge Poulsen, 'Beyond Credible Commitments: (Investment) Treaties as Focal Points', International Studies Quarterly (forthcoming).

[33] Bonnitcha et al. (n. 14).

[34] *Compañia del Desarrollo de Santa Elena S.A. v Republic of Costa Rica*, Award, ICSID Case No. ARB/96/1 (2000).

[35] Quoted in Charles Brower and Jarrod Wong, 'General Valuation Principles: The Case of Santa Elena', in Todd Weiler (ed.), *International Investment Law and Arbitration: Leading Cases From the ICSID, NAFTA, Bilateral Treaties and Customary International Law* (Cameron May, 2005), 752 n. 17. Note that IADB is the only multilateral organization where the US can veto an individual loan—and that only if it is provided through its Fund for Special Operations. When in 2012, the US was joined by Germany and Spain wanting to block a 'hard' IADB loan to Argentina—partly due to its stalling on payment of ICSID awards—the loan went ahead anyway.

[36] Poulsen (n. 32).

[37] *Case Concerning Ahmadou Sadio Diallo (Republic of Guinea v Dem. Rep. of the Congo)*, Preliminary Objections, ICJ (2007).

international lawyers argue that investment treaty arbitration has indeed replaced power politics with legalized procedures in the resolution of investment disputes. Recall that for Lowenfeld, for instance, the treaties have 'insulated' investment disputes from diplomacy and inter-state relations.

A few anecdotal correlations lend support to this. In the absence of ratified investment treaties Brazil appears to have been more inclined to use 'old-fashioned' foreign policy tools to defend Brazilian investors in neighbouring states.[38] A similar argument is made by Schwebel, who notes that if the Iranian government had consented to investment arbitration in 1951 (pursuant to a concession agreement), the political fall-outs of the expropriation of the Anglo-Iranian oil company would not have taken place.[39] More generally, and following Lowenfeld and Reisman, Maurer suggests that US investment treaties have made the US government much less involved investment disputes over the last two decades.[40]

As with all counterfactuals, however, these claims are difficult to show in practice. Maurer's work is the most comprehensive, yet his empirical evidence precedes the rise of investor–state arbitration, so it is unclear whether the reduction in aggressive forms of (American) diplomatic protection has been due to other factors than investment treaty arbitration. One obvious reason could be that the types of disputes ICSID and investment treaties were intended to depoliticize—outright expropriation—are much less frequent than during the 1960s and 1970s. The theory is also underspecified. On some occasions governments still *want* to involve themselves in investment disputes, even when investors have recourse to investment treaty arbitration. In the case of the US, Gertz documents how commercial diplomacy has been at the forefront of the American diplomatic corps after the end of the Cold War, and the US government increasingly use investment disputes as opportune moments to promote foreign policy agendas with host states.[41] Rather than seeking to avoid politicization of investment disputes, the executive branch has often explicitly encouraged it. As a result, empirical evidence from the 1990s and 2000s suggest that the presence of an investment treaty has had no systematic impact on whether the US chooses to escalate investment disputes.[42] In some of the few cases where the US government imposed economic sanctions, the investor already had recourse to investment treaty arbitration.[43] Anecdotal evidence suggests

[38] After nationalizations of Brazilian assets, Brasilia has threatened to stop paying for gas exports, block development loans, and in one case the defence minister even subtly threatened to support secessionist movements in east Bolivia. According to Maurer, the Brazilian government would have been less muscular in its approach had investment treaty arbitration been available. See Maurer (n. 24), ch. 11.

[39] Stephen Schwebel, 'In Defence of Bilateral Investment Treaties', 31 Arbitration International 181 (2015), 181–2.

[40] Maurer (n. 24), 428–33.

[41] Geoffrey Gertz, 'Commercial Diplomacy and Investment Protection: American Diplomatic Interventions to Protect US Assets Overseas Since 1990' (DPhil thesis, University of Oxford, 2016).

[42] Geoffrey Gertz, Srividya Jandhyala, and Lauge Poulsen, 'Legalization, Diplomacy, and Development: Do Investment Treaties De-politicize Investment Disputes?' 107 World Development 239 (2018).

[43] The Occidental case against Ecuador is a case in point. Here, US officials were told by the firm early on that it would file an investment treaty claim if the contract dispute was not settled, yet the American government nevertheless proceeded to cancel negotiations over a free trade agreement because of that dispute: Gertz et al. (n. 44).

that the American case is not unique in this respect. Governments in Europe, Canada, and Russia have also escalated investment disputes politically, even in the presence of investment treaties with recourse to investment treaty arbitration.[44]

At a minimum, the depoliticization thesis needs further study before being used as a robust justification for investment treaty arbitration. The separation of law and politics in the most extreme versions of the thesis is rather artificial, and—arguably—a narrow Western, or even American, view of how international law works in practice. In addition, and related, the thesis is often made based on underlying, but typically unarticulated, normative assumptions about politics being somehow inappropriate and/or ineffective for resolving investment disputes. This, too, requires more careful consideration in future work.[45]

31.2 Political justification II: host state politics and institutions

Whereas the depoliticization thesis relates to domestic politics and commercial diplomacy of *home* states, another set of political justifications focus on the domestic politics and institutions of the *host* state. From this perspective, investment treaty arbitration helps host states facilitate investment by (i) offering a credible commitment of property right protections; (ii) sending a costly signal about the nature of the investment regime; and/or (iii) improving decision-making among host-state administrative and judicial institutions. The first mechanism should promote investment by investors protected by investment treaties adopted by the host state, the second should promote investment also from states not party to investment treaties with the host state, and the third mechanism should promote both foreign and domestic investment.[46]

31.2.1 Three theories of investment treaty arbitration and investment promotion

The most prominent justification for investment treaty arbitration is that it can help resolve so-called hold-up problems.[47] Once a foreign investment is made, an initial

[44] Ibid.

[45] See e.g. Jason Webb Yackee, 'Politicized Dispute Settlement in the Pre-Investment Treaty Era: A Micro-Historical Approach', University of Wisconsin Legal Studies Research Paper 1412 (2017).

[46] A separate question is whether investment treaty arbitration allows foreign investors and host states to better manage their disputes, and thus facilitate investment *retention* in the presence of disputes; see here Rachel Wellhausen, 'International Investment Law and Foreign Direct Reinvestment', 73(4) International Organization 839–58 (2019).

[47] E.g. Anne van Aaken, 'International Investment Law Between Commitment and Flexibility: A Contract Theory Analysis', 12(2) Journal of International Economic Law 507 (2009); Jonathan Bonnitcha,

share of the costs is often used up front and cannot be recovered; i.e. it is 'sunk' within the host state. After the investment has been made, the host state therefore has an opportunity to expropriate the investment. This will allow the government to keep the entire surplus of the investment to itself (assuming it can operate the project as efficiently) as well as 'steal' the investment that was sunk. The host state is thereby faced with a 'time-inconsistency' problem—it would like to attract the investment, but is unable to credibly commit against appropriating a larger share of the investment after it has been made. The rational and fully informed investor knows this and therefore decides not to invest, which leaves both the investor and the host state worse off than if the investment had been made and the state had not expropriated it. An investment treaty with recourse to investment arbitration offers a credible commitment against such opportunistic state behaviour, as the state will now have to pay full compensation for expropriation along with additional legal and reputation costs of responding to investor claims. Knowing this, the investor now decides to proceed with the investment to the benefit of the investor and the host state.

Hold-up problems do not necessarily involve outright expropriation. In obsolescent bargaining models, for instance, the state renegotiates initial project terms or increases the tax rate after an investment has been made. Such measures allow the investor to still operate the investment—perhaps more efficiently than the host state—but to appropriate a larger share of the surplus to the host government. The government can do this because the investor would suffer a significant loss should it decide to leave (due to sunk costs) and therefore has significantly less bargaining power post-establishment.[48] Here again, investment treaty arbitration can prevent such behaviour, provided the treaty includes protections against indirect expropriation, unfair and inequitable treatment, and/or breaches of state contracts or other specific obligations (the umbrella clause).

A related but distinct hypothesis is that consent to investment treaty arbitration allows the host state to send a costly signal about the nature of its investment regime. Rather than acting as a 'substitute' for poor domestic institutions—as in the credible commitment hypothesis—the consent to investment treaty arbitration is here used to inform imperfectly informed investors about the fact that the government is 'serious' about property right protections. In this theory, countries with 'poor' investment climates are assumed to be most likely targets of investment treaty claims, and investors therefore expect that only well-governed countries would be willing to sign the treaties.[49] Importantly, the treaties thereby send a signal to all foreign investors about the nature of

'Foreign Investment, Development, and Governance: What Can International Investment Law Learn from the Empirical Literature on Investment?' 7 Journal of International Dispute Settlement 31 (2016); Jason Webb Yackee, 'Do BITs "Work"? Empirical Evidence From France', 7 Journal of International Dispute Settlement 55 (2016).

[48] Raymond Vernon, e*Sovereignty at Bay: The Multinational Spread of U.S. Enterprises* (Longman, 1971).

[49] Rodolphe Desbordes and Vincent Vicard, 'Foreign Direct Investment and Bilateral Investment Treaties: an International Political Perspective', 37 Journal of Comparative Economics 372 (2009). See also Andrew Kerner, 'Why Should I Believe You? The Costs and Consequences of Bilateral Investment Treaties', 53 International Studies Quarterly 73 (2009).

the domestic investment climate—including those investors not covered by a treaty with the host state.

Finally, investment treaty arbitration may promote investment through improvements in government decision-making. Although investment treaty arbitration rarely involves primary remedies (such as changing laws and regulations), the significant monetary awards imposed by tribunals can nevertheless incentivize states to promote domestic administrative and judicial practices that conform with their investment treaty obligations.[50] This, in turn, should help promote foreign *as well as* domestic investment.

31.2.2 Investment promotion as an important driver of investment treaty adoption

Unlike the depoliticization thesis, there is ample evidence that investment promotion was a crucial driver for investment treaty adoption—at least in developing countries.[51] North–South investment treaties were premised on a Grand Bargain: 'a *promise* of protection of capital in return for the *prospect* of more capital in the future.'[52] And indeed, the vast majority of developing country governments justified their consent to investment treaty arbitration with the argument that it would promote foreign investment.[53]

In some cases, the logic of credible commitments was used. In the case of NAFTA's Chapter 11, for instance, Mexico explicitly made reference to the fact that the obligations 'tied in' the government (and future governments) from backtracking on its promises to protect foreign investors.[54] In other cases, signalling was the main justification. The first BIT signed by South Africa, for instance, was justified by its ability to 'prove to foreign investors...that South Africa is an investor-friendly country'.[55] More generally, a former US negotiator notes about the 1990s that 'many developing countries [now saw] the BIT [as] a tangible way of signalling their captivity to foreign investment, and thus may seem to assist in attracting capital from the United states and other developed countries'.[56]

[50] E.g. Rudolf Dolzer, 'The Impact of International Investment Treaties on Domestic Administrative Law', 37 International Law and Politics 953 (2006); Roberto Echandi, 'What Do Developing Countries Expect from the International Investment Regime?' in Jose Alvarez et al. (eds), *The Evolving International Investment Regime* (Oxford University Press, 2011).

[51] Zachary Elkins, Andrew Guzman, and Beth Simmons, 'Competing for Capital: the Diffusion of Bilateral Investment Treaties, 1960–2000', 60 International Organization 811 (2006); Timm Betz and Andrew Kerner, 'The Influence of Interest: Real US Interest Rates and Bilateral Investment Treaties', 1 Review of International Organizations (2015).

[52] Jeswald Salacuse and Nicholas Sullivan, 'Do BITs Really Work? An Evaluation of Bilateral Investment Treaties and their Grand Bargain', 46 Harv. Int'l LJ 67 (2005), 77.

[53] Poulsen (n. 32).

[54] Manuel Pastor and Carol Wise, 'The Origins and Sustainability of Mexico's Free Trade Policy', 48(3) International Organization 459 (1994), 484; Maxwell Cameron and Brian Tomlin, *The Making of NAFTA: How the Deal Was Done* (Cornell University Press 2000), 101.

[55] Quoted in Poulsen (n. 32), 8.

[56] Vandevelde (n. 27), 638.

This view has also been promoted to developing countries by organizations such as ICSID[57] and UNCTAD.[58]

There is little evidence that developing countries explicitly saw investment treaty arbitration as a tool to promote better administrative and judicial decision-making (which in turn would attract investment). To the extent there was an explicit link between treaty obligations and domestic reforms, it operated through a different mechanism: many governments began consenting to investment treaty arbitration at the same time as they were implementing similar investment protection reforms in their national investment regimes.[59] The causality is here reversed, as changing domestic policies towards foreign investment resulted in the adoption of investment treaties rather than the other way around. In some cases the causal pathway is more complex, as national investment laws were inspired by the World Bank Guidelines on the Treatment of Foreign Direct Investment, which in turn were directly inspired by investment treaty obligations.[60] Here, investment treaties may have had an indirect impact on the content of domestic laws, which in turn may have helped facilitated investment, but this was not because of the shadow of investment treaty arbitration.

31.2.3 Investment promotion as a result of investment treaties?

Despite investment promotion being a core driver for developing countries participation in the investment treaty regime, empirical literature has questioned the extent to which consent to investment treaty arbitration has in fact helped developing countries attract investment.[61] Survey evidence suggest that a very large share of foreign investors find consent to investment treaty arbitration irrelevant when investing in otherwise

[57] E.g. Rudolph Dolzer and Margrete Stevens, *Bilateral Investment Treaties* (Martinus Nijhoff, 1995), 12.

[58] Poulsen (n. 32), 91–6.

[59] Jose Alvarez, *The Public International Law Regime Governing International Investment* (Brill Nijhoff, 2011); Poulsen (n. 32).

[60] Ibrahim Shihata, 'Judicial Reform in Developing Countries and the Role of the World Bank' (Inter-American Development Bank 1993).

[61] E.g. Emma Aisbett, 'Bilateral Investment Treaties and Foreign Direct Investment: Correlation versus Causation', in Karl Sauvant and Lisa Sachs (eds), *The Effect of Treaties on Foreign Direct Investment: Bilateral Investment Treaties, Double Taxation Treaties and Investment Flows* (Oxford University Press, 2009); Jason Webb Yackee, 'Do Bilateral Investment Treaties Promote Foreign Direct Investment? Some Hints from Alternative Evidence', 51(2) Virginia Journal of International Law 397 (2010); Yackee (n. 49); Andrew Kerner and Jane Lawrence, 'What's the Risk? Bilateral Investment Treaties, Political Risk and Fixed Capital Accumulation', 44(1) British Journal of Political Science 107 (2014); Srividya Jandhyala and Robert Weiner, 'Institutions sans frontières: International Agreements and Foreign Investment', 45 Journal of International Business Studies 649 (2014); Sarah Danzman, 'Contracting with Whom? The Differential Effects of Investment Treaties on FDI', 42 International Interactions 452 (2016); Emma Aisbett, Matthias Busse, and Peter Nunnenkamp, 'Bilateral Investment Treaties as Deterrents of Host-Country Discretion: The Impact of Investor–state Disputes on Foreign Direct Investment in Developing Countries', 154 Review of World Economics 119 (2017).

risky jurisdictions. A 1991 survey of investors from the United States and Western Europe, conducted by the World Bank, concluded: 'Professional advisors, such as accountants or merchant bankers, would be people to concern themselves with such minutia, only after detailed project planning was already underway.'[62] Two decades later, a survey of in-house legal counsel in large American firms found that foreign investment decisions hardly ever depended on investment treaties.[63] Equally, by 2010 underwriters in the political risk insurance industry rarely considered the treaties important for availability and pricing of political risk insurance.[64]

The treaties are undoubtedly important for investment decisions by some investors in some jurisdictions, and they may have become more important in recent years after the rise of investment treaty arbitration. Yet the effect of the treaties on foreign investment is less than what was expected by many developing country governments when joining the regime. This is for a number of reasons, some of which have to do with the underlying assumptions of the theories presented above.

With respect to credible commitment hypothesis, hold-up problems vary significantly across contexts. Mobile investments with a low share of sunk costs—e.g. light manufacturing—are much less prone to hold-up problems than natural resource or infrastructure investments.[65] Secondly, investment management can reduce the likelihood that investor–state bargains obsolesce, for instance by withholding certain benefits from the state over time[66] or making links with the domestic economy.[67] Third, hold-up problems are 'one-shot' games, whereas in practise investor–state relations are repeated games, which mean the host state is concerned with the negative reputation effects of mistreating foreign investors. Finally, hold-up problems vary depending on the nature of the host state. Empirical literature suggests that expropriation is less likely to occur in democracies, for instance, due their greater property right protections and higher number of 'veto players' that in turn increase policy stability.[68] Equally, the presence of

[62] MIGA PAS, *Industrialized Countries' Policies Affecting Foreign Direct Investment in Developing Countries*, vol. 1 (World Bank, 1991), 92.

[63] Yackee (n. 63).

[64] Lauge Poulsen, 'The Importance of BITs for Foreign Direct Investment and Political Risk Insurance: Revisiting the Evidence', in Karl Sauvant (ed.), *Yearbook of International Investment Law and Policy, 2009–2010* (Oxford University Press, 2010).

[65] Jonathan Bonnitcha, 'Foreign Investment, Development, and Governance: What Can International Investment Law Learn from the Empirical Literature on Investment?', 7 Journal of International Dispute Settlement 31 (2016); Bonnitcha et al. (n. 14).

[66] Ravi Ramamurti, 'Can Governments Make Credible Commitments? Insights from Infrastructure Projects in Developing Regions', 9 Journal of International Management 253 (2003).

[67] Witold Henisz, 'The Institutional Environment for Multinational Investment', 16 Journal of Law, Economics, and Organization 334 (2000); Leslie Johns and Rachel Wellhausen, 'Under One Roof: Supply Chains and the Protection of Foreign Investment', 110(1) American Political Science Review 32 (2016).

[68] Facundo Albornoz, Sebastian Galiani, and Daniel Haymann, 'Foreign Investment and Expropriation under Oligarchy and Democracy', 24(1) Economics & Politics 24 (2012); Nathan Jensen, 'Political Risk, Democratic Institutions, and Foreign Direct Investment', 70(4) Journal of Politics 1040 (2008). Note, of course, that only a minority of investment treaty claims relate to direct expropriation, and Williams (n. 2) finds that democracies are not less likely to be targeted by investment treaty claims.

independent and effective courts lowers the likelihood of uncompensated expropriation.[69] To the extent investment treaty arbitration acts as a crucial credible commitment device, this is the case only in very specific circumstances.

The signalling thesis is not without its challenges either. Practically all states have consented to investment treaty arbitration—including many with 'poor' investment climates—so it is unclear whether the treaties do in fact offer a useful signal about the nature of a state's domestic investment regime. Equally, whereas early investment treaties may have allowed some countries to 'stand out', there are today more than 3,000, so yet another treaty is unlikely to send a particularly costly signal about the nature of a government's investment regime.

Finally, the thesis that consent to investment treaty arbitration promotes better administrative and judicial decision-making comes with caveats as well. Here, a crucial assumption is that host states internalize the constraints imposed by investment treaties into national administrative and judicial systems. This proposition remains severely under-studied, but the work available to date suggest a very low awareness of investment treaty obligations among core officials.[70] Only few countries have institutionalized implementation of investment treaty obligations to ensure compliance—and that only recently.[71] And with respect to promoting better judicial decision-making, one could make the opposite argument as well. By giving foreign investors the right to sidestep domestic courts, investment treaty arbitration may reduce foreign investors' incentive to lobby for judicial reforms.[72] If evidence is found for that proposition, the result could be that investment treaty arbitration reduces, rather than improves, the quality of domestic legal institutions. Thus far, however, we know disappointingly little about the relationship between investment treaty arbitration and the decision-making of host state authorities.

31.3 Recent Developments: Unintended Consequences and the Power of Arbitrators

The politics of investment treaty arbitration has changed radically in recent years. Two factors are particularly important. The first is the unintended consequences of investment

[69] Douglass North and Barry Weingast, 'Constitutions and Commitment: The Evolution of Institutional Governing Public Choice in Seventeenth-Century England', 49(4) Journal of Economic History 803 (1989); Barry Weingast, 'Constitutions as Governance Structures: The Political Foundations of Secure Markets', 149(1) Journal of Institutional and Theoretical Economics 286 (1993).

[70] Mavluda Sattorova, *The Impact of Investment Treaty Law on Host states* (Hart, 2018).

[71] UNCTAD, *Investor–state Disputes: Prevention and Alternatives to Arbitration* (UNCTAD, 2010).

[72] Tom Ginsburg, 'International Substitutes for Domestic Institutions: Bilateral Investment Treaties and Governance', 25 International Review of Law and Economics 107 (2005).

treaty arbitration, which have resulted in changes in treaty practise. In order to understand this development, we need to consider how investment treaties were negotiated in the past. Secondly, the very institution of investment treaty arbitration has become controversial, not least the use of private lawyers to settle public law disputes.

31.3.1 Outcomes: the politics of unintended consequences

Investment treaties have typically been drafted in vague and open-ended terms, which left considerable flexibility to arbitrators to 'fill in the blanks'. After the recent explosion in claims, many governments have been taken by surprise about how far-reaching arbitrators have interpreted and applied vague terms, such as 'fair and equitable' or 'indirect expropriation'. The scope of jurisdiction, the lack of deference to national decision-makers, and particularly the size of some monetary awards have also prompted concerns about whether the costs—monetary, regulatory, or both—outweigh the benefits.

Given the few claims pursued at the time the investment treaty network expanded rapidly during the 1980s and 1990s, there is nothing inherently surprising about this development, and unintended consequences stemming from 'incomplete contracting' in international law is not limited to investment treaty arbitration. What is unique to this regime, however, is that many governments did not just underestimate the scope of investment treaty arbitration due to imperfect information, but often entirely failed to appreciate the very nature of the regime.

The fact that modern investment protection treaties were enforceable in practice through investment treaty arbitration was not appreciated in a large number of developing countries. Often it took a claim against governments themselves before they realized the treaties were more than just soft-law arrangements.[73] It was not just politicians who failed to appreciate the potency of the regime—including in developed countries[74]—but also many negotiators. Rather than carefully tailoring treaty obligations, officials often copy-pasted from template agreements of Western countries without much consideration, and few stakeholders paid attention. Negotiations were typically quick, and sometimes did not even involve face-to-face meetings,[75] and some developed-country negotiators had serious doubts whether their counterparts took the process seriously. A former German negotiator notes that, while some countries were well prepared, he often had the impression that developing country negotiators

> had very little knowledge about BITs. But that didn't make negotiations easy, because then we had to explain everything. And then there were countries who just wanted

[73] Lauge Poulsen and Emma Aisbett, 'When the Claim Hits: Bilateral Investment Treaties and Bounded Rational Learning', 65(2) World Politics 273 (2013); Poulsen (nn. 60, 34).

[74] See e.g. Guillermo Alvarez and William Park, 'The New Face of Investment Arbitration: NAFTA Chapter 11', 28 Yale J. Int'l L. 365 (2003), 386–3.

[75] Joachim Pohl, 'Societal Benefits and Costs of International Investment Agreements', Working Paper (OECD, 2018), n. 150.

> to sign—whatever the text, but these are extreme examples. In most cases, we were bombarded with questions. What does non-discrimination mean? What does free transfer mean? And in each negotiation we had to explain not just one, but many times.[76]

A Dutch negotiator equally notes that 'during the 1990s, developing countries often asked what even basic provisions meant',[77] and in Latin America an experienced negotiator recalls:

> Many here in Latin America thought it was harmless to sign these treaties; no-one had an idea what they meant. Many who negotiated were not lawyers, so they just signed them off within a few days, hours, or even over email because travels are too expensive... Governments want to display co-operation, and one way to do that is to sign promotion treaties that sound nice... No discussion, analysis, goes into it... And even if it gets a legal review, the lawyers don't have the experience what to check for... No-one cares until the dispute comes.[78]

Similarly, when treaties were 'negotiated' among developing countries themselves, the process occasionally went so fast that the final agreement was just a signed copy of a template. In an extreme case, officials even forgot to put the names of the two countries on the treaty.[79] As one arbitrator puts it, many developing country governments simply 'had no idea that this would have real consequences in the real world'.[80]

This may appear surprising, and to some supporters of investment treaty arbitration the suggestion that many developing country officials failed to appreciate the nature of what they were negotiating is outright offensive.[81] Yet many developing country officials work in under-resourced organizations that are often subject to a range of complex institutional pressures. Often investment treaty negotiations were only a small part of their job portfolio. In the case of South Africa, for instance, officials involved with early investment treaties were also responsible for customs unions, double taxation agreements, legal issues pertaining to Antarctica, and law of the seas.[82] Add to that career incentives for diplomats and ambassadors to promote treaties to 'show the fruit of their labor'[83] as well as broader political incentives to use treaties to promote strategic foreign policy objectives unrelated to investment,[84] and there was ample scope for investment treaties to be signed as little more than diplomatic tokens of goodwill.

[76] Quoted in Poulsen (n. 32), 156. [77] Quoted ibid. 155. [78] Quoted ibid. 148.

[79] Ibid. 181.

[80] Schreuer quoted in *Wintershall Aktiengesellschaft v Argentine Republic*, Award, ICSID Case No. ARB/04/14 (2008), para. 85.

[81] Jan Paulsson, 'Moral Hazard in International Dispute Resolution', 25 ICSID Review 339 (2010), 344; Francisco Vicuña, 'Regulatory Expropriations in International Law: Carlos Calvo, Honorary NAFTA Citizen', 11 New York University Environmental Law Journal 19 (2002), 31.

[82] Poulsen (n. 32), 170–71.

[83] Lauge Poulsen and Emma Aisbett, 'Diplomats Want Treaties: Diplomatic Agendas and Perks in the Investment Regime', 7 Journal of International Dispute Resolution 72 (2016).

[84] Ibid.; Pohl (n. 78), 70–72; Chilton (n. 31).

Moreover, opting into 'default rules' with little consideration of the potential ramifications is a well-known phenomenon.[85] In the context of contract law, for instance, Korobkin notes:

> Many of the terms commonly specified in standard form contracts govern what will happen if a low-probability risk comes to pass... If these possible but unlikely outcomes are not readily 'available' to buyers, they are likely to respond to the risk of these harms by treating them as if they do not exist at all... [Buyers] might allocate their attention elsewhere, rendering the form terms that concern low probability risks non-salient... A form term calling for arbitration of disputes in an inconvenient state, for example, is likely to be non-salient to the vast majority of buyers unless the type of contract in question commonly results in disputes.[86]

Archival records, interviews, and statistical analyses suggest that a similar development took place in the investment treaty regime.[87] The combination of (i) few investment treaty claims up through the 1980s and 1990s, (ii) a lack of expertise among relevant developing country officials, and (iii) inflated expectations about the investment impact of the treaties made for a dangerous cocktail of risk-neglect and optimism bias. There were exceptions, of course, as some developing country governments did carefully consider the ramifications of consenting to investment treaty arbitration.[88] A country like China, for instance, more carefully calibrated its investment treaty network than many other developing countries, and has in recent years pursued the treaties to protect Chinese investors abroad.[89] But for many, if not most, developing countries, the rise of investment treaty arbitration has come as a surprise. Partly for this reason, a few countries have cancelled some of their investment protection treaties and left ICSID.[90]

The majority of states have largely stuck with the regime, however, and instead sought to negotiate their agreements more carefully than in the past.[91] More recent treaties

[85] Cass Sunstein, 'Deciding by Default', 162(1) University of Pennsylvania Law Review 1 (2013); Jean Galbraith, 'Treaty Options: Towards a Behavioural Understanding of Treaty Design', 53 Virginia Journal of International Law 309 (2013); Joseph Jupille, Walter Mattli, and Duncan Snidal, *Institutional Choice in Global Commerce: Governance Strategies from the 19th Century to the Present* (Cambridge University Press, 2013).

[86] Russell Korobkin, 'Bounded Rationality, Standard Form Contracts, and Unconscionability', 70 University of Chicago Law Review 1203 (2003), 1233–4.

[87] Poulsen (n. 32).

[88] Ibid. 156–60; Luke Nottage and Sakda Thanitcul, 'The Past, Present and Future of International Investment Arbitration in Thailand', Working Paper 16/31 (Sydney Law School, 2016).

[89] Axel Berger, 'The Politics of China's Investment Treaty-Making Program', in Tomer Broude, Marc Busch, and Amy Porges (eds), *The Politics of International Economic Law* (Cambridge University Press, 2011).

[90] Clint Peinhardt and Rachel Wellhausen, 'Withdrawing from Investment Treaties But Protecting Investment', 7(4) Global Policy (2016).

[91] UNCTAD, *Investor-state Dispute Settlement and Impact on Investment Rulemaking* (UNCTAD, 2007), 91–2.

often include more precise provisions so as to provide arbitrators with more guidance.[92] Exceptions and carve-outs have also become more widespread to excuse breaches of investor rights. In some cases, such clarifications have been issued by the parties through interpretive statements about past treaties as well[93] or through renegotiation.[94]

Some of these developments can be critically important in investor–state claims. As in the 1980s and 1990s, however, investment treaties are still mostly negotiated around model agreements of developed states, which means that changes in treaty practise have primarily come from Western states.[95] The result is that most alterations remained incremental and path-dependent. Whether signed as stand-alone agreements or as part of broader free trade agreements, recent investment treaties continue to give foreign investors legal privileges that domestic investors do not have, the most important being the right to file claims outside of national courts.[96] With very few exceptions, there has been no move towards binding investor obligations.[97] With the notable exception of India, there has been no move towards extensive local remedy requirements, and with the exception of a recent model treaty of Brazil no governments have suggested removing the option of direct investor standing and instead relying only on inter-state dispute settlement. Despite the recent politicization, most governments are primarily concerned with creating slightly more 'complete contracts' rather than significantly departing from the status quo.

[92] Wolfgang Alschner, 'The Impact of Investment Arbitration on Investment Treaty Design: Myth versus Reality', 42 Yale Journal of International Law 1 (2018); Caroline Henckels, 'Protecting Regulatory Autonomy through Greater Precision in Investment Treaties: The TPP, CETA, and TTIP', 19 Journal of International Economic Law 27.

[93] Anthea Roberts, 'Power and Persuasion in Investment Treaty Interpretation: The Dual Role of states', 104(2) American Journal of International Law 179 (2010).

[94] Yoram Haftel and Alex Thompson, 'When Do states Renegotiate International Agreements? The Case of Bilateral Investment Treaties', 13 Review of International Organizations 25 (2017); Alex Thompson, Tomer Brouder, and Yoram Haftel, 'Once Bitten, Twice Shy? How Disputes Affect Regulatory Space in Investment Agreements', International Organization (forthcoming).

[95] Mark Manger and Clint Peinhardt, 'Learning and Diffusion in International Investment Agreements', Working Paper (Princeton University, 2017).

[96] It is beyond this chapter to address whether the substantive rights afforded by investment treaties exceed those in national legal systems. See e.g. Santiago Montt, *state Liability in Investment Treaty Arbitration: Global Constitutional and Administrative Law in the BIT Generation* (Hart, 2009); Parvan Parvanov and Mark Kantor, 'Comparing U.S. Law and Recent U.S. Investment Agreements: Much More Similar Than You Might Expect', in Sauvant (n. 66); Lise Johnson and Oleksandr Volkov, 'Investor–state Contracts, Host-state Commitments and the Myth of Stability in International Law', 24 Am. Rev. Int'l Arb. 361 (2013). On investor standing and remedies in investment arbitration compared to domestic jurisdictions, see e.g. David Gaukrodger, 'Investment Treaties and Shareholder Claims for Reflective Loss: Insights from Advanced Systems of Corporate Law', Working Paper (OECD, 2014); Armand de Mestral and Robin Morgan, 'Does Canadian Law Provide Remedies Equivalent to NAFTA Chapter 11 Arbitration?' CIGI Investor–state Arbitration Series 4 (2016).

[97] An arbitration practitioner has noted that many policy-makers seem to have an 'uncritical adherence' to the belief that only investors should be able to file claims, not the other way around. See Gustavo Laborde, 'The Case for Host state Claims in Investment Arbitration', 1 Journal of International Dispute Settlement 97 (2010), 102–3.

31.3.2 Inputs: the politics of arbitrators

Apart from the unexpected consequences of the investment treaty regime, the very nature of the dispute settlement mechanism has become controversial as well. In Europe, in particular, the recent politicization of the regime has evolved not simply around the nature of the substantive protections afforded by investment treaties, but also around the identity of the adjudicators and the use of arbitration to settle investment treaty disputes in the first place.

Using arbitrators that work for a profit to rule on sensitive areas of public regulation, with limited transparency and no real possibility of appeal, has become increasingly contentious.[98] Attempts have been made to address some of these challenges, for instance with respect to opacity.[99] Yet, at the heart of the criticisms is the identity and selection of adjudicators themselves. Whether the critics are correct, misguided, or a bit of both is beyond this chapter to address. From a political perspective, however, the question is ultimately immaterial, as the lack of perceived legitimacy can undermine claims to authority, which in turn may prompt non-compliance or even widespread exit from the regime. 'As the gulf deepens,' one arbitrator has lamented, 'the complaints get louder and the stability of the system gets undermined.'[100]

The role of arbitrators is not accounted for in the basic contract theory referenced above, as this assumes that third-party adjudicators are disinterested and neutral parties.[101] Yet we know from a large literature that the identity of those deciding legal disputes matters.[102] And while methodological challenges make it difficult to assess causality, an emerging research agenda is testing whether, and to what extent, the identity of arbitrators play a critical role in investment treaty arbitration.[103] Focus has been on the personal characteristics, motives, and selection processes of arbitrators.[104]

[98] For critics within the legal academy, see e.g. Gus Van Harten, *Investment Treaty Arbitration and Public Law* (Oxford University Press, 2007); Muthucumaraswamy Sornarajah, 'International Investment Law as Development Law: The Obsolescence of a Fraudulent System', in Mark Bungenberg et al. (eds), *European Yearbook of International Economic Law* (Springer, 2016), 209.

[99] Critiques about opacity have been partially addressed with transparency requirements in some recent investment protection treaties, as well as the UN Convention on Transparency in Treaty-Based Investor–state Arbitration (the 'Mauritius Convention on Transparency'). On transparency in investment arbitration, see generally Joachim Delaney and Daniel Magraw, 'Procedural Transparency', in Peter Muchlinski, Federico Ortino, and Christoph Schreuer (eds), *The Oxford Handbook of International Investment Law* (Oxford University Press, 2008).

[100] Landau (n. 3). [101] van Aaken (n. 49), 528.

[102] Cass Sunstein et al., *Are Judges Political? An Empirical Analysis of the Federal Judiciary* (Brookings Institution Press, 2007); Erik Voeten, 'The Impartiality of International Judges: Evidence from the European Court of Human Rights', 102(4) American Political Science Review 417 (2008). On investment arbitration, see also discussion in Susan Franck et al., 'The Diversity Challenge: Exploring the "Invisible College" of International Arbitration', 52 Columbia Journal of Transnational Law 429 (2015).

[103] E.g. Daphna Kapeliuk, 'Collegial Games Analyzing the Effect of Panel Composition on Outcomes in Investment Arbitration', 31 Review of Litigation 267 (2012); Franck et al. (n. 104); Todd Tucker, 'Inside the Black Box: Collegial Patterns on Investment Tribunals', 7 Journal of International Dispute Settlement 183 (2016); Michael Waibel and Yanhui Wu, 'Are Arbitrators Political?' (SSRN, 2012).

[104] E.g. Thomas Schultz, 'Arbitral Decision-Making: Legal Realism and Law & Economics', 6(2) Journal of International Dispute Settlement 231 (2015).

With respect to personal characteristics, it is notable that by 2011 only 37 individuals accounted for 50 per cent of all ICSID appointments made since 1972,[105] and more than half of all investment treaty claims had been decided by just 15 arbitrators.[106] Together, this small group of—mostly—white, wealthy, Western men trained at the same institutions have been delegated a remarkable concentration of power in global investment governance. Moreover, whereas WTO panellists tend to be former Geneva diplomats (who in turn are carefully nudged by the WTO secretariat), most investment arbitrators come from a corporate law background[107] with little embeddedness in law-making and diplomatic communities.[108] The collective biography of this small group of individuals has raised concerns whether adjudicators in the investment regime may be implicitly biased towards corporate actors, against judicial deference to national decision-makers, and against 'political' considerations in investment decision-making.[109]

In addition to their personal characteristics, concerns have been raised that arbitrators may have financial or career incentives to expand the judicial scope of the regime.[110] A broad interpretation of vague provisions will facilitate more claims by investors and thus more appointments for arbitrators. In addition, most arbitrators can earn more as counsel than as arbitrators, and the option of arbitrators to sit as counsel in similar claims has raised concerns about conflicts of interests.[111] Also, even in the absence of 'double-hatting' and revolving doors, the financial rewards for arbitrators can be significant. And in cases with particularly high fees, like the *Yukos* arbitration, it is not difficult to see the conscious or unconscious biases that can emerge, when a mere assistant to a tribunal can keep $1.7 million for himself.[112]

These concerns came to the fore in European controversies over the prospect of enshrining consent to investment treaty arbitration into the Transatlantic Trade and Investment Partnership (TTIP) agreement. As a result, the European Commission was forced to come up with a new proposal for investment treaty arbitration more palatable to European critics. This is a semi-permanent tribunal—including an appellate

105 Puig (n. 8), 407. 106 Olivier and Eberhardt (n. 6). 107 Waibel and Wu (n. 105).

108 Joost Pauwelyn, 'The Rule of Law Without the Rule of Lawyers? Why Investment Arbitrators are from Mars, Trade Adjudicators from Venus', 109 American Journal of International Law 761 (2015).

109 Franck et al. (n. 104).

110 Van Harten (n. 100). An additional concern relates to the appointment of arbitrators. Whereas one view is that party appointments is a traditional right in arbitration, and may increase the chances of compliance, others have raised concerns that it generates a 'market' for different arbitrator profiles and thereby fails to ensure neutrality and independence in the dispute settlement process. See e.g. Paulsson (n. 83). Another question is whether arbitrators have an individual incentive to favour developed respondent states as a way to 'manage' the backlash there; see Malcolm Langford and Daniel Behn, 'Managing Backlash: The Evolving Investment Treaty Arbitrator?' 29 European Journal of International Law 2 (2018).

111 Malcolm Langford, Daniel Behn, and Runar Lie, 'The Revolving Door in International Investment Arbitration', 20 Journal of International Economic Law 2 (2017); Thomas Buergenthal, 'The Proliferation of Disputes, Dispute Settlement Procedures and Respect for the Rule of Law', 22(4) Arbitration International 495 (2006); Philippe Sands, 'Conflict and Conflicts in Investment Treaty Arbitration: Ethical Standards for Counsel', in Chester Brown and Kate Miles (eds), *Evolution in Investment Treaty Law and Arbitration* (Cambridge University Press, 2011).

112 Global Arbitration Review, *The Cost of Yukos* (GAR, 2014).

body—where members are appointed by the contracting parties (not investors), must have certain public law qualifications, and are paid a fixed salary. Tribunal members are also barred from acting as counsel in investment claims. At the time of writing, the model was included in a couple of EU investment treaties and was proposed by the Commission as a template for a multilateral court, under discussion at UNCITRAL. If successful, that would be a path-breaking development, but at the time of writing it remains unclear whether there is appetite for the model in other powerful states, notably the United States and China.

Finally, it is worth noting that an additional political dimension of investment arbitrators is often overlooked in policy debates and scholarship. Many investment arbitration practitioners do not just settle legal claims but also advise governments on their investment treaty policies.[113] The most notable historical case was when the American Bar Association sent arbitration practitioners to the former Soviet bloc to advise on investment law reforms there.[114] Governments were typically told by investment lawyers to sign up to ICSID and investment protection treaties as crucial instruments to attract investment. Arbitrators have also acted as policy advisors to governments on whether and how to draft investment treaties (see Table 31.1), and some governments have appointed arbitration practitioners as their representatives to inter-state deliberations, as was the case in deliberations of the Mauritius Convention on Transparency. This political agency of investment arbitrators remains under-studied. Whereas we know that some law firms specializing in investment arbitration have begun to fund political

Table 31.1 Private lawyers as government advisors

Firm/Chambers	Examples of policy advice to developing countries	Lawyers with background in government or IO as investment treaty advisor or negotiator (n)
20 Essex Street	AILA; member of advisory committee of Chile's Ministry of Foreign Affairs.	USA, Canada, Chile
Allen & Overy	UNCTAD; AILA; Allen & Overy course to Rwanda on investment arbitration; advised 'states in Europe, Central Asia and Middle East' on negotiation and drafting investment treaties.	
Arnold & Porter	UNCTAD; advised fifteen CARICOM countries on investment chapter for external PTAs.	USA, Colomba (n), Costa Rica, ICSID
Baker Botts	UNCTAD and AILA; advised Caribbean government on its arbitration law.	ICSID
Clifford Chance	UNCTAD; IISD; AILA.	Argentina
Crow & Moring	UNCTAD; one co-director of ILI's International Investment Law Centre.	USA (n), Canada

[113] Olivier and Eberhardt (n. 6).

[114] Poulsen (n. 32), table 4.5.

Firm/Chambers	Examples of policy advice to developing countries	Lawyers with background in government or IO as investment treaty advisor or negotiator (n)
Curtis	UNCTAD; one co-director of ILI's International Investment Law Centre.	ICSID
DAP LLC	UNCTAD; advised Colombia on implementation of BIT obligations, Chile on its model BIT, and Morocco on investment provisions in US PTA.	USA (n)
Dechert	UNCTAD; ILI.	Ecuador, ICSID
Essex Court	AILA; BHR; advised Pakistan and Mauritius on their arbitration laws; advised arbitration office of Thai Ministry of Justice; UNCITRAL delegate of Mauritius.	USA, UK (n)
Foley Hoag	UNCTAD; advised South Africa on its arbitration law.	USA (n), Canada (n), Ecuador, Argentina, Ukraine (n), Inter-American Development Bank, UNCTAD
Freshfields	AILA; advised Mexico on negotiation of NAFTA Chapter 11 and South Africa on its arbitration law; UNCITRAL delegate of Bahrain.	USA
Hogan Lovells	UNCTAD; AILA.	Austria
King & Spalding	UNCTAD.	ICSID, Mexico (n)
Lalive	UNCTAD; UNITAR.	
Matrix	UNCTAD; AILA; advised 'numerous Latin American governments' on their model BITs.	MEX (n)
McNair	UNCTAD.	Germany
Salans	UNCTAD and AILA.	USA
Sidley Austin	UNCTAD; IISD; CEELI; ILI; advised several countries on investment treaty arbitration clauses.	USA (n), Bulgaria (n)
Shea. & Sterling	UNCTAD; ILI; AILA.	USA (n)
Steptoe	Advised several countries, incl. one in Asia, on BIT and PTA investment chapter negotiations.	
Weil	UNCTAD; advised on NAFTA arbitration provisions (unclear for which party).	USA (n)
White & Case	UNCTAD; ILI; AILA.	USA (n), Germany (n)

Notes: Apart from UNCTAD, list includes technical assistance for: International Law Institute (ILI); African International Legal Awareness (AILA); International Institute for Sustainable Development (IISD); United Nations Institute for Training and Research (UNITAR); and CEELI. Countries identified when possible.

Source: Robert Howse, 'International Investment Law and Arbitration: A Conceptual Framework', Working Paper 2017/1 (IILJ 2017), table 4.2 Note that many lawyers refrain from making their advisory work public.

activism—most visibly in the organization EU Investment Law and Arbitration (EFILA)—there is little available evidence on the informal interaction between arbitrators and policy-makers designing the future of the investment treaty regime.

31.4 Conclusion

Whereas few had heard of the investment treaty regime a decade ago, investment treaty arbitration has become one of the most politicized aspects of global economic governance in recent years. Until recently, the contentious debates about the regime were almost solely dominated by opinionated camps ranging from the staunchest supporters (often arbitration practitioners) to the likes of Reverend Billy—each with their own favourite studies and anecdotes. This brought more heat than light to our understanding of the distributive and rule-of-law consequences that arise from the dispute settlement mechanism. In recent years, an emerging literature has sought to fill these gaps with better theories and more robust empirical evidence, but many of the critical socio-economic questions about this crucial corner of global economic governance lack systematic and careful assessment. This chapter has alluded to four in particular.

The first is the relationship between investment treaty arbitration and diplomacy. How, and to what extent, does the increase in investor claims influence inter-state relations? Much has been said about this question—often to defend investment treaty arbitration—but very little empirical evidence has been brought to the debate. Second, what is the relationship between investment treaties and administrative and judicial decision-making in host states? This is a much more important question than the investment impact of the treaties, yet it has received hardly any scholarly attention to date. For instance, much of the debate about whether the investment treaty regime results in 'regulatory chill' remains largely abstract and anecdotal.[115] Also, whereas some recent work on settlements suggests that investors often achieve either compensation or regulatory changes in return for withdrawing their claims,[116] we have only the most superficial understanding of how the politics of foreign investment and investor–state bargaining is shaped by 'the shadow' of international investment law.

Third, and related, how do different states—and stakeholders within them—respond to decisions by arbitral tribunals? Which types of claims have political fall-outs, and why? Some interpretations and outcomes have taken not just developing countries but also developed countries by surprise, which in turn raises questions about what exactly

[115] Pohl (n. 77), 61–6. For an exception, see Carolina Moehlecke, 'The Chilling Effect of International Investment Disputes: Limited Challenges to state Sovereignty,' International Studies Quarterly (forthcoming).

[116] Robert Howse, 'International Investment Law and Arbitration: A Conceptual Framework,' Working Paper 2017/1 (IILJ, 2017).

was expected by different states when they consented to investment treaty arbitration. Historical work on this question has just begun. Finally, given that much of the controversy concerning the investment treaty regime homes in on the identity and actions of investment arbitrators, we need a better understanding of the political roles played by arbitration practitioners and firms shaping the investment treaty regime.

PART VI

PERSPECTIVES

CHAPTER 32

INTERNATIONAL COMMERCIAL ARBITRATION

The creation of a legal market

YVES DEZALAY AND BRYANT G. GARTH

32.1 Introduction

The development of international commercial arbitration is often presented as a response to the demand for law and dispute resolution created naturally by an increase in transnational commerce and investment. The International Chamber of Commerce (ICC) in Paris, consistent with this conventional history, was relatively marginal from its establishment in 1923 until the increase in global trade and commerce that came in the 1970s and 1980s. The demand naturally created the supply.

Recognizing that this market was not inevitable, Jerome Sgard argues that the rise of international commercial arbitration depended on institutional entrepreneurs around the ICC.[1] In contrast to potential competitors in London and New York, he finds, those around the ICC 'actually developed by way of experimentation the new legal technology of international arbitration'.[2] These individuals, with 'limited social and professional capital', developed a 'novel approach to cross-jurisdictional borders that solved problems of governance that were inherent to the long-run evolution of the international division of labor'.[3] The novel features and expertise, including the practice of limiting arbitration to disputes between companies from different countries and selecting

[1] Jerome Sgard, 'A Tale of Three Cities: The Construction of International Commercial Arbitration', in Gregoire Mallard and Jerome Sgard (eds), *Contractual Knowledge: One Hundred Years of Legal Experimentation in Global Markets* (Cambridge University Press, 2016).

[2] Ibid. 156. [3] Ibid. 179.

arbitrators from third countries, turned out to be a technology that businesses wanted. Accordingly, 'from the 1950s onwards, this approach to international dispute settlement was increasingly endorsed by multinational firms, who thrived on the back of the gradual reopening of international markets.'[4] Innovators from the margins created something that business wanted, and therefore it began to thrive, was imitated by others, and became accepted globally.

Our historical and sociological account shares the recognition that the development of the field of international commercial arbitration was not inevitable, but it differs in several respects. First, it focuses much more on the supply side. Rather than the creation of a technology that meets a demand, we examine how the development of international commercial arbitration relates to the history of the legal profession, to hegemonic and imperial struggles involving the US and the old European imperial powers, and to innovations or 'revolutions' that provide both change and continuity in structures of power. A key focus of this chapter is therefore how the relatively marginal group around the ICC that Sgard studies gained credibility and acceptance from both multinational enterprises and developing countries. It was not, we suggest, just because the technology worked well.

Before turning specifically to the modern story of the development of international commercial arbitration, we think it is essential to start from the imperial and legal genesis of the legal profession. The late reinvention of international law and commercial justice is built on a long historical construction. The innovations of international arbitration between states and then between private businesses as well came out of the very specific history of the legal profession. From the beginning, in medieval Italy, law-trained individuals armed with a family name, cosmopolitan capital, and legal know-how built their own careers in part by brokering and arbitrating between different interests and places.

Building on this initial history, we trace four further dimensions to this story. The first is the construction of what can be called the field of 'international justice' mainly oriented toward public international law.[5] The tremendous investment prior to the First World War in public international law and international arbitration between states—through an alliance between US corporate lawyers and their clients on one side and European professors of international law on the other side—built a credibility that the entrepreneurs of international commercial arbitration drew on. The power of the alliance shaped what came later, and made a place in which the 'marginal players' around the ICC could build credibility.

The second, relatedly, is the work of entrepreneurs in the period between the world wars building the academic side and finding a niche for the *lex mercatoria* and international commercial arbitration. They were steeped mainly in the German academic tradition but were relatively marginal, and several were even forced to leave Germany

[4] Ibid.

[5] Yves Dezalay and Bryant Garth, 'Constructing a Transatlantic Marketplace of Disputes on the Symbolic Foundations of International Justice', in Mallard and Sgard (n. 1).

because of their Jewish family background. They were the kinds of newcomers and upstarts that Berman[6] and Sacriste[7] describe as the promoters of legal change who, at the same time, rebuild the credibility of the core of the law. Their innovations served the hierarchies embedded in the law and the interests that the hierarchies in turn helped legitimate and sustain.

The third element mixes the two. The international circulation of these academic investments in international public and private law led to arbitration provisions in a number of the petroleum agreements between oil companies on one side and developing countries on the other. These provisions were inserted by international lawyers who advised the oil companies and connected to one or both sides of public international law and emerging legal doctrines for international commercial arbitration. The prestige of interstate arbitration helped these provisions to gain acceptance, putting them in place to emerge through the huge oil arbitrations of the 1960s and 1970s.

Fourth, after the initial acceptance in the wake of the oil arbitrations, we discuss the routinization of international commercial arbitration as offshore litigation through two developments. After the technology of international commercial arbitration—and the people who went with it—became accepted in some circles, diffusion was still not automatic. Again, credibility must be built among potential users. One key was activity by US law firms in particular, who were key players from the start through the transatlantic alliance, opening up new markets outside the ICC beginning with London. They sought to increase competition among the various potential forums for international commercial arbitration. The second was the gradual expansion to new sites through conferences and missionary efforts involving the co-optation of local elites.

Our conclusion notes briefly that the picture is still evolving, with the model of offshore litigation appearing to change incrementally through an increased mixing with the international law that was so important at the beginning of the story. Again, US corporate law firms are central to the story.

32.2 The History of Lawyers as Brokers and Arbitrators

The strong linkage between legal and social capital central to international commercial arbitration is a by-product of the specific competition between empires in Western Europe.[8] The Roman model for constructing and managing vast and fragmented

[6] Harold Berman, *Law and Revolution: The Formation of the Western Legal Tradition* (Harvard University Press, 1983); *Law and Revolution II: The Impact of the Protestant Reformations on the Western Legal Tradition* (Belknap Press, 2003).

[7] Guillaume Sacriste, *La république des constitutionnalistes. Professeurs de droit et légitimation de l'état en France (1870–1914)* (Sciences Po, 2011).

[8] Jane Burbank and Frederick Cooper, *Empires in World History: Power and the Politics of Difference* (Princeton University Press, 2010).

empires continued for many centuries in Constantinople, even though it was restructured very differently by the Moslem caliphate and later the Ottoman empire. But the Roman model had a different history in Western Europe. In Western Europe, the Roman institutional framework of governance became re-appropriated more or less rapidly by new ruling elites—particularly a mix of Roman Catholic elite and the landed aristocracy.[9] The rapid demise of Rome as a centralized site of power contributed to a lasting competition and fighting between peripheral regional elites, with only a few limited attempts (such as that by Charlemagne) at recreating some more coherent set of institutions and rules over a vast territory. As a result, the more ambitious rulers could only expand their territory through alliances with powerful aristocratic families, and their complex system of feudal clientelism amongst lesser nobility.

The development of the legal profession in Europe took place within this specific context, which required accepting a compromise with feudal institutions of power. That meant accommodating the family ties and capital that played a major role along with a whole process of seigneurial justice—in turn relying on a hybrid mix of customs and some remains of Roman law. The Gregorian revolution described by Brundage[10] and Martines,[11] therefore, can be seen as a kind of political compromise and institutional hybridization, constructed around the conversion and revamping of seigneurial justice into a new and more legitimate professional justice closely linked to the new rulers—the Church, kings and city-states.

The embeddedness of law in social hierarchies and capital, in short, is at the core of the historical construction of political power in Western Europe (as opposed to the completely different management of imperial power in the Ottoman empire, which carefully avoided any compromise with local elite families) and the related history of the legal profession and its relation to change. The specific broker or double-agent role of elite lawyers (and those who have followed the same model) is a product of this history.

The multiple turf battles between and among overlapping and competing state institutions provided one of the principal markets for legal experts who could interpret texts in order to justify the pretensions of one or another side, serving also as arbitrator or consultant in proceedings before powerful groups or authorities (including the Council of the Seigneurie of Florence or the Papal Courts). Martines thus noted: 'overlapping jurisdictions (are the) source of many conflicts (and) legal knowledge (represents) a useful weapon on both sides.'[12] Elite jurists positioned themselves very early as courtiers of the international in the name of universal principles of learned law valid for civil law as well as canon law. In fact, if we look deeper at the process, we see that the success of the learned capital was at the same time inseparable from investments in cosmopolitan capital. These jurists acquired their cosmopolitan capital through trips that they took at a very young age, as well as through the long years spent in prominent universities such

[9] See John Schmidhauser, 'The European Origins of Legal Imperialism and its Legacy in Legal Education in Former Colonial Regions', 18(3) International Political Science Review 337 (1997).

[10] James Brundage, *The Medieval Origins of the Legal Profession* (University of Chicago Press, 2008).

[11] Lauro Martines, *Lawyers and Statecraft in Renaissance Florence* (Princeton University Press, 1968).

[12] Ibid. 251.

as Bologna—where they met their counterparts from other cities. They took advantage of numerous opportunities to grow their international capital—whether in legal practice or in the service of the state.

A practice that assisted them was that certain judicial activities were reserved to foreign judges. This tradition, deriving from practices in the Roman empire, was justified in the name of a concern for impartiality. Judges coming from city-states not involved in a dispute were considered more neutral than their local counterparts for the purpose of deciding disputes, preventing adverse parties from mobilizing extended family and clientelist networks that would extend to legal practitioners and judges.

This imperial holdover helped build cosmopolitan connections and experience, but in fact it represented but a small part of the international market for legal expertise responding to the demands of the new states. The mix of relational and learned capital acquired by the offspring of old patrician families furnished useful instruments to the new holders of power of the city-states to manage confrontations between rival cities nourished by competition between commercial powers and their own power ambitions.

As Martines showed, these courtiers in international legal relations fulfilled many functions: negotiating and drafting treaties, drafting legal opinions where there were potential differences of interpretation, offering the services of arbitrator in order to avoid the resort to force or to settle a dispute between rival cities.[13] Finally, for the ambassadors to Rome, these jurists also fulfilled a double function: to advise and negotiate the numerous fiscal and jurisdictional relationships between the religious and state authorities; and then also to handle judicial proceedings involving important individuals before the Papacy.

This trans-frontier dimension seen in early European legal history supports a clarification of the analysis developed by Kantorowicz.[14] The reliance on multiple sites to construct cosmopolitan capital enabled legal elites to succeed in playing on two essential scales. They constructed their professional autonomy and credibility, but they also put their expertise at the service of the new holders of state power—which then allowed the acquisition of the capital of political notoriety and influence vital to continuing professional success. The descendants of aristocratic and patrician families, therefore, played a particular role in the construction of the modern state because they could rely on family resources that permitted them to connect themselves to trans-frontier power through networks situated above—but also within—the city-states. This role of international courtier was central to the genesis of the European legal field.

This brokering role is also essential to the management of change. As Berman showed in his two works of *Law and Revolution*, major or even revolutionary changes, which may be religious or political, are also opportunities for a fraction of legal elites—typically to some extent outsiders—to promote an updating or *aggiornamento* in the production of legal doctrine, getting themselves in phase with the political objectives of new ruling

[13] Ibid.

[14] Ernst Kantorowicz, *The King's Two Bodies: A Study in Medieval Political Theology* (Princeton University Press, 1997).

groups seeking allies and privileged collaborators.[15] This way, for example, as Berman indicates, law professors made an alliance with theologians and Protestant leaders in order to construct a new political-legal order—which served in large part also to reintegrate the Roman and even canon law that formed the basis of their authority.[16]

The diachronic and synchronic dimensions combine to provide an image of legal elites including professors operating a kind of ferry between regimes and places—as courtier, diplomat, mediator, arbitrator—reshaping the model of excellence and mechanisms of influence by drawing on legal capital strengthened in fights for state power or in battles between states.

32.3 The Construction of the Field of International Commercial Arbitration

The construction of the field of international commercial arbitration draws on this historical position of lawyers as brokers between different interests and places and also facilitating and legalizing societal changes. They use their capital and positions as brokers to enhance their power and status both locally and transnationally. An openness to international arbitration, which validates their learning and their cosmopolitan contacts while bolstering their stature at home, is not surprising.

32.3.1 Building the field of international justice

The development of international commercial arbitration depended on the development of a field of international justice—identified especially with public international law. The enduring patterns of exchange among lawyer brokers who combined family, cosmopolitan, academic, economic, and political capital went into the field of international law. The construction of the international here as elsewhere depends on battles that take place within national legal fields.[17] Careers historically are made at the local level or validated at that level. The local context reveals the tactical alliances put into play during the period of the genesis—alliances evident at the level of national fields of state power, as well as at the international level—between fractions of national elites whose interests converged or whose resources were complementary.

The approach here highlights the complementary forms of symbolic capital, academic, political, and philanthropic, that provided international justice with its initial

[15] Berman, *Law and Revolution* and *Law and Revolution II* (n. 6).

[16] More recent examples are in Sacriste (n. 7); Ronen Shamir, *Managing Legal Uncertainty* (Duke University Press, 1995).

[17] Yves Dezalay and Bryant Garth, *The Internationalization of Palace Wars: Lawyers, Economists, and the Contest to Transform Latin American States* (University of Chicago Press, 2002).

accumulation of expertise, mixing diplomatic skills and the professional legitimacy of the key national legal fields. The alliance had on one side Europe, with continental professors seeking to promote new learned disciplines marginalized within the doctrinal hierarchies that dominated their diplomatic milieu,[18] and on the other side of the Atlantic, a small elite of Wall Street lawyers seeking to enhance their legitimacy as colonial proconsuls newly promoted as lawyer-statesmen.[19] Building on their ties to elite legal education, they also invested the resources of their longstanding patrons, the 'robber barons', whom they had converted into philanthropists/statesmen, in learned European law idealized as an instrument of universal peace. Each had a domestic agenda that led to interest in the international.

The agents who were engaged in the creation, institutionalization, and routinization of new legal practices and institutions had in common the accumulation of multiple expertise and resources—national and cosmopolitan, jurists/diplomats and lawyer/entrepreneurs.[20] This alliance emerged in part because of these multiple roles occupied by each side—professors who also served as diplomats and practitioners with both learned and cosmopolitan resources and interests. They also had in common—even if in varying degrees—the ability to mix their learned expertise with practice in politics, diplomacy, or business affairs. These combinations—part of the habitus of elite lawyers, with national variations—made them well-suited to take part in conflicts, negotiations, or mediations that involved the overlap between different systems of national or transnational rules—a legal complexity of which they often were the principal architects.[21]

The founding fathers of international law as it gained credibility in the nineteenth century were a loose community of learned practitioners and professors who played multiple roles in order both to serve the increased competition between imperial societies and also to limit its risks by building legal channels towards the peaceful resolution of conflicts. These masters of legal rhetoric, either before or after the Second World War, were at ease with a discourse characterized by oppositions—making their skills as mediators and negotiators more valuable—between, for example, ideals such as international peace-making and realist claims for national sovereignty or even imperialism.[22]

[18] See Guillaume Sacriste and Antoine Vauchez, 'The Force of International Law: Lawyers' Diplomacy on the International Scene in the 1920s', 32 Law and Social Inquiry 83 (2007); Sacriste (n. 7); Martti Koskenniemi, *The Gentle Civilizer of Nations: The Rise and Fall of International Law 1870–1960* (Cambridge University Press, 2001), 30–32.

[19] Yves Dezalay and Bryant Garth, *Asian Legal Revivals: Lawyers in the Shadow of Empire* (University of Chicago Press, 2010).

[20] Koskenniemi (n. 18).

[21] See Robert Gordon, 'The Ideal and the Actual in the Law: Fantasies and Practices of New York City Lawyers, 1870–1910', in Gerald Gawalt (ed.), *The New High Priests: Lawyers in Post-Civil War America* (Greenwood Press, 1984), 51–74; M. J. Sklar, *The Corporate Reconstruction of American Capitalism: The Market, the Law, and Politics* (Cambridge University Press, 1988); Kantorowicz (n. 14).

[22] See Mark Mazover, *Governing the World: The History of an Idea* (Penguin, 2012), 73; Benjamin Coates, *Legalist Empire: The United States, Civilization, and International Law in the Early Twentieth Century* (Oxford University Press, 2016), 23.

Furthermore, these leaders on both sides were also directly engaged in the use of legal learning for progressive reform, whether as professors[23] or as lawyers/statesmen mobilizing the resources of financiers reconverted into philanthropists (exemplified by Elihu Root as a lawyer, and by Andrew Carnegie and John D. Rockefeller as sources of philanthropy). The new international legal practices appeared first as spaces of learned investment and academic debate that constructed an idealized representation of these—still quasi-virtual institutions—in order to show what they could or should produce. Far from international justice being born fully formed, this slow and uncertain emergence of the field is a complex process that can be understood by analysing the internal battles which these new legal elites fought within national legal fields—and also, by ricochet, the competition between national legal models played out in new transnational spaces.

This analysis requires taking into account hierarchical structures and related political alliances that are the product of very different national histories. The differentiation between the legal models is not limited, furthermore, to the classic divide between common law and civil law, analyzed by Weber as the differentiation between *Professorenrecht* and practitioners' law. The international competition between different national models of legal hierarchies and division of labour relates also to antagonistic strategies of 'clerks' of law in fields of state power. As Berman noted, the two classic political strategies are, on one side, royal officers and professors who put their competencies in the service of religious or royal bureaucracies and, on the other, learned gentlemen who mobilize their common law expertise in order to control royal power on behalf of the gentry and the rising merchant class.[24]

The continental model of jurists of the state was constituted by the Gregorian reforms[25] and the growth of royal bureaucracies (exemplified by France and Spain), then reconverted as reformist strategies with Protestant princes,[26] before settling with the politics of modernist states such as that of Bismarck[27] and imitators such as Meiji Japan.[28]

On the other side, the practitioners of the common law imposed themselves during the long English revolution around a professional and political strategy that was just the opposite of this continental model, yet was also later extended overseas through colonization by merchant enterprises. The expanding social and professional elite of barristers put their legal and parliamentary expertise at the service of the gentry and merchant classes—from which they largely came—in order to limit the absolutist pretensions of a royal power that was already weakened by civil wars and religious conflicts. This model was also exported to the British colonies, including the United States, where aspects of

[23] See Sacriste and Vauchez (n. 18); Coates (n. 22).

[24] Berman, *Law and Revolution* and *Law and Revolution II* (n. 6); See also Martines (n. 11); Brundage (n. 10).

[25] Ibid. [26] Berman, *Law and Revolution II* (n. 6).

[27] Dietrich Rueschemeyer, 'State, Capitalism, and the Organization of Legal Counsel: Examining an Extreme Case—the Prussian Bar, 1700–1914', in Terence Halliday and Lucien Karpik (eds), *Lawyers and the Rise of Western Political Liberalism: Europe and North America from the Eighteenth to Twentieth Centuries* (Oxford University Press, 1997), 207–28.

[28] Setsuo Miyazawa and Hiroshi Otsuka, 'Legal Education and the Reproduction of Hierarchy in Japan', in Yves Dezalay and Bryant Garth (eds), *Global Prescriptions: The Production, Exportation, and Importation of a New Legal Orthodoxy* (University of Michigan Press, 2002).

the model began to break down during the Jacksonian period with the attack on the old colonial legal elites.

Partly as a result, this divide has become blurred. The new hegemonic society, the United States, reinvented itself late in the nineteenth century with a de facto hybrid out of two different modes. Law professors and law schools in the US played a large role—borrowed from the civil law—in contrast to England, where the rise of the barristers led to the dismantling of law faculties for more than three centuries. The difference between the legal fields of the continental professors and the US practitioners was therefore somewhat more ambiguous than a simple Weberian opposition between practitioners' law and *Professorenrecht*.

In sum, the general competition—which does not preclude convergence—between the two models that emerged in Europe, differentiated by the hierarchy of professional positions and by the strategies of alliance of the notables of law within national fields of power, provides the context through which transnational spaces emerged out of the nineteenth century. In that period European imperial powers (the British, French, and Germans especially) fought not only over the military control of overseas territories but also over the control of the definition of international legal practices.

32.3.2 The exacerbation of imperial competition in the early twentieth century

The confrontation between the hegemonic attempts to control international law by common law and civil law practitioners coming from Europe was shaped by the rising role played by American lawyers linked to corporate power. Indeed, since US corporate lawyers controlled considerable resources—philanthropic, political, and commercial—they could deploy those resources to promote compatible conceptions of law and international justice. Those conceptions conformed to their own interests and to those of the large corporations that were their clients and patrons. Yet the professional and state strategy of these US practitioners led paradoxically to a position close to the continental model—and, more concretely, to investing in the production of learned law in the service of reformist or modernizing politics. This coming together did not occur until the beginning of the twentieth century. According to the recent history written by Coates:

> By the turn of the twentieth century, the United States had developed a tradition of promoting international law in order to maintain political non-entanglement... [T]he profession of international law in the United States, to the extent that it could be called a profession...had not yet joined with its European brethren in the promotion of overseas empire. Yet, because of how international law interacted with the politics of civilization, such a move remained a latent possibility. In 1898 the needs of the new world power would compel the appearance of an imperial international law in the United States.[29]

[29] Coates (n. 22), 38.

These practitioners and professors from elite law schools in the US were also involved deeply in reform, which aimed at importing some aspects of continental civil law traditions and incorporating them within common law practices. Their objective was to reconstruct the legitimacy of the Bar after the professional, political, and economic upheavals that characterized US history in the nineteenth century. Corporate law firms had emerged to serve the burgeoning national companies, but both the role of lawyers and the tremendous social inequalities associated with their clients were highly controversial. In this context, more investment in social reform and in the law was a strategy to ameliorate and legitimize the emerging social order in the US.

The alliance with the emerging elite Ivy League law schools at that time was part of that strategy. That emergence, however, did not mean that professors in the US achieved pre-eminence over judges—who still held a monopoly on the production of legal jurisprudence. It was much later, with the New Deal, that this hierarchy and division of labour between professors and judges in the legal field began to shift, at least marginally.[30] Nevertheless, a partial recomposition occurred that was the result of the systematic importation of scientific approaches to law from continental Europe, financed and managed by the great philanthropic foundations under the guidance of lawyer-statesmen such as Elihu Root for the Carnegie Foundation and Richard Fosdick for the Rockefeller Foundation.[31] Their objective was to import, at least partially, the learned innovations produced in Germany and France by young generations of professors who were building new legal disciplines—e.g. administrative law, public law—and new approaches to law that borrowed from the social sciences in order to educate and legitimate cadres of modernizing bureaucracies.[32]

Even though US practitioners moved closer to the strategies of the jurists of the state in the continental model, this reconversion was inscribed in their own professional and political trajectory—providing them with the supplementary legitimacy and prestige embedded in imported academic law presented as universal. A portion of the elite of the New York Bar, as part of this process, became strongly invested in the politics of US colonialism and the expansion of global trade in the service of US industrial interests.

Historical and political circumstances combined with professional dynamics to explain the relative success of these strategies of internationalization, but also their limits, as seen from the point of view of the Europeans whose work was introduced in the US market. The unequal alliance between the European academics and the alliance of Carnegie, Wall Street lawyers, the US state, and the emerging elite law schools is well-documented by Coates.[33] The turn to international law was in part a recognition that the US was not likely to expand through more colonial annexation after the Spanish-American War: 'Contemplating an expanded role for international law became a way of imagining a greater international role for the United States, one that promised heightened

[30] Shamir (n. 16).

[31] Katharina Rietzler, 'Experts for Peace: Structures and Motivations of Philanthropic Internationalism in the United States and Europe', in Daniel Laqua (ed.), *Internationalism Reconfigured: Transnational Ideas and Movements between the World Wars* (I.B. Tauris, 2011), 45–65.

[32] Sacriste (n. 7).

[33] Coates (n. 22).

influence without the political headaches of overt colonialism.'[34] Investment in international law was consistent with promoting US hegemony and influence versus the traditional European colonial powers. The collaborators across the Atlantic were therefore both competing and collaborating in building international law.

Using Carnegie Funds, in particular, Root supported James Brown Scott's activities to found the American Society of International Law and build important linkages to Europe, including the Institut de Droit International.[35] Scott's credentials reveal the alliance between the state, law, economic power and the academy. He was solicitor to the US Department of State (1906–10) and secretary of the Carnegie Endowment for International Peace (1910–40). He was one of the founders, in 1906, of the American Society of International Law, serving as editor in chief of the *American Journal of International Law*, and later president (1929–39) of the Society.

The Europeans were essential to this project. Recognition from European scholars was vital to the credibility of US scholars building the profession in the United States.[36] US lawyers kept up to date on the scholarship in Europe, and credibility in Europe could build the reputation of a US academic. Economic power counted, however. Coates documents how the US side could call the shots to a substantial degree:

> Carnegie's millions put weight on the western side of the Atlantic. For all its successes, the financial resources of the Institut de droit international were so limited... that it was unable to hold a meeting every year, and many members could not afford to attend the sessions at all. Scott suggested a deal. The Carnegie Endowment would grant the Institut an annual $20,000 subsidy. In return, the Institut would establish a permanent advisory committee to the Endowment. It seemed an ideal combination of European expertise and American capital... [Further] the Institut's stamp of approval would ease the reception of Carnegie's funds overseas.[37]

The US support for an international court beyond the Permanent Court of Arbitration gained power through Carnegie's funds as well. As Coates writes,

> [although] many members of the Institut continued to prefer the arbitral model of the Permanent Court of Arbitration... Institut voted overwhelmingly to issue an official statement in favor of a permanent international court... John Bassett Moore was sure that the support had been purchased. 'I confess that, since the Institute accepted the bounty offered it... I have felt for it a greatly diminished respect,' he wrote a few years later.[38]

Interestingly, as Coates also points out, the focus on creating an international court was in part a domestic strategy. US courts were heavily criticized for their conservatism at the time, as they resisted governmental relations in the name of property rights. There was a move by critics to recall US judges because of their alliance with businesses. Thus

[34] Ibid. 81. [35] Ibid. 66-85. [36] Ibid. 96. [37] Ibid. 97. [38] Ibid. 83.

when 'international lawyers embraced the "cult of the robe" in their arguments about courts, they implicitly defended the judiciary from its attackers'.[39]

Finally,

> The Endowment also aimed to further the judicialist vision by creating an entirely new institution: the Academy of International Law at The Hague…Scott spent $40,000 on its behalf (the greatest single contribution made by the Division of International Law), and insisted that it accord with his vision of international law. Specifically, he directed, it was 'to be an Academy in the scientific sense of the word' that could not 'ever become an organ of pacifism.' Neither should it promote a purely positivistic legal program.[40]

The limits of this alliance across the Atlantic, however, were also apparent with respect to the genesis of international law and justice at the time. Only the US partners had the power to mobilize the substantial political and economic resources required for the success of such a venture, and the continental professors found themselves in an awkward position, since US law practitioners imported their work in the US mainly for domestic purposes, to help provide legitimacy for the free trade aims of their clients along with legitimacy and stature to themselves.

More fundamentally, the US generally pursued a politics of withdrawal from international alliances after the First World War, and that affected the US side's willingness to further build alliances with Europe. The European professors were unable to rely on their own resources—consisting mainly of a still marginal academic capital and a dominated position within diplomatic arenas. As a result, they privileged a cautious strategy that essentially cantonized the institutions of The Hague, which they had developed with the support of American (and Russian) sponsors before 1914. They withdrew into the role of a small, learned, and cosmopolitan circle sustained by the support—at least financially and symbolically—of their US sponsors.[41]

The strategy of withdrawal into an ivory tower followed by European professors was also determined by the lack of opportunities for these European merchants of peace to act on the diplomatic or legal scene. The European professors, as compared to the gentlemen corporate lawyers in the US, were not at the top of their national academic and diplomatic fields. The worsening of the political and financial crisis in Europe throughout the 1920s (with the problems of hyper-inflation left by the overhang of war debts and reparations as well as the rise of Bolsheviks in Russia) accentuated the weakness—even impotence—of international forums for the handling of inter-state conflicts.

This very weak position was reinforced by an elitist and Malthusian strategy that limited access to European positions in international law to a small group of professor diplomats, expanded to include only a few learned practitioners who occupied diverse roles—which could be accumulated—including judge, lawyer, or producer of doctrine.[42] This peer group was able in this manner to accumulate the profits—which were essen-

[39] Ibid. 79. [40] Ibid. 84. [41] Koskenniemi (n. 18).
[42] See Sacriste and Vauchez (n. 18).

tially symbolic—of a small market while avoiding dissent, criticism, and even over-investment that might damage the weak credibility of their offerings and underline the impotence of what they were promoting in the face of growing political disorder. The result was that the Permanent Court—a key achievement of the alliance—served as a kind of virtual forum, barely visible outside of a few of the initiated who were making every effort to believe—and create the belief—that one day they would be able to contribute to the objectives of international peace as called for by the idealistic pronouncements of their founding fathers.

32.3.3 The transatlantic promotion of international commercial arbitration in the shadow of international justice

With respect to international commercial arbitration, the genesis—and more precisely the rebirth and relegitimation—varied in significant ways from the path of the institutions of The Hague. There were aspects of the same logic, however, and resultant similarities. Here too, in particular, there was a similar transatlantic strategy between lawyers and entrepreneurs on the US side building and borrowing European legal knowledge, with the results appearing above all in the different national legal fields. European law professors were not at the forefront, but there were pronounced links to the learned European law. The shadow of international justice helped also to provide credibility for international private justice.

As an example of the linkages, one of the lectures given in The Hague Academy of International Law in 1928, by Simon Rundstein, a member of the Committee of Experts of the League of Nations, was on 'L'arbitrage international en matière privée'.[43] Furthermore, as noted by Martin Domke in a 1957 retrospective, the notable international scholar Arthur Nussbaum, originally of the faculty of law in Berlin, was an enthusiast for international commercial arbitration as far back as 1912.[44] In 1918, he produced a draft arbitration law for Germany that was enacted into law. Later, in the 1920s, he produced *International Yearbooks on Civil and Commercial Arbitration*. The first yearbook was published in German in 1926 and translated into English by the American Arbitration Association. Nussbaum moved to Columbia in 1934, part of an exodus from Germany and Eastern Europe (including Louis Sohn and many others who wrote about arbitration) that helped to cement the transatlantic alliance. Another lecture at The Hague, this time in 1935, by Count Giorgio Balladore Pallieri, then a young professor who later in his career chaired the European Court of Human Rights, was on private arbitration in international relations.[45]

[43] S. Rundstein, 'L'arbitrage international en matière privée', 23 Recueil des cours 327 (1928).

[44] Martin Domke, 'Arthur Nussbaum: The Pioneer of International Commercial Arbitration', 57 Columbia Law Review 8 (1957).

[45] Giorgio Pallieri, 'L'arbitrage privé dans les rapports internationaux', 51 Recueil de cours 291 (1935).

The international space for commercial arbitration in the 1920s also provided important symbolic manifestations—including a cosmopolitan club that provided legitimacy and opportunities for US lawyers as well as a potential new market for legal scholars. That market included a number of international law scholars who advised not only states but also large state-connected companies, most notably oil companies, in their dealings with other states. The commercial arbitration arena maintained a relative porosity and openness that facilitated discrete alliances between the academic and business worlds—which also ultimately permitted professors to profit from their learning and their reputational capital.

The specific starting point for the (re)launch of international commercial arbitration was again a rapprochement between converging commercial and professional interests, on both sides of the Atlantic. The key promoters of these developments were business leaders (the Americans in particular) looking to mobilize their international capital to thwart the submission of merchant disputes—which in the past had often been kept or sought to be kept at the margin of the legal field—to judicial authorities (cf. the romance of the *lex mercatoria*). These recurring merchant efforts had historical highs and lows. At certain times the merchants, or more precisely their professional organizations and the relatively low-prestige legal practitioners who often were their representatives, succeeded in enlarging and gaining recognition for parajudicial practices such as arbitration; in other periods the reverse occurred and the judicial hierarchy reaffirmed its monopoly—and therefore that of the mainstream Bar—on the market for business disputes.

The late nineteenth century was a period of the restoration of the monopoly of the 'true' legal practitioners—both in the European countries and in the United States. Business lamented this turn to the judicial order, since it preferred arbitration by Chambers of Commerce—with the tacit recognition of the judicial order—as a means to manage the business conflicts of colonial and post-colonial history. It is in this context that the leaders of the US Chambers of Commerce, and especially the Chamber of Commerce of New York, sought to promote the creation in Paris of an International Chamber of Commerce in order to relaunch their campaign in favour of the statutory recognition of arbitration in the United States.

They sought to draw on the prestige and visibility of projects seeking to promote international arbitration as a means for handling inter-state conflicts. Riding this wave of public justice, they contended that this merchant justice would contribute to international peace in the same manner as the Permanent Court of Arbitration. They called themselves 'Merchants of Peace'.[46] They were strongly behind the establishment of the International Chamber of Commerce in 1920 in Paris, with its aspirations to promote international commercial arbitration, even though in fact the main strategy was to use international credibility to build domestic arbitration within the United States.[47]

[46] George Ridgeway, *Merchants of Peace* (Little, Brown, 1959).

[47] Ibid.; Imre Szalai, *Outsourcing Justice: The Rise of Modern Arbitration Laws in America* (Carolina Academic Press, 2013).

In this counter-offensive, they were able to obtain the public support of the elite of the corporate lawyer-statesmen. Elihu Root, the pillar of the corporate Bar, even co-signed a small brochure on the merits of commercial arbitration with a relatively small textile businessman, Charles Leopold Bernheim, then the leader of the US Chamber of Commerce in New York. Charles Evans Hughes, another elite corporate lawyer-statesman, signed on to the project. Owen D. Young, a business leader for General Electric, facilitated relations with the networks of the League of Nations. This counter-offensive rapidly produced effects in national spaces. The Federal Arbitration Act of 1925, which quickly followed the Geneva Protocol of 1923, reversed decades of judicial mistrust of arbitration. It allowed the enforcement of arbitration clauses in contracts that applied to disputes that emerged out of the contract.

There was a similar process in France and in most of continental Europe, where judges had been willing to enforce arbitration clauses only if entered into after the emergence of a commercial dispute and naming the arbitrators on which the parties agreed. Even when the restrictive conditions for arbitration were met, state courts still took the position that the courts could be invoked if one of the parties chose to do so. These restrictions led to the focus on international conventions as a potential solution. In France, nevertheless, the courts in 1921 recognized the enforcement of foreign arbitration awards, and the Geneva Protocol of 1923 recognized the validity of arbitration clauses for future disputes.[48]

In Great Britain, the situation was slightly different,[49] but there was also the same judicial hostility to arbitration characteristic of the era: 'From Coke, the soil of England never proved kindly to arbitration.'[50] The American commentators noted also that arbitration remained under the control of the elite practitioners, high judges, and QCs, who had imposed the rule that any commercial dispute, even if involving two foreign parties, was automatically governed by the common law. This imposition notably was also a tool and a product of the imperial hegemony of Britain—forcing disputes with foreigners into British legal terrain. Thus, it makes sense that the US entrepreneurs and lawyers would want to create something outside of British imperial reach.[51] It is also relevant that, except for routine disputes and those where the stakes were low, the parties had to resort to the very expensive services of a small number of barristers' chambers who monopolized the most lucrative commercial conflicts.

48 Ridgeway (n. 46). 49 Sgard (n. 1). 50 Gordon (n. 21).

51 Sgard makes this point even while suggesting that the hegemony did not work out, since New York did not gain dominance in arbitration. See Sgard (n. 1), 166: 'With hindsight, therefore, the emergence and expansion of international commercial arbitration in New York should have been a foretold story, one indeed of "hegemonic succession." Very soon when the industrial, financial and commercial centre of the world economy started to shift westward, private American interests showed increasing resistance to English practices and started to militate for a new and more progressive model of international market governance. The imperial dimension was however quite visible: in the future, it would be up to the Americans to organise and regulate markets, for themselves as for the rest of the world; and this would apply to capital markets, production standards, or the extra-territorial reach of domestic courts or arbitration laws.'

From this point of view, the signature of Great Britain to the Geneva protocol did nothing to change the situation of a market that was closed to American entrepreneurs and even more to their lawyers—and part of the imperial fabric of the British empire. The French, by contrast, never had far-reaching and centralized judicial institutions such as the Privy Council serving to legalize a trading empire—in part because of the reluctance of the French legal elite to become involved in trade and business. Trade disputes in the colonies were outside of the jurisdiction of the French Cour de Cassation. On the contrary, as shown below, the disdain shown by the elite of the Parisian Bar with respect to business helped make Paris open to foreign lawyers who were able to expand a kind of free harbour—where they could develop what we have called 'offshore litigation' on the basis of a heterogeneous alliance and a division of labour between the large law firms and a small group of continental professors and high court judges.[52]

The entrepreneurs of the Chamber of Commerce of New York—and their advisers—lacked the learned resources and social capital to permit them to gain recognition of the legitimacy of arbitration. They could not mobilize the combination of learned and political investment that was available for inter-state arbitration. The lawyer-statesmen who ostensibly supported them did not commit more than formal support, since the field of commercial arbitral practice was neither highly valued nor useful to their ambitions as men of state. Still, the success, even if limited, of the internationalization strategy of the jurist-diplomats gained the interest of their private law colleagues on the continent.

This interest was not based on economic motivations, since the market of international commercial arbitration was very much in its infancy, with an uncertain future except for the relatively small impact of this international recognition in domestic settings. Nevertheless, in the same way as their colleagues from public law, they sought to gain advantages from the opening of international spaces of exchange and circulation among the leaders of the business world, which was accompanied by a demand for rationalization, legitimation, and thus of learned investments, in order to valorize disciplines still in their infancy and still considered relatively marginal in the European faculties of law.[53]

The specific genesis of commercial arbitration was therefore in the shadow of the institutions of The Hague. It was a quasi-virtual institution, with symbolic capital related to international law and justice but serving mainly domestic objectives. Yet there was already some learned investment in international commercial arbitration, as evidenced by a number of lectures in The Hague already mentioned. The learned investment was not mainly from the elite of the professoriate. The leading names associated with international commercial arbitration in the period before and after the Second World War were a group of emigrants and Jews producing scholarly works that opened the way to arbitration to be adopted by the mainstream. The names included Frédéric Eisemann,

[52] Anne Boigeol and Yves Dezalay, 'De l'agent d'affaires au barreau. Les conseils juridiques et la construction d'un espace professionnel', 27 Genèses 53 (1997); Yves Dezalay and Bryant Garth, *Dealing in Virtue: International Commercial Arbitration and the Construction of a Transnational Legal Order* (University of Chicago Press, 1996).

[53] Sacriste (n. 7).

Charles Carabiber, Berthold Goldman, Martin Domke, Arthur Nussbaum, René David, and Hersch Lauterpacht.[54] They produced much of the work that could then be used to bring international commercial arbitration into the mainstream.

32.3.4 The rising importance of international commercial arbitration after the Second World War

Prior to the Great Depression and the Second World War, as we have seen, there were variations on an alliance between, on one side, US legal practitioners identified with Wall Street law firms, multinational corporations and banks, and philanthropic foundations, later termed the 'foreign policy establishment' in the United States,[55] and on the other side an emerging but still relatively marginal group of professors of law, many with some diplomatic ties as well, on the European continent. The practically virtual institutions that they supported on the international law and justice side of international arbitration and the commercial side of international arbitration stayed in place but hardly thrived—especially after the 1930s.[56] They gained energy after the Second World War, in part through the funding of the Ford Foundation as part of a Cold War strategy[57] and partly because of the US renewal of interest in commercial arbitration in the post-war period.[58]

The key events in the renewal and expansion of international commercial arbitration were crises associated with decolonization and the battles for the control of oil production in the period after the Second World War.[59] The oil companies known as the Seven Sisters—which included the Standard Oil Company created by John D. Rockefeller, British Petroleum, Texaco, and Royal Dutch Shell—had supported the movement toward expansion of global trade and investment, but there were important challenges to their power and their investments (for instance, when the US and British powers made a coup to restore the Shah in Iran after Mossadegh's 1951 decision to appropriate 51 per cent of the shares of the Anglo-Iranian oil company).

Oil nationalizations were symptomatic of the rise of nationalism and the erosion of the paternalistic relationship between the Seven Sisters oil companies and national leaders. The tensions led first to the nationalization of the Suez Canal (the main conduit for Middle East oil) in 1956, which was followed by the creation of OPEC, a cartel of oil

[54] See Sgard (n. 1) for profiles. [55] Dezalay and Garth (n. 19).

[56] With respect to the Permanent Court of Arbitration: 'All told, during the first seventy years of the PCA's existence, only twenty-five arbitrations were submitted to PCA tribunals, for a filing rate of 0.3 cases per year; even fewer nonbinding PCA conciliations or inquiries were conducted.' See Gary Born, 'A New Generation Of International Adjudication', 61 Duke Law Journal 775 (2012), 798. The ICC caseload was relatively light until the 1980s as well. There were 3,000 requests for arbitration between 1923 and 1976 and then 7,000 more between 1976 and 1998. See Lawrence Craig, William Park, and Jan Paulson, *International Chamber of Commerce Arbitration*, 3rd edn (Oceana, 2000).

[57] Giles Scott-Smith, 'Attempting to Secure an "Orderly Evolution": American Foundations, the Hague Academy of International Law, and the Third World', 41 Journal of American Studies 507 (2007).

[58] Sgard (n. 1). [59] Dezalay and Garth (n. 52).

producers modelled on the way that Texas controlled the supply and price of oil. OPEC remained dormant for ten years, but it suddenly woke up in 1973, when it was able to increase the price of oil dramatically—this decision followed Nixon's decision to let the US dollar float (and decline, which automatically led to the decline in the price of the oil barrel) and Nixon's military support of Israel in the 1973 war.

After 1973, the stakes over the control of oil profits therefore rose dramatically. But histories of the oil industry typically do not even mention law or lawyers.[60] Oil companies whose positions were threatened by nationalizations lined up the support of their home countries, and both groups invested substantial resources into rebuilding the prior lucrative positions. For most analysts, law was not at the core of the response to the crises. Managers and lawyers of the oil industry used diplomacy, the threat of gunboats, and personal relationships to respond to the nationalizations and other attacks on their position, and for the most part they were successful in maintaining their role in the production and distribution of petroleum resources.

If we pay closer attention to the role of law and lawyers in the reorganization of the oil industry that followed from the first shock of 1973, however, we realize that lawyer-entrepreneurs took advantage of the situation. The longstanding concession agreements entered into between the oil companies and the oil-producing states—most of which dated from the times of the League of Nations and its mandates—contained arbitration clauses that could be invoked. The clauses were inserted in the interwar period because of the perceived legitimacy of state–state arbitration and the role of international law experts who consulted with the large oil companies. The 1933 oil concession agreement creating the Anglo-Iranian Oil Company, for example, was drafted by Vladimar Idelson, a Russian lawyer who emigrated to England after the Russian Revolution and became a King's Counsel and international law expert.[61] He and Hersch Lauterpacht were the legal advisers to the oil company after Iran nationalized oil in 1951, and they sought to invoke the arbitration clause at that time. The arbitration clause had given appointment powers to the President of the Permanent Court of International Justice. An Iranian lawyer posited that these arbitrations involved a kind of law that in theory stood between public international law and national law.[62]

Other scholars in the 1950s, also in lectures at The Hague, examined related issues. F. Munch, a German professor of international law who began as a bank apprentice, studied abroad with a Carnegie fellowship, and served as a German delegate to the Law of the Sea negotiations in 1958, wrote, for example, on the effect of foreign nationalizations.[63] The Rt. Honorable Lord Shawcross—a barrister who served as chief prosecutor for the British at Nuremberg, was a Labour Member of Parliament, the British head of the International Committee of Jurists, and at the time of his lecture a lawyer for Royal Dutch Shell—delivered his lecture on the problems of foreign investment in international

[60] Daniel Yergin, *The Prize: The Epic Quest for Oil, Money, and Power* (Free Press, 1993).

[61] Elihu Lauterpacht, *The Life of Hersch Lauterpacht* (Cambridge University Press, 2012).

[62] Abolbashar Farmanfarma, 'The Oil Agreement between Iran and the International Oil Consortium: The Law Controlling', 34 Texas Law Review 259 (1955).

[63] F. Münch, 'Les effets d'une nationalisation à l'étranger', 98 Recueil des cours 411 (1959).

law.[64] These well-connected and scholarly individuals were definitely setting the stage for the use of arbitration to handle the disputes emerging through decolonization and a new relationship and set of potential North–South conflicts.

There were connections to the ICC as well among these learned and multi-faced individuals. Charles Carabiber, who lectured on the evolution of international commercial arbitration in 1950, was originally from Istanbul, studied there and in Paris, became a professor in Paris and an avocat at the Cour d'Appel, was adviser to the Iranian government, and was also the President of the Court of Arbitration of the ICC. When the ICC took the lead in seeking to advance international commercial arbitration with a convention on the enforcement of awards, which became the New York Convention of 1958, academics were also strongly present in the negotiations—including Pieter Sanders, a lawyer, diplomat, professor, and art collector from Rotterdam; Mario Matteucci, the director of the League of Nations Institute for the Unification of Private Law in Rome and a prestigious academic 'of highest international standing'; Benjamin Wortley, a professor of commercial law in Manchester, England; Conseiller d'État Georges Holleaux, 'a French academic in the best sense of the word, the very picture of the elegant Senior French Legal Officer, who was joined by Rene Arnaud, a true product of one of the French elite schools, a practitioner economist, and the co-founder of the ICC in 1918'; and others including Martin Domke of the American Arbitration Association.[65]

Domke was the major promoter of international commercial arbitration within the AAA in the United States until his retirement in 1967. He was a German-trained lawyer who went to the United States in 1943 and began a long career with the American Arbitration Association as Vice President.[66] Domke wrote much on domestic US arbitration, but he also sought to build up the prestige of AAA arbitration by linking arbitration to international law professors and international commercial arbitration associated with the ICC. The US arbitration movement, with close ties to the business community, built a strong alliance with European law professors to promote international commercial arbitration. The success of the New York Convention in 1958, which considerably enhanced the enforceability of international commercial arbitration, was a product of this alliance.[67]

[64] Lord Shawcross, 'The Problems of Foreign Investment in International Law', 102 Recueil des cours 335 (1961).

[65] Ottarndt Glossner, 'From New York (1958) to Geneva (1961): A Veteran's Diary', in Ottarndt Glossner, *The New York Convention: Experience and Future* (United Nations, 1999).

[66] Pieter Sanders (ed.), *International Arbitration: Liber Amicorum for Martin Domke* (Nijhoff, 1967).

[67] Hale notes that this was not the result simply of a rational demand by business interest: 'Although the initial impetus to revisit the international law on arbitration did originate with the ICC, it cannot be said to have represented the kind of groundswell of support in the business community that the cause of arbitration enjoyed in the 1920s. Instead, it was nurtured by the arbitration epistemic community around the ICC, legalistic in orientation, that had developed over the interwar period.' See Thomas Hale, *Between Interests and Law: The Politics of International Commercial Disputes* (Cambridge University Press, 2015), 152. Further, the US ratification of the Convention in 1970 also came from the legal networks, including the American Bar Association and the American Society of International Law (p. 221).

In the 1970s, according to our interviewees,[68] the oil companies chose to invoke the arbitration clauses as one additional option in the battle over the appropriation of economic profits with oil-producing states, but arbitration was very much a sideshow. Thus, they paid very little attention to the processes of arbitration, since they believed that the key to their claims remained in the hands of diplomatic and commercial negotiators.

The ties of the ICC group to the oil industry, as best one can tell, were not then very strong outside of relatively few international law professors who consulted with the oil companies; but these individuals were brought into the arbitrations and provided with what to them amounted to essentially unlimited resources. By the 1960s, as noted above, drawing in fact on the oil concession agreements existing from the 1930s, they had already produced a body of legal scholarship that could provide some of the raw material necessary to equip the field. In addition to the connections mentioned above, including Caribiber's relationship with Iran, other clear ties included Goldman 1963 (referring to oil arbitrations); Lalive 1967 (mentions that he was secretary in oil arbitrations); El-Kosheri 1975 (mentioning that he represented Kuwait).

This group included professors from the North and their students from the South, such as El-Kosheri, who were also ready to see the virtues of arbitrations that would involve their mentors and likely also themselves.[69] By 1972, Werner Goldschmidt, an international professor who resumed his career in Argentina after fleeing Germany, demonstrated the scholarly legalization of the field when he lectured at The Hague on international arbitration with such categories as 'trialistic ontology' and 'dikelogical juristic'.[70]

Partly because it was a sideshow, the arbitration lawyers on both sides were able to treat the legal disputes as epic legal battles involving grand legal principles exemplified in the Hague lectures. Lawyers in the nationalization cases developed highly formal legal arguments while the actual resolutions of the disputes proceeded by other means. The result was a series of closely reasoned arbitral opinions that have long been the staple of international law courses. They had virtually no practical impact at the time, but here as elsewhere, that lack of practical impact allowed the field to develop initially. Legal capital accumulated through the initial investments, and then later, through the outpouring of scholarship promoting, rationalizing, and elaborating the jurisprudence of the arbitration cases—and indeed making the cases central to casebooks. Those with key positions in the cases gained stature and credibility, and the combination of factors jump-started this transnational legal field and put it into a perfect position to take advantage of the disputes that then emerged in the 1970s and 1980s as petrodollars and Eurodollars were invested in major infrastructure projects leading to major arbitrations.

The oil crises, in short, provided the initial funding and credibility to a group of self-proclaimed amateurs and hobbyists who then became the backbone of what became the international commercial arbitration industry in the 1980s. They enhanced the

[68] Dezalay and Garth (n. 52). [69] Ibid. 86–7.

[70] W. Goldschmidt, 'Transactions between States and Public Firms and Foreign Private Firms: A Methodological Study', 136 Recueil des cours 203 (1972).

credibility of European law and the European law professors linked to the ICC. They made it clear that the *lex mercatoria* would serve the interests of multinational corporations, but that there was also a certain autonomy that could be emphasized by professors in the south and others anxious to participate in this field.[71] The division of labour between the 'grand old men'—mainly the European law professors but also some professors from the South—and what could be called the 'grand law firms' was a key to the success of this mode of handling commercial disputes. It is also this alliance between professionals that occupy opposing positions—as much through the very different legal traditions in which their careers are inscribed as the specific positions that they occupy in their national fields as producers of legal learning on one side and business lawyers on the other—that paradoxically explains the success of this hybrid form of international justice.

32.3.5 Petro-dollars and the routinization of international commercial arbitration

The legitimacy of international commercial arbitration—like other legal fields, such as human rights law[72]—remained relatively weak at the initial stages, when it involved some combination of idealistic European international scholarship, relatively marginal to national fields of economic and political power, and US political and economic capital. But it emerged in a strong position in the 1980s after a period of crisis-generated investment in the 1970s.

The relative success in institutionalization with respect to arbitration, coupled with the passage of time, brought a degree of routinization. Institutions such as the ICC became naturalized and decontextualized such that the particular crises and political and economic configurations that produced them initially became obscured. Instead of appearing as the product of particular strategies and configurations of interests, such as those at play in the Cold War or the oil crisis, the semi-autonomous field and its institutions came to appear much more neutral and universal. The field of international commercial arbitration in the 1960s and 1970s worked out a set of rules to enforce oil concessions against sovereign states. As noted above, the rules had little impact at the time they were developed.

But when arbitration took off in the 1980s, the so-called *lex mercatoria* developed by continental arbitrators provided a legally principled manner to treat multinational agreements with sovereign states in the Middle East and Africa as if they were private contracts. The circumstances of the genesis were by then mostly obscured. Legal doctrines, furthermore, are taught as such in the law schools, sustained and further formalized through legal scholarship, used to resolve disputes, and in general legitimated and taken for granted—treated as simply the law. As a result, the fields developed some

71 Hale (n. 67).

72 For some comparison of the two fields, see Dezalay and Garth (n. 5).

distance from the specific interests evident at the inception and embedded in the structures of the field.

Two further developments merit attention with respect to the routinization of international commercial arbitration. One key dimension was the effort to put pressure on London as a site for international commercial arbitration in which the US law firms could operate. As noted before, the alliance between the Europeans and the US corporate lawyers related to the effort of the US to shape the rules of the game of governance to those favouring US technologies and approaches. Offshore litigation served US clients and lawyers well, and they also were familiar with the concept of forum shopping through experience with the complex federal court system in the United States.

The move to open up London as a centre for international commercial arbitration was the product of an alliance in the late 1970s among British solicitors who, through participation in the oil arbitrations, could see that 'there was serious money to be made in litigation and arbitration'; US lawyers already in London emphasizing the growth of lucrative international commercial arbitration in France and Switzerland, where the courts did not interfere as much as in London; and a few individuals such as Lord Wilberforce who 'were already drawn to the ICC in Paris.[73] The result was both legislation making London a more desirable site for arbitration and innovations in the London Commercial Court that drew on international commercial arbitration. London became a much stronger competitor with Paris and Switzerland. Other centres repeated similar processes to foster competition and forum shopping to a much greater extent.

The second development relates to this proliferation of forums and sites. Through a process involving locals involved in transnational networks, conferences, and co-optation, the field of international commercial arbitration gained institutionalization in places where arbitration had been marginal or rejected, including Latin America[74] and China.[75] The field of arbitration gradually extended into new markets of disputes, and in geographical reach. International commercial arbitration therefore facilitated the relatively easy conversion of various forms of capital into arbitration, making for a relatively smooth expansion from North–South disputes to transnational contracts generally, and to new markets, such as Latin America, that had once been hostile to international arbitration. Each expansion brought new capital and subtle adjustments in the doctrine and approaches—while at the same time reinforcing the value of the core of the field.

In particular, high barriers to entry to become an arbitrator allowed the gradual co-optation of national legal notables who could provide the credibility to gain the support of the national court systems. The local notables in turn invested in the legal capital connected to international commercial arbitration as a condition of entry, again reinforcing the core while extending the field to cover new terrain. And while the local notables gained a place, the terms of exchange were quite unequal. Those at the periphery had to erase much of their local identity to be taken seriously as neutrals, while those at the core were assumed to be neutral. And those at the periphery helped also to provide the local

[73] Dezalay and Garth (n. 52), 135–6.

[74] Hale (n. 67), 299–309 on Argentinian networks.

[75] Ibid. 348–9.

legitimacy for the inner group of the arbitration 'mafia' to handle the largest and most important disputes.

Finally, the field of international commercial arbitration continues to develop. The tremendous increase in investor–state arbitration in the past fifteen years has produced a strong critical literature.[76] Critics argue that the interests of states in health and safety are neglected by arbitrators too closely tied to corporate interests and rigid contractual interpretation. At the same time, corporate law firms have begun to move increasingly into public international law along with private economic law.[77] They have continued in this way to multiply the forums that they can invoke to represent their clients—now including the proliferation of international courts. Recognizing the threat to the legitimacy of international commercial arbitration of investment arbitration seen as too pro-corporate, in addition, a number of insiders have worked to expand the group and the perspective by including more individuals with backgrounds in public international law. The field continues to thrive through this process of adaption through capital absorption.

32.6 Conclusion

This relatively strong entrenchment of international commercial arbitration came not through any single transnational institutional structure, but rather through a multiplicity of forums following the same business model. It is a strength that comes from weak links, with a highly flexible set of institutions that structure an internationalized market of legal expertise, and a very flexible use of concepts and doctrines. That market allows national legal notables to accumulate or diversify their own portfolios by exchanging their respective forms of national capital. The local impact is therefore relatively limited. There is a spill-over into national settings, but it is segmented in the way that there used to be colonial courts in Shanghai or Cairo. It is a Western justice—offshore 'litigociation' handled by corporate law firms—with a few local characteristics.

In sum, the alliances that we saw in the 1920s continued and thrived in the period following the Second World War, leading to important transnational developments in international justice and in private arbitral justice. Indeed, the transnational circulation of agents and resources that were exemplified by the moves, for example, of Lauterpacht and Lalive, moving between The Hague and international arbitration, continues. International legal practices are continuously used as spaces of strategic exchange and coalitions between specific fractions of different national fields.

[76] Cecilia Olivet and Pia Eberhardt, 'Profiting from Injustice: Challenging the Investment Arbitration Industry' (2013): <https://www.opendemocracy.net/cecilia-olivet-pia-eberhardt/profiting-from-injustice-challenging-investment-arbitration-industry>.

[77] Sara Dezalay and Yves Dezalay, 'Professionals of International Justice: From the Shadow of State Diplomacy to the Pull of the Market in Arbitration', SSRN (2016).

CHAPTER 33

THE CREATION OF INVESTOR–STATE ARBITRATION

TAYLOR ST JOHN

33.1 Introduction

Is investor–state arbitration a radical departure from earlier mechanisms for resolving disputes between foreign investors and states? On one hand, the first investment treaty arbitration was decided in 1990[1] and was 'dramatically different from anything previously known in the international sphere.'[2] On the other hand, scholars convincingly present investor–state arbitration as a direct descendant of legal practices in previous centuries, including unequal treaties and empire[3] as well as eighteenth- and nineteenth-century mixed claims commissions.[4] Scholars even show that individual arbitrations between a foreign investor and a host state in the nineteenth century have a 'strikingly modern character'.[5] Other scholars emphasize more immediate inspirations.[6]

[1] *Asian Agricultural Products Ltd (AAPL) v Republic of Sri Lanka*, ICSID Case No. ARB/87/3, Final Award (27 June 1990).

[2] Jan Paulsson, 'Arbitration Without Privity', 10 ICSID Review–FILJ 232 (1995).

[3] Kate Miles, *The Origins of International Investment Law: Empire, Environment, and the Safeguarding of Capital* (Cambridge University Press, 2013).

[4] Heather Bray, 'Understanding Change: Evolution from International Claims Commissions to Investment Treaty Arbitration', in Stephan Schill, Christian Tams, and Rainer Hofmann (eds), *International Investment Law and History* (Edward Elgar, 2018), 102.

[5] Jason Webb Yackee, 'The First Investor–State Arbitration: *The Suez Canal Company v Egypt*', 17 Journal of World Investment & Trade 401 (2016).

[6] E.g. in his history of ICSID, Parra notes World Bank mediations of investor–state disputes in the 1950s. Antonio Parra, *The History of ICSID*, 2nd edn (Oxford University Press, 2017). See also Sergio Puig, 'Emergence and Dynamism in International Organizations: ICSID, Investor–State Arbitration and International Investment Law', 44 Georgetown Journal of International Law 531 (2013).

There is no shortage of antecedents for investor–state arbitration. So why is it perceived as 'dramatically different' from what had gone before? In the second half of the twentieth century, consent to investor–state arbitration was provided prospectively (before disputes arose) and pursuant to generalized jurisdiction (for any treaty breach); this is profoundly different from previous practices.[7] Two institutional developments were crucial for creating prospective, generalized consent. First, the ICSID Convention emerged.[8] Second, provisions providing consent to investor–state arbitration were added to investment treaties. This chapter focuses on these two developments. It reconstructs the choices that officials faced, their constraints, and the reasons why they made the choice for investor–state arbitration against other alternatives. To do so, it uses primary documents from five archives: the American, British, German, and Swiss national archives as well as the World Bank archives.[9]

Section 33.2 discusses the world's first bilateral investment treaties (BITs), which were negotiated by the Federal Republic of Germany and Switzerland. These treaties did not include investor–state arbitration, despite discussions within both governments about including this form of arbitration in their treaties.

Section 33.3 introduces three multilateral institutions that were proposed while those first BITs were being signed in the 1960s: a substantive code, investment insurance, and an arbitration convention. Officials from capital-exporting countries discussed and compared these three proposals in intergovernmental settings, especially within the Organisation for Economic Co-operation and Development (OECD). The Code, widely known as the Abs–Shawcross Draft, was doomed from the start: the UK could not obey its standards, the US opposed it, and the Draft even lost its main supporters, Germany and Switzerland, after they realized they could negotiate higher standards of investment protection bilaterally. Insurance, in contrast, had strong support from governments and from investors. Puzzlingly, insurance did not emerge in the 1960s. Instead, it was only the third option, a stand-alone arbitration convention, that emerged.

Section 33.4 examines the steps that World Bank officials took to draft and disseminate this arbitration convention. World Bank General Counsel Aron Broches, observing the floundering Abs–Shawcross Draft, decided that its dispute resolution provisions could be isolated and sponsored by the World Bank as a separate convention. He believed this convention, the ICSID Convention, could be framed in a way that would appeal to both capital-importing and capital-exporting states. He also designed a new procedure

[7] Joost Pauwelyn, 'At the Edge of Chaos? Foreign Investment Law as a Complex Adaptive System, How It Emerged and How It Can Be Reformed', 29 ICSID Review–FILJ 372 (2013), 402.

[8] Convention on the Settlement of Investment Disputes Between States and Nationals of Other States, (opened for signature 18 March 1965), 575 UNTS 159 ('ICSID Convention').

[9] Archival documents cited here are available for download from the Qualitative Data Repository. Taylor St John, 'The Rise of Investor–State Arbitration' (Qualitative Data Repository, 16 March 2018): <https://doi.org/10.5064/F6UMRNAC>, accessed 1 June 2019. This chapter's analysis of these documents draws on Taylor St John, *The Rise of Investor–State Arbitration: Politics, Law, and Unintended Consequences* (Oxford University Press, 2018).

for introducing the convention to states, which foreclosed the possibility of intergovernmental deliberation, thus preventing disagreements from derailing the convention.

When the ICSID Convention came into force, it created a secretariat, and Broches became Secretary-General. This Secretariat drafted model clauses that showed states how to provide consent to investor–state arbitration in their investment treaties. Then Broches and other World Bank officials travelled with these clauses and discussed the idea of treaty-based consent with government officials. After these discussions, certain governments began adding consent to investor–state arbitration into their investment treaties. These developments are discussed in Section 33.5, which, framed provocatively, probes whether investment treaties would have included investor–state arbitration without the strong encouragement of Broches and the World Bank.

Section 33.6 concludes and discusses unintended consequences. It suggests that many of the main contours of contemporary investor–state arbitration, including a large treaty-based caseload, would not surprise officials who were heavily involved in the 1960s. Yet, due to the absence of intergovernmental deliberation and then the decentralized manner in which investor–state arbitration spread, expectations were not widely shared.

33.2 Early Bilateral Investment Treaties excluded investor–state arbitration

Providing access to investor–state arbitration is 'the real innovation' of BITs.[10] Yet BITs and investor–state arbitration emerged separately; early investment treaties did not include access to investor–state arbitration.

In 1959, the world's first BIT was signed between the Federal Republic of Germany and Pakistan. When drafting the model treaty that would be used in these negotiations, the German government considered investor–state arbitration and rejected it. In February 1959, a senior German official made notes about Article 8 of the draft BIT (which provided 'access to the International Court of Justice (ICJ) or an ad hoc arbitration tribunal') after meeting with a lawyer named Paul Krebs. The official noted, 'Dr Krebs deemed it to be essential that this access is not only open for states, but also particularly for private persons in the event of opinion disputes about the interpretation or application of the treaty under international law.'[11] A month later, in his formal minutes

[10] Franck observes: 'the real innovation of BITs was the provision of procedural rights that gave investors a mechanism to enforce the substantive rights directly.' Susan Franck, 'Foreign Direct Investment, Investment Treaty Arbitration and the Rule of Law', 19 McGeorge Global Business and Development Law Journal 337 (2007), 343.

[11] 'Entwurf einer Mustervereinbarung über Kapitalanlagen vom 2.2.1959' (Draft model on investments of 2 February 1959); 'Stellungnahme von Bankdirektor Dr Krebs zu dem Entwurf einer Mustervereinbarung' (statement by Bank Director Dr Krebs on the Draft Model Agreement), DE B102/27082.

about the BIT blueprint, the same official wrote: 'The wish of Dr Krebs to enable private individuals to appeal to arbitration judges cannot be satisfied.'[12] From this official's notes, the reason why the German government could not implement Krebs' wish was that individuals did not have standing before the ICJ. In other discussions, other reasons not to include arbitration were mentioned, including that German investors did not care about arbitration: when surveyed by the ICC in 1962, no German firms responded that the investment climate would be improved by the creation of an arbitration tribunal.[13] German officials were also afraid investor–state arbitration would politicize investment disputes.[14]

It is not a coincidence that the most influential proposals for investment protection, and the most nuanced discussions of those proposals, occurred in the Federal Republic of Germany. Every German investor or official working in the 1950s had lived through large-scale expropriations undertaken by the Reich government, hundreds of post-war restitution trials, and American, British, and Soviet expropriations of German-owned property during and after the Second World War. The central individual advancing investment protection in the Federal Republic was Hermann Josef Abs, a banker who was arguably the most experienced person in the world with regard to expropriation, with unparalleled personal experience as expropriator and as expropriatee.[15] He spearheaded the drafting of what was initially known as the 'Abs Draft' which became the Abs–Shawcross and later the OECD Draft, discussed in the next section. Many examples in the Abs Draft are European or American expropriations and many are indirect expropriations;[16] In 1954, Abs had led a mission to Washington seeking compensation for German property seized in the US,[17] despite having been 'blasted' as a 'known Nazi' on the floor of the US Senate.[18] This context is relevant for the German BIT. Paul Krebs, the lawyer who suggested individual standing in German BITs, was Abs's deputy, and his comments drew from the Abs Draft, which provides both states and individuals

[12] 'Aufzeichnung über die Hausbesprechung' (Record of the Internal Discussion), 11 March 1959, DE B102/27082.

[13] Internal Note from Dr Berger, 8 March 1962, subject: 'Vermittlungs- und Schiedsgerichtstätigkeit unter dem Schutze der Weltbank' (Mediation and Arbitration Activities under the Protection of the World Bank), DE B102/48464.

[14] Citing a German archival document, Poulsen observes that the German government feared investor–state arbitration could 'politicize investment disputes by turning "every case of expropriation into an international litigation with political relevance"'. Lauge Skovgaard Poulsen, *Bounded Rationality and Economic Diplomacy: The Politics of Investment Treaties in Developing Countries* (Cambridge University Press, 2015), 52–3.

[15] Among his many involvements, Abs was the central figure in Deutsche Bank's expropriation of Jewish property during the Second World War. Harold James, *The Deutsche Bank and the Nazi Economic War against the Jews: The Expropriation of Jewish-Owned Property* (Cambridge University Press, 2001) vii, 217. On Abs generally, see Lothar Gall, *Der Bankier Hermann Josef Abs: Eine Biographie* (Beck, 2005).

[16] Proposed International Convention for the Protection of Foreign Investors, UK T 236/5429.

[17] Letter from Ministerialdirektor Dr Berger to Botschafter Dr Heinz Krekeler, 30 December 1954, IFZ ED 135/45.

[18] Letter from Heinz L. Krekeler to Herr Ministerialdirektor Dr Löns, 17 December 1954, IFZ ED 135/45.

with standing in front of an international court for questions of law,[19] and an arbitration tribunal for compensation questions or lesser disputes.[20]

Abs did not directly influence German treaties, however; German economic diplomacy was characterized by a studied avoidance of assertiveness in the 1950s, and officials held Abs at a careful distance when considering their options. Their discussions provide useful perspective on how investor–state arbitration was perceived before the World Bank's framing of the ICSID Convention. First, German (and Swiss) officials connected investor–state arbitration and treaties when drafting the first model BITs.[21] Even in 1962, before any drafts of the ICSID Convention had been released, German officials told World Bank officials who raised the idea of ICSID that 'the arbitration court would constitute a valuable complement of the bilateral investment treaties'.[22] Yet before the World Bank drafted model clauses for BITs, no government mentioned investor–state arbitration in their treaties, as discussed later.

Second, for German officials, arbitration, insurance, and state pressure were all complementary. In April 1958, German officials noted that providing investors with access to arbitration would ease the burden on the diplomatic service. At the same time, these officials argued that in certain instances, the full weight of the German government might be needed in order to get compensation.[23] A newspaper article on the new German model BIT, written in June 1959, trumpets that insurance guarantees put the full weight of the German government behind the investor, observing that the treaty's 'most striking feature is that the partner country recognizes the federal government as the legal successor of the investors in disputes. Hence, in a situation of guarantee, the government can punch its entire political and moral weight in order to enforce the claims of the Federal Republic.'[24] The article then observes that these efforts go hand in hand with individual standing in the Abs Draft, and that government officials believe these two plans complement each other harmoniously.[25] The rhetoric that providing

[19] Art. X(1), International Convention for the Mutual Protection of Private Property in Foreign Countries 1957, UK T 236/5429.

[20] Art. X(2), International Convention for the Mutual Protection of Private Property in Foreign Countries 1957, UK T 236/5429.

[21] Switzerland is not discussed here, but in consultations between the Swiss government and industry groups, it is clear that industry group representatives understood the connection between BITs and investor–state arbitration. 'Compte rendu de la réunion du 12 octobre 1966 consacrée à un échange de vues sur la Convention pour le règlement des différends relatifs aux investissements entre Etats et ressortissants d'autres états' (Minutes of the meeting held 12 October 1966 to exchange views on the Convention on the Settlement of Investment Disputes between states' and nationals of other states), Bern, 17 October 1966, CH C.41.124.5.1 (64–7).

[22] 'Besuch von Weltbank-Präsident Black am 17. Januar 1962' (Visit of World Bank President Black, 17 January 1962), DE B102/48464.

[23] 'Übersicht über die wichtigsten Grundsätze in dem Entwurf einer Internationalen Konvention zum gegenseitigen Schutz privater Vermögensrechte im Ausland' (Overview of the main principles in the draft International Convention on the Mutual Protection of Private Property Abroad), 25 April 1958, DE B102/130141.

[24] 'Verträge zum Schutz von Auslandsanlagen' (Contracts for the Protection of Foreign Investment), Handelsblatt, No. 78, 2 June 1959, DE B102/27082.

[25] 'Verträge zum Schutz von Auslandsanlagen' (Contracts for the Protection of Foreign Investment), Handelsblatt, No. 78, 2 June 1959, DE B102/27082.

investors with access to arbitration replaces home state pressure, or 'depoliticizes', investor–state disputes emerged later, with the World Bank's framing.

33.3 Three proposed institutions for investment protection: a code, insurance, or an arbitration convention

During the first decade in which BITs were negotiated, officials in capital-exporting governments also discussed three options for multilateral investment protection: a substantive code; an investment insurance organization; and a convention on investor–state arbitration. Officials discussed all three proposals in the same fora, primarily the OECD and World Bank, and often compared the three options. In 1969, British officials heading to the Annual Meetings of the International Monetary Fund and World Bank were instructed as follows: 'We support the ICSID, have strong reservations about the [World Bank] draft Agreement for an International Investment Insurance Agency and regard the potentially useful O.E.C.D. draft Convention for the Protection of Foreign Property as a dead duck.'[26] A memo for American officials headed to the OECD Ministerial meeting in 1966 explains: 'Encouraging assistance from the private sector... is the basis for our interest in the OECD Draft Convention on the protection of private property, the proposed Multilateral Investment Guarantee Corporation and the recently established World Bank Center for the settlement of investment disputes.'[27] This section examines the two proposals that did not emerge during the 1960s, for a code and an insurance organization.

33.3.1 The code

The OECD Draft Convention on the Protection of Foreign Property is an intergovernmental, modified version of the Abs–Shawcross Draft, which was itself a modified version of the Abs Draft, as noted above.[28] While the idea of a single multilateral treaty setting out substantive standards, with a single court to interpret these standards, is intuitively appealing, at no point did this Draft Convention secure widespread support from governments in the ten years it was discussed (1956–66).

[26] 'I.M.F./I.B.R.D. Twenty-Second Annual Meeting, Settlement of Investment Disputes: Investment Insurance and Protection', brief by the Treasury, UK FCO 48/145.

[27] 'Encouraging Assistance from Private Sector', drafted by Peter F. Geithner for the OECD Ministerial Meeting, Paris, 24–5 November 1966, US 595219 Box 4.

[28] Schwarzenberger wrote of a 'toned-down' version. Georg Schwarzenberger, *Foreign Investments and International Law* (Stevens & Sons, 1969), 153.

Disagreements within the OECD were present from the start of talks. The German government did not sponsor the initial Abs Draft; they were careful to merely suggest it, as a private document, and German officials were told to adopt an attitude of 'benevolent distance' when it was deliberated.[29] Early American opposition was unequivocal: the American government stated that drafting the convention without developing country participation would hand them 'a fait accompli and imply an element of coercion'.[30] The British government was also opposed, since the UK could not participate in any endeavour that officials believed might facilitate outward investment, due to the UK's balance of payment difficulties, and since the British government did not believe it could comply with several standards in the draft.[31] Finally, the British government had grave concerns about their ability to participate in 'provisions for the reference to international arbitration of disputes over compensation paid on… foreign-owned rights or property'.[32]

The slow death of the OECD Draft began in earnest when European governments realized they could get stronger investment law standards in BITs. The evolution of the Swiss position between 1962 and 1963 illustrates this learning process. In a November 1962 speech, the main Swiss official responsible for investment protection observed that Switzerland generally preferred multilateral initiatives, but if enough BITs had been signed then a multilateral solution might become redundant.[33] By March 1963, the government position had changed: Swiss officials agreed that no action should be taken to promote the Draft, and instead they should intensify their efforts to conclude BITs.[34] In September 1963, the main official wrote that the OECD Convention is, on the one hand, the maximum possible for a multinational convention but, on the other, the minimum possible in BITs.[35] By November 1963, that Swiss official was arguing that the government should not promote the OECD Draft because it would necessarily include compromises, and these compromises would weaken the Swiss bargaining position in BIT

[29] Minutes of a meeting with Dr Krebs, 20 March 1958: 'Entwurf einer internationalen Konvention zum gegenseitigen Schutz privater Vermögensrechte im Ausland' (Draft International Convention on the Protection of Private Investment Abroad), DE B102/130141.

[30] Position paper for the OECD Ministerial Meeting, Paris, 16–17 November 1961, Convention on Protection of Foreign Property, US 595219 Box 2.

[31] 'The United Kingdom itself would in all likelihood find difficulty in two particular respects in subscribing to even the less ambitious of the various draft conventions… First, there would be the difficulty of accepting provisions at variance with our Exchange Control policy.' Anglo-German Economic Committee, Sixth Session, London, July 1958, Protection of Foreign Investors, UK T 236/5436. See also Appendix: Protection of Foreign Investments, Exchange Control Aspects of the Swiss and German Draft Conventions, July 1958, UK T 236/5436.

[32] Anglo-German Economic Committee, Sixth Session, London, July 1958, Protection of Foreign Investors, UK T 236/5436.

[33] 'Protection of Investments in International Law', by Dr E. Diez, Head of the Legal Service of the Swiss Foreign Office (US Government translation of a lecture delivered in German before the Swiss Society of International Law, Bern, 24 November 1962), CH C.41.124.5.2.

[34] Letter from Micheli to the Swiss Ambassador at the OECD, 25 March 1963, CH C.41.124.5.2.

[35] Internal note from Emanuel Diez, 23 September 1963, CH C 41.124.5.2.

negotiations.[36] In 1963, the largest capital-exporters (France, Germany, the UK, and the US) consulted developing country governments to see if they would sign the OECD Draft, or if they were more likely to sign bilateral investment treaties.[37]

By 1967, it was clear that bilateral treaties had outpaced the Draft Convention. Bowing to this reality, in 1967 the OECD Secretary-General described the Draft Convention as a model for BITs: he '[s]tressed Draft was only a model; [which] could be modified for use as bilateral treaty'.[38] By the late 1960s, it seemed that bilateral treaties were the way forward and that the Draft Convention was, as one British briefing note put it, 'dying a harmless though lingering death'.[39] While capital-exporting states were signing BITs with developing countries, they were still unable to agree within the OECD. Bargaining over the Draft Convention grew so rancorous by 1966 that it was uncertain if the OECD Council could pass even a non-binding resolution expressing support for the principles in the Draft. As the Austrian representative remarked, 'the lowest common denominator was not yet low enough'.[40] In its time, the OECD Draft was divisive.

33.3.2 The insurance

Unlike the proposal for a code, the proposal for multilateral investment insurance had widespread support from governments during the 1960s. In April 1964, the OECD prepared the 'key clauses of a convention which would set out the basis for a multilateral guaranty system'[41] and then, in June 1965, OECD governments formally instructed the World Bank to create an insurance agency on this basis.[42] Crucially, the US government supported proposals for multilateral insurance, in stark contrast to its initial stance on a multilateral code.[43] After a 1964 OECD meeting, Swiss officials noted:

> the group who wants to draft a system: Belgium, Netherlands, Italy, Denmark, the EEC [European Economic Community] Commission, and the US. Sensationally,

[36] Letter from Micheli to the Swiss Ambassador at the OECD, 25 March 1963, CH C.41.124.5.2.

[37] Information from the Haager Freundeskreis (Hague Circle of Friends), 'OECD Konvention: Reaktionen von Entwicklungsländern gemäß englischer und deutscherseits eingeholter Informationen' (OECD Convention: Reactions of Developing Countries According to English and German Information), included in letter from Robert Dunant to E. Diez, 8 July 1963, CH C.41.124.5.2.

[38] Telegram from AmEmbassy Paris to Secstate WashDC, 7 February 1967, 'Draft Convention Foreign Property', US 595219 Box 13.

[39] 'I.M.F./I.B.R.D. Twenty-Second Annual Meeting, Settlement of Investment Disputes: Investment Insurance and Protection', brief by the Treasury, UK FCO 48/145.

[40] Telegram from AmEmbassy Paris to Secstate WashDC, 17 February 1967, 'Draft Convention Protection Foreign Property', US 595219 Box 13.

[41] Background paper: 'Multilateral Investment Guarantees', OECD Ministerial Meeting, Paris, 19–20 November 1963, US 595219 Box 2.

[42] Background paper: 'Multilateral Investment Insurance Proposal and IBRD Arbitration Convention', OECD Ministerial Meeting, Paris, 24–5 November 1966, US 595219 Box 3.

[43] 'Our position is one of general support for the concept of a multilateral investment guaranty institution within the IBRD [International Bank for Reconstruction and Development] family embodying generally the principles of the OECD proposal.' Background paper (n. 42).

> the US delegate took the lead of this group and promoted the idea vocally and promised that the US would participate even though they have a national system in place.[44]

There was no opposition within the OECD; France and the UK were 'unenthusiastic, but have not come out in flat opposition.'[45] Their concerns were that multilateral insurance would cause their investors to demand a national system (France)[46] or that insurance was too effective at stimulating investment (the UK).[47] Insurance was widely seen as effective at facilitating investment, even by those who preferred other options.[48]

Multilateral insurance had strong supporters and faced little opposition, so why did it not emerge in the 1960s? One reason is that World Bank officials subtly discouraged insurance. In July 1960, the American government requested that the World Bank undertake 'a study of the feasibility of an investment guarantee program.'[49] The study was issued in March 1962, and its 'pessimistic' tone surprised governments.[50] Swiss officials, for instance, were surprised that the Bank's study found that a multilateral guarantee system would 'not trigger many new investments', as this ran counter to the widely shared view.[51] The World Bank report's pessimistic tone was additionally peculiar because the International Chamber of Commerce (ICC), which had collaborated with the World Bank in conducting the survey underlying the report, came to the opposite conclusion. In their report, the ICC 'came out strongly in support of the creation of a multilateral

[44] Letter from Montandon to the Trade Section of Economic Department, 30 April 1964, CH C.41.124.5.2.

[45] Background paper: 'Multilateral Investment Guarantees', OECD Ministerial Meeting, Paris, 19–20 November 1963, US 595219 Box 2.

[46] 'Only France was against the idea and that was because French industry would demand a national system and the French government cannot afford one since their investment is mostly in Africa, which is subject to African Nationalism.' Letter from Montandon to the Trade Section of Economic Department, 30 April 1964, CH C.41.124.5.2.

[47] 'While we do not oppose the scheme, we do not see ourselves as founder members of it, because we cannot in balance of payments terms afford the stimulus to investment that this scheme would provide.' 'I.M.F./I.B.R.D. Twenty-Second Annual Meeting, Settlement of Investment Disputes: Investment Insurance and Protection', brief by the Treasury, UK FCO 48/145.

[48] Hermann Abs, for instance, believed that investment insurance was effective at facilitating investment. 'When investors do go into such areas ["high-risk" countries] it is often because of state guarantees granted by their own governments,' he argued. Hermann Abs, 'The Safety of Capital', in James Daniel (ed.), *Private Investment: The Key to International Industrial Development. A Report of the San Francisco Conference, October 14–18, 1957* (McGraw-Hill, 1957), 72. Abs preferred a code and arbitration because he wanted the risk of expropriation to be shifted onto the shoulders of the countries receiving capital. Text of a speech by Hermann J. Abs, 'The Protection of Duly Acquired Rights in International Dealings as a European Duty: Reflections on the Development of the Suez Crisis', UK T 236/5429.

[49] Position paper on the Convention on Protection of Foreign Property, OECD Ministerial Meeting, Paris, 16–17 November 1961, US 595219 Box 2. Same reported in the German archives, letter from Dr Henckel (recipient unnamed): 'Anreise für Kapitalinvestitionen in Entwicklungsländern' (Trip regarding capital investment in developing countries), 14 August 1961, DE B102/47640.

[50] 'Bemerkungen zum Bericht der Weltbank über die multilaterale Investitionsgarantie' (Summary of the World Bank Report about a multilateral risk guarantee for investments), CH C41.124.5.2.

[51] Ibid.

insurance scheme'.[52] While World Bank officials discouraged and delayed action on insurance in the 1960s, they instead devoted resources to an arbitration convention.

33.4 The emergence of the ICSID Convention

The third option, a stand-alone multilateral arbitration convention, was 'in the air' in the 1960s, World Bank General Counsel Aron Broches would later remark.[53] The idea had been discussed in International Law Association meetings,[54] in American Bar Association committees, and of course, the Permanent Court of Arbitration could already administer investor–state arbitrations.[55] Yet it was World Bank officials, led by Broches, who had the political acumen and institutional resources to make this proposal into a reality. This section focuses on the steps that World Bank officials took to draft and disseminate the ICSID Convention. It emphasizes two points. First, the drafting of the ICSID Convention did not involve intergovernmental deliberation at any point. Second, there was strong leadership from World Bank officials at all stages of the process. Framed provocatively, this section asks: would the ICSID Convention have emerged without the strong leadership of Broches and the World Bank?

33.4.1 Consultations, not intergovernmental deliberations

Broches and the World Bank's management designed a novel procedure for the drafting of the ICSID Convention. First, the World Bank's Legal Department produced a complete draft, internally. Then World Bank officials met with Executive Directors and discussions were held about how the convention should be finalized. The idea of a diplomatic conference to negotiate the ICSID Convention was proposed repeatedly and discussed in meetings of the Executive Directors,[56] but rejected by the World Bank's

[52] EI Nwogugu, *The Legal Problems of Foreign Investment in Developing Countries* (Manchester University Press, 1965), 87, quoting ICC Doc. No. 111/114.

[53] Antonio Parra, 'Establishing ICSID: An Idea That Was "In the Air"' (OUP Blog, 8 September 2015): https://blog.oup.com/2015/09/history-of-icsid-law/, accessed 1 June 2019.

[54] Taylor St John and Yuliya Chernykh, 'Déjà vu? Investment Court Proposals from 1960 and Today' (EJIL: Talk!, 15 May 2018): https://www.ejiltalk.org/deja-vu-investment-court-proposals-from-1960-and-today/, accessed 1 June 2019.

[55] A fact the Permanent Court of Arbitration advertised in the late 1950s, which the British government raised during the creation of ICSID. Letter from Hester Boothroyd to Peter Reilly, 4 October 1961, UK T 312/251.

[56] E.g. one delegate 'felt... that an instrument of such significance ought to be discussed in a wider forum than that offered by a regional meeting'. International Centre for Settlement of Investment Disputes, *History of the Convention: Documents Concerning the Origin and the Formulation of the Convention in English*, vols 1 and 2, pts 1 and 2 (ICSID, 1970), 543.

management.[57] Yet the World Bank also knew it needed to match the representativeness of United Nations bodies, in which newly independent states had voice by the early 1960s.

The Bank's strategy was to invite experts from all member states, but keep all conferences and discussions consultative. First there were four consultative conferences in different regions of the world to introduce governments to the idea, followed by a three-week-long Legal Committee in Washington DC. Attendees were 'experts-designate' not representatives of their countries, and were expressing quasi-personal views.

33.4.2 The consultative roadshow

Between December 1963 and May 1964, the Bank's Legal Department, with help from the UN, convened four conferences in different regions of the world. As Broches explained:

> We hit on the idea of taking the show on the road to get comments from member countries, because we didn't get them through the Directors... I have to take credit for the idea of having four regional consultative meetings in the four capitals of the UN: Geneva, Santiago, Bangkok, and Addis Ababa. The Bank paid for up to two experts for one week–travel and subsistence... [these] representatives of countries were not really representing these countries, they were experts-designate.[58]

The four conferences were attended by experts from 86 countries. These experts-designate came from a mix of backgrounds: some were private lawyers, while others were professors, cabinet members, or elder statesmen who had attended Bretton Woods.[59] The Bank asked member states to prioritize legal expertise, even if that meant sending individuals who were not in government. States duly sent lawyers expert in procedure, not the individuals responsible for foreign investment policy-making. On the basis of the consultative conferences, the Bank's management believed that there would be enough support for the proposal to succeed, even though some countries would be opposed.[60]

[57] The World Bank President argued a diplomatic conference would 'unnecessarily delay and impede progress'. SID/64-3, quoted in ICSID (n. 56), 556. Parra (n. 6, 59–61) also notes this quote and discusses the ensuing meeting of the Executive Directors.

[58] Aron Broches, 'Oral History, Interview by Robert Asher' (World Bank Archives, Oral History Program, 23 May 1984), 38.

[59] E.g. this is how attendance at the Santiago conference was summarized for the Bank's board: 'Most of the delegates were lawyers, some of them of great distinction, like Mr [Guillermo] Sevilla Sacasa of Nicaragua [Ambassador to the US 1943–1979, second in succession to the President] and Mr Alfonso Espinoza of Venezuela [former Finance Minister, former President of the Central Bank, lawyer and economist by training] both veterans of Bretton Woods. Mr Roberto Ramirez, President of the Central Bank of Honduras and an old friend of the Bank, represented his country.' ICSID (n. 56), 365.

[60] Broches (n. 58), 39.

33.4.3 The 'No de Tokio' and the Legal Committee

At the 1964 Annual Meeting, the World Bank President discussed investment insurance, and then introduced investor–state arbitration as 'another approach [to facilitating foreign investment], which we have actively sponsored'.[61] He then asked the World Bank's Board of Governors to pass a resolution asking the Executive Directors to formulate a Convention on the Settlement of Investment Disputes.[62]

This resolution triggered a protest, known as the 'No de Tokio'. The Chilean Governor, Felix Ruiz, also Vice President of the Banco Central de Chile, acted as a spokesman for a group of 21 states, primarily but not exclusively Latin American, which opposed the proposal. After stating that the legal systems of all Latin Americans 'prohibit confiscation and discrimination' and require expropriation be accompanied by compensation, Ruiz focused on equality:

> The new system that has been suggested would give the foreign investor, by virtue of the fact that he is a foreigner, the right to sue a sovereign state outside its national territory, dispensing with the courts of law. This provision . . . would confer a privilege on the foreign investor, placing the nationals of the country concerned in a position of inferiority.[63]

As World Bank officials had expected, this show of opposition was not enough to derail the proposal. The resolution passed and the World Bank paid for each member state to send two experts-designate to Washington DC for three weeks in November–December 1964.

Broches opened the Legal Committee by closing off the possibility of debate on the idea of investor–state arbitration.[64] The experts-designate were there to give World Bank officials a sense of the likelihood that their governments could ratify, but were not formally representing their government's views. During the Legal Committee, as during the consultative conferences, the formal power to change the document remained with the Chair, Broches, and the World Bank. When experts-designate encountered an issue on which they disagreed, they would decide if they considered it important. If representatives felt the issue was not particularly essential, they would resolve it then and there with a show of hands. If the issue was felt to be important, it would be removed from the discussion and reported to the Executive Directors. Broches, who chaired the committee, later termed it a 'voting/non-voting system', and noted that it 'was pretty innovative' and 'worked pretty well'.[65] The system got things done. The drafting committee and remaining steps were handled efficiently: by 11 December 1964, Broches submitted a

[61] ICSID (n. 56), 605.

[62] World Bank, 'Annual Meetings of the Boards of Governors, Tokyo, 7–11 September' (World Bank, 1964), 34.

[63] ICSID (n. 56), 606.

[64] Broches said, 'The present meeting was no longer concerned with the question of the desirability of creating machinery for facilitating the settlement of investment disputes since that question had already been decided in the affirmative.' Ibid. 674.

[65] Broches (n. 58), 38–9.

Revised Draft of the ICSID Convention to the Executive Directors; then, in a series of meetings from February–March 1965, the Executive Directors discussed the Convention before approving a final version of the Convention on 18 March 1965.[66]

The World Bank's strategy to create ICSID was summarized in a November 1963 article in *The Washington Post*. Under a section titled 'Low-Key Approach', the article stated:

> Extended and enthusiastic public discussion of the mechanism has been deliberately avoided. The low-key approach is designed to reassure developing nations which might otherwise fear that the capital-exporting countries are trying to put something over on them.[67]

The World Bank's skilful navigation of sensitive terrain was recognized by other contemporary observers. In 1969, Georg Schwarzenberger wrote:

> The crucial question is the extent to which the draftsmen of the Convention considered it prudent to commit the governments of capital-importing states, without unduly rousing their susceptibilities as sovereign and equal members of the United Nations. They have come as near as is possible to the point of squaring this particular circle. With remarkable ingenuity, they have couched the minimum of legal commitments in a form which leaves everything on the level of optional undertakings, but attains as much as, in the present political climate, is likely to be attained for the protection of foreign investments through conciliation and arbitration.[68]

Schwarzenberger recognized that the drafting of the ICSID Convention was not a traditional inter-state negotiation process. The Convention was drafted by the World Bank's Executive Directors, which in practice meant the Legal Department. Broches, head of the Legal Department, later explained: 'I worked on the Convention. I was also the principal draftsman and negotiator of that treaty. It took a fair amount of my time.'[69] The World Bank's strategy boded well for success, but did not make it inevitable. Ratification was still necessary, and ratification is a political decision.

33.4.4 Ratification

To succeed, the ICSID Convention needed to be ratified by capital-importing states, especially states where property rights were considered least secure.[70] These were

[66] Parra (n. 6), 81–5 describes these meetings in detail.

[67] Bernard Nossiter, 'Foreign Fund Safeguard Program Taking Shape', *Washington Post*, 30 November 1963.

[68] Schwarzenberger (n. 28), 142.

[69] Broches was answering a general question about who administers ICSID cases; he started by explaining his involvement in the creation of ICSID. Aron Broches, 'Oral History, Interview by Robert Oliver' (World Bank Archives, Oral History Program, 7 November 1985), 7–8.

[70] When he first saw the proposal, the relevant official from the British Treasury said: 'we should see how the newly emergent and underdeveloped countries reacted to them.' Briefing for H.M. Ambassador

mainly former colonies, as one confidential British memo put it: 'what we are perhaps mainly concerned with is the likely reaction of politicians in the more difficult newly independent countries (by definition the less difficult under-developed are less of a problem).'[71] This focus remained unstated because of the political and intellectual milieu in 1964, in which dependency theory was ascendant and figures like Raul Prebisch were campaigning to strengthen the solidarity of developing countries.[72] In this context, a new organization's legitimacy was inversely related to the amount of leadership shown by former colonial powers in creating it. This position was expressed in a private memo to the US Secretary of state from an adviser, briefing him on US support for ICSID:

> The United States has at all times indicated its support for the Convention, but has deliberately not led the way, since the thought has been that this Convention, unlike the OECD Convention, should not have the appearance of being prepared by the capital exporting countries for signature by the capital importing countries.[73]

This type of language was reserved for internal discussions; American officials avoided saying anything like this publicly. Yet former colonizers did play an important role in nudging newly independent countries to ratify.

The French and British governments appear to have encouraged their former colonies to ratify ICSID, along with World Bank officials who actively encouraged ratification.[74] Years later, when an interviewer remarked: 'my impression is that initially a number of African countries, former colonial countries or countries in transition, did join ICSID early on', Georges Delaume, a French national, replied, 'Yes. They were pushed by the French.'[75] Archival records show that the Commonwealth Relations Office within the British government wrote to relevant officials in Commonwealth countries urging ratification.[76]

in Washington, result of a meeting held at the Treasury, 5 January 1962, 'Settlement of Disputes between Governments and Private Parties', UK T 312/251. German and French officials expressed similar sentiments. ICSID (n. 56), 373–4.

[71] Parenthesis in the original. Letter from Martin Reid to Hester Boothroyd, 30 January 1963, UK T 312: 545 (1962–3).

[72] Richard Toye and John Toye, *The UN and Global Political Economy: Trade, Finance, and Development* (Indiana University Press, 2004), 192, and, more generally, 191–4 and 204–5.

[73] Memo from Leonard Meeker for the Secretary of State, concerning 'Circular 175 Authority for Signature of World Bank Convention on Settlement of Investment Disputes: Action Memorandum', undated but likely March 1965. US LA: Bill S.3498.

[74] A British official noted the World Bank's efforts to encourage ratifications: 'the Bank believes that the energetic canvassing of Executive Directors representing other African countries will soon result in further ratifications.' Letter from R. E. Radford to Nicholson, Foreign Office, 18 April 1966, UK T 312/1498.

[75] Georges Delaume, 'Oral History, Interview by Robert Grathwol' (World Bank Archives, Oral History Program, 10 and 17 May 2004), 13.

[76] E.g. in April 1966, the Office wrote a letter to the High Commission for Pakistan that 'expresses hope that the Government of Pakistan will itself ratify the [ICSID] Convention in the near future'. Letter from Downing Street to the Office of the High Commissioner for Pakistan, 5 May 1966, UK T 312/1498.

States that viewed themselves as primarily capital-importing, yet developed, did not ratify quickly. The six OECD member states that did not ratify within five years were primarily capital-importers: Australia, Canada, Ireland, Portugal, Spain, and Turkey. Officials in New Zealand, for instance, waited fifteen years to ratify, and then gave interesting reasons for ratifying. They argued that ICSID would 'promote the international climate for foreign investment generally; New Zealand will acquire additional creditworthiness to the good reputation which we already have; and New Zealand will stand in better stead at the Bank... [including] her suitability as a potential borrower.'[77] If New Zealand believed ratifying would improve its likelihood of loans from the World Bank and reputation as a borrower, other countries likely did too. British officials believed the World Bank's lending was important for inducing capital-importing states to provide access to arbitration:

> The question hinges on whether, in the absence of a convention, the unwilling party (usually the state concerned) would go to arbitration. The 'real reason' namely reliance on the 'authority and lending power' of the Bank, means reliance on the power of the Bank to withhold loans. This is an argument we could not use in open debate. It is precisely what the under-developed countries are frightened of.[78]

In contrast, capital-exporting countries had an easier time supporting the proposal because they did not expect their governments to be respondents. This understanding emerges in a letter from a US State Department official to the head of the Securities and Exchange Commission, who was concerned that foreigners could use ICSID to challenge US financial regulations.

> The support of the United States for the Convention is primarily designed to establish another mechanism for peaceful settlement of investment disputes between investors and the less developed countries... Also, from the nature of the Convention, there appears to be little likelihood that claims against the United States by private investors would be suggested for decision under the Convention. The legal and administrative remedies already available to the private investor in the United States are broad and effective.[79]

When investors came to the US, they accepted that domestic law and domestic courts would govern the investment. One is reminded here of Thomas Wälde's observation that 'the Calvo-doctrine, much opposed by Western governments with respect to developing countries, has in fact been—and still is—the dominant maxim of Western countries

[77] 'Ratification of the Convention by New Zealand', internal memo, likely August 1972, NZ 241.

[78] Letter from Peter Reilly to Mr Pliatsky, 6 December 1962, UK T 312: 545 (1962–3).

[79] Letter from MacArthur to Harris, 27 March 1965. US LA: Bill S.3498. A similar statement was made by the State Department legal advisor when he testified to the relevant subcommittee. See Report on the 'Convention on the Settlement of Investment Disputes, 89th Congress, 2d Session, May 11, 1966', US LA Bill S.3498.

themselves.'[80] This understanding seems to have been shared by officials in many capital-exporting governments. Georges Delaume, a World Bank Legal Department official who translated the Convention into French, recalled: 'Politically, the Europeans were not for [ICSID]—except as potential users taking advantage of the institution to protect their investors against developing countries. So, it was all biased.'[81] Officials were careful to ensure that this understanding was rarely publicly acknowledged, since it would have reinforced perceptions of the Convention as a one-sided document.

World Bank officials, consistent with their active brokering in earlier stages of the process, followed up with governments and encouraged ratification. The British archives reveal a stream of letters and phone calls from Broches and other World Bank officials:

> *January 1966*: I enclose a copy of a memorandum we have received from the President of the World Bank about the ratification of this Convention by the U.K.[82]
>
> *May 1966*: As you probably know, Woods called on Sir Denis Rickett at the Treasury on 26 April and gave him a memorandum, of which I enclose a copy, urging early U.K. ratification.[83]
>
> *May 1966*: Since that reply [to a letter from Broches about British ratification] was sent Mr Broches has appeared again and done his own bit of lobbying, and seen the people concerned in the Foreign Office.[84]
>
> *July 1966*: We have been pressed from time to time by members of the I.B.R.D. to ratify as soon as possible.[85]
>
> *July 1966*: Several enquiries have been received from the IBRD about the timing of ratification by the U.K.[86]

The New Zealand archives show a similar stream of reminders, stretching over a ten-year period.[87] The volume of reminders demonstrates the active, consistent work of World Bank officials to promote ICSID.

[80] Thomas Wälde, 'Investment Arbitration under the Energy Charter Treaty: From Dispute Settlement to Treaty Implementation', 12 Arbitration International 429 (1996), 446.

[81] Delaume (n. 75), 52.

[82] Letter from R. E. Radford to Robins, 19 January 1966, UK T 312/1498.

[83] Letter from R. E. Radford to the Foreign Office, 9 May 1966, UK T 312/1498.

[84] Letter from J. Kelley to Mr Jenkyns, 12 May 1966, UK T 312/1498.

[85] Letter from Mr Butler to Mr Ryrie, 7 July 1966, UK T 312/1498.

[86] Draft from Mr Hildyard to Mrs White: 'Legislation in Connection with the IBRD Convention on the Settlement of Investment Disputes (undated, likely July 1966)', UK T 312/1498.

[87] Mentioned in: Letter from the Secretary of Foreign Affairs to the Secretary to the Treasury, 30 November 1971, NZ 241; Letter from the Secretary for Foreign Affairs to the Secretary for Justice, 11 August 1972, NZ 241; Letter from the Secretary to the Treasury to the Secretary, Justice Department, 31 May 1978, NZ 241.

33.5 The First Treaties with Investor–State Arbitration

After the ICSID Convention came into force in 1966, ICSID Secretariat officials began promoting the idea of consent to ICSID in contracts,[88] in domestic laws,[89] and in treaties. This section focuses on the work that ICSID Secretariat officials did to encourage consent to investor–state arbitration in investment treaties, which was revolutionary. This section, like the previous section, can be framed provocatively: would consent to investor–state arbitration have emerged in treaties without the strong backing of Broches and the World Bank? There are reasons to believe it would have emerged later, or not at all, without the work of World Bank officials.

33.5.1 The Secretariat writes model clauses for BITs

The ICSID Secretariat released a document of model clauses tailored to BITs in 1969, and then disseminated it widely.[90] Before these clauses were released, no BITs included investor–state arbitration clauses.[91] Such clauses in BITs spread only *after* the Secretariat provided model clauses and advisory help. The Secretariat's model clauses are the centralized origin of investment *treaty* arbitration.

The ICSID Secretariat advised governments on how to insert ICSID clauses into their investment treaties. In 1969, this is how Broches offered the Secretariat's assistance:

> Since foreign investments are increasingly being made with the encouragement and under the protection of investment treaties, it appears that these instruments too could become a vehicle incorporating both governmental consent to the jurisdiction of the Centre and appropriate inducements for investors to submit on their part. To assist in the formulation of such provisions, the Centre has just issued a set of Model Clauses for Insertion into Bilateral Investment Treaties.[92]

[88] In 1968, the Secretariat released a set of model clauses showing governments and investors how to consent in contracts. When Broches discussed these model clauses, he offered the Secretariat's advisory services, e.g. 'Address by Aron Broches to the Second Annual Meeting', 30 September 1968.

[89] The World Bank advocated for advance consent to be enshrined in domestic laws in the Report of the Executive Directors sent to states with the Convention. ICSID (n. 56), 1077. The Centre did not believe it appropriate to publish model clauses for legislation, but noted that it stood 'ready to advise governments on the formulation of appropriate provisions to be included in such instruments'. ICSID Fifth Annual Report, 4.

[90] These clauses were later released as Model Clauses Relating to the Convention on the Settlement of Investment Disputes Designed for Use in Bilateral Investment Agreements ICSID/6. They were released in ILM in September 1969, as 8 ILM 1341. They were also announced in the Third Annual Report, 4. These clauses, like the clauses for contracts, were drafted by Paul Szasz. Parra (n. 6), 121.

[91] There was one exception to this, the Netherlands–Indonesia BIT, discussed below.

[92] 'Address by A. Broches to the Third Annual Meeting', 29 September 1969.

33.5.2 ICSID first appears in an investment treaty

The first treaty to include a reference to ICSID was the Netherlands–Indonesia agreement of 1968.[93] The relationship between the two governments was fraught, since the treaty was negotiated following extensive, uncompensated expropriations of Dutch property in Indonesia. Indonesia had a close relationship with the World Bank[94] and Broches, who was Dutch, is remembered as having suggested an ICSID reference to the Dutch government.[95] The ICSID Secretariat was well-informed about the treaty's development, and it was celebrated in the 1968 Administrative Council meeting.[96] After that, the Netherlands began include a reference to ICSID by default; ten out of their next thirteen treaties included references.[97] The Dutch government also added protocols with ICSID references to two pre-existing treaties, with Côte d'Ivoire and Cameroon.[98] The first Dutch model treaty, drafted in 1979, also included a reference to ICSID arbitration.[99] The Dutch government acted first, but was soon joined by other European capital exporters in adding ICSID references to their treaties.

33.5.3 ICSID references slowly added to European model treaties

The spread of bilateral investment treaties can be visualized as a hub-and-spoke pattern. The hubs were the model treaties of European capital exporters, and the spokes were the actual treaties they negotiated with other governments. References to ICSID, and later to investor–state arbitration at other fora, spread through the same hub-and-spoke pattern. Once a capital-exporting government added a reference to ICSID to one of their treaties, they typically updated their practice and began inserting references to ICSID by default, meaning that it appears in most of their subsequent treaties, just like the Netherlands. The question is: what explains why capital-exporting governments inserted references to ICSID when they did?

I argue that the appearance of references to ICSID in treaties signed by European governments before 1981 can be traced to visits from Broches. A visit or several visits

[93] Article 11 of the Indonesia–Netherlands Agreement on Economic Cooperation.

[94] Indonesia had the first resident World Bank office, with 9 staff working closely with the Indonesian government. Bernard Bell, 'Oral History, Interview by John Lewis, Richard Webb, and Devesh Kapur' (World Bank Archives, Oral History Program, 21 November 1990), 8–12.

[95] An official who worked with Broches told me that Broches suggested the ICSID reference; while available evidence suggests this is extremely likely, I have not found written evidence illustrating it.

[96] ICSID Second Annual Meeting Press Release, 30 September 1968.

[97] ICSID Fifteenth Annual Report and UNCTAD, *International Investment Instruments: A Compendium*, vol. 3 (UNCTAD, 1996).

[98] Rudolf Dolzer and Margrete Stevens, *Bilateral Investment Treaties* (Martinus Nijhoff, 1995), 130, n. 362.

[99] Nico Schrijver and Vid Prislan, 'Netherlands', in Chester Brown (ed.), *Commentaries on Selected Model Investment Treaties* (Oxford University Press, 2013), 581.

from Broches was not sufficient to trigger the appearance of a reference to ICSID, and he made a large number of visits to national capitals that did not result in any such clause; but he was a persuasive, respected official who met senior government officials and encouraged them to put investor–state clauses on their agendas.

Among other trips, Broches had discussions in Italy and Belgium in 1967 and 1968.[100] In 1969, ICSID access appeared in the Italy–Chad treaty.[101] In 1970, ICSID access appeared in a treaty between Belgium and Indonesia.[102] The same dispute resolution clause appeared in the next two treaties that Belgium negotiated, with South Korea and Egypt.[103] In 1978 the wording changed, but the principle of access to ICSID remained: Belgium's subsequent treaties include 'irrevocable consent' to ICSID as a general rule, except the treaty with Romania.[104]

French treaties provide compelling evidence that the initial push for investor–state arbitration clauses came from the ICSID Secretariat. The Paris headquarters of the International Chamber of Commerce (ICC) had long been the global hub of commercial arbitration, and the ICC was one of the largest, best-organized groups in the world lobbying for the interests of international investors. If there had been lobbying by the ICC, then early French treaties would likely have included ICC access. They did not. Instead, World Bank archives show Broches visiting Paris[105] and then the French government reporting back to the ICSID Secretariat that they were including investor–state clauses in their treaties. For instance, in 1972, the French representative at the ICSID annual meeting said:

> [The French government] participated during the last year in negotiations with other countries on agreements for the protection of private investments abroad . . . Negotiations underway or already concluded have provided for reference to ICSID—explicit reference to ICSID—in the event of disputes.[106]

In 1972 the French government signed treaties with Tunisia and Zaire that included references to ICSID. Then the next year France signed treaties that included references to ICSID with Indonesia and Mauritius, then in 1974 with Egypt, Yugoslavia, then in 1975

[100] Telegram from the Swiss Embassy Washington to Bern, 6 October 1966. CH C.41.124.5.1. See also Address by A. Broches, General Counsel of the World Bank and Secretary-General of ICSID, to Institut Royal des Relations Internationales, Brussels, Belgium, 4 April 1967, WB Folder 1,651,420.

[101] Article 7 of the Chad–Italy BIT. For an explanation, see Andrew Newcombe and Lluis Paradell, *Law and Practice of Investment Treaties: Standards of Treatment* (Kluwer Law International, 2009), 45–6.

[102] Art. 10 of Belgium–Indonesia BIT.

[103] Art. 8 (Belgo-Luxembourg Economic Union–South Korea BIT) and Art. 9 (Belgo-Luxembourg Economic Union–Egypt BIT).

[104] As discussed below, Romanian treaties from this period limit arbitration to disputes over the amount of compensation only, and arbitration is only an option after local remedies have been exhausted, and within a two-year time limit. Art. 3 (Belgo-Luxembourg Economic Union–Romania BIT).

[105] Discours par Mr Aron Broches à la Société de Géographie Économique (Speech by Mr Aron Broches at the Society of Economic Geography), Paris, 14 October 1969, WB Folder 1,651,420.

[106] ICSID Sixth Annual Meeting, 5.

with Korea, Malaysia, Morocco, and Singapore. The pattern was established, and references to ICSID had become a default part of French treaties.[107]

The appearance of investor–state arbitration in the UK's treaties also attests to the influence of the Secretariat, and Broches in particular. The British negotiating brief for investment treaties tells British negotiators to mention that Broches has approved their investor–state arbitration clause. With regard to Article 8, the investor–state arbitration clause, the guidance for negotiators was:

> This [Article] may well be difficult to negotiate since prospective signatories may wish to reserve to themselves the right to decide in the case of each individual dispute whether they are prepared to have it referred to the Centre for arbitration or conciliation, but we have secured this wording in most of our IPPAs [investment treaties] and should do our best to get it in future Agreements. It could be useful to mention in negotiation that the wording of this Article has been approved by the Secretary General of ICSID.[108]

The negotiating brief then instructs officials: 'where an initialled Agreement contains an Article providing for the reference of disputes to ICSID (Article 8), a copy should be sent to the Secretary-General for his information.'[109] In his review of early British investment treaties, Poulsen also notes the heavy presence of Broches, observing, for instance: 'Broches had encouraged the United Kingdom to include ICSID clauses into economic cooperation agreements with the Ivory Coast and Congo.'[110] When negotiating partners raised concerns, the clause could be left out; one example of this is Thailand, which voiced serious concerns about investor–state arbitration and ensured an investor–state arbitration clause was not in their treaty with the UK.[111]

By 1981, when Broches retired as Secretary-General, the Secretariat knew of 67 investment treaties that included references to ICSID. Belgium, France, Italy, the Netherlands, and the UK were including ICSID references by default, and references appeared in most of their treaties.[112] Germany and Sweden had included references in a small fraction of their treaties.[113] After Romania joined ICSID in 1976, the Romanian government concluded 12 treaties with references to ICSID, although these references were limited

[107] During the 10 years from 1972 to 1982, France signed 23 treaties, and 20 of these included references to ICSID—the treaties with Malta, Panama, and the Philippines did not include references.

[108] Model Investment Promotion and Protection Agreement (April 1981 Version): General Negotiating Brief, UK FCO 69/658.

[109] Model Investment Promotion and Protection Agreement (April 1981 Version): General Negotiating Brief, UK FCO 69/658.

[110] Poulsen (n. 14), 60.

[111] In line with the opposition that Thailand's expert-designate expressed toward the ICSID Convention at the consultative conferences, 10 years earlier.

[112] Belgium 6 out of 8 treaties; France 17 out of 20; Italy 4 out of 4; Netherlands 13 out of 16; the UK 11 out of 14. The first number is drawn from the 1981 ICSID Annual Report, while the second column is drawn from UNCTAD (n. 97). The figures have been corroborated with the original treaty text wherever possible, and with Dolzer and Stevens (n. 98).

[113] Germany 3 out of 51; Sweden 2 out of 10.

to disputes concerning the amount of compensation and gave precedence to local remedies.[114] Four treaties without European participation had been signed that included references to ICSID.[115] In sum, by 1981, the practice of including ICSID references in investment treaties was established. Their early spread had been piecemeal and inconsistent, but Broches had gotten the ball rolling.

33.5.4 Arbitration other than ICSID appears in BITs

When Broches retired in 1981, access to ICSID in treaties was already transforming into access to investor–state arbitration more generally. The UN Commission on International Trade Law (UNCITRAL) Arbitration Rules were released in 1976, and after that, some governments added a reference to these rules into treaties, alongside or in place of ICSID clauses.[116] In 1979, the ICSID Additional Facility was created, which widened access to ICSID, allowing states that had not ratified the ICSID Convention to refer disputes for arbitration. In 1977, the French government inserted the first reference to a forum other than ICSID in a BIT, when they added an ICC reference.[117]

Yet capital-exporting governments still seemed to prefer ICSID: for instance, when the German government added investor–state clauses to its treaties, ICSID was the only option to appear.[118] The British government had a preference for ICSID, but if their negotiating partners could not agree to ICSID, they would investigate other arbitral fora:

> If ICSID is clearly not acceptable to a particular country, we should investigate their willingness to submit investment disputes to other international arbitration procedures such as the International Chamber of Commerce or the UNCITRAL Arbitration Rules. But omission of ICSID should only be conceded in the very last resort, or we risk undermining the reputation of the Centre.[119]

In the early 1980s, references to the ICC and the Arbitration Institute of the Stockholm Chamber of Commerce (SCC) became more common in treaties alongside ICSID, ICSID Additional Facility, and UNCITRAL Rules. The reasons for selecting or adding new institutions varied. With regard to the SCC, Dahlquist Cullborg finds that

114 E.g. Art. 4 (1) of the Pakistan–Romania BIT.

115 The 1981 ICSID Annual Report lists: Egypt–Japan (1977); Egypt–Yugoslavia (1977); Korea–Sri Lanka (1980); Singapore–Sri Lanka (1980).

116 The first treaty that refers to investor–state arbitration without mentioning ICSID says that the arbitration shall be conducted under UNCITRAL Rules. This treaty was concluded between France and Panama in 1982. Joel Dahlquist Cullborg, *The Use of 'Non-ICSID' Arbitration Rules in Investment Treaty Disputes* (Uppsala University, 2019), 76.

117 The first was the France–Syrian Arab Republic BIT (1977), which gives an investor a choice between ICSID and ICC arbitration. Ibid. 75.

118 This was true until 2008. Rudolf Dolzer and Yun-I Kim, 'Germany', in Chester Brown (ed.), *Commentaries on Selected Model Investment Treaties* (Oxford University Press, 2013).

119 Model Investment Promotion and Protection Agreement (May 1981 Version): General Negotiating Brief, UK FCO 69/662.

the SCC Arbitration Institute did not promote or advertise its services; rather, it benefited from Sweden's reputation for neutrality during the Cold War and its own experience with commercial disputes that crossed Cold War borders.[120] In the 1980s, treaty negotiators invented new permutations of advance consent clauses, including versions that fall somewhere between consent and non-consent, like giving the ICSID Secretary-General appointing authority for non-ICSID arbitrations, or giving tribunals the right to decide the amount of compensation only. The architecture for investment treaty arbitration, which had begun with the ICSID Model Clauses, became more expansive and varied in the subsequent two decades.

33.6 Conclusion: Unintended Consequences?

This chapter discusses the emergence of the ICSID Convention and the addition of investor–state arbitration references to investment treaties. These two developments enabled the exponential growth in the number of investment treaty arbitration cases that would occur in later decades. To what extent would this exponential growth have surprised officials involved with investor–state arbitration's creation in the 1960s?

The available evidence suggests that officials like Broches, who monitored developments closely, might not be too surprised at the size of the caseload. In 1984, before there had been a single investment treaty case, Broches observed that investment treaties created an 'enormous potential clientele':

> There are now about sixty treaties between states, generally industrialized and developing, which provide for access to ICSID in case of disputes about violations of the treaties. And those treaties are investment protection treaties. So, ICSID has an enormous potential clientele.[121]

The vision of a stand-alone arbitration convention, as the central node connecting a vast array of bilateral and multilateral agreements, was clear to some officials as early as 1960. A UN Report written that year, after conversations with Broches, notes: 'If such an [arbitration] agency were able to achieve a wide practice and prestige, it might in time become the natural fulcrum for the conclusion of bilateral, and possible multilateral, agreements between governments on foreign private investments.'[122] So some officials had a clear vision, and the main contours of contemporary investor–state arbitration

[120] Dahlquist Cullborg finds that most early treaties that include a reference to the SCC were concluded between an 'Eastern' and a 'Western' country, in Cold War terms. Dahlquist Cullborg (n. 116), 80–84.

[121] Broches (n. 58), 44–5.

[122] Progress Report by the Secretary-General, United Nations Economic and Social Council, 26 February 1960 (E/3325): 81.

resemble that vision to a remarkable extent. It is more difficult to assess how widely this vision was shared. The lack of intergovernmental deliberations during the drafting of the ICSID Convention and substantive standards being negotiated primarily bilaterally, rather than multilaterally, seem to have encouraged governments to underestimate the potential investment treaty caseload.

Legal institutions like investor–state arbitration do not fully determine the purposes to which they may be put, and of course consequences have emerged that even Broches could not have predicted. In particular, he seems to have underestimated the emergence of actors with strong commercial interests in investor–state arbitration. In ICSID's first decades, only a small number of firms were involved, before it was transformed into a competitive, lucrative field by a new and more entrepreneurial generation of lawyers.[123] In ICSID's first decades, the possibility of speculative finance driving arbitration claims was not even considered.

It is jarring to look back from contemporary investor–state arbitration, widely perceived as a lucrative field of legal practice, to some of the speeches Broches made as Secretary-General of ICSID. In 1973, he challenged his audience 'to help create the conditions for economic and social progress, with dignity and in freedom, remembering that the ultimate object of law is the welfare of mankind'.[124] Earlier in the same speech, he chastised international lawyers: 'We failed to meet adequately the moral obligations accepted in all civilized societies since the beginning of time, the obligations of the strong to help the weak.'[125] Broches was drawn to investor–state arbitration because he believed in the power of law to resolve disputes peacefully, and believed that rich societies had an imperative to use law to facilitate development in poorer societies. It is questionable whether those are the purposes that investor–state arbitration has come to serve.

[123] Yves Dezalay and Bryant Garth, *Dealing in Virtue: International Commercial Arbitration and the Construction of a Transnational Legal Order* (University of Chicago Press, 1996).

[124] Aron Broches, 'The Dimension of Development: Statement at the First Session of the Centenary Celebration of the International Law Association, Brussels, 30 August 1973', in *Selected Essays: World Bank, ICSID, and Other Subjects of Public and Private International Law* (Martinus Nijhoff, [1973] 1995), 516.

[125] Ibid. 514.

CHAPTER 34

INVESTMENT ARBITRATION IN THE ENERGY SECTOR

Past, present, and future

ELENA CIMA

34.1 Introduction

INVESTMENT arbitration in the energy sector has received increasing attention over the last decade. International energy investment accounts for a significant percentage of all global investments and makes up the largest portfolio of international arbitrations in the world today.[1] Energy-related disputes can take many forms: they may occur between two states, two private parties, or a private party and a state, in which case they may relate either to an investment by a foreign company in a state or to a commercial contract between a foreign company and a state.[2] In line with the theme of this volume, the present contribution will tackle only one type of energy-related dispute, namely investment disputes between a foreign investor and a state, and it will focus in particular on arbitration, which represents 'the most widely used form of dispute settlement between foreign investors and host States'.[3]

In a legal-technical sense, it has been observed that 'investment disputes in the energy sector are not fundamentally different from "regular" investment disputes'.[4] Whenever an investment dispute arises, the substantive standards of protection, as well as the rules

[1] A. T. Martin, 'Dispute Resolution in the International Energy Sector', 4 Journal of World Energy Law and Business 332 (2001), 339.

[2] E. De Brabandere, 'The Settlement of Investment Disputes in the Energy Sector', in E. De Brabandere and T. Gazzini (eds), *Foreign Investment in the Energy Sector: Balancing Private and Public Interests* (Martinus Nijhoff, 2014), 130.

[3] Ibid. 131; Martin (n. 1), 332–68.

[4] De Brabandere (n. 2), 131.

of procedures which guide the proceedings, are substantially the same, regardless of the specific industry involved.[5] At the same time, the specific characteristics of the energy sector should not be overlooked. Generally speaking, energy projects require large capital investments and, because they tend to involve long-term agreements, they are exposed over long periods of time to political risk. The latter can be defined as 'the possibility that political developments in the host state undermine the economics on which an investment decision was based',[6] ranging from the more straightforward cases of nationalization or forced renegotiation to more subtle and extensive examples of political problems a foreign investor might face.[7] Moreover, energy projects and investments often have a significant social, economic, and political impact, and raise thorny questions of energy security and state sovereignty. The level of state interference is higher than in most other sectors, and public and private interests must constantly be kept in balance. The severe uncertainty that characterizes this sector often leads to tensions between investors, who seek a stable and predictable investment climate, and host states, trying to retain sufficient policy space to protect important competing national interests.[8]

It then should be no surprise that certain rules have been developed which apply *only* to disputes related to investments in the energy sector. The adoption, in 1994, of the Energy Charter Treaty (ECT)[9] and the increasing number of disputes based on it are evidence that, although energy-related investment arbitration is not fundamentally different from 'regular' investment arbitration, it does often involve the application of ad hoc rules, it requires addressing issues and questions peculiar to this sector and, even when the general rules apply—i.e. outside of the scope of ECT—the specific characteristics of the energy industry tend to influence the reasonings and decisions of arbitral tribunals.[10]

Against this backdrop, this chapter intends to develop three simple ideas: first, access to international arbitration is particularly important for energy investors, given the high risks involved in their investments and the delicate balance between their rights and the public interest protected by the host state; second, the specific features of this economic sector have significantly contributed to the evolution of investment treaty-drafting and arbitration in this field; third, energy-related disputes have played a pivotal role in shaping the evolution of investment arbitration broadly speaking.

These three ideas will constitute the *fil rouge* of this chapter, which attempts to guide the reader through the evolution of energy investment arbitration over time. Section 34.2 explores the origins of investment arbitration in this area, stemming from the

[5] Ibid.

[6] T. W. Wälde, 'Investment Arbitration Under the Energy Charter Treaty: From Dispute Settlement to Treaty Implementation', 12(4) Arbitration International 429 (1996), 431.

[7] Ibid.

[8] K. Hobér, 'Overview of Energy Charter Treaty Cases', in M. Scherer (ed.), *International Arbitration in the Energy Sector* (Oxford University Press, 2018), 175.

[9] Energy Charter Treaty, 34 ILM 360 (1995) [hereinafter ECT].

[10] See Sections 34.3.2.1 and 34.4.2.

nationalization waves following the Second World War and the tension between states' sovereignty over their natural resources and investors' right to see their investment adequately protected. Section 34.3 will review the issues raised in the context of the ECT through an analysis of the most relevant disputes. While not all energy-related disputes have been brought and decided on the basis of this Treaty, it does represent 'a prominent tool when it comes to settling investment disputes in the energy sector',[11] and for this reason deserves special attention. Section 34.4 will discuss some of the current issues and questions as well as their potential impact on the future of energy arbitration, expanding the scope of the analysis beyond the ECT; finally, Section 34.5 will draw some conclusions.

34.2 The Past: The Early Years of Energy-Related Investment Disputes

The first discussions within the United Nations on permanent sovereignty took place amidst a 'nationalization wave' of global proportions: nationalizations of oil and gas enterprises—in the form of abrogation of concessions, increase of taxes, legislative intervention, and forced renegotiation of contracts—were taking place or being considered all over the world.[12] After the Second World War, states had decided to affirm and strengthen the control over their natural—energy—resources,[13] and the principle of permanent sovereignty contributed to the success of their efforts. At the same time foreign investors, feeling threatened by such behaviour, began to negotiate certain guarantees in their contracts with the host state, to safeguard and protect their interests abroad.

34.2.1 Decolonization, nationalization, and permanent sovereignty over natural resources

The rights of the state over its natural resources were first recognized and made explicit with the adoption by the UN General Assembly, in 1962, of Resolution 1803 on Permanent Sovereignty over Natural Resources (Resolution).[14] The origin of this famous Resolution can be traced back to the end of the Second World War and the

[11] De Brabandere (n. 2), 134.

[12] See e.g. the 1950–52 Anglo-Iranian Oil Company dispute, the nationalization of tin mines in Bolivia in 1951, and, more than a decade earlier, the Mexican oil nationalization of 1938. See N. Schrijver, *Sovereignty over Natural Resources: Balancing Rights and Duties* (Cambridge University Press, 1997), 6.

[13] Ibid. 4–7.

[14] Permanent Sovereignty over Natural Resources, G.A. Res. 1803 (XVII), U.N. Doc. A/RES/1803/XVII (14 December 1962) [hereinafter Permanent Sovereignty over Natural Resources].

beginning of the process of decolonization. The latter had provided newly independent nations with *political* independence without, however, being coupled with *economic* independence. It did not take long before the new governments of many former colonies realized that the vast majority of natural resources in their territory—the most important factor of production necessary for their economic growth and development—were being exploited by private corporations, on the basis of concession contracts and licensing agreements signed with the former colonial powers.[15] Moreover, those years were characterized by growing concerns over the scarcity of natural resources, the awareness of most states' dependence on other countries for raw materials, and the extreme vulnerability and instability of their supply lines.[16] As a result, tensions between states and foreign investors for the control of these resources began to intensify, and the Resolution was adopted precisely in response to these tensions, and to address the need of newly independent nations—enjoying a strong numerical position in the UN General Assembly—to reassert their control over the natural resources located on their territory.[17]

Accordingly, the Resolution recognized the sovereignty of states over their natural wealth and resources as an inalienable right.[18] At the same time, however, the rights of foreign investors were also acknowledged:

> Nationalization, expropriation or requisitioning shall be based on grounds or reasons of public utility, security or the national interest which are recognized as overriding purely individual or private interests, both domestic and foreign. In such cases the owner shall be paid appropriate compensation, in accordance with the rules in force in the State taking such measures in the exercise of its sovereignty and in accordance with international law.[19]

A decade later, in 1974, the UN General Assembly adopted the Declaration on the Establishment of a New International Economic Order (Declaration)[20] and the Charter of Economic Rights and Duties of States (Charter),[21] which had been part of a 'wider push by developing countries...to establish a new paradigm for economic relations

[15] See e.g. Schrijver (n. 12); K. N. Gess, 'Permanent Sovereignty over Natural Resources: An Analytical Review of the United Nations Declaration and its Genesis', 13 International and Comparative Law Quarterly 398 (1964); R. Pereira and O. Gough, 'Permanent Sovereignty over Natural Resources in the 21st Century: Natural Resources Governance and the Right to Self-Determination of Indigenous Peoples under International Law', 14 Melbourne Journal of International Law 451 (2013).

[16] Schrijver (n. 12), 4.

[17] A. Sabater and M. Stadnyk, 'International Arbitration and Energy: How Energy Disputes Shaped International Investment Dispute Resolution', in K. Talus (ed.), *Research Handbook on International Energy Law* (Edward Elgar, 2014), 202.

[18] Permanent Sovereignty over Natural Resources, preamble.

[19] Ibid. para. 4.

[20] Declaration on the Establishment of a New International Economic Order, U.N. Doc. A/RES/3201(S-VI) (1994) [hereinafter Declaration on the Establishment of a New International Economic Order].

[21] Charter of Economic Rights and Duties of States, U.N. Doc. A/RES/3281/XXIX (12 December 1974) [hereinafter Charter of Economic Rights and Duties].

between developed and developing countries.'[22] Both the Declaration and the Charter drew heavily on the Resolution, reasserting and strengthening the fundamental principle of permanent sovereignty over each state's 'natural resources and all economic activities', including 'the right to nationalization or transfer of ownership to its nationals.'[23] However, the protection afforded to foreign investors seemed to be less substantial: instead of phrasing the duty of compensation in case of expropriation as a binding obligation as it appeared in the text of the Resolution ('shall be paid'), the Charter couched this duty in hortatory terms, providing that 'appropriate compensation *should* be paid, taking into account its relevant laws and regulations and all circumstances that the State considers relevant'.[24]

Moreover, all three documents reflected the lack of agreement on the substantive standards of protection of foreign investors, in particular with regards to the treatment of the compensation due in case of expropriation. In such cases, both the Resolution and the Charter simply referred to the payment of 'appropriate compensation', while the amount was supposed to be determined by the expropriating state's own courts under its own national law.[25]

34.2.2 Legal techniques to 'level the playing field' between investors and states

The Charter indicated that disputes 'shall be settled under the domestic law of the nationalizing State and by its tribunals', unless all states decided otherwise.[26] This placed foreign investors at a disadvantage, particularly in the extractive industries, as it did not protect them from possible unilateral alterations of the contract or the legislative framework by the hand of the host state. To emerge from this position of weakness and level the playing field with their contractual counterpart, foreign investors began to negotiate agreements with the government of the host state so as to avoid the application of host-state law and the settlement of disputes by the host state's national courts.[27] These efforts resulted in the drafting of three types of clauses: *stabilization clauses*, which shielded investors from changes in the host state's legal or regulatory framework that might have affected the equilibrium of the contract; *choice of law clauses*, which replaced national law with the application of 'general principles of law' or public international law (also known as the 'internationalization' of contracts); and *dispute settlement clauses*, which

[22] S. Luttrell, 'An International Perspective on the Tanzanian Natural Wealth and Resources Acts', 36(3) Australia Resources and Energy Law Journal (2018).

[23] Declaration on the Establishment of a New International Economic Order, 4(e).

[24] Charter of Economic Rights and Duties, Art. 2(2)(c) (emphasis added).

[25] See Sabater and Stadnyk (n. 17), 202; T. Roe and M. Happold, *Settlement of Investment Disputes under the Energy Charter Treaty* (Cambridge University Press, 2011), 3.

[26] Charter of Economic Rights and Duties, Art. 2.

[27] Roe and Happold (n. 25), 4.

excluded the settlement of disputes by the host state's national courts and provided for international arbitration instead.[28]

The legal effects of these clauses, and in particular of 'internationalization' and 'stabilization clauses', have been subject to diverging interpretations, and their legal validity and effects have been among the very first controversies confronting investment arbitration tribunals in the Middle Eastern and Libyan arbitrations of the 1970s and 1980s.[29]

34.2.2.1 *Stabilization clauses*

These famous oil and gas arbitrations, such as those resulting in the 1977 award in *Texaco v Libya* and the 1982 award in *Kuwait v Aminoil,* marked a first important step towards the progressive erosion of state sovereignty,[30] partly due to the arbitrators' interpretation and application of stabilization clauses included in the text of the concession contracts. The *Texaco v Libya* arbitration originated from 14 Deeds of Concession concluded between 1955 and 1968 between Libya and two US companies. Between 1973 and 1974, the entirety of their properties, rights, and assets was nationalized because of two decrees adopted by the Libyan government, and the claimants relied on a stabilization clause in the concession agreement to argue against Libya's invocation of 'subsequent nationalization decrees'.[31] The arbitrator sided with the investors and concluded: 'a State cannot invoke its sovereignty to disregard commitments freely undertaken through the exercise of this same sovereignty and cannot, through measures belonging to its internal order, make null and void the rights of the contracting party which has performed its various obligations under the contract.'[32] The principle referred to by the arbitrator was by no means new. What *was* new was the extension of this principle to contracts between the state and a private investor: 'in respect of the international law of contracts, a nationalization cannot prevail over an internationalized contract, containing stabilization clauses, entered into between a State and a foreign private company.'[33]

The tribunal in *Kuwait v Aminoil* reached a similar conclusion. The dispute concerned a concession granted by Kuwait in 1948 for the exploration and exploitation of petroleum and natural gas. In September 1977, the Government of Kuwait issued Decree Law no. 124, terminating the agreement, and all assets and interests of the company were taken over by the state, which prompted Aminoil to initiate arbitration proceedings. The

[28] Ibid. The Resolution already referred to the possibility of the parties to agree to settle their dispute through arbitration, but it also stressed the need to exhaust local remedies first: 'In any case where the question of compensation gives rise to a controversy, the national jurisdiction of the State taking such measures shall be exhausted. However, upon agreement by sovereign States and other parties concerned, settlement of the dispute should be made through arbitration or international adjudication.'

[29] See *British Petroleum Company (Libya) Ltd v Libya* (1973) [hereinafter *BP v Libya*]; *Award on the Merits in Dispute between Texaco Overseas Petroleum Company/California Asiatic Oil Company and the Government of the Libyan Arab Republic and others,* Award of 19 January 1977, 17 ILM 1 1978 [hereinafter *Texaco v Libya*]; *Libyan American Oil Company (LIAMCO) v Libya* (1977) [hereinafter *LIAMCO v Libya*]; *In the matter of an Arbitration between the Government of the State of Kuwait and the American Independent Oil Company (Aminoil),* 21 ILM 976, 1000 (1982) [hereinafter *Kuwait v Aminoil*].

[30] Sabater and Stadnyk (n. 17), 212.

[31] Ibid.

[32] *Texaco v Libya*, Award, 24.

[33] Ibid.

tribunal began by recognizing that 'Aminoil's concessionary contract contained specific provisions in the light of which it may be queried whether the nationalization was in truth lawful'.[34] Just as in *Texaco v Libya*, the tribunal accepted *in principle* that a contract between a state and a private investor might limit the host state's right to nationalize the investor's assets.[35] However, it further clarified that this result would only be possible in the presence of 'particularly serious undertaking which would have to be expressly stipulated for, and be within the regulations governing the conclusion of State contract; and it is to be expected that it should cover only a relatively limited period.'[36] This was ultimately found to be the case in the dispute at hand, given that 'the stabilization clause in Aminoil's concession had lost its "former absolute character"... and only precluded nationalizations having a "confiscatory" character'.[37]

34.2.2.2 *Internationalized contracts*

Another key doctrine that was developed by these early Middle Eastern and Libyan oil and gas arbitrations was the 'internationalization of contracts'.[38] In the 1963 award in *Saudi Arabia v Aramco*, the tribunal held that 'general principles of law' could supplement the municipal law otherwise applying to the concession agreement.[39] Although the arbitrator rejected international law as the governing law and chose the 'general principles of law' instead, this reasoning 'has been used in several subsequent decisions as a strong precedent for rejecting municipal law'.[40] The 1970s Libyan arbitration awards were similarly instrumental in excluding the application of purely municipal law to concession contracts.[41] In *Texaco v Libya*, for instance, the tribunal concluded that 'the application of the principles of Libyan law does not have the effect of ruling out the application of the principles of international law, but quite the contrary: it simply requires us to combine the two in verifying the conformity of the first with the second.'[42]

Over time, bilateral investment treaties (BITs) have developed significantly more refined solutions than stabilization clauses and internationalized contracts to address the host state's responsibility for arbitrary and drastic changes to its municipal laws and regulations. Nevertheless, it has been argued that such developments built precisely on these clauses and on their application in the context of the above-mentioned oil and gas arbitrations.[43] Moreover, although reliance on stabilization clauses has decreased in the

[34] *Kuwait v Aminoil*, Award, 1020. The reference was in particular to Art. 17 of the 1948 Concession Agreement.

[35] Sabater and Stadnyk (n. 17), 213–14.

[36] *Kuwait v Aminoil*, Award, 1023.

[37] Sabater and Stadnyk (n. 17), 213–14. *Kuwait v Aminoil*, Award, 1023–4.

[38] Sabater and Stadnyk (n. 17), 215.

[39] *Saudi Arabia v Arabian American Oil Company (ARAMCO)*, 27 ILR 117 (1963) [hereinafter *Saudi Arabia v ARAMCO*], Award, 168.

[40] M. E. Dickstein, 'Revitalizing the International Law Governing Concession Agreements', 6(1) Berkeley Journal of International Law 54 (1988), 67, n. 58.

[41] Sabater and Stadnyk (n. 17), 215.

[42] *Texaco v Libya*, Award, 182.

[43] Sabater and Stadnyk (n. 17), 216.

recent years,[44] they are still very often present in contracts related to the extractive and energy industries.[45] As a matter of fact, today as in the 1970s, the severe uncertainty that characterizes the natural resources sector often motivates foreign investors to require the host state to safeguard the stability of their agreement, while governments may have reason to agree to them to attract promising foreign investments in their territory.

34.2.2.3 *Arbitration*

Before arbitration proved to be a viable way of settling investor–state disputes, the investor could resort either to the courts of the host state or to diplomatic protection. The Charter of Economic Rights and Duties of States indicated the host state's national courts as the appropriate forum for the settlement of disputes between foreign investors and the host state. This option, as has been observed, placed the investors in an unfavourable position, as it could rarely qualify as a neutral forum. On the other hand, diplomatic protection had its own disadvantages. First, it deprived the investor of any control over the claim, giving its state of nationality complete discretion whether to make a claim on its behalf or not. Second, espousal of a claim by a state immediately politicized it, transforming an investor–state dispute into an inter-state dispute,[46] and thus one influenced by the existing political relations and power plays between the states involved.

Arbitration proved capable of overcoming these shortcomings, offering effective remedies to the investor without, at the same time, depriving the host state of appropriate defences. After the initial scepticism of some states,[47] later awards led to a wider acceptance of international arbitration as a viable solution, paving the way for the success of the International Center for Settlement of Investment Disputes (ICSID) Convention.[48] The *Kuwait v Aminoil* award, for instance, although the tribunal ultimately ruled in favour of Kuwait, played a significant role in cementing the legitimacy of international investment arbitration, as the respondent state participated actively in the proceedings and 'satisfied the award in full promptly'.[49]

[44] R. Dolzer and C. Schreuer, *Principles of International Investment Law* (Oxford University Press, 2008), 75.

[45] See e.g. M. Erkan, *International Energy Investment Law: Stability through Contractual Clauses* (Kluwer Law International, 2010). For an assessment of stabilization clauses in general, see e.g. also T. Wälde and G. Ndi, '"Stabilizing International Investment Commitments": International Law versus Contract Integration', 31 Texas International Law Journal 215 (1996); E. Paasivirta, 'Internationalization and Stabilization of Contracts versus State Sovereignty', British Yearbook of International Law 315 (1989); and A. Al Faruque, 'Validity and Efficacy of Stabilization Clauses: Legal Protection v Functional Value', 23 Journal of International Arbitration 317 (2006).

[46] Roe and Happold (n. 25), 1–2.

[47] Such skepticism was motivated e.g. by the outcome of the 1951 Trucial Coast Arbitration. *In the matter of an Arbitration between Petroleum Development (Trucial Coast) Ltd and the Sheikh of Abu Dhabi*, 1 ILCQ 247 (1952), 250–51.

[48] Convention on the Settlement of Investment Disputes Between States and Nationals of Other States (International Centre for Settlement of Investment Disputes [ICSID]), 575 UNTS 159 [hereinafter ICSID Convention].

[49] Sabater and Stadnyk (n. 17), 205.

The ICSID Convention, adopted in 1965, built precisely on this and other similar awards,[50] in an attempt to strike a balance between the interests of the foreign investor, who obtained the benefit of a neutral forum, and the host state, who benefited from the prohibition of diplomatic protection. As clearly explained by Thomas Wälde, the contribution that arbitration made to the protection of foreign investors has been particularly important in the context of energy disputes:

> International arbitration is one of the most powerful instruments available to foreign investors to counter that part of the political risk which is within the control of the host state. First, it provides an independent setting outside host state control for settling disputes. More importantly, the prospect of international arbitration can often quite effectively discourage host states against using sovereign powers for abrogating legal and contractual rights granted to an investor...it then protects such regime against legislative and administrative intervention...much more importantly, it discourages host state agencies from interfering in the investment's contractual regime.[51]

As these paragraphs have shown, the link between the energy sector and investment arbitration is twofold. On the one hand, the specific characteristics of this sector, and in particular its highly political and sensitive nature, explain the absolute importance of access to international arbitration for energy investors,[52] replacing the more inadequate systems of diplomatic protection or settlement in the host state's domestic courts. On the other, these early oil and gas disputes have significantly contributed to the development of investment arbitration in a more general sense, having paved the way for the establishment of international arbitration as the preferred mechanism for settling investor–state disputes.

34.3 The Present: Investment Disputes under the Energy Charter Treaty

The strategic importance of the energy sector, its economic and geopolitical repercussions, and its unique characteristics led, in 1994, to the signing of a multilateral treaty offering investment protection and access to investment arbitration to international investors in the energy industry: the Energy Charter Treaty.[53] The latter represents the

[50] See e.g. *BP v Libya*, *Texaco v Libya*, and *LIAMCO v Libya*.

[51] Wälde (n. 6), 432.

[52] R. W. Bentham, 'Arbitration and Litigation in the Oil Industry', 2 Oil and Gas Law and Tax Rev. 35 (1986); S. Bond, 'Negotiating Dispute Settlement in the International Petroleum Industry', in T. Wälde and G. Ndi, *International Oil and Gas Policies* (Graham and Trotman, 1994); T. Wälde, 'Negotiating for Dispute Settlement in Transnational Mineral Contracts', 7 Denver Journal of International Law and Policy 33 (1977).

[53] De Brabandere (n. 2), 135; Hobér (n. 8), 175.

successful culmination of a series of discussions that had begun at the dawn of the 1990s on how to develop inter-governmental energy cooperation between Eastern and Western Europe. On one side, Russia and many of its neighbouring countries were rich in energy sources—in particular oil and gas—'but in great need of investments to reconstruct their economies'.[54] On the other, Western European countries were seeking ways to improve their 'energy security' by reducing their dependence on Middle Eastern oil and by diversifying their energy supply mix. The ECT would allow for such trade-off: it would guarantee Western European countries access to energy sources in the former Soviet Union,[55] protecting their investments in these strategic but volatile industries, while at the same time granting Eastern European countries access to Western markets.[56] Although it had begun as a 'European project', soon other Western countries, members of the Organization for Economic Development and Cooperation (OECD), made sure to get involved in the ECT negotiating process, to avoid the conclusion of a multilateral agreement that risked putting their investors and traders at a disadvantage.[57]

The result of these negotiations was a binding multilateral instrument aimed at promoting 'long-term co-operation in the energy field, based on complementarities and mutual benefits'.[58] Signed in 1994 and entered into force in April 1998, the Treaty counts, as of August 2019, 53 contracting parties, including the European Union and Euratom. Although it developed strands already present in the dispute settlement provisions of modern BITs, the ECT presents several important distinguishing features. The following sub-sections will provide an analysis of the dispute settlement system established by the ECT (34.3.1), focusing in particular on selected issues of jurisdiction (34.3.2) and merits (34.3.3) addressed by arbitral tribunals. Although the decisions rendered under the Treaty are still limited in number, certain issues 'of general interest for the application of the ECT'[59] are emerging, and worth exploring.

34.3.1 A framework suitable for energy

If one were to skim through the pages of the Energy Charter Treaty—and in particular Article 26 devoted to the settlement of disputes between a contracting party and a foreign investor—the resemblance to bilateral and multilateral investment treaties concluded over the last 40 years would be hard to miss.[60] Chapter 11 of the North American Free Trade Agreement (NAFTA)[61] and the UK Model BIT, in particular, seem to have served as

[54] K. Hobér, 'Investment Arbitration and the Energy Charter Treaty', 1(1) Journal of International Dispute Settlement 153 (2010), 154; Hobér (n. 8), 176.

[55] Roe and Happold (n. 25), 9. [56] Wälde (n. 6), 430.

[57] It was in particular because of the lobbying efforts of the US, afraid that the European Communities would end up monopolizing the energy sector of the former Soviet Union, that other non-European OECD countries managed to be included in the ECT membership. Roe and Happold (n. 25), 9.

[58] ECT, Art. 2. [59] Hobér (n. 54), 154. [60] Wälde (n. 6), 434.

[61] North American Free Trade Agreement, 32 ILM 298, 605 (1993) [hereinafter NAFTA].

major precedents for the ECT.[62] However, a more accurate reading would reveal that the framework introduced by the ECT does present several important distinguishing features, such as a stronger emphasis on extensive state responsibility for sub-state authorities and enterprises,[63] on the principle of *pacta sunt servanda*,[64] and on incorporating better-treatment standards from international law.[65]

However, the main element of novelty introduced by the ECT drafters is the creation of a system of compulsory jurisdiction (at the option of the investor) against the host state 'to increase the chances of effective implementation and compliance of the Treaty's significant (post-) investment obligations.'[66] The ICSID Convention is based on reciprocity and consent, requiring both parties to agree in writing for a dispute between them to be referred to ICSID. Consent occurs at two levels: first, governments have to join the ICSID Convention and, second, a specific agreement between the investor and the host state is required to trigger the arbitral mechanism.[67] The ECT introduced a new model, which replaced 'reciprocity' with compulsory jurisdiction *against the host state*, with the result of subjecting oil and gas contracts, licences, and concessions to investment arbitration, eroding the notion of state sovereignty and the Calvo doctrine, as practiced in many Western countries.[68] In this new system, reciprocity is replaced by 'asymmetry' and consent by 'unconditional consent'.

The asymmetric nature of the arbitration procedure envisaged by Article 26 of the Treaty is evident on at least two levels. First, the investor—and only the investor—can decide to submit a dispute to arbitration, if an amicable settlement has proven impossible.[69] Second, it is once again only the investor which is given the choice of one out of four alternative arbitral procedures: the 1965 ICSID Convention; the ICSID-based 'Additional Facility' (if either the home states of the investor or the host state is not a member of the ICSID Convention); sole arbitrator or an arbitral tribunal constituted according to UNCITRAL rules; or the Stockholm Chamber of Commerce (SCC) arbitration rules.[70]

The unconditional consent, which replaced the state's written consent typical of ICSID and most investment agreements, is enshrined in Article 26(3), according to which 'each contracting party hereby gives its unconditional consent to the submission of a dispute to international arbitration', and this consent, given simply by the signature

[62] T. W. Wälde, 'Energy Charter Treaty-Based Investment Arbitration: Controversial Issues', 5 Journal of World Investment and Trade 373 (2004), 376.

[63] ECT, Art. 26(8) (second sentence).

[64] ECT, Art. 10(1) (last sentence).

[65] ECT, Art. 10(1).

[66] Wälde (n. 6), 430.

[67] Ibid. 434. See G. Horlick and A. Marti, 'NAFTA, Chap. 11B-A Private Right of Action to Enforce Market Access through Investments', 14(1) Journal of International Arbitration 43 (97).

[68] Wälde (n. 6), 437–8.

[69] ECT, Art. 26(2). According to Art. 26(1), the parties should always try to settle their disputes amicably and only if this first option fails the investor can, after a period of three months, decide to proceed to arbitration. See in general, for a comprehensive analysis of each paragraph of Article 26, F. Dias Simões, 'Article 26: Settlement of Disputes between an Investor and a Contracting Party', in R. Leal-Arcas (ed.), *Commentary on the Energy Charter Treaty* (Edward Elgar, 2018).

[70] ECT, Art. 26(4(a)–(c).

of the Treaty, is considered to satisfy the requirements of the four arbitral options listed in the fourth paragraph of the same provision, as well as the 1958 New York Convention on Recognition and Enforcement of Arbitral Awards.[71] As aptly observed by Wälde, 'once the Treaty is effective and investors have carried out an investment, they have most likely obtained an arbitral right against states: states are bound [and] can withdraw only under... very restrictive conditions.'[72]

The combination of asymmetrical arbitration and the state's unconditional consent can be described using Jan Paulsson's expression, 'arbitration without privity',[73] generally used to refer to 'the right of the investor to initiate arbitration against the host state without a previous arbitration agreement'.[74] This way, the ECT introduced a method of enforcing the Treaty's investment obligations which appears to be more powerful—from the perspective of the investor—and less controllable—from that of the host state—than it used to be, in particular in comparison with arbitration clauses typically found in investment agreements concerned with petroleum or mineral development, or in oil and gas exploration and production licenses or energy licenses.[75] Moreover, the combination of Article 26 and the last sentence of Article 10(1)—'Each Contracting Party shall observe any obligations it has entered into with an Investor or an Investment of an Investor of any other Contracting Party'—extends investment arbitration to those agreements and contracts that do not include an arbitration clause.[76]

It is clear from these observations that the introduction of this system of compulsory jurisdiction stems from a careful analysis of investments in the energy sector. Not only does it enable the investor to benefit from international arbitration even when the agreements between the state of nationality and the host state or the contract with the host state do not themselves include the possibility of resort to arbitration—as has been fairly common in the oil, gas, and mining industries—but it equally allows the opportunity to counter national policies against submissions to international arbitration, especially in those countries where the Calvo doctrine is a part of local law.[77] In addition, it takes into

[71] ECT Art. 26(5)(a) and (b). See Wälde (n. 6), 450; M. M. Winkler, 'Arbitration without Privity and Russian Oil: The Yukos Case before the Houston Court', 27(1) University of Pennsylvania Journal of International Economic Law 115 (2006), 141.

[72] Wälde (n. 6).

[73] J. Paulsson, 'Arbitration without Privity', 10 ICSID Review–Foreign Investment Law Journal 232 (1995) and 'Arbitration without Privity', in T. Wälde (ed.). *The Energy Charter Treaty: An East-West Gateway for Investment and Trade* (Kluwer Law International, 1996), 422-23: 'This new world of arbitration is one where the claimant need not have a contractual relationship with the defendant, and where the tables could not be turned; the defendant could not have initiated the arbitration, nor is it certain of being able even to bring a counterclaim.'

[74] Winkler (n. 71), 135. As rightly pointed out by Winkler, because of Art. 26(4)(a)(ii), 'the state's consent can be given [even] without the host state having to undersign either the ICSID Convention or a bilateral treaty with the national state of the investor' (p. 141).

[75] Wälde (n. 52); S. M. Frank and J. Z. Barsy, 'International Energy Arbitration: Rules and Issues', 5 Energy and Natural Resources Law 245 (1987). See Wälde (n. 6), 439.

[76] Ibid. 455. [77] Ibid. 446.

account the specific situation of emerging companies in the sector, which, unlike well-established international energy companies, are given the opportunity to benefit from this system without having to bargain for it.[78] Overall, the decision to create this system—asymmetric and compulsory for the state—responds to the logic that characterizes the whole Treaty, the latter being 'primarily concerned with compliance by the state with its investment obligations... [rather than with] providing an effective mechanism for investment disputes *per se* and in general'.[79]

34.3.2 Selected jurisdictional issues

34.3.2.1 *The definition of 'investment'*

The compulsory jurisdiction against the host state introduced by Article 26 of the ECT only covers, as legitimate subject matter of the arbitration, disputes related to an *investment*.[80] 'Investment' is defined very broadly in the ECT, as it includes 'every kind of asset owned or controlled directly or indirectly by an investor'.[81] In *Plama v Bulgaria*, the tribunal defined the list contained in Article 1(6) as a 'broad, non-exhaustive list of different kinds of assets encompassing virtually any right, property or interest in money or money's worth'.[82] In *Energoalians v Moldova*, the tribunal followed the decisions rendered in the *Yukos* cases and in *Remington v Ukraine* when it concluded that the ECT provides for a 'rather broad definition of the term "Investment".'[83] Although the notion of 'Investment' is defined broadly in many BITs as well, it has been argued that the ECT contains 'the most extensive definition of "investment" to be found in modern investment promotion and protection treaties'.[84] Along these lines, the Svea Court of Appeal, asked to decide on the appeal of the award rendered in *Petrobart v Kyrgyz Republic*, observed: 'the term investment can have different meanings in different international contexts. The meaning of the term as defined in the ECT has a wider scope of application... when the ECT was negotiated it was an explicit intention to give investment a broad

[78] Ibid. 446. [79] Ibid. 452.

[80] The scope of application of Art. 26 is further limited by the fact that arbitration is only available to decide on alleged breaches of one or more obligations of the host state under Part III of the Treaty (see Section 34.3.3).

[81] ECT, Art. 1(6).

[82] *Plama Consortium Limited v Republic of Bulgaria*, ICSID Case No. ARB/03/24 [hereinafter *Plama v Bulgaria*], Decision on Jurisdiction, 8 February 2005, para. 125.

[83] *Energoalians TOB v Republic of Moldova*, UNCITRAL [hereinafter *Energoalians v Moldova*], Award, 23 October 2013, para. 227. See *also Remington Worldwide Limited v Ukraine*, SCC Case No. V(l 16/2008) [hereinafter *Remington v Ukraine*], Award, 28 April 2011, 194.

[84] S. Jagush and A. Sinclair, 'The Limits of Protection for Investments and Investors under the Energy Charter Treaty', in C. Ribeiro (ed.), *Investment Arbitration and the Energy Charter Treaty* (JurisNet, 2006). For a comparison of the definition of 'Investment' under ICSID and under the ECT, see A. Turinov, '"Investment" and "Investor" in Energy Charter Treaty Arbitration: Uncertain Jurisdiction', 26 Journal of International Arbitration 1 (2009).

application.'[85] This 'explicit intention' has been relied upon by many tribunals to explain the rather broad interpretation of the term. The tribunal in *Petrobart v Kyrgyz Republic*, for instance, stated that, precisely because 'there is no uniform definition of the term investment, but the meaning of this term varies,'[86] the term must 'be interpreted in the context of each particular treaty in which the term is used.'[87] This tribunal, and many others afterwards, relied on Article 31(1) of the Vienna Convention on the Law of Treaties (VCLT), and therefore interpreted the notion of 'Investment' 'in accordance with the ordinary meaning to be given to the terms of the Treaty in their context and in the light of its object and purpose.'

This broad definition and interpretation of the term 'Investment' is evident inter alia because of the approach adopted towards indirect and minority shareholders. According to Article 1(6), the assets that constitute an 'Investment' can be 'owned or controlled *directly or indirectly* by an investor'.[88] With this expression, it is clear that the Treaty intends to protect the interests not only of those investors who directly own or control the investment in question but also of those who simply hold it through a series of shareholdings. Accordingly, the tribunal in *Kardassopoulos v Georgia* stated that 'the indirect ownership of shares by Claimant constitutes an "investment" under...the ECT,'[89] founding its conclusion on previous awards.[90] As a matter of fact, the extension of shareholder standing to minority and indirect shareholders is provided for in many BITs concluded even before the adoption of the ECT. This constitutes a doctrinal innovation that was largely developed in the context of arbitrations related to the energy sector, starting from *CMS v Argentina*, where the tribunal made it very clear that 'there [was] indeed no requirement that an investment, in order to qualify, must necessarily be made by shareholders controlling a company or owning the majority of its shares.'[91]

The ECT does pose certain limits to the applicability of the term 'Investment'. In particular, the Treaty distinguishes between two phases in the life of an investment and

[85] *Petrobart Ltd (Gibraltar) v Kyrgyz Republic*, SCC Case No. 126/2003 [hereinafter *Petrobart v Kyrgyz Republic*], Judgment of the Svea Court of Appeal, 19 January 2007; unofficial translation in (2007) Transnational Dispute Management 4–5, as quoted in Roe and Happold (n. 25), 63.

[86] See e.g. R. Dolzer and M. Stevens, *Bilateral Investment Treaties* (Martinus Nijhoff, 1995), 25–31, and G. Sacerdoti, *Bilateral Treaties and Multilateral Instruments on Investment Protection* (The Hague Academy of International Law), 1997, 305–10/

[87] *Petrobart v Kyrgyz Republic*, Award, Section VIII.6. See *also Nykomb Synergetics Technology Holding AB, Stockholm v Republic of Latvia*, SCC Case No. 118/2001 [hereinafter *Nykomb v Latvia*], Award, 16 December 2003, para. 4.3.3.3(d).

[88] ECT, Art. 1(6) (emphasis added).

[89] See *Ioannis Kardassopoulos v Republic of Georgia*, ICSID Case No. ARB/05/18 [*Kardassopoulos v Georgia*], Decision on Jurisdiction, 6 July 2007, paras. 121–4.

[90] E.g. *Siemens A.G. v the Argentine Republic*, ICSID Case No. ARB/02/8, Decision on Jurisdiction, 3 August 2004, para. 137. The *Siemens v Argentina* tribunal stated that the Argentina–Germany BIT 'does not require that there be no interposed companies between the investment and the ultimate owner of the company'.

[91] *CMS Gas Transmission Company v Republic of Argentina*, ICSID Case No. ARB/01/8 [hereinafter *CMS v Argentina*], Decision of Jurisdiction, 17 July 2003, 51. See also *LG and E Energy Corp., LG and E Capital Corp. and LG and E International Inc. v Argentine Republic*, ICSID Case No. ARB/02/1 [hereinafter *LG and E v Argentina*], Decision of the Arbitral Tribunal on Objections to Jurisdictions, 30 April 2004, 29.

submits them to different protection mechanisms: a pre-investment and a post-investment phase.[92] While there has never been any doubt that existing investments, or investments made (post-investment), are covered by Article 26, the question has arisen as to whether the pre-investment process is equally included. It has been argued that, since Article 26 applies only to alleged breaches of obligations under Part III of the Treaty and Article 10(1)—which falls under Part III—imposes obligations that extend to both pre- and post-investment phases,[93] the former should also be justiciable under Article 26. However, the opinion of the vast majority argues its exclusion, given in particular that Article 26(1) only refers to 'Investment' and 'Investor', without mentioning disputes relating to the 'making of an investment' (Article 1(8)).[94]

Another important requirement is that the investment be associated with an economic activity in the energy sector (Article 1(6)(f)). Article 1.5 defines 'Economic Activity in the Energy Sector' as 'an economic activity concerning the exploration, extraction, refining, production, storage, land transport, transmission, distribution, trade, marketing, or sale of Energy Materials and Products except those included in Annex NI, or concerning the distribution of heat to multiple premises'—a definition which is further clarified and developed in the Understanding with respect to Article 1(5). The question arises, however, as to how closely the investment must be 'associated with' an Economic Activity in the Energy Sector. In *Amto v Ukraine*, the tribunal adopted a 'functional criterion'[95] to establish the 'association' requirement and held that

> the interpretation of the words 'associated with' involves a question of degree, and refers primarily to the *factual rather than legal* association between the alleged investment and an Economic Activity in the Energy Sector. A mere contractual relationship with an energy producer is insufficient to attract ECT protection where the subject matter of the contract has no functional relationship with the energy sector.[96]

34.3.2.2 *Provisional application of the treaty*

One important feature of the ECT is that it provides for the provisional application of the Treaty by a signatory who has signed but not yet ratified it, pending its entry into

[92] Dias Simões (n. 69), 342.

[93] T. Wälde and W. Hamida, 'The Energy Charter Treaty and Corporate Acquisition', in G. Coop and C. Ribeiro (eds), *Investment Protection and the Energy Charter Treaty* (JurisNet, 2008), 172–85.

[94] P. Andrews-Speed and T. Wälde, 'Will the Energy Charter Treaty Help International Energy Investors?' 5(3) Transnational Corporations 31 (1996), 42. Instead, the pre-investment phase comprises soft-law obligations which simply impose a duty of 'best efforts'. Wälde (n. 6), 438; Dias Simões (n. 69), 342.

[95] De Brabandere (n. 2).

[96] *Limited Liability Company Amto v Ukraine*, SCC Case No. 080/2005 [hereinafter *Amto v Ukraine*], Award, 26 March 2008, para. 42 (emphasis added). The tribunal found: 'The close association of EYUM-10 with ZAES in the provision of services directly related to energy production means that AMTO's shareholding in EYUM-10 is an "investment associated with an Economic Activity in the Energy Sector"' (para. 43).

force.[97] The concept of a treaty's provisional application is not new. Article 25 of the VCLT, for instance, provides that 'a treaty... is applied provisionally pending its entry into force if (a) the treaty itself so provides or (b) the negotiating states have in some other manner so agreed', adding that such provisional application is terminated in relation to a state 'if it notifies the other States between which the treaty is being applied provisionally of its intention not to become a party to the treaty'.[98] This provision, however, does not define the content of the specific obligations provisional application imposes, leaving it to the negotiators 'to fashion the specific mode by which provisional application of the treaty at issue will operate'.[99]

The negotiating parties to the ECT have addressed the Treaty's provisional application in Article 45 which, in the relevant part, reads:

> (1) Each signatory which applies the Energy Charter Treaty provisionally in accordance with Article 45(1) and each Contracting Party agrees to apply this Amendment provisionally pending its entry into force for such signatory or Contracting Party to the extent that such provisional application is not inconsistent with its constitution, laws or regulations.
>
> (2)(a)(i) any signatory which applies the Energy Charter Treaty provisionally or Contracting Party may deliver to the Depositary within 90 days from the date of the adoption of this Amendment by the Charter Conference a declaration that it is not able to accept the provisional application of this Amendment.

Once again, this provision falls short of defining the substance of such provisional application, and it has been up to the tribunals to analyse the exact meaning of Article 45 and the 'content of the obligations of states which have signed but not yet ratified the Treaty'.[100]

The correct interpretation and application of Article 45 was a crucial issue in the three *Yukos* interim awards on jurisdiction and admissibility rendered on 30 November 2009, given that Russia, the respondent state in the disputes, had initially signed the treaty without ratifying it and without indicating its inability to accept provisional application, giving notice, however, on 20 August 2009, of its decision to terminate its provisional application.[101]

The first question addressed by the tribunal concerned the existence of a link between the first and second paragraph of Article 45—in other words whether a declaration under Article 45(2) was necessary in order to invoke the limitation clause of Article 45(1)

[97] ECT, Art. 45(1). See A.M. Niebruegge, 'Provisional Application of the Energy Charter Treaty: The Yukos Arbitration and the Future Place of Provisional Application in International Law', 8(1) Chicago Journal of International Law 355 (2007), 356; K. Hober and S. Nappert, 'Provisional Application and the Energy Charter Treaty: the Russian Doll Provision', 10 International Arbitration Review 53 (2007); G. Hafner, 'The "Provisional Application" of the Energy Charter Treaty', in C. Binder et al. (eds), *International Investment Law for the 21st Century: Essays in Honour of Christoph Schreuer* (Oxford University Press, 2009), 593.

[98] VCLT, Art. 25(1) and (2). [99] Niebruegge (n. 97), 357. [100] De Brabandere (n. 2).

[101] Termination of the Treaty's provisional application is regulated by Art. 45(3).

('to the extent that such provisional application is not inconsistent with its constitution, laws or regulations'). Relying on the decision rendered in *Kardassopoulos v Georgia*, the *Yukos* tribunal concluded that there was no linkage between the two paragraphs.[102]

The second issue addressed by the tribunal related to whether some form of declaration or notification was required under Article 45(1). The tribunal settled this question, finding that Russia could invoke the limitation clause of the first paragraph of Article 45 to exclude the provisional application of the ECT, even though it had made no prior declaration or notification to this end.[103] A declaration is instead required if a state wishes to benefit from the second paragraph of Article 45, as well as if it wishes to terminate the Treaty's provisional application according to Article 45(3). This question was first raised in *Petrobart v the Kyrgyz Republic*, where the tribunal was very clear in stating that if the UK wished to terminate the provisional application of the ECT to Gibraltar, it should have made this clear with a notification or a declaration.[104]

The *Yukos* tribunal was faced with yet another question concerning the interpretation of Article 45(1), namely the requirement of 'consistency' with the state's constitution, laws, and regulations for the Treaty to apply on a provisional basis. Despite Russia's argument that 'the tribunal had to assess whether each and every individual provision of the ECT was consistent with Russian municipal law',[105] the tribunal 'considered that the provisional application of the ECT, applies to the treaty as a whole, and that the potential inconsistency of one particular provision with a State's constitution, laws or regulations is of no relevance'.[106] In other words, 'by signing the ECT, the Russian Federation agreed that the Treaty *as a whole* would be applied provisionally pending its entry into force unless *the principle* of provisional application itself were inconsistent "with its constitution, laws or regulations".'[107]

Finally, as to the actual content of the obligations of those states which have signed but not yet ratified the ECT, the tribunal in *Kardassopoulos v Georgia* explained that the Treaty's provisional application under Article 45(1) was equivalent to its entry into force during the period between signature and ratification: 'the provisional application of the whole treaty...imports the application of all its provisions as if they were already in

[102] *Kardassopoulos v Georgia*, Decision on Jurisdiction, para. 228, as quoted in *Hulley v Russia*, *Yukos v Russia*, and *Veteran Petroleum v Russia*, Interim Award on Jurisdiction and Admissibility, para. 269.

[103] *Hulley Enterprises Ltd v The Russian Federation*, PCA Case No. AA 226, UNCITRAL [hereinafter *Hulley v Russia*], Interim Award on Jurisdiction and Admissibility, 30 November 2009, para. 285; *Yukos Universal Limited (Isle of Man) v The Russian Federation*, PCA Case No. AA 227, UNCITRAL [hereinafter *Yukos v Russia*], Interim Award on Jurisdiction and Admissibility, 30 November 2009, para. 285; and *Veteran Petroleum Ltd v The Russian Federation*, PCA Case No. AA 228, UNCITRAL [hereinafter *Veteran v Russia*], Interim Award on Jurisdiction and Admissibility, 30 November 2009, para. 285. See T. Gazzini, 'Yukos Universal Limited (Isle of Man) v The Russian Federation: Provisional Application of the ECT in the Yukos Case', 30(2) ICSID Review 293 (2013), 296; Hobér (n. 8), 187.

[104] The tribunal added that 'the fact that the ratification...did not include Gibraltar does not justify the conclusion that the United Kingdom intended to revoke the application of the Treaty to Gibraltar on a provisional basis'. *Petrobart v Kyrgyz Republic*, Award, Section VIII.2.

[105] Hobér (n. 8) 188. [106] De Brabandere (n. 2).

[107] *Hulley v Russia*, *Yukos v Russia*, and *Veteran v Russia*, Interim Award on Jurisdiction and Admissibility, 30 November 2009, para. 301 (emphasis in original).

force, even though the treaty's proper or definitive entry into force has not yet occurred.'[108] As a matter of fact, if the opposite were true—if investments during the period of provisional application were excluded from the scope of the ECT—'such a result would strike at the heart of the clearly intended provisional application regime.'[109] This conclusion has serious repercussions on the interpretation of the term 'entry into force' set out in Article 1(6), which has accordingly to be interpreted to mean the date on which the ECT becomes provisionally applicable.[110]

34.3.2.3 *Denial of benefits*

In accordance with Article 17(1) of the ECT, each contracting party reserves the right to deny the advantages of Part III to an entity owned or controlled by investors of a state that is not a party to the ECT, if that entity has no substantial business activities in the area of the contracting party in which it is organized.[111] Recent arbitral awards of tribunals established under the ECT have clearly demonstrated that the interpretation of Article 17(1) raises difficult issues as to its meaning and effect.[112]

The first question is whether Article 17 goes to the jurisdiction of the tribunal or to the merits. In a number of cases, the respondents have been arguing the tribunal's lack of jurisdiction *ratione materiae* whenever Article 17 is invoked. The respondent in *Plama v Bulgaria*, for instance, argued that 'any issue raised under Article 17(1)... can deprive this Tribunal of all jurisdiction to decide the merits of the parties' dispute.'[113] In this case, the tribunal ruled out the respondent's argument and stated that the denial foreseen in Article 17 applies *only* to advantages under Part III of the Treaty—Article 17 itself is titled 'Non-Application of Part III in Certain Circumstances.' It would instead 'require a gross manipulation of the language to make it refer to Article 26 in Part V of the ECT.'[114] In doing so, the *Plama* tribunal rejected the idea that the application of Article 17 would affect its jurisdiction, and refused to consider it as a provision which would exclude certain categories of investors from the coverage of the Treaty, as this approach 'would clearly not accord with the ECT's object and purpose.'[115] This very same question was raised in several other disputes, including *Amto v Ukraine*, where the Tribunal referred to the competence-competence principle in international arbitration, and explained that 'a dispute regarding an obligation includes a dispute relating to the existence of an

[108] *Kardassopoulos v Georgia*, Decision on Jurisdiction, para. 219. [109] Ibid. para. 222.

[110] Hobér (n. 8), 186; De Brabandere (n. 2).

[111] Moreover, according to Art. 26(2), contracting parties can deny the advantages of Part III if it is established that the investment 'is an Investment of an Investor of a third state with or as to which the denying Contracting Party: (a) does not maintain a diplomatic relationship; or (b) adopts or maintains measures that (i) prohibit transactions with Investors of that state; or (ii) would be violated or circumvented if the benefits of this Part were accorded to Investors of that state or to their Investments.'

[112] Hobér (n. 54), 162. [113] *Plama v Bulgaria*, Decision on Jurisdiction, para. 146.

[114] Ibid. para. 147.

[115] Ibid. para. 149. As pointed out by the tribunal, 'In the absence of Article 26 as a remedy available to the covered investor (as the Respondent contends), how are such disputes to be determined between the host state and the covered investor, given that such determination is crucial to both?'

obligation',[116] which meant that Ukraine's exercise of its right to deny advantages constituted an aspect of the dispute submitted to arbitration and therefore within the jurisdiction of this arbitral tribunal.[117]

A second issue addressed by the *Plama* tribunal concerned the proper way to 'exercise' the right of denial. The question at stake was whether 'Article 17 in itself provided sufficient notice to the investor that it could not enjoy the protection of the ECT...or if further notice was required'.[118] The tribunal distinguished between the mere existence of a right and its exercise, and concluded that, given the wording of Article 17(1)—'reserves the right to deny'—any interpretation of Article 17(1) in accordance with Article 31(1) of the VCLT required that the right of denial be actively exercised by the contracting state.[119] The same conclusion was reached by the tribunal in the *Yukos* cases, whereby it was confirmed that 'Article 17(1) does not deny simpliciter the advantages of Part III of the ECT' to certain categories of investors. Rather, 'it "reserves the right" of each Contracting Party to deny the advantages of that Part to such an entity' which signifies that 'to effect denial, the Contracting Party *must exercise* the right.'[120] The tribunal in *Khan Resources v Mongolia* followed this very same reasoning, further clarifying the importance of the timing of the objection, which becomes relevant when discussing the application *ratione temporis* of the provision.[121]

A final question regarding the correct interpretation and application of Article 17 concerned its potential retrospective application. In *Plama v Bulgaria,* the respondent state only made its notice under this provision *after* the claimant had filed for arbitration and *four years after* the investment had been made. Yet, the respondent argued that its notice could apply retrospectively. In its reasoning, the tribunal once again relied on Article 31 of the VCLT and in particular made reference to the object and purpose of the ECT, finding that a retrospective application of Article 17 would not be consistent with the purpose of the Treaty to 'promote *long-term cooperation* in the energy field'.[122] The same conclusion was reached by the tribunals in the *Yukos* cases and in *Khan Resources v Mongolia.* In the former, the tribunal explained that a 'retrospective application of a denial of rights would be inconsistent with such promotion and protection and constitute treatment at odds with those terms'.[123] In the latter, the tribunal pointed out that if

[116] *Amto v Ukraine*, Award, para. 60.

[117] Ibid. This issue was similarly addressed by the tribunal in *Khan Resources v Mongolia*, where it was found that the question was one of merits, although it was discussed in the decision on jurisdiction. *Khan Resources Inc., Khan Resources B.V., and Cauc Holding Company Ltd v The Government of Mongolia*, UNCITRAL [hereinafter *Khan Resources v Mongolia*], Decision on Jurisdiction, 25 July 2012, Section H.

[118] Hobér (n. 54), 181.

[119] *Plama v Bulgaria*, Decision on Jurisdiction, para. 155.

[120] *Hulley v Russia*, Interim Award on Jurisdiction and Admissibility, para. 455; *Yukos v Russia*, Interim Award on Jurisdiction and Admissibility, para. 456; *Veteran Petroleum v Russia*, Interim Award on Jurisdiction and Admissibility, para. 512 (emphasis added).

[121] *Khan Resources v Mongolia*, Decision on Jurisdiction, para. 424.

[122] ECT, Art. 2 (emphasis added). *Plama v Bulgaria*, Decision on Jurisdiction, para. 161.

[123] *Hulley v Russia*, Interim Award on Jurisdiction and Admissibility, para. 457; *Yukos v Russia*, Interim Award on Jurisdiction and Admissibility, para. 458; *Veteran Petroleum v Russia*, Interim Award on Jurisdiction and Admissibility, para. 514.

the contrary approach were to be preferred, the investor 'would find itself in a highly unpredictable situation. This lack of certainty would impede the investor's ability to evaluate whether or not to make an investment in any particular state. This would be contrary to the Treaty's object and purpose.'[124]

34.3.3 Investment protection and promotion

Unlike the vast majority of BITs, which usually give jurisdiction to an arbitral tribunal to determine 'all' or 'any' disputes between the parties,[125] under the ECT only alleged breaches of obligations in Part III can be arbitrated. The latter contains the substantive provisions aimed at the promotion and protection of investments in the energy sector: it imposes certain obligations on the Contracting States and requires them to treat foreign investors—provided their state of nationality is a party to the Treaty—according to certain standards, the overarching goal being the creation of a 'level playing field' for investments in the energy sector and the reduction of the non-commercial risks associated with them.[126]

The core standards of protection can be found in Article 10(1):

> Each Contracting Party shall, in accordance with the provisions of this Treaty, encourage and create stable, equitable, favourable and transparent conditions for Investors of other Contracting Parties to make Investments in its Area. Such conditions shall include a commitment to accord at all times to Investments of Investors of other Contracting Parties *fair and equitable treatment*. Such Investments shall also enjoy the most constant *protection and security* and no Contracting Party shall in any way impair by *unreasonable or discriminatory* measures their management, maintenance, use, enjoyment or disposal. In no case shall such Investments be accorded treatment less favourable than that required by international law, including treaty obligations. Each Contracting Party shall *observe any obligations it has entered into* with an Investor or an Investment of an Investor of any other Contracting Party.[127]

As is evident from this provision, Part III of the ECT places particular emphasis on the principle of non-discrimination.[128] This was also the first standard to be breached under the ECT in *Nykomb v Latvia*, 'where the tribunal found that Latvia had discriminated against the Swedish investor by offering higher tariffs for produced electricity to companies other than Nykomb's Latvian subsidiary'.[129]

In *Petrobart v Kyrgyz Republic*, the tribunal, while interpreting Article 10(1), observed that it was not necessary to analyse the Kyrgyz Republic's action in relation to the

[124] *Khan Resources v Mongolia*, Decision on Jurisdiction, para. 426.

[125] See e.g. UK Model BIT (2005/6); Germany Model BIT (2005); Netherlands Model BIT (1997); France Model BIT (2006).

[126] Hobér (n. 54), 154.

[127] ECT, Art. 10(1) (emphasis added).

[128] Roe and Happold (n. 25), 15.

[129] *Nykomb v Latvia*, Award, Section 4.3.2(a). See Hobér (n. 8), 195.

various specific elements of the provision, noting instead that 'this paragraph in its entirety is intended to ensure a *fair and equitable treatment* of investments'.[130] The fair and equitable treatment or FET standard raises a number of controversial issues and one of the thorniest—the question of what sort of governmental acts generate legitimate expectations and when failure to satisfy those legitimate expectations can lead to state responsibility—has been addressed by several tribunals established under the ECT. In *Charanne v Spain*, for instance, the tribunal spoke on the issue of 'timing' of the investor's expectations, and concluded that the appropriate time for ascertaining an investor's expectations was the time when the 'investment was decided and made' by the investor: 'the question is whether the legal order in force *at the time of the investment* could in itself generate legitimate expectations'[131]—an approach that has been adopted by other tribunals in arbitration both within and outside the ECT.[132] Regarding instead the issue of 'specificity', the tribunal was faced with the question of whether regulations applying to all companies in a particular economic sector could create legitimate expectations for individual investors, or whether a more specific commitment was needed. Here the tribunal adopted a limited interpretation of legitimate expectations, and concluded that, because 'there was no specific commitment by Spain vis-à-vis the claimants' that the regime would remain unchanged for the duration of the investment, the investor could not have any 'legitimate expectations'.[133] In his dissenting opinion, Professor Tawil disagreed with this interpretation, arguing instead that such expectations 'can also derive from, or be based on, the legal system in force at the time of the investment'.[134] The *Electrabel v Hungary* tribunal reached the same conclusion, observing that 'a specific representation is not always indispensable to a claim advanced under the ECT's FET standard'.[135]

Another issue that has been raised in many arbitrations is the correct interpretation of the last sentence of Article 10(1), which contains what has been defined as 'one of the most extensive umbrella clauses'.[136] This clause reflects the principle of *pacta sunt servanda* by making it an obligation of each Contracting Party to 'observe any obligations it

[130] *Petrobart v Kyrgyz Republic*, Award, 76 (emphasis added).

[131] *Charanne B.V. and Construction Investments S.A.R.L. v Spain*, SCC Arbitration No. 062/2012, [hereinafter *Charanne v Spain*], Final Award, 21 January 2016, para. 494 (emphasis added).

[132] See e.g. the tribunal's decision in *LG and E v Argentina*: 'the fair and equitable treatment analysis involves consideration of the investor's expectations *when making its investment* in reliance on the protections to be granted by the host State.' *LG and E v Argentina*, Decision on Liability, 3 October 2006, para. 127 (emphasis added). Similarly, in *CMS v Argentina*, the tribunal found that 'the measures that are complained of did in fact entirely transform and alter the legal and business environment under which the investment was decided and made… It has also been established that the guarantees given in this connection under the legal framework and its various components were crucial for the investment decision.' *CMS v Argentina*, Award, 12 May 2005, para. 275.

[133] *Charanne v Spain*, Final Award, para. 494. See *also Isolux Infrastructure Netherlands B.V. v Spain*, SCC Arbitration No V2013/153 [hereinafter *Isolux v Spain*], Award, 17 July 2016, paras. 774–9.

[134] *Charanne v Spain*, Dissenting Opinion, para. 5.

[135] *Electrabel S.A. v Republic of Hungary*, ICSID Case No. ARB/07/19 [hereinafter *Electrabel v Hungary*], Award, 25 November 2015, para. 155. See *also LG and E v Argentina* and *CMS v Argentina*.

[136] De Brabandere (n. 2).

has entered into with an Investor or an Investment of an Investor of any other contracting party', thus transforming a simple breach of a contract or licensing agreement into a violation of the host state's obligations under the ECT. The breadth of this clause has been confirmed by the tribunal in *Amto v Ukraine*, which found that the clause imposed obligations not only on the foreign investor but also on a subsidiary company established in the host state, defining the clause itself as having 'wide character'.[137]

Article 13 contains another standard of protection commonly found in both bilateral and multilateral investment treaties—the protection against unlawful expropriation—and just like most other treaties, it lists certain conditions that can make the expropriatory behaviour 'lawful'.[138] Moreover, again like most investment treaties, the protection provided for in Article 13 extends to situations of de facto or indirect expropriation: investments 'shall not be nationalized, expropriated or subjected to a measure or measures having *effect equivalent* to nationalization or expropriation'.[139] However, Article 13 'does not itself provide a definition or standard for determining—in a specific fact situation—whether or not an indirect expropriation has occurred'.[140] Several tribunals were faced with cases of alleged indirect expropriations. In *Mamidoil v Albania*, the tribunal found that the rezoning of the claimants' tank farm in Albania was not an indirect or creeping expropriation, but an appropriate enactment of public policy and a subsequent accommodation of the claimants' interests, because, among other things, they had operated profitably until then.[141] The tribunal followed the decision is *El Paso v Argentina*, stating: 'regulations that reduce the profitability of an investment, but do not shut it down completely and leave the investor in control, will generally not qualify as indirect expropriations.'[142]

The question of what constitutes 'indirect expropriation' was also at the heart of the *Yukos* arbitrations. The analysis of the tribunal can be summarized by looking at three elements that have become traditional in determining whether the legal threshold for an indirect expropriation has been met: (i) the economic impact of the government measures on the investment, (ii) the investor's legitimate expectations, and (iii) the character of the government measures.[143] After finding, rather easily and convincingly, that the level of economic impact suffered by the claimants constituted an expropriation, and

[137] *Amto v Ukraine*, Final Award, 26 March 2008, para. 110. See De Brabandere (n. 2).

[138] Dolzer and Stevens (n. 86) 97. For a 'classic' case of direct expropriation, *see Kardassopoulos v Georgia*.

[139] ECT, Article 13(1) (emphasis added).

[140] C. S. Gibson, '*Yukos Universal Limited (Isle of Man) v. The Russian Federation*: A Classic Case of Indirect Expropriation', 30(2) ICSID Review 303 (2015), 306. See Dolzer and Stevens (n. 86), 98: 'BITs generally do not define the term expropriation or any of the other terms denoting similar measures of dispossession.'

[141] *Mamidoil Jetoil Greek Petroleum Products Societe SA v Republic of Albania*, ICSID Case No. ARB/11/24 [hereinafter *Mamidoil v Albania*], Award, 30 March 2015, para. 577. See Hobér (n. 8), 197.

[142] *El Paso Energy International Company v The Argentine Republic*, ICSID Case No. ARB/03/15 [hereinafter *El Paso v Argentina*], Award, 31 October 2011, paras. 255–6, as quoted in *Mamidoil v Albania*, Award, para. 572. The same reasoning was followed by the tribunal in *AES Summit v Hungary*.

[143] See e.g. T. Gazzini, 'Drawing the Line between Non-compensable Regulatory Powers and Indirect Expropriation of Foreign Investment: An Economic Analysis of Law Perspective', 7(3) Manchester Journal of International Economic Law 36 (2010).

that the scope and degree of the Russian authorities' responses had without any doubt generated their legitimate expectations, the tribunal turned to the difficult issue of the character of the government measure. The issue, however, proved to be difficult only on the surface, as the tribunal quickly[144] concluded that the relevant measures imposed by the Russian Federation were 'taken only under the guise of taxation, but in reality, aim[ed] to achieve an entirely unrelated purpose'.[145]

As is evident from the analysis of the jurisprudence conducted so far, it is still difficult to talk about a general approach to the substantive issues raised in each of these cases. On the other hand, one merit issue that has been dealt rather consistently is the standard of compensation in cases where the investor was successful on the merits.[146] Like the majority of investment treaties, the ECT does not contain any provision which specifies the standard of compensation in case of violation of investment protection provisions *other* than expropriation, such as those contained in Article 10(1). Thus, tribunals have relied on customary international law and, in particular, on principles of customary law as restated in the International Law Commission (ILC) Articles on State Responsibility as well as in the *Chorzów Factory* case. In *Nykomb v Latvia*, for instance, the tribunal noted that the principles of compensation provided for in Article 13(1) of the ECT, in the event of expropriation, were not applicable to the assessment of damages or losses caused by violations of Article 10, while 'the question of remedies to compensate for losses or damages... must primarily find its solution in accordance with established principles of customary international law'.[147] As a result, 'taking into regard the requirements under applicable customary international law of causation, foreseeability and the reasonableness of the result',[148] the tribunal considered that the 'reduced earnings of Windau constituted the best available basis for the assessment also of Nykomb's losses'.[149] The same approach has been followed by the tribunals in *Petrobart v Kyrgyz Republic*[150] and *Kardassopoulos v Georgia*.[151]

34.4 The Future: Recent Developments in Energy Investment Arbitration

Sections 34.2 and 34.3 have addressed, respectively, the origins of investment arbitration in the energy sector and the most salient issues—concerning both jurisdiction and merits—that have been raised in the context of energy arbitrations under the Energy

[144] It has been observed that 'while the Tribunal took some 300 pages to describe its factual findings, its legal reasoning on breach required a mere five and a half pages'. A. Newcombe, 'An Introduction to the Agora', 30(2) ICSID Review 1 (2015), 5.

[145] *Hulley v Russia*, *Yukos v Russia*, *Veteran Petroleum v Russia*, Final Award, para. 1407. See Gibson (n. 140), 311.

[146] Hobér (n. 8), 200–01.

[147] *Nykomb v Latvia*, Award, Section 5.1, 38.

[148] Ibid. section 5.2, 41.

[149] Hobér (n. 54), 187.

[150] *Petrobart v Kyrgyz Republic*, Award, 77–8.

[151] *Kardassopoulos v Georgia*, Award, para. 507.

Charter Treaty which, while not representing the entire 'universe' of energy disputes, have played an important role in shaping this field. This section aims to build on this analysis to flesh out some of the most recent developments in the landscape of energy arbitration.

34.4.1 The 'explosion' of renewable energy disputes

A first, rather self-evident development in energy investment arbitration has concerned the subject matter of the more recent disputes. The first cases surveyed in this contribution—and the first ones in chronological order—such as the Middle Eastern and Libyan arbitrations of the 1970s and 1980s, up until many of the first cases brought under the ECT or even non-ECT disputes such as those against Argentina, dealt almost exclusively with activities related to oil and gas. After 2010, although oil and gas disputes have far from disappeared, a new industry within the energy sector—the renewable energy industry—has become a major target of investment claims.

The motivation of many states to encourage both domestic and foreign investment in their renewable energy sector needs to be understood in the global context. Under the 1992 UN Framework Convention on Climate Change (UNFCCC)—and later in other climate change-related instruments—state parties have committed to a reduction of greenhouse gas emissions and to allocating resources to address climate change. As a result, many countries have begun providing a number of support measures and crucial economic incentives for the creation of a favourable renewable energy market environment. Such measures include both market-pull policies—quota systems, feed-in tariffs, and market-pull incentives for deployment—and various types of government support, for example, funds, direct loans, loan guarantees, and tax breaks.[152]

Many of these measures, however, might be seen as violating provisions of investment and trade treaties, as evidenced by the claims brought by the US company Mesa Power Group LLC (Mesa) against Canada in 2011. The claims concerned in particular the feed-in tariff programme introduced by the Government of Ontario to promote the generation and consumption of renewable energy in the province. Under this programme, renewable energy generators, if selected, would have benefited from a long-term contract guaranteeing a fixed price for electricity sold to the electricity grid above market prices. Mesa, despite having filed six separate applications, was never awarded any FIT contracts and decided to file arbitration under NAFTA Chapter 11, arguing that the programme—and in particular the requirement to satisfy certain domestic-content requirements to be able to qualify for the programme—had resulted in discrimination against the company.[153] The tribunal, however, found against the claimant, concluding that, although 'at least some criticism may be levelled at Ontario's' implementation of

[152] E. Cima, 'Caught Between Trade and Climate Change: The Economic Rationale of "Green Subsidies"', in K. Mathis and B. R. Huber (eds), *Environmental Law and Economics* (Springer, 2017), 379.

[153] *Mesa Power Group LLC v Government of Canada*, UNCITRAL, PCA Case No. 2012–17 [hereinafter *Mesa v Canada*], Award, para. 211.

the programme, 'judged in all the circumstances, this is not criticism that reaches the threshold of a violation of Canada's international obligations'.[154]

The 'explosion' of renewable energy disputes under the ECT has instead been motivated by rather different circumstances. The nearly 50 disputes filed over the last five years arose not because of the renewable energy programmes introduced by the respondent states—as in the case of *Mesa v Canada*—but rather because of these 'governments' decision to revoke the subsidies agreed to be paid for clean energy from renewable sources, as they struggled to cope financially with the [economic] crisis'.[155] Spain, Italy, and the Czech Republic in particular have found themselves facing multiple disputes after having introduced changes to their legal and regulatory framework for renewable energy investment. To this day, nine disputes have reached a final award stage and have been made public, either in full or in some redacted form.[156] The discussion on the merits has focused mostly on two standards: the requirement to provide fair and equitable treatment and the protection against expropriation. As to the former, in particular, these decisions have contributed significantly to shaping the evolution of the interpretation and application of the FET standard under the ECT. Besides what has already been described with regards to the degree of specificity of the government's commitments towards the investor, all awards have agreed that this standard cannot be read so as to prevent a state from making changes to its regulatory framework. In *Charanne v Spain*, for instance, the tribunal stated that, in the absence of a specific contractual guarantee between the investor and the state, a change in the applicable laws and regulations would not constitute a breach of the FET standard.[157] However, the tribunal added that 'subsequent changes should be made fairly, consistently and predictably, taking into account the circumstances of the investment'.[158] Along the same lines, the tribunal in *Eiser v Spain* noted that while the ECT does not prevent 'appropriate changes to the regulatory regime', it does protect investors 'against... total and unreasonable change'.[159]

34.4.2 Energy disputes and the environment: environmental counterclaims

Another development has concerned the role played by environmental considerations and environmental law in the context of recent energy arbitrations. It is widely known

[154] Ibid. para. 682.

[155] N. Gallagher, 'ECT and Renewable Energy Disputes', in Scherer (n. 8), 250.

[156] K. Parlett, 'Investment Arbitration in the Energy Sector: The European Renewables Disputes', MS with the author.

[157] *Charanne v Spain*, Final Award, para. 503.

[158] Ibid. para. 500, quoting *Electrabel v Hungary*, Award, para. 7.77.

[159] *Eiser Infrastructure Limited and Energia Solar Luxembourg S.à.r.l. v Spain*, ICSID Case No. ARB/13/36 [hereinafter *Eiser v Spain*], Award, 4 May 2017, para. 363. See also *Antaris GMBH and Michael Göde v Czech Republic*, PCA Case No. 2014–01 [hereinafter *Antaris v Czech Republic*], Award, 2 May 2018, para. 360(7); and *Masdar Solar and Wind Cooperatief U.A. v Spain* (ICSDI Case No ARB/14/1), [hereinafter *Masdar v Spain*], Award, 16 May 2018, para. 484.

that energy activities pose significant risks in terms of environmental degradation. Tensions exist between the international legal framework that regulates economic activities, including foreign investments, on the one hand, and the one governing environmental protection on the other. In particular, a tension exists between states' willingness to strengthen their domestic environmental standards and the use, by foreign investors in energy-intensive industries, of provisions in bilateral or multilateral investment treaties to challenge those standards, as they risk to negatively impact their investment's profitability. While the environment has, for a long time, played a rather marginal role in energy arbitration, recent practices, both in treaty-drafting and dispute settlement, seem to provide new avenues to mainstream environmental considerations in energy investment arbitration.

In particular, states have begun to bring environmental counterclaims in proceedings initiated by investors to try to enforce environmental law against them. This opportunity was taken by Ecuador in the context of the disputes against Perenco Ecuador (Perenco) and Burlington Resources (Burlington).[160] The two corporations, registered in France, created a consortium and obtained an oil-drilling concession in the Amazon region of Ecuador in 2002. A few years later, in 2006 and 2007, the Ecuadorian government enacted several amendments to its Hydrocarbon Law with the effect, among others, of increasing the revenues to be paid to the Ecuadorian government.[161] Once all attempts at negotiations failed, the two foreign investors launched two separate arbitral proceedings, claiming the state's breach of certain provisions contained both in their respective concession agreements and in the France–Ecuador BIT. What is relevant for our purposes is the fact that in both proceedings, Ecuador presented an environmental counterclaim against the investors, 'on the basis that its experts had determined the existence of an "environmental catastrophe" in the two oil blocks situated in the country's Amazonian rainforest that had been worked by the consortium under Perenco [and Burlington]'s operatorship'.[162] The counterclaims 'largely concerned the alleged failure of [the investors] to comply with Ecuadorian law during the time in which [they were] responsible for the oil drilling operations'.[163] Moreover, because of the strict liability regime prescribed by the 2008 Ecuadorian Constitution, the respondent state argued that it was only necessary for Ecuador to prove that damage had taken place, without having to prove causation or negligence.[164] Finally, Ecuador claimed that both Perenco

[160] *Perenco Ecuador Ltd v The Republic of Ecuador and Empresa Estatal Petróleos del Ecuador (Petroecuador)*, ICSID Case No. ARB/08/6 [hereinafter *Perenco v Ecuador*] and *Burlington Resources Inc. v Republic of Ecuador*, ICSID Case No. ARB/08/5 [hereinafter *Burlington v Ecuador*].

[161] J. Harrison, 'Environmental Counterclaims in Investor–State Arbitration', 17 Journal of World Investment and Trade 479 (2016), 480.

[162] *Perenco v Ecuador*, Decision on Jurisdiction, 30 June 2011, para. 34; Claimant's Counter-Memorial on Counterclaims dated 28 September 2012, para. 1. See *also Burlington v Ecuador*, Decision on Counterclaims, 7 February 2017, para. 80.

[163] Harrison (n. 161), 481. *Perenco v Ecuador*, Decision on Jurisdiction, paras. 36–42.

[164] *Perenco v Ecuador*, Decision on Jurisdiction, para 36; *Burlington v Ecuador*, Decision on Counterclaims, paras. 81–2 and 93–8.

and Burlington had adopted the strategy of concealing and failing to report the existence of environmental harm, and had later tried to rely on a set of environmental audits, whose results Ecuador deemed not credible, to evade their liability for environmental damages.[165]

Environmental considerations guided the tribunals throughout the analysis:

> Ecuador viewed [the environmental catastrophe caused by the investor] as an extremely serious matter deserving the most careful consideration by the Tribunal. On this point, the Tribunal cannot but agree. Proper environmental stewardship has assumed great importance in today's world. The Tribunal agrees that if a legal relationship between an investor and the State permits the filing of a claim by the State for environmental damage caused by the investor's activities and such a claim is substantiated, the State is entitled to full reparation in accordance with the requirements of the applicable law.[166]

Moreover, despite siding with the investor in the reading of the Ecuadorian Constitution, the tribunal in *Perenco* held that the 'Constitution's focus on environmental protection means that when choosing between certain disputed (but reasonable) interpretations of the Ecuadorian regulatory regime, the interpretation which most favours the protection of the environment is to be preferred'.[167] One example of this presumption in favour of environmental protection is evident in the way in which the tribunal has assigned the burden of proof. While Perenco submitted that the burden, first and foremost, remained on Ecuador to affirmatively prove the existence of a causal link, the tribunal decided to employ 'a strong rebuttable presumption that if there is a regulatory exceedance, that in itself is evidence of fault [as] any alternative approach would make it too onerous for a claimant because it would likely lack sufficient evidence to demonstrate that the operator failed in its duty of care in many if not most instances in which regulatory exceedances have occurred'.[168] As a result, in *Burlington*, the tribunal awarded US$39.2 million to Ecuador for environmental harm caused by the investor in breach of the Ecuadorian statutory environmental regulation regime.[169] In *Perenco*, despite being inclined to hold Perenco liable for some environmental contamination, the tribunal preferred to appoint its own expert to investigate the relevant sites, in the light of the significant disagreement between the party-appointed experts on the extent of contamination and Perenco's responsibility for it.[170]

[165] *Burlington v Ecuador*, Decision on Counterclaims, para. 87; *Perenco v Ecuador*, Decision on Jurisdiction, paras. 38–40.

[166] *Perenco v Ecuador*, Decision on Jurisdiction, para. 34.

[167] Ibid. para. 322.

[168] Ibid. para. 374.

[169] K. Parlett and S. Ewad, 'Protection of the Environment in Investment Arbitration: A Double-Edged Sword', 20 Essex St. Bulletin (2017).

[170] Ibid.

34.5 Conclusions

Investment arbitration in the energy sector is, in many ways, not too different from 'regular' investment arbitration. Why, then, has it attracted so much attention recently, and why has it been addressed, more and more often, almost as a sub-field of international investment law? Answering these questions was precisely the goal of this chapter, exploring and analysing what makes energy investment arbitration simply part of investment arbitration and what makes it (to a certain extent) 'different' or even 'special'.

Since the very first disputes in the early 1960s until the more recent Latin American and European cases, three points are clear: investment arbitration is especially important for energy investors, considering the specific characteristics of this industry and the particularly difficult balance to be stricken between states' and investors' interests; the specific characteristics of this sector, in turn, have contributed to the creation of a unique legal framework, applicable only to energy investments, and to a certain interpretation of investment norms by arbitral tribunals; and finally, energy disputes have played a crucial role in shaping the constant development and evolution of international investment law and arbitration, with reference not only to energy disputes but to 'regular' disputes as well.

CHAPTER 35

INTER-STATE ARBITRATION IN HISTORICAL PERSPECTIVE

ALEXIS KELLER

I have no intention of writing a new history of inter-state arbitration. The works of Dereck Roebuck on arbitration in the ancient world are well known.[1] We owe to †V. V. Veeder a vivid description of some famous arbitration cases.[2] We are also familiar with the descriptions of some historical incidents of arbitration like the discussions leading to the New York Convention or, more recently, the circumstances that led Great Britain to pass the Arbitration Act 1979, recounted by Lord Hacking in an issue of the journal of the Chartered Institute of Arbitrators.[3] The theoretical development of arbitration after the end of the Second World War has also been described in many different ways in the recently published empirical works of writers like J. L. Simpson and H. Fox, J. H. W. Verzijl, A. M. Stuyt, Ph. Fouchard, E. Gaillard and B. Goldman, J. F. Poudret and S. Besson, and even Lord Mustill and S. Boyd to mention only the most important among them.[4]

[1] Derek Roebuck, *Ancient Greek Arbitration* (Holo Books, 2001); *The Charitable Arbitrator* (Holo Books, 2002); *Roman Arbitration* (Holo Books, 2004).

[2] See †V. V. Veeder's Ch. 8 in this Handbook. See also †V. V. Veeder, 'The Lena Goldfields Arbitration: The Historical Roots of Three Ideas', 47 International and Comparative Law Quarterly 747 (1998), 747–9; 'Lloyd George, Lenin and Cannibals: The Harriman Arbitration', 16(2) Arbitration International 115 (2000), 115–19; 'The Tetihue Mining Concession: A Swiss–Russian Story', in *Autour de l'arbitrage. Liber amicorum Claude Reymond* (Pédone, 2004), 325–42.

[3] See Lord Hacking, 'The Story of the Arbitration Act 1979', 76 Chartered Institute of Arbitrators 124 (2010).

[4] John Simpson and Hazel Fox, *International Arbitration* (Praeger, 1959); J. H. W. Verzijl, *International Law in Historical Perspective* (A. W. Sijthoff-Leyden, 1970); A. M. Stuyt, *Survey of International Arbitrations 1794–1989* (Springer, 1989); Philippe Fouchard, Emmanuel Gaillard, and Berthold Goldman, *Traité de l' arbitrage commercial international* (Litec, 1996); Jean-François Poudret and Sébastian Besson, *Droit comparé de l' arbitrage commercial international* (LGDJ, 2002); Lord Mustill and Stewart Boyd, *The Law and Practice of Commercial Arbitration in England*, 2nd edn (LexisNexis, 1987).

My objective is to identify and describe the principal *moments*—called 'historical crossroads' by historians—when the definition of arbitration and the institutions and techniques associated with it underwent major changes.[5] The emphasis of this chapter is on inter-state arbitration, yet its proposed historical lessons should illuminate the entire field of international dispute settlement.

From that perspective, I will divide this history into five distinct moments. The first (Section 35.1), which could be described as the 'Greek moment', refers to the systematic use of arbitration by Greek cities to resolve their conflicts. The second second (35.2), covering the period between 1200 and 1400 AD, witnessed the emergence of the first arbitration procedures under the influence of canonical law and acknowledged the growing power of the Popes in the settlement of disputes between states. The third (35.3), marked by the Jay Treaty of 1794, initiated a major turning point in the history of arbitration as it confirmed the role of diplomatic commissions in the peaceful resolution of disputes. The fourth moment (35.4), which began with the *Alabama* case (1871), saw the establishment of the first impartial and independent tribunal. The fifth moment (35.5) began with the setting up of the Permanent Arbitration Court in 1899 and the harmonisation of arbitration procedures.

35.1 The Greek moment: the *status quo* principle

Although traditional historiography generally maintains that modern arbitration began with the Jay Treaty in 1794 (to which we will come back later), we cannot ignore the contribution of the ancient world and the Middle Ages. John Jay did not develop his ideas in a vacuum. He founded them on a well-established practice and on the works of several theoreticians of the *jus gentium*.[6]

Treating arbitration as a normal way of conflict resolution, the Greeks traced its origin to the mythological period. Strabo (IX, 3, 7) in fact attributed the establishment of the first arbitration court to Acrisius, king of Argos and father of Danae. According to Pausanias, the gods themselves set an example in this regard. Even though the examples provided by Pausanias seem to belong to the realm of literary fantasy, it is generally accepted that the arbitration procedure has existed as a positive institution since the

[5] See Pierre Rosanvallon, *Pour une histoire conceptuelle du politique* (Seuil, 2003).

[6] Jay was likely unaware of the use of arbitration during the reign of Charles VI in 1726 to resolve the dispute between the Austrians and the Dutch regarding the activities of the Dutch East India Company (the Oostindische Compagnie); similarly, he must have read Vattel, who, in book II of *Droits des gens* (1758) (The Law of People), had presented a relatively modern arbitration theory referring in particular to the practice followed in Swiss cantons. In this regard, see C. G. Roelofsen, 'The Jay Treaty and All That: Some Remarks on the Role of Arbitration in European Modern History and its Revival in 1794', in Alfred Soons (ed.), *International Arbitration: Past and Prospects* (Martinus Nijhoff, 1990), 201.

5th century BC.[7] Thucydides has preserved for posterity the texts of a large number of arbitral clauses. In addition, epigraphy provides very precise information about the composition and designation of arbitral courts and the procedures followed by them.

Almost all the major peace treaties of the 5th century BC contain a clause pertaining to the judicial settlement of disputes likely to arise between contracting parties. Thucydides makes it easy for us to reconstitute the substance of the peace treaty between Athens and Sparta concluded in 445. He claims that the Peloponnesian War was the result of Sparta's refusal to apply the treaty's provisions on dispute settlement. The Athenian delegate to the Spartan Grand Congress of 431 is supposed to have said, 'We have just told you, as long as the choice of a wise decision is for both of us to make, we should not break treaties or violate promises and resolve our disputes in accordance with conventions, through judicial processes.'[8] After having carefully considered the Athenian arguments, most of the Spartans voted for recourse to arms, except for one member, who pointed out that it would be preferable to respect the inter-Hellenic legal system and send a delegation to discuss the wrongs of which their allies claimed to be victims.

A similar clause on arbitration is seen in the truce concluded between the two cities in 423, and also in the Peace Treaty of 418 between Sparta and Argos, where it is explicitly mentioned that the parties 'would resolve their disputes through arbitration on an equal footing, in accordance with established practices'.[9] All this shows that the notion of resolving disputes through legal processes or arbitration was deeply rooted in the Hellenic conscience. Furthermore, almost all the Leagues and Confederations of this period—beginning with the Boeotian Confederation (sixth century)—believed that disputes between member cities should be resolved through arbitration. An inscription from the latter half of the fourth century discovered in Smyrna reproducing an arbitral verdict pronounced by the Assembly of Argos on the delegation of the Greek Parliament—the Corinthian League's decision-making body—shows that the Confederation's judicial powers were widely recognized.

A careful reading of these ancient texts reveals that arbitration in Greece, both in the ancient and classical periods, was essentially structured around the *status quo* principle: 'each maintains what he holds' (μενεσθαι εκατερους την εχουσι). This principle was inserted in peace treaties, armistices, and alliance treaties for the benefit of arbitrators. They could thus decide the standards of reference in territorial disputes that might arise later between the parties to the treaty. Official documents, as well as inscriptions engraved on bronze or marble detailing the clauses of treaties and arbitral decisions, show how the Greeks adhered to the principle of *status quo* for many centuries, and how it was one of the basic principles underlying the resolution of territorial disputes.

As regards the alliance treaty concluded between Sparta and Argos in 418, Thucydides reports the terms of the treaty in the Doric dialect, which guarantees the exactitude of

[7] See Marcus Tod, *International Arbitration among the Greeks* (Clarendon Press, 1913); Jackson Ralston, *International Arbitration From Athens to Locarno* (Stanford University Press, 1929); Sheila Ager, *Interstate Arbitrations in the Greek World, 337–90* BC (University of California Press, 1996).

[8] Thucydides, *The Peloponnesian War*, I, 78, 4.

[9] Ibid. V, 79.

his text. The Lacedaemonians and the Argians, having agreed to 'a peace and alliance between them for a duration of fifty years' and having decided that pending disputes would be resolved by arbitration, expected that 'the other Peloponnesian cities would be associated with the peace and alliance, even as they remained autonomous and independent, having full control over their territory'.[10] This last clause, which stands out for its brevity, refers to the continuance of territorial *status quo*. The phrase is repeated twice (§§ 1 and 2) in relation to two different groups of allies. It thus constitutes the fundamental principle determining the division of territories. In case of difficulty regarding control over some of these territories, the matter would be referred to an arbitrator, who would have to give a ruling in accordance with the principle of the continuance of the existing situation.[11]

The Roman domination over Greek cities did not bring about any fundamental changes in arbitration. The latter continued to use the *status quo* principle as the normal method of resolving territorial disputes under Rome's watchful eye. Additionally, this principle was gradually adopted by Roman law. Though it is true that Rome almost always tried to affirm its superiority in its relations with other peoples, it also resorted to the principle of *status quo* to resolve some conflicts, and the evidence available in this regard leaves no room for doubt. Carthage came under Roman rule after its defeat in the second Punic War (201 BC), but Rome granted the Carthaginians the right to 'retain the cities, towns and countryside with the boundaries they controlled before the war'.[12] The same terms were applied when Rome intervened in the conflict opposing Carthage to Massinissa, king of Numidia, even though he was an ally and protégé of the Romans.

To Titus Livius' testimony we may add the evidence found in epigraphic sources stating the terms of Roman arbitrations in more official language. A bronze plaque found in Spain preserves the text of a decree issued by the governor of Spain at the end of the second century BC, which says that the inhabitants of Turris Lascuna 'will continue to possess the territory and its fortifications as they did at that time'.[13] Here, the governor deals with the possession of land (*possidere habereque*) just as it will be treated later in Gaius' *Institutes* (II, 7) in the middle of the second century AD. He too seemed in favour of maintaining the earlier position regarding the possession of land.

The terminology used in this case is the terminology of private law. The Roman *agrimensores* of the second century AD, like Frontinus, Hyginus, Siculus Flaccus, and Aggenus Urbicus, often dealt with *controversiae agrorum* or disputes related to the boundaries of fields between private parties. They compare all these private disputes to border disputes between Greek cities. This analogy is mentioned particularly in the passage by Hyginus about *controversiae*. He refers to the 'battles' (*certamina*) between

[10] Ibid.

[11] Numerous examples of this type could be cited from more recent periods, e.g. the delimitation of the territory between Delphi and Ambryssos-Phlygonion in the 2nd c. AD.

[12] Titius Livius, *The History of Rome*, 30, 37 (*quas urbes, quosque agros quibusque finibus ante bellum tenuissent, tenerent*). The same argument is also found in Polybius' Histories, 15, 18, 1.

[13] Mentioned in Paul Girard, *Les lois des romains* (Rousseau, 1977), 344–5 (*agrum oppidumque, quod ea tempestate posedissent, item possidere habereque joussit*).

'peoples of neighbouring cities or between land-owners'.[14] Here we can underline the parallel drawn between private *controversiae agrorum* and inter-city conflicts concerning extensive territories.

We cannot rule out the possibility that arbitrations in Rome after the second century BC invoking the *status quo* clause were based on the *uti possidetis* principle. Do we need to go any further to establish the intellectual link between the *status quo* clause and the *uti possidetis* principle? Some historians have been tempted to do so because of the precedence given to inter-city arbitration and the use of the *status quo* clause. There may certainly be a link, but that is not the key issue. The 'Greek moment' made arbitration a general principle of the inter-city law based on the *status quo* clause for the resolution of conflicts. Almost all peace and alliance treaties contain this clause, which is usually drafted in identical or very similar terms in accordance with the time-honoured expression: 'each person will possess the territory as he used to earlier.' There is no reference to 'sovereignty', an idea that was alien to ancient political thought. It was more a question of real control bringing with it practical consequences, possession and use. The Latin terms used for this purpose are *habere, possidere, uti*, and *frui*. And the Greek words have the same resonance.

35.2 The Institution of Arbitration in the Middle Ages: The Role of the Papacy

Historiography has underlined the significant role played by arbitration in the legal culture of the Middle Ages.[15] Historians do not agree on the historical origins of arbitration mechanisms created in medieval times, with some giving more importance to Germanic sources and others to canonical and Roman sources, but they are all agreed that this institution was very active in Europe between the thirteenth and fifteenth centuries.

From the twelfth to the fifteenth century, the prevalence of feudal conditions and the almost total disappearance of an organized state justice system strongly favoured the growth of arbitral procedures, both in private law and in the 'law of people' (*jus gentium*). The emperor, kings and leading members of the clergy played an important role in the process of dispute settlement. There were even specialists in the area like William I, the counts of Hainaut, Holland, and Zeeland, the father-in-law of the English King Edward III, and the leader of the 'English' party in the Netherlands whose contribution led to the conclusion of numerous agreements. Louis IX, king of France, also acted as an arbitrator in the settlement of several conflicts, especially the one related to the Flemish

[14] Hyginus, *De controversiae agrorum*, 78, pp. 9–17.

[15] See Wilhelm Grewe, *The Epochs of International Law* (de Gruyter, 2000), 93–104; Stephen Neff, *Justice Among Nations: A History of International Law* (Harvard University Press, 2014), 56–9.

inheritance, the negotiation of peace with Aragon through the treaty of Corbeil in 1258 and the establishment of peace with England through the treaty of Paris in 1259.[16]

Although there was no institution in the Middle Ages comparable to the International Court of Justice, a large number of tribunals came into existence in the eleventh century. Arbitration was an important element of the law of peace in the *Res publica Christiana*. In many ways it acted as a deterrent to the feudal world's tendency to become atomized. Moreover, it is difficult to distinguish between 'private' and 'public' arbitration during this period since their mechanisms overlapped.[17] A conflict between two princes passed very often from the private sphere to the public sphere before ending up in the domain of the law of people (*jus gentium*).

Following antique practices, arbitration in the Middle Ages was essentially based on the Roman principle of *compromissum*. The details of the procedure were left to the discretion of the 'arbitrator', who could choose between a *per sententiam* and a *per judicium* procedure or between a *per concordiam* and a *per transactionem* procedure. He thus had a choice between two types of procedures. Arbitration clauses first appeared in treaties as far back as the twelfth century, but it became frequent only towards the end of the thirteenth century. It seems to have been used most frequently in Italy, and became more common in the areas to the north of the Alps in the fourteenth century. The German urban leagues included it in their fundamental laws, and its presence was noticeable in inter-regional peace agreements, notably the alliances between Flanders and Brabant in 1339 and the treaty between the prince-bishop of Liège and the count of Namur in 1342.

The Swiss case is interesting in this respect because it throws light on the multiplicity and complexity of arbitral practices in medieval times. Practically all the alliance treaties between cantons contain an arbitration clause—the pact of 1291 between the three original cantons being a typical example—and the overlapping links between cantons, cities, and communes made it almost obligatory to resolve disputes in a peaceful manner. Since 'arbitrators' or arbitral tribunals were obliged to justify their verdicts, they did so by relying on the *Bünde* and *Bürgerrechte* found in different cantons. Whenever this was not possible and they could not adduce the support of any other written text such as a constitution, a charter, or a convention, they had to turn to local customs—the *altes Herkommen*—commonly followed in Swiss cantons. They also used the *Kundschaft*, a kind of testimony to prove the existence of a custom. The historian E. Usteri cites the

[16] Jacque Le Goff, in his biography of Saint-Louis (Gallimard, 2004), 398ff., makes special mention of the arbitration conducted by the king between the King of England, Henry III, and his barons. The ruling given at Amiens in January 1264 mainly favoured the King of England, allowing him to regain full power and unrestricted sovereignty. Louis IX had then compared the famous 'Provisions of Oxford' of 1258 to 'bad customs': the king was thus able to manoeuvre between the idea of a feudal king that he continued to be, and the idea of royal sovereignty inspired by canonical law. What is important is that Saint-Louis acted in this case not as a judge but as an arbitrator, since he had obtained his power to act from both the parties that had approached him.

[17] See Hans Waser, *Das öffentlich-rechtliche Schiedsgericht and die anderen Mittel friedlicher Streiterledigung im Spätmittelalterlichen Südfranckreich* (1935), 58ff.

example of the 1425 arbitration between Lucerne and five villages (*Orte*) during which the *Obmann* (arbitrator) referred to all three categories of sources to give his ruling.[18]

In the Middle Ages, the same person could act as both mediator and arbitrator, the former acting as a conciliator not bound by the rules of law while the latter was bound by them. However, the terminology was not always precise: normally the *arbiter* resolved a dispute according to the law, while the *amicabilis compositor* settled an accord without being bound by it; but the texts contain one more term, *arbitrator*, which could cover both approaches. This was the case in a territorial conflict between the duchess of Brabant and the duke of Gueldre which was originally supposed to have been decided in 1389 by a college consisting of the duke of Lorraine, the archbishop of Cologne, the lord of Coucy, and the duke of la Trémoille. However, since the duke of Lorraine failed to present himself, it was decided to appoint a new college of twelve *arbitrators* consisting of neighbouring lords and vassals of the parties involved, who willingly accepted the college's ruling given in 1390.

The most important mediator during this period was undoubtedly the pope. After the eleventh century, his real power increased considerably. The decree of 1059 freed the papacy from secular control; around the same time, the Germanic Holy Roman Empire was exposed to the first assaults. Gregory VII entrusted the papacy with a new mission following the publication of *Dictatus Papae* in 1075 through which he affirmed the superiority of spiritual power over temporal power. The church became the 'mother of nations', and used its religious power over princes to bring them together and divide them. It set up an autonomous structure with its own internal organization, its institutions, and its laws. As for the pope, he assumed the title of Head of Christendom and was thereby authorized to arbitrate disputes.[19]

The doctrinal positions of successive supreme pontiffs regarding arbitration were naturally quite nuanced, differing according to individual viewpoints and sometimes even at a given point of time under the same pope. It nevertheless remains true that from the time of Gregory VII to the end of the Avignon papacy in 1377, the popes professed a relatively constant doctrine regarding arbitration, for at least three reasons. Firstly, for humanitarian reasons: the pope was keen to avoid the horrors of war, as mentioned in several letters. Secondly, for evangelical reasons: because it was his duty to ensure the reign of peace as promised by Christ to all men of goodwill. He had received from Christ himself the power to unite or divide, make or break emperors and kings. Finally, by altering or spoiling relations between vassals and suzerains, he felt he had the right to influence the conduct of princes.

[18] See Emil Usteri, *Das öffentlich-rechtliche Schiedgericht in der sweizerischen Eidgenossenschaft des 13–15 Jahrhunderts. Ein Beitrag zur Institutionsgeschichte und zum Völkerrecht* (1925), 268ff. See also Dietrich Schindler, 'Les traités de conciliation et d'arbitrage conclu pas la Suisse', (1925) Revue de droit international et de législation comparée 818ff.

[19] We must point out that the notion of 'Christendom' is relatively vague, as its terminology indicates. The words *populus christianus*, *gens christiana*, *orbis christianus*, *terra christianorum* appear in the texts to describe this idea. Nevertheless, all these terms refer to a united community of Christian peoples and kingdoms based on the community's commitment to their faith and obedience to the Roman Church.

Historians have often wondered about the nature of papal interventions, use of good offices, mediation, arbitration, and actual judgments. But such distinctions, which are a result of the development of modern international law, were unknown to the doctrine prevalent in the medieval era. The papacy was not called upon to resolve the same type of problems, and it is difficult for a modern historian to say whether, in a particular case, the pope had to resort to one or another of the above-mentioned types of intervention. At the most, it is possible to discern a change during the thirteenth century. Though, at the beginning of the century, the pope still tried to intervene as the head of Christendom by setting up a compulsory arbitration body, things changed somewhat in 1250. The pope could no longer intervene as the head of Christendom, as it had ceased to be a reality. The states had become bigger, and were more concerned about their independence when it came to respecting their newly acquired sovereignty. The pope's authority and his power to settle disputes by arbitration were now determined by his personal prestige and not his official position.

Pontifical arbitration was not always accepted, because it revived unpleasant memories of the subjugation of some kingdoms to the Holy See. In that case, the pope then declared that any intervention on his part would be 'in his private capacity'—as seen in the comments of de Benedict XII, who declared that he was acting *non tanquam judices vel arbitros, sed velut mediatores et amicos communes.*[20] This is what the English chronicler Adam de Murimuth affirmed in his report on the intervention of Clement VI in the dispute between France and England as *persona privata et amicus communis.*[21] Knowing that the term *amicus* invoked the notion of kinship at that time, it becomes even more obvious why such mediations were deliberately conducted in the private domain.

This form of arbitration did not remain unaffected by advances in the legal domain during that period, which produced new principles related to the problem of representation.[22] Because of his intellectual background and his experience in the political arena when he was in the service of the king of France, Clement VI was not unaware of these advances. He used them with subtlety, as seen in his statement made in the course of the 1344 negotiations, where he avers that he is not acting *ex auctoritate nostra, sed ex potestate attributa nobis a partibus.*[23] This was one way of bringing together the parties involved in the negotiation without allowing them to challenge the pope's authority.

As a matter of fact, by the end of the thirteenth century the papacy was constantly faced with the problem of lack of authority to enforce its rulings. This absence of real power was not compensated by undisputed prestige which would have allowed the pope to use his moral authority to enforce his decisions. On the contrary, the pope's prestige

[20] See Jean Gaudemet, 'Le rôle de la papauté dans le règlement des conflits entre états aux XIIIe et XIVe siècles', *La paix. Recueil de la Société Jean Bodin*, vol. 15 (1961), 95.

[21] Adae Murimuth, 'Adae Murimuth Continuatio Chronicorum (1303–1347)', in Edward Thompson (ed.), *Adae Murimuth Continuatio Chronicorum* (Cambridge University Press, 2012), 136.

[22] Like the *plena potestas* which transforms a messenger into a prosecutor or an ambassador.

[23] Eugène Déprez, 'La conférence d'Avignon (1344). L'arbitrage pontifical entre la France et l'Angleterre', in A. G. Little and Frederick Powicke (eds), *Essays in Medieval History presented to Thomas Tout* (Manchester University Press, 1925), 304, n. 3.

declined after the 1290s. Though in the thirteenth century, Innocent III could still try to impose his will as the head of Christendom, less than a century later Boniface VIII was obliged to admit that he could no longer do so. In 1300, he informed the English that there was little chance of him assuming the mantle of arbitrator. This was not only because of the 'unreasonable' demands made by the French, but even more because the latter were sure to refuse to comply with his ruling. Threats of penalty to force them to comply would be of no use, as they would refuse to pay the fine. The path of arbitration being closed, the only way out was to exercise his 'full pontifical power'. But to do so, he first had to prove the 'sin' committed by the king of France or resort to *ratione peccati* jurisdiction in compliance with the medieval doctrine; Boniface VIII was fully aware of the political risks that would arise when applying it.[24]

After the fifteenth century, the institution of arbitration—regardless of the roles played by the pope, the emperor, and papal princes—gradually lost its vitality. As the states gained sovereignty with the progressive decrease of 'private' wars and the development of independent judicial institutions, arbitration was no longer the sole method of resolving disputes peacefully. Undoubtedly, several rulings were given by arbitral tribunals between 1500 and 1700, but their number declined constantly. Arbitration clauses were no longer the norm. Arbitration as a method of preventing conflicts was no longer the order of the day. This side-lining of the arbitration process was echoed in the doctrine. In his *De Jure Belli ac Pacis* (1625), Grotius pays little attention to the question of peaceful resolution of disputes.[25] Quoting Vitoria, he suggests that a congress of Christian powers be set up to resolve conflicts and supports the possibility of involving a third party. But the terms are rather vague and, though he quotes many examples from the ancient world, it is clear that for him arbitration is no more than a hope, if not a theoretical notion far removed from reality. We have to wait until the end of the eighteenth century for a famous arbitration case—the Jay Treaty of 1794—for this institution to regain the respect it deserves.

35.3 The Birth of Modern Arbitration: the Jay Treaty (1794)

Practically all historians of international law agree that modern arbitration began with the General Treaty of Friendship, Commerce and Navigation between the United States and Great Britain, commonly known as the Jay Treaty, of 19 November 1794.[26] This

[24] The complete text is quoted by Pierre Chaplais in *Le Moyen Âge* (1951), 289. See also Pierre Chaplais, *Essays in Medieval Diplomacy and Administration* (Hambledon Press, 1981).

[25] See Hugo Grotius, *De Juri Belli ac Pacis* (1625), bk II, ch. 23, 8, and bk III, ch. 20, 46–8.

[26] 'Treaty of Amity, Commerce and Navigation, between His Britannic Majesty and The United States of America, by their President, with the advice and consent of Their Senate (1794)' (Jay Treaty), in David Miller (ed.), *Treatises and Other International Acts of the United States of America, Documents 1–40: 1776–1818* (Washington Government Printing Office, 1931), vol. 2.

historiographic tradition is, however, fairly recent. Wheaton's famous book published in 1845, *History of the Law of Nations in Europe and America from the Earliest Times to the Treaty of Washington, 1942*, contains just a few lines on the Jay Treaty. Wharton's *Digest of International Law of the United States* (3 vols, 1886) hardly mentions it. Phillimore's *Commentaries upon International Law* (4 vols, 1879–89) and Lorimer's *Institutes of the Law of Nations* (2 vols, 1883–4), barely tackles the issue. We have to wait for the publication in 1898 of J. B. Moore's great collection of arbitration cases involving the United States, followed in 1905 by the publication of *Recueil des arbitrations internationales* by Lapradelle and Politis, for this perception to change drastically.[27] The Jay Treaty became an important milestone in the history of arbitration, the beginning of a 'new era' and one of the founding myths of public international law. Signed in 1794 by Great Britain and the United States, it was an innovative agreement in many respects. Negotiated over a period of almost ten years after the end of the American War of Independence, it put an end to a tension-ridden period between Britain and the newly created United States—tensions caused by war and the way the separation between Britain and her former colonies had been resolved.

35.3.1 The context

In 1782, after many years of fighting between Britain and her American colonies, the British parliament reached the conclusion that it was time to give independence to its former possessions.[28] Opting for a policy of conciliation rather than confrontation, the British prime minister, Lord Shelburne, signed a peace treaty with the newly formed nation on 3 September 1783. In Britain, several articles of this peace treaty came under severe criticism—for example, Article 2, defining the borders of the United States.[29] According to the terms of this article, the USA would get all the land to the north-west of the River Ohio. This 'natural' border was selected because it corresponded to the waterway and gave access to a huge navigation system both to Britain, through Canada, and to the United States.[30]

In those days, in Canada as well as in the United States, navigable waterways were the New World's major routes of communication,[31] and gaining access to them was indispensable for trade and control over the continent. However, there were widespread protests in Britain against the concession of this territory to the United States. Most of

[27] John Moore, *History and Digest of the International Arbitrations to which the United States has been a Party* (U.S. Government Printing Office, 1898).

[28] See Jerald Combs, *The Jay Treaty: Political Battleground of the Founding Fathers* (University of California Press, 1970).

[29] 'The Definitive Treaty of Peace, September 30 1783', in Miller (n. 26).

[30] See Samuel Bemis, *Jay's Treaty: A Study in Commerce and Diplomacy* (Yale University Press, 1962).

[31] See Gilles Havard, 'La domestication intellectuelle des Grands Lacs par les Français dans la seconde moitié du XVIIe siècle', in Charlotte Castelnau-l'Estoile and François Regourd (eds), *Connaissances et pouvoirs. Les espaces impériaux (XVIe–XVIIIe siècles)* (Presses Universitaires de Bordeaux, 2005), 68–9.

the land on the American side was extremely fertile. The Canadians claimed that Quebec and Montreal were only trading ports that could not subsist on their own without the support of lands that once provided good economic returns but now lay on the other side of the border. Without the lands lying between the Ohio and Mississippi rivers, Canada would become dependent on Britain for its food supplies and would not be able to survive on its own. From an economic viewpoint, the delimitation of this border was thus disastrous for Britain. In addition to these fertile lands that became a part of the United States, *le Grand Portage*, a trail used by native Indians and French-Canadian settlers engaged in the fur trade, also became a part of US territory. Canada was largely dependent on the fur trade and, if deprived of access to this trading post, it was likely to bear heavy losses.

Problems connected with the demarcation of the border did not end here. On the US side of the border, there were seven forts that had once provided protection to the region and ensured the defence of the colonies. The role of these military posts was of utmost importance in the last years of the eighteenth century. The soldiers posted there did not just defend the military establishment, but also helped maintain cordial relations with the indigenous peoples living in the surrounding areas. Further, the posts also served as depots for the fur trade. They were thus multi-purpose centres supporting the economy of the entire region. By losing these forts, Canada had not only lost strategic trading posts but also access to the indigenous peoples who provided the British colonies with the security that their own soldiers, through lack of numbers, were incapable of providing. Britain was also afraid that the seizure of these forts by the United States would create more upheavals than a simple change of garrison. British authorities felt that once they had abandoned these posts, the newly formed nation would take advantage of them to expand its control over surrounding areas occupied by native Indians, and permanently destroy a source of fur on which Canadian trade was heavily dependent.[32]

It was, however, the debt problem that really aggravated the tension in both Britain and the United States. Article 4 of the Treaty states: 'It is agreed that Creditors on either Side shall meet with no lawful Impediment to the Recovery of the full Value in Sterling Money of all bona fide Debts heretofore contracted.'[33] These words refer to the debts incurred by the Americans vis-à-vis the British before the War of Independence. The peace treaty made sure that the creation of the United States would not cancel these debts, and that the Americans would have to do everything to honour their obligations. The War of Independence had led to the depreciation of the value of the dollar, making it almost impossible for the Americans to repay these debts in pounds sterling. Reluctant to honour these obligations, the Americans took refuge behind the issue of the forts mentioned in the previous paragraph. They informed Britain, through John Adams, the British envoy, that they wished to negotiate the consequences of the treaty that would set in motion their legal system for the recovery of debts only after the forts had been evacuated as envisaged in Article 2. The British replied to this formal notice by affirming that

[32] Bemis (n. 30), 9ff.

[33] 'The Definitive Treaty of Peace' (n. 29), Art. 4.

they would release the forts only after the Americans had fully paid their debts, and would order the commanders of different posts to respond with arms if they were attacked by the Americans.[34]

In the years following the conclusion of the peace treaty, both the signatory states grew more and more exasperated. The situation was made extremely tense by Article 3 related to fishing rights, Article 5 regarding the future of American 'loyalists' who continued to be faithful to the British crown, as well as by the failure of trade negotiations between the two countries.[35] But in 1793, things started moving fast. That year, Britain went to war with France. With the idea of undermining the interests of the United States, Britain passed a law on 6 November 1793 forbidding all ships from trading with French colonies.[36] This law had serious repercussions for the United States, because they were engaged in regular trade with the French West Indies. In fact, after the slaves' revolt in Saint Domingue, many landowners were obliged to export large quantities of goods to save them from destruction, and they used American ships that were very active in this trade.

In February 1794, Britain seized the French colony of Martinique and simultaneously captured more than 50 American vessels engaged in trade with the island. The ships' crews were thrown into prison and their merchandise seized in accordance with the law of 6 November. The British boarded and inspected all American ships in the vicinity of French colonies, following which they seized more than 250 ships belonging to the United States.[37] The Americans once again toyed with the idea of retaliation, and this time they declared an embargo against Britain.[38] Following the complaint from the United States regarding the seizure of its vessels, Britain modified the law of 6 November on 8 January 1794, so that such a thing would not recur.[39] However, the vessels had already been seized and damages had to be paid. The situation between the two countries deteriorated further, and the two governments feared that war would be declared.

35.3.2 The issues at stake

When Jay arrived in England to negotiate a treaty, there were numerous unresolved issues between the two nations. First and foremost, Britain and the United States wanted to avoid a war. Although treaties are usually intended to restore peace after an armed conflict, this time the two countries were keen to discuss and put an end to their disputes, which had become considerably worse since the 1783 treaty.

As we have seen in the preceding paragraphs, trade was a major cause of discord between Britain and the United States. The United States wanted to trade with the British East Indies, but this had become impossible after the signature of the 1783 treaty. The

[34] See Combs (n. 28), 13.

[35] See Reginald Horsman, *The Diplomacy of the New Republic, 1776–1815* (H. Davidson, 1985), 28–41.

[36] Joseph Fewster, 'The Jay Treaty and British Ship Seizures: The Martinique Cases', 45(3) William and Mary Quarterly 426 (1988).

[37] Ibid. 426. [38] Combs (n. 28), 144. [39] Fewster (n. 36), 427.

British found it difficult to concede this demand because they were afraid that the United States would dominate the market in this region, putting their own trade in peril.

Although the law of 6 November had been repealed, it still created problems in the realm of trade. The United States did not want to take the risk of their ships being boarded and inspected by the British. They wanted a guarantee that their ships would benefit from liberal and neutral treatment when trading with other nations. Even though they were opposed a priori to the idea of agreeing to American free trade in the East Indies, the British knew full well that they would be obliged to make certain concessions if they wanted to avoid a war.

The border between Canada and the United States was the last point of discord. The British—through Grenville, who was well-versed in the matter—were aware of the need to evacuate the disputed posts to ensure peace with the United States. A few years earlier, the latter had tried to propose a plan to resolve the disputes related to the US–Canada border, but without any success. Several possibilities were available to the negotiators to resolve the dispute. It could be internationalized through the treaty or it could be decided by a British tribunal. The Americans were opposed to the idea of submitting the dispute to a British tribunal, and the British had no faith in international mechanisms. It was finally decided to continue bilateral discussions with a view to concluding a treaty.

35.3.3 Principal innovations

I do not intend to present a detailed analysis of the contents of this treaty. Rather, I would like to point out that from a conceptual angle, Jay's treaty introduced significant innovations in the realm of arbitration, at both theoretical and practical levels.

It was one of the first treaties negotiated with the aim of preventing a war rather than bringing it to an end.[40] The Greeks had already made use of 'preventive' arbitration, but the United States and Britain went much further in this direction by developing an original and innovative model. Negotiating peace to avoid war gave negotiators much more room for manoeuvre because they did not represent 'winning' and 'losing' camps, just two countries with rights and obligations trying to work out a fair compromise.

What was strikingly new about the Jay Treaty was the use of a novel instrument in the form of independent commissions.[41] They were entrusted with the task of settling disputes that negotiators had not been able to resolve. These commissions heralded a change in the method of resolving international disputes. For the first time, negotiations through direct diplomatic channels were bypassed by setting up a sort of tribunal

[40] See Arthur Eyffinger, *La Cour Internationale de Justice. 1946–1996* (Kluwer Law International, 1999), 29ff.; Alfred Soons, 'International Arbitration in Historical Perspective: Past and Present', in Soons (n. 6), 9.

[41] See Roger Alford, 'The American Influence on International Arbitration', 19 Ohio State Journal on Dispute Resolution 69 (2003).

consisting of arbitrators acting as judges. The resolution of inter-state disputes thus took on a judicial aspect, which became widely acceptable after the nineteenth century.[42]

Indeed, the Jay Treaty arbitrations exemplify the ways in which the membership of the commissions and their rules of procedure led to a combination of legal proceedings and diplomatic negotiations. Despite being free from governmental instructions, arbitrators tended to view their mandates as an extension of diplomacy. They understood that they served in a representative capacity. Furthermore, their rules of procedure reinforced that orientation. For example, Articles 6 and 7 empowered their respective commissions to render decisions by majority vote, but called for the presence of at least one party-appointed member from each side to conduct discussions. Under these circumstances, the party-appointed members from either side held a collective veto, which they could exercise by withdrawing and bringing the proceedings to a temporary halt. This arrangement encouraged a 'high level of consensus-seeking' among arbitrators.[43] Thus, although awards were based on legal principles, these joint commissions worked best when their members blended the functions of judges and negotiators.

The Jay Treaty set up three commissions. The first, called the St. Croix River Commission, was charged with the task of resolving the border dispute (Article 5). Each party was to name a commissioner, and the two commissioners named were to agree on the choice of a third. In case of failure, each of them would select a candidate and the third commissioner would then be selected by drawing lots.[44] The first two commissioners quickly agreed on the appointment of the third member,[45] and the commission was able to give an irrevocable ruling.[46]

The second commission was charged with finding a solution to the American debt problem (Article 6). Due to the subject's importance, this commission had more members than the first: two American commissioners, two British commissioners, and a fifth commissioner to be elected by these four. Unlike the first commission, the four original members could not agree on the choice of the fifth member, and were obliged to draw lots. However, they could not find a solution to the debt problem, and this vexing problem was resolved only in 1802.

The last commission, consisting of five members, was charged with deciding the status of American ships seized by the British during the short period when the law of 6 November was in force as well as the problem of smuggling (Article 7). It was the result

[42] See Stuyt (n. 4), vii.

[43] David Bederman, 'The Glorious Past and Uncertain Future of International Claims Tribunals', in Mark Janis (ed.), *International Courts for the Twenty-First Century* (Martinus Nijhoff, 1992), 161–4.

[44] Jay Treaty (n. 26), Art. 5: 'One Commissioner shall be named by His Majesty, and one by the President of the United States, by and with the advice and Consent of the Senate thereof, and the said two Commissioners shall agree on the choice of a third, or, if they cannot so agree, They shall each propose one Person, and of the two names so proposed one shall be drawn by Lot, in the presence of the two original Commissioners...'

[45] Richard Lillich, 'The Jay Treaty Commissions', 37(2) St. John's Law Review 260 (1963), 266.

[46] The Schoodiac River would be considered as a part of the Saint Croix River according to Britain's defence, but at the time of its separation into two branches, only the northern branch would be treated as the border.

of a compromise between two interpretations of the applicable law. The United States were unwilling to argue their case before a British tribunal because the matter in hand needed to be resolved at the international level.[47] The British, on the contrary, felt that it was necessary to protect the sailors who had acted lawfully in accordance with the law of 6 November. Hence, they had the right to be judged by a national tribunal.[48] Unlike the Debt Commission, this one was a complete success, and is well known in the history of arbitration for the quality of its work and the precision of its ruling.[49]

Finally, the Jay Treaty proved to be innovative as regards the arbitrators' status and duties. They were paid by the two nations, who set up a compensation system to which they contributed equally. All the commission members were well trained in legal matters and were reputed advocates in their respective countries. The fact that they belonged to the same legal tradition simplified matters. Finally, they could also be replaced easily in the event of death or illness. Both the United States and Britain would avail themselves of this option: the former following the demise of one of its judges and the latter because one of the members of the commission set up under Article 7 was a salaried employee of a government organization and therefore subject to his government's orders.[50]

In essence, the famous treaty launched a new process leading to the 'judicialization' of international dispute settlement. The use of written depositions and testimonies (as provided for in Article 6) and the acceptance of majority rulings should be seen in this perspective. Although the first two commissions did not have much impact on the development of international law, the third soon acquired a special status in terms of doctrine by affirming that an arbitral ruling should necessarily conform to the essential principles of the law of people (*jus gentium*).[51]

After the signature of the treaty, many on both sides violently attacked its contents. In Britain, they claimed that Grenville had agreed to give up the border posts to the Americans without obtaining anything in return. Article 6, which provides for the repayment of debts, did not guarantee the payment of interest accumulated over the years following the war. It was left to a joint commission to decide the matter, which was

[47] Fewster (n. 36), 434. [48] Ibid. 436.

[49] Lillich (n. 45), 279ff. The claim of American ships to a total compensation of $11,650,000 would be accepted. Similarly, the right of British sailors, who had acted in accordance with the law then in force, would be entitled to compensation for the seized goods they had handed over to the American authorities.

[50] Georg Schwarzenberg, 'Present-Day Relevance of the Jay Treaty Arbitrations', 53 Notre Dame Law Review 713 (1978).

[51] Ibid. 724–5. It should be pointed out that the Jay Treaty, concluded more than 200 years ago, still affects the position of the indigenous peoples in both the countries. In the US, in spite of the adoption in 1815 of a policy not very favourable to a dialogue with the natives, their free movement across the border was never questioned. The rights given by the Treaty were included in an internal law, the Immigration and Naturalization Act of 1952. Natives born in Canada and those who could prove that they had at least 50% Indian blood were also permitted to cross the border without completing any of the formalities required of Canadians or nationals of other countries. This also allows these indigenous people to reside permanently in the US if they so desired. See Bryan Nickels, 'Native American Free Passage Rights under the 1794 Jay Treaty: Survival under United States Statutory Law and Canadian Common Law', 24(2) Boston College International and Comparative Law Review 313 (2001).

considered to be an inadequate guarantee.[52] Further, Article 7, providing for the appointment of a commission to resolve the issue of ships seized by the British, was not acceptable to English sailors because they believed they had acted in accordance with the prevailing regulations. Finally, permission given to the Americans to trade in the British East Indies did not please the Conservatives who, like Lord Hawkesbury, felt that this intrusion would be dangerous for their country's economy.[53]

In the United States, reactions were equally virulent. Even before the terms of the treaty became known,[54] the anti-federalists consolidated their position and reunited to oppose the treaty negotiated by a member of the opposing camp.[55] On the basis of rumours regarding the terms of the treaty, they described it as an unconditional surrender to Britain. When the articles of the treaty were finally made public, these protesters organized meetings in the country's major cities to inform the public about the agreement that, according to them, called into question the very principles of the constitution and the freedom of the United States.[56] After an intensive campaign and numerous debates, the treaty was ratified in the United States on 14 August 1795 and on 28 October of the same year in England. The treaty became operative on 29 February 1796.

35.4 The Alabama claims: Arbitration becomes a Judicial Process

The Jay Treaty marked the return of arbitration to the international stage. Even though arbitral rulings were not always followed by concrete results, their number grew considerably in the nineteenth century. It is believed that during the period extending from 1794 to 1900 there were over 177 arbitrations, more than half of which took place between 1880 and 1900.[57] It should be noted that the idea of arbitration developed after 1815 under the influence of the young republics of Latin America. The Panama Conference in 1826 and the general, permanent and absolute arbitration treaty between Colombia and Chile were important milestones on the path leading to The Hague Conference in 1899. Among the important arbitral rulings given during this period, we may note in particular the ones on the *Bering Sea* (1873), *Delagoa Bay* (1875) and the vessel *Costa Rica* (1897).

[52] Bermis (n. 30), 351.

[53] Bradford Perkins, 'Lord Hawkesbury and the Jay–Grenville Negotiations', 40(2) Mississippi Valley Historical Review 291 (1953), 292.

[54] As a matter of fact, the treaty document took time to reach the US. A French ship entrusted with the delivery of two copies of the treaty was attacked by pirates, and the documents were thrown overboard. A second ship carrying one more copy was held up by bad weather and took more than three months to cross the Atlantic to reach the US. See Combs (n. 28), 159.

[55] See Todd Estes, *The Jay Treaty Debate, Public Opinion, and the Evolution of Early American Political Culture* (University of Massachusetts Press, 2006), 61.

[56] Ibid. 71ff.

[57] See Francis Lyons, *Internationalism in Europe, 1815–1914* (A. W. Sijthoff, 1963), 385.

The case that exerted the greatest influence on arbitration doctrine during the nineteenth century was the Alabama Claims case, described by some legal historians as the biggest arbitration of modern times. Two nations, Great Britain and the United States, agreed to submit their disputes to an arbitral tribunal set up specifically to resolve the case, whose origin went back to the War of Secession. This tribunal was asked to judge the conduct of Great Britain, which, while claiming to be neutral in the conflict threatening the unity of the United States, continued to build and deliver armed ships to the Confederate States challenging the defences of the Northern States. This case is famous not only because it marked the completion of the 'judicialization' process launched by Jay's Treaty but also because it laid down the rules of international law that are in force even today.[58]

35.4.1 Context

The Alabama Claims arbitration began in the middle of the American War of Secession. Even though at the beginning of this conflict, British public opinion supported the claims of the Northern States because of their anti-slavery stand, Abraham Lincoln's early speeches refusing to ban slavery changed the situation to some extent. British feelings towards the Northern and Southern States became less clear-cut. British industrialists looked at the issue from a commercial angle and tended to support the claims of the South. It must be pointed out that the Southern States were in favour of free trade in their ports, whereas the Northern States put up prohibitive customs barriers to protect their interests. British industrial circles were thus inclined to continue their trade with

[58] Among the important writings on the Treaty of Washington and the Alabama Claims, see in particular Tom Bingham, 'The Alabama Claims Arbitration', 54 International and Comparative Law Quarterly 1 (2005); Adrian Cook, *The Alabama Claims: American Politics and Anglo-American Relations, 1865–1872* (Cornell University Press, 1975); Geneva Cantonal Archives Department, 'Alabama Files 1, 3-4, 16 & 20'; Doris Dashew, 'The Story of an Illusion: The Plan to Trade the Alabama Claims for Canada', 15(4) Civil War History 332 (1969); Geneviève Guyomar, 'L'arbitrage concernant les rapports entre états et particuliers', 5 Annuaire français de droit international 333 (1959); Frank Hackett, *Reminiscences of the Geneva Tribunal of Arbitration, 1872, the Alabama Claims* (Bibliolife, 2009); Maureen Robson, 'The Alabama Claims and the Anglo-American Reconciliation, 1865–71', 42 Canadian Historical Review 1 (1961); Gustave Rolin-Jaequemyns, 'Quelques mots sur la phase nouvelle du différend anglo-américain', 4 Revue de droit international et de législation comparée 127 (1872); Francis Ruddy, 'La portée de l'arbitrage de l'Alabama', in Walter Zurbuchen and Ladislas Mysyrowicz, *Arbitrage de l'Alabama. Genève, 1782–1972* (Chancellerie d'État, 2004), 41–3; Jay Sexton, 'The Funded Loan and the Alabama Claims', 27(4) Diplomatic History 449 (2003); Spencer Tucker, 'CSS Alabama and the Confederate Commerce Raiders during the U.S. Civil War', in Bruce Elleman and S. C. M. Paine (eds), *Commerce Raiding: Historical Case Studies, 1755–2009* (Naval War College Press, 2013), 73–88; J. P. van Niekerk, 'The Story of the CSS ("Daar kom die...") Alabama: some Legal Aspects of her Visit to the Cape of Good Hope, and her Influence on the Historical Development of the Law of War and Neutrality, International Arbitration, Salvage, and Maritime Prize', 13(2) Fundamina 175 (2007); †V. V. Veeder, 'The Historical Keystone to International Arbitration: The Party-Appointed Arbitrator: From Miami to Geneva', 107 Proceedings of the ASIL Annual Meeting 387 (2013).

this part of America despite the practice of slavery, even more so because they badly needed the cotton produced by the Confederate States.[59]

On 13 May 1861, Britain stated that the Southern States were as belligerent as the Northern States, and declared its neutrality. This meant that British citizens were banned from enlisting in the army of either of the two parties involved in the conflict. They however had the right to supply arms to both parties, given that the arms trade was not conducted by the government but by private individuals who were free to act as they pleased.[60]

At the same time, President Lincoln announced an economic blockade of ports in the Southern States so as to isolate them and cut off their supplies completely. Henceforth, all trade through these ports was deemed to be piracy, and goods were subject to seizure.[61] British industrialists ignored this announcement and continued to supply arms and British-built ships to the Southern States.[62]

The Alabama Claims case was a part of this tussle between Britain and the Northern States. In 1862, British manufacturers delivered an armed vessel named *Alabama* to the Confederates. It retained the major part of its British crew,[63] who had no intention of attacking warships of the Unionists but intended only to board merchant ships as pirates. While they were active, they burnt and plundered more than 64 American trading ships, but confronted only one enemy warship, in January 1863.[64]

It was only in June 1864 that the *Alabama* was boarded in international waters after facing fire from a Unionist cruiser. The United States then asked the British secretary of state for foreign affairs to submit for arbitration the disputes related to damages and plunder caused by CSS *Alabama* and other ships supplied to the Confederates. The latter, however, refused to consider this demand, affirming that Britain had not acted against the law.

After the War of Secession ended in 1865, the relations between Britain and the United States deteriorated further.[65] Lord Russell, the British secretary of state for foreign affairs, accepted the American demand for arbitration, but imposed certain conditions that the latter found unacceptable, and hence felt compelled to refuse his proposal.[66] However, after 1865, the balance of power between the two nations changed, since the British government began to fear American expansionism. The United States had a reliable army and a strong navy.[67] The invasion and annexation of Canada was a topic frequently discussed in political circles in Washington.[68] At the same time, the international situation in Europe became worse and there was a possibility of war breaking out any day, with Franco-Prussian rivalry threatening to involve Britain in the imminent European conflict.

In 1869, both the American Senate and British public opinion rejected the Clarendon–Johnson Convention proposing the path of arbitration, thereby accentuating the tension between the two nations. The United States claimed that assistance provided by the British

[59] Bingham (n. 58), 2–3. [60] Zurbuchen and Mysyrowicz (n. 58), 11.
[61] Van Niekerk (n. 58), 177. [62] Zurbuchen and Mysyrowicz (n. 58), 12. [63] Ibid. 14.
[64] Bingham (n. 58), 7. [65] Van Niekerk (n. 58), 221. [66] Bingham (n. 58), 11.
[67] Zurbuchen and Mysyrowicz (n. 58), 17. [68] Robson (n. 58), 3.

to the Confederates during the War of Secession was responsible for the continuation of hostilities. Had it not been for this assistance, the Unionists would have defeated the South much earlier and thus reduced the magnitude of damages.[69] The proclamation of neutrality by Britain in 1861 was also a cause of tension. The Americans considered it a treacherous act, since they believed that the British government should not have given the status of belligerents to the Confederates. The Southern States could not be deemed a nation: they were no more than a community of rebels who had revolted against the central government.[70]

Finally, the question of the warships delivered by Britain to the Southern States added to the points of discord. The *Alabama*, *Florida*, and other ships built in England were responsible for damaging American trade, which suffered severe material losses.[71] The Americans demanded compensation for these losses. They maintained that attacks by the *Alabama* had a catastrophic effect on their economy, leading to high insurance costs for seizure of ships and non-delivery of goods.

Signed on 5 May 1871 after nine weeks of negotiations, the Treaty of Washington led to a singular improvement in the relations between the two nations. Unlike the Clarendon–Johnson Convention, this treaty acknowledged Britain's responsibility in the *Alabama* affair as stated in Article 1: 'The regret felt by Her Majesty's Government for the escape, under whatever circumstances, of the Alabama and other vessels from British ports, and for the depredations committed by those vessels.'

From the arbitration point of view, the singular novelty of the Treaty of Washington lay in setting up an arbitral tribunal composed of five members, as clearly stated by Article 1:

> Now, in order to remove and adjust all complaints and claims on the part of the United States, and to provide for the speedy settlement of such claims, which are not admitted by Her Britannic Majesty's Government, the High Contracting Parties agree that all the said claims, growing out of acts committed by the aforesaid vessels and generically known as the Alabama Claims, shall be referred to a Tribunal of Arbitration...[72]

The idea of setting up a tribunal was itself an innovation. At that time, arbitration was more of a diplomatic than a judicial procedure. Undoubtedly, the Jay Treaty of 1794 had set up independent commissions charged with resolving the disputes between the two nations, but it was not a 'judicialized' version of arbitration. Setting up commissions to resolve the *Alabama* affair seemed inappropriate to the negotiators of the Treaty of Washington. The commissioners, chosen by the two parties, were usually practising advocates from their respective countries charged with tilting the balance in their favour. In the present case, the disputing parties consented for the first time in history to arbitration before a panel of jurists appointed mostly by neutral governments, charged with a mandate to apply specific legal rules, and having the capacity to transact issues by

[69] Sexton (n. 58), 457. [70] Dashew (n. 58), 334. [71] Ibid. 59.

[72] Treaty of Washington: Treaty between Her Majesty and the United States of America (1871), Art. I.

majority vote. From then on, the trajectory of arbitration shifted decisively towards a judicial model.

The prevailing intellectual environment was favourable for the introduction of this novelty. The principle of an 'arbitral tribunal' had been supported since 1860 by several leading jurists. The American advocate Thomas Blach, the German-American jurist Francis Lieber—who had suggested that the law faculties of foreign universities should be selected as arbitrators by the parties concerned to resolve their dispute[73]—and two Swiss jurists, J. K. Blüntschli and Gustave Moynier, all declared themselves in favour of an arbitral tribunal, a suggestion which was accepted by the Treaty of Washington.[74]

Being the accused party in the *Alabama* claims case, the British did not wish to subject themselves to arbitration without first understanding the legal principles on which the judges would base their decision. That is why Article 6 of the treaty laid down the rules that were to be applied by the arbitrators when analysing the case. These rules recommended how a country should behave when it had adopted a neutral position in a conflict related to the delivery of armed ships involving several belligerent parties.[75]

Article II of the treaty states that the arbitral tribunal would hold its hearings in Geneva. Though Calvin's city did not enjoy the international status that it would acquire later, it was selected because Switzerland was not involved in the conflict threatening Europe. In addition, due to its history and its institutions, Switzerland boasted a long tradition in the areas of arbitration and neutrality in conflicts.

35.4.2 The negotiators

Article I of the Treaty of Washington lays down that the *Alabama* claims case would be heard by five arbitrators belonging to five different nations. Evidently, Britain and the United States were asked to select one representative each. In addition, Switzerland, Italy, and Brazil were each asked to appoint one person capable of dealing with the claims.

The United States selected Charles Francis Adams, who had served as American ambassador in London during the War of Secession. On account of his official position in Britain at the time of the *Alabama* affair, he was thoroughly acquainted with the circumstances of the case that he was called upon to judge in Geneva. He was the son and grandson of two former American presidents, and had sided with the Unionists during the War of Secession. The choice of the American government was strongly criticized by the British, who held that because he was involved in the matter during the War of Secession, Adams would not be able to judge the *Alabama* case impartially. However, the British finally accepted the presence of this respected American judge on the tribunal.[76]

[73] Veeder (n. 58), 392. [74] Ibid. 393.

[75] For a detailed presentation of these rules (Art. VI), see below. It should be pointed out that Britain agreed to be judged retrospectively, in accordance with rules that did not exist when the conflict under arbitration occurred and which, moreover, were not a part of its legal corpus.

[76] Bingham (n. 58), 16.

The British arbitrator was Alexander Cockburn, a member of the Queen's Privy Council. He had behind him a long career as a jurist, having earlier served as advocate-general and then attorney-general before being appointed lord chief justice of England and Wales.[77] A polyglot and an excellent advocate, he was opposed to the arbitration process that he had nevertheless agreed to follow. He believed that the Treaty of Washington was a mistake, and that the three rules that had been framed could not serve as a basis of judgment for Britain whose interests were not adequately protected.[78] Cockburn was also severely critical of his Swiss, Italian, and Brazilian colleagues. He affirmed that the republican beliefs of the Swiss were likely to be prejudicial to British interests, that the Italian was enamoured of his own voice, and that the Brazilian had absolutely no knowledge of the case.[79]

The Brazilian colleague thus maligned by Cockburn was Marcos Antônio d'Araújao, a diplomat posted in Paris and a professor of law at Pernambouc University.[80] The arbitrator chosen by Switzerland was Jacques Staempfli, a former director of the Swiss National Bank, a former deputy representing Berne in the National Council, a former member of the federal tribunal, and also ex-president of the Confederation. Fervently opposed to slavery, he had sided with the Union during the War of Secession. Thanks to his vast experience in the legal and diplomatic fields, he was well-versed in the matter he was called upon to judge. Finally, the arbitrator selected by the king of Italy, who was appointed president of the arbitral tribunal, was Count Frederick Scolpis. A minister in his country, he had also been trained as a judge and advocate.[81]

The negotiations were conducted in French, which angered the British arbitrator. Since the documents were drafted in English, Alexander Cockburn demanded that the Italian, Swiss, and Brazilian judges be replaced, as they did not have sufficient mastery over the language of the parties. Article II of the Treaty of Washington also stated that Britain and the United States should each appoint an agent charged with representing them before the arbitral tribunal. The United States selected Bancroft Davis, an American diplomat posted in London and American correspondent of *The Times*, while Britain appointed Baron Tenterden, permanent undersecretary of state for foreign affairs. The two nations would also be represented by legal consultants. The United States appointed three persons: Caleb Cushing, a Democrat and advocate-general of the United States known for his Anglophobia; William Maxwell Evarts, who had also been an advocate-general and was undersecretary of state under President Hayes, and Morrison Remick Waite, who would be appointed a judge of the American Supreme Court after the arbitration of the *Alabama* case was over. As for Britain, it appointed its advocate-general, Sir Roundell Palmer, Montague Bernard, professor of law at Oxford University and Arthur Cohen, an advocate.

[77] Van Niekerk (n. 58), 230. [78] Bingham (n. 58), 17. [79] Ibid. 18.
[80] Zurbuchen and Mysyrowicz (n. 58), 20–21. [81] Van Niekerk (n. 58), 230.

This is not the place to describe in detail the ruling given in Geneva on 14 September 1872 by the first arbitral tribunal in modern history.[82] We will simply point out that Britain's responsibility was acknowledged. It was pointed out that the latter should have acted with greater haste to stop the delivery of armed ships to one of the belligerent parties in the War of Secession. In addition, Britain was also judged guilty of allowing CSS *Alabama* to enter its ports after carrying out attacks under the banner of the Southern States. The judges arrived at the same conclusions in the case of the ship *Florida*, declaring that Britain should have stopped its transport and taken action against it once its misdeeds were known.[83] These two decisions were taken by a majority of four to one, the opposition coming from Cockburn, the English judge. As for the delivery of several other ships to the Confederates, Britain was acquitted by a small majority of three to two; to compensate for the losses caused, it was asked to pay the United States a fine of $15,500,000 in gold, a sizeable sum in those days.[84]

35.4.3 The main innovations

The judgement pronounced in the *Alabama* case is of great importance for international arbitration.[85] It stands out not so much as the end of a historical era as marking the opening of a new intellectual sphere.

Firstly, at the doctrinal level, Article 6 of the Treaty of Washington introduces a whole new way of understanding the concept of neutrality and the conduct of neutral states during armed conflicts. Even though, until 1815, many countries preferred to stay away from conflicts close to their borders, the concept of neutrality was not fully established. The duties of neutral nations and their relations with belligerent states had not yet been clearly defined, and until the signature of the Treaty of Washington, the right to neutrality was not fully developed. Article 6 of the Treaty of Washington made it possible to define these rules more precisely and, what is more important, bring them to the knowledge of other nations so that they too would treat them as a part of international law.

[82] Alabama claims of the United States of America against Great Britain, Award (1872), rendered by the Tribunal of Arbitration established by Art. I of the Treaty of Washington (1871).

[83] Ibid. para. 131: 'And whereas, with respect to the vessel called the "Florida", it results from all the facts relative to the construction of the "Oreto" in the port of Liverpool, and to its issue therefrom, which facts failed to induce the authorities in Great Britain to resort to measures adequate to prevent the violation of the neutrality of that nation, notwithstanding the warnings and repeated representations of the agents of the United States, that Her Majesty's government has failed to use due diligence to fulfil the duties of neutrality; And whereas it likewise results from all the facts relative to the stay of the "Oreto" at Nassau, to her issue from that port, to her enlistment of men, to her supplies, and to her armament, with the co-operation of the British vessel "Prince Alfred," at Green Cay, that there was negligence on the part of the British colonial authorities; And whereas, notwithstanding the violation of the neutrality of Great Britain committed by the "Oreto", this same vessel, later known as the confederate cruiser "Florida", was nevertheless on several occasions freely admitted into the ports of British colonies...'

[84] Van Niekerk (n. 58), 237. [85] See Alford (n. 41), 74.

Thus, the passage stating:

> to use due diligence to prevent the fitting out, arming, or equipping, within its jurisdiction, of any vessel which it has reasonable ground to believe is intended to cruise or to carry on war against a Power with which it is at peace; and also to use like diligence to prevent the departure from its jurisdiction of any vessel intended to cruise or carry on war as above, such vessel having been specially adapted, in whole or in part, within such jurisdiction, to warlike use.[86]

would be repeated in Art. 8 of The Hague Convention on Neutrality during the maritime war of 18 October 1907. Although they were not codified under international law, the two other rules would also be treated as being part of customary international law.

Further, unlike the commissions set up by the Jay Treaty of 1794, the Treaty of Washington excluded the role of individuals in international law.[87] Only countries were allowed to plead before the arbitral tribunal, as stated in Article II: 'The Arbitrators shall ... decide all questions that shall be laid before them on the part of the Governments of the United States and Her Britannic Majesty respectively ...' If individuals wished to obtain compensation, they had to approach courts through their own governments, which would take the responsibility of acting in their name in the international sphere.

The procedure adopted by the arbitral tribunal was also new (Articles 3 and 4). The Joint Commissions set up by the Jay Treaty in 1794 to judge the dispute between Britain and the United States essentially used oral testimonies. In the judgement of the *Alabama* case, the parties submitted their arguments in writing in two stages. At the first stage, the parties submitted to the arbitrators a statement listing their claims and their position with regard to the *Alabama* claims. Four months later, the arbitrators were given a counter-statement containing their replies to the accusations of the opposite party.[88]

Finally, for the first time in history, each party was allowed to choose one arbitrator in a tribunal consisting of five members, the majority of whom were foreign nationals belonging to countries having no interest in the conflict. In 1794, when selecting the members of the commissions, the parties confined themselves to American and British arbitrators.[89] In 1871, the position was quite different: they willingly agreed to accept the ruling of the arbitral tribunal composed of a majority of foreign arbitrators. This practice, which considerably limits the influence of parties involved in the conflict, opened new possibilities in the field of arbitration.[90]

[86] Treaty of Washington: Treaty between Her Majesty and the United States of America (1871), Art. VI.

[87] Egidio Reale, *L'arbitrage international. Le règlement judiciaire du conflit de l'Alabama* (Payot, 1929), 72–4.

[88] Ibid. 76. [89] Veeder (n. 58), 393.

[90] The possibility—exploited by Cockburn, the English judge—of including a dissident viewpoint in the judgement assured the states that their position would be acknowledged.

35.5 The Hague moment: from the Permanent Court of Arbitration to the Permanent Court of International Justice

The end of the nineteenth century has been described by historians of international law 'as the age of internationalism in law'. This expression aptly describes the ideological context which gave birth to the idea of a Permanent Court of Arbitration (PCA). The need to organize international society and lay down arbitration procedures became the topic of a widespread debate after 1875 in political and business circles.[91]

But it was the peace movement that contributed the most to the emergence of this idea. Arbitration was one of the major causes supported by the peace movement since the Peace Congress in Brussels, Paris and Frankfurt during the 1840s. After 1890, the movement pinned all its hopes on arbitration as the best short-term measure to put an end to war.[92] The Interparliamentary Union, founded in Berne in 1889, supported this idea.[93] This Union organized conferences from time to time to bring together members of national legislative assemblies. Eminent personalities like Henri La Fontaine, Frederik Bajer, and Albert Gobat devoted a large part of their lives to this institution. In London, in 1890, the Union decided that the inclusion of a clause insisting on arbitration was a *sine qua non* of any treaty. Later, in Berne, during the meeting that ended in the creation of the International Bureau of Peace and the Interparliamentary Bureau, its president, Karl Schenk, declared that a general treaty would soon be concluded in order to set up a permanent court.[94]

The first official reaction to this line of thinking emerged in 1887, when the United States government requested European nations to jointly consider the possibility of setting up an International Court.[95] This proposal, received with much misgiving by the Germans and the British, was raised by the Interparliamentary Union during its

[91] For an excellent and lively account of this historical moment, though not focusing closely on legal questions, see Barbara Tuchman, *The Proud Tower: A Portrait of the World before the War, 1890–1914* (Macmillan, 1966), 265–338.

[92] See Verdiana Grossi, *Le pacifisme européen* (Bruylant, 1994); Peter Brock, *Pacifism in Europe to 1914* (Princeton University Press, 1972).

[93] See Bureau Interparlementaire, *Union interparlementaire. Son histoire, son organisation, son oeuvre* (Bureau Interparlementaire, 1925).

[94] See Bureau Interparlementaire, *Procès-verbaux des séances de la Conférence Interparlementaire* (Bureau Interparlementaire, 1892).

[95] See International Court of Justice, *The International Court of Justice: Facts and Documents about the History and Work of the Court* (International Courts Association, 2011). See also Robert Kolb, *The International Court of Justice* (Hart, 2013).

meetings in Brussels in 1895 and in Budapest in 1896.[96] On both occasions, William Randal Cremer, co-founder of the International Arbitration League and its secretary in 1870, fervently defended this idea with Frédéric Passy, a leading member of the Union. The project, later submitted to the Examination Committee of the Third Commission (in charge of arbitration) of The Hague Peace Conference, drew inspiration from a proposal already tabled by the Union.

On 24 August 1898, Czar Nicholas II published a circular inviting all nations to attend an international conference on issues related to world peace and disarmament.[97] The rapid expansion of increasingly complex military equipment, he explained, as well as its excessive burden on the economy, had slowed down the development of humanity and the social, political and intellectual progress of nations. The amassing of this military equipment had itself become a major threat to peace. He said it was necessary to beat swords into ploughshares, and that modern artillery should make way for locomotives and bridges.[98]

The proposal was received with a mixture of astonishment and mistrust.[99] The initiative was undoubtedly in line with the political tradition of the Romanovs—pacifism having deep roots in Russian history—but it satisfied the imperatives of realpolitik. The arms race had well and truly impoverished the Russian treasury. Anxieties caused by the build-up of impressive arsenals by foreign powers along Russia's western border were a favourite topic of discussion in St Petersburg. So, it is not surprising that diplomats considered this proposal a figment of the czar's imagination, a utopian idea or perhaps a shrewd political move.

In January 1899, however, Russia addressed a second letter to the European nations inviting them to a peace conference at a venue yet to be decided.[100] This new letter explained the objectives of the proposed conference: agreeing a ceiling on the progressive accumulation of arms, and studying the possibility of preventing armed conflicts through measures of peaceful resolution of disputes like mediation and arbitration available to international diplomats. Despite criticism by the Netherlands and the

[96] See Union Interparlementaire, 'Conférence du Bruxelles du 13–15 août 1895' and 'Conférence de Budapest du 23–25 septembre 1896', in *Résolutions des conférences et décisions principales du conseil*, 2nd edn (Bureau Interparlementaire, 1911), 53–60.

[97] See 'Message of the Czar, Aug. 24, 1898', repr. in *Documents Relating to the Program of the First Hague Peace Conference* (The Hague, 1921), 1–2.

[98] See Dan Morrill, 'Nicolas II and the Call for the First Hague Conference', 46(2) Journal of Modern History 296 (1974), 296.

[99] See Warren Kuehl, *Seeking World Order* (Vanderbilt University Press, 1969), 44–5; James Scott, 'The Work of the Second Hague Peace Conference', 2 American Journal of International Law 1 (1908), 8; Geoffrey Best, 'Peace Conference and the Century of Total War: The 1899 Hague Conference and What Came After', 75(3) International Affairs 619 (1999), 622.

[100] 'Circular Note of the Count Mouravieff to the Diplomatic Representatives Accredited to the Court at Petrograd' (1898), repr. in *Documents Relating to the Program of the First Hague Peace Conference* (n. 97), 2–3.

United States and the absence of the Holy See, about 100 delegates representing 26 nations were present at The Hague on 18 May 1899.[101]

This is not the place to go into the details of the results of this conference.[102] Only the deliberations of the third commission are of interest to us because it took up the issue of arbitration. Reports from this period all speak of the major role played by the Russian delegate, Frédéric de Martens. Even though he was one of the most eminent internationalists of the time, he was nonetheless extremely realistic and fully aware of the prevailing balance of power. In his *Traité de droit international*, published a few years earlier, he expressed his ideas on the creation of an arbitration court in the following words:

> What kind of future awaits international arbitration? To answer this question, it is possible to advance two different points of view: one expressing hope and one presenting the actual state of things... As for the future, we should not delude ourselves. Experience teaches us that there are many disputes and occasions of international conflicts where judicial analysis does not provide any help. Many of these difficulties are a consequence of the history of nations and can be resolved only by force and by the destruction of the prevailing order and laws. It is difficult to imagine two nations agreeing to approach an arbitration tribunal to sort out disputes that are a result of their history, and it is not possible to see how the latter could find the legal grounds on which it could base its judgements.[103]

Two questions dominated the commission's deliberations: the principle of an arbitration court (which the Germans vehemently opposed) and the status of the arbitral judgment (whether it would be binding or not). The debates were very lively. The British proposal served as the basis of negotiations. After several weeks of deliberation, there was unanimous agreement on the creation of a permanent arbitration court. The court would be competent to rule in all domains, and its members would be appointed for a term of six years. On 25 July, a convention comprising 61 articles was submitted to the conference's plenary session. The commission's efforts were crowned by an exemplary success: the arbitration system owed its conception to Britain, the enquiry commissions were inspired by Russia, the clause relating to the obligations of contracting parties came from France, and the mediation procedure from the United States.[104]

[101] The Dutch were angered by the omission of the young republics of southern Africa, and the US deplored the absence of representatives from the countries of Central and South America, particularly Carlos Calvo of Argentina, an authority on international law.

[102] There is a fairly substantial literature on the two Hague Peace Conferences. On the first Conference, see Morrill (n. 98), 296–313; Arthur Eyflinger, *The 1899 Hague Peace Conference: The Parliament of Man, the Federation of the World* (Kluwer Law International, 1999). On the role of the US at the first Conference, see Calvin Davis, *The United States and the First Hague Peace Conference* (Cornell University Press, 1962).

[103] See Friedrich de Martens, *Traité de droit international* (Chevalier-Marescq, 1887), vol. 3, 154 (author's translation).

[104] See Robert Morris, *International Arbitration and Procedure* (BiblioBazaar, 2009), 137ff.; 'Report to the Secretary of State of the Delegates to the First Hague Conference', in James Scott (ed.), *Instructions to the American Delegates to the Hague Peace Conferences and their Official Reports* (Oxford University Press, 1916), 17–22.

In the 1899 Hague Convention on the peaceful resolution of disputes, Chapters 2 and 3 of the fourth section and more particularly Sections 20–29 (corresponding to Articles 41–50 of the 1907 version—a revised version but without any fundamental changes), deal with the court of arbitration. These articles define the court's aims and objectives, its jurisdiction, judicial functions, secretarial and administrative services, and working expenses. Apart from the text's formal dimensions, what is even more striking is the use of the term 'Court', since, strictly speaking, it is neither a court nor is it an arbitration tribunal and, if it were to be considered as a court, it has nothing permanent about it.[105] The best definition that could be given to this structure is the one proposed by William Butler, who sees it as an 'institutional framework' that parties to a dispute can resort to when they so desire, or even a permanent arbitration service provided by the institution's central body, the International Bureau of Arbitration.[106] It was this bureau that drew up a list of persons of note in the legal field to be called 'members of the Court', who were in reality no more than potential arbitrators or legal advisers ready to act as arbitrators in case a dispute arose during their six-year term. This list was the only 'permanent' feature of the court, which led Martens to declare that the court was 'but an idea which occasionally assumes shape and then disappears'.[107]

The creation of the PCA in 1899 and its confirmation in 1907 were important watersheds in the history of arbitration. After the signature of the Jay Treaty (1794), the need to institutionalize the peaceful resolution of disputes and harmonize arbitration procedures was gradually accepted. Though it is true that the PCA was initially conceived as an institution without any powers, the sovereignty of the parties to the conflict was fully respected; and though it was described as utopian by many commentators,[108] it was soon accepted as a useful instrument for the prevention of inter-state conflicts. Thus in 1904, the dispute arising from the *Dogger Bank* incident between Russia and Britain involving the 'vital interests of the two parties' was resolved by an enquiry commission constituted under Article 9 of the 1899 Convention for the Peaceful Resolution of International Conflicts. A few months later, President Theodore Roosevelt of the United States invoked Article 3 of the same convention and initiated the mediation that put an end to the Russo-Japanese conflict (the Treaty of Portsmouth of 1905).

One would have expected that disagreements would be resolved by such deliberations. But despite numerous delegations to The Hague claiming to be convinced of the great success of the 1899 conference, the PCA remained a very imperfect legal institution regardless of its merits. Some still found the idea unacceptable; others felt that it did

105 See Anthony Aust, *Handbook of International Law* (Oxford University Press, 2005), 444.

106 William Butler, 'The Hague Permanent Court of Arbitration', in Janis (n. 43), 43.

107 Martens, quoted in James Scott, 'The Proposed Court of Arbitral Justice', 2 American Journal of International Law 772 (1908), 780.

108 See David Hill, 'The Net Result at The Hague', S. Doc 444 (1907), 3 (observing 'The Hague Conferences have been saluted with contempt on the one hand, and satire on the other'). See also James Scott, *The Hague Peace Conferences of 1899 and 1907* (Johns Hopkins Press, 1909), 1–2 (indicating that the great public felt that the lack of agreements on disarmament and compulsory arbitration 'involved the failure of the Conference').

not go far enough. Still others refused to accept arbitration because it was a slow, costly, and complex procedure.[109]

This criticism bore fruit when its detractors claimed that the PCA was not capable of creating jurisprudence. It was precisely for this reason that several countries proposed in 1907 to venture further and create a truly permanent institution vested with real judicial powers. This desire is expressed in the recommendation adopted by the conference almost unanimously in the following words: 'The Conference recommends that the signatory Powers pass the plan annexed to the convention regarding the establishment of a court of arbitral justice and that it be implemented as soon as there is an agreement on the choice of judges and the court's constitution.'

The draft convention relating to the establishment of a court of arbitral justice thus recommends the creation of a court 'that will be freely and easily accessible and bring together judges representing the world's diverse legal systems'.[110] The new court would be located in The Hague and would be an extension of the PCA. It would meet at least once every year. Only signatory states would have recourse to the services of this court. But there would be no directive regarding the applicable law. The convention would be valid for a period of twelve years, with automatic renewal subject to termination. But it was only during the third peace conference held in The Hague in 1915 that an attempt was made to conciliate positions regarding details and give finishing touches to the convention.

The First World War put to a severe test the basic principle of dispute settlement, as well as the idea of a Permanent Court of Arbitration. However, in 1919 Britain distributed in Paris the preliminary draft of the Society of Nations, which included the possibility of a judicial body which was none other than 'the one already in existence in The Hague' and which would be completed or modified by the Society of Nations and peace treaties.[111] An alternate version of the draft explicitly mentions the 'creation of a Permanent International Court of Justice'. What is interesting is that the decisions of this court would have the force of law and be effective only 'if they were confirmed by the report of the Conference or the Council'. To begin with, the arbitrators of the PCA would be members of this new legal body.

The British government, represented by Lord Cecil, began by pleading for the creation of a new court. According to the proposal it had presented in 'Notes on a Permanent Court',[112] five of the nine judges were to be appointed by the principal allied

[109] On the theoretical debates on the Permanent Court of Arbitration, see Martti Koskenniemi, *The Gentle Civilizer of Nations: The Rise and Fall of International Law, 1870–1960* (Cambridge University Press, 2001), chs 3–5.

[110] 'Projet d'une convention relative à l'établissement d'une cour de justice arbitrale', Titre 1, Art. 1, in Pearce Higgins (ed.), *The Hague Peace Conferences and other International Conferences concerning the Laws and Usages of War* ([1909] Cambridge University Press, 2014), 498.

[111] The same words are found in Art. 14 of the Covenant of the League of Nations.

[112] See Lord Cecil, 'Draft Convention on the League of Nations, submitted by Lord R. Cecil for the Consideration of the Plenipotentiaries, January 20, 1919', in Kenneth Bourne and D. Cameron Watt (eds), *British Documents on Foreign Affairs: Reports and Papers from the Foreign Office* (University Publications of America, 1984), 159–69.

powers and their associates. These five judges would then select the four remaining judges from a list of candidates named by other members of the Society of Nations. Expecting opposition to this idea from smaller nations, Lord Cecil declared that once they were admitted to the Society of Nations, 'these countries would have to completely give up Barbosa's theories which, as a matter of fact, they did'.[113]

All through the debates, Germany and Austria, as well as France and the United States, presented counter-proposals that did not suggest any basic changes. Thus, the final draft of the pact, which constituted Part I of the Peace Treaties concluded at Versailles on 28 June 1919, at Saint-Germain-en-Laye on 10 September 1919, at Neuilly-sur-Seine on 27 November 1919, and at Trianon on 4 June 1920, retained in Article 14 the following statement:

> The Council [of the Society of Nations] is charged with preparing the draft of a Permanent Court of International Justice and submitting it to the Society's members. This court will adjudge all disputes of an international nature submitted to it by the Parties concerned. It will also give advisory opinions on all disputes or points referred to it by the Council or Assembly.[114]

This article is of fundamental importance because it lays down for the first time the basic principles that inspire the functioning of the court even today: its judicial obligations towards member nations and its duty to perform a consultative function vis-à-vis international organizations. In addition, the institution was also given a name. Before the Paris Conference, several variants were being circulated: International High Court of Justice, International Tribunal, International Court of Law, International Court of Justice (which figured in an Italian proposal).[115] All these names were finally discarded in preference to the one that was mentioned for the first time in the British draft presented on 20 January 1919: it would be called the Permanent Court of International Justice.

This name simultaneously stressed the international character of the new institution and also its permanent nature. As we have already seen, there was nothing superficial about the desire to create a permanent court: it expressed the idea that it was necessary to go much further than in the case of the PCA. In addition, the selected name emphasized the fact that the court was a judicial body, and was no longer a question of simple arbitration. But as M. O. Hudson observes, the order of the words is not very felicitous: the institution that was to be created was actually not so much a permanent court of international justice but a 'permanent international court of justice'.[116]

At the Paris Conference, the court was manifestly perceived as a 'creature' of the Society of Nations, whose members had to be a part of the organization. Article 415 of the Versailles Treaty expressly mentions 'the Permanent Court of International Justice

[113] At the Hague in 1907, Roy Barbosa, the Brazilian delegate, defended the idea that every nation should be represented in the judicial institution.

[114] Traité de Versailles (1919), Art. 14 (author's translation).

[115] See Eyffinger (n. 40), 75.

[116] Manley Hudson, *The Permanent Court of International Justice 1920–1942: A Treatise* (Macmillan, 1943), 114.

of the Society of Nations'. As the report of the Committee of Jurists of 1920 says, being 'a judicial component of the Society of Nations, the new court could have been created only under the auspices of the Society of Nations. Because of its bond with the Society of Nations, it could not be a product of an external organisation but only of an organisation within the society.'[117]

From 1922 to 1940, during what historians call its 'active life', the Permanent Court of International Justice heard 66 cases, 36 of them litigations and 28 requests for advisory opinions. Twelve of these cases were settled amicably. All in all, the court passed 32 rulings and gave 27 advisory opinions, all of them requested by the Council of the Society of Nations.[118] With an average of four cases a year, it worked assiduously and efficiently and proved its usefulness to the international community. Even though it could not prevent the Second World War, it provided jurisprudence for the resolution of some serious international disputes and by doing so elucidated some ambiguous areas of international law. In May 1940 the court was transferred to Geneva, with the exception of its sole vice-president, Eysinga, and some Dutch officials who remained in The Hague.

In 1946, a new court was constituted as an extension of the United Nations Organization. The judges of the Permanent Court of International Justice resigned on 30 January 1946. On 18 April, the permanent court was dissolved by a resolution passed by the UN Assembly, which met to declare its closure. The inauguration of the International Court of Justice was held the same day to maintain juridical continuity by using the same structure and the same personnel.[119]

35.6 Conclusion—Inter-State Arbitration in Historical Perspective: Past and Future

Although inter-state arbitration has experienced five important moments in the course of its history, it must be admitted that since the Second World War we have seen little enthusiasm for this way of resolving disputes peacefully. We should not be misled by the growing tendency to include arbitration clauses in treaties. In actual practice, inter-state arbitration is no longer popular and, since 1945, treaties based on arbitration have

[117] Quoted by Eyffinger (n. 40), 76.

[118] See Manley Hudson, *International Tribunals: Past and Future* (Brookings Institution, 1944), 11; Terry Gill (ed.), *Rosenne's The World Court: What It Is and How it Works* (Brill, 2003), 11; Stephen Schwebel, 'Reflections on the Role of the International Court of Justice', 61 Washington Law Review 1063 (1986).

[119] Which would lead some observers to claim that it was in fact the same court, only with two different names. See J. G. Merrills, *International Dispute Settlement*, 4th edn (Cambridge University Press, 2012), 127; Pierre-Marie Dupuy, 'The Danger of Fragmentation or Unification of the International Legal System and the International Court of Justice', 31 New York University Journal of International Law and Policy 791 (1998).

become rare.[120] Some writers have established a link between the decline of the PCA and the establishment of the International Court of Justice.[121] Others have presented a very detailed analysis of the period extending from 1945 to 1990 giving multiple reasons for the decreasing use of arbitration.[122] It is true that the number of international courts has increased substantially, suggesting an almost total transition from arbitration to the judicial settlement of disputes among nations.

There is no doubt that recently the number of contracting countries approaching the PCA has increased, rising from 60 to 80 between 1960 and 1995. Nevertheless, this figure seems surprisingly small in view of the influence still exerted by the Hague Conventions on the customary rules of international law. Could it be said that nations desirous of resolving their disputes do not approach the Hague institutions more often because of the very idea and the constitutive principles of arbitration and judicial settlement, or is it for practical reasons such as those related to procedure? In other words, do the reasons behind this phenomenon lie in the nature of these institutions or are they external reasons? Are they permanent or are they cyclical? Should they modify the laws that they apply? No one can answer these questions with any certitude.

Dealing with inter-state arbitration from a historical perspective can provide some food for thought. 'The prevailing incomprehension is inevitably a result of past ignorance,' wrote the famous historian Marc Bloch.[123] It is not just a matter of appreciating the value of our heritage or 'throwing light' on the present with the help of the past. It means transforming the way individuals, nations, and other groups have handled conflict situations at a pivotal juncture in their history, and figuring out how they have coordinated their thinking on the peaceful resolution of disputes. In this sense, the history of arbitration is a functioning laboratory of our present and not just a narration of its past achievements. States should therefore question the limits of judicial settlement, not so much because of the increasing use of arbitration in private international law (particularly for the resolution of international commercial disputes among private parties) but because history provides them with a variety of arbitrations reflecting the advantages of this specific way of resolving disputes peacefully.

[120] Indeed, general arbitration treatises such as the 1948 Pact of Bogota and the European Convention for the Peaceful Settlement of Disputes are exceptional. Moreover, in addition to arbitration, both these treatises provide for other means of peaceful settlement.

[121] See Pieter Koojmans, 'International Arbitration in Historical Perspective: Past and Present (Comments on a Paper by Professor L. B. Sohn)', in Soons (n. 6), 23.

[122] Christine Gray and Benedict Kingsbury, 'Interstate Arbitration since 1945: Overview and Evaluation', in Janis (n. 43), 55–82.

[123] Marc Bloch, *Apologie pour l'histoire ou métier d'historien*, 7th edn (Armand Colin, 1974), 47.

CHAPTER 36

ARBITRATION FROM A LAW & ECONOMICS PERSPECTIVE

ANNE VAN AAKEN AND TOMER BROUDE

36.1 Introduction

International arbitration and Law & Economics (L&E) have two things in common. They have both been on the rise in the last decades; and they are both hotly contested and discussed in all their facets. Perhaps not yet cause enough to view arbitration from an L&E perspective and indeed, fifteen years ago, it was lamented that L&E had neglected arbitration to large extent;[1] it was instead focused on judicial, rather than arbitral contexts. L&E can inform (legal) discussion through explicit statements (either rational choice assumptions or empirically grounded behavioural economics) about the behaviour of arbitrators and disputants. L&E analyses law in practice and how the interaction between law and non-legal factors influences behaviour; in this respect it proceeds from the same epistemology as legal realism.[2] Once it is accepted that judges or arbitrators are neither 'la bouche qui prononce les paroles de la loi'[3] nor a 'judicial slot machine',[4] looking at the factors which determine arbitrators' decision-making becomes

[1] Bruce Benson, 'Arbitration', in Boudewijn Bouckaert and Gerrit de Geest (eds), *Encyclopedia of Law and Economics* (Edward Elgar, 2000), vol. 5, 160. Early articles were Robert Cooter, 'The Objectives of Private and Public Judges', 41 Public Choice 107 (1983); William Landes and Richard Posner, 'Adjudication as a Private Good', 8 Journal of Legal Studies 235 (1979); Steven Shavell, 'Alternative Dispute Resolution: An Economic Analysis', 24 Journal of Legal Studies 1 (1995).

[2] Thomas Schultz, 'Arbitral Decision-Making: Legal Realism and Law & Economics', 6 Journal of International Dispute Settlement 231 (2015), 239.

[3] Charles-Louis de Secondat, Baron de La Brède et de Montesquieu, *De l'esprit des lois* (1777), bk 11, ch. 6, 327.

[4] Roscoe Pound, *The Spirit of the Common Law* (Marshall Jones Company, 1921), 170.

crucial for understanding their conduct. This in turn is crucial for every party designing contracts or treaties with an arbitration clause or being involved in arbitration.

This chapter proceeds as follows. After a short introduction to the rational choice assumptions of traditional L&E, subsequent developments in behavioural economics relevant to arbitration are described (Section 36.2). We then briefly provide a general institutional economics perspective on arbitration (Section 36.3). Section 36.4 goes into greater detail concerning some questions where L&E can contribute by focusing on disputants involved in arbitration, their incentives and decision-making, including different types of dispute settlement, arbitrator appointment, incentives for settlement, and third-party funding. Section 36.5 discusses the incentives and behaviour of arbitrators, including their cognitive abilities. Section 36.6 concludes by considering the contribution of L&E to our understanding of arbitration.

36.2 L&E APPROACHES GENERALLY: TRADITIONAL AND BEHAVIOURAL

Lawyers, including international lawyers, often assume rationality of actors, explicitly or implicitly. They do so, for example, when drafting treaties or contracts taking into account the interests of the parties and their assumed incentives for different courses of action, or when considering rules on conflicts of interest in international arbitration. An elaborate version of the rationality assumption is also the basis for both positive and normative (law and) economics. Positive (neo)classical economics assumes rational actors, never denying that occasional lapses from rationality occur. However, these are deemed immaterial: traditional economics is concerned with average behaviour. Since positive economics is mainly about predicting future behaviour, arguably what matters is the predictive accuracy of models, not the reality of their assumptions.[5] But predictions by economists have also often gone wrong (sometimes because of behavioural assumptions). We briefly discuss the rationality assumption as used in L&E here and elaborate on the psychological developments in Section 36.5.

A classic definition of rationality employed by economists is by Gary Becker: 'all human behavior can be viewed as involving participants who [1] maximize their utility [2] from a stable set of preferences[6] and [3] accumulate an optimal amount of information

[5] Famously, Milton Friedman argued for this because of simplicity, in being able to predict at least as much as an alternate theory, while requiring less information, with fruitfulness in the precision and scope of predictions and the ability to generate additional research lines. See Milton Friedman, 'The Methodology of Positive Economics', in Milton Friedman (ed.), *Essays in Positive Economics* (Chicago University Press, 1953), 10–14.

[6] Stable preferences are defined by a minimal, formal rationality: first, as transitivity (i.e., if option A is preferred over option B and option B over option C, then option A must be preferred over option C), and second, completeness (i.e., the person can always say which of two alternatives they consider preferable or that neither is preferred to the other).

and other inputs in a variety of markets.'[7] The central tenets are utility maximization, stable preferences, rational expectations, and optimal processing of information. The standard rational choice model describes choice under uncertainty; the so-called expected utility theory.[8] Introducing uncertainty, of course, makes the model more accurate, since uncertainty is pervasive in our lives.

Law is considered a 'gigantic price machine'.[9] Economic analysis is incentive-based, and law shapes incentives. Law thus acts as an external restraint on the possibilities of action of human beings, like a budget constraint. Preferences are assumed to be egoistically self-regarding: *homo oeconomicus* is indifferent to others, neither envious nor malicious nor altruistic, although some economist have introduced opportunistic behaviour. The rationality assumption does not predetermine utility or preferences—these can in principle include everything—income, honour, reputation, influence, political or economic ideology, etc.—which may be important to arbitrators.

This approach to rationality is not without criticism: 'the principle of rationality, unless accompanied by extensive empirical research to identify the correct auxiliary assumptions, has little power to make valid predictions about political phenomena.'[10] And this is the crux: we do not have reliable information about what the preferences of arbitrators really are. Whereas rational choice theory *assumes* how people behave, and normative decision theory tells them how they *should* behave, the more recently evolved field of behavioural economics explores how people *do* behave, in actuality. This is important if those insights allow us to make more accurate predictions, since those are necessary for legal design, including the arbitration process but also may explain parties' behaviour.

The rational choice paradigm as employed by neoclassical economics has been thoroughly challenged since the 1970s by psychological experimental research, and has considerably changed large parts of economics.[11] Most prominent among the behavioural research pioneers in this vein have been Daniel Kahneman and Amos Tversky[12] and their sometime critic, Gerd Gigerenzer,[13] analysing systematic heuristics and biases running against the rationality assumption, searching for more realistic models of

[7] Gary Becker, *The Economic Approach to Human Behavior* (University of Chicago Press, 1976), 14.

[8] Ibid.; Gary Becker, *Accounting for Tastes* (Harvard University Press, 1996). Generally, expected utility of an option X comprises the sum of all outcomes X weighted by their probability P.

[9] Lawrence Friedman, 'Two Faces of Law', 1 Wisconsin Law Review 13 (1984).

[10] Herbert Simon, 'Human Nature in Politics: The Dialogue of Psychology with Political Science', 79 American Political Science Review 293 (1985), 293.

[11] Colin Camerer, 'Behavioral Economics: Reunifying Psychology and Economics', 96 Proceedings of the National Academy of Science 10,575 (1999); Matthew Rabin, 'Psychology and Economics', 36 Journal of Economic Literature 11 (1998).

[12] Starting with prospect theory and further extended into many other 'biases', see, Daniel Kahneman and Amos Tversky, 'Prospect Theory: An Analysis of Decisions under Risk', 47 Econometrica 312 (1979); Amos Tversky and Daniel Kahneman, 'Judgment under Uncertainty: Heuristics and Biases', 185 Science 1124 (1974).

[13] See Gerd Gigerenzer and Daniel Goldstein, 'Reasoning the Fast and Frugal Way: Models of Bounded Rationality', 103 Psychological Review 650 (1996); Gerd Gigerenzer and Reinhard Selten (eds), *Bounded Rationality: The Adaptive Toolbox* (MIT Press, 2002).

human behaviour. Some of the heuristics and biases analysed in behavioural economics which are potentially relevant to actors involved in arbitration are addressed below. A useful classification of heuristics and biases is to separate bounded rationality, bounded willpower, and bounded self-interest.[14]

The first and most central concept in the context of arbitration, bounded rationality, recognizes that the human brain systematically makes shortcuts in judgment and decision-making that diverge from expected utility theory. These shortcuts—generally known as biases and heuristics—inevitably cause human decisions that appear erroneous when compared with 'perfectly' rational outcomes. Significantly, under standard rational choice it is assumed that preferences are independent of the circumstances in which they are applied. Different descriptions and representations of alternative choices should have no influence over the decision itself: rational actors should always choose the same alternative, no matter how (objectively identical) data is presented. However, based on many experiments, prospect theory shows that this is incorrect. Individuals are loss averse, i.e. they have an asymmetrical attitude towards gains and losses (loss aversion) and whether there is a gain frame, or a loss frame depends on the representation of the problem. Their subjective utility is increased less by gains made than by losses avoided.

In other words, decisions are subject to 'framing effects', which contradict the axiom of stable preferences. Logically equivalent presentations of a choice lead individuals to different decisions. Typically, decisions vary depending on how circumstances are presented, either as positive (gain frame) or negative (loss frame), and whether the decision is taken under uncertainty or certainty.[15] Decisions about medical intervention are a typical example. The standard model would predict that patients would choose the most secure therapeutic method independently of how the choice is presented to them (as either death rates or survival rates). Death rates can theoretically function as lost profits or damages. If a relatively safe therapeutic method is presented to a patient in terms of death rate (i.e. potential loss) and an unsafe method is presented in terms of survival rate (i.e. potential gain), patients will tend to prefer the unsafe over the safe method, because potential gains are perceived to be more valuable than the avoidance of potential losses.[16] Thus, the description of a problem can lead to a demonstrably irrational decision. Depending on how a problem is presented, decisions can be considerably influenced by

[14] Christine Jolls, Cass Sunstein, and Richard Thaler, 'A Behavioral Approach to Law and Economics', 50 Stanford Law Review 1471 (1998), 1476.

[15] See Kahneman and Tversky, 'Prospect Theory' (n. 12); Amos Tversky and Daniel Kahneman, 'The Framing of Decisions and the Psychology of Choice', 211 Science 453 (1981); Daniel Kahneman, 'A Perspective on Judgment and Choice: Mapping Bounded Rationality', 58 American Psychologist 697 (2003), 703. See also James Druckmann, 'Political Preference Formation: Competition, Deliberation and the (Ir)relevance of Framing Effects', 98 American Political Science Review 671 (2004) for a description of experiments.

[16] This outcome is compatible with prospect theory. See Rabin (n. 11), 36ff., including descriptions of experiments and further references. See also Amos Tversky and Daniel Kahnemann, 'Rational Choice and the Framing of Decisions', in Robin Hogarth and Melvin Reder (eds), *Rational Choice* (University of Chicago Press, 1987), for experiments with medical students.

external elements—including law, which contains positive and negative frames in the way it is formulated.

Many more experimentally substantiated biases and heuristics are relevant to arbitration, such as the 'anchoring effect', in which people take into account irrelevant information they have been previously exposed to,[17] or the 'availability bias', wherein individuals put too much emphasis on recent events when estimating probabilities. These expressions of bounded rationality show that in many situations, individuals are incapable of rational utility maximization because of the way the human mind processes information and reacts to particular circumstances. In many cases, heuristics can be effective in reducing costs in decision-making. But at the same time, they may also lead to systematic and repeated errors. This has consequences for the design of a legal system if it aims at 'debiasing', that is, bringing actors closer to the normative ideal of rationality.

Regarding bounded self-interest, the standard economic models routinely assume that self-regarding interest (often of a material nature) is the sole motivation of all actors. But much experimental research has shown that individuals are strongly motivated by other-regarding/altruistic and social preferences.[18] Concerns for the well-being of others (for fairness and reciprocity) need to be taken into account if behaviour in social interactions is to be understood:[19] 'the real question is no longer whether many people have other-regarding preferences, but under which conditions these preferences have important economic and social effects.'[20] Fairness preferences are now well established. Those preferences may also guide arbitrators or disputants. Furthermore, individuals may punish free riders even if such action is costly for themselves;[21] this is again highly important for international arbitration, which has only a decentralized enforcement system and thus needs 'punishers' (states or non-state actors). International arbitration is, despite international conventions, costly and sometimes difficult to enforce in comparison with national legal orders. Thus, the system needs 'punishers' more than national legal systems.

In addition to bounded rationality, cognitive psychology has shown that individuals may have only bounded willpower. People sometimes act against their own interests, even when fully informed and conscious of the damage they may be inflicting upon themselves. The classic example is of habitual smokers who do not kick the habit, even if they declare that they would like to. While this may be attributable to substance addiction,

[17] See e.g. Edward Joyce and Gary Biddle, 'Anchoring and Adjustment in Probabilistic Inference in Auditing', 19 Journal of Accounting Research 120 (1981).

[18] This started with the so-called Ultimatum Game (by Werner Güth, Rolf Schmittberger, and Bernd Schwarze, 'An Experimental Analysis of Ultimatum Bargaining', (1982) 3 Journal of Economic Behavior and Organization 367), the Dictator Game, the Power to Take Game, the Third Party Punishment Game, the Gift Exchange Game and the Trust Game, etc. For details on the experiments, see Ernst Fehr and Klaus Schmidt, 'The Economics of Fairness, Reciprocity and Altruism–Experimental Evidence and New Theories', in Serge Kolm and Jean Mercier Ythier (eds), *Handbook of the Economics of Giving, Altruism and Reciprocity* (Elsevier, 2006), vol. 1, s. 2.

[19] Ibid. n. 18. [20] Ibid. 617.

[21] See, regarding retaliatory motives to punish, Armin Falk, Ernst Fehr, and Urs Fischbacher, 'Driving Forces Behind Informal Sanctions', 73 Econometrica 2017 (2005).

behaviourists have shown that bounded willpower is influential in other areas that are relevant to law, such as lack of self-control in criminal behaviour.[22] This can be relevant in circumstances that lead to arbitration, or to decisions taken by disputants in the process of arbitration.

36.3 A General Institutional Economics Perspective on Arbitration

L&E scholars tend to view dispute resolution as a market. They thus look at the supply and demand of such third-party adjudication, usually comparing litigation to arbitration. Predominantly, in the literature, there are two interrelated L&E perspectives on this: one is focused on the general welfare consequences of arbitration; the other is focused on why disputants choose one kind of third-party settlement over another. In this section, we will address only the general welfare consequences. The choice of dispute settlement of disputants is covered in Section 36.4.

Comparing the general welfare consequences of arbitration as an alternative to courts, one position is that litigation in courts and arbitration compete and differ slightly in the provision of goods and how they fulfil certain functions of third-party dispute settlement. Landes and Posner hold that:

> [a] court system (public or private) produces two types of service. One is dispute resolution—determining whether a rule has been violated. The other is rule formulation—creating rules of law, as a by-product of the dispute-settlement process. When a court resolves a dispute, its resolution, especially if embodied in a written opinion, provides information regarding the likely outcome of similar disputes in the future.[23]

Thus, traditional L&E scholars see mostly difficulties with arbitration in rule formation and production, i.e. the public good provided by adjudication despite its private nature. First, they see little incentive for arbitrators to produce precedents (writing from a common law perspective, and *a fortiori* from a civil law one), since '[t]o do so would be to confer an external, an uncompensated, benefit not only on future parties but also on competing judges'.[24] Although arbitrators may strive for a reputation for competence and impartiality and thus give reasons for their decisions, this is by no means certain. Even if they render written opinions, those might not be published and be accessible for all potential parties.

[22] See e.g. James Wilson and Allan Abrahamse, 'Does Crime Pay?' 9 Justice Quarterly 359 (1992); Roy Baumeister and John Tierney, *Willpower: Rediscovering the Greatest Human Strength* (Penguin, 2011).

[23] Landes and Posner (n. 1), 236.

[24] And, implicitly, arbitrators. See ibid. 238.

A second problem with a 'free' (arbitral) market in law production is that inconsistent decisions could destroy the value of a precedent system in guiding behaviour: 'If there are many judges, there is likely to be a bewildering profusion of precedents and no obvious method of harmonizing them.'[25] Furthermore, 'one effect of arbitration is to take out of the traditional legal system a lot of cases, which, if they remained in the formal legal system would generate published opinions, which would provide greater guidance for the future.'[26] Thus, the 'judge as the gardener of the law' is not presented with the risk that legal uncertainty raises for all prospective disputants.

Another critique is that arbitrators, since they are appointed by disputants, may take into account only the interests of the parties and not those of third parties affected by externalities of the contract. Whereas most L&E scholarship analyses the minimization of social costs by disputants choosing between arbitration and litigation, they always do so under the assumption that there are 'no third party effects'.[27] But those who relax that assumption hold that 'the main policy conclusion is that private judges should be allowed, or encouraged, to decide disputes which are truly private in the sense that the effects of the decision do not reach beyond the disputants, but public judges should have exclusive responsibility for cases such as class actions whose effects are diffuse'[28]—or for cases where there are externalities on third parties.[29] The incentive for public judges, who are assumed to be independent of reappointment considerations, will more likely take those third parties into account.

Nevertheless, in spite of these public functions of adjudication, there are many advantages to international arbitration from the disputants' perspective to which we now turn.

36.4 Disputants and Their Choices

There are many ways of resolving disputes between contractual parties: arbitration is also in competition with mediation, conciliation, litigation, and other forms of resolving disputes, including so-called 'extra-legal', socially normative ones (which can mimic formal methods, especially in close-knit groups).[30] At all junctures, disputants can choose to negotiate or settle the dispute. Most literature has focused either on the choice

[25] Ibid.

[26] Richard Posner, 'What Do Arbitrators Maximize?' in Peter Nobel, Katrin Krehan, and Philipp von Ins (eds), *Law and Economics of International Arbitration* (Schulthess, 2014), 123.

[27] Christopher Drahozal and Keith Hylton, 'The Economics of Litigation and Arbitration: An Application to Franchise Contracts', 32 Journal of Legal Studies 549 (2003), 552; Shavell (n. 1), 3.

[28] Cooter (n. 1), 108, 130: 'private judges aim for decisions which are pairwise Pareto efficient, which involves giving no weight to third parties.'

[29] On a discussion of proposals for reform of international arbitration where it involves 'public law responsibilities, see Philip McConnaughay, 'The Risks and Virtues of Lawlessness: A "Second Look" at International Commercial Arbitration', 93 Northwestern University Law Review 453 (1999).

[30] Lisa Bernstein, 'Opting Out of the Legal System: Extralegal Contractual Relations in the Diamond Industry', 21 Journal of Legal Studies 115 (1992).

between litigation and arbitration or on the influence of arbitration on negotiation and settlement between the parties.[31] We discuss those questions in Section 36.4.1. We then address other disputant choices, relating to third party funding (36.4.2) and arbitrator appointment (36.4.3).

36.4.1 Arbitration vis-à-vis other forms of dispute resolution

Why would disputants choose arbitration over other alternatives? Arbitration is an *ex ante* voluntary decision by disputants to contractually specify arbitration over litigation in the event of a dispute (although arbitration can also be agreed upon ad hoc by parties after a dispute has arisen). All contracts, particularly international contracts, have to deal with *ex post* opportunism in incomplete (the longer term, the more incomplete) contracts.[32] In order to protect themselves against this problem, parties take *ex ante* measures, such as agreed conflict resolution provisions. Nonetheless, third-party adjudication is not the focus of research in contract theory,[33] although some research has been done, on which our comments build.

Contracting parties are expected to choose the dispute resolution forum that provides the greatest (positive) difference between deterrence benefits[34] and dispute resolution costs for the parties.[35] The choice of the form of dispute resolution affects both *ex ante* incentives and dispute resolution costs. It also affects contracting costs, since parties are more likely to leave contract provisions vague, opting for relational governance, when they have chosen a forum that can be trusted to reach value-maximizing results (assumed to be arbitration). Parties may prefer more explicit contract terms if they have a high degree of confidence regarding the interpretation of those terms in court, since courts are assumed to be less trusted to interpret incomplete contracts in the sense parties intended.[36] Drahozal and Hylton find that the probability of arbitration is significantly higher when the parties are likely to rely on implicit terms for governance, and compliance with those terms is difficult to ensure[37]—which might well be the case

[31] E.g Cooter (n. 1). There are also studies which look at the choice of different methods of arbitration—e.g. conventional arbitration versus final offer arbitration and tri-offer arbitration. See Orley Ashenfelter et al., 'An Experimental Comparison of Dispute Rates in Alternative Arbitration Systems', 60 Econometrica 1407 (1992).

[32] Long-term contracts create more problems of unforeseen contingencies not dealt with in the contract, and augment potentially opportunistic behaviour of the parties. Thus, neutral third-party adjudication gains in importance.

[33] See e.g. Patrick Bolton and Mathias Dewatripont, *Contract Theory* (MIT Press, 2005); Victor Goldberg, 'Toward an Expanded Economic Theory of Contract', 10 Journal of Economic Issues 45 (1976).

[34] Deterrence benefits (or governance benefits) are defined as avoided harms net of avoidance costs. For contracting parties, the harms avoided through superior governance generally can be classified as losses due to breach of either explicit or implicit contract terms. See Drahozal and Hylton (n. 27), 550.

[35] Ibid. 550. [36] Ibid. 551. [37] Ibid.

in international business relationships as well as in international investment, in which arbitration under bilateral investment treaties (BITs) may be the default in practice.

What are some commonly identified advantages of arbitration for parties set forth by economics? First, unlike judges, arbitrators tend to specialize in particular types of dispute. Arbitrators competing for business have incentives to develop expertise and render unbiased decisions echoing those of past arbitrators, since this signals reliability in judgment and thus may lead to higher appointment rates.[38] A knowledgeable specialist can render a decision faster and with fewer information transfer from, and therefore less costs incurred by the disputants. She is also assumed to be less likely to make an error. Arbitration can thus reduce the uncertainty associated with judicial error and/or bias. The parties are assumed not to have to provide as much information to the arbitrator as they would to a judge/jury. But of course, arbitrators paid by the hour or day might have an incentive to ask for as much information as possible. Another benefit is said to arise when public courts have significant wait-times for hearings and decisions, since delay can be very costly.

Other potentially important benefits discussed in the economic literature are: (a) arbitration is generally less 'adversarial' or intensely contentious than litigation so it is more likely to allow continuation of mutually beneficial repeated-dealing relationships; (b) if desired, privacy and confidentiality can be maintained; and (c) parties may (subject to restrictions) agree to derogate from state law through contract provisions which may not be fully respected in a public court (e.g. business practice and custom rather than the statutes or judicial precedents of a particular jurisdiction). Thus, 'the potential of mutual gains (lower costs of dispute resolution and/or a larger "pie" to share in the long run) means that there clearly is a 'cooperative' element to arbitration as compared to litigation.'[39]

Furthermore, international arbitration can 'denationalize' disputes, therefore creating a level legal playing field for the parties, avoiding home-biased courts. The parties can choose not only the *lex arbitri* but also the *lex mercatoria*, which enhances their flexibility in the contractual design in choosing the rules appropriate to the question at issue—possibly those rules developed through the concerted efforts of those actors concerned with and participating in international trade, or any mix in between also national laws.[40] It bears noting that many of these benefits and advantages exist also after a dispute is manifest and parties consider their dispute resolution alternatives (i.e. deterrence benefits are moot, but dispute resolution cost considerations remain).

[38] Benson (n. 1), 162. [39] Ibid. 164.

[40] Nigel Blackaby, *Redfern and Hunter on International Arbitration*, 6th edn (Oxford University Press, 2015), 4. On the discussion of whether *lex mercatoria* is more efficient than national laws, see Christopher Drahozal, 'Busting Arbitration Myths', 56 University of Kansas Law Review 663 (2008), 669, and Christopher Drahozal's Ch. 27 in this Handbook. He finds that around 80% of ICC arbitration clauses choose national laws. This contradicts some L&E scholars' assumptions. Also, the 'common law is more efficient' hypothesis is refuted by empirical evidence. See Stefan Voigt, 'Are International Merchants Stupid? Their Choice of Law Sheds Doubt on the Legal Origin Theory', 5 Journal of Empirical Legal Studies 1 (2008).

How do arbitration clauses influence negotiation and settlement (as the most basic form of dispute resolution)? L&E scholars may object to conventional arbitration mechanisms to the extent that 'they "chill" the negotiation process which precedes arbitration. This argument is rooted in the belief that conventional arbitration awards systematically tend to be compromises between the parties' final positions, thereby providing an incentive for the parties to avoid pre-arbitration concessions.'[41] Although such compromise awards are not confirmed by the empirics,[42] it is evident that relatively fewer settlements take place during arbitration than in litigation, at least in the US.[43] The reasons remain unclear, but arguments range from the different incentives judges face (minimizing their dockets) to the fact that arbitrations are often initiated pursuant to a multi-tier clause, which means the arbitration is only filed after contractually mandated negotiation or mediation has failed, or the impact on settlement of significant pre-trial discovery in US civil courts vs the lesser quantity of discovery in commercial arbitration (both as to development of a realistic assessment of prospects for success and as to increased expense of pursuing the dispute).[44]

Moreover, L&E scholars describe negotiations to avoid a trial—and at least by extension, an arbitration—'as a bargaining game in which settlement is the cooperative solution and trial is the noncooperative solution'.[45] The threat values of the parties are then defined by their subjective predictions about the outcome of a trial. If both parties are optimistic about the trial in the sense that the defendant believes that the court award will be negligible, whereas the plaintiff believes that the award will be large, their optimism 'can make the sum of the subjective values of trial to the defendant and plaintiff exceed the stakes in the dispute'.[46] If it is then 'impossible to divide the stakes so that both parties get at least their subjective value of trial, then trial is inevitable. In technical language, a sufficient condition for trial is that the core of the game is empty.'[47] And indeed, some research has shown that parties often have 'systemic over-optimism', and underestimation of arbitration costs, that present significant obstacles to settlement.[48] In sum, it is clear that economic and behavioural factors significantly influence disputants' choices regarding arbitration vis-à-vis other methods of dispute resolution (primarily adjudication/litigation as opposed to negotiation/settlement); but these choices depend on a variety of factors and significant empirical research is still needed in this respect.

[41] David Bloom, 'Empirical Models of Arbitrator Behavior Under Conventional Arbitration', 68 Review of Economics and Statistics 578 (1986), 578.

[42] See Section 36.5.

[43] American Arbitration Association (AAA), 'B2B Dispute Resolution Impact Report: 2015 Key Statistics' (2015): <https://ssusa.s3.amazonaws.com/c/2345/media/5702c0b6ca18b/AAA186_2015_B2B_Case_Statistics.pdf>. For arbitration statistics see Thomas Stipanowich and Zachary Ulrich, 'Commercial Arbitration and Settlement: Empirical Insights into the Roles Arbitrators Play', 6 Penn State Yearbook on Arbitration and Mediation 1 (2014), for US Courts with further references on the data, which ranges between 70% and 90% of settlement or other means of avoiding a final court decision.

[44] This is suggested by Mark Kantor, 'OGEMID Post of 30 June 2016' (OGEMID, 2016).

[45] Cooter (n. 1), 109. [46] Ibid. [47] Ibid.

[48] Christian Bühring-Uhle, Lars Kirchhoff, and Gabriele Scherer, *Arbitration and Mediation in International Business*, 2nd edn (Kluwer Law International, 2006), 115.

36.4.2 Third-Party Funding

Third-Party Funding (TPF) (or 'legal financing') has recently become a subject of heated discussion in arbitration and litigation, but has hitherto to our knowledge not been analysed from an L&E perspective.[49] TPF has no commonly accepted definition, but we use the following: a (private) party (i) with no pre-existing interest in the arbitration funds a party's costs arising from the arbitral process; (ii) receives a certain amount of the sum recovered in an award or settlement; and (iii) does not receive anything in case the claim fails.[50] It is thus similar to contingency fees, and should not be considered a loan. Most commonly, the funder receives a certain percentage which—depending on the contract—can lie between 15 and 50 per cent of the recovery amount, including a settlement. If the funded party loses the trial, the funding company receives nothing, and the funded party has no obligation to repay anything.

Usually it is claimants, not respondents, who are thus funded. Most of the funding agreements are confidential.[51] The funded party may disclose to the arbitrators, but the latter may not know of other claims being funded by the funder, even if the arbitrator is counsel in another case which is funded by that very same entity. But this (missing) knowledge may influence an arbitrator's decision or components of it, such as cost allocation. The funder often has a confidentiality agreement with the client, so the funder cannot disclose to the arbitrator.[52]

What are the incentives for the different parties involved: disputants, funders,[53] and arbitrators? By some accounts, funders[54] show average returns of 17 per cent on their

[49] With the exception of Irene Röthlisberger, 'Third-Party Funding in International Arbitration: A Law and Economics Analysis' (master's thesis, University of St. Gallen, 2015), on which we draw heavily in this section.

[50] Catherine Rogers, *Ethics in International Arbitration* (Oxford University Press, 2014), 5.26; Lisa Nieuwveld and Victoria Shannon, *Third-Party Funding in International Arbitration* (Kluwer Law International, 2012), 3. The ICCA task force has published its first report in 2015, available at: <http://www.arbitration-icca.org/media/6/09700416080661/tpf_taskforce_security_for_costs_and_costs_draft_report_november_2015.pdf>.

[51] Victoria Shannon, 'Victoria Shannon Discusses The State of the Legal Funding Industry at Home and in International Arbitration' (Legal Funding Central, 2014): <http://prospectfundingcom/victoria-shannon-discusses-the-state-of-the-legal-funding-industry-at-home-and-in-international-arbitration/>: 'Usually the funding agreements are secret. The funder keeps its clients secret. The funder might not tell the arbitrator, "I'm funding these other cases, too, including this one that you're representing the other side on." The funder often has a confidentiality agreement with the client, so the funder actually can't tell the arbitrator. So, the only way the arbitrator knows is if the funded party tells the arbitrator.'

[52] Ibid.

[53] The funders' point of view is based on specialized funding companies and hedge funds. These companies are specialized in funding parties of a legal dispute, and have their own procedure in evaluating whether or not to invest by assessing the claim using an extensive due diligence process. For an overview on arbitration financing, see Christopher Bogart, 'Overview of Arbitration Finance', in Bernardo Cremades and Antonias Dimolitsa (eds), *Third-Party Funding in International Arbitration* (Kluwer Law International, 2013).

[54] William Park and Catherine Rogers, 'The Arbitration Agreement and Arbitrability: Third-Party Funding in International Arbitration. The ICCA Queen-Mary Task Force', in Christian Klausegger et al.

investment, some going as high as 25 per cent (these are much higher returns than common loans), but only select disputes receive actual funding.[55] The funders' main goal is to receive as much return on their investment as possible, and since they earn nothing if a case is lost, their significant interest is in extensive due diligence of each case, with analysis of central factors, such as: jurisdiction, merits, the respondent, potential value, costs, and the duration of the case. He bears financial risk and is also subject to a behavioural risk as well as dispute resolution risks. He typically tries to manage these risks by funding several cases and spreading the risks among different disputes.

The funder's interest in the return on investment is likely to influence the evaluation of settlement offers as well. He may act differently from its client's interests because the funder's main goal is not to achieve a win, but to optimize its return. He may prefer an early settlement, which is not as high as it might possibly be after serious negotiations, to risking a costly trial or even a loss. That choice depends on the respective investment strategy. A funder might be willing to accept a lower offer just to receive a secure payment.[56] Generally, the funder is also induced to take an earlier exit to its investment, because the longer the proceedings the smaller the return.[57] On the other hand, the funder might be induced not to take the settlement because it is not enough to reimburse its investment, and thus takes the risk to win or lose the case.[58] International arbitration, in contrast to other forms of dispute settlement, is very attractive for third-party funders because of the high sums involved, but such processes are also complex, and reportedly only around 25 companies are as yet in this business.[59]

What are the incentives for the actual disputants? For the claimant (usually the funded party), surely gaining access to justice through funding is an important benefit. Studies have shown that the high costs of arbitration are viewed as the biggest disadvantage of arbitration.[60] Using TPF, claimants are able to transfer and thus reduce their risk. The funder's due diligence provides the potential client with valuable information—for example, by correcting over-optimistic miscalculations about expected compensation, about the chances of winning, or about collection of the award from the respondent. Thus, it may be the case that concerns over those 'modern' forms of 'champerty'[61] are

(eds), *Austrian Yearbook on International Arbitration* (AYIA, 2015), 113, summarize: 'International arbitration attracts funders in part because such cases typically involve high-value claims, proceedings with no substantive appeal, potential for streamlined procedures, the ability to control litigation variables such as the arbitrator's expertise, and the enforcement mechanisms of international conventions.'

[55] Georges Affaki, 'A Financing Is a Financing Is a Financing . . .', in Cremades and Dimolitsa (n. 53).

[56] Susanna Khouri, Kate Hurford, and Clive Bowman, 'Third Party Funding International Commercial and Treaty Arbitration: A Panacea or a Plague?', 8 Transnational Dispute Management 1 (2011); Sebastian Perry, 'Third-Party Funding: the Best Thing Since Sliced Bread?' 8 Global Arbitration Review 1 (2012), 5.

[57] Maya Steinitz, 'The Litigation Finance Contract', 54 William & Mary Law Review 455 (2012), 489.

[58] Perry (n. 56), 5. [59] Shannon (n. 51).

[60] Chartered Institute of Arbitrators, 'CIArb Costs of International Arbitration Survey 2011' (2011): <https://www.international-arbitration-attorney.com/wp-content/uploads/CIArb-costs-of-International-Arbitration-Survey-2011.pdf>.

[61] The concept of champerty has a long tradition. It arose from a practice in medieval England whereby sometimes the frivolous claims of noblemen were funded, which was then criticized. The

misguided from an L&E perspective, as TPF discourages rather than encourages frivolous arbitration.[62]

There is a principal-agent relationship between the funder and the funded disputant, with significant economic aspects. Funders face the problem of information asymmetry because the disputants possess private information about the case, some of it potentially adverse. Even though funders conduct extensive due diligence, they cannot be certain of having received all pertinent information. They also face moral hazard problems from the funded disputants, who may oversell their claim, whether out of over-optimism or to gain funding, causing adverse selection. Since funders' investments are at stake, they prefer greater control over the proceedings (subject to incurring unnecessary costs of control).

All then depends on the TPF contract. Depending on the case, a funder can influence arbitrator selection. Since there are few funders and the market is small, giving market power to funders, counsel for the funded party may also prefer the interest of the funder, since there are few alternatives. The funder can also retain control, e.g. in participating in the decision of some key issues.[63] The drafting of (inter alia) the termination clause is therefore very important, as it can indirectly influence the extent of the funder's control. If the funder is able to terminate the funding relationship 'at will', the client will refrain from acting against the funder's preferences.

For the opposing disputant's side, TPF may also provide information and create signalling effects. For the funded party to take advantage of the signalling effect of TPF, the non-funded party, however, must be aware that a funding relationship exists. The opposing party clearly has an interest in knowing that a funder exists. The TPF may then have a deterrent effect—potentially influencing the strategy of the defendant and inducing him to settle. This is especially likely if the funded party is a one-shot player, since the funder turns him into a repeat player via his expertise. Assuming that funders are experienced and conduct deep due diligence of the case thus signals having a strong case. A claimant who is supported by a funding company has sufficient financial resources, more knowledge, and profits from the economies of scale effect of the legal expertise.

What about the arbitrators? Some commentators question the independence and impartiality of an arbitrator if a funder is involved,[64] and indeed, these arrangements raise important ethical questions. First, arbitrators may have a personal financial interest in increased supply of arbitration disputes, a supply generated by TPF (i.e. cases are brought which would not have brought without TPF). Second, a relatively small group of repeat players of funders, attorneys, and arbitrators is active in international arbitration. If arbitrators did not know about TPF, or had no influence over its development,

assumed encouragement of litigation was also considered as 'un-Christian'. See Bernardo Cremades, 'Third Party Litigation Funding: Investing in Arbitration', 8 Transnational Dispute Management 4 (2011).

62 On champerty and TPF, see Victoria Shannon, 'Harmonizing Third-Party Litigation Funding Regulation', 36 Cardozo Law Review 861 (2015), 875.

63 Steinitz (n. 57), 495.

64 Ibid.

there would be no special problem. Yet many arbitrators also work as counsel and thus they may act as counsel for clients who are funded by the same funder. There is thus fear expressed by some experts that arbitrators may not remain independent if they have special ties with funders.[65] Currently only the International Bar Association (IBA) Guidelines have provisions on TPF which require disclosure.[66]

36.4.3 Arbitrator selection

It is difficult to make a clean analytical cut between, on the one hand, economic elements of arbitrators' behaviour (discussed in more detail in Section 36.5) and, on the other, the L&E of arbitrator appointment. This is because of repeated interactions, often of a strategic nature, between disputant preferences regarding arbitrators' selection (whether general preferences, e.g. for expertise, efficiency and reliability; or more specific to the dispute, the disputant, or the arbitrator), and arbitrator behaviour both during arbitral proceedings and in rendering decisions. In Section 36.5 we will discuss different incentives for arbitrator behaviour, but there is no question that arbitrators have an interest in being appointed (and reappointed) to disputes. This is the case, setting aside (at least for now) the question of whether this interest is purely pecuniary (first, due to high fees paid to arbitrators, and second, because of high fees that well-established arbitrators can charge as counsel in other disputes) or involves other elements such as prestige and influence.[67] Arbitrators (and potential arbitrators interested in initial appointment) therefore have incentives to behave in ways that correlate with disputant preferences (or those preferences dictated by disputants' legal counsel). This often derives from the involvement of the parties to the arbitration in the selection of arbitrators. In any case, this creates a market for arbitrators (as suppliers of arbitration services), in which potential disputants serve as consumers. Inevitably, there is competition between arbitrators over appointment. In practice, there can be significant party calculations as well as political and cognitive biases associated with arbitrator appointment.[68]

[65] Roula Harfouche and James Searby, 'Third-Party Funding: Incentives and Outcomes', 2013 European, Middle Eastern and African Arbitration Review: <http://www.fticonsulting.com/global2/critical>; Shannon (n. 51).

[66] Particularly important are General Standards 6 and 7 of the IBA Guidelines. General Standard 7(a) requires the party to disclose the presence of a third-party funder. General Standard 6(b) allows a 'legal entity... having a controlling influence on the legal entity, or a direct economic interest in, or a duty to indemnify a party for, the award to be rendered in the arbitration, may be considered to bear the identity of such party'.

[67] See Sergio Puig, 'Social Capital in the Arbitration Market', 25(2) European Journal of International Law 387 (2014), 398, noting that, regarding ICSID arbitrations as an example, 'the financial incentives are considerable'.

[68] See ibid.; Catherine Rogers, 'The Politics of International Investment Arbitrators', 12 Santa Clara Journal of International Law 223 (2014); Michael Waibel and Yanhui Wu, 'Are Arbitrators Political?' (2012): <www.researchgate.net/publication/256023521_Are_Arbitrators_Political>.

Different arbitration agreements and facilities adopt different appointment methods that alter incentive structures. Indeed, these methods of appointment are in this respect the fundamental institutional dimension of arbitration, lending themselves easily to general rational choice analysis. One can take as a starting point Paulsson's observation:

> the fact that parties have a dispute means that each of them thinks it is right and wishes to prevail, and will act in every instant in such a way to achieve that objective; that objective is also foremost in their minds when they make the unilateral selection of an arbitrator. On that basis, one person whom the either party does not trust is surely the arbitrator chosen by its adversary.[69]

Here Paulsson refers to a common method of appointment, whereby each disputant selects one qualified arbitrator, and the two party-appointed arbitrators then decide between them on a presiding arbitrator. Although all arbitrators, regardless of who appointed them, are bound by ethical rules of independence and impartiality, in this scenario, potential appointees have incentives to develop general reputations as desirable arbitrators (such as expertise) and more specific reputations as arbitrators with normative tendencies that coincide with those of the appointing party's interests.[70] Moreover, while this type of appointment process appears to create symmetry between the disputants, respondents have structural reasons to skew it, for example, 'if one party to a dispute expects that an impartial arbitrator would rule against him, he has an incentive to drag his feet in agreeing to the appointment of an arbitrator'.[71] Other appointment methods, such as overall appointment by a third party, as in the London Court of International Arbitration (LCIA),[72] or single arbitrators appointed by both parties, can circumvent some (though not all) of these issues.

Recent empirical research, linked to the common party-appointment model, demonstrates that even professional arbitrators suffer from 'affiliation effects'—in other words, a party-appointed arbitrator, no matter how ethical, may tend to express a decision in favour of the party appointing him, and it has been suggested that arbitrators be de-biased by 'blinding', i.e. that they not be informed which party appointed them.[73] Though this is a theoretically sound option, we believe that it would be both difficult and costly to enforce such 'blinding', and that nevertheless disputants would have significant incentives to signal to arbitrators, at low cost, that they have appointed them. It might be more efficient and indeed necessary in this regard to blind the disputants instead in the appointment process—i.e. they will not know whom they appointed. Arbitrators may be drawn blindly from a list filtered according to their expertise.

[69] See Jan Paulsson's Ch. 4 in this Handbook. [70] See Puig (n. 67); Waibel and Wu (n. 68).

[71] Landes and Posner (n. 1), 245. [72] See Paulsson (n. 69).

[73] Sergio Puig and Anton Strezhnev, 'Affiliation Bias in Arbitration: An Experimental Approach', Arizona Legal Studies Discussion Paper No. 16-31 (2016), 1.

36.5 Arbitrators' behaviour: theory and empirics

Just as L&E has been enriched by behavioural economics, so has the theory and the empirics about judges' and arbitrators' behaviour. We will survey the classical approach first before turning to behavioural L&E.

36.5.1 The rational choice approach to arbitrators' behaviour

The classical approach ultimately assumes the same behavioural theory for judges and arbitrators as for everybody else.[74] According to Posner:

> there are no fundamental differences between judges, arbitrators, workers and politicians. They (or better we) all are self-interested, and I mean that not in any bad sense. It's human nature to think about one's life and an adequate income, to do a good job and to pursue, to a certain extent, also personal interests.[75]

Most analysis has been conducted regarding judges—and we will draw on those insights as well. For judges and arbitrators, the classical approach assumes that they pursue their goals rationally and maximize their utility. As Thomas Schultz puts it: 'they will take into account, in their decision-making, the factors that reasonably promote what they conceive to be in their self-interest, regardless whether these factors are of a legal or extra-legal nature.'[76] Drobak and North note: '[t]hat something beyond legal doctrine influences judicial decision-making is no surprise.'[77]

Which incentives exactly drive arbitrator decisions is still a question of theoretical debate. From the perspective of L&E, there are several possibilities. International arbitrators are well paid. Do they maximize (consciously or unconsciously) their income? Their reputation as good, impartial decision-makers (as a value per se)? Their own political views?[78] Is reputation just a means to secure more cases and generate greater

[74] Richard Posner, 'What Do Judges and Justices Maximize? (The Same Thing Everybody Else Does)', 3 Supreme Court Economic Review 1 (1993).

[75] Posner (n. 26), 123.

[76] Schultz (n. 2).

[77] John Drobak and Douglass North, 'Understanding Judicial Decision-Making: The Importance of Constraints on Non-Rational Deliberations', 26 Washington University Journal of Law & Policy 131 (2008), 135.

[78] Waibel and Wu (n. 68), finding that in ISDS arbitrators routinely appointed by the investor scrutinize the actions of host states more closely, as compared to arbitrators typically appointed by host states. Arbitrators are more lenient to host countries from their own legal family. Other aspects of the arbitrators' experience and training, such as the development status of their country of origin and whether or not they engage in full-time private practice, also play an important role in arbitration decisions.

income? For public judges, it has been assumed that they (all other things being equal to arbitrators) are driven by prestige (since being a public judge does not earn as much money as being an arbitrator) more than by income[79] (but of course public judges often become arbitrators after retirement).

In investment treaty arbitration, for example, it has been claimed that arbitrators have a structural interest in not declining jurisdiction in order to have continued income from the case. Furthermore, they may have a broader interest in preserving and expanding the system, with a due interest in giving more weight to investors' interests since those are the ones who bring claims.[80] They would then have an interest in expanding the 'industry of arbitration'.[81] What do the empirics say? Studies have explored how far professional and educational experience influence decisions of arbitrators. The hypothesis that arbitrators who belong to the same legal family, like the defendant state, are more deferential to the host country measure in question was supported by the evidence. There was also partial evidence that arbitrators with skewed appointment records favour the type of party that routinely appoints them,[82] and that arbitrators with experience in government or with a public international background are more deferential to the host state.

Further, arbitrators who depend on fees are more likely to affirm jurisdiction (which then leads to more fees on the merit decision). An often-heard hypothesis, namely that arbitrators from developed states are less deferential to host states (predominantly developing or transition countries), applying the good governance ideas of their own (mainly developed) states, was not supported by the evidence, neither was it supported that attorney-arbitrators are less deferential to host states.[83] In an experimental study regarding a survey experiment conducted on 266 arbitration professionals, evidence was found that arbitrators suffer from strong party affiliation effects—a cognitive bias in favour of the nominating party, including in cost allocation.[84]

36.5.2 Behavioural approaches to arbitrators' decision-making

The rational choice literature on judges' behaviour is legion, encompassing their preferences, their political orientation, their interaction with legislators, etc.[85] Recently,

[79] Cooter (n. 1), 130: 'public judges behave much like private judges, but some differences may arise because public judges escape market pressures.'

[80] David Gaukrodger and Kathryn Gordon, 'Inter-Governmental Evaluation of Investor–State Dispute Settlement: Recent Work at the OECD-Hosted Freedom of Investment Roundtable', in Jean Kalicki and Anna Joubin-Bret (eds), *Reshaping the Investor–State Dispute Settlement System: Journeys for the 21st Century* (Nijhoff, 2015), 606.

[81] Gus Van Harten, *Investment Treaty Arbitration and Public Law* (Oxford University Press, 2007), 152–53.

[82] See Puig (n. 67). [83] Waibel and Wu (n. 68). [84] Puig and Strezhnev (n. 73).

[85] All important contributions with a view to national law can be found in Lee Epstein (ed.), *The Economics of Judicial Behavior* (2 vols, Edward Elgar, 2013). The volumes do not include one article on the behavioural economics research concerning judges.

behavioural research has also been applied to municipal judicial actors—be it jurors or judges. The research explores how cognitive biases and heuristics impact domestic adjudication,[86] and demonstrates that cognitive biases—such as hindsight, irrelevant evidence, arbitrary numerical estimates, and incoherence in calculating damages—adversely affect the quality of judges' and jurors' decisions.

Guthrie and Rachlinski pioneered the analysis of how cognitive biases and heuristics affect the decisions of US judges.[87] Their research, using experiments with judges, demonstrated that judges often, but not always, rely upon intuition to process information and make decisions. They explored, for example, how irrelevant numerical anchors affect damage awards made by specialized judges; they considered how the framing of disputes impacts judges' evaluations; they demonstrated that judges overestimate their skills in assessing witness credibility as well as in facilitating settlement and in avoiding the influence of cognitive biases.

Their research provided a baseline for testing the cognitive biases and heuristics of international arbitrators.[88] We have tested those biases' heuristics for international arbitrators, including investment treaty arbitrators.[89] They exhibit biases and heuristics similar to judges, i.e. they are subject to the framing effect as described above, exhibit the irrelevant anchoring effect, are influenced by representativeness, and are over-optimistic concerning their own abilities.[90] This may call for de-biasing mechanisms in international procedural rules (for arbitration).[91]

Most commonly, international arbitrators do not take their decisions alone. Rather, they decide in groups or panels. This might mitigate cognitive errors, since de-biasing through group decisions is possible whenever counterfactual mindsets are presented.[92] People tend to recognize the impact of biases on the judgement of others, while failing to see the impact of biases on their own judgement (so called 'blind spot bias'), and thus group discussions may help. Also, the presentation of counterframes helps. Thus, international courts usually call for a diverse composition of adjudicators,[93] supposedly contributing

[86] For an overview of the research on judges, see David Klein and Gregory Mitchell (eds), *The Psychology of Judicial Decision Making* (Oxford University Press, 2010).

[87] Chris Guthrie, Jeffrey Rachlinski, and Andrew Wistrich, 'Inside the Judicial Mind', 86 Cornell Law Review 777 (2001); 'Blinking on the Bench: How Judges Decide Cases', 93 Cornell Law Review 1 (2007).

[88] Susan Franck, 'Empiricism and International Law: Insights for Investment Treaty Dispute Resolution', 48 Virginia Journal of International Law 767 (2008), 791 (n. 106) (mentioning the potential effect of cognitive biases on the WTO dispute settlement process); 'The ICSID Effect? Considering Potential Variations in Arbitration Awards', 51 Virginia Journal of International Law 825 (2011), 850–51 (n. 123) (mentioning cognitive psychology and its possible applications in investment treaty dispute settlement).

[89] Susan Franck et al., 'Inside the Arbitrator's Mind', 66 Emory Law Journal 1115 (2017). For US arbitrators, see Rebecca Helm, Andrew Wistrich, and Jeffrey Rachlinski, 'Are Arbitrators Human?' 13 Journal of Empirical Legal Studies 666 (2016).

[90] See also Christopher Drahozal's Ch. 27 in this Handbook.

[91] Franck et al. (n. 89); Jan-Philip Elm, 'Behavioural Insights into International Arbitration: An Analysis on How to De-Bias Arbitrators', 27 American Review of International Arbitration 75 (2016).

[92] Laura Kray and Adam Galinsky, 'The Debiasing Effect of Counterfactual Mind-Sets: Increasing the Search for Disconfirmatory Information in Group Decisions', 91 Organizational Behavior and Human Decision 69 (2003) (finding in experiments that the activation of a counterfactual mindset minimizes decision errors resulting from the failure of groups to seek disconfirming information).

[93] See e.g. in the WTO, Art. 8(2) DSU for panels and Art. 17(3) DSU for the Appellate Body.

to a potential discussion of (legal, cultural and maybe even ideological) counterframes.[94] However, there is a problem with international arbitration: international arbitrators may be more prone to share the same mindset,[95] since their diversity in terms of geography and gender is rather small[96]—which in turn might lessen the de-biasing potential of group adjudication in comparison with courts. Thus, for example, the understanding of different legal cultures might be hindered.

36.5.3 Splitting the difference

As outlined above, arbitrators are assumed to pursue their own interest. They thus have an interest in reappointment. A common criticism of arbitrators rests on the assumption that arbitrators tend to split the difference, or the 'baby'.[97] The traditional L&E perspective, a view which also 'persisted within the legal community for decades'[98] assumes that arbitrators have an incentive to split the baby,[99] since they need reappointment. They use an incentive-based theory to explain the assumed decision-making by arbitrators.[100] The main theoretical insight is that income-maximizing private judges make decisions which are Pareto-efficient (pair-wise efficient) with respect to the litigants. The exact account of the division of the stakes is developed by Cooter by using the Bayesian–Nash concept of bargaining equilibrium.[101] To cite Posner again:

> In particular the fact that they're paid by the parties is going to lead to different incentives. What I and others have conjectured is that there would be a tendency of arbitrators to split the difference between the parties rather than side entirely with one party. The reason for this is that the arbitrator, if he's a career arbitrator, has to consider what effect his decision is going to have on the future demand for his services. So, if he sides very decidedly with one party . . . the other party will not consent to his arbitrating future disputes.[102]

[94] Adam Galinsky and Laura Kray, 'From Thinking About What Might Have Been to Sharing What we Know: The Effects of Counterfactual Mind-Sets on Information Sharing in Groups', 40 Journal of Experimental Social Psychology 606 (2004) (finding in experiments that activation of a counterfactual mindset minimizes group decision errors caused by the failure of groups to discuss unshared, uniquely held information).

[95] Puig (n. 67), finding that the social structure of investor–state arbitrators is not very diverse. We find a similar result in Susan Franck et al., 'The Diversity Challenge: Exploring the "Invisible College" of International Arbitration', 53 Columbia Journal of Transnational Law 429 (2015).

[96] Ibid.

[97] Richard Posner, 'Judicial Behavior and Performance: An Economic Approach', 32 Florida State University Law Review 1259 (2005), 1261 ('We can expect, therefore, a tendency for arbitrators to "split the difference" in their awards'); Posner (n. 26), 124–25 ('[T]here would be a tendency of arbitrators to split the difference between the parties rather than side entirely with one party').

[98] Carter Greenbaum, 'Putting the Baby to Rest: Dispelling a Common Arbitration Myth', 26 American Review of International Arbitration 101 (2015), 101.

[99] Bloom (n. 41). [100] Cooter (n. 1). [101] Ibid. 107. [102] Posner (n. 26).

Under this assumption by Posner, the way in which arbitrator compensation is determined is going to have an effect on splitting. If arbitrators receive modest compensation, the incentive to split the baby, if that's a way of getting more and more arbitration business, becomes greater.[103] We deem the compensation argument unconvincing. Even if one follows the argument that splitting is a consequence of the quest for reappointment and compensation, we propose that this is an optimization problem between reappointment and compensation (otherwise, little compensation would be the way to get more reappointments, which must overcompensate for the low compensation in absolute terms). But in any case, we follow the argument that arbitrators think very carefully about what impact their decision has on their reputation—important for reappointment. But, as Judge Posner concedes, 'there is an empirical question: How often do arbitrators split the difference—consciously or unconsciously?'[104]

The empirical evidence speaks against the traditional L&E assumption. Most commonly, no splitting the difference is found.[105] Although more of it is found in B2B commercial arbitration, less is found in arbitration including a consumer.[106] Also, in experiments with international arbitrators with in-group variation in case vignettes, no across-the-board splitting was found. The case vignette's main issue was the valuation of a land property in investment arbitration. At best, there were three different paradigms for international arbitrators—a group inclined to prioritize claimant valuations, a group inclined to prioritize respondent valuation, and a group that was roughly in the middle but tended to render more respondent-favourable awards. The largest two single responses did not reflect a compromise between claims. Rather, the most common response involved arbitrators taking an 'all-or-nothing' approach. These responses undermine claims that arbitrators, as a group, 'split the baby'.[107]

The question is what drives arbitrators not to split the baby. It might be fairness considerations in arbitrations with unequal parties. In commercial arbitration, it may also be that they are indifferent as to which party appoints them. In investment arbitration, many arbitrators are appointed (chosen by the claimant or the respondent) because they are known to be pro-state or pro-investor. Splitting the baby for them would be counterproductive. For sole arbitrators of presidents of the tribunal, it might be a more successful strategy to have fairly marked 'normative inclinations'—and precisely not splitting the baby.[108] Or it may just be that they do not follow the assumptions of the L&E behavioural model, but are all instead trying to apply the law in the most faithful manner, disregarding

[103] Ibid. 130. [104] Ibid. 125.

[105] See Drahozal (n. 40), 673–77 (identifying the 'split the baby' myth of arbitration but providing contradictory empirical evidence); Stephanie Keer and Richard Naimark, 'Arbitrators Do Not "Split the Baby": Empirical Evidence from International Business Arbitrations', 18 Journal of International Arbitration 537 (2001), 574–5 (analysing arbitration awards to observe, overall, that tribunals award roughly 47–50% between amounts demanded, but instead finding a bimodal distribution where tribunals rendered awards in favour of either claimant or respondent); Greenbaum (n. 98, providing empirical data that 'the incidence of compromise awards in commercial arbitration is insignificant', testing 400 cases). The AAA has replicated the study and also found no baby-splitting. See American Arbitration Association (AAA), 'Splitting the Baby: A New AAA Study' (2007): <www.adr.org/aaa/ShowPDF?doc=ADRSTG_014040>.

[106] Greenbaum (n. 98), 101. [107] Franck et a.l (n. 89). [108] See Puig (n. 67).

their own potential interests for reappointment. Or splitting the baby does not cause more appointments because it impacts the arbitrators' reputation—a question of party behaviour.

36.6 Conclusion

Arbitration in general and international arbitration more particularly are by now a significant fixture in the contemporary globalized economy. Arbitration is, however, an ever-controversial phenomenon, as far as global governance is concerned. As a cross-border dynamic that is not usually embedded in classic Westphalian nation-state structures, and as a privatized form of dispute settlement—in contrast to public dispute settlement—its overall legitimacy is called into question. Yet for the same reasons it reduces transaction costs and increases efficiencies of dispute settlement for businesses and governments worldwide.

In this context, this chapter has been only a survey of some of the arbitration issues that L&E methods and research can illuminate, looking at both disputants and arbitrators as rational actors, as well as considering bounded rationality in their decision-making, ranging from issues of forum selection and third-party finance to arbitral decision-making. The issues we have covered are, in our opinion, the most important and also the best-researched so far. Many other issues are yet to be explored from classical and behavioural L&E perspectives. For example, we consider the absence of substantive appeal mechanisms in international arbitration worthy of further research (in particular their relationship with other dispute settlement fora), as well as the effectiveness of collection and recovery across jurisdictions, and the reduction of costs through international automated arbitration and the enabling of greater access to dispute settlement.

Arbitration has many difficulties that need to be analysed. In this respect L&E is not a panacea, but can serve as an additional analytical tool for evaluation and reform, where necessary. But for now, some of its predictions are proved wrong (splitting the baby) and some of its assumptions concerning the rational cognition of arbitrators also have to be carefully considered. We end this chapter with a call for more empirical studies which will either prove or disprove the predominant theory of rational choice. We consider this a starting point, but in order to generate reliable predictions on arbitrators and party behaviour, much more research is needed, including on what really drives arbitrator behaviour.

CHAPTER 37

ARBITRATION AND LITERATURE

FRANÇOIS OST

ARBITRATION seems to receive little attention in literary works, as opposed to justice and the judge, which form the heart of the 'law and literature' movement. This disparity is likely due to our collective fascination with the judge (with his wig, robes and gavel) as the embodiment of justice.

The air of mystery that often surrounds arbitration can also be explained by the difference between the way in which it is presented in fictional texts and in modern law. Literature does not usually apprehend arbitration in the strict understanding of a private judge chosen by the parties, who adjudicates on a dispute by rendering a final and binding award which he cannot enforce without the assistance of state courts. Yet literature's approximations in the treatment of arbitration are precisely what makes them interesting, in that they shed a welcome light on a justice that is both broader and more perennial that the justice that is rendered within the strict boundaries of the traditional court system.

For instance, literary works remind us of the infinite variety of disputes, and that their characterization as 'legal' is nothing more than a conventional and incidental construct. The work of sociologists Boltanski and Thévenot helps us understand this point by distinguishing no less than six domains of human activity, each with their own 'principles of judgment', separate and distinct from the idea of legal judgment.[1] Drawing on their work, we can think of arbitration, historically, as constituting a form of welcomed third-party intervention (if possible impartial, despite its proximity to the parties) that preceded the institution of official justice.[2] Today, we can think of it as a mechanism that

[1] Luc Boltanski and Laurent Thevenot, *De la justification* (Gallimard, 1991).

[2] For more on the beginnings of arbitration and its role as a precursor to modern institutionalized justice, see Thomas Schultz and Tom Grant, *Arbitration: A Very Short Introduction* (Oxford University Press) (forthcoming).

intervenes not only within legal relationships, when the parties choose to resort to a private method of dispute resolution, but also on the fringes of the law, in many important areas which escape the regulation of states and instituted law: areas that are perhaps without (official) rule of law, but certainly not without a need for justice. In these areas, the literary 'arbitrator' intervenes under different names, in different capacities, with different roles, and in different circumstances: he can be a counsellor, an expert, an intermediary, a mediator, or perhaps an *amicus curiae*. And, in the world of fiction, it is not rare to see the 'arbitrator' take on the persona of a wise man, the divine, or even the court jester.

Section 37.4 of this chapter will be devoted to how literature apprehends these areas at the 'fringes of justice' where the 'arbitrator' sometimes operates. Less constrained by the formal dictates of the law, fiction can help us think about: the emergence of the need for third party intervention before its official institutionalization; the continuation of this need when courts have failed; and its constant renewal at the edge of institutionalized justice. We will thus encounter the figures, among others, of the private conscience, of the superman, of the architect of justice and founder of institutions, and finally the figure of the author himself re-enacting the trial on the stage of public opinion.

Works of literary fiction also provide many valuable stories about the value and reach of decisions rendered by arbitrators. 'A bad agreement is better than a good law suit': this proverb, of which Balzac reminds us in *Lost Illusions* [*Les illusions perdues*],[3] is only a very approximate account of the merits of the arbitrator's work compared to those of the judicial decision. A laconic overview of this question, as it is apprehended in literary works (this chapter, quite obviously, does not pretend to be an exhaustive treatment of the question and only makes some soundings), rather suggests the hypothesis that the arbitral decision is sometimes more just and edifying than the ordinary decision of justice (Section 37.2) and sometimes, on the contrary, it is only a crude caricature of official justice, when it is not a corrupt or menacing version of it (Section 37.3). In short, an arbitrator's decision may be better or worse than the decision of a judge. Better because it is closer to equity, less constrained by texts and formalities and more concerned with repairing and restoring the social link which is in jeopardy. Worse because there is less guarantee that an arbitrator will act impartially (we will also encounter a few examples in which the absurdity of the arbitral decision is meant to reflect the absurdity of the dispute itself, or even the grotesqueness of the litigants).

But to appreciate the merits of third-party intervention—be it a judge or an arbitrator—we first need to know what we can expect from justice. Ricoeur's celebrated analysis will answer this question (Section 37.1), by distinguishing between justice's short-term end (distributing shares) and its long-term end (restoration of the social bond).

[3] Honoré de Balzac, *Lost Illusions* (Dodo Press, 2006).

37.1 THE TWO FUNCTIONS OF JUSTICE

Based on a sort of phenomenology of judgment, Paul Ricoeur[4] distinguishes a short-term end to the act of judging 'in virtue of which judging signifies deciding, for the purpose of ending uncertainty', to which he contrasts a long-term end, 'namely, the contribution of a judgment to public peace'.[5] In the first sense, the decision puts an end to a virtually endless debate, by a decision which will become final after the time limits for appeal, and which public authorities will then enforce. In so doing, the judge will have fulfilled the first function: he will have allocated the share belonging to each party, in application of the old adage by which the Romans defined the role of law: *suum cuique tribuere*. The judge will have allocated parts, or rectified the possession of parts improperly taken by one of the parties. He thus operates as an essential institution of society, which John Rawls describes as a vast system of the distribution of parts. In this first sense, judging is, then, the act that separates, that decides between (in German, *Urteil* 'judgment' is explicitly formed from *Teil* 'share').

However, the act of judging is not exhausted by this dividing function. If it is true that, more fundamentally, the judgment occurs against a background of social conflict and latent violence, then it is also necessary that the legal process and the judgment that closes it pursue a broader function, as an institutional alternative to violence, starting with the violence of the justice that one performs for oneself. In these circumstances, Ricoeur continues, 'it becomes clear that the horizon of the act of judging is finally social peace rather than security'.[6] Not merely the provisional pacification that would result from an arrangement imposed by the law of the strongest, but a harmony that is restored because mutual recognition has taken place: regardless of the fate of their case, each of the protagonists must be able to recognize that the judicial decision is not an act of violence, but a recognition of their respective points of view. At this stage, we have moved to a higher conception of society: no longer just a system of allocation of shares synonymous with distributive justice, but society as a system of cooperation: through distribution, but beyond it, through procedure, but beyond it, something similar to a 'common good' can be pursued, a something that creates the social bond. A good that, paradoxically, is made of eminently shareable values. At this stage, the communitarian dimension has taken over from the procedural dimension, which is itself incapable of warding off violence.

In sum, the judicial process is concerned with both distribution and sharing—the allocation of shares (which separates) and sharing the same society (which unites).[7]

[4] Paul Ricoeur, 'L'acte de juger', in Paul Ricoeur (ed.), *Le juste* (Esprit, 1995), 185–92.

[5] Ibid. 185. [6] Ibid. 190. [7] Ibid. 191.

From allocation emerges a new property, more important than the share due to each: it is the re-establishment of concord, the renewal of cooperation.[8]

If properly conducted, arbitration can satisfy this dual function of justice: the fact that the parties chose their own arbitrator means that they are more likely to accept the final decision—a decision which could also be better than the judgement of an official judge at addressing the human and social aspects of the dispute. Conversely, it is not difficult to see that when the arbitrator is careless, biased, or corrupt, because of the lack of institutional framework, his decision will not even fulfil the short-term end of judging: the simple compensation of damages, the elementary allocation of shares. In such a case, as Schultz explains, the decision, being strictly ad hoc, would not even satisfy the basic requirements of justice, neither in their substantive nor in their procedural dimension; it is also not able to produce any pedagogical or other societal effects beyond the individual case.[9]

37.2 A SUPERIOR JUSTICE

History and dreams are as old as law itself: a right superior to the law; a law not only legal, but just, and even capable of compassion. The spirit beyond the letter; in the language of Victor Hugo: law beyond the law; in the language of the social sciences of today: law in context, in touch with the human. Sometimes the arbitrator rises to these peaks, for he is more liberated from formal constraints.

My first illustration of arbitration as a superior form of justice is the famous judgement of Solomon reported in the Book of Kings (I Kgs 2:16–28). The story is well known and surprisingly simple. Two prostitutes who share the same house give birth only a few days apart. One night, one of the children dies. Distraught, the mother of the dead child switches the babies around and takes the other child as her own. In the morning the other mother realizes what she has done and demands her child back. The other mother refuses, and the case is brought before King Solomon for arbitration.

The problem for Solomon, of course, was: how was he to decide who was the child's true mother? How could he make a lawful decision in a situation where the law has so little to hold onto? Yet Solomon is divinely inspired, and plays the law against the law, pushing legalism to the extreme of absurdity to make something else come out of it.

[8] For a very precise application of this idea, see Desmond Tutu, *No Future Without Forgiveness* (Rider, 1999), 51: 'I contend that there is another kind of justice, restorative justice, which was characteristic of traditional African jurisprudence. Here the central concern is not retribution or punishment but, in the spirit of ubuntu, the healing of breaches, the redressing of imbalances, the restoration of broken relationships. This kind of justice seeks to rehabilitate both the victim and the perpetrator, who should be given the opportunity to be reintegrated into the community he or she has injured by his or her offence.'

[9] Thomas Schultz, 'The Three Pursuits of Dispute Settlement', 1 Czech & Central European Yearbook of Arbitration 227 (2011).

Since each mother claims the child is hers, since each of them demands that what is hers be given to her (*suum cuique tribuere*), well then, the child should be shared in two, cut in two (the original Hebrew text states *guizro*, which literally means to slice),[10] with each mother to get one half!

Giving his ruling, Solomon caused each of the mothers to react from the heart. The first, whose child had passed away, is so stricken with grief that she agrees with Solomon's judgment—'It will be neither mine nor yours, slice'—and reveals in this that the logic of death guides her action, a sinister law of talion implacably demanding arithmetic equality. But the true mother exclaims—'Please god no, give her the child'. In doing so, she reveals that a logic of life guides her action, that she cannot accept this murderous equality: since one of the children is already dead, let equality be established through life rather than death—even if this means giving up her legitimate claim as the child's mother. She simply cannot accept that a born child, a living being, be equated with a thing or a carcass, which indeed had to be split in two in cases of undecidable competing claims according to the Hebrew law of the time. In a surge of motherly love, the woman was able to elevate herself to a higher logic: to abandon her right so that life prevails. Yet this is exactly what Solomon expected from the real mother: reversing his decision, he cried, 'Give her the child, do not kill him. She is the mother!'

By staging this dramatic scene, and by giving his judgment in two parts, Solomon was able to restore the contested right. But he too went through a period of non-law, for Hebrew law did not permit him to order the execution of an innocent child. Just as the true mother was ready to renounce her right and have her filiation erroneously recognized in law, Solomon, 'for a higher cause', was ready to have the child executed. But from this non-law arose a law superior to the poor egalitarian rigour of the talion. Thus, a change in level took place (from appearance to reality, from jealousy to self-sacrifice, from death to life), which at the same time unlocked an undecidable situation and connected the legal rule with more positive sources (confidence in the future rather than the brooding of the talion).

The same logic can be derived from the story of the 'twelfth camel' often discussed in legal theory. Here again, the arbitrator was able to devise an ingenious solution to an apparently inextricable situation, through a moment of apparent irrationality, by going beyond the strict logic of redistribution. The Bedouin legend is as follows.[11]

A father (certain sources suggest that he was a very wealthy Bedouin sheikh), in contemplation of his impending death, made necessary arrangements for the distribution of his fortune. His herd of camels was to be divided amongst his three sons (Ahmed, Ali, and Benjamin, although the names vary from one version to another), in the following manner: the first son, by virtue of his privilege as the eldest, would receive half; the second

[10] I am here relying on the valuable interpretation of the tale by Raphaël Draï (ed.), *Le mythe du talion. Une introduction au droit hébraïque* (Alinea, 1991), 166.

[11] For a detailed commentary on the legend of the Twelfth Camel, see François Ost, 'The Twelfth Camel, or the Economics of Justice', 2 Journal of International Dispute Settlement 333 (2011).

son would inherit one quarter; whilst the youngest would have no choice but to be satisfied with one sixth. Yet, upon their father's death the sons were flustered: the distribution of the camels became an impossible task, as there were precisely eleven camels. After bickering over this unfeasible endeavour, the sons resolved to submit the dispute to the khadi, who would arbitrate their dispute. The khadi, after having heard the parties, reflected while tracing symbols in the sand, and finally declared, 'Take one of my camels, complete the distribution, and, Allah willing, return my camel to me.' Unwilling to contradict the wise man, the stupefied sons set off with the arbitrator's camel in tow. It did not take them long to appreciate the khadi's ingeniousness: with twelve camels, the distribution became extremely easy—each received his fair share and the twelfth camel was returned soon thereafter.

I cannot explain here, for want of space, the mathematical ingenuity of the arbitrator's decision. Let me merely say that in giving his decision, he was able to give each brother what he was owed, respect the wishes of the father, and save the lives of all the camels (a vital imperative in the desert). The virtual camel of justice, which symbolizes all legal fictions, is used here as the means necessary to overcome the horizontal and closed logic of strict mathematical counting, and to rise to the level of a social positive sum game, in which everyone wins. The khadi made a bet on life and concord, thus fully realizing, like Solomon, the dual function of justice: to distribute shares fairly and to (re)integrate the parties in the great social game, with no durable exclusion or frustration caused.

Of course, one could say that these are merely legends. Then again, we may read Nobel prize-winner Isaac Bashevis Singer's *In My Father's Court*, in which he recounts his personal recollections of the rabbinical justice rendered by his father in Warsaw between the two world wars.[12] There was nothing spectacular about the daily operations of this justice of the peace, except for its atmosphere of conciliation and wisdom, which in most cases worked wonders to nurture the social ties within this community on the margins of great empires. The mathematical tit-for-tat logic was not always fully safeguarded, but the essential point of justice was: the permanence of community attachment, in spite of quarrels and conflicts. The point of his intervention was pacification (the long-term ends of justice, as discussed above); 'Perhaps one can still endeavour to make peace between you too?... Peace is the foundation upon which the world stands.'[13] History abounds on examples of this kind—both real and imagined.[14]

[12] Isaac Singer, *In My Father's Court* (Farrar, Straus and Giroux, 1991). [13] Ibid. 21.

[14] E.g. in the *Odyssey*, Homer portrayed Arete, King Alcinous's wife, celebrated for her wisdom, who settled disputes arising between her subjects: 'the whole people who look upon her as a goddess, and greet her whenever she goes about the city, for she is a thoroughly good woman both in head and heart, and when any women are friends of hers, she will help their husbands also to settle their disputes.' In the same vein, Plutarch reports that the Celts called their women to their war councils, and it was they who resolved conflicts with their neighbors.

37.3 A GROTESQUE OR CORRUPT JUSTICE

Critical representations of arbitration—as well as of justice, to be sure—are not lacking in the literature. The point of criticism, however, is far from being directed exclusively at the arbitrator. In many cases his intervention, grotesque and absurd no doubt, seems perfectly 'adjusted' to the dispute, and operates like a mirror revealing the madness that unites the litigants in their improbable dispute. I provide four examples of this kind, borrowed respectively from Furetière, Rabelais, Cervantes, and Molière.

There are other cases, however, in which it is the bias of the arbitrator that is targeted. La Fontaine offered a series of noted examples. Shakespeare did too, notably in the guise of Portia, the particularly unedifying *amicus* (*amica*) *curiae* of the Merchant of Venice. As for Giraudoux's famous Busiris, he encamped the unforgettable portrait of the archetypical expert-consultant-arbitrator with a particularly flexible backbone, happy to defend successively a cause and its opposite, depending only on the prevailing political winds.

The first example, taken from the bourgeois novel of Furetière (1666),[15] illustrates the propensity, quite widespread among litigants, to 'take heaven to witness', of seeking a complacent ear, without really wanting a decision that would end the dispute. The essential objective is to prolong an infinite dispute and to continue to plead. Arbitration then represents a kind of *mise en abyme* of a dispute without beginning or end. In the novel, Collantine files one lawsuit after another against Judge Belastre: 'You owe me nothing?' yells Collantine to the ears of Belastre. 'Are you bold enough to maintain this? I will soon show you wrong.' Enter Charroselles, the writer in want of an audience. 'I rely on Monsieur,' said Collantine, pointing to Charroselles: 'he will be our judge.' At that point they began recounting in great detail all the trials and disputes they had had, as if Charroselles had been their natural judge. They spoke, pleaded, harangued, contested, both at the same time, without ever listening to one another. It is in fact a common habit of litigants to take as judge the first person who comes into sight, to plead their cause immediately before him, and to purport to do as he will say, without all this necessarily leading to a settlement or decision. This dispute, recounted over several pages in the novel, will indeed not lead to any decision—for it did not ask for one.

Sometimes, however, a decision does intervene, putting an end to a dispute that had become inextricable. Rabelais relates a feat of this kind: 'how Pantagruel judged so equitably of a controversy, which was wonderfully obscure and difficult, that, by reason of his just decree therein, he was reputed to have a most admirable judgment.'[16] The controversy, which opposed two great noblemen, Lords of Kissbreech and of Suckfist, 'was so high and difficult in law that the court of parliament could make nothing of it'. Gathered at the command of the king, the four most learned parliaments of France, eminent university professors of France and neighboring countries, and 'a rabble of other old Rabbinists' could not even put the matter in order within 46 weeks of hard labour.

[15] Antoine Furetière, *Le roman bourgeois* (Garnier-Flammarion, 2001), 285.

[16] François Rabelais, *Gargantua and His Son Rabelais* (Moray Press, 1894), bk 2, ch. 2.

In desperation, it is decided that the superhuman wisdom of Master Pantagruel is needed, and he is sent the files and acts of the trial 'which for bulk and weight were almost enough to lade four great couillard or stoned asses'. Not without humor, Pantagruel begins by inquiring whether, after so many years of litigation, the litigants are still alive. In his role as arbitrator in this dispute, he immediately summons the parties, convinced that their oral conclusions would make it possible to avoid reading through the file, which had been 'obscured ... and made ... more intricate by the frivolous, sottish, unreasonable, and foolish reasons and opinions of Accursius, Baldus, Bartolus ... and those other old mastiffs ... ignorant of all that which was needful for the understanding of the laws'.

The litigants soon throw themselves into pleadings as interminable as they are incomprehensible, as if the object of the dispute had long since been lost along the way. At the end of the exercise, Pantagruel gave judgment 'in conscience to do right to both parties, without varying or accepting of persons'. His decision is as absurd as it is convoluted, giving each of the litigants a different reason. And so, a quite extraordinary thing occurred: 'the two parties departed both contented with the decree.' The moral is: absurd in, absurd out. Or more positively: what Pantagruel had understood was that, far more than the material satisfaction of their grievances, what the parties were seeking was to be heard and acknowledged as plaintiffs. Besides, Judge Bridlegoose, another of Rabelais's creations, was probably not so far from this truth, he who played dice at the end of trials.

In the league of absurd disputes opportunely settled by a decision of equal absurdity, we may recall this passage of Don Quixote. During a peregrination of the austere knight and his companion, peasants hail them, asking them to be the judge of their quarrel. A quite heavyset man, weighing 275 pounds, had just challenged to a race a young man, weighing only 125 pounds. The rule was that they would walk 100 with equal weights. A bettor wanted the thinner man to take on 150 pounds of iron, in order to put them in equal conditions—which the young man refused energetically. Sancho steps in and renders his decision: it is the rule, he opines, that the choice of arms belongs to the one who is defied. 'My decision, therefore, is that the fat challenger prune, peel, thin, trim and correct himself, and take eleven stone of his flesh off his body, here or there, as he pleases, and as suits him best; and being in this way reduced to nine stone weight, he will make himself equal and even with nine stone of his opponent, and they will be able to run on equal terms.' This opinion was highly appreciated: 'the gentleman has spoken like a saint, and given judgment like a canon!' It was finally agreed that the best thing was not to run at all, and they drank half the wager at the tavern.[17]

[17] Miguel de Cervantes, *Don Quixote* (Project Gutenberg, 2004), pt 2, ch. 66. To be compared with a tale of Indian origin, 'Two Angry Tigers'. Two tigers quarreled about a piece of cheese discovered in the jungle. Not knowing how to settle the case without getting into a fight, they rely on the arbitration of a fox, forgetting how cunning the animal is. Looking important and superior, the fox decides to divide the cheese into two strictly equal halves. But the process is difficult, and the fox has to constantly adjust the parts, in passing eating the remains. So much so that in the end it is all gone.

In the same comic vein, we may recall the role played by Master Jacques in Molière's *The Miser* (Act IV, Scene 4).[18] The father (Harpagon) and the son (Cléante) set their sights on the same young girl, the beautiful Marianne, and want to marry her. On the verge of coming to blows, they agree to defer to the arbitration of Master Jacques, who is to judge which of them is right and wrong. Having duly placed the protagonists at the two extremities of the scene, so that they do not hear one another, Master Jacques shuttles between them, acquiescing successively to their opposite wishes. So much so that at last the malicious arbitrator concludes that he does not have to decide: 'Gentlemen, you have nothing to do but to talk quietly over the matter together; you are agreed now, and yet you were on the point of quarrelling through want of understanding each other.' Of course, the agreement rests precisely on a misunderstanding—but with this subliminal lesson gleaned in passing: many quarrels subside as soon as a third party persuades you that you are wrong in believing that your opponent despises you and intends to harm you. And then also this truth, as old as trials themselves: how easily, how hastily, and with how much complaisance we tend to trust those who reassure us that we are within our rights, inclined as we are to seek confirmation of our wishful thinking.

In some cases, the fable is less playful, and the literary satire is directed wholly against the arbitrator, who is afflicted with various vices, starting with corruption. Thus, in the work of the fabulist La Fontaine, it is common that arbitrators lead the litigants to an agreement by taking advantage of them, if not by straightforwardly devouring them. Consider these two pilgrims, who happened upon an oyster, and were in dispute over who shall eat it.

> Justice Nincompoop arrived on the scene, and to him they appealed to judge their claims. The justice very gravely took the oyster, opened it, and put it into his mouth, whilst the two claimants looked on. Having deliberately swallowed the oyster, the justice, in the portentous tones of a Lord Chief Justice, said, 'The court here awards each of you a shell, without costs. Let each go home peaceably.'[19]

We may also mention, in the same spirit but with a graver tone, the land dispute between the weasel and the young rabbit. While 'the sharp-nosed lady' pretends to squat in the rabbit's underground lodge in the name of the right of first occupant, John Rabbit invokes inheritance laws and customs. Possession against title, how to decide between the litigants? The weasel suggests to refer the dispute to Raminagrobis: 'This person was a hermit cat,/ A cat that play'd the hypocrite,/ A saintly mouser, sleek and fat,/ An arbiter of keenest wit/ John Rabbit in the judge concurr'd.' '[H]is majesty, the furr'd', who calls himself Clapperclaw (a passing reference to Rabelais), invites them to step closer, alleging deafness—but his real purpose is to bring them to an agreement 'By virtue of his

[18] Molière, *The Miser* (Project Gutenberg, 2003).

[19] Jean de La Fontaine, *The Original Fables of La Fontaine* (Project Gutenberg Ebook, 2005), bk 9, no. 9, 27 ('The Oyster and the Pleaders').

tusked jaw'.[20] He ate them! That justice is blind: fair enough. But when justice is also deaf, there is cause for concern!

Justice and arbitration are recurring themes of La Fontaine's Fables. If he often denounces the partiality of arbitrators, he equally deplores the blindness of the litigants, stuck in their quarrel, and incapable of compromise. Thus, on the decisions rendered by a given arbitrator, La Fontaine writes in *The Arbiter, the Hospitaller, and the Hermit*: 'No one was content. Arbitration pleased neither one side nor the other. According to them the judge could never succeed in holding the balance level.'

Sometimes, however, as a counterpoint to these denunciatory fables, the fabulist praises the less formalistic justice attributed to arbitration, based on common sense—this brings us back to the first point of our analysis (Section 37.2). And so, in *The Hornets and the Honeybees*, the wisdom of a wasp is instrumental in deciding between the litigants, who were arguing over the ownership of some honeycomb left vacant. Being unable to identify a title, the wasp decides to stick to utility: it has never been seen that hornets have made honey. 'Would to God we could settle all our lawsuits this way,' the fabulist concludes, 'And that, so doing, we might follow the Turkish mode! / Simple common sense would replace our present legal code.'

Let us, however, mistrust good sentiments, common sense, and the appeal to clemency or equity: invoked by the rich and the powerful, these arguments, intended to circumvent the law, the ultimate protection of the weakest, pursue most often less edifying goals. Shakespeare makes that point masterfully in *The Merchant of Venice*, in relation to the arbitration of Portia, the eulogist of mercy against the unfortunate Shylock.[21] One may recall the strange penal clause subscribed to by Antonio, the shipowner of Venice: he consented to his creditor taking a pound of his own flesh in case he, the debtor, would not be able to repay on the due date the 3,000 ducats advanced by the Jewish lender. Various shipwrecks having made the repayment impossible, Shylock claims that the terms of the contract are met. The Doge is quite embarrassed: his sympathy is naturally on Antonio's side, but it cannot be denied that the usurer has the law on his side, as well as the language of the contract.

The decision is made to appeal to the enlightenment of Balthazar, a jurist whose wisdom was prodigious. But it was the ambitious and cunning Portia, who had stirred up the whole affair, who presented herself to the tribunal, disguised as a man. A highly suspicious character she was, since she was none other than the young wife of Bassanio, the young man for whom Antonio had madly indebted himself to make his marriage possible. And so, Portia-Balthazar launches herself into a superb tirade calling Shylock to mercy. In vain: the usurer clings to the letter of his note ('I crave the law'). But our *amicus* (*amica*) *curiae* has not exhausted her resources. She releases her secret weapon—an ultra-literal interpretation of the clause: one pound of flesh I agree, but not one gram

[20] For an excellent commentary, see Loïs Cattaruzza, 'Le chat, la belette et le petit lapin. Quand le squat animalier interrogeait les fondements du droit de propriété', in Faculté de Droit et des Sciences Sociales de Poitiers, *Jean de La Fontaine Juriste?* (LGDJ, 2009), 185.

[21] For a commentary, see François Ost, *Shakespeare, la comédie de la loi* (Michalon, 2012), 65.

more, nor a drop of blood. Everything then turns against the unfortunate Shylock, soon prosecuted for attempted homicide. The clan of the Venetians can breathe, and each of them celebrate the ingenuity of the intervention of Portia—about whom, besides, posterity will remember only the superb appeal to clemency, overdetermined by the beauties of the Christian mercy opposed to narrow literalism, associated, according to a classical anti-Semitic tradition, with the Talmudic tradition. But who does not see that Portia's arbitration rests on a scandalous imposture?

In other cases, the author of fiction does not condemn the arbitrator's bias, as in the case of Portia, who had a direct interest in the outcome of the trial. It rather is his docility which is called into question—his ability to manoeuvre, which sometimes borders on spinelessness. In such cases, the expert-arbitrator becomes a mercenary, willing to endorse all causes, to support all arguments, provided they please those in power. In *The Trojan War Will Not Take Place*,[22] Jean Giraudoux provides a famous example: Busiris, a jurist, is summoned as an expert in public international law in the dramatic context of an imminent declaration of war between the Greeks and the Trojans[23] (the play, written a few years before the outbreak of the Second World War by a French diplomat in Berlin, resonates today as a desperate plea for peace). An expedition of Greek ships had appeared before the shores of Troy, exhibiting clear intentions of aggression. Busiris is consulted in urgency by the Senate: how to interpret their acts? As a declaration of war, concludes Busiris, showing the Greeks to be in breach of international law on at least three counts.

But here Hector intervenes, resolved to try the impossible to stop the inevitable: 'You are going to provide me, here and now, with an argument which will allow our Senate to say that there has been no fault whatever on the part of our visitors.' Busiris resists: 'It isn't in keeping with the facts, Hector'—which earned him Hector's famous repartee: 'My dear Busiris, all of us here know there's no better way of exercising the imagination than the study of law. No poet ever interpreted nature as freely as a lawyer interprets truth.' Busiris protests: 'The Senate asked me for an opinion: I gave it'—another famous repartee by Hector: 'And I ask you for an interpretation. An even more juridical task.' This time Busiris gets the message: 'Actually there are certain mitigating arguments,' he concedes, and proceeds to reverse each of his arguments, so that the Greek expedition ends up appearing as the most engaging of 'offers to talk'.

Clearly, the arbitrator's feathers had to be ruffled and principles had to be solicited, but it was for a good cause: 'What is the use of justice if it doesn't hammer out a shield for innocent people?' Hector asks. Alas, in Troy as in Berlin, the shield of law appears very weak in the face of mortiferous passions that come crashing down.

[22] Jean Giraudoux, *The Trojan War Will Not Take Place* (Methuen, 1983).

[23] For a commentary, see Jean Pascal Chazal, 'Antigone, Busiris, Portia. Trois images spéculaires de la doctrine', *Revue interdisciplinaire d'études juridiques* (2002), 1–43.

37.4 On the Fringes of Justice

Reflecting on literary approaches to arbitration leads inevitably to a consideration of the edges of official justice—before it, after it, next to it. What happens before it is even instituted, with its procedures, its magistrates, and its codes; what happens after it has intervened; what happens at its margins. What happens, also, when official justice is not or no longer possible. An immense domain, in sum, which by contrast makes instituted justice appear to be a modest little island, official and well-lit, in the middle of an immense ocean of conflicting passions and gestating norms. Around the core of instituted justice, there exists an inscrutable zone of penumbra in which the fuzzy but founding figure of the arbitrator stands out. I shall discuss three of his manifestations (among others certainly): the tribunal of our own conscience; the eminent character, justice's great architect; and finally, the author himself, who seeks to replay scenes of justice in the court of his readers.

To begin with, two examples of the intervention of our conscience's tribunal, which operate in parallel to the justice of men, and very often in more severe fashion. My first example is borrowed from a novel by the Hungarian writer Sándor Márai: *Divorce in Buda* [*Válás Budán*].[24] It tells the story of a judge who, although not corrupt and above suspicion, comes to the conclusion that he is not in a position to handle a case because of his involvement, which is probably largely unconscious, in the stakes of the trial. Leading an exemplary life and promised to the highest judicial functions, this judge, who currently handles divorces, is about to hear the case of a former classmate. To his surprise, the classmate in question calls on him at his home on a Sunday night, on the eve of the trial, to make a confession: he killed his wife a few hours earlier. We are given to understand that misunderstanding and disagreement had crept into the marriage, the wife becoming increasingly distant, with no apparent reason. Gradually the truth emerges from the shadows: the wife had never ceased to love the judge himself, whom she had met ('with honourable intentions', as one says in such cases) several times, a few years earlier.

Taken by surprise in the middle of the night, the judge understands at this moment that 'there is also a supreme court in which everyone, including himself, has to tell the truth'. He thus 'feels compelled, against the civil code and against rules of propriety, to hold a hearing on the spot; life sometimes violates the rules of procedure; this trial must be completed here and now.'[25] Five times the friend asks the judge: 'Have you, too, dreamed of Anna?' When the judge finally 'admits that yes, indeed, he dreamed of this woman', it is clear that has already abandoned, a few hours ago, his position as a third neutral (the impartial 'he', beyond the 'me' and the 'you', meant to characterize the law's

[24] Sándor Márai and Válás Budán (Helikon, 2013), translated into French by Georges Kassai and Zéno Bianu as Sándor Márai, *Divorce à Buda* (Biblio, 2007). At present, there is no English translation available.

[25] Ibid. 153.

spokesman).[26] And while the next day's hearing does not take place (the wife being dead), it is perhaps above all because doubt has settled in: who are we to judge?

My second example is borrowed from the novel *A Dangerous Game* [*Die Panne*] by Friedrich Dürrenmatt. It illustrates both the intervention of an unofficial tribunal, composed of retired professionals of justice, and the justice of remorse, which is more pitiless than instituted juries. During one of his travels to the countryside, a sales representative, unable to find a hotel room, is hosted by a retired judge. He is invited to join a dinner that the former judge organizes each month with a prosecutor and an advocate, who are both retired like him. During the meal, a game is improvised, to which the three friends seem well accustomed: a fictitious trial, in which the host is invited to participate. What would he have to fear: is he not a very ordinary salesman? In the course of a skilfully conducted cross-examination, it appears however that the man may have been the indirect but probable cause of a heart attack which took away his boss. Advocate and prosecutor then passionately spar over the case, and a decision is made by the judge. The game ends in high spirits, the three agents of justice cheerful at having once again been able to indulge in their favourite activity. But when they knock on the door of the salesman's room to show him the written record of his conviction, they find him hanged. Apparently, the man's conscience had proved more inflexible than the easy company of law's professionals.

On the fringes of justice, one also finds, in a quasi-demiurgic position, the figure of the great architect of justice. Sometimes he is the founder of a tribunal, ensuring the transition from vengeance to justice (Athena). Sometimes he intercedes in the midst of an incurable conflict, and combines various procedures in order to achieve an honorable solution (Luther). Sometimes, when human justice lapses, he refers the litigants to the authority of forgiveness (the father-judge).

Athena, in Aeschylus's *Oresteia*, represents the most complete incarnation of the figure of the architect of justice. Orestes, it will be recalled, killed his mother, Clytemnestra (herself the murderer of her husband, Agamemnon). Pursued by the Erinyes, implacable avengers with a long memory, Orestes presents himself, pleading, before Apollo. For the Athenian spectator of the fifth century, there is no doubt about the outcome: Orestes will not escape the private cycle of mirror revenge. But Aeschylus crafts another scenario, which prepares the judicial reforms that Athens is experiencing at the same time as democracy: the transition from private vengeance to public justice, through the establishment of an official tribunal. But the decisive intervention of a superhuman character, Athena, is required, to whom Orestes is sent by Apollo.

Refusing to hand over the fugitive to the Erinyes, as would be customary, Athena convinces the parties to appoint her as arbitrator in their dispute. After having investigated the case, she decides—a decisive passage—that Orestes will be judged, after an exchange of arguments and evidence. To do this, she establishes the human court of the

[26] This theme is finally mentioned on ibid. 154 ('all of a sudden there is no role any longer'), 156 ('I need, tonight, a judge who comes down from his lofty grounds, and takes part himself in the trial'), and 160 ('it is always someone else who makes the ruling').

Areopagus, takes the oath of the judges, lays the foundations of the procedure, and recalls the basic principles to be respected. In the end, she adds her own vote to those of the judges, causing the matricide's acquittal. More importantly, she persuades the Erinyes to accept this new regime of justice, thus sparing Athens their murderous wrath. A unique example throughout literature, Aeschylus's Athena is the author of justice par excellence—no less was required to achieve the transition which is rightly considered to be the passing of the threshold from pre-law to law: the transition from mirror vengeance to third-party justice.

In a less fundamental but nevertheless significant vein, one may mention Luther's intervention in *Michael Kohlhaas*, a novella by Heinrich von Kleist.[27] The stakes are no longer to found a court, but to intervene at the height of a popular uprising and to convince the protagonists—the righter of wrongs Michael Kohlhaas on the one hand, and the German authorities on the other—to find their way back to a judicial settlement of their dispute. After the figure of the founder of tribunals, we have here the figure of the mediator-intercessor, who pursues the same objective of preventing a maelstrom of vengeance. The story, which had begun on a very quotidian note, was now spiralling into insurrection: a simple horse-dealer, Kohlhaas, had suffered the harassment of a local squire, Wenzel von Tronka. The squire had illegally demanded a non-existent document, and was keeping Kohlhaas's horses in the meantime. The horse-trader moves heaven and earth, filing sundry lawsuits, in order to recover his horses and obtain recognition of his right. Yet, all this is in vain. The iron law of class justice closes in around him. Finally convinced that he no longer has a place in a state that knows no justice, Kohlhaas becomes an outlaw and launches into an escalation of exactions which soon puts Saxony to fire and blood.

It is in this context that Luther, to whom the rebel had requested audience, intervenes. Luther listens attentively to the avenger, recognizing his initial rights but condemning his crimes, and imagines a way to end the crisis: he promises to obtain a safe-conduct, along with impunity, for Kohlhaas, which would enable him to lay his case before the elector of Saxony. In return, Kohlhaas has to immediately lay down arms. The rebel accepts the plan, never having ceased to aspire to the recognition of the rightness of his cause. Invoking his moral authority, Luther intercedes with the elector and succeeds in convincing him too, even though this procedure means the discredit of the lesser, corrupt nobles, such as von Tronka, who gravitate around the prince. In the end, a court in Dresden reinstates Kohlhaas in his full civil rights, while the imperial court in Berlin (not bound by the impunity granted by the elector) condemns him to death for the impressive series of crimes he committed during the revolt.

Kohlhaas is nevertheless content and soothed when he walks to his death, having been restored as a subject of the rule of law. Only the intercession of a high moral figure like Luther made the restauration of the law possible, at the cost of an ingenious combination of procedures and a subtle phasing of their intervention.

[27] Heinrich von Kleist, 'Michael Kohlhaas', in Kuno Francke, *The German Classics: Masterpieces of German Literature translated into English* (German Publication Society, 1913), 308.

Another example of the intervention of a third-party architect of justice appears in Ernst Wiechert's novella *The Judge* [*Der Richter*].[28] This time the transition is from (misguided) official justice to a model of forgiveness—the final means of 'settling scores'. Here the architect of justice is both an investigating judge and a father. It is he who points out his criminal son to the parents of the victim in order to obtain another kind of justice: forgiveness.

In Nazi Germany, on the eve of the war, an investigating judge discovers that the culprit of the political assassination he is investigating is none other than his own son. He soon confronts him, and, assuming his role as a father as well as a judge, persuades the son (called—perhaps coincidentally—'Christian') to turn himself in. But in deviant Germany, where evil has taken the place of good, there is no one to prosecute him—he is instead congratulated for having done justice in taking out an opponent. It remains for the father to take Christian to the 'supreme court'—the victim's parents. Christian is eventually forgiven by them. As for the judge, he sends his letter of resignation to his superiors the next day, with this last line: 'Where there is no justice, there is place for neither law nor judge.'

I note in conclusion that the figure of the architect of justice is sometimes occupied by the author himself when he takes on a real trial, undertakes to reinvestigate it, and then submits it to the court of opinion of his readers. I am thinking of Voltaire's pamphlets (regarding the Calas affair), transforming an incident which had made the headlines into a national cause which echoed well beyond the borders of France. I am also thinking of Stendhal, replaying the trial of Antoine Berthet, who had been sentenced to death, in *The Red and the Black*; Dickens, Zola (*J'accuse…!*), Tolstoy (*Resurrection*), Gide (*Souvenirs de la cour d'assises*), Mauriac, Camus, and so many others.

Victor Hugo, whose work often addresses this theme, theorizes this position of the writer as supreme arbitrator: 'There is in my role something sacerdotal: I replace the judiciary and the clergy. I judge what judges did not; I excommunicate what priests did not.'[29] The writer, taking up the trial anew, places himself in the position of a supreme arbitrator; sometimes, like Zola, prosecuting those who thought they escaped prosecution; sometimes, like Hugo, acquitting or granting a pardon to those who should never have been prosecuted; sometimes, like Voltaire, obtaining a real rehabilitation of innocent citizens (the Sirven affair) or the removal of an unworthy judge (the Chevalier de la Barre affair); sometimes, like Tolstoy and Gide, inviting men not to judge—a prerogative reserved for God alone (Gide founded, for the French publisher Gallimard, a book series entitled 'Do Not Judge').[30]

[28] Ernst Wiechert, *Der Richter* (Desch, 1969).

[29] Victor Hugo, 'Draft Foreword for *Histoire d'un crime*, 1877–78', cited in Gérard Gengembre, 'Cette grande chose divine qu'on appelle la justice! Le droit, la loi et la justice dans *Les Misérables*', in Denis Salas (ed.), *La plume et le prétoire* (La Documentation Française, 2014), 149.

[30] Gide published two books in his own collection: *The Redureau Affair* (*L'affaire Redureau*) and *The Prisoner of Poitiers* (*La séquestrée de Poitiers*).

CHAPTER 38

ARBITRATION IN ITS PSYCHOLOGICAL CONTEXT

A contextual behavioural account of arbitral decision-making

TONY COLE, PIETRO ORTOLANI, AND SEAN WRIGHT

> As a matter of principle, humanity is precarious: each person can only believe what he recognizes to be true internally and, at the same time, nobody thinks or makes up his mind without already being caught up in certain relationships with others, which leads him to opt for a particular set of opinions.
>
> Maurice Merleau-Ponty, *The World of Perception*

38.1 Arbitration Never Happens in Isolation

While traditionally arbitration scholarship focused on practical issues, arguing for refinements of arbitration laws or attempting to identify a core of procedural 'best practices', a growing strain of arbitration scholarship has begun to focus on developing a deeper and more ambitious understanding of arbitration.[1] In this attempt to attain

[1] See e.g. Thomas Schultz, *Transnational Legality: Stateless Law and International Arbitration* (Oxford University Press, 2014); Jan Paulsson, *The Idea of Arbitration* (Oxford University Press, 2013); Emmanuel

theoretical insights into a traditionally practice-dominated field, scholars increasingly borrow epistemic tools from fields as diverse as sociology, economics, philosophy and psychology.[2]

Psychology in particular has a clear appeal as a mechanism for moving beyond discussions of black-letter law and legal practice. Arbitration, after all, is fundamentally an activity undertaken by human actors, and unlike in litigation those actors have been largely freed from pre-ordained rules, allowing personal beliefs and preferences to play the core role in the creation of the dispute resolution process. Numerous questions spontaneously ensue, for which psychology appears to offer particular expertise: Do arbitrators act like judges? Are they legal decision-makers or commercial problem-solvers? What are the parties' expectations? Are arbitrators really impartial and independent? Do arbitrators' cultural and legal backgrounds influence the reasoning patterns within a tribunal? What cognitive biases exist, and how should they be countered?[3]

The relations between arbitration and psychology, hence, are a particularly promising field of analysis: the scrutiny of the internal workings of arbitration, beyond mere formalities, is almost instinctively linked to the need to understand what happens in the heads of those who *make* arbitration. Yet interdisciplinary work always carries with it a substantial risk. Just as general guides to dispute resolution often produce little more than trite and oversimplified portrayals of arbitration, so arbitration specialists who attempt to invoke psychological research when analysing arbitration risk misunderstanding a field in which they are not themselves genuinely expert.[4]

Gaillard, *Aspects philosophiques du droit de l'arbitrage international* (Nijhoff, 2008); Bruno Oppetit, *Théorie de l'arbitrage* (PUF, 1998).

[2] See e.g. Tony Cole (ed.), *The Roles of Psychology in International Arbitration* (Kluwer Law International, 2017); Cédric Dupont and Thomas Schultz, 'Towards a New Heuristic Model: Investment Arbitration as a Political System', 7 JIDS 3 (2016); Lauge Poulsen, *Bounded Rationality and Economic Diplomacy: The Politics of Investment Treaties in Developing Countries* (Cambridge University Press, 2015); Emmanuel Gaillard, 'Sociology of International Arbitration', 31(1) Arb. Int'l 1 (2015).

[3] To date, psychological studies on arbitration have primarily been inspired by cognitive psychology (focusing on the question of whether arbitrators make good decisions) and social psychology (focusing on the question of whether arbitration is acceptable as a mechanism of dispute resolution). The principal findings of cognitive psychology indicate that arbitrators are susceptible to the same cognitive biases as judges and laypeople. See Edna Sussman, 'Biases and Heuristics in Arbitrator Decision-Making: Reflections on How to Counteract or Play to Them', in Cole (n. 2), 45. For a comparison of cognitive performance of arbitrators and judges, see Rebecca Helm, Andrew Wistrich, and Jeffrey Rachlinski, 'Are Arbitrators Human?', 13 Journal of Legal Empirical Studies 666 (2016). The social psychology research suggests that arbitration will be considered acceptable when it meets the criteria of 'procedural justice', which refer to procedures that ensure a perception of fairness in the way the dispute is resolved. See e.g. Rebecca Hollander-Blumoff and Tom Tyler, 'Procedural Justice and the Rule of Law: Fostering Legitimacy in Alternative Dispute Resolution', 2011 J. Disp. Resol. 1 (2011) (reviewing the concept of procedural justice); Alex Shaw and Kristina Olson, 'Fairness as Partiality Aversion: The Development of Procedural Justice', 119 J. Experimental Child Psychol. 40 (2014) (reporting an experimental demonstration of procedural justice effects among children).

[4] It should perhaps be emphasized at this point that, as our intent is to bridge two disciplines in an accessible way, we will use language designed to be functional for this purpose. Nonetheless, in principle all the statements in this chapter could be sensibly written in the technical language of the underlying discipline.

One central risk underlying many efforts to look at arbitration from a psychological perspective lies in the temptation to separate psychological phenomena from their context. In a nutshell, one may think that in order to understand how those involved in arbitration think, it is desirable and necessary to isolate their psychology from its surroundings. Following this line of reasoning, one could assume that by undertaking ever more sophisticated empirical studies of how successful individual arbitrators solve cases, we can finally understand how arbitration works. This methodological starting point, though, is fraught with pitfalls, as it fails to take into account the inextricable connections that always exist between the minds of human beings and the context in which those human beings operate. Any behaviour is, to a large extent, influenced and determined by the circumstances within which it takes place,[5] and reasoning itself is never free of contextual influences.

This is a particularly important point to recognize for arbitration, as arbitration never happens in isolation: from the conclusion of an arbitration agreement to the commencement of the proceedings, from the taking of evidence to the rendering of the award, all aspects of arbitration are based on complex sets of interactions between different actors.[6] Yet while arbitration's relative lack of strict rules might seem to free those actors to behave 'purely', reflecting only their personal judgments and beliefs, arbitration as a field of practice is replete with contextual influences. The absence of formal rules in arbitration has not resulted in the creation of a value-free vacuum, in which every arbitral actor is free to be him/herself, but rather in the intensification of 'softer' forms of social control,[7] in which an arbitrator's self-conception of her role, the opinions of others in the field, and the ability to demonstrate adherence to community-endorsed 'norms' of arbitration, have taken on a central importance.[8]

Without considering these influences on arbitral actors, no application of psychology to arbitration can provide real insights into arbitration as it actually functions in practice. While isolated studies of how arbitrators solve problems can provide important information, an arbitrator solving a problem during an empirical study is freed from precisely the social and professional influences that may be impacting his/her reasoning while solving actual cases.

This chapter is intended to lay out a programme for a more 'contextual' approach to the application of psychology to arbitration than has been adopted within arbitration scholarship thus far. It will not attempt to deliver an exhaustive overview of the ways that

[5] Steven Hayes and Aaron Brownstein, 'Mentalism, Behavior–Behavior Relations, and a Behavior-Analytic View of the Purposes of Science', 9(2) Behavior Analyst 175 (1986), 177 ('In behavior analysis, any event is to be understood and even defined through a contextual analysis'). See also Jack Michael, 'Establishing Operations', 16(2) Behavior Analyst 191 (1993). Radical behaviourists like Steven Hayes, continuing the work of B. F. Skinner, go further and assert that behaviour should not be viewed as mainly determined by contextual influences, but as wholly determined by them.

[6] See similarly Stavros Brekoulakis, 'Systemic Bias and Arbitral Decision-Making', in Cole (n. 2), 335.

[7] Hollander-Blumoff and Tyler (n. 3).

[8] In this respect, the tendency to comply with norms even in the absence of rigid mechanisms of enforcement must be taken into account. See e.g. Brian Sheppard, 'Norm Supercompliance and the Status of Soft Law', 62(4) Buff L. Rev. 787 (2014).

psychology can be or has been applied to arbitration, but will instead attempt to demonstrate the fruitfulness of studying behaviour 'in context'. In so doing it will rely in particular on work in the area of Contextual Behavioral Science (CBS),[9] which focuses on the 'act in context', treating behaviour as inseparable from the circumstances (historical and situational) that surround it.[10] Such a context-sensitive approach allows new light to be shed on the psychology of arbitration, while also unifying the existing literature within a new epistemic framework that offers the advantage of not only predicting but also potentially influencing the behaviour of interest in arbitration.

While psychology can be applied to arbitration in many ways, this chapter will focus on arbitrator reasoning. Section 38.2 presents contextualism as an alternative to mechanistic accounts of psychological phenomena. Section 38.3 addresses the professional context of arbitration, scrutinizing how individual conceptions of the role of the arbitrator can influence reasoning. Section 38.4 deals with the social context of arbitration, analysing the relations between the hierarchical character of the arbitration community and the existence of cognitive biases. Section 38.5 concludes.

38.2 Contextualism as an Alternative to Mechanistic Accounts of Psychological Phenomena

While psychology as a field has never ignored the impacts that other people and the environment in which we live can have on our lives, the successes of physiological research into mental operations have led cognitive psychology, the study of mental processes, to be dominated by a particular, 'mechanistic' view of mental phenomena.[11] While psychologists themselves are rarely explicit about their underlying theoretical assumptions, focusing instead on the analysis or diagnosis of particular mental phenomena, psychology's goal of scientifically analysing human behaviour is profoundly influenced by the intellectual commitments of a given psychologist's underlying philosophy of science.

Consider, for example, a man diagnosed with clinical depression who wakes up at 6 a.m., feels fatigued, thinks 'There is no point to going out today', and returns to sleep

[9] See e.g. Michael Levin, Michael Twohig, and Brooke Smith, 'Contextual Behavioral Science: An Overview', in Robert Zettle et al. (eds), *The Wiley Handbook of Contextual Behavioral Science* (Wiley, 2016).

[10] It is important to clarify that we are not relying in this chapter on the commonplace definition of 'behaviour' as only that which is publicly observable. Private events, like thoughts and emotions, also constitute behaviour. CBS examines 'the contexts that evoke private experiences and how context affects relations between internal events and other behaviours'. See ibid.

[11] Gary Hatfield, 'Psychology, Philosophy, and Cognitive Science: Reflections on the History and Philosophy of Experimental Psychology', 17 Mind & Language 207 (2002).

for several hours. Accounting for this behaviour (staying in bed) requires a choice of one of several alternative philosophies of science, each of which offers a different explanatory route. Within contemporary psychology, the most commonly chosen philosophical stance is what is often labelled *mechanism*.[12] Under this theory, explanation of human behaviour is developed through reliance on a metaphor of a human being as a form of machine: the psychologist's aim is not to understand an individual's behaviour as it unfolds in context, attempting to examine the reasoning and influences that lead him to make the decisions that he makes; rather, it is to identify 'the machine parts, their interrelations, and the forces involved in these relations'.[13]

In the example just used of the depressed man, a 'mechanistic' explanation for his behaviour might, for instance, focus upon the interactions between biological units within his body, such as an attentional bias in depression toward negative stimuli, which is mediated by different activity in brain structures including the anterior cingulate cortex, amygdala, thalamus, and pre-frontal cortex.[14] Alternatively, his behaviour could be explained as arising from a tendency toward excess sleep (hypersomnolence) caused by hypothesized 'chemical imbalances'[15] or observed gene variants that predispose him towards depression.[16] Through such explanations, psychologists relying upon a mechanistic philosophy of science are able to reduce psychological phenomena to steps in a causal chain, thereby allowing them to ground their efforts in research and diagnostic methodologies common across the physical sciences.

Importantly, while biological explanations are a prominent part of mechanism in psychology, adopting a mechanistic worldview does not require adopting a biological conception of psychology, and a mechanistic explanation can also be constructed by connecting behaviours, rather than physical processes. For example, a mechanistic explanation for the depressed man's decision to stay in bed might specify a causal relation between thoughts and experiences, rather than biological events (e.g. 'He did action X because he had previously done actions A and B, and he believes C'). The essential

[12] Sometimes called elemental realism. See e.g. Levin et al. (n. 9), 19.

[13] Anthony Biglan and Steven Hayes, 'Functional Contextualism and Contextual Behavioral Science', in Zettle et al. (n. 9), 37, 44.

[14] Seth Disner et al., 'Neural Mechanisms of the Cognitive Model of Depression', 12(8) Nature Reviews Neuroscience 467 (2011).

[15] Note that the term 'imbalance' functions to identify the brain as a machine whose forces must be balanced for proper function, typically with pharmacotherapy. The concept of depression as chemical imbalance has been widely embraced in media and in psychoeducation to clients, but has had weak research support. See e.g. Jeffrey Lacasse and Johnathan Leo, 'Serotonin and Depression: A Disconnect between the Advertisements and the Scientific Literature, 2(12) PLoS 392 (2005). Indeed, even the supposed benefits of appealing to a biological basis for depression to reduce stigma and shame have not consistently been found in the literature. See e.g. Sven Speerforck et al., 'Different Biogenetic Causal Explanations and Attitudes Towards Persons with Major Depression, Schizophrenia and Alcohol Dependence: Is the Concept of a Chemical Imbalance Beneficial?' Journal of Affective Disorders 168 (2014), 224–8.

[16] Lukas Pezawas et al., '5-HTTLPR Polymorphism Impacts Human Cingulate–Amygdala Interactions: a Genetic Susceptibility Mechanism for Depression', 8(6) Nature Neuroscience 828 (2005).

component of mechanism is the use of the metaphor of the 'machine', not any particular conception of the parts that constitute the machine.

How well does the mechanistic approach to psychology work? Unsurprisingly, given the dominance it has come to achieve in cognitive psychology, the answer is that it can work very well. Of course, judging the success of a philosophical theory requires clarifying the basis on which it can be claimed to be successful, and different theories may adopt different standards for success. Adopting, however, what Stephen Pepper has argued to be the 'truth criterion' for mechanistic theories, of 'predictive verification',[17] or the extent to which a theory can predict real-world examples of a phenomenon, mechanism has proved to be a very successful approach to the study of psychology. With respect to depression, for instance, Aaron Beck's theory that depression is caused by maladaptive patterns of thinking about the self[18] has been supported by brain scans that indicate that more depressed individuals show more activity in limbic areas of the brain when deliberately thinking negative things about themselves.[19]

Due to its tremendous success in the physical and biological sciences, the mechanistic approach has been widely adopted in psychology. Yet it is not the only approach to analysis present in contemporary psychology, and in recent decades dissatisfaction with mechanism has led to a rise in attempts to provide alternative 'contextualist' explanations for psychological phenomena. While, as described above, the root metaphor in mechanism is the 'machine', in contextualism the root metaphor is the 'act-in-context', emphasizing that human actions cannot be properly understood without consideration of the broader context in which they are undertaken.[20]

To return to the previous example of the man suffering from depression, the mechanistic explanation of this decision to stay in bed invoked a causal chain, perhaps identifying brain states and body states that connected in sequence to result in the action of staying in bed. A contextualist explanation, on the other hand, would focus on the idea that every action is 'performed by someone for some purpose in some context.'[21] Consequently, this theory argues, a proper understanding of an action cannot be gained by merely referring to certain processes that are claimed to have resulted in the action being performed. Rather, any adequate explanation must focus on the context in which the action was taken, 'context' being interpreted broadly to include not only the physical environment but relevant history, social influences, etc.[22] In the words of one commentator,

[17] Stephen Pepper, *World Hypotheses: A Study in Evidence* (University of California Press, 1942).

[18] Aaron Beck, 'The Core Problem in Depression: The Cognitive Triad', in J. H. Masserman (ed.), *Depression: Theories and Therapies* (Grune and Stratton, 1970), 47.

[19] Shinpei Yoshimura et al., 'Self-Referential Processing of Negative Stimuli within the Ventral Anterior Cingulate Gyrus and Right Amygdala', 69 Brain and Cognition 218 (2009).

[20] Pepper (n. 17).

[21] Hayne Reese, 'Contextualism and Dialectical Materialism', in Linda Hayes et al. (eds), *Varieties of Scientific Contextualism* (Context Press, 1993), 72.

[22] Hayes and Brownstein (n. 5), 185 ('No matter how dynamically one behavioral event may be intertwined with other behavioral events within the same individual, however, for a contextualist a behavior-behavior relation is a phenomenon to be explained by appealing to particular contextual arrangements (e.g. contingencies of reinforcement) that might permit prediction and control of the behavior-behavior

'the entire universe and all of time are considered part of the full context of any event.'[23] Contextualist analysis, of course, requires identifying those aspects of an act's context that have particular importance in explaining the act.

A further important difference between mechanism and contextualism relates to what has been referred to above as the 'truth condition' each philosophy adopts. As noted previously, for mechanism, what makes an explanation true is that it predicts occurrences of the phenomenon. Contextualism, on the other hand, invokes a truth condition of 'successful working', according to which '[a]nalyses are true only in terms of the accomplishment of particular goals.'[24] That is, a contextualist analysis is true if it results in effective action and the achievement of desired goals. Successful working requires, of course, accurate prediction of events, and so in this respect there is an overlap between mechanism and contextualism. However, for the contextualist mere prediction of the occurrence of an event does not suffice, as only with further contextual information is it possible to alter behaviour to achieve desired goals.

The comparison of these two truth conditions brings out an important fact about the 'choice' between mechanism and contextualism: on a factual level, the two theories are not inconsistent. A contextualist need not deny that the universe operates in accordance with laws, and consequently that all psychological events can be described as the result of causal chains, just as a mechanist would claim. Mechanism and contextualism are not metaphysical theories, positing conflicting accounts of the nature of reality or of human beings.[25] They are, rather, theories of explanation, and, in the words of philosopher Hilary Putnam, 'Explanation is an interest-relative notion.'[26] A mechanistic account of the depressed man's decision to stay in bed is true if it allows us to predict accurately when he will stay in bed. On the other hand, a contextualist explanation is true if it allows the man to alter his behavior in a desired manner. Both explanations can simultaneously be true. The important question is which is the more effective for use in psychological analysis.[27]

relation itself. A behavior-behavior relation cannot be a complete explanation of behavior, except to a mechanist, whose world view does not insist on control as a necessary goal of science').

[23] Eric Fox, 'Contextualistic Perspectives', in J. Michael Spector et al. (eds), *Handbook of Research on Educational Communications and Technology*, 3rd edn (Taylor & Francis, 2008), 55, 59.

[24] Steven Hayes, Linda Hayes, and Hayne Reese, 'Finding the Philosophical Core: A Review of Stephen C. Pepper's World Hypotheses: A Study in Evidence', 50 Journal of the Experimental Analysis of Behavior 97 (1988), 101.

[25] Functional contextualism finds this a-ontological perspective useful. R. T. Codd III, 'The Functional Contextual A-Ontological Stance and Bas C. van Fraassen's Constructive Empiricism', 4 Journal of Contextual Behavioral Science 215 (2015).

[26] Hilary Putnam, *Meaning and the Moral Sciences* (Routledge, 1978), 41. See also Sam Leigland, 'The Language of Ontology Is the Subject Matter of Behavioral Science', 4(4) Journal of Contextual Behavioral Science 231 (2015).

[27] In terms of the man suffering from depression, then, he may treat his thought that 'there is no point to going out today' as true and cite it as the literal cause of his choice to stay in bed. In this case, his thought influences his physical behaviour because it is embedded in the context of 'literality' in which the words are treated like causes of his behaviour. A therapist can effect behavioural change through a modification of the context: using a technique called 'defusion', the client can be taught to deliteralize his

It is our position that contextualism provides the more effective approach for the application of psychology to arbitration. While mechanistic approaches have resulted in great progress in cognitive and neuroscientific work, simply knowing, for example, that activity in the amygdala differs in individuals with depression does not suggest how to influence this activity to treat depression in the context of the person's environment.[28] Similarly, simply identifying the influences that lead arbitral actors to make certain decisions does not help improve decision-making within arbitration. Arbitration, however, is an applied discipline, and although understanding the mechanics behind the reasoning of arbitrators can be interesting from a purely psychological standpoint, from the perspective of the arbitration community's definition of 'successful working', such considerations are clearly less important than the goal of improving arbitrator reasoning where improvements can be made.[29]

This said, it is important to acknowledge that even within contextualism itself there are further distinctions made by psychologists, and so it is important to clarify the particular version of contextualism on which this chapter will rely. In particular, a distinction has often been drawn within psychological literature between what is termed 'descriptive contextualism' and 'functional contextualism'. It is the latter that will be used in this chapter, but the distinction needs to be clarified.

As defined by Steven C. Hayes, a leading contextualist psychologist, *descriptive contextualism* 'approaches the study of a whole organism interacting in and with a historical and situational context much as a historian'.[30] That is, a descriptive contextualist analysis

thoughts and see them simply as a string of syllables that might influence his behaviour, but certainly do not control it. See John Blackledge, 'Disrupting Verbal Processes: Cognitive Defusion in Acceptance and Commitment Therapy and Other Mindfulness-Based Psychotherapies', 57(4) Psychological Record 555 (2007); Katie Snyder, Joseph Lambert, and Michael Twohig, 'Defusion: a Behavior-Analytic Strategy for Addressing Private Events', 4(4) Behavior Analysis in Practice 4 (2011). For example, a client may be asked to read the sentence 'I cannot walk around this room' while physically walking about in order to notice that he can entertain thoughts without giving them power over his behavior. Notice that the content of thought may be entirely unchanged, but by changing the context of literality, the thought has decreased influence over the client's behaviour. The *social* context may also strongly influence behaviour. Humans are taught from an early age to verbalize acceptable reasons for their behaviour. Unacceptable reasons are socially punished. For example, the man's wife may not accept 'hating my job' as a reason to remain in bed, but would accept 'struggling with clinical depression'. Thus, the probability of the man staying in bed can be influenced through manipulations of the social context. See Matthieu Villatte, Steven Hayes, and Jennifer Villatte, *Mastering the Clinical Conversation: Language as Intervention* (Guilford, 2015); Robert Zettle and Steven Hayes, 'Dysfunctional Control by Client Verbal Behavior: The Context of Reason-Giving', 4 Analysis of Verbal Behavior 30 (1986).

[28] The mechanistic approach that is the basis of pharmacological therapies could be useful here if the aim is to intervene at the level of biological substrates. Most therapeutic approaches use the more contextually sensitive tool of language.

[29] References to 'improvements' of arbitral reasoning, in this context, should not be read as entailing that the quality of reasoning can be measured through objective, unbiased methods. To the contrary, in this context quality can only be measured by comparing the reasoning of the arbitral tribunal in a specific case with an agreed and socially shared abstract conception of what proper reasoning requires.

[30] Steven Hayes, 'Analytic Goals and the Varieties of Scientific Contextualism', in *The Act in Context: The Canonical Papers of Steven C. Hayes* (Routledge, 2016), 110.

will 'seek an active appreciation of the quality of an event by situating it in its various contextual strands'.[31] The emphasis of descriptive contextualism, then, is on creating a complex and detailed understanding of psychological phenomena. More specifically, descriptive contextualism focuses on the goal of developing a narrative that will be acceptable to the individual. Yet just as an historian may believe that a particular interpretation of an historical event will help a contemporary political dispute, so a descriptive contextualist psychologist may desire that the richly detailed narrative being sought will facilitate the individual's achievement of certain goals. Nonetheless, since descriptive contextualism does not specifically aim at the prediction and influence of behaviour, enhancing the achievement of the individual's goals is not essential to a descriptive contextual analysis, and even when possible is decidedly subsidiary to the construction of a narrative satisfactory to the individual.

This emphasis on the construction of a narrative, however, provides little benefit for the study of arbitration, and indeed would focus inappropriately on developing an account of arbitrator reasoning, for example, that would be endorsed as acceptable by arbitrators. For that reason, this chapter relies instead upon what has become known as *functional contextualism*.[32] While descriptive contextualism focuses on providing a

[31] Ibid.

[32] In recent years, functional contextualism has inspired the work of a growing community of researchers in CBS, whose collective aim is to create a science of behaviour that is adequate to address human suffering. See generally Steven Hayes, Dermot Barnes-Holmes, and Kelly Wilson, 'Contextual Behavioral Science: Creating a Science More Adequate to the Challenge of the Human Condition', 1(1) Journal of Contextual Behavioral Science 1 (2012). CBS includes basic and applied research projects that have demonstrated success influencing a wide range of human behaviour, including:

Improving individual psychological functioning (J. G. A-Tjak et al., 'A Meta-Analysis of the Efficacy of Acceptance and Commitment Therapy for Clinically Relevant Mental and Physical Health Problems', 84(1) Psychotherapy and Psychosomatics 30 (2014); Robyn Walser et al., 'Training in and Implementation of Acceptance and Commitment Therapy for Depression in the Veterans Health Administration: Therapist and Patient Outcomes', 51 Behaviour Research and Therapy 555 (2013));

Enhancing symbolic language use in individuals with autism (Ruth Rehfeldt and Yvonne Barnes-Holmes (eds), *Derived Relational Responding: Applications for Learners with Autism and other Developmental Disabilities. A Progressive Guide to Change* (New Harbinger, 2009); Carol Murphy and Dermot Barnes-Holmes, 'Establishing Complex Derived Manding with Children With and Without a Diagnosis of Autism', 60(3) Psychological Record 489 (2010));

Reducing burnout in workplaces (Frank Bond, Paul Flaxman, and Fredrik Livheim, *The Mindful and Effective Employee: An Acceptance and Commitment Therapy Training Manual for Improving Well-Being and Performance* (New Harbinger, 2013); Hillevi Brinkborg et al., 'Acceptance and Commitment Therapy for the Treatment of Stress Among Social Workers: A Randomized Controlled Trial', 49 Behaviour Research and Therapy 389 (2011); Paul Flaxman and Frank Bond, 'A Randomised Worksite Comparison of Acceptance and Commitment Therapy and Stress Inoculation Training', 48 Behaviour Research and Therapy 816 (2010));

Reducing prejudice and stigma (Jason Lillis and Steven Hayes, 'Applying Acceptance, Mindfulness, and Values to the Reduction of Prejudice: A Pilot Study', 31 Behavior Modification 389 (2007); Akihiko Masuda et al., 'The Impact of Acceptance and Commitment Therapy versus Education on Stigma Toward People with Psychological Disorders', 45(11) Behaviour Research and Therapy 2764 (2007); Steven et al., 'The Impact of Acceptance and Commitment Training and Multicultural Training on the Stigmatizing Attitudes and Professional Burnout of Substance Abuse Counsellors', 35 Behavior Therapy 821 (2004));

Increasing organizational effectiveness (Elinor Ostrom, *Governing the Commons: The Evolution of Institutions for Collective Action* (Cambridge University Press, 1990); David Wilson, Elinor Ostrom, and suitably contextualized description of events, functional contextualism emphasizes instead 'the prediction-and-influence of events'.[33] In turn, while descriptive contextualism can be understood through a parallel with the work of historians, functional contextualism parallels the work of engineers. As described by Hayes, 'Engineers have little use for knowledge in the abstract', as 'to know that a bridge will fail is not enough—we must know how to make it not fail.'[34] Functional contextualism, then, attempts to construct an analysis 'that points to features of the historical strands and current context of a psychological action that can effectively guide the behavior'[35] of an individual.[36]

Functional contextualism endorses the descriptive contextualist's attempt to find a richer explanation of psychological phenomena than is sought by mechanists, but emphasizes as well the need to use that description to affect future behaviour. For that reason it is ideally suited for the study of arbitrator psychology, the ultimate goal of which must be to improve arbitrator reasoning and practice, not merely to describe it, or to provide an explanation acceptable to arbitrators with their current practices.[37] Against this theoretical background, the remainder of this chapter will provide an initial foundation for developing a properly contextualized approach to the application of psychology to arbitration.

38.3 The context of arbitration I: The professional context of arbitrator psychology

38.3.1 What is an arbitrator? The feedback loop of arbitrator role identity

References to the importance of 'context' in understanding the reasoning of arbitrators might suggest that focus should be placed entirely on external influences on arbitrators, such as social connections or professional interests, and indeed, Section 38.4 will focus

Michael Cox, 'Generalizing the Core Design Principles for the Efficacy of Groups', 90 Journal of Economic Behavior & Organization 21 (2013); Anothony Biglan, *The Nurture Effect: How the Science of Human Behavior Can Improve Our Lives and Our World* (New Harbinger, 2015));

Evolving values-based capitalism (Anothony Biglan and Chirstine Cody, 'Integrating the Human Sciences to Evolve Effective Policies', 90 Journal of Economic Behavior & Organization 152 (2013)); and

Increasing efforts to address climate change (Mark Alavosius et al., 'A Functional Contextualist Analysis of the Behavior and Organizational Practices Relevant to Climate Change', in Zettle (n. 9, 513).

[33] Hayes (n. 30), 112. [34] Ibid. [35] Ibid.

[36] While reference is made throughout this discussion to 'individuals', it should be understood that contextual analysis can also be applied to groups.

[37] 'The explicit goal of functional contextualism is the prediction and influence of the behavior of individuals or the actions of groups or organizations': Biglan and Hayes (n. 9), 41.

precisely on such external considerations. However, as the previous section has emphasized, functional contextualism includes as context not only facts and events entirely external to an individual, but also an individual's own beliefs and mental states.[38]

This 'internal' perspective is particularly important to take into account when considering the contextual influences on arbitrators, as the job of arbitrator is one of a small proportion of jobs in which the self-conception of the individual undertaking the work stands to impact considerably on how the work is done.[39] Arbitration conferences, for example, are replete with panel discussions focusing on questions not only of arbitration practice but, more importantly, of arbitrator professional responsibility and on the structure of arbitration as a profession. Similarly, discussions of the true nature of an arbitrator, and hence of how arbitrators should pursue their roles, are not restricted solely to academics, but are engaged in even by practicing arbitrators. In short, the question 'What is an arbitrator?' is an active and important question for arbitrators in a way that 'What is a car salesman?' is not for car salesmen, or that 'What is a surgeon?' is not for surgeons.[40]

The aliveness of this question has an important consequence for understanding the context in which arbitrators perform their work. As already noted, while the word 'context' most naturally suggests influences on an individual from the environment in which he is acting, context as understood in the framework of functional contextualism also includes an individual's mental states, which will potentially impact on an individual's actions just as will external events. The aliveness of the question 'What is an arbitrator?', then, when combined with the prestige attached to the role of arbitrator within the arbitration community, creates a situation in which individual arbitrators are encouraged to develop a conception of what the role of an arbitrator is, while they are also encouraged to believe that adhering to this conception (i.e. being a 'good arbitrator') is of fundamental importance.[41]

Arbitrators, in other words, are incentivized to believe that it is important that they perform their role correctly, and they are affirmed in this view by their encounters within the arbitration community. Needless to say, to perform the role of arbitrator well it is first of all necessary to understand what an arbitrator should do. However, because the role of arbitrator is fundamentally malleable and open to different interpretations,

[38] The expression 'mental states', used in this chapter, is equivalent to the notion of 'private events' discussed in psychological scholarship.

[39] Variations on the term 'self-concept' are used here in their most general linguistic sense. In terms of Relational Frame Theory (RFT, the most prominent functional contextual theory), 'self-concept' refers to a frame of coordination between a speaker's verbal evaluation and the speaker's deictic frame of 'I', which is often described by the middle-level term, 'the conceptualized self'. For a clear introduction to RFT, see Villatte et al. (n. 27).

[40] From an RFT perspective, at the individual and perhaps even group level, we should expect a variety of psychological functions, some contributing to and some detracting from successful working, to be cued by this group debate about the 'correct' verbal description of an arbitrator.

[41] In RFT terms, this is the predicted influence of a social-verbal community (here, individuals in a particular arbitration community), which functions to socially reinforce or punish behaviours endorsed or condemned by the group.

the role itself does not provide guidance on how it should be performed. Consequently, to fill this void and provide self-assurance that they are performing the role well, arbitrators are incentivized to engage with the question 'What is an arbitrator?', adopting a particular conception of what an arbitrator is, and attempting to adhere to it.[42] Since different choices are possible within the same community, and given that each arbitrator attaches importance to the correctness of his/her choice, the arbitration community is encouraged to continue the discussion of the question 'What is an arbitrator?' This social phenomenon ultimately results in a positive feedback loop, as the importance of the question is then confirmed for arbitrators by the fact that the question is commonly debated amongst those who practise arbitration.

Understanding the nature of this feedback loop is important for identifying how psychology should be used to inform our understanding of arbitration. In particular, the feedback loop incorporates both 'internal' psychological components (i.e. the arbitrator's views on the role of an arbitrator), and 'external' social components (i.e. the arbitration community's views on the role of an arbitrator). Without both internal and external components, the feedback loop would not function, and the importance of the question would diminish.

Because of the central role that social considerations play in the feedback loop, any examination of how arbitrator self-conceptions impact on arbitrator performance must consider how that question is addressed in the arbitration community in which arbitrators are operating. For the purposes of this present chapter, then, the question becomes how the role of arbitrator is conceived within the international arbitration community.[43]

As always in discussions of arbitration, a useful place to start is a comparison with the role of judges in litigation. Arbitrators, after all, are commonly characterized both as performing a 'judicial' role in a private setting and as providing a form of dispute resolution fundamentally different from that available in court litigation. As a result, the initial steps toward developing a picture of how any arbitration community conceives of the role of an arbitrator are always fundamentally defined by negation, i.e. by delineating how an arbitrator differs from a judge.[44]

Owen Fiss has famously described state court litigation as having the function of giving 'meaning to public values, not merely [of resolving] disputes'.[45] State courts, it is argued, are an important element of the constitutional structure of the state, ensuring

[42] RFT findings that establishing and maintaining narrative 'coherence' is reinforcing might account for this effect. See e.g. Michael Bordieri et al., 'Basic Properties of Coherence: Testing a Core Assumption of Relational Frame Theory', 66 Psychological Record 83 (2016).

[43] For a methodological precedent concerning the operational approach to the development of definitions in the field of psychology, see B. F. Skinner, 'The Operational Analysis of Psychological Terms', 52(5) Psychological Review 270 (1945). For an explanation of how any term of interest can be operationalized, see Leigland (n. 26).

[44] This conceptual link between arbitrators and judges plays a role in the feedback loop described above. While understanding the role of arbitrator requires distinguishing an arbitrator from a judge, it also expressly connects arbitrators with one of the most prestigious positions in any legal system, thereby affirming the role's importance, and again feeding into the feedback loop of arbitrator role identity.

[45] Owen Fiss, 'Foreword: The Forms of Justice', 93 Harvard LR 1 (1980), 44.

that the policies enshrined in the law are translated into practical reality. This conception of court litigation as an abstracted and independent form of justice is closely connected to the idea of the judges as a state official, and with the principle of the 'natural judge'. Especially since the seventeenth century, the figure of the judge is depersonalized:[46] the judge is not important because of her personal features, but because she is a state official exerting a sovereign power. Moreover, judges are not appointed on a case-by-case basis, but instead have a continuing role within an ongoing court structure. Parties, hence, have no direct role in selecting the judge who will hear their case, beyond having the power to challenge a judge's appointment where a conflict of interest is alleged to exist. The principle of the 'natural judge', in a nutshell, requires that parties are simply told the identity of their judge, that identity being decided by the rules of the court system itself.

The role of arbitrator, on the other hand, is indisputably more 'personal' than that of judge. While judges are appointed through state-controlled mechanisms designed to emphasize the interchangeability of judges within a specific court, arbitrators are selected by one or more parties involved in the dispute they will hear, and are appointed solely for that specific case. This difference has important consequences for arbitrator self-understanding: arbitration is fundamentally rooted in the idea that arbitrators are not interchangeable, and that the style and quality of decision-making in any given arbitration depends ultimately on the identity of the members of the arbitral tribunal. Arbitrators, that is, may not have an entitlement to the sense of importance that unavoidably comes from a judge's role as an official exerting a sovereign power, but they have a compensatory sense of importance derived from the fact that while an arbitrator's role may be less publicly important than that of a judge, an arbitrator always has his/her role because of his/her personal characteristics. As a result, every appointment as arbitrator serves as a direct endorsement of an arbitrator's personal value, in a way that is not true for a judge.

It is not, however, just any of an arbitrator's characteristics that are considered in making an arbitrator appointment, but only those that are important indicators of how the arbitrator will perform his/her role. In short, an arbitrator attracts appointments thanks to those characteristics that reveal how he/she will answer the question 'What is an arbitrator?'

Yet while this conclusion appears to focus on the specific choices individual arbitrators have made regarding how the role of arbitrator is properly performed, it is precisely at this point that social considerations become important. The practical reality of international commercial arbitration is that the vast majority of decisions regarding who should be appointed as an arbitrator are made either by arbitral institutions or by the parties' counsel.[47] In other words, in international commercial arbitration, appointment decisions are overwhelmingly made by individuals within the arbitral community.

[46] For an analysis of the relations between the development of adjudicatory powers and the genesis of modern national States, see Pietro Ortolani, 'The Three Challenges of Stateless Justice', 7(3) JIDS 596 (2016), 598.

[47] In this latter case, the parties merely affirm the recommendation made by their counsel. As a result, while arbitration is dominated by the principle of party autonomy, this autonomy is in practice 'mediated'.

This fact plays an essential role in any attempt to understand arbitrator psychology, as it means that although the most important consideration in an arbitrator's ability to build a successful career is his/her answer to the question 'What is an arbitrator?', arbitrators are not entirely free to answer this question in any way they wish. Rather, the ability of any individual to build a successful career as an arbitrator depends on his/her ability to answer the question 'What is an arbitrator?' in a way that is consonant with the views of at least a substantial proportion of the arbitral community.[48] An arbitrator may well adopt a radically unpopular conception of his/her role, but individuals within the community will see little reason to appoint as arbitrator an individual who does not share their conception of how an arbitrator should perform his/her job. Consequently, such an arbitrator either will either be forced to adapt to the social context in which he/she works and adopt a more acceptable self-conception, or must accept a peripheral role in the field, and an unsuccessful career.

Within contemporary arbitration two conceptions of the role of arbitrator have come to dominate the field, both currently existing, but each having predominance in a particular era. In this chapter we will refer to these conceptions as the 'oracle' and the 'service provider'.

The 'oracle' conception of the role of an arbitrator was most famously portrayed in the 1996 book *Dealing in Virtue*, the first comprehensive sociological study of international arbitration. Relying on the work of sociologist Pierre Bourdieu, authors Yves Dezalay and Bryant Garth argued that arbitrators compete with one another primarily by accumulating 'symbolic capital'.[49] In the words of Bourdieu, the accumulation of symbolic capital corresponds to 'the acquisition of a reputation for competence and an image of respectability and honorability'.[50] Within the specific context of arbitration, Dezalay and Garth argue that symbolic capital takes the particular forms of 'academic standing, scholarly publication, particular kinds of practical experience, training in alternative dispute resolution, connections to business, connections to political power, particular language skills, proficiency in technical aspects of arbitration practice'.[51]

In short, under the 'oracle' conception, the role of arbitrator is not directly connected with the ability to reach legally correct conclusions, or to perform in accordance with the wishes of the parties. It is, rather, centred on being the type of person who can be 'trusted with your dispute'. The arbitrator has a place of prestige within the dispute resolution process because of his/her personal characteristics, and delivers to the parties a dispute resolution process reflecting his/her expertise, including a final decision drawn from his/her wisdom and knowledge. While technically the parties control the arbitral

[48] This complex interplay between individual freedom and collective constraints could be seen as an example of network power. See David Grewal, *Network Power: The Social Dynamics of Globalization* (Yale University Press, 2008).

[49] Yves Dezalay and Bryant Garth, *Dealing in Virtue: International Commercial Arbitration and the Construction of a Transnational Legal Order* (University of Chicago Press, 1996).

[50] Pierre Bourdieu, *Distinction: A Social Critique of the Judgement of Taste* (Harvard University Press, 1987), 291.

[51] Dezalay and Garth (n. 49), 19.

process, in reality they have submitted their dispute to the judgment of an individual with the symbolic capital required to earn their trust.

However accurate this picture may have been at the time of *Dealing in Virtue*, there is clear evidence that in contemporary arbitration another conception of the role of arbitrator has come to prominence, namely that of the 'service provider'. This new conception has evolved largely due to the success of arbitration and its spread far beyond the limited realm of major international transactions that characterized arbitration at the time Dezalay and Garth wrote. Arbitration, after all, is now used to resolve not only exceptionally complex elite cases, but also a multitude of cross-border and domestic disputes covering a wide range of claim sizes and prior party experience with arbitration. On a purely practical level, this has resulted in a substantial increase in the number of individuals able to act as arbitrator, as the small group of leading international arbitrators who so dominated the field in the time in which Dezalay and Garth wrote are simply incapable of handling all the available work.

The consequence of this change, however, has been not just an increase in the number of arbitrators, but also the rise to prominence of a competitor conception of the role of arbitrator, from being 'oracles dealing in virtue' to being 'service providers dealing in efficiency'. This development can clearly be seen in Joshua Karton's recent empirical work, which demonstrates the existence of a shared assumption amongst many practicing arbitrators, that they are fundamentally problem-solvers rather than policy-makers.[52] What this means in terms of the arbitrator's role self-conception is that the arbitrators' perceived duty is to stay true to the parties' mandate, rather than merely to deliver a dispute resolution process as he/she believes such a process should operate. In brief, 'meeting the expectations of the parties' is the categorical imperative of the 'service provider' arbitrator.

There are, then, two conceptions of the role of arbitrator that can be seen to fundamentally structure contemporary international arbitration: the 'oracle' and the 'service provider'. Career success as an arbitrator depends upon adopting one or the other of these self-conceptions, or else arbitrator appointments are unlikely to arise.[53] Yet the feedback loop of arbitrator self-identity ensures that these conceptions are far more than merely superficial labels arbitrators adopt to secure appointments, and instead play a central role in how arbitrators approach their work, and hence in arbitrator decision-making. The next two sections of this chapter will elaborate more clearly on how the impact of these self-conceptions on arbitral decision-making occurs.

[52] Joshua Karton, *The Culture of International Arbitration and the Evolution of Contract Law* (Oxford University Press, 2013), 76.

[53] This observation is consistent with observations by functional contextual psychotherapists that individuals often work hard to preserve a 'conceptualized self'. This can be problematic for individual psychological adaptation, but in the context of the role of arbitrator, there appears to be a clear benefit to organizing one's actions and one's verbalizations about these actions in a way that supports one of the two community-endorsed arbitrator self-concepts.

38.3.2 Fuzzy-trace theories of reasoning versus other dual process theories of reasoning

In order to understand the possible impact of arbitrator self-conceptions on arbitrator decision-making, it is important to address currently available evidence on how human decision-making works. This section will introduce what is known as 'fuzzy-trace theory', a leading empirically supported explanation of how human decision-making functions, and will argue that it provides an effective mechanism for the application of psychology to international arbitration.

One of the fundamental shared experiences of almost all human beings is what has come to be known as the 'unity of consciousness'.[54] In the words of the philosopher René Descartes: 'When I consider the mind, that is to say, myself inasmuch as I am only a thinking thing, I cannot distinguish in myself any parts, but apprehend myself to be clearly one and entire.'[55] Indeed, this experience of having a unified mind is so fundamental to ordinary human experience that individuals who claim not to experience this unity are standardly classified as having a psychological disorder.[56]

Despite this experience, a similarly long pedigree exists for the idea that human reasoning is not actually a unitary mental process, with theorists as early as Plato arguing for the fundamentally divided nature of the human mind.[57] Although traditionally such views have centred on notions of a conflict between reason and emotion, or between conscious and subconscious processes, since the 1970s empirical psychology has provided increasing evidence that the long-recognized experience of conflicting influences in human reasoning does not merely reflect the influence of non-rational processes on the rational mind, but is instead a fundamental feature of human reasoning itself.[58] In other words, that our undeniable experience that our minds are unified is actually an illusion, masking the operation of a far more complex and divided human rationality.

[54] See generally Andrew Brook and Paul Raymont, 'Unity of Consciousness' (Proceedings of the 28th Annual Conference of the Cognitive Science Society 2006): <http://http-server.carleton.ca/~abrook/papers/2006-Unity-CSS2006.pdf>; Tim Bayne and David Chalmers, 'What is the Unity of Consciousness?' in Axel Cleeremans (ed.), *The Unity of Consciousness: Binding, Integration, Dissociation* (Oxford University Press, 2003), ch 1.1.

[55] René Descartes, 'Meditation VI', in *Meditations on First Philosophy* (1641), repr. in *The Philosophical Works of Descartes*, trans. John Cottingham, Robert Stoothoff, and Dugald Murdoch (Cambridge University Press, 1967), vol. 1, 196.

[56] Exact diagnoses will, of course, vary with individual cases, but Dissociative Identity Disorder is the broad label currently included in the *Diagnostic and Statistical Manual of Mental Disorders*, 5th edn (DSM-5).

[57] For an historical overview, see Keith Frankish and Jonathan Evans, 'The Duality of Mind: An Historical Perspective', in Jonathan Evans and Keith Frankish, *In Two Minds: Dual Processes and Beyond* (Oxford University Press, 2009), 1.

[58] Gideon Keren and Yaacov Schul, 'Two Is Not Always Better Than One: A Critical Evaluation of Two-System Theories', 4(6) Perspectives on Psychological Science 533 (2009).

This insight has led to the development within psychology of a group of theories of the human mind known as 'dual process theories',[59] the most famous example being that developed by Nobel laureate Daniel Kahneman and his colleague Amos Tversky. As most prominently expounded in Kahneman's book *Thinking, Fast and Slow*,[60] this theory builds on earlier work by Kahneman and Tversky on heuristics and biases[61] to present a model of human reasoning as involving two distinct processes, labelled by Kahneman as 'System 1' and 'System 2'. System 1 is 'intuitive, automatic, unconscious, and effortless; it answers questions quickly through associations and resemblances; it is nonstatistical, gullible, and heuristic',[62] while System 2 is 'conscious, slow, controlled, deliberate, effortful, statistical, suspicious, and lazy (costly to use)'.[63] Importantly, Kahneman argues that most reasoning is made using System 1, with System 2 only being invoked in a limited subset of contexts. In essence, under this model the human mind is designed to operate quickly and efficiently, sacrificing accuracy in many cases, with serious deliberation reserved only for a minority of cases in which correctness is both essential and feasible in the circumstances.

This picture of how the two 'systems' interact positions Kahneman's theory in the core of what are known as 'default-interventionist' dual process theories. These theories acknowledge the existence within human reasoning of distinct processes, but portray these two systems as fundamentally conflicting with one another: in Kahneman's theory, System 1 is the predominant mode of reasoning, but System 2 intervenes in certain circumstances to deliver a more thorough and deliberative judgment.[64]

While default-interventionist dual process theories are certainly prominent in psychological literature,[65] a second strain also exists, originating in work by Steven Sloman,[66] commonly referred to as 'parallel-competitive' dual process theories. Under this model, both 'systems' are continually operating in all reasoning, rather than System 2 merely intervening into the operations of the 'default' System 1.

Parallel-competitive theories have been argued by some psychologists to provide an explanation of human reasoning more consistent with empirical observation, which supports the conclusion that different faculties operate within the mind simultaneously.

[59] See generally Magda Osman, 'An Evaluation of Dual Process Theories of Reasoning', 11(6) Psychonomic Bulletin & Review 988 (2005).

[60] Daniel Kahneman, *Thinking, Fast and Slow* (Farrar, Straus and Giroux, 2013).

[61] Amos Tversky and Daniel Kahneman, 'Judgment under Uncertainty: Heuristics and Biases', 185 Science 1124 (1974). See generally Thomas Gilovich and Dale Griffin, 'Introduction: Heuristics and Biases—Then and Now', in Thomas Gilovich, Dale Griffin, and Daniel Kahneman (eds), *Heuristics and Biases: The Psychology of Intuitive Judgment* (Cambridge University Press, 2002), 1.

[62] Andrei Shleifer, 'Psychologists at the Gate: A Review of Daniel Kahneman's *Thinking, Fast and Slow*', 50(4) Journal of Economic Literature 1 (2012), 3.

[63] Ibid.

[64] Simon Handley and Dries Trippas, 'Dual Processes and the Interplay between Knowledge and Structure: A New Parallel Processing Model', 62 Psychology of Learning and Motivation 33 (2015).

[65] See also e.g. Jonathan Evans and Keith Stanovich, 'Dual Process Theories of Higher Cognition: Advancing the Debate', 8 Perspectives on Psychological Science 223 (2013).

[66] Steven Sloman, 'The Empirical Case for Two Systems of Reasoning', 119 Psychological Bulletin 3 (1996).

Experimental research, for example, indicates that memories are simultaneously coded in two forms: (1) in a 'verbatim' form that focuses on surface qualities, such as exact words or pictures; and (2) in a 'gist' form that focuses on meaning, at the expense of precise detail. That is, rather than a single memory being formed that initially has significant amounts of detail, but degrades over time into a vaguer and less precise recollection, all memories are simultaneously encoded in both forms, with both types of memory then playing a role in how facts and events are remembered at any given time, and hence also in how those facts and events are deployed in decision-making.[67]

By way of example, given the statement 'the patient's risk of heart attack is 20%', the memory of this information can be stored in 'verbatim' form as '20%'—a simple and precise statement that focuses on detail, rather than deeper meaning. Simultaneously, however, a gist representation of the patient's risk of heart attack can be coded as 'moderate'—sacrificing detail for the sake of more immediately ascertainable, contextually informed meaning, i.e. whether there is reason to be concerned that the patient will suffer a heart attack.[68] In turn, whether the verbatim or the gist representation is relied upon in reasoning will depend on the specific task being undertaken, and which form of representation is more appropriate for that task.

While it is not possible within the confines of this short discussion to examine seriously the dispute between competing dual process theories, or between dual process theories and other theories of the mind's operation, one dual process theory, Valerie Reyna and Charles Brainerd's fuzzy-trace theory,[69] has achieved particular prominence within psychological literature, and will be relied upon in this chapter as an effective model for investigating arbitrator reasoning.[70]

Drawing strongly from work on human memory, fuzzy-trace theory uses as its core the evidence just discussed distinguishing between 'verbatim' and 'gist' mental representations of facts and events.[71] Its account of human reasoning then builds upon these two types of representation to describe two forms of reasoning, which can be termed 'analytic reasoning' (relying on verbatim representation) and 'intuition' (relying on gist representation). In this respect, fuzzy-trace theory resembles Kahneman's own distinction between an intuitive System 1 and a more rigorous System 2.

Importantly, however, while in Kahneman's theory an intuitive and quick System 1 serves as the 'default' form of reasoning, to be overruled by a more deliberative and

[67] Valerie Reyna, 'A New Intuitionism: Meaning, Memory, and Development in Fuzzy-Trace Theory', 7 Judgment and Decision-Making 332 (2012).

[68] Note that the emphasis on meaning entails that gist representation is dependent on context in a way that verbatim representation is not: a 20% chance of rain may be considered low, while a 20% chance of death may be considered high.

[69] Charles Brainerd and Valerie Reyna, 'Gist is the Grist: Fuzzy-Trace Theory and the New Intuitionism', 10(1) Developmental Review 3 (1990); Valerie Reyna and Charles Brainerd, 'Fuzzy-Trace Theory: An Interim Synthesis', 7 Learning & Individual Differences 1 (1995).

[70] See Reyna (n. 67) (discussing the distinction between fuzzy-trace theory and other dual process models and critical comparison tests of the models).

[71] Valerie Reyna, 'How People Make Decisions that Involve Risk: A Dual Process Approach', 13 Current Directions in Psychological Science 60 (2004), 61.

sophisticated System 2 in certain cases, fuzzy-trace theory does not prioritize either form of reasoning over the other. Instead, one of the important insights of Reyna's research has been that whether 'verbatim' or 'gist' memory representations are relied upon in reasoning is determined by the specific task individuals are attempting to perform. In other words, performance is impacted by the context of the task: if the task requires recalling and using precise details, verbatim representations will have priority over any conflicting gist representations. If meaning has priority, such as in the comprehension of metaphors, then gist representations will take priority over conflicting verbatim representations. In many cases, however, both detail and meaning will be essential for effective reasoning. In such cases, both verbatim and gist representations will play an important role: verbatim representations provide an initial foundation, but if they do not decide the matter, gist representations become important, with the decision-maker moving through progressively more precise gist representations until a decision can finally be made.[72]

Importantly, fuzzy-trace theory does not provide a uniform model claimed to be applicable to all human reasoning, as Kahneman does with his System 1 and System 2. Rather, fuzzy-trace theory allows that the nature of the interaction between verbatim and gist representations in reasoning will vary from one individual to another, and will even vary over the course of a single individual's lifetime. That is, fuzzy-trace theory allows that different individuals will rely upon verbatim and gist representations in their reasoning to different degrees. Adults, for example, have been shown to rely more substantially upon gist-based reasoning than do children.[73] Similarly, substantial empirical evidence exists that as an individual's expertise in a field increases, her reliance upon gist representations and intuition-based reasoning often also increases.[74]

Fuzzy-trace theory, then, has substantial virtues as a model for the analysis of arbitrator reasoning. Firstly, and most importantly, it is consistent with the available empirical evidence on human reasoning. Secondly, contrary to theories that view intuitive

[72] Reyna (n. 67), 337: 'Adults begin with the lowest (categorical) level of gist and only proceed to higher (more precise) levels if the lower levels do not allow them to perform the task (e.g. to differentiate between options in a choice task). For example… nominal or categorical gist (e.g. some lives are saved; some money is won; no lives are saved; no money is won) is the simplest gist of numbers, such as numerical outcomes and probability values. If categorical distinctions fail to discriminate options, ordinal distinctions (e.g. more lives are saved; more money is won; fewer lives are saved; less money is won) are used, and so on until options can be discriminated.'

[73] Valerie Reyna and Charles Brainerd, 'Dual Processes in Decision-Making and Developmental Neuroscience: A Fuzzy-Trace Model', 31 Dev. Rev. 180 (2011), 184. This developmental change is consistent with the functional contextual research demonstrating that analogical reasoning (deriving meaning not limited to surface form) develops later than other kinds of reasoning. See e.g. Franck Carpentier, Paul Smeets, and Dermot Barnes-Holmes, 'Equivalence-Equivalence as a Model of Analogy: Further Analyses', 53 Psychological Record 349 (2003).

[74] Reyna (n. 67), 337; Valerie Reyna, 'Intuition, Reasoning and Development: A Fuzzy-Trace Theory Approach', in Pierre Barrouillet and Caroline Gauffroy (eds), *The Development of Thinking and Reasoning* (Psychology Press, 2013), 193. See also Amanda Peters et al., *Examining the Influence of Context and Professional Culture on Clinical Reasoning Through Rhetorical-Narrative Analysis* (Qualitative Health Research, 2016).

judgments as merely a first-stage and 'quick and ready' form of reasoning, to be overruled by more rigorous reasoning when important questions are at stake, 'fuzzy-trace theorists place intuition at the apex of [cognitive] development rather than at the nadir',[75] providing an account of human reasoning particularly suitable for the analysis of an expertise-based field such an arbitration. Finally, psychologists using fuzzy-trace theory have developed a substantial literature aimed at facilitating gist-based reasoning by decision-makers,[76] thereby making the use of fuzzy-trace theory consistent with functional contextualism's emphasis on 'the prediction-and-influence of events'.[77] In sum, fuzzy-trace theory is a parsimonious, robustly supported theory that is consistent with the functional contextual approach that has been argued in this Chapter to be most suitable for the application of psychology to international arbitration.

38.3.3 Fuzzy-trace theory and arbitrator reasoning

Section 38.3.1 argued that the self-conceptions of arbitrators in contemporary international commercial arbitration can largely be categorized into two groups: 'oracles', who emphasize their ability to deliver a high-quality decision due to their expertise and wisdom, and 'service providers', who emphasize their ability to provide parties with a dispute resolution process that meets their particular needs. Section 38.3.2 then argued that psychological research on human reasoning has provided solid evidence for the existence of two aspects to human reasoning: analytic reasoning based on verbatim representations of facts and events, and intuitive reasoning based on gist-based representations of facts and events. This section will now demonstrate how the insights provided by fuzzy-trace theory can be used to understand the impact of arbitrator self-conceptions on arbitrator decision-making.

While it might initially seem possible to draw a simple parallel, in which 'oracle' arbitrators rely upon intuitive gist-based reasoning, while 'service provider' arbitrators rely upon analytic verbatim-based reasoning, it must be emphasized that, as described in Section 38.3.2, all human beings rely on both forms of reasoning. That said, however, fuzzy-trace theory explicitly allows that different individuals will rely to differing degrees on the two types of reasoning, and it is through this flexibility that fuzzy-trace

[75] Reyna (n. 71), 61.

[76] See e.g. Christopher Fisher et al., 'A Signal Detection Analysis of Gist-Based Discrimination of Genetic Breast Cancer Risk', 45 Behavior Research Methods 613 (2013).

[77] These efforts have largely been applied in the context of communicating medical information. See e.g. Priscila Brust-Renck, Caisa Royer, and Valerie Reyna, 'Communicating Numerical Risk: Human Factors that Aid Understanding in Health Care', 8 Reviews of Human Factors and Ergonomics 235 (2013), 240. However, recent efforts have explored how this can be extended to the legal sphere. Cornel Marian and Sean Wright, 'The Separate Awards for the Advance on Costs: Psychological Phenomena that Account for Biased Risk Assessment Generated By Early Victories and Methods for Legal Counsel to De-Bias Risk Assessment', in Cole (n. 2), 231; Valerie Reyna et al., 'The Gist of Juries: Testing a Model of Damage Award Decision Making', 21(3) Psychology, Public Policy, and Law 280 (2015) (finding that numeracy and cognitive style did not have the impact predicted by other dual process models).

theory can provide insight into the realities of arbitrator reasoning.[78] This is because, while the gist representations used in intuitive reasoning are understood by fuzzy-trace theorists to be retrieved unconsciously, verbatim representations are understood to be retrieved through a consciously controlled process.[79]

Consider, however, how an arbitrator's self-conception as 'oracle' or 'service provider' will influence her approach to information encountered during the arbitration, and to subsequent decision-making. Take the example of an arbitrator adhering to the 'oracle' conception, whereby private decision-makers are selected because of their 'wisdom', 'symbolic capital', or 'authority'. According to this narrative, an arbitrator's main duty is to stay true to her personal, distinctive viewpoints and convictions, as it is for these personal attributes that the arbitrator was selected in the first place. Operating from this starting point, an 'oracle' arbitrator can be expected to approach a case by 'looking at the big picture', focusing on the essential elements of the dispute rather than on details, and as a result making a greater effort to ascertain the 'meanings' that form the basis of gist representations, rather than the precise details that form the basis of verbatim representations. Both types of representation will be formed, but an 'oracle' arbitrator is likely to form stronger-than-usual gist representations because of the extra attention paid to meaning in the examination of the case, and weaker-than-usual verbatim representations, because of the reduced attention paid to the details.[80]

At the opposite end of the continuum, an arbitrator conceiving of her role as that of a 'service provider' prioritizes, as the reason for her appointment, not her immediate personal characteristics but her ability to be entrusted with the task of executing the parties' mandate scrupulously and to meet their requests and expectations. For such an arbitrator, her role is to provide not an insightful 'correct' decision, but rather a process that both parties see as fair, resulting in a decision that both parties recognize has taken their views into account. Operating from this starting point, a 'service provider' arbitrator can be expected to approach written submissions and oral arguments with the goal of understanding all the nuances of the case and noting all the significant details. Again, both types of representations will be formed, but the 'service provider' arbitrator's strong

[78] It may be important to distinguish between the behaviour of reasoning (which is a kind of directed interaction with internal thoughts and emotions) and the behaviour of *demonstrating* one's reasoning (e.g. reporting how one decided, writing persuasive prose). The behaviour of demonstrating or signalling the use of a certain kind of reasoning does not imply perfect correspondence with the behaviour of reasoning, as is seen in cases of coherent *ex post facto* descriptions of why one has acted in a certain way. The incentives to claim one reasons a certain way may be different from the incentives to actually reason this way.

[79] Marlène Abadie, Laurent Waroquier, and Patrice Terrier, 'Gist Memory in the Unconscious-Thought Effect', 24 Psychological Science 1253 (2013).

[80] At present this hypothesis is circumstantially supported by the diverse literature on the training and performance of experts, but it could be empirically tested with arbitrators specifically using the oracle/service provider distinction. See generally Johnathan Corbin et al., 'How Reasoning, Judgment, and Decision Making are Colored by Gist-Based Intuition: A Fuzzy-Trace Theory Approach', 4 J. Appl. Res. Mem. Cogn. 344 (2015).

focus on detail over substantive meaning will mean that the arbitrator will form weaker-than-usual gist representations and stronger-than-usual verbatim representations.

Of course, when actually reaching a decision in a case, international commercial arbitrators of both 'oracle' and 'service provider' self-conceptions will ordinarily have access to the parties' written submissions, and often to a written record of any hearings. Consequently, it may seem unimportant how an arbitrator has initially approached the case, as the arbitrator does not have only his/her memory to rely upon. There are, however, three important reasons why such a view is incorrect.

Firstly, arbitrators do not wait until all evidence is presented and all arguments made before commencing to consider their views on a case. Rather, they will have been forming views throughout the course of the proceedings, which will then strongly inform the decision ultimately reached. Consequently, the degree to which an arbitrator has attended to the details of a case or to the underlying 'meaning' will have a significant impact on the views that arbitrator has already formed prior to turning to the written materials and reaching a decision. In addition, psychological research has provided clear evidence for the existence in all human reasoning of a 'confirmation bias', in which new evidence is routinely interpreted to support pre-adopted viewpoints.[81] Consequently, the views that an arbitrator forms prior to the final decision-making phase have enormous importance for the final decision.

Secondly, both analytic verbatim-based reasoning and intuitive gist-based reasoning play a role in all decision-making, with a preference for decisions to be rendered at a verbatim level when possible. Yet the use of verbatim representations is guided consciously.[82] As a result, an arbitrator's self-conception will also determine the degree to which he/she makes a conscious effort to resolve disputes through reliance on verbatim representations. 'Oracle' arbitrators, that is, will not only have initially developed weaker-than-usual verbatim representations, which will then be less likely to resolve a case, but will also be less likely to rely on verbatim representations than would a 'service provider' arbitrator.[83] Therefore, a 'service provider' arbitrator will be more likely than an 'oracle' arbitrator to have detailed verbatim representations that are strong enough to resolve a case and thus avoid reliance upon gist. Furthermore, the role of conscious control in the recall of verbatim representations entails that a 'service provider' arbitrator will be more likely to attempt to store verbatim representations during the final review of the written record, and then to recall them. The 'oracle' arbitrator, by contrast, will again have prioritized the meaning of the evidence when reviewing the written record. As a result, each will get different things from that evidence.

[81] See generally Raymond Nickerson, 'Confirmation Bias: A Ubiquitous Phenomenon in Many Guises', 2 Review of General Psychology 175 (1998).

[82] Abadie et al. (n. 79).

[83] There is, of course, a question of temporal causation in this description that needs to be confirmed through further empirical research: to what degree does an arbitrator's self-identification as oracle/service provider shape that arbitrator's verbatim/gist repertoire, and to what degree does the repertoire shape the arbitrator's self-identification as oracle/service provider?

Thirdly, the 'oracle' arbitrator will be more likely to rely upon gist-based intuitive reasoning than the 'service provider' arbitrator, precisely because of the self-conception each has of their role as arbitrator. An 'oracle' arbitrator, then, will be more likely to conclude that the case can only be decided by looking at the general contours of the dispute, while a 'service provider' arbitrator is likely to rely heavily on specific pieces of information, rather than deciding a case on the basis of its overall 'meaning'.

Of course, the influence of the professional context of arbitration on the prioritization of verbatim or gist representations is not, in itself, problematic: as fuzzy-trace theory demonstrates, the existence of two different modes of encoding and storing information is an advantage of human reasoning, rather than something to be eradicated. However, it is important for arbitrators to be aware of the impact of their self-conception on the modes of information processing. Keeping this in mind, arbitrators can predict and counter possible risks. An arbitrator leaning towards gist representations, for instance, may risk forming an 'overall idea' of a case prematurely, and ignore subsequent inputs rather than encoding and storing them through verbatim representations. In order to ensure balance in decision-making, this type of arbitrator could make an effort to look at the details of the dispute in the initial phase of decision-making, so as to avoid the undue marginalization of relevant information. Conversely, an arbitrator relying on verbatim representations may try to develop a holistic understanding of the dispute throughout the procedure, rather than focusing exclusively on precise, measurable information. Gist representations could then be relied upon at the decision-making stage, should verbatim representations prove insufficient. In other words, by understanding the psychological phenomena underlying reasoning and the contextual factors triggering them, arbitrators can attain the development of more balanced thinking patterns.[84]

Understanding the professional context of arbitration and its influence on arbitral reasoning is also important for the purposes of forming well-balanced and effective tribunals. In particular, whenever the arbitral tribunal is composed of three members, the final decision results from the combination of the arbitrators' personal viewpoints. For this reason, the tendency of a member of the tribunal to prioritize gist representations can be counterbalanced by another member's focus on verbatim representations. If the parties have appointed two verbatim-focused arbitrators, a more gist-oriented chairman could be selected, so as to ensure balance in the modes of information-processing. Within such a tribunal, each arbitrator should not see the differences in self-conceptions

[84] Our discussion of the use of verbatim vs. gist representations for arbitrators demonstrates the potential distinction between mechanistic and contextual prediction. Specifically, it may be the case that mechanistic studies of verbatim/gist representation in the context of arbitration will not confirm our hypotheses. Nonetheless, even if the claim is not verified in subsequent decision-making research, the claim may still prove useful in the context of verbal behaviour. That is, functional statements about the use of verbatim/gist representations may contribute to successful working of a theory even if they are not verified in neuroscientific studies. While we expect our claim is contextually 'true' given the goals of arbitration, we are agnostic about it being mechanistically 'true'. To the extent that the arbitration community values agreement with biological science where possible, we hope the claims are true in both senses.

and cognitive attitudes as a problem: if understood and valued correctly, this psychological diversity can be a significant strength and distinctive feature of arbitration.

38.4 The context of arbitration II: The social context of arbitrator psychology

38.4.1 The hierarchic structure of the arbitration community

In describing the influence of arbitrator self-conceptions on arbitrator decision-making, Section 38.3 argued that individual answers to the question 'What is an arbitrator?' are not developed in isolation, but are rather the results of a complex set of influences coming from the arbitration community. This section will examine the social context of arbitration more closely, in order to determine exactly how this context can be understood to impact on arbitrator reasoning.

According to a commonly repeated narrative, those involved in international commercial arbitration can be understood as forming a relatively homogeneous social group, the 'arbitration community'. This 'community' comprises not only arbitrators, but also lawyers who specialize in international arbitration, representatives of leading arbitral institutions, and even representatives of parties who regularly participate in international arbitrations (typically, sophisticated commercial actors).[85] Moreover, the cohesive nature of this community, so it is argued, has given rise to a normative set of rules and practices for the conduct of arbitration, more and more often reflected in soft-law instruments drafted to guide arbitration practitioners.

While there is little question that there is some level of truth to this portrayal, it is a fundamentally oversimplified picture that fails to take adequate account of the centrality of local contexts and individual actors to the operation of this 'community'. Arbitration, that is, is a fundamentally unregulated form of professional practice: while arbitrators and party representatives in arbitrations are overwhelmingly lawyers, few formal restrictions are placed on who may participate in arbitration. Arbitrators and party representatives need not be nationals of any particular state, have any particular expertise, or have any legal qualifications. In addition, even if they are lawyers, arbitrators and counsel participating in an arbitration located outside the jurisdiction in which

[85] The distinction between sophisticated commercial actors and private individuals who participate in domestic arbitration highlights an important analytic principle in functional contextualism: behaviour is defined by its function rather than by its topographical form. Topographically, any form of dispute resolution (small or large, domestic or international) that is called 'arbitration' is similar. However, the function of 'arbitrating' is quite different among these variations. In this chapter, we limit our focus to international commercial arbitration.

they are licensed may not be subject to any kind of professional discipline for their actions.

One possible consequence of this governmental deregulation would be adoption by the arbitration community of regulations of its own, such as are found in parallel situations like the regulation of the broader legal profession by Bar associations. Within arbitration, however, the idea that arbitration benefits from being deregulated has itself become a norm. Consequently, not only is arbitration unregulated by governments, but it is self-consciously left unregulated by the arbitration community.

This, however, does not mean that no regulation exists within arbitration at all. Rather, arbitration has come to be regulated by a highly developed system of social recognition and professional status. Arbitration is a highly sought-after specialization, with many more individuals interested in the field than there is arbitration work to be done. As a result, those already in the field have taken on the role of informal 'gatekeepers', identifying and promoting the community's values, and providing opportunities to those individuals seen to share those values.[86]

Equally importantly, the spread of arbitration as a form of commercial dispute resolution has caused a diversification and stratification of the underlying professional community, such that multiple distinct but overlapping social groups exist. An individual engaged in arbitration in Europe may, for example, be subject to the social rules and norms of a national arbitration community (as the primary community in which he/she works), of a regional or cultural arbitration community (e.g. Scandinavian or French-speaking arbitration practitioners), of a subject-specific arbitration community (e.g. energy arbitration, construction arbitration), and of the community formed by the 'elite' practitioners of international commercial arbitration (as the community he/she seeks to join, or of which he/she is already a member). This diversity is indeed reflected quite clearly in the variations that often exist in the rules of arbitral institutions, and in the practices used in international commercial arbitration in different jurisdictions.[87]

Just as importantly as the diversity of international commercial arbitration, what this more realistic picture emphasizes is the centrality to the operation of international commercial arbitration of hierarchy. That is, rather than constituting a horizontal community of stakeholders, the 'community' of international commercial arbitration instead operates as a tiered structure, with certain individuals having particular importance as providers of opportunities for career advancement. In other words, given the importance of reputation and experience in arbitration, a small elite of highly regarded individuals

[86] See e.g. Sergio Puig, 'Social Capital in the Arbitration Market', 25 EJIL 387 (2014), 40, describing the influence of the social-verbal community, which is defined functionally (who has an impact, irrespective of formal status) rather than topographically (who is said by social convention to be a part of the community).

[87] Tony Cole, Pietro Ortolani, and Barbara Warwas, 'Arbitration in Southern Europe', 26 American Review of International Arbitration 187 (2015). Indeed, the diversity of institutions and procedures highlights a strength of arbitration: specifically, its ability to respond (behave differently) in response to user needs. This is in distinction to the 'frozen' quality of procedures in litigation.

can act as gatekeepers, determining the career progression patterns of all other individuals operating within this field of legal practice.

What this means is that the rules and practices governing arbitration are not the result of a spontaneous, peer-to-peer phenomenon of transnational norm-making, but are rather the product of choices made by a relatively small group of leading figures. From a behavioural perspective, these gatekeepers constitute an influential portion of the 'social-verbal community' which reinforces appropriate behaviour and punishes inappropriate behaviour. When an individual is attempting to 'break into' international commercial arbitration, this will usually involve accessing a relevant local arbitration community, and in particular building connections with those individuals actively involved in international commercial arbitration. After establishing a presence in, for example, 'international commercial arbitration in Portugal', that individual may wish to move into a higher tier of arbitration, and so will need to build connections with individuals involved in another tier, ideally that composed of the most prominent international arbitration practitioners, but potentially merely a tier that brings him closer to the top of the field. In order to move into this new community, however, he will again have to build connections with individuals in that community, in order to be provided with opportunities.

The important consideration with respect to this picture is that at each stage, career progression occurs though interpersonal connections. Yet given the professional context of the relationships the 'aspirant arbitrator' is attempting to build, the primary consideration as to whether he will succeed in building the connections he requires is the views he expresses regarding the proper approach to arbitration. Where these views correspond with those of a gatekeeper of the community he is attempting to enter, this significantly enhances his chances of entry; where they conflict, the gatekeeper has no reason to provide him with opportunities, for the simple reason that the gatekeeper believes the 'aspirant arbitrator' does not practice arbitration properly.

To sum up, in an initial classification we can represent the varying influence of different types of members of an international arbitration community along a spectrum. On one side of the spectrum we can locate 'marginal' stakeholders, who do not have a significant ability to determine the success (or lack thereof) of others in the field of arbitration. On the other side, we can locate 'gatekeepers', who shape the normative framework of arbitration and can regulate access to the arbitration professional market and progression therein. Benefiting from a hierarchically apical position, gatekeepers have a strong influence on all other arbitration actors. Even this picture, however, oversimplifies the reality of career development in a fundamentally socially regulated profession such as arbitration. Instead, a more accurate picture will also emphasize that different 'gatekeepers' value different things.

In order to better elucidate the scope of influence exerted by gatekeepers, it is useful to introduce a second distinction, between 'outsiders' and 'insiders'. Some actors look at arbitration from the outside: they are not interested in the outcome of a specific case, but rather in the procedural conduct of the arbitration. By way of example, arbitral institutions typically have the primary purpose of ensuring that the proceedings are conducted efficiently, with adequate management skills. By contrast, other actors are more likely to evaluate the behaviour of an arbitrator from the inside: arbitrators sitting in a three-member panel, for example, value not only the managerial skills but also the decision-making expertise of their colleagues.[88] Typically, insiders have access to the final award and form their opinions on the basis of the substance of the decision, while outsiders are mainly concerned with the conduct of the arbitration. As a consequence, outsiders mainly influence the procedural choices made by the arbitrator, but they do not generally impact the outcome of a case. Insiders, by contrast, can influence the substance of decision-making. The interrelationship between these elements of an arbitral community is pictured in Figure 38.1.

In conclusion, the degree to which an arbitrator may be influenced by a given member of an international arbitration community depends on the degree to which and the manner in which this stakeholder acts a gatekeeper within the arbitration community. By way of example, a popular arbitral institution is likely to make a significant number of arbitrator appointments, and therefore arbitrators have an incentive to comply with its

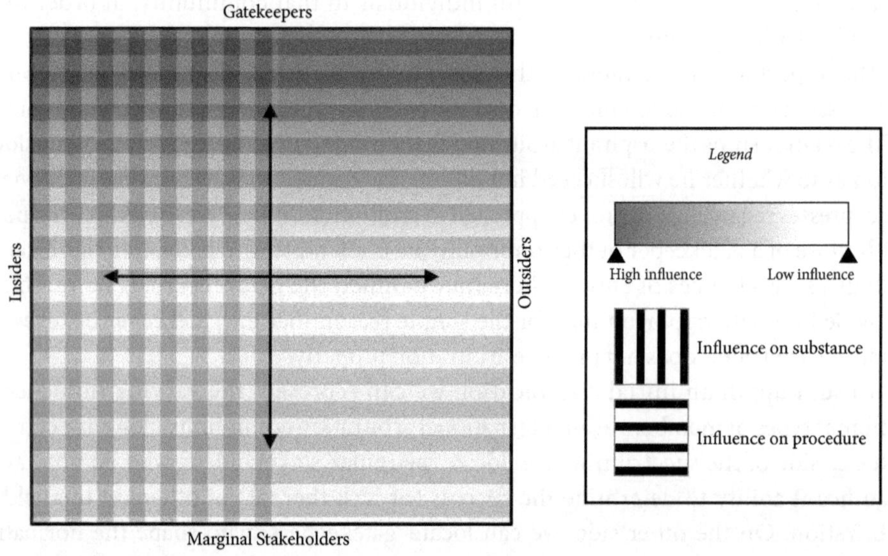

FIGURE 38.1 The influence of actors within the arbitration community.

[88] It should incidentally be noted that the distinction between outsiders and insiders depends on the circumstances of the case and is therefore subject to variations. By way of example, an arbitral institution whose exclusive concern is the efficient procedural management of the case is best qualified as an 'outsider', while an institution reviewing the contents of the award and adopting a hands-on approach to the decision-making aspect of the arbitration should be qualified as an 'insider'. Interviews conducted with representatives of arbitral institutions confirm, in fact, that some institutions adopt a hands-off approach and do not interfere with arbitral decision-making, while others scrutinize (either formally or informally) the contents of the award. See Tony Cole et al., *The Legal Instruments and Practice of Arbitration in the EU* (European Parliament, 2014), 2.2.

expectations, in order to secure future appointments. Similarly, a prominent and highly regarded co-arbitrator can be a precious social connection for a newcomer trying to establish herself as an arbitration specialist.[89] Conversely, community members that do not act as gatekeepers (such as a party involved in a single dispute) are unlikely to exert a significant influence.[90] As to the nature of the influence, it is likely to concern procedure if it comes from outsiders, and substance too if it comes from insiders. What must be emphasized, however, is that ultimately any international commercial arbitration community is best represented as a spectrum, not a simple classification. In other words, any member of that community has some ability to act as a gatekeeper, but some have much more ability than others. Similarly, any gatekeeper has some ability to influence both substance and procedure, but some have far more influence over one of these characteristics than the other.

This picture of the social context of arbitration having been developed, the question that arises is how this context influences arbitrator decision-making. There is, for example, no evidence to support a finding of a widespread practice of arbitrators consciously adapting their decisions to the expectations of gatekeepers in order to advance their careers. Indeed, the seriousness with which leading arbitrators take their self-perception as independent decision-makers would make such a practice self-defeating, as any arbitrator believed by his colleagues to engage in such a practice would be excluded from precisely the opportunities he was attempting to generate.[91] The answer, rather, stems from the very fact that gatekeepers take the role of decision-maker seriously: career progression as an arbitrator fundamentally relies upon convincing gatekeepers of the quality of one's decision-making. Each arbitrator, hence, can maximize her career potential if she can show the ability to render high-quality unbiased decisions.[92] The next

[89] Currently, our understanding of the ways behaviour is reinforced or punished through reputational effects comes mostly from anecdotal reports of arbitrators describing their own behaviour in specific instances: see William Park, 'Rules and Reliability: How Arbitrators Decide', in Cole (n. 2), 3. A comprehensive account would require specifying behaviours that increase or decrease in frequency in response to reputation contingencies.

[90] A relatively unexplored area is the impact of the arbitrator's own verbal behaviour. As an insider to arbitration, the arbitrator is in a position to judge his own behaviour by the standards of the social-verbal community as he understands them. Contextual behavioural science has developed increasingly sophisticated ways to account for 'self-discriminated behaviour', such as self-mands that encourage one to behave in a specific way ('I need to write an award that is compelling in its logic') and perspective-taking ('If I were [an esteemed arbitrator], I would do X'). One's personal history will be relevant in determining the extent to which one is influenced by the behaviour of others. E.g. a socially anxious arbitrator may allow others to have a stronger influence on his behaviour compared to a narcissistic arbitrator who is insensitive to these consequences.

[91] General support for this view comes from the various empirical studies reporting that arbitrators perform comparably to judges even though the two groups may have different incentives. Helm et al. (n. 3); Pat Chew, 'Arbitral and Judicial Proceedings: Indistinguishable Justice or Justice Denied?' 46 Wake Forest Law Review 185 (2011); Theodore Eisenberg and Elizabeth Hill, 'Arbitration and Litigation of Employment Claims: An Empirical Comparison', 58 Disp. Resol. J 44 (2003), 53.

[92] It is important not to conflate the notion of 'unbiased' in a statistical sense with the notion of 'unbiased' used in the arbitration community. Clearly, the community would prefer that its definition of 'unbiased' generally be equivalent to the statistical meaning of 'unbiased', but since this is a hard empirical

section will, therefore, focus on one of the primary obstacles to the achievement of such a goal: the problem of cognitive biases and the inherent flaws in human reasoning. Subsequently, Section 38.4.3 will illustrate how these cognitive biases can be countered through actions by and on arbitration communities

38.4.2 The impacts of cognitive biases on decision-making

One of the fundamental realities of all human reasoning is that human minds are imperfect 'rationality machines'.[93] While human minds are capable of doing remarkable things, they are fundamentally multi-purpose machines, controlling decision-making, social interaction, communication, creativity, and many other things. In light of this, it is hardly surprising that they are ultimately 'master' of none of them. The difficulty this creates in the context of arbitration is that fundamentally arbitrators are decision-makers: although high-quality reasoning is certainly not the only ability an arbitrator is expected to have, few parties involved in an arbitration will be content with a poorly reasoned award by noting that the arbitrator nonetheless had a great facility for multiple languages, or managed to be charming throughout the proceeding. An arbitrator's mind, thus, is a multi-purpose machine placed in a context in which most of its functions are now deemed to be irrelevant, and its performance will be judged almost entirely on how it undertakes a single activity, which it unavoidably performs imperfectly.

The consequences of the 'multi-function' nature of the human mind have come to be investigated in empirical psychology under the label of 'cognitive biases'.[94] While 'bias' is

question to answer, and is rarely answered in a way that meets the standard for scientific rigour, the relevant sense of 'unbiased' is what the community says it is. Arbitrators are therefore mainly *signaling* to others in the community in symbolic ways so that the community labels them unbiased. Rare is the arbitrator who reports to the psychology lab for 'bias' testing after an arbitration.

[93] Although RFT uses technical jargon to achieve its scientific goals, the theory aims to account for what a general reader would call 'reasoning' and 'decision-making'.

[94] Most studies of cognitive bias are grounded in mechanistic assumptions, rather than the contextual approach advocated in this chapter. While this issue cannot be addressed exhaustively here, it is useful to note that recent work by De Houwer on the development of a functional-cognitive framework can provide the necessary foundation to connect the two approaches. See Jan De Houwer, 'Why the Cognitive Approach in Psychology would Profit from a Functional Approach and Vice Versa', 6(2) Perspectives on Psychological Science (2011) 202; Sean Hughes, Jan De Houwer, and Marco Perugini, 'The Functional-Cognitive Framework for Psychological Research: Controversies and Resolutions', 51(1) International Journal of Psychology 4 (2016). An advantage of the functional approach is the possibility of deriving '*abstract* functional knowledge that is not restricted to a certain procedure but that can explain a wide variety of topographically different outcomes (i.e., knowledge that is both precise and far reaching)'. Hughes et al.,' Functional-Cognitive Framework', 9. De Houwer and colleagues have shown that different cognitive effects can functionally be accounted for using well-known behavioural principles. See Baptist Liefooghe and Jan De Houwer, 'A Functional Approach for Research on Cognitive Control: Analysing Cognitive Control Tasks and their Effects in Terms of Operant Conditioning', 51(1) International Journal of Psychology 28 (2016). For recent work proposing functional accounts of cognitive bias, see Marco Tagliabue, Valeria Squatrito, and Giovambattista Presti, 'Models of Cognition and Their Applications in Behavioral Economics: A Conceptual Framework for Nudging Derived from Behavior Analysis and Relational Frame Theory', 10 Frontiers in Psychology 1 (2019); Alisha Wray, Rachel Freund, and Michael

a familiar term within arbitration, it is important to emphasize that it is not used in this context to refer to a prejudice for or against a party in an arbitration. Rather, 'bias' in this context is a fundamentally normative term, referring to situations in which an individual's reasoning systematically and consistently departs from a certain standard of reasoning. In turn, the 'cognitive' element of the label refers to the fact that the flawed reasoning in question does not result from a particular factual belief held by the decision-maker, but rather is a feature of the way the human mind reaches decisions—in effect, a 'cognitive bias' is like a piece of poorly written code in a computer programme, which consistently results in the wrong decision being reached whenever it is activated. Importantly, empirical research has demonstrated that these biases are not flaws in an individual's rationality, present in those who are bad at reasoning, and absent from those who are good at it. They are, instead, inherent features of human reasoning itself—in short, there are certain things human minds do imperfectly.

While there is significant disagreement within psychology over precisely what cognitive biases exist, and how they should be classified, certain biases whose existence is supported by strong evidence have particular relevance for arbitration. Discussion of some of these biases will be the focus of the remainder of this section. However, it must be emphasized that the goal of this section is not to provide an exhaustive list of all possible biases that may affect arbitral reasoning, but merely to illustrate the evidence that such biases exist.[95]

One of the most famous cognitive biases, known as 'anchoring', affects the ability of decision-makers to reach conclusions without being affected by previously presented evidence.[96] In an early experiment by Daniel Kahneman and Amos Tversky, subjects were initially invited to spin a 'wheel of fortune' to obtain an ostensibly random (but actually experiment-chosen) number, half receiving the number 10, and half 65. Participants were then asked whether the percentage of African countries that were members of the United Nations was higher or lower than the number they had just 'randomly' spun. Next they were asked to estimate what the correct percentage was. The group that had received an initial number of 10 averaged an estimate of 25 per cent, while the group that had received an initial estimate of 65, averaged an estimate of 45 per cent.[97] What is notable in this result, of course, is that although the subjects of the experiment were clearly influenced in their estimates by the original number they had received, they would themselves deny that they had been influenced at all—the original number, after

Dougher, 'A Behavior-Analytic Account of Cognitive Bias inClinical Populations', 32(1) Behavior Analyst 29 (2009). A proper account of decision-making requires the application of traditional behavioural principles like establishing operations and reinforcement in conjunction with the effects of verbal processes like arbitrarily applicable relational responding in relational frame theory, the details of which are beyond the scope of this chapter. The interested and brave reader will find analysis of many higher-order cognitive abilities in Steven Hayes, Dermot Barnes-Holmes and Bryan Roche, *Relational Frame Theory: A Post-Skinnerian Account of Human Language and Cognition* (Springer, 2001).

[95] A thorough discussion of cognitive biases in the context of arbitration can be found in Peter Ayton and Geneviève Helleringer, 'Bias, Self-Insight, Vested Interests and Self-Deception in Judgment and Decision-Making: Challenges set by the Requirement of Arbitrator Impartiality', in Cole (n. 2), 21.

[96] Tversky and Kahneman (n. 61). [97] Ibid.

all, was just a random number. Nonetheless, the evidence is clear that they were indeed influenced.[98]

One response to this evidence, of course, would be to suggest that the experiment merely revealed the lack of self-awareness of many people about their own reasoning, but that arbitrators, as professional decision-makers, would be immune to such an effect, or at least be able to resist it. Other experiments, however, have demonstrated clearly that the same effect is evident even in the reasoning of judges, also professional decision-makers. In one leading study, judges who had been presented with inadmissible evidence, including demands made during a settlement conference and conversations protected by attorney–client privilege, were found to reach decisions significantly different from those reached by judges who had not received that evidence.[99] That is, despite their own ruling that such evidence was inadmissible, and their expertise as decision-makers, the judges in the study were clearly affected by the evidence they had consciously decided to disregard.[100]

Anchoring, of course, as already noted, is merely one of the known cognitive biases, and other biases are at least as important for decision-making in arbitration. Indeed, whereas anchoring can seem to influence only relatively technical aspects of

[98] For discussion of the anchoring bias in arbitration, see e.g. Christopher Drahozal, 'Of Rabbits and Rhinoceri: A Survey of Empirical Research on International Commercial Arbitration', 20(1) J. Int'l Arb 23 (2003). Also see Christopher Drahozal's Ch. 27 in this Handbook.

[99] Andrew Wistrich, Chris Guthrie, and Jeffrey Rachlinski, 'Can Judges Ignore Inadmissible Information? The Difficulty of Deliberately Disregarding', U. Pa. L. Rev. 1251 (2005).

[100] See also Reyna et al. (n. 77), 280, showing similar response effects on the size of hypothetical damage awards by juries when subjects were exposed to numerical anchors. In terms of the non-cognitive approach adopted in this chapter, the anchoring effect can be recast using well-known behavioural principles of motivating operations and reinforcement. Motivating operations temporarily change relevant consequencesm and potentiate behaviours associated with obtaining these consequences. See Michael (n. 5); Jack Michael, 'Distinguishing between Discriminative and Motivational Functions of Stimuli', 37(1) Journal of the Experimental Analysis of Behavior 149 (1982); 'Motivating Operations', in John Cooper, Timothy Heron, and William Heward (eds), *Applied Behavior Analysis*, 2nd edn (Prentice Hall, 2007), 374. E.g. food deprivation is a motivating operation, as it temporarily increases the reinforcing value of food and increases food-seeking behaviours; once the establishing operation is terminated, as in satiation, the behaviour changes. Cognitive applications of this concept have been termed 'motivated perception' to indicate that perception is affected by motivational operations. See Andreas Voss and Christiane Schwieren, 'The Dynamics of Motivated Perception: Effects of Control and Status on the Perception of Ambivalent Stimuli', 29(8) Cognition and Emotion 1411 (2015). In the case of anchoring, the experimental context creates an establishing operation such that the subject increases a behaviour (attempting to correctly respond) in order to achieve reinforcement (through monetary pay-offs, social approval, or self-approval). Anchoring to the initial value is an example of motivated perception. Adjustment—the process whereby subjects change their responses away from, but still as if tethered to, the anchor—can be accounted for by another strong source of reinforcement: coherence. Laboratory research supports the claim that the opportunity to make a coherent narrative that makes sense is often reinforcing: Alisha Wray et al., 'Examining the Reinforcing Properties of Making Sense: A Preliminary Investigation', 62(4) Psychological Record 599 (2012); Michael Bordieri et al., 'Basic Properties of Coherence: Testing a Core Assumption of Relational Frame Theory', 66(1) Psychological Record 83 (2016). Thus, in the anchoring experiment, subjects may have experienced an arbitrary narrative association between the anchor and their final response as more reinforcing than pay-offs for accurate responses.

decision-making, other biases have been demonstrated to impact significantly on the substance of the judgements that judicial and arbitral decision-making requires. 'Priming', for example, occurs when the existence of a particular stimulus, whether or not the subject is consciously aware of the stimulus, causes a demonstrable change in the subject's behaviour, compared to when the stimulus is absent. In the leading experiment on this bias, it was hypothesized, in accordance with what is known as Terror Management Theory,[101] that decision-makers who were reminded of their own mortality would respond exceptionally positively to individuals seen to be upholding cultural values, and negatively to individuals seen to be violating them.[102] Judges were presented with a standard case file for an individual arrested for prostitution, half the judges also being asked to complete a questionnaire prior to examining the case file, in which they were required to describe what would happen to them as they died, and what emotions the thought of their death aroused. Notably, judges who completed this questionnaire set a bail bond roughly nine times higher for the accused described in the case file than did judges who had not completed the questionnaire.[103]

Contextual effects have also been demonstrated to significantly impact decision-making, even of professionals. One study examined 1,112 judicial rulings, covering a ten-month period, by eight judges who presided over three-member parole boards.[104] Such boards sat for day-long sessions hearing a series of cases, with the day broken only by a 'late morning snack' and lunch. The study found a significant impact by comparatively minor levels of fatigue and hunger on the decisions made, with rates of granting parole decreasing from 65 per cent at the beginning of a session to essentially zero per cent by the end of each session. After a break and consumption of food, rates of granting parole immediately returned to 65 per cent, only to again decrease steadily as the session progressed. There was no difference between the cases being considered at different

[101] Terror Management Theory is based on the proposition that all human beings experience a fundamental conflict between their instinct for self-preservation and their awareness that their own death is ultimately inevitable. It proposes that the natural response to this conflict is to embrace things that, in a sense, allow one to transcend death, by connecting one's own time-limited existence with things that will continue even after one's own death, such as a particular culture, society, or religion. See e.g. Sheldon Solomon, Jeff Greenberg, and Tom Pyszczynski, *The Worm at the Core: On the Role of Death in Life* (Random House, 2015). Of course, the particular way in which this conflict manifests itself is contextually determined by an individual's specific verbal history, and so could be expressed differently for individuals with different histories.

[102] Abram Rosenblatt et al., 'Evidence for Terror Management Theory, I. The Effects of Mortality Salience on Reactions to Those Who Violate or Uphold Cultural Values', 57(4) Journal of Personality and Social Psychology 681 (1989).

[103] An average of $455, compared to $50. See ibid.

[104] Shai Danziger, Jonathan Levav, and Liora Avnaim-Pesso, 'Extraneous Factors in Judicial Decisions', 108(17) Proceedings of the National Academy of Sciences 6889 (2011). A recent study of variations in the rate of granting asylum for individual judges reported significant variation based on current weather and the previous night's football game: Daniel Chen, 'This Morning's Breakfast, Last Night's Game: Detecting Extraneous Factors in Judging', IAST Working Papers 16-49, Institute for Advanced Study in Toulouse (IAST).

times during the session that could have explained the differences in willingness to grant parole.[105]

Researchers have also identified the existence of a 'self-serving bias', which reflects the tendency to 'conflate what is fair with what benefits oneself'.[106] In mock negotiations, Lowenstein et al. demonstrated that subjects' perceptions of whether a settlement is fair are strongly tied to their own self-interest.[107] Moreover, the same researchers found a substantial discrepancy between estimates by lawyers and judges regarding the willingness of judges to allow reimbursement of lawyers' fees in bankruptcy cases, with 37 per cent of judges reporting that they usually allowed reimbursement at the 'value of the services', while only 15 per cent of lawyers reported the same thing.[108] While neither of these studies is expressly aimed at the self-interest of a decision-maker, the existence of a self-interest bias clearly connects with traditional concerns that arbitrators may be tempted to 'split the baby' in order to please both parties and maximize their chances of further work. Importantly, it would mean that this could happen even if arbitrators consciously rejected such an approach to decision-making.

Finally, in a situation particularly relevant for arbitrators, researchers have also identified the existence of a 'confirmation bias', which reflects the tendency to 'misinterpret new information as supporting previously held hypotheses',[109] even if the new information only ambiguously supports the previously held belief.[110] As explained by one group of researchers, 'there is considerable evidence that people tend to interpret subsequent evidence so as to maintain their initial beliefs. The biased assimilation processes underlying this effect may include a propensity to remember the strengths of confirming

[105] The cause of this variation is not definitively known, although the authors of the study themselves argue that it may result from the interaction of mental depletion and time impact choices. That is, parole decisions are made against a background of the 'status quo' of the prisoner remaining in jail. Decisions which alter the status quo require more time and effort than decisions which maintain it, due to the need to proffer defensible reasons for releasing the prisoner from jail. As a result, such decisions are less likely when judges are 'mentally depleted' at the end of a long session without food or a break. But see Andreas Glöckner, 'The Irrational Hungry Judge Effect Revisited: Simulations Reveal that the Magnitude of the Effect is Overestimated', 11(6) Judgment and Decision Making 601 (2016) (arguing on the basis of a computer simulation that the variations observed in the original study by Danziger et al. can be partially, but not entirely, explained by rational decisions by judges, such as to leave more difficult cases until after breaks).

[106] Linda Babcock and George Loewenstein, 'Explaining Bargaining Impasse: The Role of Self-Serving Biases', 11 J. Econ. Persp. 109 (1997), 110. See also George Lowenstein et al., 'Self-Serving Assessments of Fairness and Pretrial Bargaining,' 22 J. Legal Stud. 135 (1993).

[107] Ibid. A similar finding is the 'endowment effect' in which the same item is valued higher when it belongs to a person compared to when a person is trying to acquire the item: Daniel Kahneman, Jack Knetsch, and Richard Thaler, 'Experimental Tests of the Endowment Effect and the Coase Theorem', Journal of Political Economy 1325 (1990).

[108] Babcock and Loewenstein (n. 106), 121.

[109] Matthew Rabin and Joel Schrag, 'First Impressions Matter: A Model of Confirmatory Bias', 114 QJ Econ. 37 (1999).

[110] Hal Arkes, 'Principles in Judgment/Decision Making Research Pertinent to Legal Proceedings', 7(4) Behavioral Sciences & The Law 429 (1989); Randy Borum, Randy Otto, and Steve Golding, 'Improving Clinical Judgment and Decision Making in Forensic Evaluation', 21 Journal of Psychiatry and Law 35 (1993).

evidence but the weaknesses of disconfirming evidence, to judge confirming evidence as relevant and reliable but disconfirming evidence as irrelevant and unreliable, and to accept confirming evidence at face value while scrutinizing disconfirming evidence hypercritically.'[111] Given the extended period over which many arbitrations operate, the existence of confirmation bias obviously raises significant questions about the relative impacts of early-presented and later-presented evidence and arguments on final decisions.

Arbitrators, of course, are human, and it can hardly be a surprise that despite their role as professional decision-makers, they are nevertheless imperfect in that role. More importantly, however, it should be emphasized that the fact that the reasoning of arbitrators will consistently depart from norms of perfect reasoning is not necessarily a 'flaw' as such.[112] After all, the existence of these biases may be compensated for by strengths in other areas of the mind's operation that provide benefits to an arbitration, such as empathy, interpersonal skills, and creativity. Consequently, that human minds do not conform to a certain norm of quality reasoning should not be taken as a criticism of the individuals concerned. Indeed, the minds of those individuals may be providing benefits in other respects, that would not be gained from a more perfect 'reasoning machine'. The question becomes, however, whether decision-makers are aware of the imperfections of their reasoning, and how those imperfections can be dealt with in a way that maximizes the quality of each arbitration.

38.4.3 The social context of arbitrator psychology and the problem of cognitive bias

Section 38.4.1 focused on identifying the essentially hierarchic nature of arbitration as a field of professional practice, as well as the important role that social connections play in the development of a successful arbitral career. Neither of these might seem to have an immediate relevance to cognitive biases, as cognitive biases relate to the internal operations

[111] Charles Lord, Lee Ross, and Mark Lepper, 'Biased Assimilation and Attitude Polarization: The Effects of Prior Theories on Subsequently Considered Evidence', 37(11) Journal of Personality and Social Psychology 2098 (1979).

[112] E.g. psychologist Etienne Mullet has emphasized that standards of good reasoning are developed by human beings to resolve problems. Mullet is a forceful critic of the notion that cognitive biases constitute independent phenomena. His scepticism initially stems from the sheer number of biases that have been identified (by his count, 104 as of 2012). He argues that the extensive number of biases is likely related to the large number of procedural variations that have been established to identify deviations from normative models of decision-making. As such, it is unsurprising that humans do not adhere to these standards, as if they did, development of the standards would not have been necessary. For example, regarding Bayes' Theorem, he has argued: 'The existence of this theorem is thus a strong indication that Reverend Bayes himself was not Bayesian. If he had been Bayesian, he would not have needed to create Bayes' Theorem. He would just have used his natural Bayesian mind to solve it.' See, Etienne Mullet, 'The Superfluous Postulate of Human Rationality', 120(3) Rivista internazionale di scienze sociali 269 (2012), 275.

of the mind, while the issues discussed in Section 38.4.1 relate to external social interactions.

However, arbitrators are likely to believe that their career progression depends to a significant degree on their capacity to display good decision-making skills: 'If I am seen as being able to deliver high quality unbiased awards,' an arbitrator may think, 'then my potential to attract future appointments will increase.' For this reason, while on the one hand it is undeniable that even specialized decision-makers are subject to certain flaws in reasoning, arbitrators are structurally tempted to deny this risk, in order to preserve the image of the 'good arbitrator'. Unlike judges, who are protected by long-term appointment and can recognize their own flaws in reasoning as something to be worked upon, arbitrators endanger the ongoing viability of their careers through such revelations. In a nutshell, no one wants to hire an arbitrator who is known to have flawed reasoning, particularly when it is a predictable flaw that could be exploited by the other side. In addition, public knowledge of flaws in the reasoning of individual arbitrators can be expected to lead to a rise in arbitrator challenges, based on the alleged existence of a cognitive bias.[113]

Cognitive biases are, of course, not individualized, and so are not, as such, flaws in individual arbitrators. They are, rather, common artifacts of human reasoning, and so flaws to which all arbitrators are subject. Nonetheless, the social constraints within which arbitrators operate mean that it is unreasonable to expect individual arbitrators to take responsibility for addressing the issue, as doing so will unavoidably involve significant risk to their career.[114] Just as significantly, however, the discussion in Section 38.4.2 illustrated that in many cases cognitive biases are significantly contextual, and are tied to the way that the human brain responds to the environment in which it is currently operating. Cognitive biases are not, that is, 'machine malfunctions' of the brain taken in isolation, but are instead consequences of how cognitive functions are influenced by context. For both these reasons, while it is clearly desirable for individual arbitrators to increase their awareness of their own cognitive biases, and to take whatever measures they can to avoid indulging them, any serious attempt to address the problem of cognitive biases within arbitration must focus instead on the social structures within which arbitrators operate.

One initial step in addressing this problem, of course, is education. This cannot be sufficient as a solution, but it is nonetheless essential as a component, as only arbitrators

[113] As a cognitive bias constitutes a deviation from good reasoning, parties able to argue that an arbitrator's known cognitive bias would result in the arbitrator being more likely to rule for the other party, on grounds that cannot be rationally justified, would have solid grounds for arguing that the arbitrator was unable to resolve the dispute impartially.

[114] Just as an arbitrator taking English lessons serves both as evidence of that individual's desire to be a better arbitrator (by eliminating mistakes based on language) and as a sign that he is currently flawed as an arbitrator (i.e. he currently makes mistakes based on language), so an arbitrator taking training designed to eliminate cognitive biases serves both as evidence of his desire to be a better arbitrator (by improving his reasoning) and as a sign that he is currently flawed as an arbitrator (i.e. he currently has flawed reasoning). Such an effect will, of course, decrease as recognition of the universality and eradicability of cognitive biases increases within the arbitration community.

aware of the degree to which and ways in which they are personally influenced by cognitive biases will take steps to avoid those biases affecting their work. The difficulty is how such education could be offered in a way that would not subject arbitrators to the possible negative career consequences noted above. Arbitral institutions can play a central role in this process.

The social nature of arbitration as a field of professional practice has led to the development of a significant number of arbitral institutions throughout the world. While to those outside the field arbitral institutions often seem to be little more than providers of administrative services, in reality they often serve as a social hub for arbitral communities, providing fora in which arbitration professionals can make the social connections on which careers are built, and providing educational programmes that practitioners can undertake in order to be able to demonstrate their training in arbitral practice.

This social role of arbitral institutions creates an opportunity for addressing the training of arbitrators on cognitive biases in a way that is responsive to the social context in which arbitrators operate. That is, by providing training courses on cognitive biases, arbitral institutions would immediately legitimize such training, as the institution's central role as a norm-representer within its arbitration community would ensure that taking such a training course would be seen as adhering to the community's norms of good arbitral practice, rather than as acknowledging a personal deficiency that deviated from those norms. In addition, providing such training through arbitral institutions would mean that arbitrators who took the training would receive a credential from a reputable education-provider within their community, which they could then use to demonstrate their enhanced awareness of and ability to address cognitive biases—the identity of the education-provider serving to legitimize the training within the context of arbitration in a way that courses from non-arbitration providers would not.

Of course, as repeatedly mentioned here, training alone cannot entirely solve the problem of cognitive biases. These biases are, after all, inherent realities of human reasoning, and so will not disappear simply because arbitrators become aware of them. To give one example, while arbitrators could be trained relatively easily in the techniques of Bayesian reasoning[115]—and such training would unquestionably be useful—this would not protect against biases that occur under conditions where there is no normatively correct answer, as is standardly the situation in arbitral decision-making. Similarly, there is clear empirical evidence that simply being conscientious about trying to suppress a cognitive bias is likely to be ineffective[116] due to the existence of a 'bias blind spot',

[115] Peter Sedlmeier and Gerd Gigerenzer, 'Teaching Bayesian Reasoning in Less than Two Hours', 130(3) Journal of Experimental Psychology: General 380 (2001). Bayes' theorem derives from the work of English cleric Thomas Bayes (1701–61), and addresses the question of what level of confidence one should have in a given belief based on the evidence available, including how new evidence should change one's level of confidence in an existing belief. A useful overview of the potential benefits of Bayesian reasoning for legal decision-making is available in Norman Fenton, Martin Neil, and Daniel Berger, 'Bayes and the Law', 3 Annual Review of Statistics and Its Application 51 (2016).

[116] Daniel Wegner et al., 'Paradoxical Effects of Thought Suppression', 53(1) Journal of Personality and Social Psychology 5 (1987).

as a result of which human beings are much better at identifying the cognitive biases of others than of themselves.[117] Indeed, particularly problematically for arbitrators, there is evidence that higher intelligence appears correlated with a higher degree of blindness towards one's own biases.[118]

Training in the existence of cognitive biases, combined with exhortations to watch for bias and think clearly, is therefore unlikely to suffice. Combining such awareness with training in techniques that formalize reasoning and remove some of the subjectivity of decision-making, such as through Bayesian reasoning techniques, would be a further improvement. However, the social influences on arbitrators would remain.

If cognitive biases in arbitral reasoning are to be seriously addressed, what is required instead is a fundamental restructuring of arbitration as a field of professional practice. The current reality of arbitration is that the feedback loop of arbitrator role identity encourages arbitrators to self-identify with their role as specialized decision-makers—a situation that encourages over-confidence in their ability to make reasoned decisions;[119] the social structure of arbitration and the centrality of personal endorsement for career progression undermines the willingness of those not already at the top of the field to critique those who are;[120] the potential consequences of recognizing flaws in one's own reasoning provide incentives for arbitrators to avoid self-examination or attempts to remedy flaws; the confidentiality that dominates commercial arbitration means that the work of arbitrators receives little serious feedback, and negative views by 'outsiders' to the field have little importance to an arbitrator's career success. In short, arbitration as a field of professional practice is very poorly designed from the perspective of encouraging high-quality arbitral reasoning.

This does not mean that there must be a 'revolution' in arbitration (if only because such an event is extraordinarily unlikely to occur). But awareness of the structural problems with arbitration as a field of professional practice can indicate some workable alterations to conventional arbitral practice that will help address cognitive biases in arbitrator reasoning.

[117] Emily Pronin, Daniel Lin, and Lee Ross, 'The Bias Blind Spot: Perceptions of Bias in Self versus Others', 28(3) Personality and Social Psychology Bulletin 369 (2002); Richard West, Russell Meserve, and Keith Stanovich, 'Cognitive Sophistication Does Not Attenuate the Bias Blind Spot', 103 J. Pers. Soc. Psychol. 506 (2012).

[118] Ibid.

[119] Several cognitive biases contribute to overconfidence, including the self-serving bias, confirmation bias, hindsight bias, and cognitive dissonance. See e.g. Marian and Wright (n. 77), 243–7; Baruch Fischoff, Paul Slovic, and Sarah Lichtenstein, 'Knowing with Certainty: The Appropriateness of Extreme Confidence', 3 Journal of Experimental Psychology: Human Perception and Performance 552 (1977).

[120] While it might seem that the mechanics of market competition would encourage criticism of leading arbitrators by those attempting to become arbitrators, as a means of emphasizing the need for their own services, this effect is undermined by the central role of leading arbitrators in arbitration communities, and the central role of arbitration communities in the development of arbitral careers. As a result, while those seeking to enter the field have an incentive to display their intelligence and ability, there are equally strong incentives to do so in ways that do not involve undermining and alienating leading figures in their community through direct strong criticism.

For example, one arbitral institution has recently adopted a process of 'screened' arbitrator appointments, under which arbitrators are not informed of which party appointed them to the tribunal,[121] and a recent empirical study has indicated that such a procedure does indeed help reduce bias in arbitral decision-making.[122] However, while such an approach addresses intra-arbitration dynamics, it does not address the broader social context in which arbitrator selection occurs. In some cases, for example, it will nonetheless be clear to an arbitrator which of the two parties was most likely to have appointed him/her. In addition, it does not remove the incentives that arbitrators have to develop good impressions with parties likely to be involved in future arbitrations, and so likely to make future appointments, or with arbitral institutions, which also play a large role in making arbitral appointments. This broader social context can only be addressed by altering the role played by parties and arbitral institutions in the arbitrator selection process. Party selection of arbitrators is, of course, a central feature of arbitration, and provides parties with confidence that at least one member of the tribunal deciding their case understands their perspective. Consequently, removal of party selection would undermine the ability of arbitration to serve as an effective mechanism for the resolution of disputes.[123]

An alternative is to combine 'screened' appointments with party selection from lists of potential arbitrators, 'cab rank' nomination to lists, and institutional nomination to lists of arbitrators judged to be particularly appropriate for the case in question.[124] Pursuant to this system, parties are presented with a short list of arbitrators, and are permitted to select any arbitrator from that list. Half the members of the list are selected through a 'cab rank' process, in which names are drawn from a larger list of arbitrators, in order, without discretion. The other half of the list is selected by an arbitral institution, based on the particular suitability of those arbitrators for the case in question. No indication is given as to whether an arbitrator is a 'cab rank' or 'institutional' addition to the list. Once selected, arbitrators are then screened from information revealing which party selected them.

While this process does not retain full party discretion in arbitrator selection, it affords parties enough involvement in the selection process that they can be confident in

[121] See e.g. the discussion at: <https://www.cpradr.org/news-publications/press-releases/2016-03-02-cpr-captures-2016-gar-innovation-award-press-release>.

[122] Sergio Puig and Anton Strezhnev, 'Affiliation Bias in Arbitration: An Experimental Approach', Arizona Legal Studies Discussion Paper No. 16–31 (2016).

[123] It should be noted that party appointments have recently been criticized by some prominent commentators. See e.g. Jan Paulsson's Ch. 4 in this Handbook. See also Jan Paulsson, 'Moral Hazard in International Dispute Resolution', 25 ICSID Rev. 339 (2010); Albert Jan van den Berg, 'Dissenting Opinions by Party-Appointed Arbitrators in Investment Arbitration', in Mahnoush Arsanjani et al. (eds), *Looking to the Future: Essays on International Law in Honor of W. Michael Reisman* (Brill, 2011). By contrast, the importance of party-appointed arbitrators has been underlined by Charles Brower and Charles Rosenberg, 'The Death of the Two-Headed Nightingale: Why the Paulsson–van den Berg Presumption that Party-Appointed Arbitrators are Untrustworthy is Wrongheaded', 29(1) Arb. Int'l 7 (2014); Tony Cole, 'Authority and Contemporary International Arbitration', 70 Louisiana Law Review 801 (2010).

[124] A 'non-screened' version of this procedure was adopted by the International Expedited Arbitration Centre on the recommendation of Tony Cole, one of the authors of this chapter.

the constitution of the tribunal. Similarly, while it allows arbitral institutions to use their expertise to assist parties in the selection process, it guarantees arbitrators a place on a list whatever their relationship with the institution, and thereby reduces the importance of social connections in the appointment process.

In addition to alterations to the process of the appointment of arbitrators, increased publication of appropriately redacted arbitral awards would also help reduce the impact of certain cognitive biases on arbitral decision-making. One of the unfortunate consequences of the confidentiality of arbitral awards is that the reasoning of arbitrators is only evaluated by the limited group of individuals who actually participate in an arbitration with them. As a result, the reality of cognitive biases means that arbitrators are incentivized to align their reasoning with the most influential participants in an arbitration, whether another arbitrator, an arbitral institution, or even a representative of a party. Broad publication of redacted awards would reduce such incentives by ensuring that information on an arbitrator's reasoning is available to all individuals considering that arbitrator for possible appointment, thereby reducing the importance of the approval of prominent individuals for success as an arbitrator.

There are, of course, other recommendations that could be made, and more 'revolutionary' suggestions would centre on continuing and enhancing current efforts to more effectively 'democratize' arbitration, by encouraging greater diversity in terms of gender, ethnicity, and age of arbitrators. However, the guiding point behind this discussion is a simple one: arbitration is a field that promotes itself on the quality of dispute resolution that it provides, and yet the structures through which the field operates actively undermine the quality of arbitral decision-making. Only by recognizing the reality of cognitive biases, and of the influences on arbitrator reasoning of the context in which arbitrators reach their decisions, can changes be implemented to ensure that the context of arbitration actually supports high-quality arbitral decision-making, rather than undermining it.

38.5 Conclusion

This chapter has attempted to achieve two aims. Firstly, to introduce non-psychologists to certain elements of psychological research and psychological theory that have a particular relevance for the practice of arbitration. Secondly, to develop the idea that in approaching the application of psychology to arbitration, it is essential to maintain a focus on the contextual realities of arbitration as a field of professional practice. Arbitrations do not occur in a vacuum, and an accurate understanding of arbitrator reasoning can only be achieved by combining the insights available from traditional psychological research with an awareness of the social influences that play a central role in structuring the profession.

To achieve that goal, we have briefly described the differences between mechanistic and functional contextual approaches to psychology and have suggested that functional contextualism is most suitable for analysing the psychological aspects of arbitration, due to its focus on attaining practical results while at the same time accounting for the complexity of human behaviour. We have also examined the professional context of arbitration and, in particular, the impact of arbitrator self-conceptions on arbitrator decision-making. Relying on fuzzy-trace theory, we have argued that arbitrators who adhere to the 'oracle' self-conception are more likely to rely strongly on gist representations, while arbitrators who see themselves as 'service providers' are likely to prioritize verbatim representations. Finally, we have examined the social context of arbitration and its influence on cognitive biases, emphasizing in particular the impact on arbitrator decision-making of the hierarchical nature of arbitration as a field of professional practice, in which the approval of 'gatekeepers' is fundamental for individual success.

The application of psychology to arbitration remains at an early stage of development, and it is certainly to be hoped that it will progress far beyond the relatively rudimentary observations made in this chapter. However, the foundations on which a discussion is built play a fundamental role in how that discussion develops, and the ultimate goal of this chapter has been to make a case for the benefits to be gained from adopting a contextual approach that relies on solid empirical research, but applies the results of that research with a developed understanding of the social realities in which arbitrators function.

Index

Note: Tables and figures are indicated by an italic "*t*" and "*f*", respectively, following the page number.

F

G

J

O

P

T